Index to the 1800 Massachusetts Federal Census
for the County of
Essex

Rebecca M. Sullivan
Deborah Lee Larsson

Index to the 1800 Massachusetts Federal Census
for the County of
Essex

October 2014

ISBN: 978-1502737458

FOREWARD:

This is the third volume of several containing the heads of household that were enumerated in the 1800 United States Federal Census in Massachusetts. Our third volume is comprised of those towns in Essex County. In order to make it easy for the researcher, towns are alphabetized, followed by an alphabetical index of Essex county.

We have made every attempt at correctly transcribing each town. However, many of these documents are torn, covered with ink, tape marks, rips and poor handwriting. Spelling errors have been left as they were originally written. Any names & enumerations illegible are denoted with an asterisk.

This book should be used as a guide and research aid. When possible the actual image should be obtained for proper verification and citation. Visit the National Archives website to find out more on how to obtain census images. www.archives.gov/research/census.

In order to get all of the information on one page to make for easy reading we had to reduce the size of the font.

Drop us a line, we'd love to hear what you're researching:
rsulli1219@aol.com

Becky & Deb
October 2014

Check out our other books:

Index to the 1800 Massachusetts Federal Census for the Counties of Barnstable, Dukes & Nantucket, Volume 1

Index to the 1800 Massachusetts Federal Census for the County of Worcester, Volume 2

INDEX

Essex County

Amesbury	page 7-11
Andover	page 12-18
Beverly	page 19-28
Boxford	page 29-30
Bradford	page 31-33
Danvers	page 34-40
Gloucester	page 41-52
Hamilton	page 53-54
Haverhill	page 55-60
Ipswich	page 61-68
Lynn	page 69-75
Lynnfield	page 76-77
Manchester	page 78-80
Marblehead	page 81-93
Methuen	page 94-96
Middleton	page 97-98
Newbury	page 99-106
Newburyport	page 107-119
Rowley	page 120-123
Salem	page 124-143
Salisbury	page 144-148
Topsfield	page 149-150
Wenham	page 151-152
Index	page 153-287

Essex County Stats

Microfilm Reel Number: M32-14

Town:	Page Numbers:	Enumerated By:
Amesbury	35-47	Unknown
Andover	89-103	John Farnum
Beverly	289-306	Joseph Wood
Boxford	133-136	Joseph Wood
Bradford	121-126	Unknown
Danvers	2-15	Eleazer Putnam
Gloucester	55-86	James Day
Hamilton	284-287	Unknown
Haverhill	142-152	Nathaniel Marsh
Ipswich	273-283	Unknown
Lynn	223-234	Henry Oliver
Lynnfield	235-237	Henry Oliver
Manchester	49-55	Unknown
Marblehead	238-270	Isaac Mansfield
Methuen	152-156	Eleazer Putnam
Middleton	15-18	Eleazer Putnam
Newbury	105-120	Unknown
Newburyport	157-181	Nathaniel Marsh
Rowley	127-132	Ivory Hovey
Salem	183-221	Jonathan Waldo
Salisbury	24-34	Samuel Nye
Topsfield	18-22	Unknown
Wenham	308-311	Joseph Wood

TOWN	PG#	LN#	LAST NAME	FIRST NAME	FREE WHITE MALES					FREE WHITE FEMALES					TOTAL ALL OTHER	TOTAL SLAVES	TOTALS	DISTRICT/ TOWNSHIP	NOTES
					under 10	10 to 16	16 to 26	26 to 45	45 and over	under 10	10 to 16	16 to 26	26 to 45	45 and over					
Amesbury	35	1	Burrough	Josiah	1		1			3			1				6		
Amesbury	35	2	Blasdell	Lewis	2		1			1			1				5		
Amesbury	35	3	Birkam	Willm B.	1		1			2			1				5		
Amesbury	35	4	Baley	James	2	2	3	1				1		1			10		
Amesbury	35	5	Bagley	Jeremiah	1		1			1			1	1			5		
Amesbury	35	6	Barnard	Molly Wid						2	1	1		1			5		
Amesbury	35	7	Badger	John		1	1	1	1		1			1			6		
Amesbury	35	8	Bartlett	Nicholus		1	1		1		1			1			5		
Amesbury	35	9	Bagley	Enoch			2	1	1		1	3		1			9		
Amesbury	35	10	Bartlett	Wm Capt				1		2	1		1				5		
Amesbury	35	11	Burrough	George Capt		1	1		1				1	1			5		
Amesbury	35	12	Bagley	David	3		1	1		1	1		1				8		
Amesbury	35	13	Bagley	Jacob Capt	4	1		1		1	1		1				9		
Amesbury	35	14	Barnard	Mary Wid										1			1		
Amesbury	35	15	Bartlett	Nathan	2	1	1		1			1		1			7		
Amesbury	35	16	Bagley	Isaac	1		1	1				1	1	1			6		
Amesbury	35	17	Bartlett	Ruth Wid									1	2			3		
Amesbury	35	18	Bartlett	Samuel	1		1						1				3		
Amesbury	36	1	Blasdell	Ruth Wid						1			1				2		
Amesbury	36	2	Bartlett	Enoch	3		2	1			1		1				8		
Amesbury	36	3	Blasdell	Stephen				1					1				2		
Amesbury	36	4	Blasdell	Ephraim Junr		1		1			1		1				4		
Amesbury	36	5	Blasdell	Ephraim				1					1				2		
Amesbury	36	6	Blasdell	John	3			1					1				5		
Amesbury	36	7	Blasdell	Richd				1		1			1				3		
Amesbury	36	8	Blasdell	Joseph	2			1		1		1					5		
Amesbury	36	9	Blasdell	Oliver	1				1	1		2		1			6		
Amesbury	36	10	Bartlett	Rachel Wid	1							1	1				3		
Amesbury	36	11	Bartlett	John			1		1			1		1			4		
Amesbury	36	12	Bartlett	Jacob	3	1		1		1			1				7		
Amesbury	36	13	Bartlett	Joseph			1		2	1			1	1			6		
Amesbury	36	14	Brown	Richd	2	1		1		2			1				7		
Amesbury	36	15	Barnard	Willm		1	1		1	1			1				5		
Amesbury	36	16	Barnard	Jona Capt	1	1		1		1	1		1				6		
Amesbury	36	17	Barnard	Jona				1						1			2		
Amesbury	36	18	Barnard	John	1		2	1		1		2		1			8		
Amesbury	36	19	Brown	Ebenz	2	2		1		1			1				7		
Amesbury	36	20	Barnard	Isaac				1	1			2		1			5		
Amesbury	36	21	Badger	Obadiah		1	1		1				1	1			5		
Amesbury	36	22	Barnard	Joseph	1				1	3			1	1			7		
Amesbury	36	23	Barnard	Daniel					1			1					2		
Amesbury	36	24	Barnard	Jacob	1			1		1	1		1				5		
Amesbury	36	25	Bartlett	Hannah Wid			1						2	1			4		
Amesbury	36	26	Bagley	Orlando			2		1			1		1			5		
Amesbury	36	27	Barker	Samuel	2	1		1		1	2		1				8		
Amesbury	36	28	Bagley	Sargent	1		2		1			1	1				6		
Amesbury	36	29	Bootman	Elias		1		1			1		1				4		
Amesbury	36	30	Bagley	Vallentine Capt	1			1				1	1				4		
Amesbury	37	1	Chalace	Wid			1					1		1			3		
Amesbury	37	2	Colbey	Adonijah					1					1			2		
Amesbury	37	3	Colbey	John	4			1		1			1				7		
Amesbury	37	4	Colbey	John W.	1			1					1				3		
Amesbury	37	5	Chalace	Timothy					1				1				2		
Amesbury	37	6	Chase	Mary Wid										1			1		
Amesbury	37	7	Currier	David		1		1		1			1	2			6		
Amesbury	37	8	Currier	Jacob		1			1	2	3	1		1			9		
Amesbury	37	9	Colbey	Obadiah Dr.		2		1	1				1	1			6		
Amesbury	37	10	Colbey	Obadiah Junr	4	1		1				2	1				9		
Amesbury	37	11	Curtis	Anna Wid								1		1			2		
Amesbury	37	12	Currier	Daniel		1	1		1			1		1			5		
Amesbury	37	13	Colbey	Allice										1			1		
Amesbury	37	14	Colbey	Judith Wid										1			1		
Amesbury	37	15	Chandler	Hannah Wid			1			1			1	1			4		
Amesbury	37	16	Curtis	Daniel	1		1						1				3		
Amesbury	37	17	Cleves	Marchant		1			1				1	1			4		
Amesbury	37	18	Currier	Michd	2		4		1		2	1		1			11		
Amesbury	37	19	Currier	David Junr	1			1					1				3		
Amesbury	37	20	Colbey	Benj					1				1	1			3		
Amesbury	37	21	Colbey	Aaron	1	1	2		1	1	1			2			9		
Amesbury	37	22	Currier	Timothy			2	1					1	1			5		
Amesbury	37	23	Currier	Levi		2	1		1				1				5		
Amesbury	37	24	Colbey	Thomas		1		1		1			1				4		
Amesbury	37	25	Colbey	Vallentine					1	1		1		1			4		
Amesbury	37	26	Colbey	Vallentine Junr	1		1						1				3		
Amesbury	37	27	Colbey	Jonathan					1				1				2		
Amesbury	37	28	Currier	John Capt			1	1				1		1			4		
Amesbury	37	29	Currier	Dorothy Wid		1							1				2		
Amesbury	37	30	Chalace	Samuel			1	1		1		2		1			6		
Amesbury	37	31	Colbey	Wm Capt.	1					1		1					4		

TOWN	PG#	LN#	LAST NAME	FIRST NAME	FREE WHITE MALES under 10	10 to 16	16 to 26	26 to 45	45 and over	FREE WHITE FEMALES under 10	10 to 16	16 to 26	26 to 45	45 and over	TOTAL ALL OTHER	TOTAL SLAVES	TOTALS	DISTRICT/TOWNSHIP	NOTES
Amesbury	37	32	Currier	Thomas		1		1						2			4		
Amesbury	37	33	Currier	Willm				1					1				2		
Amesbury	37	34	Chalace	Thomas		1	1	1					3	1			7		
Amesbury	38	1	Chalace	John	1		1		1	1	2			1			7		
Amesbury	38	2	Chalace	Elizabeth Wid									2	1			3		
Amesbury	38	3	Clough	John				1				1		1			3		
Amesbury	38	4	Clough	David	1	1		1		1		1					5		
Amesbury	38	5	Clough	Elijah	1			1						1			3		
Amesbury	38	6	Clough	Baley			1			1		1					3		
Amesbury	38	7	Colbey	Gideon				1				1	1				3		
Amesbury	38	8	Colbey	Aaron		1	1	1		1	1	2		1			8		
Amesbury	38	9	Currier	Nathan	1	1	1	1		1			2				7		
Amesbury	38	10	Currier	Abigail Wid		1								2			3		
Amesbury	38	11	Currier	Allice Wid							1			2			3		
Amesbury	38	12	Currier	Joseph			1			2			1				4		
Amesbury	38	13	Currer	Rachel Wid	2		1					2	1				6		
Amesbury	38	14	Clement	Jacob	1	1		1		2	1		1	2			9		
Amesbury	38	15	Chace	Mary Wid										1			1		
Amesbury	38	16	Chace	Amos		1	1	1		1		2	1	1			8		
Amesbury	38	17	Colbey	Barzilla				1					1	1			3		
Amesbury	38	18	Colbey	Barzilla Junr		1							1				2		
Amesbury	38	19	Colbey	Woodman				1					1				2		
Amesbury	38	20	Colbey	Joshua	2			1		1	2		1				7		
Amesbury	38	21	Currier	Seth		1						1					2		
Amesbury	38	22	Dennie	John		1		1		1			1				4		
Amesbury	38	23	Davis	John		1	1					1		2			5		
Amesbury	38	24	Davis	Elijah				1		1		1	1	2			6		
Amesbury	38	25	Davis	Ephm			3		1			1		1			6		
Amesbury	38	26	Davis	Joseph	1	1	1		1	1	1			1			7		
Amesbury	38	27	Davis	Enoch		1		1						1			3		
Amesbury	39	1	Flanders	Deborah Wid		1							3	1			5		
Amesbury	39	2	Follembe	Samuel	1	1		1			1	1		1			6		
Amesbury	39	3	Follembe	Berzia Wid						1			1				2		
Amesbury	39	4	Fobes	Levi	1		1	1		1		1	1				6		
Amesbury	39	5	Foot	Theophilus	3	1	1	1				1		1			8		
Amesbury	39	6	Foot	Ephm	1		1					1					3		
Amesbury	39	7	Follembe	David Capt	1	1	1					1					4		
Amesbury	39	8	Foster	Robert		2						1					3		
Amesbury	39	9	Farrington	Ebenz				1				1		1			3		
Amesbury	39	10	Farrington	Ebenz Junr	1		1	1		2	2	2		1			10		
Amesbury	39	11	Farrington	Saml		2		1				2		1			6		
Amesbury	39	12	Gould	Theophilus			1							1			2		
Amesbury	39	13	Gale	Ely Capt		1	3	1		2			1				8		
Amesbury	39	14	Gale	Beza			1				1						2		
Amesbury	39	15	Goodrich	Willm	1	1		1	1	2			1	1			8		
Amesbury	39	16	Goodwin	Levi	2	1	1	1		1			1				7		
Amesbury	39	17	Gale	John	1			1		1		1					4		
Amesbury	39	18	Gordon	Mirriam Wid									1				1		
Amesbury	39	19	Googin	Richard			1			3		1					5		
Amesbury	39	20	Gould	Philip			1	1						3			5		
Amesbury	39	21	Gould	Elihu		1		1						3			5		
Amesbury	39	22	Goodwin	Susanna									1	1			2		
Amesbury	39	23	Goodwin	Mons		1		1					1	1			4		
Amesbury	39	24	Goodwin	Ephm	1		1						1				3		
Amesbury	39	25	Goodwin	William	4		1	1			1		1				8		
Amesbury	39	26	Goodwin	Isaac				1		1		2		1			5		
Amesbury	39	27	Goodwin	Isaac Junr	2	1		1					1				5		
Amesbury	39	28	Goodwin	Ezra				1		1			1				3		
Amesbury	39	29	Goodwin	Thomas		1	1			1	1	1	1				6		
Amesbury	40	1	Goodwin	Thomas Junr		1		1		2			1				5		
Amesbury	40	2	Harket	Mehitable Wid	3								1				4		
Amesbury	40	3	Hoyt	Joseph Capt		2	1				1		1	1			6		
Amesbury	40	4	Hunt	Merriam Wid							1		1				2		
Amesbury	40	5	Hoyt	Willoughby				1		1	1		1				4		
Amesbury	40	6	Harket	Joseph		1				1		1					3		
Amesbury	40	7	Hoyt	Stephen		1		1		4			1				7		
Amesbury	40	8	Hoyt	Moses Junr				1						1			2		
Amesbury	40	9	Hoyt	Aaron			1			1		1					3		
Amesbury	40	10	Hoyt	Lydia Wid	1					3			1	1			6		
Amesbury	40	11	Hoyt	Enoch		1						1		1			3		
Amesbury	40	12	Hoyt	Moses				1				1		2			4		
Amesbury	40	13	Hull	Stephen Revd	1		1						2				4		
Amesbury	40	14	Hoyt	Levi		1		1		2	1	1	1				7		
Amesbury	40	15	Hunniford	John	1			1					1				3		
Amesbury	40	16	Huntington	Willm		2	1	1					1				5		
Amesbury	40	17	Huntington	Willm Junr			1			1		1					3		
Amesbury	40	18	Huntington	Moses	2			1				1	1				5		
Amesbury	40	19	Hartings	Robert		1		1						1			3		
Amesbury	40	20	Hoyt	Moses		1		1		1	1		1				5		

TOWN	PG#	LN#	LAST NAME	FIRST NAME	\<10	10–16	16–26	26–45	45+	\<10	10–16	16–26	26–45	45+	TOTAL ALL OTHER	TOTAL SLAVES	TOTALS	DISTRICT/ TOWNSHIP	NOTES
Amesbury	40	21	Hoyt	Daniel		1			1	1	2			1			6		
Amesbury	40	22	Hoyt	Judith Wid	1		2							1			4		
Amesbury	40	23	Hoyt	Hannah Wid									2	1			3		
Amesbury	40	24	Hoyt	Sarah Wid		1			1				2	1			5		
Amesbury	40	25	Huntington	Elijah	2	1			1	3	1			1			9		
Amesbury	40	26	Huntington	David	1			2						1			4		
Amesbury	40	27	Huntington	John				1				1	3	1			6		
Amesbury	40	28	Huntington	Amos		1		1					2	1			5		
Amesbury	40	29	Huntington	Isaac				1					1	1			3		
Amesbury	40	30	Hoyt	Zenos	1			1					1				3		
Amesbury	41	1	Hoyt	Joseph			1	1	1	3			1	1			8		
Amesbury	41	2	Hoyt	Timothy				1					2				3		
Amesbury	41	3	Hoyt	William			1	1					1	1			4		
Amesbury	41	4	Hoyt	Daniel		1	1	1					1	1			5		
Amesbury	41	5	Hoyt	Thomas Junr			1						1				2		
Amesbury	41	6	Hoyt	Matthias		1		1	1	1		1	2	1			8		
Amesbury	41	7	Hine	Nathan Dr		1		1	1					2			5		
Amesbury	41	8	Hine	Nathan Junr	1			1					1				3		
Amesbury	41	9	Harvey	Jacob	2	1		1		1			1				6		
Amesbury	41	10	Hoyt	Robert			2		1				1				4		
Amesbury	41	11	Hoyt	Jacob Junr		1		2					1				4		
Amesbury	41	12	Hoyt	John				1						1			2		
Amesbury	41	13	Hoyt	Humphrey		1		1		2			1				5		
Amesbury	41	14	Hoyt	Jacob	3	1		1					1				6		
Amesbury	41	15	Hoyt	Joseph Junr	1			1		2			1				5		
Amesbury	41	16	Hoyt	John Junr				1					1				2		
Amesbury	41	17	Jones	Ezekiel Junr		1	1					1					3		
Amesbury	41	18	Jones	Ezekiel				1				1		1			3		
Amesbury	41	19	Jones	Philip		1		1		2		1	1				6		
Amesbury	41	20	Jones	Abner		1		1	2	1		1	1				7		
Amesbury	41	21	Kindrick	Samuel			1		1				1				3		
Amesbury	41	22	Kenniston	Moses				1					2				3		
Amesbury	41	23	Kent	John	1			1	1	1			1				5		
Amesbury	41	24	Kelley	John			2		1			2		1			6		
Amesbury	41	25	Kelley	Louis			1					2		1			4		
Amesbury	41	26	Kelley	Stephen	1	1	3	1		1		1	1				9		
Amesbury	41	27	Kelly	Anthony	1	1		1	1	1		1	1	1			8		
Amesbury	41	28	Kendrick	Seth		1		1				2	1	1			6		
Amesbury	41	29	Kimbal	John			1							1			2		
Amesbury	42	1	Lowell	Barnard	4	2		1		1			1				9		
Amesbury	42	2	Lowell	Ezra Capt				1			1	1	1	1			5		
Amesbury	42	3	Lowell	James Capt	1	1		1				1					4		
Amesbury	42	4	Long	Nathan	3	1	2	2		2		1	1				12		
Amesbury	42	5	Lowell	David	1	1	1	1				3	1				8		
Amesbury	42	6	Lowell	Eliphalet				1						1			2		
Amesbury	42	7	Lowvey	Benj Capt				2					1	1			4		
Amesbury	42	8	Lane	Hannah Wid	1					1		1					3		
Amesbury	42	9	Lewin	John	1		1			1		1					4		
Amesbury	42	10	Lowvey	Wm Capt	3		2	1				2	1				9		
Amesbury	42	11	Little	Willm C		2	1		1			1	1	1			7		
Amesbury	42	12	Little	John		1	1			2		1					5		
Amesbury	42	13	Lancster	Jacob	1	2		1		3	1		1				9		
Amesbury	42	14	Martin	John	2		1	1					2	1			7		
Amesbury	42	15	Martin	Eliphalet				1						1			2		
Amesbury	42	16	Morse	Joseph	3	1	1	1		2			1				9		
Amesbury	42	17	Maxfield	Judith		1						1		1			3		
Amesbury	42	18	Merrill	Benja	1		1	1		2	1		1	1			8		
Amesbury	42	19	Moses	David	3		1	1		1				1			7		
Amesbury	42	20	Morrill	Adam			2		1			1	1				5		
Amesbury	42	21	Morrill	Sarah Wid								2	1				3		
Amesbury	42	22	Morrill	John			1			1		1					3		
Amesbury	42	23	Morrill	Wid										2			2		
Amesbury	42	24	Morrill	Jona Capt	3	2	1	1				3	1				11		
Amesbury	42	25	Morrison	Michael	1			1		2			2				6		
Amesbury	42	26	Merrill	Jacob	1		2	1	1	1	1	1		1			9		
Amesbury	42	27	March	Ichabod		1		1						1			3		
Amesbury	42	28	Merrill	Joseph	3	1		1		2	1	1	1				10		
Amesbury	42	29	Martin	Isaac	1	1	1	1				1		1			6		
Amesbury	42	30	Martin	Aquilla			2	1				2	2	1			9		
Amesbury	42	31	Merrill	Isaac		1		1	1	1	1	1		1			7		
Amesbury	43	1	Merrill	John Capt		1	2	1					2				6		
Amesbury	43	2	Moulton	Jonathan				1		1				1			3		
Amesbury	43	3	Moody	Cutting		1		1				1	1				4		
Amesbury	43	4	Moody	Joseph		1	2				1	1		1			7		
Amesbury	43	5	Morse	John	1	1	2		1		1	1		1			8		
Amesbury	43	6	Merrill	Hannah Wid										1			1		
Amesbury	43	7	Moulton	David				1						1			2		
Amesbury	43	8	Matron	Dorothy Wid						1				1			2		
Amesbury	43	9	Noyes	Eliphalet		1						1					2		

TOWN	PG#	LN#	LAST NAME	FIRST NAME	FREE WHITE MALES under 10	10 to 16	16 to 26	26 to 45	45 and over	FREE WHITE FEMALES under 10	10 to 16	16 to 26	26 to 45	45 and over	TOTAL ALL OTHER	TOTAL SLAVES	TOTALS	DISTRICT/TOWNSHIP	NOTES
Amesbury	43	10	Nichols	Moses		1		1						1			3		
Amesbury	43	11	Nichols	Daniel				1						1			2		
Amesbury	43	12	Nichols	Enoch		1		1		1		1		1			5		
Amesbury	43	13	Nichols	Stephen	4			1		2	2	1					10		
Amesbury	43	14	Nichols	Hezekiah	2	1		1			1	1		1			7		
Amesbury	43	15	Osgood	Samuel				1		1				1			3		
Amesbury	43	16	Osgood	Abel	1			1		2			1				5		
Amesbury	43	17	Ordway	Saml Dr		1	3		1				2	1			8		
Amesbury	43	18	Osgood	Timothy				1		2	1	1					5		
Amesbury	43	19	Patten	Jona	3		1	1		2			2				9		
Amesbury	43	20	Propey	Jona				1						1			2		
Amesbury	43	21	Propey	John	3	1		1		1	1		1				8		
Amesbury	43	22	Propey	Joseph			1						1				3		
Amesbury	43	23	Propey	Hezekiah	1	1		1					1				4		
Amesbury	44	1	Prouter	Nathl		2	1						1				4		
Amesbury	44	2	Propey	Chalare		2		1		1			1				5		
Amesbury	44	3	Parker	Willm Dr		1	1			4	4	1	1				12		
Amesbury	44	4	Plummer	Moses	2	1		1		1	1	1		1			8		
Amesbury	44	5	Patten	Willis Dr		1	2	1					2	1			8		
Amesbury	44	6	Patten	John		1		1		2	1		1				6		
Amesbury	44	7	Patten	Mary Wid	1		1	1		1			1				5		
Amesbury	44	8	Patten	Willis Junr	1			1		2			1				5		
Amesbury	44	9	Patty	Moody		1		1		1			1				4		
Amesbury	44	10	Plummer	Joshua				1				1		1			3		
Amesbury	44	11	Plummer	John				1									1		
Amesbury	44	12	Pillsbury	Samuel	1			1					1				3		
Amesbury	44	13	Randall	Isaac Capt				1						1			2		
Amesbury	44	14	Rogers	Sarah Wid	2								1	1			4		
Amesbury	44	15	Ring	David				1					1				3		
Amesbury	44	16	Rogers	Enoch		1		1			1	1	1				5		
Amesbury	44	17	Ramsey	Charles	1			1					1				3		
Amesbury	44	18	Smith	Judith Wid									1	1			2		
Amesbury	44	19	Sweat	Enoch	3			1		2			1				7		
Amesbury	44	20	Sweat	Benja				1						1			2		
Amesbury	44	21	Sweat	Willm			1			2		1					4		
Amesbury	44	22	Souter	Samuel	2	1		1		1	1		1				7		
Amesbury	44	23	Shoars	Matthew			1					1					2		
Amesbury	44	24	Standring	Benja	1	1		1		2			1				6		
Amesbury	44	25	Shepherd	Samuel				1						1			2		
Amesbury	44	26	Sargent	Ichabod	3	1		1		1			1	1			8		
Amesbury	44	27	Sargent	Stephen	2		1	1					1				5		
Amesbury	45	1	Sargent	Zebulon	1			1				2	1				5		
Amesbury	45	2	Sargent	Orlando Esqr		1							2	2			6		
Amesbury	45	3	Sargent	Orlando Junr	1			1		1			1				4		
Amesbury	45	4	Sargent	Moses			2	1		3	1	2		1			10		
Amesbury	45	5	Sargent	Moses Junr	1	1		1		2	2	1	1	1			10		
Amesbury	45	6	Sargent	Robert Capt	1			1		2			1				5		
Amesbury	45	7	Sargent	Josiah				1				1	1	1			4		
Amesbury	45	8	Sargent	Christopher Esqr		1		1					2	1			5		
Amesbury	45	9	Sargent	Nehemiah				1						1			2		
Amesbury	45	10	Sargent	Nehemiah Junr	3			1			1		1	1			7		
Amesbury	45	11	Sargent	Ezekiel	1	2			1	3			1				8		
Amesbury	45	12	Sargent	Amos	4	3	2	1		1			2				13		
Amesbury	45	13	Sargent	Amasa	1	3	1		1			1		1			8		
Amesbury	45	14	Sargent	Joshua	2	2	2	1		2			1	1			11		
Amesbury	45	15	Sargent	Sarah Wid									1	2			3		
Amesbury	45	16	Sargent	Thomas	1		2	1		3	1		1				9		
Amesbury	45	17	Sargent	Judith Wid								1	2	1			4		
Amesbury	45	18	Sargent	Jacob	1			1		3	1		1				7		
Amesbury	45	19	Sargent	Joshua Junr	2			1		1			1				5		
Amesbury	45	20	Sargent	Joshua				1						1			2		
Amesbury	45	21	Sargent	Seth	1			1					1				3		
Amesbury	45	22	Sargent	Jona Junr	1		2						1				4		
Amesbury	45	23	Sargent	Hezekiah		1	1		1		1	1		1			6		
Amesbury	45	24	Sargent	Jona	2			2		1	1		1				7		
Amesbury	45	25	Smith	David Revd	1			1		2	2		1				7		
Amesbury	45	26	Sawyer	John Capt		1		1	1	2			1				6		
Amesbury	45	27	Sawyer	Michl			1	1	1					1			4		
Amesbury	45	28	Sawyer	Willm	1		1					1					3		
Amesbury	45	29	Sawyer	John	2			2		2	3		1				10		
Amesbury	45	30	Sawyer	Aaron Dr			1		1					1			3		
Amesbury	45	31	Sawyer	Stephen	1			1		3			1				6		
Amesbury	45	32	Short	David	2			1		1			1				5		
Amesbury	45	33	Sargent	Christopher Junr	3			1					1				5		
Amesbury	45	34	Savory	Daniel	1	1	1		1	1	1	1	1				8		
Amesbury	45	35	Stowker	Marshal		1			1					1			3		
Amesbury	45	36	Savory	Daniel Junr			1					1					2		
Amesbury	45	1	Sargent	Dorothy Wid									2	1			3		
Amesbury	46	2	Trupell	Moses			1			1							3		
Amesbury	46	3	Trupell	Henry		1			1					1			3		

TOWN	PG#	LN#	LAST NAME	FIRST NAME	FREE WHITE MALES					FREE WHITE FEMALES					TOTAL ALL OTHER	TOTAL SLAVES	TOTALS	DISTRICT/ TOWNSHIP	NOTES
					under 10	10 to 16	16 to 26	26 to 45	45 and over	under 10	10 to 16	16 to 26	26 to 45	45 and over					
Amesbury	46	4	Taylor	Archibald Capt		1			1	1	1		1	1			6		
Amesbury	46	5	Titromb	Ichabod	1			1		2		1					5		
Amesbury	46	6	Titromb	Anna Wid									1	1			2		
Amesbury	46	7	Tilton	Samuel	1			1		3			1				6		
Amesbury	46	8	Tewksbury	Isaac	3		1		1		2	2	1				10		
Amesbury	46	9	Tewksbury	John			1		1			1					3		
Amesbury	46	10	Tewksbury	Moses	1		1	1		2	2		1				8		
Amesbury	46	11	Tewksbury	Daniel			1		1	2	2			3			9		
Amesbury	46	12	Tucker	Elisha			1			1		1					3		
Amesbury	46	13	Webster	David	1		1			2			1				5		
Amesbury	46	14	Whitten	Rhoda Wid						1			1				2		
Amesbury	46	15	Worthen	Ezra		1	1		1			2		1			6		
Amesbury	46	16	Webster	Stephen Capt	2		1				1	1					5		
Amesbury	46	17	Wait	John	1		1			1	1		1				5		
Amesbury	46	18	Webb	Samuel			1						1				2		
Amesbury	46	19	Worthen	Ezekiel Capt	2	1			1					1			5		
Amesbury	46	20	Wait	Daniel	1				1	2	1			1			6		
Amesbury	46	21	Welsh	Jonathan				2					1	1			4		
Amesbury	46	22	Wait	Sylvanus	1		1						1				3		
Amesbury	46	23	Weed	Charles					1	2			1	1			5		
Amesbury	46	24	Weed	Elijah				1		1			1				3		
Amesbury	46	25	Weed	Ephm Capt		1	2	1	1			1		1			7		
Amesbury	46	26	Weed	Ephm					1					1			2		
Amesbury	46	27	Weed	Isaac			1		1			2		1			5		
Amesbury	46	28	Weed	David		1	1		1			1		1			5		
Amesbury	46	29	Worthen	Willm	1			1		2			1				5		
Amesbury	46	30	Worthen	Hannah Wid									1	1			2		
Amesbury	47	1	Worthen	Thomas				1	1			1	1				4		
Amesbury	47	2	Worthen	George	1	1	2		1			1		1			7		
Amesbury	47	3	Williams	Dorothy Wid			1						1	1			3		
Amesbury	47	4	Weld	Elias Dr.			1			1			1				3		
Amesbury	47	5	Whittier	Isaac Major	2	2	1		1		1	1		1			9		
Amesbury	47	6	Williams	William			2		1				1	1			5		
Amesbury	47	7	Wilcomb	Hezekiah Wid	1	1							1				3		
Amesbury	47	8	Whittier	Maurice		1			1			1		1			4		

11

TOWN	PG#	LN#	LAST NAME	FIRST NAME	FREE WHITE MALES					FREE WHITE FEMALES					TOTAL ALL OTHER	TOTAL SLAVES	TOTALS	DISTRICT/ TOWNSHIP	NOTES
					under 10	10 to 16	16 to 26	26 to 45	45 and over	under 10	10 to 16	16 to 26	26 to 45	45 and over					
Andover	89	1	Adams	John	1				1		1	1		2			6		
Andover	89	2	Adams	John Jnr	2	1	2	1		3			2				11		
Andover	89	3	Adams	John 3d		1	2			1	1	1					6		
Andover	89	4	Austin	John	1			1		4			1				7		
Andover	89	5	Austin	Samuel	1			1					1				3		
Andover	89	6	Abbott	Samuel Esq			2		1		1	2		1			7		
Andover	89	7	Abbott	Henry	1	1	1		1			1	1	1	1		8		
Andover	89	8	Abbott	John		1	2		1	1			1	2			8		
Andover	89	9	Abbott	Moses	1		2	2	1		1	4	2	1			14		
Andover	89	10	Abbott	John L		6	2	1		3	1	2	1	1			17		
Andover	89	11	Abbott	Ezra	1	5	1	1				2					10		
Andover	89	12	Abbott	Nathan	3	2	2		1	1		1	1	1			12		
Andover	89	13	Abbott	Timothy	1	3		1	1			2		2			10		
Andover	89	14	Abbott	Jonathan Junr			1		1	1		1	1				5		
Andover	89	15	Abbott	Benjamin Junr	1	1	1					1					4		
Andover	89	16	Abbott	Moses Junr		4		1		1		1	1				8		
Andover	89	17	Abbott	Isaac		1	1		1			1					4		
Andover	89	18	Abbott	Nehemiah Junr			1		1			1					3		
Andover	89	19	Abbott	Benjamin Junr	1	2		1				3	3				11		
Andover	89	20	Allen	Asa	1								1				2		
Andover	89	21	Allen	Deborah						1				3			4		
Andover	90	1	Abbott	Phebe Wid								1		1			2		
Andover	90	2	Abbott	Caleb	1	1			1	3		1	1				8		
Andover	90	3	Abbott	Thomas				1					2				3		
Andover	90	4	Averil	Paul		1	1		1	2			1	1			7		
Andover	90	5	Ames	Spafford	2	3			1	1		1	1				9		
Andover	90	6	Abbott	Nehemiah	1	2	6	1	1	1	1		3	1	1		18		
Andover	90	7	Abbott	Jonathan				1					3				6		
Andover	90	8	Abbott	Jeduthum		1	2		1	1	3	1	2				11		
Andover	90	9	Abbott	Ephraim		1	1		1	1	1	1	1				7		
Andover	90	10	Abbott	Bixby	2	2			1			1					6		
Andover	90	11	Abbott	William Junr			1				1						2		
Andover	90	12	Abbott	Zebadiah			2			2	1		2	1			8		
Andover	90	13	Abbott	Jonathan 3d			1				1						2		
Andover	90	14	Abbott	David	3			1		1	1		1				7		
Andover	90	15	Abbott	Nathan Junr	1	1		1				1					4		
Andover	90	16	Abbott	Solomon			1			1	1						3		
Andover	90	17	Abbott	Benjamin	1		1			2		1					5		
Andover	90	18	Ames	Benjamin	1		1	1		2	1		1	1	1		9		
Andover	90	19	Bridges	Moody		2	1		1	1	1	1	1	1			9		
Andover	90	20	Barker	Mehetabel									2				2		
Andover	90	21	Barker	Phinehas			2		1	1			1				5		
Andover	90	22	Barker	Stephen	3	1	1	1		1	1	1		1			11		
Andover	90	23	Bradley	Joseph	3	1			1	1			1		1		8		
Andover	90	24	Barker	John	2		1		1	2	2	2		1			11		
Andover	90	25	Barker	Isaac	1		1	1		3		1	1				8		
Andover	90	26	Barker	Mehetabel Wid	1	1					1	2	2				7		
Andover	90	27	Barker	Nathan	1	1		1		1	1	1	1				7		
Andover	90	28	Bradley	Jonathan	3	2	1		1	1		2	1				11		
Andover	90	29	Barnard	John		1		1				1	1				4		
Andover	90	30	Bridges	James			1	1									2		
Andover	90	31	Bridges	James Jr		2	1	1	1	5	2	1	1				14		
Andover	90	32	Berry	Nathanael		2						1					3		
Andover	90	33	Blunt	Mary Wid		1				1		1	1				4		
Andover	90	34	Blunt	Isaac	2	1	1	1		2		1	2				10		
Andover	90	35	Barker	Sarah									2				2		
Andover	90	36	Balard	Hezekiah	1	1		1	1	2	1		1	1			9		
Andover	90	37	Barker	Henry Gray	1		1	1		1		1					5		
Andover	91	1	Blunt	David		2		1		1	1		1				6		
Andover	91	2	Bowlman	John	2			1		1			1				5		
Andover	91	3	Blanchard	Josiah			1					1					2		
Andover	91	4	Butters	Benjamin				1		1			1				3		
Andover	91	5	Barnum	Thaddeus		1		1			1						3		
Andover	91	6	Barker	Samuel			1	1	1	1	1		1				6		
Andover	91	7	Berry	John		1	1	1		2			1				6		
Andover	91	8	Berry	Ruth Wid		2							2				4		
Andover	91	9	Bowman	John	1		1		1	2		1					6		
Andover	91	10	Beverly	John	3			1		1	1		1				8		
Andover	91	11	Bragg	Ingal		1											1		
Andover	91	12	Burt	Joseph		1		1	1	1	1		1	1			7		
Andover	91	13	Barnard	James	2			2	1	1			2	1			9		
Andover	91	14	Baker	Symonds			1		1			1	1		1		5		
Andover	91	15	Bailey	Moses		1	2		1		1	1		2			8		
Andover	91	16	Bailey	William		1	1		1	1	1	1		1			7		
Andover	91	17	Boynton	Thomas		1	3		1	2		3		1			11		
Andover	91	18	Bailey	James	3	1		1		1		1	1	1			8		
Andover	91	19	Ballard	Timothy	2	1		1	1	1	1	4	1		1		13		
Andover	91	20	Bailey	Joshua	1			1		1			1				4		
Andover	91	21	Burt	Ebenezer	2		2	1		2		2	1	1			11		

TOWN	PG#	LN#	LAST NAME	FIRST NAME	FREE WHITE MALES					FREE WHITE FEMALES					TOTAL ALL OTHER	TOTAL SLAVES	TOTALS	DISTRICT/ TOWNSHIP	NOTES
					under 10	10 to 16	16 to 26	26 to 45	45 and over	under 10	10 to 16	16 to 26	26 to 45	45 and over					
Andover	91	22	Burt	Joseph Junr	3	1		1			1		1				7		
Andover	91	23	Bickford	Jonathan				1						1			2		
Andover	91	24	Bailey	Samuel	2			1		1			1				5		
Andover	91	25	Buck	Asa				1					1	1			3		
Andover	91	26	Bailey	Daniel	1	2		1		3	1		1				9		
Andover	91	27	Bailey	Luther		1		1			1	1		1			5		
Andover	91	28	Barnard	John Jr	5			1					1				7		
Andover	91	29	Bartlett	Daniel			2			1	1	1					5		
Andover	91	30	Barnard	Mehetabel										1			1		
Andover	91	31	Barker	Richard				1									1		
Andover	91	32	Blanchard	Amos	3	1	1	1		2			1	1			10		
Andover	92	1	Carlton	Isaac				2				1		1			4		
Andover	92	2	Carlton	Benjamin		2	1			3			1				8		
Andover	92	3	Chickering	Samuel	2	2		2	1			2	1	2			12		
Andover	92	4	Chickering	Dean	3	1		1		1			1				7		
Andover	92	5	Currier	David		1											1		
Andover	92	6	Cutler	Adam		1		1		2		1					5		
Andover	92	7	Clark	Micah		1	1	1					1				4		
Andover	92	8	Chandler	Hannah Wid									1		2		3		
Andover	92	9	Chandler	Isaac		1		1		2	1		1				6		
Andover	92	10	Cummings	Jonathan		1	2		1	1	1		1				7		
Andover	92	11	Cheever	Peter		1		1	1			1		1			5		
Andover	92	12	Chandler	Bekah Wid			1						1	1			3		
Andover	92	13	Cogswell	Samuel	2			1	1	2		1		1			8		
Andover	92	14	Cummings	Samuel		1	2						1				5		
Andover	92	15	Chandler	John	1		1	1		3			1	1			8		
Andover	92	16	Clark	Lemuel	3			1					1				5		
Andover	92	17	Chandler	Phebe Wid									1	1			2		
Andover	92	18	Carlton	Peter		1	1		1			2		1			6		
Andover	92	19	Carlton	Daniel				2				1		2			5		
Andover	92	20	Carlton	Ezekiel		1	2		1	1		1	2	1			9		
Andover	92	21	Carlton	Christopher			1	1		1	1		1				5		
Andover	92	22	Carlton	Daniel Junr	2	1	1	1		1	1	1	1				9		
Andover	92	23	Carlton	Dean	1	1		1				1	1				5		
Andover	92	24	Carlton	Michael			1			1		1	1				4		
Andover	92	25	Carlton	Israel	1			1			1		1				4		
Andover	92	26	Cazneau	Isaac			1						1				2		
Andover	92	27	Cummings	Deborah Wid						2	1		1				4		
Andover	92	28	Carlton	Amos	1			1		1		1					4		
Andover	92	29	Curtise	Israel	2	1			1	3		1	1				9		
Andover	92	30	Chandler	Joshua		1		1	1	2		1	1	1			8		
Andover	92	31	Crosby	Simon				1						1			2		
Andover	92	32	Crosby	John	4			1		1							7		
Andover	92	33	Chandler	Abiel	2	1	1	1	1	2		1	3	1			13		
Andover	92	34	Clark	Abijah			3		1	1	1			1			8		
Andover	92	35	Chase	Enoch		2		1		1		1		1			6		
Andover	92	36	Clark	Thomas		1		2				1		1			5		
Andover	92	37	Cochran	James	2	2			1	3	1	1		1			11		
Andover	92	38	Chandler	James	2	2		1		2	1	1	1				10		
Andover	92	39	Chandler	Zebadiah	2	1	1		2	2	1	2		1			12		
Andover	93	1	Chandler	Joseph	2	1	1	1		2	1		1				9		
Andover	93	2	Crosby	Timothy			1					1					2		
Andover	93	3	Clark	Samuel	1	1	1		1		1		1				6		
Andover	93	4	Corey	Ephraim				1					1				2		
Andover	93	5	Corey	Mary									1				1		
Andover	93	6	McCrobia	William			1			1		1					3		
Andover	93	7	Dilliway	William			1	1				1		1			4		
Andover	93	8	Duntenn	Nathanael	4			1		2	2		1				10		
Andover	93	9	Delap	John				1					1				2		
Andover	93	10	Davidson	Phinehas		1											1		
Andover	93	11	Dole	Casar											3		3		
Andover	93	12	Dane	John	1			2	2	1		1	1	2			10		
Andover	93	13	Dane	Joseph		1			1					2			4		
Andover	93	14	Dane	James		1		1					1				3		
Andover	93	15	Downing	Palfrey	2		1	1			2		1				7		
Andover	93	16	Durant	Amos	1	1			1	1	1	2	1				8		
Andover	93	17	Dane	Moses	1			1		3		1	1				7		
Andover	93	18	Farnum	Isaac		1	1		1	1		3		1			8		
Andover	93	19	Farnum	Isaac Jr				1		1		1					3		
Andover	93	20	Foster	Daniel 3d		1	1					2	2	1			7		
Andover	93	21	Frost	William	2	1			1	2	1	1	1				9		
Andover	93	22	Fowler	Dolly Wid	1								1	1			3		
Andover	93	23	Foster	David			1		1			1		1			4		
Andover	93	24	Foster	Charles			1	1		1	1		1	1			6		
Andover	93	25	Frye	Phillip		1		1				2	2				6		
Andover	93	26	Freeman	Cato											7		7		
Andover	93	27	French	Jonathan Revd		5	2		1	1		2		2	2		15		
Andover	93	28	Foster	William	6	11		1	1			2		1			22		
Andover	93	29	Fisk	John			1	1	1								4		

TOWN	PG#	LN#	LAST NAME	FIRST NAME	FREE WHITE MALES					FREE WHITE FEMALES					TOTAL ALL OTHER	TOTAL SLAVES	TOTALS	DISTRICT/ TOWNSHIP	NOTES
					under 10	10 to 16	16 to 26	26 to 45	45 and over	under 10	10 to 16	16 to 26	26 to 45	45 and over					
Andover	93	30	Foster	Jacob		1	1		2	1	2		2	2			11		
Andover	93	31	Foster	Joseph				1		1	1		1				4		
Andover	93	32	Foster	Daniel	1		4	1		2		1	1				10		
Andover	93	33	Foster	Davis		1		1		1		1					4		
Andover	93	34	Faulkner	Abiel		1	1	1				1		2			6		
Andover	93	35	Frye	Elizabeth Wid										1			1		
Andover	94	1	Foster	John 3d				1		1			1				3		
Andover	94	2	Flood	William	1			1		1	1	1		1			6		
Andover	94	3	Follambee	Moody			1										1		
Andover	94	4	Farnum	Benjmain				1			1	2	1	1			6		
Andover	94	5	Farnum	John	2			1		1		1		1			6		
Andover	94	6	Farnum	Sarah Wid										1			1		
Andover	94	7	Farnum	Peter	3	1		1		1		1		1			8		
Andover	94	8	Farnum	Daniel		1		1		1	2	1		1			7		
Andover	94	9	Farnum	Jedediah		2	1	1				1		1			6		
Andover	94	10	Farnum	Jedediah Jr		1		1		1		1					4		
Andover	94	11	Farnum	Jacob		2				1		2					5		
Andover	94	12	Farnum	Moses		1											1		
Andover	94	13	Farnum	James	1	1	1		1	1	1	1					8		
Andover	94	14	Farnum	Timothy	2	1		1		3	1		1				9		
Andover	94	15	Farnum	Benja Jr		1		1		3		1	1				7		
Andover	94	16	Farington	Phillip		2		1	1	1		2		1			8		
Andover	94	17	Farington	Benja		1				2		1					4		
Andover	94	18	Fuller	Abijah		2		1			1		1				5		
Andover	94	19	Faulkner	Hannah Wid								1		1			2		
Andover	94	20	Faulkner	Daniel			2	1			1			1			5		
Andover	94	21	Fish	Benjamin	3	1		1		2				1			8		
Andover	94	22	Foster	William Junr			2	1	1				1	3			8		
Andover	94	23	Foster	Simeon		1	1	1					1	1			5		
Andover	94	24	Foster	John	1			1		3	1	1	1				8		
Andover	94	25	Foster	Nathan	2		1	1		3		1	1				9		
Andover	94	26	Foster	Daniel Junr	2		1	1		1		1	1				7		
Andover	94	27	Foster	Andrew				1						1			2		
Andover	94	28	Foster	Peter		2	1	1		3			1				8		
Andover	94	29	Frye	James			1	1				1		1			4		
Andover	94	30	Frye	John	1			1			1	2		1			6		
Andover	94	31	Frye	Joshua	1			1		2			1				5		
Andover	94	32	Frye	Peter			1			2			1				4		
Andover	94	33	Frye	John Junr	1			1			1	1		2			6		
Andover	94	34	Frye	John 3rd	3	1		1		3	2	1	1	1			13		
Andover	94	35	Frye	Sarah Wid										1			1		
Andover	94	36	Frye	Samuel Junr	1			1		1			1				4		
Andover	94	37	Frye	Samuel				1						1			2		
Andover	95	1	Frye	Theophilus	3	2	1		1	2		1		1			11		
Andover	95	2	Frye	Samuel 3rd	2			1		3			1				7		
Andover	95	3	Frye	Enoch	1		1					1					3		
Andover	95	4	Frye	Amos			1										1		
Andover	95	5	Frye	Joseph				1		1			1				3		
Andover	95	6	Frye	Timothy		1		1	1	2			2				7		
Andover	95	7	Foster	Gideon	2			1		1		2		1			7		
Andover	95	8	Furbush	Simeon		1		1			1		1				4		
Andover	95	9	Furbush	Solomon	1		1			1			3	1			7		
Andover	95	10	Flint	Samuel				1					1				2		
Andover	95	11	Flint	John	2	1		1		1		2					7		
Andover	95	12	French	Jacob	2	2	1	1			1	1	1				9		
Andover	95	13	French	Peter	1			1		1			1				4		
Andover	95	14	Foster	John Junr				1					1				2		
Andover	95	15	Grainger	Sarah Wid									1	1			2		
Andover	95	16	Griffen	Joseph			1										1		
Andover	95	17	Gardner	Jonathan	1	1	2		1				1	4			10		
Andover	95	18	Gage	Nathanael	1		1	1		4		1	1				9		
Andover	95	19	Goldsmith	William		2	2	1						1			6		
Andover	95	20	Gray	Thomas	2		1	1			1		1				6		
Andover	95	21	Gray	David	1	1		1		1	1		2				7		
Andover	95	22	Goldsmith	Benja		1	1	1		1	1	1	2				8		
Andover	95	23	Goldsmith	Jeremiah	2			1		4		1	1				9		
Andover	95	24	Goldsmith	Zacheus	2	1		1		3	1		1				9		
Andover	95	25	Griffin	Jonathan	2		1	1		1			1	1			7		
Andover	95	26	Griffin	William Junr			1						1				2		
Andover	95	27	Goodhue	Phineas	2	1		1		1				1			6		
Andover	95	28	Gray	Daniel	4	1		1		1	1		1	1			10		
Andover	95	29	Goldsmith	John	2	1	1			1		1					6		
Andover	95	30	Griffin	William				1				1	1	1			4		
Andover	95	31	Griffin	Daniel			2						1				3		
Andover	95	32	Gleason	Jonathan		1	1						1	1			4		
Andover	95	33	Holt	Phebe Wid		1	2					1		1	1		6		
Andover	95	34	Holt	Nathanel Junr	3			1		2			1				7		
Andover	96	1	Hill	John	3		1	1		1	2		1				9		
Andover	96	2	Holt	George	2			1		4			1				11		

14

TOWN	PG#	LN#	LAST NAME	FIRST NAME	FREE WHITE MALES					FREE WHITE FEMALES					TOTAL ALL OTHER	TOTAL SLAVES	TOTALS	DISTRICT/ TOWNSHIP	NOTES
					under 10	10 to 16	16 to 26	26 to 45	45 and over	under 10	10 to 16	16 to 26	26 to 45	45 and over					
Andover	96	3	Holt	Joseph Junr	2			1					1				4		
Andover	96	4	Holt	Jonathan				1			1		1				3		
Andover	96	5	Holt	Dane	1		1	1	1		1	1	1				7		
Andover	96	6	Holt	Joseph			1		2	1		1	1				6		
Andover	96	7	Holt	Abiel Junr			1						1				2		
Andover	96	8	Holt	James Junr			1		1	2		2	1				7		
Andover	96	9	Holt	Isaac Junr	2			1	1	3			1	1			9		
Andover	96	10	Holt	David	1		1		1		1	1	1				6		
Andover	96	11	Holt	Abiel				1		1			1				3		
Andover	96	12	Holt	Timothy	1	2			1	1	2		1				8		
Andover	96	13	Holt	Peter			1		1			1	1				4		
Andover	96	14	Holt	Ezra	1			1		1			1	1			5		
Andover	96	15	Holt	Abigail Wid	2								1				3		
Andover	96	16	Holt	Henry	2			1		1			1				6		
Andover	96	17	Haywood	Nehemiah		1		1		1	2		1				6		
Andover	96	18	Hardy	Ezekiel				1					1				2		
Andover	96	19	Houghton	Euclid	3	1		1		2	1		1				9		
Andover	96	20	Hall	Christa B. Wid						1			1				2		
Andover	96	21	Holt	John				1					1	2			4		
Andover	96	22	Holt	Kimball		1						2					3		
Andover	96	23	Hawley	William		1	1	1		2			1				6		
Andover	96	24	Harden	John	1			2		2			1				6		
Andover	96	25	Holt	David Junr				1					1				2		
Andover	96	26	Holt	Nathl				1					1				2		
Andover	96	27	Holt	James			1		2			1		2			6		
Andover	96	28	Holt	Joshua Esq	1	2		1	1			2		1			8		
Andover	96	29	Holt	Zebadiah	2	2		1		1	1		1				8		
Andover	96	30	Hunt	Reul			1		1	1	1	1					5		
Andover	96	31	Hardy	James		1	1		1					1			4		
Andover	96	32	Hardy	John			1						2				3		
Andover	96	33	Hardy	Ezekiel Junr			3	1		1		3	4				12		
Andover	96	34	Holt	Isaac			1					1	1				3		
Andover	96	35	Hill	William	1			1					1				3		
Andover	96	36	Hunt	Anna Wid		1							1				2		
Andover	96	37	Hazeltine	Botfer						1			1				2		
Andover	97	1	Johnson	Samuel		1		1	1			4		1			8		
Andover	97	2	Johnson	Peter		1			1				1				3		
Andover	97	3	Johnson	Benjamin	2	1	1	1		1		1	2	1			10		
Andover	97	4	Johnson	Joshua	3	1	1	1		1	1		1				9		
Andover	97	5	Johnson	Asa	2			1		2			1	1			7		
Andover	97	6	Johnson	Samuel Jr	1			1					1				3		
Andover	97	7	Johnson	Edmund		1				1			1				3		
Andover	97	8	Johnson	Stephen				1						1			2		
Andover	97	9	Jones	Jacob		1		1	1			2		1			6		
Andover	97	10	Jenkins	Samuel			2					3		1			6		
Andover	97	11	Jenkins	Benja	1	2	1	1			1	1	1				8		
Andover	97	12	Jenkins	Joel	2	1	1		1	1	1	1		1			9		
Andover	97	13	Jones	Nathan	2			1		2	1		1				7		
Andover	97	14	Jordan	Richard			1			1			1				4		
Andover	97	15	Ingals	Henry			1	1	1			1	1	1	1		7		
Andover	97	16	Ingals	John		1		1	1			2	1				6		
Andover	97	17	Ingals	Jonathan	2			1		1		1	1				6		
Andover	97	18	Ingals	Elizabeth Wid									2				2		
Andover	97	19	Ingals	Lydia Wid						2		1	1				4		
Andover	97	20	Ingals	Hutchinson	1			1				4	1				7		
Andover	97	21	Johnson	William	2		2		1	3	1			2			11		
Andover	97	22	Johnson	Ebenezer				1		1			1	1			4		
Andover	97	23	Johnson	Mary		1							1	1			3		
Andover	97	24	Jenkins	Benja Jr	2		2	1				1	1				8		
Andover	97	25	Johnson	Jacob	1		1		1			2	1				6		
Andover	97	26	Ingals	Ezra			1	1				1					3		
Andover	97	27	Johnson	James	1			1				1		1			4		
Andover	97	28	Ingals	Isaac				1					1				2		
Andover	97	29	Johnson	Phillip	3	1			1	1	1		1				8		
Andover	98	1	Kitteridge	Thomas			4		1	1	1	1	1	1	4		14		
Andover	98	2	Kitteridge	John	1		1	1				2	1				6		
Andover	98	3	Kimball	Moses Junr				1		2	1	1		1			6		
Andover	98	4	Kimball	William	1		2					1					4		
Andover	98	5	Kneeland	John		2			1			1		1			5		
Andover	98	6	Kimball	Moses			1		1			1	1				4		
Andover	98	7	Kimball	John				1				3		1	1		6		
Andover	98	8	Kimball	Thomas			1			1		1					3		
Andover	98	9	Kimball	Daniel	2	2			1		2	1	1				10		
Andover	98	10	Kimball	Esther Wid									2				2		
Andover	98	11	Kendall	Ephraim	3	2			1	1		1	2	1			11		
Andover	98	12	Lee	John		2			1			1		1	1		6		
Andover	98	13	Lovejoy	Isaac				2		1			1	1			5		
Andover	98	14	Lovejoy	Joshua				1					1				2		
Andover	98	15	Lovejoy	Joseph		2		1			1	1					6		
Andover	98	16	Lovejoy	Isaac 3rd	3		1	1		1		2	1	1			10		

15

TOWN	PG#	LN#	LAST NAME	FIRST NAME	FREE WHITE MALES under 10	10 to 16	16 to 26	26 to 45	45 and over	FREE WHITE FEMALES under 10	10 to 16	16 to 26	26 to 45	45 and over	TOTAL ALL OTHER	TOTAL SLAVES	TOTALS	DISTRICT/ TOWNSHIP	NOTES
Andover	98	17	Lovejoy	John			1										1		
Andover	98	18	Lovejoy	Nathaniel Esq	1		1	1				1	1				5		
Andover	98	19	Lacy	Ephraim	2		1	1			2	1	1				8		
Andover	98	20	Lacy	John		1		1		1	1		1	1			6		
Andover	98	21	Long	John			1		1			1		2			5		
Andover	98	22	Long	John Junr	1			1		1		1					4		
Andover	98	23	Long	Stephen					1								1		
Andover	98	24	Lovejoy	Jeremiah	1		1					1		1			5		
Andover	98	25	Lovejoy	Isaac Junr	1	2		1	1	2	1		1	1			10		
Andover	98	26	Lovejoy	Ebenezer	4		1					1					6		
Andover	98	27	Lummus	Joseph	4			1					1				7		
Andover	98	28	Merrill	Ebenz	1		1	1		2			1	1			7		
Andover	98	29	Marble	Cyrus			1	1	1	1		1	2	1			8		
Andover	98	30	Montgomery	Alexander		1		1						1			3		
Andover	98	31	Meacham	Benja	2		1	1		1		1					6		
Andover	98	32	March	Daniel			1										1		
Andover	98	33	Merrill	Benja			1										1		
Andover	98	34	McLaughlin	Mary	2								1				3		
Andover	98	35	Manning	Thomas	1	4	1		1			1		1			9		
Andover	99	1	Mooar	Isaac		1		1		2				1			5		
Andover	99	2	Mooar	Martha Wid								1		1			2		
Andover	99	3	Moary	Thomas	1			1		1			1				4		
Andover	99	4	Martin	Joseph				1						1			2		
Andover	99	5	Mason	Robert			1						1				2		
Andover	99	6	Martin	Solomon	2			1		3	1		1				8		
Andover	99	7	Mooar	Timothy				1					1				2		
Andover	99	8	Mare	Isaac				1					1	1			3		
Andover	99	9	Mare	Jonathan	2		1			1			1				5		
Andover	99	10	Merrill	Enoch	1			1		3	2		1				8		
Andover	99	11	Merrill	John		1		1				3		1			6		
Andover	99	12	Merrill	John Junr	1			1		3		1					6		
Andover	99	13	Malcoy	John				1						1			2		
Andover	99	14	Marshall	Jacob	1	1		1	1			1		1			6		
Andover	99	15	Manning	Thomas Jr		1											1		
Andover	99	16	Noyes	Ward				1		2	2	1		1			7		
Andover	99	17	Noyes	Timothy			1	1						1			3		
Andover	99	18	Noyes	Nicholas			1						1				2		
Andover	99	19	Newman	Mark	1	1		1			1		1				5		
Andover	99	20	Nicholson	Francis				1			1		1				3		
Andover	99	21	Nichols	John		1		1		1			1				4		
Andover	99	22	Nichols	John Junr	2			1		1		1	1	1			7		
Andover	99	23	Nichols	Phillip			1			1			1				3		
Andover	99	24	Noyes	Aaron	1	2	1	1		2	1	1	1				10		
Andover	99	25	Osgood	Peter		1	2	1					1	1			6		
Andover	99	26	Osgood	Timothy Junr	4		1	1		1	2	1		1			11		
Andover	99	27	Osgood	George	2		2	1		1	1	1	1				9		
Andover	99	28	Osgood	Peter Junr	1	3	1		1	2	2	4	1				15		
Andover	99	29	Osgood	Timothy		1	1	1	1		1	2	1	2			10		
Andover	99	30	Osgood	Huldah Wid										1			1		
Andover	99	31	Osgood	Samuel			1	1			1	1	1				5		
Andover	99	32	Osgood	Thomas	1		2	1		3			1				8		
Andover	99	33	Osgood	Jacob		1	2	1			1	1					6		
Andover	99	34	Osgood	Aaron			1						1				2		
Andover	99	35	Parker	Asa			1	2	1	2	1		1	2			10		
Andover	99	36	Parker	Michael		1	2	1			1	2	1	1			9		
Andover	100	1	Peters	Andrew			1	1	2			1	1				6		
Andover	100	2	Peters	Joseph	3			1		1			2	1			8		
Andover	100	3	Poor	John Junr		2	2		2			2		2			10		
Andover	100	4	Poor	Abraham		1	2	1		1	2			1			8		
Andover	100	5	Poor	Isaac	3			1		2			1				7		
Andover	100	6	Poor	Theodore	1			1		3		1					6		
Andover	100	7	Poor	Ebenz	3		1	1		1			1				7		
Andover	100	8	Poor	Stephen	1	1		1		1		1	1				6		
Andover	100	9	Poor	Lemuel	1	1		1		1			1				5		
Andover	100	10	Poor	Peter				1						1			2		
Andover	100	11	Poor	Susanna										1			1		
Andover	100	12	Phillips	John Junr			4			1	2	2	1				11		
Andover	100	13	Phillips	John		1		1	1			1	1	1			6		
Andover	100	14	Peabody	Mary										1			1		
Andover	100	15	Peabody	Deborah Wid										1			1		
Andover	100	16	Phelps	Joseph				1		1				1			3		
Andover	100	17	Phelps	Elisha			1						1				2		
Andover	100	18	Phillips	Samuel Esq Honble		1	2	2	1			1	2	1			10		
Andover	100	19	Poor	Daniel		6	3		1		1	2		1	1		15		
Andover	100	20	Parson	Abiel	1	1		1		2		1					6		
Andover	100	21	Phelps	Joseph Junr				1		1			1				3		
Andover	100	22	Parker	Carlton	1			1	1	1	1		1				6		
Andover	100	23	Parker	James				1					1		1		3		
Andover	100	24	Parker	Kendall		1							1				2		
Andover	100	25	Phelps	Isaac			1	1					2				4		
Andover	100	26	Pitcher	Wm						3			1				4		
Andover	100	27	Patten	Elijah			1			1			1	1			4		
Andover	100	28	Page	Daniel				1				1		2			4		
Andover	100	29	Parker	Isaac	2		1		1	4	3		1				12		
Andover	100	30	Parker	Jonathan				1	1	1		1		2			5		
Andover	100	31	Parker	Benja				1					1				2		
Andover	100	32	Phelps	Joshua	2	1		1					1	1			6		
Andover	100	33	Phelps	Henry		1	1		1			1		1			5		
Andover	100	34	Phelps	Mary Wid							1	1		1			3		

TOWN	PG#	LN#	HEADS OF HOUSEHOLD LAST NAME	HEADS OF HOUSEHOLD FIRST NAME	FREE WHITE MALES under 10	FREE WHITE MALES 10 to 16	FREE WHITE MALES 16 to 26	FREE WHITE MALES 26 to 45	FREE WHITE MALES 45 and over	FREE WHITE FEMALES under 10	FREE WHITE FEMALES 10 to 16	FREE WHITE FEMALES 16 to 26	FREE WHITE FEMALES 26 to 45	FREE WHITE FEMALES 45 and over	TOTAL ALL OTHER	TOTAL SLAVES	TOTALS	DISTRICT/ TOWNSHIP	NOTES
Andover	100	35	Robinson	John	1	2	1	1	1	1		2	1	1			11		
Andover	101	1	Richardson	Caleb	1			1		2		1	1				6		
Andover	101	2	Russel	John			1		1	1		2		1			6		
Andover	101	3	Russel	Uriah		1	3		1	1	1		1				8		
Andover	101	4	Russel	John Junr	1		1					1					3		
Andover	101	5	Richardson	William	2	1	1	1		2			1				8		
Andover	101	6	Russel	Abigail Wid										2			2		
Andover	101	7	Russel	Sarah Wid										1			1		
Andover	101	8	Russel	Prudence Wid									1	1			2		
Andover	101	9	Rea	Daniel		1						1					2		
Andover	101	10	Richardson	Abigail	1								1				2		
Andover	101	11	Rand	Ebenz				1						1	1		3		
Andover	101	12	Robinson	John Junr		1						1					2		
Andover	101	13	Stevens	Lydia Wid		1								2			3		
Andover	101	14	Stevens	Mary Wid										1			1		
Andover	101	15	Stevens	James	2	1	2	1		1	1	1					9		
Andover	101	16	Sargeant	Benja	2	1		1		3			1				8		
Andover	101	17	Stevens	Timothy		1		2		2		1	1	1			8		
Andover	101	18	Stevens	Peter	2	1		1		1	1		1				7		
Andover	101	19	Stevens	Phebe									1				1		
Andover	101	20	Symmes	William Revd		1		1		1			1		1		5		
Andover	101	21	Stevens	Phillip			1			1			1				3		
Andover	101	22	Stevens	Jonathan Junr	1		1	1		2			1				6		
Andover	101	23	Stevens	Amos		2	2		1			1	1	1			8		
Andover	101	24	Stevens	Jonathan	3	1			1	1	2		1				9		
Andover	101	25	Spafford	Moody	3		1		1	2	1	1	1				10		
Andover	101	26	Spafford	Isaac	3	1	1	1		1			1	1			9		
Andover	101	27	Stickney	John		1	1		1			1		1			5		
Andover	101	28	Stevens	Edward	2			1		2			1				6		
Andover	101	29	Stevens	Joseph	1		1		1	1	1		1				6		
Andover	101	30	Swift	Jonathan	1		3	1				1	1				7		
Andover	101	31	Stevens	David	1			1		1			1				4		
Andover	101	32	Stevens	Thomas	1			1						1			3		
Andover	101	33	Stevens	Ebenz		1			1	1	1			1			5		
Andover	101	34	Stevens	Joseph Junr	3			1				1	1				6		
Andover	101	35	Stevens	Abigail									1	1			2		
Andover	101	36	Swan	Robert			2		1	4		1	1				9		
Andover	101	37	Smith	Eliakim	2		1	1					1				5		
Andover	101	38	Shattuck	Isaac Junr	3	2		1		1	1		1				9		
Andover	101	39	Stevens	Simeon		1		1	1	2		1	1	1			8		
Andover	102	1	Stevens	Samuel Junr	2	1	3	1	1				1	1			10		
Andover	102	2	Stevens	Joshua	3	1		1		2	2		1				10		
Andover	102	3	Shattuck	Jebadiah		2			1			2		2			7		
Andover	102	4	Shattuck	Isaac	2			1	1				1	2			7		
Andover	102	5	Shattuck	Joseph	2			1		1			1				5		
Andover	102	6	Shattuck	Peter	1		1	1		1		1		1			6		
Andover	102	7	Stickney	Abraham	3	1	2	1		1		2	1				11		
Andover	102	8	Tyler	Jonathan			1	1		3	1	1					7		
Andover	102	9	Thompson	John				1		2			1				4		
Andover	102	10	Town	Asa	4	1	5	1		1		1	1				14		
Andover	102	11	Tucker	William	1	1		1		3			1				7		
Andover	102	12	Tucker	Martha Wid									1	1			2		
Andover	102	13	Town	Nathan	1	2			1	1	1	1					7		
Andover	102	14	Town	Peter		1	3		1	1	2		1				9		
Andover	102	15	Town	Simeon			1			3		1	1				6		
Andover	102	16	Town	Aaron				1				1		1			3		
Andover	102	17	Town	Aaron Junr	1			1				1	1				4		
Andover	102	18	Town	Elijah	2	1	1					1	1				6		
Andover	102	19	Trow	John Junr	1		1	1		3	1		1	1			9		
Andover	102	20	Town	Mary								1	1	1			3		
Andover	102	21	Thurton	Stephen	1			1		2			1				5		
Andover	102	22	Trow	John	3	1	1		1		2	2		2			12		
Andover	102	23	Trull	Levi			1			1		1					3		
Andover	102	24	Townsend	Dennis	2		1	1		3			1				8		
Andover	102	25	Trow	Dudley	1		1			1	1		1				5		
Andover	102	26	Upton	Abiel	3	1		1			1		2				8		
Andover	102	27	Wilson	Joshua	2	3			1			1	1		3		11		
Andover	102	28	Woods	John			1			1	1						3		
Andover	102	29	Wardwell	Nathan	2			1		3			1				7		
Andover	102	30	Wardwell	Simon	3	2	2		1	3		1	1				13		
Andover	102	31	Woodbridge	Benja	3	1	1			1	2		1				9		
Andover	103	1	Woodbridge	Dudley	2	1		1		2			1				7		
Andover	103	2	Wardwell	Daniel		1				1		1					3		
Andover	103	3	Wardwell	Ezekiel	1		1	2		1	1			2			8		
Andover	103	4	Walker	Abbot	1			1		1			1				4		
Andover	103	5	Wight	John				1						1			2		
Andover	103	6	Wardwell	Joshua	1			1						1			3		
Andover	103	7	Wardwell	Ruth									1				1		
Andover	103	8	Wardwell	Jeremiah			1										1		
Andover	103	9	Wood	David				1				1	1	1			4		
Andover	103	10	Wardwell	John	2			1					2				5		
Andover	103	11	Wood	John	1			1		2	2						7		
Andover	103	12	Wood	Obadiah		1			1					1			3		
Andover	103	13	Winchester	Samuel	2	1		1		2	2		1				9		
Andover	103	14	Woodberry	Wm			1	1				1		1			4		
Andover	103	15	Wilkins	Moses	1		1	1		3		2					8		
Andover	103	16	Ames	Prince											7		7		
Andover	103	17	Cordaner	Amos											4		4		
Andover	103	18	Freman	Cesar											7		7		
Andover	103	19	Johnson	Benito											5		5		

TOWN	PG#	LN#	LAST NAME	FIRST NAME	FREE WHITE MALES					FREE WHITE FEMALES					TOTAL ALL OTHER	TOTAL SLAVES	TOTALS	DISTRICT/ TOWNSHIP	NOTES
					under 10	10 to 16	16 to 26	26 to 45	45 and over	under 10	10 to 16	16 to 26	26 to 45	45 and over					
Andover	103	20	Middleton	Douglas											1		1		
Andover	103	21	Walker	Prince											3		3		
Andover	103	22	Marshall	Jeremiah			1						1		2		4		
Andover	103	23	Richardson	Allen											6		6		
Andover	103	24	Simpson	Cesar											2		2		
Andover	103	25	Elisha	John								1			2		3		
Andover	103	26	Toby	Dinah											2		2		
Andover	103	27		Boos											5		5		
Andover	103	28	Lovejoy	Momp											3		3		
Andover	103	29	Poor	Nancy											2		2		

TOWN	PG#	LN#	LAST NAME	FIRST NAME	FREE WHITE MALES					FREE WHITE FEMALES					TOTAL ALL OTHER	TOTAL SLAVES	TOTALS	DISTRICT/ TOWNSHIP	NOTES
					under 10	10 to 16	16 to 26	26 to 45	45 and over	under 10	10 to 16	16 to 26	26 to 45	45 and over					
Beverly	289	1	Thorndike	Israel Esq	6	3			1				3		1		14		
Beverly	289	2	Oliver	Daniel Rvd		1			1	4	1		1		2		10		
Beverly	289	3	McKeen	Joseph Rvd	1	2		1			1	1	1				7		
Beverly	289	4	Fisher	Joshua Revd				1				1	1				3		
Beverly	289	5	Dane	Nathan Esq			2		1			2		1			6		
Beverly	289	6	Cleaver	Benjamin		1			1				2	1			5		
Beverly	289	7	Stephens	Anne			2						2	1			5		
Beverly	289	8	Stephens	John	1	1		1		2	1		1				7		
Beverly	289	9	Busby	William		1	1	1	1	1	2		3				10		
Beverly	289	10	Woodbery	Thomas		1			1		1	2		1			6		
Beverly	289	11	Woodbery	Thomas Jun	1		1				1	1					4		
Beverly	289	12	Heman	William Esq	2	1			1	2	1	2	1	1	1		12		
Beverly	289	13	Batchelder	Josiah Esq					1				1	1	1		4		
Beverly	289	14	Batchelder	Josiah Jr			1			1			1				3		
Beverly	289	15	Wood	Joseph		1	2		1			1		1			6		
Beverly	289	16	Herrick	Asa		1		1	1			1		1			5		
Beverly	289	17	Wood	Judith									1				1		
Beverly	289	18	Beckford	Benjamin		2	2	1		2	1	1	1				10		
Beverly	289	19	Porter	Hannah										1			1		
Beverly	289	20	Smith	Hasadiah				1					1	1			3		
Beverly	289	21	Smith	Francis		1	1		1				1	1			5		
Beverly	289	22	Pickett	Joseph Jr	2			1		1		1					5		
Beverly	289	23	Pickett	Joseph				1	1	1		1					4		
Beverly	290	1	Smith	*	1			1					1				3		
Beverly	290	2	Hovey	Thomas			3	1	1			2	1				8		
Beverly	290	3	Smith	James			2	1		2		1					6		
Beverly	290	4	Woodberry	Benja 3d	2		1					1					4		
Beverly	290	5	Webber	Nathll		1				2		1					4		
Beverly	290	6	Smith	Mary						1		1					2		
Beverly	290	7	Batchelder	Joseph	2			1				1					4		
Beverly	290	8	Porter	John		1	1				1	1					4		
Beverly	290	9	Clark	Peter	3			1				1					5		
Beverly	290	10	Grind	Robert	2			1		2		1					6		
Beverly	290	11	Herrick	James				1		1		1					3		
Beverly	290	12	Beckford	Elizabeth				1					1				2		
Beverly	290	13	Baker	Eunice	1	1				1		1					4		
Beverly	290	14	Herrick	Deborah		1						1	1				3		
Beverly	290	15	Pickett	John	2	1	1		1	1	2		1				9		
Beverly	290	16	Morgan	William 2d		1		2					1				4		
Beverly	290	17	Evelith	Anna		1	2				1		1				5		
Beverly	290	18	Tayler	Asa			1						1				2		
Beverly	290	19	Foster	Edward		1			1	1	2	1					6		
Beverly	290	20	Smith	Asa	2			1		1							4		
Beverly	290	21	Goodridge	Hannah			2	1					1				4		
Beverly	290	22	Twess	Robert		1			1			2	1	1			6		
Beverly	290	23	Raymond	Mary						2		1					3		
Beverly	290	24	Kinneson	Aphria									1				1		
Beverly	290	25	Twiss	Mehitable								1	1				2		
Beverly	290	26	Laskey	James	1		1					1					3		
Beverly	290	27	Trask	Osman			3		1	2		3	1				10		
Beverly	290	28	Batchelder	Eliza	1					1		1					3		
Beverly	290	29	Verry	Mary	3							1					4		
Beverly	290	30	Robertson	John			1				1		1				3		
Beverly	290	31	Elliott	Andrew	1		3		1		2		2		1		10		
Beverly	290	32	Woodbery	Nicholas		2	3		1	2	1		2				11		
Beverly	290	33	Prince	John	2			1		1	1		1				6		
Beverly	290	34	Woodbery	Curtice			1		1			2		1	2		7		
Beverly	290	35	Thissel	Paul	2			1		1			1				5		
Beverly	290	36	Thissel	Jeffrey	1	1	2	1		1	1	1	1				9		
Beverly	290	37	Thissel	Sarah		1								1			2		
Beverly	290	38		Pompe Negro											4		4		
Beverly	290	39	Patch	Nicholas			2	1		1	1		1				6		
Beverly	290	40	Thissel	Mary						1			1	2			4		
Beverly	290	41	Saxby	James		1	1		1			1		1			5		
Beverly	290	42	Standly	Robert		1	1		1		1			1			5		
Beverly	290	43	Thissel	Sarah 2d	1					3	1						5		
Beverly	291	1	Herrick	Anna			1				1		2	1			5		
Beverly	291	2	Dodge	Jonathan				1					1				2		
Beverly	291	3	Dodge	Cornelius	1	1	3		1	1		2		1			10		
Beverly	291	4	Woodbery	Sarah	3	2	1				1		2	1			10		
Beverly	291	5	Clark	John				1				1	1				3		
Beverly	291	6	Clark	Jonathan	1			1					1				3		
Beverly	291	7	Arnold	Robert Negro											4		4		
Beverly	291	8	Thissel	Ebenezer		1	1		1			1	1	1			7		
Beverly	291	9	Cleaver	Titus											5		5		
Beverly	291	10	Cleaver	Andrew	1	1	2	1	1	1	1		3	1			12		
Beverly	291	11	Dodge	Israel	1			1		1	1		1				5		
Beverly	291	12	Lefeaver	Anna		1	1					1	1	1			5		
Beverly	291	13	Lefeaver	Amos	1			1					1				3		

TOWN	PG#	LN#	LAST NAME	FIRST NAME	FREE WHITE MALES					FREE WHITE FEMALES					TOTAL ALL OTHER	TOTAL SLAVES	TOTALS	DISTRICT/ TOWNSHIP	NOTES
					under 10	10 to 16	16 to 26	26 to 45	45 and over	under 10	10 to 16	16 to 26	26 to 45	45 and over					
Beverly	291	14	Cole	Samuel	2	1			1	1		2	1				8		
Beverly	291	15	Glover	Benjamin	2			1		2			1				6		
Beverly	291	16	Morgan	Abigail	1		1					1	1	1			5		
Beverly	291	17	Morgan	Israel	1	1		1	1				1				5		
Beverly	291	18	Cole	Abigail									1				1		
Beverly	291	19	Woodbery	Mary		1						1	1				3		
Beverly	291	20	Woodbery	William			1					1					2		
Beverly	291	21	Morgan	Josiah				1						2			3		
Beverly	291	22	Morgan	William 3d	2	1	2	1		2			1				9		
Beverly	291	23	Stone	Josiah			1						1				2		
Beverly	291	24	Stone	Josiah Jun	1	1		1		3	1		1				8		
Beverly	291	25	Edward	Robert				1					1				2		
Beverly	291	26	Standly	William			2	1					1				4		
Beverly	291	27	Standly	Timothy	2			1		1			1				5		
Beverly	291	28	Patch	James	1			1			1		1				4		
Beverly	291	29	Bradford	Marian		1							1	1			3		
Beverly	291	30	West	Anna	1	2	2						2	2			9		
Beverly	291	31	Patch	William	2	1		1		2	2		1				9		
Beverly	291	32	Roberts	Mary						1	1		1				3		
Beverly	291	33	Roberts	Nathaniel	1			1				1	1				4		
Beverly	291	34	Standly	Sands	2			1		3			1				7		
Beverly	291	35	Standly	John	1			1		1			1	1			5		
Beverly	291	36	Standly	William Jur	2	1		1		1			1				6		
Beverly	291	37	Butman	Benjamin	2			1		1	2	1	1	1			9		
Beverly	291	38	Grose	George Jun	2			1		1			1				5		
Beverly	291	39	Patch	Joseph	3			1		1			1				6		
Beverly	291	40	Grose	George		1	1						1				3		
Beverly	291	41	Hull	Isaac	2	1	1			2	1		1				8		
Beverly	291	42	Tucker	Henry	1		1			2			1				5		
Beverly	291	43	Standly	David	1			1			1		1				4		
Beverly	291	44	Appleton	Thomas	1		1	1			3		1				7		
Beverly	292	1	Hull	Theophilus			1				2		1				4		
Beverly	292	2	Morgan	Zachariah 2d	2		1	1					3				7		
Beverly	292	3	Corning	Peter			1						1				2		
Beverly	292	4	Smith	Francis Jun	3			1		2			1				7		
Beverly	292	5	Elliott	Andrew Jr		1					1						2		
Beverly	292	6	Creesy	Noah	3			1					1				5		
Beverly	292	7	Herrick	Mary		1							1				2		
Beverly	292	8	Herrick	Thomas	2		1	1		1		1					6		
Beverly	292	9	Roundy	Benja			1	1					1				3		
Beverly	292	10	Smith	William	2		1			1			1				5		
Beverly	292	11	Prince	Mary		1							1				2		
Beverly	292	12	Goodridge	William		1	1	1		2		1					6		
Beverly	292	13	Smith	Ebenz			1	1					1				3		
Beverly	292	14	Newbury	Tryphena						2		1					3		
Beverly	292	15	Batchelder	Nathanl	3	1	1	1		1	1		1		1		10		
Beverly	292	16	Roundy	Robert				1									1		
Beverly	292	17	Burchsted	Henry	4	1	1	1		1	1		1				10		
Beverly	292	18	Trask	Retire	1			1					1	1			4		
Beverly	292	19	Trask	Benja			1						1				2		
Beverly	292	20	Goodridge	Eliza									1				1		
Beverly	292	21	Cole	Eliza									2	2			4		
Beverly	292	22	Trask	Jeremiah	4	3	1	1		1	1		2				13		
Beverly	292	23	Glidden	John	2	1		1					1				5		
Beverly	292	24	Smith	Joseph	4		1	1					1				7		
Beverly	292	25	Smith	Job			1	1						1			3		
Beverly	292	26	Pickard	Ephraim		1	2	1			2		1	1	1		8		
Beverly	292	27	Woodberry	Lucy		1							1	1			3		
Beverly	292	28	Standly	Benja	1	2		1		2			1				7		
Beverly	292	29	Ober	Josiah	1			1		1	2	2	1				8		
Beverly	292	30	Bowers	Ishmael											1		1		
Beverly	292	31	Herrick	William		1	2	1				1		1			6		
Beverly	292	32	Lovett	Joseph			1	1				1	1	1			6		
Beverly	292	33	Woodberry	Asa	1		2		1	1	3			2			10		
Beverly	292	34	McLallan	George			1			2			1				4		
Beverly	292	35	Brown	Simeon	1			1					1				3		
Beverly	292	36	Trask	Osman 2d		2	2	1				1					7		
Beverly	292	37	Woodberry	Martha									1				1		
Beverly	292	38	Toutam	Ruth						1			2				3		
Beverly	292	39	Woodberry	Esther									1				1		
Beverly	292	40	Green	Moses	4	1		1		1	1		1	1			10		
Beverly	292	41	Green	Joanna		2							2	1			5		
Beverly	292	42	Lovett	Eliza		1	1					3	1	1			7		
Beverly	292	43	Lovett	Jonathan H			1			1		1					3		
Beverly	292	44	Lovett	John	1			1		1	1		2				6		
Beverly	292	45	Thorndike	Henry	1	1		1		4	2		1				10		
Beverly	293	1	Stickny	Seilas	2			1					2				5		
Beverly	293	2	Lee	Joanna		3	2			1		2	1				10		
Beverly	293	3	Obear	Zebulon		1	1	2		1		1	2	1			9		

TOWN	PG#	LN#	HEADS OF HOUSEHOLD		FREE WHITE MALES					FREE WHITE FEMALES					TOTAL ALL OTHER	TOTAL SLAVES	TOTALS	DISTRICT/ TOWNSHIP	NOTES
			LAST NAME	FIRST NAME	under 10	10 to 16	16 to 26	26 to 45	45 and over	under 10	10 to 16	16 to 26	26 to 45	45 and over					
Beverly	293	4	Simonds	Thomas			1	1				2		1			5		
Beverly	293	5	Williams	Thomas 2d			1										1		
Beverly	293	6	Morgan	Zachariah	2	1		1		1		1	1				7		
Beverly	293	7	Goodridge	Samuel		1	1	1			1	3	1				8		
Beverly	293	8	Woodberry	Zebulon		1				1		1					3		
Beverly	293	9	Negro	Philip											2		2		
Beverly	293	10	Carries	Alexander		1		1					1				3		
Beverly	293	11	Carries	Thomas		1				1		1					3		
Beverly	293	12	Turkin	Abigail		1							1	1			3		
Beverly	293	13	Wallis	James	2			1		1			1				5		
Beverly	293	14	Smith	Nehemiah			2	1						1			4		
Beverly	293	15	Smith	Ezra			1			3							4		
Beverly	293	16	Green	Joanna 2d	1					2			1				4		
Beverly	293	17	Fornice	David		2	1	1					2	1	1		8		
Beverly	293	18	Babsob	Ruth						1				1			2		
Beverly	293	19	Fisk	John	3	1		1					1	1			7		
Beverly	293	20	Stone	Joanna		1				1	1			1			4		
Beverly	293	21	Knowlton	Mark	1		1			1			1				4		
Beverly	293	22	Standly	Thomas		1							1				2		
Beverly	293	23	Stone	Mary 2d									1	1			2		
Beverly	293	24	Stone	Abner C	2			1		2	1		1				7		
Beverly	293	25	Woodberry	Joseph		1	2	1	1				1	1			7		
Beverly	293	26	Frances	Aaron	2		2	1				1		1			7		
Beverly	293	27	Brown	Asa	1	1		1		1			1				5		
Beverly	293	28	Dodge	Joshua				1			1		1				3		
Beverly	293	29	Brown	Eliza		1	1					1		1			4		
Beverly	293	30	Porter	Billy Esq				1					1				2		
Beverly	293	31	Friend	Hannah										1			1		
Beverly	293	32	Knowlton	Jonathan			1			1			1				3		
Beverly	293	33	Batchelder	William	3			1		1	3		1				9		
Beverly	293	34	Coffin	Abner		1							1				2		
Beverly	293	35	Conant	Samuel Jr				1		2			1				4		
Beverly	293	36	Trow	Josiah	1			1					1				3		
Beverly	293	37	Batchelder	Zachariah	1	2		1		4			1				9		
Beverly	293	38	Batchelder	Mehitable									2				2		
Beverly	293	39	Wyman	Joshua	4		1			3			1				9		
Beverly	293	40	Trask	Bartholomew	1		2	1				1		1			6		
Beverly	293	41	Chipman	Joseph		1	1	2				1	1				6		
Beverly	293	42	Dodge	William		1	1	1		1	1	1	1				7		
Beverly	293	43	Dodge	Asa				2					1				3		
Beverly	293	44	Dodge	Asa R	1		1			2			1				5		
Beverly	293	45	Edwards	Asa B	1		1			2	1						5		
Beverly	293	46	Dodge	Thomas				1		3	1		1				6		
Beverly	293	47	Dodge	Rebecca										2			2		
Beverly	293	48	Edwards	John		1	1	1		1	1		1				6		
Beverly	293	49	Wilkins	Sylester		1				1		1					3		
Beverly	293	50	Edwards	Jacob		1	2	1		1	1		1				7		
Beverly	293	51	Conant	John		2	1	1	1			2	2	1			10		
Beverly	294	1	Perkins	Mary										2			2		
Beverly	294	2	Goodwin	Mary									1	1			2		
Beverly	294	3	Conant	Lot		1		1						1			3		
Beverly	294	4	Conant	Lydia						2	1		1				4		
Beverly	294	5	Dodge	Charles	1	2	1	1				3	1	1			10		
Beverly	294	6	Elliott	William 2d	1	1	1	1		5	1		1	1			12		
Beverly	294	7	Nash	Morish			1			2		1		2			6		
Beverly	294	8	Creesy	John 2nd	1		2			1			1				5		
Beverly	294	9	Herrick	John	1		1						1				3		
Beverly	294	10	Buckston	Anthony				1						1			2		
Beverly	294	11	Woodman	Hannah									1	1			2		
Beverly	294	12	Curtice	William	3			1		3			1				8		
Beverly	294	13	Fisher	Anna									1	1			2		
Beverly	294	14	Dodge	Levi				1					1	1			4		
Beverly	294	15	Trask	Deborah	1								1	1			3		
Beverly	294	16	Trask	Barnabas		1	1	1						1			4		
Beverly	294	17	Dodge	Jacob		1	1		1	2	1		1				7		
Beverly	294	18	Twiss	Dimon C			1			1			1				3		
Beverly	294	19	Woodberry	Hannah		1	2				1		1				5		
Beverly	294	20	Grant	Joseph			1			1			1				3		
Beverly	294	21	Bowles	Rebecca								1	1	1			3		
Beverly	294	22	Cleaver	Benja				1		2			1				4		
Beverly	294	23	Price	Joanna									1				1		
Beverly	294	24	Wallis	Mary		2							1	1			4		
Beverly	294	25	Brown	Walis	1		1			2			2				6		
Beverly	294	26	Allin	John B	1	1		1	1			1	1				6		
Beverly	294	27	Kinney	Israel		1		1		1		1	1				5		
Beverly	294	28	Allin	Daniel	4	1		1		1			1				8		
Beverly	294	29	Champney	Thomas		1		1			1		1				4		
Beverly	294	30	Hill	Peter	1	1		1		2			1	1			7		
Beverly	294	31	Tuck	Samuel	2			1		1			1	1			6		

TOWN	PG#	LN#	HEADS OF HOUSEHOLD LAST NAME	FIRST NAME	FREE WHITE MALES under 10	10 to 16	16 to 26	26 to 45	45 and over	FREE WHITE FEMALES under 10	10 to 16	16 to 26	26 to 45	45 and over	TOTAL ALL OTHER	TOTAL SLAVES	TOTALS	DISTRICT/ TOWNSHIP	NOTES
Beverly	294	32	Glover	Peter		1		1	1			3		1			7		
Beverly	294	33	Rose	Benjamin											2		2		
Beverly	294	34	Cook	William 2d			1			2		1					4		
Beverly	294	35	Dial	Rachel								2		2			4		
Beverly	294	36		Pompe Negro											7		7		
Beverly	294	37	Lovett	Joseph 3d	2			1		2			1				6		
Beverly	294	38	Lovett	William 2d	1			1		2	1		1				6		
Beverly	294	39	Tarbell	William	2				1				1		1		5		
Beverly	294	40	Woodberry	Jeremiah				1					1				2		
Beverly	294	41	Woodberry	Martha									1	2			3		
Beverly	294	42	Presson	Allice	1						1		2	1			5		
Beverly	294	43	Presson	Benjamin	1			1		2			1				5		
Beverly	294	44	Preston	Thankfull										1			1		
Beverly	294	45	Price	John				1						1			2		
Beverly	294	46	Peirce	William			1					1	1				3		
Beverly	294	47	Poland	Joseph				1				1	2	1			5		
Beverly	294	48	Wyat	George		1		1		3	1		1				7		
Beverly	294	49	Pierce	Nicholas			1			2		1					4		
Beverly	294	50	Standly	George				1						1			2		
Beverly	294	51	Peirce	John Jr			1						1				2		
Beverly	294	52	Preston	Elizabeth			1							1			2		
Beverly	294	53	Preston	Richard		1						1					2		
Beverly	294	54	Standly	Robert 2nd	5			1		1	2		1				10		
Beverly	295	1	Standly	Jonathan			1		1	1	1			1			5		
Beverly	295	2	Lascome	Francis W			1			2			1				4		
Beverly	295	3	Smith	Nellie								1		2			3		
Beverly	295	4	Smith	Isaac W			1			1			1				3		
Beverly	295	5	Standly	Nehemiah	1			1		2			1				5		
Beverly	295	6	Woodberry	Hannah			1		1					1			3		
Beverly	295	7	Trout	Abraham	2			1		3	1		1				8		
Beverly	295	8	Obear	Isaac	2			1		1			1				5		
Beverly	295	9	May	James	1			1		2			1	1			6		
Beverly	295	10	Woodberry	Robert	2	1	1		1		1	3		2			11		
Beverly	295	11	Knowlton	Benja 2nd	1	2		1			1		1				6		
Beverly	295	12	Knowlton	Benjamin	2			1		1			1				5		
Beverly	295	13	Perry	Mary			2						1	1			4		
Beverly	295	14	Perry	Robert	1			1					1				3		
Beverly	295	15	Woodberry	Malachi		1			1	1	2	1		1			7		
Beverly	295	16	Ober	Richard			1		1				1	1			4		
Beverly	295	17	Ober	Richard 3d	1			1		3	1		1				7		
Beverly	295	18	Woodberry	James				1					1				2		
Beverly	295	19	Trask	Molly	1									1			2		
Beverly	295	20	Marshel	Timothy	4	1	1		1				1				8		
Beverly	295	21	Preston	Thomas	1			1		1		1					4		
Beverly	295	22	Larcom	Priscill			1							1			2		
Beverly	295	23	Larcom	Henry			1			1		1	1				4		
Beverly	295	24	Mors	William				1		1				1			3		
Beverly	295	25	Roberts	Andrew	1		1	1		3	3		1				10		
Beverly	295	26	Hilton	Benjamin			1			2		1	1	1			6		
Beverly	295	27	Ormon	Asa	2		1					1					4		
Beverly	295	28	Osmond	Jane			1							1			2		
Beverly	295	29	Smith	Jonathan	1	1		1		2			1				6		
Beverly	295	30	Buckman	John			1			1		1	1				4		
Beverly	295	31	Manning	Wm S	1	1			1	3			1				7		
Beverly	295	32	Woodberry	Joseph			1					1					2		
Beverly	295	33	Glidden	Joseph				1					1	1			3		
Beverly	295	34	Cavandish	John			1							1			2		
Beverly	295	35	Roundy	Stephen	2			1					2	2			7		
Beverly	295	36	Hart	Jacob				1		1	2	1	1				6		
Beverly	295	37	Batchelder	Asa	1	2		1		2	1	1	1				9		
Beverly	295	38	Gouldsberry	Joseph			1			1		2					4		
Beverly	295	39	Boison	William			1					1					2		
Beverly	295	40	Low	John	3	1	1		1	2	2		1				11		
Beverly	295	41	Stone	Rachel		1				1	2		1				5		
Beverly	295	42	Foster	Sarah		1						1		1			3		
Beverly	295	43	Fornice	David Jr	2			1		1			1				5		
Beverly	295	44	Wallis	Hezekiah	1					4	1		1				8		
Beverly	295	45	Chapman	Prescilla							1	1		1			3		
Beverly	295	46	Conant	Israel			1						1				2		
Beverly	295	47	Woodbery	Willm C	1			1		2			1				5		
Beverly	295	48	Chapman	Abner	1	1	1	1		2		1	1				8		
Beverly	295	49	Sawyer	Amasa	1	1	2			1			1				6		
Beverly	295	50	Gage	Judith	1								1	2			4		
Beverly	295	51	Moulton	Billy	1		1			1		1					4		
Beverly	295	52	Abbott	Nathl			1	1		1				1			4		
Beverly	296	1	Smith	Benjamin	1		1					1		1			4		
Beverly	296	2	Ellinwood	John	2	1	1	1	1					2			8		
Beverly	296	3	Raymond	Thomas		1	1					2					4		
Beverly	296	4	Smith	Thomas	2			1		1	1		1				6		
Beverly	296	5	Baker	Joseph		1			1					1			3		

TOWN	PG#	LN#	HEADS OF HOUSEHOLD		FREE WHITE MALES					FREE WHITE FEMALES					TOTAL ALL OTHER	TOTAL SLAVES	TOTALS	DISTRICT/ TOWNSHIP	NOTES
			LAST NAME	FIRST NAME	under 10	10 to 16	16 to 26	26 to 45	45 and over	under 10	10 to 16	16 to 26	26 to 45	45 and over					
Beverly	296	6	Ober	Oliver			1						1				2		
Beverly	296	7	Odlin	Samuel					1	3			1				5		
Beverly	296	8	Fornice	John				1		1			2				4		
Beverly	296	9	Obear	Eliza	1					1			1				3		
Beverly	296	10	Baker	Lucy	1	1				1			1				4		
Beverly	296	11	Wallis	John		2	1	1		3	1	1	1				10		
Beverly	296	12	Wallis	Hannah	2	2	2		1	2	1		1				11		
Beverly	296	13	Down	Betsey									2	1			3		
Beverly	296	14	Abbitt	Dudly	3			1		1			1				6		
Beverly	296	15	Mann	Perez	1	1	1	1		3			1				8		
Beverly	296	16	Haskell	Israel	1			1		1			1				4		
Beverly	296	17	Wallis	Ebenezer	1		1	1		2			1				6		
Beverly	296	18	Gouldsberry	Asa				1		2			1				4		
Beverly	296	19	Herrick	James Jr	1		1			3		1	1				7		
Beverly	296	20	Wales	David	2			1		1	1						5		
Beverly	296	21	Grusts	Philip	1		1			1		1					4		
Beverly	296	22	Herrick	Lemmon				1		1	1		1				4		
Beverly	296	23	Raymond	Benjamin		1	1	1					1				4		
Beverly	296	24	Stewart	Mary							1		2				3		
Beverly	296	25	Hatch	John			1						1				2		
Beverly	296	26	Hatch	Gamaleal		1	1						1				3		
Beverly	296	27	Poulling	Edward			1			1			1				3		
Beverly	296	28	Trask	William 2d	2			1					1				4		
Beverly	296	29	Cleaver	Ambroas		1			1	1			1				4		
Beverly	296	30	Carries	Benjamin	2			1		1			1				5		
Beverly	296	31	Wallis	Barthm	1	1	2		1	1	1			1			8		
Beverly	296	32	Oliver	Anna			1						1	1			3		
Beverly	296	33	Raymond	William	3	4	1	1		1			1	1			12		
Beverly	296	34	Down	John	1			1					1				3		
Beverly	296	35	Murray	Eliza			1					1	1				3		
Beverly	296	36	Dike	John	2		1		1		1	2		1			8		
Beverly	296	37	Fornice	William	2		1	1		1			1	1			7		
Beverly	296	38	Burchsted	John	1			1	1				2	1			6		
Beverly	296	39	Lovett	Mary			1						1	1			3		
Beverly	296	40	Rae	John	2			1				3		1			7		
Beverly	296	41	Woodberry	Obed	3		1			1			1				6		
Beverly	296	42	Woodberry	Benjamin		1		1					1	1			4		
Beverly	296	43	Elliott	William	1	1		1		5	1	1	1				11		
Beverly	296	44	Ober	Asa	1			1		2			1				5		
Beverly	296	45	Miller	Isaac	3			1		1			1				6		
Beverly	296	46	Woodberry	Joseph 3d	2			1		1			1				5		
Beverly	296	47	Woodberry	Anna										1			1		
Beverly	296	48	Haskell	Isaac			1			2		1					4		
Beverly	296	49	Haskel	Nathaniel			1			1		1		1			4		
Beverly	297	1	Haskell	Nathaniel Jr			1			1		1					3		
Beverly	297	2	Haskel	William		1	2		1	2			1				7		
Beverly	297	3	Haskel	James W	3	1			1	2		1	1				9		
Beverly	297	4	Larcom	Juno Negro											11		11		
Beverly	297	5	Larcom	Abigail			3			1			1	1			6		
Beverly	297	6	Adams	Asa				1		2			1				4		
Beverly	297	7	Pride	Peter	1				1	1	1	2		1			7		
Beverly	297	8	Woodberry	Hephzibah			3						1	1			5		
Beverly	297	9	Ober	Jerusha						1			1	1			3		
Beverly	297	10	Thissel	James		2			1			1	2	1			7		
Beverly	297	11	Thissel	Lucy		1	1			2	2	1	1	1			9		
Beverly	297	12	Thissel	James Jr			1						1				2		
Beverly	297	13	Thissel	John	1			1				1	1				4		
Beverly	297	14	Russel	Ceaser											6		6		
Beverly	297	15	Smith	Isaac	1	1		1		2	2		1	1			9		
Beverly	297	16	Byler	Betsy								3					3		
Beverly	297	17	Obear	Peter			1	1		1			1	1			5		
Beverly	297	18	Bisson	Lucy						1	1	1	1	1			5		
Beverly	297	19	Ober	Mary										1			1		
Beverly	297	20	Obear	Samuel 2d	1		1			1		1					4		
Beverly	297	21	Byler	Mary	1		1						1	1			4		
Beverly	297	22	Byler	Alexander	1		1						1				3		
Beverly	297	23	Pedrich	Richard			1			2		1	1				5		
Beverly	297	24	Standly	David	1		1	1		2			1				6		
Beverly	297	25	Lovett	Joseph		1		1		1			1				4		
Beverly	297	26	Larcome	Cornelius		1				1			1				3		
Beverly	297	27	Elliott	James	2	1		1		1			1				6		
Beverly	297	28	Mors	Ebenezer					1				1	1			3		
Beverly	297	29	Foster	Jeremiah		1	2		1		2			1			7		
Beverly	297	30	Crampesee	Isaac	2	2		1		1			1				7		
Beverly	297	31	Parker	James	1	1		1		1				1			5		
Beverly	297	32	Chapman	Rebeca						1			2	1			4		
Beverly	297	33	Harris	Jonathan	1			1				1					3		
Beverly	297	34	Prince	Brackbry	2	2		1		1	1		1				8		
Beverly	297	35	Clark	Richard				1					1				2		
Beverly	297	36	Foster	Jeremiah Jr			1						1				2		
Beverly	297	37	Prince	Abigail									1				1		
Beverly	297	38	Wales	Mary						1				1			2		
Beverly	297	39	Woodberry	Priscilla									2	2			4		
Beverly	297	40	Foster	Josiah	2	2		1		2	2		1				10		
Beverly	297	41	Young	William	3	1		1		2	1		1				9		
Beverly	297	42	Woodberry	Eliza									1	1			2		
Beverly	297	43	Chapman	Josiah F	1			1		1			1				4		
Beverly	297	44	Kent	Josiah			1			1		1					3		
Beverly	297	45	Foster	Joshua	2	1	1	1		2	1	1	1				10		

23

TOWN	PG#	LN#	HEADS OF HOUSEHOLD		FREE WHITE MALES					FREE WHITE FEMALES					TOTAL ALL OTHER	TOTAL SLAVES	TOTALS	DISTRICT/ TOWNSHIP	NOTES
			LAST NAME	FIRST NAME	under 10	10 to 16	16 to 26	26 to 45	45 and over	under 10	10 to 16	16 to 26	26 to 45	45 and over					
Beverly	297	46	Cole	Asa					1				1				2		
Beverly	297	47	Adams	Daniel		1	1		1	1	1		1	1			7		
Beverly	298	1	Sumner	Benja C	3	2		1		2	1		1				10		
Beverly	298	2	Averit	Sarah								1	1	1			3		
Beverly	298	3	Thompson	Peter				1					1	1	1		3		
Beverly	298	4	Givens	Lydia	2	1							1	1			5		
Beverly	298	5	Haskell	Stephen	2	1		1		1			1				6		
Beverly	298	6	Giles	Hannah		2							1	2			5		
Beverly	298	7	Obear	Joseph		1		1		1			1				4		
Beverly	298	8	Clark	William			1	1				1					3		
Beverly	298	9	Clark	Nathanl				1						2			3		
Beverly	298	10	Ward	William				1			1			2			4		
Beverly	298	11	Foster	Daniel		1	3	1			2			1			8		
Beverly	298	12	Foster	Joseph		2		1				1		1			5		
Beverly	298	13	Sumner	James	3	1		1		1			1				7		
Beverly	298	14	Daland	Benjamin	3			1					1				5		
Beverly	298	15	Wallis	Bartholomew Jr		1				1			1				3		
Beverly	298	16	Strickland	Allin	3			1		2	1		1				8		
Beverly	298	17	Chapman	George D				1		1			1				3		
Beverly	298	18	Knowlton	Caleb		1							1				2		
Beverly	298	19	Campbell	Duncan		1	1						1	3			6		
Beverly	298	20	Brimter	Daniel	1	1			1	3			1	2			9		
Beverly	298	21	Lamson	Nathan	2	2	2		1	5	1	1	1				15		
Beverly	298	22	Whyer	Joseph				1		1				1			3		
Beverly	298	23	Giles	Eleazer		1	1		1	1	1			1			6		
Beverly	298	24	Lemmon	John	1			1					1				3		
Beverly	298	25	Giles	Ebenezer			1						1				2		
Beverly	298	26	Vickeree	Knot	1	1	1	1		3	2		1				10		
Beverly	298	27	Herrick	William 2d	2	1	2	1			1	1	1				9		
Beverly	298	28	Vickeree	Richard	4			1		1			1				7		
Beverly	298	29	Haskel	Robert	3	2		1		3	1		1	1			12		
Beverly	298	30	Vickeree	William	1					3			1	1			6		
Beverly	298	31	Porter	William	1	2	3	1						1			8		
Beverly	298	32	Porter	Rachel		1	1					1		2			5		
Beverly	298	33	Fielder	John Jr	3			1		1			1				6		
Beverly	298	34	Hannon	George	2			1					1	1			5		
Beverly	298	35	Vickeree	John			1		1	1		2		1			6		
Beverly	298	36	Cox	Osmon				1				1	1	1			4		
Beverly	298	37	Fielder	Willm H	3	1	1	1					1	1			8		
Beverly	298	38	Fielder	John				1		1			1	1			4		
Beverly	298	39	Adams	William Jr	1		1			3			1				6		
Beverly	298	40	Wallis	Benja			1			1	1	1					4		
Beverly	298	41	Row	Seth			1			1		1					3		
Beverly	298	42	Calf	John		1				1			1	1			4		
Beverly	298	43	Adams	William		1		1				2		1			5		
Beverly	298	44	Adams	Charles	2	1						1					4		
Beverly	298	45	Whittridge	Livemore		1		1		1	2		1				6		
Beverly	299	1	Whittridge	Livemore Jr	2			1		2			1				6		
Beverly	299	2	Leech	Nathan				1					1	1			3		
Beverly	299	3	Cabot	Huldah									1	1			2		
Beverly	299	4	Leech	William	1	1	1	1		2		1	1	1			9		
Beverly	299	5	Porter	Robert		2	2	1				1		1			7		
Beverly	299	6	Hall	Hugh	5				1			1	1	2			10		
Beverly	299	7	Willson	James	1	1		2					1				5		
Beverly	299	8	Herrick	Daniel		1		1				1		1			4		
Beverly	299	9	Wiles	Michael		1							1				2		
Beverly	299	10	Bridger	Thomas		1		1					1				3		
Beverly	299	11	Bridger	Benja	2			1					1	1			5		
Beverly	299	12	Poland	Joseph	1		1	1			1		1				5		
Beverly	299	13	Bulloch	Betsey						3			1				4		
Beverly	299	14	Waters	Stephen				1			1	1					3		
Beverly	299	15	Williams	James						2		1	1	1	1	1	7		
Beverly	299	16	Craft	Richard	2			1					1				4		
Beverly	299	17	Harvey	Dover											6		6		
Beverly	299	18	Hill	Eliza	2		1			2	2	1	2				10		
Beverly	299	19	Adams	John			1			1		1					3		
Beverly	299	20	Webber	Samuel	1		1	1				1		1			5		
Beverly	299	21	Pike	Sally	1							1	1	1			4		
Beverly	299	22	Trask	Nehemiah		1						1	2				4		
Beverly	299	23	Chadwick	Abijah	2		1	1		2	2		1				9		
Beverly	299	24	Cole	Andrew	1			1					1		1		4		
Beverly	299	25	Hale	Mary	1	1	1					1	1	1			6		
Beverly	299	26	Woodberry	Joseph 2d				1						2			3		
Beverly	299	27	Harmon	John	1	1	1			1			1				5		
Beverly	299	28	Burbank	Willm		2							1				3		
Beverly	299	29	Froathingham	Ruth		1				1	1		1	1			5		
Beverly	299	30	Treadwell	Nathl	1		1	1		1		1	1	1			7		
Beverly	299	31	Worrly	James		1		1			1	1					4		
Beverly	299	32	Norton	Wm		1	1				1	1					4		
Beverly	299	33	Meservey	John	1		1						1				3		
Beverly	299	34	Lugue	Anthony	2			1					1				4		
Beverly	299	35	Green	Lydia								2	1				3		
Beverly	299	36	Nours	Rufus	1			1		1			1				4		
Beverly	299	37	White	Henry	1	1		1		2	1		1				8		
Beverly	299	38	williams	Thomas				1		1			1				3		
Beverly	299	39	Quiner	Abraham Jr	2		1			2			1				6		
Beverly	299	40	Dempsey	Rogger	1	1		1		1			1				5		
Beverly	299	41	Stone	Abigail									1	1			2		
Beverly	299	42	Leach	Asa	1	1		1				1	2	1			8		
Beverly	299	43	Wittemore	Joseph	1	1		1		4	2	1	1				11		

TOWN	PG#	LN#	LAST NAME	FIRST NAME	FREE WHITE MALES					FREE WHITE FEMALES					TOTAL ALL OTHER	TOTAL SLAVES	TOTALS	DISTRICT/ TOWNSHIP	NOTES
					under 10	10 to 16	16 to 26	26 to 45	45 and over	under 10	10 to 16	16 to 26	26 to 45	45 and over					
Beverly	299	44	Wakefield	Nathl	1	1	1			1			1				5		
Beverly	300	1	Franch	Sarah		1	1					1	1	1			5		
Beverly	300	2	Calla	John			1			1			1				3		
Beverly	300	3	Black	Nathl		1		1		3	1		1				7		
Beverly	300	4	Remmond	Robert	2	1		1		1			1				6		
Beverly	300	5	Brown	Benja				1					1				2		
Beverly	300	6	Wallis	Eleazer	1	2		1				1	2				7		
Beverly	300	7	Brown	Benja 2nd	2		1	1				1		1			6		
Beverly	300	8	Sanders	John			1					1	1				3		
Beverly	300	9	Herick	Jonathan	2		2			2			1				7		
Beverly	300	10	Landen	Rebecca				1					1	1			3		
Beverly	300	11	Wallis	Nathl			1					1	1	1			4		
Beverly	300	12	Moulton	Tarbox			1										1		
Beverly	300	13	Ellinwood	Joanna	1								1	1			3		
Beverly	300	14	Hurly	Abigail	1		1						1	1			4		
Beverly	300	15	Carrico	John				1						1			2		
Beverly	300	16	Dale	Archalus		1	1		1	1	1		1				6		
Beverly	300	17	Smith	Daniel G	1			1		2		1					5		
Beverly	300	18	Selman	Jacob				1		2			1				4		
Beverly	300	19	Mange	Sarah								1	1				2		
Beverly	300	20	Pouslin	Thomas		1							1				2		
Beverly	300	21	Ellinwood	Wm			1					1	1				3		
Beverly	300	22	Goodwin	Nathaniel		3	2	1					1		1		8		
Beverly	300	23	Denis	Charles			1			1		1	1				4		
Beverly	300	24	Ashton	John		1		1		2			1				5		
Beverly	300	25	Eaton	Joseph	1	1		1		1	2		1				7		
Beverly	300	26	Stephens	George				1					1				2		
Beverly	300	27	Benson	Francis	2		2	1		2	1	1	1				10		
Beverly	300	28	Ellinwood	Sarah									1				1		
Beverly	300	29	Cox	Samuel	1		1						1				3		
Beverly	300	30	Creely	Nicholas			1			2	2	1					6		
Beverly	300	31	Thorndike	Elizabeth									1	1			2		
Beverly	300	32	Thissel	Lydia		1	1			2	1	1					6		
Beverly	300	33	Rae	Mehitable									1				1		
Beverly	300	34	Rae	Ebenz	2		1	1		1	2		1				8		
Beverly	300	35	Ober	Samuel	1	1		1		2	1		1				7		
Beverly	300	36	Foster	Samuel		1				1		1					3		
Beverly	300	37	Foster	Mary		3	2				1		1				7		
Beverly	300	38	Haskell	Daniel		1						1					2		
Beverly	300	39	Thorndike	Jeremiah			1					1					2		
Beverly	300	40	Woodberry	Mark	1		1			2			1				5		
Beverly	300	41	Quiner	Mary	1								1				2		
Beverly	300	42	Ford	Edward			1						1				2		
Beverly	300	43	Rae	Gideon	2	1		1		1			1	1			7		
Beverly	300	44	Rae	Isaac			1						1				2		
Beverly	300	45	Corning	Anna										1			1		
Beverly	301	1	Corning	Jonathan			1						1				2		
Beverly	301	2	Woodberry	Richard	1		1						1				3		
Beverly	301	3	Wales	John		1							1				2		
Beverly	301	4	Lovett	Ebenezer		1	1	1		3	1		1				8		
Beverly	301	5	Ober	Richard 2nd		1	1	1				1	1				5		
Beverly	301	6	Lovett	Joanna	1									1			2		
Beverly	301	7	Lovett	Josiah		1						1					2		
Beverly	301	8	Lovett	Benja B					1				1				2		
Beverly	301	9	Gale	Jonas		1							1				2		
Beverly	301	10	Woodberry	Freeborn	1		1			1			1				4		
Beverly	301	11	Anderson	Job			1			1			1				3		
Beverly	301	12	Dawling	James	1		1			2			1				5		
Beverly	301	13	Ober	Andrew	1		1			1			2				5		
Beverly	301	14	Hart	Sarah								1	2	1			4		
Beverly	301	15	Dodge	Thomas	1		1						1				3		
Beverly	301	16	Gallop	William	1		2		1	1	1		1				7		
Beverly	301	17	Wood	Cornelius			1	1					1	1			4		
Beverly	301	18	Hammon	Philip	1		1			2			1				5		
Beverly	301	19	Robertson	Rawling		1		1		1			1				4		
Beverly	301	20	Hogins	Thomas	1	2	1	1	3	3			1				12		
Beverly	301	21	Burk	Thomas			1			1			1				3		
Beverly	301	22	Bisson	Israel		1	1						2				4		
Beverly	301	23	Woodbery	Martha									1				1		
Beverly	301	24	Woodbery	Gideon	3			1		1		1					6		
Beverly	301	25	Cox	Judith	2	1							1				4		
Beverly	301	26	Glover	Peter Jr				1		1			1				3		
Beverly	301	27	Woodbery	Myhill	1				1				3				5		
Beverly	301	28	Lovett	Jonathan		1		1			1		1				4		
Beverly	301	29	Lovett	Judith										1			1		
Beverly	301	30	Arbuckle	John	1		1						1				3		
Beverly	301	31	Matter	John			1				1						2		
Beverly	301	32	Matter	Samuel		1						1					2		
Beverly	301	33	Woodbery	Josiah		2	1		2				1				6		
Beverly	301	34	Lakeman	Rachel		2	1						1				4		
Beverly	301	35	Buckman	Elizabeth										1			1		
Beverly	301	36	Harris	Charles S				1		3			1				5		
Beverly	301	37	Cook	Samuel		1											1		
Beverly	301	38	Ober	Lydia			1							1			2		
Beverly	301	39	Ober	Jonathn P		1	1			3			1				6		
Beverly	301	40	Woodberry	Elisha			1			1		1					3		
Beverly	301	41	Grover	John			1					1	1				3		
Beverly	301	42	Grover	Abigail								2		2			4		
Beverly	301	43	Harris	Hannah		1						1	1	1			4		
Beverly	301	44	Lovett	Samuel		1	1			2			1	1			6		

TOWN	PG#	LN#	HEADS OF HOUSEHOLD		FREE WHITE MALES					FREE WHITE FEMALES					TOTAL ALL OTHER	TOTAL SLAVES	TOTALS	DISTRICT/ TOWNSHIP	NOTES
			LAST NAME	FIRST NAME	under 10	10 to 16	16 to 26	26 to 45	45 and over	under 10	10 to 16	16 to 26	26 to 45	45 and over					
Beverly	302	1	Butman	Samuel	2			1					1				4		
Beverly	302	2	Thissel	Hannah	1								1				2		
Beverly	302	3	Butman	Mary									1	1			2		
Beverly	302	4	Sergant	John			1						1				2		
Beverly	302	5	Wadden	Isaac			1						1				2		
Beverly	302	6	Bunker	Daniel	1		1	1		1	2		1	1			8		
Beverly	302	7	Woodberry	Nathl				1									1		
Beverly	302	8	Seward	Henry	2			1					1				4		
Beverly	302	9	How	Daniel	1	1		1		2			1	1			7		
Beverly	302	10	Mors	Mark	1	1	1	1					1	1			6		
Beverly	302	11	Black	Anna									1	1			2		
Beverly	302	12	Knowlton	Joseph				1		1			1	1			4		
Beverly	302	13	Cook	William			1						1				2		
Beverly	302	14	Bodoin	Thomas	2			1					1				4		
Beverly	302	15	Standly	Andrew	1			1		1			1				4		
Beverly	302	16	Claxton	Philip	3			1		1			1				6		
Beverly	302	17	Butman	Lucy									1				1		
Beverly	302	18	Fellows	Isaac			1			1			1				3		
Beverly	302	19	Burrows	Elizabeth									1				1		
Beverly	302	20	Bartlet	Sipio											1		1		
Beverly	302	21	Smith	Elias				1					1				2		
Beverly	302	22	Coben	Jack Negro											4		4		
Beverly	302	23	Claxton	Matthias				1					1				2		
Beverly	302	24	Walls	Thomas	1	2		1					1				5		
Beverly	302	25	Allin	Davis			1	1				1		1			4		
Beverly	302	26	Foster	Josiah Jr	2			1					1	1			5		
Beverly	302	27	Ford	Charity									1				1		
Beverly	302	28	Jones	David	1			1		3	2		1	1			9		
Beverly	302	29	Dane	John				1			1		1	1	1		4		
Beverly	302	30	Cleaver	Ezra			1	1		1			1				3		
Beverly	302	31	Bradshaw	John	1	2		1		1	1	1		1			8		
Beverly	302	32	Stickney	Joseph	3			1		1			1				6		
Beverly	302	33	Tarbox	Daniel	1			1		1			1				4		
Beverly	302	34	Lamson	Samuel	2			1					1				4		
Beverly	302	35	Roundy	Nehemiah 2d		2		1				1					4		
Beverly	302	36	Thomas	David	1			1		3			1				6		
Beverly	302	37	Wells	Nathaniel	1			1		1		1					4		
Beverly	302	38	Peirce	Benja			2			2		1	1				6		
Beverly	302	39	Currel	Nicholas	2			1		1			1				5		
Beverly	302	40	Woodbery	Samuel				1						1			2		
Beverly	302	41	Roggers	Ebenezer				1						1			2		
Beverly	302	42	Roggers	Benja			1			1		1					3		
Beverly	302	43	Griffin	Jonathan	2	2	1						1				6		
Beverly	302	44	Ober	Issacher	1		1			1			1				4		
Beverly	302	45	Dodge	Nicholas		1	5	1			1	1		1			10		
Beverly	303	1	Thompson	James	2			1					1	1			5		
Beverly	303	2	Gardner	William											2		2		
Beverly	303	3	Brown	Benja 3d	1			1					1				3		
Beverly	303	4	Tisser	Abigail			1			1			1				3		
Beverly	303	5	Thorndike	Eleanor		1	1				1		1				4		
Beverly	303	6	Thorndike	Nicholas	2			1		2		1	1				7		
Beverly	303	7	Thomson	Jacob	1			1		2			1	1			6		
Beverly	303	8	Endicott	Robert	2	2		1				1	1				7		
Beverly	303	9	Larnard	David	3	1		1		2			1				8		
Beverly	303	10	Nichols	John				1						1			2		
Beverly	303	11	Pender	John			1				1	1					3		
Beverly	303	12	Hilton	Hale				1									1		
Beverly	303	13	Masury	John	1			1		1			1				4		
Beverly	303	14	Gray	Molly								1		1			2		
Beverly	303	15	Quiner	Abrahm					1			2		1			4		
Beverly	303	16	Frost	Benja	1			1		1			1				4		
Beverly	303	17	Lamson	Francis		2		1		3	1			1			8		
Beverly	303	18	Pickett	Thomas	1	2	2	1		2	2	2	1				13		
Beverly	303	19	Beckford	William			1						1				2		
Beverly	303	20	Stone	Mary				1					1	1			3		
Beverly	303	21	Woodbery	Peter	3		2	1		1			1				8		
Beverly	303	22	Leech	Nathan 2d	1		1	1		1		1	1				6		
Beverly	303	23	Foster	Samuel 2d	1			1		1			1				4		
Beverly	303	24	Fowler	Benja	1		1	1						1			4		
Beverly	303	25	Stickney	Samuel	1		3	1		2	1	2					10		
Beverly	303	26	Castle	Samuel		2		1				1	1				6		
Beverly	303	27	Lovett	Benja Jr	3	3	2	1		2	2	1	2				16		
Beverly	303	28	Cox	Mary									1				1		
Beverly	303	29	Lamson	Asa	1			1		1			1				4		
Beverly	303	30	Cox	William				1				2	1				4		
Beverly	303	31	Glover	John			1			1			1				3		
Beverly	303	32	Ingersol	Samuel	2	2		1	1		1	2	1	1			11		
Beverly	303	33	Eaton	Joseph 2nd				1					1	1			3		
Beverly	303	34	Brown	Eliza									1				1		
Beverly	303	35	Brown	Moses Esq	2			1				1	2		1		7		
Beverly	303	36	Kilham	Abraham			1				1	2					4		
Beverly	303	37	Tittle	John		2	1	1		3			1	1	1		10		
Beverly	303	38	Gardner	John	1		1			1			2				5		
Beverly	303	39	Barrett	Thomas		1		1				3	1	1			7		
Beverly	303	40	Chapman	Eliza									1	1			2		
Beverly	303	41	Lamson	Jonathn	3			1					1				5		
Beverly	303	42	Lovett	William	2			1		1	2		1				7		
Beverly	303	43	Haskel	William	2			1		1			1				5		
Beverly	303	44	Standly	Betsy			1				2		1				4		
Beverly	303	45	Standly	Peter	2	1		1			1		1				6		

TOWN	PG#	LN#	LAST NAME	FIRST NAME	FREE WHITE MALES					FREE WHITE FEMALES					TOTAL ALL OTHER	TOTAL SLAVES	TOTALS	DISTRICT/ TOWNSHIP	NOTES
					under 10	10 to 16	16 to 26	26 to 45	45 and over	under 10	10 to 16	16 to 26	26 to 45	45 and over					
Beverly	303	46	Briant	Benja	2	1		1		2			1				7		
Beverly	303	47	Appleton	Isaac		1	2					1					4		
Beverly	304	1	Lovett	Ezra		1		1		2			1				5		
Beverly	304	2	Lovett	Hannah								1		1			2		
Beverly	304	3	Lovett	Jeremiah	1	1	1	1		1			1	1			7		
Beverly	304	4	Peirce	Samuel	2			1		1			1				5		
Beverly	304	5	Whitney	Elisha Eaq	2	1	1		1	2	1	2	2				12		
Beverly	304	6	Dyson	John	1				1	2	2	2		1			9		
Beverly	304	7	Anderson	Jacob			1						1	2			4		
Beverly	304	8	Batchelder	Hannah										1			1		
Beverly	304	9	Larcome	Jonathan	1			1		1			1				4		
Beverly	304	10	Lovett	Hezekiah	1		1	1		3			1				7		
Beverly	304	11	Richardson	Philip		1			1		1	1	1				5		
Beverly	304	12	Dike	Solomon	1			1		3			1				6		
Beverly	304	13	Cabot	Lydia			3			1	2	4	1				11		
Beverly	304	14	Shale	Andrew	1				1	2	1	1	1				7		
Beverly	304	15	Wyer	William	2			1		1			1				5		
Beverly	304	16	Hammon	Eliza		2	1			2				1			6		
Beverly	304	17	Cabott	John			1		1	1	1	1	1				6		
Beverly	304	18	Sugden	Lucy								1	1				2		
Beverly	304	19	Webster	Sarah		1								1			2		
Beverly	304	20	Howard	Moses		1					1						2		
Beverly	304	21	Roundy	Nehemiah	2	1	1		1	1	1		1				8		
Beverly	304	22	Trask	Eliza										1			1		
Beverly	304	23	Lee	Joseph					1			4	2		1		8		
Beverly	304	24	Smith	Ebenezer Jr		2	3	1		1		2					9		
Beverly	304	25	Wallis	Daniel		1	1	1	1		1	1	1	1			8		
Beverly	304	26	Little	Hannah						2			1				3		
Beverly	304	27	Abott	Eliza						1	1		1				3		
Beverly	304	28	Mackey	Samuel G			1					1					2		
Beverly	304	29	Ives	Eliza		1					1	1		2			5		
Beverly	304	30	Gould	Joseph	4		1	1		1			1	1			9		
Beverly	304	31	Gage	Andrew					1				1				2		
Beverly	304	32	Webber	William Jr	2		1						1				4		
Beverly	304	33	Wadden	Hannah			1						1	2			4		
Beverly	304	34	Gage	Henry	1			1		2			1				5		
Beverly	304	35	Gage	Zachariah	1		1		1				1	1			5		
Beverly	304	36	Wood	Eliza		3							1				4		
Beverly	304	37	Gage	William			1										1		
Beverly	304	38	Lovett	Benjamin		2			1	2	1	2	1				9		
Beverly	304	39	Stone	John	1	2	2		1	3			1	1			11		
Beverly	304	40	Davis	Thomas					1					1			2		
Beverly	304	41	Davis	Thomas Jr	2	2			1	2	1		2				10		
Beverly	304	42	Perry	William			1	1									2		
Beverly	304	43	Raymond	Nathan					1	1	2		1				5		
Beverly	304	44	Trask	John	1		1	1		2	1		1				7		
Beverly	304	45	Spencer	William	3	1	2	1		1		1					9		
Beverly	305	1	Porter	Nathan	1	3				1				1			7		
Beverly	305	2	Dobben	John	2				1	1	1		1				6		
Beverly	305	3	Balch	Joshua					1				1	2			4		
Beverly	305	4	Andrews	Thomas	5	1		1		1			1				9		
Beverly	305	5	Baker	Belle			1			1	1		2				5		
Beverly	305	6	Twiss	Benjamin	1		1			2			1				5		
Beverly	305	7	Creesy	John	2			1		1			1				5		
Beverly	305	8	Creesy	Jonathan			1		1		1			1			4		
Beverly	305	9	Debman	William			1				1		1				3		
Beverly	305	10	Gray	James	2			1		1		1					5		
Beverly	305	11	Creesy	Nathl		1			2		1	2		1			7		
Beverly	305	12	Friend	Nathl	1		1		1	3	1	1	1				9		
Beverly	305	13	Leeds	Richard					1								1		
Beverly	305	14	Friend	Caleb			1			1			1				3		
Beverly	305	15	Putnam	Rufus	3			1					1				5		
Beverly	305	16	Foster	Benja			1			1			1				3		
Beverly	305	17	Hovey	Hannah								2		1			3		
Beverly	305	18	Friend	William	2	1	1					1	1				7		
Beverly	305	19	Patch	Abigail								2	1				3		
Beverly	305	20	Peirce	Nathanl		2		1		5	1		1				10		
Beverly	305	21	Creesy	Benja	1			1	1				2				5		
Beverly	305	22	Trask	William		1			1					1			3		
Beverly	305	23	Cook	Samuel		1							1				2		
Beverly	305	24	Cook	Joseph			1							1			2		
Beverly	305	25	Woodberry	Peter			1						1	1			3		
Beverly	305	26	Stickney	Samuel	1	2			1				1	1			6		
Beverly	305	27	Batchelder	John			1						1	1			3		
Beverly	305	28	Trask	Ebenezer	1	1			1			2		1			6		
Beverly	305	29	Trask	Ebenezer Jr	4			1		2			1				8		
Beverly	305	30	Safford	John		1	1		1	1		1	1				6		
Beverly	305	31	Dodge	Barnabas					1				1	2			3		
Beverly	305	32	Dodge	John		1	1			1			1	2			6		
Beverly	305	33	Waters	Silus	1				1	1	1		1				5		
Beverly	305	34	Dodge	Jonathan 2d		2		1		1				1			5		
Beverly	305	35	Baker	John	1	1		1		1	2	1					8		
Beverly	305	36	Batchelder	James				1						1			2		
Beverly	305	37	Batchelder	Anna									1	1			2		
Beverly	305	38	Conant	Samuel					1				1				2		
Beverly	305	39	Conant	Nathanl	2			1		3			1				7		
Beverly	305	40	Woodberry	John		1			1			1	1	1			5		
Beverly	305	41	Pennel	John	1			1			2			1			5		
Beverly	305	42	Herick	Joshua	2			1		2	1		2	1			9		
Beverly	305	43	Batchelder	Cornelius	2			1		1			1				5		

27

TOWN	PG#	LN#	LAST NAME	FIRST NAME	FREE WHITE MALES					FREE WHITE FEMALES					TOTAL ALL OTHER	TOTAL SLAVES	TOTALS	DISTRICT/ TOWNSHIP	NOTES
					under 10	10 to 16	16 to 26	26 to 45	45 and over	under 10	10 to 16	16 to 26	26 to 45	45 and over					
Beverly	305	44	Ford	Sarah	1					2			1				4		
Beverly	306	1	Raymond	John				1		3		1	1				6		
Beverly	306	2	Raymond	Hannah									1	1			2		
Beverly	306	3	Webber	William	2	2	1		1	1	1	1		1			10		
Beverly	306	4	Raymond	Joseph							1		1	1			4		
Beverly	306	5	Raymond	George				1	1								2		
Beverly	306	6	Raymond	David			1		1	2			1				5		
Beverly	306	7	Pouslas	John	1		2	1		3	1	1	1				10		
Beverly	306	8	Pouslas	John Jr	2		1			1		1					5		
Beverly	306	9	Chandler	Isaac	2	1		1			2	1		1			8		
Beverly	306	10	Shaw	Peter	1		1	1		3			1				7		
Beverly	306	11	Davison	Patiance										1			1		
Beverly	306	12	Cordwell	Abraham	1			1					1	1			4		
Beverly	306	13	Derby	Edith										1			1		
Beverly	306	14	Gardner	Nancy						1			1	2	1		5		
Beverly	306	15	Chapman	John			1		1	1		3		1			7		
Beverly	306	16	Mors	Sally						1			1				2		
Beverly	306	17	Burnham	James Esq	2	1		1			2	1	1				8		
Beverly	306	18	Ely	John Francis		1	2	1	1	1	1	2	1				10		
Beverly	306	19	Woodberry	Isaac		1	2	1		3	1		1				9		
Beverly	306	20	Edwards	Robert Jr	1			1		3			1				6		
Beverly	306	21	Thursting	Enoch	1				1				1				3		
Beverly	306	22	Creesy	Henry	1		1	1		1	1		1				6		
Beverly	306	23	Babson	Eleanor										1			1		
Beverly	306	24	Sheldon	John	5	1	1	1		2	1	1	1				13		
Beverly	306	25	Batchelder	John Jr		1			1		1	2		1			6		
Beverly	306	26	Bradborne	James			1			2		1					4		
Beverly	306	27	Dodge	Samuel	1	2			1	3			1				8		
Beverly	306	28	Standly	Wells			1					1	1				4		
Beverly	306	29	Baker	Robert					1	1		3		1			6		
Beverly	306	30	Woodberry	Benja 2d	2	1			1					1			5		
Beverly	306	31	Woodberry	Daniel	1				1	1			1	1			5		
Beverly	306	32	Baker	Robert Jun	1		1					1					3		
Beverly	306	33	Freeman	Cato Negro											5		5		

TOWN	PG#	LN#	LAST NAME	FIRST NAME	FREE WHITE MALES under 10	10 to 16	16 to 26	26 to 45	45 and over	FREE WHITE FEMALES under 10	10 to 16	16 to 26	26 to 45	45 and over	TOTAL ALL OTHER	TOTAL SLAVES	TOTALS	DISTRICT/ TOWNSHIP	NOTES
Boxford	133	1	Hovey	John					1					1			2		
Boxford	133	2	Parker	William	2			1		2	1			1			7		
Boxford	133	3	Hovey	Richard				1					1	1			3		
Boxford	133	4	Hovey	John	1		1			1		1					4		
Boxford	133	5	Kimball	David		1		1				2	1	1			6		
Boxford	133	6	Kimball	Micijah	1		1					2					4		
Boxford	133	7	Cole	Moses	2			1		1		1	1	1			7		
Boxford	133	8	Peabody	Daniel			1							1			2		
Boxford	133	9	Tyler	Broadst	3	1	1	1			1	2	1				10		
Boxford	133	10	Tyler	Joshua			2			1		2					5		
Boxford	133	11	Sessions	Nathll			1						1	1			3		
Boxford	133	12	Runnels	Samuel		1	2	1				1	1	1			7		
Boxford	133	13	Runnels	Jonathan			1			1			1				3		
Boxford	133	14	Runnels	Enos	2	1	3	1		2	1	1	1	1			13		
Boxford	133	15	Peabody	Ebenezr	1	1	1		1	2	1	2	1	1			11		
Boxford	133	16	Pearl	John	1		2		1	2	2	1		1			10		
Boxford	133	17	Pearl	John	1			1				1	1	1			5		
Boxford	133	18	Coburn	David		2		1				1	1				5		
Boxford	133	19	Wood	Joseph		1		1					1	1			4		
Boxford	133	20	Wood	Joseph			1			1		1					3		
Boxford	134	1	Hovey	Hannah		1	5			1	3	2	1	1			14		
Boxford	134	2	Robinson	John		1		1				2	2				6		
Boxford	134	3	Robinson	Aaron	1			1		1		1	1				5		
Boxford	134	4	Eaton	Peter	2			1		1	1		1		1		7		
Boxford	134	5	Hovey	Ivory		2		1			1	2	1				7		
Boxford	134	6	Wood	Lemuel	2		1	1		2	1		1		1		9		
Boxford	134	7	Hovey	Joseph	1	1	1	1			1	3	1				9		
Boxford	134	8	Chadwick	Moses	1			2		1		1	1		1		7		
Boxford	134	9	Chadwick	Samuel			1	1		1	1	1			1		6		
Boxford	134	10	Chadwick	Thos	1			1		2			1		1		6		
Boxford	134	11	Chadwick	Isaac			1						1		1		3		
Boxford	134	12	Herriman	Jereh		1	1	1		1	1	2	1				8		
Boxford	134	13	Porter	Moses			1	1	1			1	1				5		
Boxford	134	14	Cole	Thos			1	1		1		1					4		
Boxford	134	15	Cole	Phineas				2		1			1				4		
Boxford	134	16	Parker	Jacob	1			1		1			1		1		5		
Boxford	134	17	Cole	Simeon	2	1	1	1	1	2		1	1				10		
Boxford	134	18	Butrick	William	1			1		1		1	1				5		
Boxford	134	19	Merril	Dorcas						1		1					2		
Boxford	134	20	Robinson	Benj	2			1		2		1					6		
Boxford	134	21	Carlston	Samuel	1	2			2	3	1	2	1	1			13		
Boxford	134	22	Carlston	Moses	1			1				1	1				4		
Boxford	134	23	Long	Nathll		1				1	2		1	1			6		
Boxford	134	24	Porter	Mary						1		1	1	2			5		
Boxford	134	25	Palmer	John				1					1				2		
Boxford	134	26	Kimball	Amos	1	1		1		1	1	1					6		
Boxford	134	27	Tyler	John	1	1	2	1		3		1	2	2			13		
Boxford	134	28	Kimball	John	1			1		1		1	1				5		
Boxford	134	29	Freeman	Simon											2		2		
Boxford	134	30	Foster	Ephm	1	1	1		1	1		1		1			7		
Boxford	134	31	Foster	Jonathan	1				1			1		1			4		
Boxford	134	32	Kimball	Stephen	1		1			3		1					6		
Boxford	134	33	Kimball	Nathan				1			1			1			3		
Boxford	134	34	Foster	Israel	1	1		1	1	3			1	1	1		10		
Boxford	134	35	Kimball	Enoch	1		2		1	3	1	1		2			11		
Boxford	134	36	Kimball	Asa		1		1					2	1			5		
Boxford	134	37	Foster	Jereh		1	1	1				1	1				5		
Boxford	134	38	Kimball	Samuel	1	1	1	1				2	1				7		
Boxford	134	39	Kimball	David		3	2	1				2	1				9		
Boxford	134	40	Foster	Jonathn		1	1	1				1					4		
Boxford	134	41	Kimball	Daniel	1	1			1	1				1			5		
Boxford	134	42	Dorman	John	1			1	1	3		1	1				8		
Boxford	134	43	Adams	Israel		2		1				1		1			5		
Boxford	134	44	Spofford	Amos				1					2				3		
Boxford	134	45	Spofford	Thos	2			1				1					4		
Boxford	134	46	Spofford	Samuel		1		1	1			1					4		
Boxford	134	47	Spofford	Stephen		1		1	1				1				4		
Boxford	134	48	Carleton	Joseph		2	1	1		2		1	1	1			9		
Boxford	134	49	Kimball	Samuel	2	1		1		2	1		1				8		
Boxford	134	50	Tyler	Abraham	1		1		1			1	1	1			6		
Boxford	134	51	Wood	Nathan				1					1				2		
Boxford	134	52	Wood	Moses	2		2	1		3	1	1	1				12		
Boxford	134	53	Stickney	Jedidiah				1			1			1			3		
Boxford	134	54	Stickney	Ariel		1		1			1		1				4		
Boxford	135	1	Spofford	Parker	5	2		1		2	1	1	1				13		
Boxford	135	2	Herrick	Nathll	1	1		1		4			1				8		
Boxford	135	3	Perley	Moody	2			1		1	1		1				6		
Boxford	135	4	Wood	Solomon		1		1		3	1		1				7		
Boxford	135	5	Perley	Eliphalet			1					1					2		

TOWN	PG#	LN#	HEADS OF HOUSEHOLD		FREE WHITE MALES					FREE WHITE FEMALES					TOTAL ALL OTHER	TOTAL SLAVES	TOTALS	DISTRICT/ TOWNSHIP	NOTES
			LAST NAME	FIRST NAME	under 10	10 to 16	16 to 26	26 to 45	45 and over	under 10	10 to 16	16 to 26	26 to 45	45 and over					
Boxford	135	6	Dresser	Thos	1		3	1		1			2				8		
Boxford	135	7	Perley	Phineas	2			2		2	1	1	1				9		
Boxford	135	8	Perley	Nathll			1		1		1			1			4		
Boxford	135	9	Low	Nathan	1		3	1						1			6		
Boxford	135	10	Jackson	Joshua				1			1		1				3		
Boxford	135	11	Chapman	Daniel		1		2			1		1				5		
Boxford	135	12	Spofford	Benja		2		1		2			2				7		
Boxford	135	13	Perley	Amos	3			1		2	1	1	1				9		
Boxford	135	14	Perley	Aaron	3	2		1	2		1		1	1			11		
Boxford	135	15	Hale	Joseph		1		1		2			1	1			6		
Boxford	135	16	Perley	Asa	1			1	1			1		2			6		
Boxford	135	17	Perley	Jesse	3			1					2	1			7		
Boxford	135	18	Wood	Margret									1	1			2		
Boxford	135	19	Gould	Daniel	2			1		1	1	3	1				9		
Boxford	135	20	Peabody	Stephen		1		1		1			1				4		
Boxford	135	21	Peabody	Richard			1		1	1	1		1				5		
Boxford	135	22	Herrick	Israel		1		1	1	1			2	1			7		
Boxford	135	23	Butman	David		1			1	1			1	1			5		
Boxford	135	24	Holyoke	Elizar				1	1			1		2	2		7		
Boxford	135	25	Peabody	Asa			1		1	1				1			4		
Boxford	135	26	Stiles	John					2					1			3		
Boxford	135	27	Peabody	Samll				1					1				2		
Boxford	135	28	Dorman	Moses				1				1	2	1			5		
Boxford	135	29	Dorman	Timothy		2	1	1					1	1			6		
Boxford	135	30	Andrews	Nathan				1					1	1			3		
Boxford	135	31	Andrews	Nathan	3	1		1		2			1				8		
Boxford	135	32	Foster	Phineas		1							1		1		3		
Boxford	135	33	Smith	Nathll				1					1	2			4		
Boxford	135	34	Smith	Joseph		1	1			1			1				4		
Boxford	135	35	Symonds	Stephen	1		1					1	2	1			6		
Boxford	135	36	Andrews	Jacob		1		1		1	1	1	1				6		
Boxford	135	37	Bixby	Gideon	2	2		1		1	2	1					9		
Boxford	135	38	Gould	Cornelus	1			1		3			1				6		
Boxford	135	39	Giddens	John	2	2		1				1		1			7		
Boxford	135	40	Gould	Jacob		1		1			1	1	1				5		
Boxford	135	41	Folensbee		4	1		1			1		1				8		No first name
Boxford	135	42	Curtice	John				1		2			1				4		
Boxford	135	43	Foster	Richard	1			1	1			3		1			7		
Boxford	135	44	Gould	Jacob	1			1		1		1	1				5		
Boxford	135	45	Grant			1						1					2		No first name
Boxford	135	46	Killam	John		1	2	1					1	1			6		
Boxford	135	47	Gould	Samuel	4			1	1	1	1	1					9		
Boxford	135	48	Russell	James	1	2	1	1				2		1			8		
Boxford	135	49	Peabody	Bimsley	1		1	1					1	1			5		
Boxford	135	50	Stiles	Simeon		2		1		1		2		1			7		
Boxford	135	51	Peabody	Moses		1		1		1	2		1				6		
Boxford	135	52	Herrick	Edmond	1	1		1		3	2		1				9		
Boxford	135	53	Symonds	Joseph	1		1	1		3	1	1	1	1			10		
Boxford	135	54	Town	John	2		2	1				1	1				7		
Boxford	136	1	Rea	Joshua		1	1	1		1	1	1	2				8		
Boxford	136	2	Foster	John	2		1	1			1	1	1	1			8		
Boxford	136	3	Town	John		1	1	1		1		1		1			6		
Boxford	136	4	Hening	Asa											4		4		
Boxford	136	5	Perley	Henry	2	1		1		1	2		1				8		
Boxford	136	6	Tyler	Stephen	2	1		1		2			1				7		
Boxford	136	7	Burnam	Rufus		1		1			2		1				5		
Boxford	136	8	Perley	William			2		1			2	1	1			7		
Boxford	136	9	Brown	Parker		2	2			1	2	1	1				9		
Boxford	136	10	Smith	John		1			1	2	1		1				6		
Boxford	136	11	Wood	John	1			1		2			1				5		

Town	PG#	LN#	LAST NAME	FIRST NAME	FREE WHITE MALES					FREE WHITE FEMALES					TOTAL ALL OTHER	TOTAL SLAVES	TOTALS	DISTRICT/ TOWNSHIP	NOTES
					under 10	10 to 16	16 to 26	26 to 45	45 and over	under 10	10 to 16	16 to 26	26 to 45	45 and over					
Bradford	121	1	Munnds	John			1		1			2		1			5		
Bradford	121	2	Burnell	James		1	1			3		1					6		
Bradford	121	3	Haggit	Moses		1		1					1				3		
Bradford	121	4	Phillips	Samuel	2			1		2			1				6		
Bradford	121	5	Phillips	Timo	1	1	3	1				1	1				8		
Bradford	121	6	Carlton	David		1		1		3	1		1	1			8		
Bradford	121	7	Day	Bailey	3	1		1				1	1				7		
Bradford	121	8	Hall	Moses	1			1		4			1		1		8		
Bradford	121	9	Carlton	Stephen				1						1			2		
Bradford	121	10	Carlton	Margea*	1			1		3			1				6		
Bradford	121	11	Day	Joseph		1		1				1		1			4		
Bradford	121	12	Day	John		1		1	1	1		1	1	3			9		
Bradford	121	13	Day	John			1			1		1					3		
Bradford	121	14	Bradley	Thos	2		1					1	1	1			6		
Bradford	121	15	Gage	Daniel		1		1		2		1		1			6		
Bradford	122	1	Hazzeltine	Amos	1	1			1	1	2			1			7		
Bradford	122	2	Gage	Peter			1		1	1	1	2		1			7		
Bradford	122	3	Gage	Asa		1		1	1	3		1	1	1			9		
Bradford	122	4	Kimball	Nathan	1	2	2	1			1	1	1				9		
Bradford	122	5	Kimball	Elijah	1		2	1				1	1				6		
Bradford	122	6	Kimball	Nathan			1	1				2	1				5		
Bradford	122	7	Kimball	Asa		3	1			2	1		1				8		
Bradford	122	8	Gage	Uriah			3		1	3	1	1	1	1			11		
Bradford	122	9	Gage	Jeremiah		1	1	1	1			2					6		
Bradford	122	10	Kimball	Abraham	1			1			3	1	1				7		
Bradford	122	11	Kimball	Benja	1	1				1	1	2					6		
Bradford	122	12	Kimball	Benja	1			1				1	1				4		
Bradford	122	13	Head	Reuben	2	1		1		1	2		1				9		
Bradford	122	14	Head	Amos			1			1	1		1				4		
Bradford	122	15	Campbell	James	1			1	1	1		1	1	1			7		
Bradford	122	16	Tenney	John				1			1	1		2			5		
Bradford	122	17	Carlton	David		1	4	1		1	1		1				9		
Bradford	122	18	Kimball	Jereh				1				1		2			4		
Bradford	122	19	Day	Abraham		1		1		1	1		1				5		
Bradford	122	20	Kimball	Daniel	2	1		1		1	1	1	2	1			10		
Bradford	122	21	Griffin	John		3		1		1				1			6		
Bradford	122	22	Griffin	Ebenezr	1	2	1	1			1	1	1				8		
Bradford	122	23	Webster	Moses		1		1		2	1		1				6		
Bradford	122	24	Buswell	Daniel		1		1			1	1		2			6		
Bradford	122	25	Carlton	Dudley		1		1			1	1	1		1		6		
Bradford	122	26	Webster	Thomas			1		1	1		1					4		
Bradford	122	27	Webster	Samuel		1		2		1	1	1	1				7		
Bradford	122	28	Kimball	Edward	3	1	2		1	1	2		2				12		
Bradford	122	29	Kimball	Obadiah			1	1	1		1			1			5		
Bradford	122	30	Kimball	James	2	1	1		2	2	3	2	1				14		
Bradford	122	31	Porter	Moses	1			1		1			1				4		
Bradford	122	32	Tenny	Shubal			3		1	1	1		1				7		
Bradford	122	33	West	Isaac			1	1					1				3		
Bradford	122	34	Gage	Abijah		1			1		1	2		2			7		
Bradford	122	35	Hergeyethine	John	1	1		1			3	1	1				8		
Bradford	122	36	Gardner	Samuel	1	1	3	1					1				7		
Bradford	122	37	Allen	Jonathan				1			1	1		1	1		5		
Bradford	122	38	Chadwick	James	4	2	1	1		1	1		1				11		
Bradford	122	39	Trask	Samuel				1					1	1			3		
Bradford	122	40	Trask	Samuel		1	2	1		1			1				6		
Bradford	122	41	Chadwick	Samuel			1	1					1	1			4		
Bradford	122	42	Smiley	John	2	1	2	1				1					7		
Bradford	122	43	Kimball	Amos	1		1	1		2			1				6		
Bradford	122	44	Trask	Ezzra				1		4	1	1	1				8		
Bradford	122	45	Palmer	William				1		1			1	1			4		
Bradford	122	46	Wyman	Daniel	1		2	2					2				7		
Bradford	122	47	Kimball	Jacob				1					2	1			4		
Bradford	123	1	Kimball	Moses		1	1				1			1			4		
Bradford	123	2	Peabody	John	3		1	1		2	1		1				9		
Bradford	123	3	Kimball	Abel	1			1		2	1	1	1				7		
Bradford	123	4	Kimball	Phineas		2	1						2	2			7		
Bradford	123	5	Kimball	Nathl		1	2			1	2	1		1			8		
Bradford	123	6	Kimball	Richd		1		1				1		1			4		
Bradford	123	7	Kimball	Edward	3	1		1	1	2		2					10		
Bradford	123	8	Chadwick	Jonathan				1					1	1			3		
Bradford	123	9	Chadwick	Joseph	2		1	1		1	2	1	1				9		
Bradford	123	10	Merril	Dortha	2		1				1	2		1			7		
Bradford	123	11	Hovey	Stephen			1					1					2		
Bradford	123	12	Perry	David			1					1					2		
Bradford	123	13	Hibbart	Thomas			1			2			1				4		
Bradford	123	14	Carlton	Jos		2		1			1			1			5		
Bradford	123	15	Carlton	Reuben				1						1			2		
Bradford	123	16	Carlton	Reuben Jr	1		1			1		1					4		
Bradford	123	17	David	Daniel	2			1		1			1				5		

31

TOWN	PG#	LN#	HEADS OF HOUSEHOLD		FREE WHITE MALES					FREE WHITE FEMALES					TOTAL ALL OTHER	TOTAL SLAVES	TOTALS	DISTRICT/ TOWNSHIP	NOTES
			LAST NAME	FIRST NAME	under 10	10 to 16	16 to 26	26 to 45	45 and over	under 10	10 to 16	16 to 26	26 to 45	45 and over					
Bradford	123	18	Walker	Benjamin	2	1		1	1		1	1	1				8		
Bradford	123	19	Kimball	Francis	1		1			1	1	1					5		
Bradford	123	20	Walker	Richard		1	1					1		3			7		
Bradford	123	21	Woodman	Phineas			1	1		3			1	1			7		
Bradford	123	22	Thurston	Daniel		1	1	1		3	1		1				8		
Bradford	123	23	Stiles	Samll	1	1		1		2			1	1			7		
Bradford	123	24	Thurston	Nathll	2	1	1	1	1			3					9		
Bradford	123	25	Thurston	Daniel		1		1	1	1			1				5		
Bradford	123	26	Payton	Elliot		1	1	3			1	1		1			8		
Bradford	123	27	Frost	Caleb	2				1	2	2	1	1				9		
Bradford	123	28	Marble	Joseph				2	1				1	1			5		
Bradford	123	29	Hovey	John		1	1		1				1	2			6		
Bradford	123	30	Kimball	Jonathn	1	1	2	1	1	3	1	1					11		
Bradford	123	31	Greenough	James				1		1	2		1				5		
Bradford	123	32	Kimball	Joseph	2			3	1	2			3	1			12		
Bradford	123	33	Johnson	Samll				1					1				2		
Bradford	123	34	Peabody	Andrew	1	1		1		3	1	1		1			9		
Bradford	123	35	Dodge	Abel				1	1	1	1	2	4	1			11		
Bradford	123	36	Kimball	Daniel			1	1	1				1				4		
Bradford	123	37	Curtice	William	1		1	2		1		1	1				7		
Bradford	123	38	Carlton	Phineas		3	1		1			3	1	1			10		
Bradford	123	39	Hows	Thos	2	2	2		1	1		1	1	1			11		
Bradford	123	40	Morse	Benja	3	1		1				2	1	1			9		
Bradford	123	41	Parker	Aaron	1	2	1	1		1		2					8		
Bradford	123	42	Parker	Nathll			4			1		1		1			7		
Bradford	123	43	Pimberton	Abel	1	2		1					2				6		
Bradford	123	44	Parker	William	1	1	5	1		1		2	1				12		
Bradford	123	45	Curtice	John				1		1			1				3		
Bradford	123	46	Morse	Benja	1	1		1		1	3		1				8		
Bradford	123	47	Hardy	Solomon		1			1			1		2			5		
Bradford	123	48	Hardy	Phineas		2	2	1				1	1				7		
Bradford	124	1	Parker	Samuel	1			1	1	1			1				4		
Bradford	124	2	Parker	Stephen	2	1	2		1		2			2			10		
Bradford	124	3	Parker	Paul				1		2			1	1			5		
Bradford	124	4	Goodridge	James	3	2	2	1		1		1					10		
Bradford	124	5	Greenough	William	2	1		1		3	2	1	1				11		
Bradford	124	6	Attwood	William				1					1				2		
Bradford	124	7	Burbank	William	1			1		1		1					4		
Bradford	124	8	Jennings	John	4			1		1			1				7		
Bradford	124	9	Holden	John	1								1	1			3		
Bradford	124	10	Parker	Sarah	1							2	1				4		
Bradford	124	11	Greenough	Bayley		1				1		1	2	1			6		
Bradford	124	12	Hardy	Samuel	2			1				1	2	1			7		
Bradford	124	13	Parker	Moses									2				2		
Bradford	124	14	Parker	Chesen	1			1		3			1				6		
Bradford	124	15	Burbank	Stephen				2	1			1		1			5		
Bradford	124	16	Rollings	Eliphalet	1			1					1				3		
Bradford	124	17	Mitchel	Peter				1					1				2		
Bradford	124	18	Little	Enoch			4	1		2		2					9		
Bradford	124	19	Mitchel	Joseph				1		1		1		1			4		
Bradford	124	20	Tilden	Niles	2	1		1					1				5		
Bradford	124	21	Greenough	John	2			1		1		2	1				7		
Bradford	124	22	Mitchel	Day		1						1					3		
Bradford	124	23	Hardy	Enoch	2		2	1	1	2	1	1	1	1			12		
Bradford	124	24	Rollings	Joseph	1		1	1		1	1	1					6		
Bradford	124	25	Stevens	Jonathan	2	2	3		1			2		1			11		
Bradford	124	26	Parker	Trace Grove	1		1		1	1		1		1			6		
Bradford	124	27	Parker	William	1		2		1	1	1	1		1			8		
Bradford	124	28	Russell	Peter				1			1	2		1			5		
Bradford	124	29	Shuff	John		1		1		1		1					4		
Bradford	124	30	Hardy	Reuben	1	1				2	1	1					6		
Bradford	124	31	Bayley	Moses		1				1							2		
Bradford	124	32	Mardin	David				1			1	1	1				4		
Bradford	124	33	Dutch	Ebenezr			2		2	1	1	1	1				8		
Bradford	124	34	Attwood	Jesse	1	2			1				2				6		
Bradford	124	35	Hardy	Silvanus			1			1		1					3		
Bradford	124	36	Hardy	Timothy				1						1			2		
Bradford	124	37	Hardy	Parker	1		1			1		1					5		
Bradford	124	38	Hardy	Simon			1			1		1					3		
Bradford	124	39	Bacon	Josiah				1				1	1				3		
Bradford	124	40	Lapham	King		3		1		1			1				6		
Bradford	124	41	Foot	Rowel	1			1		3			1				6		
Bradford	124	42	Burbank	Benja	2			1		1		1	1				6		
Bradford	124	43	Johnson	Thos				1		2		1	1				5		
Bradford	124	44	Attwood	Simon	2			1		1			1				5		
Bradford	124	45	Tyler	Samuel	1		1	1		1		2					6		
Bradford	124	46	Lutice	Joshua	1	2		1	1				4	1			10		
Bradford	125	1	Parker	Moses	1	1		1		1	1	1	1				7		
Bradford	125	2	Hardy	Joshua	2	2		1					2				7		

TOWN	PG#	LN#	LAST NAME	FIRST NAME	FREE WHITE MALES					FREE WHITE FEMALES					TOTAL ALL OTHER	TOTAL SLAVES	TOTALS	DISTRICT/ TOWNSHIP	NOTES
					under 10	10 to 16	16 to 26	26 to 45	45 and over	under 10	10 to 16	16 to 26	26 to 45	45 and over					
Bradford	125	3	Foster	Stephen	2	1	3	1	1		1	2		1			12		
Bradford	125	4	Stickney	Thos			1	1	1			2	1	1			7		
Bradford	125	5	Hopkinson	Silas	2	1	1	2		2		1	1	1			11		
Bradford	125	6	Balch	Jonathan	2			1		1		1	1				6		
Bradford	125	7	Palmer	David					1	2	1	1	1				6		
Bradford	125	8	Hopkinson	Ebenzr		1	1		1			1		1			5		
Bradford	125	9	Savory	John	1	1	1	1		1	1	1	1				8		
Bradford	125	10	Savory	Benja	3		1	1		1	1		1				8		
Bradford	125	11	Savory	Eliphalet		1		1					1				3		
Bradford	125	12	Wood	Samuel	4		1	1	1	2	3	1	1	1			15		
Bradford	125	13	Tenny	Samuel	1	2		1	1	2	1	1					9		
Bradford	125	14	Foot	David	1			2		2		2					7		
Bradford	125	15	Pine	David			1	1	1		1	1	1				6		
Bradford	125	16	Smith	John		1		1				1			1		4		
Bradford	125	17	Colby	John			1				2	2	1				6		
Bradford	125	18	Burbank	Elipht	4		2	1		1	1	1	1				11		
Bradford	125	19	Tenny	Solomon		2		1	1		1	1	1				7		
Bradford	125	20	Hardy	Henry	2	1		1		3	2		1	1			11		
Bradford	125	21	Chaplin	Aaron	1	2		1					1				5		
Bradford	125	22	Herriman	Samll			1				1		1				3		
Bradford	125	23	Hale	Jonath	1	1	1	1			1		1	1			7		
Bradford	125	24	Herriman	Nathll	1			1		1			1				4		
Bradford	125	25	Hale	Eliphalet	3		2	1	1	2		1	1	1			12		
Bradford	125	26	Cheney	Daniel				1		1	1						3		
Bradford	125	27	Jackman	Timothy		1	1		1	1		1		1			6		
Bradford	125	28	Adams	Samuel	2		1		1	2			1	1			8		
Bradford	125	29	Burbank	John	1			1	1	1	1	1	2	1			9		
Bradford	125	30	Burbank	Caleb	3		1			1		1	1				7		
Bradford	125	31	Stickney	Ebenzr		1	1		1			1		1			5		
Bradford	125	32	Hardy	Joshua	1	1	1		2	2				1			8		
Bradford	125	33	Boynton	Samuel		1			1			2		1			5		
Bradford	125	34	Hardy	Simon	1			1				1					3		
Bradford	125	35	Hardy	Joseph	3		1					1					5		
Bradford	125	36	Herriman	Enoch	2	1		1		2		1					7		
Bradford	125	37	Hardy	Elijah	2				1	2				1			6		
Bradford	125	38	Hardy	Jacob	1			1		3			3	1			9		
Bradford	125	39	Parker	Broadst	1	1		1	1	1		1	1				7		
Bradford	125	40	Greenough	Moses	1			1		2		1					5		
Bradford	125	41	Stickney	Daniel	1			1		2	1		1				6		
Bradford	125	42	Hardy	David	1	1			1	2	1	1		1			8		
Bradford	125	43	Jaquish	Benja		1	1		1			2		1			6		
Bradford	125	44	Jaquish	Noyce	1			1		3			1				6		
Bradford	125	45	Savory	Thomas		1	3					2	1	1			8		
Bradford	125	46	Tenny	William		1		1		1			1				4		
Bradford	125	47	Tenny	William		1		1				2		1			5		
Bradford	125	48	Tenn	Silas	2	1		1		1			1				6		
Bradford	125	49	Palmer	Samuel		2	1	1		1	2		1	1			9		
Bradford	125	50	Savory	Thomas	3		2	1		3		1	1	1			12		
Bradford	126	1	Wood	Moses		1		1				1					3		
Bradford	126	2	Wallingford	Nathll		1	1			1		1		1			5		
Bradford	126	3	Wood	Thomas			3		1	1	1	1		1			8		
Bradford	126	4	Bayley	Jonathan			1		1					1			3		
Bradford	126	5	Little	William	1			1				1					3		
Bradford	126	6	Bayley	William			1						1				2		
Bradford	126	7	Sanders	Moses	1	1		1	4			1		1			9		
Bradford	126	8	Hopkinson	Daniel		1	1		1	1				2			6		
Bradford	126	9	Hopkinson	Nathll			1		1					1			3		
Bradford	126	10	Morse	Stephen			2		1			2		1			6		
Bradford	126	11	Richardson	Daniel				1		1	1	1					5		
Bradford	126	12	Dwinel	Abigal			1						1	1			3		
Bradford	126	13	Wallingford	James		1							2				3		
Bradford	126	14	Platts	Abigal										2			2		
Bradford	126	15	Richardson	Dorithy	1					1			1	2			5		
Bradford	126	16	Balch	William		1	1		1			1	1	2			7		
Bradford	126	17	Foster	Runnels			1	1		1				1			4		
Bradford	126	18	Woodman	Richard	1		1		1	1			2	2			8		
Bradford	126	19	Kimball	Francis	1	1	1		1		2	1		1			8		

TOWN	PG#	LN#	LAST NAME	FIRST NAME	FREE WHITE MALES					FREE WHITE FEMALES					TOTAL ALL OTHER	TOTAL SLAVES	TOTALS	DISTRICT/ TOWNSHIP	NOTES
					under 10	10 to 16	16 to 26	26 to 45	45 and over	under 10	10 to 16	16 to 26	26 to 45	45 and over					
Danvers	2	1	Holten	Samuel		1		1		1			2	1			6		
Danvers	2	2	Wadsworth	Benjm Revd	2				1				2		1		6		
Danvers	2	3	Ingersoll	Jonathan	1		2	2	1	1	1	2					10		
Danvers	2	4	Cross	Peter			1	2	1	1		1		2			8		
Danvers	2	5	Preston	John		1	2		1	1		1	2	1			9		
Danvers	2	6	Putnam	Daniel	1	1	1		1				1	1			6		
Danvers	2	7	Chase	Benjamin				1	1				2				4		
Danvers	2	8	Kettell	John	1	2	1		1	2			1				8		
Danvers	2	9	Dodge	Ephraim	1		1	1		1	1						5		
Danvers	2	10	Towne	William		1			1				1	1			4		
Danvers	2	11	Demsey	Isaac	1			1					1				3		
Danvers	2	12	Clark	Caleb			1		1				1				3		
Danvers	2	13	Clark	Caleb Junr	2			1		1			1				5		
Danvers	2	14	Demsy	Bartholw	3			1		1			1	1			7		
Danvers	2	15	Tapley	Asa	2	2	1	1		1	1		1				9		
Danvers	2	16	Putnam	James		1			1	1	1		1				5		
Danvers	2	17	Tapley	Amos	2	2	1		1	1	1	1	1	1			11		
Danvers	2	18	Flint	Elijah	1	2	1	1		1	1		1		1		9		
Danvers	2	19	Flint	Herzekiah	1	1		2		2			1				7		
Danvers	2	20	Patch	Mahue	1	1		1		1			1	1			6		
Danvers	2	21	Flint	Samuel		1							1				2		
Danvers	2	22	Putnam	Israel Jur	2			1		1			1				5		
Danvers	2	23	Smith	George G				1		2			1				4		
Danvers	2	24	Upton	George				1				2		1			4		
Danvers	2	25	Wiatt	George				1	1					2			4		
Danvers	2	26	Cheever	Israel Jur		1	2		1					1			5		
Danvers	2	27	Cheever	Israel Jur					1				1	1			3		
Danvers	2	28	Nichols	Andrew	1	1	1	1		1			1	1			7		
Danvers	2	29	Putnam	Phinehas				1					1	1			3		
Danvers	2	30	Putnam	Joseph 3rd		1		1		1			1				4		
Danvers	2	31	Cheever	Samuel					1								1		
Danvers	3	1	Cheever	Nathan	4			1					1				6		
Danvers	3	2	Preston	Levi	3	1	1	1	1	2	1	1	1				12		
Danvers	3	3	White	John	1	2	1		1				1	1			7		
Danvers	3	4	Putnam	Eleazer	2	1	1	1			2		1				8		
Danvers	3	5	Dale	Margaret		1								1			2		
Danvers	3	6	Dale	Eben			2						1				3		
Danvers	3	7	Small	George		1		1					1	1			4		
Danvers	3	8	Hutchinson	John	1		1	1	1	2		1	1	1			9		
Danvers	3	9	Swinerton	John	1		1		1				1	1			5		
Danvers	3	10	Tapley	Gilbert				1		1			1				3		
Danvers	3	11	Buxton	Amos Junr		1	1		1				1	1	1		6		
Danvers	3	12	Goodale	James		1		1	1			1	1	1			6		
Danvers	3	13	Goodale	James Junr		1		3					1				5		
Danvers	3	14	Crain	Ralp		2		1					2				5		
Danvers	3	15	Gardner	Samuel			3		1	1			1				6		
Danvers	3	16	Shelden	Amos		2		1		2	1		1				7		
Danvers	3	17	Shelden	Elisabeth										2			2		
Danvers	3	18	Smith	Susanna	1	1	1			3	1	1	1				9		
Danvers	3	19	Tayler	Daniel		1	2	1						1			5		
Danvers	3	20	Tayler	Samuel				1		1			1				3		
Danvers	3	21	Flint	Amos		1		1	1	2	2		1				8		
Danvers	3	22	Tayler	Daniel Junr	1		1	1					3	1			7		
Danvers	3	23	Flint	William	4			1		1				1			7		
Danvers	3	24	Laribee	Hannah	1					2	1		1				5		
Danvers	3	25	Laribee	Ephraim		1				1		1					3		
Danvers	3	26	Curtis	Allen	1			1		3			1				6		
Danvers	3	27	Curtis	Molly									1	1			2		
Danvers	3	28	Green	Samuel				1					1				2		
Danvers	3	29	Green	Meribah									1	1			2		
Danvers	3	30	Moulton	Ebenezer		1							1	2			4		
Danvers	3	31	Moulton	Ebenezer Jr		1							1				2		
Danvers	3	32	Moulton	Benjamin					1				1	1			3		
Danvers	3	33	King	John	1	1			1	1	1		2				7		
Danvers	3	34	Thornton	John	2		1	1					1				5		
Danvers	3	35	Laribee	Ephriem	1		1		1	1			1				5		
Danvers	3	36	Laribee	Ephriem		1				1			1				3		
Danvers	4	1	Putney	Stephen	4			1					1				6		
Danvers	4	2	Douty	Thomas		2		1						1			4		
Danvers	4	3	Douty	James				1					1	1			3		
Danvers	4	4	Douty	Joseph	1	1	1					1	1	1			6		
Danvers	4	5	Twiss	Peter		1		1	1	2							5		
Danvers	4	6	Mansfield	Andrew		1	1	1		1			1	2			7		
Danvers	4	7	Mansfield	John		1	1						1				3		
Danvers	4	8	Newhall	David	1				1	1			1	1			5		
Danvers	4	9	Newhall	Nathaniel			1	1						1			3		
Danvers	4	10	Newhall	Nathaniel Jun			1						1				2		
Danvers	4	11	Newhall	Joseph	3	1			1	1		1	2				9		
Danvers	4	12	Newhall	Joseph Jun	1		1	1					1				4		

TOWN	PG#	LN#	LAST NAME	FIRST NAME	FREE WHITE MALES					FREE WHITE FEMALES					TOTAL ALL OTHER	TOTAL SLAVES	TOTALS	DISTRICT/ TOWNSHIP	NOTES
					under 10	10 to 16	16 to 26	26 to 45	45 and over	under 10	10 to 16	16 to 26	26 to 45	45 and over					
Danvers	4	13	Nurse	Nathaniel	1		1	2			1	1	1	1			8		
Danvers	4	14	Nurse	Jonathan		1	1		1		1	1		1			6		
Danvers	4	15	Boyce	Jonathan				1					1				2		
Danvers	4	16	Williams	Henry	1		2			1			1				5		
Danvers	4	17	Twiss	Joseph				1		1		1		1			4		
Danvers	4	18	Verry	William	2			1		2	2	1		1			9		
Danvers	4	19	Pepper	John	1			1		1		1	1	1			5		
Danvers	4	20	Davis	Nathaniel	1			1		2			1				5		
Danvers	4	21	Putnam	Israel				1				1		2			4		
Danvers	4	22	Putnam	Daniel Junr	1			2				2					5		
Danvers	4	23	Putnam	Joseph	1		1		1			1		1			5		
Danvers	4	24	Putnam	Jethro	2		1	1		2		1					7		
Danvers	4	25	Putnam	Timothy	2	1	3	1	1			1					9		
Danvers	4	26	Porter	Hannah									1				1		
Danvers	4	27	Putnam	Henry				1					1				2		
Danvers	4	28	Marsh	Rhode wife of John Marsh	2							1	1				4		
Danvers	4	29	Putnam	Gideon	1		1		1	1				1			5		
Danvers	4	30	Page	Jeremiah			3		1			1		1			6		
Danvers	4	31	Webb	Nathl	2	1	2		1	3		1	1				11		
Danvers	4	32	Clinton	Prudence									1	2			3		
Danvers	4	33	Skidmore	Richard Jr			1			2		1	1				5		
Danvers	4	34	Waitt	Jonathan	2			1		1	1		1				6		
Danvers	4	35	Porter	Hitte	1					1		1					3		
Danvers	4	36	Stickney	Asa	1	1	1		1	3		1		1			9		
Danvers	4	37	Fowler	John			2					1					3		
Danvers	5	1	Dole	Benjamin		1	2					1		1			5		
Danvers	5	2	Tapley	David		1	1			2		1	1				6		
Danvers	5	3	Putnam	Edmund Junr	2			1		1		2					6		
Danvers	5	4	Putnam	Amos		1		1	2			2		3			9		
Danvers	5	5	Dodge	Joshua		1			1				1	1			4		
Danvers	5	6	Holt	James	2			1				1		1			5		
Danvers	5	7	Hayward	Levi		1			1			1	1	1			5		
Danvers	5	8	Perry	John				2					1				3		
Danvers	5	9	Williams	John				1					1				2		
Danvers	5	10	Hutnam	Matthew		1	1	1		4		1		1			9		
Danvers	5	11	Page	Samuel	1	2			1	1	1	3		1			10		
Danvers	5	12	Needham	John			1	1				1	1		1		5		
Danvers	5	13	Seldon	Elizabeth	1					1	1		1				4		
Danvers	5	14	Towne	Samuel	1		1	1		1		1	1				6		
Danvers	5	15	Gray	Rebech Wido									1				1		
Danvers	5	16	Shelden	Amos 2nd	2			1	1	2		1	1				8		
Danvers	5	17	Putnam	Aaron		1	1		1	1	1	1		2			8		
Danvers	5	18	Cutter	Solomon	3			1		1			1				6		
Danvers	5	19	Porter	Zorubbable	2		4	1		1		1	1				10		
Danvers	5	20	Porter	Benjamin				1					1				2		
Danvers	5	21	Putnam	Israel3rd		2		1	1	1			2	1			8		
Danvers	5	22	Batchelder	Ezra Junr	2	1		1		1			1				6		
Danvers	5	23	Whipple	Marey								1	1				2		
Danvers	5	24	Batchelder	Ezra Junr	1	1	2	1	1	1		1		1			9		
Danvers	5	25	Putnam	Ezra				2				1					3		
Danvers	5	26	Rea	Archelaus			1	1					1				3		
Danvers	5	27	Preston	Moses	1	1		1			1		1				5		
Danvers	5	28	Felton	Nathl	2			1		1	1		1	1			7		
Danvers	5	29	Goodale	Phebe	1	1				1	1	1		1			6		
Danvers	5	30	Felton	Mary									1	1			2		
Danvers	5	31	Felton	Sarah	1	1	1			3			1				7		
Danvers	5	32	Felton	Timothy		1	2		1		1	1	1	1			8		
Danvers	5	33	Felton	Eunice									2				2		
Danvers	5	34	Pierce	Abigail								1	1				2		
Danvers	5	35	Dodge	John			1					1					2		
Danvers	5	36	Richardson	Jedediah			1			3			1				5		
Danvers	5	37	Leach	Timothy			1	1		1			1	1			4		
Danvers	5	38	Verry	Joseph			1	1					1				3		
Danvers	5	39	Jaques	Nathan			1			3			1				5		
Danvers	6	1	Prince	James	4			1			1		1				7		
Danvers	6	2	Whitten	William Jr		2	1		2			1	1				7		
Danvers	6	3	Bodge	Samuel	2		1	1					1				5		
Danvers	6	4	Fuller	Timothy	3	2			1	1	1	2		1	1		12		
Danvers	6	5	Hutchinson	Jeremiah			1	1	1				2				5		
Danvers	6	6	Hutchinson	Ebenezer	2			1		1			1				5		
Danvers	6	7	White	Samuel	3			1		2	1		1				8		
Danvers	6	8	Goodale	Sarah									2				2		
Danvers	6	9	Putnam	Asa	1			1		1			1	1			5		
Danvers	6	10	Hutchinson	Job		1	2					1		1			5		
Danvers	6	11	Hutchinson	Abijah		1						1					2		
Danvers	6	12	Mudge	Simon		2				1	2		1				6		
Danvers	6	13	Butler	Richard				1		2			1				4		
Danvers	6	14	Putnam	Elisha				1			3		2				6		
Danvers	6	15	Smith	mAry									2				2		

TOWN	PG#	LN#	LAST NAME	FIRST NAME	FREE WHITE MALES					FREE WHITE FEMALES					TOTAL ALL OTHER	TOTAL SLAVES	TOTALS	DISTRICT/ TOWNSHIP	NOTES
					under 10	10 to 16	16 to 26	26 to 45	45 and over	under 10	10 to 16	16 to 26	26 to 45	45 and over					
Danvers	6	16	Gifford	Lydia							1			1			2		
Danvers	6	17	Gifford	Sarah						2	1	1					4		
Danvers	6	18	Russell	Jethro			1	1				1		1			4		
Danvers	6	19	Macentire	Aaron	2			1		1			1				5		
Danvers	6	20	Russell	Benjamin					1					2			3		
Danvers	6	21	Russell	Benjamin Junr	1		1	1		1	1			2			7		
Danvers	6	22	Russell	John					1					1			2		
Danvers	6	23	Russell	Enoch			1					1					2		
Danvers	6	24	Russell	John Junr	2		1						1				4		
Danvers	6	25	Upton	Asa		1		1				1		2			5		
Danvers	6	26	Upton	Eli	1			2		1		1	1				6		
Danvers	6	27	Upton	Jesse	3		2	2				2	1				10		
Danvers	6	28	Danforth	Benjamin			1	1		3		1					6		
Danvers	6	29	Brown	John				1		1			1				3		
Danvers	6	30	Foster	James			2	1				1	1				5		
Danvers	6	31	Brown	Mary			1					1	1				3		
Danvers	6	32	Southwick	George				1		1			1				3		
Danvers	6	33	Southwick	Nathan		1	1			2		1					5		
Danvers	6	34	Southwick	George Junr	1	2		1		1	1		1	1			8		
Danvers	6	35	Southwick	Hannah	1					1				2			4		
Danvers	6	36	Gowen	Gideon	1			1						2			4		
Danvers	6	37	Trask	Ezra				1									1		
Danvers	6	38	Brown	William	1		1			3		1							
Danvers	6	39	Herrod	Ezra	1			1		3	2	1					8		
Danvers	6	40	Macenture	Judith									1	2			3		
Danvers	7	1	Marsh	Ezekiel	1		1	1				2					5		
Danvers	7	2	Marsh	Ezekiel Junr	1			1		1			1				4		
Danvers	7	3	Munro	Andrew	2	3	1		1	3	1	1	1				13		
Danvers	7	4	King	Amos	1	2			1	2	1	1	1				9		
Danvers	7	5	Gifford	Simeon	1	1		1		4	1		1				9		
Danvers	7	6	Procter	Keziah			1					1		1			3		
Danvers	7	7	Procter	Frances	2			1					1	1			5		
Danvers	7	8	Procter	Johnson	2		1	1		2		1	1				8		
Danvers	7	9	Goodale	Daniel Junr		1	1			1		1					4		
Danvers	7	10	Marble	Enoch				1									1		
Danvers	7	11	Procter	Jonathan	1	1	1		1			1	1	2			8		
Danvers	7	12	Gardner	John			1	1					3	1			6		
Danvers	7	13	Needham	Lydia									1	1			2		
Danvers	7	14	Needham	John Junr	1			1		1			1				4		
Danvers	7	15	Needham	Stephen	3	1		1	1			1	1	1			9		
Danvers	7	16	Pope	Elijah	1			1	1	3			2	1			9		
Danvers	7	17	Walcut	John	3	1		1	1		1		1	1			9		
Danvers	7	18	Marsh	Daniel	1			1		2			2				6		
Danvers	7	19	Jacobs	Henry				1					1				2		
Danvers	7	20	Jacobs	John	1		1	1		2		1	1				7		
Danvers	7	21	Marsh	Ebenezer				1					1				2		
Danvers	7	22	Marsh	Aaron			1			1	1						3		
Danvers	7	23	Dunklen	Ezekiel				1				1		1			3		
Danvers	7	24	Goodale	Eleazer		2		1		1		2		1			7		
Danvers	7	25	Gilford	Aaron			1			1			1				3		
Danvers	7	26	Swinerton	John Junr	1	1		1		3			2				8		
Danvers	7	27	Swinerton	Ede								1	1		1		2		
Danvers	7	28	Goodale	Daniel	4			1					1				6		
Danvers	7	29	Swinerton	Ruth	1			1		1		1		1			5		
Danvers	7	30	Swinerton	James			1	1					2	1			5		
Danvers	7	31	Prince	Joseph		1		1				1		2			5		
Danvers	7	32	Prince	Caleb		1	1	1					1				4		
Danvers	7	33	Putnam	Peter			1		1		2			1			5		
Danvers	7	34	Putnam	Ruth									1	1			2		
Danvers	7	35	Brown	Joseph				1					1	1			3		
Danvers	7	36	Brown	Ebenezer	2			1		2			1				6		
Danvers	7	37	Putnam	Hannah										1			1		
Danvers	7	38	Putnam	William	1		1			1		1		2			7		
Danvers	7	39	Putnam	Eben	1			1		2			1				5		
Danvers	7	40	Putnam	Porter			1	1		1			1				4		
Danvers	7	41	Putnam	Mary	1						1	1	2				5		
Danvers	7	42	Putnam	Rebecca										1			1		
Danvers	7	43	Porter	Joseph Junr		1		1					1				3		
Danvers	7	44	Putnam	Benja			1		1	2	2		1				7		
Danvers	8	1	Putnam	Sarah			1						1	1			3		
Danvers	8	2	Peasley	Ruben			1						1				2		
Danvers	8	3	Shelden	Jonathan		1		2		3			1	1			8		
Danvers	8	4	Putnam	Stephen		3	3	1	1		1	1		2			13		
Danvers	8	5	Putnam	David	1	2		1	2	1		1		2			10		
Danvers	8	6	Andrew	Israel				1						1			2		
Danvers	8	7	White	Joseph	2			1		2				1			6		
Danvers	8	8	Wilkins	Zadock	2		1	1		4			1	1			11		
Danvers	8	9	Butman	Daniel				1						1			2		
Danvers	8	10	Porter	Jonathan Junr	1			1	1	2	1		1	1			8		

TOWN	PG#	LN#	LAST NAME	FIRST NAME	FREE WHITE MALES under 10	10 to 16	16 to 26	26 to 45	45 and over	FREE WHITE FEMALES under 10	10 to 16	16 to 26	26 to 45	45 and over	TOTAL ALL OTHER	TOTAL SLAVES	TOTALS	DISTRICT/ TOWNSHIP	NOTES
Danvers	8	11	Towne	Thomas	1			1	1				1	1			5		
Danvers	8	12	Gowdy	James					1					1			2		
Danvers	8	13	Dwinell	Joseph			1		1			1	1				5		
Danvers	8	14	Gloyad	Hannah										2			2		
Danvers	8	15	Dwinell	Joseph Junr	1	1		1				1	1				5		
Danvers	8	16	Smith	Israel	1				1	3			1				6		
Danvers	8	17	Endicott	Elias			1	1		2		1	1				6		
Danvers	8	18	Harris	Ephriem				1				2					3		
Danvers	8	19	Porter	Ruth Widow										2			2		
Danvers	8	20	Porter	Joseph				1				1	1				3		
Danvers	8	21	Porter	Jonathan 3rd	1		1			1	1						4		
Danvers	8	22	Porter	Israel Junr			1	1		3		1					6		
Danvers	8	23	Porter	Israel		1			1			1					4		
Danvers	8	24	Porter	Abigail			1					1	1				3		
Danvers	8	25	Porter	Abijah		1				1		1					3		
Danvers	8	26	Caroll	Amey									1				1		
Danvers	8	27	Usher	Daniel	1			1		1			1				4		
Danvers	8	28	Caroll	William	1			1		2			1				5		
Danvers	8	29	Kent	Benjan			2	1					1				4		
Danvers	8	30	Burch	Sarah									1				1		
Danvers	8	31	Kent	Benjan Junr	2			1		2			1				6		
Danvers	8	32	Hook	Humphrey		1		1	1	1			1				5		
Danvers	8	33	Karr	James Junr	1			1					1				3		
Danvers	8	34	Karr	James				1		1	1		1				4		
Danvers	8	35	Wells	Willebie	2	1	1					2					6		
Danvers	8	36	Thurston	Ebenezer		1				1		1					3		
Danvers	8	37	Skidmore	Richard	1		2		1	2	1		1				8		
Danvers	8	38	Smith	Epriem	2			1		1		1	1				6		
Danvers	8	39	Putnam	Thomas	5			1		1		1	2				10		
Danvers	8	40	Oaks	Caleb	1		2	1			1		1				6		
Danvers	8	41	Hilbert	Nathan			1			1		1					3		
Danvers	8	42	Endicott	Israel	1			1					1				3		
Danvers	8	43	Johnson	William	2			1		1	1		1				6		
Danvers	9	1	Cheever	Simon			1	1	1					1			4		
Danvers	9	2	Putnam	Nathaniel Jr		1		1		1	1	1					5		
Danvers	9	3	Fowler	Samuel Junr	1		4					1					6		
Danvers	9	4	Trask	William		1		1		1	1						4		
Danvers	9	5	Porter	James				1				1					2		
Danvers	9	6	Dutch	Samuel				1					1				2		
Danvers	9	7	Putnam	Jeremiah				1		1		1	1				4		
Danvers	9	8	Porter	Daniel				1		3	1		1				6		
Danvers	9	9	Fowler	Anna						1	2		1				4		
Danvers	9	10	True	Corier				1				1					2		
Danvers	9	11	Welch	Betty	1		2			1			1				5		
Danvers	9	12	Floyd	Stephen				1		2	1	1					5		
Danvers	9	13	Hutchinson	Israel				1				1	2				4		
Danvers	9	14	Hutchinson	Israel Junr	2	1		1		3	2		1				10		
Danvers	9	15	Putnam	Nathaniel		1	1		1	4	1	1	1				10		
Danvers	9	16	Endicott	Moses	1	1		1		1	1		1				6		
Danvers	9	17	Gray	James				1					1				2		
Danvers	9	18	Fowler	Samuel				1			1	1		1			4		
Danvers	9	19	Smith	Joseph				1					1				2		
Danvers	9	20	Putnam	Rachel								1	1				2		
Danvers	9	21	Cora	Thomas	1			1		2	2		1				7		
Danvers	9	22	Pinder	Simon	1		1		1		1	1		1			6		
Danvers	9	23	Endicott	John Junr	3	1		1		1		1	1				8		
Danvers	9	24	Giddins	Solomon	3		1		1				1				6		
Danvers	9	25	Anger	Sarah									1				1		
Danvers	9	26	Bishop	James	3			1					1				5		
Danvers	9	27	Fuller	Andrew			1			4			1				6		
Danvers	9	28	Allen	Jonathan	1		1			1		1					4		
Danvers	9	29	Cutler	William	1			1		1			1				4		
Danvers	9	30	Macintire	Samuel	1	2		1		2	1		1				8		
Danvers	9	31	Robbins	Jonathan	1		1	1		1			1	1			6		
Danvers	9	32	Macintire	John				1				1		1			3		
Danvers	9	33	Osgood	Jonathan			1			1		1					3		
Danvers	9	34	Pinder	Samuel	1		1			1		1					4		
Danvers	9	35	Fairfield	Samuel				1					1				2		
Danvers	9	36	Endicott	Joseph			1	1				1	2				5		
Danvers	9	37	Endicott	John		1	1	1				1	2		1		7		
Danvers	9	38	Reed	Nathan			2	1		2		1	1				7		
Danvers	9	39	Josling	John	1	1		1		4	2		1				10		
Danvers	9	40	Waters	Lydia									1				1		
Danvers	9	41	Richardson	Seth	1	1		1		1	1		1				6		
Danvers	9	42	Page	Jeremiah Junr		1	2	1					1				5		
Danvers	10	1	Hilbert	William				4					1				5		
Danvers	10	2	Skilson	Seth				1				1					2		
Danvers	10	3	Jacobs	Elizabeth		1					1		1				3		
Danvers	10	4	Jacobs	Ebenezer	2	2			1			1	1	1			8		
Danvers	10	5	Gardner	John			5	1	1				1				8		

TOWN	PG#	LN#	LAST NAME	FIRST NAME	FREE WHITE MALES					FREE WHITE FEMALES					TOTAL ALL OTHER	TOTAL SLAVES	TOTALS	DISTRICT/ TOWNSHIP	NOTES
					under 10	10 to 16	16 to 26	26 to 45	45 and over	under 10	10 to 16	16 to 26	26 to 45	45 and over					
Danvers	10	6	Saltmarsh	Seth			1						1	1			3		
Danvers	10	7	Jacobs	Daniel				1						1			2		
Danvers	10	8	Whittemore	Hannah									1	1			2		
Danvers	10	9	Rea	Mary										1			1		
Danvers	10	10	Holt	Job				1						1			2		
Danvers	10	11	Batchelder	Asa			1			3			1				5		
Danvers	10	12	Collins	Benajah		1	1	1					4	1	4		12		
Danvers	10	13	Wood	Israel	1			1		2	2		1				7		
Danvers	10	14	Abbott	John Moody				1					1				2		
Danvers	10	15	Procter	Stephen			1	1				1	1	1			5		
Danvers	10	16	Procter	David	2			1		2	1		1				8		
Danvers	10	17	Procter	Sarah									1				1		
Danvers	10	18	Procter	Jonathan Junr			1			1			1				3		
Danvers	10	19	Willson	Jonathan	3	1		1		2	2		1				10		
Danvers	10	20	Darby	Zilpher											1		1		
Danvers	10	21	Willson	Isaac	1	1		1		2	2	2	1				10		
Danvers	10	22	Willson	Sarah Junr		1	1			2		1					5		
Danvers	10	23	Felton	Jonathan			1	1						2			4		
Danvers	10	24	Willson	Robert			1					1					2		
Danvers	10	25	Willson	Sarah		1	1			1		2		1			6		
Danvers	10	26	Willson	Newhall	2		1				1	2					6		
Danvers	10	27	Moulton	Elizabeth									1				1		
Danvers	10	28	Dalan	Benjamin				1					2				3		
Danvers	10	29	Reeves	Samuel				1					1				2		
Danvers	10	30	Kenny	Jonathan			1	2					1	1			5		
Danvers	10	31	Whittemore	Daniel				1					1				2		
Danvers	10	32	Whittemore	Joseph				1			1		1				3		
Danvers	10	33	Stephens	Benjamin		1	2	1		1			1				6		
Danvers	10	34	Winn	Joshua		2	1	1				1		1			7		
Danvers	10	35	Epes	William	1	1		1		3	2	1	1				10		
Danvers	10	36	Willson	Elisha	1	1							1				3		
Danvers	10	37	Bushby	John Jr	2		1			1			1				5		
Danvers	10	38	Bushby	John				1					1				2		
Danvers	10	39	Richardson	Samuel			1	1		1			1				4		
Danvers	10	40	Osborn	Anna									1	1			2		
Danvers	10	41	Osborn	Susanna		1	2			1	1	1	1	1			8		
Danvers	10	42	Willson	Clark	1			1		1			1				4		
Danvers	11	1	Willson	Benjamin		1		1					2	1			5		
Danvers	11	2	Poor	James	2			1		2		1	1				7		
Danvers	11	3	Osborn	John	1		1	1				1	1	1			6		
Danvers	11	4	Osborn	Paul	1		1	1		3	1		1				9		
Danvers	11	5	Willson	Isaac				2					2				4		
Danvers	11	6	Osborn	Daniel				2					2				4		
Danvers	11	7	Buxton	Jonathan Junr	2			1		2		1	1				7		
Danvers	11	8	Buxton	Jonathan			1	1					2	1			5		
Danvers	11	9	Mead	Samuel Revd	1			1				1		1			4		
Danvers	11	10	Osborn	Richard	1			1					1	1			4		
Danvers	11	11	Osborn	John Jr	2	1		1		1	2		1				8		
Danvers	11	12	Osborn	James			2	1			1	1					5		
Danvers	11	13	Osborn	Aaron	1			1					1				3		
Danvers	11	14	Osborn	Samuel		1	2	1			2	1	1				8		
Danvers	11	15	Osborn	Patience									1	1			2		
Danvers	11	16	Osborn	Abraham			1	1					1	1			4		
Danvers	11	17	Pike	Eben				1						1			2		
Danvers	11	18	Richardson	James				1						2			3		
Danvers	11	19	Willington	Thaddeus	1	1		1		3	1	3	1				11		
Danvers	11	20	Convers	Elizabeth	1					1	1		1				4		
Danvers	11	21	Macintire	Solomon			2			1			1				4		
Danvers	11	22	Laribee	Stephen	3	1	1	1					1				7		
Danvers	11	23	Day	Jonathan	2		1	1					1				5		
Danvers	11	24	Day	John			1			2			1				4		
Danvers	11	25	Frye	William	1		1						1				3		
Danvers	11	26	Trask	Henry			1			1		1					3		
Danvers	11	27	Stinson	John			2	1		2				3			8		
Danvers	11	28	Palmer	Jeremiah	1		1			1		1					4		
Danvers	11	29	Purington	Amos			1	1		1			1	1			5		
Danvers	11	30	Purington	Samuel		1		1					1	1			4		
Danvers	11	31	Purington	Abijah			1			1	1		1				4		
Danvers	11	32	Marshal	Robert	1	1		1		2			1				6		
Danvers	11	33	Hayward	Archelaus	2			1		1	1		1				6		
Danvers	11	34	Eden	Mary									1	1			2		
Danvers	11	35	Trask	Lydia	1							1	1	2			5		
Danvers	11	36	Towne	William			1			1		1					3		
Danvers	11	37	Trask	Daniel			1										1		
Danvers	11	38	Shillaber	Robert		1		1	1			1		1			5		
Danvers	11	39	Shillaber	William		1		1				1		2			5		
Danvers	11	40	Low	Caleb			2	1						1			4		
Danvers	11	41	Frost	John	3	2	1	1		1	1		1				10		
Danvers	11	42	Low	Stephen	5		1					1	1				8		
Danvers	11	43	Tucker	Sarah								1	1	1			3		
Danvers	12	1	Smith	Jabez	1	3	2					1					7		
Danvers	12	2	Dunkle	Ezekiel			1			2			1				4		
Danvers	12	3	Ston	Benjamin	2	1	1						1				6		
Danvers	12	4	Trask	Mehitable				1					1				2		
Danvers	12	5	Trask	William	1			1					1				3		
Danvers	12	6	Goldthwait	Benjamin	1		1				2		1				5		
Danvers	12	7	Smothers	Sarah			3					1	1	1			6		
Danvers	12	8	Willson	William	3		1				1	2	1				8		
Danvers	12	9	Pool	Elizabeth		1	1				1		1				4		

TOWN	PG#	LN#	LAST NAME	FIRST NAME	FWM under 10	FWM 10 to 16	FWM 16 to 26	FWM 26 to 45	FWM 45 and over	FWF under 10	FWF 10 to 16	FWF 16 to 26	FWF 26 to 45	FWF 45 and over	TOTAL ALL OTHER	TOTAL SLAVES	TOTALS	DISTRICT/ TOWNSHIP	NOTES
Danvers	12	10	Torry	Joseph	2			1					1		1		5		
Danvers	12	11	Derby	Samuel				1					1				2		
Danvers	12	12	Roles	Rebecca			1					1	1				3		
Danvers	12	13	White	Lucreece		1				3		1					5		
Danvers	12	14	Adams	Joseph	1			1		1		1	1				5		
Danvers	12	15	Darby	Charles				1			2	1	2	1			7		
Danvers	12	16	Porters	Mary									1	1			2		
Danvers	12	17	Johnson	William				1					1				2		
Danvers	12	18	Foster	Gideon		1	2		1		1	1		1			7		
Danvers	12	19	Southwick	Sarah									1	1			2		
Danvers	12	20	Hilbert	William	1			1	1	1		1					5		
Danvers	12	21	Hammond	Benjamin	1				1					1			3		
Danvers	12	22	Shove	Squiers	2		4	1		2	1		1				11		
Danvers	12	23	Sprague	Ebenezer					1					1			2		
Danvers	12	24	Sprague	Ebenezer Jr		1	1	1		1		1					5		
Danvers	12	25	Pierce	John		1		1				1					3		
Danvers	12	26	Verry	Joseph			2		1			1					4		
Danvers	12	27	Verry	Ephriem	3			1					1				5		
Danvers	12	28	Felton	David		1		1				1	1				4		
Danvers	12	29	Osborn	Sylvester	1		2	1		1	1	1	2				9		
Danvers	12	30	Wyman	Francis	1			1		1	1		1				5		
Danvers	12	31	Southwick	Edward	3		1	1		2			2				9		
Danvers	12	32	Trask	Jonathan	1	1			1	1			1	1			6		
Danvers	12	33	Souter	Sally			1						1				2		
Danvers	12	34	Trask	Joseph			1	1					2				4		
Danvers	12	35	Southwick	Joseph			1	1				1					3		
Danvers	12	36	Wallis	Dennison			2	1	1				1	2			7		
Danvers	12	37	Stone	Edmund Junr		1		1		4	2			1			9		
Danvers	12	38	Bell	Daniel		1		1		3		1					6		
Danvers	12	39	Upton	John Junr	1			1		1			1				4		
Danvers	12	40	Dodge	Daniel			1					1					2		
Danvers	12	41	Upton	John		1	1		1					1			4		
Danvers	12	42	Smith	Richard				1					1	2			4		
Danvers	12	43	Reed	Daniel Junr				1		1			1				3		
Danvers	12	44	Reed	Daniel				1			1			1			3		
Danvers	13	1	Saivl	Curtis	1			1					1				3		
Danvers	13	2	Wyman	Solomon					1					1			2		
Danvers	13	3	Mills	James				1					1				2		
Danvers	13	4	Osborn	Joseph Junr		2	1	1		2			2				8		
Danvers	13	5	Kimball	Richard		1		1	1					1			4		
Danvers	13	6	Saunders	John				1					1				2		
Danvers	13	7	Symonds	Samuel	2			1		1	1		1				6		
Danvers	13	8	Foster	David		1	1	1		1			1				5		
Danvers	13	9	Osborn	Lydia			1					1	1	1			4		
Danvers	13	10	Jones	William	2			1		1			1				5		
Danvers	13	11	Procter	Daniel Junr				1					1				2		
Danvers	13	12	Osborn	John Junr				1					1				2		
Danvers	13	13	Trask	John	1		1						1				3		
Danvers	13	14	Stone	George	1		1			3	1		1				7		
Danvers	13	15	Procter	Sylvester			1	1					1				3		
Danvers	13	16	Procter	Mehitable								2		1			3		
Danvers	13	17	Southwick	Simon	2			1		2			1				6		
Danvers	13	18	Downes	Experience									1				1		
Danvers	13	19	Sarle	Richard			1					1					2		
Danvers	13	20	Sprague	Betsy						1			1	1			3		
Danvers	13	21	Daniels	David	2		1	1		2	1		1				8		
Danvers	13	22	Reed	William	2				1		1	1		2			7		
Danvers	13	23	Reed	Benjamin	1		1						1				3		
Danvers	13	24	Goldthwait	William					1			2	1	1			5		
Danvers	13	25	Goldthwait	William Jr	1		1						1				3		
Danvers	13	26	Foster	Joseph	1				1	1	1	1	1				6		
Danvers	13	27	Cook	Henry	1		1	1		3		1	1				8		
Danvers	13	28	Pool	Ward	2		2	1				1	1				7		
Danvers	13	29	Child	Lemuel		2		1			1			1			5		
Danvers	13	30	Dodge	Tammerson										1			1		
Danvers	13	31	Tewksbury	Henry			1	1		2	1		1				6		
Danvers	13	32	Hammond	John	2	2		1		2	1		1				9		
Danvers	13	33	Osborn	James 3rd	2			1		1			1				5		
Danvers	13	34	Osborn	Daniel Junr			1	1					1	1			4		
Danvers	13	35	Peabody	Thomas	1	1		1		2			1				6		
Danvers	13	36	Snow	Asa	2			1		1	1		1				6		
Danvers	13	37	Curtis	Amos			1		1	1			1				4		
Danvers	13	38	Emmerson	Timothy	2	1	2		1	1	1	1		1			10		
Danvers	13	39	Emmerson	Thomas			1							1	1		3		
Danvers	13	40	Cook	George	1	1	1		1	3			1				8		
Danvers	13	41	Tapley	Betsy	2					1			1				4		
Danvers	13	42	Biggs	Eunice		1	1			1		1		1			5		
Danvers	14	1	Verry	Amos	1			1		2			1	1			6		
Danvers	14	2	Laribee	Anna			2	1	1				1	1			6		
Danvers	14	3	Dodge	Jeremiah			2		1	1	1		1				6		
Danvers	14	4	Needham	John	1			1		1	1		1		1		8		
Danvers	14	5	Boyce	Stephen						1				1			2		
Danvers	14	6	Marsh	John			1							2			3		
Danvers	14	7	Shaw	William		2		1		2		2		1			8		
Danvers	14	8	Rodes	Edmund			1	1	1			1		1			5		
Danvers	14	9	Rodes	Joseph			1			1			1				3		
Danvers	14	10	Herrod	Jonathan				1						1			2		
Danvers	14	11	Pickering	James	1		1					1					3		
Danvers	14	12	Rodes	Samuel	1			1	1	4		2	1				10		
Danvers	14	13	Osborn	Caleb	2	1		1		1	1		1				7		

TOWN	PG#	LN#	LAST NAME	FIRST NAME	FREE WHITE MALES					FREE WHITE FEMALES					TOTAL ALL OTHER	TOTAL SLAVES	TOTALS	DISTRICT/ TOWNSHIP	NOTES
					under 10	10 to 16	16 to 26	26 to 45	45 and over	under 10	10 to 16	16 to 26	26 to 45	45 and over					
Danvers	14	14	Goldthwait	Daniel				1		1			1				3		
Danvers	14	15	Goldthwait	John	1			1		2			1	1			6		
Danvers	14	16	Goldthwait	Nathaniel		1				1	2		1	1			6		
Danvers	14	17	Southwick	James Junr	3	1	1	1		1			2		1		10		
Danvers	14	18	Southwick	Ebenz		2			1			1	1	1			6		
Danvers	14	19	King	Zachariah Junr	2			1									3		
Danvers	14	20	Stone	Robert	2	2		1					1				6		
Danvers	14	21	Southwick	George 3rd	1			1		2		1	1				6		
Danvers	14	22	Smith	Elizabeth									1	1			2		
Danvers	14	23	King	Jonathan					1				1				2		
Danvers	14	24	Finney	Filemon		1		1					1				3		
Danvers	14	25	Southwick	William	3	1	1		1	1	1	1	1				10		
Danvers	14	26	Southwick	James				1		2	2		1				6		
Danvers	14	27	Southwick	Stephen	1	1		1		1	1		1				6		
Danvers	14	28	Shaw	Esther									1	1			2		
Danvers	14	29	Shaw	Joseph	1	1	1	1		3	1	1	1				10		
Danvers	14	30	King	Daniel		1		1			1	1					4		
Danvers	14	31	King	Zacheriah		1	3		1			1		1			7		
Danvers	14	32	King	Sarah										2			2		
Danvers	14	33	Bushby	Asa	2			1		1	1		1				6		
Danvers	14	34	Poor	Joseph	2			1				1	1				5		
Danvers	14	35	Messer	Asa Swan	1		1	1		1			1				5		
Danvers	14	36	Breed	Priscill						1		1					2		
Danvers	14	37	Burnham	Timothy				1		2		1					4		
Danvers	14	38	Buxton	John			1	1	1			1	1				5		
Danvers	14	39	Buxton	Sarah				1					1				2		
Danvers	14	40	Buxton	Joseph	2			1		2			1				6		
Danvers	14	41	Buxton	Henry		1	1		1			2		1			6		
Danvers	14	42	Buxton	Amos			1				1	1	1				5		
Danvers	14	43	Poor	Joseph	2	2	2		1	1	1	2		1			12		
Danvers	14	44	Reed	Desiah		1							1				2		
Danvers	15	1	Southwick	Hepsy	1								1	1			3		
Danvers	15	2	Hires	John			1	1		2			1				5		
Danvers	15	3	Osborn	Jonathan	1	1		1		1	1		1				6		
Danvers	15	4	Stephens	Jonas				1					1				2		
Danvers	15	5	Laird	Margaret	1		1							1			3		
Danvers	15	6	Upton	Elizabeth		2						1	1	1			5		
Danvers	15	7	Osborn	Joseph					1			1	1				3		
Danvers	15	8	Osborn	Amos	1		1			1		1					4		
Danvers	15	9	Procter	Esther	1			1			1			2			5		
Danvers	15	10	Osborn	Benjamin			1	1					3	1			6		
Danvers	15	11	Jacobs	Primas											4		4		
Danvers	15	12	Murphy	Milon											3		3		
Danvers	15	13	Pool	Milo											4		4		

TOWN	PG#	LN#	HEADS OF HOUSEHOLD LAST NAME	FIRST NAME	FREE WHITE MALES under 10	10 to 16	16 to 26	26 to 45	45 and over	FREE WHITE FEMALES under 10	10 to 16	16 to 26	26 to 45	45 and over	TOTAL ALL OTHER	TOTAL SLAVES	TOTALS	DISTRICT/ TOWNSHIP	NOTES
Gloucester	55	1	Adams	James			1			2		1					4		
Gloucester	55	2	Andrews	Jona	2			1		2		1	1				7		
Gloucester	55	3	Bray	Samuel			2		1				1	1			5		
Gloucester	55	4	Bray	Mark		2	1		1			2		1			7		
Gloucester	55	5	Bray	Isaac	2	1	1		1	1	1	2	1	1			11		
Gloucester	55	6	Bray	Willm		1		1		1			1				4		
Gloucester	55	7	Burnham	Ebenz		1	1	1			1	1		1			6		
Gloucester	55	8	Bray	Idea Wd		1	1			1	1	2		1			7		
Gloucester	55	9	Bray	Samuel Jun				1		2	2	2	1				8		
Gloucester	55	10	Bray	Silas	2			1		1			1				5		
Gloucester	55	11	Bray	Daniel	3			1				1	1				6		
Gloucester	55	12	Bray	Ebenz	3			1		2	1		1				8		
Gloucester	55	13	Butler	Jona	3		1			1				1			6		
Gloucester	55	14	Bray	Aaron	1		1			2		1					5		
Gloucester	55	15	Coghlin	Peter Esq			3		1	1	2						7		
Gloucester	55	16	Choate	Josiah				1					1				2		
Gloucester	55	17	Currier	Isiah		1		1		1		1		1			5		
Gloucester	55	18	Collins	Nathl				1					1				2		
Gloucester	55	19	Clark	George Junr	1		1					1					3		
Gloucester	56	1	Choate	Judith Wd		1	1					1		1			4		
Gloucester	56	2	Bray	Theo Doctr				1						1			2		
Gloucester	56	3	Cole	Weden		1	1							1			3		
Gloucester	56	4	Cole	Weden Junr	2	1						1					4		
Gloucester	56	5	Choate	Adonjo	1		1							1			3		
Gloucester	56	6	Ayers	Abigal Widw	2					1	1		1	1			6		
Gloucester	56	7	Courtney	Samuel	1		1			1			1				4		
Gloucester	56	8	Cole	Annie Wd	2								1				3		
Gloucester	56	9	Currier	Adonjo		1				1			1				3		
Gloucester	56	10	Dennen	Joseph	1			1		2	2	1	1				8		
Gloucester	56	11	Dennen	Joseph Junr	2		1			1			1				5		
Gloucester	56	12	Davis	Timothy	2		1			1			1				5		
Gloucester	56	13	Eveleth	Joseph				1						2			3		
Gloucester	56	14	Eveleth	Isaac Majo		1		1				1					3		
Gloucester	56	15	Fuller	Danl Revd	1	1	2	1				1	1	1			8		
Gloucester	56	16	Ford	John	1			1		2			1	1			6		
Gloucester	56	17	Gilbert	Jona				1		1				1			3		
Gloucester	56	18	Gilbert	Willa	1		3	1		2	5		1	1			14		
Gloucester	56	19	Gilbert	Jona Junr	2		1					1					4		
Gloucester	56	20	Haskell	Nathl Deac				1						1			2		
Gloucester	56	21	Haskell	William				1						1			2		
Gloucester	56	22	Haskell	Aaron		2	4	1	1	1	1		1	2			13		
Gloucester	56	23	Haskell	Daniel				1				1					2		
Gloucester	56	24	Haskell	Danl Jun	2	1		1		1		1					6		
Gloucester	56	25	Haskell	Stephen	2			1		3			1				7		
Gloucester	56	26	Haskell	Elias	1		2	1		2	2		1				9		
Gloucester	56	27	Haskell	Zebulon	1		1	2	1	2	2		1				10		
Gloucester	56	28	Haskell	Zebulon Junr	1		1	1		2			1				6		
Gloucester	56	29	Herrick	Joseph				1					1				2		
Gloucester	56	30	Herrick	Joseph Junr			1						1				2		
Gloucester	56	31	Herrick	Willm A.		2	1			3			2				8		
Gloucester	56	32	Herrick	Danl		1	1	1		2		1		1			7		
Gloucester	56	33	Haskell	Adonj	1		1			1			1				4		
Gloucester	56	34	Haskell	Moses	3	1	2	1		2	1		1				11		
Gloucester	56	35	Haskell	Stephen Junr	1			1			1	1					4		
Gloucester	56	36	Herrick	Thos				1			1	1		1			4		
Gloucester	56	37	Haskell	Abraham	2			1					1				4		
Gloucester	56	38	Herrick	Richard	2			1					1				4		
Gloucester	56	39	Haskell	Amoss		1	1		1	1				1			5		
Gloucester	57	1	Haskell	Amoss Junr			1			1			1				3		
Gloucester	57	2	Haskell	Enoch	1		1						1				3		
Gloucester	57	3	Knight	Joseph				1				1		1			3		
Gloucester	57	4	Knghts	Thos			1			1			1				3		
Gloucester	57	5	Knowlton	Moses	2		1	1		1	2		1				9		
Gloucester	57	6	Lufkins	Thos	2		1	1		1	1	1	1	1			9		
Gloucester	57	7	Pulcifer	Nathl		2	1	1		1				1			6		
Gloucester	57	8	Pulcifer	Jacob			1						1				2		
Gloucester	57	9	Pulcifer	Jabez		1		1						1			3		
Gloucester	57	10	Pulcifer	Daniel	2			1		1			2				6		
Gloucester	57	11	Pulcifer	Taba Wd				1			1	1		1			4		
Gloucester	57	12	Procter	Willm	1	1	1	1						2			6		
Gloucester	57	13	Rust	Benja	2	1	1	1		2		1					8		
Gloucester	57	14	Roberts	Jacob	1			1				1					3		
Gloucester	57	15	Roberts	Ephm	1			1						1			3		
Gloucester	57	16	Roberts	Levi	1	1	1		1			1		1			6		
Gloucester	57	17	Roberts	John	3	2	1		1				1				8		
Gloucester	57	18	Rust	Israel	2		1			3		2		1			9		
Gloucester	57	19	Riggs	Aaron	2		1					1					4		
Gloucester	57	20	Rust	Anna Wd								1		1			2		
Gloucester	57	21	Sargent	Thos Doct	3				1	1				1			4	West Parish	

41

TOWN	PG#	LN#	LAST NAME	FIRST NAME	FREE WHITE MALES					FREE WHITE FEMALES					TOTAL ALL OTHER	TOTAL SLAVES	TOTALS	DISTRICT/ TOWNSHIP	NOTES
					under 10	10 to 16	16 to 26	26 to 45	45 and over	under 10	10 to 16	16 to 26	26 to 45	45 and over					
Gloucester	57	22	Steel	Sarah Wd			2	1						1			4	West Parish	
Gloucester	57	23	Steel	John	1			1		1				1			4	West Parish	
Gloucester	57	24	Steel	Danl	1		1			2		1	1				7	West Parish	
Gloucester	57	25	Stanwood	Zebulon Junr			1			1	1	1					4	West Parish	
Gloucester	57	26	Steel	Joseph	1		1			1	1	1	1				6	West Parish	
Gloucester	57	27	Sargent	Dudlay	1		1			1		1					4	West Parish	
Gloucester	57	28	Trask	Ebenz		2			1	1				1			5	West Parish	
Gloucester	57	29	Wallace	Joseph	3	1		1		1	2	1	1				10	West Parish	
Gloucester	57	30	Woodbery	Winthrop	1		1			1	1	1		1			6	West Parish	
Gloucester	57	31	Woodbery	Seth			1						1	1			3	West Parish	
Gloucester	57	32	Morgan	William			1				1	2		2			6	West Parish	
Gloucester	57	33	Haskell	Isaac				1						1			2	West Parish	
Gloucester	57	34	Greene	Negro											4		4	West Parish	
Gloucester	57	35	Haskell	Cornelius											12		12	West Parish	
Gloucester	57	36	Dodge	Nathll		1	1		1					1			4	West Parish	
Gloucester	57	37	Clarke	George		1			1					1			3	West Parish	
Gloucester	57	38	Roberts	Eliphalet	1	1	1		1					1			5	West Parish	
Gloucester	57	39	Stevens	Ebenz					1				1	1			3	West Parish	
Gloucester	58	1	Robbins	Nathl		1	3	1	1	1	1			2			10		
Gloucester	58	2	Roberts	Jeru Wo								1		2			3		
Gloucester	58	3	Roberts	Estr Wo							1	1		1			3		
Gloucester	58	4	Pulcifer	Edmand	1			1		1		1		1			5		
Gloucester	58	5	Boyanton	Eliphl				1						1			2		
Gloucester	58	6	Boyanton	John		1	1	1				1					4		
Gloucester	58	7	Hannon	John			1			2			1				4		
Gloucester	58	8	Hadock	Hannah Wo			1							1			2		
Gloucester	58	9	Roberts	Mary Wo							1	1		1			3		
Gloucester	58	10	Bray	Abigail Wo			2							1			3		
Gloucester	58	11	Bray	Enoch Junr				1		4	2		1				8		
Gloucester	58	12	Bray	Enoch				1						1			2		
Gloucester	58	13	Perrin	Eliza Wo							1	2		1			4		
Gloucester	58	14	Pulcifer	Nathll Junr				1					1				2		
Gloucester	58	15	Davy	Mark	1		1						1				3		
Gloucester	58	16	Drews	Eleazer	1		1			2			1				5		
Gloucester	58	17	Davy	Patty Widow									1	2			3		
Gloucester	58	18	Burgan	John	1			1		2			1	1			6		
Gloucester	58	19	Allen	Solomon Junr				1		1		1		1			4		
Gloucester	58	20	Allen	Solomon 3d	1	1		1		3	1	1	1				9		
Gloucester	58	21	Allen	William Junr			1			1		1					3		
Gloucester	58	22	Appleton	William	1			1		1			1	1			5		
Gloucester	58	23	Allen	Sarah Widow			2					1	1				4		
Gloucester	58	24	Appleton	John	1			1						1			3		
Gloucester	58	25	Brinick	James	1									1			2		
Gloucester	58	26	Thomas	Nehemiah	1		1			1		1					4		
Gloucester	58	27	Brown	Jona Junr	1		1		1		1	1		1			6		
Gloucester	58	28	Brown	Jona 3d	3	1	1	1		2		1	1				10		
Gloucester	58	29	Brown	Jon Cap					1				1	1			3		
Gloucester	58	30	Bond	Samuel		2			1					1			4		
Gloucester	58	31	Babson	Dolly Wo			1					2		1			4		
Gloucester	58	32	Burnham	Aaron	1	1	1	1			1		1				6		
Gloucester	58	33	Brown	Stephen		2		1		3	1		1				8		
Gloucester	58	34	Bishop	Benja			1	1						1			3		
Gloucester	58	35	Barker	Nathll	2			1		1			2	1			7		
Gloucester	58	36	Clough	Elias			1						1				2		
Gloucester	58	37	Clough	Martha Wo									1				1		
Gloucester	58	38	Calder	Samuel	2			1		1		1		1			6		
Gloucester	59	1	Coffin	Willa Doct	2	2	2	1		2	3	2	1				15		
Gloucester	59	2	Coffin	Dolly Widw		1						1		1			3		
Gloucester	59	3	Cushing	Zenias	1			1		2			1				5		
Gloucester	59	4	Wharfe	Sarah Widw	2							2		1			5		
Gloucester	59	5	Davis	Moses	1			1		1			1				4		
Gloucester	59	6	Dodge	Jona	2	1		1		2		1	1				8		
Gloucester	59	7	Dexter	William	3	2		1		1		2	1				10		
Gloucester	59	8	Davis	Elipt Colo	4	2	1	1		1	2	2	1				14		
Gloucester	59	9	Dane	William		1			1				2				4		
Gloucester	59	10	Dennis	John			1	1						1			3		
Gloucester	59	11	Dawson	Elias	1			1			1	1					4		
Gloucester	59	12	Ellery	Abigale Wo									1	1			2		
Gloucester	59	13	Ellery	Nathll	2			1					1				4		
Gloucester	59	14	Discal	Jeremiah			1		1					1			3		
Gloucester	59	15	Elwell	Isaac	1	3	1		1			2		3			11		
Gloucester	59	16	Fredericks	Jabez		2	2	1				2		1			8		
Gloucester	59	17	Griffen	William	1			1		4			1	1			8		
Gloucester	59	18	Forbes	Eli Revd		1			1		1	1		1			5		
Gloucester	59	19	Gould	John				1		1		1					3		
Gloucester	59	20	Gaffnay	Michl	5			1		2	1		1				10		
Gloucester	59	21	Greenleaf	William	2			1			1	1		1			6		
Gloucester	59	22	Haskell	Nathll	1		1	1		2	1		1				7		
Gloucester	59	23	Hodgkins	Jacob	2			1					1	1			5		

TOWN	PG#	LN#	LAST NAME	FIRST NAME	M under 10	M 10 to 16	M 16 to 26	M 26 to 45	M 45 and over	F under 10	F 10 to 16	F 16 to 26	F 26 to 45	F 45 and over	TOTAL ALL OTHER	TOTAL SLAVES	TOTALS	DISTRICT/ TOWNSHIP	NOTES
Gloucester	59	24	Haskell	Nathll Junr		1	2		1			1	1	1			7		
Gloucester	59	25	Hibbard	Jacob	2		1	1		1	3	1					9		
Gloucester	59	26	Hayes	James		1	1	1		1	2	1	1				8		
Gloucester	59	27	Hall	Aaron	2	3			1	1	1		1				9		
Gloucester	59	28	Haskell	Josiah	1	1	1		1		2			1			7		
Gloucester	59	29	Hough	Benja				1		1	2	1	1				6		
Gloucester	59	30	Hayes	James Junr	1		1				2						4		
Gloucester	59	31	Jones	Joseph	1			1		2			1	1			6		
Gloucester	59	32	Indersol	William	1	1	1					1	1				5		
Gloucester	59	33	Johnson	John	1		2					1	1				5		
Gloucester	59	34	Knight	Stephen	2		1						2				5		
Gloucester	59	35	Knight	Abigl Widow		1	1					2		1			5		
Gloucester	59	36	Low	Jonathan	1	2		2		2		1	1				9		
Gloucester	59	37	Low	Frances	1			1						1			3		
Gloucester	59	38	Low	John Junr	2	1		1		1			1	1			7		
Gloucester	59	39	Logan	John				1						1			2		
Gloucester	59	40	Lutkin	David	1			1		1	1	3	1	1			9		
Gloucester	60	1	Lincoln	Richard	2		1				1		1				5		
Gloucester	60	2	Marble	Benja	3			1		2			1				7		
Gloucester	60	3	Morey	Thomas	2	2		1			1	3	1				10		
Gloucester	60	4	Morgan	Willa				1			1	1	1				4		
Gloucester	60	5	Morey	Joseph		1		1		1		1	1				5		
Gloucester	60	6	Murphy	William				1					1				2		
Gloucester	60	7	Morehead	Samll			1				2		1				4		
Gloucester	60	8	Mansfield	James	1		1	1		2	1		2				8		
Gloucester	60	9	Mittell	Joseph	2		1				1						4		
Gloucester	60	10	Marshall	John			1	1		1	1	1					5		
Gloucester	60	11	Marshall	Solomon	2		1					1	1				6		
Gloucester	60	12	Marshall	Samuel			1			3	2		1				7		
Gloucester	60	13	Mason	John	2		1				1		1				5		
Gloucester	60	14	Millatt	Thos			1	2		3				1			7		
Gloucester	60	15	Oben	Jona	2	1		1		1	2	2	1				10		
Gloucester	60	16	Parsons	Solomon				1			2	2		1			6		
Gloucester	60	17	Presson	William		1		1			1	1		1			5		
Gloucester	60	18	Procter	Isaac		2		2				1		1			6		
Gloucester	60	19	Peirced	David Capt				1		2		3					6		
Gloucester	60	20	Procter	Joseph		1	2	1				2		1			7		
Gloucester	60	21	Parsons	Jona	1		1			3		1					6		
Gloucester	60	22	Sawyer	Abraham Jun		1		1		1	1		1				5		
Gloucester	60	23	Parsons	Aaron Capt	2			1		2			1				6		
Gloucester	60	24	Parsons	Andrew	2			1		1	1	1		1			7		
Gloucester	60	25	Parsons	Nehemiah	1	1		1		1	1	1		1			7		
Gloucester	60	26	Parsons	Michael	1			1		1	1	1	1	1			7		
Gloucester	60	27	Pew	William			1					1					2		
Gloucester	60	28	Phelps	Henry Doct	1	1		1		2		1		1			7		
Gloucester	60	29	Procter	Danl & Epes	1	1		1		3	1		2				9		
Gloucester	60	30	Peirce	Will C Col	1	2	5	1		1	1	2	2				15		
Gloucester	60	31	Rust	John					1					2			3		
Gloucester	60	32	Rust	Morey		1	2	1		1		1		1			7		
Gloucester	60	33	Robinson	Samuel			1	1		1			1	1			5		
Gloucester	60	34	Rogers	Charles Capt	1	2		1		3		3					10		
Gloucester	60	35	Rogers	Daniel			3					2			1		6		
Gloucester	60	36	Rogers	Rachel Wd			5		1	1	2	3		1			13		
Gloucester	60	37	Piper	Marth Wd			1					1		2			4		
Gloucester	60	38	Rogers	John Maj	3			1		2	1	1	1				9		
Gloucester	60	39	Robinson	Jno Junr	1	1		1		1			1	1			6		
Gloucester	60	40	Sawyer	Abraham		1		1				1		1			4		
Gloucester	61	1	Stacy	Nymphus Dea				1						1			2		
Gloucester	61	2	Stanwood	Aaron		1	1						1	1			4		
Gloucester	61	3	Stevens	Eliza Wd		1					2	4	1				8		
Gloucester	61	4	Stacy	Lucy Wd		2			1	1	1	2		1			7		
Gloucester	61	5	Stacy	Benja	3	1		1			1		1				7		
Gloucester	61	6	Sargent	Nathll							1	2	1				5		
Gloucester	61	7	Stanwood	Zebulon	1	2	2	1	1		2		1				10		
Gloucester	61	8	Saunders	Joseph Capt			1				1	1	1				4		
Gloucester	61	9	Somes	John Capt		1		1			1		2				5		
Gloucester	61	10	Stevens	Zacha	2	1		1		1	1	2		1			10		
Gloucester	61	11	Smith	Jacob	2	1	3	1		2	1	1	1	1			13		
Gloucester	61	12	Smith	Charles	3		1						2				6		
Gloucester	61	13	Smith	Joseph	2		1						2				5		
Gloucester	61	14	Slatery	Henry	2		1					1					4		
Gloucester	61	15	Steal	James	3	2		1		1		1	1				9		
Gloucester	61	16	Sawyer	James	2		1	1			1	1		1			8		
Gloucester	61	17	Somes	John 4th Capt	1		1	1			1		1	1			6		
Gloucester	61	18	Somes	John Jun	1		1			1			1				4		
Gloucester	61	19	Sargent	Abimh	2		1			2		1	1				7		
Gloucester	61	20	Stevens	Cyrus	1	1	1			1		2					6		
Gloucester	61	21	Sawyer	James Junr	1	1	1			2	1		1				7		
Gloucester	61	22	Shackelford	Willm	1		1			4							7		

TOWN	PG#	LN#	LAST NAME	FIRST NAME	FREE WHITE MALES					FREE WHITE FEMALES					TOTAL ALL OTHER	TOTAL SLAVES	TOTALS	DISTRICT/ TOWNSHIP	NOTES
					under 10	10 to 16	16 to 26	26 to 45	45 and over	under 10	10 to 16	16 to 26	26 to 45	45 and over					
Gloucester	61	23	Stanwood	Thos	1	1	1			1		1	1		1		7		
Gloucester	61	24	Trask	Abigal Widw						1		1	1	1			4		
Gloucester	61	25	Trewboday	John	1			1	2				2	1			8		
Gloucester	61	26	Tayler	Thomas			1			1	1	1					4		
Gloucester	61	27	Tucker	Nathl	1	1		1		2			1	1			7		
Gloucester	61	28	Tarr	David	2	1		1					1				5		
Gloucester	61	29	Tappan	James	1					3	1	2					8		
Gloucester	61	30	Whittemore	Samll Esq		1	1	1	1	1	3	1	2				11		
Gloucester	62	1	Webber	Benja	2	3	1			1	1	2	1				11		
Gloucester	62	2	Webber	Ignatius	2	1		1		1	2	1	1				9		
Gloucester	62	3	Wharfe	Isaac	1				1	2	1		1	1			7		
Gloucester	62	4	Woodberry	John	1					2		1	1				6		
Gloucester	62	5	Whittemore	Joshua	1					1	1	1	1				6		
Gloucester	62	6	Winchester	John	3			1					1				5		
Gloucester	62	7	West	Benja	1	2	1	1	1	5	1	2		1			15		
Gloucester	62	8	Parsons	Joshua	2	1	1	1		1			1				7		
Gloucester	62	9	Cushing	Polly								1					1		
Gloucester	62	10	Ellery	William		1						1					2		
Gloucester	62	11	Low	Elias Junr		1				1		1					3		
Gloucester	62	12	Parsons	Obed Esq		2		1		2		1					6		
Gloucester	62	13	saunders	Nath	2		1			1		1					5		
Gloucester	62	14	Millett	Isaac	1		1					1					3		
Gloucester	62	15	Ingersole	David	1			1		1		1					4		
Gloucester	62	16	Davis	Judith Wd			3				1		1				5		
Gloucester	62	17	Honners	Robert	1		4		1	1		1		1			9		
Gloucester	62	18	Harken	Hannah Wd	1		2			1		1	1	1			7		
Gloucester	62	19	Selah	Mathew				1			1		1	1			4		
Gloucester	62	20	Stanwood	Lemuel				1					1				2		
Gloucester	62	21	Parsons	Enoch	1			1					1	1			4		
Gloucester	62	22	Locke	Joseph		1		1		1			1				4		
Gloucester	62	23	Saunders	Bradbury		1					2	1					4		
Gloucester	62	24	Atkins	Benja	1		1					1		1			4		
Gloucester	62	25	Wotton	Henry	1			1		3	3	1	1				10		
Gloucester	62	26	Wotton	Joseph	1			1		1	1		1				5		
Gloucester	62	27	Andrews	Andrew	1	1			1	2	1		1				7		
Gloucester	62	28	Jones	Agnes Wo	1					1		1		1			4		
Gloucester	62	29	Trask	Abigal Wo	1	1				2		1					6		
Gloucester	62	30	Marshall	William	3			1					1				5		
Gloucester	63	1	Baley	Nathl				1		1				1			3	West Ward	
Gloucester	63	2	Pain	Richard		1	1		1					1			4	West Ward	
Gloucester	63	3	Day	David			1						2				3	West Ward	
Gloucester	63	4	Robinson	Jona	1			1		1			1	1			5	West Ward	
Gloucester	63	5	Bryer	John			1				1		1				3	West Ward	
Gloucester	63	6	Gray	William	1			1					1				3	West Ward	
Gloucester	63	7	Andrews	Mary Wo			1						1				2	West Ward	
Gloucester	63	8	Bond	Hannah Wo	2					1		2	1				6	West Ward	
Gloucester	63	9	Parsons	Ezekial	2	1			1	1			1				6	West Ward	
Gloucester	63	10	Day	Isaac		2		1		2	1		1				7	West Ward	
Gloucester	63	11	Barrett	William	2			1		1			1				5	West Ward	
Gloucester	63	12	Day	Anna Wo								2	1				3	West Ward	
Gloucester	63	13	Tyler	John	2	1		1			1		1				6	West Ward	
Gloucester	63	14	Morse	Humphrey	2	2		1					1				6	West Ward	
Gloucester	63	15	Emons	Daniel			1				1		1				3	West Ward	
Gloucester	63	16	Adams	Joseph	2	2	3		1	1			1				10	East Ward	
Gloucester	63	17	Babson	Samuel Cap		1	1				1		1				4	East Ward	
Gloucester	63	18	Brown	Elisha				1			3						4	East Ward	
Gloucester	63	19	Bates	Henry	1		1			1	1		1				5	East Ward	
Gloucester	63	20	Bennett	Noah	2		1		1	1	1	1					7	East Ward	
Gloucester	63	21	Coas	William	2		1			2	2	1					8	East Ward	
Gloucester	63	22	Coas	Jeren	2		1			1				1			5	East Ward	
Gloucester	63	23	Coffin	James Capt	1	1		1		1	1	1		1			7	East Ward	
Gloucester	63	24	Chellis	Gideon		1	1	1			2	1		1			7	East Ward	
Gloucester	63	25	Collins	Daniel Colo	2	1	2		1	1	1	2	1				11	East Ward	
Gloucester	63	26	Caswell	Samuel		1	1			2		1					5	East Ward	
Gloucester	63	27	Doliver	William Cap	2		1	1		1			1				6	East Ward	
Gloucester	63	28	Day	Samuel	1	1		1		3			1				7	East Ward	
Gloucester	63	29	Dane	Abigal Wo				1					1				2	East Ward	
Gloucester	64	1	Dane	Joshua	1			1			1						4		
Gloucester	64	2	Day	David Junr	1			1		2		1					5		
Gloucester	64	3	Doliver	William Cap				1					1		2		4		
Gloucester	64	4	Davis	Elias Capt	3	1	1		1		3			1			10		
Gloucester	64	5	Elwell	Jona 3d	1			1		1		3		1			7		
Gloucester	64	6	Everton	Joseph		3			1		2	2	1				9		
Gloucester	64	7	Elwell	Robert Junr			2	1	1			1	1	1			7		
Gloucester	64	8	Ellery	Esther Wo			1				1	1	2				5		
Gloucester	64	9	Elwell	Solomon		1			1	1	1						4		
Gloucester	64	10	Elwell	Robert 3d	1	1	1	1		4			1				9		
Gloucester	64	11	Elwell	Elias	1	2	1	1			2	1	1				9		
Gloucester	64	12	Foster	Joseph Colo		2		1			3		2				8		
Gloucester	64	13	Foster	Joseph Junr Cap	2	1		1		1	2		1	1			9		

TOWN	PG#	LN#	LAST NAME	FIRST NAME	FREE WHITE MALES under 10	10 to 16	16 to 26	26 to 45	45 and over	FREE WHITE FEMALES under 10	10 to 16	16 to 26	26 to 45	45 and over	TOTAL ALL OTHER	TOTAL SLAVES	TOTALS	DISTRICT/ TOWNSHIP	NOTES
Gloucester	64	14	Foster	Jereh Capt	2	1			1	3	2	1	1	1			12		
Gloucester	64	15	Friend	Richard	2	1		1		2	1		1				8		
Gloucester	64	16	Foster	Elijah		1			1	3				1			6		
Gloucester	64	17	Grover	Eleazer	2			1		3	1		1	1			9		
Gloucester	64	18	Goodhue	Sarah Wo										1			1		
Gloucester	64	19	Grimes	William			1	1	1			2		1			6		
Gloucester	64	20	Grimes	William Junr				1					1				2		
Gloucester	64	21	Harradan	David		2	1	2	1				2	1			9		
Gloucester	64	22	Haskell	Hubbard Dea				1						1			2		
Gloucester	64	23	Haskell	William	3	2		1		1	1	1	1				10		
Gloucester	64	24	Harrick	Josiah	1			1		2	2	1	1				8		
Gloucester	64	25	Haskell	John	1	1		1		2	1	1	1				8		
Gloucester	64	26	Haskell	Thomas	1		1			2		1					5		
Gloucester	64	27	Hudgen	John G.	1	1	2	1	1	2	3	1					12		
Gloucester	64	28	Hutchings	Willm Capt	2	1	1	1		2	2	1					10		
Gloucester	64	29	Hardy	William				1		1			1	1			4		
Gloucester	65	1	Ingalls	Joseph	1	1		1		1	1		1				6		
Gloucester	65	2	Kingsman	Nathaniel					1			2	1	2			6		
Gloucester	65	3	Kingsbury	Aaron					1					1			2		
Gloucester	65	4	Kinsman	William	1		1	1		1	1		1				6		
Gloucester	65	5	Littlehale	Richard		1	2	1	1		1	2	1				9		
Gloucester	65	6	Lincoln	Obed Esq		1		1			1		1				4		
Gloucester	65	7	Haskell	Zebulon	1		1					1					3		
Gloucester	65	8	Lamson	Daniel	1		1			1			1				4		
Gloucester	65	9	Low	Lydia Wo	2	2				2	1	1					8		
Gloucester	65	10	Atkins	John		1					1		1				3		
Gloucester	65	11	Medox	James	1		1			1		1					4		
Gloucester	65	12	Millett	James	1	2	1	1		3	1		1				10		
Gloucester	65	13	Medox	John	2			1					1				4		
Gloucester	65	14	Norwood	Solomon Junr	2		1			1		1					5		
Gloucester	65	15	Newman	John	1	1	2	1	1	1	1	1	1				10		
Gloucester	65	16	Oakes	John	2	1		1		2		2		1			9		
Gloucester	65	17	Oakes	William	3		1						1				5		
Gloucester	65	18	Pearson	Samuel	2		1			2			1				6		
Gloucester	65	19	Parsons	Jereh				1					1				2		
Gloucester	65	20	Parsons	Thomas Capt		1	1	1				2	1				6		
Gloucester	65	21	Pearson	William Cap	1	1	1		2	1	1	2	1				10		
Gloucester	65	22	Prindle	Eldad				1						2			3		
Gloucester	65	23	Plummer	David		2	3	1			1	2	1				10		
Gloucester	65	24	Parsons	James	1		1			2	1		1	1			7		
Gloucester	65	25	Prindle	Eliakim	3	1		1		1	1	1	1				9		
Gloucester	65	26	Pasa	Richard G.	2		1			1			1				5		
Gloucester	65	27	Parsons	Samuel	2		1			1			1				5		
Gloucester	66	1	Qualls	William	1		1			2			1				5		
Gloucester	66	2	Rowe	David	1	1	1	1						1			5		
Gloucester	66	3	Rowe	Joseph	1	1		1						2			5		
Gloucester	66	4	Rogers	John	1	2		1		1	1	1	1				8		
Gloucester	66	5	Rand	Thomas	1		1	1			3		1				7		
Gloucester	66	6	Rowe	William	2	1		1		2			1				7		
Gloucester	66	7	Robinson	Andrew	2	1		1				1					5		
Gloucester	66	8	Rowe	Abraham		2		1		1			1	1			6		
Gloucester	66	9	Reding	William	1		1	1		2	1						7		
Gloucester	66	10	Riggs	Asa		1							1				2		
Gloucester	66	11	Sullivan	Michael	1			1					1				3		
Gloucester	66	12	Ingersole	Abigail Wo		1	1				1	1					4		
Gloucester	66	13	Sargent	Ignatius Majr	2			1		1	3						7		
Gloucester	66	14	Torres	Benj Capt				1					2				3		
Gloucester	66	15	Sayward	Henry		1					1			1			3		
Gloucester	66	16	Saunders	John Capt		2	1						1				4		
Gloucester	66	17	Sayward	James Junr	1		1			2	1		1				6		
Gloucester	66	18	Somes	Abigal Widw		1	2			2	1		1				7		
Gloucester	66	19	Smith	John			1			1			1				3		
Gloucester	66	20	Somes	John 3d	4		1	1		1	1	1					9		
Gloucester	66	21	Sargent	Jonan		2	3	1		1	1		1				9		
Gloucester	66	22	Saunders	Joseph Junr	3	2		1		1	1		1				9		
Gloucester	66	23	Sayward	James S. Capt			1			3				1			5		
Gloucester	66	24	Sargent	Fit* W. Capt	2		1	1		4	1		2	1			12		
Gloucester	66	25	Sayward	Daniel			1			3	1	1					6		
Gloucester	66	26	Smith	Benjm Jun	1		1			1			1				4		
Gloucester	66	27	Smith	Henry Cap	1	1		1		3	1	1	1				9		
Gloucester	66	28	Sayward	William	1	1		1		1			1				5		
Gloucester	67	1	Sargent	David				1					1				2		
Gloucester	67	2	Stacy	John Capt	1		1			2		1	1				6		
Gloucester	67	3	Sayward	John	1		1			2			1	1			6		
Gloucester	67	4	Tucker	John Maj		1		1		2	1		1				6		
Gloucester	67	5	Thomas	William	1	1	1	1		1	2		1				8		
Gloucester	67	6	Tyler	James	1		1						1				3		
Gloucester	67	7	T*	Marry Widw		1							1				2		
Gloucester	67	8	Tarbox	Benja		1		1			2			1			5		
Gloucester	67	9	Trask	Israel Cap	2		1			3	1		1				8		
Gloucester	67	10	Tarr	Abraham	2								1				3		
Gloucester	67	11	Thompson	James	1		1	1		2		1	1				7		
Gloucester	67	12	Warren	Willm Capt	1		1						1				3		
Gloucester	67	13	Witham	Edward		2		1				1		1			5		
Gloucester	67	14	Hutching	Benja			1			1			1				3		
Gloucester	67	15	Hutchins	Rachal Wo		1								1			2		
Gloucester	67	16	Warren	Danl Colo			1	2			1		1				5		
Gloucester	67	17	Brown	Vincent	1		1			1			1				4		
Gloucester	67	18	Watson	Robert	1	2			1	1							6		

TOWN	PG#	LN#	HEADS OF HOUSEHOLD LAST NAME	FIRST NAME	FREE WHITE MALES under 10	10 to 16	16 to 26	26 to 45	45 and over	FREE WHITE FEMALES under 10	10 to 16	16 to 26	26 to 45	45 and over	TOTAL ALL OTHER	TOTAL SLAVES	TOTALS	DISTRICT/ TOWNSHIP	NOTES
Gloucester	67	19	Witham	Dorcas Wo			3			2				1			6		
Gloucester	67	20	Witham	Danl		1	2		1	2		1		1			8		
Gloucester	67	21	Wallace	David		1			1			1		1			4		
Gloucester	67	22	Witham	Benja	1	1			1			1					4		
Gloucester	67	23	Witham	Benja 3d				1		1			1				3		
Gloucester	67	24	Williams	Nathl	2			1		1	1		1				6		
Gloucester	67	25	Wonson	Saml Junr	2		2			2		2					8		
Gloucester	67	26	Sorey	Nancy Wo	1		1						1	1			4		
Gloucester	67	27	Wonson	Charles	2		1						1				4		
Gloucester	67	28	Whipple	David	1		1			2			1				5		
Gloucester	68	1	Williams	Abraham	2			2		1	1		1	1			8		
Gloucester	68	2	Witham	Thos	1			1			1		1				4		
Gloucester	68	3	Witham	Abraham			1			1			1				3		
Gloucester	68	4	Winter	William	1		1			1			1	1			5		
Gloucester	68	5	White	Jos Doct	1			1		2		1	1				6		
Gloucester	68	6	Woodbery	Joshua	2	1		1		1		1	1				7		
Gloucester	68	7	Kinsman	John			1						1				2		
Gloucester	68	8	Babson	Charles			1						1				2		
Gloucester	68	9	Somes	John Junr	3	1		1		3	1		1				10		
Gloucester	68	10	Robinson	Abigal Wo										1			1		
Gloucester	68	11	Haller	Mary Wo									1	1			2		
Gloucester	68	12	Joseph	Mathew			1			1		1		1			4		
Gloucester	68	13	Thomas	Anna Wo		1	1						2	1			5		
Gloucester	68	14	Dresson	Moses		3	1	1		2		1	1				9		
Gloucester	68	15	Cristee	John			2			1			2				5		
Gloucester	68	16	Claywood	James	1			1	1	1			1				5		
Gloucester	68	17	Harday	John		1		1				2		1			5		
Gloucester	68	18	Storey	John	1			1		2			1	1			6		
Gloucester	68	19	Smith	Nathl			1			1	1	1					4		
Gloucester	68	20	Martin	Sarah Wo			1						1				2		
Gloucester	68	21	Brown	John	3			1		1			1				6		
Gloucester	68	22	Card	Mary Wo						1			1				2		
Gloucester	68	23	Rowe	Abraham		1			1				2				4		
Gloucester	68	24	Rowe	Abraham Junr	1			1		2			1				5		
Gloucester	68	25	Watson	John			1					1					2		
Gloucester	68	26	Wonson	Saml	1					2				2			6		
Gloucester	68	27	Duglass	John				1					1				2		
Gloucester	68	28	Storey	Amos			1			1			1	1			4		
Gloucester	69	1	Duglass	Danl	1		1						1				3		
Gloucester	69	2	Lufkins	Moses											10		10		
Gloucester	69	3	Lakay	Lucy Wd	1					1	2		1				5		
Gloucester	69	4	Tarr	Solomon	1	1		1		1	1	1					6		
Gloucester	69	5	Norwood	Solomon	3		1	1		2	2		1				10		
Gloucester	69	6	Smith	Daniel				1					1	1	1		3		
Gloucester	69	7	Clark	Bacokus Sargent			1	1					1	1	4		8		
Gloucester	69	8	Dean	Nathl		1		1					1				3		
Gloucester	69	9	Gilbert	Moses		1						1					2		
Gloucester	69	10	Goodrich	Joseph	1		1	1	1	4			1				9		
Gloucester	69	11	Ingersol	Lydia Wo		1	2					1	1				5		
Gloucester	69	12	Haskell	Josiah Junr	1			1					1				3		
Gloucester	69	13	Lakay	James		1			1			2		2			6		
Gloucester	69	14	Lang	James	2			1		1	1	1					6		
Gloucester	69	15	Loyd	John	2			1		1			1				5		
Gloucester	69	16	Gloucester												4		4		
Gloucester	69	17	Knight	Thomas	3				1				1				5		
Gloucester	69	18	Sayward	Steven	1			1		1		1	1	1			6		
Gloucester	69	19	Ingersol	Robt Wo		1				1			2				4		
Gloucester	69	20	Horton	Elijah Junr	1		1						1				3		
Gloucester	69	21	Babson	Joseph	1		2						1				4		
Gloucester	69	22	Babson	Hanh Wo		1	2			1	1						6		
Gloucester	69	23	Huffon	Cathr Widw									1	1			2		
Gloucester	70	1	Carter	William	3			1		3			1	1			9		
Gloucester	70	2	Allen	Thomas	4				1		2	2	1				10		
Gloucester	70	3	Allen	Solomon			2			1			1	1			5		
Gloucester	70	4	Allen	William					1				1	1			3		
Gloucester	70	5	Rowe	John Esq	1	1		1		1	1	2		1			8		
Gloucester	70	6	Low	David Capt	2	1			1	2			2	1			9		
Gloucester	70	7	Lowe	John	2	2	4		1			1	3	1			14		
Gloucester	70	8	Rogers	William	2	1		1		2		1	1	1			9		
Gloucester	70	9	Hubbard	Sarah Wo			2			1	1			1			5		
Gloucester	70	10	Baker	Martha Wo			2						2	1			5		
Gloucester	70	11	Bennett	Moses	3	2	3			1		1	1				11		
Gloucester	70	12	Smith	George G Cao	3			1	1	1	1	1	1				9		
Gloucester	70	13	Turner	Daniel	1			1		3			1				6		
Gloucester	70	14	Noble	Joseph			1						1				2		
Gloucester	70	15	Survey	Abigal Wo			2						1	1			4		
Gloucester	70	16	Riggs	Aaron	1	2	2		1	1	2			1			10		
Gloucester	70	17	Millett	Susanh Wo									1	1			2		
Gloucester	70	18	Millett	Dorcas Wo								1	0	2			3		
Gloucester	70	19	Grimes	Mark	1	1		1		3			1	1			8		
Gloucester	70	20	Riggs	Pela Widow										2			2		
Gloucester	70	21	Riggs	Mary Wo										1			1		
Gloucester	70	22	Harvey	Benja	1	2	2		1	2			2	1			11		
Gloucester	70	23	Riggs	Saml Capt	1	1		1					1				4		
Gloucester	70	24	Ingersol	Samuel	2		1	1		2	1	1		1			10		
Gloucester	70	25	Davis	Zebulon	2	1			1	3	1			1			9		
Gloucester	71	1	Brown	Ephraim	3			1		3	1		1				9		
Gloucester	71	2	Tucker	William	3	2			1	1		1		1			9		
Gloucester	71	3	Tucker	Pegy Wo	1		1						1	1			4		
Gloucester	71	4	Hodgkins	Saml	2	1	2		1	1			1	1			9		

TOWN	PG#	LN#	LAST NAME	FIRST NAME	FREE WHITE MALES under 10	10 to 16	16 to 26	26 to 45	45 and over	FREE WHITE FEMALES under 10	10 to 16	16 to 26	26 to 45	45 and over	TOTAL ALL OTHER	TOTAL SLAVES	TOTALS	DISTRICT/ TOWNSHIP	NOTES
Gloucester	71	5	Hodgkins	James	2	1	1	1				1		1			7		
Gloucester	71	6	Millette	Anna Wo								2	1				3		
Gloucester	71	7	Day	Israel	1	1		1		2	1	1					7		
Gloucester	71	8	Rust	Nathl				1		2			1				4		
Gloucester	71	9	Baley	Lucy Wo			1						1				2		
Gloucester	71	10	Robinson	Abigal Wo			1						2	1			4		
Gloucester	71	11	Wharfe	Saml			1		1			1		1			4		
Gloucester	71	12	Stanwood	Goss	1		1			1		1					4		
Gloucester	71	13	Ellott	Andrew					1					1			2		
Gloucester	71	14	Pulcifer	William	1	1		1	0			1					4		
Gloucester	71	15	Plummer	Moses	3			1					1				5		
Gloucester	71	16	Witham	Benja 4				1				2		1			4		
Gloucester	71	17	Riggs	Sarah Widw								1		2			3		
Gloucester	71	18	Babson	Mary Wo			1					2		1			4		
Gloucester	71	19	Knights	David	3			1		2			1				7		
Gloucester	71	20	Button	Henry			1						1				2		
Gloucester	71	21	Low	Judith Wo										1			1		
Gloucester	71	22	Perry	Hannah Wo		1	1							1			3		
Gloucester	71	23	Davis	Andrew			1			1			2	1			5		
Gloucester	71	24	Lowe	Elias	3	1			1	1	2		1				9		
Gloucester	71	25	Davis	Saml		1			1	2		1	1				6		
Gloucester	71	26	Tucker	Mary Wo						1	1			1			3		
Gloucester	72	1	Miller	Sarah Wo						1	1			1			3		
Gloucester	72	2	Ellery	Benja	2	2	2	1			1	1	1				10		
Gloucester	72	3	Allen	Eliza Wo			1						1				2		
Gloucester	72	4	Tucker	Nathl		2		1		2			1				6		
Gloucester	72	5	Stanwood	David	1		1			1		1					4		
Gloucester	72	6	Babson	Hannah Wo		1	1					1		1			4		
Gloucester	72	7	How	Rachel Wo						1			2				3		
Gloucester	72	8	Lane	James	1			1		2		1					5		
Gloucester	72	9	Wood	Ruth	1							1	2				4		
Gloucester	72	10	Coffin	Tristram	1		1					1					3		
Gloucester	72	11	Ged	Willm Capt		3		1		1	1		1				7		
Gloucester	72	12	Lamson	Caleb			1					1					2		
Gloucester	72	13	Foster	Betty Wo						1		1					2		
Gloucester	72	14	Tarbox	Esther Wo		1		1		2							4		
Gloucester	72	15	Tarbox	Dorcas Wo				1						1			2		
Gloucester	72	16	Wallace	John				1					1				2		
Gloucester	72	17	Wallace	Saml		1			1	3			1				6		
Gloucester	72	18	Millett	Nathl	2	1	1							1			6		*
Gloucester	72	19	Day	Danl Jr	2		1			1		1		1			6		
Gloucester	72	20	Allen	Andrew	2	1		1		2		3					9		
Gloucester	72	21	White	James	1					3			1				6		
Gloucester	72	22	Stanwood	Susa Wo			1					1		1			3		
Gloucester	72	23	Noble	Mary Wo	1	1				1	1		1				5		
Gloucester	72	24	Wharfe	David	3	1		1		2	2	1	1				11		
Gloucester	72	25	Huse	John	2			1	1	2	1		1				8		
Gloucester	72	26	Clark	John	1			1		3			1				6		
Gloucester	73	1	Lamson	Henry			1			1		1					3		
Gloucester	73	2	Stanwood	Nehemiah	1			1		1			1	1			5		
Gloucester	73	3	Carter	John	1			1		1		1		1			5		
Gloucester	73	4	Wharfe	Arther				1						1			2		
Gloucester	73	5	Wharfe	Abraham		1		1		3			1	1			7		
Gloucester	73	6	Tucker	Joseph				1				1	2				4		
Gloucester	73	7	Lurvey	Jacob				1						1			2		
Gloucester	73	8	Jeffs	Thos				1						1			2		
Gloucester	73	9	Stanwood	John	1		1			1		1		1			5		
Gloucester	73	10	Hale	Lydia Wo			1	1				1		1			4		
Gloucester	73	11	Carter	Anna Wo	1		1	1		1			2				8		
Gloucester	73	12	White	Anna Wo	2	2	1			1		2		1			9		
Gloucester	73	13	Fips	Abigal Wo										3			3		
Gloucester	73	14	Priestly	James	2			1		1			1	1			6		
Gloucester	73	15	Davis	Moses	4			1					1				6	Town Parish	
Gloucester	73	16	Riggs	Sarah									1	2			3	Town Parish	
Gloucester	73	17	Merritt	James	1		2						1	1			5	Town Parish	
Gloucester	73	18	Smith	Thos	1			1					1				3	Town Parish	
Gloucester	73	19	Davis	Isaac	1					1			1				4	Town Parish	
Gloucester	73	20	Millette	Jona		2		1	1			2		1			7	Town Parish	
Gloucester	73	21	Davis	William	1		1		1	1			1	1			6	Squam Parish	
Gloucester	73	22	Babson	Willa	1	1	2		1	2	1	1		1			10	Squam Parish	
Gloucester	73	23	Woodbery	Asa	1	1		1		2			1				6	Squam Parish	
Gloucester	73	24	Hodgkins	Timothy		1		1		1			1	1			5	Squam Parish	
Gloucester	73	25	Lane	Solomon	1			1		2		1	1	1			7	Squam Parish	
Gloucester	74	1	Lane	Cornelius	3			1				1		1			6	Squam Parish	
Gloucester	74	2	Lavall	Thos	3			1				1	1	1			7	Squam Parish	
Gloucester	74	3	Griffen	Dudly	2			1				1	1	1			6	Squam Parish	
Gloucester	74	4	Haraden	John	1			1		3			1				6	Squam Parish	
Gloucester	74	5	Davis	George	3			1		1			1				6	Squam Parish	
Gloucester	74	6	Davis	Epes	1	1	1			1		1					5	Squam Parish	
Gloucester	74	7	Parsons	Jonah				1		1			1				3	Squam Parish	
Gloucester	74	8	Whitteredge	Oliver	1					1			1	1			4	Squam Parish	
Gloucester	74	9	Whitteredge	Richd			1			2			1	1			5	Squam Parish	
Gloucester	74	10	Griffen	Nathll	2			1	1	1			1	1			7	Squam Parish	
Gloucester	74	11	Haraden	Joseph	1	1	2			2		1	2				10	Squam Parish	
Gloucester	74	12	Lane	Gedeon	2			1		2			1				6	Squam Parish	
Gloucester	74	13	Choate	Stephen	1			1				1		1			4	Squam Parish	
Gloucester	74	14	Choate	David	1			1		2	1		1				6	Squam Parish	
Gloucester	74	15	Griffen	Gustaves		1				1		1	1				4		
Gloucester	74	16	Sargent	Gustaves			1			1		1					6		
Gloucester	74	17	Haraden	James	5			1		1			2				9		

TOWN	PG#	LN#	LAST NAME	FIRST NAME	FREE WHITE MALES					FREE WHITE FEMALES					TOTAL ALL OTHER	TOTAL SLAVES	TOTALS	DISTRICT/ TOWNSHIP	NOTES
					under 10	10 to 16	16 to 26	26 to 45	45 and over	under 10	10 to 16	16 to 26	26 to 45	45 and over					
Gloucester	74	18	Griffen	Mary Wo		1	2						1	1			5		
Gloucester	74	19	Griffen	Oliver		1	1		1			1	1	1			6		
Gloucester	74	20	Dennis	John			4	1						1			6		
Gloucester	74	21	Griffen	Andrew	1	2	1	1		3		1		1			10		
Gloucester	74	22	Griffen	James	1		2		1	1	3	3		1			12		
Gloucester	74	23	Davis	Mark		1	1	1					1	1			5		
Gloucester	74	24	Sargent	Michael	1		1			1		1					4		
Gloucester	74	25	Atkins	John				1						1			2		
Gloucester	74	26	Jusomin	Peter			1						1				2		
Gloucester	74	27	Peirce	Andrew	4		1			2		1					8		
Gloucester	75	1	Dennis	Saml			1			1		1					3		
Gloucester	75	2	Day	James		2		1		1			1				5		
Gloucester	75	3	Day	George	2		1			1			1				5		
Gloucester	75	4	Kimball	Jona	3		1			3	1	1	1				10		
Gloucester	75	5	Griffen	Epes	2		1			1			1				5		
Gloucester	75	6	Merhcant	Jabez	1	1		1		2		2	1	1			9		
Gloucester	75	7	Jones	Ambrose		2		1		1	4		1				9		
Gloucester	75	8	Nevans	William	1		1			3			1				6		
Gloucester	75	9	Sargent	David		1	1	1						1			4		
Gloucester	75	10	Phips	Willm Capt	1		1			2			1				5		
Gloucester	75	11	Merchant	Daniel			1			1		1					3		
Gloucester	75	12	Marsh	Elles Wo	2									1			3		
Gloucester	75	13	Higgens	Edward	1	1	1		1		1	2	1				8		
Gloucester	75	14	Norwood	Gustaves	2	2	1		1		2	2	1				11		
Gloucester	75	15	Lane	Judith Wo	1	1	1		1					1			5		
Gloucester	75	16	Gott	James Junr	1			1		2		1	1				6		
Gloucester	75	17	Knowlton	John	2			1		1	1		1				6		
Gloucester	75	18	Lane	Lydia Wo			2							1			3		
Gloucester	75	19	Sargent	John Lane	2			1		1			1	1			6		
Gloucester	75	20	Norwood	Eliza Wo		1	2			2	2	1	1				9		
Gloucester	75	21	Butler	John	1	3	1		1	1		2	1				10		
Gloucester	75	22	Baker	Joseph	2		1		1				1	1			6		
Gloucester	75	23	Merchant	Daniel					1					1			2		
Gloucester	75	24	Norwood	Mary Wo						3			1				4		
Gloucester	75	25	Dennison	Isaac	1				1					1			3		
Gloucester	75	26	Dennison	James		1		1		1		1					4		
Gloucester	75	27	Gott	Abner		1			1	1	1		1				5		
Gloucester	75	28	Dennison	Isaac Junr	4	2		1		1	1		1				10		
Gloucester	75	29	Savell	Jese		2	1	1		1	1			1			7		
Gloucester	75	30	Savell	James			1			1		1					3		
Gloucester	75	31	Burnham	Jona	2	2	1			1		1	1				8		
Gloucester	76	1	Gott	Charles			1			2		1					4		
Gloucester	76	2	Lane	Gedeon	1		1			1			1				4		
Gloucester	76	3	Day	James Junr			1			4	1		1				7		
Gloucester	76	4	Butram	Jona		1		1		2		1					5		
Gloucester	76	5	Norwood	Nathan				1		0				2			3		
Gloucester	76	6	Hodgkins	Moses	1			1		3			1				6		
Gloucester	76	7	Clarke	Samuel	2		1	1		3				1			8		
Gloucester	76	8	Griffen	Sam			1	1				1	3	1			7		
Gloucester	76	9	Griffen	Joel	1		1			1		1					4		
Gloucester	76	10	Herring	Thos	1			1		2	1		1				6		
Gloucester	76	11	Lane	Caleb	2	3	1	1		1			1				9		
Gloucester	76	12	Griffen	Eliphalet	2			1		3			1				7		
Gloucester	76	13	Lane	Aaron	1			1		1			1				4		
Gloucester	76	14	Lane	Joseph Junr	1			1		4			1				7		
Gloucester	76	15	Duly	Michael		2	1		1	1				2			7		
Gloucester	76	16	Davis	Joseph					1				1	1			3		
Gloucester	76	17	Bassett	Sarah Wo	1					1		1					3		
Gloucester	76	18	Griffen	William	1			1		1	1	1					5		
Gloucester	76	19	Sargent	David Junr	2			1		1		1					5		
Gloucester	76	20	Peirce	John				1						1			2		
Gloucester	76	21	Sargent	Solo Junr	2			1		3			1				7		
Gloucester	76	22	Sargent	Solo	2			1						1			4		
Gloucester	76	23	Sargent	Benja	2		1			1			1				5		
Gloucester	76	24	Sargent	Samll	1		1	1		1				1			5		
Gloucester	76	25	Sargent	Andrew	1	1		1						2			5		
Gloucester	76	26	Sargent	Epes	2		1			1			1				5		
Gloucester	76	27	Sargent	Jona				1						1			2		
Gloucester	76	28	Robinson	Jona				1					1				2		
Gloucester	76	29	Griffen	James	1	1		1		1		1	1				6		
Gloucester	76	30	Clarke	Martha Wo	2							1	1				4		
Gloucester	76	31	Sargent	Peter		1	2		1	1			1				6		
Gloucester	76	32	Phips	John				1		2			1				4		
Gloucester	76	33	Robinson	Jona Junr	2	2		1		3	1	1	1				11		
Gloucester	76	34	Wheeler	Aaron	2	2		1	1	1		2	1	1			11		
Gloucester	76	35	Sargent	Winthrop	2		2	1		2	3		1				11		
Gloucester	76	36	Lane	David Junr			1			1	1	1					4		
Gloucester	76	37	Lane	David	1	1		1		1	1	2	1	1			9		
Gloucester	76	38	Lane	John	1		1			2		1					5		
Gloucester	77	1	Lane	Joseph	1		1			2	3	1		1			10		
Gloucester	77	2	Lane	Jona		2		1		2	1		1				7		
Gloucester	77	3	Lansford	John	3	2		1		2	1	1	1				11		
Gloucester	77	4	Morgan	Paul	1	2		1		1		2	1				8		
Gloucester	77	5	Morgan	Nathan F.	1		1			1			1				3		
Gloucester	77	6	Whalen	Michael	1		1			1	1	1					5		
Gloucester	77	7	Phips	Amos	1		1			1			1				4		
Gloucester	77	8	Young	Daniel	1		1						1				3		
Gloucester	77	9	Young	Heteh Wo	2	2							1	1	1		6		
Gloucester	77	10	Robinson	Abraham	1		1						1				3		
Gloucester	77	11	Gott	James			1	1				1					3		

TOWN	PG#	LN#	LAST NAME	FIRST NAME	FREE WHITE MALES under 10	10 to 16	16 to 26	26 to 45	45 and over	FREE WHITE FEMALES under 10	10 to 16	16 to 26	26 to 45	45 and over	TOTAL ALL OTHER	TOTAL SLAVES	TOTALS	DISTRICT/TOWNSHIP	NOTES
Gloucester	77	12	Jumper	Joseph		1	1	1		2	2	1		1			9		
Gloucester	77	13	Parsons	Eliza Wo		1	1	1			2	1		1			7		
Gloucester	77	14	Bray	Benja How	3			1		2			1				7		
Gloucester	77	15	Woodbery	Susannah Wo		1	1	2			2	1		1			8		
Gloucester	77	16	Lane	Nathl			1			2		1					4		
Gloucester	77	17	Woodbery	Epes		0		1		3			1				5		
Gloucester	77	18	Woodbery	Walter		1		1		5				1			8		
Gloucester	77	19	Merchant	Daniel Junr			1		1			1					3		
Gloucester	77	20	Norwood	James	1		2		1				2				7		
Gloucester	77	21	Gott	Joshua	1		2		1	2	1	1	1				9		
Gloucester	77	22	Parsons	Esther Wo			1						1				2		
Gloucester	77	23	Thurston	Stephen	1			1		1	3		1				7		
Gloucester	77	24	Woodberry	Peter	1			1		1			1				4		
Gloucester	77	25	Storey	James	2	1		1		3	1		1				9		
Gloucester	77	26	Knight	Job	3	1		1		2			1	1			9		
Gloucester	77	27	Babson	David			1	1					1	1			4		
Gloucester	77	28	Knutsford	Stephen	3	1			1	2			1	1			9		
Gloucester	77	29	Hodgkins	Mary Wido		1	1			1		1	1				5		
Gloucester	77	30	Blanchford	John					1					1			2		
Gloucester	77	31	Wheeler	Moses		1	2		1	4	1	1	1	1			12		
Gloucester	77	32	Whitham	Jonah	2			1		1			1				5		
Gloucester	77	33	Wheeler	Benja		1	1		1					1			4		
Gloucester	77	34	Wheeler	Daniel		1	1					1					3		
Gloucester	77	35	Wheeler	John D.	2	1		1		1			1				6		
Gloucester	78	1	Wheeler	Saml	2	1		1		1			1				6		
Gloucester	78	2	Norwood	William	1		1			1		1					4		
Gloucester	78	3	Liscomb	Gedion	2			1		2			1				6		
Gloucester	78	4	White	Henry			1		1		1			1			4		
Gloucester	78	5	Hartly	Saml	2		1	1	1	1		1		1			8		
Gloucester	78	6	Davis	Lydia Wo	1	1	2					1		1			6		
Gloucester	78	7	Rowe	John Majr		1	1		1			1		1			5		
Gloucester	78	8	Baley	Joseph	2	1		1				1	1	1			7		
Gloucester	78	9	Saunders	John	1		1	1		4	2			1			10		
Gloucester	78	10	Saunders	George	1	1						1					3		
Gloucester	78	11	Tyork	Tammy Widw						2		1					3		
Gloucester	78	12	Lears	William	3	1			1	1	3	1					10		
Gloucester	78	13	Carter	Gideon	2	3		1		3			1				10		
Gloucester	78	14	Merchant	William	1	1	2		1				1				6		
Gloucester	78	15	Merchant	Willm Junr			1			1			1				3		
Gloucester	78	16	Kendal	Jona	2			1					1	1			5		
Gloucester	78	17	Andrews	William		2		1		3		2		1	2		11	Sandy Bay Parish	
Gloucester	78	18	Abbot	James		2		1		2	1	1	1				8	Sandy Bay Parish	
Gloucester	78	19	Blatchford	Henry	3			1		2			1				7	Sandy Bay Parish	
Gloucester	78	20	Blatchford	Saml	1	1		1		1			1				5	Sandy Bay Parish	
Gloucester	78	21	Boyd	Abra			1	1		1		1					4	Sandy Bay Parish	
Gloucester	78	22	Butram	Jeremiah		1	1		1		2		1				6	Sandy Bay Parish	
Gloucester	78	23	Butram	Jerea Junr			1			1		1					3	Sandy Bay Parish	
Gloucester	78	24	Bradstreet	Ezekh	2			1		3				1			7	Sandy Bay Parish	
Gloucester	78	25	Boyenton	Eleaz	2			1		3				1			7	Sandy Bay Parish	
Gloucester	78	26	Burns	John	2			1		1		1	1				6	Sandy Bay Parish	
Gloucester	78	27	Brooks	Ruben	2			1		1			1				5	Sandy Bay Parish	
Gloucester	78	28	Brooks	David	1		1						1				3	Sandy Bay Parish	
Gloucester	78	29	Brown	James	1		1			1							3	Sandy Bay Parish	
Gloucester	78	30	Haskins	Willm	1		3		1					1			6	Sandy Bay Parish	
Gloucester	78	31	Broughton	Danl	1			1		2		1					5	Sandy Bay Parish	
Gloucester	78	32	Cleavland	Ebenz Junr					1				1				2	Sandy Bay Parish	
Gloucester	79	1	Clarke	Henry Junr			1			1	1	1					4		
Gloucester	79	2	Card	William	2			1		3	1	1	1				9		
Gloucester	79	3	Clarke	Mary P.	1	1		1		1			1				5		
Gloucester	79	4	Clarke	Joshua	4	1		1		1	1		1				9		
Gloucester	79	5	Clarke	Benja			1		1	3		1	1				7		
Gloucester	79	6	Cunningham	John	2		1	1		2		1	1				8		
Gloucester	79	7	Clarke	Ebenz	2	1		1		2			1				7		
Gloucester	79	8	Corey	Jack			1							1			2		
Gloucester	79	9	Choate	Sola	1	1	1						1				4		
Gloucester	79	10	Cleavland	Ebenz Revd				1		1				1			3		
Gloucester	79	11	Davis	Benj	1	2	1	1		2			1				9		
Gloucester	79	12	Doyal	Felex	2	1		1		1	1		1				7		
Gloucester	79	13	Davis	Oliver	1		1						1				3		
Gloucester	79	14	Dresser	Richard	2	2						1		1			7		
Gloucester	79	15	Dresser	Dorcas Wo									1	1			2		
Gloucester	79	16	Elwell	David			1			2		2					5		
Gloucester	79	17	Foster	Nathl	1	1		1	1	3	1		1				9		
Gloucester	79	18	Marshall	Benja	1	1		1		1	2	1		1			8		
Gloucester	79	19	Gott	John	1	1	1			1	2		1				8		
Gloucester	79	20	Gott	Betty Wo	1	3	1			1				1			7		
Gloucester	79	21	Grover	Ebenz Junr	1			1	1	1			1	1			6		
Gloucester	79	22	Grover	Neha Junr	2		1						1				4		
Gloucester	79	23	Goss	James Doct	2			1		1			1	1			6		
Gloucester	79	24	Goss	William	3			1		1	3		1				9		
Gloucester	79	25	Goss	Richard	2			1		1				1			5		
Gloucester	79	26	Gamage	John		2	2	2	1			1		1			9		
Gloucester	79	27	Gamage	John Junr			1			3			1				5		
Gloucester	79	28	Gott	William	1	1		1		3			1				7		
Gloucester	79	29	Giles	Mary Wo	1	2	1					1		1			7		
Gloucester	79	30	Hustens	Saml	2			1		3			1				7		
Gloucester	79	31	Hale	Benja	1	1	2		2	3	2	1	1				13		
Gloucester	79	32	Haskins	John	1					2			2				6		
Gloucester	80	1	Haskall	Josiah	2			1		1		1					5		
Gloucester	80	2	Hampson	John			1	1					1	1			4		

49

TOWN	PG#	LN#	LAST NAME	FIRST NAME	FREE WHITE MALES					FREE WHITE FEMALES					TOTAL ALL OTHER	TOTAL SLAVES	TOTALS	DISTRICT/ TOWNSHIP	NOTES
					under 10	10 to 16	16 to 26	26 to 45	45 and over	under 10	10 to 16	16 to 26	26 to 45	45 and over					
Gloucester	80	3	Haskins	Bennett	2				1				1				4		
Gloucester	80	4	Knight	Willm				1		2			1				4		
Gloucester	80	5	Knights	Thos	1		1			1		1					4		
Gloucester	80	6	Kimball	David				1				1	2				4		
Gloucester	80	7	Knowlton	Nehemiah	3	1	2	1				2	1				10		
Gloucester	80	8	Lowe	Willm	3	2	2		1	1		2	1				12		
Gloucester	80	9	Lutterel	Hughes				1		4			1				6		
Gloucester	80	10	Marshall	Benja			1			1		1					3		
Gloucester	80	11	Manning	Jno Doct	1	2		1					2				6		
Gloucester	80	12	Norwood	Caleb				1					1	1			3		
Gloucester	80	13	Cook	Mary Wo		1						1	1				3		
Gloucester	80	14	Norwood	Francis Jr	1	1		1		3	1		1				8		
Gloucester	80	15	Noble	Francis		1		1		2			1				5		
Gloucester	80	16	Norwood	Francis		2			1				1	1			5		
Gloucester	80	17	Oakes	Thos	3		1	1		2			1	1			9		
Gloucester	80	18	Oakes	John			1						1				2		
Gloucester	80	19	Oakes	Ebenz		1	1						1	1			3		
Gloucester	80	20	Pool	Sarh Widow		1	1			1	1		1				5		
Gloucester	80	21	Parsons	James		1				1			1				3		
Gloucester	80	22	Parsons	Jona P.	3			1		1			1				6		
Gloucester	80	23	Parsons	Thos	4			1					1				6		
Gloucester	80	24	Parsons	Ebenz Junr	1		1	1		2		2		1			8		
Gloucester	80	25	Pool	Ebenz	1		1	1				1	3	1			8		
Gloucester	80	26	Pool	Isaac		1		0	1			2	1	2			7		
Gloucester	80	27	Pool	Francis		3		1	1	1	1			1			8		
Gloucester	80	28	Pool	Jona	1	1	2	1		2			1				8		
Gloucester	80	29	Pool	Stephen				1					2				3		
Gloucester	80	30	Pool	Caleb		1		1		1	1			1			5		
Gloucester	80	31	Pool	Caleb Junr	1		1			1			1				4		
Gloucester	80	32	Pool	John	2			1	1	2	1	2	1				10		
Gloucester	80	33	Pool	John Junr	2			1		2	1	1	1				8		
Gloucester	81	1	Pool	Abraham	2	2		1		3			1				9		
Gloucester	81	2	Pool	Stephen Junr	2	2	1	1		2			1				9		
Gloucester	81	3	Pool	Ebenz Junr		1		1				1	1				4		
Gloucester	81	4	Pool	Joseph		1						1					2		
Gloucester	81	5	Pool	Mark Maj		2		1		1			1	1			6		
Gloucester	81	6	Pool	Mark			1			2			1				4		
Gloucester	81	7	Pool	Aaron	2		1						1				4		
Gloucester	81	8	Pool	Moses		1	1	1		1	1		1				6		
Gloucester	81	9	Witham	Ebenz		1			1					1			3		
Gloucester	81	10	Phips	John	1	1		1		2	1		1				7		
Gloucester	81	11	Parsons	Vinery	3			1		1			1				6		
Gloucester	81	12	Parsons	Jeffery	1			1		1		1	1				5		
Gloucester	81	13	Parkhurst	Willa		1	1			3	1	1					7		
Gloucester	81	14	Presse	Willm		1				1			1				3		
Gloucester	81	15	Rowe	Willm	3	1	1	1		1	1		1				9		
Gloucester	81	16	Roberts	Thos Junr	4	1		1		2	2		1				11		
Gloucester	81	17	Roberts	Thomas			1	1					1	1			4		
Gloucester	81	18	Rollins	John	1	1		1		1		2	1				7		
Gloucester	81	19	Rowe	Jabez Deac	1	1		1		1			1	1			6		
Gloucester	81	20	Rowe	Jabez Junr	2		1			2			1				6		
Gloucester	81	21	Rowe	Ebenzr	3	1		1		1			1	1			8		
Gloucester	81	22	Rowe	Thomas		2			1				1	1			5		
Gloucester	81	23	Rowe	Thos Junr	2			1						1			4		
Gloucester	81	24	Rowe	Benja		1		1		2	1		1				6		
Gloucester	81	25	Rowe	Isaac		2	1	1		2			1	1			8		
Gloucester	81	26	Richardson	Simeon		1		1		1			1				4		
Gloucester	81	27	Robins	Nathll	2		1						1				4		
Gloucester	81	28	Rowe	Daniel	1	1							1				3		
Gloucester	81	29	Knights	Satah Wo	2					1		2	1				6		
Gloucester	81	30	Smith	Joseph	1	1		1		2		1	1				7		
Gloucester	81	31	Sargent	Aaron			1					1	1				3		
Gloucester	81	32	Smith	Willa	1	1	1	1		1			1	1			7		
Gloucester	82	1	Stevens	Oliver	1			1		1			1				5		
Gloucester	82	2	Stilman	Peter	2			1				1	1				5		
Gloucester	82	3	Stilman	Danl		1	1		1	1			4	1			9		
Gloucester	82	4	Lavell	William	2								1				4		
Gloucester	82	5	Slownan	Josiah				1		4			1				6		
Gloucester	82	6	Smith	Willa Junr	1		1			1			1				4		
Gloucester	82	7	Stevens	Robert	1			1		1			1				4		
Gloucester	82	8	Tarr	Benja		1			1	1			1				5		
Gloucester	82	9	Tarr	Benja Junr			1	1			1	1	1				5		
Gloucester	82	10	Tarr	Jabez	1	1		1		4	2	1	1				11		
Gloucester	82	11	Tarr	Francis	2		1			1	1	1					6		
Gloucester	82	12	Tarr	Andrew	1			1		1			1				4		
Gloucester	82	13	Tarr	David	1	1		1		2	1		1				7		
Gloucester	82	14	Tarr	Danl B.	1	1		1		1	1		1				6		
Gloucester	82	15	Smith	Polly Wo									1		1		2		
Gloucester	82	16	Tarr	Ebenz	2	2	1		1	2		1	2	1			12		
Gloucester	82	17	Tarr	Nathl	3	1		1				1	1	1			8		
Gloucester	82	18	Tarr	Oliver	1			1				1	1	1			5		
Gloucester	82	19	Tarr	Job	2		1	1		3			1	1			9		
Gloucester	82	20	Tarr	Epes	1			1					1				3		
Gloucester	82	21	Tarr	Jona	3			1		1			1	1			7		
Gloucester	82	22	Todd	Sarah Wo	2			1		1			1	1			6		
Gloucester	82	23	Tarr	Benja 3d	1	1	1			1	1		1				6		
Gloucester	82	24	Tarr	John	4			1				1	2	1			9		
Gloucester	82	25	Tarr	Saml	2				1	3		1	1	1			9		
Gloucester	82	26	Turner	John Junr				1		2	1			1			5		
Gloucester	82	27	Turner	John		2			1					1			4		

TOWN	PG#	LN#	LAST NAME	FIRST NAME	under 10	10 to 16	16 to 26	26 to 45	45 and over	under 10	10 to 16	16 to 26	26 to 45	45 and over	TOTAL ALL OTHER	TOTAL SLAVES	TOTALS	DISTRICT/ TOWNSHIP	NOTES
							FREE WHITE MALES					FREE WHITE FEMALES							
Gloucester	82	28	Tucker	Joseph	1				1		2		1				5		
Gloucester	82	29	Tucker	Willa	2			1		2			1				6		
Gloucester	82	30	Thurston	Danl	3			3	1				2	1			10		
Gloucester	82	31	Grover	E* Wd			1						1				2		
Gloucester	83	1	Thurston	Saml	1		1			1		1					4		
Gloucester	83	2	Thurston	Joseph				1					1				2		
Gloucester	83	3	Thurston	Joseph Junr			2	1				1	1				5		
Gloucester	83	4	Thurston	Ambrose	3	1		1		1	2	1					9		
Gloucester	83	5	Tarr	James				1					1				2		
Gloucester	83	6	Smith	James				1					1				2		
Gloucester	83	7	Tarr	Anna Wo				1		1			1				3		
Gloucester	83	8	Witham	Zebulon	1	1		1		1	1		1				6		
Gloucester	83	9	Witham	Henry	1	1		1				1	1				5		
Gloucester	83	10	Witham	Henry Junr		1						1					2		
Gloucester	83	11	Woodbery	Andrew		1		1		1	1		1				5		
Gloucester	83	12	Webster	Joshua	3		1			1	2	1					8		
Gloucester	83	13	Witham	Joshua	1	1				2		1					5		
Gloucester	83	14	Witham	Thos	1		2			1		1					5		
Gloucester	83	15	Wonson	Patience Wo									1				1		
Gloucester	83	16	York	Thos	1		1			2	1	1					6		
Gloucester	83	17	Hayward	Jona Capt	2			1				1	1				5		
Gloucester	83	18	Grover	Nehemiah		1		1		1	1	1					5		
Gloucester	83	19	Lane	Andrew		1				1		1					3		
Gloucester	83	20		Dick Negro				0					0		2		2		
Gloucester	83	21	Parsons	Moses			1					1					2		
Gloucester	83	22	Tarr	Betty Wo		1	1						1				3		
Gloucester	83	23	Tarr	Charles		1				1		1					3		
Gloucester	83	24	Tarr	Eunice										2			2		
Gloucester	83	25	Lane	George	3			1		2			1				7		
Gloucester	83	26	Jumper	William				1		2	3		1				7		
Gloucester	83	27	Witham	Mark				1									1		
Gloucester	83	28	Parsons	Daniel		1		1		1			1				4		
Gloucester	83	29	Wainright	Thomas	3			1		1		1					6		
Gloucester	83	30	Butnam	Joseph			1	0		1	1	1					4		
Gloucester	83	31	Pool	Rachel Wo								1	1				2		
Gloucester	84	1	Ball	Isaac				1					1				2		
Gloucester	84	2	Ingersol	Andrew	1	1		1		2	1	1					7		
Gloucester	84	3	Lakeman	Nathl Doct			1				1	1					3		
Gloucester	84	4	Lane	Dennison		1					1						2		
Gloucester	84	5	Allen	William Junr				1		1			1				3		
Gloucester	84	6	Somes	Reba Wo	1								1				2		
Gloucester	84	7	Akers	Mathew		1		1			1		1				4		
Gloucester	84	8	Maskell	Joseph	1		1					1	1				4		
Gloucester	84	9	Elwell	Mary Widow	2	2	2						2	1			9		
Gloucester	84	10	Burnham	Eliz Widw		1				1			1				3		
Gloucester	84	11	Denning	John				1					1				2		
Gloucester	84	12	Plumer	Mary Wo		1	2	1					1	1			6		
Gloucester	84	13	Rowe	Solomon	2	1	1	1				1	1				7		
Gloucester	84	14	Youlen	John				1						3			4		
Gloucester	84	15	Parsons	David			2						1	1			4		
Gloucester	84	16	Mason	Joseph			2	1				2	1				6		
Gloucester	84	17	Parsons	John	4			1		2	1	1	1				10		
Gloucester	84	18	Sawyer	George			1			1	1						3		
Gloucester	84	19	Dunahew	David	1			1		2			1				5		
Gloucester	84	20	Wharfe	Abraham Junr	1	1		1		2	1		1				7		
Gloucester	84	21	Sawyer	Anna Wo		1							1	1			3		
Gloucester	84	22	Masters	Charles G	2			1		3	1		1				8		
Gloucester	84	23	Coat	Susa Wo									1	1			2		
Gloucester	84	24	Robinson	Stephen	2			1			1		1				5		
Gloucester	84	25	Stevens	Bethh Wo	1					1			1				3		
Gloucester	84	26	Smith	Susa Wo									1	1			2		
Gloucester	84	27	Perkens	Richard		1				1	1	1					4		
Gloucester	84	28	Gardner	Robert		1		1					1				3		
Gloucester	84	29	Elwell	Saml		1						1					2		
Gloucester	84	30	Batten	Rolen		1						1					2		
Gloucester	84	31	Stevens	Joseph	0	2		1		3		0	1				7		
Gloucester	84	32	Wharfe	Sarah Wo	2							2					4		
Gloucester	84	33	Younger	Willard	1			1					1	2			5		
Gloucester	84	34	Worley	William	1									2			3		
Gloucester	85	1	Wharfe	John		2		1		2		1	1	1			8		
Gloucester	85	2	Noble	Benja			1				1	1					3		
Gloucester	85	3	Day	Nathl		2		1		1			1				5		
Gloucester	85	4	Day	Mary Wo	1					2			1				4		
Gloucester	85	5	Wharfe	Noby Wo	W		1						1	1			3		
Gloucester	85	6	Hodgkins	Patty Wo	1								1	1			3		
Gloucester	85	7	Tayler	William				1				1	1				3		
Gloucester	85	8	White	William		1		1		1	1		1				5		
Gloucester	85	9	Goodrich	Mary Wo									1				1		
Gloucester	85	10	Joseph	Dorcas Wid	1					1			1				3		
Gloucester	85	11	Newcomb	Mary Wo		1							1				2		
Gloucester	85	12	Smith	Charles	1		1						1	1			4		
Gloucester	85	13	Batten	Ebenz		2		1		1	1	2	1				8		
Gloucester	85	14	Smith	James				1									1		
Gloucester	85	15	Turner	Willm		1				1		1					3		
Gloucester	85	16	Brown	Jon	1			1		1			1				4		
Gloucester	85	17	Medler	Susa Wo		1					1		1				3		
Gloucester	85	18	Medler	Enoch			1			2		1					4		
Gloucester	85	19	Busten	Esther Wo								2	1				3		
Gloucester	85	20	William	Abraham	1			1				2	1	1			6		
Gloucester	85	21	Rowe	David		1	1	2				1	1				6		

TOWN	PG#	LN#	LAST NAME	FIRST NAME	FREE WHITE MALES					FREE WHITE FEMALES					TOTAL ALL OTHER	TOTAL SLAVES	TOTALS	DISTRICT/ TOWNSHIP	NOTES
					under 10	10 to 16	16 to 26	26 to 45	45 and over	under 10	10 to 16	16 to 26	26 to 45	45 and over					
Gloucester	85	22	Dunfield	Phil	2			1		2			1				6		
Gloucester	85	23	Row	James		1			1					1			3		
Gloucester	85	24	Fears	Patty Wo		1	2							1			4		
Gloucester	85	25	Dogett	William	1	1		1		1	1		1				6		
Gloucester	85	26	Jeffs	Joseph			1	1		2	1	1	1				7		
Gloucester	85	27	Ballard	Daniel			1						1				2		
Gloucester	85	28	Levenear	Lewis1			1			1			1				3		
Gloucester	85	29	Elwell	Job	2			1		1	2			1			7		
Gloucester	85	30	Elwell	Andrew		1	1	1		1		1	1				6		
Gloucester	85	31	Wood	Charles	2			1		1	1		1	1			4		
Gloucester	85	32	Anness	Abr		1	1		1		1		2	1			7		
Gloucester	85	33	Luteral	Hughes	1			1		2	1	1	1				7		
Gloucester	86	1	Hadley	John				1				1		1			3		
Gloucester	86	2	Rowe	Robert				1		2		1					4		
Gloucester	86	3	Leighton	Esther Wo		2	2	1				1		1			7		
Gloucester	86	4	Letour	Doly Wo									1	1			2		
Gloucester	86	5	Noble	Daniel	1			1		1			1				4		
Gloucester	86	6	Rowe	Abra 3d	1			1			1		1				4		
Gloucester	86	7	Smith	Mary Wo	2							2	2	1			7		
Gloucester	86	8	Brown	Vincent	1			1		1			1				4		
Gloucester	86	9	Card	Benja				1					1				2		
Gloucester	86	10	Abbott	Lydia Wo									1	1			2		
Gloucester	86	11	Robinson	Jona 3d			1	1			1	1	1				5		
Gloucester	86	12	Gardner	Ebenz	1				1	2			1				5		
Gloucester	86	13	Gearix	Edward	1				1	1		2		1			6		
Gloucester	86	14	Gearix	Edward Jn	3	0	1						1				5		
Gloucester	86	15	Close	John					1			2	1				4		
Gloucester	86	16	Thomas	Samuel			1						1				2		
Gloucester	86	17	Thomas	Sara Wo	1	2								1			4		
Gloucester	86	18	Haycock	Joseph	1	1		1			1		1	0			5		
Gloucester	86	19	Clarke	Lydia Wo						1			1				2		
Gloucester	86	20	Thorp	Sarah Wo	1			1		1				1			4		
Gloucester	86	21	Elwell	Zebulon	3	2	2		1	2				1			11		
Gloucester	86	22	Freeman	Robt blk											12		12		
Gloucester	86	23	Allen	Joseph	5			3	15	7		3	6	17	1		57		Listed as work house
Gloucester	86	24	Segurs	John				1					1				2		
Gloucester	86	25	Lufkin	Moses	3	2		1				1	1				5		
Gloucester	86	26	Blackfield	Nathl	2	1	2	1		3		2	1				12		

TOWN	PG#	LN#	LAST NAME	FIRST NAME	FREE WHITE MALES under 10	10 to 16	16 to 26	26 to 45	45 and over	FREE WHITE FEMALES under 10	10 to 16	16 to 26	26 to 45	45 and over	TOTAL ALL OTHER	TOTAL SLAVES	TOTALS	DISTRICT/ TOWNSHIP	NOTES
Hamilton	284	1	Whipple	William		1	1		1	1	4			1			9		
Hamilton	284	2	Brown	Stephen			1		1			3		1			6		
Hamilton	284	3	Brown	Ami			1			1			1				3		
Hamilton	284	4	Roberts	Francis		1			4	3	1			1			10		
Hamilton	284	5	Stone	John			1	1				1	1	1			5		
Hamilton	284	6	Woodbury	John	2			1	1				1				5		
Hamilton	284	7	Woodbury	Benjamin				1	1			1		1			4		
Hamilton	284	8	Woodbury	Isiah	1				1			1	2	1			6		
Hamilton	284	9	Knowlton	Edmund			2	1	1	1		1		1			7		
Hamilton	284	10	Woodbury	Eliot			2			2		1					5		
Hamilton	284	11	Patch	James					1			1		1			3		
Hamilton	284	12	Brown	Simon					1		1			1			3		
Hamilton	284	13	Knowlton	Nathaniel	1			1	1				1				4		
Hamilton	284	14	Knowlton	Nehemiah		1	2		1	1		1		1			7		
Hamilton	284	15	Knowlton	Melicah		1	1	1			1		1				5		
Hamilton	284	16	Knowlton	Ezra			2		1					1			4		
Hamilton	284	17	Dennis	Lucy	2						1	1					4		
Hamilton	284	18	Knowlton	John	2						1	1					4		
Hamilton	284	19	Woodbury	John Jun	2	1		1		3			1				8		
Hamilton	284	20	Patch	James				2						1			3		
Hamilton	284	21	Patch	Joseph	1	2		1		1	2		1				8		
Hamilton	284	22	Woodbury	Isaac	1				1	2	1		1				6		
Hamilton	284	23	Knowlton	William			1			1	1						3		
Hamilton	284	24	Woodbury	James	1			1		3			1				6		
Hamilton	284	25	Woodbury	Barnet		1			1		1			1			4		
Hamilton	285	1	Woodbury	Andrew	1	1		1		2	1		1				7		
Hamilton	285	2	Brown	Nathaniel					1			2	1				4		
Hamilton	285	3	Brown	Jacob		1	1		1			1		1			5		
Hamilton	285	4	Poland	Francis					1			1		1			3		
Hamilton	285	5	Poland	Samuel		1			1					1			3		
Hamilton	285	6	Poland	Joseph			1	1	1	2	1			1			7		
Hamilton	285	7	Dodge	Barnabas	1		1	1	1				1	1			6		
Hamilton	285	8	Dodge	Andrew	1			1				1	1				4		
Hamilton	285	9	Brown	Joseph	1		1			1		1		1			5		
Hamilton	285	10	Patch	Paul	1		1					1					3		
Hamilton	285	11	Lampen	Abigail								2	1				3		
Hamilton	285	12	Adams	Samuel	1			2	1			1		1			6		
Hamilton	285	13	Adams	Stephen	3	1		2		1	1		2				10		
Hamilton	285	14	Wallice	David		1		1		3	1		1				7		
Hamilton	285	15	Goodhue	John					1					1			2		
Hamilton	285	16	Goodhue	John Junr		2		1		1		1					5		
Hamilton	285	17	Bowles	Abigail		1								1			2		
Hamilton	285	18	Wallis	Lidia								1		1			2		
Hamilton	285	19	Adams	Thomas	3	1	1	1			1		1				8		
Hamilton	285	20	Adams	Elizabeth								1	2				3		
Hamilton	285	21	Safford	Samuel	1	2	1		1				1	1			7		
Hamilton	285	22	Patch	Benjamin	2			1		1			1				5		
Hamilton	285	23	Baker	James		1	2					1					4		
Hamilton	285	24	Wilredge	John		1		1	1	1				1			5		
Hamilton	285	25	Adams	Nathaniel		1	1	1		1		1	1				6		
Hamilton	285	26	Whitfield	Thomas					1		1			1			3		
Hamilton	285	27	Patch	Edmund	1				1	1	1			1			5		
Hamilton	285	28	Howard	Anna									1	1			2		
Hamilton	285	29	Lamson	Edward			1	1				1	1				4		
Hamilton	285	30	Lamson	Sarah			1					1	1				3		
Hamilton	285	31	Lamson	Jonathan		1	1	2			1		1				6		
Hamilton	285	32	Adams	Samuel Junr		1	1			3		1					6		
Hamilton	285	33	Dodge	George	1	3		1		2	1	1	2				11		
Hamilton	285	34	Dodge	Jonathan Junr	2		1			1	1	1					6		
Hamilton	285	35	Smith	Ruben	1	1	1	1			1		1				6		
Hamilton	285	36	Smith	John	1		1					1					3		
Hamilton	285	37	Dodge	Jonathan	1	1	1	1		1	1	4		1			12		
Hamilton	285	38	Dodge	Ephraim			1				2						3		
Hamilton	285	39	Dodge	Luke				2					2				4		
Hamilton	285	40	Brewer	John	1			1		1	1		1				5		
Hamilton	285	41	Dodge	Livermore	2			1		2			1				6		
Hamilton	285	42	Dodge	Thomas				1		2			1				4		
Hamilton	285	43	Cleaves	Nathaniel	1	1			1	1	1		1				7		
Hamilton	285	44	Baker	Moses	1	1			1	4	2		1		4		14		
Hamilton	285	45	Lovering	Ebenezer			1	1				1		1			4		
Hamilton	285	46	Lovering	John		1	1		1	1	1		1				6		
Hamilton	285	47	Lovering	Joseph	1	1				2			1				6		
Hamilton	285	48	Dodge	Mighill	2				1	1	1		1				6		
Hamilton	285	49	Dean	John	1		1		1		1		1				5		
Hamilton	285	50	Dean	William			1		1	1			1				3		
Hamilton	285	51	Annable	Jacob		1			1		1	1	1				5		
Hamilton	285	52	Dean	Eloner							1	1		1			3		
Hamilton	285	53	Adams	Ezekiel				1					1				2		
Hamilton	285	54	Giddings	Abigail									1				1		

TOWN	PG#	LN#	LAST NAME	FIRST NAME	FREE WHITE MALES under 10	10 to 16	16 to 26	26 to 45	45 and over	FREE WHITE FEMALES under 10	10 to 16	16 to 26	26 to 45	45 and over	TOTAL ALL OTHER	TOTAL SLAVES	TOTALS	DISTRICT/ TOWNSHIP	NOTES
Hamilton	285	55	Brown	Ephraim		1		1	1	1			2				6		
Hamilton	285	56	Brown	William					1			1		1			3		
Hamilton	285	57	Brown	William Junr		2			2			1	1	2			8		
Hamilton	285	58	Cole	Anna	1	1	1			1	1	1		1			7		
Hamilton	285	59	Appleton	Benjamin			1		1	1	2			1			6		
Hamilton	285	60	Annable	Robert		1	1		1			1		1			5		
Hamilton	285	61	Annable	Robert Junr				1					1	1			3		
Hamilton	285	62	Annable	John	1			1				1					3		
Hamilton	285	63	Annable	Daniel	1		1					1					3		
Hamilton	285	64	Whipple	Jonathan	3		1		1	1	2	1		1			10		
Hamilton	285	65	Tuttle	John			1		1			1		2			5		
Hamilton	285	66	Patch	Benjamin	2		1		1	1	2	1		1			9		
Hamilton	285	67	Kinsman	William	1				1	1		1	1				5		
Hamilton	285	68	Clinton	Samuel	1				1					1			3		
Hamilton	285	69	Annable	John Junr	2			1				1	1				5		
Hamilton	285	70	Kinsman	Mary									2	1	6		9		
Hamilton	285	71	Annable	Whipple	2			1		2			1				6		
Hamilton	285	72	Caldwell	Stephen				1		1			1				3		
Hamilton	285	73	Whipple	Matthew		2		1		1			1				5		
Hamilton	285	74	Whipple	John	1		1		1			1	1	1			6		
Hamilton	285	75	Harden	Isaac			1			2		2					5		
Hamilton	285	76	Patch	Benjamin	1				1	1	1	1		1			6		
Hamilton	285	77	Whipple	Nathaniel		1			1				3	1			6		
Hamilton	285	78	Whipple	John		1			1	1		1		1			5		
Hamilton	285	79	Whipple	Sarah										2			2		
Hamilton	285	80	Dodge	Isaac		1	1	1				1	1				5		
Hamilton	285	81	Sands	Susanna									1				1		
Hamilton	285	82	Porter	Dudley	2			1					1				4		
Hamilton	285	83	Poland	Nathan			1	1	1		2			1			6		
Hamilton	285	84	Dean	Anna									1	1			2		
Hamilton	285	85	Giddings	Joshua			1	1		1				1			4		
Hamilton	285	86	Adams	George				1						1			2		
Hamilton	285	87	Brown	James		1		1						1			3		
Hamilton	285	88	Whipple	Samuel	1			1					1				3		
Hamilton	285	89	Brown	Daniel	1		2	1		1	1	1					7		
Hamilton	285	90	Wilkins	Abijah			1			2	1		1				5		
Hamilton	285	91	Cutler	Manasseth			2	1				1		1	1		6		
Hamilton	285	92	Roberts	David			1		1				1				3		
Hamilton	285	93	Roberts	Samuel		1	1		1				1				4		
Hamilton	285	94	Patch	Nehemiah		1		1				1		1			4		
Hamilton	285	95	White	William	2			1		1			1				5		
Hamilton	285	96	Patch	Isaac		1						1					2		
Hamilton	285	97	Quales	Hipsabah									2				2		
Hamilton	285	98	Foster	William	1			1					1				3		
Hamilton	285	99	Brown	Stephen		1	1	1		3	1	2	1				10		
Hamilton	285	100	Rust	Daniel	2			1		2			1				6		
Hamilton	285	101	Brown	Lemuel	1	1		1				1					4		
Hamilton	285	102	Brown	Sarah									1	2			3		
Hamilton	285	103	Brown	Benjamin				1				1			1		3		
Hamilton	285	104	Porter	Samuel	1	1	2	1				2		1			8		
Hamilton	285	105	Potter	William	3		3	1			1		1	1			10		
Hamilton	285	106	Patch	Abraham	2	1		1		3			1	1			9		
Hamilton	285	107	Quales	Francis				1				1	1	1			4		
Hamilton	285	108	Fairfield	Elijah				1						2			3		
Hamilton	285	109	Knowlton	Ephraim	1			1		1		2		1			6		
Hamilton	285	110	Smith	Job			2			1	1		1				5		
Hamilton	285	111	Whitmarsh	Zakariah			1						1				2		
Hamilton	285	112	Patch	John				1									1		
Hamilton	285	113	Patch	John Junr				1				1		1			3		
Hamilton	285	114	Brown	John	1			1				1		1			4		
Hamilton	285	115	Potter	Nathaniel	2			1					1				4		
Hamilton	287	1	Lovering	John		1		1				2		1			5		
Hamilton	287	2	Dodge	Robert		1		1						4			6		
Hamilton	287	3	Dodge	John A	3			1			1		1				6		
Hamilton	287	4	Poland	Nehemiah			1			1			1	1			4		
Hamilton	287	5	Dodge	William	3		1	1				1		1			7		
Hamilton	287	6	Dodge	Ephraim		1	1			1		1					4		
Hamilton	287	7	Dodge	Henry	2	1	1	1		1	1						7		
Hamilton	287	8	Roberts	Joseph			2	1	1				2	1			7		
Hamilton	287	9	Woodbury	Nicholas	1		1	1					1				4		

TOWN	PG#	LN#	LAST NAME	FIRST NAME	FREE WHITE MALES under 10	10 to 16	16 to 26	26 to 45	45 and over	FREE WHITE FEMALES under 10	10 to 16	16 to 26	26 to 45	45 and over	TOTAL ALL OTHER	TOTAL SLAVES	TOTALS	DISTRICT/TOWNSHIP	NOTES
Haverhill	142	1	Adams	Phineas				1	1					1			3		
Haverhill	142	2	Abbot	Abiel			1			2	1		2				6		
Haverhill	142	3	Ayer	Samuel	1	2	1		1	2	1	1	1				10		
Haverhill	142	4	Ayer	James Jun	3	2		2		1	1	1	1				11		
Haverhill	142	5	Appleton	Daniel		1	3		1		2	2		1			10		
Haverhill	142	6	Appleton	Mary										2			2		
Haverhill	142	7	Ayer	John		1		1		1	1		1	2			7		
Haverhill	142	8	Ayer	Nathan	1	1		2		2		2	1				9		
Haverhill	142	9	Ayer	James 3d	1		1	1		1	1	1					6		
Haverhill	142	10	Atwood	Moses	1		1	2		5	2		2				13		
Haverhill	142	11	Atwood	Joseph				1		3				1			5		
Haverhill	142	12	Alley	John			3			3			1	1			8		
Haverhill	142	13	Ayer	Moses	1	2		1				2		1			7		
Haverhill	142	14	Ayer	Obadiah		1	1	1		2	1	2	1				9		
Haverhill	142	15	Ayer	James	2			1		1	2	1	1				8		
Haverhill	142	16	Ayer	James	2			1		1	2	1	1				8		
Haverhill	142	17	Ayer	Jonathan	1		1	1	1		2	1		1			8		
Haverhill	142	18	Ayer	Mary	1			1				1		1			4		
Haverhill	142	19	Ayer	John	3	1	1	1			1		1				8		
Haverhill	142	20	Ayer	Timothy	2		2					1					5		
Haverhill	142	21	Atwood	Abijah		2			1		1	1		1			6		
Haverhill	142	22	Ayer	Peter	3			1		2	1		1				8		
Haverhill	142	23	Ayer	Simon		1	1		2	1	3			2			10		
Haverhill	142	24	Adams	Daniel	2	1		1		1	1		1				7		
Haverhill	142	25	Appleton	Thomas R.			1	1		2			1	1			6		
Haverhill	143	1	Bradley	Samuel	3	1	1	1		1			1				8		
Haverhill	143	2	Brown	John	2			1					1				4		
Haverhill	143	3	Bradbury	Daniel	1			1		3			1				6		
Haverhill	143	4	Bradbury	Samuel	1	1			1	1		1	1	1			7		
Haverhill	143	5	Brown	Edmund				1				1	1				3		
Haverhill	143	6	Brown	John Jun	2			1					1				4		
Haverhill	143	7	Brickett	James		1	1		1	2	1		1				7		
Haverhill	143	8	Brickett	Daniel				1		3	3	1					8		
Haverhill	143	9	Bartlett	Bailey	3			1		4	3	1	1				13		
Haverhill	143	10	Bartlett	Israel	1	1	3		1		1			2	1		10		
Haverhill	143	11	Barnard	Sarah									1	1			2		
Haverhill	143	12	Bradley	Nathaniel		1	1		2	2		2					8		
Haverhill	143	13	Bradley	Peter	1			1	1				1	1			5		
Haverhill	143	14	Bradley	Francis			1			2			1				4		
Haverhill	143	15	Bradley	Maehetable									2	1			3		
Haverhill	143	16	Baker	Jonathan				1						2			3		
Haverhill	143	17	Bailey	Nathan			1		1	1	1			1			5		
Haverhill	143	18	Brooks	Cotton B.	2	1		1		1			1	1			7		
Haverhill	143	19	Burrell	Joseph	2			1		3			1				7		
Haverhill	143	20	Ballard	Ebenzr				1						1			2		
Haverhill	143	21	Bailey	Nathll			1			2			1				4		
Haverhill	143	22	Bailey	Benjm	1		2		2		1	1	1	1			9		
Haverhill	143	23	Bradley	Benjm		1	1	1		3	2		1	1			10		
Haverhill	143	24	Bradley	Joseph	3		1	1				1		1			7		
Haverhill	143	25	Briant	Ann	1		2				1	1	1	1			7		
Haverhill	143	26	Brickett	Barnard		2		1						2			5		
Haverhill	143	27	Bray	Thomas R.	1	1		1		1			1				5		
Haverhill	143	28	Bartlett	John	3			1		1	1		1				7		
Haverhill	143	29	Buswell	Mary									1	1			2		
Haverhill	143	30	Blanchard	Samuel	1	1		1		2	1			1			7		
Haverhill	143	31	Balch	Wesley	2		1	1		1		2					7		
Haverhill	143	32	Buck	Eliphalet	1	2		1		4		1	1				10		
Haverhill	143	33	Badger	Abigail							1		1				2		
Haverhill	143	34	Brickett	John	2	1	1	1		1	2		1				9		
Haverhill	143	35	Bradley	Dudley			1			3			1				5		
Haverhill	143	36	Bradley	Daniel				1					1	1			3		
Haverhill	143	37	Bradley	Daniel Jun	1			1		2		1	1				6		
Haverhill	143	38	Bradley	David		1		1		2			1	1			6		
Haverhill	143	39	Barber	Samuel		1		1					2	1			5		
Haverhill	143	40	Bradley	Josiah	2	2		1		2			1				8		
Haverhill	143	41	Bailey	Nathan Jun	1			1		1			1				4		
Haverhill	143	42	Bacheldor	William	2	1		1		2	1	3		1			11		
Haverhill	143	43	Bradbury	David	3			1					1				5		
Haverhill	143	44	Bradley	Enoch		2	2	1				1		2			8		
Haverhill	143	45	Bailey	Lewis	3	3		2		2			1				11		
Haverhill	143	46	Bailey	Jonathan	1	1		1	1	3			1	1			9		
Haverhill	144	1	Bartlett	Nathll	1			1		1	1		1				5		
Haverhill	144	2	Copps	Simeon	1			1					1				3		
Haverhill	144	3	Chase	Daniel	2			1		1			1				5		
Haverhill	144	4	Chase	Daniel Jun				1		1			1				3		
Haverhill	144	5	Carr	Francis	2	1	1		1	2	1	1					9		
Haverhill	144	6	Chase	Anthony		1		1		1	1			1			5		
Haverhill	144	7	Chase	Woodman	1	1		1		3		1	1				9		
Haverhill	144	8	Chase	Joseph	1		1	1		2		1	1				7		

TOWN	PG#	LN#	LAST NAME	FIRST NAME	FREE WHITE MALES under 10	10 to 16	16 to 26	26 to 45	45 and over	FREE WHITE FEMALES under 10	10 to 16	16 to 26	26 to 45	45 and over	TOTAL ALL OTHER	TOTAL SLAVES	TOTALS	DISTRICT/ TOWNSHIP	NOTES
Haverhill	144	9	Chase	John	1			1				1					3		
Haverhill	144	10	Chase	Leonard	1	1			1			1		2			6		
Haverhill	144	11	Chase	Jonah	2	1		1		1	2	1	1				9		
Haverhill	144	12	Chase	Ephraim	1			1		2			1				5		
Haverhill	144	13	Chase	William	1		1	1		2	1	1	2				9		
Haverhill	144	14	Colby	Ephraim		2	1		1		1			2			7		
Haverhill	144	15	Currier	Reuben		2	2		1		1	1		1			8		
Haverhill	144	16	Cottle	Thomas				1			1	1	1				4		
Haverhill	144	17	Cottle	William				1	1	1			2				4		
Haverhill	144	18	Carleton	Enos	2	2		1		3	1		1				10		
Haverhill	144	19	Chase	Theoph	1		1			2		1					5		
Haverhill	144	20	Clement	Samuel				1				1					2		
Haverhill	144	21	Clement	Moses	1	2		1		3			1				8		
Haverhill	144	22	Clement	Amos			1			1		1					3		
Haverhill	144	23	Clement	Ebenzr	2		1			1		1					5		
Haverhill	144	24	Cogswell	John	2	1		1	1	2	2		1				10		
Haverhill	144	25	Cogswell	Thomas	1			1		3		1	1				7		
Haverhill	144	26	Chase	Amos	1			1		2	2						6		
Haverhill	144	27	Carleton	Phineas	1			1		1	4	1	1		1		10		
Haverhill	144	28	Carleton	Kimball		1		1		1		1		1			5		
Haverhill	144	29	Carleton	Jonathan		1	1			1	1						4		
Haverhill	144	30	Carleton	Michael	2			1					1				4		
Haverhill	144	31	Chamberlain	Wilson	2	1	2	1		1			1				8		
Haverhill	144	32	Chickering	John		1	1		1		1	2		1			7		
Haverhill	144	33	Case	William			1		1				1				3		
Haverhill	144	34	Colby	Theoph			1			1		1					3		
Haverhill	144	35	Cordwell	Enoch	2			2		2	3	1	1				12		
Haverhill	144	36	Chase	Benjamin	2	1	1	1		3	1		1				10		
Haverhill	144	37	Colby	Nicolus	1		1			1		1					4		
Haverhill	144	38	Carleton	Aaron		1	1	1			1	1	1				6		
Haverhill	144	39	Clement	John	3		1		1	1	1	1	2				11		
Haverhill	144	40	Clement	Benjamin		2	1			1		1	1				6		
Haverhill	144	41	Cushing	Moses				1		1			1				3		
Haverhill	144	42	Clark	Nathaniel			1	2					1				4		
Haverhill	144	43	Carleton	Israel	2		1	1		3	1	1	1				10		
Haverhill	144	44	Currier	Jonathan	1	1	3				1	1					7		
Haverhill	144	45	Chase	James		1		1	1		1		1				5		
Haverhill	144	46	Corlis	Ephraim		2		1	1		1	1	1				7		
Haverhill	145	1	Corlis	John	2			1		2			1				6		
Haverhill	145	2	Cook	Benjamin	1			1		2			1				5		
Haverhill	145	3	Corlis	John S.	1	1		1	1	1	1		1	1			8		
Haverhill	145	4	Cloud	Daniel	3			1					1				5		
Haverhill	145	5	Clark	Elijah			1						1				2		
Haverhill	145	6	Davis	Amos	1			1		1			1				4		
Haverhill	145	7	Davis	James	1			2		1	1		1	2			8		
Haverhill	145	8	Duncan	James		1			1		1	1	1				5		
Haverhill	145	9	Duncan	James Jr	2	1	1	2		1			2				9		
Haverhill	145	10	Dodge	Joseph				1					1				2		
Haverhill	145	11	Durton	Thomas		1		1		4	1		1	1			9		
Haverhill	145	12	Dunnels	Joseph	3			1		1			1				6		
Haverhill	145	13	Dunton	Ruth			2						1				3		
Haverhill	145	14	Davis	William	3	1			1	2	1		1	1			10		
Haverhill	145	15	Downing	John		2		1		1			1				5		
Haverhill	145	16	Davis	Prince									1		4		5		
Haverhill	145	17	Corlis	Stephen		1		1		2			1				5		
Haverhill	145	18	Ela	Jacob				1		1	1		1		1		5		
Haverhill	145	19	Eliot	Thomas				1			1	1	1				4		
Haverhill	145	20	Eliot	Ephraim	1	1	1	1		2			2				9		
Haverhill	145	21	Ela	Jonathan		1		1		1			1				4		
Haverhill	145	22	Easterbrooks	Hannah	1			1		1			1				4		
Haverhill	145	23	Emery	Ephraim	1	1		1		1		1					5		
Haverhill	145	24	Emerson	Amos	1		1					1					3		
Haverhill	145	25	Emerson	Nehemiah	2	1	2	1	1	3		1	1		1		13		
Haverhill	145	26	Emerson	Susana			2	1				1		1			5		
Haverhill	145	27	Eames	Samuel		2	1		1	1		1	3	1			10		
Haverhill	145	28	Eaton	Ward			3					1					4		
Haverhill	145	29	Eaton	Timothy		1			1			1	1				4		
Haverhill	145	30	Eaton	Joseph			1	1			1	2	1		1		7		
Haverhill	145	31	Emery	John		1	1	1			4		1				9		
Haverhill	145	32	Emerson	Ithamar			2		1	2	1		1				7		
Haverhill	145	33	Eaton	Rebeckah	2		1	1		1	1	3		1			10		
Haverhill	145	34	Emerson	Nathan	2			1		1			1				5		
Haverhill	145	35	Emerson	Abraham	1	1	2		1			2		1			8		
Haverhill	145	36	Emerson	Moses	3	1		1		2		1	1				9		
Haverhill	145	37	Eaton	Timothy Jun	2	2	4	1		3		1	1				14		
Haverhill	145	38	Emerson	Daniel	4	1		1					1				7		
Haverhill	145	39	Emerson	Josiah		2			1	1		1	1				6		
Haverhill	145	40	Emerson	John		1	1			1	2		1				7		
Haverhill	145	41	Emery	Moses	2			1		1	2		1				8		

TOWN	PG#	LN#	LAST NAME	FIRST NAME	FREE WHITE MALES					FREE WHITE FEMALES					TOTAL ALL OTHER	TOTAL SLAVES	TOTALS	DISTRICT/TOWNSHIP	NOTES
					under 10	10 to 16	16 to 26	26 to 45	45 and over	under 10	10 to 16	16 to 26	26 to 45	45 and over					
Haverhill	145	42	Edwards	William	2		1	1		1		1	1				7		
Haverhill	145	43	Emerson	Nehemiah Jun			1					1					2		
Haverhill	145	44	Emer	Micah			1							1			2		
Haverhill	145	45	Eaton	Phineas	1		2	1				1					5		
Haverhill	145	46	Eaton	Amos	1	2			1	1	1		1				7		
Haverhill	146	1	McFarland	Moses	1	1	1		1			2		1			7		
Haverhill	146	2	Foster	Nathll			1			2			1	1			5		
Haverhill	146	3	Frink	Elizabeth						2				1			3		
Haverhill	146	4	Frink	Samuel	2				1	2	2		1				9		
Haverhill	146	5	Foster	John	1		1	1					1				4		
Haverhill	146	6	Fitts	Jeremiah	2				1	2	1		1				7		
Haverhill	146	7	George	Amos	1	2	1		1	2	1	1		1			10		
Haverhill	146	8	George	Lewis	1	1	2		1	2	1	1	1				10		
Haverhill	146	9	George	Austin	3	1		1		1	1	1	1	1			10		
Haverhill	146	10	George	Hezekiah			1			2		1					4		
Haverhill	146	11	Greeley	Joseph				1		1			1	1			4		
Haverhill	146	12	Grover	Joseph		1	1	1					1				4		
Haverhill	146	13	Gay	Joseph		2		1			1		1				5		
Haverhill	146	14	Gale	Moses				2	1	2	1	1					8		
Haverhill	146	15	Greeley	Clement	1	1		1					1				4		
Haverhill	146	16	Greenleaf	William	1	1		1	1	3	1	1	1	2			12		
Haverhill	146	17	Gage	Thomas					1	1	4	1	1				8		
Haverhill	146	18	Gage	Ebenezer			2	1	1	1							5		
Haverhill	146	19	Greenough	Polly			1							2			3		
Haverhill	146	20	Goodridge	Barnabas	2			1		1			1				5		
Haverhill	146	21	Green	John				1				1		1			3		
Haverhill	146	22	Green	Moses	1			1		1		1	1				5		
Haverhill	146	23	Gile	James	1	1		1		2	1		1				7		
Haverhill	146	24	Gile	Amos	1		1		1	3				2			8		
Haverhill	146	25	George	Richard	3			1		1			1				6		
Haverhill	146	26	George	Timothy			2		1		1			1			5		
Haverhill	146	27	Greenleaf	Caleb	2	2		1		1	1		1	1			9		
Haverhill	146	28	Gile	John R	3			1		1			1				6		
Haverhill	146	29	Gile	Samuel	2		2	1					1	1			7		
Haverhill	146	30	Gleason	David	2		2	1					1	1			7		
Haverhill	146	31	Gale	Ephraim	3	1		1		1			1				7		
Haverhill	146	32	Godkins	Stephen	2			1					1				4		
Haverhill	146	33	Goodridge	John	1			1		1			1	1			5		
Haverhill	146	34	Greenleaf	Sarah	1	1				1			1	1			5		
Haverhill	146	35	Hunkins	Jonathan	1		1		1				3	2			8		
Haverhill	146	36	Hunkins	David	3	2		1				1	2				10		
Haverhill	146	37	How	david	2	2	2	2		1	1	2	2				14		
Haverhill	146	38	Haseltine	James Jun	1	1	1		1	1	1		1				7		
Haverhill	146	39	Haseltine	James 4th	1			1				1					3		
Haverhill	146	40	Harrod	Joseph	1	1	1		2	1	4	1	1				12		
Haverhill	146	41	Haddack	James	2		1	1		2			1				7		
Haverhill	146	42	Haynes	Thomas	1	2			1	2	1	1		1			9		
Haverhill	146	43	Hale	Ezzekiel	3	1	1	1		2		1	2				11		
Haverhill	146	44	Huse	John	2			1		1			1				5		
Haverhill	146	45	Harding	Jesse	1		1			2		1	1	1			7		
Haverhill	147	1	Hickey	Volentine		1	1		1					1			4		
Haverhill	147	2	Holland	Joseph	1	1	1		1		1	2	1				8		
Haverhill	147	3	Harding	Thomas	1		1					1					3		
Haverhill	147	4	Harriman	Joel			1	1	1				2	1			6		
Haverhill	147	5	Hazeltine	John	2	1	1		1	1	1	2		1			10		
Haverhill	147	6	Hazeltine	Ladd	4	3		1		1	1	1	1				12		
Haverhill	147	7	Haynes	Joseph		1	1	2	1				2	1	1		9		
Haverhill	147	8	Haynes	Ammi			1	1					3	1			6		
Haverhill	147	9	Haynes	Jonathan			1	1		3	1	1					8		
Haverhill	147	10	How	Isaac	2	1	2	1		2	2	1	2				13		
Haverhill	147	11	Hill	George W.	2	1	1			1		1					6		
Haverhill	147	12	Hoyt	John	2	1		1		1			1				6		
Haverhill	147	13	Hastings	Richard	2			1						1			4		
Haverhill	147	14	Hill	Nathll		1	1					1		1			4		
Haverhill	147	15	Hale	Joshua			1					1					2		
Haverhill	147	16	Hill	Edmund				1						1			2		
Haverhill	147	17	Haddack	Dileverc						1	1	1					3		
Haverhill	147	18	Harriman	Joseph		1		1		2	1		1				6		
Haverhill	147	19	Hastings	John		1	1					1					3		
Haverhill	147	20	Haynes	Warren	2		1						1	1			5		
Haverhill	147	21	Hazeltine	James				1				2		1			4		
Haverhill	147	22	Hazeltine	James 3d	3		3	1		1	1		1				10		
Haverhill	147	23	Ingalls	Henry	2		1		1	1	1		1				7		
Haverhill	147	24	Johnson	Thomas	4		1			1			1				7		
Haverhill	147	25	Johnson	Nathll	3	1	1					1					6		
Haverhill	147	26	Johnson	John	2		1				1		1				6		
Haverhill	147	27	Johnson	Hannah			1			1				1			3		
Haverhill	147	28	Johnson	John Jur			1			1		1					3		
Haverhill	147	29	Johnson	Elias			1	2					2	1			7		

TOWN	PG#	LN#	HEADS OF HOUSEHOLD		FREE WHITE MALES					FREE WHITE FEMALES					TOTAL ALL OTHER	TOTAL SLAVES	TOTALS	DISTRICT/ TOWNSHIP	NOTES
			LAST NAME	FIRST NAME	under 10	10 to 16	16 to 26	26 to 45	45 and over	under 10	10 to 16	16 to 26	26 to 45	45 and over					
Haverhill	147	30	Ingersol	Zebulon		1		1		1	3		1				7		
Haverhill	147	31	Johnston	John			1		1		3		1				6		
Haverhill	147	32	Kelley	Moses	1		1			1		1					4		
Haverhill	147	33	Kelley	Joseph		1	1	1			1		2				6		
Haverhill	147	34	Kimball	Cotton	2	3		1		2		1					9		
Haverhill	147	35	Kimball	Solomon	1			1		2			1	1			6		
Haverhill	147	36	Kimball	David		3	2	1				2		1			9		
Haverhill	147	37	Kimball	Moses	1			1		2			1				5		
Haverhill	147	38	Kimball	John		1		1					1				3		
Haverhill	147	39	Kimball	Jonathan Jnr		1				1		1					3		
Haverhill	147	40	Kendrick	John	5			1					1				7		
Haverhill	147	41	Kendrick	Abner	2		1	1		2		1	1				8		
Haverhill	147	42	Kent	Justin	2		1			2		2	1				8		
Haverhill	147	43	Kezer	Timothy				1					1				2		
Haverhill	147	44	Kendal	Asaph	2			1		1		1	1				6		
Haverhill	147	45	Knight	Stephen		1	1			2		1	1				6		
Haverhill	147	46	Kimball	Richard	2	1	3	1		2			2				11		
Haverhill	147	47	Kimball	Jonathan	1	2			1		1	2					7		
Haverhill	147	48	Kimball	Benjan	3	1	1	1		2			1				9		
Haverhill	148	1	Kelley	Abijah		1		1		1			1				4		
Haverhill	148	2	Kelley	Willm			1	1					1				3		
Haverhill	148	3	Kimball	Samuel				1					1				2		
Haverhill	148	4	Ladd	Nathll	3	1		1		1	2		1				9		
Haverhill	148	5	Lake	Joseph	4			1		1			1				7		
Haverhill	148	6	Little	William	1		4	1				1	1				8		
Haverhill	148	7	Low	Hannah	2		2			2			1				7		
Haverhill	148	8	Ladd	Dudley				1		1		1	1				4		
Haverhill	148	9	Leborquet	Caleb		1	1	1		1			1		1		6		
Haverhill	148	10	Leborquet	John				1	1	1		1	1				5		
Haverhill	148	11	Leborquet	Ebenezr			1			1		1					3		
Haverhill	148	12	Luftkin	Mehitable		2							2	1			5		
Haverhill	148	13	Lecount	William	1	1	1			1			1	2			7		
Haverhill	148	14	Leach	Benjamin	2		1			2			1	1			7		
Haverhill	148	15	Loud	William	3			1		1			1				6		
Haverhill	148	16	Long	Joshua				1		1	1	1					4		
Haverhill	148	17	Martin	Oliver	2			2		3	1	1	1				10		
Haverhill	148	18	Moody	Moses		1		1		1			1				4		
Haverhill	148	19	Morse	Henry		1		1						1			3		
Haverhill	148	20	Morse	David		1		1		3		1	1				7		
Haverhill	148	21	Morse	Oliver		1		1		2			1	1			6		
Haverhill	148	22	Manfise	Hannah									2				2		
Haverhill	148	23	Manfise	Simon		2	1		1	1			1	1			7		
Haverhill	148	24	Manfise	Cornelus		2	1		1	1			1	1			7		
Haverhill	148	25	Moores	Jonathan				1		2	1						5		
Haverhill	148	26	Marsh	David				3						2			5		
Haverhill	148	27	Marsh	Moses		1	1	1	1			1	1	1			7		
Haverhill	148	28	Marsh	David Junr	1			1					1				3		
Haverhill	148	29	Moody	Abigail						1				1			2		
Haverhill	148	30	Moody	Moses Junr	2	2		1		2	1		1				9		
Haverhill	148	31	Mullen	Robert	1	1		2			1		1				6		
Haverhill	148	32	Marsh	Cutting	1			1			1			1			4		
Haverhill	148	33	Marsh	Moses Junr	2		1	1		1	1		1				7		
Haverhill	148	34	Marsh	Robert	2			1					1				4		
Haverhill	148	35	Moore	Seth H.	3			1		1		1	1				7		
Haverhill	148	36	Mahana	John	1		1	1		1				1			5		
Haverhill	148	37	Morse	Moses	2		2						2				6		
Haverhill	148	38	McRoy	John	1			1		1			1				4		
Haverhill	148	39	Middleton	Samuel				1		4			1	1			7		
Haverhill	148	40	Morse	David	3		4	1				1	1				10		
Haverhill	148	41	Mayhew	Nathll			1			3		1		2			7		
Haverhill	148	42	Miliken	Susanna			1							1			2		
Haverhill	148	43	Morrill	Israel		1		1						1			3		
Haverhill	148	44	Merrill	Samuel			4	2	1		1			3			11		
Haverhill	148	45	Marble	Samuel	1			1		1			2				5		
Haverhill	148	46	Mitchel	James		1		1		3	2	2	1	1			11		
Haverhill	148	47	Merrill	Giles		2	1		1	2	3		1				10		
Haverhill	148	48	Marble	John	1			1				1	1	2			6		
Haverhill	148	49	Merrill	Jonathn		1		1					1				3		
Haverhill	149	1	Nichols	Phineas				1			1		1	1			4		
Haverhill	149	2	Nichols	Dottey	2			1				1	1	1			6		
Haverhill	149	3	Nichols	Thomas	3			1		2	1	1	1				9		
Haverhill	149	4	Nichols	Benjamin			1			1			1				3		
Haverhill	149	5	Hoyes	Parker		2					1	2	1				6		
Haverhill	149	6	Hoyes	Eliphalet	2			1		1			1				5		
Haverhill	149	7	Ordway	Benjamin				1			1	1	1				4		
Haverhill	149	8	Ordway	James	1			1					1				3		
Haverhill	149	9	Osgood	Abigail		1	1	2			2			2			8		
Haverhill	149	10	Osgood	Peter	1		1	1		2			1				6		
Haverhill	149	11	Osgood	Henry		2		2		1			1				6		
Haverhill	149	12	Ordway	Benjamin Jun	1		1	1	1			2	1	2			9		

TOWN	PG#	LN#	LAST NAME	FIRST NAME	FREE WHITE MALES					FREE WHITE FEMALES					TOTAL ALL OTHER	TOTAL SLAVES	TOTALS	DISTRICT/ TOWNSHIP	NOTES
					under 10	10 to 16	16 to 26	26 to 45	45 and over	under 10	10 to 16	16 to 26	26 to 45	45 and over					
Haverhill	149	13	Ordway	Edward	1	1	2		1		1	1		1			8		
Haverhill	149	14	Parker	Frederick		2		1				1					4		
Haverhill	149	15	Poor	Timothy				1			1		1				3		
Haverhill	149	16	Pike	James				1					1				2		
Haverhill	149	17	Page	Caleb	1			1		1	1		1				5		
Haverhill	149	18	Page	John C.		1	1	1				2		1			6		
Haverhill	149	19	Page	Stephen W	1			1		1			1				4		
Haverhill	149	20	Page	Joshua		2	1		1	1		3		1			9		
Haverhill	149	21	Page	Samuel	1			1				1					3		
Haverhill	149	22	Page	Joshia Junr		1				1		1					3		
Haverhill	149	23	Page	Jonathan		1	1						1				3		
Haverhill	149	24	Putman	Oliver	2	1			1	2	1	1	1				9		
Haverhill	149	25	Plummer	Asa	1	1			1	1	1	1	1				7		
Haverhill	149	26	Plummer	Thomas			2	1		1	2	1	1				8		
Haverhill	149	27	Plummer	Silas	1	2	1	1		2		1	1				9		
Haverhill	149	28	Poor	John	1		1		1	2			1				6		
Haverhill	149	29	Petingall	Mathew	1			1		3			1	2			8		
Haverhill	149	30	Peabody	Josiah	1				2	1		1	1				6		
Haverhill	149	31	Peabody	Joseph	2	1		1		1	1						6		
Haverhill	149	32	Porter	Dudley				1		1	1						3		
Haverhill	149	33	Pearley	Nathan		1	1		1	2	1			1			7		
Haverhill	149	34	Pecker	Daniel			1			5		1					7		
Haverhill	149	35	Pecker	Ruth	1		1			1	1		1				5		
Haverhill	149	36	Peabody	Jonah G.	1	1		1				1					4		
Haverhill	149	37	Pettingall	Jedediah	1			1		1			1				4		
Haverhill	149	38	Petty	Abigail									1				1		
Haverhill	149	39	Palmer	James	2			1		1			1				5		
Haverhill	149	40	Robertson	Joseph				1				1	1		1		4		
Haverhill	149	41	Rollins	John	1		2					3					6		
Haverhill	149	42	Runnels	Hannah						1		1	1				3		
Haverhill	149	43	Runnels	Thomas	1		1	1		3		1					7		
Haverhill	149	44	Russell	John	1							1	1				4		
Haverhill	149	45	Rogers	Hannah							1	1	1				3		
Haverhill	149	46	Russell	Joseph	1		1	1		1	1						5		
Haverhill	149	47	Silleway	Reuben			1						1				2		
Haverhill	149	48	Sargent	Elias		1			1			1	1				4		
Haverhill	150	1	Sanders	Samuel					1				1				2		
Haverhill	150	2	Swan	Francis	3	1			1	2	1		1				9		
Haverhill	150	3	Sargent	Amos			1			2		1	1				5		
Haverhill	150	4	Sawyer	Joshua		2		1		1			1				5		
Haverhill	150	5	Sanders	Timothy		2		1		1			1				5		
Haverhill	150	6	Spollet	Henry	2			1		1		1					5		
Haverhill	150	7	Stephens	Judith	1					1		1					3		
Haverhill	150	8	Tuexbury	Jonathan			1			1	1						3		
Haverhill	150	9	Sargent	Sarah						1			1				2		
Haverhill	150	10	Smiley	William	1	1	3		1		1		1				8		
Haverhill	150	11	Smith	Hezekiah		1			1		2		1				5		
Haverhill	150	12	Straw	Sherburn	1			1		2		1					5		
Haverhill	150	13	Sawyer	Amos	2	1		1		1		1	1				7		
Haverhill	150	14	Stickney	Jeremiah		2	1			3	1	1					8		
Haverhill	150	15	Scoffield	James	1	1		1		3	1	1					8		
Haverhill	150	16	Sanders	Subtle	2		1		1	1		2	1				9		
Haverhill	150	17	Stearns	Benjamin	1	1						1					3		
Haverhill	150	18	Sargent	Jonathan			1	2				1	1				5		
Haverhill	150	19	Swett	Nathan		1					1						2		
Haverhill	150	20	Simpson	James	1	2		1				1					6		
Haverhill	150	21	Sortridge	William			2			2		1					5		
Haverhill	150	22	Soley	Nathll	2	1		1				1					5		
Haverhill	150	23	Sawyer	Ruth								1	1				2		
Haverhill	150	24	Smith	William	2	1	1	1		1	1		1				8		
Haverhill	150	25	Straw	Abigail		1				1	1		1	1			5		
Haverhill	150	26	Sargent	Mary								1	2	1			4		
Haverhill	150	27	Saltonstall	Nathll	1	2	1		1	2		3	1	1			12		
Haverhill	150	28	Souther	Samuel	1	1	1		1	1			2				7		
Haverhill	150	29	Smith	Jonathan			1			1		1					3		
Haverhill	150	30	Smiley	Mary			2						2				4		
Haverhill	150	31	Sargent	Moses	1		1			1		1					4		
Haverhill	150	32	Souther	Jonathan	2	1		1		1	1		1				7		
Haverhill	150	33	Sawyer	William	1	1	2		1	3	1	1					11		
Haverhill	150	34	Smiley	James		2	1	1		1		1	1				7		
Haverhill	150	35	Simmons	Nehemiah		1	1		1	1		1		1			6		
Haverhill	150	36	Simmons	Nehemiah Junr	1		1					1					3		
Haverhill	150	37	Swett	Abraham		1	1	1				1		1			5		
Haverhill	150	38	Swett	Daniel			1			3	1	1					6		
Haverhill	150	39	Sweesy	Appleton	1			1				1		1			4		
Haverhill	150	40	Silver	Daniel	1			1		2			1				5		
Haverhill	150	41	Silver	John	2			1				1					5		
Haverhill	150	42	Silver	Susanna									2				2		
Haverhill	150	43	Stephens	Ephraim	1	1		1		3	1		1				8		
Haverhill	150	44	Smith	John		1							1				3		
Haverhill	150	45	Smith	Walker		1	1		1	3	2		1				9		
Haverhill	150	46	Silver	John Junr	1		1					1					3		
Haverhill	150	47	Tomkins	Isaac		1		1		2		2					6		
Haverhill	150	48	Tucker	Henry	1			1				1					3		
Haverhill	150	49	Tylor	Job	1	1			1	4		1	1		1		10		
Haverhill	151	1	Tylor	Joseph	1		1			1	1						4		
Haverhill	151	2	Tucker	Ihabod		1	1			2	1						5		Probably Ichabod
Haverhill	151	3	Tapley	William				1					1				2		
Haverhill	151	4	Walker	James		1		1				1					3		

TOWN	PG#	LN#	LAST NAME	FIRST NAME	FREE WHITE MALES					FREE WHITE FEMALES					TOTAL ALL OTHER	TOTAL SLAVES	TOTALS	DISTRICT/ TOWNSHIP	NOTES
					under 10	10 to 16	16 to 26	26 to 45	45 and over	under 10	10 to 16	16 to 26	26 to 45	45 and over					
Haverhill	151	5	Whittier	Joseph		1		3				2	1	1			8		
Haverhill	151	6	Walker	Nathll		2	1	1	1			3		1			9		
Haverhill	151	7	White	Samuel		2	2		1	1		2	1				9		
Haverhill	151	8	White	Leonard	1			2		3		3	3	2	1		15		
Haverhill	151	9	Willis	Benjamin		2		1		1	2		2				8		
Haverhill	151	10	Willis	Benjan Junr	4	1	1	1			1		1				9		
Haverhill	151	11	White	Samuel Junr		1		1		4			1				7		
Haverhill	151	12	West	Henry	1		2		1	2	1		1	2			10		
Haverhill	151	13	West	Mary			3	1					1	1			6		
Haverhill	151	14	Whittier	Thomas		1	1		1	1		3		1			8		
Haverhill	151	15	Wells	David				1		1				1			3		
Haverhill	151	16	Woodbury	Hannah	2		1					3	1				7		
Haverhill	151	17	Wied	Joshua			1				1		1				3		
Haverhill	151	18	Wilson	John	1		1	1		2		1		1			7		
Haverhill	151	19	Winn	David	1	1	1	1		2			1				7		
Haverhill	151	20	Wyman	Jacob				1						1			2		
Haverhill	151	21	Walker	Samuel	1			1						1			3		
Haverhill	151	22	Williams	John M.		1		1		1	1						4		
Haverhill	151	23	Webb	Daniel				1					1				2		
Haverhill	151	24	Wingate	William				1				1					2		
Haverhill	151	25	Wingate	Paine	2		1	1		2			1				7		
Haverhill	151	26	Wingate	Moses			1			1			1				3		
Haverhill	151	27	Williams	Isaac F.			1	1		2	2		1				6		
Haverhill	151	28	Whiting	John				1					1	1			3		
Haverhill	151	29	Wyman	Reuben			1						1				2		
Haverhill	151	30	Whittier	William	1		1					1		1			4		
Haverhill	151	31	West	Richard	1		1			1		1					4		
Haverhill	151	32	Whittier	Daniel	3			1		1			1				6		
Haverhill	151	33	White	Thomas M.			1						1		1		3		
Haverhill	151	34	Whittier	Thomas Junr	1		2						1				4		
Haverhill	151	35	Whitaker	William	2	1		1		2			1				7		
Haverhill	151	36	Whitaker	Peter	2			1	1	1			1				6		
Haverhill	151	37	Webster	Jonathan		2		1			1	1	1				6		
Haverhill	151	38	Webster	Moses			2		1			2		1	1		7		
Haverhill	151	39	Webster	Joshua	5	2	1		1	1		1	1				12		
Haverhill	151	40	Webster	Moses Junr		1	2		1			2		1			7		
Haverhill	151	41	Webster	Stephen 3d	1		1	1	1		1			2			7		
Haverhill	151	42	Webster	David		1			1	1		1		2			6		
Haverhill	151	43	Webster	Stephen	2	1	1	1	1	1			1				8		
Haverhill	151	44	Webster	Stephen Junr	2		2		1	1	2	1		2			11		
Haverhill	151	45	Webster	Stephen 4th	2			1					1				4		
Haverhill	151	46	Webster	Isaac	1		1		1	1				1			5		
Haverhill	151	47	Webster	Caleb	2	3		1		2			1				9		
Haverhill	151	48	West	Thomas	2		1	1		2			1				7		
Haverhill	152	1	Walker	John	2			1					1				4		
Haverhill	152	2	Mitchel	John		1		1		1			1				4		
Haverhill	152	3	Mitchel	John Junr		1						1					2		
Haverhill	152	4	Mitchel	Mehetable						1			1				2		

TOWN	PG#	LN#	HEADS OF HOUSEHOLD		FREE WHITE MALES					FREE WHITE FEMALES					TOTAL ALL OTHER	TOTAL SLAVES	TOTALS	DISTRICT/ TOWNSHIP	NOTES
			LAST NAME	FIRST NAME	under 10	10 to 16	16 to 26	26 to 45	45 and over	under 10	10 to 16	16 to 26	26 to 45	45 and over					
Ipswich	273	1	Bradstreet	Nathaniel			1		1		1	2		1			6		
Ipswich	273	2	Jewett	Edward	2			1		1			1				5		
Ipswich	273	3	Bailey	Peirce	2			1		1		1	1				6		
Ipswich	273	4	Bailey	Hannah									2	1			3		
Ipswich	273	5	Pearson	Nathan		1		1		1			1	1			5		
Ipswich	273	6	Pearson	Sarah										1			1		
Ipswich	273	7	Pearson	Stephen	2			1		1			1				5		
Ipswich	273	8	Tresser	Daniel		1		1					1				3		
Ipswich	273	9	Jewett	Aaron			2		1	2			1	1			7		
Ipswich	273	10	Jewett	Abigail									4				4		
Ipswich	273	11	Jewett	Nehemiah Junr			1						1				2		
Ipswich	273	12	Jewett	Nehemiah				1			1			1			3		
Ipswich	273	13	Jewett	Katharine	1									1			2		
Ipswich	273	14	Jewett	Purchase			1	1						1			3		
Ipswich	273	15	Jewett	Mehitable			1										1		
Ipswich	273	16	Jewett	Abraham			1					1					2		
Ipswich	273	17	Nurse	Daniel			1	2	1			1		1			6		
Ipswich	273	18	Smith	Isaac	3			1		2			1				7		
Ipswich	273	19	Poller	John Jur	1	2		1		3	1		1				9		
Ipswich	273	20	Baker	Robert	1			1		1			2				5		
Ipswich	273	21	Linneus	John Jur			1	1	1				2				5		
Ipswich	273	22	Haskell	Mark		2		1				1		1	1		6		
Ipswich	273	23	Hodgkins	John	1			1					1				3		
Ipswich	273	24	Day	Jeremiah		1		1				1		1			4		
Ipswich	273	25	Lord	Charles		1		1	1	1	1		1				6		
Ipswich	273	26	Kimball	Jeremiah	1	1							1				3		
Ipswich	273	27	Lord	Moses								1					1		
Ipswich	273	28	Safford	Ebenezer				1				1	1	1			4		
Ipswich	273	29	Lord	David	1	2		1		2			1				7		
Ipswich	273	30	Russell	Story Jun	1	1		1		2	1		1				7		
Ipswich	273	31	Lord	Benjamin	2			1		1	2		1				7		
Ipswich	273	32	Potter	John				1					1	1			3		
Ipswich	273	33	Kimball	Sarah										1			1		
Ipswich	273	34	Kimball	Jeremiah	2	1	1		1	1	1	3		1			11		
Ipswich	273	35	Russell	Stery		1		1					1	1			4		
Ipswich	273	36	Fowler	Joseph			1	1				1			1		4		
Ipswich	273	37	Jewett	John C.	1	2	1	1					1	1			7		
Ipswich	273	38	Fowler	Joseph Jun		1	2	1				1	3				9		
Ipswich	273	39	Poiles	Charles			1						1				2		
Ipswich	273	40	Lord	Daniel		1		1					1	1			4		
Ipswich	273	41	Lord	John	1			1					1	1			4		
Ipswich	273	42	Shotswell	Richard				1					1	1			3		
Ipswich	273	43	Shotswell	Nathaniel				1		1		1	1				4		
Ipswich	273	44	Shotswell	Moses	1			1		2			1				5		
Ipswich	273	45	Lord	Isaac	1	3		1					1	1			7		
Ipswich	273	46	Kimball	Isaac	1		1			2			1				5		
Ipswich	273	47	Lord	Elizabeth		1						2		1			4		
Ipswich	273	48	Hart	Mary										1			1		
Ipswich	273	49	Burga	Sarah										1			1		
Ipswich	273	50	Sweet	Jabez				1				1		1			3		
Ipswich	273	51	Smith	Simon			2	1			1		1	1			6		
Ipswich	273	52	Low	Sarah										1			1		
Ipswich	273	53	Jewett	Moses	2		1						1				4		
Ipswich	273	54	Lakeman	William			1			2			1				4		
Ipswich	274	1	Stocker	Robert	1			1	1	1			1	1			6		
Ipswich	274	2	Wise	Joseph			1						1				2		
Ipswich	274	3	Wise	Elizabeth			1							1			2		
Ipswich	274	4	Kimball	Nathaniel		1	1	1		1			2	1			7		
Ipswich	274	5	Choate	Daniel				1					1	1			3		
Ipswich	274	6	Lord	Samuel				1		2				1			4		
Ipswich	274	7	Peters	Mary									1				1		
Ipswich	274	8	Jewett	Epes	1	2		1		1	1		1	1			8		
Ipswich	274	9	Gould	Major			1	1					1				3		
Ipswich	274	10	Gould	Thomas	1			1		1			1				4		
Ipswich	274	11	Harris	John	1		3		1	2	3			1			11		
Ipswich	274	12	Obrian	John				1						1			2		
Ipswich	274	13	Wells	Elizabeth									2				2		
Ipswich	274	14	Spiller	William	1			1		2			1		7		12		
Ipswich	274	15	Lakeman	John			1	1				1		1			4		
Ipswich	274	16	Lord	Abraham			1						1				2		
Ipswich	274	17	Lakeman	Martha										1			1		
Ipswich	274	18	Lord	Elizabeth								1		1			2		
Ipswich	274	19	Caldwell	Martha										1			1		
Ipswich	274	20	Harris	Nathaniel			1			1		1					3		
Ipswich	274	21	Galloway	Sarah									2	1			3		
Ipswich	274	22	Ripley	Kimball				1		3				1			5		
Ipswich	274	23	Stone	Robert	1		1			2			1				5		
Ipswich	274	24	Lummus	Isaac		1		1						1			3		
Ipswich	274	25	Hodgkins	John 3d		1		1		1			1				4		

TOWN	PG#	LN#	LAST NAME	FIRST NAME	FREE WHITE MALES					FREE WHITE FEMALES					TOTAL ALL OTHER	TOTAL SLAVES	TOTALS	DISTRICT/ TOWNSHIP	NOTES
					under 10	10 to 16	16 to 26	26 to 45	45 and over	under 10	10 to 16	16 to 26	26 to 45	45 and over					
Ipswich	274	26	Baker	Stephen			1			1		1					3		
Ipswich	274	27	Lord	Daniel	3			1		1			1				6		
Ipswich	274	28	Goodhue	Daniel	2			1						1			4		
Ipswich	274	29	Baker	Sarah	1								1	1			3		
Ipswich	274	30	Goodhue	Daniel Jur			1						1				2		
Ipswich	274	31	Lummus	Daniel Jur			1	1					1				3		
Ipswich	274	32	Ridge	John		2		1		3			1				7		
Ipswich	274	33	Newman	Elisha				1				1	1				3		
Ipswich	274	34	Baker	Samuel	1		1	1		1	1	2	1				8		
Ipswich	274	35	Rindge	Mary									1				1		
Ipswich	274	36	March	Nathaniel Jun			1			2		1					4		
Ipswich	274	37	Perkins	Elizabeth										2			2		
Ipswich	274	38	Caldwell	Benjamin		1		1				2					4		
Ipswich	274	39	Dodge	Thomas			1			2			1	1			5		
Ipswich	274	40	Caldwell	John	1	1		1				4	1	1			9		
Ipswich	274	41	Grow	John			1			1			1				3		
Ipswich	274	42	Smith	Daniel B.	2	1		1		1	3		1				9		
Ipswich	274	43	Lord	Ebenezer Jun	1		1			1		1					4		
Ipswich	274	44	Lord	Daniel	2		1						1				4		
Ipswich	274	45	Thornton	Lydia										2			2		
Ipswich	274	46	Lord	Joseph	2		1			1	1	1					6		
Ipswich	274	47	Moss	Thomas	3	1		1		1		1					7		
Ipswich	274	48	Smith	Annie			1			1		1					3		
Ipswich	274	49	Kimball	James	1		1						1				3		
Ipswich	274	50	Lord	Ebenezer		1		1		1	1		1				5		
Ipswich	274	51	Lord	Nathaniel	1		1	1		2	2		1				8		
Ipswich	274	52	Lord	Aaron	1			1					1	1			4		
Ipswich	274	53	Lord	Samuel 3d			1	1					3	1			6		
Ipswich	274	54	Lord	Daniel B.	2		1			2			1				6		
Ipswich	274	55	Lord	Samuel 4th	2		2	1		2			1				8		
Ipswich	274	56	Andrews	Asa	1	1		1		1		1	2		1		8		
Ipswich	274	57	Lord	Caleb				1			1						2		
Ipswich	274	58	Lord	Robert	1			1		1	1		1				5		
Ipswich	275	1	Lord	Samuel	1	1		1	1	2			1				7		
Ipswich	275	2	Willcomb	Sarah									1				1		
Ipswich	275	3	Willcomb	William	1			1		2	1		1				6		
Ipswich	275	4	Treadwell	Nathaniel	1			1		1		1	1				5		
Ipswich	275	5	Caldwell	Thomas	1	1		3		2	1		3	18	1		30		
Ipswich	275	6	Harris	James	2	3		1		1			1				8		
Ipswich	275	7	Newman	Samuel		1		1		1	1		1				5		
Ipswich	275	8	Newman	William			1			1		1					3		
Ipswich	275	9	Manning	John		1	5	1		2		4	1				14		
Ipswich	275	10	Williams	Joshua				1					1				2		
Ipswich	275	11	Hodgkins	John Junr	1	1	1	1		3	1	1	1		1		11		
Ipswich	275	12	Smith	Nathaniel		1		1				3	1				6		
Ipswich	275	13	Dodge	Bethiah		1						2	1				4		
Ipswich	275	14	Emmons	Daniel		1				1			1	1			4		
Ipswich	275	15	Staniford	James			1						1				2		
Ipswich	275	16	Sawyer	George W.		1		1					1				3		
Ipswich	275	17	Treadwell	Nathaniel Jr	1			1					1		1		4		
Ipswich	275	18	Smith	Joshua		1		1	1	1	1	1		1			7		
Ipswich	275	19	Gains	Thomas				1		2			1				4		
Ipswich	275	20	Perkins	James				1		1		1	1				5		
Ipswich	275	21	Kindall	Ephraim		2	2	1	1			1	3	1			11		
Ipswich	275	22	Kindall	Ephraim Jur	1			1				1	1				4		
Ipswich	275	23	Staniford	Aaron		1		1		2	1		1				6		
Ipswich	275	24	Goodhue	Jeremiah	2	1		1		1	1		1				7		
Ipswich	275	25	Smith	Samuel	1	2		1		2	1		1				8		
Ipswich	275	26	Staniford	Thomas	1		1						1				3		
Ipswich	275	27	Day	John			1						1				2		
Ipswich	275	28	Dodge	Ezekiel	2	2		1		2			1				8		
Ipswich	275	29	Kimball	Thomas	1	2		1		2			1				7		
Ipswich	275	30	Perkins	Sarah		1						3	1				5		
Ipswich	275	31	Perkins	Aaron		3		1				1	1	1			7		
Ipswich	275	32	Perkins	Aaron Jr	2			1					1				4		
Ipswich	275	33	Shatswell	Martha									1				1		
Ipswich	275	34	Pulsipher	David	2			1		2			1				6		
Ipswich	275	35	Fitts	Mary	1								1	1			3		
Ipswich	275	36	Staniford	Jeremiah Jur			5			2	1	1	1				10		
Ipswich	275	37	Jones	Nathaniel				1					1				2		
Ipswich	275	38	Beal	Mary									1	1			2		
Ipswich	275	39	Graves	John	2			1	1				1	1			6		
Ipswich	275	40	Harris	Mary								1	1				2		
Ipswich	275	41	Dutch	Nathaniel	1			1		1	1		1				5		
Ipswich	275	42	Dutch	Daniel	1	1		1		2			1				6		
Ipswich	275	43	Farley	Michiel	1			1				1	1				4		
Ipswich	275	44	Foster	James				1					1				2		
Ipswich	275	45	Treadwell	Jacob	2	1		2		2			2		1		10		
Ipswich	275	46	Treadwell	Moses		1	1	1			1	2	1				7		

TOWN	PG#	LN#	LAST NAME	FIRST NAME	FREE WHITE MALES					FREE WHITE FEMALES					TOTAL ALL OTHER	TOTAL SLAVES	TOTALS	DISTRICT/ TOWNSHIP	NOTES
					under 10	10 to 16	16 to 26	26 to 45	45 and over	under 10	10 to 16	16 to 26	26 to 45	45 and over					
Ipswich	275	47	Thorndike	Mary						1			2	1			4		
Ipswich	275	48	Lord	Stephen	2		1			2			1				6		
Ipswich	275	49	Ross	Jeremiah	3		1			1			1				6		
Ipswich	275	50	Dennis	Rebecca									1	1			2		
Ipswich	275	51	Day	Aaron				1		2	1			1			5		
Ipswich	275	52	Fuller	Elizabeth										1			1		
Ipswich	275	53	Ross	Samuel	1		1			1		1					4		
Ipswich	275	54	Ross	Sarah								1	2	2			5		
Ipswich	275	55	Brown	Elizabeth										1			1		
Ipswich	275	56	Knowlton	Thomas			1						2				3		
Ipswich	275	57	Chapman	Joanna										1			1		
Ipswich	275	58	Barley	Abigail										1			1		
Ipswich	275	59	Rogers	Daniel		1	2		1			3	2	1			10		
Ipswich	275	60	Noyes	Daniel	1		1	1	1					1			5		
Ipswich	275	61	Dennis	William			1		1				1	2			5		
Ipswich	276	1	Treadwell	William			1						1	1			3		
Ipswich	276	2	Waite	Judith		2	2					1		1			6		
Ipswich	276	3	Jewett	Richard D.	2			1				1	1				5		
Ipswich	276	4	Spiller	Moses	2		1						1				4		
Ipswich	276	5	Dutch	Martha									1				1		
Ipswich	276	6	Hodgkins	Sarah									1				1		
Ipswich	276	7	Lord	Moses Jun	2	1	1	1		1			1	1			8		
Ipswich	276	8	Caldwell	Samuel			1						1	1			3		
Ipswich	276	9	Baker	John Junr		1	1						2				4		
Ipswich	276	10	Jewett	John	2	1		1		2		1	1				8		
Ipswich	276	11	Farley	Jabez	4	1	3	1		1	1	1			1		13		
Ipswich	276	12	Farley	Robert		1		1		3	2		1	1			9		
Ipswich	276	13	Heard	Samuel			1	2						2			5		
Ipswich	276	14	Tibbets	Timothy	1	1		1				1					4		
Ipswich	276	15	Kimball	Ebenezer				1				1					2		
Ipswich	276	16	Heard	Nathaniel		1		1	1					1			4		
Ipswich	276	17	Goodhue	Moses		2	1						1	1			5		
Ipswich	276	18	Burnham	Judith	2			1		1			1	1			6		
Ipswich	276	19	Kinsman	Eunice									2				2		
Ipswich	276	20	Kimball	Aaron	1	1	1	1	1			2		2			9		
Ipswich	276	21	Clinton	James	1			1				1		1			4		
Ipswich	276	22	Smith	Aaron	1			1		1			1				4		
Ipswich	276	23	Treadwell	Lidia	1	1						1	2	1			6		
Ipswich	276	24	Treadwell	Priscilla										1			1		
Ipswich	276	25	Newman	Michiel				1		1	1			1			4		
Ipswich	276	26	Crocker	John		1		1	1			1		1			5		
Ipswich	276	27	Pearson	Enoch		1		1	1	1	2	3		1			10		
Ipswich	276	28	Pearson	Lemual	4			1		1	2		1				9		
Ipswich	276	29	Farley	Mary			2					1	2				5		
Ipswich	276	30	Lealand	John	2			1		2			1				6		
Ipswich	276	31	Safford	Simeon	2	2			1				2	1			8		
Ipswich	276	32	Jefts	John	1		3						1				5		
Ipswich	276	33	Stacey	Edward		1			1	1	1	2		1			7		
Ipswich	276	34	Pinder	Moses	1				1		1			1			4		
Ipswich	276	35	Burnham	Thomas		2			1	2			2				7		
Ipswich	276	36	Thurston	Daniel					1					1			2		
Ipswich	276	37	Roberts	Easter										2			2		
Ipswich	276	38	Grant	Nathaniel				1						2			3		
Ipswich	276	39	Ross	Daniel			1			2	1	2	1				7		
Ipswich	276	40	Tucker	David	2		1			1				1			5		
Ipswich	276	41	Heard	John	1	1	1		1	2		3		2	1		12		
Ipswich	276	42	Spiller	Jeremiah				1						1			2		
Ipswich	276	43	Choate	John	2		2				1		1				6		
Ipswich	276	44	Giddings	Joshua	1		2			1		2		1			7		
Ipswich	276	45	Ingersoll	Jonathan				1				1		1			3		
Ipswich	276	46	Dodge	Elizabeth									1	1			2		
Ipswich	276	47	Jewett	Martha						1			1	1			3		
Ipswich	276	48	Fitts	Jeremiah				1						1			2		
Ipswich	276	49	Caldwell	John				1		1				1			3		
Ipswich	276	50	Caldwell	Ebenezer	1	1	1		1	2	2	2		1			11		
Ipswich	276	51	Farley	Jonathan	3			1		1	2			1			8		
Ipswich	276	52	Appleton	Sarah				1		2			2				5		
Ipswich	276	53	Appleton	William	1				1			1		1	1		5		
Ipswich	276	54	Hall	Charles	1	1			1			1	1	1			7		
Ipswich	276	55	Foster	Mary										1			1		
Ipswich	276	56	Hodgkins	Thomas	1				1	1			1	1			5		
Ipswich	276	57	Stanwood	Isaac	2			1		1	1		1				6		
Ipswich	276	58	Perkins	Elizabeth										1			1		
Ipswich	276	59	Appleton	Aaron			1						1				2		
Ipswich	276	60	Frisbie	Levie		1	1		1	1		1	1	1			7		
Ipswich	277	1	Knowlton	Sarah								1	3	1			5		
Ipswich	277	2	Lord	John	3			1		1	1			1			7		
Ipswich	277	3	Warner	William				1			1			1			3		
Ipswich	277	4	Holland	Daniel				1					1				2		

TOWN	PG#	LN#	HEADS OF HOUSEHOLD		FREE WHITE MALES					FREE WHITE FEMALES					TOTAL ALL OTHER	TOTAL SLAVES	TOTALS	DISTRICT/ TOWNSHIP	NOTES
			LAST NAME	FIRST NAME	under 10	10 to 16	16 to 26	26 to 45	45 and over	under 10	10 to 16	16 to 26	26 to 45	45 and over					
Ipswich	277	5	Wells	Jonathan			1			1		1					3		
Ipswich	277	6	Dennis	Mary	1					2	1	1					5		
Ipswich	277	7	Martain	Edward	1			1		1	2		1				6		
Ipswich	277	8	Hammon	Phillip				1					1				2		
Ipswich	277	9	Kimball	Abraham	1			1		4			1				7		
Ipswich	277	10	Lakeman	Deborah			1				1	1		1			4		
Ipswich	277	11	Sevard	John		1		1		3			1				6		
Ipswich	277	12	Lakeman	Richard	1		1	1						1			4		
Ipswich	277	13	Leatherland	William	2			1		2			1				6		
Ipswich	277	14	Hunt	Deborah									1				1		
Ipswich	277	15	Kinsman	Nathaniel		1		1		3		1		1			7		
Ipswich	277	16	Stone	Samu				1			1			1			3		
Ipswich	277	17	Whyett	Stephen	1			1		1			1	1			5		
Ipswich	277	18	Kimball	Benjamin Jr	1			1		1				1			4		
Ipswich	277	19	Sutton	Richard				1			1			1			3		
Ipswich	277	20	Russell	Daniel	3			1				1					5		
Ipswich	277	21	March	Nathaniel		1		1				1		1			4		
Ipswich	277	22	Eveleth	Samuel		1		1		3	1		1				7		
Ipswich	277	23	Coleman	Samuel				1						1			2		
Ipswich	277	24	Caldwell	Moses	5	1		1			1		1				9		
Ipswich	277	25	Roberts	William	1		1					2		1			5		
Ipswich	277	26	Saniford	Ebenezer	1			1		1	1		1				5		
Ipswich	277	27	Staniford	Jeremiah			1	1					1	1			4		
Ipswich	277	28	Hinderson	Thomas	2			1					1	1			5		
Ipswich	277	29	Smith	James	2	1		1			1		1	1			7		
Ipswich	277	30	Hammon	Abigail	2						1			1			4		
Ipswich	277	31	Sawyer	Samuel		1	2	1		1			2	1			8		
Ipswich	277	32	Hovey	Ebenezer	2			1		1			1				5		
Ipswich	277	33	Dennis	Nathaniel			1						1				2		
Ipswich	277	34	Homes	Sarah						1			1	1			3		
Ipswich	277	35	Hodgkins	Thomas	1			1		3			1				6		
Ipswich	277	36	Harris	John	1		2	1		1			1	1			7		
Ipswich	277	37	Harris	Samuel	1				2	1	1	1		1			7		
Ipswich	277	38	Spiller	Mary								1	1	1			3		
Ipswich	277	39	Stone	William	1			1		1			1				4		
Ipswich	277	40	Appleton	Joseph				1				1		1			3		
Ipswich	277	41	Harris	David	3			1		1			1				6		
Ipswich	277	42	Wickins	Abraham	1		1						1				3		
Ipswich	277	43	Hovey	Francis	1		1	1		1		3	1	1			9		
Ipswich	277	44	Ellice	George				1				1		1			3		
Ipswich	277	45	Pulsipher	Lucey										1			1		
Ipswich	277	46	Fuller	Mary										2			2		
Ipswich	277	47	Mansfield	Abigail									1	1			2		
Ipswich	277	48	Harris	Samuel Jun			1						1	1			3		
Ipswich	277	49	Stanwood	John		1		1		1			1	1			5		
Ipswich	277	50	Galloway	Abigail								1	1	1			3		
Ipswich	277	51	Perkins	Abraham	1			1		2	1			1			6		
Ipswich	277	52	Pulsipher	Anna				1					1	1			3		
Ipswich	277	53	Pulsipher	Bickford	1			1					1				3		
Ipswich	277	54	Averill	Benjamin	1			1		1			1				4		
Ipswich	277	55	Harris	Tabathy									1	1			2		
Ipswich	277	56	Glazer	John	1			1		2			1				5		
Ipswich	277	57	Smith	Jeremiah	1			1					1				3		
Ipswich	277	58	Hodkins	Abigail		1					1	1		1			4		
Ipswich	277	59	Stanwood	Nathaniel	1	1		1		1				1			5		
Ipswich	278	1	Sweet	Aaron	1		1						1				3		
Ipswich	278	2	Spiller	John	4	1	1			1			1				8		
Ipswich	278	3	Holland	Hannah										1			1		
Ipswich	278	4	Perkins	Charlotte	1					1			1				3		
Ipswich	278	5	Green	Benjamin			1			2			1				4		
Ipswich	278	6	Seward	John	1			1		2	2			1			7		
Ipswich	278	7	Kinder	Benjamin		1	1						1	1			4		
Ipswich	278	8	Kimball	Jacob	2			1		2			1				6		
Ipswich	278	9	Hodgkins	Sarah									2	1			3		
Ipswich	278	10	Glazer	Benjamin			1			2			1				4		
Ipswich	278	11	Fuller	Nathaniel	1			1		5	2		1				10		
Ipswich	278	12	Perkins	Nathaniel		1		1				1		1			4		
Ipswich	278	13	Sweet	John		1		1			2	2		1			7		
Ipswich	278	14	Stone	Samuel Junr	2			1		2			1				6		
Ipswich	278	15	Lakeman	Samuel Junr		1		1		2	1		1				6		
Ipswich	278	16	Lakeman	Richard		1		1		1			1				4		
Ipswich	278	17	Lakeman	Jonathan				1		1		1			5		8		
Ipswich	278	18	Parker	Mary									1				1		
Ipswich	278	19	Newmarck	Hannah									2				2		
Ipswich	278	20	Boardman	Daniel		1	1			1	2	1	1				7		
Ipswich	278	21	Holland	Richard				1				1	1				3		
Ipswich	278	22	Newmarck	John		1	1	1			1		1	1			6		
Ipswich	278	23	Martain	Mary			1						1	2			4		
Ipswich	278	24	Caldwell	Thomas	2	1	2		1				1	1			8		
Ipswich	278	25	Treadwell	Aaron			1	1		1				1			4		

TOWN	PG#	LN#	HEADS OF HOUSEHOLD		FREE WHITE MALES					FREE WHITE FEMALES					TOTAL ALL OTHER	TOTAL SLAVES	TOTALS	DISTRICT/ TOWNSHIP	NOTES
			LAST NAME	FIRST NAME	under 10	10 to 16	16 to 26	26 to 45	45 and over	under 10	10 to 16	16 to 26	26 to 45	45 and over					
Ipswich	278	26	Summers	William	2	1		1		1			2				7		
Ipswich	278	27	Treadwell	Aaron Junr				1		1			1				3		
Ipswich	278	28	Kilborn	Joseph		1	1						1				4		
Ipswich	278	29	Smith	Moses			2		1	3	1		1				8		
Ipswich	278	30	Perkins	Bensley				1					2				3		
Ipswich	278	31	Kimball	John				1			1		1	1			4		
Ipswich	278	32	Southier	Timothy	3			1		1			2				7		
Ipswich	278	33	Rust	Nathanl	1	1	3	1	1			2		1			10		
Ipswich	278	34	Cogswell	Antice		1						2		1	1		5		
Ipswich	278	35	Jones	Thomas				1		1		1		1			4		
Ipswich	278	36	Jones	Amos			1						1				2		
Ipswich	278	37	Baker	Asa	1	2	1		1	1	3	1	1				11		
Ipswich	278	38	Farley	Nathaniel				1					1				2		
Ipswich	278	39	Hodgkins	Joseph		1	2		2	1	2		1		2		11		
Ipswich	278	40	Choate	Stephen		1		1		1		2	1		1		7		
Ipswich	278	41	Dana	Joseph	2	1	1		1		1	2		1			9		
Ipswich	278	42	Smith	Aaron		2		1			1	1		1			6		
Ipswich	278	43	Baker	Eunice									2	1			3		
Ipswich	278	44	Baker	Mary	3		2			1	1		1				8		
Ipswich	278	45	Wade	Nathaniel	1	1		1	1	1	1	1					8		
Ipswich	278	46	Wade	Thomas	3			1			1		1				6		
Ipswich	278	47	Wade	Ruth									2				2		
Ipswich	278	48	Wade	John	1	1	1	1		2			1				7		
Ipswich	278	49	Appleton	Thomas				1					1				2		
Ipswich	278	50	Manning	Jacob	1	1		1		2	2		1				8		
Ipswich	278	51	Farley	John			2	1					1				4		
Ipswich	278	52	Burnham	Isaac	1		2	1				1		1			6		
Ipswich	278	53	Fuller	Daniel				1			1		1				3		
Ipswich	278	54	Lakeman	Samuel				1		2			2				5		
Ipswich	278	55	Treadwell	Jabez	1	1		1	1				1				5		
Ipswich	278	56	Radford	Benjamin	1			1				1	1				4		
Ipswich	278	57	Merrifield	Francis Jr			1						1				2		
Ipswich	278	58	Merrifield	Francis		1		1					1				3		
Ipswich	278	59	Spiller	Henry				1			1		2	1			5		
Ipswich	278	60	Seward	Abraham	2			1		1	1		1				6		
Ipswich	278	61	Fuller	William	3			1		1	1		1				7		
Ipswich	279	1	Woodbury	Major		1		1		1			1	1			5		
Ipswich	279	2	Andrews	William F.		1	1	1					1				4		
Ipswich	279	3	Andrews	David				1					1	1			3		
Ipswich	279	4	Dodge	William			2	1		1	1		1	1			7		
Ipswich	279	5	Patch	Abigail									1				1		
Ipswich	279	6	Heard	Nathaniel Jun	2			1		3		1	1				8		
Ipswich	279	7	Lakeman	Richard Jun	2			1		2			1				6		
Ipswich	279	8	Swasey	Joseph	1				1	1	1	1	2				7		
Ipswich	279	9	Lakeman	Jonas	2	2	1		1	1	1	1		1			10		
Ipswich	279	10	Choate	Stephen Jun	1	1	2		1	1	1	1		1			9		
Ipswich	279	11	Brown	Tristram	1		2			1	1	1					6		
Ipswich	279	12	Tilton	Anna			1					1		1			3		
Ipswich	279	13	Burnham	Josiah			1	1					1				3		
Ipswich	279	14	Kinsman	Samuel		2		1		1		1		1			6		
Ipswich	279	15	Wells	John	1			1				1		1			4		
Ipswich	279	16	Hobson	Clarek	5			1			1		1		5		13		
Ipswich	279	17	Merrifield	Thomas	1		1					1					3		
Ipswich	279	18	Kinsman	Mary	1	1				1	1		1				5		
Ipswich	279	19	Cross	Benjamin			1	1				1		1			4		
Ipswich	279	20	Cross	Nathaniel		1		1				1	1				4		
Ipswich	279	21	Lord	Ebenezer		1	1		1			1	1				5		
Ipswich	279	22	Lord	Phillip				1									1		
Ipswich	279	23	Summers	Daniel				1			1	2		1			5		
Ipswich	279	24	Kimball	Benjamin		1		1				1	2				5		
Ipswich	279	25	Scott	Benjamin	1	1		1		2	2		1				8		
Ipswich	279	26	Calef	Jeddediah	1		1					1					3		
Ipswich	279	27	Kimball	Caleb	1			1		2	3		1				8		
Ipswich	279	28	Chapman	Jedediah	1	2		2	1			1	2				9		
Ipswich	279	29	Day	Thomas				1		1			1	1			4		
Ipswich	279	30	Day	Moses			1	2					3	1			7		
Ipswich	279	31	Davis	Charles	1	1	1				1	1		1			7		
Ipswich	279	32	Medcalf	Joseph				1			1		1				3		
Ipswich	279	33	Smith	Josiah			1			1		1					3		
Ipswich	279	34	Chapman	Joseph			1					2	1				4		
Ipswich	279	35	Kimball	Nathaniel	3	2		1		1	2		1				10		
Ipswich	279	36	Conant	William		1	2		1			1		1			6		
Ipswich	279	37	Fowler	John	1	1	2		1	1	1		1				9		
Ipswich	279	38	Foster	Allen	2		2		1		1		1				7		
Ipswich	279	39	Smith	James		1		1				1		1			4		
Ipswich	279	40	Foster	Thomas			1			3	1		1				6		
Ipswich	279	41	Foster	Mehitable								1	1				2		
Ipswich	279	42	Foster	Hannah									2				2		
Ipswich	279	43	Tenny	Elijah			1					1					2		
Ipswich	279	44	Moss	Timothy		1	1		1				1				4		
Ipswich	279	45	Howe	Elenor		2					1		1	1			5		
Ipswich	279	46	Foster	Ebenezer	1	1			1	1	1	1					6		
Ipswich	279	47	Howe	Joseph	2			1		2			2	1			8		
Ipswich	279	48	Howe	Nathaniel			1	1	1				1				4		
Ipswich	279	49	Foster	Philemon				1			1	1		1			4		
Ipswich	279	50	Foster	Jonathan		1			1			1	1				4		
Ipswich	279	51	Foster	Philemon Jun			1					1					2		
Ipswich	279	52	Perley	Allen Jun	3	1		1		1			1				7		
Ipswich	279	53	Perley	Allen				1				1	1				3		

TOWN	PG#	LN#	HEADS OF HOUSEHOLD		FREE WHITE MALES					FREE WHITE FEMALES					TOTAL ALL OTHER	TOTAL SLAVES	TOTALS	DISTRICT/ TOWNSHIP	NOTES
			LAST NAME	FIRST NAME	under 10	10 to 16	16 to 26	26 to 45	45 and over	under 10	10 to 16	16 to 26	26 to 45	45 and over					
Ipswich	279	54	Perley	Jacob			1			1		1					3		
Ipswich	279	55	Perley	John	1			1		1		1					4		
Ipswich	279	56	Conant	Lot			1	1					1				3		
Ipswich	279	57	Potter	Ezekiel				1					1				2		
Ipswich	279	58	Potter	Nathaniel	1		1	1				1					4		
Ipswich	279	59	Potter	Isaac	3			1		2			1				7		
Ipswich	279	60	Howe	Jacob		1		1					1	1			4		
Ipswich	279	61	Barnsdale	John			1	1						2			4		
Ipswich	279	62	Ross	Jabez	1	1	1		1	1		1		2			8		
Ipswich	280	1	Potter	Ezekiel Jun		1		1						1			3		
Ipswich	280	2	Smith	Elizabeth								1		1			2		
Ipswich	280	3	Goodhue	Jude		1		1	1				2	1			6		
Ipswich	280	4	Goodhue	Aaron	2		1	1		1	1		2	1			9		
Ipswich	280	5	Warner	William	2	1	2	1				1	1	2			10		
Ipswich	280	6	Wallice	Aaron	2		1			4			1				8		
Ipswich	280	7	Wallice	Robert	1			1						2			4		
Ipswich	280	8	Cogswell	Daniel			2						1		1		4		
Ipswich	280	9	Smith	John		1		1					1				3		
Ipswich	280	10	Fuller	James			1						1				2		
Ipswich	280	11	Kimball	Joseph				1					1				2		
Ipswich	280	12	Fellows	Mary								1		1			2		
Ipswich	280	13	Waite	Aaron	3	1		1		2	1		1	1			10		
Ipswich	280	14	Treadwell	Nathl	2			1						1			4		
Ipswich	280	15	Kimball	Ebenezer	5			1			1	1					8		
Ipswich	280	16	Baker	Allen	1	2	1		1		1	2	1	1			10		
Ipswich	280	17	Baker	John		2		1	1		1	2		1			8		
Ipswich	280	18	Kinsman	Aaron	1		1	1		2			1	1			7		
Ipswich	280	19	Day	Abner	2	1	2		1	3	2	3	1				15		
Ipswich	280	20	Smith	Adam		1	1	1					1	1			5		
Ipswich	280	21	Cogswell	Ebenezer	2	1	1	1		2		2	1	1	1		12		
Ipswich	280	22	Smith	Asa	3	1		2		3	1		1				11		
Ipswich	280	23	Wells	Nathaniel		1			2			1		1	1		6		
Ipswich	280	24	Patch	John			2				1	1					4		
Ipswich	280	25	Kinsman	Moses	2		1		1	4	2	1	1				12		
Ipswich	280	26	Brown	Nehemiah	2			1			2		1	1			7		
Ipswich	280	27	Brown	Abner				1					1	1			3		
Ipswich	280	28	Brown	David				1			1		1				3		
Ipswich	280	29	Caldwell	Francis			1	1					1	2			5		
Ipswich	280	30	Day	Abigail										2			2		
Ipswich	280	31	Burnham	Elizabeth									1	1			2		
Ipswich	280	32	Brown	Judith							1	1	1	1			4		
Ipswich	281	1	Lakeman	William Jr			1			2		1					4		
Ipswich	281	2	Lakeman	William		2		1						1			4		
Ipswich	281	3	Meedy	Thomas	1	1	1		1			2	1	1			8		
Ipswich	281	4	Brown	Benjamin Jr	3			1		2			1				7		
Ipswich	281	5	Brown	Benjamin		1	2	1					1				5		
Ipswich	281	6	Brown	Nathaniel		2		1						1			4		
Ipswich	281	7	Troop	Lucy	1	1						3	2	1			8		
Ipswich	281	8	Potter	Daniel Jun	1			1	1	1	1	1					6		
Ipswich	281	9	Brown	Stephen		1	2		1	1	2	1	1	1			10		
Ipswich	281	10	Potter	Jonathan	4		1						1				6		
Ipswich	281	11	Lano	John	1			1		1		1					4		
Ipswich	281	12	Willett	John		1	1	1					2	1			7		
Ipswich	281	13	Manning	John Junr	1		1		1	1		1	1	1			7		
Ipswich	281	14	Underhill	Jeremiah			1			1			1	1			4		
Ipswich	281	15	Appleton	Oliver	4			1		2	1		1				9		
Ipswich	281	16	Smith	Samuel	2		1	1		2		1	1	2			10		
Ipswich	281	17	Lord	Aaron Junr		1		1		2	1	1	1				7		
Ipswich	281	18	Manning	John 3d			1			1			1				3		
Ipswich	281	19	Fellows	Israel	2	1		1		2	1	1	1				9		
Ipswich	281	20	Fellows	John			1	1				1		1			4		
Ipswich	281	21	Fellows	Isaac	1		1	1					1	1			5		
Ipswich	281	22	Fellows	Nathan	1	1		1		4	4		1				12		
Ipswich	281	23	Brown	Nathan	2	1		1		1		2	1				8		
Ipswich	281	24	Brown	Abraham		1		1		1		1	1	1			6		
Ipswich	281	25	Brown	John	1			1		5			1				8		
Ipswich	281	26	Brown	James	1	1		1				1	2				7		
Ipswich	281	27	Brown	Joseph	1	1	1					1	1	1			7		
Ipswich	281	28	Brown	Elisha	3		1			1			1				6		
Ipswich	281	29	Brown	Ephraim	3		1			1			2				7		
Ipswich	281	30	Boardman	John H	1			3		1			2	1			8		
Ipswich	281	31	Patch	Samuel		2	1					3	1				7		
Ipswich	281	32	Kinsman	Jeremiah				1					1				2		
Ipswich	281	33	Kinsman	William		2		1				1					4		
Ipswich	281	34	Cogswell	William		1	1	2	1			2		1			8		
Ipswich	281	35	Low	Ebenezer	1	1	1	1	1				1				6		
Ipswich	281	36	Dodge	Grover		1		1					1				3		
Ipswich	281	37	Hodgkins	Christopher				1					1	1			3		
Ipswich	281	38	Spiller	Thomas	6		1		1	1			1				10		
Ipswich	281	39	Sutton	Ebenezer			1	1				1		1			4		
Ipswich	281	40	Brown	Elizabeth			1					1	1	1			4		
Ipswich	281	41	Andrews	John				1	1	1		1					4		
Ipswich	281	42	Giddings	Thomas Junr			1			1			1				3		
Ipswich	281	43	Giddings	Samuel			1	1		2			1				5		
Ipswich	281	44	Dodge	Nehemiah			1			1		1					3		
Ipswich	281	45	Hardy	Samuel	3	1		1		1	2		1				9		
Ipswich	281	46	Poland	Josiah	3		1			2			1				7		
Ipswich	281	47	Giddings	Thomas				1						1			2		
Ipswich	281	48	Giddings	Aaron		1		1		2	1		1				6		
Ipswich	281	49	Choate	George	3	1	1	1			1	1	1				9		

TOWN	PG#	LN#	LAST NAME	FIRST NAME	FWM under 10	FWM 10 to 16	FWM 16 to 26	FWM 26 to 45	FWM 45 and over	FWF under 10	FWF 10 to 16	FWF 16 to 26	FWF 26 to 45	FWF 45 and over	TOTAL ALL OTHER	TOTAL SLAVES	TOTALS	DISTRICT/ TOWNSHIP	NOTES
Ipswich	281	50	Martain	Nathaniel					1					1			2		
Ipswich	281	51	Cogswell	Mary	1									1			2		
Ipswich	281	52	Peirce	George		1	1		1	4	2			1			10		
Ipswich	281	53	Burnham	Anna	2					2		1	1				6		
Ipswich	281	54	Choate	John			2						1				3		
Ipswich	281	55	Andrews	Jacob		2	2	3	1	2			1	1			12		
Ipswich	281	56	Lord	Thomas	2	1	3		1		1	1		2			11		
Ipswich	281	57	Low	William	1	2	2		1	2		1	1				10		
Ipswich	281	58	Smith	John				1		1		1		1			4		
Ipswich	281	59	Goodhue	Nancy								1		1			2		
Ipswich	281	60	Rust	Parker				1									1		
Ipswich	281	61	Cogswell	Jonathan				1	1					1			3		
Ipswich	281	62	Cogswell	Benjamin	2	1		1					1				5		
Ipswich	281	63	Cogswell	Nathaniel	2			1					1				4		
Ipswich	281	64	Cavis	John				1	1					1			3		
Ipswich	281	65	Boyd	Adam	5					1			1				8		
Ipswich	281	66	Choate	David	2		1	1		2			1	1			8		
Ipswich	281	67	Perkins	Joseph		1	1	1	2	1	2	2		1			11		
Ipswich	281	68	Holmes	Nathaniel	1			1		3			1				6		
Ipswich	281	69	Holmes	William	3			1			1		1				6		
Ipswich	281	70	Low	Daniel	1	1	2	1	1		1	1		1			9		
Ipswich	281	71	Boardman	Stephen			2	1		4			1				8		
Ipswich	281	72	Burnham	Amos	3	1		1					1				6		
Ipswich	281	73	Marshall	Moses	2	2		1		2			1	1			9		
Ipswich	281	74	Dexter	John	2		1				1	1					5		
Ipswich	281	75	Burnham	Charles				1					1				2		
Ipswich	281	76	Burnham	Thomas M.	3	2		1		1			1				8		
Ipswich	281	77	Alion	Joseph			1					1					2		
Ipswich	281	78	Dodge	John			1						1				2		
Ipswich	281	79	Burnham	William 3d				1		2			1				4		
Ipswich	281	80	Andrews	Sarah									1				1		
Ipswich	281	81	Low	Elizabeth	1					1	1		1				4		
Ipswich	281	82	Choate	Thomas	2	1		1	1		1	1	1				8		
Ipswich	281	83	Burnham	David				1		2	1	1					5		
Ipswich	281	84	Andrews	Moses			1			2		1					4		
Ipswich	282	1	Burnham	Nathan	2	2		1		1	1		1				8		
Ipswich	282	2	Burnham	Aaron	1			1		2			1				5		
Ipswich	282	3	Quincy	Samuel	3	2		1		2	1	1	1				11		
Ipswich	282	4	Proctor	Samuel			1	1		3		1	1	1	1		9		
Ipswich	282	5	Butler	John			1	1		5	4		1	1			13		
Ipswich	282	6	Lufkin	Nathaniel				1				1		1	1		4		
Ipswich	282	7	Lufkin	William	2	1	1		1	2	2			1			10		
Ipswich	282	8	Lufkin	Jonathan			1			1		1					3		
Ipswich	282	9	Emerton	Oliver		1		1		1			1	1			5		
Ipswich	282	10	Cogswell	John	3		1		1		2		1		9		17		
Ipswich	282	11	Andrews	Elias		1	1			1			1				4		
Ipswich	282	12	Andrews	Joseph				1				1	1				3		
Ipswich	282	13	Burnham	William		2	1	2	1	2	1	3		1			13		
Ipswich	282	14	Haskell	Enoch				1					1	1			3		
Ipswich	282	15	Haskell	Ebenezer	1	1		1		3		1	1				8		
Ipswich	282	16	Burnham	Jesse	2			1		2			1				6		
Ipswich	282	17	Herriden	Sarah			1	1			1	1	1				5		
Ipswich	282	18	Harlow	John	4			1		1	2		1				9		
Ipswich	282	19	Burnham	Joshua	2			1		1			1				5		
Ipswich	282	20	Burnham	Moses				1		1			1				3		
Ipswich	282	21	Burnham	Eunice								1		1			2		
Ipswich	282	22	Andrews	Jacob	2	1		1		1			1				7		
Ipswich	282	23	Andrews	Joanna			1			1	1	1		1			5		
Ipswich	282	24	Andrews	Levi	1			1		1			1				4		
Ipswich	282	25	Andrews	Solomon			1			3			1				5		
Ipswich	282	26	Low	Aaron	2	1	1		1	3			1	1			10		
Ipswich	282	27	Burnham	William	1				1		1	1	2	1			7		
Ipswich	282	28	Andrews	Mark	1		1			1		1					4		
Ipswich	282	29	Goodhue	Lucy									1				1		
Ipswich	282	30	Cogswell	Jacob Junr			1	1					2				4		
Ipswich	282	31	Burnham	Isaac	1		1	1				1		1			5		
Ipswich	282	32	Burnham	Joseph			1	1		1		3		1			7		
Ipswich	282	33	Norton	George		1	1	1						2			5		
Ipswich	282	34	Burnham	Nathan			1			1		1					3		
Ipswich	282	35	Smith	Mary				1				1		1			3		
Ipswich	282	36	Smith	Mary							3	1		1			5		
Ipswich	282	37	Burnham	James			1						1				2		
Ipswich	282	38	Burnham	Sarah									1	2			3		
Ipswich	282	39	Lufkin	Mary			2						1	1			4		
Ipswich	282	40	Burnham	David Junr	2		1		1			1					6		
Ipswich	282	41	Burnham	Ezra			1			2			1				4		
Ipswich	282	42	Burnham	Benjamin		1	1		1	1	1			1			6		
Ipswich	282	43	Burnham	David				1					1				2		
Ipswich	282	44	Burnham	Westley	1	1	3		1	1	1			1			9		
Ipswich	282	45	Burnham	Parker	1			1		3	2		1				8		
Ipswich	282	46	Rust	Robert	1			1		1			1				4		
Ipswich	282	47	Burnham	Nathaniel	2	1	3		1	3	1	1	1				13		
Ipswich	282	48	Burnham	Francis				1					2	1			4		
Ipswich	282	49	Burnham	Jacob		2		1	1	2	2			1			8		
Ipswich	282	50	Storey	Jacob	3	1	2	1		3			1				11		
Ipswich	282	51	Allen	Isaac	3		1						1				5		
Ipswich	282	52	Emerson	John	2			1		1			3				7		
Ipswich	282	53	Burnham	Mehitable							1			1			2		
Ipswich	282	54	Foster	Thomas	1	1		1		3	1		1				8		
Ipswich	282	55	Haskell	Aaron	1			1		1		1					4		

TOWN	PG#	LN#	LAST NAME	FIRST NAME	FREE WHITE MALES under 10	10 to 16	16 to 26	26 to 45	45 and over	FREE WHITE FEMALES under 10	10 to 16	16 to 26	26 to 45	45 and over	TOTAL ALL OTHER	TOTAL SLAVES	TOTALS	DISTRICT/ TOWNSHIP	NOTES
Ipswich	282	56	Storey	Jonathan	2		2		1			3		1			9		
Ipswich	282	57	Evelett	Aaron	1		3		2	1	1	1		1			10		
Ipswich	282	58	Ross	Timothy	1				1		2	2		1			7		
Ipswich	282	59	Evelett	Lucy									1		1		2		
Ipswich	283	1	Perkins	Abraham		1			1		1	2		1			6		
Ipswich	283	2	Perkins	Abraham Junr				1		1		1			1		4		
Ipswich	283	3	Storey	Elizabeth	1					1			1	1			4		
Ipswich	283	4	Burnham	Ebenezer		2	1	1		2	1		1				8		
Ipswich	283	5	Andrews	Benjamin	1	1			1				1				4		
Ipswich	283	6	Craft	Aaron					1			3	1				5		
Ipswich	283	7	Andrews	James	3	1		1		1	1		1	1			9		
Ipswich	283	8	Andrews	Anna			1						1	1			3		
Ipswich	283	9	Poland	Abner Junr	2	2		1		1	1	2	1				10		
Ipswich	283	10	Poland	Abner				1					1	1			3		
Ipswich	283	11	Mears	Alexander	3		2		1	1	1		1				9		
Ipswich	283	12	Burnham	John	2			1		3	1	2	1				10		
Ipswich	283	13	Burnham	Martha									2	1			3		
Ipswich	283	14	Low	Stephen				1		1			1				3		
Ipswich	283	15	Low	Rufus				1		1			1		1		4		
Ipswich	283	16	Marshall	Sarah									2	1			3		
Ipswich	283	17	Cogswell	Jonathan Junr		1		1			2	1	1		1		7		
Ipswich	283	18	Webster	Josiah		1				1			1				2		
Ipswich	283	19	Foster	Aaron				1					1	1			3		
Ipswich	283	20	Foster	Zebulun	1			1		1			1	1			5		
Ipswich	283	21	Storey	Nathan		1	1		1	1	1			1			6		
Ipswich	283	22	Storey	Nehemiah				1						1			2		
Ipswich	283	23	Choate	Solomon	3		1	1	1	2	1		1	1			11		
Ipswich	283	24	Choate	Nathan				1	1			1	1	1	1		6		
Ipswich	283	25	Foster	Moses	3	1	1	2		1		1	1	1			11		
Ipswich	283	26	Storey	Jesse	1			1		1				1			4		
Ipswich	283	27	Storey	Elizabeth		1							1	1			3		
Ipswich	283	28	Storey	Stephen	3	1		1		1			1				7		
Ipswich	283	29	Low	Isaac			1					1					2		
Ipswich	283	30	Low	Einice									1				1		
Ipswich	283	31	Burnham	Moses			1						1				2		
Ipswich	283	32	Norton	Oliver	2		1			1		1					5		
Ipswich	283	33	Mears	John		1				1		1					3		
Ipswich	283	34	Storey	Hannah		1						1	1				3		
Ipswich	283	35	Storey	Anna								1	1				2		
Ipswich	283	36	Burnham	Westley	2			1				1					4		
Ipswich	283	37	Jones	Abraham		1				1		1					3		
Ipswich	283	38	Storey	Elisha	1			1		2	2		1		1		8		
Ipswich	283	39	Storey	Jonathan	2			1		1			1				5		
Ipswich	283	40	Storey	Ebenezer			1	1				1		1			4		
Ipswich	283	41	Burnham	Enoch	2		2	1		1			2				8		
Ipswich	283	42	Burnham	Jonathan	3	2		1					1				7		
Ipswich	283	43	Storey	Deborah								1		1			2		
Ipswich	283	44	Smith	John				1				1		1			3		
Ipswich	283	45	Choate	Solomon Junr			1			2		1	2	1			7		
Ipswich	283	46	Butter	Ralph	1	1		1		2		1					6		

TOWN	PG#	LN#	LAST NAME	FIRST NAME	FREE WHITE MALES					FREE WHITE FEMALES					TOTAL ALL OTHER	TOTAL SLAVES	TOTALS	DISTRICT/ TOWNSHIP	NOTES
					under 10	10 to 16	16 to 26	26 to 45	45 and over	under 10	10 to 16	16 to 26	26 to 45	45 and over					
Lynn	223	1	Alley	Nathan	3	2	3		1	2			1				12		
Lynn	223	2	Breed	Nathan				1					1	1			3		
Lynn	223	3	Lewis	Isaac					1				1				2		
Lynn	223	4	Alley	Abigail				1					2	1	1		5		
Lynn	223	5	Breed	James Jun	2	1		1		1	1		1				7		
Lynn	223	6	Pratt	John	2	1	1	1		1	1	1	1				9		
Lynn	223	7	Collins	Abijah				1			1		1				3		
Lynn	223	8	Phillips	Zacheus		1		1		3			1				6		
Lynn	223	9	Rich	James	3			1		1	1		1				7		
Lynn	223	10	Breed	Abraham			1		1	2	1		1				6		
Lynn	223	11	Breed	James	1				1			1		1			4		
Lynn	223	12	Fuller	Joseph 3d	1		1	1				1	1				5		
Lynn	223	13	Stover	John Junr			1	1		1			1				4		
Lynn	223	14	Johnson	David	1	1	1	1				1	1				6		
Lynn	223	15	Johnson	Richard				1					1				2		
Lynn	223	16	Purinton	Jedh	1	1	2		1	2	1			1			9		
Lynn	223	17	Tilsbe	Saml				1				1					2		
Lynn	223	18	Tilsbe	Nehemiah	2		1	1					1				5		
Lynn	223	19	Tilsbe	Sarah		1		1					3	1			6		
Lynn	223	20	Chase	Saml	2		1	1		2			1				7		
Lynn	223	21	Hanson	Bitfield			1	1				1	1				4		
Lynn	223	22	Tufts	Anne	2		1			3		1		1			8		
Lynn	223	23	Richards	Crispus		1		1				1	1				4		
Lynn	223	24	Alley	Micajah		1	1		1			1	1				5		
Lynn	223	25	Alley	Timothy	2			1		1		2	1				7		
Lynn	223	26	Alley	Hulday								1		1			2		
Lynn	223	27	Newhall	Rufus Jr	1			1		2			1				5		
Lynn	223	28	Richards	William				1				2	1				4		
Lynn	223	29	Newhall	Richard			1	1		1			2				5		
Lynn	223	30	Munroe	Timothy	1		2	1		1			1				6		
Lynn	223	31	Newhall	Hanson				1						1			2		
Lynn	223	32	Newhall	Allen	2			1		1		1					5		
Lynn	223	33	Alley	Benj 3d	3	1		1		3	2		1				11		
Lynn	223	34	Alley	Solomon	2			1					1				4		
Lynn	223	35	Alley	John			1		1					1			3		
Lynn	223	36	Newhall	Lois						1			1				2		
Lynn	223	37	Reed	Thomas			1			1			1				3		
Lynn	223	38	Baker	Ezra	1			1				1					3		
Lynn	223	39	Newhall	Lois						1			1				2		
Lynn	223	40	Reed	Thomas			1			1			1				3		
Lynn	223	41	Baker	Ezra	1			1				1					3		
Lynn	223	42	Baker	Elisha				1		1			1				3		
Lynn	223	43	Newhall	Winthrop	2			1		1			1				5		
Lynn	223	44	Boyce	Jonathan	1			1		1	1		1				5		
Lynn	223	45	Alley	Samuel Junr			1					1					2		
Lynn	223	46	Alley	James				1				1		1			3		
Lynn	223	47	Alley	James Junr			1					1					2		
Lynn	223	48	Chase	Benj		1		1		1		2		1			6		
Lynn	223	49	Breed	Simeon	2		1	1		2	1		1				8		
Lynn	223	50	Pratt	Richd Jn	2			1		1	2		1				7		
Lynn	223	51	Alley	Benj	1	2		1	1	2		1	1	1			10		
Lynn	223	52	Williams	Jerusha		2				3			1				6		
Lynn	223	53	Johnson	Benj B.			1	1		2			1				5		
Lynn	223	54	Stickney	Enoch			1			1		1					3		
Lynn	223	55	Jones	Nathl	1			1				1					3		
Lynn	223	56	Smith	Stephn	1	1			1				1				4		
Lynn	223	57	Shorey	Miles	1			1		1			1				4		
Lynn	223	58	Johnson	Benj Jn	2			1		3			1				7		
Lynn	223	59	Johnson	Benj		1	1		1			1		1			5		
Lynn	223	60	Johnson	John L	3	1		1		1			2				8		
Lynn	223	61	Oliver	Henry Jr	1			1				1					3		
Lynn	223	62	Johnson	Joseph	1	1		1		2		1	1				7		
Lynn	223	63	Johnson	Timy	2			1		1			1				5		
Lynn	223	64	Johnson	Saml	2	1	1	2			2		1	1			10		
Lynn	224	1	Breed	B Newhall	1			1		3			1				6		
Lynn	224	2	Chase	Jacob	2			1					1				4		
Lynn	224	3	Newhall	Mary									1	1			2		
Lynn	224	4	Burrill	John Jr		1			1			1	1				4		
Lynn	224	5	Breed	Aaron	3			1		3	3		1	1			12		
Lynn	224	6	Breed	Theoph Jr			2	1		2		2	1				8		
Lynn	224	7	Hitchings	Thos	2	2		1		3			1				9		
Lynn	224	8	Spinney	Thos	1			1		2			1				5		
Lynn	224	9	Lyndsey	Mary				1						1			2		
Lynn	224	10	Lyndsey	Daniel		2			1	3				2			8		
Lynn	224	11	Alley	Ephm	2	1	3		1	3				1			11		
Lynn	224	12	Martin	Jonathan			1		1					1			3		
Lynn	224	13	Hallowell	Henry		1	2		1	1	2		1				8		
Lynn	224	14	Newhall	James Jr			1	1		2	1		1				6		
Lynn	224	15	Hallowell	Theoph	1	1	2		1			1	2	1			9		

TOWN	PG#	LN#	HEADS OF HOUSEHOLD LAST NAME	FIRST NAME	FREE WHITE MALES under 10	10 to 16	16 to 26	26 to 45	45 and over	FREE WHITE FEMALES under 10	10 to 16	16 to 26	26 to 45	45 and over	TOTAL ALL OTHER	TOTAL SLAVES	TOTALS	DISTRICT/ TOWNSHIP	NOTES
Lynn	224	16	Alley	Moses B	1		2	1					1				5		
Lynn	224	17	Oliver	Willm			1	1				1					3		
Lynn	224	18	Rose	Willm		1	3	1			1		1				7		
Lynn	224	19	Wesson	George	2			1		1			1				5		
Lynn	224	20	Newhall	Aaron		1	3	1	1			1		2			9		
Lynn	224	21	Alley	John Esq	1	1		1		1			1				5		
Lynn	224	22	Bacheller	James	3	1			1		2		1				8		
Lynn	224	23	Bacheller	Samll	2	2	1	1		1		1	1				9		
Lynn	224	24	Breedeen	John				1				1					2		
Lynn	224	25	Nichols	John	2			1				1					4		
Lynn	224	26	Burrage	Susanna		1							1				2		
Lynn	224	27	Ramsdell	Kimbal	1			1				1					3		
Lynn	224	28	Newhall	Joseph	1			1		1		1					4		
Lynn	224	29	Atwill	Zacheus	3	1	3	1		1	2		1				12		
Lynn	224	30	Witt	Benj		1		1		1	1		1				5		
Lynn	224	31	Allen	Ezra	3			1		2	1		1				8		
Lynn	224	32	Breed	Mattw	4	2		1		2	1	1	1				12		
Lynn	224	33	Farrington	Theph		1		1		3		1					6		
Lynn	224	34	Mudge	John			2	1		1	1	1					6		
Lynn	224	35	Newhall	Micajah	1	2	3	1		3	1	1	1				13		
Lynn	224	36	Mudge	Enoch	1	1	2		1		2			1			8		
Lynn	224	37	Minick	John		1						1					2		
Lynn	224	38	Nichols	Andrew	1			1		1			1				4		
Lynn	224	39	Lummus	Aaron	4			1		1	2		1				9		
Lynn	224	40	Hatcher	Thos C		1		1		2			2				6		
Lynn	224	41	Chever	Thos					1		1		1				3		
Lynn	225	1	Lewis	Thos	2	1		1				1					5		
Lynn	225	2	Chever	Thos Jr	1	1		1		1		1					5		
Lynn	225	3	Newhall	John Esq	2	1		1		2			1				7		
Lynn	225	4	Bulfinch	Jerh	4	1		1		1	3	1	1				12		
Lynn	225	5	Lye	Joseph	2	1	1	1		2	2		1				10		
Lynn	225	6	Fuller	Abigail	1	1				2	1		1				6		
Lynn	225	7	Witt	Danl P				1		1			1				3		
Lynn	225	8	Farrington	Danl Jr	1		1	1		2			1				6		
Lynn	225	9	Newhall	Nathan		1		1		1				1			4		
Lynn	225	10	Breed	Theoph Sen		1		1	2				1	1			6		
Lynn	225	11	Alley	Benj Jn		1	1							1			3		
Lynn	225	12	Breed	Ephm				2			1		1	1			5		
Lynn	225	13	Breed	Josh 3d	1			1		2		1			1		6		
Lynn	225	14	Bacheller	Theoph	1	1			1	2	1	1	1				8		
Lynn	225	15	Chadwell	Moses	1			1					1				3		
Lynn	225	16	Chadwell	Harris		1	1		1	2	1		1				7		
Lynn	225	17	Rhodes	John			1		1	1	1	1	1				6		
Lynn	225	18	Newhall	John B	1	1		1		3		1					7		
Lynn	225	19	Smith	John	2			1					1				4		
Lynn	225	20	Mansfield	Robt Jr		1							1				2		
Lynn	225	21	Stone	John		1						1	1				3		
Lynn	225	22	Emmerton	Jeremiah		1				1		1					3		
Lynn	225	23	Goodwin	Amaziah		1				1		1					3		
Lynn	225	24	Williams	John Junr	1			1	1	2		1					6		
Lynn	225	25	Bacheller	Rufus	1		1					1					3		
Lynn	225	26	Breed	Anne		1		1		1	1	1	1				6		
Lynn	225	27	Breed	Willm		1		1					1	1			4		
Lynn	225	28	Breed	Benj	1			1		3	1		1	1			8		
Lynn	225	29	Alley	Saml				1					1				2		
Lynn	225	30	Breed	Joseph Jn	2	1		1		1			1				6		
Lynn	225	31	Breed	Samuel		1	1	1		1		1	1				6		
Lynn	225	32	Walden	Nathl	4			1		1			1				7		
Lynn	225	33	Breed	Charles	2			1		1			1				5		
Lynn	225	34	Breed	Nathan		1		1		1			1				4		
Lynn	225	35	Breed	Willm 3d	1		1	1			1	1					5		
Lynn	225	36	Breed	Ezra		1		1	1			1	1	1			6		
Lynn	225	37	Smith	Saml	2	1			1	1			1				6		
Lynn	225	38	Rhodes	Thos		2	2		1	1		1		1			8		
Lynn	225	39	Alley	Willm	2	1		1		2			1				7		
Lynn	225	40	Green	James Jr	1		1						1				3		
Lynn	225	41	Floyd	Hugh		2		1		2	2		1				8		
Lynn	225	42	Dunn	David				2					1				3		
Lynn	225	43	Ramsdel	Eliza									1				1		
Lynn	225	44	Tuffts	David	3			1		1	1		1	1			8		
Lynn	226	1	Johnson	Enoch	2		1	1		1			1				6		
Lynn	226	2	Fanington	John				1	1	1				1			3		
Lynn	226	3	Walker	David			1						1				2		
Lynn	226	4	Massey	John	1	1	1	1	1	2			1				8		
Lynn	226	5	Newhall	John			1	1					1				3		
Lynn	226	6	Downing	John	1	1		1		2	1		1				7		
Lynn	226	7	Seylon	James	1			1		2			1				5		
Lynn	226	8	Tuffts	Grimes	1			1				1					3		
Lynn	226	9	Hitchings	Ezra		1	1	1	1				1	1			6		

TOWN	PG#	LN#	LAST NAME	FIRST NAME	\<10 M	10–16 M	16–26 M	26–45 M	45+ M	\<10 F	10–16 F	16–26 F	26–45 F	45+ F	TOTAL ALL OTHER	TOTAL SLAVES	TOTALS	DISTRICT/TOWNSHIP	NOTES
Lynn	226	10	Ballard	Mary & Mary Tuffts					1		1			2			4		
Lynn	226	11	Bowler	Thos	2	2		1		2			1				8		
Lynn	226	12	Brown	John			1			1			1				3		
Lynn	226	13	Phillips	Benj H	2	1	1	1		1	1	1	1	1			10		
Lynn	226	14	Hood	Martha		1							1	1			3		
Lynn	226	15	Phillips	Jonathan	1		1	1		2			1				6		
Lynn	226	16	Breed	Isaiah		1		1						3			5		
Lynn	226	17	Holder	Richd	3		3	1		1	1		1				10		
Lynn	226	18	Mover	John				1					1				2		
Lynn	226	19	Newhall	Eliza										2			2		
Lynn	226	20	Newhall	Pharaoh		1		1	1			1		1			5		
Lynn	226	21	Newhall	Saml	2	1		1					1				5		
Lynn	226	22	Bassett	Isaac	2		3	1	1		1	1					10		
Lynn	226	23	Bassett	Neheh		1		1						2			4		
Lynn	226	24	Newhall	Estes	2	1	1	1				1	1				7		
Lynn	226	25	Breed	James 3d				1					1				2		
Lynn	226	26	Mover	Enoch	1			1		2			1				5		
Lynn	226	27	Rich	Thos			1	1		2			1				5		
Lynn	226	28	Rich	Robert			1					1					2		
Lynn	226	29	Oliver	Henry	1	2	1		1		1			1			7		
Lynn	226	30	Estes	Mark			1		1				1	1			4		
Lynn	226	31	Estes	Willm			1	1				1					3		
Lynn	226	32	Breed	Amos				1	1			2					4		
Lynn	226	33	Pitcher	Robert		1	1		1				1	1			5		
Lynn	226	34	Johnson	Hannah			1			1				1			3		
Lynn	226	35	Newhall	Timy	2			1		1			1				5		
Lynn	226	36	Burrill	Micajah	4	1		1			1		1				8		
Lynn	226	37	Ireson	John Junr	3	1		1					1	1			7		
Lynn	226	38	Curtin	John	1	2		1		1	1	1	1				8		
Lynn	226	39	Ingals	Henry	4	1		1		1	1		1				9		
Lynn	226	40	Larabe	Isaac Jr	2			1		1			1				5		
Lynn	226	41	Ingals	Amos					1								1		
Lynn	226	42	Watts	Daniel	5	1		1		1			1				9		
Lynn	226	43	Ashton	Saml		1		1					1				3		
Lynn	226	44	Collins	Zacheus	1			1		1		1	1				5		
Lynn	227	1	Ramsdel	Eliza	1	1			1				1				4		
Lynn	227	2	Ingals	Abner	3			1					2				6		
Lynn	227	3	Watts	Jacob	1			1		1			1				4		
Lynn	227	4	Watts	John Junr			1			1		1					3		
Lynn	227	5	Collins	Saml Junr			2		2			2		2			8		
Lynn	227	6	Mudge	Nathan	3	3	2	1		2	2	1	1				15		
Lynn	227	7	Newhall	Abijah				1					1	1			3		
Lynn	227	8	Perkins	Jona	1			1		1		1					4		
Lynn	227	9	Curtin	Martha									1	1			2		
Lynn	227	10	Kippontall	France			1						1				2		
Lynn	227	11	Mansfield	Ebenz	2			1		1		1					5		
Lynn	227	12	Burrill	John 4th	1			1		3			1				6		
Lynn	227	13	Collins	Jacob		2	1	1				1		1			7		
Lynn	227	14	Banup	Rufus L.	1			2		1			1				5		
Lynn	227	15	Tilsbe	Henry			2	1				2					5		
Lynn	227	16	Ireson	Saml			2	1	1	1		1	1	1			8		
Lynn	227	17	Ireson	Benj	1	1	3	1		4	2		1				13		
Lynn	227	18	Ireson	Edwd		1						1					2		
Lynn	227	19	Brown	Ephm	1			1		2			1				5		
Lynn	227	20	Burrill	Theoph	1			1			1	1	1				5		
Lynn	227	21	Atwill	John D	2		1	1		1	1	1					7		
Lynn	227	22	Ingals	Jacob	1	1			1					1			4		
Lynn	227	23	Ingals	Edmd	1			1		3	1						7		
Lynn	227	24	Ingals	Nathl				1						1			2		
Lynn	227	25	Ingals	Nathl Junr	2			1		1			1				5		
Lynn	227	26	Ingals	Rebekah	1	1				1			1				4		
Lynn	227	27	Panott	Benja Jun	2			1		3			1				7		
Lynn	227	28	Ingals	Jona				1	1	3			1				6		
Lynn	227	29	Panott	Benja Jun		1	1		1	1				1			5		
Lynn	227	30	Panott	Jane	1	1		1		1			1				5		
Lynn	227	31	Porter	Thos	1	1	2						1	1			6		
Lynn	227	32	Mudge	Nathl Jr	1		1					1					3		
Lynn	227	33	Lewis	Willm	2			1		1							4		
Lynn	227	34	Chase	Charles	2		1	1				1					5		
Lynn	227	35	Lewis	Robert			1			1		1					3		
Lynn	227	36	Chase	Daniel	1			1					1				3		
Lynn	227	37	Trevitt	Richd				1				1		1			3		
Lynn	227	38	Newhall	Rufus	1	2			1	3			1				8		
Lynn	227	39	Breed	Jabez		2	1	1			1			1			6		
Lynn	227	40	Lewis	Edmd	1				1	1	3			1			7		
Lynn	227	41	Lewis	Nath	2			1		2			1				6		
Lynn	227	42	Lewis	James	1			1		2			1				5		
Lynn	227	43	Lewis	John	3	1	2	1				1		1			9		
Lynn	227	44	Goldsmith	Joseph	1								1				3		

71

TOWN	PG#	LN#	LAST NAME	FIRST NAME	FREE WHITE MALES					FREE WHITE FEMALES					TOTAL ALL OTHER	TOTAL SLAVES	TOTALS	DISTRICT/ TOWNSHIP	NOTES
					under 10	10 to 16	16 to 26	26 to 45	45 and over	under 10	10 to 16	16 to 26	26 to 45	45 and over					
Lynn	227	45	Stone	Caleb	4		2		1	1	1		1				10		
Lynn	228	1	Lewis	John 3d	1		1					1					3		
Lynn	228	2	Phillips	John	3	1	1	2		3	1	1	1				13		
Lynn	228	3	Northey	Willm			2		1		1			1			5		
Lynn	228	4	Stanley	Thos	1	1	3	1		4			2				12		
Lynn	228	5	Phillips	Content								1	1	1			3		
Lynn	228	6	Phillips	Anne			1						1	1			3		
Lynn	228	7	Collins	Zach		2			1		1	1		1			6		
Lynn	228	8	Waitt	Jabez	1			1						1			3		
Lynn	228	9	Carriage	Willm	1	1		1		1			1				5		
Lynn	228	10	Collins	Jacob Jr			2	1			1		1				5		
Lynn	228	11	Hawkes	Delliverance										2			2		
Lynn	228	12	Lewis	W Burk			1			1		1					3		
Lynn	228	13	Collins	Saml			1	1					1				3		
Lynn	228	14	Burrill	Benja			1	1					1				3		
Lynn	228	15	Tarbox	David	5		1	1					1	1			9		
Lynn	228	16	Panott	Danl			1		1	1		1		1			5		
Lynn	228	17	Panott	Joseph	1		1	1		2			1				6		
Lynn	228	18	Randel	Abijah			2		1			1		2			6		
Lynn	228	19	Panott	Eleazr	1		1			2			1				5		
Lynn	228	20	Rhodes	Jona	1		1		1	1		1					5		
Lynn	228	21	Williams	James	1	1	1		1	1		1	1				7		
Lynn	228	22	Fern	Saml	2			1		1	1		1	1			7		
Lynn	228	23	Graves	Ran				2					1				3		
Lynn	228	24	Graves	Saml	2	1		1					1				5		
Lynn	228	25	Graves	Benja			1	1				1					3		
Lynn	228	26	Goodridge	Moses			2	1		2			1				6		
Lynn	228	27	Ramsdel	Willm	1	1		1		4			1				8		
Lynn	228	28	Ramsdel	Abijah Jn	2	1	1	1		2			1				8		
Lynn	228	29	Nouse	James	1	3		1		3			1				9		
Lynn	228	30	Kenney	Ebenz	1			1		2			1				5		
Lynn	228	31	Richardson	Eleazr	1			1		1		1					4		
Lynn	228	32	Mansfield	Robert	1		4		1		1	1		1			9		
Lynn	228	33	Larabee	Elias			1			1		1					3		
Lynn	228	34	Moulton	Jacob			1					1					2		
Lynn	228	35	Willis	John				1					1				2		
Lynn	228	36	Larabee	Ebenz C	1			1				1					3		
Lynn	228	37	Whittemore	Willm				1					1				2		
Lynn	228	38	Hall	Thos	2			1			1		1	1			6		
Lynn	228	39	Farrington	Willm			1	1					1				3		
Lynn	228	40	Farrington	Amos	1			1					1				3		
Lynn	228	41	Mansfield	Saml			2	1			1	1					5		
Lynn	228	42	Newhall	Ebenzr	1	1	1	1		1				2			8		
Lynn	228	43	Newhall	Benj Jr				1		1			1				3		
Lynn	228	44	Ramsdel	Joseph	1	1	1	1		2			1				7		
Lynn	229	1	Chever	Abijah	2			1					1				4		
Lynn	229	2	Hocker	Martha			2							1			3		
Lynn	229	3	Mansfield	Willm			2	1	1	2	1	1					9		
Lynn	229	4	Rhodes	Ezra			1			5			1				4		
Lynn	229	5	Newhall	Sarah						1			1				2		
Lynn	229	6	Organ	Isaac	1			1		3	1		1				7		
Lynn	229	7	Newhall	Daniel AB			1			1			1				3		
Lynn	229	8	Brimbleson	Saml	1		1			1			1				4		
Lynn	229	9	Smith	Ephm			1			1			1				3		
Lynn	229	10	Atwill	Joanne			1				1		1				3		
Lynn	229	11	Newhall	Polly	2								1				3		
Lynn	229	12	Newhall	Joel	3	1	3		1	1		1	1				11		
Lynn	229	13	Rhodes	Jesse	1		1	1		1	3		1				8		
Lynn	229	14	Winship	Saml	2	1	2	1				1	1				8		
Lynn	229	15	Breed	Fredk		1	4	1			3		1				10		
Lynn	229	16	Halsey	Benj	2	1		1		3	2		1				10		
Lynn	229	17	Mansfield	Eliza	1		2					1	1				6		
Lynn	229	18	Moulton	Joseph	1		1	1		1		1					5		
Lynn	229	19	Newhall	Daniel		1	2	1		1				2			7		
Lynn	229	20	Newhall	Amos	1		1			2		1					5		
Lynn	229	21	Carnes	John Esq				1					1	1			3		
Lynn	229	22	Gardner	James Esq	2			1		1	1		1	1			7		
Lynn	229	23	Robinson	James Esq	3	1	1	2		1		1	2				11		
Lynn	229	24	Newhall	Israel	1		1			1		1					4		
Lynn	229	25	Merry	Sarah	1	1							1	1			4		
Lynn	229	26	Mansfield	Jona			1						1				2		
Lynn	229	27	Rhodes	Amos	2		1	1		2	1		2				9		
Lynn	229	28	Haney	Martin	2			1					1				4		
Lynn	229	29	Rhodes	Jona Jr	1		1					1					3		
Lynn	229	30	Welman	Caleb	1			1						1			3		
Lynn	229	31	Newhall	Increase				1						1			2		
Lynn	229	32	Tarbox	Willm	2	1							1				5		
Lynn	229	33	Phillips	Benj	1	2	1	1		5	1		1				12		
Lynn	229	34	Mansfield	Rufus			3		1		1			1			6		
Lynn	229	35	Mansfield	Rufus Jr				1		1		1					3		

TOWN	PG#	LN#	LAST NAME	FIRST NAME	FREE WHITE MALES					FREE WHITE FEMALES					TOTAL ALL OTHER	TOTAL SLAVES	TOTALS	DISTRICT/ TOWNSHIP	NOTES
					under 10	10 to 16	16 to 26	26 to 45	45 and over	under 10	10 to 16	16 to 26	26 to 45	45 and over					
Lynn	229	36	Meeks	George		1				1		1					3		
Lynn	229	37	Tarbox	Nathl		1		2		1	2		2				8		
Lynn	229	38	Wyman	Ebenz		1				1		1					3		
Lynn	229	39	Goudey	Levi	2			1		1		1					5		
Lynn	229	40	Pratt	Joseph		1				2			1				4		
Lynn	229	41	Pratt	Nathn G	1		1			2			1				5		
Lynn	229	42	Quiner	John			1	1									2		
Lynn	229	43	Fuller	Joseph Junr		2		2				1		1			7		
Lynn	230	1	Hart	Joseph		1		1				2		1			5		
Lynn	230	2	Newhall	Willm	1			1		1				1			4		
Lynn	230	3	Lewis	Hannible											5		5		
Lynn	230	4	Newhall	Benj			1			1	1		1				4		
Lynn	230	5	Ramsdel	Nathl			1	1		3		1	1	3			10		
Lynn	230	6	Kirbey	John			1	1		2		1	1				6		
Lynn	230	7	Aborn	James			1					1					2		
Lynn	230	8	Brown	Abram			1			1		1					3		
Lynn	230	9	Downing	Elijah			1					1					2		
Lynn	230	10	Moulton	Ezekl	2	1	2	1						1			7		
Lynn	230	11	Skinner	Abigail				1						1			2		
Lynn	230	12	Green	James				1						1			2		
Lynn	230	13	Larabe	Isaac	1	2		1						1			5		
Lynn	230	14	Skinner	Willm	2		1	1			1		1				6		
Lynn	230	15	Hitchings	John	3			1		2			1				7		
Lynn	230	16	Moulton	Ezra				1						1			2		
Lynn	230	17	Hitchings	Ezra Jr			1	1					1				3		
Lynn	230	18	Massey	Nathl			1				1	1					3		
Lynn	230	19	Newhall	Jedh	2		1	1		1	2			1			8		
Lynn	230	20	Newhall	Willm 3d	4			1					1	1			7		
Lynn	230	21	Hart	Lois										1			1		
Lynn	230	22	Seargant	Salley	1	1	1						1	1			5		
Lynn	230	23	Newhall	Willm Jr	1	3	2		1	3	2	1	1				14		
Lynn	230	24	Milliken	Saml	3	1	1	1		1	1		1				9		
Lynn	230	25	Ramsdel	Nehh				1					1				2		
Lynn	230	26	Rand	Ezekiel		1						1					2		
Lynn	230	27	Rand	Ezra				1				1					2		
Lynn	230	28	Newhall	Charles	1	1	3	1	1					1			8		
Lynn	230	29	Walton	Willm	1	1	1	1					1				5		
Lynn	230	30	Atwill	Nathan	1	1	2		1	1			1	1			8		
Lynn	230	31	Burchstead	Henry		1	2	1					1	1			6		
Lynn	230	32	Green	Nehh	3	1	1						1				6		
Lynn	230	33	Burrill	John 3d			4	1		2			1				8		
Lynn	230	34	Burrill	Thomson	3	1	1	1		1			1				8		
Lynn	230	35	Yell	John			1			1			1				3		
Lynn	230	36	Gipson	Mary										1			1		
Lynn	230	37	Newhall	James Esq		1	1	2	1			1		1			7		
Lynn	230	38	Newhall	Thos	1		2	1	1	1				2			8		
Lynn	230	39	Hawkes	Mattw		2	1		1	1		2		1			8		
Lynn	230	40	Hawkes	John Jr	3		1		2		1		1				8		
Lynn	230	41	Rhodes	Josiah			1		2				1				5		
Lynn	230	42	Oakman	Ebenz	2		2	1		3			1				9		
Lynn	230	43	Hawkes	Joseph			1	1		1		1					4		
Lynn	230	44	Newhall	James 3d			1	1		2		1					4		
Lynn	231	1	Newman	Thos				1						1			2		
Lynn	231	2	Brown	Willm	3		1						1	1			6		
Lynn	231	3	Woodbury	John	1		1			1	2		1				6		
Lynn	231	4	Hudson	Benj	4	2				1			1	1			10		
Lynn	231	5	Meecham	Ruth									1				1		
Lynn	231	6	Hudson	Jona	1		1	1		2			1				6		
Lynn	231	7	Berry	Joseph	1			1		3			1				6		
Lynn	231	8	Hudson	Hannah										1			1		
Lynn	231	9	Phillips	Alice	1		1	2			1	1	1				7		
Lynn	231	10	Phillips	Willm				1					1				2		
Lynn	231	11	Phillips	Walter		2		1			1		1				5		
Lynn	231	12	Ingals	John	2		1	1		2	2		1				9		
Lynn	231	13	Fuller	Joseph Jr			2						1				3		
Lynn	231	14	Fuller	Jona			1			1		1					3		
Lynn	231	15	Watts	John		1		1					1	1			4		
Lynn	231	16	Blaney	Joseph		1	2	1						1			5		
Lynn	231	17	Blaney	Eliza	2								1				3		
Lynn	231	18	Seegar	Willm	1	1	1		1	1	1		1	1			8		
Lynn	231	19	Richards	Richd			2	1					1	1			5		
Lynn	231	20	Richards	Henry	2	1		1		2	1		1	1			9		
Lynn	231	21	Richards	Joseph	2	1			1	1	1	1					8		
Lynn	231	22	Burrill	Ebenz			1	2				1		2			6		
Lynn	231	23	Parrott	Rufus	2			1					1				4		
Lynn	231	24	Graves	Mark	1			1					1	1			4		
Lynn	231	25	Proctor	Willm			1	1				1		1			4		
Lynn	231	26	Proctor	Willm Jr	2			1					1				4		
Lynn	231	27	Clark	Edmd				1			1			1			3		
Lynn	231	28	Lewis	Nathl Jr	2			1		3			1				7		
Lynn	231	29	Lewis	John Junr	1			1		1		1					4		
Lynn	231	30	Proctor	Joseph				1									1		
Lynn	231	31	Jackson	George	1		1			1		1					4		
Lynn	231	32	Proctor	Isaac	2		1						1				4		
Lynn	231	33	Collins	Nathl		2		2		1	1	1		1			8		
Lynn	231	34	Ingals	Eleazr		1	1	1					1	1			5		
Lynn	231	35	Hood	Abner	2	1	1			1	1	1	1	1			9		
Lynn	231	36	Breed	Nehemiah & Son		2		1	1	1		1	1	1			8		
Lynn	231	37	Johnson	Jona		1		1						1			3		

TOWN	PG#	LN#	LAST NAME	FIRST NAME	FREE WHITE MALES					FREE WHITE FEMALES					TOTAL ALL OTHER	TOTAL SLAVES	TOTALS	DISTRICT/ TOWNSHIP	NOTES
					under 10	10 to 16	16 to 26	26 to 45	45 and over	under 10	10 to 16	16 to 26	26 to 45	45 and over					
Lynn	231	38	Johnson	Caleb			1			1		1					3		
Lynn	231	39	Johnson	Joseph Junr		1				2	1	1	1				6		
Lynn	231	40	Ingals	Edmd Junr	3			1		1	1	1					7		
Lynn	231	41	Chase	John	2		1						1				4		
Lynn	231	42	Curtin	James	1		1						1				3		
Lynn	231	43	Clark	Theophl	2		1						1				4		
Lynn	231	44	Lewis	Benj	1	1		1		2			1				6		
Lynn	232	1	Bacheller	Henry				1					1				2		
Lynn	232	2	Richardson	Ebenz	1	2		1		1		1	1				6		
Lynn	232	3	Bacheller	Henry Jr			1			1		1					3		
Lynn	232	4	Williams	Joseph				1					1				2		
Lynn	232	5	Rhodes	Joseph	1		1						1				3		
Lynn	232	6	Markpiece	Jona			1			1			2				4		
Lynn	232	7	Larabee	Lydia							1	1	1				3		
Lynn	232	8	Moulton	Joshua		2		1		2	1	1	1				8		
Lynn	232	9	Gallusha	Simeon	1		1						1				3		
Lynn	232	10	Ramsdel	Giddeon			1			1	1		1	1			5		
Lynn	232	11	Tarbox	Ebenz		3		1		3	1		1				9		
Lynn	232	12	Battees	John				1		1				2			4		
Lynn	232	13	Newhall	Asa			1			1	1	1	1				5		
Lynn	232	14	Lyndsey	John	1			1		3			1				6		
Lynn	232	15	Lyndsey	Phebe									1	3			4		
Lynn	232	16	Chamberlain	Mary		1				1	1		1				4		
Lynn	232	17	Newhall	Jacob 3d	4			1					1	1			7	West Parish	
Lynn	232	18	Ballard	John				1		1			1				3	West Parish	
Lynn	232	19	Newhall	Jacob Jun				1		1	2	1	1				6	West Parish	
Lynn	232	20	Tuttle	Thomas	1	1	1			1			1				5	West Parish	
Lynn	232	21	Redding	Thos	1		1	1		1			1				5	West Parish	
Lynn	232	22	Burrll	Isaac		1	1						1				3	West Parish	
Lynn	232	23	Pennison	John	2		2			1			1				6	West Parish	
Lynn	232	24	Burrill	John Junr		1		1		1			1				4	West Parish	
Lynn	232	25	Burrill	Willm		1						1					2	West Parish	
Lynn	232	26	Burrill	John 5th	3		1			2			1				7	West Parish	
Lynn	232	27	Grover	John			1			2		1					4	West Parish	
Lynn	232	28	Newhall	Willm 5th	3		1						1				5	West Parish	
Lynn	232	29	Boardman	Saml	2	2	1			3			1				9	West Parish	
Lynn	232	30	Newhall	Jacob		4	2	2				3		1			12	West Parish	
Lynn	232	31	Florence	Thos		1		1									2	West Parish	
Lynn	232	32	Whitney	Isaiah				1		1			1				3	West Parish	
Lynn	232	33	Dampney	John	2		1			1			1				5	West Parish	
Lynn	232	34	Parker	David			2	1				2					5	West Parish	
Lynn	232	35	Root	Eliza		1							1				2	West Parish	
Lynn	232	36	Oliver	Saml	3	1		1		1			1				7	West Parish	
Lynn	232	37	Stocker	Amos Junr	1		2	1		1			1	1			7	West Parish	
Lynn	232	38	Stocker	Amos				1				1	1				3	West Parish	
Lynn	232	39	Stocker	John				1					2		2		5	West Parish	
Lynn	232	40	Stocker	Ruth									2				2	West Parish	
Lynn	232	41	Bancroft	Ebenz	2	1	3				1	1					8	West Parish	
Lynn	233	1	Stocker	Susanna							1	1	1	1			4		
Lynn	233	2	Seargant	Saml				1		2	1	1	1				6		
Lynn	233	3	Stocker	Ebenz	1	2	1	1		2			2				9		
Lynn	233	4	Bruce	Lewis	3			1		1		1	1				7		
Lynn	233	5	Coats	Joseph	1			2		1			1				5		
Lynn	233	6	Danforth	Joshua Junr		2		1		4	2		1				10		
Lynn	233	7	Sweetser	Willm	2	1		1		1	1	2	1				9		
Lynn	233	8	Boynton	Nathl	1	1		1	1			1	1	1			7		
Lynn	233	9	Batts	John	1	1		1		2			1				6		
Lynn	233	10	Batts	John Junr	5		1	1	1	1			1				10		
Lynn	233	11	Breeden	Saml				1			1		1	2			5		
Lynn	233	12	Allen	Lemuel				1			1	1	1				3		
Lynn	233	13	Chever	Abner	1	1		2		2	1		1	1			9		
Lynn	233	14	Perkins	Jenny									1	1	1		2		
Lynn	233	15	Harrington	Eliza									1				1		
Lynn	233	16	Burrill	Micajah Jn	1			1					1				3		
Lynn	233	17	Chever	Eliza									2				2		
Lynn	233	18	Chever	Ezekiel	1			1		2			2				6		
Lynn	233	19	Chever	James	1			1		2		1	1				6		
Lynn	233	20	Brown	Ezra	3	1			1	2	1	2	1				11		
Lynn	233	21	Tudors	Willm Family in Lynn		1	1						1		1		4		
Lynn	233	22	Mansfield	Saml 3d	1	2		1	1	3			1				9		
Lynn	233	23	Grover	Asa	2			1				1	1	1			6		
Lynn	233	24	Vinning	Saml		2	1	1					2				6		
Lynn	233	25	Smith	Abram				1					1				2	West Parish	
Lynn	233	26	Smith	Frances	1	1		1		1			1				5	West Parish	
Lynn	233	27	Hawkes	Eunice								1	1	1			3	West Parish	
Lynn	233	28	Boardman	Saml			2	1		1		1	1				6	West Parish	
Lynn	233	29	Howard	Lydia	2	2							1				5	West Parish	
Lynn	233	30	Howard	Ezekiel	1	2		1		1	1			2			8	West Parish	
Lynn	233	31	Downing	Caleb			3			1		1	1	1			7	West Parish	
Lynn	233	32	Sweetser	Asa	2			1		2	1		1				7	West Parish	
Lynn	233	33	Sweetser	Joseph	1	1		1		3			1				7	West Parish	
Lynn	233	34	Mansfield	Thos				1					1	1			3	West Parish	
Lynn	233	35	Willson	Benj	2	1		1		1	1		1				7	West Parish	
Lynn	233	36	Sweetser	Saml Junr			1						2				3	West Parish	
Lynn	233	37	Sweetser	Saml			1					1		1			4	West Parish	
Lynn	233	38	Hitchings	Nathan		2		1					1	1			5	West Parish	
Lynn	233	39	Hitchings	Eunice		2					1	1	1				5	West Parish	
Lynn	233	40	Knights	Thos K	1	1		1		1			1				5	West Parish	
Lynn	233	41	Hawkes	Ebenz		1		1				1	1				4	West Parish	
Lynn	233	42	Hawkes	Nathan		1	3		1		1	2		1			9	West Parish	

74

TOWN	PG#	LN#	LAST NAME	FIRST NAME	Free White Males under 10	10 to 16	16 to 26	26 to 45	45 and over	Free White Females under 10	10 to 16	16 to 26	26 to 45	45 and over	TOTAL ALL OTHER	TOTAL SLAVES	TOTALS	DISTRICT/ TOWNSHIP	NOTES
Lynn	233	43	Hakes	Rebekah			1	2			1	3	1	1			9	West Parish	
Lynn	233	44	Hawkes	Nathan		1	3		1		1	2		1			9	West Parish	
Lynn	233	45	Sweetser	Willm			1		1				1	1			4	West Parish	
Lynn	233	46	Redding	Benj		1	3		1					1			6	West Parish	
Lynn	233	47	Pool	Thos			1			1		1					3	West Parish	
Lynn	233	48	Redding	John	1		2	1		1			1				6	West Parish	
Lynn	233	49	Sweetser	Ephm			1					1					2	West Parish	
Lynn	234	1	Tuttle	Willm				1		3	1		1	1			7		
Lynn	234	2	Hawkes	Joseph	2			1		2			1				6		
Lynn	234	3	Burrill	Saml	1			1				1					3		
Lynn	234	4	Pool	Susanna			1	1	1				1	1			5		
Lynn	234	5	Parker	Willm				1		1			1				3		
Lynn	234	6	Parker	Timy				1		1			1				3		
Lynn	234	7	Sweetser	Benj			1	1			2		1				5		
Lynn	234	8	Whitman	Joseph	1			1		2			1				5		
Lynn	234	9	Danforth	Joshua					1			1		1			3		
Lynn	234	10	Lewis	Caleb	4			1		1			1	1			8		
Lynn	234	11	Downing	Joseph					1					1			2		
Lynn	234	12	Mansfield	Benj	1		2		1	1	1			1			7		
Lynn	234	13	Mansfield	Nathl	1		1	1					1				4		
Lynn	234	14	Howard	Nathl			1					1					2		
Lynn	234	15	Mansfield	Richard		1	1	1		2			1				6		
Lynn	234	16	Mansfield	Saml		1	2		1				1				5		
Lynn	234	17	Mansfield	Thomas Jr	1	2	2	1		2	1	1	1				11		
Lynn	234	18	Mansfield	Moses		1	2	1				2					6		
Lynn	234	19	Carter	Loami	1		1					1		2			5		
Lynn	234	20	Newhall	James 3d	2			1		3			1				7		
Lynn	234	21	Newhall	Jona	1	1			1	1	1		1				6		
Lynn	234	22		Alexander a Black Man										1	1		2		

TOWN	PG#	LN#	HEADS OF HOUSEHOLD		FREE WHITE MALES					FREE WHITE FEMALES					TOTAL ALL OTHER	TOTAL SLAVES	TOTALS	DISTRICT/ TOWNSHIP	NOTES
			LAST NAME	FIRST NAME	under 10	10 to 16	16 to 26	26 to 45	45 and over	under 10	10 to 16	16 to 26	26 to 45	45 and over					
Lynnfield	235	1	Newhall	David	1			1					1				3		
Lynnfield	235	2	Newhall	Amos	1	1	1	1					1				5		
Lynnfield	235	3	Tarbel	Jona				1					1				2		
Lynnfield	235	4	Tarbel	Jona Junr				1				1	1	1			4		
Lynnfield	235	5	Newhall	Phebe										2			2		
Lynnfield	235	6	Newhall	Willm				1		2			1	1			5		
Lynnfield	235	7	Peas	James			1			1			1				3		
Lynnfield	235	8	Moulton	Eliza	1			1		1			1				4		
Lynnfield	235	9	Mansfield	Jane			3				1	3		1			8		
Lynnfield	235	10	Newhall	Matthew				1		1				2			4		
Lynnfield	235	11	Newhall	Wright	3			1		1			1	1			7		
Lynnfield	235	12	Newhall	Aaron	1		1	1		1			1	1			6		
Lynnfield	235	13	Newhall	Jacob	3			1					4	1			9		
Lynnfield	235	14	Newhall	Ezekl		1	2	1		1		2		2			9		
Lynnfield	235	15	Larabee	Willm	2			1		3	1		1	1			9		
Lynnfield	235	16	Newhall	Noah	1			1		3	2		1				8		
Lynnfield	235	17	Lawrence	Ebenr			1	1						1			3		
Lynnfield	235	18	Mansfield	Willm		1		1		1	1		1				5		
Lynnfield	235	19	Brown	James	2	1		1		1			1	1			7		
Lynnfield	235	20	Walton	Nathan				1		1			1	1			4		
Lynnfield	235	21	Welman	Jona				1					2	1			4		
Lynnfield	235	22	Walton	Josiah	3			1		1			1				6		
Lynnfield	235	23	Mansfield	Andrw	1			1		1			1	1			5		
Lynnfield	235	24	Hawkes	John	2			1		3	3		1				10		
Lynnfield	235	25	Munroe	Timy	1			1				1	1	1			5		
Lynnfield	235	26	Flint	Phebe	1						1			1			3		
Lynnfield	235	27	Reed	Isaac	1			1			1		1				4		
Lynnfield	235	28	Burnham	Joshua	2	3	4	1		2		2	1				15		
Lynnfield	235	29	Pearsons	Saml	1			1		2	2		1				7		
Lynnfield	235	30	Shelden	Jerh	1		1	1		2		1	1				7		
Lynnfield	235	31	Parker	Ebenz	4			1		1			1				7		
Lynnfield	235	32	Eaton	Timy	1			1		2			1				5		
Lynnfield	235	33	Hart	John				1				1	1	1			4		
Lynnfield	235	34	Hart	Joseph	1			1		1			1				4		
Lynnfield	235	35	Hart	George	1		1						3	1			6		
Lynnfield	235	36	Hart	Ebenz	2			1		3			1				7		
Lynnfield	235	37	Smith	Abigail									1				1		
Lynnfield	235	38	Smith	Walter		1	1				1						3		
Lynnfield	235	39	McIntire	John	1		1	1		1				1			5		
Lynnfield	235	40	Sherman	Nathl		1		1						1			3		
Lynnfield	235	41	Peabody	Willm			1			2			1				4		
Lynnfield	235	42	Sherman	Hannah										2			2		
Lynnfield	235	43	Swinnerton	Lucy										1			1		
Lynnfield	235	44	Needham	Daniel	1	1		1		2	1		1				7		
Lynnfield	235	45	Burnham	John	1		1	1				2		1			6		
Lynnfield	235	46	Perkins	John Esq		1		1	1				2	1	1		7		
Lynnfield	236	1	Riplon	John	1				1			1	1	1			6		
Lynnfield	236	2	Adams	Benja	1			1		1	1		1				5		
Lynnfield	236	3	Richardson	Elias			1			1			1				3		
Lynnfield	236	4	Lakeman	James	1		1						1				3		
Lynnfield	236	5	Putnam	James			1						1				2		
Lynnfield	236	6	Orne	John		1		1		2		2		1			7		
Lynnfield	236	7	Aborn	Saml	2	1	2	2		2			1	1			11		
Lynnfield	236	8	Fogg	Nathl	1		1	1		3			1				7		
Lynnfield	236	9	Willey	Benj	1	3		1				1	1				7		
Lynnfield	236	10	Mead	John				1						1			2		
Lynnfield	236	11	Perry	John				1		2			1				4		
Lynnfield	236	12	Mottey	Joseph		1		1		2	1		1				6		
Lynnfield	236	13	Parsons	Ebenz	2			1		2			1	1			7		
Lynnfield	236	14	Flagg	Theodore	1			1		1		1					4		
Lynnfield	236	15	Gowen	Joseph				1					1	1			3		
Lynnfield	236	16	Miriam	Jona	2			1		2			1				6		
Lynnfield	236	17	Dodge	Thos				1					1				2		
Lynnfield	236	18	Bancroft	Nathl		1		1					2	1			5		
Lynnfield	236	19	Johnson	James				1			1		1				3		
Lynnfield	236	20	Bancroft	James				1					1				2		
Lynnfield	236	21	Smith	Stephen	1			1		3			1	1			7		
Lynnfield	236	22	Mansfield	Willm Jr				1					1				2		
Lynnfield	236	23	Townshend	Daniel	3			1		2			1				7		
Lynnfield	236	24	Hewes	John	1	2	2		1		1			1			8		
Lynnfield	237	1	Bancroft	Thos	4		1	1		1			1	1			9		
Lynnfield	237	2	Welman	Mehetable								1	2	2			5		
Lynnfield	237	3	Briant	John		1		1				2	1		1		6		
Lynnfield	237	4	Derby	Sarah								3	1	1			5		
Lynnfield	237	5	Putnam	Saml			3	1		2				1			7		
Lynnfield	237	6	Norwood	John	1		2	1		1		1	1	1			8		
Lynnfield	237	7	Gowen	Ezra	3	1		1		2		1	1	1			10		
Lynnfield	237	8	Willey	Ephm	2	1		1					2				6		
Lynnfield	237	9	Aborn	Joseph	2	1	1		1	3	1		1				10		

TOWN	PG#	LN#	LAST NAME	FIRST NAME	FREE WHITE MALES					FREE WHITE FEMALES					TOTAL ALL OTHER	TOTAL SLAVES	TOTALS	DISTRICT/ TOWNSHIP	NOTES
					under 10	10 to 16	16 to 26	26 to 45	45 and over	under 10	10 to 16	16 to 26	26 to 45	45 and over					
Lynnfield	237	10	Aborn	Ebenz	2			1		2	2		1				8		
Lynnfield	237	11	Bragg	Josiah					1				1	1			3		
Lynnfield	237	12	Aborn	Cathrne	2									1			3		
Lynnfield	237	13	Aborn	Benj					1					1			2		
Lynnfield	237	14	Gowen	Nathl	1			1		2	1		1	1			7		
Lynnfield	237	15	Butler	Amos	1				1	2				1			5		
Lynnfield	237	16	Brown	Joseph	3			1		1			1				6		
Lynnfield	237	17	Perry	Thaddeus			1		1			1					3		
Lynnfield	237	18	Ramsdel	Timy					1					1			2		

TOWN	PG#	LN#	HEADS OF HOUSEHOLD		FREE WHITE MALES					FREE WHITE FEMALES					TOTAL ALL OTHER	TOTAL SLAVES	TOTALS	DISTRICT/ TOWNSHIP	NOTES
			LAST NAME	FIRST NAME	under 10	10 to 16	16 to 26	26 to 45	45 and over	under 10	10 to 16	16 to 26	26 to 45	45 and over					
Manchester	49	1	Allen	Samuel				1						1			2		
Manchester	49	2	Allen	Nathl M.	2		1			2		1					6		
Manchester	49	3	Allen	Hooper	1		1			2		1					5		
Manchester	49	4	Allen	Milichi			2	1		1		1		2			7		
Manchester	49	5	Allen	Wo Sarah		1							2	1			4		
Manchester	49	6	Allen	Jacob				1		1	1			1			4		
Manchester	49	7	Allen	Nathan	3			1		2	1	1					8		
Manchester	49	8	Allen	Stephen Jun	1	1		1		3	1	1					8		
Manchester	49	9	Allen	Nabby Wo									1	1			2		
Manchester	49	10	Ayers	John	4			1		2	1		1				9		
Manchester	49	11	Driver	Andw	1			1					1				3		
Manchester	49	12	Allen	Abner	3			1					1				5		
Manchester	49	13	Driver	Bethiah Wo									1	1			2		
Manchester	49	14	Allen	Betty Wo			1			1		1	1				4		
Manchester	49	15	Allen	John Junr	2	1	1	1		2	1		1				9		
Manchester	49	16	Allen	William	1	1		1		1	1	2	1				8		
Manchester	49	17	Babcock	William	2			1					1				4		
Manchester	49	18	Allen	Elizh Wo										1			4		
Manchester	49	19	Richards	John				1		2		1					4		
Manchester	49	20	Allen	William 2d				1		3			1				5		
Manchester	49	21	Beare	Sarah Wo									1	1			2		
Manchester	50	1	Baker	Jemima Wo		1				1				1			3		
Manchester	50	2	Lanbord	John	3			1		1		1					6		
Manchester	50	3	Allen	Isaac		1		1		1			4	1			8		
Manchester	50	4	Bigham	Delucena L.	2	1		1		4	1			1			10		
Manchester	50	5	Brown	Lydia Wo	1							1	1	2			5		
Manchester	50	6	Prentice	Jana	1		1			1		1					4		
Manchester	50	7	Babcock	Thos		1	2	1		1	1			1			7		
Manchester	50	8	Baker	John		1		1				1		1			4		
Manchester	50	9	Brown	Willm	1	2		1		2	1	1	1				9		
Manchester	50	10	Bennett	Saml	1	2	1			2	1	1		1			9		
Manchester	50	11	Carmen	John		1						1		1			3		
Manchester	50	12	Babcock	Jno	1			1		1			1				4		
Manchester	50	13	Babcock	Josh		1	1						1				3		
Manchester	50	14	Dow	Jereh		1		1					2	1			5		
Manchester	50	15	Cheever	Ezeh		2	1	1				1		1			6		
Manchester	50	16	McCartney	Jas	1	1	1			1			1				5		
Manchester	50	17	Craft	Estr Wo										1			1		
Manchester	50	18	Burges	Abial		2		1		3	1	1	1				9		
Manchester	50	19	Carter	Nathan	1			1		2			1				5		
Manchester	50	20	Cheever	Sarah Wo			1			1				1	2		5		
Manchester	50	21	Craft	Benja			1					2		1			4		
Manchester	50	22	Cheever	John	1	1		1		1	1						5		
Manchester	50	23	Hart	Ruth Wo								1					1		
Manchester	50	24	Craft	David			1	1		1							3		
Manchester	50	25	Colby	Davd Maj	1			1				2					4		
Manchester	50	26	Craft	Willm	4			1					1				6		
Manchester	50	27	Craft	Eliza Wo										1			1		
Manchester	50	28	Allen	Aaron	1			1		1	1		1				5		
Manchester	50	29	Craft	Eleazer	3			1					1				5		
Manchester	50	30	Carter	Obed Junr	1		1	1		1			1				5		
Manchester	50	31	Collins	Mary Wo										1			1		
Manchester	50	32	Dodge	Sarah Wo										1			1		
Manchester	50	33	Allen	Nathl	3			1		1			1				6		
Manchester	50	34	Day	Joseph Junr		1						1					2		
Manchester	50	35	Dewer	Solomon		2	1		1			2	1	2			9		
Manchester	50	36	Donels	Asa	1		1			2			1				5		
Manchester	50	37	Dow	Hanh Wo	4	1					1		1				7		
Manchester	50	38	Dow	Jacob	2			1		2			1				6		
Manchester	51	1	Driver	Andrew	1			1					1				3		
Manchester	51	2	Driver	John	2			1		1			1				5		
Manchester	51	3	Edwards	Willa	3			1				1	1	1			7		
Manchester	51	4	Jones	Benja				1					1				3		
Manchester	51	5	Edwards	Samll	2	1							1	1			5		
Manchester	51	6	Edwards	John Junr				1				1					2		
Manchester	51	7	Edwards	Willm Jun	1		2	1			1	1					6		
Manchester	51	8	Edwards	John Jun					1		1	1					3		
Manchester	51	9	Edwards	John 3d	2				1	1	1	1					6		
Manchester	51	10	Day	Joseph Junr					1			1		1			3		
Manchester	51	11	Foster	Betha Wo			1							1			2		
Manchester	51	12	Foster	Benja				1		2			1				4		
Manchester	51	13	Fowler	Jacob	2			1		2			1				6		
Manchester	51	14	Eastcot	Philip	1	1		1		3			1				7		
Manchester	51	15	Roberts	Marcy Wo			1				1	2		1			5		
Manchester	51	16	Flours	Wm			1			1		1					3		
Manchester	51	17	Farriss	Mary Wo	1					1			1				3		
Manchester	51	18	Flowers	Barthl	1		2	1				1	1				6		
Manchester	51	19	Flowers	John			1	1		4			1				7		
Manchester	51	20	Gurley	John		1		1		2	2		1				7		

78

| TOWN | PG# | LN# | LAST NAME | FIRST NAME | FREE WHITE MALES | | | | | FREE WHITE FEMALES | | | | | TOTAL ALL OTHER | TOTAL SLAVES | TOTALS | DISTRICT/ TOWNSHIP | NOTES |
					under 10	10 to 16	16 to 26	26 to 45	45 and over	under 10	10 to 16	16 to 26	26 to 45	45 and over					
Manchester	51	21	Gurley	George	2	1		1			1	2	1				8		
Manchester	51	22	Goldsmith	Gifford	1	1	1	1	1	3	2	1	1	1			13		
Manchester	51	23	Hossim	Willm			2		1		2		1				6		
Manchester	51	24	Hilton	Susa Wo									1				1		
Manchester	51	25	Hilton	Nathl Jun	1		1			1		1					4		
Manchester	51	26	Cromby	Benja	1	1		1		2		1					6		
Manchester	51	27	Hilton	Nathll Jun		1			1	1	1		1				5		
Manchester	51	28	Rogers	Nathll				1									1		
Manchester	51	29	Hilton	Hilton				1		2	2	2	1				8		
Manchester	51	30	Hall	Abigalk Wo		1					1	3	2	1			8		
Manchester	51	31	Hossim	Joseph				1		1	2	1	1				6		
Manchester	51	32	Hill	Sarah Wo	1									1			2		
Manchester	51	33	Hill	John			1			2		2					5		
Manchester	51	34	Hilton	Abig Wo	1	1	1			1		1					5		
Manchester	51	35	Hill	Benja		1				1		1					3		
Manchester	51	36	Hill	Margt Wo							1		1				2		
Manchester	51	37	Hilton	Aphice Wo	1	1					1		1				4		
Manchester	52	1	Haskell	Benja		1			1		1	1	1				5		
Manchester	52	2	Hossim	Josiah	1			1		3			1				6		
Manchester	52	3	Jones	Mary										1			1		
Manchester	52	4	Hooper	William				1			2		1				4		
Manchester	52	5	Hooper	John	1			1					1				3		
Manchester	52	6	Hooper	William Jun	1			1		1			1				4		
Manchester	52	7	Hooper	Jacob		1		1	1	1			1				5		
Manchester	52	8	Hooper	Nathll	2			1		1			1				5		
Manchester	52	9	Knight	John	3	2	1	1		1	1	1	1				11		
Manchester	52	10	Kilham	Joseph			1			3			1				5		
Manchester	52	11	Crop	Lucy Wo							1		1				2		
Manchester	52	12	Kilham	William			1			1		1					3		
Manchester	52	13	Danford	Lucy Wo			1					1		1			3		
Manchester	52	14	Danford	Stepn	1			1				1					3		
Manchester	52	15	Kitfield	Lydia Wo						1			1	1			3		
Manchester	52	16	Lee	Israel	1	1		1		2			1				6		
Manchester	52	17	Lee	Henry				1		5	1	1	1				9		
Manchester	52	18	Lee	Winthrop				1		1							2		
Manchester	52	19	Leach	Bethh										1			1		
Manchester	52	20	Lee	Elizabh Wo	1		2			1		1					5		
Manchester	52	21	Leach	Annie Wo										1			1		
Manchester	52	22	Allen	John 3d			1			1		1					3		
Manchester	52	23	Lee	Aaron		1	1	1					1				4		
Manchester	52	24	Lee	Nathll Junr	2	1		1		2		1	1				8		
Manchester	52	25	Leach	Benja	1	1		1		2			1				6		
Manchester	52	26	Low	Daniel	1	1	1	1		3		1					8		
Manchester	52	27	Lee	Sol	1	2		1		1			1				6		
Manchester	52	28	Lee	William	2			1		2		1					6		
Manchester	52	29	Lee	Joseph	1	1		1		3	1	2	1				10		
Manchester	52	30	Lee	Nathan	2	1		1		2			1				7		
Manchester	52	31	Leach	Daniel	1			1		1	3	1	1				8		
Manchester	52	32	Lee	Andrew		1					1			1			4		
Manchester	52	33	Morre	Mary Widw		1					1	1	1				4		
Manchester	52	34	Lendal	John	3	1	2	1		2			1				10		
Manchester	52	35	Leach	Marian Wo							1	1	1				3		
Manchester	52	36	Lee	Lydia Wo									2		1		3		
Manchester	52	37	Leach	Ezehl		1	3	1		1	2	1					10		
Manchester	53	1	Lee	Sarah Wo									1		1		2		
Manchester	53	2	Lee	Josiah	2	2		1					1				6		
Manchester	53	3	Lee	Isaac	1	1	2	1	1	1	1		1				9		
Manchester	53	4	Lee	John Junr		1				1							2		
Manchester	53	5	Lee	Amoss	2			1		3			1				7		
Manchester	53	6	Lendal	Eunice Wo			2			1		1		1			5		
Manchester	53	7	Lee	Isaac Junr	2	1		1		2	1		1				8		
Manchester	53	8	Lee	Nathll			1					1		1			3		
Manchester	53	9	Carter	Benja	1	1		1		1			1				5		
Manchester	53	10	Babcock	Thomas Jun			1			1		1					3		
Manchester	53	11	Cross	George Jun	2			1		3			1				7		
Manchester	53	12	Cross	George		2			1	1				1			5		
Manchester	53	13	Craft	Benja Jun			1					1	1				3		
Manchester	53	14	Camp	William	2			1		1			1	1			6		
Manchester	53	15	carter	Oben				1					1	1			3		
Manchester	53	16	Crowell	Benja	3		1		1			1		1			7		
Manchester	53	17	Marston	Andrew		1						1					2		
Manchester	53	18	Morgan	Israel	1	2	1	1		1			1				7		
Manchester	53	19	May	Jon		1		1		1			1				4		
Manchester	53	20	May	Sarah Wo	2	1							2	1			6		
Manchester	53	21	Babcock	Nicholas		1						1					2		
Manchester	53	22	Morse	Samll	1		1			2			1	1			6		
Manchester	53	23	Morgan	Polly Wo	1		1						1				3		
Manchester	53	24	Manning	Prisc Wo	1								2				3		
Manchester	53	25	Morse	David	1		1			1			1	1			6		

TOWN	PG#	LN#	LAST NAME	FIRST NAME	FREE WHITE MALES					FREE WHITE FEMALES					TOTAL ALL OTHER	TOTAL SLAVES	TOTALS	DISTRICT/ TOWNSHIP	NOTES
					under 10	10 to 16	16 to 26	26 to 45	45 and over	under 10	10 to 16	16 to 26	26 to 45	45 and over					
Manchester	53	26	May	Annie Wo							1			1			2		
Manchester	53	27	Marston	Betty Wo								1	1	1			3		
Manchester	53	28	May	Jona Jun		1		1		1			1				4		
Manchester	53	29	Morgan	Israel			1			1		1					3		
Manchester	53	30	Morgan	Loes Wo			1					1		1			3		
Manchester	53	31	Morgan	Edward	1			1		1			1				4		
Manchester	53	32	Norton	George			1						1				2		
Manchester	53	33	Gurley	Willm			1						1				2		
Manchester	53	34	Norwood	Davd Doct		1	1	1		1	1	1					7		
Manchester	53	35	Miller	Simeon		1	1		1	1	1						5		
Manchester	53	36	Morgan	Anna Wo						1	1			1			3		
Manchester	53	37	Davis	Nancy Wo	1					1		1					3		
Manchester	53	38	Hosman	John			1						1				2		
Manchester	54	1	Ober	Benja		1			1	1				1			4		
Manchester	54	2	Parsons	Tyler	1	1	1			1		1					5		
Manchester	54	3	Presson	Isaac	1			1		1		1					4		
Manchester	54	4	Peirce	Abial Wo		1				1			1	1			4		
Manchester	54	5	Perry	Elizh Wo	2								1	1			4		
Manchester	54	6	Prince	Saml1	1		1						1				3		
Manchester	54	7	Procter	Francis	1	3	1		1	4			1	1			12		
Manchester	54	8	Part	Saml1	2			1					1				4		
Manchester	54	9	Part	Richd		1	1	3	1			1	1	1			9		
Manchester	54	10	Russell	William	1	1			1	2			2	1			8		
Manchester	54	11	Russell	Isaac	1		1			1		1	1	1			6		
Manchester	54	12	Smith	Stephn	2	1	1						1				5		
Manchester	54	13	Storey	Nathll				1		1			1				3		
Manchester	54	14	Driver	Saml1			1						1				2		
Manchester	54	15	Storey	Henry Maj	1	2			1	2				1			8		
Manchester	54	16	Sinnett	Willm				1		2			1	1			5		
Manchester	54	17	Simmons	Andrew	2			1					1				4		
Manchester	54	18	Simmons	Ruth Wo									1	1			2		
Manchester	54	19	Smith	Barly	1		1						1				3		
Manchester	54	20	Stevens	Moses	1		1						1				3		
Manchester	54	21	Stone	Willa Senr					1	1	1			1			4		
Manchester	54	22	Morgan	David	1			1		2			1	1			6		
Manchester	54	23	Stone	Samuel	1				1	3		1					6		
Manchester	54	24	Stone	Abraham	2	1		1		1			1				6		
Manchester	54	25	Bishop	Willm	1			1		2			1				5		
Manchester	54	26	Stiles	Thomas	1	1		1		2			1				6		
Manchester	54	27	Stares	Philip			1					1	1				3		
Manchester	54	28	Tappon	Ebenz	4			1		1	1		2	1			10		
Manchester	54	29	Tuck	Saml1	2			1		1			1				5		
Manchester	54	30	Davey	Ephm Doct		1		1		1	1	1					6		
Manchester	54	31	Tuck	William Esq	2	1	1		1	1			2				8		
Manchester	54	32	Thompson	Benja	1		1						1				3		
Manchester	54	33	Tuck	John Junr	1			1		1			1	1			5		
Manchester	54	34	Tuck	John		1		1		1	2			1			6		
Manchester	54	35	Tewxbury	Jacob Deac					1					1			2		
Manchester	54	36	Tewxbury	Jacob Junr	1				1				1				3		
Manchester	54	37	Warner	Abrm			1			1			1				3		
Manchester	54	38	Woodbery	David	1		1			3	1	1					7		
Manchester	54	39	Woodbery	Andrew				1						1			2		
Manchester	55	1	Morse	William			1			2			1				4		
Manchester	55	2	West	John	2			2		2				1			7		
Manchester	55	3	Stanwood	Mary						1			2	1			4		
Manchester	55	4	Ayers	Lydia Wo		1		1				1	1	1			5		
Manchester	55	5	Allen	Rebc Wo	1							1	1	1			4		
Manchester	55	6	Allen	Mary Wo	2			1					2	1			6		
Manchester	55	7	Allen	Richard	1			1					1	1			4		
Manchester	55	8	Abbot	Nathll		2		1		2			1				6		
Manchester	55	9	Burges	David	2	2	2	1		1	1	1	1				11		
Manchester	55	10	Baker	Joseph	1		1						1				3		
Manchester	55	11	Brown	Andrew	1		1						1				3		
Manchester	55	12	Brown	James			1						1				2		
Manchester	55	13	Bonason	Betty						2		1					3		
Manchester	55	14	Widgen	Joseph	3			1		1			1				6		
Manchester	55	15	Woodbery	Mary Widow									1	1			2		
Manchester	55	16	Allen	Ruth Wo			1						1	1			3		

TOWN	PG#	LN#	LAST NAME	FIRST NAME	FWM under 10	FWM 10 to 16	FWM 16 to 26	FWM 26 to 45	FWM 45 and over	FWF under 10	FWF 10 to 16	FWF 16 to 26	FWF 26 to 45	FWF 45 and over	TOTAL ALL OTHER	TOTAL SLAVES	TOTALS	DISTRICT/ TOWNSHIP	NOTES
Marblehead	238	1	Abraham	Woodward		1			1				1	1			4		
Marblehead	238	2	Abraham	Woodward Jun	1			1			1		1				4		
Marblehead	238	3	Anderson	Benjamin			1			1		1					3		
Marblehead	238	4	Adams	John	2	2		1		1		1					7		
Marblehead	238	5	Ashton	William		1							1				2		
Marblehead	238	6	Atkins	Joseph			1						1				2		
Marblehead	238	7	Atkins	Elizaneth		1	2							1			4		
Marblehead	238	8	Abbott	Anna										1			1		
Marblehead	238	9	Allen	Moses	3			1		1			1				6		
Marblehead	238	10	Aborn	Benjamin		1		1		3		1	1	1			8		
Marblehead	238	11	Adams	Nathaniel	1	1		1		1			1				5		
Marblehead	238	12	Adams	Rebecca	1									2			3		
Marblehead	238	13	Ashton	Samuel		1	2		1	2	1	1		1			9		
Marblehead	238	14	Andrews	Betty										1			1		
Marblehead	238	15	Arbuncle	William		1		1		1	1		1	1			6		
Marblehead	238	16	Ashton	Hannah								1		1			2		
Marblehead	238	17	Ashton	Benjamin			1			1		1					3		
Marblehead	238	18	Ashton	Mary										1			1		
Marblehead	238	19	Adams	Mary	1								1	1			3		
Marblehead	238	20	Ashton	Philip	2	1		1		2			1				7		
Marblehead	238	21	Anderton	Thomas	1	1		1				1					4		
Marblehead	238	22	Abbott	Benjamin	1			1		1			1				4		
Marblehead	238	23	Atkins	Robert		1	1						1	1			5		
Marblehead	239	1	Andrews	Eleanor									1	1			2		
Marblehead	239	2	Andrews	Mary									1	1			2		
Marblehead	239	3	Andrews	John															Enumeration left blank
Marblehead	239	4	Aborns	James				1			1	1		1			4		
Marblehead	239	5	Anderton	Elizaneth									1				1		
Marblehead	239	6	Allen	Ambrose			1			2			1				4		
Marblehead	239	7	Blackler	William	2		3		1	1	3	2		1			13		
Marblehead	239	8	Bruce	Joseph	1			1					1				3		
Marblehead	239	9	Bonnler	William	1					2			1				5		
Marblehead	239	10	Brown	Hannah	2	1						2	1				6		
Marblehead	239	11	Brown	Ebenezer	3	3	1	1					1				9		
Marblehead	239	12	Bassett	John			1			1		1					3		
Marblehead	239	13	Woodward	Abraham		1							1	1			4		
Marblehead	239	14	Woodward	Abraham Junr	1			1		1		1					4		
Marblehead	239	15	Andrews	Benjamin			1			1		1					3		
Marblehead	239	16	Adams	John	2	2		1		1		1					7		
Marblehead	239	17	Brown	Joseph											2		2		
Marblehead	239	18	Brown	Jane											2		2		
Marblehead	239	19	Bartoll	Samuel	1	1		1		1		1	1				6		
Marblehead	239	20	Girdler	Richard	1		1			1		1					4		
Marblehead	239	21	Selman	Joseph	2			1					1				4		
Marblehead	239	22	Collyer	Isaac Junr			1						1				2		
Marblehead	239	23	Dodd	Cornelius	4	1		1					1				7		
Marblehead	239	24	Stevens	Mary		3		1		1							5		
Marblehead	239	25	Doak	Francis			1			2		1					4		
Marblehead	239	26	Craw	Mary		1								1			2		
Marblehead	239	27	Witham	Susanna		2				2			1				5		
Marblehead	239	28	Martin	John			1		1	1	1			1			5		
Marblehead	239	29	Melvill	John		1		1		3				1			6		
Marblehead	239	30	Pedrick	William			1			2			1				4		
Marblehead	239	31	Tidder	John	1		2			1			1	1			6		
Marblehead	239	32	Parker	Richard	5			1					1				7		
Marblehead	239	33	Crips	Tabitha		1				1	1		1				4		
Marblehead	240	1	Venning	Mary				1					1				2		
Marblehead	240	2	Reed	John	4			1		1	1		1				8		
Marblehead	240	3	Pearson	Lucretia	1	1						1		1			4		
Marblehead	240	4	Clone	Thomas	1	1			1				1				4		
Marblehead	240	5	Horton	Samuel	2		1		1	4		2	1				11		
Marblehead	240	6	Dennis	Benjamin			1						1				2		
Marblehead	240	7	Morse	Abraham	3	1		1		1			1				7		
Marblehead	240	8	Pritchard	Benjamin			1					1					2		
Marblehead	240	9	Hilton	Richard				1						1			2		
Marblehead	240	10	Reed	Elizabeth										1			1		
Marblehead	240	11	Foster	Joshua					1		1						2		
Marblehead	240	12	Waitt	Jacob					1	3	3	1	1				9		
Marblehead	240	13	Cocklin	John		1		1		1			1				4		
Marblehead	240	14	Collyer	Isaac		3	1	1		1			1	1	1		9		
Marblehead	240	15	Reed	Annie									1				1		
Marblehead	240	16	Vickery	Alice	1	1				1			1	1			5		
Marblehead	240	17	Smethurst	John	1			1		2			1				5		
Marblehead	240	18	Smith	Benjamin	1			1		2			1				5		
Marblehead	240	19	Tucker	Nicholas Junr			1			1		1					3		
Marblehead	240	20	Tucker	Nicholas		1	2		1	1	2		1				8		
Marblehead	240	21	Walker	Moses			1	1						1			3		
Marblehead	240	22	Wilkins	William			1			2		1					4		
Marblehead	240	23	LeMaster	Thomas	1				1	2	2		1				7		
Marblehead	240	24	Bartoll	William	1		1		1	3	2			1			9		
Marblehead	240	25	Glover	Edmund	2			1					1				4		
Marblehead	240	26	Call	Henry P.	1			1		2		1					5		
Marblehead	240	27	Quinen	Henry		1				2		1					4		
Marblehead	240	28	Riddan	John			1	1					1				3		
Marblehead	240	29	Parsons	Samuel				1					1				2		
Marblehead	240	30	Burgean	William	1			1					1				3		
Marblehead	240	31	Hodson	Peter			1										1		
Marblehead	240	32	Lee	William				1		2	1	2					6		
Marblehead	240	33	Hooper	John			1			1		2					4		
Marblehead	240	34	Greenwood	Mary									1				1		

TOWN	PG#	LN#	LAST NAME	FIRST NAME	FREE WHITE MALES					FREE WHITE FEMALES					TOTAL ALL OTHER	TOTAL SLAVES	TOTALS	DISTRICT/ TOWNSHIP	NOTES
					under 10	10 to 16	16 to 26	26 to 45	45 and over	under 10	10 to 16	16 to 26	26 to 45	45 and over					
Marblehead	240	35	Poor	John			1					1					2		
Marblehead	240	36	Craw	Benjamin			1					1					2		
Marblehead	240	37	Hooper	Elizabeth								1		2			3		
Marblehead	240	38	Woodridge	John	2	2		1		1	1	1	1				9		
Marblehead	241	1	Homan	Nathaniel					1			2					3		
Marblehead	241	2	Fowle	Mart	1								1				2		
Marblehead	241	3	Devereux	Peggy									1				1		
Marblehead	241	4	Frail	John		2		1		2	1	1	1	1			9		
Marblehead	241	5	Gilbert	Thomas	3			1		1		1					6		
Marblehead	241	6	Roads	Samuel	3			1					1				5		
Marblehead	241	7	Harris	William	1	1	1	1		2	1	2	1				10		
Marblehead	241	8	Greaves	William	2			1		1			1				5		
Marblehead	241	9	Hanover	Hannah										1			1		
Marblehead	241	10	Megan	Susannah	3								1	1			5		
Marblehead	241	11	Dennis	Charity									1	1			2		
Marblehead	241	12	Roundey	Joseph		1	1		1	1		1	1				6		
Marblehead	241	13	Dennis	Sarah		1							1				2		
Marblehead	241	14	Youngs	Stephen			1						1				2		
Marblehead	241	15	Williams	Abigail	1		1			1		1	1				5		
Marblehead	241	16	Prince	Cato											5		5		
Marblehead	241	17	Lewis	Jack											2		2		
Marblehead	241	18	Thomas	Isaac											3		3		
Marblehead	241	19	Foster	Pompey											5		5		
Marblehead	241	20	Gardner	Peter											5		5		
Marblehead	241	21	Dutton	Peter				1		2			1				4		
Marblehead	241	22	Church	George			1					1					2		
Marblehead	241	23	Jackson	Elizabeth	1	2							1				4		
Marblehead	241	24	Jackson	George			1						1				2		
Marblehead	241	25	Sparhawk	John	3			1		1			1				6		
Marblehead	241	26	Martin	John			1			1			1				3		
Marblehead	241	27	Bowen	Nathaniel	1	1		1		1	1	1	1				7		
Marblehead	241	28	Rousland	William	1	1		1		2			1	1			7		
Marblehead	241	29	Wooldridge	Margaret								2	1				3		
Marblehead	241	30	Berry	Ebenezer			1						1		1		3		
Marblehead	241	31	Russell	John	1			1		1			1	1			5		
Marblehead	241	32	Rea	Henry	2			1		1				2			6		
Marblehead	241	33	Mann	Lydia	2	1	1			1	1		1				7		
Marblehead	242	1	Fuller	Thomas			1						1				2		
Marblehead	242	2	Bartoll	Sally						1		1					2		
Marblehead	242	3	Story	William			1			1		2					4		
Marblehead	242	4	Hubbard	Ebenezer Revd	3	2		1		1	2		2				11		
Marblehead	242	5	Newhall	Samuel	2	1	2		1	2	2						10		
Marblehead	242	6	Redrick	Thomas		1	1	1					1				5		
Marblehead	242	7	Redrick	James											5		5		
Marblehead	242	8	Putman	Jacob	2	1	1	1		2	1	1	1				10		
Marblehead	242	9	Dodd	Thomas			1						1				2		
Marblehead	242	10	Brimblecome	Charity									1	1			2		
Marblehead	242	11	Brimblecome	Nathaniel	1		1			2			1				5		
Marblehead	242	12	Mason	William				1					1				2		
Marblehead	242	13	Orne	John	2			1		1			1				5		
Marblehead	242	14	Proctor	Jonathan	1			1					1				3		
Marblehead	242	15	Hadley	Nathaniel				1		1			1	1			4		
Marblehead	242	16	Halen	Elias	1			1		1	1						4		
Marblehead	242	17	Francis	Charles											4		4		
Marblehead	242	18	Peach	Abraham F.											4		4		
Marblehead	242	19	Bradstreet	Sarah		1				1	1		1				4		
Marblehead	242	20	Blackler	William Junr				1		4		1	1				7		
Marblehead	242	21	Rolls	Alden	2		1						1				4		
Marblehead	242	22	Mason	Mary									1		2		3		
Marblehead	242	23	Francis	Abraham			1			2		1					4		
Marblehead	242	24	Pedrick	John		1		1		1			1	1			5		
Marblehead	242	25	Grant	Thomas	2			1		2	1		1				7		
Marblehead	242	26	Bean	James				1		1			1				3		
Marblehead	242	27	Grant	Christopher		1		1		4			1				7		
Marblehead	242	28	Bartlett	Mary		1							1	1			3		
Marblehead	242	29	Hulen	John	3	1		1		1	1		1				8		
Marblehead	242	30	Weld	Payson	2								1				4		
Marblehead	242	31	Homan	Richard			1	1		1	1		1				6		
Marblehead	242	32	Hendley	John		1		1					1				3		
Marblehead	243	1	Woodridge	Mary								1	1				2		
Marblehead	243	2	Gilbert	John	1			1					1				3		
Marblehead	243	3	Freeman	Cesar											6		6		
Marblehead	243	4	Hatch	Naler	1	1	1			1		1					5		
Marblehead	243	5	Lord	Benjamin	2	2			1				1				6		
Marblehead	243	6	Martin	Amorlold		2	1	1			1		1				6		
Marblehead	243	7	Dixey	Rebecca		1	1	1				1	2	1			7		
Marblehead	243	8	Francis	Christopher			1			1			1				3		
Marblehead	243	9	Lefarrow	Elizabeth	3	3		1		2		1	1				11		
Marblehead	243	10	Scott	John				1					1				2		
Marblehead	243	11	Robinson	Elizabeth									1				1		
Marblehead	243	12	Doliber	John	3	1							1				7		
Marblehead	243	13	Hammon	Elizabeth								1	1				2		
Marblehead	243	14	Hulen	Elias				1				1	1				3		
Marblehead	243	15	Dimon	Elizabeth	2					1	2		1				6		
Marblehead	243	16	Stanley	Thomas			1							1			2		
Marblehead	243	17	Thrasher	Sarah										2			2		
Marblehead	243	18	Hubbard	Ruth								1	1				2		
Marblehead	243	19	Pedrick	John					1				1				2		
Marblehead	243	20	Stacey	William	3			1					1				5		
Marblehead	243	21	Stacey	Mary			2					1		1			4		

TOWN	PG#	LN#	LAST NAME	FIRST NAME	FREE WHITE MALES					FREE WHITE FEMALES					TOTAL ALL OTHER	TOTAL SLAVES	TOTALS	DISTRICT/TOWNSHIP	NOTES
					under 10	10 to 16	16 to 26	26 to 45	45 and over	under 10	10 to 16	16 to 26	26 to 45	45 and over					
Marblehead	243	22	Trefry	John	2			1		2			1				6		
Marblehead	243	23	Devereaux	Susanna									1	1			2		
Marblehead	243	24	Furniss	Anthony		1	1		1				2	1			6		
Marblehead	243	25	Wooldridge	Robert	1				1			2		1			5		
Marblehead	243	26	Knight	Robert				1	1					1			3		
Marblehead	243	27	Knight	George	1	1			1	4			1				8		
Marblehead	243	28	Dixey	Peter	1			1		2			1				5		
Marblehead	243	29	Elkins	Thomas		1	1		1	1	1		1				6		
Marblehead	244	1	Vickery	William	2			1		1			1				5		
Marblehead	244	2	Brown	Tameson									1	1			2		
Marblehead	244	3	Riddan	Rachel			1							1			2		
Marblehead	244	4	Gilbert	John	1		1						1				3		
Marblehead	244	5	Patten	Elizabeth	2	1				1	1	1		1			7		
Marblehead	244	6	Woodfine	Richard L.	3	1		1	1	2			1				9		
Marblehead	244	7	Eaton	Hannah	1		2						1				4		
Marblehead	244	8	Pritchard	John	3	1		1		1			1				7		
Marblehead	244	9	Pritchard	Elizabeth	2	1	2						1				6		
Marblehead	244	10	Bowen	William		1		1		2			1				5		
Marblehead	244	11	Trefry	Sarah	1	1							1				3		
Marblehead	244	12	Hooper	Asa		1	1	1		3			1				7		
Marblehead	244	13	Hooper	Mary								2	1				3		
Marblehead	244	14	Pedrick	Thomas Junr	1		1					1					3		
Marblehead	244	15	Bailey	John	2	1		1		1		1	1	1			8		
Marblehead	244	16	Devereux	Robert			2		1		1	1		1			6		
Marblehead	244	17	Poorhouse	Keeper of	2				12	1		1	1	37			54		
Marblehead	244	18	Story	Isaac Revd				1		1	1	3		1			7		
Marblehead	244	19	Johnson	Benrice		2		1		1	1						5		
Marblehead	244	20	Picker	Nicholas	1		1		1	2		2	2	2			11		
Marblehead	244	21	Besome	Philip	1			1		3	1	2	1		1		10		
Marblehead	244	22	Barjona	Cato											4		4		
Marblehead	244	23	Ingalls	Thomas	1	1		1		1			1				5		
Marblehead	244	24	Russell	Elizabeth	1						2		1				4		
Marblehead	244	25	Scobie	James	2			1		2		2					7		
Marblehead	244	26	Grater	Francis	2	1	1		1			1	1				7		
Marblehead	244	27	Hooker	Philip	1		1		1	3	1	2	1				10		
Marblehead	244	28	Standley	Peter	2		1	1			2		1				7		
Marblehead	244	29	Standley	William	2	1	1		1	3	1	1	1				11		
Marblehead	245	1	Orne	John	1			1					1				3		
Marblehead	245	2	Doliber	Peter				1		1			1	1			4		
Marblehead	245	3	Besom	John	2	1	1	1		3			1	1			10		
Marblehead	245	4	Brown	John 4th		1				1		1					3		
Marblehead	245	5	Strong	William	2			1		1			1				5		
Marblehead	245	6	Barker	Sarah	1						1			1			3		
Marblehead	245	7	Martin	Richard		1	2		1	2	2	1	1	1			11		
Marblehead	245	8	Oliver	James	2			1					1				4		
Marblehead	245	9	Wipping	George	3			1				3	1				8		
Marblehead	245	10	Bartlett	John	2	1			1	1		2					8		
Marblehead	245	11	Picker	Sally									1				1		
Marblehead	245	12	Bray	Edmund	2			1		2			1				6		
Marblehead	245	13	Williams	Mary								2	1				3		
Marblehead	245	14	Lindsey	Joseph	1			1		2			1				5		
Marblehead	245	15	Cowell	Hannah	1	1		1		1		1					5		
Marblehead	245	16	Brown	William	1	1		1		2			1				6		
Marblehead	245	17	Garrison	Fanny						1		1					2		
Marblehead	245	18	Deruff	Lemie	1		1			1		1					4		
Marblehead	245	19	Plaisted	Lucy									1				1		
Marblehead	245	20	Rotch	George			1					1					2		
Marblehead	245	21	Story	Elisha	3		1		1	2	2	2	1				12		
Marblehead	245	22	Devereux	Samuel		1	1		1			1	1	2			7		
Marblehead	245	23	Martin	Mary		1				1	1	1					4		
Marblehead	245	24	Besome	Rebecca	1	1				1			1				4		
Marblehead	245	25	Humphreys	Amos	3	1		1		1	1		1				8		
Marblehead	245	26	Smith	Thomas G.		1						1					2		
Marblehead	245	27	Bowen	Ashley	1		1		1			1		1			5		
Marblehead	245	28	Furniss	Alice									1				1		
Marblehead	245	29	Widger	Thomas	1		1						1				3		
Marblehead	245	30	Glover	Hannah									1				1		
Marblehead	245	31	Downing	William			1			1			1				4		
Marblehead	245	32	Florence	Charles	3	1		1		1	1		1				8		
Marblehead	245	33	Vikery	Elisabeth									1				1		
Marblehead	245	34	Hammond	John	3			1		1	1		1				7		
Marblehead	245	35	Bacon	William				1					1				2		
Marblehead	246	1	Mason	William	1	1	1		1			2		1			7		
Marblehead	246	2	Pearce	Hannah	1							1					2		
Marblehead	246	3	Pedrick	Mary	1		1			3			1				6		
Marblehead	246	4	Tewksbury	James		1	1			2			1	1			6		
Marblehead	246	5	Wadden	Jacob		1						1	1				3		
Marblehead	246	6	Dennis	Erasmus		1							1				2		
Marblehead	246	7	Homan	Thomas	1	1		1		1	1	1	1				7		
Marblehead	246	8	Walfrey	John	1		1						1				3		
Marblehead	246	9	Burroughs	William		1	1					1					3		
Marblehead	246	10	Hine	John		2		1				1	1				5		
Marblehead	246	11	Homan	Hannah									1				1		
Marblehead	246	12	Homan	Edward		1		1		1			1				4		
Marblehead	246	13	Freeto	Francis	3	1	1	1		2	2		1	1			12		
Marblehead	246	14	Dennis	Thomas	1			1		3			1				6		
Marblehead	246	15	Thompson	Benjn 3rd			1			1		1					3		
Marblehead	246	16	Lawrece	Joseph H.		1			1	1			1				4		
Marblehead	246	17	Salter	Joseph				1					1				2		
Marblehead	246	18	Doliber	William			1			1			1				3		

TOWN	PG#	LN#	HEADS OF HOUSEHOLD LAST NAME	FIRST NAME	FREE WHITE MALES under 10	10 to 16	16 to 26	26 to 45	45 and over	FREE WHITE FEMALES under 10	10 to 16	16 to 26	26 to 45	45 and over	TOTAL ALL OTHER	TOTAL SLAVES	TOTALS	DISTRICT/ TOWNSHIP	NOTES
Marblehead	246	19	Smith	Thomas	1		1						1				3		
Marblehead	246	20	Pitman	Thomas					1	1				1			3		
Marblehead	246	21	Salter	Joseph	1	2		1		2			1				7		
Marblehead	246	22	Doliber	Thomas P.	1	1		1		1		1	1				6		
Marblehead	246	23	Brown	John Jun	1		2		1	3	1		1				9		
Marblehead	246	24	Nimblet	Robert			2		1	3			1				7		
Marblehead	246	25	Broughton	Nicholson	3	1		1			1	1					7		
Marblehead	246	26	Curtis	William	1	2	1		2				1				7		
Marblehead	246	27	Quill	Robert		2			1				1				4		
Marblehead	246	28	Topham	James			1		1			1	1				4		
Marblehead	246	29	Green	Peter					1				1				2		
Marblehead	246	30	Boden	Elizabeth									1	1			2		
Marblehead	246	31	Boardman	Francis		2		1					1				4		
Marblehead	246	32	Thompson	George	1			1		1		1					4		
Marblehead	246	33	Rolf	Samuel				1					1				2		
Marblehead	246	34	Florence	John	1			1		1		1					4		
Marblehead	246	35	Willard	Thomas				1				1	1				3		
Marblehead	246	36	Conway	Peter			1			1		1					3		
Marblehead	247	1	Barton	Susannah						1			1				2		
Marblehead	247	2	Doak	James				1			1	1					3		
Marblehead	247	3	Smith	Moses	2			2		1	1	1					7		
Marblehead	247	4	Lee	John	2	1		1		1		1					6		
Marblehead	247	5	Bowen	David	2			1		2			1				6		
Marblehead	247	6	Snell	Joseph		1		1					1				3		
Marblehead	247	7	Vickery	Eli				1			1		1				3		
Marblehead	247	8	Tidder	Volentine			2	1				1	1				5		
Marblehead	247	9	Wilson	Joseph	1	1		1		2		1	1				7		
Marblehead	247	10	Reed	Mary			3	1		1	1	1	1				8		
Marblehead	247	11	Besome	Phillip	1			1		3	1	2	1		1		10		
Marblehead	247	12	Hooper	Samuel			2	1	2	1			1	1			8		
Marblehead	247	13	Bond	John			2	1		2			1	1			7		
Marblehead	247	14	Powers	John		1	1	1		2	3			1			9		
Marblehead	247	15	Hooper	Phillip	1		1		1	3	1	2	1				10		
Marblehead	247	16	Ingalls	Thomas	1	1		1		1			1				5		
Marblehead	247	17	Russell	Elizabeth	1							2		2			5		
Marblehead	247	18	Foster	Israel					1				2	2			5		
Marblehead	247	19	Russell	John			2	1		1	1		1				6		
Marblehead	247	20	Kelly	John	1	1		1		1		1	1				6		
Marblehead	247	21	Hammond	Elizabeth	2	1	1						1	1			6		
Marblehead	247	22	Edney	James	1	1		1		1			1				5		
Marblehead	247	23	Tucker	George		1	1		1		1	1		1			6		
Marblehead	247	24	Bubier	Hannah									1				1		
Marblehead	247	25	Cloutman	John				1		3		2	1				7		
Marblehead	247	26	Humphries	Sarah								1		1			2		
Marblehead	247	27	Stevens	Sarah	1	1	2			3	1	1		2			11		
Marblehead	247	28	Jarvis	John	3			1		1	1	1	1				8		
Marblehead	247	29	Hanty	Mary								1		1			2		
Marblehead	247	30	Roads	Henry				1			1		1				3		
Marblehead	247	31	Follett	Elizabeth									1				1		
Marblehead	247	32	Tucker	George Junr	1			1					1	1			4		
Marblehead	247	33	LeWorthy	Thomas				1					1				2		
Marblehead	247	34	Stevens	Silvester		1							1				2		
Marblehead	247	35	Stevens	John				1				1	1	1			4		
Marblehead	247	36	Conway	Martha	1		1			1			1				4		
Marblehead	247	37	Prebble	Nathaniel			1						1				2		
Marblehead	247	38	Pearce	William	3			1			1		1				6		
Marblehead	248	1	Caryll	Jane	1					2	2		1	1			7		
Marblehead	248	2	Burroughs	Alice									1				1		
Marblehead	248	3	Prentiss	Henry	2	1		1		3			1	1			9		
Marblehead	248	4	Hooper	Nathaniel	1		1	1		3		1	1				9		
Marblehead	248	5	Wood	Elizabeth	1					1			1				3		
Marblehead	248	6	Richardson	John	3	1		1		1			1	1			8		
Marblehead	248	7	Skinner	William				1				1		1			3		
Marblehead	248	8	Lewis	Edmund	1	1			1	2		1	2	1			9		
Marblehead	248	9	Phillips	Stephen				1					1	1			3		
Marblehead	248	10	Grifle	John				1					1	1			3		
Marblehead	248	11	Prince	Richard	2	1		1		2	2	1	1				10		
Marblehead	248	12	Snell	Martha									2				2		
Marblehead	248	13	Meek	Thomas	2	3	3	1		3	1	1	1	1			16		
Marblehead	248	14	Putnam	Stephen		1				1			1				3		
Marblehead	248	15	Osgood	Hooker				1					1				2		
Marblehead	248	16	Ollyer	John	1			1		1			1				4		
Marblehead	248	17	Brindlecome	Samuel	1			1		1			1				4		
Marblehead	248	18	Waitt	William					1					2			3		
Marblehead	248	19	Story	Abiel			1						1	1	1		4		
Marblehead	248	20	Widger	William		1						1					2		
Marblehead	248	21	Waitt	John		2	2	1	1		1	2		1			10		
Marblehead	248	22	Bray	Benjamin	1	1							1				3		
Marblehead	248	23	Peach	John	3			1		1		1	1	1			8		
Marblehead	248	24	Sargeant	Francis	1		1						1				3		
Marblehead	248	25	Beal	Mary	2	1				1			1				5		
Marblehead	248	26	Blair	John	2	2	1	1					1				7		
Marblehead	248	27	Stacey	John	2			1				1					4		
Marblehead	248	28	Cole	William	2	1		1		1			1				6		
Marblehead	248	29	Snow	Samuel	3	2		1		1			1				8		
Marblehead	248	30	Snow	Mary										1			1		
Marblehead	248	31	Griffen	Alice		1					1	1		1			4		
Marblehead	248	32	Green	Sarah						1			1				2		
Marblehead	248	33	Russell	Wilson H.	2			1					1	1			5		
Marblehead	248	34	Cooks	James	1	2	1	2			2		1	1			10		

TOWN	PG#	LN#	LAST NAME	FIRST NAME	FREE WHITE MALES under 10	10 to 16	16 to 26	26 to 45	45 and over	FREE WHITE FEMALES under 10	10 to 16	16 to 26	26 to 45	45 and over	TOTAL ALL OTHER	TOTAL SLAVES	TOTALS	DISTRICT/ TOWNSHIP	NOTES
Marblehead	248	35	Doliber	Sarah			2						1	1			4		
Marblehead	248	36	Powers	John	1		1	1					1				4		
Marblehead	248	37	Green	John	1		2		1	1	1		1				7		
Marblehead	248	38	Gregory	Joseph	4	1		1					1				7		
Marblehead	249	1	Dodd	Mary			2							1			3		
Marblehead	249	2	Stacey	Elizabeth										1			1		
Marblehead	249	3	Green	Alexander			1						1				2		
Marblehead	249	4	Thomas	Redding			1			1		1					3		
Marblehead	249	5	Oakes	Jacob	1	1			1	1		2	1				7		
Marblehead	249	6	Brooks	John				1		1			1				3		
Marblehead	249	7	Girdler	Lewis	2			1		1			1				5		
Marblehead	249	8	Knowland	Andrew	2			1					1				4		
Marblehead	249	9	Miller	John				1				1	1				3		
Marblehead	249	10	Goldsmith	Lucy			2				2		1				5		
Marblehead	249	11	Green	Elizabeth						2	1		1				4		
Marblehead	249	12	Tishoe	John		3			1	1		2	1				8		
Marblehead	249	13	Gready	Samuel	2	1		1					1				5		
Marblehead	249	14	Denais	Anna									1				1		
Marblehead	249	15	Clark	Sarah									1				1		
Marblehead	249	16	Curtis	William			1	1					1	1			4		
Marblehead	249	17	Snelling	Abigail									1				1		
Marblehead	249	18	Girdler	Benjamin			1	1				1	1	1			5		
Marblehead	249	19	Carney	Susannah	2					3			1				6		
Marblehead	249	20	Doliber	Thomas	2		1	1		1	1		1	1			8		
Marblehead	249	21	Severy	Clement	2	1		1		1			1				6		
Marblehead	249	22	Greaves	Samuel			1			1		1					3		
Marblehead	249	23	Upton	Thomas	4	2		1		1	1		1				10		
Marblehead	249	24	Peach	Thomas				1						2			3		
Marblehead	249	25	Peach	Joseph		1		1					1				3		
Marblehead	249	26	Dennis	John	1			1						2			4		
Marblehead	249	27	Ireson	Robert	1			1		1			1				4		
Marblehead	249	28	Trefry	Edward	1	1		1		1			1				5		
Marblehead	249	29	Doliber	Joseph	1			1				1					4		
Marblehead	249	30	Oliver	Sarah										2			2		
Marblehead	249	31	Trefry	Elizabeth									1				1		
Marblehead	249	32	Russell	Martha									1				1		
Marblehead	249	33	Pearce	Robert		1			1		1	1					5		
Marblehead	249	34	Hammond	John	2			1		1	1		1				6		
Marblehead	249	35	Dennis	Archable		1							1				2		
Marblehead	249	36	Proctor	Mary										1			1		
Marblehead	250	1	Cheever	Peter D.	2	1		1		2			1				7		
Marblehead	250	2	Salter	Mary		1	1						1				3		
Marblehead	250	3	Frost	Joshua		1				1		1					3		
Marblehead	250	4	Oliver	Sarah							2	1		2			5		
Marblehead	250	5	Cloutman	Sukey	1					1			1				3		
Marblehead	250	6	Swetland	Benjamin		1					1	1					3		
Marblehead	250	7	Stevens	Joseph			1			2			1				4		
Marblehead	250	8	Calley	Samuel		1							1				2		
Marblehead	250	9	Clough	Ebenezer	2	1		1		1			1				6		
Marblehead	250	10	Martin	Ebenezer	2	2	2	1		3		2	1				13		
Marblehead	250	11	Martin	Prudence								1		2			3		
Marblehead	250	12	James	Richard				1					1				2		
Marblehead	250	13	Crocker	Uriel	2		1			2			1				6		
Marblehead	250	14	Severance	Sarah								1		1			2		
Marblehead	250	15	Fettyplace	Edward Junr		3	2		1	1			1	1			6		
Marblehead	250	16	Perry	Hannah			1						1				2		
Marblehead	250	17	Perry	George			1					1					3		
Marblehead	250	18	Snell	Stephen	1			1		2	1	1	1				7		
Marblehead	250	19	Hawks	Willia	1			1		4		1					7		
Marblehead	250	20	Feller	Hannah									1				1		
Marblehead	250	21	Knight	Benjamin	3			1		1	1		1				7		
Marblehead	250	22	Snell	Samuel	3	2		1					1				7		
Marblehead	250	23	Rexford	Jordan	1			1		1			1				4		
Marblehead	250	24	Doble	Thomas	1	1			1					1			4		
Marblehead	250	25	Knapp	Peter	1			1		3			1				6		
Marblehead	250	26	Maine	William			1	1		1			1	1			5		
Marblehead	250	27	Kanpp	Samuel	2			1		1			1				5		
Marblehead	250	28	Girdler	Hannah									1				1		
Marblehead	250	29	Coombs	Nicholas				1		2			1				4		
Marblehead	250	30	Goss	Joshua Jun	1			1		1			1				4		
Marblehead	250	31	Tucker	Deborah								2					2		
Marblehead	250	32	Wittam	John		1		1				1		1			4		
Marblehead	250	33	Carell	Mary	2					2			1				5		
Marblehead	250	34	Bowden	Benjamin				1									1		
Marblehead	250	35	Bowden	Samuel		1		1						1			3		
Marblehead	251	1	Smethurst	John	3	1		1		3	1		1				10		
Marblehead	251	2	Bettis	Mary	1								1				2		
Marblehead	251	3	Severy	Mary						2		3	1				6		
Marblehead	251	4	Lee	Elizabeth									1				1		
Marblehead	251	5	Clothey	Joseph	2			1		2	1		1	1			8		
Marblehead	251	6	Bartlett	Hannah	1	1				1			1				4		
Marblehead	251	7	Bettis	Elizabeth		1							1				2		
Marblehead	251	8	Savage	John	2		1						1				4		
Marblehead	251	9	Prebble	Nehemiah	1		1			2		1					5		
Marblehead	251	10	Stacey	Edward	3			1		1	1		1				7		
Marblehead	251	11	Melzard	Mary									1				1		
Marblehead	251	12	Brimblecome	Thomas			1			4			1				6		
Marblehead	251	13	Bridges	George			1			1		1					3		
Marblehead	251	14	Brown	Thomas		1		1			1		1				4		
Marblehead	251	15	Porter	Abigail									1				1		

TOWN	PG#	LN#	LAST NAME	FIRST NAME	FREE WHITE MALES					FREE WHITE FEMALES					TOTAL ALL OTHER	TOTAL SLAVES	TOTALS	DISTRICT/ TOWNSHIP	NOTES
					under 10	10 to 16	16 to 26	26 to 45	45 and over	under 10	10 to 16	16 to 26	26 to 45	45 and over					
Marblehead	251	16	Stacey	John		2		1		1			1				5		
Marblehead	251	17	Felton	John H.			1						1				2		
Marblehead	251	18	Brimblecome	David	2		1						1				4		
Marblehead	251	19	Dodd	William				1					1				2		
Marblehead	251	20	Houghton	Joseph				1		1			1				3		
Marblehead	251	21	Martin	Polly	1					1			1				3		
Marblehead	251	22	Swaysey	Samuel			1			2			1				4		
Marblehead	251	23	Martin	Nathan B	1		1	1		2			1	1			7		
Marblehead	251	24	Lyons	James	4	2						1	1	1			10		
Marblehead	251	25	Robinson	Benjamin		1	1	1		3			1				7		
Marblehead	251	26	Curtis	Joseph				1					1				2		
Marblehead	251	27	Kitchens	Samuel			1						1				2		
Marblehead	251	28	Goodwin	Hannah	3	1							1				5		
Marblehead	251	29	Prentiss	Joshua	1	2		1		2			1				7		
Marblehead	251	30	Selman	Archa	4	1		1		1	1						8		
Marblehead	251	31	Green	Mary	1	1							1				3		
Marblehead	251	32	Thompson	Samuel	4		1		1	1	2		1				10		
Marblehead	251	33	Selman	John			3		1	2			1	1			8		
Marblehead	252	1	Kitchens	Lilla									1	1			2		
Marblehead	252	2	Hiram	Richar			1						1				2		
Marblehead	252	3	Porter	Thomas	1	2		1		2			1				7		
Marblehead	252	4	Bray	Rebecca			1				1	2		2			6		
Marblehead	252	5	Goodwin	William	1		1						1				3		
Marblehead	252	6	Roundy	Jonathan Junr			1						1				2		
Marblehead	252	7	Megear	John				1		1			1				3		
Marblehead	252	8	Stevens	Benjamin	1	1		1					1	1			5		
Marblehead	252	9	Frost	Grace		1							1				2		
Marblehead	252	10	Hooper	John	1			1		1			1	1			5		
Marblehead	252	11	Calley	William	3	1		1		2	1		1				9		
Marblehead	252	12	Cheever	John	2	1		1		1	1		1				7		
Marblehead	252	13	Hall	Prince								1			1		2		
Marblehead	252	14	Matthews	William			1						1				2		
Marblehead	252	15	Collins	Lydia	1	1				2	1		1				6		
Marblehead	252	16	Stacey	John		1	1	1					1				4		
Marblehead	252	17	Roundey	Jonathan Junr		1	1	1		1	1		1				6		
Marblehead	252	18	Frost	Richard	1			1		4	1		1				8		
Marblehead	252	19	Valentine	Andrew	3	1		1		2	2		1				10		
Marblehead	252	20	Roundey	Francis	2			1		2			1				6		
Marblehead	252	21	Casden	Joseph				1					2				3		
Marblehead	252	22	Roundey	John	1		1						1	1			4		
Marblehead	252	23	Mugford	Lidia									1	2			3		
Marblehead	252	24	Willisten	Thomas			2	1	1	1							5		
Marblehead	252	25	Thompson	Abigail									1				1		
Marblehead	252	26	Martin	Ambrose			1	1		1	1	1					5		
Marblehead	252	27	Deveraux	Lidia		1					1	1					3		
Marblehead	252	28	Gerry	Samuel R		1	2		1		1	1	1				7		
Marblehead	252	29	Lane	Henry	2	2	1	1		1	1	1					9		
Marblehead	252	30	Pedrick	Richard		3	1	2		1	1		1				9		
Marblehead	253	1	Doak	Benjamin	2	1		1		1			1				6		
Marblehead	253	2	Elkins	Thomas			1						1				2		
Marblehead	253	3	Goodwin	Samuel		1	1		1		1	2		1			7		
Marblehead	253	4	Shirley	William	1	2			1	3	1	1		1			10		
Marblehead	253	5	Foster	Annis	1								1				2		
Marblehead	253	6	Carryll	Jane	1					3			2	1			8		
Marblehead	253	7	Evens	Ebenezer G.	2	1	1					2	1				8		
Marblehead	253	8	Horten	Richard Junr			1			1			1				3		
Marblehead	253	9	Horten	Richard				1					1				2		
Marblehead	253	10	Vinsent	John				1					1				2		
Marblehead	253	11	Caswell	William	4	1		1					1				7		
Marblehead	253	12	Neck	Elizabeth		1							1	1			3		
Marblehead	253	13	Rogers	William	2	1	1	1					1				6		
Marblehead	253	14	Blaney	Asa	2			1		4	1		1				9		
Marblehead	253	15	Reynolds	Andrew	1			1		2	1		1				6		
Marblehead	253	16	Millet	Abigail			2						1				3		
Marblehead	253	17	Striker	Samuel			1						1				2		
Marblehead	253	18	Proctor	Joseph	1	1	1		1	1	1	1					7		
Marblehead	253	19	Barnes	Nancy						1		1					2		
Marblehead	253	20	Hawkes	Benjamin	2			1		1	1		1				6		
Marblehead	253	21	Trefry	James	1			1		1			1				4		
Marblehead	253	22	Kimball	Daniel	1		1	1		2			2				7		
Marblehead	253	23	Caruth	Thomas				1				2		1			4		
Marblehead	253	24	Follett	Thomas	2	1	2	1		1	1		1	1			10		
Marblehead	253	25	Proctor	*us		1				1			1						
Marblehead	253	26	Fundy	Nicholas			1			3			1				5		
Marblehead	253	27	Newhall	Sarah	2					2	1		1				6		
Marblehead	253	28	Bowler	*mes		3			1	1	1		1				7		
Marblehead	253	29	Bird	Daniel			1			3	1						6		
Marblehead	253	30	Mitchell	*en			1			2		1					4		
Marblehead	253	31	Bradeen	*n	1		1						1				3		
Marblehead	253	32	Swasey	Susannah										1			1		
Marblehead	253	33	Hooper	*an	1					3	1	1	1				8		
Marblehead	253	34	Kenning	*				1		1			1	1			4		
Marblehead	253	35	Goss	William			1			2		1					4		
Marblehead	254	1	Thompson	William	1	1				2	2		1				8		
Marblehead	254	2	Wormstead	Benjamin		1		1					1	1			4		
Marblehead	254	3	Goss	Joshua	2		1		1	1	1	2		1			9		
Marblehead	254	4	Tucker	Andrew		1				1			1				3		
Marblehead	254	5	Greaves	Ebenezer Junr				1				1	1				4		
Marblehead	254	6	Howe	Nathaniel			1						1				2		
Marblehead	254	7	Greene	Peter Junr			1			1			1	1			4		

TOWN	PG#	LN#	HEADS OF HOUSEHOLD		FREE WHITE MALES					FREE WHITE FEMALES					TOTAL ALL OTHER	TOTAL SLAVES	TOTALS	DISTRICT/ TOWNSHIP	NOTES
			LAST NAME	FIRST NAME	under 10	10 to 16	16 to 26	26 to 45	45 and over	under 10	10 to 16	16 to 26	26 to 45	45 and over					
Marblehead	254	8	Flory	John			1	1		1							3		
Marblehead	254	9	Greene	Samuel			1					1	1				3		
Marblehead	254	10	Giles	Samuel	1	1	1			4			1				8		
Marblehead	254	11	Coombs	Nicholas	3		1					1					5		
Marblehead	254	12	Bartlett	Jonathan					1	1	2	1		1			6		
Marblehead	254	13	Smith	Samuel	1	2			1	3	1		1				9		
Marblehead	254	14	Peyton	Mary										1			1		
Marblehead	254	15	Wortey	Elizabeth						1	2	1		1			5		
Marblehead	254	16	Thompson	Richard	2	1			1	1			1	1			7		
Marblehead	254	17	Clark	George		1			1			1		1			4		
Marblehead	254	18	Greaves	Ebenezer	1	1	2		1	1	1			1			8		
Marblehead	254	19	Stenness	Samuel	2		1						2				5		
Marblehead	254	20	Russell	Samuel	3			1		2			1				7		
Marblehead	254	21	Bowden	Benjamin	1			1		1			1				4		
Marblehead	254	22	Bruce	Hannah	1									1			2		
Marblehead	254	23	Homan	Benjamin	2			1		2			1	1			7		
Marblehead	254	24	Tishoe	Peter				1						1			2		
Marblehead	254	25	Brooks	William				1					1				2		
Marblehead	254	26	Dennis	Elizabeth		1						1	2				4		
Marblehead	254	27	James	Mary		1	1						1	1			4		
Marblehead	254	28	Metzard	Benjamin		1				2			1				4		
Marblehead	254	29	Roundy	Elizabeth										1			1		
Marblehead	254	30	Simonds	Daniel	2			1					1				4		
Marblehead	254	31	Brooks	Edward	2			1		3	1		1				8		
Marblehead	254	32	Wadden	John B.	3			1		1	1		1				7		
Marblehead	254	33	Horton	George	2		1						1				4		
Marblehead	254	34	Newhall	Peter	1		2		1	2				1			7		
Marblehead	255	1	*att	Elizabeth										1			1		
Marblehead	255	2	Condon	Jane	1								1				2		
Marblehead	255	3	Green	John			1						1				2		
Marblehead	255	4	Hines	Nancy						1	1		1				3		
Marblehead	255	5	Dupree	Thomas	1		1						1				3		
Marblehead	255	6	Smith	Mary						2		1	1				4		
Marblehead	255	7	Proctor	William	2		1						1	1			5		
Marblehead	255	8	Bartlett	John	1		1			1			1				4		
Marblehead	255	9	Pitman	Benjamin	2		1			2			1				6		
Marblehead	255	10	Johnson	Benjamin				1						1			2		
Marblehead	255	11	Bowden	Mary	1					1			1				3		
Marblehead	255	12	Skinner	John	1	1	1			1	1		1				6		
Marblehead	255	13	Twisden	Samuel	2	2		1		1	1	1	1				9		
Marblehead	255	14	Twisden	Sarah			2						1	1			4		
Marblehead	255	15	Greaves	John	1	2			1	2			1	1			8		
Marblehead	255	16	Devereaux	Benjamin P.		2			1	1	1	1	1				7		
Marblehead	255	17	Iveson	Benjamin			1						1				2		
Marblehead	255	18	Skinner	Richard	2			1		1	1		1				6		
Marblehead	255	19	Stevens	Christopher		1				1	1	1					4		
Marblehead	255	20	Merrett	John	1	1	1	1						2			6		
Marblehead	255	21	Brimblecome	Marrett	1			1		2	1		1	1			7		
Marblehead	255	22	Jones	Sarah		1	1						2	1			5		
Marblehead	255	23	Maley	Daniel	2	1	2		1	2			1	1			10		
Marblehead	255	24	Chambers	John			1						1				2		
Marblehead	255	25	Smith	John	2			1		2			1				6		
Marblehead	255	26	Cash	Hannah		1				1				1			3		
Marblehead	255	27	Neel	John	1		1						1	1			4		
Marblehead	255	28	Holder	Daniel	2			1					1				4		
Marblehead	255	29	Holder	Susanna									1	1			2		
Marblehead	255	30	Dennis	Sally						1			1				2		
Marblehead	255	31	Stiles	Desire									1	1			2		
Marblehead	255	32	Butman	Joseph	2			1		1			1				5		
Marblehead	255	33	Merrett	Francis	2			1					1				4		
Marblehead	256	1	Martin	Knott					1	1			1				3		
Marblehead	256	2	Stevens	Thomas	1	1		1		1	1		1	1			7		
Marblehead	256	3	Curtis	John				1					1				2		
Marblehead	256	4	Gardner	Benjamin			1			1		1					3		
Marblehead	256	5	Gardner	John			2	1	1					1			5		
Marblehead	256	6	Brown	Thomas Junr				1		2			1				4		
Marblehead	256	7	Candler	John	3	2	2	1		1	1		1				11		
Marblehead	256	8	Stacey	John	1	2		1		2	1	1		1			9		
Marblehead	256	9	Stacey	Elizabeth										1			1		
Marblehead	256	10	Delone	Rebecca								1	1				2		
Marblehead	256	11	Homan	Ambrose		1		1									2		
Marblehead	256	12	Pearce	George	1		1						1				3		
Marblehead	256	13	Wills	Elizabeth		1	1						1				3		
Marblehead	256	14	Handley	Joseph				1									1		
Marblehead	256	15	LeCrane	William		2		1		2			1				6		
Marblehead	256	16	LeCrane	John	2			1		2			1				6		
Marblehead	256	17	Hooper	John	1		1						1				3		
Marblehead	256	18	Pedrick	Thomas	1			1		2	1	1					6		
Marblehead	256	19	Russell	Thomas	2			1		3			1				7		
Marblehead	256	20	Ellis	Francis					1	1				1			3		
Marblehead	256	21	Hendley	Abigail										1			1		
Marblehead	256	22	Battes	John Jr			1			2			1	1			5		
Marblehead	256	23	Flaitt	Michael	1			1					1				3		
Marblehead	256	24	LeGron	Philip				1					1				2		
Marblehead	256	25	Duncan	Joseph	1			1		1	1		1				5		
Marblehead	256	26	Chambers	Ephraim	1	2	1		1	1				2			8		
Marblehead	256	27	Cotitle	Philippe		2		1					1				4		
Marblehead	256	28	Liscolm	Richard	1			1		1			1				4		
Marblehead	256	29	Breed	Micajah		1		1					1				3		
Marblehead	256	30	Lewis	Aaron		1			1	1				1			4		

TOWN	PG#	LN#	LAST NAME	FIRST NAME	FREE WHITE MALES under 10	10 to 16	16 to 26	26 to 45	45 and over	FREE WHITE FEMALES under 10	10 to 16	16 to 26	26 to 45	45 and over	TOTAL ALL OTHER	TOTAL SLAVES	TOTALS	DISTRICT/ TOWNSHIP	NOTES
Marblehead	256	31	George	Hannah	1					1			1				3		
Marblehead	256	32	Prebble	Nathaniel		2	1		1				1	1			6		
Marblehead	256	33	Meservy	William		2			1				1				4		
Marblehead	256	34	Pope	Joseph				1						1			2		
Marblehead	257	1	Curtis	Richard				1						1			2		
Marblehead	257	2	Brown	Samuel	1			1		2			1				5		
Marblehead	257	3	Brown	Anna										2			2		
Marblehead	257	4	Bradeen	Joseph				1						1			2		
Marblehead	257	5	Ireson	Elizabeth										1			1		
Marblehead	257	6	Doak	George			1						1				2		
Marblehead	257	7	Hooper	John	1		1	1			2			1			6		
Marblehead	257	8	Fowler	Thomas			1					1					2		
Marblehead	257	9	Goodwin	Hephzibah										2			2		
Marblehead	257	10	Williams	Hannah			1						1				2		
Marblehead	257	11	Martin	Mary			1						1				2		
Marblehead	257	12	Newhall	Philip	3		1					1					5		
Marblehead	257	13	Doak	Deliverance	1					1			1				3		
Marblehead	257	14	Ross	Rebecca		2						1		1			4		
Marblehead	257	15	Bowden	Samuel			1	1						1			3		
Marblehead	257	16	Leach	Eleazer	2			1					1				4		
Marblehead	257	17	Selman	Joseph	2	1	2		1	1	1			1			9		
Marblehead	257	18	Capell	William	1	2			1	2	3	2		1			12		
Marblehead	257	19	Trefry	William	2		1			1			1				5		
Marblehead	257	20	Bowden	Joseph			1			1		1					3		
Marblehead	257	21	Bowden	Samuel 4th			1			1			1				3		
Marblehead	257	22	Morse	Thomas			1			3			1				5		
Marblehead	257	23	Garney	Thomas	1	3			1	2		2	2	1			10		
Marblehead	257	24	Tenly	Thomas	1		1			1			1				4		
Marblehead	257	25	Desmore	Joseph	2		1						1				4		
Marblehead	257	26	Pedrick	William		2	2		1		1	1	1	1			9		
Marblehead	257	27	Bowden	William	1			1		2			1				5		
Marblehead	257	28	Hammond	William	2			1		1			1				5		
Marblehead	257	29	Knight	Samuel	4			1				1		1			7		
Marblehead	257	30	Page	*hel	3			1		1	2		1				8		
Marblehead	257	31	French	Chase W		1				2		1					4		
Marblehead	257	32	Nicholson	Thomas	3	2	2	1			2			1			11		
Marblehead	257	33	Felton	Daniel				1					1	1			3		
Marblehead	257	34	Basset	Michael	2			1						1			4		
Marblehead	257	35	Chinn	Samuel Junr		1		1		2			1				5		
Marblehead	257	36	Petey	Mary		1	1				1	1	1				5		
Marblehead	258	1	Bowden	Thomas	1		2		1	1	1			1			7		
Marblehead	258	2	Fowler	John			1	1					1	1			4		
Marblehead	258	3	Lashey	James	1			1					1	1			4		
Marblehead	258	4	Desmore	Joseph P.	3			1		3	1		1	1			10		
Marblehead	258	5	Williston	Thomas Junr			1						1				2		
Marblehead	258	6	Cash	Mary										1			1		
Marblehead	258	7	Doliber	John	3	1		1		1			1				7		
Marblehead	258	8	Scott	John				1						1			2		
Marblehead	258	9	Robinson	Elizabeth									1				1		
Marblehead	258	10	Melzard	George		1	1		1				1	1			5		
Marblehead	258	11	Besome	Richard Junr	2	1	1			1		1	1				7		
Marblehead	258	12	Russell	Richard	1	1		1		2		1	1				7		
Marblehead	258	13	Bowden	John				1			1	1		1			4		
Marblehead	258	14	Mann	Thomas				1					1				2		
Marblehead	258	15	*man	John		1						1					2		
Marblehead	258	16	Russell	Benjamin		2		1					1				4		
Marblehead	258	17	Hubbard	*tha									1				1		
Marblehead	258	18	Doliber	Deborah									1				1		
Marblehead	258	19	Hubbard	Sarah									1				1		
Marblehead	258	20	Chinn	Samuel		1	2	1	1				1	1			7		
Marblehead	258	21	Flint	Elizabeth	1								1				2		
Marblehead	258	22	Cloutman	Hannah	1					1			1				3		
Marblehead	258	23	Bridgam	Phillip		1	1	1		3	2		1				9		
Marblehead	258	24	Goodwin	Samuel	3			1		2			1				7		
Marblehead	258	25	Northey	John	2			1		2			1				6		
Marblehead	258	26	Doliber	John	1		1						1				3		
Marblehead	258	27	Gamey	Margaret										1			1		
Marblehead	258	28	Reed	Nancy	1								1				2		
Marblehead	258	29	Ball	Nancy								1	1				2		
Marblehead	258	30	Brown	John Junr	1	1		1		3	2		1				9		
Marblehead	258	31	Homan	William	2	2	1			1			1				7		
Marblehead	258	32	Waitt	Elias				1		1			1				3		
Marblehead	258	33	Ramsdell	Phillip	3			1		2			1				7		
Marblehead	259	1	Besome	Richard		1		1	1					2			5		
Marblehead	259	2	Bowers	John				1						1			2		
Marblehead	259	3	Freetoe	John				1						1			2		
Marblehead	259	4	Newhall	Joseph				1		3			1				5		
Marblehead	259	5	Sanitt	Samuel	2	1		1		1			1				6		
Marblehead	259	6	Veal	Charles				1			1		1				3		
Marblehead	259	7	Scores	Edward	1			1		3			1				6		
Marblehead	259	8	Goodwin	William			1					1					2		
Marblehead	259	9	Cross	John	2			1					1				4		
Marblehead	259	10	Leach	Henry		1			1		2			1			5		
Marblehead	259	11	Chittenden	Thomas				1			1			1			3		
Marblehead	259	12	Barker	Ruth										3			3		
Marblehead	259	13	Barker	Francis	1	2	1						1				5		
Marblehead	259	14	Ashton	Sarah		1	1			2		1	1				6		
Marblehead	259	15	Ball	John				1					1	1			3		
Marblehead	259	16	Doliber	Elizabeth										1			1		
Marblehead	259	17	Grons	Elizabeth		2							1				3		

Town	PG#	LN#	Last Name	First Name	FREE WHITE MALES					FREE WHITE FEMALES					TOTAL ALL OTHER	TOTAL SLAVES	TOTALS	DISTRICT/ TOWNSHIP	NOTES
					under 10	10 to 16	16 to 26	26 to 45	45 and over	under 10	10 to 16	16 to 26	26 to 45	45 and over					
Marblehead	259	18	Bean	William	1	1			1	1	2	2	1				9		
Marblehead	259	19	Selman	Mary									1				1		
Marblehead	259	20	Miller	Patience									1				1		
Marblehead	259	21	Brown	John			1	1					1				3		
Marblehead	259	22	Curtis	Mary			1					1					2		
Marblehead	259	23	Dennis	Jonas		1		1			1	1		1			5		
Marblehead	259	24	Pearce	Benjamin				1						1			2		
Marblehead	259	25	Green	Thomas			1			2			1				4		
Marblehead	259	26	Severy	Nicholas				1						2			3		
Marblehead	259	27	Crowningshield	Edward	1			1		3			1				6		
Marblehead	259	28	Hackleton	John1			1	1				1					3		
Marblehead	259	29	Miller	Joseph			1					1					2		
Marblehead	259	30	Bowden	Joshua Orne			1			1		1					3		
Marblehead	259	31	High	John			1	1		1			1				4		
Marblehead	259	32	Brimblecome	Joseph	1		1			2			1				5		
Marblehead	259	33	Hammond	Jane	1								1				2		
Marblehead	259	34	Thompson	Benjamin				2						1			3		
Marblehead	260	1	Ross	Sarah								1	1	1			3		
Marblehead	260	2	Fettyplace	Edward		2		1				1		1			5		
Marblehead	260	3	Orne	Jonathan Junr	2		1			1			1				5		
Marblehead	260	4	Butman	Joseph				1						1			2		
Marblehead	260	5	Butman	John			1			1			1				3		
Marblehead	260	6	Pope	Joseph			1					1					2		
Marblehead	260	7	Doak	Benjamin			1	1				1	1	1			5		
Marblehead	260	8	Dennis	John D. Junr	2		1			1		1					5		
Marblehead	260	9	Dennis	John D.		2	3	1		1	1			2			10		
Marblehead	260	10	Wooldridge	Benjamin	2		1			1							4		
Marblehead	260	11	Cash	George	1		1	1		1	1	1					6		
Marblehead	260	12	Horgan	Anna			1				1			1			3		
Marblehead	260	13	Green	John		1		1				1		1			4		
Marblehead	260	14	Dennis	Thomas	3	1		1		3			1				9		
Marblehead	260	15	Lewis	Edward	1			1		2		1					5		
Marblehead	260	16	Thompson	William		1		1		2		1		1			6		
Marblehead	260	17	Thompson	Cornelius			1							1			2		
Marblehead	260	18	Nutting	John				1		2	1			2			6		
Marblehead	260	19	Trefry	William	1	1		1		1	2		1				7		
Marblehead	260	20	Downs	John			1	1						2			4		
Marblehead	260	21	Seveny	Joseph			1			1			1				3		
Marblehead	260	22	Gifford	*ah	1		1							1			3		
Marblehead	260	23	Smith	John	1		1						1				3		
Marblehead	260	24	Cash	Moses	2		2	1			1	1		1			8		
Marblehead	260	25	Frost	William	1		1						1				3		
Marblehead	260	26	Girdler	Robert				1	1				1	1			4		
Marblehead	260	27	Girdler	Joseph	3	1		1		2			1				8		
Marblehead	260	28	Quinner	Peter				1					1	1			3		
Marblehead	260	29	Cole	Nicholas				1				1		1			3		
Marblehead	260	30	Hammond	Thomas F	1	1	1		1		1			1			6		
Marblehead	260	31	Felton	Thomas	1			1		1			1	1			5		
Marblehead	260	32	Felton	James	2			1		1		1					5		
Marblehead	260	33	Chapman	Jane								2		1			3		
Marblehead	260	34	Lewis	Edmund	3			1		1		1					6		
Marblehead	260	35	Jones	James	1			1		1	1		1				5		
Marblehead	260	36	Brown	Mehitable									1				1		
Marblehead	261	1	Mulley	Susannah									1				1		
Marblehead	261	2	Pearce	William	3			1			1		1				6		
Marblehead	261	3	Smith	Jeremiah			1					1					2		
Marblehead	261	4	Dixey	John	3			1		2			1				7		
Marblehead	261	5	Ingalls	William				1		2		1					4		
Marblehead	261	6	Tucker	Elizabeth	2	1	2			1	1			1			8		
Marblehead	261	7	Flack	Martha								2		1			3		
Marblehead	261	8	Widger	William	2	1			1	1	1	1		1			8		
Marblehead	261	9	Canell	James	1			1		1	1		1				5		
Marblehead	261	10	Stevens	Francis				1		1		1					3		
Marblehead	261	11	Melzard	John	2	1	2		1	1				1			9		
Marblehead	261	12	Brooks	Elizabeth										1			1		
Marblehead	261	13	Trasher	John		1	2		1	4	1	1	1				11		
Marblehead	261	14	Burrage	Robert	1			1		3	1		1				7		
Marblehead	261	15	Caswell	John	1		1	1	1			1		1			6		
Marblehead	261	16	Melzard	Richard			1					1					2		
Marblehead	261	17	Smith	John			1							2			4		
Marblehead	261	18	Williams	John	1	1		1		2	1		1				7		
Marblehead	261	19	Howard	Rachel							2			1			3		
Marblehead	261	20	Cole	Nicholas		1						1					2		
Marblehead	261	21	Humphries	Hannah	1		1				1	2		1			6		
Marblehead	261	22	Humphries	Samuel		1						1					2		
Marblehead	261	23	Reynolds	Nathaniel		3		1		1	1			1			7		
Marblehead	261	24		Simon											4		4		Last name left blank
Marblehead	261	25	Gerry	Cato											2		2		
Marblehead	261	26	Dennis	Hannah		2						1		1			4		
Marblehead	261	27	Savage	John	1			1			1						3		
Marblehead	261	28	Hooper	Robert Junr	4			1		2	1	1	1				10		
Marblehead	261	29	Salkins	Thomas	1	1	2		1	1			1				7		
Marblehead	261	30	Barker	George	2			1			1	1					5		
Marblehead	262	1	Barker	Joseph		1		1		4	1	1	1				9		
Marblehead	262	2	Barker	Charity										1			1		
Marblehead	262	3	Baker	Hannah	1	1					2		1				52		
Marblehead	262	4	Barker	Thomas			1		1		2	2		1			7		
Marblehead	262	5	Bartlett	Abijah	2		1	1		2			1	1			8		
Marblehead	262	6	Bartlett	Thomas	3	1		1		1			1				7		
Marblehead	262	7	Bartlett	Nicholas	2	1			1	1	2	2	1				10		

TOWN	PG#	LN#	HEADS OF HOUSEHOLD		FREE WHITE MALES					FREE WHITE FEMALES					TOTAL ALL OTHER	TOTAL SLAVES	TOTALS	DISTRICT/ TOWNSHIP	NOTES
			LAST NAME	FIRST NAME	under 10	10 to 16	16 to 26	26 to 45	45 and over	under 10	10 to 16	16 to 26	26 to 45	45 and over					
Marblehead	262	8	Blanchard	Jesse	2		1	1					1				5		
Marblehead	262	9	Bessett	Richard	1		1	1		1							4		
Marblehead	262	10	Besome	Nicholas	3			1		1	1		1				7		
Marblehead	262	11	Blaney	Ruth		1	1			2	1			1			6		
Marblehead	262	12	Boden	William	1			1		3	2		1				8		
Marblehead	262	13	Bowen	Deborah									1				1		
Marblehead	262	14	Hinkley	Joseph					1	2	2		2				7		
Marblehead	262	15	Boden	Lidia	1					2		1	1				5		
Marblehead	262	16	Bowden	Francis			2		1	2	2	2	1				10		
Marblehead	262	17	Briars	Elias			1			1		1					3		
Marblehead	262	18	Briars	Annis		2	1						2				5		
Marblehead	262	19	Oliver	Elizabeth									2	2			4		
Marblehead	262	20	Burnam	Mary	1	1	1					1	1	1			6		
Marblehead	262	21	Chapman	John	1			1		1		1					4		
Marblehead	262	22	Chapman	Daniel	2			1		2	3	1	1				10		
Marblehead	262	23	Chapman	Samuel	1			1		1			1				4		
Marblehead	262	24	Chapman	Stephen	1		1			1		1					4		
Marblehead	262	25	Curtis	Benjamin	1			1		3			1	1			7		
Marblehead	262	26	Clark	Rebecca	1	1							1				3		
Marblehead	262	27	Clemmons	Alice							2		1				3		
Marblehead	262	28	Curtis	Mary		2	1					1	1				5		
Marblehead	262	29	Church	Anna									1				1		
Marblehead	262	30	Clothey	Betty		1						1	1				3		
Marblehead	262	31	Clone	Sarah		1							1				2		
Marblehead	262	32	Cylebee	John		1						1					2		
Marblehead	263	1	Coombs	Elizabeth	1					1		1					3		
Marblehead	263	2	Coombs	Meriam		1							1				2		
Marblehead	263	3	Thomas	Reddin		1				1		1					3		
Marblehead	263	4	Smethurst	Alice									1				1		
Marblehead	263	5	Coombs	Joshua	2	2		1		1			1				7		
Marblehead	263	6	Coombs	Michael				1		1			1				3		
Marblehead	263	7	Goss	Katherine	1	1				2			1				5		
Marblehead	263	8	Clone	John	1				1				1				3		
Marblehead	263	9	Dennis	Benjamin			2	1				1	1				5		
Marblehead	263	10	Dailey	Elizabeth		1				2			1				4		
Marblehead	263	11	Dixey	John Junr	4		1		1		1	1	1				9		
Marblehead	263	12	Fish	Daniel		1		1		1	1		1				5		
Marblehead	263	13	Fortune	Francis	2			1					1				4		
Marblehead	263	14	Gale	Mary								1	1				2		
Marblehead	263	15	Gibson	Alice	2							1					3		
Marblehead	263	16	Gordon	Nicholas	1			1		1			2	1			6		
Marblehead	263	17	Goss	William		2	1	1		2			1		5		12		
Marblehead	263	18	Grandy	Mary		1							1				2		
Marblehead	263	19	Grant	Thomas			2	1				1					4		
Marblehead	263	20	Grant	William	1			1		1			1				4		
Marblehead	263	21	Greaves	Samuel		1				2			1				4		
Marblehead	263	22	Goldsmith	Samuel	2			1		2			1				6		
Marblehead	263	23	Green	Mercy										2			2		
Marblehead	263	24	Hamson	Henry	2	1	2		1	1	1	1	1				10		
Marblehead	263	25	Greenough	Emanuel				1						1			2		
Marblehead	263	26	Hayden	William				1					1				2		
Marblehead	263	27	Hammond	Edward	4			1		1			1				7		
Marblehead	263	28	Hilliard	George	2			1		1			1				5		
Marblehead	263	29	Hooper	Robert			1	1	1				2	2			7		
Marblehead	263	30	Jarvis	John	3			1		1	1		1				7		
Marblehead	263	31	Jarvis	Manjural	1								1				2		
Marblehead	263	32	Ingalls	Thomas	1	1		1		1			1				5		
Marblehead	263	33	Ireson	Joseph	2	1		1		3			1				8		
Marblehead	264	1	Knowland	Andrew	2			1		2			1				6		
Marblehead	264	2	Laskey	Mary	3		1						1				6		
Marblehead	264	3	LeCrans	Philip			2		1	2	1	2	1	1			10		
Marblehead	264	4	Lee	William R.		1			1		1	2		2			7		
Marblehead	264	5	Lee	Samuel		1						2					3		
Marblehead	264	6	Lewis	Thomas	1			1		3	1		1		1		8		
Marblehead	264	7	Mansfield	Isaac		1		1		1			2				5		
Marblehead	264	8	Martin	Hannah				1				1	1				3		
Marblehead	264	9	Millett	Zebulun	1	2	1	1		3	1		1				10		
Marblehead	264	10	Nantz	Henry			1				1		1				3		
Marblehead	264	11	Knowland	James	2			1		2			1				6		
Marblehead	264	12	Oakes	Hannah	2			1		1			1				5		
Marblehead	264	13	Follett	Elizabeth									1				1		
Marblehead	264	14	Ogleby	Martha								1	1				2		
Marblehead	264	15	Orne	Joshua	1	3	1	1		1			2	1			10		
Marblehead	264	16	Paine	Martha		2							1				3		
Marblehead	264	17	Paine	James	1		1						1				3		
Marblehead	264	18	Paine	John	1		1	1					1	1			5		
Marblehead	264	19	Pedrick	Knott		1		1		1	3	1	1				8		
Marblehead	264	20	Phillips	Richard	2	1		1		1	1		1				7		
Marblehead	264	21	Pitman	Thomas	2			1		2	1		1				7		
Marblehead	264	22	Powers	Thomas	1	2		1		3	2		1				10		
Marblehead	264	23	Powers	Sarah		2							1				3		
Marblehead	264	24	Prince	John	1			1		2			1				5		
Marblehead	264	25	Prince	Anna								1	1				2		
Marblehead	264	26	Ramsdile	James	3	1		1		2		1	2				10		
Marblehead	264	27	Reynolds	William H.	2	1	1		1	1		2	1				9		
Marblehead	264	28	Roads	Henry				1					1				2		
Marblehead	264	29	Rogers	William	2	1	1	1					1				6		
Marblehead	264	30	Russell	Elizabeth						1	1	1	1				4		
Marblehead	264	31	Roundey	Joseph	5	1		1					1				8		
Marblehead	264	32	Roundey	Samuel	3			1					1				5		

TOWN	PG#	LN#	HEADS OF HOUSEHOLD LAST NAME	FIRST NAME	FREE WHITE MALES under 10	10 to 16	16 to 26	26 to 45	45 and over	FREE WHITE FEMALES under 10	10 to 16	16 to 26	26 to 45	45 and over	TOTAL ALL OTHER	TOTAL SLAVES	TOTALS	DISTRICT/ TOWNSHIP	NOTES
Marblehead	264	33	Russell	William	2	1		1		2	1		1				8		
Marblehead	264	34	Russell	John	3		2	1		1	2	1					10		
Marblehead	265	1	Russell	Joseph		2		1					1				4		
Marblehead	265	2	Sanden	William					1			1		1			3		
Marblehead	265	3	Smith	James	1			1		1	1	1	1				6		
Marblehead	265	4	Stacey	Mary			1			3	1		1				6		
Marblehead	265	5	Roundey	John			1	1		1	1		1				5		
Marblehead	265	6	Swan	John P.	1		1	1		3	1		2				9		
Marblehead	265	7	Swan	Robert	1	1			1	1	1	1					6		
Marblehead	265	8	Thayer	Isaac	1		1					1					3		
Marblehead	265	9	Thompson	Thomas	4	1		1		1	1		1				9		
Marblehead	265	10	Turner	Samuel	1	1	3	1		3		3					12		
Marblehead	265	11	Vickery	Samuel	2			1		1	1	1					7		
Marblehead	265	12	Waitt	Peter	1		1			1		1					4		
Marblehead	265	13	Wyman	Isaac				1	1					1			3		
Marblehead	265	14	Wooldridge	Thomas	2	2		1		1			1				7		
Marblehead	265	15	Walker	Mary	3								1				4		
Marblehead	265	16	Welsh	Deborah		1						1		1			3		
Marblehead	265	17	Wilford	George	1	2		1		1			1				6		
Marblehead	265	18	Warren	John	1			1		1							3		
Marblehead	265	19	Wheeler	Richard		1		1		1		1	1				5		
Marblehead	265	20	Grow	Jane	1						1		1				3		
Marblehead	265	21	Gardner	Molly										1			1		
Marblehead	265	22	Garner	Grace		1						1					2		
Marblehead	265	23	Pedrick	Joseph	1	2		1		1			1				6		
Marblehead	265	24	Florey	Nicholas	1			1		1			1				4		
Marblehead	265	25	Felton	Francis			1					1					2		
Marblehead	265	26	Getchell	Samuel				1	1				1	1			4		
Marblehead	265	27	Getchell	Jeremiah	2			1	1	2			1	1			8		
Marblehead	265	28	Doliber	William		1	1					1					3		
Marblehead	265	29	Stone	Nehemiah	1		2		1		1		1	1			7		
Marblehead	265	30	Nantz	Nicholas			1							1			2		
Marblehead	265	31	Phillips	William		1						1		1			4		
Marblehead	265	32	Phillips	Jacob	2		1			3		1	1				8		
Marblehead	265	33	Bartlett	William		1	1		1		1	1		1			6		
Marblehead	266	1	Stone	James	2	2		1		1				1			7		
Marblehead	266	2	Boynton	Nathaniel	1		1	1		1		1					5		
Marblehead	266	3	Brown	Samuel		1	1	1				1		1			5		
Marblehead	266	4	Getchell	Mary							1			1			2		
Marblehead	266	5	Ingalls	John		1		1			1	1	1				5		
Marblehead	266	6	Symmes	John			1			1	1						3		
Marblehead	266	7	Grant	Amos	1		1	1		1				2			6		
Marblehead	266	8	Morse	Abraham	3	1		1		1			1				7		
Marblehead	266	9	Davis	William	1			1		1			1				4		
Marblehead	266	10	Stacey	Samuel	2			1		1			1				5		
Marblehead	266	11	Conway	John	2			1		1			1				5		
Marblehead	266	12	Blancy	Sarah								1					1		
Marblehead	266	13	Oakes	Hannah	2					1			1				4		
Marblehead	266	14	Pickel	Moses A.					1								1		
Marblehead	266	15	Follett	Elizabeth	1			1						1			3		
Marblehead	266	16	Humphries	John	1	1		1		4	2	1	1				11		
Marblehead	266	17	Drury	John	2	1	1	2		1			1				8		
Marblehead	266	18	Warner	Elizabeth	1		2			1	2		1	1			8		
Marblehead	266	19	Stacey	Rebecca	1					1			1	1			4		
Marblehead	266	20	Creesy	Usine										1			1		
Marblehead	266	21	Glover	Sarah		1			1		2		1				5		
Marblehead	266	22	Gilley	William		1	1	1					2				5		
Marblehead	266	23	Mitchell	John	1		3	1						1			7		
Marblehead	266	24	Webster	Ambrose				1		1		1					3		
Marblehead	266	25	County	Mary				1		1							2		
Marblehead	266	26	Caryll	Susanna		2								1			3		
Marblehead	266	27	Bubin	Deborah								1		1			2		
Marblehead	266	28	Johnson	Benoice	1	3		1		2			1				8		
Marblehead	266	29	Eaton	Israel			1		1	1	1		1				5		
Marblehead	266	30	Harris	John	2	2	1		1	1	1	1					9		
Marblehead	266	31	Stevenson	David	2	1			1	2		3	1	1			11		
Marblehead	266	32	Wood	Richard					1					1			2		
Marblehead	266	33	Dodd	Benjamin					1	3		1					5		
Marblehead	266	34	Bowden	Nicholson		1	1			1		1		1			5		
Marblehead	267	1	Brimblecome	Cornelius		1						1					2		
Marblehead	267	2	Lefavour	Philip		1						1					2		
Marblehead	267	3	Bowden	Richard				1						1			2		
Marblehead	267	4	Goldsmith	Elizabeth		1						1		1			3		
Marblehead	267	5	Laskey	William			1						1				2		
Marblehead	267	6	Bowden	Thomas	1	1			1		1	2	1				7		
Marblehead	267	7	Johnson	Charity	1	2								1			4		
Marblehead	267	8	Barnard	Hannah	1					1	1		1				4		
Marblehead	267	9	Cloutman	Joseph	2			1		3			1				7		
Marblehead	267	10	Phillips	Nathaniel	3	1		1		1	1	1	1				9		
Marblehead	267	11	Bowler	Sarah						1		1					2		
Marblehead	267	12	Barnes	Peter W.	2	1			1	1	2	2		1			10		
Marblehead	267	13	Barnes	Woodin	1			1				1	1				4		
Marblehead	267	14	Devereux	Nathaniel	3			1		2			1				7		
Marblehead	267	15	Roundey	Thomas	1	1		1		2			1				6		
Marblehead	267	16	Roles	Jeremiah		1			1			1		1			4		
Marblehead	267	17	Bridges	Mary										1			1		
Marblehead	267	18	Bartlett	William	1	2	2		1		3		1				10		
Marblehead	267	19	Nicholson	Thomas	1			1		2			1	1			6		
Marblehead	267	20	Homan	John	3	2		1		1							8		
Marblehead	267	21	Nicholson	William			2		1			1	1	1			6		

TOWN	PG#	LN#	LAST NAME	FIRST NAME	FREE WHITE MALES					FREE WHITE FEMALES					TOTAL ALL OTHER	TOTAL SLAVES	TOTALS	DISTRICT/ TOWNSHIP	NOTES
					under 10	10 to 16	16 to 26	26 to 45	45 and over	under 10	10 to 16	16 to 26	26 to 45	45 and over					
Marblehead	267	22	Martin	Thomas Junr	1	1	1	1		1	1						6		
Marblehead	267	23	Thompson	John	1	2	1		1	1	1	1		2			10		
Marblehead	267	24	Cloutman	Robert	2			1					1				4		
Marblehead	267	25	Wells	Polly						1			1				2		
Marblehead	267	26	Leach	Sarah										1			1		
Marblehead	267	27	Brimblecome	Leanard				1			1			1			3		
Marblehead	267	28	Waitt	John	1	2		1		3		1	1				9		
Marblehead	267	29	Calley	Thomas				1		1		1					3		
Marblehead	267	30	Boden	Samuel				2	1				1				4		
Marblehead	267	31	Brimblecome	Samuel			1		1		1			1			4		
Marblehead	267	32	Martin	Thomas	1		1		1		1			1			5		
Marblehead	267	33	Cruss	Lewis	1	3	1		1	1				1			8		
Marblehead	267	34	Dennis	Thomas	1			1					1				3		
Marblehead	267	35	Cloutman	Hannah	1					1		1					3		
Marblehead	268	1	Prentiss	Joshua				1						1			2		
Marblehead	268	2	Cloutman	Thomas Junr	1	1		1			1			1			5		
Marblehead	268	3	Ashton	Philip				1						1			2		
Marblehead	268	4	Sweet	Nathaniel	1			1		3			1				6		
Marblehead	268	5	Harris	John				1		1		1					3		
Marblehead	268	6	Standley	Thomas		1	2		1		1			1			6		
Marblehead	268	7	Cross	Thomas				1		3			1				5		
Marblehead	268	8	Laskey	Benjamin	3			1						1			5		
Marblehead	268	9	Cross	Mary		1	1							1			3		
Marblehead	268	10	Morse	Stephen				1		1			1	1			4		
Marblehead	268	11	Peach	William				1					1				2		
Marblehead	268	12	Cloutman	Ebenezer B.				1					1				2		
Marblehead	268	13	Harris	William				1									1		
Marblehead	268	14	Homan	Edward	3	1			1		2			1			8		
Marblehead	268	15	Gale	Ambrose				1				1	1				3		
Marblehead	268	16	Harris	William Revd				1		5	1	1		1			9		
Marblehead	268	17	Doliber	Elizabeth	1					1	2			1			5		
Marblehead	268	18	Martin	Bartholomew	2			1		3	1			1			8		
Marblehead	268	19	Benson	Eleanor			2						1				3		
Marblehead	268	20	Gale	Samuel	1	2		1		1	1			1			7		
Marblehead	268	21	Boden	John				1					1				2		
Marblehead	268	22	Gardiner	Benjamin			1		1	2	1			1			6		
Marblehead	268	23	Doliber	William	1			1		1		1					4		
Marblehead	268	24	Peltro	Hannah	1							1		1			3		
Marblehead	268	25	Evans	Elizabeth		2						1		1			4		
Marblehead	268	26	Greaves	Joseph	1		1			1		1					4		
Marblehead	268	27	Blaney	Benjamin	1			1		3			1				6		
Marblehead	268	28	Harris	Robert		1	1						2				4		
Marblehead	268	29	Curtis	Rebecca	2								1				3		
Marblehead	268	30	Harris	Mason		2	1		1		2	2		2			10		
Marblehead	268	31	Wooldridge	William	3	1			1	2	1		1				9		
Marblehead	268	32	Barber	Martha	2								1	1			4		
Marblehead	268	33	Grush	Thomas	2	2		1		3	1	1					10		
Marblehead	268	34	Davis	Job		1		1					1	1			4		
Marblehead	268	35	Fletcher	William	2			1		2			1	1			7		
Marblehead	268	36	Phillips	John	2			1		2			1				6		
Marblehead	269	1	Collins	Moses A.				1					1	1			3		
Marblehead	269	2	Merrich	Elizabeth		1								1			2		
Marblehead	269	3	Darling	Hannah								2		1			3		
Marblehead	269	4	Thomas	Martha		1	1						1	1			4		
Marblehead	269	5	Brown	Sarah	1					1	1		1				4		
Marblehead	269	6	Thayer	Jeremiah				1				2		1			4		
Marblehead	269	7	Barker	Hannah	1					1			1	1			4		
Marblehead	269	8	Quiner	Nicholas		2		1		2	1		1				7		
Marblehead	269	9	Andrews	John		2	1		3		1	1	1				9		
Marblehead	269	10	Sewall	Samuel	2	2		1		3		1	1				10		
Marblehead	269	11	Collier	John			1		1		1	2		1			6		
Marblehead	269	12	Coleman	Ann		1							1	1			3		
Marblehead	269	13	Haskoll	William			1							1			2		
Marblehead	269	14	Calley	Hannah			1							1			2		
Marblehead	269	15	Calley	Rebecca										1			1		
Marblehead	269	16	Proctor	John	3		1						1				5		
Marblehead	269	17	Hathaway	John Gardner	3	2	1		1	2	1		1				11		
Marblehead	269	18	Webber	George	1			1				1					4		
Marblehead	269	19	Ingalls	Mary			1						1	1			3		
Marblehead	269	20	Butman	Benjamin	2	2		1		1	2		1				9		
Marblehead	269	21	Haskoll	Mark		1		1	1				2	1			6		
Marblehead	269	22	Morse	Elizabeth										1			1		
Marblehead	269	23	Hiler	Samuel		1		1		1			1				4		
Marblehead	269	24	Pearce	Robert	2			1						1			4		
Marblehead	269	25	Dixey	Mary										1			1		
Marblehead	269	26	Haskell	Thomas	2			1		1	1		1				6		
Marblehead	269	27	Cloutman	Thomas				1				1		1			3		
Marblehead	269	28	Cloutman	Robert				1				1		1			3		
Marblehead	269	29	Peach	Elizabeth		1	3					1	1	1			7		
Marblehead	269	30	Gallison	Henry		1	1						1				3		
Marblehead	269	31	Hichings	Nancy										1			1		
Marblehead	269	32	Waitt	Sarah	1					1			1				3		
Marblehead	269	33	Sheldon	Francis			1						1	1			3		
Marblehead	269	34	Covell	James	2			1		2			1				6		
Marblehead	270	1	Stevens	Joseph				1			3			1			5		
Marblehead	270	2	Deacon	Jonathan	1			1					1	2			5		
Marblehead	270	3	Griffin	William	1			1					1				3		
Marblehead	270	4	Lindsey	Sarah			3					2	2	1			8		
Marblehead	270	5	Cahill	William											3		3		
Marblehead	270	6	Robinson	John											4		4		

TOWN	PG#	LN#	LAST NAME	FIRST NAME	FREE WHITE MALES					FREE WHITE FEMALES					TOTAL ALL OTHER	TOTAL SLAVES	TOTALS	DISTRICT/ TOWNSHIP	NOTES
					under 10	10 to 16	16 to 26	26 to 45	45 and over	under 10	10 to 16	16 to 26	26 to 45	45 and over					
Marblehead	270	7	Chapell	Mary								2		1			3		
Marblehead	270	8	Marston	Sarah	1	1						2	1	1			6		
Marblehead	270	9	Lee	Richard	2	1	1	1		1			1				7		
Marblehead	270	10	Thorner	Sarah	1								1	1			3		
Marblehead	270	11	Thorner	Sarah			2						1				3		
Marblehead	270	12	Stone	Hannah	2	1	2			2		1	1				9		
Marblehead	270	13	Card	Nathaniel				1					1				2		
Marblehead	270	14	Peck	Benjamin				1		3			1				5		
Marblehead	270	15	Lindsey	Nathaniel	2			1		1		1	1				6		
Marblehead	270	16	Besome	Sarah	1		1				1			1	1		5		
Marblehead	270	17	Glover	Jonathan			1		1	2	1	1	1				7		
Marblehead	270	18	Mann	Abijah	2	1	2	2		1	1						9		
Marblehead	270	19	Francis	Richard	1	1		1		5			1				9		
Marblehead	270	20	Hunt	Job	1	1		1		3			1				7		
Marblehead	270	21	Swan	Aaron					1				1	1			3		
Marblehead	270	22	Greaves	Mark		1			1				1	1			4		
Marblehead	270	23	Greaves	Crispus	1		1						1				3		
Marblehead	270	24	Jones	Mary									1				1		
Marblehead	270	25	Coleby	Benjamin	1			1		1			1				4		
Marblehead	270	26	Lloyd	Thomas		1		1		2			1				5		
Marblehead	270	27	Proctor	Thomas				1		4			1	1			7		
Marblehead	270	28	Lear	Alexander				1					1				2		
Marblehead	270	29	Chapman	Annie		1	1							1			3		
Marblehead	270	30	Moriatt	Hugh	1			1				1					3		
Marblehead	270	31	Hiller	Thomas	2	1		1					1				5		
Marblehead	270	32	Chapman	Jane				1						1			2		

TOWN	PG#	LN#	HEADS OF HOUSEHOLD LAST NAME	FIRST NAME	FREE WHITE MALES under 10	10 to 16	16 to 26	26 to 45	45 and over	FREE WHITE FEMALES under 10	10 to 16	16 to 26	26 to 45	45 and over	TOTAL ALL OTHER	TOTAL SLAVES	TOTALS	DISTRICT/ TOWNSHIP	NOTES
Methuen	152	1	Austin	Isaac	2	1			1	2		2	1				9		
Methuen	152	2	Bodwell	Isaac	2			1		1	1	1	1				7		
Methuen	152	3	Bodwell	Henry Junr				1		3			1				5		
Methuen	152	4	Bixby	Dudley	2	2		1				2	1				8		
Methuen	152	5	Bodwell	Parker	1		1					1					3		
Methuen	152	6	Bodwell	Daniel				1				1		1			3		
Methuen	152	7	Bodwell	Alpheus	2	1		1		1			1				6		
Methuen	152	8	Bodwell	Henry				1		1	1			2			5		
Methuen	152	9	Bodwell	William			2		1			2		1			6		
Methuen	152	10	Bodwell	William Junr	1		1			1		1					4		
Methuen	152	11	Bodwell	Stephen				1					2	1			4		
Methuen	152	12	Bodwell	John L.	1			3		2			1				7		
Methuen	152	13	Bodwell	Daniel Junr	1	1		1		1	1			1			6		
Methuen	152	14	Bodwell	Joseph	1		1	1		1			1				5		
Methuen	152	15	Barker	Stephen	2	1	1		1	2		1	1				9		
Methuen	152	16	Barker	Amos	1		2	1				1	1				6		
Methuen	152	17	Barker	Ebenezer			1	1				1	1				4		
Methuen	152	18	Barker	John				1		2			1				4		
Methuen	152	19	Boynton	David	1			1				1	3				6		
Methuen	152	20	Bolls	Reuben	2		1		1	2		1		1			8		
Methuen	152	21	Brown	Thomas	1		1	1				1					4		
Methuen	152	22	Bolls	Reuben Junr	1		1					1	1				4		
Methuen	152	23	Bartlett	Daniel	1		1	1					2				5		
Methuen	152	24	Baswell	Joshua	2		1					1					4		
Methuen	152	25	Bernard	Theodor			1					1					2		
Methuen	152	26	Blodget	Asa			1						1				2		
Methuen	153	1	Carleton	Ebenezr			3	1	1		1	1	1	1			9		
Methuen	153	2	Carleton	Ebenezr Junr	2	1		1		2	1	1	1				9		
Methuen	153	3	Carleton	Elijah	2	2	1		1		1	2		1			10		
Methuen	153	4	Currier	Stephen	1	1			1		2	1	2				8		
Methuen	153	5	Currier	Asa		2			1		2		2				7		
Methuen	153	6	Currier	Richard	1	1			1	2	1	1	1				8		
Methuen	153	7	Carleton	Daniel		1	1					2		1			5		
Methuen	153	8	Crop	Abijah	3	1		1	1	2	2		1	1			12		
Methuen	153	9	Currier	Daniel			1					1					2		
Methuen	153	10	Chickering	Samuel	3			1		1	2		1				8		
Methuen	153	11	Crop	Daniel		1			1		1	3		1			7		
Methuen	153	12	Clark	Samuel	4				1	1	1	1	1	1			10		
Methuen	153	13	Clark	Joseph	2	1	1					1					5		
Methuen	153	14	Carleton	Samuel	3		1	1		1			1				7		
Methuen	153	15	Davis	John		1	2	1				1		1			6		
Methuen	153	16	Davis	James		2		1				1	1				5		
Methuen	153	17	Davis	Joshua			1			2		1					4		
Methuen	153	18	Davis	William	2			1		3			1				7		
Methuen	153	19	Eaton	Timothy		1	3		1			2		1			8		
Methuen	153	20	Emerson	Timothy	1	1		2		1	1		1	3			10		
Methuen	153	21	Emerson	Oliver		1	2		1	2	1		1				8		
Methuen	153	22	Emerson	Day	2	1		1		3			1				8		
Methuen	153	23	Frye	James		1	2	1	1			1		1	1		8		
Methuen	153	24	Frye	Robertson	1	1		1		1	1		1	1			7		
Methuen	153	25	Frye	Daniel		2		1				1					4		
Methuen	153	26	Farnum	William	1	2	1		1			2	1	1			9		
Methuen	153	27	Flint	Miles			1	1		2		1	1				6		
Methuen	153	28	Gage	Micah	2		1	1		1			1				6		
Methuen	153	29	Gage	John	1	1	1	1		2	2		2	1			11		
Methuen	153	30	Gibbon	Samuel	3			1					1				5		
Methuen	153	31	Griffin	Joseph			3	1	1		1	1		1			8		
Methuen	153	32	Griffin	Joseph Junr	1	1		1			1		1				5		
Methuen	153	33	Griffin	Jonathan	2	1		1					1				5		
Methuen	153	34	Gutterson	William	2				2	2	2	1	1				10		
Methuen	153	35	Gutterson	James	3			1					2				6		
Methuen	153	36	How	Joseph				1		2	1		1	1			6		
Methuen	153	37	How	Joseph Junr	4	1						1					8		
Methuen	153	38	How	Abial			1		1				1	1			4		
Methuen	153	39	How	Abial Junr			1	1		3			1				6		
Methuen	153	40	How	John		1			1				1	1			4		
Methuen	153	41	How	James	1	1	1		1	2			2	1			9		
Methuen	153	42	Hastings	Simeon	1				2				1	1			5		
Methuen	153	43	Haseltine	Mehetable		1	1					1		1			4		
Methuen	153	44	Harris	Ralph	1	1	2	1		2	1	1	1				10		
Methuen	153	45	Herrick	Thomas				1		1			1	1	1		5		
Methuen	153	46	Herrick	George D.	1	1		1					1				4		
Methuen	154	1	Hubbard	Daniel	1				1	2			1	1			6		
Methuen	154	2	Huse	John		1	2	1	1		1	2		4			12		
Methuen	154	3	Huse	Stephen	1	1		1		1			1	1			6		
Methuen	154	4	Hildrith	Samuel	1	1	1		1	1	1	1		1			8		
Methuen	154	5	Huse	Daniel			1				1		1				3		
Methuen	154	6	How	Jacob		1	1		1			2		1			6		
Methuen	154	7	Hastings	Robert			1		1					2			4		

TOWN	PG#	LN#	HEADS OF HOUSEHOLD LAST NAME	FIRST NAME	FREE WHITE MALES under 10	10 to 16	16 to 26	26 to 45	45 and over	FREE WHITE FEMALES under 10	10 to 16	16 to 26	26 to 45	45 and over	TOTAL ALL OTHER	TOTAL SLAVES	TOTALS	DISTRICT/ TOWNSHIP	NOTES
Methuen	154	8	Hall	Elizabeth									1	1			2		
Methuen	154	9	Hibberd	John		1		1		1		1	1	2			7		
Methuen	154	10	Hibberd	William		1			1			3		1			6		
Methuen	154	11	Hibberd	Nathl		1	1		1		2	3		1			9		
Methuen	154	12	Hibberd	Ebenezer		1		1	1	1			1	1			6		
Methuen	154	13	Harris	Samuel	3	1		1	1	3	1	1	1	1			13		
Methuen	154	14	Harris	John			1	2				1	1	1			6		
Methuen	154	15	Heath	Abial	1	1		1		1		1	1				6		
Methuen	154	16	Harris	Heman			1			1	1	1					4		
Methuen	154	17	Hase	Samuel			1	1	1			2		1			6		
Methuen	154	18	Haynes	James	2	2		1		2			1	1			9		
Methuen	154	19	Hall	Jacob	3			1		1	1	1	1				8		
Methuen	154	20	How	Jonathan	1		1		1			1		1			5		
Methuen	154	21	Ingalls	James	1		1	1	1	3			2				9		
Methuen	154	22	Jones	James			1	1		1		2	1	1			7		
Methuen	154	23	Jennings	Solomon				1		4	1		1				7		
Methuen	154	24	Kelley	John		1			1			1		1			4		
Methuen	154	25	Ladd	John		1			1					1			3		
Methuen	154	26	Merrill	Samuel	3	1		1	1			2					8		
Methuen	154	27	Merrill	John			1		1	1		1		1			5		
Methuen	154	28	Messer	Asa		1			1		1	2		1			6		
Methuen	154	29	Messer	Nathl	2			1		1		2					6		
Methuen	154	30	Messer	William	1		1	1		1	1	1					6		
Methuen	154	31	Messer	Phineas			1	1	1	4	1	1		1			10		
Methuen	154	32	Messer	Jacob		1			1		1	1	1	1			6		
Methuen	154	33	Morse	David		1			1		1			1			4		
Methuen	154	34	Messer	Alpheus	2		2	1		1	1	1					8		
Methuen	154	35	Marsten	Peter		4			1	2			1	2			11		
Methuen	154	36	Morse	Asa	3		2	1		3		1	1				11		
Methuen	154	37	Messer	Jacob Jun			1					1					2		
Methuen	154	38	Morse	Paine	2	1	1		1	1	2	2		1			11		
Methuen	154	39	Morse	Amos	4	2		1		2	1		1				11		
Methuen	154	40	Morse	Joseph					1	1	1		1				4		
Methuen	154	41	Morse	Daniel	1				1	3			1				6		
Methuen	154	42	Morse	Samuel	2			1	1		1	1	1	1			8		
Methuen	154	43	Messer	James	2	1		1			2		1				7		
Methuen	154	44	Messer	Cyrus	3		1	1		1			1	1			8		
Methuen	154	45	Merrill	Jonathan	2		1	1		2	1		1	1			9		
Methuen	154	46	McClary	David			2		1				1	1			5		
Methuen	154	47	Morrill	Ezekiel		1						1	1	2			5		
Methuen	155	1	Melone	Kendal	1		1	1		1		1					5		
Methuen	155	2	Melone	James	1			1		1			1				4		
Methuen	155	3	Mansur	Elijah	3			1		1			1				6		
Methuen	155	4	Osgood	Benjamin	2	1	3	1		1	1	1	1	1			12		
Methuen	155	5	Osgood	Joseph	3			1					1				5		
Methuen	155	6	Ordway	James	1		1		2		1	1		1			7		
Methuen	155	7	Pike	Thomas	1			1		1		1					4		
Methuen	155	8	Pettery	Edward			1			1			2				4		
Methuen	155	9	Pearley	Humphrey			1			1			1	1			4		
Methuen	155	10	Poor	Thomas		1	2		1			1		2			7		
Methuen	155	11	Perkins	Elisha		1	1		1			2		1			6		
Methuen	155	12	Pingrey	Job		1			1			1		1			4		
Methuen	155	13	Pingrey	John	2		2	1		1		1	1				8		
Methuen	155	14	Pingrey	Moses				1				1	1				3		
Methuen	155	15	Picker	John	1	1	2		1	1	1	1		1			9		
Methuen	155	16	Pace	Thomas				1						1			2		
Methuen	155	17	Percy	John	1			1		3			1	1			7		
Methuen	155	18	Parker	John			2		1		1	1		1			6		
Methuen	155	19	Parker	Elisha	1	2		1		4	1		1				10		
Methuen	155	20	Parker	Joseph K	4	1		1		1			2				9		
Methuen	155	21	Palmer	Asa			1						1	2			4		
Methuen	155	22	Palmer	John	2	1			1	1	1	1		1			8		
Methuen	155	23	Pettingall	John	1	1		1	1	3	2		1	1			11		
Methuen	155	24	Pettingall	Asa	2	1	1	1		2	1		1				9		
Methuen	155	25	Peabody	Ephraim	1	1		1					1	1			5		
Methuen	155	26	Runnels	William		1	1		1	1		2		1			7		
Methuen	155	27	Russ	William			2		1		1	1		1			6		
Methuen	155	28	Russ	John		1	1					1					4		
Methuen	155	29	Russell	Isaac				1						1			2		
Methuen	155	30	Richardson	John	3	1			1	1	2			3			11		
Methuen	155	31	Richardson	Thomas			3	1		2		1		1			8		
Methuen	155	32	Richardson	Francis	1			1	1			2	1				7		
Methuen	155	33	Richardson	Elisha	1	1		1		2	1	1					7		
Methuen	155	34	Richardson	Samuel	2	1	1		1	2	1			1			10		
Methuen	155	35	Richardson	Edward	3			1	3	2			2	1			12		
Methuen	155	36	Swan	Dorcas	1	1				1	1	1		1			6		
Methuen	155	37	Swan	William	2	2		1		3			2	1			11		
Methuen	155	38	Sargent	James			1	1		1			1	1			5		
Methuen	155	39	Swan	Joshua	1	1				3	1						8		

TOWN	PG#	LN#	LAST NAME	FIRST NAME	FREE WHITE MALES					FREE WHITE FEMALES					TOTAL ALL OTHER	TOTAL SLAVES	TOTALS	DISTRICT/ TOWNSHIP	NOTES
					under 10	10 to 16	16 to 26	26 to 45	45 and over	under 10	10 to 16	16 to 26	26 to 45	45 and over					
Methuen	155	40	Swan	John	1			1	1	3			1	1			8		
Methuen	155	41	Stephens	Noah	1			1		3		2	1	1			9		
Methuen	155	42	Sawyer	Caleb			1	1						2			4		
Methuen	155	43	Smith	Aaron				1					1				2		
Methuen	155	44	Sargent	John	3	1	1		1	1		3		1			11		
Methuen	155	45	Sargent	James Jun	1			3	1			1		1			7		
Methuen	155	46	Sargent	Nathl	3			1					1	1			6		
Methuen	155	47	Sawyer	Benjamin	1			1		3			1	1			7		
Methuen	155	48	Sawyer	Aaron			1	1		3			1				6		
Methuen	156	1	Stephens	Jeremiah	3			2	1	2			2	2			12		
Methuen	156	2	Spafford	Amos	1			1		1			1				4		
Methuen	156	3	Searl	John		1	2	1					3	1			8		
Methuen	156	4	Sargent	Jacob	1			1		1	1		1				5		
Methuen	156	5	Tylor	Jesse	3	1			1	2	1	1		1			10		
Methuen	156	6	Tylor	Jacob	5				1	1	2		1				10		
Methuen	156	7	Tylor	Jacob Junr	2		2	1		1			1				7		
Methuen	156	8	Town	Benjamin		1	3		1		1	1		1			8		
Methuen	156	9	Tippet	John	2	2		1	1	3	1	1	1	1			13		
Methuen	156	10	Whittier	William Junr	1	1		1		3		2	1				9		
Methuen	156	11	Whittier	Nathl	1	2	1	1		2	1		1				9		
Methuen	156	12	Willson	James			1	1	1				1	1			5		
Methuen	156	13	Webber	Benjamin	1	1	2		1	1	1		1	1			9		
Methuen	156	14	Webber	Daniel	3			1		3			2				9		
Methuen	156	15	Willson	John	1	1		1					1				4		
Methuen	156	16	White	Elizabeth	1	1	1	2		3	1	1		1			11		
Methuen	156	17	Whittier	William				1				1		1			3		
Methuen	156	18	Whittier	John		2		1		1	1	2		1			8		
Methuen	156	19	Whittier	William 3d	1	1	1					2					5		
Methuen	156	20	Willson	Benjamin	1			1				1					3		

TOWN	PG#	LN#	HEADS OF HOUSEHOLD		FREE WHITE MALES					FREE WHITE FEMALES					TOTAL ALL OTHER	TOTAL SLAVES	TOTALS	DISTRICT/ TOWNSHIP	NOTES
			LAST NAME	FIRST NAME	under 10	10 to 16	16 to 26	26 to 45	45 and over	under 10	10 to 16	16 to 26	26 to 45	45 and over					
Middleton	15	1	Hutchinson	Joseph		1	1	1		3			1				7		
Middleton	15	2	Hutchinson	Keziah								1		1			2		
Middleton	15	3	Richardson	Stephen	2	2	1		1			1	2				9		
Middleton	15	4	Hutchinson	Josiah	2	1		1		1			1				6		
Middleton	15	5	Richardson	Mary	1	3	1			2		1	1				9		
Middleton	15	6	Richardson	John	1			2		1	1		1				6		
Middleton	15	7	Hoping	John	1			1					1				3		
Middleton	15	8	Kenney	Asa	1		1			1		2					5		
Middleton	15	9	Kenney	Eunice			1							1			2		
Middleton	15	10	Fuller	Betty										1			1		
Middleton	15	11	Fuller	Daniel	2			1				2					5		
Middleton	15	12	Flint	Jeremiah	1	2	3	1		2		1	1	1			12		
Middleton	15	13	Flint	John	1		1		1	2	2	1					9		
Middleton	15	14	Russell	David	1			1		1	1		1				5		
Middleton	15	15	Russell	Joseph	2			1					1				4		
Middleton	15	16	Lemon	Jonathan		1		1	1				2	2			7		
Middleton	15	17	Wilkins	Jonathan			1		1			1	1	2			6		
Middleton	15	18	Thomas	Israel		1							1				3		
Middleton	15	19	Estey	Samuel		1							1				2		
Middleton	15	20	Johnson	Tabitha						1			1	2	1		5		
Middleton	15	21	Wilkins	Benjamin		2			1	1	1		1				6		
Middleton	15	22	Thomas	Rebecca									1				1		
Middleton	16	1	Wilkins	Enos		1			1			1		1			4		
Middleton	16	2	Wilkins	Pelatiah			1			1		1					3		
Middleton	16	3	Berry	Nathaniel	1			1			1	1	1				5		
Middleton	16	4	Berry	Jonathan	2		1				1	1					5		
Middleton	16	5	Fuller	Elijah	1			1					1				3		
Middleton	16	6	Estey	John	1	2	1	1	1	1		2	1				10		
Middleton	16	7	Meriam	Silas		2		1		3			2				8		
Middleton	16	8	Kenney	Archelaus				1		1			1				3		
Middleton	16	9	Fuller	Elisha			1	1				1					3		
Middleton	16	10	Thomas	Richard	3	2		1					1				7		
Middleton	16	11	Wilkins	Solomon			1	1			1		1				4		
Middleton	16	12	Bradstreet	Abigail			1						1				2		
Middleton	16	13	Adams	Solomon Revd	1		1			2		1	1				6		
Middleton	16	14	Fuller	Andrew				1				1	1				3		
Middleton	16	15	Fuller	John		2		1			1		1				5		
Middleton	16	16	Lamon	Lydia							1		1				2		
Middleton	16	17	Stiles	John	1			1		1			1				4		
Middleton	16	18	Giddings	Zacheus			1			4	3	1	1				10		
Middleton	16	19	Elliot	Rachel									2				2		
Middleton	16	20	Perkins	Timothy				1			1		1				3		
Middleton	16	21	Johnson	John	3			1		2	1		1				8		
Middleton	16	22	Fuller	Sarah		1	1						2	1			5		
Middleton	16	23	Putman	Joseph	1	1		1					1				4		
Middleton	16	24	Fuller	Jerusha								1	1				2		
Middleton	16	25	Fuller	David	1			1					1				3		
Middleton	16	26	Thomas	William				1						1			2		
Middleton	16	27	Gray	William	3			1					1				5		
Middleton	16	28	Knight	Joseph			2	1						1			4		
Middleton	16	29	Peabody	Benjamin			1	1	1	1	1		1	1			7		
Middleton	16	30	Wright	Joseph				1		2		1					4		
Middleton	16	31	Hobbs	Elizabeth									1				1		
Middleton	16	32	Peabody	Francis	1	1	1	1	1	2	1	1	1				10		
Middleton	16	33	Fuller	David 2nd	2	2		1		2	1		2				10		
Middleton	16	34	Peabody	Joseph 2nd				1			3		1				5		
Middleton	16	35	Averell	Mark	1		1		2					2			6		
Middleton	16	36	Averell	Joseph	1	1	3	1		1	1		1				10		
Middleton	16	37	Wilkins	Elias		1	2	1		2		1					7		
Middleton	16	38	Symonds	Joseph	1		1	1		4		1	1				9		
Middleton	16	39	Peabody	Andrew		1			1			1		2			5		
Middleton	16	40	Peabody	David		2	1	1		3		2	1				10		
Middleton	16	41	Peabody	Joseph		1			1				1				3		
Middleton	16	42	Peabody	Nathaniel	1			1		3		1					6		
Middleton	17	1	Small	Samuel			1	1		1	1		1				5		
Middleton	17	2	Wilkins	Nehemiah	1	1			1		1	3		1			8		
Middleton	17	3	Eliott	Stephen			1						1				2		
Middleton	17	4	Elliot	Roger	1			1		2			1				5		
Middleton	17	5	Nichols	Jerusha									2				2		
Middleton	17	6	Gage	Abraham	2			1			1	1					5		
Middleton	17	7	Nichols	Joseph				1					3	1			5		
Middleton	17	8	Elliot	Ruth		1				1	1		1	1			5		
Middleton	17	9	Elliot	Andrew	1			1					1				3		
Middleton	17	10	Nichols	Stephen	1			1	1	1		2					6		
Middleton	17	11	Berry	Samuel				1				1		1			3		
Middleton	17	12	Elliot	Asa		1			1			1	1	1			5		
Middleton	17	13	Elliot	John			1					1	1				3		
Middleton	17	14	Wilkins	Jonathan		1			1			1	1				4		
Middleton	17	15	Rea	Jonathan Frye			1					1					2		

97

TOWN	PG#	LN#	LAST NAME	FIRST NAME	FREE WHITE MALES under 10	10 to 16	16 to 26	26 to 45	45 and over	FREE WHITE FEMALES under 10	10 to 16	16 to 26	26 to 45	45 and over	TOTAL ALL OTHER	TOTAL SLAVES	TOTALS	DISTRICT/ TOWNSHIP	NOTES
Middleton	17	16	Wilkins	Icabod					1				1	1			3		
Middleton	17	17	Wilkins	Samuel		1	1		1	1	2	1	1				8		
Middleton	17	18	How	Asa	2	1	1	1		1	1	1	1				9		
Middleton	17	19	How	Eunice									1				1		
Middleton	17	20	Kimball	Moses	3			1		1	1		1				7		
Middleton	17	21	Curtis	Hannah						2			1				3		
Middleton	17	22	Bancroft	Abigail								1	1				2		
Middleton	17	23	Ingals	Theodor	2	2		1					1				6		
Middleton	17	24	Berry	Nehemiah	1			1		2	2		1				7		
Middleton	17	25	Giddings	Isaac				1					1				2		
Middleton	17	26	Perkins	Oliver Junr	2			1				1					4		
Middleton	17	27	Fuller	Simeon	2		1	1		2			1				7		
Middleton	17	28	Upton	Jeremiah	1			1		1	1		1	1			7		
Middleton	17	29	Peabody	Joseph 3rd		1	1	1				1					4		
Middleton	17	30	Stiles	Mary		1						1		1			3		
Middleton	17	31	Stiles	Daniel		2		1					1	2			6		
Middleton	17	32	Stiles	Meriam	2	2	1				1		1	1			8		
Middleton	17	33	Berry	Bartholomew		1		1				1		1			4		
Middleton	17	34	Berry	Andrew	3			1		1			1				6		
Middleton	17	35	Cave	Amos	2		1	1		1		1	1		1		8		
Middleton	17	36	Cave	Silvester			1										1		
Middleton	17	37	Gould	Solomon				1						1			2		
Middleton	17	38	Gould	Nathaniel	1	1		1		1			1				5		
Middleton	17	39	Wilkins	Elijah	2	1		1		4			1				9		
Middleton	17	40	Perkins	Andrew	1			1		2	1			1			6		
Middleton	17	41	Perkins	Oliver Junr		1	1	1				2	1	1			7		
Middleton	17	42	Felton	Amos	2		1	1		2	1		1				8		
Middleton	18	1	Whitford	William	1		1	1					1				4		
Middleton	18	2	Giddings	Isaac Junr	1	1		1		4			1	1			9		
Middleton	18	3	Watts	Mary										1			1		
Middleton	18	4	Peabody	Amos	3	1		1		2			1	1			9		
Middleton	18	5	Whittemore	Edmund				1									1		
Middleton	18	6	Nichols	John		1	1	1					1	1			5		
Middleton	18	7	Peabody	Frances Jun		1		1		4			1				7		
Middleton	18	8	Kenney	Asa		1		1					1	1			4		
Middleton	18	9	Kenney	Simeon			1		1		1	1		1			5		
Middleton	18	10	Gould	Andrew			1			1		1					3		
Middleton	18	11	Frances	Frank											6		6		
Middleton	18	12	Frances	Snow											3		3		
Middleton	18	13	Frances	Charles											5		5		

TOWN	PG#	LN#	LAST NAME	FIRST NAME	FREE WHITE MALES under 10	10 to 16	16 to 26	26 to 45	45 and over	FREE WHITE FEMALES under 10	10 to 16	16 to 26	26 to 45	45 and over	TOTAL ALL OTHER	TOTAL SLAVES	TOTALS	DISTRICT/ TOWNSHIP	NOTES
Newbury	105	1	Smith	Thomas	1		1			1	1	1	1				6		
Newbury	105	2	Thurston	Stephen		1	1	1		3		3					9		
Newbury	105	3	Colman	Benjamin			2		1	1			1	1			6		
Newbury	105	4	Parish	Elijah				1	1	1			1		1		5		
Newbury	105	5	Martin	James					1			1		1			3		
Newbury	105	6	Colman	Moses		2	1	2	1			1	1	1	1		10		
Newbury	105	7	Parson	Obadiah				1		1			1				3		
Newbury	105	8	Pike	Thomas			1	1		1			2				5		
Newbury	105	9	Colman	William	2	1	2	2		3	1		1				12		
Newbury	105	10	Dummer	Shuball		1		1	1			1	2	1			7		
Newbury	105	11	Dummer	William		1	2						2	1			6		
Newbury	105	12	Dummer	Richard					1					1			2		
Newbury	105	13	Dummer	Richard			1			2			1				4		
Newbury	105	14	Derby	Jacob	2	2	1			1	2		1				9		
Newbury	105	15	Noyce	Lemuel	1	1	1		2	1		1	2	1			10		
Newbury	105	16	Martin	Jonathan			1			2		1	1				5		
Newbury	105	17	Dole	Moses			1	1		1	1		1				5		
Newbury	105	18	Northern	Samuel	1	4	4	2		1		1	1	1			15		
Newbury	105	19	Hale	Joseph	1		3	1	1	1		1	1	1			10		
Newbury	105	20	Adams	Moses	2		1			2			1				6		
Newbury	105	21	Plumer	Nathaniel	1				1	1	1		1	2			7		
Newbury	105	22	Boynton	Enoch		1		1					1				3		
Newbury	105	23	Adams	Simeon				1		1			1				3		
Newbury	106	1	Adams	George	1			1		2			1				5		
Newbury	106	2	Adams	John		1	3		1	1			1	1			8		
Newbury	106	3	Noyce	John				2				2					4		
Newbury	106	4	Woodman	Jewel		1		1		1			2	1			6		
Newbury	106	5	Goodridge	Edward		1		1		1	1	1	1				6		
Newbury	106	6	Rogers	John	4	1		1		2		2	1				11		
Newbury	106	7	Burbank	Mary							1	1		1			3		
Newbury	106	8	Flood	Enoch					1					1			2		
Newbury	106	9	Tictman	Simeon	3	1		1		1	1	1	1	1			10		
Newbury	106	10	Tictman	Caleb	1	1		1		4	2		1				10		
Newbury	106	11	Longfellow	John	2			1		1		1	1	1			7		
Newbury	106	12	Adams	Stephen	2	2		2	1	2	1	1	1	1			13		
Newbury	106	13	Longfellow	Nathan	1		2	1		1			1	1			7		
Newbury	106	14	Anderson	James	2	1		2	1	3	1	1					11		
Newbury	106	15	Moody	Paul	2		4		1			2	1				10		
Newbury	106	16	Henshinfield	John			1							1			2		
Newbury	106	17	Lewis	John	1			1		1		1	1				5		
Newbury	106	18	Dennit	Mary	1						1		1				3		
Newbury	106	19	Woodman	William			1	1		1	1		1				5		
Newbury	106	20	Woodman	Abner	1	1	1	1						1			5		
Newbury	106	21	Person	Ebenezer	1		1	1		1			1	1			6		
Newbury	106	22	Person	David				1						1			2		
Newbury	106	23	Person	Benjamin	2	1	1		1	1	2	2	1	1			12		
Newbury	106	24	Person	Joseph	1			1					1				3		
Newbury	106	25	Thurlow	Simeon			1		1				2	1			5		
Newbury	106	26	Dummer	Samuel	1			1		1			2	1			7		
Newbury	106	27	Lunt	Stephen	1		1		1				1	1			5		
Newbury	106	28	Flood	Joseph			2		1	2			1				6		
Newbury	106	29	Goodridge	Oliver	1			1		1			1				4		
Newbury	106	30	Cheney	John			1	2	1			2	2	1			9		
Newbury	106	31	Person	Jeremiah		1	2		1				1	2			7		
Newbury	106	32	Jaquish	Parker			1		1				1	2			5		
Newbury	106	33	Noyce	Follensbee	3	1			1	2		1					8		
Newbury	106	34	Richardson	Joseph	2			1			1	1		1			6		
Newbury	106	35	Jaquish	Moses	1	1			1					4			7		
Newbury	106	36	Ames	Sarah								2		1			3		
Newbury	106	37	Noyce	Ephraim	2	1			1	1		1					6		
Newbury	106	38	Dole	Stephen			2		1		1			1			5		
Newbury	106	39	Follensbee	Jeremiah		1		1		1	2	1	1				7		
Newbury	106	40	Bayley	Samuel					1			1		3			5		
Newbury	106	41	Bayley	Ezekiel					2		1		4				7		
Newbury	106	42	Bayley	Ephraim			1			1	2		1				5		
Newbury	106	43	Noyce	Enoch		1	2		1	2			1				7		
Newbury	106	44	Bayley	Samuel	2			1		2							6		
Newbury	106	45	Bayley	Asa		1	1		2			2	1				7		
Newbury	106	46	Follensbee	John		1	2		1	1	1	1	1				8		
Newbury	106	47	Noyce	Joseph	1				1				1				3		
Newbury	106	48	Carleton	Amos			2	1			1	1					5		
Newbury	106	49	Noyce	John		1		1		2	2		1				7		
Newbury	107	1	Chase	Moses			1						1				2		
Newbury	107	2	Jacquish	Samuel	1		1		1	3		2	1	1			10		
Newbury	107	3	Chase	Somesby	2	1	1	1		1	2	1	1				10		
Newbury	107	4	George	James	1	1		1		2			1	1			7		
Newbury	107	5	Newal	Joseph	1		2	2		1	1	2	1				11		
Newbury	107	6	Pilsbury	Silas			1			1		1					3		
Newbury	107	7	Hill	Josiah	3	1	5	3		1			3				16		
Newbury	107	8	Chase	Trustham	1		2	1					1				5		
Newbury	107	9	Bayley	John		1	2	1			1		1				6		
Newbury	107	10	Osgood	John		4	3		1	1		2	1				12		
Newbury	107	11	Noyce	William		1				1		2	1				5		
Newbury	107	12	Woodman	Edward		1		1	3			2	1	1			9		
Newbury	107	13	Chase	Joseph	1	1		1		2	2		1				8		
Newbury	107	14	Chase	Parker	1		1		1				1				4		
Newbury	107	15	Chase	Moses			1	1		2			1				5		
Newbury	107	16	Davies	Stephen			1	1		2			1				4		
Newbury	107	17	Chase	John				1		1			1				3		
Newbury	107	18	Carr	John			1					1					2		

TOWN	PG#	LN#	HEADS OF HOUSEHOLD		FREE WHITE MALES					FREE WHITE FEMALES					TOTAL ALL OTHER	TOTAL SLAVES	TOTALS	DISTRICT/ TOWNSHIP	NOTES
			LAST NAME	FIRST NAME	under 10	10 to 16	16 to 26	26 to 45	45 and over	under 10	10 to 16	16 to 26	26 to 45	45 and over					
Newbury	107	19	Hills	Eliphalet		1			1			1		1			4		
Newbury	107	20	Hills	William			1	1						1			3		
Newbury	107	21	Noyce	Stephen			1	1			1	1		1			5		
Newbury	107	22	Pilsbury	Moses				1		1		2					4		
Newbury	107	23	Pilsbury	William			1						1				2		
Newbury	107	24	Woods	Lenord Revd	1		1					2	1				5		
Newbury	107	25	Noyce	Moses			1			1			1	1			4		
Newbury	107	26	Poor	Daniel	1			1		1	1		1				5		
Newbury	107	27	Hill	Thomas				1				1	1				3		
Newbury	107	28	Sawyer	Enoch		1		1			1	2					5		
Newbury	107	29	Noyce	Thomas			1	1		1				1			4		
Newbury	107	30	Carr	Daniel	1		1	1				1	2	1			7		
Newbury	107	31	Brewster	John		2						2					4		
Newbury	107	32	Bayley	Joshua				2						1			3		
Newbury	107	33	Bayley	Moses	1		1					1	1				4		
Newbury	107	34	Bayley	Esther		1							1	1			3		
Newbury	107	35	Baley	Daniel	1		1	1		3	2	1	1				10		
Newbury	107	36	Bayley	Anna									1	1			2		
Newbury	107	37	Chase	Caleb			1						1				2		
Newbury	107	38	Bayley	Stephen	1	1		1		2		2	1				8		
Newbury	107	39	North	Edmond		1		1				3	1	1			7		
Newbury	107	40	Woodman	Mark		2	1	1		1	1	2	1				9		
Newbury	107	41	Chase	David		1	1			1		1	1				5		
Newbury	107	42	Morse	Daniel	3	3	1	1		1	1	1	1				12		
Newbury	107	43	Pilsbury	Chase				1		1			1				3		
Newbury	107	44	Chase	Joseph		1	1			1			1				4		
Newbury	107	45	Sawyer	Joseph	1			1		2	2	1					7		
Newbury	107	46	Chase	Jonathan	1	1		1		1			1				5		
Newbury	107	47	Chase	David				1									1		
Newbury	107	48	Bayley	Paul	1	2		1		1			1				6		
Newbury	108	1	Bartlett	Enos		1	1	1		1			1				5		
Newbury	108	2	Carr	Samuel	2		1	1		1		1					6		
Newbury	108	3	Carr	John	1		1	1		2		1					6		
Newbury	108	4	Kelly	Nathan	1		1						1				3		
Newbury	108	5	Brown	Elizabeth							1	3		1			5		
Newbury	108	6	Carr	samuel			1	1		1		1	1	1			6		
Newbury	108	7	Carr	Josiah			1	1					1				3		
Newbury	108	8	Bartlett	Jonas		1							1	1			3		
Newbury	108	9	Haskell	Alexander				1					1				2		
Newbury	108	10	Quimby	Phillip		1	1			1			1				4		
Newbury	108	11	Stonewood	Peter	1			1		2			1				5		
Newbury	108	12	Knight	Joseph		1							1				2		
Newbury	108	13	Brown	Joshua		1	1	1					1				5		
Newbury	108	14	Sawyer	Mary						1			2				3		
Newbury	108	15	Brickett	John		1				3			1				5		
Newbury	108	16	Morse	Moses		1	1						1				3		
Newbury	108	17	Dyke	William		1							1				2		
Newbury	108	18	Foster	Mary						1		1	2	2			6		
Newbury	108	19	Moody	Samuel	1	1	2	1		3			1				9		
Newbury	108	20	Stanwood	Joseph	2		4		3	4	1	3	1	1			19		
Newbury	108	21	Bayley	Edward	1	1		1	1	2		1		1			8		
Newbury	108	22	Hooper	Stephen		1	2	1	1		1		1	2			9		
Newbury	108	23	Tomb	Samuel		1	1			3	1		1				8		
Newbury	108	24	Hale	Nathaniel				1									1		
Newbury	108	25	Emery	Moody	2	1		1					1				5		
Newbury	108	26	Moody	Moses	1			1		1	1	1	1	1			7		
Newbury	108	27	Greenleaf	Nathaniel		2	3						1				6		
Newbury	108	28	Ordway	Eliphalet	1	1	1					1	2				6		
Newbury	108	29	House	Thomas	1			1		1			1		2		6		
Newbury	108	30	Emery	Nathaniel		2	1						1				4		
Newbury	108	31	Cheney	John			1			2			1				4		
Newbury	108	32	Emerson	Abel	1			1				2	1				5		
Newbury	108	33	Greenleaf	Abner	2	1	6	1	1	2	2		1	1			17		
Newbury	108	34	Brown	Joseph			1	1				1			1		4		
Newbury	108	35	Emerey	Stephen	1	1		1		1		1	1				6		
Newbury	108	36	Chase	John				1					2	1			4		
Newbury	108	37	Kimball	Caleb		1		1				2		1			5		
Newbury	108	38	Kimball	John	2		1					1					4		
Newbury	108	39	Kimball	Thomas	2		1			1		1					5		
Newbury	108	40	Williams	Thomas						1	1	3	2				8		
Newbury	108	41	Emerey	Samuel	1		1	1	1			2	1				7		
Newbury	108	42	Quimby	Moses	1		1			2			1				5		
Newbury	108	43	Chase	Nathan	1		1						1				3		
Newbury	108	44	Chase	Nathan		1	1			3			1				6		
Newbury	108	45	Cooper	Simeon	1			1					1				3		
Newbury	108	46	Cooper	Moses		1		1					2		1		5		
Newbury	108	47	Chismore	David			2	1					2	1			6		
Newbury	108	48	Cohies	Thomas	3	2		1		3	2		2				13		
Newbury	108	49	Morse	David		1		1		1		1		1			5		
Newbury	109	1	Brown	Anna				1			1	2	1	1			6		
Newbury	109	2	Chase	Samuel	1	1	1	1		2		1	1				9		
Newbury	109	3	Chase	Amos	3	2	1						1				7		
Newbury	109	4	Emery	Nathaniel		2		1			1	2	2				8		
Newbury	109	5	Quimby	Henry		1		1		1							3		
Newbury	109	6	Morse	Humphrey		2		1				2		1			6		
Newbury	109	7	Sawyer	Hannah	2					1	1		1				5		
Newbury	109	8	Ordway	Peter		1	1				1		1				4		
Newbury	109	9	Ordway	Benjamin	1	2	1	1						3			8		
Newbury	109	10	Ordway	James			1			1		1					3		
Newbury	109	11	Jackman	John			1			1				2			4		

100

TOWN	PG#	LN#	LAST NAME	FIRST NAME	FWM under 10	FWM 10 to 16	FWM 16 to 26	FWM 26 to 45	FWM 45 and over	FWF under 10	FWF 10 to 16	FWF 16 to 26	FWF 26 to 45	FWF 45 and over	TOTAL ALL OTHER	TOTAL SLAVES	TOTALS	DISTRICT/TOWNSHIP	NOTES
Newbury	109	12	Hatch	John			1						1				2		
Newbury	109	13	Whitmore	Daniel		1		1					3	1			6		
Newbury	109	14	Person	David		2		1		2	1		1				7		
Newbury	109	15	Jackman	Matthias	2		1			2		1					6		
Newbury	109	16	Wise	David	1		1		1	2		1		1			7		
Newbury	109	17	Jackman	Elias	2	1		1		2		1	1				8		
Newbury	109	18	Jackman	Stephen	1	1			1			1	1	1			6		
Newbury	109	19	Davis	Ebenezer				1				2		1			4		
Newbury	109	20	Morse	John	2		1		1	2			1	1			8		
Newbury	109	21	Jackman	David			4	1					3	1			9		
Newbury	109	22	Currier	John		1		1									2		
Newbury	109	23	Chase	Aquilla	4	2		1		2	2		1				12		
Newbury	109	24	Molton	John	2			1		2			1				6		
Newbury	109	25	Bartlett	Nehemiah	2			1		2			1	1			7		
Newbury	109	26	Bartlett	Moses		1		1	1	1			1				5		
Newbury	109	27	Bartlett	Humphrey	2	1		1		1			1				6		
Newbury	109	28	Bartlett	Jacob			1				1			1			3		
Newbury	109	29	Bartlett	Joseph			1			3			1				5		
Newbury	109	30	Jackman	Richard	1		1	1		2		1	1				7		
Newbury	109	31	Moses	Jonathan	1				1					1			3		
Newbury	109	32	Rogers	Peter		2	1	1		2	1	1					8		
Newbury	109	33	Knight	John	1		1			4			1	1			8		
Newbury	109	34	Spillar	Josiah	3	1				1		1		1			7		
Newbury	109	35	Currier	Isaac		1	2		1	1	3		1				9		
Newbury	109	36	Sawyer	Joseph			1			1		1	1	1			5		
Newbury	109	37	Woodman	Merriam									1	1			2		
Newbury	109	38	Merril	Henry	1	1	2		2	2	1		1				10		
Newbury	109	39	Morril	Enoch	1	2	1	1		2		3	1	1			12		
Newbury	109	40	Tappan	Enoch	2		1	1		2	1		1	1			9		
Newbury	109	41	Tappan	Stephen	2	1	2		1	2	1		1				10		
Newbury	109	42	Harris	John		1	1	1		2			1	1			7		
Newbury	109	43	Tyng	Dudley	2	1		1		2			1	2			9		
Newbury	109	44	Atkinson	Matthias		1			1				2	1			5		
Newbury	109	45	Lovering	Richard		1	2	1		1	1	1					7		
Newbury	110	1	Dodge	Robert		3	1			1			2				7		
Newbury	110	2	Cammel	Alexander	2	1		1		4			1				9		
Newbury	110	3	Rogers	Samuel	1		4	1		1			1				8		
Newbury	110	4	Conner	Gideon	1		1	1					3	1			7		
Newbury	110	5	Little	Jacob	3	1		2		2	1	1	1				11		
Newbury	110	6	Merril	Olander	3	1		1				1	1				7		
Newbury	110	7	Atkinson	Amos	1	4	4		1	1			1	1			13		
Newbury	110	8	Atkinson	Moses	1		1		1				2				5		
Newbury	110	9	How	Varnum	1	1	2	7		2			1	2			16		
Newbury	110	10	Hale	Thomas	3	3	4	1			1		1				13		
Newbury	110	11	Ordway	Joseph			1			1			1				3		
Newbury	110	12	Ridgeway	Joseph	4		3	1					1	1			10		
Newbury	110	13	Gorden	Timothy	3	2		1			1		1				8		
Newbury	110	14	Atkinson	Theodore	1	1	1			1			1				5		
Newbury	110	15	Reed	Phillip	2		1			2			1				6		
Newbury	110	16	Fuller	Nathan	1			1		2		1	1				6		
Newbury	110	17	Sawyer	Elijah		1		1					2				4		
Newbury	110	18	Sawyer	Hannah		1							1	1			3		
Newbury	110	19	Whitemore	Ebenezer	2			1		2			1				6		
Newbury	110	20	Emery	Thomas	2	1	1						1				6		
Newbury	110	21	Sawyer	Enoch	2	1	1	1		2	1		3				11		
Newbury	110	22	Lunt	Sarah			1						2	1			4		
Newbury	110	23	Coffin	Lemuel	2			1		1	1		1				6		
Newbury	110	24	Tucker	Jacob		1	1						1	1			4		
Newbury	110	25	Merril	Abel		1			1					1			3		
Newbury	110	26	Dial	Charles			1			3			1				5		
Newbury	110	27	Calwell	David	2		1	1		2	1		1				8		
Newbury	110	28	Merril	Nathan			2				1	2		1			6		
Newbury	110	29	Currier	John	1			1		1			1				4		
Newbury	110	30	Coffin	Tristam					1				3	1			5		
Newbury	110	31	Coffin	John	1	1	1						1				4		
Newbury	110	32	Greenleaf	Samuel	2			1		1			1				5		
Newbury	110	33	Coffin	Amos	3		1	1		1				1			7		
Newbury	110	34	Coffin	Stephen		1		1					1				3		
Newbury	110	35	Atkinson	John	1	1	1		1			1	2	1			8		
Newbury	110	36	Sawyer	Elijah	1		1						1				3		
Newbury	110	37	Flanders	Daniel	2			1		3	1		1	1			9		
Newbury	110	38	Merril	Joseph	1		1			1			1				4		
Newbury	110	39	Atkinson	Ichobed					1		1	1					3		
Newbury	110	40	Merril	Jacob	2			1			1	1		1			6		
Newbury	110	41	Norton	John		1		1						1			3		
Newbury	110	42	Williams	Eliphalet			1			3			1				5		
Newbury	110	43	Little	Stephen	2		3	1		1		1	1				9		
Newbury	111	1	Carr	Richard	1				1	1	1						4		
Newbury	111	2	Pilsbury	David				1									1		
Newbury	111	3	Pirce	John	1	1		1			1		1				5		
Newbury	111	4	Pilsbury	Timo	2	1						1	1	1	1		7		
Newbury	111	5	Coffin	Jacob	1	1	1	1		2	1		1				8		
Newbury	111	6	Warner	Lucy	1	1		1			1		1				5		
Newbury	111	7	Somerbe	Nathan	1		1	1		1	1		1	1			7		
Newbury	111	8	Dean	Oliver			1			1		1					3		
Newbury	111	9	Whitmore	Amos		1		1			1	2	1				6		
Newbury	111	10	Person	John				1				1		1			3		
Newbury	111	11	Wise	Jonathan		1							1				3		
Newbury	111	12	Merril	Nathan	1		1	1					1				4		
Newbury	111	13	Merril	Jonathan	1			1					1				3		

TOWN	PG#	LN#	LAST NAME	FIRST NAME	FWM under 10	FWM 10 to 16	FWM 16 to 26	FWM 26 to 45	FWM 45 and over	FWF under 10	FWF 10 to 16	FWF 16 to 26	FWF 26 to 45	FWF 45 and over	TOTAL ALL OTHER	TOTAL SLAVES	TOTALS	DISTRICT/TOWNSHIP	NOTES
Newbury	111	14	Magridge	John					1	2	2	1					6		
Newbury	111	15	Coffin	Abel		1						1	3	1			6		
Newbury	111	16	Remmix	Samuel		1	1	1		4	1		1				9		
Newbury	111	17	Moody	Moses				1				1	1	1			4		
Newbury	111	18	Huse	Samuel	1			1		2	1		1				6		
Newbury	111	19	Harvey	Thomas				1					1				2		
Newbury	111	20	Moody	Cutting		1	2	1					3	1			8		
Newbury	111	21	Downing	John		1		1		1		1	1	1			5		
Newbury	111	22	Stickney	David	1		1			1			1				5		
Newbury	111	23	How	Benjamin	1		1	1			1	1	1				6		
Newbury	111	24	Moody	Enoch		1		1		1		1	1				5		
Newbury	111	25	Printice	Stanton	2	2			1		1			1			7		
Newbury	111	26	Pilsbury	Samuel				1									1		
Newbury	111	27	Adkins	Sarah			1	1		3		1		1			7		
Newbury	111	28	Atkinson	Theodore	1	1	1			1			1				5		
Newbury	111	29	Greenleaf	Ebenezer	1	1	1			1		1	1				6		
Newbury	111	30	Corey	Michael	1	1		1		3	1		1				8		
Newbury	111	31	Francis	Hannah	1					1	1		1				4		
Newbury	111	32	Stocker	Ebenezer		1	2	1		2	2		3	1			12		
Newbury	111	33	Wheelwright	Ebenezer	2	1		1		4	1		2				11		
Newbury	111	34	Dodge	William				1					1				2		
Newbury	111	35	Sawyer	George											2		2		
Newbury	111	36	Haskell	Solomon	1	2		1		3		1	2				10		
Newbury	111	37	Pike	Richard			2			1		1	1				5		
Newbury	111	38	Obrian	John	2	1	1		1	1		3	2				11		
Newbury	111	39	Tappan	Samuel	1			1		1	1		1				5		
Newbury	111	40	Combs	Phillip	1		2			1		2	1	1			8		
Newbury	111	41	Hunt	Elias	3	1			1	1	2		1	1			10		
Newbury	111	42	Coffin	Abigal	2			1					1				4		
Newbury	111	43	Johnson	John	2			1		1		1	1				6		
Newbury	111	44	Kilburn	Thomas	2			1					1				4		
Newbury	111	45	Coffin	Charles	1	1	1		1			1	2				7		
Newbury	111	46	Lunt	Benja	1			1		1	1		1				5		
Newbury	111	47	Lunt	Woodbridge	2			1		1		1					5		
Newbury	111	48	Adams	Henry	1	1		1					1				4		
Newbury	111	49	Hawks	John		1		1			1		1				4		
Newbury	112	1	Gould	Silas	1			1	1	2			1	2			9		
Newbury	112	2	Greenfield	Nathll				1					1				2		
Newbury	112	3	Hale	Moses	1		1			1	1	1					5		
Newbury	112	4	Howard	Nathan	1	1		1		3	1		1				8		
Newbury	112	5	Perkins	Jacob				1					1				2		
Newbury	112	6	Garrish	Enoch		1		1				3	2				7		
Newbury	112	7	Garrish	Mayhue	2		1			1		1					5		
Newbury	112	8	Brown	Parson	1			1				3	2				7		
Newbury	112	9	Garrish	Paul				1					1				2		
Newbury	112	10	Garrish	William			1	1					1				3		
Newbury	112	11	Somerbe	Henry	1			1		1	1			1			6		
Newbury	112	12	Knight	Joseph			1			1			1				3		
Newbury	112	13	Lunt	Lydia						1			1				2		
Newbury	112	14	Chapman	William				1					1				2		
Newbury	112	15	Pirce	Henry	2	1		1		1		1					6		
Newbury	112	16	Stocker	Samuel	2			1					1				4		
Newbury	112	17	Thurlow	Joseph	3		2	1		1		2	1				10		
Newbury	112	18	Thurlow	Lydia	1	1		1		1	1	1	1				8		
Newbury	112	19	Wise	William	1		1			1		1		1			5		
Newbury	112	20	Lunt	Enoch	1	1			1	3		1	1				8		
Newbury	112	21	Lunt	Tristam			1						1				2		
Newbury	112	22	Pettengill	David			2		1	3		2	2				10		
Newbury	112	23	Pettengill	Benjn	1		2	1		3	1	2	1				11		
Newbury	112	24	Safford	John			1	1					1				3		
Newbury	112	25	Stickney	Rebecca								1	2				3		
Newbury	112	26	Woodwell	John	1	3		1		1			4				10		
Newbury	112	27	Woodwell	Gideon	1		1		1	1	2	2	1	1			10		
Newbury	112	28	Adams	Smith	1			1		2			1	1			6		
Newbury	112	29	Price	Elizabeth		2							1				3		
Newbury	112	30	Knight	Thomas	2			1		2	1		1				7		
Newbury	112	31	Obbin	Joseph	1		1	1					1	1			5		
Newbury	112	32	Knight	Unice										1			1		
Newbury	112	33	Aisworth	Moses				1		2			2	1			6		
Newbury	112	34	Knight	Barzuliel				1					1				2		
Newbury	112	35	Wells	Daniel			1						1				2		
Newbury	112	36	Dole	John	1		2			2	1	2		1			9		
Newbury	112	37	Hidden	Anny		1						1		1			3		
Newbury	112	38	Hidden	Icabod	1		1						1				3		
Newbury	112	39	Marshal	Isaac			1		1				1				3		
Newbury	112	40	Addams	Jacub				1					1				2		
Newbury	112	41	Allen	Jacub	2			1				1					4		
Newbury	112	42	Lunt	Samuel	1			1		2			1	1			6		
Newbury	112	43	Hale	Enoch	4	1		1		1	2		1	1			11		
Newbury	112	44	Blanchard	Jeremiah	1			1		3	2		1				8		
Newbury	112	45	Finney	George	2			1		2			1				6		
Newbury	112	46	Greenlieff	Thomas			1	1	1					1			4		
Newbury	112	47	Lunt	Ambrose	2		1			1		2					6		
Newbury	113	1	Berry	Joseph	3			1		2			1				7		
Newbury	113	2	Hunt	Bart	2		1						1				4		
Newbury	113	3	Phurlo	Paul		1		1		4		1	1				8		
Newbury	113	4	Hunt	Nathl	2		1			1	1	1					6		
Newbury	113	5	Stickney	Hannah							1	1	1				3		
Newbury	113	6	Brocking	Samuel	1		1						1				3		
Newbury	113	7	Phurlo	John	1			1		1			1				4		

TOWN	PG#	LN#	LAST NAME	FIRST NAME	M under 10	M 10 to 16	M 16 to 26	M 26 to 45	M 45 and over	F under 10	F 10 to 16	F 16 to 26	F 26 to 45	F 45 and over	TOTAL ALL OTHER	TOTAL SLAVES	TOTALS	DISTRICT/ TOWNSHIP	NOTES
Newbury	113	8	Pettingall	Anny			1			1		1		1			4		
Newbury	113	9	Robinson	Isaac	3			1					1				5		
Newbury	113	10	Deepwall	John	2			1					1				4		
Newbury	113	11	Colby	Joseph	1			1		1		1		1			5		
Newbury	113	12	Pappen	Anny									1				1		
Newbury	113	13	Smith	John	3	1		1		1			1	1			8		
Newbury	113	14	Roges	Budley	1		1					1			1		4		
Newbury	113	15	Slarter	Thomas				1				1					2		
Newbury	113	16	Lane	Humphrey	1		1			1		1					4		
Newbury	113	17	Elwall	Samuel				1					1				2		
Newbury	113	18	Lunt	Elijah	1	1				1	1		1				5		
Newbury	113	19	Pettingall	Thomas	2	1		1				1					5		
Newbury	113	20	Perkins	Joseph	2	1	1					1					5		
Newbury	113	21	Lunt	Thomas	1			1		1		1	1				5		
Newbury	113	22	Colbey	Joseph		1		1		4	1		1				8		
Newbury	113	23	Harker	Mary	1	1							1	1			4		
Newbury	113	24	Jester	Anny						1			1				2		
Newbury	113	25	Stanwood	William	3		1			1		1					6		
Newbury	113	26	Stodder	Daniel				1				1		1			3		
Newbury	113	27	Pappon	Moses	1			1		3	1		1				7		
Newbury	113	28	Hoyt	Samuel			1	1		1			1				4		
Newbury	113	29	Ramsey	William	1			1		4			2				8		
Newbury	113	30	Atkinson	Richard	1		1			1			1				4		
Newbury	113	31	Mitchel	Stephen				1					1				2		
Newbury	113	32	Downs	Solomon				1			2		1				4		
Newbury	113	33	Callwall	John				1			1		1				3		
Newbury	113	34	Smith	Joanna	1		1						1				3		
Newbury	113	35	Colbey	Eliza	1	2	2						1				6		
Newbury	113	36	Hunt	Josiah	1			1		1			1	1			5		
Newbury	113	37	Dugan	John	3		1			1		1					6		
Newbury	113	38	Lovering	Enis		2							1				3		
Newbury	113	39	Pettingell	Moses	1	2	1	1	1	1	1		1				9		
Newbury	113	40	Gooding	Amos	1		3	1					1	1			7		
Newbury	113	41	Gooding	Samuel			1					1					2		
Newbury	113	42	Jenkins	Robert	2			1					1				4		
Newbury	113	43	Flood	James	1		1	1		1	1	1					6		
Newbury	113	44	Lunt	Richard				1		2			1	1			5		
Newbury	113	45	Gooding	Stephen	1			1		3	1		1				7		
Newbury	113	46	Downer	Jesse			1						1				2		
Newbury	113	47	Flood	Aaron		1	2						1				4		
Newbury	113	48	Jenkins	Lenord				1					1	1			3		
Newbury	114	1	Smith	John		1		1		1	2	1	1				7		
Newbury	114	2	Brocking	Eliza	1		1				1		1	1	1		6		
Newbury	114	3	Cadwall	Robert			1			1			1				3		
Newbury	114	4	Townsen	Anny	1								1				2		
Newbury	114	5	Addams	Henry	1				1	1		1	1	1			6		
Newbury	114	6	Weld	Daniel		1		1		1		1	1				5		
Newbury	114	7	Flood	William	2	1	1		1	1		1		1			8		
Newbury	114	8	Mace	Joseph	1	1		1		1			1				5		
Newbury	114	9	Cheney	Moses	1	1		1		1		2	1				7		
Newbury	114	10	Bennet	Laban	1						1		1	1			4		
Newbury	114	11	Hale	Eliza						1		1	1				3		
Newbury	114	12	Pears	Ebnz		2							1				3		
Newbury	114	13	Jackman	William	2	1		1		1	1		1				7		
Newbury	114	14	Pears	John				1		3			1				5		
Newbury	114	15	Jackman	Hannah		1				1		2					4		
Newbury	114	16	Ball	James	3			1		2		1	1				8		
Newbury	114	17	Bookman	Joseph			2					2					4		
Newbury	114	18	Reed	William	3			1				1	1				6		
Newbury	114	19	Casy	Ammy	1							1	1	1			5		
Newbury	114	20	Cammil	Jack											3		3		
Newbury	114	21	Horton	Aaron	2			1		1	2	2					8		
Newbury	114	22	Phillips	William											3		3		
Newbury	114	23	Mace	William				1		1			1				3		
Newbury	114	24	Jackman	Benja	1			1	1					1			4		
Newbury	114	25	Black	Henry	1			1	1		1		2	1			7		
Newbury	114	26	Little	John			2							2			3		
Newbury	114	27	Bordman	Ollin		2	1		1	3				1			8		
Newbury	114	28	Stickney	William	2			1		1		1	1				6		
Newbury	114	29	Stickney	Benja	2			1		1			1				5		
Newbury	114	30	Stickney	Richard	1			1				1	1				4		
Newbury	114	31	Stickney	Theoder		1		1					1	1			4		
Newbury	114	32	Thomas	Joseph				1						1			2		
Newbury	114	33	Stickney	Amos		1		1						1			3		
Newbury	114	34	Tucker	Sarah									2	2	1		5		
Newbury	114	35	Pettingall	Nicol		1		1	1				1	1			5		
Newbury	114	36	Johnson	Benja				1				2	1				4		
Newbury	114	37	Hale	Ezra				1		1		1	1				4		
Newbury	114	38	March	Ebenezer		1		1					1				4		
Newbury	114	39	Smith	Lydia									1	1			2		
Newbury	114	40	Evons	Thomas	2		2	1		2	1		1				9		
Newbury	114	41	Shannon	Robert	1	2			1	1	1			1			7		
Newbury	114	42	Mors	Abraham			1			2	1		1				5		
Newbury	114	43	Jaquith	John			1	1				1		1			4		
Newbury	114	44	Moors	John	1		1	1		1			1				5		
Newbury	114	45	Jaquith	Enos		1			1			1	1				4		
Newbury	114	46	Smith	Richard	1	1		1		1	1		1				6		
Newbury	114	47	Smith	John															Enumeration left blank
Newbury	114	48	Fish	Samuel	2			1		2	1		1	3			10		
Newbury	114	49	Addams	Charles				1			2			1			4		

			HEADS OF HOUSEHOLD		FREE WHITE MALES					FREE WHITE FEMALES					TOTAL ALL OTHER	TOTAL SLAVES	TOTALS	DISTRICT/ TOWNSHIP	NOTES
TOWN	PG#	LN#	LAST NAME	FIRST NAME	under 10	10 to 16	16 to 26	26 to 45	45 and over	under 10	10 to 16	16 to 26	26 to 45	45 and over					
Newbury	115	1	Ilsley	Isaiah		2		1		1	1		1				6		
Newbury	115	2	Ilsley	Joshua	2		1					1					4		
Newbury	115	3	Ilsley	Stephen			1						1	1			3		
Newbury	115	4	Lunt	Henry	1	1	1		1	1	1		1				7		
Newbury	115	5	Jaquith	Eliphelet				1									1		
Newbury	115	6	Jaquith	Parker		1	1	1		2	1	1		1			8		
Newbury	115	7	Addams	Silas				1			1		1	1			4		
Newbury	115	8	Pappin	Joseph		1		1					1				3		
Newbury	115	9	Coffin	Joseph	2			1		1	1		1				6		
Newbury	115	10	Coffin	Edmund	2		1			1	1		1				6		
Newbury	115	11	Knight	Addams	1		1					1		1			4		
Newbury	115	12	Knight	John	1				1	1	1		1	1			6		
Newbury	115	13	Tory	John	1	1		1		1			1	1	1		7		
Newbury	115	14	Jaquith	Richard		1		1					1				3		
Newbury	115	15	Lunt	Paul		1		1		2			1				5		
Newbury	115	16	Little	Paul		1							1				3		
Newbury	115	17	Flood	Moses	1	1	1						1				4		
Newbury	115	18	Noyes	John		1		1				1					3		
Newbury	115	19	Noyes	Sarah	2					1	2						5		
Newbury	115	20	Little	Richard			1	1		3		2		1			8		
Newbury	115	21	Little	David	1	1	1	1		2	1		1		1		9		
Newbury	115	22	Flood	John		1	3	1				2	1				8		
Newbury	115	23	Short	Moses	2	1	1	1					1				6		
Newbury	115	24	Rogers	Mary	1						1		1		1		4		
Newbury	115	25	Chase	Daniel	1			1		1	1		1				5		
Newbury	115	26	Chase	Nathl	1			1		1			1				4		
Newbury	115	27	Cooper	John	1			1	1	1	2		1				7		
Newbury	115	28	Hoys	Joseph	1			1					1				3		
Newbury	115	29	Goodridge	Joseph	1			1		3			1				6		
Newbury	115	30	Gooding	Nath	1	2	2		1			2	1	1			10		
Newbury	115	31	Gooding	Moses	1			1				1					3		
Newbury	115	32	Hills	Nath	1		2		1	1	1	1	1				8		
Newbury	115	33	Hills	Amos	1			1	1	3			1				7		
Newbury	115	34	Little	Joseph		1	1		1			1		1			5		
Newbury	115	35	Addams	Robert	1		1					1					3		
Newbury	115	36	Little	Edmund				1				1		1			3		
Newbury	115	37	Little	Enoch			1	1		1				1			3		
Newbury	115	38	Little	Moses		1						1					2		
Newbury	115	39	Little	John				1						1			2		
Newbury	115	40	Pilsbury	Moses	5		1					2	1				10		
Newbury	115	41	Smith	James	2		1			1			1				5		
Newbury	115	42	Smith	Enoch	3		1					2					6		
Newbury	115	43	Thurlow	Samuel		1	1	1				1		1			5		
Newbury	115	44	Dole	Oliver	4		1	1		1			1				8		
Newbury	115	45	Dike	Ann		1		2						3			6		
Newbury	115	46	Smith	Parker	1	1		1				2	1				6		
Newbury	116	1	Melton	Silas	1		1						1				4		
Newbury	116	2	Brickett	James	1		1	1	1			2	1				7		
Newbury	116	3	Ilsley	Jonathan		2		1				2	1				6		
Newbury	116	4	Addams	Israel		1	1					2	1	1			6		
Newbury	116	5	Chase	Able			1					2	2	1			6		
Newbury	116	6	Chase	Jeremiah	1		1	1		3	2		1	1			10		
Newbury	116	7	Hills	Benja	2		1		1	3	2		1				10		
Newbury	116	8	Barlett	Joseph		1	1					2		1			5		
Newbury	116	9	Little	Stephen	1		1			1		1					4		
Newbury	116	10	Bartlett	Joseph		1	1	1	1	5	1	1	1				12		
Newbury	116	11	Peeksbury	Jonathan	3			1		1			1				6		
Newbury	116	12	Pinny	Samuel	1		1		1	1	2	3		1	1		11		
Newbury	116	13	Morse	John				1				1	1				3		
Newbury	116	14	Follingbe	Moody		1		1	1			3	1				7		
Newbury	116	15	Kindrick	Samuel	1		1	1		1		1					5		
Newbury	116	16	Fallingbe	Samuel			1					1					2		
Newbury	116	17	Woodman	Samuel		1		1				2		1			5		
Newbury	116	18	Chase	Tristam			1		1	1	1	3	1				8		
Newbury	116	19	Bartlett	Josiah		1	1	1				1	1	1			6		
Newbury	116	20	Chase	Semien			1			1			1				3		
Newbury	116	21	Little	Coleman	1			1		2			1				5		
Newbury	116	22	Morrill	John		1		1				1	1				4		
Newbury	116	23	Ordway	Stephen	2	1		1		2	1		1				8		
Newbury	116	24	Jaquith	Stephen	2	1	1	1		2		1	1	1			10		
Newbury	116	25	Dole	Samuel		1	1	1		1		1	1				6		
Newbury	116	26	Smith	John	2			2	1		1	1		1			8		
Newbury	116	27	Tictcomb	Joseph		2	1	1	1	1		2	1				9		
Newbury	116	28	Pettengall	Stephn		1						1		1			3		
Newbury	116	29	Noyes	John		1		1				1		1			4		
Newbury	116	30	Knight	Edmund		1	2		1			2		1			7		
Newbury	116	31	Addams	Nathll	1			1		1			1				4		
Newbury	116	32	Lunt	Paul	1			1				1					3		
Newbury	116	33	Russell	Joseph			1					2	1				4		
Newbury	116	34	Little	Amos		1		1		3	1		1				7		
Newbury	116	35	Little	Nathll	1			1	1	1	1	1					7		
Newbury	116	36	Little	Silas	1			1		3	1		1				7		
Newbury	116	37	Jaquith	Stephen		1		1				2	1				5		
Newbury	116	38	Noyes	Mary				1			1		1	1			4		
Newbury	116	39	Parson	Silas	1		1	1		1		1					6		
Newbury	116	40	Kent	Stephen	1	1		1	1			1		2			7		
Newbury	116	41	Kent	Paul		1		1		1		1	1				5		
Newbury	116	42	Noyes	Nicolas	1							2	2				6		
Newbury	116	43	Moody	Nathll	1	1		3		2		1	1	2			11		
Newbury	116	44	Short	Henry		1	1		1			1		1			5		

TOWN	PG#	LN#	HEADS OF HOUSEHOLD		FREE WHITE MALES					FREE WHITE FEMALES					TOTAL ALL OTHER	TOTAL SLAVES	TOTALS	DISTRICT/ TOWNSHIP	NOTES
			LAST NAME	FIRST NAME	under 10	10 to 16	16 to 26	26 to 45	45 and over	under 10	10 to 16	16 to 26	26 to 45	45 and over					
Newbury	116	45	Short	Silas		1	1	1	1		1	1	1	1			8		
Newbury	116	46	Short	Richard		1	1		1	1	1	1		1			7		
Newbury	117	1	Addams	Asa	1	1		1		1			1	1			6		
Newbury	117	2	Addams	Ebenez	1	1		1		1		1					5		
Newbury	117	3	Lumbart	Abigall	2					1	1	1	1				6		
Newbury	117	4	Kal*sh	Moses		1						1	1				3		
Newbury	117	5	Knight	Richard	1	2			1	3			1				8		
Newbury	117	6	Hoyes	Noah			1	1					1	1			4		
Newbury	117	7	Howes	Amos				1		3	1	1		1			7		
Newbury	117	8	Black	Samuel	1			1		2	1	1	1	1			8		
Newbury	117	9	Isley	Stephen		1		1					1	1			4		
Newbury	117	10	Chapman	Jonath		1							1	1			3		
Newbury	117	11	Knight	Eunice	1	1	2			2	1	1		2			10		
Newbury	117	12	Plummer	Jonath		1	1	1					1	1			5		
Newbury	117	13	Lunt	Nicolas			1	1				4	1	2			9		
Newbury	117	14	Lunt	Samuel			1						1				2		
Newbury	117	15	Hale	Amos	1		2						2	2			7		
Newbury	117	16	Addams	Daniel	2	1		1		3	1			1			9		
Newbury	117	17	Addams	Paul		2	1			3			2	1			9		
Newbury	117	18	Isley	Paul	2							1		1			5		
Newbury	117	19	Isley	Ansel	2			1		4	2		1	2			12		
Newbury	117	20	Rummer	Simion		1	1	1			3	1	2				9		
Newbury	117	21	Hale	Joshua	1			1		1		1					4		
Newbury	117	22	Plummer	Isaiah	1		1			2		1		1			6		
Newbury	117	23	Dole	Henry	1		1	1				2		2			7		
Newbury	117	24	Plummer	Richard			1	1		1		1	1				5		
Newbury	117	25	Boynton	Edmund	2			1		2		1		1			7		
Newbury	117	26	Lowrey	Peter	2			1		2	1		1				7		
Newbury	117	27	Dalby	Thomas			1			3			1				5		
Newbury	117	28	Perkins	Bimsley	4			1		1	7		1				14		
Newbury	117	29	Flood	Jonath		1							1				2		
Newbury	117	30	Plummer	Paul	1	1	1		1	1	1	1		1			8		
Newbury	117	31	Kent	Moses	1			1		1			1	1			5		
Newbury	117	32	Hale	John					1		1			1			3		
Newbury	117	33	Plummer	Seth				1			1	1	1				4		
Newbury	117	34	Dole	David		1		1			1		1				4		
Newbury	117	35	Dole	Enoch	1	2		1		1			1				6		
Newbury	117	36	Plummer	Paul			1			2	2	1					6		
Newbury	117	37	Plummer	Hannah								2		1			3		
Newbury	117	38	Hale	Isaac			1	1		3	2	1					9		
Newbury	117	39	Dole	William	2			1		1			1				5		
Newbury	117	40	Poor	Stephen	1	2		1		2	2	2	1				11		
Newbury	117	41	Plummer	Benja				1					1	1			3		
Newbury	117	42	Plummer	Benja	1		3	1				3					8		
Newbury	117	43	Plummer	Joseph	1	1		1		1			1				5		
Newbury	117	44	Woodman	Joseph	3	1		1		2	1		1				9		
Newbury	117	45	Poor	Jonathan		1		1		1			1				4		
Newbury	118	1	Thurston	Benjamin		2		1		1	1		1				6		
Newbury	118	2	Plummer	Mark				1						1			2		
Newbury	118	3	Plummer	John	2		1			1			1				5		
Newbury	118	4	Plummer	David	1	2					1		3	1			8		
Newbury	118	5	Thurston	John	2	1		1		1			1	1			7		
Newbury	118	6	Huse	Amos	2	1		1		1			1	1			7		
Newbury	118	7	Kilborn	Jedediah					1		1	1		1			5		
Newbury	118	8	Greenleaf	Abner					1		1	1	1	1			5		
Newbury	118	9	Coffen	Eliphalet		1	1	1		1			1	1			6		
Newbury	118	10	Chase	Johanna		1		1					1	1			4		
Newbury	118	11	Greenliff	Josiah			1			1		1					3		
Newbury	118	12	Papin	Daniel			1			2	2	1	1				7		
Newbury	118	13	Bartlett	Hannah	2		1			1			1				5		
Newbury	118	14	Davis	Mary										1			1		
Newbury	118	15	Chase	John	3	1		1		2	1	1					9		
Newbury	118	16	Bartlett	John				2		1	1		1	2			7		
Newbury	118	17	Bartlett	David	3		1			2			1				7		
Newbury	118	18	Davis	John	2	2	2			1	1		1				9		
Newbury	118	19	Bartlett	Isaac	1	1		1		1	2		2				8		
Newbury	118	20	Colby	John				1									1		
Newbury	118	21	Noyes	Silas		1		1		2	1						5		
Newbury	118	22	Noyes	Thomas		2	3	1					1	1			8		
Newbury	118	23	Noyes	Amos			1	1				1	1	1	2		7		
Newbury	118	24	Brown	Samuel			1						1				2		
Newbury	118	25	Rogers	Ester				1						2			3		
Newbury	118	26	Noyes	Nathan		1		1					1	1			4		
Newbury	118	27	Noyes	Nathll															Enumeration left blank
Newbury	118	28	Killey	John			1			1			1				3		
Newbury	118	29	Brown	Stephen	2	2		1		1	3			1			10		
Newbury	118	30	Brown	Thomas		1				1		1					3		
Newbury	118	31	Hills	Josiah			1	1						3			5		
Newbury	118	32	Brickett	Moses		2		1				1	1	1			6		
Newbury	118	33	Morrill	Able				1		1	1		1		1		5		
Newbury	118	34	Hills	Benja	2					1	3	1	1				9		
Newbury	118	35	Isley	Jonathan		2		1		2			1				6		
Newbury	118	36	Chase	Joseph	1			1	1	3	2		1	1			10		
Newbury	118	37	Chase	Able		1			1			1	2				5		
Newbury	118	38	Chase	Thomas			1						1				2		
Newbury	118	39	Brickett	Nathll				1						1			2		
Newbury	118	40	Molton	Silas	1		1	1					1				4		
Newbury	118	41	Brickett	Amos	1	1	1	1					1				5		
Newbury	118	42	Noyes	Silas				2						1			3		
Newbury	118	43	Noyes	Jacob	2		1			1			1				5		

TOWN	PG#	LN#	LAST NAME	FIRST NAME	Free White Males under 10	10 to 16	16 to 26	26 to 45	45 and over	Free White Females under 10	10 to 16	16 to 26	26 to 45	45 and over	TOTAL ALL OTHER	TOTAL SLAVES	TOTALS	DISTRICT/ TOWNSHIP	NOTES
Newbury	118	44	Merrill	Jacub	1	1	2		1				1	1			7		
Newbury	118	45	Downs	Stephen					1			1		1			3		
Newbury	118	46	Gould	Joseph	2			1		1	2			1			7		
Newbury	118	47	Noyes	Paul	3	1		1		1			1				7		
Newbury	119	1	Noyes	Samuel	4	1		1		3	1		1				11		
Newbury	119	2	Morss	Greenlif	1	1		1	1			1	1				7		
Newbury	119	3	Pinny	Moses	1		2			1			1	1			6		
Newbury	119	4	Coffin	Ecabod			1		1	1			1				4		
Newbury	119	5	Coffin	Richard			1			1		1					3		
Newbury	119	6	Coffin	Stephen	1			1	1	2			1	1			5		
Newbury	119	7	Pilsbury	Semion	2			1		1			1				5		
Newbury	119	8	Pilsbury	Amos		1		1				1	1	1			5		
Newbury	119	9	Downer	Daniel	1			1		1			1				4		
Newbury	119	10	Noyes	Abner			1			1			1				3		
Newbury	119	11	Pearson	Nathan			1				1		1				3		
Newbury	119	12	Poor	Amos			1						1	1			3		
Newbury	119	13	Currier	Mary										1			1		
Newbury	119	14	Danford	John	1			1	1	1	1	1					6		
Newbury	119	15	Noyes	Ezekiel	4	3		1		1	1		1				11		
Newbury	119	16	Turner	William				1					1				2		
Newbury	119	17	Turner	Israel				1	1	2	3		1				8		
Newbury	119	18	Noyes	Gedion	1	3	1		1	3	2		1				12		
Newbury	119	19	Colby	Charles		1		1				1		1			4		
Newbury	119	20	Rogers	Aaron	1			1		3	2		1				9		
Newbury	119	21	Perry	William		2		1		2			1				6		
Newbury	119	22	Duty	John			1	1	1	2		2	1				8		
Newbury	119	23	Danford	Joseph		1		1						1			3		
Newbury	119	24	Downer	Anna		1						1	1	1			4		
Newbury	119	25	Noyes	Thomas	1			1		2		1					5		
Newbury	119	26	Poor	John		1				1	1	1					5		
Newbury	119	27	Poor	Samuel				1		2			1				4		
Newbury	119	28	Poor	Micajah	1	1		1	1		1	1		2			8		
Newbury	119	29	Poor	Moses	1		1	1		4			1				8		
Newbury	119	30	Sawyer	Micajah	1	2			1	3			1				8		
Newbury	119	31	Poor	Benja			7		1				3	3			14		
Newbury	119	32	Callwall	Joshua			1			1		1	1	1			5		
Newbury	119	33	Callwall	Nathll			1					1					2		
Newbury	119	34	Callwall	Josiah			1					1					2		
Newbury	119	35	Callwall	David		1	1			2	2			2			9		
Newbury	119	36	Emerson	John		1		1					1				3		
Newbury	119	37	Hale	Oliver		2		1					2				5		
Newbury	119	38	Hale	Oliver	2	1	1	1	1		2	2	1	1			12		
Newbury	119	39	Colway	Nathan			1					1	1				3		
Newbury	119	40	Colway	Enoch	2			1		1			1				5		
Newbury	119	41	Rollins	Joseph		1		1				1		1			4		
Newbury	119	42	Baley	Abner		1	1	1			1		1				5		
Newbury	119	43	Baley	Abner	2		1	1		1		2	1				8		
Newbury	119	44	Hills	Obediah	3	1	1		1	1	2	2	1				12		
Newbury	119	45	Goodridge	Jonathan	1			1		1			1	1			5		
Newbury	119	46	Goodridge	Joseph		1		1						1			3		
Newbury	119	47	Sawyer	Bootfield				1				1		1			3		
Newbury	120	1	Coffin	Samuel				1						1			2		
Newbury	120	2	Thurlow	Enoch	2			1					1				4		
Newbury	120	3	Lunt	Enoch			1					1		1			3		
Newbury	120	4	Smith	John	1	1		1						1			4		
Newbury	120	5	Smith	John	2		1						1				5		
Newbury	120	6	Titcomb	Joseph		2		1		1	1	2		1			8		
Newbury	120	7	Pettingill	Sarah				1						1			2		
Newbury	120	8	Jaquish	Joseph	1			1	1			1		1			5		
Newbury	120	9	Jaquish	Enoch	1			1		1	1		1				5		
Newbury	120	10	Noyes	John			1						1				3		
Newbury	120	11	Addams	Nathll		1		1		1			1				4		
Newbury	120	12	Lunt	Paul	1	1							1				3		
Newbury	120	13	Russell	John			1						1	2			4		
Newbury	120	14	Little	Amos		1		1		2	2		1				7		
Newbury	120	15	Little	Nathll		2			1	1	1	1	1				7		
Newbury	120	16	Little	Silas	1	2		1				1					6		
Newbury	120	17	Noyes	Stephen			1				1	1		1			5		
Newbury	120	18	Noyes	Mary			1			1		1	1				4		
Newbury	120	19	Parson	Silas	1		1	1	1	1		2	1	2			10		
Newbury	120	20	Noyes	Samuel		1	1	1				1	2	1			7		
Newbury	120	21	Noyes	Samuel	2		1			1		1	1				6		
Newbury	120	22	Addams	Daniel	1	1		1		1	1	1					7		
Newbury	120	23	Addams	Israel				1				1	1	1			4		
Newbury	120	24	Adams	Eliphelet		1		1	1			1	1				5		
Newbury	120	25	Chase	Josiah	1	3	1		1	4	1	1	1	1			14		
Newbury	120	26	Little	Joshua			1					1	1				3		
Newbury	120	27	Little	Moses	3	1		1		1		2	1	1			10		
Newbury	120	28	Little	Josiah	1	2			1	1		2		1			8		
Newbury	120	29	Brown	Stephen			1	3	1		1	3		1			10		
Newbury	120	30	Brown	Thomas	1	1	1						1				4		
Newbury	120	31	Savory	Ebenzr			1	1		3		1	1				7		
Newbury	120	32	Pike	Mathew		1					1		1	1			4		
Newbury	120	33	Lunt	Amos	1		1			1		1					4		
Newbury	120	34	Chase	Joshua	1	2		1		1		2	1	1			9		
Newbury	120	35	Noyes	John	1	1	2	1			1						6		

TOWN	PG#	LN#	LAST NAME	FIRST NAME	FREE WHITE MALES					FREE WHITE FEMALES					TOTAL ALL OTHER	TOTAL SLAVES	TOTALS	DISTRICT/ TOWNSHIP	NOTES
					under 10	10 to 16	16 to 26	26 to 45	45 and over	under 10	10 to 16	16 to 26	26 to 45	45 and over					
Newburyport	157	1	Andrews	John Revd	1	1		1		1		1	2	1			8		
Newburyport	157	2	Aubin	Philip	1	2			1		1		1	1			7		
Newburyport	157	3	Adams	Abraham					1					1			2		
Newburyport	157	4	Adams	Benjamin	1	1		1		1		1	1				6		
Newburyport	157	5	Adams	Isaac				1					1				2		
Newburyport	157	6	Adams	Richard	1	1	1		1	2	1		1				8		
Newburyport	157	7	Akerman	Noah			1				1		1				3		
Newburyport	157	8	Akerman	Joshua	2	1	1		1			1		1			7		
Newburyport	157	9	Akerman	John Jr	1			1		1		1					4		
Newburyport	157	10	Appleton	Joseph				1		1			1				3		
Newburyport	157	11	Appleton	Nathaniel	1			1				1					3		
Newburyport	157	12	Alexander	William		1		1				2	2	1			7		
Newburyport	157	13	Atwood	John		1	1	1	1	1	1	1	1				8		
Newburyport	157	14	Atwood	Margaret Wid	2							1	1				4		
Newburyport	157	15	Abbot	Benjamin	3			1		3	2		1	1			11		
Newburyport	157	16	Ash	Nathaniel			1						1				2		
Newburyport	157	17	Abbot	James	1			2		2			2				7		
Newburyport	157	18	Ayers	Richard				1						1			2		
Newburyport	157	19	Arther	Wilson	1			1					1				3		
Newburyport	157	20	Aramatage	Samuel	2	1		1					1				5		
Newburyport	157	21	Aubin	Nathaniel			2		1	2		1	1				7		
Newburyport	157	22	Atkins	Mary						1			3				4		
Newburyport	158	1	Allgreen	Thomas			1			1			1				3		
Newburyport	158	2	Bass	Edward R.R. Bishop				1						3	1		5		
Newburyport	158	3	Bass	Edward Jr	1			1					2				4		
Newburyport	158	4	Boardman	Offin		1		1					1	1			4		
Newburyport	158	5	Boardman	Jonathan		1		1		1	2		1				6		
Newburyport	158	6	Boardman	William	2	3		1		1			1	1			9		
Newburyport	158	7	Boardman	John	2		1	1		2		1	1				8		
Newburyport	158	8	Boardman	Abel	3		1	1		1	1		1				8		
Newburyport	158	9	Boardman	Wido Mary	1	1					1		1				4		
Newburyport	158	10	Boardman	Martha						1	3		1				5		
Newburyport	158	11	Boardman	Wido Ann			1					2		1			4		
Newburyport	158	12	Bartlet	Edmond		1			1	1				1			4		
Newburyport	158	13	Bartlet	Richard	1		2	1		2	1		2				9		
Newburyport	158	14	Bartlet	Richard Jr	1			1		1	1	1	1				6		
Newburyport	158	15	Bartlet	William		2	4		1		1		2	1			11		
Newburyport	158	16	Bartlet	William Jr				1				1					2		
Newburyport	158	17	Bartlet	Abel	1	1	2		1	3		1	1	1			11		
Newburyport	158	18	Bartlet	Stephen		1	2	1				2	1				7		
Newburyport	158	19	Bartlet	Samuel		1	3					2					6		
Newburyport	158	20	Bemes	Daniel	1		1					1					3		
Newburyport	158	21	Bayley	Samuel		1		1		1			1	1			4		
Newburyport	158	22	Bayley	William			1			2			2	3			8		
Newburyport	158	23	Bayley	Nathaniel			1			1			1				3		
Newburyport	158	24	Bayley	Stephen			1			1		1					3		
Newburyport	158	25	Bayley	Elizabeth Wido						1	1			1			3		
Newburyport	158	26	Bayley	Thomas	2		1	1				1	1				6		
Newburyport	158	27	Bayley	William Wido of	2								1				3		
Newburyport	158	28	Beck	Jonathan				1				1	1				3		
Newburyport	158	29	Beck	Jonathan Jr	3	1	2		1	2		1	1				11		
Newburyport	158	30	Balch	Benjamin				1		1			1				3		
Newburyport	158	31	Balch	John		1	1	2	2	5	2	3	1	1			18		
Newburyport	158	32	Balch	Daniel	2	2		1			3		1				9		
Newburyport	158	33	Balch	Thomas H			1			2	1		1				5		
Newburyport	158	34	Balch	Daniel Wido of		1							1				2		
Newburyport	158	35	Brown	Moses Mercht		1	1	1	1	1	1	1		2			9		
Newburyport	158	36	Brown	Moses Capt	1		2		1			1		1			6		
Newburyport	158	37	Brown	Ebenezer		1		1						2			4		
Newburyport	158	38	Brown	Thomas		1			1			3		1	1		7		
Newburyport	158	39	Brown	Josiah		1							1				2		
Newburyport	159	1	Brown	Jacob	1			1		1	1		1				5		
Newburyport	159	2	Brown	James	2			2				1	1				6		
Newburyport	159	3	Brown	Nicolas	1	3	2		1	3	1	1	1				13		
Newburyport	159	4	Brown	Henry			1						1				2		
Newburyport	159	5	Brown	Edward				1					1	2			4		
Newburyport	159	6	Brown	Joseph	1	2	2		1	1	1		1				9		
Newburyport	159	7	Brown	John Jr			1	1						2			4		
Newburyport	159	8	Brown	John			2	1		1			2	1			7		
Newburyport	159	9	Brown	Zebulon R	1			1					1				3		
Newburyport	159	10	Brown	Obadiah	5		2			1			1	2			11		
Newburyport	159	11	Brown	Samuel	2	2	1		1	2		1	1				10		
Newburyport	159	12	Brown	Samuel Jr			1			1		2					4		
Newburyport	159	13	Brown	Nathaniel	2			1	1			1	1				6		
Newburyport	159	14	Brown	Tristram			1						1				2		
Newburyport	159	15	Brown	Hannah Wido		1						1	1	1			4		
Newburyport	159	16	Brown	William			1			2			1	1			5		
Newburyport	159	17	Brown	Eliphalet		1						1					2		
Newburyport	159	18	Barber	Daniel				1					1	1			3		

107

TOWN	PG#	LN#	LAST NAME	FIRST NAME	FREE WHITE MALES under 10	10 to 16	16 to 26	26 to 45	45 and over	FREE WHITE FEMALES under 10	10 to 16	16 to 26	26 to 45	45 and over	TOTAL ALL OTHER	TOTAL SLAVES	TOTALS	DISTRICT/ TOWNSHIP	NOTES
Newburyport	159	19	Bond	John		2	1		1		2	1		1			8		
Newburyport	159	20	Brocheway	Pardon		2	1	1		3		1	1				9		
Newburyport	159	21	Bray	Aaron			3					1		1			6		
Newburyport	159	22	Brickell	Nathaniel	2	1			1	1				1			6		
Newburyport	159	23	Batchelder	Samuel					1			2		1			4		
Newburyport	159	24	Burnham	Daniel	1			1		1			1		1		5		
Newburyport	159	25	Banford	Joseph				1		2		1					4		
Newburyport	159	26	Brazier	Simeon				1	2				1				4		
Newburyport	159	27	Burril	Samuel				1					1				2		
Newburyport	159	28	Burril	Samuel Jr	2		1	1		1		1	1				7		
Newburyport	159	29	Burril	Thomas	1	1		1		1	1		1				6		
Newburyport	159	30	Burril	John	2	1		1		2	1		1				8		
Newburyport	159	31	Betty	John	3			1		1	1	2	1	4			13		
Newburyport	159	32	Bagley	Philip	1	2	2	2		1	1	2					12		
Newburyport	159	33	Barker	George				1					1				2		
Newburyport	159	34	Brett	John				1		1		1	1				4		
Newburyport	159	35	Burt	Elizabeth Wdo						1			2				3		
Newburyport	159	36	Burrage	Hannah Wdo	1			1		1			1	1			5		
Newburyport	159	37	Blunt	Edmund M	2		2	1		1		1	1				8		
Newburyport	159	38	Blunt	Elizabeth Wdo		1					1	3		1			6		
Newburyport	159	39	Babson	Joseph		2		1		1	2		1				7		
Newburyport	159	40	Buck	John				1		1	1		1				4		
Newburyport	159	41	Bragdon	Joseph	1			1		3			1				6		
Newburyport	160	1	Berry	Aron	1		1	1		1	1	1	1				7		
Newburyport	160	2	Berry	Abigail Wdo	1					3	1		1				6		
Newburyport	160	3	Bassett	Christopher Jr				1					1				2		
Newburyport	160	4	Bassett	Christopher	1		1			2	1		1				6		
Newburyport	160	5	Buswell	John	1	1		1		1		1					5		
Newburyport	160	6	Bunton	Thomas	1		1	1		1		1	1				6		
Newburyport	160	7	Bradbury	Theophilus	1	1			1	2	1	1		1			8		
Newburyport	160	8	Bradbury	Theophilus Jr				1		2	1	1					5		
Newburyport	160	9	Bradbury	Theophilus 3d	1			1		1		1					4		
Newburyport	160	10	Bradbury	George				1					1				2		
Newburyport	160	11	Bradbury	Jonathan			1	1						1			3		
Newburyport	160	12	Butler	Philip		1	1		1	1	1			1			6		
Newburyport	160	13	Butler	William	1			1		3	1		1	1			8		
Newburyport	160	14	Butler	William Junr	1			1					1	1			4		
Newburyport	160	15	Butman	Jonathan	1		1		1				1				4		
Newburyport	160	16	Baker	Thomas		1	2							1			4		
Newburyport	160	17	Baker	Thomas H			1							1			2		
Newburyport	160	18	Baker	Mary Wdo	1									1			2		
Newburyport	160	19	Baker	Zacheriah	2		4	5	1	2	2		1	1			18		
Newburyport	160	20	Blodgett	William	1			1		1		1	1				5		
Newburyport	160	21	Burbank	Daniel	3	2		2		1	1		1				10		
Newburyport	160	22	Bodily	John Revd	2	1		1		1		3	1				9		
Newburyport	160	23	Bennett	David	2			1		1			1				5		
Newburyport	160	24	Balentine	Robert	2			1		1			1				5		
Newburyport	160	25	Barrett	William	1	1	1	1		3	1	1	1				10		
Newburyport	160	26	Bowley	William Wdo of	2					2			1				5		
Newburyport	160	27	Barbe	Wyatt S		1		1				1		1			4		
Newburyport	160	28	Blompy	Aaron	1	1		1			1	1		1			6		
Newburyport	160	29	Bragg	Robert	2		1	1				1	1				6		
Newburyport	160	30	Bowers	Abigail Wido	1					1		1					3		
Newburyport	160	31	Baldwin	Ann Wdo	1					2	1		1				5		
Newburyport	160	32	Bradstreet	Elizabeth								1	1				2		
Newburyport	160	33	Cary	Thomas Revd	1	1	1		1		1		1	1			7		
Newburyport	160	34	Coffin	David	3	2	1	1			1		1	2			11		
Newburyport	160	35	Coffin	David Jr	1	2	1	1			1	2	1				9		
Newburyport	160	36	Coffin	Samuel		1	3		1	1	2	2		2			12		
Newburyport	160	37	Coffin	Tristram			1	1	1		1	1	1	1	1		8		
Newburyport	160	38	Coffin	Sussanah Wdo			1				1	2	1				5		
Newburyport	160	39	Coffin	Lemuel	2		1	1		2	1	1					10		
Newburyport	160	40	Coffin	Benjamin	1				1				1				3		
Newburyport	161	1	Coffin	Joseph			1	1					1				3		
Newburyport	161	2	Coffin	Joseph Jr	2			1		1			1				5		
Newburyport	161	3	Coffin	Moses Mercht			1	1					1				3		
Newburyport	161	4	Coffin	Charles	1	1	1					2	1				7		
Newburyport	161	5	Coombs	William			1	1		2	2	1	2				10		
Newburyport	161	6	Coombs	John		1	2		1		1	1		1			7		
Newburyport	161	7	Cross	Stephen		1	1		1			3	1	1			8		
Newburyport	161	8	Cross	Stephen Junr	4			1		1		1	1				8		
Newburyport	161	9	Cross	Ralph			1	1				1	1				4		
Newburyport	161	10	Cross	William	4			1		2	2	1	1				11		
Newburyport	161	11	Cross	Thomas	2		1	1		1			1				6		
Newburyport	161	12	Cross	Benjamin	1		1	1					1				4		
Newburyport	161	13	Carter	Nathaniel	1	2	1	1		2	1		2				10		
Newburyport	161	14	Carter	Joshua	2		1	2		2	1		2				10		
Newburyport	161	15	Carter	Benjamin				1		2			1				4		
Newburyport	161	16	Cook	Charles				1					1				2		

TOWN	PG#	LN#	LAST NAME	FIRST NAME	FREE WHITE MALES under 10	10 to 16	16 to 26	26 to 45	45 and over	FREE WHITE FEMALES under 10	10 to 16	16 to 26	26 to 45	45 and over	TOTAL ALL OTHER	TOTAL SLAVES	TOTALS	DISTRICT/ TOWNSHIP	NOTES
Newburyport	161	17	Cook	Charles Junr		1	2		1			1		1			6		
Newburyport	161	18	Cook	William	2	1	1	1		1		1	1				8		
Newburyport	161	19	Cook	John	3	1			1	1		1	1	1			9		
Newburyport	161	20	Cook	Zebedee	2	1	1	1		2	1	1	1				10		
Newburyport	161	21	Cook	Elias	3	1	1		1	1	1	1		1			10		
Newburyport	161	22	Currier	William 3d		1	2		1	1	1						6		
Newburyport	161	23	Currier	Mathew	2		2		1	1	1	1		1			9		
Newburyport	161	24	Currier	Nicolas		1		1		3			1				6		
Newburyport	161	25	Currier	Nathaniel	2			1		2			1				6		
Newburyport	161	26	Currier	Joseph	2			1		1	2		1				7		
Newburyport	161	27	Currier	Mark	1		1					1					3		
Newburyport	161	28	Currier	Susannah Wido						3			1				4		
Newburyport	161	29	Currier	William	1			1		1			1				4		
Newburyport	161	30	Cotton	Benjamin					1					1			2		
Newburyport	161	31	Cotton	Joel	1	1			1				1				4		
Newburyport	161	32	Chase	Ezra			1					1					2		
Newburyport	161	33	Chase	William		1		1		2		2					6		
Newburyport	161	34	Chase	James		1		1	1	2			1				6		
Newburyport	161	35	Chase	James Junr	1			1		1		1					4		
Newburyport	161	36	Chase	Somerby	2		2		1	1	1	1					8		
Newburyport	161	37	Chase	Samuel	1			1		1		2					5		
Newburyport	161	38	Chase	Benjamin		1						1					2		
Newburyport	161	39	Cheever	Moses		1	1	1	1			1		1			6		
Newburyport	162	1	Cheever	John	4	2	1		1	1				1			10		
Newburyport	162	2	Cheever	Benjamin H	1			1		1			1				4		
Newburyport	162	3	Cheever	William					1					1			2		
Newburyport	162	4	Chase	William Jr		1				2		1	1	1			6		
Newburyport	162	5	Clarkson	James	1				1			1		1			4		
Newburyport	162	6	Couch	Joseph	1	2	1		1			2		1			8		
Newburyport	162	7	Couch	John		1				1		1					3		
Newburyport	162	8	Clark	Greenleaf		1		1		1	3			2			8		
Newburyport	162	9	Clark	Robert		1	2					1					4		
Newburyport	162	10	Clark	Christopher		1		1			1		1				4		
Newburyport	162	11	Clark	Thomas M	1			1		1			2				6		
Newburyport	162	12	Clark	Moses	3	1		1		1			1				7		
Newburyport	162	13	Clark	John P	2			1					1				4		
Newburyport	162	14	Clark	Samuel				1			1			1			3		
Newburyport	162	15	Clark	Stephen				1						1			2		
Newburyport	162	16	Cummins	William			2	1				1	1				5		
Newburyport	162	17	Call	Jonathan	1	2	1		1	3	1	3					12		
Newburyport	162	18	Calman	William			1			1		1	1				4		
Newburyport	162	19	Condry	Timothy				1						1			2		
Newburyport	162	20	Condry	Dennis	1			1		3	1	3					9		
Newburyport	162	21	Clannin	Benjamin	1			1		1		1					4		
Newburyport	162	22	Colby	John			2			1		1					4		
Newburyport	162	23	Calef	Elizabeth Wido		1	1							1			3		
Newburyport	162	24	Cresey	Francis		1		1		1		2	2				7		
Newburyport	162	25	Cresey	William	3			1			1		1				6		
Newburyport	162	26	Calley	Israel		1		1		2		1					5		
Newburyport	162	27	Caldwell	William		1		1		1	1	2		1			7		
Newburyport	162	28	Caldwell	Alexander	2	2	1		1			3		1			10		
Newburyport	162	29	Cutter	Jacob	1	1	1					1					4		
Newburyport	162	30	Cutter	Ebenezer	2	1		1		1		1					7		
Newburyport	162	31	Coolidge	Jonathan		2			1	1	2	1	1				8		
Newburyport	162	32	Choate	Ebenezer	4	1		1		2	1	1	1				11		
Newburyport	162	33	Choate	Benjamin		1	1			2		2					6		
Newburyport	162	34	Carlton	John			2					2					4		
Newburyport	162	35	Cutler	Joseph		2		1		1	1	1	1				7		
Newburyport	162	36	Cutler	Samuel				1		2	1		1				5		
Newburyport	162	37	Cutler	William	1			1		2			1		1		6		
Newburyport	162	38	Cheney	Moses	2	1		1		2	1		1				8		
Newburyport	162	39	Curtis	Samuel	1		1	1		1	1		1				6		
Newburyport	162	40	Curtis	Timothy		1		1		3		1	1				7		
Newburyport	162	41	Curtis	Henry			2										2		
Newburyport	163	1	Clements	Samuel		1		1				1	1				4		
Newburyport	163	2	Clements	Joseph		1							1				2		
Newburyport	163	3	Cooper	David	2		1	1	1			2	1	1			9		
Newburyport	163	4	Coverly	Thomas		1				1		1					3		
Newburyport	163	5	Connor	William	3			1					1				5		
Newburyport	163	6	Connor	Joseph		1		1						1			3		
Newburyport	163	7	Collins	Joseph			1		1	1	1		1	2			6		
Newburyport	163	8	Carrol	Philip		1						1		1			3		
Newburyport	163	9	Coburn	Jacob		1						1					2		
Newburyport	163	10	Campbell	James		1		1				3		1			6		
Newburyport	163	11	Connell	George			1			1		1	1	1			5		
Newburyport	163	12	Dana	Daniel Revd		1		1				2					4		
Newburyport	163	13	Davenport	Anthnony	2		2		1	2	3	3	1				14		
Newburyport	163	14	Davenport	Moses		1	2	1			1	2	1	1			9		
Newburyport	163	15	Dodge	Daniel					1				1				6		

TOWN	PG#	LN#	LAST NAME	FIRST NAME	FREE WHITE MALES under 10	10 to 16	16 to 26	26 to 45	45 and over	FREE WHITE FEMALES under 10	10 to 16	16 to 26	26 to 45	45 and over	TOTAL ALL OTHER	TOTAL SLAVES	TOTALS	DISTRICT/ TOWNSHIP	NOTES
Newburyport	163	16	Dodge	Thomas	3	1	1	1		1	1		1				9		
Newburyport	163	17	Dodge	Abraham	3	1	2	1		2	2		1				12		
Newburyport	163	18	Dodge	Hannah Wido		1							1				2		
Newburyport	163	19	Dowe	William			1						1				2		
Newburyport	163	20	Dossett	Florence			1						1				2		
Newburyport	163	21	Davis	Elias J		1				1		1					3		
Newburyport	163	22	Davis	Edmund			1						1				2		
Newburyport	163	23	Davis	Moses	1				1		1	1		1			5		
Newburyport	163	24	Davis	Moses Junr	1			1		1			1				4		
Newburyport	163	25	Davis	Asa	1	1		1		1	1		1				6		
Newburyport	163	26	Davis	Samuel	1			1					1				3		
Newburyport	163	27	Davis	Samuel Jr		2					1	1					4		
Newburyport	163	28	Davis	Joseph					1					1			2		
Newburyport	163	29	Davis	Joseph Jr	2				1	2	1		2				8		
Newburyport	163	30	Davis	William	1			1		1			1				5		
Newburyport	163	31	Davis	Aaron		2	1		1		1	1	1	1			8		
Newburyport	163	32	Davis	James	1			1		1			1	1			5		
Newburyport	163	33	Davis	Andrew			1	1					1	1			4		
Newburyport	163	34	Davis	Benjamin			1	2					2	1			6		
Newburyport	163	35	Davis	Benjamin Jr			1			2			1				4		
Newburyport	163	36	Davis	Ambros			1					1		1			3		
Newburyport	163	37	Davis	Elizabeth Wido	2	1							1				4		
Newburyport	163	38	Davison	John		1		1					1				3		
Newburyport	163	39	Danforth	Enoch	1			1		1			1				4		
Newburyport	163	40	Dowell	David	1				1	3			1				6		
Newburyport	164	1	Downes	Thomas			1						1				2		
Newburyport	164	2	Downes	Sarah Wido	1								1				2		
Newburyport	164	3	Downer	Hannah								2	1	1			4		
Newburyport	164	4	Dole	Jonathan Jr	1	1		1		2			1				6		
Newburyport	164	5	Dole	Benjamin			1						1	1			3		
Newburyport	164	6	Dole	Friend			1			1			1				3		
Newburyport	164	7	Dole	William		1				1		1					3		
Newburyport	164	8	Dole	Ebenezer		3							1				4		
Newburyport	164	9	Delany	William				1		2			1				4		
Newburyport	164	10	Dorman	Jesse			1						1				2		
Newburyport	164	11	Dennis	James R			1			1				1			3		
Newburyport	164	12	Dennis	Samuel	1			1		1			1				4		
Newburyport	164	13	Doggett	Joseph	3			1		1			1				6		
Newburyport	164	14	Dalton	Jonathan	1			1				1	1				4		
Newburyport	164	15	Dillaway	Thomas				1					1				2		
Newburyport	164	16	Dutton	Stephen	1			1		1			1				4		
Newburyport	164	17	Desmazes	John B	1			1		1			1				4		
Newburyport	164	18	Dudley	Elias	2		1	1		2		1	1				8		
Newburyport	164	19	Dexter	Timothy			1	1					1	1	1		5		
Newburyport	164	20	Downers	Prince Lambart	1			1		1			1				4		
Newburyport	164	21	Emerson	Bulkeley				1					3	1			5		
Newburyport	164	22	Emerson	Bulkeley Jr	4			1			1		1	1			8		
Newburyport	164	23	Emerson	Samuel		2	1						1				4		
Newburyport	164	24	Emerson	Joseph			1						1	1			3		
Newburyport	164	25	Edmunds	Barnabas				1						1			2		
Newburyport	164	26	Eliot	Jeremiah			1			2			1	1			5		
Newburyport	164	27	Elsworth	Jeremiah		1		1					1	1			4		
Newburyport	164	28	Elwell	David			1			1			1				3		
Newburyport	164	29	Ellis	Rachael Wido	2					1			1				4		
Newburyport	164	30	Edwards	John				1					1				2		
Newburyport	164	31	Edwards	Abraham	1			1		1		1		1			5		
Newburyport	164	32	Edwards	Benjamin	2		1					2					5		
Newburyport	164	33	Edwards	Thomas	1	1							1				3		
Newburyport	164	34	Edwards	Edward	2		1			1		1					5		
Newburyport	164	35	Edwards	William	2	1		1		1	1		1				7		
Newburyport	164	36	Edwards	Moses R			2					2	1				5		
Newburyport	164	37	Eustice	William	1	1		1					1	1			6		
Newburyport	164	38	Edes	Isaac	1			1		2			1				5		
Newburyport	164	39	Eaton	Benjamin				1					1	1			3		
Newburyport	164	40	Eaton	Stephen		1		1				1					3		
Newburyport	165	1	England	Francis	1	1	1	1						1			5		
Newburyport	165	2	England	Samuel Jr	1			1		2			1				5		
Newburyport	165	3	Ervins	John	3			1		1	1		1				8		
Newburyport	165	4	Faris	William	1		1		1	3	2		2	1			11		
Newburyport	165	5	Fitz	Mark		1	2	2	1				1	1			8		
Newburyport	165	6	Fitz	John	2	1		1		2			1	1			8		
Newburyport	165	7	Fitz	William	2			1					1				4		
Newburyport	165	8	Follansbee	Thomas M		1		1	1	2	1		1	1			8		
Newburyport	165	9	Follansbee	John N				1		3			1				5		
Newburyport	165	10	Follansbee	Amos Jr		1	1										2		
Newburyport	165	11	Farley	Daniel	1	1	1	1		1			1	2			8		
Newburyport	165	12	Farley	John D				1					2				3		
Newburyport	165	13	Furber	John D		1	1	1		1			1				5		
Newburyport	165	14	Furgeson	Elizabeth Wido	1		2	2		2	1		3	1			12		
Newburyport	165	15	Foster	Samuel	2		1		1		2	1		1			8		

110

TOWN	PG#	LN#	LAST NAME	FIRST NAME	FREE WHITE MALES					FREE WHITE FEMALES					TOTAL ALL OTHER	TOTAL SLAVES	TOTALS	DISTRICT/ TOWNSHIP	NOTES
					under 10	10 to 16	16 to 26	26 to 45	45 and over	under 10	10 to 16	16 to 26	26 to 45	45 and over					
Newburyport	165	16	Foster	Samuel Jr	1		1	1			1	1					5		
Newburyport	165	17	Foster	Samuel 3d	1		1	4				1	1				8		
Newburyport	165	18	Fowler	Samuel			1						1				2		
Newburyport	165	19	Folsom	Jeremiah		1		1					1				3		
Newburyport	165	20	Fry	Zachariah	1	2		1		1			1				6		
Newburyport	165	21	Frothingham	Andrew		1	3		1		1	2	1	1			10		
Newburyport	165	22	Frothingham	Andrew Jr		1	1					1	1				4		
Newburyport	165	23	Frothingham	Benjamin					1	3		1	2				7		
Newburyport	165	24	Frothingham	Gilman		1	1	1		2		2					7		
Newburyport	165	25	Frothingham	Stephen	2	1		1				1	1				6		
Newburyport	165	26	Friend	Henry					1		1	1					3		
Newburyport	165	27	Friend	John					1					2			3		
Newburyport	165	28	Friend	Elizabeth Wido			2							1			3		
Newburyport	165	29	Farnham	William	3			1		3		2	1		1		11		
Newburyport	165	30	Farnham	Zebedee		1			1		1	1		1			5		
Newburyport	165	31	Farnham	Peter	1			1					1	1			4		
Newburyport	165	32	Farnham	David				1					1				2		
Newburyport	165	33	Flanders	Nehemiah	3	1	2		1	1	2	1		1			12		
Newburyport	165	34	Flanders	John			2					1	1				4		
Newburyport	165	35	Fletcher	Uriah		1	2		1			1		1			6		
Newburyport	165	36	Fletcher	Nathaniel		1	1					1					3		
Newburyport	165	37	Foss	John	1			1					1				3		
Newburyport	165	38	French	Samuel Jr	3	1	1	1	1	2		1		1	1		12		
Newburyport	165	39	Ford	Timothy T				1					1				2		
Newburyport	165	40	Favorer	Daniel				1			1	1		2			5		
Newburyport	165	41	Felton	Samuel			1		1				1				3		
Newburyport	166	1	Francis	William	2	1	4	6		1	1		1				16		
Newburyport	166	2	Francis	James	1		1	1		1			1				5		
Newburyport	166	3	Francis	Hannah Wido	1	1	2			1				1			6		
Newburyport	166	4	Francis	Ann Wido								1		2			3		
Newburyport	166	5	Furlong	Laurence		1		1					1	1			4		
Newburyport	166	6	Frazier	Elizabeth Wido		1	1			1		2	1				7		
Newburyport	166	7	Foster	Mary Wido									1	2			3		
Newburyport	166	8	Greenleaf	John			1	1	1	1	1	3					8		
Newburyport	166	9	Greenleaf	John Jr	1			1		3	1	1					7		
Newburyport	166	10	Greenleaf	Jonathan				1					1				2		
Newburyport	166	11	Greenleaf	Abel	1	1		1	1	1	1	2	1		2		11		
Newburyport	166	12	Greenleaf	Abner				1					1				2		
Newburyport	166	13	Greenleaf	Joshua	1	1		1		2		1	1				7		
Newburyport	166	14	Greenleaf	Edmund C	4	1		1			1		2				9		
Newburyport	166	15	Greenleaf	Woodbridge	2			1		1			1				5		
Newburyport	166	16	Greenleaf	Jacob				1				1	1				3		
Newburyport	166	17	Greenleaf	Richard	1			1		3			1	1			7		
Newburyport	166	18	Greenleaf	Lucy Wido						1		1	4	1			7		
Newburyport	166	19	Greenleaf	Elizabeth									1	1			2		
Newburyport	166	20	Greenleaf	Dorothy Wido		1				2			1				4		
Newburyport	166	21	Gunnison	Ebenezer	1	1	2	1		1	1	1	2				10		
Newburyport	166	22	Gallishan	Abraham				1					1				2		
Newburyport	166	23	Gallishan	Abraham Jr		1	2	1		1	1	1					8		
Newburyport	166	24	Gurney	Elisha	2			1		2			1				6		
Newburyport	166	25	Gardner	Benjamin	1		1		1	2	2	1		1			9		
Newburyport	166	26	Gardner	Cristopher		1		1		1	1	1					5		
Newburyport	166	27	Gardner	Robert	2	1		1		2			2				8		
Newburyport	166	28	Granger	Joseph	1			1		3			1				6		
Newburyport	166	29	Gordon	Elisha	2			1		2	1		1				7		
Newburyport	166	30	Gearing	Jabez	1			1					1	1			4		
Newburyport	166	31	Goodrich	Charles				1		2	2	1					7		
Newburyport	166	32	Goodrich	Moses	1	1	1	1		1	1		1	1			8		
Newburyport	166	33	Goodrich	Edward	4			1				1	1				7		
Newburyport	166	34	Goodwin	John		1			1		1		1				4		
Newburyport	166	35	McGaw	John	1	1		1			1		1				5		
Newburyport	166	36	Gotham	Edward		1							1				2		
Newburyport	166	37	Gilman	Arthur		1		1		1	2			1			7		
Newburyport	166	38	Gerrish	oses			1	1				1		1			4		
Newburyport	166	39	Gerrish	Stephen			2	1				3		1			7		
Newburyport	166	40	Giles	Samuel	1	1	1	1		1			1				6		
Newburyport	166	41	Goodhue	Joseph	1	2		1		2			1				7		
Newburyport	166	42	Goodhue	Hezekiah			2		1		1	2		1			7		
Newburyport	166	43	Goodhue	Sarah Wido								1					1		
Newburyport	167	1	Gibson	John	2				1	1			1				5		
Newburyport	167	2	Gage	Jonathan				1			2	1		1			5		
Newburyport	167	3	Greenough	Joseph		1	1	1			1	1		1			6		
Newburyport	167	4	Greenough	John				1		2		2					5		
Newburyport	167	5	George	Benjamin	3		1	1		3	2		1				11		
Newburyport	167	6	George	James				1		3			1				5		
Newburyport	167	7	Greely	Stephen	2		3	2			1		2				10		
Newburyport	167	8	Griffith	Sarah Wido		2	2			1			1				6		
Newburyport	167	9	Griffith	William	1	2		1			1			2			7		
Newburyport	167	10	Geiger	Henry	1		2	1					1				5		
Newburyport	167	11	Green	Joseph	2	1			1	2		1	1				9		
Newburyport	167	12	Haskell	Nehemiah		2		1				1	1				5		
Newburyport	167	13	Haskell	Caleb				1					1	1			3		
Newburyport	167	14	Haskell	John			1			1			1				3		
Newburyport	167	15	Haskell	Hubbard		1	1		1	1		3					8		
Newburyport	167	16	Haskell	Hubbard Jr	2			1		1			1				5		
Newburyport	167	17	Haskell	Jeremiah	3		2	1					1				7		
Newburyport	167	18	Haskell	William		1		1		1							4		
Newburyport	167	19	Hindson	Henry		2			2		1	1		2			8		
Newburyport	167	20	Huse	Joseph	1		2	1		1			1				6		

TOWN	PG#	LN#	LAST NAME	FIRST NAME	FREE WHITE MALES under 10	10 to 16	16 to 26	26 to 45	45 and over	FREE WHITE FEMALES under 10	10 to 16	16 to 26	26 to 45	45 and over	TOTAL ALL OTHER	TOTAL SLAVES	TOTALS	DISTRICT/ TOWNSHIP	NOTES
Newburyport	167	21	Huse	William	2			1			1		2	1			7		
Newburyport	167	22	Huse	Samuel	2	1	5	1		2			1				12		
Newburyport	167	23	Hodgkins	Jacob		1		1					1				3		
Newburyport	167	24	Hunt	Zebedee			1	1	1		1	1		1			6		
Newburyport	167	25	Hunt	Elizabeth Wido	1		5	5		2	4	3	1	1			22		
Newburyport	167	26	Harris	Giles	1			1		1			2	1			6		
Newburyport	167	27	Hale	Jacob	1		1		1				1	1			5		
Newburyport	167	28	Hale	Jacob Jr	3		1	1		1			1	1			8		
Newburyport	167	29	Hale	Joseph			1							1			2		
Newburyport	167	30	Hale	Samuel				1		2			1	1			5		
Newburyport	167	31	Hale	Ebenezer	3		2		1	1			1	1			9		
Newburyport	167	32	Hale	David Wido of										1			1		
Newburyport	167	33	Howard	Stephen	2	2		1		1	1		1	1			9		
Newburyport	167	34	Howard	Mary Wido			4	5		1	1	1		1			13		
Newburyport	167	35	Howard	William		1		1		1		2		1	1		7		
Newburyport	167	36	Hale	Paul	3	1		1		1			1				7		
Newburyport	167	37	Haskell	Elizabeth Wido			1						3	1			5		
Newburyport	167	38	Hale	Robert			1						1	2			4		
Newburyport	167	39	Hillier	Edward	2	1		1		2			1				7		
Newburyport	167	40	Hastings	Susannah Wido									1	1			2		
Newburyport	167	41	Holland	Stephen	2	1		1		1	1	1	1				8		
Newburyport	167	42	Holland	Samuel				1					1	1			3		
Newburyport	167	43	Hillier	Joshua			2						1				3		
Newburyport	167	44	Hillier	Caleb	1		1	1		1			1				5		
Newburyport	168	1	Hawley	William	1				1	2			1				5		
Newburyport	168	2	Harrod	John		1	1					2	3	1	1		10		
Newburyport	168	3	Harrison	John	1			1		2			2				6		
Newburyport	168	4	Hidden	John	1			1		1			1				4		
Newburyport	168	5	Hidden	David				1		1			2				4		
Newburyport	168	6	Honniwell	Daniel			3						1	1			5		
Newburyport	168	7	Honniwell	Richard	1			1		1			1	1	1		6		
Newburyport	168	8	Horton	Samuel	1				1			2		1			5		
Newburyport	168	9	Horton	James			2			1			1				4		
Newburyport	168	10	Horton	Obadiah				1					2	1			4		
Newburyport	168	11	Horton	Obadiah Jr	1			1		2			1				5		
Newburyport	168	12	Horton	Daniel		1	2	1					2	1			7		
Newburyport	168	13	Hoyt	Moses		1		1	1					4			7		
Newburyport	168	14	Hoyt	Moses Jr	1		1		1	1		1	1	1			7		
Newburyport	168	15	Hoyt	Nathan		1			1	2	3	2		2			11		
Newburyport	168	16	Hoyt	Ebenezer		1		1		2	1			1			6		
Newburyport	168	17	Hoyt	David				1					1	1			3		
Newburyport	168	18	Hoyt	Joseph				1		1			1				3		
Newburyport	168	19	Hoyt	William		1				1		1					3		
Newburyport	168	20	Hoyt	Dototthy Wido			1	1					1	1	1		5		
Newburyport	168	21	Ham	Thomas	2			1		1			1	1			6		
Newburyport	168	22	Howard	William			1			1			1				3		
Newburyport	168	23	Hodge	Michael		1	3		1		2	2	1	1			11		
Newburyport	168	24	Hodge	James	1	1	3	1		2			1	1			10		
Newburyport	168	25	Hodge	Nicolas				1					2	2			5		
Newburyport	168	26	Hodge	William			1							1			2		
Newburyport	168	27	Herbett	Charles		2	1	2		1		2	1				9		
Newburyport	168	28	Harton	George C			1			1			1				3		
Newburyport	168	29	Harvey	Thomas	3	1	1	2		1	1	1	1	2			13		
Newburyport	168	30	Harvey	David	2			1					1				4		
Newburyport	168	31	Harvey	William				1			1		1				3		
Newburyport	168	32	Hardin	John	1			1		2		1					5		
Newburyport	168	33	Hardy	Dudley				1		1			1				3		
Newburyport	168	34	Holt	Joseph	1			1					1				3		
Newburyport	168	35	Higgins	Josiah	2			1		1			1				5		
Newburyport	168	36	Holliday	William			2	2					1	1			6		
Newburyport	168	37	Head	Richard					2		1			1			4		
Newburyport	168	38	Hand	William		1		1	1				1				4		
Newburyport	168	39	Herrick	Hannah Wido	1	1							1	1			4		
Newburyport	168	40	Johnson	William P	2	2	1		1				3		1		10		
Newburyport	168	41	Johnson	Nicolas	4	1	1		1		2	3		1			13		
Newburyport	168	42	Johnson	Philip	1		1	1		2			1				6		
Newburyport	168	43	Johnson	John B	1			1					1				3		
Newburyport	169	1	Johnson	Bradford				1						1			2		
Newburyport	169	2	Johnson	Eleazer			1						1				2		
Newburyport	169	3	Johnson	Eleazer Jr	1	2	2						2				7		
Newburyport	169	4	Johnson	Isaac		1		1		1	1		1				5		
Newburyport	169	5	Johnson	Joseph		1	1		1				3		1		7		
Newburyport	169	6	Johnson	Daniel				1						1			2		
Newburyport	169	7	Johnson	Daniel C	1			2	1	2			1	1			8		
Newburyport	169	8	Johnson	Joanna Wido								2	2				4		
Newburyport	169	9	Johnson	William		1			1		1	1		1			5		
Newburyport	169	10	Ingalls	Ann Wido	1			1					1				5		
Newburyport	169	11	Ingalls	Susannah Wido		1	1						1	2			5		
Newburyport	169	12	Jackson	Abraham			2		1	3		3	1				10		
Newburyport	169	13	Jackson	Charles			1				1	1	1				4		
Newburyport	169	14	Jackman	Benjamin	1			1					1				3		
Newburyport	169	15	Jenkins	John			1		1				1	1			4		
Newburyport	169	16	Jenkins	George		1		1		1		2					5		
Newburyport	169	17	Jenkins	Mary Wido								1	2	1			4		
Newburyport	169	18	Jenkins	Ruth Wido								1	1	1			3		
Newburyport	169	19	Ilsley	David	1			1		1			1				4		
Newburyport	169	20	Jewett	Seth	2	1		1			1	1	1				7		
Newburyport	169	21	Jaques	Theophilus	2			1		2		1	1	1			9		
Newburyport	169	22	Johns	Samuel	2			1				1	1	2			7		
Newburyport	169	23	Jacobs	Mary Wido		1				2			1				4		

112

TOWN	PG#	LN#	HEADS OF HOUSEHOLD		FREE WHITE MALES					FREE WHITE FEMALES					TOTAL ALL OTHER	TOTAL SLAVES	TOTALS	DISTRICT/ TOWNSHIP	NOTES
			LAST NAME	FIRST NAME	under 10	10 to 16	16 to 26	26 to 45	45 and over	under 10	10 to 16	16 to 26	26 to 45	45 and over					
Newburyport	169	24	Jones	Reuben				1					1				2		
Newburyport	169	25	Jones	Samuel		2		1				1		1			5		
Newburyport	169	26	Jones	Abraham				1					1	1			3		
Newburyport	169	27	Kettell	James		1			1	1	1	1	1	1			7		
Newburyport	169	28	Kettell	James Jr		1	1	1		1	1	1					6		
Newburyport	169	29	Kettell	Jonathan		1	1	1		3		1	1				8		
Newburyport	169	30	Kilborn	George		1	1		1	1	1	1		2			8		
Newburyport	169	31	Kilborn	Robert	2			1				1					4		
Newburyport	169	32	Knap	Nathaniel		1	2		1		1			1			6		
Newburyport	169	33	Knap	Nathaniel Jr	2	1	1	1		2		1	1				9		
Newburyport	169	34	Knap	Isaac	1			1		1		1					4		
Newburyport	169	35	Knap	Hannah Wido			1					1		1			3		
Newburyport	169	36	Knap	Benoni E					1		1	1		1			4		
Newburyport	169	37	Knap	Anthony	1			1		1			1	1			5		
Newburyport	169	38	Knap	John	1			1		2		1	1	1			7		
Newburyport	169	39	Knap	Samuel				1						2			3		
Newburyport	169	40	Knap	Philip C	2	1	1	1		1		1	1				8		
Newburyport	169	41	Knap	William			1	1				2		2			6		
Newburyport	169	42	Knap	William Jr	1			1				1	1	1			5		
Newburyport	169	43	Knap	Benjamin	1	2	2	1		1		1	1				9		
Newburyport	169	44	Knap	Ebenezer			1					2		1			4		
Newburyport	170	1	Knap	Tristram			1					1					2		
Newburyport	170	2	Kimball	Benjamin	4		4	1		2		1	1				13		
Newburyport	170	3	Kimball	Amos	2		2	1				1	1				7		
Newburyport	170	4	Kimball	Edmund	1			1		2		1	1				6		
Newburyport	170	5	Kimball	William	1			1		2	1		1				6		
Newburyport	170	6	Kimball	Moses	1		2				2	1		1			7		
Newburyport	170	7	Keezer	Eleazer				1		2			2	1			6		
Newburyport	170	8	Keezer	Nathaniel	3			1		1			1				6		
Newburyport	170	9	Knight	Ann Wido	2	2						1	1	1			7		
Newburyport	170	10	Knight	Elizabeth Wido		2				1			1				4		
Newburyport	170	11	Knight	Amos			1	2				1		1			5		
Newburyport	170	12	Knight	Daniel	1			2		2		1		1			7		
Newburyport	170	13	Knight	Daniel Jr			1					1					2		
Newburyport	170	14	Knight	Hale	2		1	1				1	1				6		
Newburyport	170	15	King	Thomas	1			1				1					3		
Newburyport	170	16	Kent	Joseph	1		2		1	2				1			7		
Newburyport	170	17	Kent	Joshua	1				1					1			3		
Newburyport	170	18	Kent	Moses	1		1	1		2		1		1			7		
Newburyport	170	19	Kent	Daniel	2			1		1	1		1	1			7		
Newburyport	170	20	Kuhn	Jacob		1			1	1	1	2		1			7		
Newburyport	170	21	Knowlton	John	1	1	3	1		2		1	1				10		
Newburyport	170	22	Keiff	William	3			1				1					5		
Newburyport	170	23	Lunt	Benjamin	2	1		1	1	2	3	1	1				12		
Newburyport	170	24	Lunt	Samuel		1			1	1	1	2		2			8		
Newburyport	170	25	Lunt	Abel	2			1		1		1	3				8		
Newburyport	170	26	Lunt	William P				1				1	1				3		
Newburyport	170	27	Lunt	Benjamin S	1	1	1					1					4		
Newburyport	170	28	Lunt	Silas			1					1		1			3		
Newburyport	170	29	Lunt	Josiah	2			1		3			1				7		
Newburyport	170	30	Loring	Richard					1	2	1			1			5		
Newburyport	170	31	Lane	David		1	1					1					3		
Newburyport	170	32	Lane	Francis	3	2		1			1		1				8		
Newburyport	170	33	Lane	Benjamin Jr	2			1		2			1				6		
Newburyport	170	34	Leigh	Benjamin	2	1	1		1	1	1	2		1			10		
Newburyport	170	35	Lakeman	Ann Wido							1			1			2		
Newburyport	170	36	Lake	John				1				1					2		
Newburyport	170	37	LeBreton	Peter		1	1		1	1		1	1	1			7		
Newburyport	170	38	Long	Robert	1	3	2		1		3	1		1			12		
Newburyport	170	39	Long	Judith		1				1			1				3		
Newburyport	170	40	Lander	John	1	1		1		1			1				5		
Newburyport	170	41	Lancaster	Henry	1	2	2	1		1	1		1				9		
Newburyport	170	42	Lancaster	Thomas		1		1		1		2	1				6		
Newburyport	170	43	Lowe	John	1		1	1						1			4		
Newburyport	170	44	Little	Hazen			2					1	1				4		
Newburyport	170	45	Laurence	David	2	1		1		2			1	1			8		
Newburyport	170	46	Laird	Robert	1			1		3		1	1				7		
Newburyport	171	1	Leonard	William B				1									1		
Newburyport	171	2	Lewis	Anthony	2			1					1	1			5		
Newburyport	171	3	Lewis	John	2				1	1				3			7		
Newburyport	171	4	Lucas	Thomas	2			1					1				4		
Newburyport	171	5	Libby	John	2			1		1	1		1				6		
Newburyport	171	6	Lanagin	Ann Wido						1			1				2		
Newburyport	171	7	Lenox	James					1			1		1			3		
Newburyport	171	8	Leach	Benjamin	2	1			1	1		1	1	1			8		
Newburyport	171	9	Leach	Sarah Wido			1					1		1			3		
Newburyport	171	10	Lowell	Ebenezer	1			1						1			3		
Newburyport	171	11	Larcum	Luke				2				1					3		
Newburyport	171	12	Marsh	Jonathan	1			1				1	1	1			5		
Newburyport	171	13	Morland	William		1		1				1					3		
Newburyport	171	14	March	Angier		1	3	1		1			1				8		
Newburyport	171	15	Mayhew	Elijah		1		5			1	1	1				9		
Newburyport	171	16	Middleton	William	1			1		2			1				5		
Newburyport	171	17	Milbery	William	1	1		1		2			1				6		
Newburyport	171	18	Moffett	Samuel	1			1					1				3		
Newburyport	171	19	Marchmore	Jeffrey	1				1		1			1			4		
Newburyport	171	20	Marchmore	John		1			1			1		1			4		
Newburyport	171	21	Mulliken	Samuel					1	1			1				3		
Newburyport	171	22	Milton	Charles W Revd	1			1		1	1		2				6		
Newburyport	171	23	Margerand	Joseph	1	1			1	2	2	2	1	1			11		

113

TOWN	PG#	LN#	LAST NAME	FIRST NAME	FREE WHITE MALES under 10	10 to 16	16 to 26	26 to 45	45 and over	FREE WHITE FEMALES under 10	10 to 16	16 to 26	26 to 45	45 and over	TOTAL ALL OTHER	TOTAL SLAVES	TOTALS	DISTRICT/ TOWNSHIP	NOTES
Newburyport	171	24	Moody	David				1	1					2			4		
Newburyport	171	25	Moody	John		1		1					1				3		
Newburyport	171	26	Moody	Joseph		1		1					1	1			4		
Newburyport	171	27	Moody	Benjamin			2	1					1	2			6		
Newburyport	171	28	Moody	Daniel			3			1		1					5		
Newburyport	171	29	Moody	Moses		1								2			3		
Newburyport	171	30	Morse	Jonathan		1	2		1					1			5		
Newburyport	171	31	Morse	Edmund		2			1				1	1			5		
Newburyport	171	32	Morse	Samuel N				1		2			1				4		
Newburyport	171	33	Morse	William	2			1					1				4		
Newburyport	171	34	Morse	Sarah Wido									1	1			2		
Newburyport	171	35	Mersevy	Mary Wido						1		2		1			4		
Newburyport	171	36	Moulton	Joseph		2	2		1		1	2	1	1			10		
Newburyport	171	37	Moulton	Joseph Jr	2	1		1		3		1					8		
Newburyport	171	38	Moulton	Jonathan	2			1				1					4		
Newburyport	171	39	Morris	John	1			1		2			1				5		
Newburyport	171	40	Morris	William				1									1		
Newburyport	171	41	Morrison	Ebenezer	1			1					1				3		
Newburyport	171	42	Morrison	Ebenezer Jr	3	1		1		1			1				7		
Newburyport	171	43	Morrison	Thomas	1			1		1			1				4		
Newburyport	171	44	Morrison	William			1					1					2		
Newburyport	171	45	Morrison	Allen			1						1				2		
Newburyport	172	1	Mills	Levi			1	1		2			1				5		
Newburyport	172	2	Myers	James	1			1					1				3		
Newburyport	172	3	Murry	Elizabeth Wido		1	1						4				6		
Newburyport	172	4	Montgomery	Mary Wido						1	1		1				3		
Newburyport	172	5	Montgomery	Moody				1						1			2		
Newburyport	172	6	Morrill	Micajah	1			1		2			1				5		
Newburyport	172	7	Morrill	Ezekiel		1	4		1			1		1			8		
Newburyport	172	8	Morrill	Benjamin				1					1	1			3		
Newburyport	172	9	Merrill	Robert		1	1	1									3		
Newburyport	172	10	Merrill	Thomas				1		1	1			1			4		
Newburyport	172	11	Merrill	Thomas Jr				1		1	2	1		1			6		
Newburyport	172	12	Merrill	James		1		1			2	1		1			6		
Newburyport	172	13	Merrill	Jonathan			1			2			1				4		
Newburyport	172	14	Merrill	Thomas P	1			1					1				3		
Newburyport	172	15	Merrill	Daniel		1		1		2				1			5		
Newburyport	172	16	Merrill	Ezra	1		1						1				3		
Newburyport	172	17	Mace	Bernard				1						1			2		
Newburyport	172	18	Mace	Abraham	1	1		1		2	1	1		2			9		
Newburyport	172	19	Minor	Francis		1	2						1				4		
Newburyport	172	20	Marchant	Samuel		1		1				1	1				4		
Newburyport	172	21	Murry	John	1			1	1	1	2	1	1				8		
Newburyport	172	22	Mitchell	Josiah		1		1			1		1				4		
Newburyport	172	23	Mitchell	Rachel Wido		2	4	1					1				8		
Newburyport	172	24	Mansfield	David	1			1		1			1				4		
Newburyport	172	25	Marston	John	1		2			1			1				5		
Newburyport	172	26	McDaniel	Ruth Wido									1				1		
Newburyport	172	27	Mercy	Anthony	1			1		1			1				4		
Newburyport	172	28	Manser	Samuel				1				1	1				3		
Newburyport	172	29	Myrick	Jacob	2	1		1					1	1			6		
Newburyport	172	30	Merrill	Sarah Wido									1				1		
Newburyport	172	31	Martin	Mary Wido									1	1			2		
Newburyport	172	32	Noyes	Joseph	1		1	2	1				1	1			7		
Newburyport	172	33	Noyes	Joseph Jr	1			1		2			1	1			6		
Newburyport	172	34	Noyes	Joseph 3	1			1		2			1				5		
Newburyport	172	35	Noyes	Josepth 4th			2			1		1					4		
Newburyport	172	36	Noyes	Nathaniel	2	2		1		2		1	1				9		
Newburyport	172	37	Noyes	Samuel				1						4			5		
Newburyport	172	38	Noyes	Samuel Jr	2	1		1		2			1				7		
Newburyport	172	39	Noyes	William			1	1					1				3		
Newburyport	172	40	Noyes	Isaac				1						1			2		
Newburyport	172	41	Noyes	Richard S.	4			1		1	1		1				8		
Newburyport	172	42	Noyes	Amos	3	1	1	1				2	1				9		
Newburyport	172	43	Noyes	Timothy	3			1					1				5		
Newburyport	173	1	Noyes	Jacob				1			1		1				3		
Newburyport	173	2	Noyes	Dorcas Wido										1			1		
Newburyport	173	3	Noyes	John M	2			1		1		1					5		
Newburyport	173	4	Noyes	Paul			2		2		1		2	1			8		
Newburyport	173	5	Noyes	Enoch	1	1	1					1					4		
Newburyport	173	6	Noyes	Ebenezer	1	1	5					2	1	1			11		
Newburyport	173	7	Noyes	Eliphalet				1					1	1			3		
Newburyport	173	8	Noyes	Nathan			1						1				2		
Newburyport	173	9	Nutting	William	1			1					2				4		
Newburyport	173	10	Nellage	Duncan			1										1		
Newburyport	173	11	Nicolls	John				1					1				2		
Newburyport	173	12	Nicolls	Mary Wido		1	1					1	1				4		
Newburyport	173	13	Norton	Bishop	1	1		1	1	1		2	2	1			10		
Newburyport	173	14	Norton	George			1			1		1	1	1			5		
Newburyport	173	15	Norton	Benjamin	3	2	1		1	2		2		2			13		
Newburyport	173	16	Norton	John	2	1		1		1			1				6		
Newburyport	173	17	Norton	Michael	2			1		1			1				5		
Newburyport	173	18	Norton	Constantine			1						1				2		
Newburyport	173	19	Norwood	Judith Wido	1	2	2	1		2			1				9		
Newburyport	173	20	Newmarsh	Joseph	1	1							2				5		
Newburyport	173	21	Nelson	Samuel			1							1			2		
Newburyport	173	22	Newman	Elizabeth Wido				1			1		1				3		
Newburyport	173	23	Newman	John	1			1			1		1	1			5		
Newburyport	173	24	Newman	Nathaniel				1						3			4		
Newburyport	173	25	Newman	Nathaniel Jr			1		1		1	2	2	1			8		

TOWN	PG#	LN#	LAST NAME	FIRST NAME	FREE WHITE MALES					FREE WHITE FEMALES					TOTAL ALL OTHER	TOTAL SLAVES	TOTALS	DISTRICT/ TOWNSHIP	NOTES
					under 10	10 to 16	16 to 26	26 to 45	45 and over	under 10	10 to 16	16 to 26	26 to 45	45 and over					
Newburyport	173	26	Newman	Samuel				1					1	2			4		
Newburyport	173	27	Newman	Joseph	1			1		1	1		1				5		
Newburyport	173	28	Newman	Timothy		1	1					2	1				5		
Newburyport	173	29	Newman	Benjamin	1			1		1			1	1			5		
Newburyport	173	30	Nowell	George	2			1		2			1	1			7		
Newburyport	173	31	Nowell	Silas		1	1	1					2				5		
Newburyport	173	32	Nowell	Joseph			1	1		1	1	1		1			6		
Newburyport	173	33	Nowell	Samuel		1		1		1				1			4		
Newburyport	173	34	Nowell	Joseph Jr	1			1					1	2			5		
Newburyport	173	35	Nowell	Richard		1	1						2				4		
Newburyport	173	36	Obrien	John	2	2	2	1	1	2	1	1	1	1			14		
Newburyport	173	37	OBrien	Joseph	2	2		1					2				7		
Newburyport	173	38	Otis	Samuel A	2	1		1					2	1			7		
Newburyport	173	39	Osgood	Alfred			2	1					1				4		
Newburyport	173	40	Orne	William	1			1		2			1	1			6		
Newburyport	173	41	Orne	John		1	1			1							4		
Newburyport	173	42	O'Neill	Mercy Wido									1	1			2		
Newburyport	173	43	Osborne	Mary Wido	4							1	1				6		
Newburyport	173	44	Over	Rhoda Wido						1		1	1	1			4		
Newburyport	174	1	Plummer	Joseph		1	2	1					1				5		
Newburyport	174	2	Plummer	Josiah				1				1	1				3		
Newburyport	174	3	Plummer	Daniel		1	2							2			5		
Newburyport	174	4	Plummer	Samuel	2		1	1		2	2		1				9		
Newburyport	174	5	Plummer	Enoch	1	1		1			1	2					6		
Newburyport	174	6	Plummer	Tristram		1	1				1	2		3			8		
Newburyport	174	7	Plummer	Nathan			1			1		2					4		
Newburyport	174	8	Plummer	Seth	2	1	1					2					6		
Newburyport	174	9	Pearson	John	1	1		1					1				4		
Newburyport	174	10	Pearson	John Jn	3	1	2	1		2		1	2				12		
Newburyport	174	11	Pearson	Jonathan					1	2	1		1				5		
Newburyport	174	12	Pearson	Thomas	1				1	1	2		1				6		
Newburyport	174	13	Pearson	David		1		1		2			1				5		
Newburyport	174	14	Pearson	Amos			1	1		1	1						4		
Newburyport	174	15	Pearson	Moses	3	1		1		2			1	1			9		
Newburyport	174	16	Pearson	Jethro	1		3						1				5		
Newburyport	174	17	Pearson	Theodore	2		1		1	1	3	1	1				10		
Newburyport	174	18	Pearson	Benjamin		1		1		1			1				4		
Newburyport	174	19	Pearson	Isaac G	1	1	3		1			1	4	3			14		
Newburyport	174	20	Pearson	Hannah Wido								1	1	1			3		
Newburyport	174	21	Pearson	Simeon	2			1		2	3		1				9		
Newburyport	174	22	Perkins	Mathew				1					1				2		
Newburyport	174	23	Perkins	Benjamin				1		1	1		2				5		
Newburyport	174	24	Perkins	Jacob	2	1		1		2	1		1				8		
Newburyport	174	25	Perkins	Abraham	3	2	1	1				1	1				9		
Newburyport	174	26	Peirce	Nathan					1				2	1			4		
Newburyport	174	27	Peirce	Nathan for the work hous	1		2	6	6			1	9	10	1		36		
Newburyport	174	28	Peirce	Henry			1	1					2	1			5		
Newburyport	174	29	Peirce	Enoch	1	1	1	1	3	1		1	1				10		
Newburyport	174	30	Peirce	Benjamin		1		1		4		1	1				8		
Newburyport	174	31	Peirce	Nicolas	1	2		1					1				5		
Newburyport	174	32	Piper	Walter		1	2	1		1		2	1				8		
Newburyport	174	33	Piper	Walter Jr	2	1		1		2			1				7		
Newburyport	174	34	Piper	William			1			1		1					3		
Newburyport	174	35	Pettingel	Edmund				1					1				2		
Newburyport	174	36	Pettingel	Joshua			2	1		1	2		1				7		
Newburyport	174	37	Pettingel	Mathew		1		1		1	2		1				6		
Newburyport	174	38	Pettingel	John		1		1				3	1				6		
Newburyport	174	39	Pardee	Aaron	2	1		1		1		1	1				7		
Newburyport	174	40	Pritchard	Hugh		2	1	1		1			1				6		
Newburyport	174	41	Palmer	Timothy	1			1					1				3		
Newburyport	174	42	Palmer	Andras	1		2	1		1	1		1				7		
Newburyport	174	43	Paris	Peter				1				1					2		
Newburyport	174	44	Pulsifer	Ebenezer				1					1				2		
Newburyport	175	1	Prince	James	1		3		1	1	2	2	2	1			13		
Newburyport	175	2	Prince	Ezekiel	2	1	2	1		3	1		2				12		
Newburyport	175	3	Prince	John	2			1		1			1				5		
Newburyport	175	4	Pike	Nicolas		1		1						1	1		4		
Newburyport	175	5	Pike	Martha Wido	2	1				1				1			5		
Newburyport	175	6	Pike	Martha Wido Junr	1					1	1		1	1	1		6		
Newburyport	175	7	Pike	Joseph	4			1					1				6		
Newburyport	175	8	Pike	Daniel				1					1				2		
Newburyport	175	9	Pike	Daniel Jr	3	1		1		1			1				7		
Newburyport	175	10	Pike	Enoch	1		1	1		1		1	1				6		
Newburyport	175	11	Pike	William			1			1		1					3		
Newburyport	175	12	Pike	Josiah			1			1		1					3		
Newburyport	175	13	Poor	Nathan			2	1	1		1			1			6		
Newburyport	175	14	Poor	William			1	1	1		1			3			7		
Newburyport	175	15	Potter	Thomas	2	1		1		1	1	4		1			12		
Newburyport	175	16	Paine	Thomas			1			2		1	1				5		
Newburyport	175	17	Parsons	Theophilus	2		1	1	1	1	2	3	2	1	1		15		
Newburyport	175	18	Parsons	Harry		1		1					1	1			4		
Newburyport	175	19	Parsons	Thomas	1	1		1		1	1		1				6		
Newburyport	175	20	Parsons	Jonathan			2						1				3		
Newburyport	175	21	Putman	Billings	2		2	1		2	1						8		
Newburyport	175	22	Pidgeon	Benjamin				2						2			4		
Newburyport	175	23	Prout	William M		1	1				1	2			1		6		
Newburyport	175	24	Potter	William	1		1						1				3		
Newburyport	175	25	Potter	James			2	1			1	1					5		
Newburyport	175	26	Peters	Richard	2	1		1					1				6		
Newburyport	175	27	Peters	John			1					1					2		

TOWN	PG#	LN#	LAST NAME	FIRST NAME	FREE WHITE MALES under 10	10 to 16	16 to 26	26 to 45	45 and over	FREE WHITE FEMALES under 10	10 to 16	16 to 26	26 to 45	45 and over	TOTAL ALL OTHER	TOTAL SLAVES	TOTALS	DISTRICT/ TOWNSHIP	NOTES
Newburyport	175	28	Pilsbury	Samuel		1		1	1		1		1	1			6		
Newburyport	175	29	Pilsbury	Samuel Jr	2		1			2	1		1				7		
Newburyport	175	30	Pilsbury	John	1			1	1	1	1	2		1			7		
Newburyport	175	31	Pilsbury	Michael	2	1		1		1		1	2	1			9		
Newburyport	175	32	Pilsbury	Benjamin	2			1					2				5		
Newburyport	175	33	Phillemore	Samuel	1		1						1				3		
Newburyport	175	34	Pickett	William	1	3			1	2		1	1				9		
Newburyport	175	35	Parker	Silas	1	1	1		1		2	1		1			8		
Newburyport	175	36	Parker	George	1			1			1	1					4		
Newburyport	175	37	Packer	Thomas	2	1	1		1			1	1				7		
Newburyport	175	38	Platt	Thomas	1	2			1				1				5		
Newburyport	175	39	Pingree	Daniel R	1			2				1					4		
Newburyport	175	40	Patch	Joseph	2			1				1					4		
Newburyport	175	41	Page	Daniel	1			1		1			1				4		
Newburyport	175	42	Perry	Joseph	2			1		1			2	1			7		
Newburyport	175	43	Parry	Samuel H	2			1					1				4		
Newburyport	175	44	Parchard	Samuel	2		2			1		2					7		
Newburyport	176	1	Peabody	Jona	1	1	1	1		2	1		1				8		
Newburyport	176	2	Quimby	Henry	1		1	1		2							5		
Newburyport	176	3	Raboteau	Charles C				1		2	1		2				6		
Newburyport	176	4	Reed	Joseph	1			1		1			3	1			7		
Newburyport	176	5	Ryan	Augustus	1	1		1		1		1	1				6		
Newburyport	176	6	Racklyeth	Benjamin	1	1	2		1	1	1			2			9		
Newburyport	176	7	Rand	Edward		2	1		1	1	1	1	1				8		
Newburyport	176	8	Rogers	Robert				1			1		1				3		
Newburyport	176	9	Rogers	Robery Jr	3	1	1	1			2		1				9		
Newburyport	176	10	Rogers	Benjamin				1					1				2		
Newburyport	176	11	Rogers	Benjamin Jr	2			1		1			1				5		
Newburyport	176	12	Rogers	George W	1		1	1		2			1				6		
Newburyport	176	13	Rogers	Mary Wido						4		1	1				6		
Newburyport	176	14	Rogers	Moses Wido of									1				1		
Newburyport	176	15	Rogers	Moses Wido of Jr		2	3			1			1				7		
Newburyport	176	16	Rogers	Amos				1		1			1				3		
Newburyport	176	17	Rowell	Olive Wido		1				1			2				4		
Newburyport	176	18	Raynes	John	1			1					1				3		
Newburyport	176	19	Remick	William				1		1		1	1				4		
Newburyport	176	20	Robinson	John		1	1	1		1			1	1			6		
Newburyport	176	21	Robinson	Daniel				1					1				2		
Newburyport	176	22	Richards	Daniel		1	1	1		1			1				5		
Newburyport	176	23	Richards	James	1			1					1				3		
Newburyport	176	24	Richardson	Samuel			1	3		1		1	1		2		9		
Newburyport	176	25	Richardson	Thomas	1			1		3			1				6		
Newburyport	176	26	Richardson	Ann Wido		2				2			1				5		
Newburyport	176	27	Rutley	Henry	1				1	1		2	3				8		
Newburyport	176	28	Rose	Eber	2			1		2			1				6		
Newburyport	176	29	Rolf	Samuel				1		3		1					5		
Newburyport	176	30	Russell	William		1	1	1			1	2		1			8		
Newburyport	176	31	Russell	John				1		1	1		1	1			5		
Newburyport	176	32	Rappal	George	1		1	1				2		1			6		
Newburyport	176	33	Rutherford	Alexander				1				2					3		
Newburyport	176	34	Rutherford	John	1			1					1				3		
Newburyport	176	35	Rutherford	Joseph	2			1		1		1	1	1			7		
Newburyport	176	36	Spring	Samuel Revd	5	1			1		1	2	1				11		
Newburyport	176	37	Smith	Leonard		3	4		1	1		2		3			14		
Newburyport	176	38	Smith	Richard				1					1				2		
Newburyport	176	39	Smith	Nathaniel	1	1		1				2					5		
Newburyport	176	40	Smith	Thomas	2			1		1	1						5		
Newburyport	177	1	Smith	Josiah		1	1		1	1	2	1		1			8		
Newburyport	177	2	Smith	James			2	1		1				2			6		
Newburyport	177	3	Smith	Michael	1		1	1		1			1				5		
Newburyport	177	4	Smith	Samuel				1					1				2		
Newburyport	177	5	Smith	Elizabeth Wido		2	2			2			1				7		
Newburyport	177	6	Stone	John		3		1					1				5		
Newburyport	177	7	Stone	Jacob	1			1		1		1					4		
Newburyport	177	8	Stone	Isaac		1	2			1		1	1				6		
Newburyport	177	9	Stone	Ebenezer	2	1			1	2	1	1	1				9		
Newburyport	177	10	Stone	Daniel		1		1					1				3		
Newburyport	177	11	Stone	Benjamin	1			1		1			1				4		
Newburyport	177	12	Stone	Sarah Wido								1		1			2		
Newburyport	177	13	Stanwood	Joseph	3	1			1	1	2		1				9		
Newburyport	177	14	Stanwood	Abel		1		1		2	1	1	1				7		
Newburyport	177	15	Stanwood	Thomas	2	1		1		3	1		1				9		
Newburyport	177	16	Stanwood	Nathaniel				1					1				2		
Newburyport	177	17	Stanwood	John	2	2			1	1		1					7		
Newburyport	177	18	Stanwood	Philip	1			1		1		1					4		
Newburyport	177	19	Seward	Samuel Wido of	2		3	4	1	2		1		1			14		
Newburyport	177	20	Spiller	Henry				1		4		1		2			8		
Newburyport	177	21	Scott	Joel	2			1		3			1				7		
Newburyport	177	22	Swasey	Edward	3	1		1		3	2	1	1				12		
Newburyport	177	23	Swasey	Joseph		1	1		1			2		1			6		
Newburyport	177	24	Swasey	Joseph Jr	1			1		2			1				5		
Newburyport	177	25	Swasey	Stephen		1			1	1		1		1			5		
Newburyport	177	26	Stickney	William			2		1	1		1	2				7		
Newburyport	177	27	Stickney	William Jr		1			1			3		1			6		
Newburyport	177	28	Stickney	Jonathan		1	1		1				1				4		
Newburyport	177	29	Stickney	Jonathan Jr				1		3	2		1				7		
Newburyport	177	30	Stickney	John		2			1			1	1				5		
Newburyport	177	31	Stickney	John Jr	2			1		4			1				8		
Newburyport	177	32	Stickney	Moses	1	1		1		2	1		1				7		
Newburyport	177	33	Stickney	Jacob	1			1		1			1				4		

TOWN	PG#	LN#	LAST NAME	FIRST NAME	FREE WHITE MALES under 10	10 to 16	16 to 26	26 to 45	45 and over	FREE WHITE FEMALES under 10	10 to 16	16 to 26	26 to 45	45 and over	TOTAL ALL OTHER	TOTAL SLAVES	TOTALS	DISTRICT/ TOWNSHIP	NOTES
Newburyport	177	34	Stickney	Jacob Jr			2			2		1					5		
Newburyport	177	35	Stickney	Ebenezer	1			1		2			1				5		
Newburyport	177	36	Stickney	Thomas	3		1	1					2				7		
Newburyport	177	37	Stickney	Gideon W		1	1			1			1				4		
Newburyport	177	38	Stickney	Sarah Wido									1	2			3		
Newburyport	177	39	Stickney	Alice Wido	1	1	1						1				4		
Newburyport	177	40	Stickney	Sarah Wido Jr				1		1	2	2		1			7		
Newburyport	177	41	Searle	Mary Wido	1	1				2		3		1			8		
Newburyport	177	42	Small	Elisha	2			1					1	1			5		
Newburyport	177	43	Shanks	Benjamin		1		1					1				3		
Newburyport	178	1	Swett	Edmund		2	1		1	1	1	1		1			8		
Newburyport	178	2	Swett	Samuel		1	1						2				4		
Newburyport	178	3	Swett	Jacob	2	2	1	1					2				8		
Newburyport	178	4	Simpson	David	1			1		2			1	1			6		
Newburyport	178	5	Somerby	Thomas		1		1		1			1				4		
Newburyport	178	6	Somerby	Thomas Jr				1				1		1			3		
Newburyport	178	7	Somerby	John					1			1	1				3		
Newburyport	178	8	Somerby	John F	2	1	1			1		1	2	1			9		
Newburyport	178	9	Somerby	Sarah Wido									1	1			2		
Newburyport	178	10	Somerby	Abraham				1						1			2		
Newburyport	178	11	Somerby	Daniel	2	1	1		1	2				1			8		
Newburyport	178	12	Somerby	Benjamin	2		1	1		2	3		1	1			11		
Newburyport	178	13	Somerby	Moses	3	1		1				1		1			7		
Newburyport	178	14	Somerby	Enoch				1		3			2	1			7		
Newburyport	178	15	Salter	Francis				1		2		1					4		
Newburyport	178	16	Salter	Ebenezer	1			1				1					3		
Newburyport	178	17	Stevenson	Robert					1		1		3				5		
Newburyport	178	18	Sargent	Ebenezer					1	4		1		2	1		9		
Newburyport	178	19	Sargent	Amos	1			1		2			1				5		
Newburyport	178	20	Shackford	Levi	2	1		1		1			1	1			7		
Newburyport	178	21	Steele	Ebenezer				1				1	1				3		
Newburyport	178	22	Somerby	Margaret Wido	1								1				2		
Newburyport	178	23	Swain	Edward Wid of	2		2			2		2		1			9		
Newburyport	178	24	Sanborn	Enoch		2	2		1	2				1			8		
Newburyport	178	25	Sawyer	Micajah		1			1		2	1		2	1		8		
Newburyport	178	26	Sawyer	Jeremiah		1		1					1				3		
Newburyport	178	27	Spooner	Bartholomew				1			4	1	1				7		
Newburyport	178	28	Sevier	Joseph		3		1		3	1		1				9		
Newburyport	178	29	Short	Sarah Wido	2				1		1		1				5		
Newburyport	178	30	Short	Elizabeth Wido	1					2		1	1				5		
Newburyport	178	31	Short	Joseph	3	1		1		1				1			7		
Newburyport	178	32	Short	William	1	1		1		2	1		1				7		
Newburyport	178	33	Stewart	James	1			1		2			1				5		
Newburyport	178	34	Sumner	Ebenezer	1		2		1	2	1	1		1			9		
Newburyport	178	35	Stoves	David					1	1	1			1			4		
Newburyport	178	36	Stover	William			1					1					2		
Newburyport	178	37	Stover	Sarah Wido	4		2	1				1	1	1			10		
Newburyport	178	38	Sylvester	Adam	1			1		2			1				5		
Newburyport	178	39	Shaw	Samuel	1	1			1	2			1				6		
Newburyport	178	40	Shaw	Andrew		1		1		2		1	1				6		
Newburyport	178	41	Stevens	Samuel	2	1		1					1	1			6		
Newburyport	178	42	Spafford	Daniel	1	1	2	1		2			1	2			10		
Newburyport	178	43	Spalding	Jeptha	1	1		1				1	1				5		
Newburyport	178	44	Soward	Henry			1						1	1			3		
Newburyport	178	45	Sweetser	Seth			1			1	1	1					4		
Newburyport	179	1	Sillaway	John			1			2	1	1	1				6		
Newburyport	179	2	Sillaway	Daniel	2	1	1			2			1				7		
Newburyport	179	3	Stockman	John	1		1					2		1			5		
Newburyport	179	4	Story	William		1			1	1		2	1	1			7		
Newburyport	179	5	Toppan	Sewell	2			1		1		2	1				7		
Newburyport	179	6	Toppan	Benjamin	3	1		1		1	1	1	1	1			10		
Newburyport	179	7	Toppan	Benjamin H	1			1					1				3		
Newburyport	179	8	Toppan	Joshua	3			1		2	1		1				8		
Newburyport	179	9	Toppan	Enoch		1	1	3		5			1				12		
Newburyport	179	10	Toppan	Joseph	1	2	1		1		1	2		1			9		
Newburyport	179	11	Toppan	Amos	1		4	1			1	1	1				9		
Newburyport	179	12	Toppan	Edward	3	1			1	1		2	1	1			10		
Newburyport	179	13	Toppan	Abner	2	1	2	1		1		1	1				9		
Newburyport	179	14	Toppan	William	1	2		1		4			1				9		
Newburyport	179	15	Toppan	John	2			1		2		1	1	1			8		
Newburyport	179	16	Toppan	Samuel	2			1		2			1				6		
Newburyport	179	17	Toppan	Elizabeth Wido								1	1				2		
Newburyport	179	18	Todd	William	4	2	1		1		1	1		1			11		
Newburyport	179	19	Todd	Jeremy		3		1		1	1	1		1			8		
Newburyport	179	20	Todd	Joanna Wido	2		3	2		1			1	1			10		
Newburyport	179	21	Todd	William Wido of								1	1				2		
Newburyport	179	22	Tyler	Joseph	2			1		1	1		1				6		
Newburyport	179	23	Thompson	Thomas		1	2					2	1	2			9		
Newburyport	179	24	Thompson	Samuel Wido of		3				1		2					6		
Newburyport	179	25	Thompson	Charles			1			2			1				4		
Newburyport	179	26	Titcomb	Michael					1			2		2			5		
Newburyport	179	27	Titcomb	Michael Jr					1			1		1			3		
Newburyport	179	28	Titcomb	Jonathan					1	1		2		1			5		
Newburyport	179	29	Titcomb	Jonathan Jr	2			1		1	1		1				6		
Newburyport	179	30	Titcomb	Richard					1				2				3		
Newburyport	179	31	Titcomb	Richard Jr	2		1						1				4		
Newburyport	179	32	Titcomb	William	1	1	1		1	1	1	1		2			9		
Newburyport	179	33	Titcomb	William Jr	2			1		1			1				5		
Newburyport	179	34	Titcomb	John B	2		1	1		1		1	1				7		
Newburyport	179	35	Titcomb	John L	3	1		1		1			1				7		

TOWN	PG#	LN#	LAST NAME	FIRST NAME	FREE WHITE MALES under 10	10 to 16	16 to 26	26 to 45	45 and over	FREE WHITE FEMALES under 10	10 to 16	16 to 26	26 to 45	45 and over	TOTAL ALL OTHER	TOTAL SLAVES	TOTALS	DISTRICT/ TOWNSHIP	NOTES
Newburyport	179	36	Titcomb	Benariah					1			1	3	1			6		
Newburyport	179	37	Titcomb	Nicolas	1	1	4			3		2		1			12		
Newburyport	179	38	Titcomb	Enoch		3	1		1	3		2	1				11		
Newburyport	179	39	Titcomb	Joshua					1	2	1	2		1			7		
Newburyport	179	40	Titcomb	Samuel		1	1	1		1	1		1	2			8		
Newburyport	179	41	Titcomb	Henry	2		1				1		1				5		
Newburyport	179	42	Titcomb	Mary Wido			1						1	1			3		
Newburyport	179	43	Titcomb	Sarah Wido								1		1			2		
Newburyport	179	44	Titcomb	Ann Wido		2				2			1		1		6		
Newburyport	179	45	Tucker	William			1			3			1				5		
Newburyport	179	46	Tucker	John		1	1						1	1			4		
Newburyport	179	47	Tucker	George		1	1			3			1				6		
Newburyport	180	1	Teed	Nathaniel	1			1		1		1		1			5		
Newburyport	180	2	Tufts	John	1		2		1		1			1			6		
Newburyport	180	3	Tufts	Abigail Wido	1									1			2		
Newburyport	180	4	Tracy	Merian Wido				1				1	1	1			4		
Newburyport	180	5	Tracy	Mary Wido	1		1			1	3	3		1			10		
Newburyport	180	6	Tracy	John	2	1	1	1	2		3	1	2	1			14		
Newburyport	180	7	Tracy	Nicolas		1	1			2			2				6		
Newburyport	180	8	Teel	Joseph		1	2				1	2		1			7		
Newburyport	180	9	Teel	John Wido of		1				1		1		1			4		
Newburyport	180	10	Truesdale	Samuel	1		1			1	1		1				5		
Newburyport	180	11	Truesdale	Richard	1	1	1							1			4		
Newburyport	180	12	Thurston	Enoch	1	3	1			2			1	1			9		
Newburyport	180	13	Tenny	Richard	1	2	2						2				7		
Newburyport	180	14	Tenny	Samuel	1		1					1	1				4		
Newburyport	180	15	Talbot	Nathaniel			1						1				2		
Newburyport	180	16	Thing	Josiah	1		1	1					1				4		
Newburyport	180	17	Tarbox	William				1		1				1			3		
Newburyport	180	18	Trainer	James				1		1							3		
Newburyport	180	19	Thomas	William	1		1	1					1				4		
Newburyport	180	20	Thomas	Thomas	1		1			1	1	1					5		
Newburyport	180	21	Toppan	John Wido of							1	1		1			3		
Newburyport	180	22	Vezie	Lydia							1			1			2		
Newburyport	180	23	Whittemore	Joseph		1	1		1		1	1		1			6		
Newburyport	180	24	Whitmore	Joseph	2		1						1				4		
Newburyport	180	25	Whitmore	Jonathan			1	1				1		1			4		
Newburyport	180	26	Wheeler	Moses	1	1	1				1		1				5		
Newburyport	180	27	Wheeler	Samuel	3	1	1			2			1				8		
Newburyport	180	28	Woodman	Jonathan		2	1		1	1			1	1	1		8		
Newburyport	180	29	Woodman	Joseph H	3		1			2		1	1				8		
Newburyport	180	30	Woodman	William		1	1			1			1				4		
Newburyport	180	31	Walsh	Michael	1		1			2	3		1				8		
Newburyport	180	32	Walsh	Richard	1		1	1		1		1	1	1			7		
Newburyport	180	33	Wells	John		1		1					1	1			4		
Newburyport	180	34	Wells	John Jr	1	1	1	1				1	1	1			7		
Newburyport	180	35	Wells	David				1		2				1			4		
Newburyport	180	36	Wells	Moses	2		1			1	1	1					6		
Newburyport	180	37	Wyatt	Benjamin	1			1		2	2		1	2			9		
Newburyport	180	38	Wyatt	Josiah	1		1					1					3		
Newburyport	180	39	Warker	Charles	2	1		1					1	1			6		
Newburyport	180	40	Warner	Groye	2	1		1					1	1			6		
Newburyport	180	41	Wheelwright	Abraham	3	1	1		1	2	1	1	2				12		
Newburyport	180	42	Wigglesworth	Michael				2		3		1	1	1			8		
Newburyport	180	43	Willard	Josiah				2				1	1				4		
Newburyport	181	1	Woodwell	Jacob				1		1		2					4		
Newburyport	181	2	Wessell	James Wido of				3		1	1		1				6		
Newburyport	181	3	Williams	Richard				2			1		1	1			5		
Newburyport	181	4	Williams	George	1		1					1					3		
Newburyport	181	5	Whitcher	Elizabeth Wido										2			2		
Newburyport	181	6	Williams	Joseph	2	2		1		1		2		1			9		
Newburyport	181	7	Williams	Lucy Wido		1	1						1				3		
Newburyport	181	8	Wood	Abner	2	1	1	1		2	1		2				10		
Newburyport	181	9	Wood	John Jr	1		1	1				1	1				5		
Newburyport	181	10	Wood	David			1	2	1	2	1		2	1			10		
Newburyport	181	11	Wood	Thomas	2	1		1		1			1				6		
Newburyport	181	12	Wood	Joseph				1		1			1				3		
Newburyport	181	13	Wood	William	3	1	1	1		1			2	1			10		
Newburyport	181	14	Woart	William				1		1		2	1				5		
Newburyport	181	15	Work	William	1	1	4	1		1			1	1			10		
Newburyport	181	16	Work	John				2						1			3		
Newburyport	181	17	Waterman	Luther			2	1					2				5		
Newburyport	181	18	Whitney	Elisha		1			1			2	1	1			6		
Newburyport	181	19	Wakefield	William				1		2		1					4		
Newburyport	181	20	Whittleton	William	3			1	1	1				1			7		
Newburyport	181	21	Wyer	William		1	1		1		1		1	1			6		
Newburyport	181	22	Wyer	William Jr	2	1		1		2			1	1			8		
Newburyport	181	23	Wyer	Nathaniel			1	1				1		1			4		
Newburyport	181	24	Whiting	Joseph				1					1				2		
Newburyport	181	25	White	Gilman	3		1	1		1		1	1	1			9		
Newburyport	181	26	Watkins	William				1					1	3			6		
Newburyport	181	27	Wallace	Samuel				1					1				2		
Newburyport	181	28	Wallace	Robert	1		1		1	1				3			7		
Newburyport	181	29	Warden	Martha Wido	1					2		1					4		
Newburyport	181	30	Witham	Thomas	3	1		1					1				6		
Newburyport	181	31	Weed	William	1	1	1	1		2			1				7		
Newburyport	181	32	Whitehouse	Stephen	3			1					1				5		
Newburyport	181	33	Wilson	Andrew	1			1				1		1			4		
Newburyport	181	34	Whelpley	Anson				1					1				2		
Newburyport	181	35	Wise	William	1			1		1			1				4		

TOWN	PG#	LN#	LAST NAME	FIRST NAME	under 10	10 to 16	16 to 26	26 to 45	45 and over	under 10	10 to 16	16 to 26	26 to 45	45 and over	TOTAL ALL OTHER	TOTAL SLAVES	TOTALS	DISTRICT/ TOWNSHIP	NOTES
			HEADS OF HOUSEHOLD		FREE WHITE MALES					FREE WHITE FEMALES									
Newburyport	181	36	Wingate	Edmund	1				1	1	1	1	1				6		
Newburyport	181	37	Young	Israel	2			1		1			1				5		
Newburyport	181	38	Young	Jonathan	1	1	1	1	1			1		1			7		
Newburyport	181	39	Young	Joseph	2			1		2			1				6		
Newburyport	181	40	Young	Reuben				1					2				3		

TOWN	PG#	LN#	HEADS OF HOUSEHOLD LAST NAME	FIRST NAME	FREE WHITE MALES under 10	10 to 16	16 to 26	26 to 45	45 and over	FREE WHITE FEMALES under 10	10 to 16	16 to 26	26 to 45	45 and over	TOTAL ALL OTHER	TOTAL SLAVES	TOTALS	DISTRICT/ TOWNSHIP	NOTES
Rowley	127	1	Holmes	Samuel			1		1			1		1			4		
Rowley	127	2	Herriman	Enoch				1	1				1	1	1		5		
Rowley	127	3	Adams	Benjo		1	1		1				1	1			5		
Rowley	127	4	Hardy	Benja	3			2					1				6		
Rowley	127	5	Ross	William	2	3		1		2	1		1				10		
Rowley	127	6	Dole	William	1	1		1		1			1				5		
Rowley	127	7	Pilsbury	Dole		1	1					1		1			4		
Rowley	127	8	Tenny	David	1			1				1	1				4		
Rowley	127	9	Hardy	Enos	1			1		1			1				4		
Rowley	127	10	Brown	John	2			1		1			1	1			6		
Rowley	127	11	Wallingford	Benja	1				1					2			4		
Rowley	127	12	Brooklebank	John		2			1			1		1			5		
Rowley	127	13	Chapin	Jonathn			2	1	1			1	1	2			8		
Rowley	127	14	Pilsbury	Amos		1			1			1		2			5		
Rowley	127	15	Nelson	Paul		1	2										3		
Rowley	127	16	Nelson	Solomon				1						3			4		
Rowley	127	17	Spofford	Moses			2			1	2			1			7		
Rowley	127	18	Warren	Jonas				1	1	2			1				4		
Rowley	127	19	Spofford	Joseph	1			1		2	1		1				6		
Rowley	127	20	Spofford	William	1	1	2		1	1	1	1	1				9		
Rowley	127	21	Spofford	Zach		1		1		1	1	2	1				7		
Rowley	127	22	Spofford	Moody		1	2				2	1	1				8		
Rowley	127	23	Spofford	Jacob	1	1			1	2	1	2	1				9		
Rowley	127	24	Dole	Greenleaf		3		1		2	2	1	1				10		
Rowley	127	25	Spofford	Amos	3	2	2		1		1	2	1				12		
Rowley	127	26	Spofford	Daniel				1					1				2		
Rowley	127	27	Spofford	Moses Dole			1			1		2					4		
Rowley	127	28	Braymon	Isaac	1	1		1		1			1		1		6		
Rowley	127	29	Boynton	Moses	1		1		1	3			1	2			9		
Rowley	127	30	Boynton	Moses									2		4		6		
Rowley	127	31	Dole	Silas	1		2		1	1	1	1	1				8		
Rowley	127	32	Dole	Ruth	1					1		1	1	1	1		6		
Rowley	127	33	Dole	Peabody			1	1					2				4		
Rowley	127	34	Nelson	Nathll		1	1	1		2			1	1			7		
Rowley	127	35	Nelson	Amos	1		2		1	1			2	1			8		
Rowley	127	36	Adams	Benja	1		1	1			1	1					5		
Rowley	127	37	Adams	Benja		2	2		1		1	1		1			8		
Rowley	127	38	Chaplin	Asa		1	2		1		1			1			6		
Rowley	127	39	Clark	Hannah		1								1			2		
Rowley	127	40	Nelson	Asa		1	3	1	1				3	3			12		
Rowley	127	41	Bailey	Asa	3	1		1		1			1				7		
Rowley	127	42	Lancaster	Thos			1						1				2		
Rowley	127	43	Mighill	David	1	1			1				1	1			5		
Rowley	127	44	Bridges	John					1				1	1			3		
Rowley	127	45	Nelson	Moses	2		3	1		1			1	1			9		
Rowley	127	46	Nelson	Amos					1				1	1			3		
Rowley	127	47	Perley	Nathan	2	1		1	1	2	1	1	1				10		
Rowley	127	48	Plummer	Samuel				1	1				1	1			4		
Rowley	127	49	Plummer	Samuel				1					1				2		
Rowley	128	1	Lovewell	Shuball	1			1		1			1				4		
Rowley	128	2	Herriman	Jonathn		1	2					1	1				5		
Rowley	128	3	Herriman	Samll			1		1				1	1			4		
Rowley	128	4	Adams	Israel	1	1			1		1		1	1			6		
Rowley	128	5	Stickney	Paul		2			1					1			4		
Rowley	128	6	Wood	John		1	1						1				3		
Rowley	128	7	Crowling	Peter		1							1				2		
Rowley	128	8	Person	Isaac	1		1	1		1			1	1			6		
Rowley	128	9	Poor	Joseph	1			1		1			1	1	1		6		
Rowley	128	10	Poor	Moses			1						1				2		
Rowley	128	11	Poor	David	2			1		2			1				6		
Rowley	128	12	Poor	Jeremiah		1		1	1	1	1			1			6		
Rowley	128	13	Longfellow	Stepn		3	2		1	1			1	1			9		
Rowley	128	14	Tenney	Oliver	1	1		1					1				4		
Rowley	128	15	Jackman	Anna										1			1		
Rowley	128	16	Jewet	Jeremiah		2		1		1	1			1			6		
Rowley	128	17	Jackman	Benja		3		1		1			1	1			7		
Rowley	128	18	Corey	John	1	1							1				4		
Rowley	128	19	Poor	Eliphalet			1						1	1			3		
Rowley	128	20	Sawyer	Lydia				2					2				4		
Rowley	128	21	Thurlow	Eliphalet	1			1		1			1	1			5		
Rowley	128	22	Mores	Elizabeth		1								1			2		
Rowley	128	23	Thurlow	Mark	1	1	1		1	2		1	1	1			9		
Rowley	128	24	Cheney	Jonathan	1			1					1	1			5		
Rowley	128	25	Person	Jacob		1	1		1				1				4		
Rowley	128	26	Cheney	Mark	1		1						1				3		
Rowley	128	27	Brown	Caleb	1			1		1			1				4		
Rowley	128	28	Jewit	David				1		1			1				3		
Rowley	128	29	Lull	Thomas		2		1	1			1	1	1			7		
Rowley	128	30	Adams	Israel	1	1			1			2	1	4			10		

TOWN	PG#	LN#	LAST NAME	FIRST NAME	FREE WHITE MALES					FREE WHITE FEMALES					TOTAL ALL OTHER	TOTAL SLAVES	TOTALS	DISTRICT/ TOWNSHIP	NOTES
					under 10	10 to 16	16 to 26	26 to 45	45 and over	under 10	10 to 16	16 to 26	26 to 45	45 and over					
Rowley	128	31	Tenny	Oliver	2		1	1	2		1		1	2			10		
Rowley	128	32	Thurlow	John				1				1	1	1			4		
Rowley	128	33	Brown	Joseph		1	1		1	2	1	1		2			9		
Rowley	128	34	Jewet	Jonathan	1			1		1			1				4		
Rowley	128	35	Wheeler	Jonathn			1		1			1		1			4		
Rowley	128	36	Chute	David			1			3			2				6		
Rowley	128	37	Stickney	Amos	1			1	1			1	1	1	1		7		
Rowley	128	38	Jewet	William	1	2	1					1		1			6		
Rowley	128	39	Chute	James		2	2		1	1	1	2	2				11		
Rowley	128	40	Merril	Thomas		1	1			1	2	1					6		
Rowley	128	41	Poor	Benja	2			1			2		1				6		
Rowley	128	42	Jewet	Maximillion		1	1		1	1	2	1	1				8		
Rowley	128	43	Cleveland	Parker	1			1		1		1	1				5		
Rowley	128	44	Piker	Thomas			2		1				1				4		
Rowley	128	45	Rogers	Jacob		1	1		1	1	1	1		1			7		
Rowley	128	46	Tenny	David		1		1		2		1	1				6		
Rowley	128	47	Smith	Anthony			1						2				3		
Rowley	128	48	Dole	Moses	1		1		1	1			1	1			6		
Rowley	128	49	Dole	Henry	1			1					1				4		
Rowley	128	50	Dole	Thomas		1	1			1			1				4		
Rowley	128	51	Sarle	Mehitabel							1	1	1				3		
Rowley	128	52	Dole	Stephen	1	1		1	1	2	1	1	3				11		
Rowley	128	53	Smith	James	1			1		1			1				4		
Rowley	128	54	Smith	Isaac		1	1		1		1			1	2		7		
Rowley	128	55	Lambert	Nathan			1		1					1			3		
Rowley	129	1	Hobson	Moses	1			1		1			1				4		
Rowley	129	2	Bishop	Benja	1	1	2						2				6		
Rowley	129	3	Bayley	John			1		1		1	1		1			5		
Rowley	129	4	Allwell	Samuel	1			1		3			1				6		
Rowley	129	5	Narker	Nathan	1				2					2			5		
Rowley	129	6	Dwinel	Amos	1			1				2					4		
Rowley	129	7	Hobson	John				1						4			5		
Rowley	129	8	Jewet	Joseph	2	1	1		1	1			1				8		
Rowley	129	9	Merrit	Thomas			1		1	1			2	1			5		
Rowley	129	10	Richards	Moses		2	1						1				4		
Rowley	129	11	Cressey	Mark	1	1			1	1	1			1			6		
Rowley	129	12	Jewet	Jacob	1				1	2	2		2				8		
Rowley	129	13	White	Anna	1		1					1	1				4		
Rowley	129	14	Clark	Amos	2			1		1		1					5		
Rowley	129	15	Clark	Moses			1			2			1				4		
Rowley	129	16	Richard	David	1	2		1	1	3			2				10		
Rowley	129	17	Richard	John		1			1	1		1					4		
Rowley	129	18	Lambert	Jonathn	1			1				1		1	1		5		
Rowley	129	19	Lambert	Alfia			1			1		2	1				5		
Rowley	129	20	Todd	George	1	1			1	1	1			1			6		
Rowley	129	21	Iselley	Thomas				1						1			2		
Rowley	129	22	Todd	Jonathn	1	1			1	1	1			1			6		
Rowley	129	23	Todd	Benja		3	2		1		1	1	1				9		
Rowley	129	24	Smith	Joseph	3	1		1		1	1		1				8		
Rowley	129	25	Richard	Joshua					1	1	2	2		1			7		
Rowley	129	26	Perley	John					1	2	1	1		2			7		
Rowley	129	27	Pickard	Joseph	3			1		1	2		1	1			9		
Rowley	129	28	Lambert	Nathan			1		1				1				3		
Rowley	129	29	Hobson	Moses	1	1		1		1			1				5		
Rowley	129	30	Hobson	Samuel	2		1	1		2			1				7		
Rowley	129	31	Smith	Benja		1	1			1		1					4		
Rowley	129	32	Pickard	Jacob	1	1		1	1			1		1			6		
Rowley	129	33	Pickard	Francis				1					1				2		
Rowley	129	34	Sanders	David			1			1		1	1				4		
Rowley	129	35	Jewet	Jonathn			1			1	3	1	1				7		
Rowley	129	36	Theyar	Samuel		1			2	1		1					5		
Rowley	129	37	Haris	John	1		1		1			2					5		
Rowley	129	38	Haris	Timothy			2	1	1					1			5		
Rowley	129	39	Cogswell	Nathll	1	1			1		2	2	2		2		12		
Rowley	129	40	Broadstreet	Moses		1	2		1	1	2	3		1			11		
Rowley	129	41	Kilborn	Ebenezr					1			2	3				6		
Rowley	129	42	Hale	Pemberton	1			1		1			1				4		
Rowley	129	43	Saunders	John		1	3		1			2	1				8		
Rowley	129	44	Crafford	John	3			1				1	1	1			7		
Rowley	129	45	Gage	Thos	2		1		1	3			1	1			9		
Rowley	129	46	Saunders	Edward	2		1		1	1	1		1				7		
Rowley	129	47	Broadstreet	Moses					1			1		1			3		
Rowley	129	48	Gage	Thos	2			1		2		1	1				7		
Rowley	129	49	Gage	Thos		1	1						1				3		
Rowley	129	50	Plummer	Samuel			1		1	2		2	1				7		
Rowley	129	51	Johnson	Nathll	3		2	1		1	3		1				11		
Rowley	129	52	Todd	David	1		1		1	1	1			2			7		
Rowley	129	53	Todd	Nathan			1		1	1	1		1				5		
Rowley	130	1	Todd	William	1		1	1	1	1			1				7		

TOWN	PG#	LN#	LAST NAME	FIRST NAME	FREE WHITE MALES under 10	10 to 16	16 to 26	26 to 45	45 and over	FREE WHITE FEMALES under 10	10 to 16	16 to 26	26 to 45	45 and over	TOTAL ALL OTHER	TOTAL SLAVES	TOTALS	DISTRICT/ TOWNSHIP	NOTES
Rowley	130	2	Johnson	Daniel			2		1					3			6		
Rowley	130	3	Cressey	Richard			1			3		1	1				6		
Rowley	130	4	Jewet	John				1					1				2		
Rowley	130	5	Jewet	Daniel	1			1					1	1			4		
Rowley	130	6	Johnson	Moses			1						1				2		
Rowley	130	7	Jewet	George			1				1			2			4		
Rowley	130	8	Gage	John	1			1		1			1	1			5		
Rowley	130	9	Todd	Nelson		1	1	2		1	1	2	1				9		
Rowley	130	10	Hobson	Thomas	1			1		1		1	3	1			8		
Rowley	130	11	Perley	William	2		1	1		1			1				6		
Rowley	130	12	Foster	Daniel	3	3	3	1		1	1		1				13		
Rowley	130	13	Foster	John				1						1			2		
Rowley	130	14	Chapman	Joseph			1				1	1		1			4		
Rowley	130	15	Pingree	Francis		1		1				2		1			5		
Rowley	130	16	Williams	Gilbert T	3			1		1			1				6		
Rowley	130	17	Pingree	Daniel	1			1					2	1			5		
Rowley	130	18	Allsworth	Daniel				1				2		1			4		
Rowley	130	19	Jackson	Caleb	1	1				1	1	1					6		
Rowley	130	20	Dwinel	Israel	2		1			1		1	1	1			7		
Rowley	130	21	Perley	Samuel			2					1		1			4		
Rowley	130	22	Perley	John			1		1					2			4		
Rowley	130	23	Pingree	Asa	1			1	1	1			1	1			6		
Rowley	130	24	Pingree	Clement			1				1	1					3		
Rowley	130	25	Merril	Moses		1		1		2	1		1				6		
Rowley	130	26	Adams	Benja	1	1	2	1		1	1	1	1		1		10		
Rowley	130	27	Morril	Samuel		1		1		2		1					5		
Rowley	130	28	Burpee	Nathll	2	1		1		1			1				6		
Rowley	130	29	Pingree	Asa				1					1				2		
Rowley	130	30	Pingree	Asa	1			1		1			1				4		
Rowley	130	31	Dodge	Phineas		1		1			2	1			1		6		
Rowley	130	32	Dodge	Solomon		1					1						2		
Rowley	130	33	Dodge	Phineas	1	1		1		2			1				6		
Rowley	130	34	Dickerson	William		1	1	1		2	1		1				7		
Rowley	130	35	Phillips	Nathan			1			1			1				3		
Rowley	130	36	Phillips	David	1		1						1				3		
Rowley	130	37	Dresser	Daniel		1			1	1		1					4		
Rowley	130	38	Lancaster	Paul					1	1			1				3		
Rowley	130	39	Wood	Jonathan	1	2		1				2		1			7		
Rowley	130	40	Wood	Jonathn					1	1			1				3		
Rowley	130	41	Dickerson	Joshua		1	1	1		1	1			1			6		
Rowley	130	42	Dresser	Joseph		1		1					1				3		
Rowley	130	43	Smith	Isaac	1		2	1				1		1			6		
Rowley	130	44	Pickard	John		1		1				1	1				4		
Rowley	130	45	How	George			1			1			1				3		
Rowley	130	46	Fuller	John	2		2						1				5		
Rowley	130	47	Bishop	Benja		1	1		1	1		1					6		
Rowley	130	48	Chaplin	Moses	1		2	2		1	1			2			9		
Rowley	130	49	Chaplin	Joseph			1		1			1		1			4		
Rowley	130	50	How	Philemon				1			1	1	1				4		
Rowley	130	51	How	Reuben	2	1		1		2	1		1	1			9		
Rowley	130	52	Bishop	Edward	1	1	2	1				1	1				7		
Rowley	131	1	Marshall	Thomas	1	1		1		2		1	1				7		
Rowley	131	2	Bayley	Abner		2	1				1	3					7		
Rowley	131	3	Hobson	Humphrey	2		2			1	1	1					8		
Rowley	131	4	Stickney	Hannah									2				2		
Rowley	131	5	Stickney	Josiah	2		1	1		1	1		1				7		
Rowley	131	6	Hobson	David				1				1		1			3		
Rowley	131	7	Brookelbank	Nathan		1		1					1				3		
Rowley	131	8	Kilborn	Joseph	1			1		1			1	1			5		
Rowley	131	9	Nelson	Stephen		1	1	1		2		1					6		
Rowley	131	10	Bradford	Ebenezr Revd		3	1		1	1			1	1			8		
Rowley	131	11	Pilsbury	Samuel		1	1	1		1	1						5		
Rowley	131	12	Scot	Moses			1	1					1	1			4		
Rowley	131	13	Cressey	John	3			1					1				5		
Rowley	131	14	Cressey	Richard			1			3			1	1			6		
Rowley	131	15	Boynton	Ebenezr	1			1		1			1	1			5		
Rowley	131	16	Prang	Mary	1						1		1				3		
Rowley	131	17	Jewet	Paul		1		1	1	1		1	1	1			7		
Rowley	131	18	Payson	Thos			1						1				2		
Rowley	131	19	Mighill	Thos		1			1			2		1			5		
Rowley	131	20	Todd	Daniel		1		1				1	1				4		
Rowley	131	21	Payson	Moses		1		1			1	2	1				6		
Rowley	131	22	Palmer	Moses	1			1				1		1			4		
Rowley	131	23	Lowel	Solomon	1		1			1			1				4		
Rowley	131	24	Palmer	Stephen				1					2				3		
Rowley	131	25	Scott	Samuel	2			1	1	1			1				6		
Rowley	131	26	Gage	Nathll				1					1	1			3		
Rowley	131	27	Perley	Darius	2	1		2	1	2	1	2	1				12		
Rowley	131	28	Jewet	Nehemiah	1		2	2	1	1			1	1			9		

122

TOWN	PG#	LN#	LAST NAME	FIRST NAME	FREE WHITE MALES					FREE WHITE FEMALES					TOTAL ALL OTHER	TOTAL SLAVES	TOTALS	DISTRICT/ TOWNSHIP	NOTES
					under 10	10 to 16	16 to 26	26 to 45	45 and over	under 10	10 to 16	16 to 26	26 to 45	45 and over					
Rowley	131	29	Person	Solomon			1	1					1	1			4		
Rowley	131	30	Williams	William	1		1		1	1			1				5		
Rowley	131	31	Person	John	1				1		1	2		1			6		
Rowley	131	32	Dole	John		1		1		2	2		1	1			8		
Rowley	131	33	Person	Reuben		1		1			2		4				8		
Rowley	131	34	Hale	Daniel	2	1		1		1		1	2				8		
Rowley	131	35	Nelson	David		3		1		1			1				6		
Rowley	131	36	Nelson	David		1	1		1			2	1				6		
Rowley	131	37	Jewet	Joseh				1	1			1	1				4		
Rowley	131	38	Taylor	Jonathan	1		1	1				2					5		
Rowley	131	39	Rose	Paul	2			1		1	1		1				6		
Rowley	131	40	Dole	Joseph	1		1		1	1	1	2	1				8		
Rowley	131	41	Todd	James			2	1				1	1	1			6		
Rowley	131	42	Spiller	Samll	3		1	1		1	1						7		
Rowley	131	43	Daniel	John	1	1		1	1			1	1				6		
Rowley	131	44	Searle	Joseph	2	2		1			1	1	1				8		
Rowley	131	45	Stickney	Jedidiah			1	1	1		1	1	1				6		
Rowley	131	46	Stickney	Benja		1	2	1	1			1	1	2			9		
Rowley	131	47	Batice	Robert	1		1			1		1	1				5		
Rowley	131	48	Dickerson	Oliver		1			1			1	1				4		
Rowley	131	49	Stickney	Moses		1				1		1					3		
Rowley	131	50	Pike	Joseph	2	1	1	1	1			2	1				9		
Rowley	131	51	Tenny	Nathl	1	1		1	1	1	1	3		1			10		
Rowley	131	52	Stickney	Dudley	1			2				1		1			5		
Rowley	132	1	Crombie	Aaron	1			1		1			2				5		
Rowley	132	2	Rogers	Nathll			1	1					3				5		
Rowley	132	3	Searle	Jereh				1				1	1				3		
Rowley	132	4	Tenny	Richard	1		2		1			2	1				7		
Rowley	132	5	Platts	John		1	1	1		2	1		1				7		
Rowley	132	6	Saunders	Benja	2				1	1				2			6		
Rowley	132	7	Palmer	John	1		1	1			1	2	1				7		
Rowley	132	8	Merril	Thos		1	2		1		1		1		1		7		
Rowley	132	9	Merril	John				1		2	1		1				5		
Rowley	132	10	Pilsbury	Amos	1		1				1		1				4		
Rowley	132	11	Nelson	Solomon				1			1		1	1			4		
Rowley	132	12	Bickle	Benja				1		2			1				4		
Rowley	132	13	Brookelbank	Job		1		1		1	1		1				5		
Rowley	132	14	Smith	John				1	1				1	1			4		
Rowley	132	15	Poor	David				1		1		1	1				4		
Rowley	132	16	Poor	Daniel				1		1	1	1					4		
Rowley	132	17	Saunders	Benjamin	2			1	1	1				1			6		

TOWN	PG#	LN#	LAST NAME	FIRST NAME	M under 10	M 10–16	M 16–26	M 26–45	M 45 & over	F under 10	F 10–16	F 16–26	F 26–45	F 45 & over	TOTAL ALL OTHER	TOTAL SLAVES	TOTALS	DISTRICT/ TOWNSHIP	NOTES
Salem	183	1	Pope	John	3	1			1	1	1	2	1				10		
Salem	183	2	Grant	Joshua Jr	1	1	1		1	3	1		1				9		
Salem	183	3	Gardner	Hannah	1						1	1	1				4		
Salem	183	4	Aspinwall	Ellis				1		1							2		
Salem	183	5	Clough	Joseph				1						1			2		
Salem	183	6	Hooper	Mary										1			1		
Salem	183	7	Alley	Rufus			1			2		1					4		
Salem	183	8	Johnson	Micajah	4		1			2			1	1			9		
Salem	183	9	Hibbert	Eliza									2				2		
Salem	183	10	Currier	Jacob			1			2			1	1			5		
Salem	183	11	Grant	Joshua Jr			1		1				1	1			4		
Salem	183	12	Proctor	William	1	2	1	1				2	1	1			9		
Salem	183	13	Abbot	Elias			1						1	1			3		
Salem	183	14	Luther	Nathan			2	1		1			1				5		
Salem	183	15	Lambert	Mary										2			2		
Salem	183	16	Merrit	Samuel		2		1		2			1				6		
Salem	183	17	Woodbury	Nath		2	1		1				1	1			7		
Salem	183	18	Purinton	Mathew	1		1						1	1			4		
Salem	183	19	Johnson	Edward			1		1	1	2	1	1				7		
Salem	183	20	Pope	Joshua	3	1	3	2		1	1	1	1				13		
Salem	183	21	Osborne	Eliza			1							1			2		
Salem	183	22	Buffum	Isaac			2	1				1	1	1			6		
Salem	183	23	Proctor	Robert		1	2	1		1		1	1				7		
Salem	183	24	Nichols	Stephen	1		2	1					1	1			6		
Salem	183	25	Day	Elisha	2		1			2			1	1			7		
Salem	183	26	Goldthwait	James			1	1					1	1			4		
Salem	183	27	Stimpson	Thadeus	1	1	1		1				1	1			6		
Salem	188	1	Adams	John	1		1		1				1	1			5		
Salem	188	2	Peele	Robert	3		1						1	1			6		
Salem	188	3	Perkins	Eunice		2		1					1	1			5		
Salem	188	4	Peirce	Jerath		1	2	1		2	1		1				8		
Salem	188	5	Williams	Mehitable		1	2					3	1				7		
Salem	188	6	Howard	Phebe									1				1		
Salem	188	7	Kendal	Abm	2	1	2						1				6		
Salem	188	8	Curtis	Abm	1	1	2			2			1				7		
Salem	188	9	Richards	Joseph		1	1			2	1	1					6		
Salem	188	10	Glison	Ichabod			1	1		1	2		1				6		
Salem	188	11	Giffords	Samuel			1			1	1	3	1				7		
Salem	188	12	Cliff	Peter	4			1				2	1				8		
Salem	188	13	Aspinwall	John	2		1			1	2		1				7		
Salem	188	14	Cook	Stephen		1	3	1	1	1			1				8		
Salem	188	15	Tate	Thos	2			1		2			1				6		
Salem	188	16	Peirce	Joshua				1						1			2		
Salem	188	17	Frye	Deborah								2	1	1			4		
Salem	188	18	Ryan	James	1		1	1						1			4		
Salem	188	19	Odel	James	1	1	1			1	1		1				6		
Salem	188	20	Peters	Eliza			1					1	1	1			4		
Salem	188	21	Barr	William	3			1		4			1				9		
Salem	188	22	Cook	Lydia									1	1			2		
Salem	188	23	Watson	Nath			1			1			1				3		
Salem	188	24	Briggs	Susanna						1			1	1			3		
Salem	188	25	Cabot	Thos	1	1	1			1			1				5		
Salem	188	26	Briggs	Lemuel	1			1					1				3		
Salem	188	27	Hascol	William	2			1		2			1				6		
Salem	188	28	Epes	William	1			1		1		1	1				5		
Salem	188	29	Peabody	Oliver	1	1	2			1		1					6		
Salem	188	30	Francis	John	1			1		3	1		1				7		
Salem	188	31	Ward	William	1	1		1		1	2	1	1				8		
Salem	188	32	Pope	Folger	2	3	3	1				1		1			11		
Salem	188	33	Burrell	Ebenz	2		1	2	1	3	1		1				11		
Salem	188	34	Cabot	Rebecca							1	1	1	1			4		
Salem	188	35	Manfield	Joseph				1				1					2		
Salem	188	36	Newhall	Thomas	3	1	1			2			1		1		10		
Salem	188	37	Browne	Edward	2	1	2	1			1	1	1				9		
Salem	188	38	Smith	Caleb	1	2			1	1		2	2	1	1		11		
Salem	188	39	Browne	Bart		1	2						1				4		
Salem	188	40	Mead	Benja		1	1						1				3		
Salem	188	41	Kane	Eliza		2				1			1				4		
Salem	188	42	Gavete	John	3	4	3	1		2		2		1			16		
Salem	188	43	Smith	David	2		1						1				4		
Salem	188	44	Andrews	James				1						1			2		
Salem	189	1	Andrews	Joseph	1		1			1			1				4		
Salem	189	2	Whitford	Samuel	1		1			1	1		1				5		
Salem	189	3	Barr	John	2		1			2	1	1	1				8		
Salem	189	4	Newhall	Gilbert		1							1				2		
Salem	189	5	Stearns	William	1	5	1		1	4			1	2			15		
Salem	189	6	Crosby	Nicholas		3			1	1	1	1	1				8		
Salem	189	7	Mansfield	Daniel R	1		1			1	1	1	1				7		
Salem	189	8	Clark	John		1	1		1	3			1	1			8		

Census table — Salem

TOWN	PG#	LN#	LAST NAME	FIRST NAME	FWM under 10	FWM 10 to 16	FWM 16 to 26	FWM 26 to 45	FWM 45 and over	FWF under 10	FWF 10 to 16	FWF 16 to 26	FWF 26 to 45	FWF 45 and over	TOTAL ALL OTHER	TOTAL SLAVES	TOTALS	DISTRICT/TOWNSHIP	NOTES
Salem	189	9	Waldo	Jonathan		2	1		1	1	1	1	1				8		
Salem	189	10	Saunders	Daniel R	1		1			2			1				5		
Salem	189	11	Buffinton	John	1				1			2		1			5		
Salem	189	12	Smith	Hannah			3				1		1	1			6		
Salem	189	13	Fisher	James	3			1		3	1		1				9		
Salem	189	14	Falen	Esther			1				1		1	1			4		
Salem	189	15	Diamond	Sarah	1	1	2			1		1		1			7		
Salem	189	16	Kenfield	Eliz	1					3		1	1				6		
Salem	189	17	Phillips	Richd	1			1				1					3		
Salem	189	18	Clough	Peter	1	1	1		1	1	2		1				8		
Salem	189	19	Atkinson	Hannah						3		1	1				5		
Salem	189	20	Gray	Benja		1		1		3		1	1				7		
Salem	189	21	Dalton	Sarah	2					3		1	1				8		
Salem	189	22	Shebrock	Abigl									1				1		
Salem	189	23	Buffum	Sarah						1		1	1				3		
Salem	189	24	Fuller	Rachel									2				2		
Salem	189	25	Leache	Eliza									1	2			3		
Salem	189	26	Fabens	Tho	4			1					1				6		
Salem	189	27	Beckford	Mary	3						1		1				5		
Salem	189	28	Henderson	Benjn	1			1			1	1					4		
Salem	189	29	Woodbury	Josiah	1	1	1		1	1	1		1				7		
Salem	189	30	Smith	Edward			1			1	1		1				4		
Salem	189	31	Kelley	Darkes	1	1						1		1			4		
Salem	189	32	Johnston	Jonathan				1				1		1			3		
Salem	189	33	Freeman	Fortune											4		4		
Salem	189	34	Newport	John											7		7		
Salem	189	35	Endicot	Samuel											5		5		
Salem	189	36	Champlin	London											2		2		
Salem	189	37	Foster	Cato											3		3		
Salem	189	38	Patterson	Isaac											2		2		
Salem	189	39	Lake	John											2		2		
Salem	189	40	Seward	Jack											6		6		
Salem	189	41	Oliver	Mary											2		2		
Salem	189	42	Smith	Aaron											1		1		
Salem	189	43	Lancaster	John											2		2		
Salem	189	44	Deukinfield	Thos											3		3		
Salem	189	45	Thurston	Henry											3		3		
Salem	190	1	Carner	Samuel				1		2		1	1				5		
Salem	190	2	Smith	Robert											4		4		
Salem	190	3	Chissee	Emanuel	1			1		1				1			4		
Salem	190	4	Waite	Edmund	2			1		2			1	1			7		
Salem	190	5	Gallushe	Jacob	1		3			2		1					7		
Salem	190	6	Brown	Samuel	1	1				1	3		1				7		
Salem	190	7	Shillaber	Walter			1		1	3				1			6		
Salem	190	8	Hathorne	William		1	1			1	3		1				7		
Salem	190	9	Archer	Nath			1			1			1				3		
Salem	190	10	Smith	Jesse	1			1		1	1	1	1	1			7		
Salem	190	11	Cleveland	Williams				1				1	1				3		
Salem	190	12	Shillaber	Benja	1			1	2		1	1	1	1			8		
Salem	190	13	Cook	Mary									1	1			2		
Salem	190	14	Tarrant	Susanna									1	1			2		
Salem	190	15	Leach	Geo			1			3	1	1					6		
Salem	190	16	Cowan	Robt		3	1	1		2	1	1					9		
Salem	190	17	Needham	Nath		1	1	1					1				4		
Salem	190	18	Smith	Geo		1	1	1		1		1					5		
Salem	190	19	Warden	John			1			1				1			3		
Salem	190	20	Francis	Thos		1	1	1		1				1			5		
Salem	190	21	Pickering	William				1		1	1	1	1	1			6		
Salem	190	22	Archer	Sarah								1	1				2		
Salem	190	23	Pickering	Joseph	1	3	1	1		2			1				9		
Salem	190	24	Felch	Rebecca								1	1	2			4		
Salem	190	25	Foster	Amos	1			1		1			1				4		
Salem	190	26	Cleveland	Stephen		3		1				2	1				7		
Salem	190	27	Symonds	Joseph	1	1		2				1		2			8		
Salem	190	28	Pitnam	Hannah	1			1			1	1		1			5		
Salem	190	29	Osborne	William			1				1	1	1				4		
Salem	190	30	Sander	Abigail							1	1		1			3		
Salem	190	31	Howard	Sarah								1		1			2		
Salem	190	32	Compton	Sarah									2				2		
Salem	190	33	Smith	John	1	1			1	1	2	3	1				10		
Salem	190	34	Archer	Nathl		1				1		1					3		
Salem	190	35	Benjamin	Sally	2		1						1	1			5		
Salem	190	36	Bruce	George	2	1	1	1			1	1	1				8		
Salem	190	37	Buffington	Nehemh				1				1	1				3		
Salem	190	38	Treadwell	John			1	1		1	1	1					5		
Salem	190	39	Meek	Timothy	2			1		2			1				6		
Salem	190	40	Hyer	Elias				1		1	2	1					5		
Salem	190	41	Upton	Edmund	2	2		1		2	1		1				9		
Salem	190	42	Galway	Samuel	1	4				1			1				8		

125

			HEADS OF HOUSEHOLD		FREE WHITE MALES					FREE WHITE FEMALES									
TOWN	PG#	LN#	LAST NAME	FIRST NAME	under 10	10 to 16	16 to 26	26 to 45	45 and over	under 10	10 to 16	16 to 26	26 to 45	45 and over	TOTAL ALL OTHER	TOTAL SLAVES	TOTALS	DISTRICT/ TOWNSHIP	NOTES
Salem	190	43	Hunt	John			1			2			1				4		
Salem	190	44	Johnson	Polly	2							2	1				5		
Salem	191	1	Osborne	Stephen		1		1					2	1			5		
Salem	191	2	French	Joshua		2	4	1		3	1		1		1		13		
Salem	191	3	Kimball	John			1					1					2		
Salem	191	4	Penchard	John	2	1	2	1		2	1		2				11		
Salem	191	5	Clifton	John	1			1	1	1			1	1			6		
Salem	191	6	Holman	Gabriel		1		1	1			1	1				5		
Salem	191	7	Holman	Samuel	3		2	1		3			2	1			12		
Salem	191	8	Follete	William			1						1				2		
Salem	191	9	Knight	Daniel				1						1			2		
Salem	191	10	Hathorne	Mary									1	3			4		
Salem	191	11	McCarthy	Justin	2			1		3			1	1			8		
Salem	191	12	Reed	Thos	1			1		1		1					4		
Salem	191	13	Waters	Robert	2			1		1		1	1	2			8		
Salem	191	14	Kerrik	William	1	1		1		4			1				8		
Salem	191	15	Ridor	Joseph				1			1	2		1			5		
Salem	191	16	Goodale	Mary	1		1				3	2		1			8		
Salem	191	17	Dawes	Stephen	2			1		1			1				5		
Salem	191	18	Daland	John	1			1		2	1		1				6		
Salem	191	19	Marston	Mary		1	1			1				1			4		
Salem	191	20	Ashby	Martha		1	1			1				1			4		
Salem	191	21	Daland	Benja	3	1		1	1	1	2	1	2		1		14		
Salem	191	22	Hook	Robert		2	1						1				4		
Salem	191	23	Popes	Ebenz		3	2	1	1	1	2	1	1	1			13		
Salem	191	24	Blythe	Sally		1				2	1	1	1				6		
Salem	191	25	Hodges	Jonathan	2			1		2	2		2				9		
Salem	191	26	Heman	Jos	2			1		4	3		1				11		
Salem	191	27	Brady	James				1				1					2		
Salem	191	28	Neale	Benja	1			1		3			1				6		
Salem	191	29	Russell	John	2			1		2			1				6		
Salem	191	30	Peirce	Daniel		1	1	1		1	1	1	1				7		
Salem	191	31	Mudge	Joseph	1		1					1	1				4		
Salem	191	32	Abbot	Priscilla			1				2	2	3	1			9		
Salem	191	33	Clarke	Henry	2			1		1	1						5		
Salem	191	34	Carnes	Jonathan		1		1		3			1	1			7		
Salem	191	35	Pike	Mary									1	2			3		
Salem	191	36	Norris	Phillip	1		1				1	1					4		
Salem	191	37	Felt	Mary	1	1	1	1		1			1	1			7		
Salem	191	38	Potter	Hannah									1				1		
Salem	191	39	Wallis	Moses			1						1				2		
Salem	191	40	Trumbel	Nath	2	3		1		1			1				8		
Salem	191	41	Ashton	Mary								1	1	1			3		
Salem	191	42	Williamson	Saml								1		1			2		
Salem	192	1	Rileman	Benjamn		1	1		1			2	1	2			8		
Salem	192	2	Carlis	Joseph			1		2		1						4		
Salem	192	3	Robey	Thos				1		1			1	1			4		
Salem	192	4	Repes	Nathl	1			1		2	1	1	1	1			8		
Salem	192	5	Ward	Saml	3						1	1	1				6		
Salem	192	6	Clevland	Abigail						1		2					3		
Salem	192	7	Liscomb	Jno	2		1						1				4		
Salem	192	8	Gibbs	Mary	2	1							1	1			5		
Salem	192	9	Blanchard	Benja	1	1		1		2			1				7		
Salem	192	10	Ward	Richd	1		2		1	1		2	2	2	1		12		
Salem	192	11	Weston	Nathl	2	1		1		2	3	1	1				11		
Salem	192	12	Richardson	Phin				1									1		
Salem	192	13	Reed	Thos	4		5	3		2			1				15		
Salem	192	14	Cummins	Nathl	2		1	1		2			1				7		
Salem	192	15	Miller	Peter			1			1		1					3		
Salem	192	16	Gavet	Jon		1		1	1	2			1				6		
Salem	192	17	Foster	Nath		1	1						1				3		
Salem	192	18	Millit	Eliza	1	1							3				5		
Salem	192	19	Johnson	Edmund	2		6			1	1	1					11		
Salem	192	20	Welch	Thos			1	1					1				3		
Salem	192	21	Tuttle	Eliza								1	1				2		
Salem	192	22	Goodhue	Abner	2		3			1	2		1				9		
Salem	192	23	Smith	Emmons			1						1				2		
Salem	192	24	Briggs	Jeremh	2			1					1				4		
Salem	192	25	Cleveland	Charles			1			1	1		1				4		
Salem	192	26	Felt	Joseph	3		1	1	2	1			1	1			10		
Salem	192	27	Farrinton	William	1			1				1	1				4		
Salem	192	28	Martin	Geo W			4			1		1	1				7		
Salem	192	29	Bullock	Isaac		3	2			1			1	1			9		
Salem	192	30	Harredan	Andrew				1					1				2		
Salem	192	31	Hascal	Epes		1	2			1	1						5		
Salem	192	32	Bullock	Jona				1			2						3		
Salem	192	33	Archer	Samuel	1	2	1			1	1	1	1				8		
Salem	192	34	Gould	James				1						1			2		
Salem	192	35	Hacker	Isaac Jr			1						1				2		

TOWN	PG#	LN#	LAST NAME	FIRST NAME	FWM under 10	FWM 10 to 16	FWM 16 to 26	FWM 26 to 45	FWM 45 and over	FWF under 10	FWF 10 to 16	FWF 16 to 26	FWF 26 to 45	FWF 45 and over	TOTAL ALL OTHER	TOTAL SLAVES	TOTALS	DISTRICT/ TOWNSHIP	NOTES
Salem	192	36	Buffinton	Jas Jr	1			1					1				3		
Salem	192	37	Bickford	Benja			1					1	1				3		
Salem	192	38	Hilliard	Marg								1	1				2		
Salem	192	39	McIntyre	Eliza										3			3		
Salem	192	40	Osgood	Joseph		2	1		1	2	2		1	1			10		
Salem	192	41	Watts	Hannah									1				1		
Salem	192	42	Stevens	Nath			1						1				2		
Salem	192	43	Derby	Sam	2	3		1		1			1				8		
Salem	193	1	Eustes	Jotham	2	1	2	2		3	2	1					13		
Salem	193	2	Gerrick	Samuel	1		3	1	1	1	1	1	2				11		
Salem	193	3	Chisholm	Willm	2			1		2	2	1					8		
Salem	193	4	Groves	Thad	1			1	1	2		1		1			7		
Salem	193	5	Burns	John				1				1		1			3		
Salem	193	6	Nource	Samuel	1		1	2			1	1	1				8		
Salem	193	7	Tucker	Susanna		1	1						1				3		
Salem	193	8	Smith	Ebenz	1			1		2			1				5		
Salem	193	9	Ross	Josep	2			1				1	1				5		
Salem	193	10	Karns	Samuel	1	1	1					1	1				5		
Salem	193	11	Emerston	Ephraim				1			1	1	1				4		
Salem	193	12	Cross	Joshua	1	1			1	2	2	1		1			9		
Salem	193	13	Cleveland	William	2	1	1	1		1	1	1					8		
Salem	193	14	Fisher	Nathl		1	2		1	1			1				6		
Salem	193	15	Cross	Violet											2		2		
Salem	193	16	Jackson	John											3		3		
Salem	193	17	Connor	Edwd											3		3		
Salem	193	18	Francis	Peter											7		7		
Salem	193	19	Wellman	Ezekl	1	1		1	1			2		1			7		
Salem	193	20	Buffum	Caleb			1				1		1	1			4		
Salem	193	21	Buffum	Jona	1	1		1		1	1		1	1			7		
Salem	193	22	Benson	Eliza	1		2					3	1	1			8		
Salem	193	23	Brown	Joseph			1						1				2		
Salem	193	24	Mason	Susanna						1			1				2		
Salem	193	25	Lang	William		1			1	3	3	1		2	1		12		
Salem	193	26	Maxcy	Levi	2			1					1				4		
Salem	193	27	Tufts	Richd	2			1		2			1				6		
Salem	193	28	Body	Mary		2				1	1		1				5		
Salem	193	29	Janes	Mary	1	2		2		3	1		1	1			11		
Salem	193	30	Janes	John	2			1		1			1				5		
Salem	193	31	Cheever	Ebenz	1			1				1	1				4		
Salem	193	32	Kimball	Nathan			1		1	1	4	3	1				11		
Salem	193	33	Bacon	Joseph	1			1									2		
Salem	193	34	Peters	Samuel	2			1		1		1	1				6		
Salem	193	35	Bowditch	Thos		3		1					1	1			6		
Salem	193	36	Putnam	Fred	2			1					1				4		
Salem	193	37	Black	Primus											4		4		
Salem	193	38	Flanders	Asa		3							1				4		
Salem	193	39	Putnam	Samuel	1			1		1	1	1	1		1		7		
Salem	193	40	Chamberlain	Nath	3	2			1				1	1			8		
Salem	193	41	Hook	William	1		4					1					6		
Salem	193	42	Waldo	Jona Jur			1						1				2		
Salem	193	43	Bancroft	Daniel	1	1	1	1	1	4	2	3		1			15		
Salem	193	44	Boyce	David		3		1					1				5		
Salem	194	1	Bancroft	Job		2				1		1	1				5		
Salem	194	2	Chandler	William	1			1		1	3		1				7		
Salem	194	3	Freeman	Israel											2		2		
Salem	194	4	Holman	William			2		1		1	3	2	1			10		
Salem	194	5	Driver	Stephen			2	1	1		3		1				8		
Salem	194	6	Brook	Lydia										2			2		
Salem	194	7	Lamson	Amos	1			1		2			1				5		
Salem	194	8	Eliotte	Mary						3		2		1			6		
Salem	194	9	Dalrymple	James	1		1			1			1				4		
Salem	194	10	Woodberry	Josiah	2	2	1		1	2	1	1	1				11		
Salem	194	11	Jenkins	John				1					1				2		
Salem	194	12	Miller	Joseph			1			1			1				3		
Salem	194	13	Punchard	Benja	1			1					1	1			4		
Salem	194	14	Beckford	Sarah									1				1		
Salem	194	15	Osgood	Joseph	2		1	1			1	1	1				7		
Salem	194	16	Dodge	John	2	3	2	1		1		1	1				11		
Salem	194	17	Cushing	Thos	3		4	1		2			1				11		
Salem	194	18	Clarke	Eliza		1								1			2		
Salem	194	19	Holt	Lemuel	3			1	1	1	1	2	2	1			12		
Salem	194	20	Davis	William				1		1							2		
Salem	194	21	Boden	William	1	2	1		1	3			1				9		
Salem	194	22	Orne	William	2	1		1		2		1	1				8		
Salem	194	23	Henderson	Joseph	2			1		1			1				5		
Salem	194	24	Beckford	Lydia				1		1			1	1			4		
Salem	194	25	Beckford	Pymont	1		1				1		1				4		
Salem	194	26	Beckford	Joshua	1		1			1		1	1				5		
Salem	194	27	Holman	William Jr	1	1				2		1					5		
Salem	194	28	Punchard	William	2		1			1	2		1				7		

TOWN	PG#	LN#	HEADS OF HOUSEHOLD LAST NAME	HEADS OF HOUSEHOLD FIRST NAME	FREE WHITE MALES under 10	FREE WHITE MALES 10 to 16	FREE WHITE MALES 16 to 26	FREE WHITE MALES 26 to 45	FREE WHITE MALES 45 and over	FREE WHITE FEMALES under 10	FREE WHITE FEMALES 10 to 16	FREE WHITE FEMALES 16 to 26	FREE WHITE FEMALES 26 to 45	FREE WHITE FEMALES 45 and over	TOTAL ALL OTHER	TOTAL SLAVES	TOTALS	DISTRICT/ TOWNSHIP	NOTES
Salem	194	29	Beckford	David	2			1		1			1				5		
Salem	194	30	Killam	Asa	2	1	3	1			2		1				10		
Salem	194	31	Chandler	John		1	1		1		1		1				5		
Salem	194	32	Epes	Samuel		1	4		1	1	2		1				10		
Salem	194	33	Goold	Mary			1			1			1				3		
Salem	194	34	Ireland	Jona	1		1		1	1	2		1				7		
Salem	194	35	Dickason	Obed											11		11		
Salem	194	36	Sanderson	Elijah	1	1	3	1	1		3	1	1				12		
Salem	194	37	Sanderson	Jacob	1	1	4	1		1	1	1	1				11		
Salem	194	38	Leach	John	4		2		1	1	1	2	1				12		
Salem	194	39	Shillaber	Ebenz	2		1	1			2		1				7		
Salem	194	40	Page	John	2	1	4		1	1	2		1				12		
Salem	194	41	Hathorne	William		1	1					4		1			7		
Salem	194	42	Prince	John	1	2	1		1		1	1	1				8		
Salem	194	43	Coates	John		1		1		1			1				4		
Salem	194	44	Bryant	John			1			3			1				5		
Salem	194	45	Sutton	Rebecca									2				2		
Salem	194	46	Hensler	George	1			1		2			1				5		
Salem	195	1	Smithhurst	Micha	1			1		2	1	1	2				8		
Salem	195	2	Taylor	Geo	1	1		1		1			1	1			6		
Salem	195	3	Landers	William	3			1			1		1				6		
Salem	195	4	Davis	Tobias			1			1							2		
Salem	195	5	Browne	Barth	2	3			1	3			1				10		
Salem	195	6	Chamberlain	Eliz	1							1	1				3		
Salem	195	7	Farrinton	Daniel	3					2			1	1			7		
Salem	195	8	Morgan	Eunice			1			1		1	1				4		
Salem	195	9	Smith	Moses		1	1	1					1				4		
Salem	195	10	Masurey	Thoms	1			1					1				3		
Salem	195	11	Lamson	Thos	2	1	2						1				6		
Salem	195	12	Lord	Jacob		1	1			1	1						4		
Salem	195	13	Punchard	James		1	1				1	1	1				5		
Salem	195	14	Smith	Samuel	2	1	1				1	1	1				7		
Salem	195	15	Browne	John	1		1			3		1	1	1			8		
Salem	195	16	Beckford	Mehit	2							1	1				4		
Salem	195	17	Hopkins	Daniel		1		1		1	1	1	1				6		
Salem	195	18	Batcheldor	Nathl	1			1		3			1	1			7		
Salem	195	19	Cooper	Eunice						1			1				2		
Salem	195	20	Lang	Richard				1									1		
Salem	195	21	Clarke	Daniel		1	3	1					1				6		
Salem	195	22	King	Nathl	1		1	1		1		2	1				7		
Salem	195	23	Gordon	John	2			1		3			1				7		
Salem	195	24	Shed	Henry			1			1	1						4		
Salem	195	25	Barnard	Thos		1			1			1	1	1			5		
Salem	195	26	Austin	Josiah	1		2	2	1			3	1		1		11		
Salem	195	27	Gardner	Henry		1			1			3	1	1			7		
Salem	195	28	Thayer	Benja			1			1	1	1					4		
Salem	195	29	Goodhue	Benja		1	1	1	1	1	2	3	1				11		
Salem	195	30	Pettingel	Joseph	1		3	1		1	2		1				9		
Salem	195	31	Oliver	Hubbard				1		2	1	1					5		
Salem	195	32	Eldridge	Joshua	1			1		1	1	1					5		
Salem	195	33	Waitt	Aaron		1	1	1					1	1			5		
Salem	195	34	Williams	Israel			1			1	2	1	1				6		
Salem	195	35	Treadwell	John			1	1		1	1		1				5		
Salem	195	36	Fisk	Sarah		3	1			2		2	1	1			10		
Salem	195	37	Higginson	Mehita								1	1	1			3		
Salem	195	38	Very	Eliza		1						1	1				4		
Salem	195	39	Ropes	Timothy	1		1				1	1					4		
Salem	195	40	Prescott	William	1	1		1		1		3	1				8		
Salem	195	41	Homes	Sarah			1						1				2		
Salem	195	42	Richards	Richard			1					1					2		
Salem	195	43	Thayer	Stephen	1		2	1					1				5		
Salem	195	44	Parker	Phil				1		1				1			3		
Salem	195	45	Pitnam	Mark		1				1		1					3		
Salem	195	46	Brooks	Zach	2		1						1				4		
Salem	195	47	Pitnam	Polly									2				2		
Salem	195	48	Gardner	Abel	1	2		1		1			1				7		
Salem	196	1	Phips	John	2	1	4		1	2	1		1				12		
Salem	196	2	Homes	Willm		1		1			2		1				5		
Salem	196	3	Dollison	Rebecca	1						1		1				3		
Salem	196	4	Smith	Hannah		2	1			2		2		2			9		
Salem	196	5	Pickering	John	1			1	1	1	1	1	1				7		
Salem	196	6	Sanderson	James	1		1			1	1	1					5		
Salem	196	7	Gardner	Joseph	3	2							1				7		
Salem	196	8	Neale	David			1						1				2		
Salem	196	9	Neale	Jona	1	1		1					1				4		
Salem	196	10	Town	Amos	1			1					1				3		
Salem	196	11	Knight	Nath	1			1					1				3		
Salem	196	12	Portsmouth												5		5		
Salem	196	13	Brinley	John	1			1			2		1				5		
Salem	196	14	Kempton	Eliza								2	1				3		
Salem	196	15	Chaplin	Solo	1	1	1	1		2			1	1			8		
Salem	196	16	Wellman	Mary								1	1				2		
Salem	196	17	Bowditch	Mary							1		1				2		
Salem	196	18	Smith	Benjamin			1			1		1	1				4		
Salem	196	19	Richardson	Addison		1	3	1				1	1				7		
Salem	196	20	Ferguson	John	2	1	1				1	1					6		
Salem	196	21	Sprague	Joseph		1		1				1	1		2		6		
Salem	196	22	Osborne	Geo				1				1	1				3		
Salem	196	23	Plummer	Oliver		3	1				1	2	1				8		

TOWN	PG#	LN#	HEADS OF HOUSEHOLD		FREE WHITE MALES					FREE WHITE FEMALES					TOTAL ALL OTHER	TOTAL SLAVES	TOTALS	DISTRICT/ TOWNSHIP	NOTES
			LAST NAME	FIRST NAME	under 10	10 to 16	16 to 26	26 to 45	45 and over	under 10	10 to 16	16 to 26	26 to 45	45 and over					
Salem	196	24	Wallis	Robt	1	1		1		1			1				5		
Salem	196	25	Gray	William	1	1		1			1	1	1				3		
Salem	196	26	Maurey	Hannah		2					1			1			4		
Salem	196	27	Rolle	James	1	1	4		1		2	1		1			11		
Salem	196	28	Coverly	Nath			1					1					2		
Salem	196	29	Richardson	Addison Senr			1	1	1		1			1			5		
Salem	196	30	Bacon	Jacob					1		1			1			3		
Salem	196	31	Foster	Robert		2	1		1		1	2		1			8		
Salem	196	32	Sherry	Francis	1				1		2	1		1			6		
Salem	196	33	Symonds	Samuel	3			1		1			1				6		
Salem	196	34	Rowell	Adam	3	1			1	2	1	2		1			11		
Salem	196	35	Chandler	John			1				1		1				3		
Salem	196	36	Symonds	Thorndike	3	1		1		2	1		1				9		
Salem	196	37	Symonds	Lydia										1			1		
Salem	196	38	Cooke	Samuel		1	1	1			1	2	1				7		
Salem	196	39	Symonds	Ebenz	4		1	1			1		1				8		
Salem	196	40	Symonds	Abigail			1			3			1				5		
Salem	196	41	Symonds	Eliza			1					1	1				3		
Salem	196	42	Ropes	Benja			1	1					1				3		
Salem	196	43	Symonds	William	1		1				1	1					4		
Salem	196	44	Symonds	Hannah			1	1			1		1				4		
Salem	196	45	Reeves	Asa	1			1		1			1				4		
Salem	197	1	Symonds	Thos				1	1	1		3	1	1			7		
Salem	197	2	Swan	Sarah	1		2				1		1				5		
Salem	197	3	Baldwin	Loammi	1		1					1					3		
Salem	197	4	Wilson	James											4		4		
Salem	197	5	Symonds	William	1		3		1	1	1	1		1			9		
Salem	197	6	Symonds	James		1			1		1			1			4		
Salem	197	7	Smith	Samuel	1		1			1			1	1			5		
Salem	197	8	Jackson	Joseph	2	2		1		1			1				7		
Salem	197	9	Kendinson	Joseph	3	2	1	1		2	1		1				11		
Salem	197	10	Fuller	Samuel	1		2		1	3	2	1					10		
Salem	197	11	Goldthwaite	Ezekl	1		1			1			1				4		
Salem	197	12	Groce	Obadh	2	1			1		2	1	1				8		
Salem	197	13	Grant	Elias		2	1	1				1	1				6		
Salem	197	14	Hutchinson	John		1			1		1	1	1				5		
Salem	197	15	Palmer	Saml	5	2		1		2	2						12		
Salem	197	16	Bradish	Sarah				1				1	1				3		
Salem	197	17	Wheeler	Thos	3	1		1		1	2		1				9		
Salem	197	18	James	Sam											5		5		
Salem	197	19	Wilkins	Reuben	4		2	1		1	1		1				10		
Salem	197	20	Symonds	Nath	3				1	2	3	1		2			12		
Salem	197	21	Fisk	Benja	2			1		1		1	1		1		7		
Salem	197	22	Symonds	John				1		3	1		1				6		
Salem	197	23	Hardwick	Mehita								1	1				2		
Salem	197	24	Telford	William	2	2			1	1			1				7		
Salem	197	25	Webb	Joanna	1								2				3		
Salem	197	26	Silver	Benjamin			1			1		1	1				4		
Salem	197	27	Silver	William			1			3	1		1				6		
Salem	197	28	Purinton	Daniel				1				1					2		
Salem	197	29	Birch	Benja											3		3		
Salem	197	30	Smally	Samuel				1		1	1		1	1			5		
Salem	197	31	Meeks	Tho				1		1			1	1			4		
Salem	197	32	Thomas	Jethro				1					1				2		
Salem	197	33	Trask	Mary	1						2		1	2			6		
Salem	197	34	Peabody	Samuel		2	1	1		1	1		1				7		
Salem	197	35	Jant	Jona					1					1			2		
Salem	197	36	Richards	Richard					1			1		1			3		
Salem	197	37	Wheeler	Joseph	1			1		1	1		1				5		
Salem	197	38	Aborn	Sarah							1	3	1				5		
Salem	197	39	Hill	Prince											5		5		
Salem	197	40	Harrinton	Charles	1			1			1		1				4		
Salem	197	41	Stone	Samuel					1				1				2		
Salem	197	42	Stone	Benjamin	3				1				1				5		
Salem	197	43	Tewksbury	Mary	2	1			1		1		1	1			7		
Salem	197	44	Silver	James	1			1		1			1	1			5		
Salem	197	45	Annabal	Benja		1	1					1					3		
Salem	197	46	Peters	Benja					1				1				2		
Salem	197	47	Peters	Jona		1	1	1			2	2	1				8		
Salem	197	48	Pratt	Caesar											2		2		
Salem	198	1	Frothinham	James	3	2		1		2			1				9		
Salem	198	2	Fullingham	Jonathn			1	1				2					4		
Salem	198	3	Reeves	John	1		1					1					3		
Salem	198	4	Southwick	Eliza			1					1		1			3		
Salem	198	5	Nutting	John	2			1		1			1				5		
Salem	198	6	Southwick	John	2				1				1				4		
Salem	198	7	Trosater	Samuel	3			1		2			1				7		
Salem	198	8	Tucker	Andrew	3		1				2	1					7		
Salem	198	9	Nichols	Ichabod	1		2	1		1	1	1					7		
Salem	198	10	Pope	Gertrude							1			1			2		
Salem	198	11	Munro	Phips			1			1	1	1					4		
Salem	198	12	Pope	Eleazer	2		1		1	2		1		1			8		
Salem	198	13	Faye	Daniel	1		4	1			2	1	1	1			11		
Salem	198	14	Pope	Enos	1			1	1			1	1				5		
Salem	198	15	Smith	Samuel		2		1					1				4		
Salem	198	16	Briggs	Elijah	1			1		1			1				4		
Salem	198	17	Buffinton	James	1			1					1				3		
Salem	198	18	Palmer	Jona		1	2						1	4			8		
Salem	198	19	Cooke	Robt				1				1	1				3		
Salem	198	20	Osborne	Eliza										2			2		

129

TOWN	PG#	LN#	LAST NAME	FIRST NAME	FREE WHITE MALES under 10	10 to 16	16 to 26	26 to 45	45 and over	FREE WHITE FEMALES under 10	10 to 16	16 to 26	26 to 45	45 and over	TOTAL ALL OTHER	TOTAL SLAVES	TOTALS	DISTRICT/ TOWNSHIP	NOTES
Salem	198	21	Goodhue	Stephn	2			1	1	1	1	1	2		1		10		
Salem	198	22	Nicholls	Thos		2			1	1	2			1			7		
Salem	198	23	Tucker	Geo			3	2	1		1	1	1	1			10		
Salem	198	24	Osborne	Robt	2	1	1	1		2		1	1	1			10		
Salem	198	25	McIntyer	Nathl	1			1		4	2		1	1			10		
Salem	198	26	Fowler	Ezekiel				1					2	1			4		
Salem	198	27	Wittridge	Tho	2		1	1		1			1	1			7		
Salem	198	28	Dean	Jona	1		1	1		2			1	1			7		
Salem	198	29	Hawker	Isaac	1	2	1		1	2			1	1			9		
Salem	198	30	Vickery	David	2	3		1		2			1	1			10		
Salem	198	31	Cheever	Samuel	1			1		1			1	1	1		6		
Salem	198	32	Tuttle	James C.			1	1					1				3		
Salem	198	33	Dean	John			3		1				1	1			6		
Salem	198	34	Johnson	Jedih	1	1	1	1				1	2	1			8		
Salem	198	35	Austin	Richard	1		1	1		1			1				5		
Salem	198	36	Johnson	Elijah	1	2			1	3				1			8		
Salem	198	37	Daland	John		1		1						1			3		
Salem	198	38	Vanderford	John	2			1					1				4		
Salem	198	39	Proctor	Ebenz		2		1				1		1			5		
Salem	198	40	Pitman	William	1		1						1				4		
Salem	198	41	Shillaber	John	1			1		3	3		1				9		
Salem	198	42	Gallushe	John	1		1						1				3		
Salem	198	43	Fowler	Samuel				1		1			1				3		
Salem	198	44	Frye	Moses	1			1		1		1					4		
Salem	199	1	Bishop	John		1		1		2			1				5		
Salem	199	2	Pitman	Michael	4		1	1		1			1	1			9		
Salem	199	3	Churchill	Zacheus	1		1						1				3		
Salem	199	4	Thomas	Mary										1			1		
Salem	199	5	Frye	Benja	2	2	1		1				3	1			10		
Salem	199	6	Tucker	Desire		1						1	3	1			6		
Salem	199	7	Wardwell	Abiel			1			1			1				3		
Salem	199	8	Tucker	Edward		3	2	1	1	2			2	1			12		
Salem	199	9	Saunders	Daniel	1		1	1		1			1	1			6		
Salem	199	10	Mann	Ebenz	3			1	4	1			1	1			11		
Salem	199	11	Goodale	Samuel		1		1		2	1		1				6		
Salem	199	12	Richardson	James		1		1					1				3		
Salem	199	13	Shillaber	William		1		1					1				3		
Salem	199	14	Frye	William					1	2	3	1	1				8		
Salem	199	15	Winchester	Jacob	4	2		1		2			1				10		
Salem	199	16	Trask	Benja		1	1			1			1				5		
Salem	199	17	Marshal	Samuel			1	1					1	1			5		
Salem	199	18	Peck	John			1			1			1	1			4		
Salem	199	19	Marshal	Samuel	1			1		1	1	1	1				6		
Salem	199	20	Goodale	Ezekiel	4			1					1				6		
Salem	199	21	Goodale	Enoch				1						1			2		
Salem	199	22	Bancroft	William	3	1		1		1			1	1			8		
Salem	199	23	More	Alexr		2		1		1	1		1				6		
Salem	199	24	Reed	Jacob				1				1					2		
Salem	199	25	Fowler	Ezekl Jr	2	2	1	1		1			1				8		
Salem	199	26	Brooks	Samuel	2			1					1				4		
Salem	199	27	Blanchard	Daniel	3	1		1		2	3		1				11		
Salem	199	28	Very	Samuel	1		1	1		2	1	2	1				9		
Salem	199	29	Bend	Mary			1			1	1			1			4		
Salem	199	30	Foster	Abram		2	1						1	1			6		
Salem	199	31	Day	Dorcas	1	3			1	1							6		
Salem	199	32	Williams	Samuel					1				1	1			3		
Salem	199	33	Ward	Nath	1		1						1				3		
Salem	199	34	Marshall	Rufus		1				1							2		
Salem	199	35	Hillor	Joseph		1			1	1	5		1				9		
Salem	199	36	Chace	Abner	1		1	1		1			2	1			7		
Salem	199	37	Osborne	Henry			1						1	1			3		
Salem	199	38	Sanderson	David	1		1	1					1	1			6		
Salem	199	39	Fabens	Sarah										1			1		
Salem	199	40	Fuller	Mary									1				1		
Salem	199	41	Chapman	Sarah		1								1			2		
Salem	200	1	Ives	William	2	1						1	1	1			6		
Salem	200	2	Crane	Hannah		2								1			3		
Salem	200	3	Dowse	William				1						1			2		
Salem	200	4	Symonds	Mary		2						2	1	1			6		
Salem	200	5	Skerry	Ephrm		1	1	1					1	1			5		
Salem	200	6	Gardner	James	3			1		1			1				6		
Salem	200	7	Cary	Joseph	2		1			1			1				5		
Salem	200	8	Skerry	John	1		1		1	3			1	1			8		
Salem	200	9	Silver	Samuel	1		1			1			1				4		
Salem	200	10	Symonds	John	1		2		1				1				6		
Salem	200	11	Symonds	Benjamin				1		2	1			1			5		
Salem	200	12	Symonds	Jonathan	1	2	1		1	3				1			9		
Salem	200	13	Deland	Benja	1			1		1		1	1				5		
Salem	200	14	Symonds	John				1						1			2		
Salem	200	15	Swan	Robt	1	4	3		1			2		1			12		
Salem	200	16	Cooke	Robt								1		1			3		
Salem	200	17	Clarke	Daniel		2							1				4		
Salem	200	18	Deland	Susanna								1	1				2		
Salem	200	19	Dennis	Fral B.		3		1		2	2			1			9		
Salem	200	20	Dennis	Willm	2	1							1				4		
Salem	200	21	Dale	Phillip			1		3				1				5		
Salem	200	22	Deland	Benja	1		1		1				1	1			5		
Salem	200	23	Symonds	Nancy										1			1		
Salem	200	24	Symonds	John	2			1		1	1		1				6		
Salem	200	25	Sheldon	Ephrm	1		1					1					3		

TOWN	PG#	LN#	LAST NAME	FIRST NAME	\<10	10 to 16	16 to 26	26 to 45	45 and over	\<10	10 to 16	16 to 26	26 to 45	45 and over	TOTAL ALL OTHER	TOTAL SLAVES	TOTALS	DISTRICT/ TOWNSHIP	NOTES
Salem	200	26	Symonds	Mehitl	1								1	1			3		
Salem	200	27	Symonds	Jacob			1						1				2		
Salem	200	28	Groce	Danl			1						1				2		
Salem	200	29	Lany	Nath		3		1				1	1				6		
Salem	200	30	Cambell	Arthur	2			1					1				4		
Salem	200	31	Estes	Nath	2	1	1		1			1	1				7		
Salem	200	32	McPherson	Duncan		1	1	1						1			4		
Salem	200	33	Browne	Jonathan	2			1	1	2	3		1	1			11		
Salem	200	34	Morgan	Israel	1			1						1			3		
Salem	200	35	Collins	Pickering		1	1		1	1	1			1			6		
Salem	200	36	Osgood	Chas	1	2	3		1	2		2		1			12		
Salem	200	37	Horton	Lemuel	1	4		1		2			1				9		
Salem	200	38	Mead	Jacob	1		2						1				4		
Salem	200	39	Britton	Edward	1	1		1		2	1		1				7		
Salem	200	40	Wright	David		1							1				2		
Salem	200	41	Dixson	Joseph	1			1					1				3		
Salem	200	42	Rawson	John					1				1				2		
Salem	200	43	Williams	Joseph	1			1		2			1	1			6		
Salem	200	44	Floid	William	1			1	1	1	1			1			6		
Salem	200	45	Phillips	Walter		1		1			2		1				5		
Salem	200	46	Fowler	Samuel		1		1		1							3		
Salem	200	47	Peach	John		1		1		2		1					5		
Salem	200	48	Upton	Paul	3	3	2	1			2	1					12		
Salem	200	49	Derby	Zeb											2		2		
Salem	200	50	Porter	Aaron	1	2	1	1		2	1		1				9		
Salem	200	51	Hower	Isaac											9		9		
Salem	201	1	Fobler	Wilson											10		10		
Salem	201	2	Putnam	Isaac			1						1				2		
Salem	201	3	Trask	Ben	1	2	2			1			1				7		
Salem	201	4	Ireland	Jona	1	2	2			2	1	1					9		
Salem	201	5	Snow	James	1	1		1		5	1		1				10		
Salem	201	6	Diamond	Benja	2			1		1			1				5		
Salem	201	7	Hayward	John					1				1	1			3		
Salem	201	8	Browne	Mary									1	1			2		
Salem	201	9	Ingalls	Collins	3			1		2	1		1				8		
Salem	201	10	Fuller	James	1			1				1					3		
Salem	201	11	Ashby	Jona	2	1		1			1		1				6		
Salem	201	12	Stoddard	Richard	1		1			1		1					4		
Salem	201	13	Phipps	Eliza	2		1										3		
Salem	201	14	Fuller	Thos	2	1		1					1				5		
Salem	201	15	Ropes	Jonathn		1	1		1		1	2		1			7		
Salem	201	16	Pitman	John			1	1			1	1	1	1			6		
Salem	201	17	Bowditch	Thos	2					3	1		1				8		
Salem	201	18	Briggs	Enos		1	8	9	1	2	2	3	1				27		
Salem	201	19	Ludden	Michael	2	1		1		1			1				6		
Salem	201	20	Pratt	Jas		1		1					1	1			4		
Salem	201	21	Basson	Patty				1					1	1			3		
Salem	201	22	Luscomb	Benja			1	1		1	3		1				7		
Salem	201	23	Luscomb	Henry	2	2		1		1			1				7		
Salem	201	24	Gould	Sarah	1								1				2		
Salem	201	25	Law	Peter	1		1						1				3		
Salem	201	26	Ingalls	Thos			1		1					1			3		
Salem	201	27	Mugford	William	2			1		2		1	1	1			8		
Salem	201	28	Lerrock	Ebenz	1		1			2		1					5		
Salem	201	29	Tay	Ebenz			1	1				1	1				4		
Salem	201	30	Mansfield	Joseph	2	2		1			1		1				7		
Salem	201	31	Kenfield	Peter					1			1	1				3		
Salem	201	32	Arington	James	2			1			1		1				5		
Salem	201	33	Moore	Jona											6		6		
Salem	201	34	Glover	John	1	1	1	1					1	1			6		
Salem	201	35	Tucker	Robt	3			1		1			1				6		
Salem	201	36	Maloon	Judy	1					1			1	1			4		
Salem	201	37	Currier	Mary		3	2						1				6		
Salem	201	38	Colvill	John	2			1		2			1	1			7		
Salem	201	39	Boulas	Eunice							1	1	1				3		
Salem	201	40	Geyer	John											2		2		
Salem	201	41	Foster	Zach											4		4		
Salem	201	42	Bowen	Jack											4		4		
Salem	201	43	Tuffts	Grimes	1		1	1					1				4		
Salem	201	44	Meservey	Hannah		1					1	1					3		
Salem	201	45	Wood	Nathan		3	1		3	1							8		
Salem	201	46	Reddington	James											5		5		
Salem	201	47	Brister	David											3		3		
Salem	201	48	Slewman	Simon	1	1		1		2			1				6		
Salem	201	49	Keeton	Francis											5		5		
Salem	202	1	Chamberlain	Samuel	1	1	1					1					4		
Salem	202	2	Erving	Geo		1	1		1	1	2			1			7		
Salem	202	3	McIntyre	Nath	1			1		2			1				5		
Salem	202	4	Gray	Willm 4th	1			1		1	1	2					6		
Salem	202	5	Clough	William	1				1	2		1					5		
Salem	202	6	Hamills	Stephen	1				1	1	2	1	2	1			9		
Salem	202	7	Borden	Sarah	2						1		1				4		
Salem	202	8	Nutting	Joseph	1			1		2		1					5		
Salem	202	9	Bowman	James		1			1					1			3		
Salem	202	10	Ward	Andrew	1		1						1				3		
Salem	202	11	Tucker	Saml	2	1	1			1			1				6		
Salem	202	12	Oakman	Samuel	1			1		2	2	1	1				8		
Salem	202	13	Joseph	Fras			1				1			1			3		
Salem	202	14	Burgess	William	1	1	1	1		2	1		1				8		
Salem	202	15	Larock	John			1							1			2		

131

TOWN	PG#	LN#	LAST NAME	FIRST NAME	FWM under 10	FWM 10 to 16	FWM 16 to 26	FWM 26 to 45	FWM 45 and over	FWF under 10	FWF 10 to 16	FWF 16 to 26	FWF 26 to 45	FWF 45 and over	TOTAL ALL OTHER	TOTAL SLAVES	TOTALS	DISTRICT/ TOWNSHIP	NOTES
Salem	202	16	Hasan	Peter		1		1		2		1					5		
Salem	202	17	Smithurst	Thos	2	1		1		2			1				7		
Salem	202	18	Barr	Arch	1			1			2	1	1				6		
Salem	202	19	Clemens	Saml	2	2		1		2			1				8		
Salem	202	20	Lane	Salem											6		6		
Salem	202	21	Butler	Thos											2		2		
Salem	202	22	Williams	Andrew											5		5		
Salem	202	23	Pratt	John	1	1	1			1		1					5		
Salem	202	24	Conway	Sarah								1	1				2		
Salem	202	25	Clemens	John	1	1		1		1			1				5		
Salem	202	26	McMillan	Arch	1	1		1		1	1		1				6		
Salem	202	27	Daniels	Benja				1					1				2		
Salem	202	28	Lewis	Benja		1				2		2					5		
Salem	202	29	Pearson	Elijah	2	2		1		1			1				7		
Salem	202	30	Fabens	William	1	1	1	1		2	1	2	1				10		
Salem	202	31	Wood	Hannah						1		1	1				4		
Salem	202	32	Daniels	Mary		1	1							1			3		
Salem	202	33	Roland	Jacob	1	1		1				1		1			5		
Salem	202	34	Symonds	Willm	4	1		1				1	1				8		
Salem	202	35	Riding	Jacob		1		1				1	1				4		
Salem	202	36	Brewer	Thos	1	1	1	1		3	1		1	1			10		
Salem	202	37	Galey	William	2		1						1				4		
Salem	202	38	Bacon	Ruth						2			1				3		
Salem	202	39	Daniels	Stephen				1						1			2		
Salem	202	40	Obear	William	4		1						1				6		
Salem	202	41	Swasey	Rachel	3							2	2	1			8		
Salem	202	42	Richards	Benja	1	1	1	1					1	2			7		
Salem	202	43	Marston	William			1						1				2		
Salem	202	44	Getchell	Mary									2	1			3		
Salem	202	45	Ingalls	James	2	1		1		1	1		1				7		
Salem	202	46	Patterson	Willm	3	1		1		2			1				8		
Salem	203	1	Whitefoot	Sarah	2	3							1				6		
Salem	203	2	Jenks	John				1					1				2		
Salem	203	3	Williams	John		1	1					2	1				5		
Salem	203	4	Magredge	Rachel		2		1					1				4		
Salem	203	5	Tucker	Mary		1				1	1	1	1				5		
Salem	203	6	Nicholls	James	1		1			2	1		1				6		
Salem	203	7	Brookhouse	Mary	2	1	1						1	1			6		
Salem	203	8	Huddle	William		1				2	1						4		
Salem	203	9	Preston	Hannah	2	1				1	1	1	1				7		
Salem	203	10	Dowst	John	3		1			1	1		1				7		
Salem	203	11	Thornton	Thos				1					2				3		
Salem	203	12	Swasey	Richd	1	2	1					1	1				7		
Salem	203	13	Martin	Mary		1	1					1	1				4		
Salem	203	14	Rust	Jacob	3		1					1	1				6		
Salem	203	15	Newhall	Samuel	1		1					1	1				4		
Salem	203	16	Lambert	Jonathan		2	2	1					1				7		
Salem	203	17	Lambert	Saml	1		1					1					3		
Salem	203	18	Hunt	Mary	2	3				3		2	1				11		
Salem	203	19	Hunt	Sarah									1				1		
Salem	203	20	Hartshorn	Thos				1				1	1				3		
Salem	203	21	Rand	Mary		1				1			1	1			4		
Salem	203	22	Beckford	Ebenezer		2		1				1	1	1			6		
Salem	203	23	Fell	Kathn										1			1		
Salem	203	24	Fell	Geo W.	1		1					1	1				4		
Salem	203	25	Barr	James				1		1	3	3	1	1			10		
Salem	203	26	Tucker	Lewis	1		2	1		1		1	1				7		
Salem	203	27	King	Benja		1		1			1	2		1			6		
Salem	203	28	Frothingham	Nath	1		6			2		1	1				11		
Salem	203	29	Millet	John	1		1			1			1				4		
Salem	203	30	Rowell	Eliza			2			2	1	1	1				7		
Salem	203	31	Boyard	Joseph		1	1				2		1				5		
Salem	203	32	Hartshorn	Joseph	1	1	1						1				4		
Salem	203	33	Barr	James			1							1			2		
Salem	203	34	Watkins	Benja		3	1						1				5		
Salem	203	35	Daland	John	1	1	1	1					1				5		
Salem	203	36	Peele	Willard		1		1			1		1				4		
Salem	203	37	Ward	James			1						1				2		
Salem	203	38	Anderson	Debh F.							1	1	1				3		
Salem	203	39	Clarke	Martha	1		1			1	3	2	1				9		
Salem	203	40	Williams	Isaac							1	3	1	2			7		
Salem	203	41	Oliver	Sarah		3	1			2	4	4	1				15		
Salem	203	42	Orne	Eliza		2					1	1	1	1			6		
Salem	203	43	Osgood	Isaac	2	1		1		1	1	1	1				9		
Salem	203	44	Grant	John		1	1	1		2		1	1				7		
Salem	204	1	Needham	Isaac		2	1		2		2	2		1			10		
Salem	204	2	Simmons	John											4		4		
Salem	204	3	Laffege	Thos											2		2		
Salem	204	4	Laffege	Peter											2		2		
Salem	204	5	Felt	Benja		2		1			2	1		1			7		
Salem	204	6	Parnell	Jonas		2		1					1				4		
Salem	204	7	Burns	Tarrant	1	1		1		4	2		1				10		
Salem	204	8	Richards	David	2	3		1			1			1			8		
Salem	204	9	Atkinson	Joseph		1	1	1		1	1	2	1				8		
Salem	204	10	Cooke	Jona	1		1						1				3		
Salem	204	11	Low	Daniel	1		2	1		1	3	2		1			11		
Salem	204	12	Tink	Thos	1	2	1			1			1				6		
Salem	204	13	Ryan	Anna									1				4		
Salem	204	14	Chipman	Thos	1	1		2		3	1		2				10		
Salem	204	15	Fauzel	John		1		2					1	1			5		

132

TOWN	PG#	LN#	LAST NAME	FIRST NAME	FREE WHITE MALES under 10	10 to 16	16 to 26	26 to 45	45 and over	FREE WHITE FEMALES under 10	10 to 16	16 to 26	26 to 45	45 and over	TOTAL ALL OTHER	TOTAL SLAVES	TOTALS	DISTRICT/ TOWNSHIP	NOTES
Salem	204	16	Harrington	James				1		1			2				4		
Salem	204	17	Glover	Hannah							1	2	1				4		
Salem	204	18	Harrington	Joseph				1		1			1				3		
Salem	204	19	Price	William	1		1						1				3		
Salem	204	20	Callum	John		1		1		3			1	1			7		
Salem	204	21	Cleland	Clark			1						1				2		
Salem	204	22	Godhsaw	William	1	1		1		2			1		1		7		
Salem	204	23	Marston	Mary									1	1			2		
Salem	204	24	Trask	Mary										2			2		
Salem	204	25	Cook	Joseph	1	1	1						1				4		
Salem	204	26	Willson	Robt	1			1		1			1				4		
Salem	204	27	Erving	John				1			1		1				3		
Salem	204	28	Townsend	Thos				1		3			1				5		
Salem	204	29	Munday	William					1	1	1			1			4		
Salem	204	30	Gilbert	James	1		1			1			1				4		
Salem	204	31	Peirce	John					1	2			2		1		6		
Salem	204	32	Lamb	Simon					1					1			2		
Salem	204	33	Lamb	Simon Jr	1			1		1	1	1	1				6		
Salem	204	34	Munday	Willm	2			1		1	2		1				7		
Salem	204	35	Bartholomew	Benja	1	1		1		1		1	1				6		
Salem	204	36	Ruck	Mary	1								1				2		
Salem	204	37	Cook	Wm				1		3			1	1			6		
Salem	204	38	Smithurst	Peter		1		1		3	2		1	2			10		
Salem	204	39	Eaton	Charles	2	1		1		2			1				7		
Salem	204	40	Felt	Nath	2	1	1	1		3	1	1					10		
Salem	204	41	Parker	Saml		1				2		1					4		
Salem	204	42	Mansfield	Mary	2					1	1		1				5		
Salem	204	43	Dolliver	William		1	2						1				4		
Salem	204	44	McIntyer	Joseph	1	1		1					1				4		
Salem	204	45	McIntyer	Sarah								2	1				3		
Salem	204	46	McIntyer	Anger	1	2		1		2			1				7		
Salem	205	1	Willson	John	2		1						1				4		
Salem	205	2	Luscomb	Saml					1					1			2		
Salem	205	3	Thompson	Joseph	1	2		1		3			1	1			9		
Salem	205	4	Manning	Anstis									1	1			2		
Salem	205	5	Kenny	Adam		1		1		1			1				4		
Salem	205	6	Felt	David			1	1					2				4		
Salem	205	7	Stone	John			1			1			1				3		
Salem	205	8	Felt	Joseph			1			1			1				3		
Salem	205	9	Felt	John		3		1		2			1	1			8		
Salem	205	10	Converse	Nabby	1								1				3		
Salem	205	11	Cox	Eliza			1						1	1			3		
Salem	205	12	Dowse	Saml	1	1		1		1			1	1			6		
Salem	205	13	Parnell	James	1	2		1					1				5		
Salem	205	14	Tay	Benja			1			1			2				4		
Salem	205	15	Luscomb	Willm	1	2			1	1	1			1			7		
Salem	205	16	Luscomb	Willm Jr	2	2	1			2	1	1					9		
Salem	205	17	Muley	Rebecca			1							1			2		
Salem	205	18	Greely	Philip			1			1		1					3		
Salem	205	19	Bridgon	Josa			1			1			1				3		
Salem	205	20	Brad	Thos			1						1				2		
Salem	205	21	Cook	Love										1			1		
Salem	205	22	Feel	Joseph			1						1				2		
Salem	205	23	Derby	John			1					1					2		
Salem	205	24	Spalding	Joshua	2		1			1		1	1				6		
Salem	205	25	Pease	Minor	1	1			1		1			1			5		
Salem	205	26	Smithers	Tobias					1			1		1			3		
Salem	205	27	Leach	Paul	2	1		1		3	1		1				9		
Salem	205	28	Pease	Samuel	1			1		1			1				4		
Salem	205	29	Halden	Charles	1			1					1				3		
Salem	205	30	Ireland	Samuel	1			1					1				3		
Salem	205	31	Honeys	Israel	1			1		3	1		1				7		
Salem	205	32	McIntyer	Samuel		1	1			1			2				5		
Salem	205	33	Kennedy	James		1	1	1			2	3					8		
Salem	205	34	Browne	David	1	1							1				3		
Salem	205	35	Cummins	John	1			1					1				3		
Salem	205	36	Smith	Geo		1				1			1				3		
Salem	205	37	Ellsy	Hipsabh							1	1	1	1			4		
Salem	205	38	Brecome	Margaret		3				1			1				5		
Salem	205	39	Cox	MAry			1					1	2	1			5		
Salem	205	40	Alley	Reuben	1		1		1	1		2		1			7		
Salem	205	41	Archer	Joseph			1			1		1					3		
Salem	205	42	Ropes	Susanna									1	1			2		
Salem	205	43	Cloutman	Abigail	1					1			1				3		
Salem	205	44	Pease	Richard			1						1				2		
Salem	205	45	Cox	Ben				1						1			2		
Salem	205	46	Dowse	Joseph			1			1			1	1			4		
Salem	205	47	Wiggins	Joseph	2	2	1		1	1			1	1			9		
Salem	205	48	Williams	John				1					1				2		
Salem	205	49	Pease	Jona	1		1						1				3		
Salem	205	50	Foster	John					1				1				3		
Salem	205	51	Kenny	John			1			1			1				3		
Salem	205	52	Green	John		1	2	1			1	1					6		
Salem	205	53	Rebour	Peter L	1		1	1			1	1	1				6		
Salem	206	1	Whittamore	Saml		1	1					2		1			6		
Salem	206	2	Brodies	Ebenzr	2			1		1			1				5		
Salem	206	3	Chammins	John	1			1		1			1				4		
Salem	206	4	Bryant	Timo		1		1		2		1		1			6		
Salem	206	5	Felt	Jane		1				1	1		1				4		
Salem	206	6	Mikels	Andrew			1						1				2		

133

TOWN	PG#	LN#	LAST NAME	FIRST NAME	FREE WHITE MALES					FREE WHITE FEMALES					TOTAL ALL OTHER	TOTAL SLAVES	TOTALS	DISTRICT/ TOWNSHIP	NOTES
					under 10	10 to 16	16 to 26	26 to 45	45 and over	under 10	10 to 16	16 to 26	26 to 45	45 and over					
Salem	206	7	Leach	Robt			2		1	2	4		2				11		
Salem	206	8	Bradshaw	Wm	3			1		1	2		1				8		
Salem	206	9	Ward	Joshua				1			1	2		1			5		
Salem	206	10	Ward	Joshua Junr			1			1	1	1	1				5		
Salem	206	11	Ropes	John	1	1	1	1		2	1	1	1				9		
Salem	206	12	Neal	Jona	2		1				1	2	1				7		
Salem	206	13	Lawrence	Abel	1	2	2		1	4	1	2	2				15		
Salem	206	14	Carpenter	Benja		1		1	1		1	2		1			7		
Salem	206	15	Silsbee	Enoch				1		1	1	1					4		
Salem	206	16	Sweeten	James				1				1		1			3		
Salem	206	17	Cox	Anna						1	1		1				3		
Salem	206	18	Peterson	Hanse				1		1	1	1					4		
Salem	206	19	Slewman	Margt		1	2			1			1				6		
Salem	206	20	Goldthwaite	Anna	2	3					1	2		1			9		
Salem	206	21	Harris	Robt		1		1			1						3		
Salem	206	22	Bowker	Joel			1	1				1					3		
Salem	206	23	Marston	William		1	2		1	3							8		
Salem	206	24	Winn	John			1					1					2		
Salem	206	25	Nicholls	Ichabod	3	2	2		1	2	2		2				14		
Salem	206	26	Newhall	Joseph			4	1		2	1		1				9		
Salem	206	27	Gale	Edmund	1	2			1	3	1	1	1				10		
Salem	206	28	Ropes	David	3	2	2	1		1		1		1			11		
Salem	206	29	Rust	Henry					1		1	2	1				5		
Salem	206	30	Appleton	John	1	1	3	1	1			1	1	1			10		
Salem	206	31	Hathorne	John		2	1		1	2	2	1		2			11		
Salem	206	32	Norris	John			1		1	1	1	1					5		
Salem	206	33	Derby	Martha	1	1				1		3					7		
Salem	206	34	Derby	John	3	1		1				3					8		
Salem	206	35	Derby	Ezekiel H.	2		1	1		2		2	2				10		
Salem	206	36	Derby	Elias H.	1	1		1		1		3					8		
Salem	206	37	Jenks	John		1	1	1		3	2	2	1	1			12		
Salem	206	38	Lee	Thos		2	1	1	1		2	1	1		1		10		
Salem	206	39	Saunders	Daniel	1	1		1		1			1				5		
Salem	206	40	Clarke	Eliza		1				1			1				3		
Salem	206	41	Frye	John	2			1		1	1		1				6		
Salem	206	42	Gavet	Jona	2			1		1			1				5		
Salem	206	43	Mansfield	Ellis				1		2	2		1				6		
Salem	206	44	Bowditch	Ebenz		1		1					1				3		
Salem	206	45	Berril	Alden		1	1	1		3	1						7		
Salem	206	46	Rea	Mary		2				1	3		1				7		
Salem	206	47	Savage	Ezekiel	2			1		1	2	1	1				8		
Salem	206	48	Jenks	Daniel				1		1	3		1				6		
Salem	206	49	Wing	Cornielius			1	1				1	1				4		
Salem	206	50	Norris	Edward	1	1	3		1			1		1			8		
Salem	206	51	Northey	Abijah		1		1		2		2	1	1			8		
Salem	206	52	West	William				1					2	2			5		
Salem	206	53	West	Edward	1			1		1		2	1				7		
Salem	206	54	King	James		3			1	1	1	4	1	1			12		
Salem	206	55	Mansfield	Mathew				1		1		1					3		
Salem	206	56	Jeffry	James				2			1		1				4		
Salem	206	57	Mansfield	Joseph	1		1					1					3		
Salem	206	58	Dennis	Samuel		1	1					1					3		
Salem	206	59	Grant	Eliza								2	1	1			4		
Salem	207	1	Shaw	John	4			1		2		1					8		
Salem	207	2	Dodge	Pian	1		1			1	1	1					5		
Salem	207	3	Burns	Edward				1			2		1				4		
Salem	207	4	Robinson	Samuel			3	1		1	1		1				7		
Salem	207	5	Pulling	Mary						1		1	1				3		
Salem	207	6	Ashton	Jacob		1	2		1	3	2	1	1				11		
Salem	207	7	Derby	John	3	2	2					1	1				9		
Salem	207	8	Cross	Moses	1		1			1		1					4		
Salem	207	9	West	Nath	1	3		1		2	1	1	3				12		
Salem	207	10	Gray	Samuel	1	2	2	1		2			1				9		
Salem	207	11	Mous	Ben				1			1		1				3		
Salem	207	12	Muse	Mary	2						1		1				4		
Salem	207	13	Yew	Mosis			1			2		1					4		
Salem	207	14	Harvey	John	3		1	1		1	1	1					8		
Salem	207	15	Dewing	Joseph	1		1				2	1					5		
Salem	207	16	Horton	eo	1		1			2		1					5		
Salem	207	17	Very	Jona				1				1	1				3		
Salem	207	18	Valpey	Abram	4	1						1					7		
Salem	207	19	Osgood	Benja			1	1					1				3		
Salem	207	20	Osborne	Betsey	1					1		1					3		
Salem	207	21	Osgood	Benja Jr			1			1	1	1					4		
Salem	207	22	Driver	Ben	1	1		1		1	1						6		
Salem	207	23	Driver	Sarah									1				1		
Salem	207	24	Driver	Robt			1			1							2		
Salem	207	25	Valpey	Joseph	4							1					6		
Salem	207	26	Hodgson	Saml		1				1		1					3		
Salem	207	27	Dutch	John	1	2						1	1				5		
Salem	207	28	Yew	Eliza	1						1	1	1				4		
Salem	207	29	Newhall	Rebecca		1							1				2		
Salem	207	30	Croel	James	1		1			2		1					5		
Salem	207	31	Culbertson	John	1	1						1					3		
Salem	207	32	Yell	Mehihl									1				1		
Salem	207	33	Moses	Benja			1			1		1					3		
Salem	207	34	Joseph	John	1		1			1		1					4		
Salem	207	35	Smith	Geo				1		1							3		
Salem	207	36	Silver	Sarah		1							1				2		
Salem	207	37	Gowen	Charles		2		1			1	1					5		

TOWN	PG#	LN#	LAST NAME	FIRST NAME	FREE WHITE MALES					FREE WHITE FEMALES					TOTAL ALL OTHER	TOTAL SLAVES	TOTALS	DISTRICT/ TOWNSHIP	NOTES
					under 10	10 to 16	16 to 26	26 to 45	45 and over	under 10	10 to 16	16 to 26	26 to 45	45 and over					
Salem	207	38	Mansfield	Jona	2			1		1	1	1					6		
Salem	207	39	Barthman	Zacha	1		3	1	1	2	1		1				10		
Salem	207	40	Putnam	Ebenz	2	1		1			1	1	1				7		
Salem	207	41	Arne	William	1	3	3		1		2		2				12		
Salem	207	42	Ropes	Joseph		1		1		1			2				5		
Salem	207	43	Orne	Josiah	3	1		1		1	1	2	1				10		
Salem	207	44	Buffinton	Deborah		2	1					3		1			7		
Salem	207	45	Chase	Rebc		1	3			2		1	1	1			9		
Salem	207	46	Abbot	Stephen		2			1			4		1	1		9		
Salem	207	47	Rust	Henry	1	1		1		2		2	1				8		
Salem	207	48	Chace	Abijah	1		1	1		1	1		1				6		
Salem	207	49	Herrick	Barnebas				1					1				2		
Salem	207	50	Herrick	Peter			1	1		2			1				5		
Salem	207	51	Rust	John		1		1		1	1	2					6		
Salem	207	52	Webb	Michael	2	1		1		1	1	1	1				8		
Salem	207	53	Daland	Thoms	1	1		1		2	3	1		1			10		
Salem	207	54	Rose	Brackly	1			1		2	1		1				6		
Salem	207	55	Perkins	Elijah	2			1		2	2	2	1				10		
Salem	207	56	Browne	Eunice									1	1			2		
Salem	207	57	Giles	Sarah								1	1	1			3		
Salem	207	58	Peabody	Ezra	2			1		2	1		1				7		
Salem	207	59	Darant	Edwd	2	1		1		1			1	1			7		
Salem	207	60	Robinson	Patty	1	2	1			2			1	1			8		
Salem	207	61	Bacall	Samuel				1		2			1				4		
Salem	208	1	Phillips	Asa			1	1					1				3		
Salem	208	2	Shelden	Ephm		1			1	1		1	1				5		
Salem	208	3	Brit	Michl	1			1					1				3		
Salem	208	4	Collier	Isaac		1		1		1	1	3	1				8		
Salem	208	5	Nicholls	Jno	3		2	1		2	2		1				11		
Salem	208	6	Fowler	Robt	1	2	2	1		1	3		1				11		
Salem	208	7	Teague	Wm	2			1	1	1	2		1				8		
Salem	208	8	Farlis	Thos	1	2		1			1	2		2			9		
Salem	208	9	Towne	Saml	1			1		1			1				4		
Salem	208	10	Derby	Saml	5		1	1		3	1	2	2				15		
Salem	208	11	Millet	Abram	1		1						1				3		
Salem	208	12	Ruste	Danl				1		2	1	1					5		
Salem	208	13	Pope	James		1	1	1		1	1		1				6		
Salem	208	14	Perkins	David	3	1	1	1		2			1	1			10		
Salem	208	15	Cheever	Samuel	2	1			1	1	1	1					7		
Salem	208	16	Seagar	Nath	1		1	1		1	1	1					6		
Salem	208	17	Hooper	Abiel								1	1				2		
Salem	208	18	Carwick	Henry	3			1		1	2		1				8		
Salem	208	19	Barton	Margaret			1				1	1	1	1			5		
Salem	208	20	Alley	Rufus	1		1			2		1					5		
Salem	208	21	Bruce	James	1			1		2			1				5		
Salem	208	22	McElroy	Benja					1					1	1		2		
Salem	208	23	Pain	Dinah											1		1		
Salem	208	24	Gardner	Newberry											2		2		
Salem	208	25	Augustus	Samson											3		3		
Salem	208	26	Martin	Thos											2		2		
Salem	208	27	Blydon	Peter											7		7		
Salem	208	28	Upton	Flora											6		6		
Salem	208	29	Poynton	Nelly											1		1		
Salem	208	30	Manuel	Peter											4		4		
Salem	208	31	Bray	Silvia											6		6		
Salem	208	32	Gomez	Emanuel	2			1					1				4		
Salem	208	33	Cardwell	Jacob	2			1				1					4		
Salem	208	34	Browne	John				1		1	1			1			4		
Salem	208	35	Worldly	William				1		1		1					3		
Salem	208	36	Redfield	James				1		1		1	1				4		
Salem	208	37	Robinson	Mary						1		1	1				3		
Salem	208	38	Arter	John				1				1	1	1			4		
Salem	208	39	Wakefield	John	2	1		1		1	2	2	1				10		
Salem	208	40	Williams	Anna	1						1	1	1				4		
Salem	208	41	Goodridge	Lydia		1					1		1				3		
Salem	208	42	Munyan	Gabriel				1		2			1				4		
Salem	208	43	Holman	Robt			1						1				2		
Salem	208	44	Powell	Abigail		1						1		1			3		
Salem	208	45	Ramsden	Anthony	2			1		2			1				6		
Salem	208	46	Waters	Sarah						2			1				3		
Salem	208	47	Ocum	Lydia		1							1				2		
Salem	208	48	Cardwell	Eliza		1						1		1			3		
Salem	208	49	Edwards	John			1			1			1				3		
Salem	208	50	Webb	Benja			1						1				2		
Salem	208	51	Kenny	Hannah		2						1	1				4		
Salem	208	52	Southwick	John			1	1									2		
Salem	208	53	Goodale	John			1						1				2		
Salem	208	54	Prince	Richard	1		1			1			1				4		
Salem	208	55	Cain	Thos	1		1			2			1				5		
Salem	208	56	Kinman	Thos			1			4			1				6		
Salem	208	57	Tarbox	Thos			1					1	1				3		
Salem	208	58	Cook	Eunice								1					1		
Salem	208	59	Flood	Mary										1			1		
Salem	208	60	Clemens	Henry	2			1				2					5		
Salem	208	61	Richards	Jona	1	1		1		1		1	1				6		
Salem	208	62	Levans	Richard			1			1		1		1			4		
Salem	209	1	Ward	Benja										1			1		
Salem	209	2	Very	James	1		1			1		1	1				5		
Salem	209	3	Porter	Abigail								1		1			2		
Salem	209	4	Manning	William	1		1			1		1		1			5		

TOWN	PG#	LN#	LAST NAME	FIRST NAME	FREE WHITE MALES under 10	10 to 16	16 to 26	26 to 45	45 and over	FREE WHITE FEMALES under 10	10 to 16	16 to 26	26 to 45	45 and over	TOTAL ALL OTHER	TOTAL SLAVES	TOTALS	DISTRICT/ TOWNSHIP	NOTES
Salem	209	5	Hutson	John		1		1		2		2	1				7		
Salem	209	6	Peabody	Jona	1	1	1	1		2			1				7		
Salem	209	7	Ward	Samuel	1	3	2		1	2		2	1	1			13		
Salem	209	8	Joplin	Mary	1			1		2		1	1	1			7		
Salem	209	9	Knap	John	1			1		1		1					4		
Salem	209	10	Gower	Eliza									1				1		
Salem	209	11	Barry	John	1	1	1					1					4		
Salem	209	12	Dunkle	John	2		1	1				1					5		
Salem	209	13	Dagget	Elisha		1	2	1		3	1	2	1				11		
Salem	209	14	Hendy	John				1					1				2		
Salem	209	15	Henick	Jona	2	1		1		1			1				6		
Salem	209	16	Butman	Ruth			1							1			2		
Salem	209	17	Still	Mary		1							1				2		
Salem	209	18	Butman	Eliza		1								1			2		
Salem	209	19	Barnard	Samuel		1	1	1		1	1	1					6		
Salem	209	20	Sweetser	Samuel	1	1			1	2	1	2	1	1			10		
Salem	209	21	Tuffts	Ivory	1		2			1		1					5		
Salem	209	22	McIntyre	Eliza				1				1					2		
Salem	209	23	Burroughs	Giles	1								1	1			3		
Salem	209	24	Shool	Priscilla		1							1				2		
Salem	209	25	Archer	Samuel	1			1				1		1			4		
Salem	209	26	Glover	Priscilla	1	1						1	1				4		
Salem	209	27	Patterson	Saml			3			1		1	1				6		
Salem	209	28	Patterson	Thos	2		1			1			1	1			6		
Salem	209	29	Gavete	James		1				1		1					3		
Salem	209	30	Lampaul	Hannah									2	1			3		
Salem	209	31	Tibbet	Henry	1	2		1		1		1					6		
Salem	209	32	Veal	Mich		1				1		1					3		
Salem	209	33	Pitnam	William	3		1						1				5		
Salem	209	34	Penny	Saml			1						1				2		
Salem	209	35	Barr	Robt	3		1						1				5		
Salem	209	36	Hodges	Priscilla								1	1	1			3		
Salem	209	37	Bancroft	Thos	1	1		1				2		1			6		
Salem	209	38	Tussel	Joseph	2	2			1	2	1	2	1				11		
Salem	209	39	Osgood	John		2	1	1		3	2	1	2	2			14		
Salem	209	40	Webb	Stephen		1	1	1		1	1	2	1				8		
Salem	209	41	Patterson	William	2			1		2			1		1		7		
Salem	209	42	Waters	Joseph	2			1		2	2	2		1			10		
Salem	209	43	Patterson	Robt				1					2				3		
Salem	209	44	Chard	Mary									1				1		
Salem	209	45	Bolton	John	1			1		1			1				4		
Salem	209	46	Gerde	Benja			1					1					2		
Salem	209	47	Smith	Joseph		1			1		1	1		1			5		
Salem	209	48	Richardson	Jesse			1			1		2					4		
Salem	209	49	Putnam	Barthl		1		1				1		1			4		
Salem	209	50	Adams	Nehemiah		2	3	3	1	4		2	2	1			18		
Salem	209	51	Lang	Edward		1	1	1			1	2		1			7		
Salem	209	52	Pulsifer	Fras	1	1	3			3	1		1				11		
Salem	209	53	Gwynn	Thaddeus	3	2	1	1		1		3	1				12		
Salem	209	54	Gray	Albert	2	3	2			1		2	1				11		
Salem	209	55	Ross	Hannah		2						1		1			4		
Salem	209	56	Punchard	Samuel	2			1		2	1	2	1				9		
Salem	209	57	Taley	William	3		1					1					5		
Salem	210	1	Taylor	Samuel			1			2		1					4		
Salem	210	2	Johnson	Charles		1						1					2		
Salem	210	3	Tuttle	Edward	1		1			2	1	1					6		
Salem	210	4	Lander	Charles	1		1					1					3		
Salem	210	5	Horton	Jona	2		1					1					4		
Salem	210	6	Dupar	Elias	1		1			1		1					4		
Salem	210	7	Thomas	Moses		2	2	1		3	1	1					10		
Salem	210	8	Deval	Michael	2		1					1					4		
Salem	210	9	Abbot	Phillip	1	2	2	1				1					7		
Salem	210	10	Anderson	Andrew		1					1	1					3		
Salem	210	11	Gale	Samuel	3	2	1			2	1	1	1				11		
Salem	210	12	Abbot	Daniel	1		1			1		1					4		
Salem	210	13	Williams	Henry	1	1		1		1			1				5		
Salem	210	14	Downing	Thos	1			1				1					3		
Salem	210	15	Very	Isaac	3		1			1		1	1				7		
Salem	210	16	Miller	Joseph		1				1		1					3		
Salem	210	17	Collins	Mary	3	1						1	1				6		
Salem	210	18	Coombs	William	1			1		3			1				6		
Salem	210	19	Steele	Robert		1						1					2		
Salem	210	20	Fairfield	William	1			1		2			1	1			6		
Salem	210	21	Maley	Lydia	1							1	1				3		
Salem	210	22	Elkins	Henry			1				1	1					3		
Salem	210	23	Sheppard	David		1						1					2		
Salem	210	24	Devereux	Thos	3		1			2			1				7		
Salem	210	25	Barnes	Thos		2		1		3	1		1	1			9		
Salem	210	26	Boden	William	2		1			2		1					6		
Salem	210	27	Knights	Enoch	1			1		1		1					4		
Salem	210	28	Hawkins	Samuel		1						1	1				3		
Salem	210	29	Wright	James		1	1						1		1		4		
Salem	210	30	Cheever	Samuel				1					1				2		
Salem	210	31	Townsend	Pen			1			2		1	1				5		
Salem	210	32	Cheever	Benja		1		1		1	3		1				7		
Salem	210	33	Browne	Margaret		1				1		1					3		
Salem	210	34	Edwards	John	2		1					1					4		
Salem	210	35	Browne	Thos			1			3		1					5		
Salem	210	36	Hovey	Thos		1	2	1				3	1				8		
Salem	210	37	Skerry	Samuel	1		1				1	1					4		

136

TOWN	PG#	LN#	LAST NAME	FIRST NAME	FREE WHITE MALES under 10	10 to 16	16 to 26	26 to 45	45 and over	FREE WHITE FEMALES under 10	10 to 16	16 to 26	26 to 45	45 and over	TOTAL ALL OTHER	TOTAL SLAVES	TOTALS	DISTRICT/ TOWNSHIP	NOTES
Salem	210	38	Newham	Daniel		2	1		1			1		1			6		
Salem	210	39	Endicott	Samuel	1			1		2	1		1				6		
Salem	210	40	Phippen	David	1		1			1		1					4		
Salem	210	41	Needham	Edmund				1				1		1			3		
Salem	210	42	Blakeney	James			1			1			1				3		
Salem	210	43	Gardner	Joseph	2		1	1		3	1	2	1				11		
Salem	210	44	Mathews	Abigail									1				1		
Salem	210	45	Dodge	Josiah	2			1		1			1				5		
Salem	210	46	Smith	Isaac			1			1	1	1					4		
Salem	210	47	Lewis	Thos	2		1					1					4		
Salem	210	48	Odell	Samuel	1		1					1					3		
Salem	210	49	Nick	Jona	2			1		1			1				5		
Salem	210	50	Cook	Joseph			1			1	1	1					4		
Salem	210	51	Barras	Peter		1		1		1		1	1				5		
Salem	210	52	Miller	Leonard			1			2		1					4		
Salem	210	53	Peters	Sarah								1		1			2		
Salem	210	54	Henry	Samuel		1		1				2		1			5		
Salem	210	55	Ropes	Priscilla									1				1		
Salem	210	56	Noyes	Simeon			1						1				2		
Salem	210	57	Corey	Peleg	1		1					1					3		
Salem	210	58	Symonds	Eliza									1				1		
Salem	211	1	Smith	Robert				1		1			1				3		
Salem	211	2	Waters	Esther	1								1				2		
Salem	211	3	Ward	Eben B.	1	1	1	1		1	1		1				7		
Salem	211	4	Caldwell	Daniel	2		1			1		1					5		
Salem	211	5	Green	William	1	1		1					1				4		
Salem	211	6	Carrel	Edward		1		1			1	1	1				5		
Salem	211	7	Davison	Anna						1		1					2		
Salem	211	8	Daniels	Eliza	2		1			2		1	1				7		
Salem	211	9	Bartlet	Cornielius	2		1	1		1		1	1				7		
Salem	211	10	Elsworth	William	1		1					1					3		
Salem	211	11	McGuay	John	1		1	1		4	1		1				9		
Salem	211	12	Hacklin	William		1						1					2		
Salem	211	13	Beel	Saml	3		1			1		1					6		
Salem	211	14	Buxton	Thos			1					1					2		
Salem	211	15	Browne	Pelatiah			1			4		1					6		
Salem	211	16	Gardner	Richard	1		1	1				2					5		
Salem	211	17	Franks	Joseph			1	1					1				3		
Salem	211	18	Franks	Joseph Jr			1					1					2		
Salem	211	19	Browne	Benja	1		1	1		4			1				8		
Salem	211	20	Vincent	Joseph		3	1			1		1	1				7		
Salem	211	21	Walden	Joseph	3	1		1		1			1				7		
Salem	211	22	Emerton	Jeremiah	1	2			1	1		1	1				7		
Salem	211	23	Arter	Mary						1			1				2		
Salem	211	24	Moria	Robt			1			1	1		1				4		
Salem	211	25	Briggs	Thos		7	1				1	2	1				12		
Salem	211	26	Vincent	Joseph			2		1	1	1	1		3			9		
Salem	211	27	Bowman	Mary		1				2	1		1				5		
Salem	211	28	Rogers	Mary	1	3				1	3	2	2				12		
Salem	211	29	Bartlett	Walter P				1		1	1		1				4		
Salem	211	30	Webb	Hannah			1					1		1	1		4		
Salem	211	31	Widen	Charles			1			1		1					3		
Salem	211	32	Richardson	Eunice		2	1			1	1	1		1			7		
Salem	211	33	Cromby	Benja		3	4			2		1	1				11		
Salem	211	34	Pettingel	Joseph	1		1					1					3		
Salem	211	35	Hathorne	Eliza			1					2		1			4		
Salem	211	36	Purbeck	Aaron	1			1		1			1				4		
Salem	211	37	Cook	Caleb	2			1			1		1				5		
Salem	211	38	Leich	Mary										1			1		
Salem	211	39	Bowditch	Eliza									2	1			3		
Salem	211	40	Brown	John	2			1					1				4		
Salem	211	41	Winn	Joseph	2			1		2		1	1				7		
Salem	211	42	Howard	John	1	2	3	1		1	3	2		1			14		
Salem	211	43	Pittman	William			1		1			1	2				5		
Salem	211	44	Gould	Josiah				1		1			1				3		
Salem	211	45	Waters	John	1		1					1					3		
Salem	211	46	Sheppard	Jeremiah	1	2	4	1				2		1			11		
Salem	211	47	Ropes	Ruth									1				1		
Salem	211	48	Snelling	John			1				1		1				3		
Salem	211	49	Henderson	Benja	2	2	1						1				6		
Salem	211	50	Dalton	Edward			1			1		1					3		
Salem	211	51	Cahon	Aaron	1		1			1		1					4		
Salem	211	52	Bray	Mary			1						1				2		
Salem	211	53	Willis	John	1	1		1		1			1				5		
Salem	211	54	Wright	Mary								2	2				4		
Salem	212	1	Gardner	John	3	1		1		1	1	1	2				10		
Salem	212	2	Gardner	Jonathan	1		1	1				1	1		1		6		
Salem	212	3	Richardson	William	2	1		1		4	1	1	1				11		
Salem	212	4	Peabody	Joseph	2		1	1			2	1	1		1		9		
Salem	212	5	Andrews	Cathr			2			1			1				4		
Salem	212	6	Williams	Lycia						1	2		1				4		
Salem	212	7	Lewis	Martha		2				2	1	1					6		
Salem	212	8	Ropes	Dan				1					1				2		
Salem	212	9	Archer	James	1			1				1					3		
Salem	212	10	Webb	Benja	1	1	7	4	2	4		1	1		1		22		
Salem	212	11	Newhall	Else		1	2					1		2			6		
Salem	212	12	White	Joseph			2	1				1	1		1		6		
Salem	212	13	King	Seth	1			1		1			1				4		
Salem	212	14	Chapman	Isaac N			1	1		1		1	1				5		
Salem	212	15	Ball	William	2	1	1		1		2		1				8		

TOWN	PG#	LN#	LAST NAME	FIRST NAME	FREE WHITE MALES under 10	10 to 16	16 to 26	26 to 45	45 and over	FREE WHITE FEMALES under 10	10 to 16	16 to 26	26 to 45	45 and over	TOTAL ALL OTHER	TOTAL SLAVES	TOTALS	DISTRICT/ TOWNSHIP	NOTES
Salem	212	16	Carlton	William		3	1	1		1	1			1	1		9		
Salem	212	17	Crowninshield	Benja	1	1				1	3	1					8		
Salem	212	18	Crowninshield	Hannah			2				1		1	1	1		5		
Salem	212	19	Babbige	John	2	2	2	1		3			1				11		
Salem	212	20	Babbige	Susanna								1	1				2		
Salem	212	21	Webb	Ben	3	2		1		1		1	1	1			10		
Salem	212	22	Bray	Robt			1	1		3			1	1			7		
Salem	212	23	Gray	William				1				1		1			3		
Salem	212	24	Moley	John			1				1	1		1			4		
Salem	212	25	Flint	Susanna									1	1			2		
Salem	212	26	Flint	John	2	1		1		3	2	2	1				12		
Salem	212	27	Burrel	Mansfield Jr	2		1	1		2			1				7		
Salem	212	28	Southwick	John	1			1					1	1			4		
Salem	212	29	Hascol	Elisha				1		2	1		1	1			6		
Salem	212	30	Cloutman	Mary								1	1				2		
Salem	212	31	Martin	Mary						1		1	1				3		
Salem	212	32	Burrel	William	1		2			2			1				6		
Salem	212	33	Burrel	Mansfield Sen	1	1		1		2		3	1	1			10		
Salem	212	34	Kimball	Jacob		1							1				2		
Salem	212	35	Ropes	William	1		2	1		3	1		2				10		
Salem	212	36	King	Gedney		2		1				1		1			5		
Salem	212	37	Cheever	Mary									1				1		
Salem	212	38	McMillan	John			1	1				1		1			4		
Salem	212	39	Palfry	Richard	1		1			1		1					4		
Salem	212	40	Joy	Joseph	2	1		1					1				5		
Salem	212	41	Gale	Anna										2			2		
Salem	212	42	Peters	John	1	1		1		1			2				6		
Salem	212	43	Webb	Henrh				1		2			1				4		
Salem	212	44	Archer	James	1	1		1		2			1				6		
Salem	212	45	Millet	William	2			1		4			1				8		
Salem	212	46	Archer	Bethiah			1						1				2		
Salem	212	47	Knight	Nath	2			1		2	2		1	1			9		
Salem	212	48	Very	Samuel	2			1		1			1				5		
Salem	212	49	Ward	Benja	1			1						1			3		
Salem	212	50	Elkins	Mary	1					1			1	1			5		
Salem	212	51	Cheever	James	4		1	1		2	1	1	1				11		
Salem	212	52	Goldsmith	Thos	1		1			1	1		1				5		
Salem	212	53	Crispin	William	1			1		4	2	2	1				11		
Salem	212	54	Cloutman	Hannah			1					3	1				5		
Salem	212	55	Fairfield	Rebecca		2					1	2	1				6		
Salem	213	1	Inglish	Andrew		1		1		1		1	1				5		
Salem	213	2	Brown	Hannah			1					1	1	1			4		
Salem	213	3	Eusis	Lydia								1	1	1					
Salem	213	4	Wellman	Mary	1	1						1	1	1			6		
Salem	213	5	White	Chrisr											7		7		
Salem	213	6	Murphy	David		1	2	1		1			1	1			7		
Salem	213	7	Shipen	Sarah		1	2						2				4		
Salem	213	8	Longway	Mary			1			1		1	2		1		6		
Salem	213	9	Rue	Anna			1						1	1			3		
Salem	213	10	Foy	William	1	3				1	1	2	1				10		
Salem	213	11	Inglish	Phillip				1		1		1	1				4		
Salem	213	12	Atkins	William	4	2		1				1		1			9		
Salem	213	13	Tiplady	Elizabeth	2								1				3		
Salem	213	14	Gray	James		1			1				1				3		
Salem	213	15	Dawson	John					1				1				2		
Salem	213	16	Wood	Mary		1	2	1					1				5		
Salem	213	17	Peirce	Jona					1				1				2		
Salem	213	18	Henfield	John				2									2		
Salem	213	19	Chapman	John	3			1					1				5		
Salem	213	20	Ward	Andrew		1			1	1			1				4		
Salem	213	21	Butman	Thos		1	3			1		1	1				7		
Salem	213	22	Smith	Hannah									1				1		
Salem	213	23	Gale	Mary									1				1		
Salem	213	24	Anthony	Nath	3	2		1		1			1				8		
Salem	213	25	Daby	James			1					1					2		
Salem	213	26	Henfield	Joseph		2		1			1	2	1				7		
Salem	213	27	Bott	John	1		1					1	1				5		
Salem	213	28	Crowell	Samuel			1				1		1				3		
Salem	213	29	Glover	Jona	2		1						1				4		
Salem	213	30	Dodge	Israel		2	1	1		2	1	1	1				9		
Salem	213	31	Jones	Hannah	1	1				1			2	1			6		
Salem	213	32	Safford	William	1	5	1					3	1				11		
Salem	213	33	Russel	Edward	2			1		1			1	1			6		
Salem	213	34	Hathorne	Mary								1	1	1			3		
Salem	213	35	Leach	Mathew		1		1		1			1				4		
Salem	213	36	Knight	Aaron		1							1				2		
Salem	213	37	Newhall	Thomas		1				1			1				2		
Salem	213	38	Ward	Nath	1		1						1				3		
Salem	213	39	Fisher	James	1	1	1						1				4		
Salem	213	40	Porter	Ruth	2	1				1	2	1	1				8		
Salem	213	41	Young	Joseph	1		1	1		2			1				6		
Salem	213	42	Baldwin	Abigail			1			1				1	1		4		
Salem	213	43	Thompson	Mary	1		1					2	1				5		
Salem	213	44	Holyoke	Edwd A			1		1		1		2	1	1		7		
Salem	213	45	Dodge	Geo					1				2				3		
Salem	213	46	Bowditch	Nath			1			1				2			4		
Salem	213	47	Appleton	William		5	3	1				1		2			12		
Salem	213	48	Gray	Saumuel	1	1		1		4	3	1	2				13		
Salem	213	49	Pickman	Benja Jr	3	1		1		2	1		3				11		
Salem	213	50	Foster	John	2			1		1	2		2				8		

TOWN	PG#	LN#	LAST NAME	FIRST NAME	FREE WHITE MALES under 10	10 to 16	16 to 26	26 to 45	45 and over	FREE WHITE FEMALES under 10	10 to 16	16 to 26	26 to 45	45 and over	TOTAL ALL OTHER	TOTAL SLAVES	TOTALS	DISTRICT/TOWNSHIP	NOTES
Salem	213	51	Long	Willliam	1		1	1		1		2		1			7		
Salem	213	52	Stickney	Judith		2	2	2				1	1	1			9		
Salem	213	53	Hunt	Lydia		1	2	1				3	1	1			9		
Salem	214	1	Briggs	John			1	1		1			1				4		
Salem	214	2	Peabody	Samuel		1	2	1				2					6		
Salem	214	3	Hascoll	Ephm			1			1		1					3		
Salem	214	4	Mylor	Mary										1			1		
Salem	214	5	Wellman	Timothy	3	1		1		1		1	2	1			10		
Salem	214	6	Brooks	Luke	1							1	1				4		
Salem	214	7	Skerry	Henry	2	2	1	1		1	1		1				9		
Salem	214	8	Russel	William	1	1	1	1		2		1	1		1		9		
Salem	214	9	Safford	Nath	1	2	1	1		1		1					7		
Salem	214	10	Oliver	Mary				2				1		2			5		
Salem	214	11	Hathorne	William					1			1		1			3		
Salem	214	12	Parons	Josiah			1					1	1				3		
Salem	214	13	Chadwick	Gilbert	2	2		1	2	3			2	1			13		
Salem	214	14	Landers	Peter		1	2		1		2	3	3	1			13		
Salem	214	15	Ward	Geo	1			1		1		1					4		
Salem	214	16	Sheppard	Jona			1					1					2		
Salem	214	17	Parker	Danl	2	1			1	1			1				6		
Salem	214	18	Grafton	Woodbe	1			1		2	1		1	1			7		
Salem	214	19	Peck	Jona			1		1			1		1			4		
Salem	214	20	Tatum	Jas	2	1		1			1		1				6		
Salem	214	21	Dage	Henry	1		1		1	1		1					5		
Salem	214	22	Morong	Sus								1		1			2		
Salem	214	23	Martin	Thos			1					1					2		
Salem	214	24	Robinson	John				1					1				2		
Salem	214	25	Norfolk	John			1		1					1			3		
Salem	214	26	Boylston	Hannah	1		3					1					5		
Salem	214	27	Ashby	Benja	1		1					2		1			5		
Salem	214	28	Shippen	Atwater				1					1				2		
Salem	214	29	Ashby	David			1	1			1		1				4		
Salem	214	30	Morong	John		1		1		5		1	1	1			10		
Salem	214	31	Saul	Joseph	3	1			1			1	1				7		
Salem	214	32	Frye	Peter				1		2	1		1				5		
Salem	214	33	Morong	John	2		1	1		1		1	1	1			8		
Salem	214	34	Black	John											7		7		
Salem	214	35	Black	John Jr											11		11		
Salem	214	36	Mansfield	James	2			1		2		1					6		
Salem	214	37	Felt	James	1		1					1		1			4		
Salem	214	38	Felt	Phebe									1				1		
Salem	214	39	Felt	Henry	1		1										2		
Salem	214	40	Boden	Charles			1			1		1					3		
Salem	214	41	Felton	James	1	1		1		2			1				6		
Salem	214	42	Brown	Margt	1							1		1			3		
Salem	214	43	Leech	Mary										1			1		
Salem	214	44	Carnes	Hannah								1	1	3			5		
Salem	214	45	Hull	John	3	1		1		2		1	1				9		
Salem	214	46	Masury	Samuel	3			1		2		1	1				8		
Salem	214	47	Eveleth	Joseph	1	2	4	1	2	2	2	2		1			17		
Salem	214	48	Buffum	Joshua			1				1	1					3		
Salem	214	49	Chipman	John	1	1	1		1		2						6		
Salem	214	50	Kennedy	Andrew			1					1					2		
Salem	214	51	Heather	Martha									1				1		
Salem	214	52	Reeves	Nath			1			1		1					3		
Salem	214	53	Buffum	Sanml Jr			1			1		1		1			4		
Salem	214	54	Buffum	Sam Senr	1	2	3		1		1	1		1			10		
Salem	215	1	Warren	Sarah	1	1				1				1			4		
Salem	215	2	Bartlet	Robt	2			1					1				4		
Salem	215	3	Upton	Jed	2	2	1	1			2		1				9		
Salem	215	4	Porter	Duddy	2		2	1		1		1					7		
Salem	215	5	Killin	Edws				1						1			2		
Salem	215	6	Brooks	Timothy	5	2	1	1		1	1	3	1				15		
Salem	215	7	Woodbridge	Darkis	1							1	1				3		
Salem	215	8	Phillips	Stephen			1			1	1		1				4		
Salem	215	9	Peirce	Asa	2	1		1		2		2	2				10		
Salem	215	10	Peirce	Nathan		1	1		1	1	2	3		1	1		11		
Salem	215	11	Mason	Jona	2	1			1	1		2	1	1			9		
Salem	215	12	Manning	Thos	3	1			1	1	3	3	1				13		
Salem	215	13	Beckett	William			1			1			1				3		
Salem	215	14	Waters	Mary									1	1			2		
Salem	215	15	Harnadan	Jona		1	1		1	1		3	1				9		
Salem	215	16	Dabny	John	1	1		1		1		1	1				6		
Salem	215	17	Murphy	Margt			1				1	1	1				4		
Salem	215	18	Phippen	Anstis									1				1		
Salem	215	19	Brooks	Samuel	1			1		2		1	1	1			7		
Salem	215	20	Fenno	Joseph	1			1		2	1	1	1				7		
Salem	215	21	Richardson	Josiah		1	2		1		1	3					9		
Salem	215	22	Barnard	Edwd			1	1					1				3		
Salem	215	23	West	Benja			1	1	1		2	1					6		
Salem	215	24	Quarles	William	1		1	1	1	2	2	1					9		
Salem	215	25	Edwards	John				1			1		1				3		
Salem	215	26	Edwards	John Jr	1			1		1			1				4		
Salem	215	27	Phippen	Thos			3		1		1	1	1				7		
Salem	215	28	Richrdson	Josiah Jr	1		1	1		1		1	1				6		
Salem	215	29	Phippen	Nath		1		1			1		1				4		
Salem	215	30	Giles	Priscilla										1			1		
Salem	215	31	Grafton	Mary								2		2			4		
Salem	215	32	Little	Moses		1		1		1		2					5		
Salem	215	33	Mason	Thos				1			1	1					3		

TOWN	PG#	LN#	HEADS OF HOUSEHOLD		FREE WHITE MALES					FREE WHITE FEMALES					TOTAL ALL OTHER	TOTAL SLAVES	TOTALS	DISTRICT/ TOWNSHIP	NOTES
			LAST NAME	FIRST NAME	under 10	10 to 16	16 to 26	26 to 45	45 and over	under 10	10 to 16	16 to 26	26 to 45	45 and over					
Salem	215	34	Bigelow	William			2	1		3	1	2					9		
Salem	215	35	Ayers	Eliza								2		1			3		
Salem	215	36	Short	James			1			1			1				3		
Salem	215	37	Thorn	William			1			1			1				3		
Salem	215	38	Robinson	John			1			1			1				3		
Salem	215	39	Cross	Joseph	3	1	1			1			1				7		
Salem	215	40	Caldwell	Mary	1	1					1	2	1				6		
Salem	215	41	Gibant	Edwd			1	1				1		1			4		
Salem	215	42	Kenny	Ebenz	1		1			2		1					5		
Salem	215	43	King	Saml	1		1			1			1				4		
Salem	215	44	Story	Saml		1	1							1			3		
Salem	215	45	Wood	Sarah										1			1		
Salem	215	46	Ramsdell	William	2		1			1		1	1				6		
Salem	215	47	Gray	John	2		1			2	2		1				8		
Salem	215	48	Smith	Jona		1	2	1				1	1	1			7		
Salem	215	49	Hobart	Noah	2	1		1		2	2		1				9		
Salem	215	50	Archer	Samuel 3d	1	1		1		4			1				8		
Salem	215	51	Archer	Rebecca		1	2				1						4		
Salem	215	52	Kerring	Samuel	1		3	1					1				6		
Salem	216	1	Phippen	Mary		1						1		1			3		
Salem	216	2	Russel	Benja			2			1			1				4		
Salem	216	3	Phippen	Anna	1		7			1	1	1		1			12		
Salem	216	4	Erving	Hugh			1						1				2		
Salem	216	5	Atwell	Ebenz	2		1	1					1				5		
Salem	216	6	Hodges	Geo	1			1		2	1		1				6		
Salem	216	7	Peele	Geo				1						2			3		
Salem	216	8	Archer	Jona	2	3		1		4	2	1	1				14		
Salem	216	9	Jenkins	Wm			1			2	1		1				5		
Salem	216	10	Thomas	Eliza		2					2	1					5		
Salem	216	11	Matoon	Hubartus				1					1				2		
Salem	216	12	Baker	John	1		1			1			1				4		
Salem	216	13	Smith	Hannah									1				1		
Salem	216	14	Gould	Solomon	1		1			1			1				4		
Salem	216	15	Allen	Edward Jr	1		1			1	1		1	1	1		7		
Salem	216	16	Archer	Hannah			1				2		1				4		
Salem	216	17	Southward	Lydia						1		1					2		
Salem	216	18	Perkins	Nathan		1		1			1		1				4		
Salem	216	19	Shelty	James			1			1			1				3		
Salem	216	20	Towser	Ebenzr		1	1	1		2			1				6		
Salem	216	21	Fearson	Margt		1	1						1				3		
Salem	216	22	Ashby	Thos	2		1			3		1	1				8		
Salem	216	23	Phelps	Wm	2		1	1		2			1				7		
Salem	216	24	Perkins	John			1			1		1	1				4		
Salem	216	25	Carlton	Samuel		1	1	1					2	1			6		
Salem	216	26	Rufus	Geo	3	1	1			2		1	1				9		
Salem	216	27	Millet	Sarah		2				1				1			4		
Salem	216	28	Manning	Richard				2				1		3			6		
Salem	216	29	Ring	Seth			1			3		1					5		
Salem	216	30	Felt	Benja		5	1			3			1				10		
Salem	216	31	Lafavor	Daniel	1		1					1					3		
Salem	216	32	Pitman	Sarah									1				1		
Salem	216	33	Read	Martha	1	1		2		1	2		1				8		
Salem	216	34	Fowler	Robt	1		1						1				3		
Salem	216	35	Phelps	Jonathan									1				1		
Salem	216	36	Southward	Geo		1		1	1			3		1			7		
Salem	216	37	Lewis	Ebed	1	1		1			1		1				5		
Salem	216	38	Safford	Thos	3	1		1		1			1				7		
Salem	216	39	Briggs	Ruth	1	2	3			2	1	1	1				11		
Salem	216	40	Moratty	Deborah		1	1	4			1		1	1			9		
Salem	216	41	Becket	Mary			1			1			1				3		
Salem	216	42	Brown	Rebecca									1				1		
Salem	216	43	Watson	John	1	1	1		1	2	2		1				9		
Salem	216	44	Parker	Willm B		2		1			2						5		
Salem	216	45	Williams	Abigail		1					1		1				3		
Salem	216	46	Brown	Margt			1						1				2		
Salem	216	47	Stewart	James		1							1				2		
Salem	216	48	Manning	Richard Jr	1	3	2	1			1	3		1			12		
Salem	216	49	Hathorne	Rachel	1			2		2		1	4	1			11		
Salem	216	50	Williams	Thos			1			2			1	1			5		
Salem	216	51	Holt	Esther		1	2	2				1	1				7		
Salem	216	52	Crowninshield	Jacob			1	1		1	1	1	1				6		
Salem	216	53	Collins	John	3		1		1	1	1		1				8		
Salem	216	54	Millet	Benja	1		1			2		1					5		
Salem	216	55	Proctor	Daniel			1					1	1				3		
Salem	216	56	Morely	Eliza	1	2				2	1	2	1				9		
Salem	217	1	Strout	Joseph	3	1	1				1		1				7		
Salem	217	2	Beckford	Jona			1			1		1	1				4		
Salem	217	3	Brown	John	1		1		1	1			1				5		
Salem	217	4	Meriam	William	1	4	1			1		1	1	1			10		
Salem	217	5	Brown	James	2	1				2		1	1				8		
Salem	217	6	Gray	William	2	1	1	1		1		2	1				10		
Salem	217	7	Byrnee	Clifford			1	1	1			1		1			5		
Salem	217	8	Forrester	Simon	2	1	2		1	2		3	1		1		13		
Salem	217	9	Byrnee	Clifford Jr			1			2			1				4		
Salem	217	10	Baker	Mehit L									1				1		
Salem	217	11	Archer	Edwd	1		1			1			1				4		
Salem	217	12	Babbidge	Ben	1		1				1	1	1				5		
Salem	217	13	Eddy	Margt	2			1		2		1	1				7		
Salem	217	14	Brooks	Abigail		1	1			1			1				4		
Salem	217	15	Brown	William				1		1		1		1			4		

TOWN	PG#	LN#	HEADS OF HOUSEHOLD		FREE WHITE MALES					FREE WHITE FEMALES					TOTAL ALL OTHER	TOTAL SLAVES	TOTALS	DISTRICT/ TOWNSHIP	NOTES
			LAST NAME	FIRST NAME	under 10	10 to 16	16 to 26	26 to 45	45 and over	under 10	10 to 16	16 to 26	26 to 45	45 and over					
Salem	217	16	Brown	James Jr				1		1			1				3		
Salem	217	17	Crowninshield	Geo			3	2	1		2	3		1			12		
Salem	217	18	Prince	Henry	2	1		1		1	1	1	1				8		
Salem	217	19	Palfray	Thos	3	1		1					1				6		
Salem	217	20	Palfray	Deborah								1		1			2		
Salem	217	21	Shed	Cathr	1					2			1				4		
Salem	217	22	Meservey	Eliza								1	1				2		
Salem	217	23	Devereux	James	1			1		2		1	1				6		
Salem	217	24	Mcannister	John A	1			1				1	1				4		
Salem	217	25	Palfray	Hemlock		1	1		1				1				4		
Salem	217	26	Swasey	Samuel			2		1	1		1	1	1			7		
Salem	217	27	Bailey	Jacob	1			1		1			1				4		
Salem	217	28	March	Thos	1		1						1				3		
Salem	217	29	Diver	Mary		1	1					1	1				4		
Salem	217	30	Webb	Samuel	1			1		2		1		1			6		
Salem	217	31	Young	Margt										1			1		
Salem	217	32	Sage	William			1		1								2		
Salem	217	33	Silsber	Saml Jr	3	2	6	1				2		1			15		
Salem	217	34	Estes	William	1		1						1				3		
Salem	217	35	Hodges	Benja		1	1		1	4	2	1	1	1			12		
Salem	217	36	Very	Mary	1		1					1	1				4		
Salem	217	37	Batten	Sarah						1			1				2		
Salem	217	38	Barry	Abigail							1			1			2		
Salem	217	39	Ford	James			1						1				2		
Salem	217	40	Berry	John				1		1				1			3		
Salem	217	41	Webb	Stephen			1			3			1				5		
Salem	217	42	Ropes	Danl	1	1		1		1			1				5		
Salem	217	43	Row	Benja			1			3		1					5		
Salem	217	44	Underwood	Sarah			1			1			1	1			4		
Salem	217	45	Cook	Willm	1		1		1			1	1				5		
Salem	217	46	Brown	Joseph	3	1		1		1		1					7		
Salem	217	47	Presson	Mary		1	1			1		1	1				5		
Salem	217	48	Holland	Charles			1					1					2		
Salem	217	49	Townsend	Samuel	2	1		1		1			1				6		
Salem	217	50	Andrews	Mary			2							1			3		
Salem	217	51	Vincent	Mathew	2	2		1		1		1	1				8		
Salem	217	52	Hodges	Gaml	2	1		1		2		1	1				8		
Salem	217	53	Sage	Danl	1	1		1		2		1	1				7		
Salem	217	54	Silsber	Saml		1		1	1	1	1			1			6		
Salem	217	55	Webb	Thos			1						1				2		
Salem	217	56	Hanscom	Willm	4			1		1			1	1			8		
Salem	217	57	Daland	Eliza									1				1		
Salem	217	58	Todd	Benja			1			2			1	1			5		
Salem	217	59	Gardner	Nancy	1								1				2		
Salem	218	1	Henry	John				1						1			2		
Salem	218	2	Curtis	Abigail										1			1		
Salem	218	3	Jenkins	Abigail										1			1		
Salem	218	4	Goss	Thos	1			1		1	1	2	1				7		
Salem	218	5	Nichols	John			1			1		1					3		
Salem	218	6	Jeffrey	Walter P				1		2	1		1				5		
Salem	218	7	Odberry	John	2		1	1		1			1				6		
Salem	218	8	Goodhue	Saml		2		1		3	1		1				8		
Salem	218	9	Dean	Benja		1			1			3		1			6		
Salem	218	10	Luscomb	William	2			1		2			1				6		
Salem	218	11	Clough	Susanna				1						1			2		
Salem	218	12	Flagg	Josiah				1		2		1					4		
Salem	218	13	Metzard	Nancy	1					1		1					3		
Salem	218	14	Hice	Sarah	2					1	1		1				5		
Salem	218	15	Price	Thos		1			1		1			1			4		
Salem	218	16	Heard	Luke	1			1					1				3		
Salem	218	17	Murray	Eliza								1	1				2		
Salem	218	18	Becket	Benja	2			1		1			1				5		
Salem	218	19	Brown	John	1	1	2					2					6		
Salem	218	20	Knight	Thos	2		2	1		2		1	1				9		
Salem	218	21	Hawks	Benja	1	1	1	1		3			1	1			9		
Salem	218	22	Webb	Wm	2			1		2			1				6		
Salem	218	23	Stevens	Mary						1	1		1				3		
Salem	218	24	Leach	Samuel	2	1		1		1			1				6		
Salem	218	25	Gaines	Eliza									1				1		
Salem	218	26	Collins	Richd		1		1				1		1			4		
Salem	218	27	Gale	Saml		1		1		1	3		1				7		
Salem	218	28	Bray	Benja	1		1			2			1				5		
Salem	218	29	Callum	Sarah	2	2				1			1				6		
Salem	218	30	Millet	Jona	4		1			1			1				7		
Salem	218	31	Stone	Robt	1		1		1			3		1			9		
Salem	218	32	Dean	Lydia		1					1	1	1				4		
Salem	218	33	Dean	Thos	2			1	1	1			1				6		
Salem	218	34	Barker	John			5	1		2	1	1	1				11		
Salem	218	35	Peal	Robt	2			1		1			1				5		
Salem	218	36	Merchant	Nath	3			1		1			1				6		
Salem	218	37	Whittemore	Mary		1								1			2		
Salem	218	38	Ackinson	Geo		1		1					1				3		
Salem	218	39	Rutlidge	Winslow	2			1		1			1				5		
Salem	218	40	Roxan	Maria									1				1		
Salem	218	41	Tabor	David	1			1					1				3		
Salem	218	42	Major	Susanna						1			1				2		
Salem	218	43	Duliver	John			1					1					2		
Salem	218	44	Bateman	Mich		1		1		2	1		1	1			7		
Salem	218	45	Deal	Susanna		1				1			1	1			4		
Salem	218	46	Ravel	Thos	3	2	2	1			2		1				11		

TOWN	PG#	LN#	LAST NAME	FIRST NAME	FREE WHITE MALES					FREE WHITE FEMALES					TOTAL ALL OTHER	TOTAL SLAVES	TOTALS	DISTRICT/ TOWNSHIP	NOTES
					under 10	10 to 16	16 to 26	26 to 45	45 and over	under 10	10 to 16	16 to 26	26 to 45	45 and over					
Salem	218	47	Slocum	Ebenr	1			1		1	1		1				5		
Salem	218	48	Boyd	William	2			1					1				4		
Salem	218	49	Murray	Lydia								1					1		
Salem	218	50	White	Margt									1				1		
Salem	218	51	Perry	John	2	2		1		1			1	1			8		
Salem	218	52	Peirce	Lydia			1						1				2		
Salem	218	53	Fairfield	John			1					1					2		
Salem	218	54	Whitford	John			1					1					2		
Salem	218	55	Peele	Josh	1		1			1		1					4		
Salem	218	56	Southward	Geo	2	2		1		2			1	1			9		
Salem	218	57	Morse	Joseph	1		1					1					3		
Salem	218	58	Lufkin	Solomon	1	1			1	1		2	1				7		
Salem	219	1	Collins	John	1	1	1	1		1	1	1					7		
Salem	219	2	McDonald	Benja			1			2			1	1			5		
Salem	219	3	Knight	Sarah									1				1		
Salem	219	4	Bowlin	Hannah						1		1					2		
Salem	219	5	Waters	Thos	1		1					1					3		
Salem	219	6	Ellison	John				1					2				3		
Salem	219	7	Beadle	Susanna									1				1		
Salem	219	8	Lane	William		1		1		2		1					5		
Salem	219	9	Brown	Nancy								1		1			2		
Salem	219	10	Bishop	Samuel	1			1		3			1				6		
Salem	219	11	Lefavour	Eliza		1	4	3		1	1	1	1				12		
Salem	219	12	McPherson	John	1	1		1		1	1	1	1				7		
Salem	219	13	Kimball	Mary		1							2				3		
Salem	219	14	Foster	Wm			1					1					2		
Salem	219	15	Donnegan	Thos	1	1		1		1	1	1					6		
Salem	219	16	Creely	James		1		1		3		1					6		
Salem	219	17	Hitchins	Abijah	2		1			1		1					5		
Salem	219	18	Murray	Peter				1				1					2		
Salem	219	19	Fairfield	Eliza			3					1	1				5		
Salem	219	20	Ransom	Cato											6		6		
Salem	219	21	Webb	Joseph			1			3	1		1				6		
Salem	219	22	Sheehan	Danl	2		1			2			1				6		
Salem	219	23	Barns	Lucy											3		3		
Salem	219	24	Wild	Michael	1		1			1		2	2				7		
Salem	219	25	Williams	John		1		1			1	1	1				5		
Salem	219	26	Parker	Eliph		1		1			2	1					5		
Salem	219	27	Wellman	Mary								1	1				2		
Salem	219	28	Mascol	Hannah				1				1					2		
Salem	219	29	Mascol	Stephen			1			1		1					3		
Salem	219	30	Kerny	Jesse	1		1			1			1				4		
Salem	219	31	Floyd	Thos	2		1					1	1				5		
Salem	219	32	Stoddard	Ebed	3	2		1		1	1		1				9		
Salem	219	33	Hanscom	James			1				1	1	1				4		
Salem	219	34	Selsbee	Sarah		2	1			1	1	1		1			7		
Salem	219	35	Trow	Nath	1		1			1		1					4		
Salem	219	36	Trask	Joseph			1			2			1				4		
Salem	219	37	Knap	Mary		1				1			1	1			4		
Salem	219	38	Webb	John				1					1				2		
Salem	219	39	Carrie	James				1		3	1	3		1			9		
Salem	219	40	Browne	Nath	1			1		1			1				4		
Salem	219	41	Collins	John		3		1		1		2					8		
Salem	219	42	Hovey	Amos				1		1	1		1				4		
Salem	219	43	Towsend	Moses			1	1		2	2	1	1	1			9		
Salem	219	44	Wellman	Timothy			1					1					2		
Salem	219	45	Fogg	Joseph			1				1		1				3		
Salem	219	46	Mallia	Marcello			1				1		1				3		
Salem	219	47	Bean	sarah									1				1		
Salem	219	48	Bushal	Josa		1				1			1				3		
Salem	219	49	Wellman	Timo	1	1	1	1		3	1	2	1				11		
Salem	219	50	Allen	Edwd	1		2		1	1	1	2		1	1		10		
Salem	219	51	Richardson	Robt		1	4		1	1		3		1			11		
Salem	219	52	Hunt	Thos		1		1		3			1				6		
Salem	219	53	Johnson	Geo	1		1			2			1				5		
Salem	219	54	Price	Thos	1	1		1			1	2					6		
Salem	219	55	Phippen	Joshua	1	1	7		1			1	1	1			13		
Salem	219	56	Phippen	Nath	2	2		1		2			1				8		
Salem	219	57	Phippen	Joshua Jr			1			1		1					3		
Salem	220	1	Webb	Joshua	1		1	1					1				4		
Salem	220	2	LeFavour	Amos	1			1		4			1				7		
Salem	220	3	Brooks	Thos		1	4	1		2	1		1				10		
Salem	220	4	Berry	Jacob			1					1					2		
Salem	220	5	Emerton	John	1		1	1		1	2		1	1			8		
Salem	220	6	Hutchinson	Benja	5		1					1					7		
Salem	220	7	Hutchinson	Margt			1				2		1				4		
Salem	220	8	Rogers	Joseph	1		1					1					3		
Salem	220	9	Ingersol	Samuel		1		1		1	1		1				5		
Salem	220	10	Towsend	Martha									1				1		
Salem	220	11	Peirce	John		1	1			3			1				6		
Salem	220	12	Perkins	James		1		1	1	1	1						4		
Salem	220	13	Kenny	Danl	2	1	1	2		1		1					9		
Salem	220	14	Searle	John	1	1			1	1				2			6		
Salem	220	15	Hitchins	Nath		1	1		1	1	1	2	2				9		
Salem	220	16	Bullock	Benja	2			1		1	1						5		
Salem	220	17	Bailey	Thos	2			1		1		1					5		
Salem	220	18	Jefferds	John			1						1				2		
Salem	220	19	Knap	Joseph			1			1	1	1					4		
Salem	220	20	Burdet	Abigail	1	1				1	1	1					6		
Salem	220	21	Dodge	Joshua	1		1	1		1		2	1	1			8		

TOWN	PG#	LN#	LAST NAME	FIRST NAME	FREE WHITE MALES under 10	10 to 16	16 to 26	26 to 45	45 and over	FREE WHITE FEMALES under 10	10 to 16	16 to 26	26 to 45	45 and over	TOTAL ALL OTHER	TOTAL SLAVES	TOTALS	DISTRICT/ TOWNSHIP	NOTES
Salem	220	22	Lane	Nicholas	1	1			2	5	3	1	1				14		
Salem	220	23	Wing	William					1		2		1				4		
Salem	220	24	Ropes	Samuel	1	2	1	1		2	1		1				9		
Salem	220	25	Palfray	Richard	2		2	1		1	2	1					9		
Salem	220	26	Lambert	Joseph		1		1		1	1	1	1				6		
Salem	220	27	Hitchins	Nath Jr			1			1	1						3		
Salem	220	28	Atwell	Josiah	1		1				1		2				5		
Salem	220	29	Babbidge	Chrisr	2		1	1		2			1				7		
Salem	220	30	Ward	Andrew	3			1		1			1				6		
Salem	220	31	Cahoo	Samuel				1		1		1					3		
Salem	220	32	Hitchins	Abijah			5	1		1		2	1				10		
Salem	220	33	Murray	Mary								1	1				2		
Salem	220	34	Cassan	Samuel	1		1					1					3		
Salem	220	35	Walkins	Saml				1						1			2		
Salem	220	36	Palfray	Jona		1		1		2			1				5		
Salem	220	37	Crookshanks	Mary			1		1	1				1			4		
Salem	220	38	Peele	William					1			2		1			4		
Salem	220	39	Dawson	Alexr			1						1				2		
Salem	220	40	Becket	John		1	2		1	2	1	1					8		
Salem	220	41	Delano	Nathl				1		1		1					3		
Salem	220	42	Nutting	Eben					1			1		1			3		
Salem	220	43	Searle	John	1			1					1				3		
Salem	220	44	Han	Mary	1	2					1		1				5		
Salem	220	45	Obear	Abigail				1						1			2		
Salem	220	46	Cloutman	Stephen	2	2	2	1		3	1		1				12		
Salem	220	47	Becket	James	1	1	1	1		2	2		1				9		
Salem	220	48	Beaten	John					1				1				2		
Salem	220	49	Goss	Richard					1				1				2		
Salem	220	50	Gray	John	2			1		1			1				5		
Salem	220	51	Becket	Retier	1	1	9	1				1	2				15		
Salem	220	52	Fuller	James	1			1				1					3		
Salem	220	53	Perkins	Robt	1	1	1	1		2	1	1	1				9		
Salem	220	54	Whittmore	James	1			1				1					3		
Salem	220	55	Presson	Sarah	2	1				1	1		1				6		
Salem	220	56	Perkins	John		1	2		1			1	1				6		
Salem	220	57	Brown	Jona	1	1	1	1		1		1	1				7		
Salem	220	58	Wood	Phalie		1		1					1				3		
Salem	220	59	Fuller	James				1			2		1				4		
Salem	221	1	Peirce	Jona				1					1				2		
Salem	221	2	Perkins	Isaac Jr		1	1	1			1	1					5		
Salem	221	3	Perkins	Isaac				1					1				2		
Salem	221	4	Cloutman	Eliza	2	1				1	1	2	1				8		
Salem	221	5	Oliver	William	2			1		1			2				6		
Salem	221	6	Pratt	William	3			1		1	1		1				7		
Salem	221	7	Smith	Emmons	2		2	1				1					6		
Salem	221	8	Cuffby	William											4		4		
Salem	221	9	Mumford	John											6		6		
Salem	221	10	Twist	John				1					1				2		
Salem	221	11	Archer	Bena	1			1		3			1				6		
Salem	221	12	Pascue	Joseph				1				1					2		
Salem	221	13	Kinman	Nath	2			1				1	1				5		
Salem	221	14	Wood	Anna				1		2		1		1			5		
Salem	221	15	Paterson	John			1	1		3		1	1				7		
Salem	221	16	Collins	Daniel			1			1		1					3		
Salem	221	17	Masury	Samuel	2	1	1	1		2	1		1				9		
Salem	221	18	Gardner	Samuel			1					1					2		
Salem	221	19	Perkins	Willm	2	2		1		1	1		1				8		
Salem	221	20	Martin	Israel			1					1		1			3		
Salem	221	21	Getchel	Josiah	1		1					1					3		
Salem	221	22	Symes	Pely D	1		3	3				1	1				9		
Salem	221	23	Emerton	Jeremiah Master Salem Poor House	9	2	3	7	23	4	1	6	15	36	19		125		

TOWN	PG#	LN#	LAST NAME	FIRST NAME	FREE WHITE MALES under 10	10 to 16	16 to 26	26 to 45	45 and over	FREE WHITE FEMALES under 10	10 to 16	16 to 26	26 to 45	45 and over	TOTAL ALL OTHER	TOTAL SLAVES	TOTALS	DISTRICT/ TOWNSHIP	NOTES
Salisbury	24	1	Beach	James					1	1				1			3		
Salisbury	24	2	Bennet	Moses					1				1	1			3		
Salisbury	24	3	Bragg	Henry			1						1				2		
Salisbury	24	4	Baker	Samuel Junr	3			1		1			1				6		
Salisbury	24	5	Boswell	Asa	1			1		1		1					4		
Salisbury	24	6	Bradbury	Roland				1					1				2		
Salisbury	24	7	Bagley	Stephen	2	1		1		3	1		1				9		
Salisbury	24	8	Bagley	Seth	1	1			1		1			1			5		
Salisbury	24	9	Bagley	Thomas	1	1		1						1			4		
Salisbury	24	10	Bagley	True			1						1	2			4		
Salisbury	24	11	Brown	Abraham	1	1		1				1					4		
Salisbury	24	12	Beattie	Andrew Revd				1		1		1	1				4		
Salisbury	24	13	Burwell	Walker			1	1	1			1		1			5		
Salisbury	24	14	Burwell	Jacob					1	1	1	1	1	1			6		
Salisbury	24	15	Burwell	Jacob Junr	1			1		1			1				4		
Salisbury	24	16	Burwell	Moses				1						1			2		
Salisbury	24	17	Baker	Samuel Junr				1						1			2		
Salisbury	24	18	Baker	James		1		1		1			1				4		
Salisbury	24	19	Brown	Jeremiah	1	1		1		2			1	1			7		
Salisbury	25	1	Brown	Hannah Wd									1	1			2		
Salisbury	25	2	Brown	William				1					1				2		
Salisbury	25	3	Brown	Enos				1				1		1			3		
Salisbury	25	4	Blasdel	Rachel Wd						1				1			2		
Salisbury	25	5	Bradbury	James Capt	1		1	1		1	2		1				7		
Salisbury	25	6	Bachelder	Israel		1						1					2		
Salisbury	25	7	Bagley	John Capt	1			1		2	1		1				6		
Salisbury	25	8	Bartlet	John	1	1	1		1	1	1	1	1				8		
Salisbury	25	9	Boardman	Joseph		1						1					2		
Salisbury	25	10	Brown	Willm Junr	1			1						1			3		
Salisbury	25	11	Balch	Samuel	2	1		1		2			1				7		
Salisbury	25	12	Boardman	Thomas	2	1			1	4	1		2	1			12		
Salisbury	25	13	Brown	Jacob Esq	4	2			1		1	1	1				10		
Salisbury	25	14	Brown	Ephraim	4		1	1			1		1				8		
Salisbury	25	15	Boardman	Nathl		1		1						1			3		
Salisbury	25	16	Celey	Betty Wd									1				1		
Salisbury	25	17	Cushing	John	1		1					2					4		
Salisbury	25	18	Carr	Samuel	2	1		1		1			1	1			7		
Salisbury	25	19	Coffin	Stephen			1		1	1		2	2				8		
Salisbury	25	20	Coffin	Stephen Junr		1		1						1			3		
Salisbury	25	21	Coffin	John	4			1					1				6		
Salisbury	25	22	Chase	Charles	1			1		1			2				5		
Salisbury	25	23	Cutler	Joseph	1	1								1			3		
Salisbury	25	24	Carr	Jesse	3	2		1		1	1		1				9		
Salisbury	25	25	Cushing	Benja		1		1			1	1					4		
Salisbury	25	26	Carr	Osgood		1		1					1	1			4		
Salisbury	25	27	Carr	Robert	1	1		1					1	1			5		
Salisbury	25	28	Clough	Aaron				1					3	1			5		
Salisbury	25	29	Clough	Jonathn		1	2	1				2		2			8		
Salisbury	25	30	Collins	Enoch	1	1		1	1	1		1	1				7		
Salisbury	25	31	Collins	Samuel				1					1				2		
Salisbury	25	32	Collins	Moses		1	1	1						1			4		
Salisbury	25	33	Collins	Benja		1	1					1		1			4		
Salisbury	25	34	Crain	Elijah				1				1		1			3		
Salisbury	26	1	Currier	Thomas				1				1					2		
Salisbury	26	2	Currier	Israel				1						2			3		
Salisbury	26	3	Currier	Jacob		1	1	1		1	1		1				6		
Salisbury	26	4	Carr	James				1					3				4		
Salisbury	26	5	Carr	Levi	1			1				1					3		
Salisbury	26	6	Colbey	Molly Wd								1	1				2		
Salisbury	26	7	Coffin	Tristam	1			1									2		
Salisbury	26	8	Currier	Molly									1				1		
Salisbury	26	9	Currier	Susanna Wd										1			1		
Salisbury	26	10	Currier	Israel Junr	1	1		1		1			1				5		
Salisbury	26	11	Clark	Seth				1		1			1				3		
Salisbury	26	12	Colbey	Ger Capt		2		1	1	1	1		1				7		
Salisbury	26	13	Crocker	Richard	2			1		1			1				5		
Salisbury	26	14	Crown	Joseph Capt				1		1		1					3		
Salisbury	26	15	Chase	Baley Capt	3	1						1	1				7		
Salisbury	26	16	Carr	Benja				2						1			3		
Salisbury	26	17	Carr	Charles	1			1		1			1				4		
Salisbury	26	18	Cronk	John		1	1					1					3		
Salisbury	26	19	Currier	David	3	1	3		1			1	2	1			12		
Salisbury	26	20	Currier	Benja		1		1		3			1				6		
Salisbury	26	21	Chandler	Elizabeth Wd										1			1		
Salisbury	26	22	Colbey	Samuel				1						1			2		
Salisbury	26	23	Colbey	Philip		1		1			1		2				5		
Salisbury	26	24	Dale	Moses		1	1	1				1	1	1			3		
Salisbury	26	25	Dow	Patience Wd			1							1			2		
Salisbury	26	26	Dow	Samuel				2			1		1	1			5		

TOWN	PG#	LN#	LAST NAME	FIRST NAME	FREE WHITE MALES under 10	10 to 16	16 to 26	26 to 45	45 and over	FREE WHITE FEMALES under 10	10 to 16	16 to 26	26 to 45	45 and over	TOTAL ALL OTHER	TOTAL SLAVES	TOTALS	DISTRICT/ TOWNSHIP	NOTES
Salisbury	26	27	Dow	Aaron	1	1	1	1		1	1		1				7		
Salisbury	26	28	Dow	Joseph	1		1		1	2		1		1			7		
Salisbury	26	29	Dole	Jemima Wd	2		1			1		1	1				6		
Salisbury	26	30	Dalton	Hannah Wd						2			1	1			4		
Salisbury	26	31	Dollar	Samuel			1							1			2		
Salisbury	26	32	Dorr	Edward	1		1		1	2			1				6		
Salisbury	26	33	Davis	William			1			1		1					3		
Salisbury	27	1	Eaton	Abel		2		1				1		1			5		
Salisbury	27	2	Eaton	Anna Wd										2			2		
Salisbury	27	3	Eaton	James	1	1	2	1		2	2		1				10		
Salisbury	27	4	Eaton	William				1					1				2		
Salisbury	27	5	Eaton	Saml Capt		1	2	2	1				2	2			10		
Salisbury	27	6	Eaton	Abigail Wd			1					1	2	1			5		
Salisbury	27	7	Eaton	Henry		1	1						1				3		
Salisbury	27	8	Eaton	Caleb			1	1	1	1	1		1				6		
Salisbury	27	9	Evans	Ezekiel	2	1	1		1		1	1		1			8		
Salisbury	27	10	Eastman	Jeremiah		1			1		1	1		1			5		
Salisbury	27	11	Evans	John	2			1		2			1	1			7		
Salisbury	27	12	Evans	Jona Junr				1					1				2		
Salisbury	27	13	Evans	Jona Colo		1			1	1	1			1			5		
Salisbury	27	14	Eastman	Moses	1			1		1			1				4		
Salisbury	27	15	Edwards	Moses	1			1		1			1				4		
Salisbury	27	16	Edwards	Rise	1			1		1			1	1			5		
Salisbury	27	17	Edwards	Reuben	3	1	2	1			1	1		1			10		
Salisbury	27	18	Evans	David				1		1			1				3		
Salisbury	27	19	Eastman	Thomas Capt				1				1		1			3		
Salisbury	27	20	Eastman	Daniel	1			1		2			1				5		
Salisbury	27	21	Eastman	Hannah Wd	2	1			1	1				1			6		
Salisbury	27	22	Eastman	Wd										2			2		
Salisbury	27	23	Eastman	Ephrm	3			1		1			1				6		
Salisbury	27	24	Easton	Wheeler				1		1			1				3		
Salisbury	27	25	Evans	Benja Esq		1			1	1	1			1			5		
Salisbury	27	26	French	Nicholas			2		1	1				1			5		
Salisbury	27	27	French	Andrew	2			1					1				4		
Salisbury	27	28	French	Mary Wd										2			2		
Salisbury	27	29	French	Josiah	2	1	2		1		1	2		1			10		
Salisbury	27	30	French	Joshua Capt				1		2	1			1			5		
Salisbury	27	31	French	Amos		1	1		1	2	3			1			9		
Salisbury	27	32	French	Eliza Wd									2	1			3		
Salisbury	27	33	French	Benja			2	1				2	1	1			7		
Salisbury	27	34	Felch	Samuel	1	1		1				1	1				5		
Salisbury	27	35	Fellows	Samuel	1	1		1	1				2	1			7		
Salisbury	27	36	Flanders	John	1			1		2	1		1				6		
Salisbury	27	37	Flanders	Betty Wd								1	1	1			3		
Salisbury	27	38	Follensbe	Thos Capt				1				2					3		
Salisbury	28	1	Fowler	Elijah Junr	1	1		1		3	1		1				8		
Salisbury	28	2	Fowler	Elijah				1		1			2	1			5		
Salisbury	28	3	Fowler	Thomas			1						1				2		
Salisbury	28	4	Fowler	Jacob	1			1		3		1	1				7		
Salisbury	28	5	Fowler	Samuel	3			1		1	2		1				8		
Salisbury	28	6	Fowler	Robert	1	2		1		3		1	1				9		
Salisbury	28	7	Fowler	Saml Capt	1	1	1	1		1	1	1					7		
Salisbury	28	8	Follensbe	Robert Capt		1		1					1				3		
Salisbury	28	9	Fowler	Daniel	2		1	1		1			1				6		
Salisbury	28	10	Fowler	Ezekiel		1			1			2		1			5		
Salisbury	28	11	Fowler	Ezekiel Junr		1							1				2		
Salisbury	28	12	Flanders	Merrill	1	1		1						1			4		
Salisbury	28	13	Flanders	Timothy				1		4		1	1				7		
Salisbury	28	14	Flanders	Joseph				1		2		1	1				5		
Salisbury	28	15	Follensbe	Daniel	1			1		3	1		1				7		
Salisbury	28	16	Follensbe	Anna Wd				1		1			1	1			4		
Salisbury	28	17	Flanders	Nathan		2	1		1					1			5		
Salisbury	28	18	Flanders	Nathan Junr			1			1		1					3		
Salisbury	28	19	Flanders	Jacob	1	2	1					1		1			7		
Salisbury	28	20	Flanders	Bennet				1		3			1				5		
Salisbury	28	21	Flanders	Benaiah	2			1		1			1	1			6		
Salisbury	28	22	Follensbe	Ws Abl	2					1			1				4		
Salisbury	28	23	Follensbe	Benja		2	1		1	1			1	1			7		
Salisbury	28	24	Follensbe	Joshua		1	1		1			1	1	1			6		
Salisbury	28	25	Fitts	Joseph		1	1		1	2	3	1	1				10		
Salisbury	28	26	Griffin	Wm Capt				1					1				2		
Salisbury	28	27	Griffin	Daniel Capt	1		1						2				4		
Salisbury	28	28	Griffin	Benja Capt			1		1				1	1			4		
Salisbury	28	29	Griffin	Benja Junr Capt	2			1		2			1				6		
Salisbury	28	30	Graves	Mark		2		1					1				4		
Salisbury	28	31	Grant	Eliza Wd										2			2		
Salisbury	28	32	Gerish	Richd	3	1		1			1	1	1				8		
Salisbury	28	33	Gerish	Prudence Wd				1					2	1			4		
Salisbury	28	34	Gerren	Joseph		1		1		2		1					6		

TOWN	PG#	LN#	LAST NAME	FIRST NAME	FREE WHITE MALES					FREE WHITE FEMALES					TOTAL ALL OTHER	TOTAL SLAVES	TOTALS	DISTRICT/ TOWNSHIP	NOTES
					under 10	10 to 16	16 to 26	26 to 45	45 and over	under 10	10 to 16	16 to 26	26 to 45	45 and over					
Salisbury	28	35	Greely	John			2		1	1		1					5		
Salisbury	28	36	Greely	David			1			1		1					3		
Salisbury	28	37	Gill	Ruth Wd			1					1		1			3		
Salisbury	28	38	Gill	Samuel				1	1					1			3		
Salisbury	29	1	Greely	Philip	1	1		1		2	2	1	1	1			10		
Salisbury	29	2	Green	Sarah Wd										1			1		
Salisbury	29	3	Goodwin	Henry			2	1						3			6		
Salisbury	29	4	Greely	Jona		1		1		1			1				4		
Salisbury	29	5	George	Nathl		2		1				1		1			5		
Salisbury	29	6	George	Ebenz			1			3		1					5		
Salisbury	29	7	Greely	Samuel		1	1	1		2	1		1				7		
Salisbury	29	8	Greely	Judith Wd								1		1			2		
Salisbury	29	9	Hinkson	John			1			1		1					3		
Salisbury	29	10	Hook	Jonah Capt			1	1					2	1			5		
Salisbury	29	11	Hook	Anna Wd	1		1			1		3	1	1			8		
Salisbury	29	12	Hubbard	Joseph			1						1	1			3		
Salisbury	29	13	Hacket	Benja		1	1					1					3		
Salisbury	29	14	Hacket	John			1	1		1	1			2			6		
Salisbury	29	15	Hall	Joseph	1			1		1			1	1			5		
Salisbury	29	16	Hacket	Wm Capt			1		1	1		1	3	1			8		
Salisbury	29	17	Hoyt	Benja Capt	2			1		1	1		1				6		
Salisbury	29	18	Hacket	John Junr	1			1		2			1				5		
Salisbury	29	19	Hacket	Wm Junr Capt				1		2			1				4		
Salisbury	29	20	Hoyt	Moses	1	1		1		2			1	1			7		
Salisbury	29	21	Harbert	James			1		1					1			3		
Salisbury	29	22	Harbert	Sarah Wd	1	1	1				2	1		1			7		
Salisbury	29	23	Joy	David				1						1			2		
Salisbury	29	24	Jackman	Nathl		1		1					1				3		
Salisbury	29	25	Jackman	Levi		1		1		2			1				5		
Salisbury	29	26	Jackman	Eleanor Wd							1	1		1			3		
Salisbury	29	27	Joy	Benja				1						2			3		
Salisbury	29	28	Joy	Benja Junr		1		2		1			1				5		
Salisbury	29	29	Jones	Richd	1	1		1					1				4		
Salisbury	29	30	Jones	Merrill	2			1			1		1				5		
Salisbury	29	31	Jewett	Joseph	1	1	1	1			1	1					6		
Salisbury	29	32	Knight	Lemuel	1		1	1				1					4		
Salisbury	29	33	Knap	John		1	1		1			1	1	1			6		
Salisbury	30	1	Lowell	Simeon	1		1		1	1	3		1				9		
Salisbury	30	2	Lowell	Stephen			1			1		1					3		
Salisbury	30	3	Lowell	Lewis	1			1		2	1		1				6		
Salisbury	30	4	Locke	James	2			1		1			1				5		
Salisbury	30	5	Lombard	Barzilla Capt				1		1	1	1					4		
Salisbury	30	6	March	Samuel		1	1	1		2	1		1	1			8		
Salisbury	30	7	March	John				1	1				1	1			4		
Salisbury	30	8	Moody	William	2	1	2		1	2	1	1		1			11		
Salisbury	30	9	Merrill	Benja		2			1	2				1			6		
Salisbury	30	10	Merrill	Sarah Wd		2				1	2		1				6		
Salisbury	30	11	Merrill	Margaret Wd										1			1		
Salisbury	30	12	Merrill	John Junr	1	1		1		1		1	1				6		
Salisbury	30	13	Merrill	John Capt		1			1					1			3		
Salisbury	30	14	Merrill	Samuel			1				1		1				3		
Salisbury	30	15	Moody	Daniel		2			1	1				1			5		
Salisbury	30	16	Moody	Judith Wd		1	3			1			1	1			7		
Salisbury	30	17	Moody	Joshua			1					1					2		
Salisbury	30	18	Merrill	Moses	1			1		2			1	1			6		
Salisbury	30	19	Merrill	Samuel	1	1		1		2	1	1	1	1			9		
Salisbury	30	20	Merrill	Daniel			1		1	1	1	1	2				7		
Salisbury	30	21	Merrill	Ezra		1	3		1				1				6		
Salisbury	30	22	Morrill	Abraham			1			1	2	1	1	1			7		
Salisbury	30	23	Morrill	Samuel 3d	3			1		1			1				6		
Salisbury	30	24	Morrill	Sarah Wd	1									1			2		
Salisbury	30	25	Morrill	Philip	1	1			1	2	2	1	1	1			10		
Salisbury	30	26	Morse	Martha Wd										1			1		
Salisbury	30	27	Manfield	Dudley			2		1					3			6		
Salisbury	30	28	Morrill	Stephen	4			1					1				6		
Salisbury	30	29	Merrill	Rhoda Wd									2	1			3		
Salisbury	30	30	Morrill	Enoch			1	1		3			2				7		
Salisbury	30	31	Morrill	Israel Capt	2	1	1	1		2		1	1				9		
Salisbury	30	32	Manfield	John	1		1		2	2	1	1					8		
Salisbury	30	33	Manfield	Wd									2				2		
Salisbury	30	34	Merrill	Melatiah				1					2				3		
Salisbury	31	1	Merrill	Ezra Capt			1						1				2		
Salisbury	31	2	Merrill	Wm Capt	2			1				1	1				5		
Salisbury	31	3	Merrill	Robert		1	2	1					1				5		
Salisbury	31	4	Mann	Dolly Wd						1			1				2		
Salisbury	31	5	Morrill	True				1				1		1			3		
Salisbury	31	6	Morrill	Timothy		2	1	1			1	1		1			7		
Salisbury	31	7	Morrill	David Junr	2	1	1	1		2			1				8		
Salisbury	31	8	Morrill	Jonathn	1	2				2	1	1	1				9		

TOWN	PG#	LN#	LAST NAME	FIRST NAME	FREE WHITE MALES					FREE WHITE FEMALES					TOTAL ALL OTHER	TOTAL SLAVES	TOTALS	DISTRICT/ TOWNSHIP	NOTES
					under 10	10 to 16	16 to 26	26 to 45	45 and over	under 10	10 to 16	16 to 26	26 to 45	45 and over					
Salisbury	31	9	Morrill	Ephrm	3			1		1			1				6		
Salisbury	31	10	Morrill	Elanor Wd				1				1	1				3		
Salisbury	31	11	Morrill	Willm	1	1		1		1	1		1				6		
Salisbury	31	12	Morrill	Mary Wd	1		1			2		1	1				6		
Salisbury	31	13	Morrill	Moses S	1			1		1	1	2	1	1			8		
Salisbury	31	14	Morrill	John	1	1		1		2	2	1	1				9		
Salisbury	31	15	Morrill	David				1				1	1				3		
Salisbury	31	16	Morrill	Aaron			1					2	1				4		
Salisbury	31	17	Morrill	Thomas	1		1						1				3		
Salisbury	31	18	Morse	Reuben	2			1					1				4		
Salisbury	31	19	Morrill	Wm Junr		2				1		1					4		
Salisbury	31	20	Morrill	Bradbury	2			1					1				4		
Salisbury	31	21	Morrill	Daniel Dr					1				1				2		
Salisbury	31	22	Morrill	Amos	2			1		2	1		1				7		
Salisbury	31	23	Morrill	Israel Junr			1					1	1				3		
Salisbury	31	24	Morrill	Judith										2			2		
Salisbury	31	25	Morrill	Benja	2			1		1			1				5		
Salisbury	31	26	Morrill	Anhelm			2		1					1			4		
Salisbury	31	27	Morrill	Sarah Wd		3							2	1			6		
Salisbury	31	28	Noyes	Edmund Esq				2	1			1		1			5		
Salisbury	31	29	Noyes	Judith Wd		1						1		1			3		
Salisbury	31	30	Nye	Samuel		2		1		1	1		1				6		
Salisbury	31	31	Norwell	Henry				1					1				2		
Salisbury	31	32	Osgood	Ruth Wd								1	1				2		
Salisbury	31	33	Osgood	Benjamin		1		1				1	3				6		
Salisbury	31	34	Osgood	Elijah			1			1		1					3		
Salisbury	31	35	Osgood	Willm		1	1	1				1	1				5		
Salisbury	32	1	Osgood	Winthrop Dr				1		1			1				3		
Salisbury	32	2	Osgood	Oliver Capt		2	2	1		1		1	1				8		
Salisbury	32	3	Osgood	Stephen	1			1		2			1				5		
Salisbury	32	4	Osgood	Jacob Capt	2		1	1			1		1				6		
Salisbury	32	5	Osgood	Abigail Wd		1						2		1			4		
Salisbury	32	6	Osgood	Moses	1		1			1		1					4		
Salisbury	32	7	Osgood	James			1			2			1				4		
Salisbury	32	8	Osgood	Willm Junr	2	1		1		1	1		1				7		
Salisbury	32	9	Osgood	John	1	1	1		1	1				1			6		
Salisbury	32	10	Osgood	Thomas	3			1				1	1				6		
Salisbury	32	11	Osgood	Joseph Capt		1	1		1		1			1			5		
Salisbury	32	12	Osgood	Joseph				1						1			2		
Salisbury	32	13	Osgood	Peter	1		1						1				3		
Salisbury	32	14	Pettingill	Joseph	1		1		1	1			1	1			6		
Salisbury	32	15	Pike	Elias Junr	1		1	1		1	2	1	1				8		
Salisbury	32	16	Pike	Caleb Junr			1				1		1				3		
Salisbury	32	17	Pike	Moses	3	1		1				2	1				9		
Salisbury	32	18	Pike	Elias			1	1		1	1		1				5		
Salisbury	32	19	Pike	Henry			1			4			1				6		
Salisbury	32	20	Pike	Abl Wd						1			1				2		
Salisbury	32	21	Pike	Jacob	1			1		2			1				5		
Salisbury	32	22	Pike	Francis			1		1				1				3		
Salisbury	32	23	Pike	Mary Wd		2	1					2		1			6		
Salisbury	32	24	Pike	John	2			1		1		1					5		
Salisbury	32	25	Pecker	James	2		1	1		3	1		1				9		
Salisbury	32	26	Purrington	Wd			1							2			3		
Salisbury	32	27	Pike	Caleb		1	1		1	3	1	3	1	1			12		
Salisbury	32	28	Pike	Joshua			1			1		2	1	2			7		
Salisbury	32	29	Pettingill	Amos			1		1					1			3		
Salisbury	32	30	Pearson	Ebenezer	1	1		1		3	1	3	1				11		
Salisbury	32	31	Page	Dorothy Wd						1		2	1	1			5		
Salisbury	32	32	Pearly	Samuel		1				1	1	1					4		
Salisbury	32	33	Pearly	Ebenzr Capt		1		1		3		2					7		
Salisbury	32	34	Pensen	John			1						1	1			3		
Salisbury	33	1	Ring	Page		2		1				2	1	1			7		
Salisbury	33	2	Ring	Reuben F.	2			1		1			1				5		
Salisbury	33	3	Rowell	Jacob		2	1	1					1	1			6		
Salisbury	33	4	Rowell	Philip	1			1		1			1				4		
Salisbury	33	5	Rowell	Mark		1	1						1	1			4		
Salisbury	33	6	Ring	Daniel				1				1		1			3		
Salisbury	33	7	Ring	Abner		1		1				1		1			4		
Salisbury	33	8	Ring	Nathl	1	1		1	1	1		1	1				8		
Salisbury	33	9	Stevens	Benja				1		1	1		1				4		
Salisbury	33	10	Stevens	Joseph	2			1		2	2		3				10		
Salisbury	33	11	Smith	Jona Colo	2	1		1		2	2	3	1				12		
Salisbury	33	12	Smith	John	1			1		2			1				5		
Salisbury	33	13	Stevens	Samuel				1					1				2		
Salisbury	33	14	Sawyer	John			1	1					1	3			6		
Salisbury	33	15	Smith	Rufus	2			1		1			1				5		
Salisbury	33	16	Stickney	Joseph				1		1			1				3		
Salisbury	33	17	Stevens	Jona	2	1		1					1				5		
Salisbury	33	18	Storkman	Joseph					1			1		1			3		
Salisbury	33	19	Storkman	Joseph Junr	1			1		1			1				4		

TOWN	PG#	LN#	LAST NAME	FIRST NAME	FREE WHITE MALES					FREE WHITE FEMALES					TOTAL ALL OTHER	TOTAL SLAVES	TOTALS	DISTRICT/ TOWNSHIP	NOTES
					under 10	10 to 16	16 to 26	26 to 45	45 and over	under 10	10 to 16	16 to 26	26 to 45	45 and over					
Salisbury	33	20	Stevens	Samuel Junr				1		2			1				4		
Salisbury	33	21	Swain	Roger					1	1	1		1	1			5		
Salisbury	33	22	Sweat	Aaron	1			1	1		1		1				5		
Salisbury	33	23	Stevens	Jeremiah					1		1	1		1			4		
Salisbury	33	24	Stevens	Ruth Wd						2		1		1			4		
Salisbury	33	25	Stevens	Jacob			1	1		1	2		1				6		
Salisbury	33	26	Stevens	John Junr	1				1		1			1			4		

TOWN	PG#	LN#	LAST NAME	FIRST NAME	FREE WHITE MALES					FREE WHITE FEMALES					TOTAL ALL OTHER	TOTAL SLAVES	TOTALS	DISTRICT/ TOWNSHIP	NOTES
					under 10	10 to 16	16 to 26	26 to 45	45 and over	under 10	10 to 16	16 to 26	26 to 45	45 and over					
Topsfield	18	1	Towne	David		1	2		1			2		1			7		
Topsfield	18	2	Bixby	Daniel		1		1	1		1	1		1			6		
Topsfield	18	3	Pike	Benjamin	1	1	1		1	4		1	1				10		
Topsfield	18	4	Porter	Daniel	1		2	1	1		1	2					9		
Topsfield	18	5	Cummings	David	2	2	1	1			2		2				10		
Topsfield	18	6	Tenney	Thomas	3	1			1		2		1				8		
Topsfield	18	7	Towne	Ephriem		1		1			1		1				4		
Topsfield	18	8	Balch	Roger	1			1					1		1		4		
Topsfield	18	9	Balch	John		1	1		1	1		2		1			7		
Topsfield	18	10	Perkins	Moses				1		1		1		1			4		
Topsfield	18	11	Perkins	Daniel	2	1		1		2	1	1	1				9		
Topsfield	18	12	Estey	Daniel		1		1	1		3	1	2		2		11		
Topsfield	18	13	Peabody	John			1		1			2	1				5		
Topsfield	18	14	Peabody	John Junr	1	1	1	1		2		1	1				8		
Topsfield	18	15	Blaisdel	Samuel	1			1				1					3		
Topsfield	18	16	Balch	Daniel			1			1		1					3		
Topsfield	18	17	Towne	Joseph				1	2				1		1		5		
Topsfield	18	18	Rea	Israel	1		1	1		2	1		2	1			9		
Topsfield	18	19	Rea	John	1			1		1		2		1			6		
Topsfield	18	20	Dwinell	John			1		1			1	1	1			5		
Topsfield	18	21	Estey	Enos								1					1		
Topsfield	19	1	Towne	Jacob Junr	1	2			1			1		2			7		
Topsfield	19	2	Fisk	Nathaniel			2		1			1		1			5		
Topsfield	19	3	Towne	Joshua	2	1	1		1	1	1	1	1				9		
Topsfield	19	4	Conant	John	2	1		1		2			1	1			8		
Topsfield	19	5	Towne	Elijah				1					1				2		
Topsfield	19	6	Cree	Cornelius			1				1		1				3		
Topsfield	19	7	Foster	Priscilla			1					1		1			3		
Topsfield	19	8	Foster	Amos		1		1				1					3		
Topsfield	19	9	Kimball	Jacob		1	1	1	1	1	1		1				7		
Topsfield	19	10	Kimball	Benjamin	1		1						1				3		
Topsfield	19	11	Hood	Samuel	2	1		1		2		1					7		
Topsfield	19	12	Baker	John			1	1			2		1				5		
Topsfield	19	13	Perkins	Thomas Junr	2	1		1		2			1				7		
Topsfield	19	14	Cleaveland	Nehemiah	2	1	1	1		1		1	1				8		
Topsfield	19	15	Conant	Aaron	1			1				1		1			4		
Topsfield	19	16	Moore	Dominick			1			2	1		1				5		
Topsfield	19	17	Balch	David	1	1		1	1	2			1				7		
Topsfield	19	18	Balch	Esther									1				1		
Topsfield	19	19	Cree	Joseph	1			1		1	1	1	1				6		
Topsfield	19	20	Cree	Martha			1					1		1			3		
Topsfield	19	21	Gould	Amos	1		1					1					3		
Topsfield	19	22	Dexter	Mehitable										1			1		
Topsfield	19	23	Cummings	Joseph				1					1				2		
Topsfield	19	24	Cummings	Jonathan	1			1		1	1	1					5		
Topsfield	19	25	Cummings	Thomas			1		1				1				3		
Topsfield	19	26	Cummings	Elijah		1		1		1		1	1				5		
Topsfield	19	27	Cummings	Jonas	1			1	1	1	2		1				7		
Topsfield	19	28	Lamson	Anna									2	1			3		
Topsfield	19	29	Lamson	Josiah		2			1	1		1	1				6		
Topsfield	19	30	Clark	Ruth										1			1		
Topsfield	19	31	Clark	Israel	2			1					1	1			5		
Topsfield	19	32	Kneeland	Aaron	3	1	3	1	1			1	1				11		
Topsfield	19	33	Kneeland	Aaron Jun		1						1					2		
Topsfield	19	34	Kneeland	Daniel			1	1		1			1	1			5		
Topsfield	19	35	Chapman	John		2	1		1	1				1			6		
Topsfield	19	36	Foster	Nathaniel	1			1					1				3		
Topsfield	19	37	Wildes	Dudley		1	2	1						2			7		
Topsfield	19	38	Hobbs	Benjamin		1	1		1	1	1		1				6		
Topsfield	19	39	Hobbs	David		1	1		2			1	1				6		
Topsfield	19	40	Hobbs	Abraham		1		1		1	1	3	3	1			11		
Topsfield	19	41	Perkins	Daniel		1		1					2				4		
Topsfield	20	1	Conant	Darkus		1							1				2		
Topsfield	20	2	Symonds	Jacob		1	1		1	1	1		1				6		
Topsfield	20	3	Batchelder	John		1		1					1				3		
Topsfield	20	4	Peabody	Jacob		1	1		1			1		1			5		
Topsfield	20	5	Peabody	Jacob Junr		1		1		4	1		1				8		
Topsfield	20	6	Boardman	Danel	1		3		1	1	1			1			8		
Topsfield	20	7	Cummings	Thomas Junr	1			1				1	1				4		
Topsfield	20	8	Porter	Asa				1					1				2		
Topsfield	20	9	Cleaves	Nehemiah	1			1				2					4		
Topsfield	20	10	Batchelder	Joseph	2			1			1		1				5		
Topsfield	20	11	Batchelder	John Junr			1			1			1				3		
Topsfield	20	12	Averell	Nathaniel P.	2		1			2	1		1	1			8		
Topsfield	20	13	Wildes	Ephriem			1	1						2			4		
Topsfield	20	14	Bradstreet	Moses			1			3			1				5		
Topsfield	20	15	Averell	Sarah						1			2				3		
Topsfield	20	16	Averell	Isaac			1	1	1		1			1			5		
Topsfield	20	17	Averell	Jacob				1				1	1				3		

TOWN	PG#	LN#	LAST NAME	FIRST NAME	FREE WHITE MALES					FREE WHITE FEMALES					TOTAL ALL OTHER	TOTAL SLAVES	TOTALS	DISTRICT/ TOWNSHIP	NOTES
					under 10	10 to 16	16 to 26	26 to 45	45 and over	under 10	10 to 16	16 to 26	26 to 45	45 and over					
Topsfield	20	18	Averell	Solomon	1			1		1			1				4		
Topsfield	20	19	Averell	Daniel				1					1	1			3		
Topsfield	20	20	Averell	Daniel Junr	2			1					1	1			5		
Topsfield	20	21	Averell	Nathaniel		1	1	1				2		1			6		
Topsfield	20	22	Averell	Azariah		1				1		1					3		
Topsfield	20	23	Wildes	Moses	1	1	3	1				1	1				8		
Topsfield	20	24	Dodge	Solomon		1	1	2		2	1		2				9		
Topsfield	20	25	Perkins	Robert Junr	2	2	3	1		1	1	3		1			14		
Topsfield	20	26	Perkins	Robert				1					3	1			5		
Topsfield	20	27	Perkins	Amos				1						2			3		
Topsfield	20	28	Wildes	Daniel	1			1		1			1				4		
Topsfield	20	29	Parker	Edmand	2			1		2			1				6		
Topsfield	20	30	Perkins	Deborah				1					1				2		
Topsfield	20	31	Bradstreet	Samuel	2	1	1	1		1	1		1				8		
Topsfield	20	32	Bradstreet	John				1						1			2		
Topsfield	20	33	Bradstreet	Dudley	2	1		1		1			1				6		
Topsfield	20	34	Dorman	Joseph			1					1	1				3		
Topsfield	20	35	Dorman	Ephriem				1									1		
Topsfield	20	36	Hovey	Ivery	1	1		1				1	1				5		
Topsfield	20	37	Gallop	Amos		2	1	1		3	3		1				11		
Topsfield	20	38	Hood	John				1						1			2		
Topsfield	20	39	Hood	John Junr	3			1		3			1				8		
Topsfield	20	40	Meriam	John		2		1		1			1				5		
Topsfield	21	1	Perkins	Thomas			1	1					2				4		
Topsfield	21	2	Meriam	Jonas		1		1		2			1				5		
Topsfield	21	3	Andrew	Elizabeth						1			1				2		
Topsfield	21	4	Gallop	William				1						3			4		
Topsfield	21	5	Emmerson	Thomas			3	1	1	2	1		1	1	2		12		
Topsfield	21	6	Bixby	Benjamin	1	1	1	1		1		1	1				8		
Topsfield	21	7	Moneys	William				1						1			2		
Topsfield	21	8	Moneys	William Junr	1		1	1		1			1				5		
Topsfield	21	9	Parker	Lucy						1			1				2		
Topsfield	21	10	Perley	Stephen				1			2		1				4		
Topsfield	21	11	Averell	Elijah				1		2	1		1				5		
Topsfield	21	12	Gould	John		1		1		1	1	1		1			6		
Topsfield	21	13	Huntington	Asahel Revd	3			1		1	1	1		1			8		
Topsfield	21	14	Gould	John Junr	1			1		1	1	1		1			6		
Topsfield	21	15	Gould	Joseph				1						1			2		
Topsfield	21	16	Gould	Joseph Junr			1			1	1						3		
Topsfield	21	17	Gould	Asa				1				1		1			3		
Topsfield	21	18	Majery	Hannah										1			1		
Topsfield	21	19	Gould	Nathaniel	3	2		1		2		2	1	1			12		
Topsfield	21	20	Gould	Simon				1					1				2		
Topsfield	21	21	Gould	Elijah			1					1					2		
Topsfield	21	22	Gould	Simon Junr	1	1		1		1			1				5		
Topsfield	21	23	Gould	Zacheus	3	1	1	1		2	2	1	1				12		
Topsfield	21	24	Bradstreet	Henry		1		1				1		1			4		
Topsfield	21	25	Lake	Eleazer		3	2	1				1		1			8		
Topsfield	21	26	Lake	Robert	2			1					2				5		
Topsfield	21	27	Balch	Thomas		1	1	1					1				4		
Topsfield	21	28	Balch	Joshua		1	1				1			1			4		
Topsfield	21	29	Bradstreet	John Junr	2			1		2			1	1			7		
Topsfield	21	30	Moore	Thomas				1						1			2		
Topsfield	21	31	Bickford	Silas	2			1		1			1				5		
Topsfield	21	32	Wildes	Sylvanus		2		1		1	2	3		2			11		
Topsfield	21	33	Wildes	Mary								2	1				3		
Topsfield	21	34	Perkins	Asa				1		2	1		1				5		
Topsfield	21	35	Towne	Daniel				1						1			2		
Topsfield	21	36	Andrew	Dorothy								1		1			2		
Topsfield	21	37	Andrew	Joseph	1			1					1				3		
Topsfield	21	38	Andrew	Ephriem			1						1				2		
Topsfield	22	1	Lefavour	John	1	1		1			2		1				6		
Topsfield	22	2	Brown	Eleazer		1	1			3			1				6		
Topsfield	22	3	Durant	Isaac	2			1		2	1		1				7		
Topsfield	22	4	Perkins	Samuel			1	1						1			3		
Topsfield	22	5	Perkins	Elijah	1			1		1			1				4		
Topsfield	22	6	Hammond	Nathaniel		1	1	1		1		1	1	1			7		
Topsfield	22	7	Perkins	David	2	1	1	2		1		1		1			9		
Topsfield	22	8	Perkins	David Junr	2	1	2	1		1	2	1	1				11		
Topsfield	22	9	Perkins	Elijah		1	1	1		1	1	1	1				7		
Topsfield	22	10	Perkins	Zebulon	1			1	1	1	2	1		1			8		
Topsfield	22	11	Towne	Jacob			1	1				1		1			4		

TOWN	PG#	LN#	LAST NAME	FIRST NAME	FREE WHITE MALES					FREE WHITE FEMALES					TOTAL ALL OTHER	TOTAL SLAVES	TOTALS	DISTRICT/ TOWNSHIP	NOTES
					under 10	10 to 16	16 to 26	26 to 45	45 and over	under 10	10 to 16	16 to 26	26 to 45	45 and over					
Wenham	307	1	Porter	Paul	1		1			1		2					5		
Wenham	307	2	Wheeler	Ruben	2			1		2	1		1				7		
Wenham	307	3	Porter	Isaac	1			1	1	1			1	2			7		
Wenham	307	4	Graften	Pattee		2						1	1				4		
Wenham	307	5	Kimball	Nathaniel	2			1	1		1		1	2			8		
Wenham	307	6	Dodge	John 2nd		3	1		1	2		2	1				10		
Wenham	307	7	Dodge	Uszial	1			2				1					4		
Wenham	307	8	Kerbe	Hanna	1					1			1				3		
Wenham	307	9	Herrick	Joshua		1	1	1		1	1		1				6		
Wenham	307	10	Greenwood	Elizabeth										1			1		
Wenham	307	11	Lambord	Priscilla										1			1		
Wenham	307	12	Fish	Samuel				1						1			2		
Wenham	307	13	Hobb	Jonathan	1	1			1	1	1	1					7		
Wenham	307	14	Perkins	Edward	1	1		1		2	1		1				7		
Wenham	307	15	Seirley	Eleanor		1				1			1				3		
Wenham	307	16	Porter	Tyler Esquire				1					2		1		4		
Wenham	307	17	Porter	John 2nd	1			1		1	1		1				5		
Wenham	307	18	Fowls	Nathaniel	1			1					1				3		
Wenham	307	19	Trivett	Samuel R		2	2		1	1		1		1			8		
Wenham	307	20	Lee	Aaron	2			1		1	2	3		1			10		
Wenham	308	1	Dodge	Jacob	1			2		3	1		1				8		
Wenham	308	2	Dodge	Abraham			1			1	1		1	1	1		6		
Wenham	308	3	Brown	Nathan		2	1		1	1		1		1			7		
Wenham	308	4	Brown	Nathan Jr			1					1					2		
Wenham	308	5	Dodge	Stephen				1				1		1			3		
Wenham	308	6	Dodge	Hannah	1	1	1			2	1	1					7		
Wenham	308	7	Dodge	John		2		1	1		1		1	1	1		8		
Wenham	308	8	Dodge	Peter	1			1		3			1				6		
Wenham	308	9	Dodge	Elizabeth			1					2		1			4		
Wenham	308	10	Quoles	Jerusha			1			1			1				3		
Wenham	308	11	Gently	Molly		3	1						1				5		
Wenham	308	12	Dowling	Mary										1			1		
Wenham	308	13	Dodge	John F		2		1		4			1				8		
Wenham	308	14	Dodge	John 3d	2			1			1		1				5		
Wenham	308	15	Hooker	John	1	1			1			1	1				5		
Wenham	308	16	Dodge	Simon	1		1		1			1	1	1			6		
Wenham	308	17	Dodge	Nichols			2								1		3		
Wenham	308	18	Edwards	Abraham	2		1	1		2		1					7		
Wenham	308	19	Knowlton	Anna								1		1			2		
Wenham	308	20	Edwards	Benjamin		2		1		3		1	1	1			9		
Wenham	308	21	Dodge	Benja				1					1				2		
Wenham	308	22	Brown	William			1			1		2					4		
Wenham	308	23	Dodge	Israel		1					1		1				5		
Wenham	308	24	Orne	Joshua	2			1		1			1				5		
Wenham	308	25	Orne	Mary			1						1				2		
Wenham	308	26	Shatten	John	1		1						1				3		
Wenham	308	27	Dodge	William	3	3	1			1		2	1				11		
Wenham	308	28	Kimball	Thomas Jr	1	1				3	1		1				8		
Wenham	308	29	Tucker	Barnard			1						1	1			3		
Wenham	308	30	Kimball	James				1			1			1			3		
Wenham	308	31	Kimball	Caleb			1			1			1				3		
Wenham	308	32	Kimball	Huldah		1							1				2		
Wenham	308	33	Freind	Hannah		1							1	1			3		
Wenham	308	34	Freind	Israel				1		1			1				3		
Wenham	308	35	Freeman	Sippes											4		4		
Wenham	308	36	Freind	James		1			1			3		1			6		
Wenham	308	37	Butman	Daniel	1			1		3			1				6		
Wenham	308	38	Dodge	Israel A	1	2			1	1		2		1			8		
Wenham	309	1	Hood	Josiah M			1					1					2		
Wenham	309	2	Dodge	Oliver	1		2					1					4		
Wenham	309	3	Fairfield	Joseph	1	1	1	1			1		1				6		
Wenham	309	4	Hood	Richard		1			1			2	1				5		
Wenham	309	5	Fisk	Samuel Jun				1		1		2					4		
Wenham	309	6	Potter	Benja	3			1					1				5		
Wenham	309	7	Peirce	Molly									2				2		
Wenham	309	8	Porter	Nathaniel		2		1				1	1				5		
Wenham	309	9	Porter	Hannah						1		1	2				4		
Wenham	309	10	Baker	Cornelus	1		1		1		1		1				6		
Wenham	309	11	Baker	John	1			1		1	1		1				5		
Wenham	309	12	Obear	Samuel	1		1		1			1	2	1			7		
Wenham	309	13	Moulton	John	2	1		1					1	1			6		
Wenham	309	14	Gallop	Enos				1		1			1				3		
Wenham	309	15	Redington	Adams	2			1		1			1				5		
Wenham	309	16	Webber	Elizabeth	1						1		1				3		
Wenham	309	17	Batchelder	Samuel				1					1	1			3		
Wenham	309	18	Moulton	Jonathan					1					1			2		
Wenham	309	19	Moulton	Daniel	1			1					1				3		
Wenham	309	20	Kimball	Thomas		1	1	1					1				4		
Wenham	309	21	Batchelder	Edmond	2					1		1					6		

TOWN	PG#	LN#	LAST NAME	FIRST NAME	FREE WHITE MALES					FREE WHITE FEMALES					TOTAL ALL OTHER	TOTAL SLAVES	TOTALS	DISTRICT/ TOWNSHIP	NOTES
					under 10	10 to 16	16 to 26	26 to 45	45 and over	under 10	10 to 16	16 to 26	26 to 45	45 and over					
Wenham	309	22	Dodge	Richard Esquire					1		1			1			3		
Wenham	309	23	Wyat	Abraham					1				1				2		
Wenham	309	24	Wyat	Simon	2			1		2	1		1				7		
Wenham	309	25	Wyat	William	3			1		2		1					7		
Wenham	309	26	Wyat	Jonathan	1			1			1		1				4		
Wenham	309	27	Wyat	Jane	1	1				1				1			4		
Wenham	309	28	Wyat	Thankful	2								1				3		
Wenham	309	29	Higgans	Timothy		1	1	1			1		1				5		
Wenham	309	30	Knowlton	Jonathan		1	1		1	1	1	1	1				7		
Wenham	309	31	Cleaver	John				1		2		1					4		
Wenham	309	32	Knowlton	Abraham	1		1		1		2	1	1				7		
Wenham	309	33	Batchelder	Amos					1		1			1			3		
Wenham	309	34	Perkins	John	1		1		1	1				1			5		
Wenham	309	35	Perkins	Nehemiah	1			1		2	1		1				6		
Wenham	309	36	Brown	Palahiah		1			1				1	1			4		
Wenham	309	37	Killham	Daniel		1		1		1			1				4		
Wenham	309	38	Freind	Joseph			1						1				2		
Wenham	309	39	Sands	Isaac					1				1	1			3		
Wenham	310	1	Gardner	John	1				1		1	1		1			5		
Wenham	310	2	Blanchard	Samuel			3	1		1		2	1				8		

TOWN	PG#	LN#	LAST NAME	FIRST NAME	FREE WHITE MALES					FREE WHITE FEMALES					TOTAL ALL OTHER	TOTAL SLAVES	TOTALS	DISTRICT/ TOWNSHIP	NOTES
					under 10	10 to 16	16 to 26	26 to 45	45 and over	under 10	10 to 16	16 to 26	26 to 45	45 and over					
Marblehead	255	1	*att	Elizabeth										1			1		
Marblehead	258	15	*man	John		1							1				2		
Beverly	296	14	Abbitt	Dudly	3		1			1			1				6		
Haverhill	142	2	Abbot	Abiel			1			2	1		2				6		
Newburyport	157	15	Abbot	Benjamin	3		1			3	2		1	1			11		
Salem	210	12	Abbot	Daniel	1		1			1		1					4		
Salem	183	13	Abbot	Elias			1						1	1			3		
Gloucester	78	18	Abbot	James		2		1		2	1	1	1				8	Sandy Bay Parish	
Newburyport	157	17	Abbot	James	1			2		2			2				7		
Manchester	55	8	Abbot	Nathll		2		1		2			1				6		
Salem	210	9	Abbot	Phillip	1	2	2		1				1				7		
Salem	191	32	Abbot	Priscilla			1				2	2	3	1			9		
Salem	207	46	Abbot	Stephen		2			1				4	1	1		9		
Marblehead	238	8	Abbott	Anna										1			1		
Marblehead	238	22	Abbott	Benjamin	1		1			1			1				4		
Andover	90	17	Abbott	Benjamin	1		1			2			1				5		
Andover	89	15	Abbott	Benjamin Junr	1	1	1					1					4		
Andover	89	19	Abbott	Benjamin Junr	1	2	1		1			3	3				11		
Andover	90	10	Abbott	Bixby	2	2		1					1				6		
Andover	90	2	Abbott	Caleb	1	1		1		3		1	1				8		
Andover	90	14	Abbott	David	3			1		1	1		1				7		
Andover	90	9	Abbott	Ephraim		1	1		1	1	1	1	1				7		
Andover	89	11	Abbott	Ezra	1	5	1	1				2					10		
Andover	89	7	Abbott	Henry	1	1	1		1			1	1	1	1		8		
Andover	89	17	Abbott	Isaac		1	1	1					1				4		
Andover	90	8	Abbott	Jeduthum		1	2	1			1	3	1	2			11		
Andover	89	8	Abbott	John		1	2	1		1			1	2			8		
Andover	89	10	Abbott	John L		6	2	1		3	1	2	1	1			17		
Danvers	10	14	Abbott	John Moody			1						1				2		
Andover	90	7	Abbott	Jonathan				1				2		3			6		
Andover	90	13	Abbott	Jonathan 3d			1					1					2		
Andover	89	14	Abbott	Jonathan Junr		1		1		1			1	1			5		
Gloucester	86	10	Abbott	Lydia Wo									1	1			2		
Andover	89	9	Abbott	Moses	1		2	2	1			1	4	2	1		14		
Andover	89	16	Abbott	Moses Junr		4	1			1		1	1				8		
Andover	89	12	Abbott	Nathan	3	2	2	1		1		1	1	1			12		
Andover	90	15	Abbott	Nathan Junr	1	1	1						1				4		
Beverly	295	52	Abbott	Nathl			1	1		1			1				4		
Andover	90	6	Abbott	Nehemiah	1	2	6	1	1	1	1		3	1	1		18		
Andover	89	18	Abbott	Nehemiah Junr			1	1					1				3		
Andover	90	1	Abbott	Phebe Wid								1		1			2		
Andover	89	6	Abbott	Samuel Esq			2	1		1	2		1				7		
Andover	90	16	Abbott	Solomon			1			1			1				3		
Andover	90	3	Abbott	Thomas				1						2			3		
Andover	89	13	Abbott	Timothy	1	3		1	1			2		2			10		
Andover	90	11	Abbott	William Junr			1					1					2		
Andover	90	12	Abbott	Zebadiah			2			2	1		2	1			8		
Lynnfield	237	13	Aborn	Benj				1						1			2		
Marblehead	238	10	Aborn	Benjamin		1		1		3		1	1	1			8		
Lynnfield	237	12	Aborn	Cathrne	2									1			3		
Lynnfield	237	10	Aborn	Ebenz	2		1			2	2		1				8		
Lynn	230	7	Aborn	James			1					1					2		
Lynnfield	237	9	Aborn	Joseph	2	1	1		1	3	1		1				10		
Lynnfield	236	7	Aborn	Saml	2	1	2	2		2		1	1				11		
Salem	197	38	Aborn	Sarah							1	3	1				5		
Marblehead	239	4	Aborns	James					1		1	1		1			4		
Beverly	304	27	Abott	Eliza						1	1		1				3		
Marblehead	238	1	Abraham	Woodward		1		1					1	1			4		
Marblehead	238	2	Abraham	Woodward Jun	1		1					1		1			4		
Salem	218	38	Ackinson	Geo		1	1						1				3		
Newburyport	157	3	Adams	Abraham				1					1				2		
Beverly	297	6	Adams	Asa			1			2			1				4		
Lynnfield	236	2	Adams	Benja	1					1		1					5		
Rowley	127	36	Adams	Benja	1		1	1				1	1				5		
Rowley	127	37	Adams	Benja		2	2			1	1		1				8		
Rowley	130	26	Adams	Benja	1	1	2	1		1		1	1	1	1		10		
Newburyport	157	4	Adams	Benjamin	1	1		1		1		1	1				6		
Rowley	127	3	Adams	Benjo		1	1		1			1	1				5		
Beverly	298	44	Adams	Charles	2		1					1					4		
Beverly	297	47	Adams	Daniel		1	1		1	1	1	1		1			7		
Haverhill	142	24	Adams	Daniel	2	1		1		1	1		1				7		
Newbury	120	24	Adams	Eliphelet		1		1	1			1	1				5		
Hamilton	285	20	Adams	Elizabeth									1	2			3		
Hamilton	285	53	Adams	Ezekiel				1						1			2		
Hamilton	285	86	Adams	George				1						1			2		
Newbury	106	1	Adams	George	1			1		2			1				5		
Newbury	111	48	Adams	Henry	1	1		1					1				4		
Newburyport	157	5	Adams	Isaac				1						1			2		
Boxford	134	43	Adams	Israel		2		1				1		1			5		
Rowley	128	4	Adams	Israel	1	1			1	1		1	1				6		
Rowley	128	30	Adams	Israel	1	1			1			2	1	4			10		
Gloucester	55	1	Adams	James						2							4		

TOWN	PG#	LN#	LAST NAME	FIRST NAME	FWM under 10	FWM 10 to 16	FWM 16 to 26	FWM 26 to 45	FWM 45 and over	FWF under 10	FWF 10 to 16	FWF 16 to 26	FWF 26 to 45	FWF 45 and over	TOTAL ALL OTHER	TOTAL SLAVES	TOTALS	DISTRICT/ TOWNSHIP	NOTES
Andover	89	1	Adams	John	1				1	1	1			2			6		
Beverly	299	19	Adams	John			1			1		1					3		
Marblehead	238	4	Adams	John	2	2		1		1		1					7		
Marblehead	239	16	Adams	John	2	2		1		1		1					7		
Newbury	106	2	Adams	John		1	3		1	1			1	1			8		
Salem	188	1	Adams	John	1	1		1		1		1					5		
Andover	89	3	Adams	John 3d		1	2			1	1	1					6		
Andover	89	2	Adams	John Jnr	2	1	2	1		3			2				11		
Danvers	12	14	Adams	Joseph	1			1		1		1		1			5		
Gloucester	63	16	Adams	Joseph	2	2	3		1	1				1			10	East Ward	
Marblehead	238	19	Adams	Mary	1								1	1			3		
Newbury	105	20	Adams	Moses	2			1		2			1				6		
Hamilton	285	25	Adams	Nathaniel		1	1	1		1		1	1				6		
Marblehead	238	11	Adams	Nathaniel	1	1		1		1		1					5		
Salem	209	50	Adams	Nehemiah		2	3	3	1	4		2	2	1			18		
Haverhill	142	1	Adams	Phineas				1		1	1			1			3		
Marblehead	238	12	Adams	Rebecca	1									2			3		
Newburyport	157	6	Adams	Richard	1	1	1		1	2	1		1				8		
Bradford	125	28	Adams	Samuel	2		1			2			1	1			8		
Hamilton	285	12	Adams	Samuel	1			2	1			1		1			6		
Hamilton	285	32	Adams	Samuel Junr			1	1		3			1				6		
Newbury	105	23	Adams	Simeon			1			1			1				3		
Newbury	112	28	Adams	Smith	1			1		2			1	1			6		
Middleton	16	13	Adams	Solomon Revd	1			1		2		1	1				6		
Hamilton	285	13	Adams	Stephen	3	1		2		1	1		2				10		
Newbury	106	12	Adams	Stephen	2	2		2	1	2	1	1	1	1			13		
Hamilton	285	19	Adams	Thomas	3	1	1			1		1					8		
Beverly	298	43	Adams	William		1		1			2		1				5		
Beverly	298	39	Adams	William Jr	1		1			3			1				6		
Newbury	117	1	Addams	Asa	1	1		1		1			1	1			6		
Newbury	114	49	Addams	Charles			1				2		1				4		
Newbury	117	16	Addams	Daniel	2	1		1		3	1		1				9		
Newbury	120	22	Addams	Daniel	1	1		1		1	1	1	1				7		
Newbury	117	2	Addams	Ebenez	1	1		1		1			1				5		
Newbury	114	5	Addams	Henry	1				1	1		1	1	1			6		
Newbury	116	4	Addams	Israel			1	1			2	1	1				6		
Newbury	120	23	Addams	Israel				1		1		1	1				4		
Newbury	112	40	Addams	Jacub			1						1				2		
Newbury	116	31	Addams	Nathll	1			1		1				1			4		
Newbury	120	11	Addams	Nathll		1		1		1				1			4		
Newbury	117	17	Addams	Paul			2	1		3		2	1				9		
Newbury	115	35	Addams	Robert	1	1							1				3		
Newbury	115	7	Addams	Silas				1		1		1	1				4		
Newbury	111	27	Adkins	Sarah		1	1			3		1		1			7		
Newbury	112	33	Aisworth	Moses			1			2			2	1			6		
Newburyport	157	9	Akerman	John Jr	1			1		1		1					4		
Newburyport	157	8	Akerman	Joshua	2	1	1		1			1		1			7		
Newburyport	157	7	Akerman	Noah			1			1		1					3		
Gloucester	84	7	Akers	Mathew		1		1		1			1				4		
Newburyport	157	12	Alexander	William			1		1			2	2	1			7		
Ipswich	281	77	Alion	Joseph		1						1					2		
Manchester	50	28	Allen	Aaron	1			1		1	1		1				5		
Manchester	49	12	Allen	Abner	3			1					1				5		
Marblehead	239	6	Allen	Ambrose				1		2			1				4		
Gloucester	72	20	Allen	Andrew	2	1		1		2		3					9		
Andover	89	20	Allen	Asa	1								1				2		
Manchester	49	14	Allen	Betty Wo			1			1		1	1				4		
Andover	89	21	Allen	Deborah						1				3			4		
Salem	216	15	Allen	Edward Jr	1			1		1	1		1	1	1		7		
Salem	219	50	Allen	Edwd	1		2		1	1	1	2		1	1		10		
Gloucester	72	3	Allen	Eliza Wo		1							1				2		
Manchester	49	18	Allen	Elizh Wo									1				1		
Lynn	224	31	Allen	Ezra	3			1		2	1		1				8		
Manchester	49	3	Allen	Hooper	1			1		2			1				5		
Ipswich	282	51	Allen	Isaac	3			1					1				5		
Manchester	50	3	Allen	Isaac		1		1		1			4	1			8		
Manchester	49	6	Allen	Jacob				1		1	1		1				4		
Newbury	112	41	Allen	Jacub	2			1					1				4		
Manchester	52	22	Allen	John 3d		1				1		1					3		
Manchester	49	15	Allen	John Junr	2	1	1	1		2	1		1				9		
Bradford	122	37	Allen	Jonathan				1		1	1		1	1	1		5		
Danvers	9	28	Allen	Jonathan	1		1			1		1					4		
Gloucester	86	23	Allen	Joseph	5			3	15	7		3	6	17	1		57		Listed as work house
Lynn	233	12	Allen	Lemuel			1						1	1			3		
Manchester	55	6	Allen	Mary Wo	2			1					2	1			6		
Manchester	49	4	Allen	Milichi		2		1		1		1		2			7		
Marblehead	238	9	Allen	Moses	3			1		1				1			6		
Manchester	49	9	Allen	Nabby Wo									1	1			2		
Manchester	49	7	Allen	Nathan	3			1		2			1				8		
Manchester	50	33	Allen	Nathl	3			1		1			1				6		
Manchester	49	2	Allen	Nathl M.	2			1		2			1				6		
Manchester	55	5	Allen	Rebc Wo	1						1		1	1			4		
Manchester	55	7	Allen	Richard	1			1					1	1			4		
Manchester	55	16	Allen	Ruth Wo			1										3		

TOWN	PG#	LN#	HEADS OF HOUSEHOLD		FREE WHITE MALES					FREE WHITE FEMALES					TOTAL ALL OTHER	TOTAL SLAVES	TOTALS	DISTRICT/ TOWNSHIP	NOTES
			LAST NAME	FIRST NAME	under 10	10 to 16	16 to 26	26 to 45	45 and over	under 10	10 to 16	16 to 26	26 to 45	45 and over					
Manchester	49	1	Allen	Samuel				1						1			2		
Gloucester	58	23	Allen	Sarah Widow			2						1	1			4		
Gloucester	70	3	Allen	Solomon			2	1					1	1			5		
Gloucester	58	20	Allen	Solomon 3d	1	1		1		3	1	1	1				9		
Gloucester	58	19	Allen	Solomon Junr				1		1			1	1			4		
Manchester	49	8	Allen	Stephen Jun	1	1		1		3	1		1				8		
Gloucester	70	2	Allen	Thomas	4			1			2	2	1				10		
Gloucester	70	4	Allen	William				1					1	1			3		
Manchester	49	16	Allen	William	1	1		1		1	1	2	1				8		
Manchester	49	20	Allen	William 2d				1		3			1				5		
Gloucester	58	21	Allen	William Junr			1			1		1					3		
Gloucester	84	5	Allen	William Junr				1			1			1			3		
Manchester	49	5	Allen	Wo Sarah			1						2	1			4		
Lynn	223	4	Alley	Abigail				1					2	1	1		5		
Lynn	223	51	Alley	Benj	1	2		1	1	2		1	1	1			10		
Lynn	223	33	Alley	Benj 3d	3	1		1		3	2		1				11		
Lynn	225	11	Alley	Benj Jn			1	1						1			3		
Lynn	224	11	Alley	Ephm	2	1	3		1	3				1			11		
Lynn	223	26	Alley	Hulday								1		1			2		
Lynn	223	46	Alley	James				1				1		1			3		
Lynn	223	47	Alley	James Junr			1						1				2		
Haverhill	142	12	Alley	John			3			3			1	1			8		
Lynn	223	35	Alley	John		1		1						1			3		
Lynn	224	21	Alley	John Esq	1	1		1		1			1				5		
Lynn	223	24	Alley	Micajah		1	1	1			1		1				5		
Lynn	224	16	Alley	Moses B	1		2	1					1				5		
Lynn	223	1	Alley	Nathan	3	2	3	1		2			1				12		
Salem	205	40	Alley	Reuben	1		1	1		1	2			1			7		
Salem	183	7	Alley	Rufus		1				2		1					4		
Salem	208	20	Alley	Rufus	1	1				2		1					5		
Lynn	225	29	Alley	Saml				1						1			2		
Lynn	223	45	Alley	Samuel Junr			1					1					2		
Lynn	223	34	Alley	Solomon	2		1						1				4		
Lynn	223	25	Alley	Timothy	2		1			1	2		1				7		
Lynn	225	39	Alley	Willm	2	1	1			2			1				7		
Newburyport	158	1	Allgreen	Thomas				1		1			1				3		
Beverly	294	28	Allin	Daniel	4	1		1		1			1				8		
Beverly	302	25	Allin	Davis			1	1				1		1			4		
Beverly	294	26	Allin	John B	1	1		1	1			1	1				6		
Rowley	130	18	Allsworth	Daniel			1					2		1			4		
Rowley	129	4	Allwell	Samuel	1		1			3			1				6		
Andover	90	18	Ames	Benjamin	1		1	1		2	1		1	1	1		9		
Andover	103	16	Ames	Prince											7		7		
Newbury	106	36	Ames	Sarah								2		1			3		
Andover	90	5	Ames	Spafford	2	3			1	1			1	1			9		
Salem	210	10	Anderson	Andrew				1			1	1					3		
Marblehead	238	3	Anderson	Benjamin			1			1			1				3		
Salem	203	38	Anderson	Debh F.							1	1	1				3		
Beverly	304	7	Anderson	Jacob				1					1	2			4		
Newbury	106	14	Anderson	James	2	1		2	1		3	1	1				11		
Beverly	301	11	Anderson	Job				1		1			1				3		
Marblehead	239	5	Anderton	Elizaneth									1				1		
Marblehead	238	21	Anderton	Thomas	1	1		1					1				4		
Topsfield	21	36	Andrew	Dorothy							1			1			2		
Topsfield	21	3	Andrew	Elizabeth							1		1				2		
Topsfield	21	38	Andrew	Ephriem			1						1				2		
Danvers	8	6	Andrew	Israel			1							1			2		
Topsfield	21	37	Andrew	Joseph	1		1						1				3		
Gloucester	62	27	Andrews	Andrew	1	1			1	2	1			1			7		
Ipswich	283	8	Andrews	Anna			1						1	1			3		
Ipswich	274	56	Andrews	Asa	1	1		1		1	1		2		1		8		
Ipswich	283	5	Andrews	Benjamin	1	1		1						1			4		
Marblehead	239	15	Andrews	Benjamin			1			1		1					3		
Marblehead	238	14	Andrews	Betty										1			1		
Salem	212	5	Andrews	Cathr			2				1						3		
Ipswich	279	3	Andrews	David				1				1	1				3		
Marblehead	239	1	Andrews	Eleanor								1	1				2		
Ipswich	282	11	Andrews	Elias			1	1		1			1				4		
Boxford	135	36	Andrews	Jacob		1		1		1	1	1	1				6		
Ipswich	281	55	Andrews	Jacob		2	2	3	1	2		1		1			12		
Ipswich	282	22	Andrews	Jacob	2	1	1		1	1			1				7		
Ipswich	283	7	Andrews	James	3	1		1		1		1	1	1			9		
Salem	188	44	Andrews	James				1					1				2		
Ipswich	282	23	Andrews	Joanna			1			1	1	1		1			5		
Ipswich	281	41	Andrews	John						1	1		1	1			4		
Marblehead	239	3	Andrews	John															Enumeration left blank
Marblehead	269	9	Andrews	John		2	1		3		1	1	1				9		
Newburyport	157	1	Andrews	John Revd	1	1		1		1		1	2	1			8		
Gloucester	55	2	Andrews	Jona	2			1		2			1	1			7		
Ipswich	282	12	Andrews	Joseph				1				1	1				3		
Salem	189	1	Andrews	Joseph	1			1		1		1					4		
Ipswich	282	24	Andrews	Levi	1			1		1			1				4		
Ipswich	282	28	Andrews	Mark	1			1				1					4		
Marblehead	239	2	Andrews	Mary								1		1			2		

TOWN	PG#	LN#	HEADS OF HOUSEHOLD		FREE WHITE MALES					FREE WHITE FEMALES					TOTAL ALL OTHER	TOTAL SLAVES	TOTALS	DISTRICT/ TOWNSHIP	NOTES
			LAST NAME	FIRST NAME	under 10	10 to 16	16 to 26	26 to 45	45 and over	under 10	10 to 16	16 to 26	26 to 45	45 and over					
Salem	217	50	Andrews	Mary			2							1			3		
Gloucester	63	7	Andrews	Mary Wo			1							1			2	West Ward	
Ipswich	281	84	Andrews	Moses			1			2	1						4		
Boxford	135	30	Andrews	Nathan				1				1	1				3		
Boxford	135	31	Andrews	Nathan	3	1		1		2		1					8		
Ipswich	281	80	Andrews	Sarah								1					1		
Ipswich	282	25	Andrews	Solomon			1			3		1					5		
Beverly	305	4	Andrews	Thomas	5	1		1		1		1					9		
Gloucester	78	17	Andrews	William		2		1		3		2		1	2		11	Sandy Bay Parish	
Ipswich	279	2	Andrews	William F.	1	1	1					1					4		
Danvers	9	25	Anger	Sarah									1				1		
Salem	197	45	Annabal	Benja		1	1				1						3		
Hamilton	285	63	Annable	Daniel	1		1			1							3		
Hamilton	285	51	Annable	Jacob		1		1			1	1	1				5		
Hamilton	285	62	Annable	John	1			1		1							3		
Hamilton	285	69	Annable	John Junr	2			1		1	1						5		
Hamilton	285	60	Annable	Robert		1	1		1	1			1				5		
Hamilton	285	61	Annable	Robert Junr			1				1		1				3		
Hamilton	285	71	Annable	Whipple	2			1		2			1				6		
Gloucester	85	32	Anness	Abr		1	1	1		1		2	1				7		
Salem	213	24	Anthony	Nath	3	2		1		1			1				8		
Ipswich	276	59	Appleton	Aaron			1				1						2		
Hamilton	285	59	Appleton	Benjamin			1	1	1	1	2			1			6		
Haverhill	142	5	Appleton	Daniel		1	3	1		2	2		1				10		
Beverly	303	47	Appleton	Isaac		1	2					1					4		
Gloucester	58	24	Appleton	John	1			1				1					3		
Salem	206	30	Appleton	John	1	1	3	1	1			1	1	1			10		
Ipswich	277	40	Appleton	Joseph			1				1		1				3		
Newburyport	157	10	Appleton	Joseph			1			1			1				3		
Haverhill	142	6	Appleton	Mary										2			2		
Newburyport	157	11	Appleton	Nathaniel	1		1					1					3		
Ipswich	281	15	Appleton	Oliver	4			1		2	1		1				9		
Ipswich	276	52	Appleton	Sarah				1		2			2				5		
Beverly	291	44	Appleton	Thomas	1		1	1			3		1				7		
Ipswich	278	49	Appleton	Thomas				1					1				2		
Haverhill	142	25	Appleton	Thomas R.		1	1			2			1	1			6		
Gloucester	58	22	Appleton	William	1		1			1			1	1			5		
Ipswich	276	53	Appleton	William	1			1		1		1	1				5		
Salem	213	47	Appleton	William		5	3	1			1		2				12		
Newburyport	157	20	Aramatage	Samuel	2	1		1					1				5		
Beverly	301	30	Arbuckle	John	1		1				1						3		
Marblehead	238	15	Arbuncle	William		1		1		1	1		1	1			6		
Salem	221	11	Archer	Bena	1			1		3			1				6		
Salem	212	46	Archer	Bethiah		1							1				2		
Salem	217	11	Archer	Edwd	1			1		1			1				4		
Salem	216	16	Archer	Hannah			1				2		1				4		
Salem	212	9	Archer	James	1			1					1				3		
Salem	212	44	Archer	James	1	1		1		2			1				6		
Salem	216	8	Archer	Jona	2	3		1		4	2	1	1				14		
Salem	205	41	Archer	Joseph			1			1		1					3		
Salem	190	9	Archer	Nath			1			1			1				3		
Salem	190	34	Archer	Nathl		1				1		1					3		
Salem	215	51	Archer	Rebecca		1	2			1							4		
Salem	192	33	Archer	Samuel	1	2	1			1	1	1	1				8		
Salem	209	25	Archer	Samuel	1			1			1		1				4		
Salem	215	50	Archer	Samuel 3d	1	1		1		4			1				8		
Salem	190	22	Archer	Sarah							1		1				2		
Salem	201	32	Arington	James	2			1		1		1					5		
Salem	207	41	Arne	William	1	3	3	1		2		2					12		
Beverly	291	7	Arnold	Robert Negro											4		4		
Salem	208	38	Arter	John			1			1	1	1					4		
Salem	211	23	Arter	Mary						1			1				2		
Newburyport	157	19	Arther	Wilson	1		1					1					3		
Newburyport	157	16	Ash	Nathaniel			1					1					2		
Salem	214	27	Ashby	Benja	1		1				2		1				5		
Salem	214	29	Ashby	David		1	1			1		1					4		
Salem	201	11	Ashby	Jona	2	1		1		1		1					6		
Salem	191	20	Ashby	Martha		1	1			1			1				4		
Salem	216	22	Ashby	Thos	2			1		3		1	1				8		
Marblehead	238	17	Ashton	Benjamin		1				1		1					3		
Marblehead	238	16	Ashton	Hannah								1	1				2		
Salem	207	6	Ashton	Jacob		1	2	1		3	2	1	1				11		
Beverly	300	24	Ashton	John		1		1		2			1				5		
Marblehead	238	18	Ashton	Mary									1				1		
Salem	191	41	Ashton	Mary							1	1	1				3		
Marblehead	238	20	Ashton	Philip	2	1		1		2			1				7		
Marblehead	268	3	Ashton	Philip				1					1				2		
Lynn	226	43	Ashton	Saml		1	1					1					3		
Marblehead	238	13	Ashton	Samuel		1	2	1		2	1	1	1				9		
Marblehead	259	14	Ashton	Sarah		1	1			2		1	1				6		
Marblehead	238	5	Ashton	William		1						1					2		
Salem	183	4	Aspinwall	Ellis				1		1							2		
Salem	188	13	Aspinwall	John	2			1		1	2		1				7		
Gloucester	62	24	Atkins	Benja	1		1				1		1				4		
Marblehead	238	7	Atkins	Elizaneth		1	2					1					4		

156

TOWN	PG#	LN#	LAST NAME	FIRST NAME	FREE WHITE MALES					FREE WHITE FEMALES					TOTAL ALL OTHER	TOTAL SLAVES	TOTALS	DISTRICT/ TOWNSHIP	NOTES
					under 10	10 to 16	16 to 26	26 to 45	45 and over	under 10	10 to 16	16 to 26	26 to 45	45 and over					
Gloucester	65	10	Atkins	John			1					1		1			3		
Gloucester	74	25	Atkins	John				1						1			2		
Marblehead	238	6	Atkins	Joseph			1						1				2		
Newburyport	157	22	Atkins	Mary						1			3				4		
Marblehead	238	23	Atkins	Robert		1	1	1				1		1			5		
Salem	213	12	Atkins	William	4	2		1				1		1			9		
Newbury	110	7	Atkinson	Amos	1	4	4		1	1		1		1			13		
Salem	189	19	Atkinson	Hannah							3		1	1			5		
Newbury	110	39	Atkinson	Ichobed				1			1	1					3		
Newbury	110	35	Atkinson	John	1	1	1				1	2		1			8		
Salem	204	9	Atkinson	Joseph		1	1		1	1		1	2	1			8		
Newbury	109	44	Atkinson	Matthias		1			1			2		1			5		
Newbury	110	8	Atkinson	Moses	1		1		1				2				5		
Newbury	113	30	Atkinson	Richard	1		1			1		1					4		
Newbury	110	14	Atkinson	Theodore	1	1	1			1		1					5		
Newbury	111	28	Atkinson	Theodore	1	1	1			1			1				5		
Bradford	124	34	Attwood	Jesse	1	2			1				2				6		
Bradford	124	44	Attwood	Simon	2			1		1			1				5		
Bradford	124	6	Attwood	William				1						1			2		
Salem	216	5	Atwell	Ebenz	2		1	1				1					5		
Salem	220	28	Atwell	Josiah	1		1				1		2				5		
Lynn	229	10	Atwill	Joanne				1			1	1					3		
Lynn	227	21	Atwill	John D	2		1	1		1	1	1					7		
Lynn	230	30	Atwill	Nathan	1	1	2		1	1			1	1			8		
Lynn	224	29	Atwill	Zacheus	3	1	3	1		1	2		1				12		
Haverhill	142	21	Atwood	Abijah		2			1	1	1		1				6		
Newburyport	157	13	Atwood	John		1	1	1	1	1	1	1	1				8		
Haverhill	142	11	Atwood	Joseph				1		3				1			5		
Newburyport	157	14	Atwood	Margaret Wid	2							1	1				4		
Haverhill	142	10	Atwood	Moses	1		1	2		5	2		2				13		
Newburyport	157	21	Aubin	Nathaniel			2		1	2			1	1			7		
Newburyport	157	2	Aubin	Philip	1	2			1	1			1	1			7		
Salem	208	25	Augustus	Samson											3		3		
Methuen	152	1	Austin	Isaac	2	1			1	2		2	1				9		
Andover	89	4	Austin	John	1			1		4			1				7		
Salem	195	26	Austin	Josiah	1		2	2	1			3	1		1		11		
Salem	198	35	Austin	Richard	1		1	1		1		1					5		
Andover	89	5	Austin	Samuel	1			1					1				3		
Topsfield	20	22	Averell	Azariah			1			1			1				3		
Topsfield	20	19	Averell	Daniel				1					1	1			3		
Topsfield	20	20	Averell	Daniel Junr	2			1					1	1			5		
Topsfield	21	11	Averell	Elijah				1		2	1		1				5		
Topsfield	20	16	Averell	Isaac		1	1	1			1			1			5		
Topsfield	20	17	Averell	Jacob				1					1	1			3		
Middleton	16	36	Averell	Joseph	1	1	3		1	1	1	1		1			10		
Middleton	16	35	Averell	Mark	1		1		2					2			6		
Topsfield	20	21	Averell	Nathaniel		1	1		1			2		1			6		
Topsfield	20	12	Averell	Nathaniel P.	2		1			2	1		1	1			8		
Topsfield	20	15	Averell	Sarah								1		2			3		
Topsfield	20	18	Averell	Solomon	1			1		1			1				4		
Andover	90	4	Averil	Paul		1	1		1	2			1	1			7		
Ipswich	277	54	Averill	Benjamin	1			1		1			1				4		
Beverly	298	2	Averit	Sarah								1	1	1			3		
Haverhill	142	15	Ayer	James	2				1	1	2	1	1				8		
Haverhill	142	16	Ayer	James	2				1	1	2	1	1				8		
Haverhill	142	9	Ayer	James 3d	1		1	1		1	1	1					6		
Haverhill	142	4	Ayer	James Jun	3	2		2		1	1	1	1				11		
Haverhill	142	7	Ayer	John		1		1		1	1		1	2			7		
Haverhill	142	19	Ayer	John	3	1	1		1	1	1						8		
Haverhill	142	17	Ayer	Jonathan	1		1	1	1		2	1		1			8		
Haverhill	142	18	Ayer	Mary	1				1			1		1			4		
Haverhill	142	13	Ayer	Moses	1	2						2		1			7		
Haverhill	142	8	Ayer	Nathan	1		1		2	2		2	1				9		
Haverhill	142	14	Ayer	Obadiah		1	1		1	2	1	2	1				9		
Haverhill	142	22	Ayer	Peter	3			1		2	1		1				8		
Haverhill	142	3	Ayer	Samuel	1	2	1		1	2	1	1					10		
Haverhill	142	23	Ayer	Simon		1	1		2	1	3			2			10		
Haverhill	142	20	Ayer	Timothy	2		2						1				5		
Gloucester	56	6	Ayers	Abigal Widw	2					1	1		1	1			6		
Salem	215	35	Ayers	Eliza							2			1			3		
Manchester	49	10	Ayers	John	4			1		2	1		1				9		
Manchester	55	4	Ayers	Lydia Wo		1		1			1	1		1			5		
Newburyport	157	18	Ayers	Richard					1					1			2		
Salem	217	12	Babbidge	Ben	1			1			1	1	1				5		
Salem	220	29	Babbidge	Chrisr	2		1	1		2			1				7		
Salem	212	19	Babbige	John	2	2	2	1		3			1				11		
Salem	212	20	Babbige	Susanna								1		1			2		
Manchester	50	12	Babcock	Jno	1			1		1			1				4		
Manchester	50	13	Babcock	Josh			1	1						1			3		
Manchester	53	21	Babcock	Nicholas		1							1				2		
Manchester	53	10	Babcock	Thomas Jun		1				1		1					3		
Manchester	50	7	Babcock	Thos		1	2		1	1	1			1			7		

TOWN	PG#	LN#	LAST NAME	FIRST NAME	FREE WHITE MALES under 10	10 to 16	16 to 26	26 to 45	45 and over	FREE WHITE FEMALES under 10	10 to 16	16 to 26	26 to 45	45 and over	TOTAL ALL OTHER	TOTAL SLAVES	TOTALS	DISTRICT/ TOWNSHIP	NOTES
Manchester	49	17	Babcock	William	2			1					1				4		
Beverly	293	18	Babsob	Ruth						1			1				2		
Gloucester	68	8	Babson	Charles			1					1					2		
Gloucester	77	27	Babson	David			1	1					1	1			4		
Gloucester	58	31	Babson	Dolly Wo			1						2	1			4		
Beverly	306	23	Babson	Eleanor										1			1		
Gloucester	69	22	Babson	Hanh Wo		1	2			1	1			1			6		
Gloucester	72	6	Babson	Hannah Wo		1	1					1		1			4		
Gloucester	69	21	Babson	Joseph	1		2						1				4		
Newburyport	159	39	Babson	Joseph		2		1		2				1			7		
Gloucester	71	18	Babson	Mary Wo		1						2		1			4		
Gloucester	63	17	Babson	Samuel Cap		1	1					1		1			4	East Ward	
Gloucester	73	22	Babson	Willa	1	1	2		1	2	1	1		1			10	Squam Parish	
Salem	207	61	Bacall	Samuel			1					2		1			4		
Salisbury	25	6	Bachelder	Israel		1						1					2		
Haverhill	143	42	Bacheldor	William	2	1		1		2	1	3		1			11		
Lynn	232	1	Bacheller	Henry				1					1				2		
Lynn	232	3	Bacheller	Henry Jr			1			1		1					3		
Lynn	224	22	Bacheller	James	3	1		1		2		1					8		
Lynn	225	25	Bacheller	Rufus	1		1					1					3		
Lynn	224	23	Bacheller	Samll	2	2	1	1		1		1	1				9		
Lynn	225	14	Bacheller	Theoph	1	1			1	2	1	1	1				8		
Salem	196	30	Bacon	Jacob				1			1		1				3		
Salem	193	33	Bacon	Joseph	1			1									2		
Bradford	124	39	Bacon	Josiah				1					1	1			3		
Salem	202	38	Bacon	Ruth						2			1				3		
Marblehead	245	35	Bacon	William				1						1			2		
Haverhill	143	33	Badger	Abigail						1			1				2		
Amesbury	35	7	Badger	John		1	1	1	1	1				1			6		
Amesbury	36	21	Badger	Obadiah		1	1		1				1	1			5		
Amesbury	35	12	Bagley	David	3		1	1		1		1		1			8		
Amesbury	35	9	Bagley	Enoch			2	1	1		1	3		1			9		
Amesbury	35	16	Bagley	Isaac	1		1	1				1	1	1			6		
Amesbury	35	13	Bagley	Jacob Capt	4	1		1		1	1		1				9		
Amesbury	35	5	Bagley	Jeremiah	1		1			1		1	1				5		
Salisbury	25	7	Bagley	John Capt	1		1			2	1	1					6		
Amesbury	36	26	Bagley	Orlando			2	1				1		1			5		
Newburyport	159	32	Bagley	Philip	1	2	2	2		1		1	1	2			12		
Amesbury	36	28	Bagley	Sargent	1		2		1			1		1			6		
Salisbury	24	8	Bagley	Seth	1	1			1		1			1			5		
Salisbury	24	7	Bagley	Stephen	2	1		1		3	1		1				9		
Salisbury	24	9	Bagley	Thomas	1	1		1						1			4		
Salisbury	24	10	Bagley	True				1					1	2			4		
Amesbury	36	30	Bagley	Vallentine Capt	1			1		1	1						4		
Rowley	127	41	Bailey	Asa	3	1		1			1		1				7		
Haverhill	143	22	Bailey	Benjm	1		2		2		1	1	1	1			9		
Andover	91	26	Bailey	Daniel	1		2	1		3	1		1				9		
Ipswich	273	4	Bailey	Hannah								2	1				3		
Salem	217	27	Bailey	Jacob	1			1		1			1				4		
Andover	91	18	Bailey	James	3	1		1		1	1		1				8		
Marblehead	244	15	Bailey	John	2	1		1		1		1	1	1			8		
Haverhill	143	46	Bailey	Jonathan	1	1		1	1	3			1	1			9		
Andover	91	20	Bailey	Joshua	1			1		1			1				4		
Haverhill	143	45	Bailey	Lewis	3	3			2	2			1				11		
Andover	91	27	Bailey	Luther		1		1		1	1		1				5		
Andover	91	15	Bailey	Moses		1	2	1		1	1		2				8		
Haverhill	143	17	Bailey	Nathan		1		1	1	1			1				5		
Haverhill	143	41	Bailey	Nathan Jun	1			1		1			1				4		
Haverhill	143	21	Bailey	Nathll		1				2			1				4		
Ipswich	273	3	Bailey	Peirce	2			1		1		1	1				6		
Andover	91	24	Bailey	Samuel	2			1		1			1				5		
Salem	220	17	Bailey	Thos	2			1		1		1					5		
Andover	91	16	Bailey	William		1	1		1	1	1	1		1			7		
Ipswich	280	16	Baker	Allen	1	2	1		1		1	2	1	1			10		
Ipswich	278	37	Baker	Asa	1	2	1		1		3	1	1				11		
Beverly	305	5	Baker	Belle			1			1			2				5		
Wenham	309	10	Baker	Cornelus	1		1		1		1		1	1			6		
Lynn	223	42	Baker	Elisha				1		1		1					3		
Beverly	290	13	Baker	Eunice	1	1				1			1				4		
Ipswich	278	43	Baker	Eunice									2	1			3		
Lynn	223	38	Baker	Ezra	1			1					1				3		
Lynn	223	41	Baker	Ezra	1			1					1				3		
Marblehead	262	3	Baker	Hannah	1	1						2		1			52		
Hamilton	285	23	Baker	James		1	2						1				4		
Salisbury	24	18	Baker	James		1		1		1			1				4		
Manchester	50	1	Baker	Jemima Wo		1					1			1			3		
Beverly	305	35	Baker	John	1	1		1		1	2	1	1				8		
Ipswich	280	17	Baker	John		2			1	1	1	2		1			8		
Manchester	50	8	Baker	John			1		1				1	1			4		
Salem	216	12	Baker	John	1			1		1			1				4		
Topsfield	19	12	Baker	John			1	1				2		1			5		
Wenham	309	11	Baker	John	1			1		1		1		1			5		

TOWN	PG#	LN#	LAST NAME	FIRST NAME	FREE WHITE MALES under 10	10 to 16	16 to 26	26 to 45	45 and over	FREE WHITE FEMALES under 10	10 to 16	16 to 26	26 to 45	45 and over	TOTAL ALL OTHER	TOTAL SLAVES	TOTALS	DISTRICT/ TOWNSHIP	NOTES
Ipswich	276	9	Baker	John Junr		1		1					2				4		
Haverhill	143	16	Baker	Jonathan					1					2			3		
Beverly	296	5	Baker	Joseph		1		1					1				3		
Gloucester	75	22	Baker	Joseph	2		1	1					1	1			6		
Manchester	55	10	Baker	Joseph	1		1					1					3		
Beverly	296	10	Baker	Lucy	1	1				1			1				4		
Gloucester	70	10	Baker	Martha Wo			2					2	1				5		
Ipswich	278	44	Baker	Mary	3		2			1	1	1					8		
Newburyport	160	18	Baker	Mary Wdo	1								1				2		
Salem	217	10	Baker	Mehit L									1				1		
Hamilton	285	44	Baker	Moses	1	1		1		4	2		1		4		14		
Beverly	306	29	Baker	Robert				1	1	1		3					6		
Ipswich	273	20	Baker	Robert	1			1		1			2				5		
Beverly	306	32	Baker	Robert Jun	1		1					1					3		
Ipswich	274	34	Baker	Samuel	1		1		1	1	1	2	1				8		
Salisbury	24	4	Baker	Samuel Junr	3			1		1			1				6		
Salisbury	24	17	Baker	Samuel Junr				1					1				2		
Ipswich	274	29	Baker	Sarah	1							1	1				3		
Ipswich	274	26	Baker	Stephen			1			1		1					3		
Andover	91	14	Baker	Symonds			1		1			1	1		1		5		
Newburyport	160	16	Baker	Thomas		1	2						1				4		
Newburyport	160	17	Baker	Thomas H				1					1				2		
Newburyport	160	19	Baker	Zacheriah	2		4	5	1	2	2		1	1			18		
Andover	90	36	Balard	Hezekiah	1	1		1	1	2	1		1	1			9		
Newburyport	158	30	Balch	Benjamin				1			1		1				3		
Newburyport	158	32	Balch	Daniel	2	2		1				3		1			9		
Topsfield	18	16	Balch	Daniel			1				1		1				3		
Newburyport	158	34	Balch	Daniel Wido of			1						1				2		
Topsfield	19	17	Balch	David	1	1		1	1	2			1				7		
Topsfield	19	18	Balch	Esther										1			1		
Newburyport	158	31	Balch	John		1	1	2	2	5	2	3	1	1			18		
Topsfield	18	9	Balch	John		1	1		1	1		2		1			7		
Bradford	125	6	Balch	Jonathan	2			1		1		1	1				6		
Beverly	305	3	Balch	Joshua				1				1	2				4		
Topsfield	21	28	Balch	Joshua			1	1			1		1				4		
Topsfield	18	8	Balch	Roger	1			1				1			1		4		
Salisbury	25	11	Balch	Samuel	2	1		1		2			1				7		
Topsfield	21	27	Balch	Thomas		1	1	1					1				4		
Newburyport	158	33	Balch	Thomas H				1		2	1		1				5		
Haverhill	143	31	Balch	Wesley	2		1	1		1		2					7		
Bradford	126	16	Balch	William		1	1		1			1	1	2			7		
Salem	213	42	Baldwin	Abigail			1			1				1	1		4		
Newburyport	160	31	Baldwin	Ann Wdo	1					2	1		1				5		
Salem	197	3	Baldwin	Loammi	1		1					1					3		
Newburyport	160	24	Balentine	Robert	2			1		1			1				5		
Newbury	119	42	Baley	Abner		1	1	1			1		1				5		
Newbury	119	43	Baley	Abner	2		1	1		1		2	1				8		
Newbury	107	35	Baley	Daniel	1		1		1	3	2	1	1				10		
Amesbury	35	4	Baley	James	2	2	3		1		1		1				10		
Gloucester	78	8	Baley	Joseph	2	1		1			1		1	1			7		
Gloucester	71	9	Baley	Lucy Wo			1						1				2		
Gloucester	63	1	Baley	Nathl				1		1				1			3	West Ward	
Gloucester	84	1	Ball	Isaac				1					1				2		
Newbury	114	16	Ball	James	3			1		2		1	1				8		
Marblehead	259	15	Ball	John				1				1	1				3		
Marblehead	258	29	Ball	Nancy							1		1				2		
Salem	212	15	Ball	William	2	1	1	1		2		1					8		
Gloucester	85	27	Ballard	Daniel			1					1					2		
Haverhill	143	20	Ballard	Ebenzr				1					1				2		
Lynn	232	18	Ballard	John				1	1				1				3	West Parish	
Lynn	226	10	Ballard	Mary & Mary Tuffts				1			1		2				4		
Andover	91	19	Ballard	Timothy	2	1		1	1	1	1	4	1	1	1		13		
Middleton	17	22	Bancroft	Abigail							1	1					2		
Salem	193	43	Bancroft	Daniel	1	1	1	1	1	4	2	3		1			15		
Lynn	232	41	Bancroft	Ebenz	2	1	3				1	1					8	West Parish	
Lynnfield	236	20	Bancroft	James				1					1				2		
Salem	194	1	Bancroft	Job		2				1		1		1			5		
Lynnfield	236	18	Bancroft	Nathl		1		1				2	1				5		
Lynnfield	237	1	Bancroft	Thos	4		1	1		1		1	1				9		
Salem	209	37	Bancroft	Thos	1	1		1				2		1			6		
Salem	199	22	Bancroft	William	3	1		1		1		1	1				8		
Newburyport	159	25	Banford	Joseph				1			2		1				4		
Lynn	227	14	Banup	Rufus L.	1		2			1			1				5		
Newburyport	160	27	Barbe	Wyatt S		1			1			1		1			4		
Newburyport	159	18	Barber	Daniel				1				1	1				3		
Marblehead	268	32	Barber	Martha	2							1		1			4		
Haverhill	143	39	Barber	Samuel		1		1				2	1				5		
Marblehead	244	22	Barjona	Cato											4		4		
Methuen	152	16	Barker	Amos	1		2	1				1	1				6		
Marblehead	262	2	Barker	Charity									1				1		
Methuen	152	17	Barker	Ebenezer			1	1				1	1				4		
Marblehead	259	13	Barker	Francis	1	2		1				1					5		
Marblehead	261	30	Barker	George	2			1			1	1					5		

159

TOWN	PG#	LN#	LAST NAME	FIRST NAME	FREE WHITE MALES under 10	10 to 16	16 to 26	26 to 45	45 and over	FREE WHITE FEMALES under 10	10 to 16	16 to 26	26 to 45	45 and over	TOTAL ALL OTHER	TOTAL SLAVES	TOTALS	DISTRICT/ TOWNSHIP	NOTES
Newburyport	159	33	Barker	George				1						1			2		
Marblehead	269	7	Barker	Hannah	1					1			1	1			4		
Andover	90	37	Barker	Henry Gray	1		1	1			1		1				5		
Andover	90	25	Barker	Isaac	1		1	1		3		1	1				8		
Andover	90	24	Barker	John	2		1		1	2	2	2		1			11		
Salem	218	34	Barker	John			5	1		2	1	1	1				11		
Methuen	152	18	Barker	John				1		2				1			4		
Marblehead	262	1	Barker	Joseph		1		1		4	1	1	1				9		
Andover	90	20	Barker	Mehetabel										2			2		
Andover	90	26	Barker	Mehetabel Wid	1	1						1	2	2			7		
Andover	90	27	Barker	Nathan	1	1		1		1	1	1					7		
Gloucester	58	35	Barker	Nathll	2			1		1			2	1			7		
Andover	90	21	Barker	Phinehas			2		1		1			1			5		
Andover	91	31	Barker	Richard				1									1		
Marblehead	259	12	Barker	Ruth										3			3		
Amesbury	36	27	Barker	Samuel	2	1		1		1	2		1				8		
Andover	91	6	Barker	Samuel			1	1	1			1	1	1			6		
Andover	90	35	Barker	Sarah										2			2		
Marblehead	245	6	Barker	Sarah	1							1		1			3		
Andover	90	22	Barker	Stephen	3	1	1	1	1		1	1	1				11		
Methuen	152	15	Barker	Stephen	2	1		1		2		1	1				9		
Marblehead	262	4	Barker	Thomas			1		1		2	2		1			7		
Newbury	116	8	Bartlett	Joseph			1	1					2	1			5		
Ipswich	275	58	Barley	Abigail									1				1		
Amesbury	36	23	Barnard	Daniel				1				1					2		
Salem	215	22	Barnard	Edwd			1	1					1				3		
Marblehead	267	8	Barnard	Hannah	1					1	1		1				4		
Amesbury	36	20	Barnard	Isaac			1	1				2		1			5		
Amesbury	36	24	Barnard	Jacob	1		1			1	1			1			5		
Andover	91	13	Barnard	James	2		2	1		1			2	1			9		
Amesbury	36	18	Barnard	John	1		2	1		1		2		1			8		
Andover	90	29	Barnard	John		1		1					1	1			4		
Andover	91	28	Barnard	John Jr	5			1					1				7		
Amesbury	36	17	Barnard	Jona				1					1				2		
Amesbury	36	16	Barnard	Jona Capt	1	1		1		1	1		1				6		
Amesbury	36	22	Barnard	Joseph	1			1		3			1	1			7		
Amesbury	35	14	Barnard	Mary Wid									1				1		
Andover	91	30	Barnard	Mehetabel									1				1		
Amesbury	35	6	Barnard	Molly Wid						2	1	1		1			5		
Salem	209	19	Barnard	Samuel		1	1	1		1	1	1					6		
Haverhill	143	11	Barnard	Sarah									1	1			2		
Salem	195	25	Barnard	Thos		1		1				1	1	1			5		
Amesbury	36	15	Barnard	Willm	1	1		1					1				5		
Marblehead	253	19	Barnes	Nancy						1		1					2		
Marblehead	267	12	Barnes	Peter W.	2	1			1	1	2	2		1			10		
Salem	210	25	Barnes	Thos			2		1	3	1		1	1			9		
Marblehead	267	13	Barnes	Woodin	1			1		1			1				4		
Salem	219	23	Barns	Lucy											3		3		
Ipswich	279	61	Barnsdale	John			1	1						2			4		
Andover	91	5	Barnum	Thaddeus		1		1				1					3		
Salem	202	18	Barr	Arch	1			1			2	1	1				6		
Salem	203	25	Barr	James				1		1	3	3	1	1			10		
Salem	203	33	Barr	James				1					1				2		
Salem	189	3	Barr	John	2			1		2	1	1	1				8		
Salem	188	21	Barr	William	3			1		4			1				9		
Salem	209	35	Barr	Robt	3			1					1				5		
Salem	210	51	Barras	Peter		1		1		1		1	1				5		
Beverly	303	39	Barrett	Thomas		1		1		3		1	1				7		
Gloucester	63	11	Barrett	William	2			1		1			1				5	West Ward	
Newburyport	160	25	Barrett	William	1	1	1	1		3	1	1	1				10		
Salem	217	38	Barry	Abigail							1		1				2		
Salem	209	11	Barry	John	1	1	1					1					4		
Salem	207	39	Barthman	Zacha	1		3	1	1		2	1		1			10		
Salem	204	35	Bartholomew	Benja	1	1		1		1			1	1			6		
Newburyport	158	17	Bartlet	Abel	1	1	2	1		3		1	1	1			11		
Salem	211	9	Bartlet	Cornielius	2		1	1		1			1	1			7		
Newburyport	158	12	Bartlet	Edmond		1		1		1			1				4		
Salisbury	25	8	Bartlet	John	1	1	1		1	1	1	1	1				8		
Newburyport	158	13	Bartlet	Richard	1		2	1		2	1		2				9		
Newburyport	158	14	Bartlet	Richard Jr	1					1	1	1	1				6		
Salem	215	2	Bartlet	Robt	2			1					1				4		
Newburyport	158	19	Bartlet	Samuel		1	3					2					6		
Beverly	302	20	Bartlet	Sipio											1		1		
Newburyport	158	18	Bartlet	Stephen		1	2	1				2	1				7		
Newburyport	158	15	Bartlet	William		2	4	1			1	2	1				11		
Newburyport	158	16	Bartlet	William Jr			1				1						2		
Marblehead	262	5	Bartlett	Abijah	2		1	1		2			1	1			8		
Haverhill	143	9	Bartlett	Bailey	3			1		4	3	1	1				13		
Andover	91	29	Bartlett	Daniel		2				1	1	1					5		
Methuen	152	23	Bartlett	Daniel	1		1	1					2				5		
Newbury	118	17	Bartlett	David	3			1			2		1				7		
Amesbury	36	2	Bartlett	Enoch	3		2	1			1		1				8		
Newbury	108	1	Bartlett	Enos			1	1		1			1	1			5		

160

TOWN	PG#	LN#	LAST NAME	FIRST NAME	FREE WHITE MALES					FREE WHITE FEMALES					TOTAL ALL OTHER	TOTAL SLAVES	TOTALS	DISTRICT/ TOWNSHIP	NOTES
					under 10	10 to 16	16 to 26	26 to 45	45 and over	under 10	10 to 16	16 to 26	26 to 45	45 and over					
Marblehead	251	6	Bartlett	Hannah	1	1				1			1				4		
Newbury	118	13	Bartlett	Hannah	2		1			1			1				5		
Amesbury	36	25	Bartlett	Hannah Wid			1						2	1			4		
Newbury	109	27	Bartlett	Humphrey	2	1		1		1			1				6		
Newbury	118	19	Bartlett	Isaac	1	1			1			1	2	2			8		
Haverhill	143	10	Bartlett	Israel	1	1	3		1			1		2	1		10		
Amesbury	36	12	Bartlett	Jacob	3	1		1		1				1			7		
Newbury	109	28	Bartlett	Jacob			1					1		1			3		
Amesbury	36	11	Bartlett	John			1		1				1	1			4		
Haverhill	143	28	Bartlett	John	3			1		1	1		1				7		
Marblehead	245	10	Bartlett	John	2	1			1	1			2	1			8		
Marblehead	255	8	Bartlett	John	1			1		1			1				4		
Newbury	118	16	Bartlett	John					2	1	1		1	2			7		
Newbury	108	8	Bartlett	Jonas			1						1	1			3		
Marblehead	254	12	Bartlett	Jonathan					1	1	2	1		1			6		
Amesbury	36	13	Bartlett	Joseph			1	2		1			1	1			6		
Newbury	109	29	Bartlett	Joseph			1			3			1				5		
Newbury	116	10	Bartlett	Joseph		1	1	1	1	5	1		1	1			12		
Newbury	116	19	Bartlett	Josiah		1	1	1				1	1	1			6		
Marblehead	242	28	Bartlett	Mary			1						1	1			3		
Newbury	109	26	Bartlett	Moses			1	1		1			1	1			5		
Amesbury	35	15	Bartlett	Nathan	2	1	1					1	1	1			7		
Haverhill	144	1	Bartlett	Nathll	1				1	1	1		1				5		
Newbury	109	25	Bartlett	Nehemiah	2		1			2			1	1			7		
Marblehead	262	7	Bartlett	Nicholas	2	1			1	1	2	2	1				10		
Amesbury	35	8	Bartlett	Nicholus		1	1		1	1			1				5		
Amesbury	36	10	Bartlett	Rachel Wid	1							1	1				3		
Amesbury	35	17	Bartlett	Ruth Wid									1	2			3		
Amesbury	35	18	Bartlett	Samuel	1		1						1				3		
Marblehead	262	6	Bartlett	Thomas	3	1		1		1			1				7		
Salem	211	29	Bartlett	Walter P				1			1	1		1			4		
Marblehead	265	33	Bartlett	William		1	1		1		1	1		1			6		
Marblehead	267	18	Bartlett	William	1	2	2	1		3			1				10		
Amesbury	35	10	Bartlett	Wm Capt			1			2	1		1				5		
Marblehead	242	2	Bartoll	Sally						1		1					2		
Marblehead	239	19	Bartoll	Samuel	1	1		1		1	1	1					6		
Marblehead	240	24	Bartoll	William	1		1		1	3	2			1			9		
Salem	208	19	Barton	Margaret			1				1	1	1	1			5		
Marblehead	247	1	Barton	Susannah			1							1			2		
Newburyport	158	3	Bass	Edward Jr	1		1						2				4		
Newburyport	158	2	Bass	Edward R.R. Bishop				1					3		1		5		
Marblehead	257	34	Basset	Michael	2		1							1			4		
Newburyport	160	4	Bassett	Christopher	1		1					2	1	1			6		
Newburyport	160	3	Bassett	Christopher Jr			1							1			2		
Lynn	226	22	Bassett	Isaac	2		3	1	1	1	1			1			10		
Marblehead	239	12	Bassett	John			1			1		1					3		
Lynn	226	23	Bassett	Neheh		1		1						2			4		
Gloucester	76	17	Bassett	Sarah Wo	1							1	1				3		
Salem	201	21	Basson	Patty			1						1	1			3		
Methuen	152	24	Baswell	Joshua	2		1						1				4		
Wenham	309	33	Batchelder	Amos				1			1			1			3		
Beverly	305	37	Batchelder	Anna									1	1			2		
Beverly	295	37	Batchelder	Asa	1	2		1		2	1	1	1				9		
Danvers	10	11	Batchelder	Asa			1			3			1				5		
Beverly	305	43	Batchelder	Cornelius	2			1		1			1				5		
Wenham	309	21	Batchelder	Edmond	2			1		1	1		1				6		
Beverly	290	28	Batchelder	Eliza	1					1			1				3		
Danvers	5	22	Batchelder	Ezra Junr	2	1		1		1			1				6		
Danvers	5	24	Batchelder	Ezra Junr	1	1	2	1	1	1			1	1			9		
Beverly	304	8	Batchelder	Hannah										1			1		
Beverly	305	36	Batchelder	James				1						1			2		
Beverly	305	27	Batchelder	John				1				1		1			3		
Topsfield	20	3	Batchelder	John		1		1						1			3		
Beverly	306	25	Batchelder	John Jr		1		1			1	2		1			6		
Topsfield	20	11	Batchelder	John Junr			1			1			1				3		
Beverly	290	7	Batchelder	Joseph	2		1						1				4		
Topsfield	20	10	Batchelder	Joseph	2		1				1		1				5		
Beverly	289	13	Batchelder	Josiah Esq				1					1	1	1		4		
Beverly	289	14	Batchelder	Josiah Jr			1			1			1				3		
Beverly	293	38	Batchelder	Mehitable										2			2		
Beverly	292	15	Batchelder	Nathanl	3	1	1	1		1	1		1		1		10		
Newburyport	159	23	Batchelder	Samuel				1				2		1			4		
Wenham	309	17	Batchelder	Samuel			1					1	1				3		
Beverly	293	33	Batchelder	William	3			1		1	3		1				9		
Beverly	293	37	Batchelder	Zachariah	1	2		1		4			1				9		
Salem	195	18	Batcheldor	Nathl	1			1		3			1	1			7		
Salem	218	44	Bateman	Mich		1		1		2	1		1	1			7		
Gloucester	63	19	Bates	Henry	1			1		1	1		1				5	East Ward	
Rowley	131	47	Batice	Robert	1		1			1		1	1				5		
Lynn	232	12	Battees	John				1					1	2			4		
Gloucester	85	13	Batten	Ebenz		2		1		1		1	2	1			8		
Gloucester	84	30	Batten	Rolen		1						1					2		
Salem	217	37	Batten	Sarah						1			1				2		
Marblehead	256	22	Battes	John Jr			1			2			1	1			5		

TOWN	PG#	LN#	LAST NAME	FIRST NAME	FWM under 10	FWM 10 to 16	FWM 16 to 26	FWM 26 to 45	FWM 45 and over	FWF under 10	FWF 10 to 16	FWF 16 to 26	FWF 26 to 45	FWF 45 and over	TOTAL ALL OTHER	TOTAL SLAVES	TOTALS	DISTRICT/ TOWNSHIP	NOTES
Lynn	233	9	Batts	John	1	1			1	2			1				6		
Lynn	233	10	Batts	John Junr	5		1	1	1	1			1				10		
Rowley	131	2	Bayley	Abner			2	1					1	3			7		
Newbury	107	36	Bayley	Anna									1	1			2		
Newbury	106	45	Bayley	Asa		1	1		2			2	1				7		
Newbury	108	21	Bayley	Edward	1	1		1	1	2		1		1			8		
Newburyport	158	25	Bayley	Elizabeth Wido						1	1			1			3		
Newbury	106	42	Bayley	Ephraim			1			1	2		1				5		
Newbury	107	34	Bayley	Esther		1						1		1			3		
Newbury	106	41	Bayley	Ezekiel				2			1	4					7		
Newbury	107	9	Bayley	John		1	2	1			1		1				6		
Rowley	129	3	Bayley	John		1		1		1	1		1				5		
Bradford	126	4	Bayley	Jonathan		1		1					1				3		
Newbury	107	32	Bayley	Joshua				2					1				3		
Bradford	124	31	Bayley	Moses		1				1							2		
Newbury	107	33	Bayley	Moses	1			1				1	1				4		
Newburyport	158	23	Bayley	Nathaniel			1			1			1				3		
Newbury	107	48	Bayley	Paul	1	2		1			1		1				6		
Newbury	106	40	Bayley	Samuel				1				1		3			5		
Newbury	106	44	Bayley	Samuel	2		1			2			1				6		
Newburyport	158	21	Bayley	Samuel			1	1				1	1				4		
Newbury	107	38	Bayley	Stephen	1	1		1		2		2	1				8		
Newburyport	158	24	Bayley	Stephen			1			1		1					3		
Newburyport	158	26	Bayley	Thomas	2		1	1				1	1				6		
Bradford	126	6	Bayley	William			1						1				2		
Newburyport	158	22	Bayley	William			1			2			2	3			8		
Newburyport	158	27	Bayley	William Wido of	2								1				3		
Salisbury	24	1	Beach	James				1		1			1				3		
Salem	219	7	Beadle	Susanna										1			1		
Ipswich	275	38	Beal	Mary									1	1			2		
Marblehead	248	25	Beal	Mary	2	1				1			1				5		
Marblehead	242	26	Bean	James			1			1			1				3		
Salem	219	47	Bean	sarah									1				1		
Marblehead	259	18	Bean	William	1	1		1		2	2	1		1			9		
Manchester	49	21	Beare	Sarah Wo									1	1			2		
Salem	220	48	Beaten	John			1						1				2		
Salisbury	24	12	Beattie	Andrew Revd			1			1		1	1				4		
Newburyport	158	28	Beck	Jonathan				1				1	1				3		
Newburyport	158	29	Beck	Jonathan Jr	3	1	2	1		2		1	1				11		
Salem	218	18	Becket	Benja	2		1			1			1				5		
Salem	220	47	Becket	James	1	1	1	1		2	2		1				9		
Salem	220	40	Becket	John		1	2	1		2	1	1					8		
Salem	220	51	Becket	Retier	1	1	9	1				1	2				15		
Salem	216	41	Becket	Mary			1			1			1				3		
Salem	215	13	Beckett	William			1			1			1				3		
Beverly	289	18	Beckford	Benjamin		2	2	1		2	1	1	1				10		
Salem	194	29	Beckford	David	2		1			1			1				5		
Salem	203	22	Beckford	Ebenezer		2		1				1	1	1			6		
Beverly	290	12	Beckford	Elizabeth			1							1			2		
Salem	217	2	Beckford	Jona				1		1		1	1				4		
Salem	194	26	Beckford	Joshua	1		1			1		1	1				5		
Salem	194	24	Beckford	Lydia				1		1			1	1			4		
Salem	189	27	Beckford	Mary	3						1			1			5		
Salem	195	16	Beckford	Mehit	2								1	1			4		
Salem	194	25	Beckford	Pymont	1			1			1		1				4		
Salem	194	14	Beckford	Sarah									1				1		
Beverly	303	19	Beckford	William		1					1						2		
Salem	211	13	Beel	Saml	3			1			1	1					6		
Danvers	12	38	Bell	Daniel		1		1			3		1				6		
Newburyport	158	20	Bemes	Daniel	1		1					1					3		
Salem	199	29	Bend	Mary			1			1	1		1				4		
Salem	190	35	Benjamin	Sally	2		1						1	1			5		
Newbury	114	10	Bennet	Laban	1							1	1	1			4		
Salisbury	24	2	Bennet	Moses				1					1	1			3		
Newburyport	160	23	Bennett	David	2		1			1			1				5		
Gloucester	70	11	Bennett	Moses	3	2	3			1	1	1					11		
Gloucester	63	20	Bennett	Noah	2		1		1	1	1	1					7	East Ward	
Manchester	50	10	Bennett	Saml	1		2	1		2	1	1		1			9		
Marblehead	268	19	Benson	Eleanor		2						1					3		
Salem	193	22	Benson	Eliza	1	2						3	1	1			8		
Beverly	300	27	Benson	Francis	2		2	1		2	1	1	1				10		
Methuen	152	25	Bernard	Theodor			1					1					2		
Salem	206	45	Berril	Alden		1	1	1		3	1						7		
Newburyport	160	2	Berry	Abigail Wdo	1					3	1		1				6		
Middleton	17	34	Berry	Andrew	3			1		1			1				6		
Newburyport	160	1	Berry	Aron	1		1	1		1	1	1					7		
Middleton	17	33	Berry	Bartholomew		1		1				1		1			4		
Marblehead	241	30	Berry	Ebenezer			1					1			1		3		
Salem	220	4	Berry	Jacob		1											2		
Andover	91	7	Berry	John		1	1	1		2			1				6		
Salem	217	40	Berry	John				1		1			1				3		
Middleton	16	4	Berry	Jonathan	2		1					1	1				5		
Lynn	231	7	Berry	Joseph	1		1			3			1				6		
Newbury	113	1	Berry	Joseph	3			1		2			1				7		

TOWN	PG#	LN#	LAST NAME	FIRST NAME	under 10	10 to 16	16 to 26	26 to 45	45 and over	under 10	10 to 16	16 to 26	26 to 45	45 and over	TOTAL ALL OTHER	TOTAL SLAVES	TOTALS	DISTRICT/ TOWNSHIP	NOTES
			HEADS OF HOUSEHOLD		FREE WHITE MALES					FREE WHITE FEMALES									
Andover	90	32	Berry	Nathanael		2						1					3		
Middleton	16	3	Berry	Nathaniel	1			1				1	1	1			5		
Middleton	17	24	Berry	Nehemiah	1		1			2	2		1				7		
Andover	91	8	Berry	Ruth Wid		2								2			4		
Middleton	17	11	Berry	Samuel				1				1		1			3		
Marblehead	245	3	Besom	John	2	1	1	1		3		1	1				10		
Marblehead	262	10	Besome	Nicholas	3			1		1	1		1				7		
Marblehead	244	21	Besome	Philip	1			1		3	1	2	1		1		10		
Marblehead	247	11	Besome	Phillip	1			1		3	1	2	1		1		10		
Marblehead	245	24	Besome	Rebecca	1	1				1			1				4		
Marblehead	259	1	Besome	Richard		1		1	1					2			5		
Marblehead	258	11	Besome	Richard Junr	2	1	1			1		1	1				7		
Marblehead	270	16	Besome	Sarah	1		1				1			1	1		5		
Marblehead	262	9	Bessett	Richard	1		1	1		1							4		
Marblehead	251	7	Bettis	Elizabeth		1							1				2		
Marblehead	251	2	Bettis	Mary	1								1				2		
Newburyport	159	31	Betty	John	3			1		1	1	2	1	4			13		
Andover	91	10	Beverly	John	3			1		1	1	1		1			8		
Salem	192	37	Bickford	Benja				1				1	1				3		
Andover	91	23	Bickford	Jonathan				1					1				2		
Topsfield	21	31	Bickford	Silas	2			1		1			1				5		
Rowley	132	12	Bickle	Benja				1		2			1				4		
Salem	215	34	Bigelow	William			2	1		3	1		2				9		
Danvers	13	42	Biggs	Eunice		1	1			1		1		1			5		
Manchester	50	4	Bigham	Delucena L.	2	1		1		4	1		1				10		
Salem	197	29	Birch	Benja											3		3		
Marblehead	253	29	Bird	Daniel			1			3	1		1				6		
Amesbury	35	3	Birkam	Willm B.	1			1		2			1				5		
Gloucester	58	34	Bishop	Benja			1	1					1				3		
Rowley	129	2	Bishop	Benja	1	1	2						2				6		
Rowley	130	47	Bishop	Benja		1	1	1		1			1				6		
Rowley	130	52	Bishop	Edward	1	1	2	1				1	1				7		
Danvers	9	26	Bishop	James	3			1					1				5		
Salem	199	1	Bishop	John		1		1		2			1				5		
Salem	219	10	Bishop	Samuel	1			1		3			1				6		
Manchester	54	25	Bishop	Willm	1			1		2			1				5		
Beverly	301	22	Bisson	Israel			1	1					2				4		
Beverly	297	18	Bisson	Lucy						1	1	1	1	1			5		
Topsfield	21	6	Bixby	Benjamin	1	1	1	1	1		1		1	1			8		
Topsfield	18	2	Bixby	Daniel		1	1	1		1	1		1				6		
Methuen	152	4	Bixby	Dudley	2	2		1					2	1			8		
Boxford	135	37	Bixby	Gideon	2	2		1		1	2		1				9		
Beverly	302	11	Black	Anna									1	1			2		
Newbury	114	25	Black	Henry	1		1	1		1		2	1				7		
Salem	214	34	Black	John											7		7		
Salem	214	35	Black	John Jr											11		11		
Beverly	300	3	Black	Nathl		1		1		3	1		1				7		
Salem	193	37	Black	Primus											4		4		
Newbury	117	8	Black	Samuel	1			1		2	1	1	1	1			8		
Gloucester	86	26	Blackfield	Nathl	2	1	2	1		3		2	1				12		
Marblehead	239	7	Blackler	William	2		3		1	1	3	2	1				13		
Marblehead	242	20	Blackler	William Junr				1		4		1	1				7		
Marblehead	248	26	Blair	John	2	2	1	1					1				7		
Topsfield	18	15	Blaisdel	Samuel	1			1					1				3		
Salem	210	42	Blakeney	James				1		1			1				3		
Andover	91	32	Blanchard	Amos	3	1	1	1		2			1	1			10		
Salem	192	9	Blanchard	Benja	1	1		1		2			2				7		
Salem	199	27	Blanchard	Daniel	3	1		1		2	3		1				11		
Newbury	112	44	Blanchard	Jeremiah	1			1		3	2		1				8		
Marblehead	262	8	Blanchard	Jesse	2		1	1					1				5		
Andover	91	3	Blanchard	Josiah				1					1				2		
Haverhill	143	30	Blanchard	Samuel	1	1			1	2	1			1			7		
Wenham	310	2	Blanchard	Samuel			3	1				2	1				8		
Gloucester	77	30	Blanchford	John					1					1			2		
Marblehead	266	12	Blancy	Sarah								1					1		
Marblehead	253	14	Blaney	Asa	2			1		4	1		1				9		
Marblehead	268	27	Blaney	Benjamin	1			1		3							5		
Lynn	231	17	Blaney	Eliza	2								1				3		
Lynn	231	16	Blaney	Joseph		1	2	1						1			5		
Marblehead	262	11	Blaney	Ruth		1	1			2	1			1			6		
Salisbury	25	4	Blasdel	Rachel Wd						1			1				2		
Amesbury	36	5	Blasdell	Ephraim				1					1				2		
Amesbury	36	4	Blasdell	Ephraim Junr		1		1		1			1				4		
Amesbury	36	6	Blasdell	John	3			1					1				5		
Amesbury	36	8	Blasdell	Joseph	2			1		1			1				5		
Amesbury	35	2	Blasdell	Lewis	2			1		1			1				5		
Amesbury	36	9	Blasdell	Oliver	1			1		1		2		1			6		
Amesbury	36	7	Blasdell	Richd			1			1			1				3		
Amesbury	36	1	Blasdell	Ruth Wid						1			1				2		
Amesbury	36	3	Blasdell	Stephen					1					1			2		
Gloucester	78	19	Blatchford	Henry	3			1		2			1				7	Sandy Bay Parish	
Gloucester	78	20	Blatchford	Saml	1	1		1		1			1				5	Sandy Bay Parish	
Methuen	152	26	Blodget	Asa				1					1				2		
Newburyport	160	20	Blodgett	William	1			1		1			1				5		

163

TOWN	PG#	LN#	LAST NAME	FIRST NAME	FREE WHITE MALES					FREE WHITE FEMALES					TOTAL ALL OTHER	TOTAL SLAVES	TOTALS	DISTRICT/ TOWNSHIP	NOTES
					under 10	10 to 16	16 to 26	26 to 45	45 and over	under 10	10 to 16	16 to 26	26 to 45	45 and over					
Newburyport	160	28	Blompy	Aaron	1	1			1		1	1		1			6		
Andover	91	1	Blunt	David			2		1	1	1			1			6		
Newburyport	159	37	Blunt	Edmund M	2		2	1		1		1	1				8		
Newburyport	159	38	Blunt	Elizabeth Wdo		1					1	3		1			6		
Andover	90	34	Blunt	Isaac	2	1	1	1		2		1	2				10		
Andover	90	33	Blunt	Mary Wid		1					1		1	1			4		
Salem	208	27	Blydon	Peter											7		7		
Salem	191	24	Blythe	Sally		1				2	1	1	1				6		
Newburyport	158	8	Boardman	Abel	3		1	1		1	1		1				8		
Topsfield	20	6	Boardman	Danel	1		3		1	1	1			1			8		
Ipswich	278	20	Boardman	Daniel			1	1		1	2	1	1				7		
Marblehead	246	31	Boardman	Francis		2		1					1				4		
Newburyport	158	7	Boardman	John	2		1	1		2		1	1				8		
Ipswich	281	30	Boardman	John H	1				3	1			2	1			8		
Newburyport	158	5	Boardman	Jonathan			1	1		1	2		1				6		
Salisbury	25	9	Boardman	Joseph		1							1				2		
Newburyport	158	10	Boardman	Martha						1	3		1				5		
Salisbury	25	15	Boardman	Nathl		1		1					1				3		
Newburyport	158	4	Boardman	Offin		1		1					1	1			4		
Lynn	232	29	Boardman	Saml	2	2		1		3			1				9	West Parish	
Lynn	233	28	Boardman	Saml			2	1		1		1	1				6	West Parish	
Ipswich	281	71	Boardman	Stephen			2	1		4			1				8		
Salisbury	25	12	Boardman	Thomas	2	1		1		4	1		2	1			12		
Newburyport	158	11	Boardman	Wido Ann		1						2		1			4		
Newburyport	158	9	Boardman	Wido Mary	1	1						1		1			4		
Newburyport	158	6	Boardman	William	2	3		1		1		1	1				9		
Salem	214	40	Boden	Charles		1				1		1					3		
Marblehead	246	30	Boden	Elizabeth								1	1				2		
Marblehead	268	21	Boden	John			1						1				2		
Marblehead	262	15	Boden	Lidia	1					2		1	1				5		
Marblehead	267	30	Boden	Samuel			2	1						1			4		
Marblehead	262	12	Boden	William	1			1		3	2		1				8		
Salem	194	21	Boden	William	1	2	1			3			1				9		
Salem	210	26	Boden	William	2		1			2		1					6		
Danvers	6	3	Bodge	Samuel	2		1	1					1				5		
Newburyport	160	22	Bodily	John Revd	2	1		1		3	1						9		
Beverly	302	14	Bodoin	Thomas	2		1						1				4		
Methuen	152	7	Bodwell	Alpheus	2	1		1					1				6		
Methuen	152	6	Bodwell	Daniel				1				1		1			3		
Methuen	152	13	Bodwell	Daniel Junr	1	1		1		1	1			1			6		
Methuen	152	8	Bodwell	Henry				1		1		1		2			5		
Methuen	152	3	Bodwell	Henry Junr			1			3			1				5		
Methuen	152	2	Bodwell	Isaac	2		1			1	1	1					7		
Methuen	152	12	Bodwell	John L.	1		3			2			1				7		
Methuen	152	14	Bodwell	Joseph	1		1	1		1			1				5		
Methuen	152	5	Bodwell	Parker	1		1						1				3		
Methuen	152	11	Bodwell	Stephen				1					2	1			4		
Methuen	152	9	Bodwell	William			2	1					2	1			6		
Methuen	152	10	Bodwell	William Junr	1		1			1			1				4		
Salem	193	28	Body	Mary		2				1	1		1				5		
Beverly	295	39	Boison	William		1						1					2		
Methuen	152	20	Bolls	Reuben	2		1	1		2		1		1			8		
Methuen	152	22	Bolls	Reuben Junr	1		1					1	1				4		
Salem	209	45	Bolton	John	1			1		1			1				4		
Manchester	55	13	Bonason	Betty						2		1					3		
Gloucester	63	8	Bond	Hannah Wo	2					1		2	1				6	West Ward	
Marblehead	247	13	Bond	John			2	1		2			1				7		
Newburyport	159	19	Bond	John		2	1		1	2	1			1			8		
Gloucester	58	30	Bond	Samuel		2			1					1			4		
Marblehead	239	9	Bonnler	William	1			1		2			1				5		
Newbury	114	17	Bookman	Joseph			2						2				4		
Amesbury	36	29	Bootman	Elias		1		1		1			1				4		
Salem	202	7	Borden	Sarah	2					1			1				4		
Newbury	114	27	Bordman	Ollin		2	1		1	3				1			8		
Salisbury	24	5	Boswell	Asa	1			1		1			1				4		
Salem	213	27	Bott	John	1		1			1	1	1					5		
Salem	201	39	Boulas	Eunice							1	1	1				3		
Marblehead	250	34	Bowden	Benjamin				1									1		
Marblehead	254	21	Bowden	Benjamin	1			1		1			1				4		
Marblehead	262	16	Bowden	Francis		2		1		2	2	2	1				10		
Marblehead	258	13	Bowden	John				1		1		1		1			4		
Marblehead	257	20	Bowden	Joseph		1				1		1					3		
Marblehead	259	30	Bowden	Joshua Orne		1				1		1					3		
Marblehead	255	11	Bowden	Mary	1					1			1				3		
Marblehead	266	34	Bowden	Nicholson		1	1			1		1		1			5		
Marblehead	267	3	Bowden	Richard				1						1			2		
Marblehead	250	35	Bowden	Samuel		1		1						1			3		
Marblehead	257	15	Bowden	Samuel		1		1						1			3		
Marblehead	257	21	Bowden	Samuel 4th			1			1			1				3		
Marblehead	258	1	Bowden	Thomas	1		2	1		1	1			1			7		
Marblehead	267	6	Bowden	Thomas	1	1		1		1	2	1					7		
Marblehead	257	27	Bowden	William	1			1		2			1				5		
Salem	206	44	Bowditch	Ebenz		1		1					1				3		
Salem	211	39	Bowditch	Eliza								2	1				3		

TOWN	PG#	LN#	HEADS OF HOUSEHOLD		FREE WHITE MALES					FREE WHITE FEMALES					TOTAL ALL OTHER	TOTAL SLAVES	TOTALS	DISTRICT/ TOWNSHIP	NOTES
			LAST NAME	FIRST NAME	under 10	10 to 16	16 to 26	26 to 45	45 and over	under 10	10 to 16	16 to 26	26 to 45	45 and over					
Salem	196	17	Bowditch	Mary								1		1			2		
Salem	213	46	Bowditch	Nath				1		1			2				4		
Salem	193	35	Bowditch	Thos			3		1			1		1			6		
Salem	201	17	Bowditch	Thos	2			1		3	1		1				8		
Marblehead	245	27	Bowen	Ashley	1		1		1			1		1			5		
Marblehead	247	5	Bowen	David	2			1		2			1				6		
Marblehead	262	13	Bowen	Deborah									1				1		
Salem	201	42	Bowen	Jack											4		4		
Marblehead	241	27	Bowen	Nathaniel	1	1			1	1	1	1	1				7		
Marblehead	244	10	Bowen	William			1		1		2			1			5		
Newburyport	160	30	Bowers	Abigail Wido	1					1			1				3		
Beverly	292	30	Bowers	Ishmael											1		1		
Marblehead	259	2	Bowers	John				1					1				2		
Salem	206	22	Bowker	Joel			1	1				1					3		
Marblehead	253	28	Bowler	*mes		3			1	1	1		1				7		
Marblehead	267	11	Bowler	Sarah						1		1					2		
Lynn	226	11	Bowler	Thos	2	2		1		2			1				8		
Hamilton	285	17	Bowles	Abigail		1							1				2		
Beverly	294	21	Bowles	Rebecca							1	1	1				3		
Newburyport	160	26	Bowley	William Wdo of	2					2			1				5		
Salem	219	4	Bowlin	Hannah						1			1				2		
Andover	91	2	Bowlman	John	2				1	1			1				5		
Salem	202	9	Bowman	James		1		1						1			3		
Andover	91	9	Bowman	John	1		1		1	2			1				6		
Salem	211	27	Bowman	Mary		1					2	1		1			5		
Gloucester	58	5	Boyanton	Eliphl				1					1				2		
Gloucester	58	6	Boyanton	John		1	1	1				1					4		
Salem	203	31	Boyard	Joseph			1	1			2		1				5		
Salem	193	44	Boyce	David			3		1				1				5		
Danvers	4	15	Boyce	Jonathan					1				1				2		
Lynn	223	44	Boyce	Jonathan	1			1		1	1		1				5		
Danvers	14	5	Boyce	Stephen					1				1				2		
Gloucester	78	21	Boyd	Abra			1	1		1		1					4	Sandy Bay Parish	
Ipswich	281	65	Boyd	Adam	5			1		1			1				8		
Salem	218	48	Boyd	William	2			1					1				4		
Gloucester	78	25	Boyenton	Eleaz	2			1		3			1				7	Sandy Bay Parish	
Salem	214	26	Boylston	Hannah	1	3							1				5		
Methuen	152	19	Boynton	David	1			1					1	3			6		
Rowley	131	15	Boynton	Ebenezr	1			1		1			1	1			5		
Newbury	117	25	Boynton	Edmund	2			1		2		1	1				7		
Newbury	105	22	Boynton	Enoch		1		1					1				3		
Rowley	127	29	Boynton	Moses	1		1		1	3			1	2			9		
Rowley	127	30	Boynton	Moses									2	4			6		
Marblehead	266	2	Boynton	Nathaniel	1		1	1		1		1					5		
Lynn	233	8	Boynton	Nathl	1	1		1	1			1	1	1			7		
Bradford	125	33	Boynton	Samuel			1		1				2	1			6		
Andover	91	17	Boynton	Thomas		1	3		1	2		3		1			11		
Salem	205	20	Brad	Thos		1							1				2		
Beverly	306	26	Bradborne	James		1				2		1					4		
Haverhill	143	3	Bradbury	Daniel	1			1		3			1				6		
Haverhill	143	43	Bradbury	David	3			1					1				5		
Newburyport	160	10	Bradbury	George			1						1				2		
Salisbury	25	5	Bradbury	James Capt	1		1	1		1	2		1				7		
Newburyport	160	11	Bradbury	Jonathan			1	1						1			3		
Salisbury	24	6	Bradbury	Roland				1						1			2		
Haverhill	143	4	Bradbury	Samuel	1	1		1		1		1	1	1			7		
Newburyport	160	7	Bradbury	Theophilus	1	1			1	2	1	1		1			8		
Newburyport	160	9	Bradbury	Theophilus 3d	1			1		1		1					4		
Newburyport	160	8	Bradbury	Theophilus Jr				1		2	1	1					5		
Marblehead	253	31	Bradeen	*n	1			1					1				3		
Marblehead	257	4	Bradeen	Joseph					1					1			2		
Rowley	131	10	Bradford	Ebenezr Revd		3	1		1	1		1		1			8		
Beverly	291	29	Bradford	Marian		1							1	1			3		
Salem	197	16	Bradish	Sarah			1					1	1				3		
Haverhill	143	23	Bradley	Benjm		1	1	1		1	3	2		1			10		
Haverhill	143	36	Bradley	Daniel				1				1	1				3		
Haverhill	143	37	Bradley	Daniel Jun	1			1		2		1	1				6		
Haverhill	143	38	Bradley	David			1	1		2		1	1				6		
Haverhill	143	35	Bradley	Dudley			1			3		1					5		
Haverhill	143	44	Bradley	Enoch		2	2		1			1		2			8		
Haverhill	143	14	Bradley	Francis			1			2		1					4		
Andover	90	28	Bradley	Jonathan	3	2	1		1	1		2	1				11		
Andover	90	23	Bradley	Joseph	3	1			1		1			1	1		8		
Haverhill	143	24	Bradley	Joseph	3		1	1			1		1				7		
Haverhill	143	40	Bradley	Josiah	2	2		1		2			1				8		
Haverhill	143	15	Bradley	Maehetable									2	1			3		
Haverhill	143	12	Bradley	Nathaniel		1	1		2		2	2					8		
Haverhill	143	13	Bradley	Peter	1			1	1			1		1			5		
Haverhill	143	1	Bradley	Samuel	3	1	1			1			1				8		
Bradford	121	14	Bradley	Thos	2		1					1	1	1			6		
Beverly	302	31	Bradshaw	John	1	2		1		1	1	1		1			8		
Salem	206	8	Bradshaw	Wm	3			1		1	2		1				8		
Middleton	16	12	Bradstreet	Abigail									1				2		

TOWN	PG#	LN#	LAST NAME	FIRST NAME	FREE WHITE MALES					FREE WHITE FEMALES					TOTAL ALL OTHER	TOTAL SLAVES	TOTALS	DISTRICT/ TOWNSHIP	NOTES
					under 10	10 to 16	16 to 26	26 to 45	45 and over	under 10	10 to 16	16 to 26	26 to 45	45 and over					
Topsfield	20	33	Bradstreet	Dudley	2	1		1		1			1				6		
Newburyport	160	32	Bradstreet	Elizabeth									1	1			2		
Gloucester	78	24	Bradstreet	Ezekh	2			1		3				1			7	Sandy Bay Parish	
Topsfield	21	24	Bradstreet	Henry			1	1				1	1				4		
Topsfield	20	32	Bradstreet	John				1						1			2		
Topsfield	21	29	Bradstreet	John Junr	2			1		2			1	1			7		
Topsfield	20	14	Bradstreet	Moses				1		3			1				5		
Ipswich	273	1	Bradstreet	Nathaniel		1		1		1	2		1				6		
Topsfield	20	31	Bradstreet	Samuel	2	1	1	1		1	1		1				8		
Marblehead	242	19	Bradstreet	Sarah		1					1	1		1			4		
Salem	191	27	Brady	James			1					1					2		
Newburyport	159	41	Bragdon	Joseph	1			1		3			1				6		
Salisbury	24	3	Bragg	Henry			1							1			2		
Andover	91	11	Bragg	Ingal		1											1		
Lynnfield	237	11	Bragg	Josiah				1					1	1			3		
Newburyport	160	29	Bragg	Robert	2		1	1					1	1			6		
Gloucester	55	14	Bray	Aaron	1		1			2			1				5		
Newburyport	159	21	Bray	Aaron		3		1					1	1			6		
Gloucester	58	10	Bray	Abigail Wo		2								1			3		
Salem	218	28	Bray	Benja	1		1			2		1					5		
Gloucester	77	14	Bray	Benja How	3			1		2				1			7		
Marblehead	248	22	Bray	Benjamin	1		1						1				3		
Gloucester	55	11	Bray	Daniel	3			1					1	1			6		
Gloucester	55	12	Bray	Ebenz	3			1		2	1		1				8		
Marblehead	245	12	Bray	Edmund	2			1		2			1				6		
Gloucester	58	12	Bray	Enoch				1						1			2		
Gloucester	58	11	Bray	Enoch Junr				1		4	2		1				8		
Gloucester	55	8	Bray	Idea Wd		1	1			1	1	2		1			7		
Gloucester	55	5	Bray	Isaac	2	1	1		1	1	1	2	1	1			11		
Gloucester	55	4	Bray	Mark		2	1					2	1	1			7		
Salem	211	52	Bray	Mary		1								1			2		
Marblehead	252	4	Bray	Rebecca		1					1	2		2			6		
Salem	212	22	Bray	Robt			1	1		3			1	1			7		
Gloucester	55	3	Bray	Samuel		2	1						1				5		
Gloucester	55	9	Bray	Samuel Jun				1		2	2	2		1			8		
Gloucester	55	10	Bray	Silas	2			1		1			1				5		
Salem	208	31	Bray	Silvia											6		6		
Gloucester	56	2	Bray	Theo Doctr				1						1			2		
Haverhill	143	27	Bray	Thomas R.	1	1		1		1			1				5		
Gloucester	55	6	Bray	Willm		1		1		1			1				4		
Rowley	127	28	Braymon	Isaac	1	1		1		1			1		1		6		
Newburyport	159	26	Brazier	Simeon			1	2					1				4		
Salem	205	38	Brecome	Margaret		3							1				5		
Lynn	224	5	Breed	Aaron	3			1		3	3		1	1			12		
Lynn	223	10	Breed	Abraham		1		1		2	1		1				6		
Lynn	226	32	Breed	Amos		1	1						2				4		
Lynn	225	26	Breed	Anne		1		1		1	1	1	1				6		
Lynn	224	1	Breed	B Newhall	1					3			1				6		
Lynn	225	28	Breed	Benj	1			1		3	1		1				8		
Lynn	225	33	Breed	Charles	2		1			1			1				5		
Lynn	225	12	Breed	Ephm				2			1		1	1			5		
Lynn	225	36	Breed	Ezra		1		1	1	1			1	1			6		
Lynn	229	15	Breed	Fredk		1	4	1		3		1					10		
Lynn	226	16	Breed	Isaiah		1	1							3			5		
Lynn	227	39	Breed	Jabez		2	1	1		1			1				6		
Lynn	223	11	Breed	James	1			1				1	1				4		
Lynn	226	25	Breed	James 3d			1						1				2		
Lynn	223	5	Breed	James Jun	2	1		1		1	1		1				7		
Lynn	225	30	Breed	Joseph Jn	2	1		1		1			1				6		
Lynn	225	13	Breed	Josh 3d	1			1		2		1			1		6		
Lynn	224	32	Breed	Mattw	4	2		1		2	1	1	1				12		
Marblehead	256	29	Breed	Micajah		1		1					1				3		
Lynn	223	2	Breed	Nathan				1						1			2		
Lynn	225	34	Breed	Nathan		1		1		1			1				4		
Lynn	231	36	Breed	Nehemiah & Son		2		1	1	1		1	1	1			8		
Danvers	14	36	Breed	Priscill						1		1					2		
Lynn	225	31	Breed	Samuel		1	1			1			1	1			6		
Lynn	223	49	Breed	Simeon	2		1	1		2	1		1				8		
Lynn	224	6	Breed	Theoph Jr		2	1			2		2	1				8		
Lynn	225	10	Breed	Theoph Sen		1		1	2				1	1			6		
Lynn	225	27	Breed	Willm		1		1					1	1			4		
Lynn	225	35	Breed	Willm 3d	1			1		1	1						5		
Lynn	224	24	Breedeen	John			1						1				2		
Lynn	233	11	Breeden	Saml				1			1		1	2			5		
Newburyport	159	34	Brett	John				1		1		1	1				4		
Hamilton	285	40	Brewer	John	1			1		1			1				5		
Salem	202	36	Brewer	Thos	1	1	1	1		3			1	1			10		
Newbury	107	31	Brewster	John		2							2				4		
Haverhill	143	25	Briant	Ann	1	2					1	1	1	1			7		
Beverly	303	46	Briant	Benja	2	1		1		2			1				7		
Lynnfield	237	3	Briant	John		1		1		2	1		1				6		
Marblehead	262	18	Briars	Annis		2	1						2				5		

166

TOWN	PG#	LN#	LAST NAME	FIRST NAME	FREE WHITE MALES under 10	10 to 16	16 to 26	26 to 45	45 and over	FREE WHITE FEMALES under 10	10 to 16	16 to 26	26 to 45	45 and over	TOTAL ALL OTHER	TOTAL SLAVES	TOTALS	DISTRICT/ TOWNSHIP	NOTES
Marblehead	262	17	Briars	Elias				1		1		1					3		
Newburyport	159	22	Brickell	Nathaniel	2	1			1	1				1			6		
Newbury	118	41	Brickett	Amos	1	1	1	1				1					5		
Haverhill	143	26	Brickett	Barnard			2	1					2				5		
Haverhill	143	8	Brickett	Daniel				1		3	3		1				8		
Haverhill	143	7	Brickett	James		1	1	1		2		1		1			7		
Newbury	116	2	Brickett	James	1		1	1					2	1			7		
Haverhill	143	34	Brickett	John	2	1	1	1		1	2	1					9		
Newbury	108	15	Brickett	John		1				3		1					5		
Newbury	118	32	Brickett	Moses			2		1		1	1		1			6		
Newbury	118	39	Brickett	Nathll					1					1			2		
Marblehead	258	23	Bridgam	Phillip		1	1	1		3	2		1				9		
Beverly	299	11	Bridger	Benja	2			1					1	1			5		
Beverly	299	10	Bridger	Thomas		1			1				1				3		
Marblehead	251	13	Bridges	George				1		1			1				3		
Andover	90	30	Bridges	James				1	1								2		
Andover	90	31	Bridges	James Jr		2	1	1	1	5	2	1	1				14		
Rowley	127	44	Bridges	John				1				1		1			3		
Marblehead	267	17	Bridges	Mary										1			1		
Andover	90	19	Bridges	Moody		2	1		1	1	1	1	1	1			9		
Salem	205	19	Bridgon	Josa			1			1			1				3		
Salem	198	16	Briggs	Elijah	1		1			1			1				4		
Salem	201	18	Briggs	Enos		1	8	9	1	2	2	3	1				27		
Salem	192	24	Briggs	Jeremh	2			1					1				4		
Salem	214	1	Briggs	John			1	1		1			1				4		
Salem	188	26	Briggs	Lemuel	1			1					1				3		
Salem	216	39	Briggs	Ruth	1	2	3			2	1	1	1				11		
Salem	188	24	Briggs	Susanna							1		1	1			3		
Salem	211	25	Briggs	Thos			7	1		1	2		1				12		
Marblehead	242	10	Brimblecome	Charity									1	1			2		
Marblehead	267	1	Brimblecome	Cornelius		1							1				2		
Marblehead	251	18	Brimblecome	David	2	1							1				4		
Marblehead	259	32	Brimblecome	Joseph	1			1		2			1				5		
Marblehead	267	27	Brimblecome	Leanard					1		1			1			3		
Marblehead	255	21	Brimblecome	Marrett	1			1		2	1		1	1			7		
Marblehead	242	11	Brimblecome	Nathaniel	1		1			2		1					5		
Marblehead	267	31	Brimblecome	Samuel		1		1				1		1			4		
Marblehead	251	12	Brimblecome	Thomas				1		4			1				6		
Lynn	229	8	Brimbleson	Saml	1			1		1			1				4		
Beverly	298	20	Brimter	Daniel	1	1			1	3		1	2				9		
Marblehead	248	17	Brindlecome	Samuel	1			1		1			1				4		
Gloucester	58	25	Brinick	James	1								1				2		
Salem	196	13	Brinley	John	1			1			2		1				5		
Salem	201	47	Brister	David											3		3		
Salem	208	3	Brit	Michl	1		1						1				3		
Salem	200	39	Britton	Edward	1	1		1		2	1		1				7		
Rowley	129	40	Broadstreet	Moses		1	2	1		1	2	3		1			11		
Rowley	129	47	Broadstreet	Moses				1					1	1			3		
Newburyport	159	20	Brocheway	Pardon		2	1	1		3			1	1			9		
Newbury	114	2	Brocking	Eliza	1		1					1	1	1	1		6		
Newbury	113	6	Brocking	Samuel	1		1						1				3		
Salem	206	2	Brodies	Ebenzr	2		1						1				5		
Salem	194	6	Brook	Lydia										2			2		
Rowley	132	13	Brookelbank	Job		1		1		1	1			1			5		
Rowley	131	7	Brookelbank	Nathan		1		1					1				3		
Salem	203	7	Brookhouse	Mary	2	1	1					1	1				6		
Rowley	127	12	Brooklebank	John		2			1				1	1			5		
Salem	217	14	Brooks	Abigail			1	1		1			1				4		
Haverhill	143	18	Brooks	Cotton B.	2	1		1		1			1	1			7		
Gloucester	78	28	Brooks	David	1		1						1				3	Sandy Bay Parish	
Marblehead	254	31	Brooks	Edward	2			1		3	1		1				8		
Marblehead	261	12	Brooks	Elizabeth										1			1		
Marblehead	249	6	Brooks	John				1		1				1			3		
Salem	214	6	Brooks	Luke	1			1				1	1				4		
Gloucester	78	27	Brooks	Ruben	2			1		1			1				5	Sandy Bay Parish	
Salem	199	26	Brooks	Samuel	2			1					1				4		
Salem	215	19	Brooks	Samuel	1			1		2		1	1	1			7		
Salem	220	3	Brooks	Thos		1	4	1		2	1		1				10		
Salem	215	6	Brooks	Timothy	5	2	1	1		1	1	3	1				15		
Marblehead	254	25	Brooks	William			1						1				2		
Salem	195	46	Brooks	Zach	2			1						1			4		
Gloucester	78	31	Broughton	Danl	1			1		2			1				5	Sandy Bay Parish	
Marblehead	246	25	Broughton	Nicholson	3	1		1				1	1				7		
Ipswich	280	27	Brown	Abner					1				1	1			3		
Ipswich	281	24	Brown	Abraham		1		1		1			1	1			6		
Salisbury	24	11	Brown	Abraham	1	1	1						1				4		
Lynn	230	8	Brown	Abram		1				1		1					3		
Hamilton	284	3	Brown	Ami		1				1			1				3		
Manchester	55	11	Brown	Andrew		1						1					3		
Marblehead	257	3	Brown	Anna										2			2		
Newbury	109	1	Brown	Anna			1				1	2	1	1			6		
Beverly	293	27	Brown	Asa	1	1			1	1			1				5		
Beverly	300	5	Brown	Benja				1						1			2		
Beverly	300	7	Brown	Benja 2nd	2		1	1				1		1			6		
Beverly	303	3	Brown	Benja 3d	1			1					1				3		
Hamilton	285	103	Brown	Benjamin					1						1		3		

167

TOWN	PG#	LN#	LAST NAME	FIRST NAME	FREE WHITE MALES under 10	10 to 16	16 to 26	26 to 45	45 and over	FREE WHITE FEMALES under 10	10 to 16	16 to 26	26 to 45	45 and over	TOTAL ALL OTHER	TOTAL SLAVES	TOTALS	DISTRICT/ TOWNSHIP	NOTES
Ipswich	281	5	Brown	Benjamin		1	2	1						1			5		
Ipswich	281	4	Brown	Benjamin Jr	3			1		2			1				7		
Rowley	128	27	Brown	Caleb	1			1		1			1				4		
Hamilton	285	89	Brown	Daniel	1		2		1		1	1	1				7		
Ipswich	280	28	Brown	David				1			1		1				3		
Danvers	7	36	Brown	Ebenezer	2			1		2			1				6		
Marblehead	239	11	Brown	Ebenezer	3	3	1	1					1				9		
Newburyport	158	37	Brown	Ebenezer		1			1					2			4		
Amesbury	36	19	Brown	Ebenz	2	2		1		1			1				7		
Haverhill	143	5	Brown	Edmund				1				1	1				3		
Newburyport	159	5	Brown	Edward				1					1	2			4		
Topsfield	22	2	Brown	Eleazer		1		1		3			1				6		
Newburyport	159	17	Brown	Eliphalet		1						1					2		
Gloucester	63	18	Brown	Elisha				1		3							4	East Ward	
Ipswich	281	28	Brown	Elisha	3			1		1			1				6		
Beverly	293	29	Brown	Eliza		1	1					1		1			4		
Beverly	303	34	Brown	Eliza									1				1		
Ipswich	275	55	Brown	Elizabeth										1			1		
Ipswich	281	40	Brown	Elizabeth		1				1			1	1			4		
Newbury	108	5	Brown	Elizabeth							1	3		1			5		
Salisbury	25	3	Brown	Enos			1						1	1			3		
Lynn	227	19	Brown	Ephm	1			1		2			1				5		
Gloucester	71	1	Brown	Ephraim	3			1		3	1		1				9		
Hamilton	285	55	Brown	Ephraim		1		1	1	1			2				6		
Ipswich	281	29	Brown	Ephraim	3			1		1			2				7		
Salisbury	25	14	Brown	Ephraim	4		1	1		1			1				8		
Lynn	233	20	Brown	Ezra	3	1		1		2	1	2	1				11		
Marblehead	239	10	Brown	Hannah	2	1				2			1				6		
Salem	213	2	Brown	Hannah			1					1	1	1			4		
Salisbury	25	1	Brown	Hannah Wd									1	1			2		
Newburyport	159	15	Brown	Hannah Wido		1						1	1	1			4		
Newburyport	159	4	Brown	Henry			1						1				2		
Hamilton	285	3	Brown	Jacob		1	1		1			1		1			5		
Newburyport	159	1	Brown	Jacob	1			1		1	1		1				5		
Salisbury	25	13	Brown	Jacob Esq	4	2			1		1	1	1				10		
Gloucester	78	29	Brown	James	1		1						1				3	Sandy Bay Parish	
Hamilton	285	87	Brown	James		1		1						1			3		
Ipswich	281	26	Brown	James	1	1	1		1			2		1			7		
Lynnfield	235	19	Brown	James	2	1		1	1			1		1			7		
Manchester	55	12	Brown	James			1						1				2		
Newburyport	159	2	Brown	James	2		2			1			1				6		
Salem	217	5	Brown	James	2	1		1		2	1		1				8		
Salem	217	16	Brown	James Jr			1			1			1				3		
Marblehead	239	18	Brown	Jane										2			2		
Salisbury	24	19	Brown	Jeremiah	1	1		1		2			1				7		
Danvers	6	29	Brown	John				1		1			1				3		
Gloucester	68	21	Brown	John	3		1		1			1					6		
Hamilton	285	114	Brown	John	1			1				1	1				4		
Haverhill	143	2	Brown	John	2		1						1				4		
Ipswich	281	25	Brown	John	1		1		5			1					8		
Lynn	226	12	Brown	John			1		1			1					3		
Marblehead	259	21	Brown	John		1	1						1				3		
Newburyport	159	8	Brown	John			2	1				2	1				7		
Rowley	127	10	Brown	John	2		1		1			1	1				6		
Salem	217	3	Brown	John	1		1	1		1			1	1			5		
Salem	218	19	Brown	John	1	1	2					2					6		
Marblehead	245	4	Brown	John 4th		1		1			1	1					3		
Newburyport	159	7	Brown	John Jr			1	1						2			4		
Haverhill	143	6	Brown	John Jun	2		1						1				4		
Marblehead	246	23	Brown	John Jun	1		2		1	3	1		1				9		
Marblehead	258	30	Brown	John Junr	1	1		1		3	2		1				9		
Gloucester	85	16	Brown	Jon	1			1		1			1				4		
Gloucester	58	29	Brown	Jon Cap				1					1	1			3		
Salem	220	57	Brown	Jona	1	1	1		1			1	1				7		
Gloucester	58	28	Brown	Jona 3d	3	1	1	1		2			1	1			10		
Gloucester	58	27	Brown	Jona Junr	1			1		1	1		1				4		
Danvers	7	35	Brown	Joseph				1					1	1			3		
Hamilton	285	9	Brown	Joseph	1		1		1			1	1				5		
Ipswich	281	27	Brown	Joseph	1	1	1		1	1	1		1				7		
Lynnfield	237	16	Brown	Joseph	3			1		1			1				6		
Marblehead	239	17	Brown	Joseph										2			2		
Newbury	108	34	Brown	Joseph			1	1					1		1		4		
Newburyport	159	6	Brown	Joseph	1	2	2		1	1	1		1				9		
Rowley	128	33	Brown	Joseph		1	1	1		2	1	1		2			9		
Salem	193	23	Brown	Joseph			1						1				2		
Salem	217	46	Brown	Joseph	3	1		1		1			1				7		
Newbury	108	13	Brown	Joshua		1	1		1				1	1			5		
Newburyport	158	39	Brown	Josiah			1						1				2		
Ipswich	280	32	Brown	Judith						1	1	1	1				4		
Hamilton	285	101	Brown	Lemuel	1	1		1					1				4		
Manchester	50	5	Brown	Lydia Wo	1							1	1	2			5		
Salem	214	42	Brown	Margt	1									1			2		
Salem	216	46	Brown	Margt			1							1			2		
Danvers	6	31	Brown	Mary			1					1		1			3		

TOWN	PG#	LN#	LAST NAME	FIRST NAME	FREE WHITE MALES					FREE WHITE FEMALES					TOTAL ALL OTHER	TOTAL SLAVES	TOTALS	DISTRICT/ TOWNSHIP	NOTES
					under 10	10 to 16	16 to 26	26 to 45	45 and over	under 10	10 to 16	16 to 26	26 to 45	45 and over					
Marblehead	260	36	Brown	Mehitable										1			1		
Newburyport	158	36	Brown	Moses Capt	1		2		1			1		1			6		
Beverly	303	35	Brown	Moses Esq	2				1			1	2		1		7		
Newburyport	158	35	Brown	Moses Mercht		1	1	1	1	1	1	1		2			9		
Salem	219	9	Brown	Nancy								1	1				2		
Ipswich	281	23	Brown	Nathan	2	1			1	1		2	1				8		
Wenham	308	3	Brown	Nathan		2	1		1	1			1	1			7		
Wenham	308	4	Brown	Nathan Jr			1					1					2		
Hamilton	285	2	Brown	Nathaniel					1				2	1			4		
Ipswich	281	6	Brown	Nathaniel		2			1					1			4		
Newburyport	159	13	Brown	Nathaniel	2			1	1			1	1				6		
Ipswich	280	26	Brown	Nehemiah	2				1		2		1	1			7		
Newburyport	159	3	Brown	Nicolas	1	3	2		1	3	1	1	1				13		
Newburyport	159	10	Brown	Obadiah	5		2			1		1	2				11		
Wenham	309	36	Brown	Palahiah		1			1				1	1			4		
Boxford	136	9	Brown	Parker		2	2			1	2		1				9		
Newbury	112	8	Brown	Parson	1			1			3		2				7		
Salem	216	42	Brown	Rebecca									1				1		
Amesbury	36	14	Brown	Richd	2	1		1		2			1				7		
Marblehead	257	2	Brown	Samuel	1		1			2			1				5		
Marblehead	266	3	Brown	Samuel		1	1		1			1		1			5		
Newbury	118	24	Brown	Samuel			1						1				2		
Newburyport	159	11	Brown	Samuel	2	2	1			2			1	1			10		
Salem	190	6	Brown	Samuel	1	1				1	3		1				7		
Newburyport	159	12	Brown	Samuel Jr			1			1		2					4		
Hamilton	285	102	Brown	Sarah									1	2			3		
Marblehead	269	5	Brown	Sarah	1					1	1		1				4		
Beverly	292	35	Brown	Simeon	1				1				1				3		
Hamilton	284	12	Brown	Simon					1		1			1			3		
Gloucester	58	33	Brown	Stephen		2		1		3	1		1				8		
Hamilton	284	2	Brown	Stephen			1		1			3		1			6		
Hamilton	285	99	Brown	Stephen		1	1	1		3	1	2	1				10		
Ipswich	281	9	Brown	Stephen		1	2		1	1	2	1	1	1			10		
Newbury	118	29	Brown	Stephen	2	2			1	1	3			1			10		
Newbury	120	29	Brown	Stephen		1	3	1		1	3			1			10		
Marblehead	244	2	Brown	Tameson									1	1			2		
Marblehead	251	14	Brown	Thomas		1			1	1			1				4		
Methuen	152	21	Brown	Thomas	1		1	1				1					4		
Newbury	118	30	Brown	Thomas		1				1			1				3		
Newbury	120	30	Brown	Thomas	1	1	1						1				4		
Newburyport	158	38	Brown	Thomas		1			1			3		1	1		7		
Marblehead	256	6	Brown	Thomas Junr			1			2			1				4		
Ipswich	279	11	Brown	Tristram	1		2			1	1	1					6		
Newburyport	159	14	Brown	Tristram		1						1					2		
Gloucester	67	17	Brown	Vincent	1			1		1			1				4		
Gloucester	86	8	Brown	Vincent	1			1		1			1				4		
Beverly	294	25	Brown	Walis	1			1		2			2				6		
Danvers	6	38	Brown	William	1			1		3			1				6		
Hamilton	285	56	Brown	William					1			1		1			3		
Marblehead	245	16	Brown	William	1	1		1		2			1				6		
Newburyport	159	16	Brown	William					1	2			1	1			5		
Salem	217	15	Brown	William	1			1		1		1		1			4		
Salisbury	25	2	Brown	William					1					1			2		
Wenham	308	22	Brown	William			1			1		2					4		
Hamilton	285	57	Brown	William Junr		2			2		1	1		2			8		
Lynn	231	2	Brown	Willm	3			1					1	1			6		
Manchester	50	9	Brown	Willm	1	2			1	2	1	1	1				9		
Salisbury	25	10	Brown	Willm Junr	1				1					1			3		
Newburyport	159	9	Brown	Zebulon R	1				1				1				3		
Salem	211	40	Brown	John	2			1					1				4		
Salem	188	39	Browne	Bart		1	2						1				4		
Salem	195	5	Browne	Barth	2	3			1	3			1				10		
Salem	211	19	Browne	Benja	1		1	1		4			1				8		
Salem	205	34	Browne	David	1		1						1				3		
Salem	188	37	Browne	Edward	2	1	2	1			1	1	1				9		
Salem	207	56	Browne	Eunice									1	1			2		
Salem	195	15	Browne	John	1			1		3		1	1	1			8		
Salem	208	34	Browne	John					1	1	1		1				4		
Salem	200	33	Browne	Jonathan	2			1	1	2	3		1	1			11		
Salem	210	33	Browne	Margaret		1				1			1				3		
Salem	201	8	Browne	Mary									1	1			2		
Salem	219	40	Browne	Nath	1			1		1			1				4		
Salem	211	15	Browne	Pelatiah			1			4			1				6		
Salem	210	35	Browne	Thos		1				3		1					5		
Salem	190	36	Bruce	George	2	1	1	1		1		1	1				8		
Marblehead	254	22	Bruce	Hannah	1									1			2		
Salem	208	21	Bruce	James	1		1			2			1				5		
Marblehead	239	8	Bruce	Joseph	1		1						1				3		
Lynn	233	4	Bruce	Lewis	3		1			1		1	1				7		
Salem	194	44	Bryant	John			1			3			1				5		
Salem	206	4	Bryant	Timo		1	1			2		1		1			6		
Gloucester	63	5	Bryer	John		1						1	1				3	West Ward	
Marblehead	247	24	Bubier	Hannah									1				1		
Marblehead	266	27	Bubin	Deborah								1		1			2		
Andover	91	25	Buck	Asa					1				1	1			3		

TOWN	PG#	LN#	LAST NAME	FIRST NAME	FREE WHITE MALES					FREE WHITE FEMALES					TOTAL ALL OTHER	TOTAL SLAVES	TOTALS	DISTRICT/ TOWNSHIP	NOTES
					under 10	10 to 16	16 to 26	26 to 45	45 and over	under 10	10 to 16	16 to 26	26 to 45	45 and over					
Haverhill	143	32	Buck	Eliphalet	1	2		1		4		1	1				10		
Newburyport	159	40	Buck	John			1			1	1		1				4		
Beverly	301	35	Buckman	Elizabeth										1			1		
Beverly	295	30	Buckman	John			1			1		1	1				4		
Beverly	294	10	Buckston	Anthony				1						1			2		
Salem	190	37	Buffington	Nehemh				1					1	1			3		
Salem	207	44	Buffinton	Deborah		2	1						3	1			7		
Salem	198	17	Buffinton	James	1			1					1				3		
Salem	192	36	Buffinton	Jas Jr	1			1					1				3		
Salem	189	11	Buffinton	John	1			1				2		1			5		
Salem	193	20	Buffum	Caleb				1			1		1	1			4		
Salem	183	22	Buffum	Isaac			2	1				1	1	1			6		
Salem	193	21	Buffum	Jona	1	1		1		1	1		1	1			7		
Salem	214	48	Buffum	Joshua		1				1		1					3		
Salem	214	54	Buffum	Sam Senr	1	2	3		1		1	1		1			10		
Salem	214	53	Buffum	Sanml Jr		1						1	1	1			4		
Salem	189	23	Buffum	Sarah								1	1	1			3		
Lynn	225	4	Bulfinch	Jerh	4	1		1		1	3	1	1				12		
Beverly	299	13	Bulloch	Betsey								3	1				4		
Salem	220	16	Bullock	Benja	2			1		1	1						5		
Salem	192	29	Bullock	Isaac		3	2		1	1		1	1				9		
Salem	192	32	Bullock	Jona				1		2							3		
Beverly	302	6	Bunker	Daniel	1		1	1		1	2		1	1			8		
Newburyport	160	6	Bunton	Thomas	1		1	1			1		1	1			6		
Bradford	124	42	Burbank	Benja	2			1		1		1	1				6		
Bradford	125	30	Burbank	Caleb	3			1		1		1	1				7		
Newburyport	160	21	Burbank	Daniel	3	2			2	1	1			1			10		
Bradford	125	18	Burbank	Elipht	4		2	1		1	1	1	1				11		
Bradford	125	29	Burbank	John	1		1	1		1		1	2	1			9		
Newbury	106	7	Burbank	Mary								1	1	1			3		
Bradford	124	15	Burbank	Stephen			2	1				1		1			5		
Bradford	124	7	Burbank	William	1			1			1		1				4		
Beverly	299	28	Burbank	Willm			2						1				3		
Danvers	8	30	Burch	Sarah									1				1		
Lynn	230	31	Burchstead	Henry		1	2	1					1	1			6		
Beverly	292	17	Burchsted	Henry	4	1	1	1		1	1		1				10		
Beverly	296	38	Burchsted	John	1		1	1				2	1				6		
Salem	220	20	Burdet	Abigail	1	1				1	1	1					6		
Ipswich	273	49	Burga	Sarah									1				1		
Gloucester	58	18	Burgan	John	1		1			2			1	1			6		
Marblehead	240	30	Burgean	William			1						1				3		
Manchester	50	18	Burges	Abial		2		1		3	1	1					9		
Manchester	55	9	Burges	David	2	2	2	1		1	1	1	1				11		
Salem	202	14	Burgess	William	1	1	1	1		2	1		1				8		
Beverly	301	21	Burk	Thomas			1			1			1				3		
Marblehead	262	20	Burnam	Mary	1	1	1				1	1		1			6		
Boxford	136	7	Burnam	Rufus		1		1		2		1					5		
Bradford	121	2	Burnell	James		1	1			3		1					6		
Gloucester	58	32	Burnham	Aaron	1	1	1	1			1		1				6		
Ipswich	282	2	Burnham	Aaron	1		1			2			1				5		
Ipswich	281	72	Burnham	Amos	3	1		1					1				6		
Ipswich	281	53	Burnham	Anna	2					2		1	1				6		
Ipswich	282	42	Burnham	Benjamin		1	1		1	1	1			1			6		
Ipswich	281	75	Burnham	Charles			1						1				2		
Newburyport	159	24	Burnham	Daniel	1		1			1			1		1		5		
Ipswich	281	83	Burnham	David			1			2	1	1					5		
Ipswich	282	43	Burnham	David				1					1				2		
Ipswich	282	40	Burnham	David Junr	2		1					1	1				6		
Ipswich	283	4	Burnham	Ebenezer		2	1	1		2		1					8		
Gloucester	55	7	Burnham	Ebenz		1	1	1		1	1		1				6		
Gloucester	84	10	Burnham	Eliz Widw		1					1		1				3		
Ipswich	280	31	Burnham	Elizabeth							1		1				2		
Ipswich	283	41	Burnham	Enoch	2		2	1		1			2				8		
Ipswich	282	21	Burnham	Eunice								1		1			2		
Ipswich	282	41	Burnham	Ezra			1			2			1				4		
Ipswich	282	48	Burnham	Francis				1					2	1			4		
Ipswich	278	52	Burnham	Isaac	1		2	1				1		1			6		
Ipswich	282	31	Burnham	Isaac	1		1	1				1		1			5		
Ipswich	282	49	Burnham	Jacob		2		1		2	2		1				8		
Ipswich	282	37	Burnham	James			1						1				2		
Beverly	306	17	Burnham	James Esq	2	1		1			2	1	1				8		
Ipswich	282	16	Burnham	Jesse	2			1		2			1				6		
Ipswich	283	12	Burnham	John	2			1		3	1	2	1				10		
Lynnfield	235	45	Burnham	John	1		1		1			2		1			6		
Gloucester	75	31	Burnham	Jona	2	2		1		1		1	1				8		
Ipswich	283	42	Burnham	Jonathan	3	2		1					1				7		
Ipswich	282	32	Burnham	Joseph			1	1		1		3		1			7		
Ipswich	282	19	Burnham	Joshua	2			1		1			1				5		
Lynnfield	235	28	Burnham	Joshua	2	3	4	1			2	2	1				15		
Ipswich	279	13	Burnham	Josiah		1	1							1			3		
Ipswich	276	18	Burnham	Judith	2			1		1			1	1			6		
Ipswich	283	13	Burnham	Martha									2	1			3		
Ipswich	282	53	Burnham	Mehitable							1			1			2		
Ipswich	282	20	Burnham	Moses			1			1			1				3		
Ipswich	283	31	Burnham	Moses					1				1				2		

			HEADS OF HOUSEHOLD		FREE WHITE MALES					FREE WHITE FEMALES									
TOWN	PG#	LN#	LAST NAME	FIRST NAME	under 10	10 to 16	16 to 26	26 to 45	45 and over	under 10	10 to 16	16 to 26	26 to 45	45 and over	TOTAL ALL OTHER	TOTAL SLAVES	TOTALS	DISTRICT/ TOWNSHIP	NOTES
Ipswich	282	1	Burnham	Nathan	2	2		1		1	1		1				8		
Ipswich	282	34	Burnham	Nathan			1			1		1					3		
Ipswich	282	47	Burnham	Nathaniel	2	1	3		1	3	1	1	1				13		
Ipswich	282	45	Burnham	Parker	1			1		3	2		1				8		
Ipswich	282	38	Burnham	Sarah									1	2			3		
Ipswich	276	35	Burnham	Thomas		2			1	2			2				7		
Ipswich	281	76	Burnham	Thomas M.	3	2		1		1			1				8		
Danvers	14	37	Burnham	Timothy				1		2		1					4		
Ipswich	282	44	Burnham	Westley	1	1	3		1	1	1		1	1			9		
Ipswich	283	36	Burnham	Westley	2			1					1				4		
Ipswich	282	13	Burnham	William		2	1	2	1	2	1	3		1			13		
Ipswich	282	27	Burnham	William	1				1		1	1	2	1			7		
Ipswich	281	79	Burnham	William 3d					1	2			1				4		
Salem	207	3	Burns	Edward			1				2	1					4		
Gloucester	78	26	Burns	John	2		1			1		1	1				6	Sandy Bay Parish	
Salem	193	5	Burns	John				1				1		1			3		
Salem	204	7	Burns	Tarrant	1	1		1		4	2		1				10		
Rowley	130	28	Burpee	Nathll	2	1		1		1			1				6		
Newburyport	159	36	Burrage	Hannah Wdo	1				1	1			1	1			5		
Marblehead	261	14	Burrage	Robert	1			1		3	1		1				7		
Lynn	224	26	Burrage	Susanna			1							1			2		
Salem	212	27	Burrel	Mansfield Jr	2		1	1		2			1				7		
Salem	212	33	Burrel	Mansfield Sen	1	1			1	2		3	1	1			10		
Salem	212	32	Burrel	William	1			2		2			1				6		
Salem	188	33	Burrell	Ebenz	2		1	2	1	3	1		1				11		
Haverhill	143	19	Burrell	Joseph	2		1			3			1				7		
Newburyport	159	30	Burril	John	2	1		1		2	1		1				8		
Newburyport	159	27	Burril	Samuel				1						1			2		
Newburyport	159	28	Burril	Samuel Jr	2		1	1		1			1	1			7		
Newburyport	159	29	Burril	Thomas	1	1		1		1	1		1				6		
Lynn	228	14	Burrill	Benja		1		1					1				3		
Lynn	231	22	Burrill	Ebenz		1		2				1		2			6		
Lynn	230	33	Burrill	John 3d		4		1			2			1			8		
Lynn	227	12	Burrill	John 4th	1		1			3			1				6		
Lynn	232	26	Burrill	John 5th	3			1		2			1				7	West Parish	
Lynn	224	4	Burrill	John Jr		1		1				1		1			4		
Lynn	232	24	Burrill	John Junr		1		1		1				1			4	West Parish	
Lynn	226	36	Burrill	Micajah	4	1		1			1			1			8		
Lynn	233	16	Burrill	Micajah Jn	1		1						1				3		
Lynn	234	3	Burrill	Saml	1		1					1					3		
Lynn	227	20	Burrill	Theoph	1		1				1	1	1				5		
Lynn	230	34	Burrill	Thomson	3	1	1		1	1			1				8		
Lynn	232	25	Burrill	Willm		1						1					2	West Parish	
Lynn	232	22	Burrll	Isaac		1		1						1			3	West Parish	
Amesbury	35	11	Burrough	George Capt		1	1		1				1	1			5		
Amesbury	35	1	Burrough	Josiah	1			1		3			1				6		
Marblehead	248	2	Burroughs	Alice									1				1		
Salem	209	23	Burroughs	Giles	1			1					1				3		
Marblehead	246	9	Burroughs	William		1	1						1				3		
Beverly	302	19	Burrows	Elizabeth									1				1		
Andover	91	21	Burt	Ebenezer	2		2	1		2	2	1	1				11		
Newburyport	159	35	Burt	Elizabeth Wdo						1				2			3		
Andover	91	12	Burt	Joseph		1		1	1	1	1		1	1			7		
Andover	91	22	Burt	Joseph Junr	3	1		1			1		1				7		
Salisbury	24	14	Burwell	Jacob				1		1	1	1		1			6		
Salisbury	24	15	Burwell	Jacob Junr	1			1		1			1				4		
Salisbury	24	16	Burwell	Moses				1						1			2		
Salisbury	24	13	Burwell	Walker		1	1	1				1		1			5		
Beverly	289	9	Busby	William		1	1	1	1	1		2		3			10		
Salem	219	48	Bushal	Josa		1				1				1			3		
Danvers	14	33	Bushby	Asa	2		1			1	1		1				6		
Danvers	10	38	Bushby	John				1						1			2		
Danvers	10	37	Bushby	John Jr	2		1			1			1				5		
Gloucester	85	19	Busten	Esther Wo								2		1			3		
Bradford	122	24	Buswell	Daniel		1			1	1	1			2			6		
Newburyport	160	5	Buswell	John	1	1		1		1		1					5		
Haverhill	143	29	Buswell	Mary									1	1			2		
Lynnfield	237	15	Butler	Amos	1			1		2			1				5		
Gloucester	75	21	Butler	John	1	3	1		1	1		2	1				10		
Ipswich	282	5	Butler	John			1	1		5	4		1	1			13		
Gloucester	55	13	Butler	Jona	3		1			1			1				6		
Newburyport	160	12	Butler	Philip		1		1		1	1		1				6		
Danvers	6	13	Butler	Richard				1		2			1				4		
Salem	202	21	Butler	Thos											2		2		
Newburyport	160	13	Butler	William	1		1			3	1		1	1			8		
Newburyport	160	14	Butler	William Junr	1		1					1	1				4		
Beverly	291	37	Butman	Benjamin	2			1		1	2	1	1	1			9		
Marblehead	269	20	Butman	Benjamin	2	2		1		1	2		1				9		
Danvers	8	9	Butman	Daniel				1						1			2		
Wenham	308	37	Butman	Daniel	1		1			3			1				6		
Boxford	135	23	Butman	David		1			1			1	1	1			5		
Salem	209	18	Butman	Eliza		1								1			2		
Marblehead	260	5	Butman	John		1				1			1				3		
Newburyport	160	15	Butman	Jonathan	1												4		

TOWN	PG#	LN#	LAST NAME	FIRST NAME	FREE WHITE MALES					FREE WHITE FEMALES					TOTAL ALL OTHER	TOTAL SLAVES	TOTALS	DISTRICT/ TOWNSHIP	NOTES
					under 10	10 to 16	16 to 26	26 to 45	45 and over	under 10	10 to 16	16 to 26	26 to 45	45 and over					
Marblehead	255	32	Butman	Joseph	2			1		1			1				5		
Marblehead	260	4	Butman	Joseph			1							1			2		
Beverly	302	17	Butman	Lucy										1			1		
Beverly	302	3	Butman	Mary									1	1			2		
Salem	209	16	Butman	Ruth			1							1			2		
Beverly	302	1	Butman	Samuel	2			1					1				4		
Salem	213	21	Butman	Thos		1	3			1	1		1				7		
Gloucester	83	30	Butnam	Joseph			1	0		1	1	1					4		
Gloucester	78	23	Butram	Jerea Junr			1			1		1					3		Sandy Bay Parish
Gloucester	78	22	Butram	Jeremiah		1	1	1		2			1				6		Sandy Bay Parish
Gloucester	76	4	Butram	Jona		1		1		2		1					5		
Boxford	134	18	Butrick	William	1			1		1		2					5		
Ipswich	283	46	Butter	Ralph	1	1		1		2		1					6		
Andover	91	4	Butters	Benjamin				1		1			1				3		
Gloucester	71	20	Button	Henry			1					1					2		
Danvers	14	42	Buxton	Amos		1		1		1	1		1				5		
Danvers	3	11	Buxton	Amos Junr		1	1	1				1	1		1		6		
Danvers	14	41	Buxton	Henry	1	1		1				2		1			6		
Danvers	14	38	Buxton	John		1	1	1					1	1			5		
Danvers	11	8	Buxton	Jonathan			1	1					2	1			5		
Danvers	11	7	Buxton	Jonathan Junr	2			1		2			1	1			7		
Danvers	14	40	Buxton	Joseph	2			1		2				1			6		
Danvers	14	39	Buxton	Sarah				1						1			2		
Salem	211	14	Buxton	Thos			1						1				2		
Beverly	297	22	Byler	Alexander	1		1						1				3		
Beverly	297	16	Byler	Betsy									3				3		
Beverly	297	21	Byler	Mary	1		1						1	1			4		
Salem	217	7	Byrnee	Clifford		1	1	1				1		1			5		
Salem	217	9	Byrnee	Clifford Jr			1			2		1					4		
Beverly	299	3	Cabot	Huldah								1	1				2		
Beverly	304	13	Cabot	Lydia			3			1	2	4	1				11		
Salem	188	34	Cabot	Rebecca							1	1	1	1			4		
Salem	188	25	Cabot	Thos	1	1	1				1		1				5		
Beverly	304	17	Cabott	John		1		1		1	1	1	1				6		
Newbury	114	3	Cadwall	Robert		1				1		1					3		
Marblehead	270	5	Cahill	William											3		3		
Salem	211	51	Cahon	Aaron	1		1			1		1					4		
Salem	220	31	Cahoo	Samuel				1		1		1					3		
Salem	208	55	Cain	Thos	1		1			2			1				5		
Gloucester	58	38	Calder	Samuel	2		1			1			1	1			6		
Newburyport	162	28	Caldwell	Alexander	2	2	1		1			3		1			10		
Ipswich	274	38	Caldwell	Benjamin		1		1				2					4		
Salem	211	4	Caldwell	Daniel	2		1			1		1					5		
Ipswich	276	50	Caldwell	Ebenezer	1	1	1		1	2	2	2		1			11		
Ipswich	280	29	Caldwell	Francis			1	1			1	2					5		
Ipswich	274	40	Caldwell	John	1	1		1			4	1	1				9		
Ipswich	276	49	Caldwell	John			1	1					1				3		
Ipswich	274	19	Caldwell	Martha									1				1		
Salem	215	40	Caldwell	Mary	1	1				1	2	1					6		
Ipswich	277	24	Caldwell	Moses	5	1		1		1		1					9		
Ipswich	276	8	Caldwell	Samuel				1				1	1				3		
Hamilton	285	72	Caldwell	Stephen			1			1		1					3		
Ipswich	275	5	Caldwell	Thomas	1	1		3		2	1		3	18	1		30		
Ipswich	278	24	Caldwell	Thomas	2	1	2	1				1	1				8		
Newburyport	162	27	Caldwell	William		1		1	1		1	2		1			7		
Newburyport	162	23	Calef	Elizabeth Wido		1	1						1				3		
Ipswich	279	26	Calef	Jeddediah	1		1					1					3		
Beverly	298	42	Calf	John		1				1			1	1			4		
Marblehead	240	26	Call	Henry P.	1		1			2		1					5		
Newburyport	162	17	Call	Jonathan	1	2	1		1	3	1	3					12		
Beverly	300	2	Calla	John			1			1		1					3		
Marblehead	269	14	Calley	Hannah			1						1				2		
Newburyport	162	26	Calley	Israel		1		1		2			1				5		
Marblehead	269	15	Calley	Rebecca										1			1		
Marblehead	250	8	Calley	Samuel		1						1					2		
Marblehead	267	29	Calley	Thomas			1			1		1					3		
Marblehead	252	11	Calley	William	3	1		1		2	1		1				9		
Salem	204	20	Callum	John		1		1		3			1	1			7		
Salem	218	29	Callum	Sarah	2	2				1			1				6		
Newbury	119	35	Callwall	David		1	1		1	2	2		2				9		
Newbury	113	33	Callwall	John			1			1		1					3		
Newbury	119	32	Callwall	Joshua			1	1		1		1	1				5		
Newbury	119	34	Callwall	Josiah			1						1				2		
Newbury	119	33	Callwall	Nathll			1						1				2		
Newburyport	162	18	Calman	William			1			1		1	1				4		
Newbury	110	27	Calwell	David	2		1	1		2	1		1				8		
Salem	200	30	Cambell	Arthur	2			1					1				4		
Newbury	110	2	Cammel	Alexander	2		1	1		4			1				9		
Newbury	114	20	Cammil	Jack											3		3		
Manchester	53	14	Camp	William	2			1		1			1	1			6		
Beverly	298	19	Campbell	Duncan		1	1						1	3			6		
Bradford	122	15	Campbell	James	1		1	1		1		1	1	1			7		
Newburyport	163	10	Campbell	James			1	1				3		1			6		
Marblehead	256	7	Candler	John	3	2	2	1		1	1		1				11		
Marblehead	261	9	Canell	James	1			1		1	1		1				5		
Marblehead	257	18	Capell	William	1	2			1	2	3	2		1			12		
Gloucester	86	9	Card	Benja			1					1					2		

TOWN	PG#	LN#	LAST NAME	FIRST NAME	M under 10	M 10 to 16	M 16 to 26	M 26 to 45	M 45 and over	F under 10	F 10 to 16	F 16 to 26	F 26 to 45	F 45 and over	TOTAL ALL OTHER	TOTAL SLAVES	TOTALS	DISTRICT/ TOWNSHIP	NOTES
Gloucester	68	22	Card	Mary Wo							1			1			2		
Marblehead	270	13	Card	Nathaniel			1						1				2		
Gloucester	79	2	Card	William	2		1			3	1	1	1				9		
Salem	208	48	Cardwell	Eliza			1					1		1			3		
Salem	208	33	Cardwell	Jacob	2		1					1					4		
Marblehead	250	33	Carell	Mary	2					2			1				5		
Haverhill	144	38	Carleton	Aaron		1	1	1			1	1	1				6		
Newbury	106	48	Carleton	Amos		2	1			1	1						5		
Methuen	153	7	Carleton	Daniel	1		1					2		1			5		
Methuen	153	1	Carleton	Ebenezr		3	1	1		1	1	1		1			9		
Methuen	153	2	Carleton	Ebenezr Junr	2	1		1		2	1	1	1				9		
Methuen	153	3	Carleton	Elijah	2	2	1		1		1	2		1			10		
Haverhill	144	18	Carleton	Enos	2	2		1		3	1		1				10		
Haverhill	144	43	Carleton	Israel	2		1	1		3	1	1	1				10		
Haverhill	144	29	Carleton	Jonathan			1	1			1	1					4		
Boxford	134	48	Carleton	Joseph		2	1		1	2		1	1	1			9		
Haverhill	144	28	Carleton	Kimball		1			1	1		1		1			5		
Haverhill	144	30	Carleton	Michael	2			1					1				4		
Haverhill	144	27	Carleton	Phineas	1				1	1		4	1	1	1		10		
Methuen	153	14	Carleton	Samuel	3		1	1		1			1				7		
Salem	192	2	Carlis	Joseph			1			2		1					4		
Boxford	134	22	Carlston	Moses	1			1			1		1				4		
Boxford	134	21	Carlston	Samuel	1	2			2	3	1	2	1	1			13		
Andover	92	28	Carlton	Amos	1			1		1		1					4		
Andover	92	2	Carlton	Benjamin		2	1	1		3			1				8		
Andover	92	21	Carlton	Christopher			1	1			1	1		1			5		
Andover	92	19	Carlton	Daniel					2			1		2			5		
Andover	92	22	Carlton	Daniel Junr	2	1	1	1		1	1	1	1				9		
Bradford	121	6	Carlton	David		1		1		3			1	1			8		
Bradford	122	17	Carlton	David		1	4	1		1		1					9		
Andover	92	23	Carlton	Dean	1	1		1				1	1				5		
Bradford	122	25	Carlton	Dudley		1			1		1	1	1		1		6		
Andover	92	20	Carlton	Ezekiel		1	2		1	1		1	2	1			9		
Andover	92	1	Carlton	Isaac					2			1		1			4		
Andover	92	25	Carlton	Israel	1			1		1		1					4		
Newburyport	162	34	Carlton	John			2					2					4		
Bradford	123	14	Carlton	Jos		2		1		1			1				5		
Bradford	121	10	Carlton	Margea*	1			1		3			1				6		
Andover	92	24	Carlton	Michael				1		1		1	1				4		
Andover	92	18	Carlton	Peter		1	1		1			2		1			6		
Bradford	123	38	Carlton	Phineas		3	1		1	3	1	1					10		
Bradford	123	15	Carlton	Reuben					1					1			2		
Bradford	123	16	Carlton	Reuben Jr	1		1			1		1					4		
Salem	216	25	Carlton	Samuel		1		1	1				2	1			6		
Bradford	121	9	Carlton	Stephen				1					1				2		
Salem	212	16	Carlton	William		3	1	1		1	1			1	1		9		
Manchester	50	11	Carmen	John		1					1		1				3		
Salem	190	1	Carner	Samuel			1			2		1	1				5		
Salem	214	44	Carnes	Hannah							1	1	3				5		
Lynn	229	21	Carnes	John Esq				1				1	1				3		
Salem	191	34	Carnes	Jonathan		1		1		3		1	1				7		
Marblehead	249	19	Carney	Susannah	2					3		1					6		
Danvers	8	26	Caroll	Amey									1				1		
Danvers	8	28	Caroll	William	1			1		2		1					5		
Salem	206	14	Carpenter	Benja		1		1	1		1	2		1			7		
Salisbury	26	16	Carr	Benja					2				1				3		
Salisbury	26	17	Carr	Charles	1			1		1			1				4		
Newbury	107	30	Carr	Daniel	1		1		1		1	2	1				7		
Haverhill	144	5	Carr	Francis	2	1	1		1	2	1	1					9		
Salisbury	26	4	Carr	James					1			3					4		
Salisbury	25	24	Carr	Jesse	3	2			1	1		1	1				9		
Newbury	107	18	Carr	John		1						1					2		
Newbury	108	3	Carr	John	1		1	1		2		1					6		
Newbury	108	7	Carr	Josiah			1	1					1				3		
Salisbury	26	5	Carr	Levi	1			1				1					3		
Salisbury	25	26	Carr	Osgood			1		1				1	1			4		
Newbury	111	1	Carr	Richard	1			1			1	1					4		
Salisbury	25	27	Carr	Robert	1	1			1				1	1			5		
Newbury	108	2	Carr	Samuel	2		1	1		1		1					6		
Newbury	108	6	Carr	samuel			1	1	1		1		1	1			6		
Salisbury	25	18	Carr	Samuel	2	1		1		1			1	1			7		
Salem	211	6	Carrel	Edward		1			1			1	1	1			5		
Lynn	228	9	Carriage	Willm	1	1		1		1			1				5		
Beverly	300	15	Carrico	John					1					1			2		
Salem	219	39	Carrie	James					1	3	1	3		1			9		
Beverly	293	10	Carries	Alexander			1	1						1			3		
Beverly	296	30	Carries	Benjamin	2			1		1			1				5		
Beverly	293	11	Carries	Thomas			1			1		1					3		
Newburyport	163	8	Carrol	Philip			1					1		1			3		
Marblehead	253	6	Carryll	Jane	1					3	1		2	1			8		
Gloucester	73	11	Carter	Anna Wo	1		1		1	1			2				8		
Manchester	53	9	Carter	Benja	1	1		1		1			1				5		

TOWN	PG#	LN#	LAST NAME	FIRST NAME	FREE WHITE MALES					FREE WHITE FEMALES					TOTAL ALL OTHER	TOTAL SLAVES	TOTALS	DISTRICT/ TOWNSHIP	NOTES
					under 10	10 to 16	16 to 26	26 to 45	45 and over	under 10	10 to 16	16 to 26	26 to 45	45 and over					
Newburyport	161	15	Carter	Benjamin			1			2			1				4		
Gloucester	78	13	Carter	Gideon	2	3		1		3			1				10		
Gloucester	73	3	Carter	John	1		1			1		1	1				5		
Newburyport	161	14	Carter	Joshua	2		1	2		2	1		2				10		
Lynn	234	19	Carter	Loami	1		1					1		2			5		
Manchester	50	19	Carter	Nathan	1		1			2			1				5		
Newburyport	161	13	Carter	Nathaniel	1	2	1	1		2	1		1				10		
Manchester	50	30	Carter	Obed Junr	1		1	1		1			1				5		
Manchester	53	15	carter	Oben				1			1		1				3		
Gloucester	70	1	Carter	William	3		1			3			1	1			9		
Marblehead	253	23	Caruth	Thomas				1				2		1			4		
Salem	208	18	Carwick	Henry	3		1			1	2		1				8		
Salem	200	7	Cary	Joseph	2		1			1			1				5		
Newburyport	160	33	Cary	Thomas Revd	1	1	1		1		1		1	1			7		
Marblehead	248	1	Caryll	Jane	1					2	2		1	1			7		
Marblehead	266	26	Caryll	Susanna			2						1				3		
Marblehead	252	21	Casden	Joseph				1					2				3		
Haverhill	144	33	Case	William			1	1					1				3		
Marblehead	260	11	Cash	George	1		1			1	1	1					6		
Marblehead	255	26	Cash	Hannah			1				1			1			3		
Marblehead	258	6	Cash	Mary										1			1		
Marblehead	260	24	Cash	Moses	2		2		1	1	1			1			8		
Salem	220	34	Cassan	Samuel	1		1						1				3		
Beverly	303	26	Castle	Samuel		2	1		1			1	1				6		
Marblehead	261	15	Caswell	John	1		1	1	1				1	1			6		
Gloucester	63	26	Caswell	Samuel			1	1		2			1				5	East Ward	
Marblehead	253	11	Caswell	William	4	1		1					1				7		
Newbury	114	19	Casy	Ammy	1						1	1	1	1			5		
Beverly	295	34	Cavendish	John			1						1				2		
Middleton	17	35	Cave	Amos	2		1	1		1		1	1	1			8		
Middleton	17	36	Cave	Silvester			1										1		
Ipswich	281	64	Cavis	John			1	1					1				3		
Andover	92	26	Cazneau	Isaac			1						1				2		
Salisbury	25	16	Celey	Betty Wd									1				1		
Salem	207	48	Chace	Abijah	1		1	1		1		1	1				6		
Salem	199	36	Chace	Abner	1		1	1		1			2	1			7		
Amesbury	38	16	Chace	Amos			1	1	1	1		2	1	1			8		
Amesbury	38	15	Chace	Mary Wid										1			1		
Lynn	225	16	Chadwell	Harris		1	1		1			2	1	1			7		
Lynn	225	15	Chadwell	Moses	1		1						1				3		
Beverly	299	23	Chadwick	Abijah	2		1		1	2	2		1				9		
Salem	214	13	Chadwick	Gilbert	2	2	2		1	3			2	1			13		
Boxford	134	11	Chadwick	Isaac			1						1		1		3		
Bradford	122	38	Chadwick	James	4	2	1	1		1	1		1				11		
Bradford	123	8	Chadwick	Jonathan				1					1	1			3		
Bradford	123	9	Chadwick	Joseph	2		1	1		1	2	1	1				9		
Boxford	134	8	Chadwick	Moses	1		2			1	2		1				7		
Boxford	134	9	Chadwick	Samuel			1	1		1	1	1			1		6		
Bradford	122	41	Chadwick	Samuel			1	1					1	1			4		
Boxford	134	10	Chadwick	Thos	1			1		2			1		1		6		
Amesbury	38	2	Chalace	Elizabeth Wid									2	1			3		
Amesbury	38	1	Chalace	John	1		1	1		1	2			1			7		
Amesbury	37	30	Chalace	Samuel			1	1		1		2		1			6		
Amesbury	37	34	Chalace	Thomas		1	1	1					3	1			7		
Amesbury	37	5	Chalace	Timothy				1					1				2		
Amesbury	37	1	Chalace	Wid			1			1				1			3		
Salem	195	6	Chamberlain	Eliz	1							1	1				3		
Lynn	232	16	Chamberlain	Mary		1				1	1	1					4		
Salem	193	40	Chamberlain	Nath	3	2			1		1		1				8		
Salem	202	1	Chamberlain	Samuel	1	1	1						1				4		
Haverhill	144	31	Chamberlain	Wilson	2	1	2	1		1			1				8		
Marblehead	256	26	Chambers	Ephraim	1	2	1		1	1			2				8		
Marblehead	255	24	Chambers	John			1				1						2		
Salem	206	3	Chammins	John	1			1		1			1				4		
Salem	189	36	Champlin	London												2	2		
Beverly	294	29	Champney	Thomas			1		1			1		1			4		
Andover	92	33	Chandler	Abiel	2	1	1	1	1	2		1	3	1			13		
Andover	92	12	Chandler	Bekah Wid		1							1	1			3		
Salisbury	26	21	Chandler	Elizabeth Wd									1				1		
Amesbury	37	15	Chandler	Hannah Wid			1			1			1	1			4		
Andover	92	8	Chandler	Hannah Wid									1	1	2		3		
Andover	92	9	Chandler	Isaac			1		1	2	1		1				6		
Beverly	306	9	Chandler	Isaac	2	1		1		2	1		1				8		
Andover	92	38	Chandler	James	2	2		1		2	1	1	1				10		
Andover	92	15	Chandler	John	1		1	1		3		1	1				8		
Salem	194	31	Chandler	John		1	1		1				1	1			5		
Salem	196	35	Chandler	John		1				1			1				3		
Andover	93	1	Chandler	Joseph	2	1	1	1		2		1	1				9		
Andover	92	30	Chandler	Joshua		1		1	1	2			1				8		
Andover	92	17	Chandler	Phebe Wid									1	1			2		
Salem	194	2	Chandler	William	1			1		1	3		1				7		
Andover	92	39	Chandler	Zebadiah	2	1	1		2	2	1	2		1			12		
Marblehead	270	7	Chapell	Mary								2		1			3		

174

TOWN	PG#	LN#	LAST NAME	FIRST NAME	FREE WHITE MALES					FREE WHITE FEMALES					TOTAL ALL OTHER	TOTAL SLAVES	TOTALS	DISTRICT/ TOWNSHIP	NOTES
					under 10	10 to 16	16 to 26	26 to 45	45 and over	under 10	10 to 16	16 to 26	26 to 45	45 and over					
Rowley	127	13	Chapin	Jonathn			2	1	1			1	1	2			8		
Bradford	125	21	Chaplin	Aaron	1	2		1					1				5		
Rowley	127	38	Chaplin	Asa		1	2		1		1			1			6		
Rowley	130	49	Chaplin	Joseph			1		1			1		1			4		
Rowley	130	48	Chaplin	Moses	1		2		2	1	1			2			9		
Salem	196	15	Chaplin	Solo	1	1	1	1		2			1	1			8		
Beverly	295	48	Chapman	Abner	1	1	1	1		2		1	1				8		
Marblehead	270	29	Chapman	Annie		1	1							1			3		
Boxford	135	11	Chapman	Daniel		1		2				1		1			5		
Marblehead	262	22	Chapman	Daniel	2			1		2	3	1	1				10		
Beverly	303	40	Chapman	Eliza								1		1			2		
Beverly	298	17	Chapman	George D			1			1		1					3		
Salem	212	14	Chapman	Isaac N			1	1		1		1	1				5		
Marblehead	260	33	Chapman	Jane							2		1				3		
Marblehead	270	32	Chapman	Jane			1						1				2		
Ipswich	279	28	Chapman	Jedediah	1	2		2	1			1	2				9		
Ipswich	275	57	Chapman	Joanna									1				1		
Beverly	306	15	Chapman	John		1		1	1	1		3		1			7		
Marblehead	262	21	Chapman	John	1		1			1		1					4		
Salem	213	19	Chapman	John	3		1						1				5		
Topsfield	19	35	Chapman	John		2	1		1	1				1			6		
Newbury	117	10	Chapman	Jonath		1						1	1				3		
Ipswich	279	34	Chapman	Joseph		1					2		1				4		
Rowley	130	14	Chapman	Joseph			1			1	1		1				4		
Beverly	297	43	Chapman	Josiah F	1		1			1			1				4		
Beverly	295	45	Chapman	Prescilla						1	1		1				3		
Beverly	297	32	Chapman	Rebeca						1		2	1				4		
Marblehead	262	23	Chapman	Samuel	1		1			1		1					4		
Salem	199	41	Chapman	Sarah		1							1				2		
Marblehead	262	24	Chapman	Stephen	1		1			1		1					4		
Newbury	112	14	Chapman	William		1						1					2		
Salem	209	44	Chard	Mary									1				1		
Newbury	116	5	Chase	Able			1				2	2	1				6		
Newbury	118	37	Chase	Able		1			1	1	2						5		
Haverhill	144	26	Chase	Amos	1		1			2		2					6		
Newbury	109	3	Chase	Amos	3	2		1					1				7		
Haverhill	144	6	Chase	Anthony		1		1	1	1	1		1				5		
Newbury	109	23	Chase	Aquilla	4	2		1		2	2		1				12		
Salisbury	26	15	Chase	Baley Capt	3	1		1				1	1				7		
Lynn	223	48	Chase	Benj		1		1		1		2		1			6		
Danvers	2	7	Chase	Benjamin			1	1				2					4		
Haverhill	144	36	Chase	Benjamin	2	1	1			3	1		1				10		
Newburyport	161	38	Chase	Benjamin		1						1					2		
Newbury	107	37	Chase	Caleb			1					1					2		
Lynn	227	34	Chase	Charles	2		1	1				1					5		
Salisbury	25	22	Chase	Charles	1		1			1		2					5		
Haverhill	144	3	Chase	Daniel	2		1			1		1					5		
Lynn	227	36	Chase	Daniel	1		1					1					3		
Newbury	115	25	Chase	Daniel	1		1			1	1		1				5		
Haverhill	144	4	Chase	Daniel Jun			1			1			1				3		
Newbury	107	41	Chase	David		1		1		1		1	1				5		
Newbury	107	47	Chase	David				1									1		
Andover	92	35	Chase	Enoch		2			1	1		1		1			6		
Haverhill	144	12	Chase	Ephraim	1			1		2			1				5		
Newburyport	161	32	Chase	Ezra			1					1					2		
Lynn	224	2	Chase	Jacob	2			1					1				4		
Haverhill	144	45	Chase	James		1		1		1		1		1			5		
Newburyport	161	34	Chase	James		1		1	1	2				1			6		
Newburyport	161	35	Chase	James Junr	1			1		1			1				4		
Newbury	116	6	Chase	Jeremiah	1			1	1	3	2		1				10		
Newbury	118	10	Chase	Johanna		1		1				1	1				4		
Haverhill	144	9	Chase	John	1		1					1					3		
Lynn	231	41	Chase	John	2		1						1				4		
Newbury	107	17	Chase	John				1		1			1				3		
Newbury	108	36	Chase	John				1				2	1				4		
Newbury	118	15	Chase	John	3	1		1			2	1	1				9		
Haverhill	144	11	Chase	Jonah	2	1		1		2	1	1					9		
Newbury	107	46	Chase	Jonathan	1	1		1		1			1				5		
Haverhill	144	8	Chase	Joseph	1		1	1		2		1	1				7		
Newbury	107	13	Chase	Joseph	1	1		1		2	2		1				8		
Newbury	107	44	Chase	Joseph		1		1		1			1				4		
Newbury	118	36	Chase	Joseph	1			1	1	3	2		1	1			10		
Newbury	120	34	Chase	Joshua	1	2		1		1	2	1	1				9		
Newbury	120	25	Chase	Josiah	1	3	1	1		4	1	1	1	1			14		
Haverhill	144	10	Chase	Leonard	1	1			1				1	2			6		
Amesbury	37	6	Chase	Mary Wid									1				1		
Newbury	107	1	Chase	Moses			1					1					2		
Newbury	107	15	Chase	Moses			1	1		2			1				5		
Newbury	108	43	Chase	Nathan	1			1				1					3		
Newbury	108	44	Chase	Nathan		1	1			3			1				6		
Newbury	115	26	Chase	Nathl	1			1		1			1				4		
Newbury	107	14	Chase	Parker	1		1	1					1				4		
Salem	207	45	Chase	Rebc		1	3			2		1	1	1			9		
Lynn	223	20	Chase	Saml	2		1	1			2		1				7		
Newbury	109	2	Chase	Samuel	1	1	1	1	1	2		1	1				9		

TOWN	PG#	LN#	LAST NAME	FIRST NAME	M under 10	M 10 to 16	M 16 to 26	M 26 to 45	M 45 and over	F under 10	F 10 to 16	F 16 to 26	F 26 to 45	F 45 and over	TOTAL ALL OTHER	TOTAL SLAVES	TOTALS	DISTRICT/ TOWNSHIP	NOTES
Newburyport	161	37	Chase	Samuel	1			1		1		2					5		
Newbury	116	20	Chase	Semien				1		1			1				3		
Newburyport	161	36	Chase	Somerby	2		2		1		1	1	1				8		
Newbury	107	3	Chase	Somesby	2	1	1	1		1	2	1	1				10		
Haverhill	144	19	Chase	Theoph	1			1		2			1				5		
Newbury	118	38	Chase	Thomas				1					1				2		
Newbury	116	18	Chase	Tristam				1	1		1	1	3	1			8		
Newbury	107	8	Chase	Trustham	1		2	1					1				5		
Haverhill	144	13	Chase	William	1		1	1		2	1	1	2				9		
Newburyport	161	33	Chase	William		1			2				2				6		
Newburyport	162	4	Chase	William Jr			1			2		1	1	1			6		
Haverhill	144	7	Chase	Woodman	1	1		1		3	1	1	1				9		
Salem	210	32	Cheever	Benja		1		1		1	3		1				7		
Newburyport	162	2	Cheever	Benjamin H	1			1		1			1				4		
Salem	193	31	Cheever	Ebenz	1			1				1	1				4		
Manchester	50	15	Cheever	Ezeh		2	1		1			1		1			6		
Danvers	2	26	Cheever	Israel Jur		1	2		1				1				5		
Danvers	2	27	Cheever	Israel Jur					1			1	1				3		
Salem	212	51	Cheever	James	4		1	1			2	1	1	1			11		
Manchester	50	22	Cheever	John	1	1			1	1	1						5		
Marblehead	252	12	Cheever	John	2	1		1		1	1		1				7		
Newburyport	162	1	Cheever	John	4	2	1		1			1		1			10		
Salem	212	37	Cheever	Mary									1				1		
Newburyport	161	39	Cheever	Moses		1	1	1	1			1	1				6		
Danvers	3	1	Cheever	Nathan	4			1					1				6		
Andover	92	11	Cheever	Peter		1		1	1			1	1				5		
Marblehead	250	1	Cheever	Peter D.	2	1		1		2			1				7		
Danvers	2	31	Cheever	Samuel				1									1		
Salem	198	31	Cheever	Samuel	1			1		1		1	1	1			6		
Salem	208	15	Cheever	Samuel	2	1		1			1	1	1				7		
Salem	210	30	Cheever	Samuel				1					1				2		
Manchester	50	20	Cheever	Sarah Wo				1		1			1		2		5		
Danvers	9	1	Cheever	Simon			1	1	1				1				4		
Newburyport	162	3	Cheever	William				1					1				2		
Gloucester	63	24	Chellis	Gideon		1	1	1			2	1		1			7	East Ward	
Bradford	125	26	Cheney	Daniel				1		1	1						3		
Newbury	106	30	Cheney	John		1	2	1			2	2	1				9		
Newbury	108	31	Cheney	John		1				2			1				4		
Rowley	128	24	Cheney	Jonathan	1		1		1			1	1				5		
Rowley	128	26	Cheney	Mark	1		1						1				3		
Newbury	114	9	Cheney	Moses	1	1		1		1		2	1				7		
Newburyport	162	38	Cheney	Moses	2	1		1		2	1		1				8		
Lynn	229	1	Chever	Abijah	2			1					1				4		
Lynn	233	13	Chever	Abner	1	1		2		2	1		1		1		9		
Lynn	233	17	Chever	Eliza										2			2		
Lynn	233	18	Chever	Ezekiel	1			1		2			2				6		
Lynn	233	19	Chever	James	1			1		2			1	1			6		
Lynn	224	41	Chever	Thos					1			1		1			3		
Lynn	225	2	Chever	Thos Jr	1	1		1		1			1				5		
Andover	92	4	Chickering	Dean	3	1		1		1			1				7		
Haverhill	144	32	Chickering	John		1	1		1		1	2		1			7		
Andover	92	3	Chickering	Samuel	2	2		2	1			2	1	2			12		
Methuen	153	10	Chickering	Samuel	3			1		1	2		1				8		
Danvers	13	29	Child	Lemuel		2		1		1			1				5		
Marblehead	258	20	Chinn	Samuel		1	2	1	1			1		1			7		
Marblehead	257	35	Chinn	Samuel Junr		1		1		2			1				5		
Salem	214	49	Chipman	John	1	1	1		1		2						6		
Beverly	293	41	Chipman	Joseph		1	1		2			1	1				6		
Salem	204	14	Chipman	Thos	1	1		2		3	1		2				10		
Salem	193	3	Chisholm	Willm	2			1		2	2	1					8		
Newbury	108	47	Chismore	David		2	1			2			1				6		
Salem	190	3	Chissee	Emanuel	1			1				1		1			4		
Marblehead	259	11	Chittenden	Thomas				1			1			1			3		
Gloucester	56	5	Choate	Adonjo	1			1						1			3		
Newburyport	162	33	Choate	Benjamin		1	1		2		2						6		
Ipswich	274	5	Choate	Daniel				1					1	1			3		
Gloucester	74	14	Choate	David	1			1		2	1		1				6	Squam Parish	
Ipswich	281	66	Choate	David	2		1	1		2			1	1			8		
Newburyport	162	32	Choate	Ebenezer	4	1		1		2	1	1	1				11		
Ipswich	281	49	Choate	George	3	1	1	1			1	1	1				9		
Ipswich	276	43	Choate	John	2			2			1		1				6		
Ipswich	281	54	Choate	John		2						1					3		
Gloucester	55	16	Choate	Josiah				1					1				2		
Gloucester	56	1	Choate	Judith Wd		1	1			1			1				4		
Ipswich	283	24	Choate	Nathan			1	1			1	1	1	1	1		6		
Gloucester	79	9	Choate	Sola	1	1	1						1				4		
Ipswich	283	23	Choate	Solomon	3		1	1		2		1	1	1			11		
Ipswich	283	45	Choate	Solomon Junr			1		1	2		1	2	1			7		
Gloucester	74	13	Choate	Stephen	1			1			1		1				4	Squam Parish	
Ipswich	278	40	Choate	Stephen		1		1	1	1		2	1	1	1		7		
Ipswich	279	10	Choate	Stephen Jun	1	1	2			1	1	1		1			9		
Ipswich	281	82	Choate	Thomas	2	1		1	1		1	1	1				8		
Marblehead	262	29	Church	Anna									1				1		
Marblehead	241	22	Church	George			1						1				2		

TOWN	PG#	LN#	LAST NAME	FIRST NAME	FREE WHITE MALES under 10	10 to 16	16 to 26	26 to 45	45 and over	FREE WHITE FEMALES under 10	10 to 16	16 to 26	26 to 45	45 and over	TOTAL ALL OTHER	TOTAL SLAVES	TOTALS	DISTRICT/ TOWNSHIP	NOTES
Salem	199	3	Churchill	Zacheus	1		1						1				3		
Rowley	128	36	Chute	David				1		3			2				6		
Rowley	128	39	Chute	James		2	2	1		1	1	2	2				11		
Newburyport	162	21	Clannin	Benjamin	1			1		1		1					4		
Andover	92	34	Clark	Abijah			3		1	1	1	1		1			8		
Rowley	129	14	Clark	Amos	2			1		1			1				5		
Gloucester	69	7	Clark	Bacokus Sargent			1	1					1	1	4		8		
Danvers	2	12	Clark	Caleb			1	1					1				3		
Danvers	2	13	Clark	Caleb Junr	2			1		1			1				5		
Newburyport	162	10	Clark	Christopher		1			1		1			1			4		
Lynn	231	27	Clark	Edmd				1			1			1			3		
Haverhill	145	5	Clark	Elijah			1						1				2		
Marblehead	254	17	Clark	George		1		1			1			1			4		
Gloucester	55	19	Clark	George Junr	1		1						1				3		
Rowley	127	39	Clark	Hannah		1								1			2		
Topsfield	19	31	Clark	Israel	2			1					1	1			5		
Beverly	291	5	Clark	John				1					1	1			3		
Gloucester	72	26	Clark	John	1			1		3			1				6		
Salem	189	8	Clark	John		1	1		1		3		1	1			8		
Newburyport	162	13	Clark	John P	2			1					1				4		
Beverly	291	6	Clark	Jonathan	1			1					1				3		
Methuen	153	13	Clark	Joseph	2	1	1						1				5		
Andover	92	16	Clark	Lemuel	3			1					1				5		
Andover	92	7	Clark	Micah		1	1		1					1			4		
Newburyport	162	12	Clark	Moses	3	1		1		1			1				7		
Rowley	129	15	Clark	Moses				1		2			1				4		
Haverhill	144	42	Clark	Nathaniel			1	2						1			4		
Beverly	298	9	Clark	Nathanl				1						2			3		
Beverly	290	9	Clark	Peter	3			1					1				5		
Marblehead	262	26	Clark	Rebecca	1	1								1			3		
Beverly	297	35	Clark	Richard			1						1				2		
Newburyport	162	9	Clark	Robert		1	2					1					4		
Topsfield	19	30	Clark	Ruth										1			1		
Andover	93	3	Clark	Samuel	1	1	1		1				1	1			6		
Methuen	153	12	Clark	Samuel	4	1						1	1	1			10		
Newburyport	162	14	Clark	Samuel				1			1			1			3		
Marblehead	249	15	Clark	Sarah										1			1		
Salisbury	26	11	Clark	Seth			1		1				1				3		
Newburyport	162	15	Clark	Stephen				1						1			2		
Lynn	231	43	Clark	Theophl	2		1						1				4		
Andover	92	36	Clark	Thomas			1	2					1	1			5		
Newburyport	162	11	Clark	Thomas M	1	1		1		1			2				6		
Beverly	298	8	Clark	William			1	1					1				3		
Newburyport	162	8	Clark	Greenleaf			1		1	1	3			2			8		
Gloucester	79	5	Clarke	Benja			1		1	3		1	1				7		
Salem	195	21	Clarke	Daniel		1	3	1					1				6		
Salem	200	17	Clarke	Daniel			2			1		1					4		
Gloucester	79	7	Clarke	Ebenz	2	1		1		2			1				7		
Salem	194	18	Clarke	Eliza		1								1			2		
Salem	206	40	Clarke	Eliza		1						1		1			3		
Gloucester	57	37	Clarke	George		1		1						1			3	West Parish	
Salem	191	33	Clarke	Henry	2			1			1	1					5		
Gloucester	79	1	Clarke	Henry Junr			1			1	1	1					4		
Gloucester	79	4	Clarke	Joshua	4	1		1		1	1		1				9		
Gloucester	86	19	Clarke	Lydia Wo								1					2		
Salem	203	39	Clarke	Martha	1		1			1	3	2	1				9		
Gloucester	76	30	Clarke	Martha Wo	2							1	1				4		
Gloucester	79	3	Clarke	Mary P.	1	1		1		1			1				5		
Gloucester	76	7	Clarke	Samuel	2		1	1		3				1			8		
Newburyport	162	5	Clarkson	James	1			1				1		1			4		
Beverly	302	23	Claxton	Matthias				1						1			2		
Beverly	302	16	Claxton	Philip	3			1		1			1				6		
Gloucester	68	16	Claywood	James	1			1	1	1			1				5		
Topsfield	19	14	Cleaveland	Nehemiah	2	1	1	1		1		1	1				8		
Beverly	296	29	Cleaver	Ambroas		1			1	1			1				4		
Beverly	291	10	Cleaver	Andrew	1	1	2	1	1	1		1	3	1			12		
Beverly	294	22	Cleaver	Benja				1		2			1				4		
Beverly	289	6	Cleaver	Benjamin		1			1				2	1			5		
Beverly	302	30	Cleaver	Ezra			1	1		1			1				3		
Wenham	309	31	Cleaver	John			1			2			1				4		
Beverly	291	9	Cleaver	Titus											5		5		
Hamilton	285	43	Cleaves	Nathaniel	1	1			1	1	1	1		1			7		
Topsfield	20	9	Cleaves	Nehemiah	1			1					2				4		
Gloucester	78	32	Cleavland	Ebenz Junr				1				1					2	Sandy Bay Parish	
Gloucester	79	10	Cleavland	Ebenz Revd			1	1					1				3		
Salem	204	21	Cleland	Clark		1						1					2		
Salem	208	60	Clemens	Henry	2			1					2				5		
Salem	202	25	Clemens	John	1	1		1		1			1				5		
Salem	202	19	Clemens	Saml	2	2		1		2			1				8		
Haverhill	144	22	Clement	Amos				1			1		1				3		
Haverhill	144	40	Clement	Benjamin			2	1		1		1	1				6		
Haverhill	144	23	Clement	Ebenzr	2			1		1			1				5		
Amesbury	38	14	Clement	Jacob	1			1		2			1	2			9		

TOWN	PG#	LN#	LAST NAME	FIRST NAME	FREE WHITE MALES					FREE WHITE FEMALES					TOTAL ALL OTHER	TOTAL SLAVES	TOTALS	DISTRICT/ TOWNSHIP	NOTES
					under 10	10 to 16	16 to 26	26 to 45	45 and over	under 10	10 to 16	16 to 26	26 to 45	45 and over					
Haverhill	144	39	Clement	John	3		1		1	1	1	1	1	2			11		
Haverhill	144	21	Clement	Moses	1	2		1		3				1			8		
Haverhill	144	20	Clement	Samuel				1					1				2		
Newburyport	163	2	Clements	Joseph			1						1				2		
Newburyport	163	1	Clements	Samuel			1	1					1	1			4		
Marblehead	262	27	Clemmons	Alice								2		1			3		
Salem	192	25	Cleveland	Charles			1			1	1		1				4		
Rowley	128	43	Cleveland	Parker	1			1		1		1	1				5		
Salem	190	26	Cleveland	Stephen			3	1				2	1				7		
Salem	193	13	Cleveland	William	2	1	1	1			1	1	1				8		
Salem	190	11	Cleveland	Williams				1				1	1				3		
Amesbury	37	17	Cleves	Marchant		1		1				1		1			4		
Salem	192	6	Clevland	Abigail							1		2				3		
Salem	188	12	Cliff	Peter	4			1				2	1				8		
Salem	191	5	Clifton	John	1			1	1	1			1	1			6		
Ipswich	276	21	Clinton	James	1			1				1		1			4		
Danvers	4	32	Clinton	Prudence									1	2			3		
Hamilton	285	68	Clinton	Samuel	1			1					1				3		
Marblehead	263	8	Clone	John	1			1					1				3		
Marblehead	262	31	Clone	Sarah			1							1			2		
Marblehead	240	4	Clone	Thomas	1	1		1						1			4		
Gloucester	86	15	Close	John				1				2	1				4		
Marblehead	262	30	Clothey	Betty		1							1	1			3		
Marblehead	251	5	Clothey	Joseph	2			1		2	1		1	1			8		
Haverhill	145	4	Cloud	Daniel	3			1					1				5		
Salisbury	25	28	Clough	Aaron				1				3	1				5		
Amesbury	38	6	Clough	Baley				1		1			1				3		
Amesbury	38	4	Clough	David	1	1		1		1		1					5		
Marblehead	250	9	Clough	Ebenezer	2	1		1		1			1				6		
Gloucester	58	36	Clough	Elias			1						1				2		
Amesbury	38	5	Clough	Elijah	1			1						1			3		
Amesbury	38	3	Clough	John				1				1		1			3		
Salisbury	25	29	Clough	Jonathn		1	2	1				2		2			8		
Salem	183	5	Clough	Joseph				1						1			2		
Gloucester	58	37	Clough	Martha Wo										1			1		
Salem	189	18	Clough	Peter	1	1	1	1				1	2	1			8		
Salem	218	11	Clough	Susanna			1							1			2		
Salem	202	5	Clough	William	1			1	2			1					5		
Salem	205	43	Cloutman	Abigail	1			1					1				3		
Marblehead	268	12	Cloutman	Ebenezer B.			1						1				2		
Salem	221	4	Cloutman	Eliza	2	1				1	1	2	1				8		
Marblehead	258	22	Cloutman	Hannah	1					1			1				3		
Marblehead	267	35	Cloutman	Hannah	1					1		1					3		
Salem	212	54	Cloutman	Hannah		1							3	1			5		
Marblehead	247	25	Cloutman	John			1			3		2	1				7		
Marblehead	267	9	Cloutman	Joseph	2		1			3			1				7		
Salem	212	30	Cloutman	Mary								1	1				2		
Marblehead	267	24	Cloutman	Robert	2		1						1				4		
Marblehead	269	28	Cloutman	Robert				1				1		1			3		
Salem	220	46	Cloutman	Stephen	2	2	2	1		3	1		1				12		
Marblehead	250	5	Cloutman	Sukey	1					1			1				3		
Marblehead	269	27	Cloutman	Thomas				1			1		1				3		
Marblehead	268	2	Cloutman	Thomas Junr	1	1		1			1			1			5		
Gloucester	63	22	Coas	Jeren	2			1		1				1			5	East Ward	
Gloucester	63	21	Coas	William	2			1		2	2		1				8	East Ward	
Gloucester	84	23	Coat	Susa Wo									1	1			2		
Salem	194	43	Coates	John		1		1		1				1			4		
Lynn	233	5	Coats	Joseph	1		2			1			1				5		
Beverly	302	22	Coben	Jack Negro											4		4		
Boxford	133	18	Coburn	David		2		1		1			1				5		
Newburyport	163	9	Coburn	Jacob			1						1				2		
Andover	92	37	Cochran	James	2	2		1		3	1	1	1				11		
Marblehead	240	13	Cocklin	John		1		1		1			1				4		
Newbury	118	9	Coffen	Eliphalet			1	1	1	1			1	1			6		
Newbury	111	15	Coffin	Abel		1				1			3	1			6		
Newbury	111	42	Coffin	Abigal	2			1					1				4		
Beverly	293	34	Coffin	Abner		1							1				2		
Newbury	110	33	Coffin	Amos	3	1		1		1			1				7		
Newburyport	160	40	Coffin	Benjamin	1			1						1			3		
Newbury	111	45	Coffin	Charles	1	1	1	1				1	2				7		
Newburyport	161	4	Coffin	Charles	1	1	1	1					2	1			7		
Newburyport	160	34	Coffin	David	3	2	1	1		1			1	2			11		
Newburyport	160	35	Coffin	David Jr	1	2	1	1		1			2	1			9		
Gloucester	59	2	Coffin	Dolly Widw		1							1	1			3		
Newbury	119	4	Coffin	Ecabod		1	1	1					1				4		
Newbury	115	10	Coffin	Edmund	2			1		1	1		1				6		
Newbury	111	5	Coffin	Jacob	1	1	1	1		2		1	1				8		
Gloucester	63	23	Coffin	James Capt	1	1		1		1	1	1		1			7	East Ward	
Newbury	110	31	Coffin	John	1	1	1						1				4		
Salisbury	25	21	Coffin	John	4			1					1				6		
Newbury	115	9	Coffin	Joseph	2			1		1	1		1				6		
Newburyport	161	1	Coffin	Joseph			1	1					1				3		
Newburyport	161	2	Coffin	Joseph Jr	2			1		1			1				5		
Newbury	110	23	Coffin	Lemuel	2			1		1	1		1				6		

TOWN	PG#	LN#	HEADS OF HOUSEHOLD		FREE WHITE MALES					FREE WHITE FEMALES					TOTAL ALL OTHER	TOTAL SLAVES	TOTALS	DISTRICT/ TOWNSHIP	NOTES
			LAST NAME	FIRST NAME	under 10	10 to 16	16 to 26	26 to 45	45 and over	under 10	10 to 16	16 to 26	26 to 45	45 and over					
Newburyport	160	39	Coffin	Lemuel	2	1	1	1		2	1	1	1				10		
Newburyport	161	3	Coffin	Moses Mercht			1	1					1				3		
Newbury	119	5	Coffin	Richard			1			1		1					3		
Newbury	120	1	Coffin	Samuel				1						1			2		
Newburyport	160	36	Coffin	Samuel		1	3		1	1	2	2		2			12		
Newbury	110	34	Coffin	Stephen		1		1					1				3		
Newbury	119	6	Coffin	Stephen	1		1	1		2		1	1				5		
Salisbury	25	19	Coffin	Stephen		1		1		1		2	2	1			8		
Salisbury	25	20	Coffin	Stephen Junr		1		1					1				3		
Newburyport	160	38	Coffin	Sussanah Wdo			1				1	2	1				5		
Newbury	110	30	Coffin	Tristam				1				3	1				5		
Salisbury	26	7	Coffin	Tristam	1			1									2		
Gloucester	72	10	Coffin	Tristram	1			1				1					3		
Newburyport	160	37	Coffin	Tristram			1	1	1		1	1	1	1	1		8		
Gloucester	59	1	Coffin	Willa Doct	2	2	2	1		2	3	2	1				15		
Gloucester	55	15	Coghlin	Peter Esq			3	1		1	2						7		
Ipswich	278	34	Cogswell	Antice		1						2	1	1			5		
Ipswich	281	62	Cogswell	Benjamin	2	1		1				1					5		
Ipswich	280	8	Cogswell	Daniel			2					1	1				4		
Ipswich	280	21	Cogswell	Ebenezer	2	1	1	1		2		2	1	1	1		12		
Ipswich	282	30	Cogswell	Jacob Junr				1	1			2					4		
Haverhill	144	24	Cogswell	John	2	1		1	1	2	2		1				10		
Ipswich	282	10	Cogswell	John	3		1				2		1		9		17		
Ipswich	281	61	Cogswell	Jonathan				1	1					1			3		
Ipswich	283	17	Cogswell	Jonathan Junr			1		1			2	1	1	1		7		
Ipswich	281	51	Cogswell	Mary	1								1				2		
Ipswich	281	63	Cogswell	Nathaniel	2		1						1				4		
Rowley	129	39	Cogswell	Nathll	1	1	1		1			2	2	2	2		12		
Andover	92	13	Cogswell	Samuel	2			1	1	2		1		1			8		
Haverhill	144	25	Cogswell	Thomas	1			1		3		1	1				7		
Ipswich	281	34	Cogswell	William		1	1	2	1			2		1			8		
Newbury	108	48	Cohies	Thomas	3	2		1		3	2		2				13		
Amesbury	37	21	Colbey	Aaron	1	1	2		1	1	1			2			9		
Amesbury	38	8	Colbey	Aaron		1	1		1	1	1	2		1			8		
Amesbury	37	2	Colbey	Adonijah				1					1				2		
Amesbury	37	13	Colbey	Allice									1				1		
Amesbury	38	17	Colbey	Barzilla				1				1	1				3		
Amesbury	38	18	Colbey	Barzilla Junr			1					1					2		
Amesbury	37	20	Colbey	Benj				1				1	1				3		
Newbury	113	35	Colbey	Eliza	1	2	2						1				6		
Salisbury	26	12	Colbey	Ger Capt		2		1	1	1	1		1				7		
Amesbury	38	7	Colbey	Gideon				1				1	1				3		
Amesbury	37	3	Colbey	John	4			1		1			1				7		
Amesbury	37	4	Colbey	John W.	1			1					1				3		
Amesbury	37	27	Colbey	Jonathan				1					1				2		
Newbury	113	22	Colbey	Joseph		1		1		4	1		1				8		
Amesbury	38	20	Colbey	Joshua	2			1		1	2		1				7		
Amesbury	37	14	Colbey	Judith Wid										1			1		
Salisbury	26	6	Colbey	Molly Wd							1	1					2		
Amesbury	37	9	Colbey	Obadiah Dr.		2		1	1			1	1				6		
Amesbury	37	10	Colbey	Obadiah Junr	4	1		1			2		1				9		
Salisbury	26	23	Colbey	Philip		1		1			1	2					5		
Salisbury	26	22	Colbey	Samuel				1						1			2		
Amesbury	37	24	Colbey	Thomas		1		1		1		1					4		
Amesbury	37	25	Colbey	Vallentine					1	1		1		1			4		
Amesbury	37	26	Colbey	Vallentine Junr	1			1				1					3		
Amesbury	37	31	Colbey	Wm Capt.	1			1		1		1					4		
Amesbury	38	19	Colbey	Woodman				1				1					2		
Newbury	119	19	Colby	Charles		1		1				1		1			4		
Manchester	50	25	Colby	Davd Maj	1			1				2					4		
Haverhill	144	14	Colby	Ephraim		2	1		1		1		2				7		
Bradford	125	17	Colby	John		1					2	2	1				6		
Newbury	118	20	Colby	John				1									1		
Newburyport	162	22	Colby	John			2			1			1				4		
Newbury	113	11	Colby	Joseph	1			1		1		1		1			5		
Haverhill	144	37	Colby	Nicolus	1		1			1		1					4		
Haverhill	144	34	Colby	Theoph				1		1		1					3		
Beverly	291	18	Cole	Abigail									1				1		
Beverly	299	24	Cole	Andrew	1			1				1			1		4		
Hamilton	285	58	Cole	Anna	1	1	1			1	1	1		1			7		
Gloucester	56	8	Cole	Annie Wd	2								1				3		
Beverly	297	46	Cole	Asa					1				1				2		
Beverly	292	21	Cole	Eliza								2	2				4		
Boxford	133	7	Cole	Moses	2			1		1			1	1	1		7		
Marblehead	260	29	Cole	Nicholas				1				1		1			3		
Marblehead	261	20	Cole	Nicholas		1						1					2		
Boxford	134	15	Cole	Phineas					2	1				1			4		
Beverly	291	14	Cole	Samuel	2	1			1	1		2	1				8		
Boxford	134	17	Cole	Simeon	2	1	1	1		1		2	1				10		
Boxford	134	14	Cole	Thos			1	1		1		1					4		
Gloucester	56	3	Cole	Weden		1		1						1			3		
Gloucester	56	4	Cole	Weden Junr	2		1					1					4		
Marblehead	248	28	Cole	William	2	1		1		1			1				6		

TOWN	PG#	LN#	LAST NAME	FIRST NAME	FREE WHITE MALES					FREE WHITE FEMALES					TOTAL ALL OTHER	TOTAL SLAVES	TOTALS	DISTRICT/ TOWNSHIP	NOTES
					under 10	10 to 16	16 to 26	26 to 45	45 and over	under 10	10 to 16	16 to 26	26 to 45	45 and over					
Marblehead	270	25	Coleby	Benjamin	1			1		1			1				4		
Marblehead	269	12	Coleman	Ann		1							1	1			3		
Ipswich	277	23	Coleman	Samuel				1					1				2		
Salem	208	4	Collier	Isaac		1		1		1	1	3	1				8		
Marblehead	269	11	Collier	John		1		1			1	2		1			6		
Lynn	223	7	Collins	Abijah				1				1	1				3		
Danvers	10	12	Collins	Benajah		1	1	1				4		1	4		12		
Salisbury	25	33	Collins	Benja		1	1			1			1				4		
Salem	221	16	Collins	Daniel		1				1		1					3		
Gloucester	63	25	Collins	Daniel Colo	2	1	2		1	1	1	2	1				11	East Ward	
Salisbury	25	30	Collins	Enoch	1	1		1	1	1		1	1				7		
Lynn	227	13	Collins	Jacob		2	1	1	1			1		1			7		
Lynn	228	10	Collins	Jacob Jr		2		1		1			1				5		
Salem	216	53	Collins	John	3		1		1	1	1			1			8		
Salem	219	1	Collins	John	1	1	1	1		1	1			1			7		
Salem	219	41	Collins	John		3		1	1	1		2		1			8		
Newburyport	163	7	Collins	Joseph			1		1	1		1	2				6		
Marblehead	252	15	Collins	Lydia	1	1					2	1	1				6		
Salem	210	17	Collins	Mary	3	1						1	1				6		
Manchester	50	31	Collins	Mary Wo									1				1		
Salisbury	25	32	Collins	Moses		1	1	1					1				4		
Marblehead	269	1	Collins	Moses A.		1					1		1				3		
Gloucester	55	18	Collins	Nathl		1					1						2		
Lynn	231	33	Collins	Nathl		2		2		1	1	1		1			8		
Salem	200	35	Collins	Pickering	1	1		1		1	1			1			6		
Salem	218	26	Collins	Richd		1		1				1		1			4		
Lynn	228	13	Collins	Saml		1		1					1				3		
Lynn	227	5	Collins	Saml Junr		2		2				2		2			8		
Salisbury	25	31	Collins	Samuel				1						1			2		
Lynn	228	7	Collins	Zach		2		1		1	1		1				6		
Lynn	226	44	Collins	Zacheus	1			1		1		1	1				5		
Marblehead	240	14	Collyer	Isaac			3	1	1		1		1	1	1		9		
Marblehead	239	22	Collyer	Isaac Junr		1						1					2		
Newbury	105	3	Colman	Benjamin		2		1		1			1	1			6		
Newbury	105	6	Colman	Moses		2	2	1		1	1		1	1	1		10		
Newbury	105	9	Colman	William	2	1	2	2		3	1		1				12		
Salem	201	38	Colvill	John	2			1		2			1	1			7		
Newbury	119	40	Colway	Enoch	2			1		1			1				5		
Newbury	119	39	Colway	Nathan				1					1	1			3		
Newbury	111	40	Combs	Phillip	1			2		1		2	1	1			8		
Salem	190	32	Compton	Sarah								2					2		
Topsfield	19	15	Conant	Aaron	1			1				1	1				4		
Topsfield	20	1	Conant	Darkus		1							1				2		
Beverly	295	46	Conant	Israel				1				1					2		
Beverly	293	51	Conant	John		2	1	1	1			2	2	1			10		
Topsfield	19	4	Conant	John	2	1		1		2			1	1			8		
Beverly	294	3	Conant	Lot		1		1					1				3		
Ipswich	279	56	Conant	Lot			1	1					1				3		
Beverly	294	4	Conant	Lydia						2	1		1				4		
Beverly	305	39	Conant	Nathanl	2			1		3			1				7		
Beverly	305	38	Conant	Samuel					1				1				2		
Beverly	293	35	Conant	Samuel Jr				1			2			1			4		
Ipswich	279	36	Conant	William		1	2		1			1		1			6		
Marblehead	255	2	Condon	Jane	1							1					2		
Newburyport	162	20	Condry	Dennis	1			1		3	1		3				9		
Newburyport	162	19	Condry	Timothy				1						1			2		
Newburyport	163	11	Connell	George				1		1			1	1	1		5		
Newbury	110	4	Conner	Gideon	1		1	1					3	1			7		
Salem	193	17	Connor	Edwd											3		3		
Newburyport	163	6	Connor	Joseph		1		1						1			3		
Newburyport	163	5	Connor	William	3			1						1			5		
Danvers	11	20	Convers	Elizabeth	1					1	1		1				4		
Salem	205	10	Converse	Nabby	1					1		1					3		
Marblehead	266	11	Conway	John	2			1		1			1				5		
Marblehead	247	36	Conway	Martha	1		1			1			1				4		
Marblehead	246	36	Conway	Peter			1			1		1					3		
Salem	202	24	Conway	Sarah								1		1			2		
Haverhill	145	2	Cook	Benjamin	1			1		2			1				5		
Salem	211	37	Cook	Caleb	2			1			1		1				5		
Newburyport	161	16	Cook	Charles				1						1			2		
Newburyport	161	17	Cook	Charles Junr		1	2	1				1		1			6		
Newburyport	161	21	Cook	Elias	3	1	1		1	1	1		1	1			10		
Salem	208	58	Cook	Eunice									1				1		
Danvers	13	40	Cook	George	1	1	1		1	3			1				8		
Danvers	13	27	Cook	Henry	1		1	1		3		1	1				8		
Newburyport	161	19	Cook	John	3	1			1	1	1	1		1			9		
Beverly	305	24	Cook	Joseph				1						1			2		
Salem	210	50	Cook	Joseph			1			1	1	1					4		
Salem	205	21	Cook	Love										1			1		
Salem	188	22	Cook	Lydia								1		1			2		
Salem	190	13	Cook	Mary									1	1			2		
Gloucester	80	13	Cook	Mary Wo		1					1	1					3		
Beverly	301	37	Cook	Samuel			1										1		
Beverly	305	23	Cook	Samuel		1							1				2		
Salem	188	14	Cook	Stephen		1	3	1	1		1			1			8		

TOWN	PG#	LN#	LAST NAME	FIRST NAME	FREE WHITE MALES					FREE WHITE FEMALES					TOTAL ALL OTHER	TOTAL SLAVES	TOTALS	DISTRICT/ TOWNSHIP	NOTES
					under 10	10 to 16	16 to 26	26 to 45	45 and over	under 10	10 to 16	16 to 26	26 to 45	45 and over					
Beverly	302	13	Cook	William			1						1				2		
Newburyport	161	18	Cook	William	2	1	1	1		1		1	1				8		
Beverly	294	34	Cook	William 2d			1			2		1					4		
Salem	217	45	Cook	Willm	1		1	1				1	1				5		
Salem	204	37	Cook	Wm			1			3			1	1			6		
Newburyport	161	20	Cook	Zebedee	2	1	1	1		2	1	1	1				10		
Salem	204	25	Cook	Joseph	1	1	1						1				4		
Salem	204	10	Cooke	Jona	1		1					1					3		
Salem	198	19	Cooke	Robt					1				1	1			3		
Salem	200	16	Cooke	Robt					1					1			3		
Salem	196	38	Cooke	Samuel		1	1		1			1	2	1			7		
Marblehead	248	34	Cooks	James	1	2	1	2			2		1	1			10		
Newburyport	162	31	Coolidge	Jonathan		2		1		1	2	1	1				8		
Marblehead	263	1	Coombs	Elizabeth	1					1				1			3		
Newburyport	161	6	Coombs	John		1	2		1	1	1		1				7		
Marblehead	263	5	Coombs	Joshua	2	2		1		1			1				7		
Marblehead	263	2	Coombs	Meriam		1								1			2		
Marblehead	263	6	Coombs	Michael				1			1			1			3		
Marblehead	250	29	Coombs	Nicholas				1			2			1			4		
Marblehead	254	11	Coombs	Nicholas	3		1					1					5		
Newburyport	161	5	Coombs	William		1	1	1			2	2	1	2			10		
Salem	210	18	Coombs	William	1		1			3			1				6		
Newburyport	163	3	Cooper	David	2		1	1				2	1	1			9		
Salem	195	19	Cooper	Eunice						1			1				2		
Newbury	115	27	Cooper	John	1			1	1	1	2		1				7		
Newbury	108	46	Cooper	Moses		1			1				2		1		5		
Newbury	108	45	Cooper	Simeon	1			1					1				3		
Haverhill	144	2	Copps	Simeon	1			1					1				3		
Danvers	9	21	Cora	Thomas	1			1		2	2			1			7		
Andover	103	17	Cordaner	Amos											4		4		
Beverly	306	12	Cordwell	Abraham	1			1					1	1			4		
Haverhill	144	35	Cordwell	Enoch	2			2		2	3	1	1	1			12		
Andover	93	4	Corey	Ephraim					1				1				2		
Gloucester	79	8	Corey	Jack			1						1				2		
Rowley	128	18	Corey	John	1	1		1					1				4		
Andover	93	5	Corey	Mary									1				1		
Newbury	111	30	Corey	Michael	1	1		1		3	1		1				8		
Salem	210	57	Corey	Peleg	1		1					1					3		
Haverhill	144	46	Corlis	Ephraim		2		1		1		1	1	1			7		
Haverhill	145	1	Corlis	John	2			1		2			1				6		
Haverhill	145	3	Corlis	John S.	1	1		1	1	1	1		1	1			8		
Haverhill	145	17	Corlis	Stephen		1		1		2			1				5		
Beverly	300	45	Corning	Anna									1				1		
Beverly	301	1	Corning	Jonathan			1						1				2		
Beverly	292	3	Corning	Peter				1					1				2		
Marblehead	256	27	Cotitle	Philippe		2		1					1				4		
Haverhill	144	16	Cottle	Thomas				1			1		1	1			4		
Haverhill	144	17	Cottle	William				1		1				2			4		
Newburyport	161	30	Cotton	Benjamin				1						1			2		
Newburyport	161	31	Cotton	Joel	1	1		1					1				4		
Newburyport	162	7	Couch	John			1			1		1					3		
Newburyport	162	6	Couch	Joseph	1	2	1		1			2		1			8		
Marblehead	266	25	County	Mary			1			1							2		
Gloucester	56	7	Courtney	Samuel	1		1			1		1					4		
Marblehead	269	34	Covell	James	2		1			2		1					6		
Salem	196	28	Coverly	Nath			1			1							2		
Newburyport	163	4	Coverly	Thomas			1			1		1					3		
Salem	190	16	Cowan	Robt		3	1	1		2	1		1				9		
Marblehead	245	15	Cowell	Hannah	1	1		1		1		1					5		
Salem	206	17	Cox	Anna						1	1		1				3		
Salem	205	45	Cox	Ben					1					1			2		
Salem	205	11	Cox	Eliza			1					1	1				3		
Beverly	301	25	Cox	Judith	2	1							1				4		
Beverly	303	28	Cox	Mary										1			1		
Salem	205	39	Cox	MAry				1				1	2	1			5		
Beverly	298	36	Cox	Osmon				1				1	1	1			4		
Beverly	300	29	Cox	Samuel	1			1					1				3		
Beverly	303	30	Cox	William				1			2		1				4		
Rowley	129	44	Crafford	John	3			1				1	1	1			7		
Ipswich	283	6	Craft	Aaron				1			3	1					5		
Manchester	50	21	Craft	Benja				1			2		1				4		
Manchester	53	13	Craft	Benja Jun			1						1	1			3		
Manchester	50	24	Craft	David			1	1		1							3		
Manchester	50	29	Craft	Eleazer	3			1					1				5		
Manchester	50	27	Craft	Eliza Wo										1			1		
Manchester	50	17	Craft	Estr Wo										1			1		
Beverly	299	16	Craft	Richard	2			1					1				4		
Manchester	50	26	Craft	Willm	4			1					1				6		
Salisbury	25	34	Crain	Elijah				1			1		1				3		
Danvers	3	14	Crain	Ralp		2		1					2				5		
Beverly	297	30	Crampesee	Isaac	2	2		1		1			1				7		
Salem	200	2	Crane	Hannah			2							1			3		
Marblehead	240	36	Craw	Benjamin		1						1					2		
Marblehead	239	26	Craw	Mary	1									1			2		
Topsfield	19	6	Cree	Cornelius			1										3		

TOWN	PG#	LN#	HEADS OF HOUSEHOLD		FREE WHITE MALES					FREE WHITE FEMALES					TOTAL ALL OTHER	TOTAL SLAVES	TOTALS	DISTRICT/ TOWNSHIP	NOTES
			LAST NAME	FIRST NAME	under 10	10 to 16	16 to 26	26 to 45	45 and over	under 10	10 to 16	16 to 26	26 to 45	45 and over					
Topsfield	19	19	Cree	Joseph	1				1	1	1	1	1				6		
Topsfield	19	20	Cree	Martha			1						1	1			3		
Salem	219	16	Creely	James		1		1		3			1				6		
Beverly	300	30	Creely	Nicholas			1				2	2	1				6		
Beverly	305	21	Creesy	Benja	1			1	1				2				5		
Beverly	306	22	Creesy	Henry	1		1	1		1	1		1				6		
Beverly	305	7	Creesy	John	2			1		1			1				5		
Beverly	294	8	Creesy	John 2nd	1			2		1		1					5		
Beverly	305	8	Creesy	Jonathan			1		1		1			1			4		
Beverly	305	11	Creesy	Nathl		1			2		1	2		1			7		
Beverly	292	6	Creesy	Noah	3			1					1				5		
Marblehead	266	20	Creesy	Usine									1				1		
Newburyport	162	24	Cresey	Francis			1		1		1		2	2			7		
Newburyport	162	25	Cresey	William	3			1			1		1				6		
Rowley	131	13	Cressey	John	3			1					1				5		
Rowley	129	11	Cressey	Mark	1	1		1		1	1		1				6		
Rowley	130	3	Cressey	Richard			1			3		1	1				6		
Rowley	131	14	Cressey	Richard			1			3		1	1	1			6		
Marblehead	239	33	Crips	Tabitha		1				1	1		1				4		
Salem	212	53	Crispin	William	1			1		4	2	2	1				11		
Gloucester	68	15	Cristee	John			2			1			2				5		
Ipswich	276	26	Crocker	John		1		1	1			1		1			5		
Salisbury	26	13	Crocker	Richard	2			1	1	1			1				5		
Marblehead	250	13	Crocker	Uriel	2			1		2		1					6		
Salem	207	30	Croel	James	1			1		2		1					5		
Rowley	132	1	Crombie	Aaron	1			1		1			2				5		
Manchester	51	26	Cromby	Benja	1	1		1		2			1				6		
Salem	211	33	Cromby	Benja			3	4		2		1	1				11		
Salisbury	26	18	Cronk	John		1	1					1					3		
Salem	220	37	Crookshanks	Mary		1		1		1				1			4		
Methuen	153	8	Crop	Abijah	3	1		1	1	2	2		1	1			12		
Methuen	153	11	Crop	Daniel		1						1	3	1			7		
Manchester	52	11	Crop	Lucy Wo								1		1			2		
Andover	92	32	Crosby	John	4			1		1			1				7		
Salem	189	6	Crosby	Nicholas		3			1	1	1	1	1				8		
Andover	92	31	Crosby	Simon				1					1				2		
Andover	93	2	Crosby	Timothy			1						1				2		
Ipswich	279	19	Cross	Benjamin			1	1				1	1				4		
Newburyport	161	12	Cross	Benjamin	1		1	1					1				4		
Manchester	53	12	Cross	George		2		1	1				1				5		
Manchester	53	11	Cross	George Jun	2			1		3			1				7		
Marblehead	259	9	Cross	John	2			1					1				4		
Salem	215	39	Cross	Joseph	3	1		1		1			1				7		
Salem	193	12	Cross	Joshua	1	1			1	2	2	1		1			9		
Marblehead	268	9	Cross	Mary		1	1						1				3		
Salem	207	8	Cross	Moses	1		1			1		1					4		
Ipswich	279	20	Cross	Nathaniel		1		1					1	1			4		
Danvers	2	4	Cross	Peter		1	2	1		1		1		2			8		
Newburyport	161	9	Cross	Ralph			1	1				1	1				4		
Newburyport	161	7	Cross	Stephen		1	1		1			3	1	1			8		
Newburyport	161	8	Cross	Stephen Junr	4			1		1		1	1				8		
Marblehead	268	7	Cross	Thomas			1			3			1				5		
Newburyport	161	11	Cross	Thomas	2		1	1		1			1				6		
Salem	193	15	Cross	Violet											2		2		
Newburyport	161	10	Cross	William	4			1		2	2	1	1				11		
Manchester	53	16	Crowell	Benja	3		1		1				1	1			7		
Salem	213	28	Crowell	Samuel			1			1		1					3		
Rowley	128	7	Crowling	Peter			1						1				2		
Salisbury	26	14	Crown	Joseph Capt			1			1		1					3		
Marblehead	259	27	Crowningshield	Edward	1			1		3			1				6		
Salem	212	17	Crowninshield	Benja	1	1		1		1	3		1				8		
Salem	217	17	Crowninshield	Geo			3	2	1		2	3		1			12		
Salem	212	18	Crowninshield	Hannah			2				1		1	1	1		5		
Salem	216	52	Crowninshield	Jacob			1	1		1	1	1	1				6		
Marblehead	267	33	Cruss	Lewis	1	3	1		1	1			1				8		
Salem	221	8	Cuffby	William											4		4		
Salem	207	31	Culbertson	John	1		1						1				3		
Topsfield	18	5	Cummings	David	2	2	1	1			2		2				10		
Andover	92	27	Cummings	Deborah Wid						2	1		1				4		
Topsfield	19	26	Cummings	Elijah		1		1		1		1	1				5		
Topsfield	19	27	Cummings	Jonas	1			1	1	1	2	1					7		
Andover	92	10	Cummings	Jonathan		1	2		1		1	1		1			7		
Topsfield	19	24	Cummings	Jonathan	1			1		1	1	1					5		
Topsfield	19	23	Cummings	Joseph					1					1			2		
Andover	92	14	Cummings	Samuel		1	2					1		1			5		
Topsfield	19	25	Cummings	Thomas			1		1					1			3		
Topsfield	20	7	Cummings	Thomas Junr	1			1				1	1				4		
Salem	205	35	Cummins	John	1			1					1				3		
Salem	192	14	Cummins	Nathl	2		1	1		2			1				7		
Newburyport	162	16	Cummins	William		2	1						1	1			5		
Gloucester	79	6	Cunningham	John	2		1	1		2			1	1			8		
Beverly	302	39	Currel	Nicholas	2			1		1			1				5		
Amesbury	38	13	Currer	Rachel Wid	2							2	1				6		

182

TOWN	PG#	LN#	LAST NAME	FIRST NAME	FREE WHITE MALES					FREE WHITE FEMALES					TOTAL ALL OTHER	TOTAL SLAVES	TOTALS	DISTRICT/ TOWNSHIP	NOTES
					under 10	10 to 16	16 to 26	26 to 45	45 and over	under 10	10 to 16	16 to 26	26 to 45	45 and over					
Amesbury	38	10	Currier	Abigail Wid			1							2			3		
Gloucester	56	9	Currier	Adonjo			1			1			1				3		
Amesbury	38	11	Currier	Allice Wid							1			2			3		
Methuen	153	5	Currier	Asa		2		1				2		2			7		
Salisbury	26	20	Currier	Benja		1		1		3			1				6		
Amesbury	37	12	Currier	Daniel		1	1	1		1			1				5		
Methuen	153	9	Currier	Daniel			1				1						2		
Amesbury	37	7	Currier	David		1		1		1			1	2			6		
Andover	92	5	Currier	David			1										1		
Salisbury	26	19	Currier	David	3	1	3		1		1		2	1			12		
Amesbury	37	19	Currier	David Junr	1			1					1				3		
Amesbury	37	29	Currier	Dorothy Wid		1							1				2		
Newbury	109	35	Currier	Isaac		1	2		1	3			1				9		
Gloucester	55	17	Currier	Isiah		1		1		1		1		1			5		
Salisbury	26	2	Currier	Israel				1						2			3		
Salisbury	26	10	Currier	Israel Junr	1	1		1		1			1				5		
Amesbury	37	8	Currier	Jacob		1		1		2	3	1					9		
Salem	183	10	Currier	Jacob			1			2		1	1				5		
Salisbury	26	3	Currier	Jacob		1	1	1		1	1		1				6		
Newbury	109	22	Currier	John		1		1									2		
Newbury	110	29	Currier	John	1			1		1			1				4		
Amesbury	37	28	Currier	John Capt			1	1					1	1			4		
Haverhill	144	44	Currier	Jonathan	1	1	3				1	1					7		
Amesbury	38	12	Currier	Joseph				1		2			1				4		
Newburyport	161	26	Currier	Joseph	2			1		1	2		1				7		
Amesbury	37	23	Currier	Levi		2	1	1					1				5		
Newburyport	161	27	Currier	Mark	1		1					1					3		
Newbury	119	13	Currier	Mary										1			1		
Salem	201	37	Currier	Mary		3	2						1				6		
Newburyport	161	23	Currier	Mathew	2		2		1	1	1	1		1			9		
Amesbury	37	18	Currier	Michd	2		4		1		2	1		1			11		
Salisbury	26	8	Currier	Molly									1				1		
Amesbury	38	9	Currier	Nathan	1	1	1		1	1			2				7		
Newburyport	161	25	Currier	Nathaniel	2			1		2			1				6		
Newburyport	161	24	Currier	Nicolas		1		1		3			1				6		
Haverhill	144	15	Currier	Reuben		2	2		1	1	1			1			8		
Methuen	153	6	Currier	Richard	1	1			1	2	1	1	1				8		
Amesbury	38	21	Currier	Seth			1						1				2		
Methuen	153	4	Currier	Stephen	1	1			1			2	1	2			8		
Salisbury	26	9	Currier	Susanna Wd										1			1		
Newburyport	161	28	Currier	Susannah Wido						3			1				4		
Amesbury	37	32	Currier	Thomas			1	1						2			4		
Salisbury	26	1	Currier	Thomas				1					1				2		
Amesbury	37	22	Currier	Timothy			2	1					1	1			5		
Newburyport	161	29	Currier	William	1			1		1			1				4		
Newburyport	161	22	Currier	William 3d		1	2		1	1	1		1				6		
Amesbury	37	33	Currier	Willm				1					1				2		
Boxford	135	42	Curtice	John				1		2			1				4		
Bradford	123	45	Curtice	John					1	1			1				3		
Beverly	294	12	Curtice	William	3			1		3			1				8		
Bradford	123	37	Curtice	William	1		1	2				1	1				7		
Lynn	231	42	Curtin	James	1			1					1				3		
Lynn	226	38	Curtin	John	1	2		1		1	1	1	1				8		
Lynn	227	9	Curtin	Martha								1	1				2		
Salem	218	2	Curtis	Abigail									1				1		
Salem	188	8	Curtis	Abm	1	1	2			2		1					7		
Danvers	3	26	Curtis	Allen	1			1		3			1				6		
Danvers	13	37	Curtis	Amos			1		1	1			1				4		
Amesbury	37	11	Curtis	Anna Wid								1		1			2		
Marblehead	262	25	Curtis	Benjamin	1			1		3			1	1			7		
Amesbury	37	16	Curtis	Daniel	1		1						1				3		
Middleton	17	21	Curtis	Hannah						2				1			3		
Newburyport	162	41	Curtis	Henry				2									2		
Marblehead	256	3	Curtis	John			1					1					2		
Marblehead	251	26	Curtis	Joseph			1						1				2		
Marblehead	259	22	Curtis	Mary		1							1				2		
Marblehead	262	28	Curtis	Mary	2	1						1	1				5		
Danvers	3	27	Curtis	Molly								1		1			2		
Marblehead	268	29	Curtis	Rebecca	2								1				3		
Marblehead	257	1	Curtis	Richard				1						1			2		
Newburyport	162	39	Curtis	Samuel	1		1	1		1	1		1				6		
Newburyport	162	40	Curtis	Timothy		1		1		3		1	1				7		
Marblehead	246	26	Curtis	William	1	2	1		2					1			7		
Marblehead	249	16	Curtis	William			1	1					1	1			4		
Andover	92	29	Curtise	Israel	2	1			1	3		1	1				9		
Salisbury	25	25	Cushing	Benja		1		1		1	1						4		
Salisbury	25	17	Cushing	John	1		1						2				4		
Haverhill	144	41	Cushing	Moses				1		1				1			3		
Gloucester	62	9	Cushing	Polly								1					1		
Salem	194	17	Cushing	Thos	3		4	1		2			1				11		
Gloucester	59	3	Cushing	Zenias	1			1		2			1				5		

TOWN	PG#	LN#	LAST NAME	FIRST NAME	FREE WHITE MALES					FREE WHITE FEMALES					TOTAL ALL OTHER	TOTAL SLAVES	TOTALS	DISTRICT/ TOWNSHIP	NOTES
					under 10	10 to 16	16 to 26	26 to 45	45 and over	under 10	10 to 16	16 to 26	26 to 45	45 and over					
Andover	92	6	Cutler	Adam		1		1		2		1					5		
Newburyport	162	35	Cutler	Joseph			2	1		1	1	1	1				7		
Salisbury	25	23	Cutler	Joseph	1		1							1			3		
Hamilton	285	91	Cutler	Manasseth			2	1				1	1		1		6		
Newburyport	162	36	Cutler	Samuel				1		2	1		1				5		
Danvers	9	29	Cutler	William	1			1		1			1				4		
Newburyport	162	37	Cutler	William	1			1		2			1		1		6		
Newburyport	162	30	Cutter	Ebenezer	2	1				1	1		1				7		
Newburyport	162	29	Cutter	Jacob	1	1							1				4		
Danvers	5	18	Cutter	Solomon	3			1		1			1				6		
Marblehead	262	32	Cylebee	John			1					1					2		
Salem	215	16	Dabny	John	1	1		1		1		1	1				6		
Salem	213	25	Daby	James			1					1					2		
Salem	214	21	Dage	Henry	1		1		1	1		1					5		
Salem	209	13	Dagget	Elisha		1	2	1		3	1	2	1				11		
Marblehead	263	10	Dailey	Elizabeth			1			2			1				4		
Danvers	10	28	Dalan	Benjamin				1						2			3		
Salem	191	21	Daland	Benja	3	1		1	1	1	2	1	1	2	1		14		
Beverly	298	14	Daland	Benjamin	3			1					1				5		
Salem	217	57	Daland	Eliza									1				1		
Salem	191	18	Daland	John	1			1		2	1		1				6		
Salem	198	37	Daland	John		1		1						1			3		
Salem	203	35	Daland	John	1	1	1	1				1					5		
Salem	207	53	Daland	Thoms	1	1		1		2	3	1	1				10		
Newbury	117	27	Dalby	Thomas			1			3			1				5		
Beverly	300	16	Dale	Archalus		1	1	1		1	1		1				6		
Danvers	3	6	Dale	Eben				2				1					3		
Danvers	3	5	Dale	Margaret		1								1			2		
Salisbury	26	24	Dale	Moses			1	1	1			1	1	1			3		
Salem	200	21	Dale	Phillip			1			3		1					5		
Salem	194	9	Dalrymple	James	1			1		1		1					4		
Salem	211	50	Dalton	Edward			1			1		1					3		
Salisbury	26	30	Dalton	Hannah Wd						2			1	1			4		
Newburyport	164	14	Dalton	Jonathan	1			1				1	1				4		
Salem	189	21	Dalton	Sarah	2					3			1	1			8		
Lynn	232	33	Dampney	John	2			1		1			1				5	West Parish	
Newburyport	163	12	Dana	Daniel Revd		1		1				2					4		
Ipswich	278	41	Dana	Joseph	2	1	1		1		1	2		1			9		
Gloucester	63	29	Dane	Abigal Wo				1						1			2	East Ward	
Andover	93	14	Dane	James		1	1						1				3		
Andover	93	12	Dane	John	1		2	2		1		1	1	2			10		
Beverly	302	29	Dane	John				1			1			1	1		4		
Andover	93	13	Dane	Joseph		1		1						2			4		
Gloucester	64	1	Dane	Joshua	1			1		1			1				4		
Andover	93	17	Dane	Moses	1			1		3		1	1				7		
Beverly	289	5	Dane	Nathan Esq			2		1			2		1			6		
Gloucester	59	9	Dane	William		1		1				2					4		
Newbury	119	14	Danford	John	1			1	1	1	1	1					6		
Newbury	119	23	Danford	Joseph			1							1			3		
Manchester	52	13	Danford	Lucy Wo			1					1	1				3		
Manchester	52	14	Danford	Stepn	1			1				1					3		
Danvers	6	28	Danforth	Benjamin			1	1		3			1				6		
Newburyport	163	39	Danforth	Enoch	1			1		1			1				4		
Lynn	234	9	Danforth	Joshua					1			1		1			3		
Lynn	233	6	Danforth	Joshua Junr		2		1		4	2		1				10		
Rowley	131	43	Daniel	John	1	1		1	1			1	1				6		
Salem	202	27	Daniels	Benja			1					1					2		
Danvers	13	21	Daniels	David	2		1	1		2		1	1				8		
Salem	211	8	Daniels	Eliza	2		1			2		1	1				7		
Salem	202	32	Daniels	Mary		1	1							1			3		
Salem	202	39	Daniels	Stephen				1						1			2		
Salem	207	59	Darant	Edwd	2	1		1		1			1	1			7		
Danvers	12	15	Darby	Charles			1				2	1	2	1			7		
Danvers	10	20	Darby	Zilpher											1		1		
Marblehead	269	3	Darling	Hannah						2			1				3		
Newburyport	163	13	Davenport	Anthnony	2		2		1	2	3	3	1				14		
Newburyport	163	14	Davenport	Moses		1	2	1			1	2	1	1			9		
Manchester	54	30	Davey	Ephm Doct		1		1		1	1	1	1				6		
Bradford	123	17	David	Daniel	2			1					1				4		
Andover	93	10	Davidson	Phinehas			1										1		
Newbury	107	16	Davies	Stephen				1		2			1				4		
Newburyport	163	31	Davis	Aaron		2	1		1		1	1	1	1			8		
Newburyport	163	36	Davis	Ambros			1					1	1				3		
Haverhill	145	6	Davis	Amos	1			1		1			1				4		
Gloucester	71	23	Davis	Andrew			1			1			2	1			5		
Newburyport	163	33	Davis	Andrew			1	1					1	1			4		
Newburyport	163	25	Davis	Asa	1	1		1		1			1				6		
Gloucester	79	11	Davis	Benj	1	2	1	1		2		1	1				9		
Newburyport	163	34	Davis	Benjamin			1	2					2	1			6		
Newburyport	163	35	Davis	Benjamin Jr			1	2		2			1				4		
Ipswich	279	31	Davis	Charles	1	1	1		1		1	1		1			7		
Newbury	109	19	Davis	Ebenezer			1				2		1				4		
Newburyport	163	22	Davis	Edmund			1							1			2		
Gloucester	64	4	Davis	Elias Capt	3	1	1		1	3				1			10		

184

TOWN	PG#	LN#	HEADS OF HOUSEHOLD		FREE WHITE MALES					FREE WHITE FEMALES					TOTAL ALL OTHER	TOTAL SLAVES	TOTALS	DISTRICT/ TOWNSHIP	NOTES
			LAST NAME	FIRST NAME	under 10	10 to 16	16 to 26	26 to 45	45 and over	under 10	10 to 16	16 to 26	26 to 45	45 and over					
Newburyport	163	21	Davis	Elias J			1			1		1					3		
Amesbury	38	24	Davis	Elijah			1			1		1	1	2			6		
Gloucester	59	8	Davis	Elipt Colo	4	2	1	1		1	2	2	1				14		
Newburyport	163	37	Davis	Elizabeth Wido	2	1							1				4		
Amesbury	38	27	Davis	Enoch			1		1					1			3		
Gloucester	74	6	Davis	Epes	1	1	1			1		1					5		Squam Parish
Amesbury	38	25	Davis	Ephm		3		1				1	1				6		
Gloucester	74	5	Davis	George	3			1		1			1				6		Squam Parish
Gloucester	73	19	Davis	Isaac	1			1		1			1				4		Town Parish
Haverhill	145	7	Davis	James	1			2		1	1		1	2			8		
Methuen	153	16	Davis	James		2		1				1	1				5		
Newburyport	163	32	Davis	James	1			1		1			1	1			5		
Marblehead	268	34	Davis	Job		1		1					1	1			4		
Amesbury	38	23	Davis	John			1	1				1		2			5		
Methuen	153	15	Davis	John		1	2	1				1		1			6		
Newbury	118	18	Davis	John				2		1	1		1				9		
Amesbury	38	26	Davis	Joseph	1	1	1		1	1	1			1			7		
Gloucester	76	16	Davis	Joseph				1				1	1				3		
Newburyport	163	28	Davis	Joseph				1						1			2		
Newburyport	163	29	Davis	Joseph Jr	2					2	1		2				8		
Methuen	153	17	Davis	Joshua			1			2			1				4		
Gloucester	62	16	Davis	Judith Wd			3				1		1				5		
Gloucester	78	6	Davis	Lydia Wo	1	1	2				1			1			6		
Gloucester	74	23	Davis	Mark		1	1		1				1	1			5		
Newbury	118	14	Davis	Mary									1				1		
Gloucester	59	5	Davis	Moses	1			1		1		1					4		
Gloucester	73	15	Davis	Moses	4			1					1				6		Town Parish
Newburyport	163	23	Davis	Moses	1			1			1	1	1				5		
Newburyport	163	24	Davis	Moses Junr	1			1		1			1				4		
Manchester	53	37	Davis	Nancy Wo	1					1		1					3		
Danvers	4	20	Davis	Nathaniel	1			1		2			1				5		
Gloucester	79	13	Davis	Oliver	1		1					1					3		
Haverhill	145	16	Davis	Prince									1		4		5		
Gloucester	71	25	Davis	Saml		1		1		2		1	1				6		
Newburyport	163	26	Davis	Samuel	1		1						1				3		
Newburyport	163	27	Davis	Samuel Jr		2				1	1						4		
Beverly	304	40	Davis	Thomas				1					1				2		
Beverly	304	41	Davis	Thomas Jr	2	2		1		2	1		2				10		
Gloucester	56	12	Davis	Timothy	2			1		1			1				5		
Salem	195	4	Davis	Tobias		1				1							2		
Gloucester	73	21	Davis	William	1		1		1	1			1	1			6		Squam Parish
Haverhill	145	14	Davis	William	3	1			1	2	1		1	1			10		
Marblehead	266	9	Davis	William	1			1		1			1				4		
Methuen	153	18	Davis	William	2			1		3			1				7		
Newburyport	163	30	Davis	William	1		1		1		1		1				5		
Salem	194	20	Davis	William				1		1							2		
Salisbury	26	33	Davis	William				1		1		1					3		
Gloucester	70	25	Davis	Zebulon	2	1			1	3	1		1				9		
Salem	211	7	Davison	Anna						1			1				2		
Newburyport	163	38	Davison	John		1		1						1			3		
Beverly	306	11	Davison	Patiance										1			1		
Gloucester	58	15	Davy	Mark	1		1						1				3		
Gloucester	58	17	Davy	Patty Widow									1	2			3		
Salem	191	17	Dawes	Stephen	2			1		1			1				5		
Beverly	301	12	Dawling	James	1			1		2			1				5		
Salem	220	39	Dawson	Alexr		1						1					2		
Gloucester	59	11	Dawson	Elias	1			1		1	1						4		
Salem	213	15	Dawson	John					1					1			2		
Ipswich	275	51	Day	Aaron				1		2	1		1				5		
Ipswich	280	30	Day	Abigail									2				2		
Ipswich	280	19	Day	Abner	2	1	2		1	3	2	3	1				15		
Bradford	122	19	Day	Abraham		1						1	1		1		5		
Gloucester	63	12	Day	Anna Wo									2	1			3		West Ward
Bradford	121	7	Day	Bailey	3	1		1				1	1				7		
Gloucester	72	19	Day	Danl Jr	2		1			1		1		1			6		
Gloucester	63	3	Day	David				1						2			3		West Ward
Gloucester	64	2	Day	David Junr	1			1		2			1				5		
Salem	199	31	Day	Dorcas	1	3			1		1						6		
Salem	183	25	Day	Elisha	2			1		2			1	1			7		
Gloucester	75	3	Day	George	2			1		1			1				5		
Gloucester	63	10	Day	Isaac		2		1		2	1		1				7		West Ward
Gloucester	71	7	Day	Israel	1	1		1		2	1	1					7		
Gloucester	75	2	Day	James			2		1	1			1				5		
Gloucester	76	3	Day	James Junr				1		4	1		1				7		
Ipswich	273	24	Day	Jeremiah			1		1				1	1			4		
Bradford	121	12	Day	John		1		1	1	1		1	1	3			9		
Bradford	121	13	Day	John		1				1			1				3		
Danvers	11	24	Day	John				1		2			1				4		
Ipswich	275	27	Day	John				1					1				2		
Danvers	11	23	Day	Jonathan	2		1	1					1				5		
Bradford	121	11	Day	Joseph		1		1				1		1			4		
Manchester	50	34	Day	Joseph Junr		1						1					2		
Manchester	51	10	Day	Joseph Junr					1				1				3		

TOWN	PG#	LN#	LAST NAME	FIRST NAME	FREE WHITE MALES under 10	10 to 16	16 to 26	26 to 45	45 and over	FREE WHITE FEMALES under 10	10 to 16	16 to 26	26 to 45	45 and over	TOTAL ALL OTHER	TOTAL SLAVES	TOTALS	DISTRICT/ TOWNSHIP	NOTES
Gloucester	85	4	Day	Mary Wo	1					2			1				4		
Ipswich	279	30	Day	Moses				1	2				3	1			7		
Gloucester	85	3	Day	Nathl			2		1			1		1			5		
Gloucester	63	28	Day	Samuel	1	1		1		3			1				7	East Ward	
Ipswich	279	29	Day	Thomas					1	1			1	1			4		
Marblehead	270	2	Deacon	Jonathan	1			1					1	2			5		
Salem	218	45	Deal	Susanna		1						1	1	1			4		
Hamilton	285	84	Dean	Anna									1	1			2		
Salem	218	9	Dean	Benja		1		1				3		1			6		
Hamilton	285	52	Dean	Eloner							1	1		1			3		
Hamilton	285	49	Dean	John	1		1		1	1			1				5		
Salem	198	33	Dean	John			3		1			1		1			6		
Salem	198	28	Dean	Jona	1		1	1		2			1	1			7		
Salem	218	32	Dean	Lydia		1						1	1	1			4		
Gloucester	69	8	Dean	Nathl		1		1						1			3		
Newbury	111	8	Dean	Oliver		1				1		1					3		
Salem	218	33	Dean	Thos	2			1	1				1	1			6		
Hamilton	285	50	Dean	William			1			1			1				3		
Beverly	305	9	Debman	William			1			1			1				3		
Newbury	113	10	Deepwall	John	2		1						1				4		
Salem	200	13	Deland	Benja	1		1			1		1	1				5		
Salem	200	22	Deland	Benja	1		1			1			1	1			5		
Salem	200	18	Deland	Susanna									1	1			2		
Salem	220	41	Delano	Nathl			1			1			1				3		
Newburyport	164	9	Delany	William				1		2			1				4		
Andover	93	9	Delap	John				1						1			2		
Marblehead	256	10	Delone	Rebecca							1		1				2		
Beverly	299	40	Dempsey	Rogger	1	1		1	1	1				1			5		
Danvers	2	11	Demsey	Isaac	1		1						1				3		
Danvers	2	14	Demsy	Bartholw	3		1			1		1		1			7		
Marblehead	249	14	Denais	Anna										1			1		
Beverly	300	23	Denis	Charles			1			1	1		1				4		
Gloucester	56	10	Dennen	Joseph	1			1		2	2	1		1			8		
Gloucester	56	11	Dennen	Joseph Junr	2		1			1			1				5		
Amesbury	38	22	Dennie	John		1	1			1			1				4		
Gloucester	84	11	Denning	John			1						1				2		
Marblehead	249	35	Dennis	Archable		1					1						2		
Marblehead	240	6	Dennis	Benjamin		1						1					2		
Marblehead	263	9	Dennis	Benjamin		2	1				1		1				5		
Marblehead	241	11	Dennis	Charity								1	1				2		
Marblehead	254	26	Dennis	Elizabeth	1					1	2						4		
Marblehead	246	6	Dennis	Erasmus	1						1						2		
Salem	200	19	Dennis	Fral B.		3	1	2		2			1				9		
Marblehead	261	26	Dennis	Hannah	2						1		1				4		
Newburyport	164	11	Dennis	James R		1		1				1					3		
Gloucester	59	10	Dennis	John	1	1							1				3		
Gloucester	74	20	Dennis	John		4	1						1				6		
Marblehead	249	26	Dennis	John	1		1						2				4		
Marblehead	260	8	Dennis	John D. Junr	2		1				1	1					5		
Marblehead	259	23	Dennis	Jonas		1	1			1	1		1				5		
Hamilton	284	17	Dennis	Lucy	2			1		1							4		
Ipswich	277	6	Dennis	Mary	1					2			1	1			5		
Ipswich	277	33	Dennis	Nathaniel			1						1				2		
Ipswich	275	50	Dennis	Rebecca									1	1			2		
Marblehead	255	30	Dennis	Sally							1		1				2		
Gloucester	75	1	Dennis	Saml			1			1			1				3		
Newburyport	164	12	Dennis	Samuel	1		1			1			1				4		
Salem	206	58	Dennis	Samuel		1	1					1					3		
Marblehead	241	13	Dennis	Sarah		1							1				2		
Marblehead	246	14	Dennis	Thomas	1			1		3			1				6		
Marblehead	260	14	Dennis	Thomas	3	1		1		3			1				9		
Marblehead	267	34	Dennis	Thomas	1			1					1				3		
Ipswich	275	61	Dennis	William			1		1				1	2			5		
Salem	200	20	Dennis	Willm	2		1						1				4		
Marblehead	260	9	Dennis	John D.		2	3		1	1	1			2			10		
Gloucester	75	25	Dennison	Isaac	1			1						1			3		
Gloucester	75	28	Dennison	Isaac Junr	4	2		1		1	1		1				10		
Gloucester	75	26	Dennison	James		1		1		1		1					4		
Newbury	106	18	Dennit	Mary	1							1	1				3		
Beverly	306	13	Derby	Edith										1			1		
Salem	206	36	Derby	Elias H.	1	1	1	1					1	3			8		
Salem	206	35	Derby	Ezekiel H.	2		1	1		2			2	2			10		
Newbury	105	14	Derby	Jacob	2	2		1		1	2		1				9		
Salem	205	23	Derby	John			1						1				2		
Salem	206	34	Derby	John	3	1	1						3				8		
Salem	207	7	Derby	John	3	2	2						1	1			9		
Salem	206	33	Derby	Martha	1	1						1	3				7		
Salem	192	43	Derby	Sam	2	3		1		1			1				8		
Salem	208	10	Derby	Saml	5		1	1		3	1	2	2				15		
Danvers	12	11	Derby	Samuel				1						1			2		
Lynnfield	237	4	Derby	Sarah							3	1		1			5		
Salem	200	49	Derby	Zeb											2		2		
Marblehead	245	18	Deruff	Lemie	1		1			1			1				4		
Newburyport	164	17	Desmazes	John B	1		1			1			1				4		
Marblehead	257	25	Desmore	Joseph	2		1						1				4		
Marblehead	258	4	Desmore	Joseph P.	3			1		3		1	1	1			10		
Salem	189	44	Deukinfield	Thos												3	3		

TOWN	PG#	LN#	LAST NAME	FIRST NAME	FREE WHITE MALES					FREE WHITE FEMALES					TOTAL ALL OTHER	TOTAL SLAVES	TOTALS	DISTRICT/ TOWNSHIP	NOTES
					under 10	10 to 16	16 to 26	26 to 45	45 and over	under 10	10 to 16	16 to 26	26 to 45	45 and over					
Salem	210	8	Deval	Michael	2		1					1					4		
Marblehead	252	27	Deveraux	Lidia		1						1	1				3		
Marblehead	255	16	Devereaux	Benjamin P.		2		1		1	1	1	1				7		
Marblehead	243	23	Devereaux	Susanna									1	1			2		
Salem	217	23	Devereux	James	1			1		2	1		1				6		
Marblehead	267	14	Devereux	Nathaniel	3			1		2			1				7		
Marblehead	241	3	Devereux	Peggy										1			1		
Marblehead	244	16	Devereux	Robert			2		1		1	1		1			6		
Marblehead	245	22	Devereux	Samuel		1	1	1			1	1	2				7		
Salem	210	24	Devereux	Thos	3			1		2			1				7		
Manchester	50	35	Dewer	Solomon		2	1	1			2	1	2				9		
Salem	207	15	Dewing	Joseph	1			1		2		1					5		
Ipswich	281	74	Dexter	John	2		1			1	1						5		
Topsfield	19	22	Dexter	Mehitable										1			1		
Newburyport	164	19	Dexter	Timothy			1	1				1	1		1		5		
Gloucester	59	7	Dexter	William	3	2		1		1		2	1				10		
Newbury	110	26	Dial	Charles			1			3			1				5		
Beverly	294	35	Dial	Rachel								2		2			4		
Salem	201	6	Diamond	Benja	2			1		1			1				5		
Salem	189	15	Diamond	Sarah	1	1	2			1		1		1			7		
Salem	194	35	Dickason	Obed											11		11		
Rowley	130	41	Dickerson	Joshua		1	1	1		1	1		1				6		
Rowley	131	48	Dickerson	Oliver		1		1				1	1				4		
Rowley	130	34	Dickerson	William		1	1	1		2	1		1				7		
Newbury	115	45	Dike	Ann			1	2						3			6		
Beverly	296	36	Dike	John	2		1	1		1	2		1				8		
Beverly	304	12	Dike	Solomon	1			1		3			1				6		
Newburyport	164	15	Dillaway	Thomas				1					1				2		
Andover	93	7	Dilliway	William			1	1				1	1				4		
Marblehead	243	15	Dimon	Elizabeth	2					1	2	1					6		
Gloucester	59	14	Discal	Jeremiah		1		1						1			3		
Salem	217	29	Diver	Mary		1	1					1	1				4		
Marblehead	261	4	Dixey	John	3			1		2			1				7		
Marblehead	263	11	Dixey	John Junr	4		1				1	1		1			9		
Marblehead	269	25	Dixey	Mary										1			1		
Marblehead	243	28	Dixey	Peter	1			1		2			1				5		
Marblehead	243	7	Dixey	Rebecca		1	1	1			1	2		1			7		
Salem	200	41	Dixson	Joseph	1			1				1					3		
Marblehead	253	1	Doak	Benjamin	2	1		1		1			1				6		
Marblehead	260	7	Doak	Benjamin			1		1			1	1	1			5		
Marblehead	257	13	Doak	Deliverance	1					1			1				3		
Marblehead	239	25	Doak	Francis				1		2		1					4		
Marblehead	257	6	Doak	George				1					1				2		
Marblehead	247	2	Doak	James					1			1	1				3		
Beverly	305	2	Dobben	John	2			1		1	1		1				6		
Marblehead	250	24	Doble	Thomas	1	1		1						1			4		
Marblehead	266	33	Dodd	Benjamin			1			3			1				5		
Marblehead	239	23	Dodd	Cornelius	4	1		1					1				7		
Marblehead	249	1	Dodd	Mary			2							1			3		
Marblehead	242	9	Dodd	Thomas				1					1				2		
Marblehead	251	19	Dodd	William				1					1				2		
Bradford	123	35	Dodge	Abel			1	1		1	1	2	4	1			11		
Newburyport	163	17	Dodge	Abraham	3	1	2	1		2	2		1				12		
Wenham	308	2	Dodge	Abraham				1		1	1		1	1	1		6		
Hamilton	285	8	Dodge	Andrew	1			1				1	1				4		
Beverly	293	43	Dodge	Asa				2						1			3		
Beverly	293	44	Dodge	Asa R	1			1		2			1				5		
Beverly	305	31	Dodge	Barnabas				1				1		1			3		
Hamilton	285	7	Dodge	Barnabas	1		1	1	1			1	1				6		
Wenham	308	21	Dodge	Benja				1						1			2		
Ipswich	275	13	Dodge	Bethiah			1					2		1			4		
Beverly	294	5	Dodge	Charles	1	2	1	1				3	1	1			10		
Beverly	291	3	Dodge	Cornelius	1	1	3	1		1		2	1				10		
Danvers	12	40	Dodge	Daniel			1										2		
Newburyport	163	15	Dodge	Daniel	1	2		1					1	1			6		
Ipswich	276	46	Dodge	Elizabeth								1	1				2		
Wenham	308	9	Dodge	Elizabeth			1						2	1			4		
Danvers	2	9	Dodge	Ephraim	1		1	1			1	1					5		
Hamilton	285	38	Dodge	Ephraim			1						2				3		
Hamilton	287	6	Dodge	Ephraim		1	1			1		1					4		
Ipswich	275	28	Dodge	Ezekiel	2	2		1			2		1				8		
Salem	213	45	Dodge	Geo				1				2					3		
Hamilton	285	33	Dodge	George	1		3	1		2	1	1	2				11		
Ipswich	281	36	Dodge	Grover		1		1						1			3		
Wenham	308	6	Dodge	Hannah	1	1	1					2	1	1			7		
Newburyport	163	18	Dodge	Hannah Wido		1							1				2		
Hamilton	287	7	Dodge	Henry	2	1	1	1				1	1				7		
Hamilton	285	80	Dodge	Isaac		1	1	1				1	1				5		
Salem	213	30	Dodge	Israel			2	1		2		1	1	1			9		
Wenham	308	23	Dodge	Israel		1		1				1		1	1		5		
Beverly	291	11	Dodge	Israel	1			1		1	1		1				5		
Wenham	308	38	Dodge	Israel A	1	2		1		1		2		1			8		
Beverly	294	17	Dodge	Jacob		1	1	1		2			1				7		
Wenham	308	1	Dodge	Jacob	1			2		3		1					8		
Danvers	14	3	Dodge	Jeremiah			2		1	1		1		1			6		

TOWN	PG#	LN#	LAST NAME	FIRST NAME	M under 10	M 10-16	M 16-26	M 26-45	M 45+	F under 10	F 10-16	F 16-26	F 26-45	F 45+	TOTAL ALL OTHER	TOTAL SLAVES	TOTALS	DISTRICT/ TOWNSHIP	NOTES
Beverly	305	32	Dodge	John		1	1		1	1				2			6		
Danvers	5	35	Dodge	John		1							1				2		
Ipswich	281	78	Dodge	John			1						1				2		
Salem	194	16	Dodge	John	2	3	2	1		1			1	1			11		
Wenham	308	7	Dodge	John		2		1	1	1			1	1	1		8		
Wenham	307	6	Dodge	John 2nd		3	1		1	2			2	1			10		
Wenham	308	14	Dodge	John 3d	2			1				1	1				5		
Hamilton	287	3	Dodge	John A	3			1				1	1				6		
Wenham	308	13	Dodge	John F		2		1		4				1			8		
Gloucester	59	6	Dodge	Jona	2	1		1		2		1	1				8		
Beverly	291	2	Dodge	Jonathan				1						1			2		
Hamilton	285	37	Dodge	Jonathan	1	1	1	1		1	1	4		1			12		
Beverly	305	34	Dodge	Jonathan 2d	2			1		1				1			5		
Hamilton	285	34	Dodge	Jonathan Junr	2			1		1	1	1					6		
Haverhill	145	10	Dodge	Joseph				1						1			2		
Beverly	293	28	Dodge	Joshua				1				1		1			3		
Danvers	5	5	Dodge	Joshua		1		1					1	1			4		
Salem	220	21	Dodge	Joshua	1		1	1		1	2	1	1				8		
Salem	210	45	Dodge	Josiah	2			1		1				1			5		
Beverly	294	14	Dodge	Levi				1		2				1			4		
Hamilton	285	41	Dodge	Livermore	2			1		2				1			6		
Hamilton	285	39	Dodge	Luke					2					2			4		
Hamilton	285	48	Dodge	Mighill	2			1		1	1			1			6		
Gloucester	57	36	Dodge	Nathll		1	1		1					1			4	West Parish	
Ipswich	281	44	Dodge	Nehemiah			1					1	1				3		
Beverly	302	45	Dodge	Nicholas	1	5		1		1	1			1			10		
Wenham	308	17	Dodge	Nichols		2									1		3		
Wenham	309	2	Dodge	Oliver	1	2						1					4		
Wenham	308	8	Dodge	Peter	1		1			3				1			6		
Rowley	130	31	Dodge	Phineas		1		1				2	1		1		6		
Rowley	130	33	Dodge	Phineas	1	1		1		2			1				6		
Salem	207	2	Dodge	Pian	1		1			1	1	1					5		
Beverly	293	47	Dodge	Rebecca									2				2		
Wenham	309	22	Dodge	Richard Esquire				1				1		1			3		
Hamilton	287	2	Dodge	Robert			1	1					4				6		
Newbury	110	1	Dodge	Robert		3	1			1			2				7		
Beverly	306	27	Dodge	Samuel	1	2		1		3			1				8		
Manchester	50	32	Dodge	Sarah Wo									1				1		
Wenham	308	16	Dodge	Simon	1		1		1			1	1	1			6		
Rowley	130	32	Dodge	Solomon		1							1				2		
Topsfield	20	24	Dodge	Solomon	1	1		2		2	1		2				9		
Wenham	308	5	Dodge	Stephen				1				1		1			3		
Danvers	13	30	Dodge	Tammerson									1				1		
Beverly	293	46	Dodge	Thomas				1		3	1		1				6		
Beverly	301	15	Dodge	Thomas	1			1				1					3		
Hamilton	285	42	Dodge	Thomas				1		2			1				4		
Ipswich	274	39	Dodge	Thomas				1		2			1	1			5		
Newburyport	163	16	Dodge	Thomas	3	1	1	1		1	1			1			9		
Lynnfield	236	17	Dodge	Thos			1						1				2		
Wenham	307	7	Dodge	Uszial	1		2					1					4		
Beverly	293	42	Dodge	William		1	1		1	1	1	1	1				7		
Hamilton	287	5	Dodge	William	3			1	1	1				1			7		
Ipswich	279	4	Dodge	William			2	1		1	1		1	1			7		
Newbury	111	34	Dodge	William			1						1				2		
Wenham	308	27	Dodge	William	3	3		1		1		2	1				11		
Gloucester	85	25	Dogett	William	1	1		1		1	1			1			6		
Newburyport	164	13	Doggett	Joseph	3		1			1			1				6		
Danvers	5	1	Dole	Benjamin		1	2					1		1			5		
Newburyport	164	5	Dole	Benjamin			1					1	1				3		
Andover	93	11	Dole	Casar											3		3		
Newbury	117	34	Dole	David		1		1		1			1				4		
Newburyport	164	8	Dole	Ebenezer		3							1				4		
Newbury	117	35	Dole	Enoch	1	2		1		1			1				6		
Newburyport	164	6	Dole	Friend			1						1	1			3		
Rowley	127	24	Dole	Greenleaf		3		1		2	2	1	1				10		
Newbury	117	23	Dole	Henry	1		1		1			2		2			7		
Rowley	128	49	Dole	Henry	1		1			1			1				4		
Salisbury	26	29	Dole	Jemima Wd	2		1			1		1	1				6		
Newbury	112	36	Dole	John	1		2			2	1	2		1			9		
Rowley	131	32	Dole	John		1		1		2	2		1	1			8		
Newburyport	164	4	Dole	Jonathan Jr	1	1		1		2			1				6		
Rowley	131	40	Dole	Joseph	1		1		1	1	1	2	1				8		
Newbury	105	17	Dole	Moses			1	1		1	1		1				5		
Rowley	128	48	Dole	Moses	1		1		1	1			1	1			6		
Newbury	115	44	Dole	Oliver	4		1	1		1				1			8		
Rowley	127	33	Dole	Peabody		1	1					2					4		
Rowley	127	32	Dole	Ruth	1					1	1		1	1	1		6		
Newbury	116	25	Dole	Samuel		1	1		1			1	1	1			6		
Rowley	127	31	Dole	Silas	1		2		1	1	1	1					8		
Newbury	106	38	Dole	Stephen		2		1		1				1			5		
Rowley	128	52	Dole	Stephen	1	1		1	1	2	1	1	3				11		
Rowley	128	50	Dole	Thomas		1											4		

TOWN	PG#	LN#	LAST NAME	FIRST NAME	FREE WHITE MALES under 10	10 to 16	16 to 26	26 to 45	45 and over	FREE WHITE FEMALES under 10	10 to 16	16 to 26	26 to 45	45 and over	TOTAL ALL OTHER	TOTAL SLAVES	TOTALS	DISTRICT/ TOWNSHIP	NOTES
Newbury	117	39	Dole	William	2			1		1			1				5		
Newburyport	164	7	Dole	William			1			1		1					3		
Rowley	127	6	Dole	William	1	1		1		1		1					5		
Marblehead	258	18	Doliber	Deborah										1			1		
Marblehead	259	16	Doliber	Elizabeth										1			1		
Marblehead	268	17	Doliber	Elizabeth	1					1	2			1			5		
Marblehead	243	12	Doliber	John	3	1		1		1			1				7		
Marblehead	258	7	Doliber	John	3	1		1		1			1				7		
Marblehead	258	26	Doliber	John	1		1						1				3		
Marblehead	249	29	Doliber	Joseph	1			1		1			1				4		
Marblehead	245	2	Doliber	Peter					1		1		1	1			4		
Marblehead	248	35	Doliber	Sarah			2						1	1			4		
Marblehead	249	20	Doliber	Thomas	2		1	1			1	1	1	1			8		
Marblehead	246	22	Doliber	Thomas P.	1	1		1		1			1	1			6		
Marblehead	246	18	Doliber	William			1			1			1				3		
Marblehead	265	28	Doliber	William		1	1						1				3		
Marblehead	268	23	Doliber	William	1			1				1	1				4		
Gloucester	63	27	Doliver	William Cap	2		1	1		1			1				6	East Ward	
Gloucester	64	3	Doliver	William Cap				1						1	2		4		
Salisbury	26	31	Dollar	Samuel			1							1			2		
Salem	196	3	Dollison	Rebecca	1					1			1				3		
Salem	204	43	Dolliver	William		1	2					1					4		
Manchester	50	36	Donels	Asa	1		1			2			1				5		
Salem	219	15	Donnegan	Thos	1	1		1		1	1	1					6		
Topsfield	20	35	Dorman	Ephriem				1									1		
Newburyport	164	10	Dorman	Jesse			1						1				2		
Boxford	134	42	Dorman	John	1			1	1	3		1	1				8		
Topsfield	20	34	Dorman	Joseph			1					1	1				3		
Boxford	135	28	Dorman	Moses			1					1	2	1			5		
Boxford	135	29	Dorman	Timothy		2	1	1				1	1				6		
Salisbury	26	32	Dorr	Edward	1		1	1		2			1				6		
Newburyport	163	20	Dossett	Florence			1						1				2		
Danvers	4	3	Douty	James			1						1	1			3		
Danvers	4	4	Douty	Joseph	1	1	1					1	1	1			6		
Danvers	4	2	Douty	Thomas			2						1	1			4		
Salisbury	26	27	Dow	Aaron	1	1	1	1		1	1		1				7		
Salisbury	26	28	Dow	Joseph	1		1		1	2		1		1			7		
Salisbury	26	25	Dow	Patience Wd			1						1				2		
Salisbury	26	26	Dow	Samuel				2		1			1	1			5		
Manchester	50	37	Dow	Hanh Wo	4	1						1	1				7		
Manchester	50	38	Dow	Jacob	2		1			2			1				6		
Manchester	50	14	Dow	Jereh		1		1					2	1			5		
Newburyport	163	19	Dowe	William			1						1				2		
Newburyport	163	40	Dowell	David	1			1		3			1				6		
Wenham	308	12	Dowling	Mary										1			1		
Beverly	296	13	Down	Betsey								2	1				3		
Beverly	296	34	Down	John	1		1						1				3		
Newbury	119	24	Downer	Anna		1						1	1	1			4		
Newbury	119	9	Downer	Daniel	1		1			1			1				4		
Newburyport	164	3	Downer	Hannah								2	1	1			4		
Newbury	113	46	Downer	Jesse		1						1					2		
Newburyport	164	20	Downers	Prince Lambart	1		1			1			1				4		
Danvers	13	18	Downes	Experience									1				1		
Newburyport	164	2	Downes	Sarah Wido	1								1				2		
Newburyport	164	1	Downes	Thomas			1						1				2		
Lynn	233	31	Downing	Caleb			3				1	1	1	1			7	West Parish	
Lynn	230	9	Downing	Elijah			1						1				2		
Haverhill	145	15	Downing	John		2		1		1			1				5		
Lynn	226	6	Downing	John	1	1		1		2	1		1				7		
Newbury	111	21	Downing	John		1		1		1		1		1			5		
Lynn	234	11	Downing	Joseph				1					1				2		
Andover	93	15	Downing	Palfrey	2		1	1		2			1				7		
Salem	210	14	Downing	Thos	1		1						1				3		
Marblehead	245	31	Downing	William			1			1			1	1			4		
Marblehead	260	20	Downs	John			1	1						2			4		
Newbury	113	32	Downs	Solomon				1			2		1				4		
Newbury	118	45	Downs	Stephen				1				1	1				3		
Salem	205	46	Dowse	Joseph			1			1		1	1				4		
Salem	205	12	Dowse	Saml	1	1		1		1		1	1				6		
Salem	200	3	Dowse	William			1							1			2		
Salem	203	10	Dowst	John	3			1		1	1		1				7		
Gloucester	79	12	Doyal	Felex	2	1		1		1	1		1				7		
Rowley	130	37	Dresser	Daniel		1		1			1		1				4		
Gloucester	79	15	Dresser	Dorcas Wo									1	1			2		
Rowley	130	42	Dresser	Joseph			1						1	1			3		
Gloucester	79	14	Dresser	Richard	2	2		1				1	1				7		
Boxford	135	6	Dresser	Thos	1		3	1		1			2				8		
Gloucester	68	14	Dresson	Moses		3	1	1		2		1	1				9		
Gloucester	58	16	Drews	Eleazer	1		1			2		1					5		
Manchester	51	1	Driver	Andrew	1			1					1				3		
Manchester	49	11	Driver	Andw	1			1					1				3		
Salem	207	22	Driver	Ben	1	1		1		1	1		1				6		
Manchester	49	13	Driver	Bethiah Wo									1	1			2		
Manchester	51	2	Driver	John	2			1		1			1				5		

189

TOWN	PG#	LN#	LAST NAME	FIRST NAME	FREE WHITE MALES					FREE WHITE FEMALES					TOTAL ALL OTHER	TOTAL SLAVES	TOTALS	DISTRICT/ TOWNSHIP	NOTES
					under 10	10 to 16	16 to 26	26 to 45	45 and over	under 10	10 to 16	16 to 26	26 to 45	45 and over					
Salem	207	24	Driver	Robt			1			1							2		
Manchester	54	14	Driver	Samll		1							1				2		
Salem	207	23	Driver	Sarah										1			1		
Salem	194	5	Driver	Stephen			2	1	1				3	1			8		
Marblehead	266	17	Drury	John	2	1	1	2		1			1				8		
Newburyport	164	18	Dudley	Elias	2		1	1		2		1	1				8		
Newbury	113	37	Dugan	John	3		1			1			1				6		
Gloucester	69	1	Duglass	Danl	1		1						1				3		
Gloucester	68	27	Duglass	John				1					1				2		
Salem	218	43	Duliver	John			1						1				2		
Gloucester	76	15	Duly	Michael		2	1		1	1				2			7		
Newbury	105	12	Dummer	Richard				1						1			2		
Newbury	105	13	Dummer	Richard			1			2			1				4		
Newbury	106	26	Dummer	Samuel	1		1			1	1		2	1			7		
Newbury	105	10	Dummer	Shuball		1	1	1				1	2	1			7		
Newbury	105	11	Dummer	William			1	2					2	1			6		
Gloucester	84	19	Dunahew	David	1			1		2				1			5		
Haverhill	145	8	Duncan	James		1		1				1	1	1			5		
Haverhill	145	9	Duncan	James Jr	2	1	1	2		1			2				9		
Marblehead	256	25	Duncan	Joseph	1			1		1	1		1				5		
Gloucester	85	22	Dunfield	Phil	2			1		2			1				6		
Salem	209	12	Dunkle	John	2		1	1					1				5		
Danvers	12	2	Dunkle	Ezekiel			1			2			1				4		
Danvers	7	23	Dunklen	Ezekiel				1				1		1			3		
Lynn	225	42	Dunn	David				2						1			3		
Haverhill	145	12	Dunnels	Joseph	3			1		1			1				6		
Andover	93	8	Duntenn	Nathanael	4			1		2	2		1				10		
Haverhill	145	13	Dunton	Ruth		2								1			3		
Salem	210	6	Dupar	Elias	1		1			1			1				4		
Marblehead	255	5	Dupree	Thomas	1		1						1				3		
Andover	93	16	Durant	Amos	1	1		1		1	1	2	1				8		
Topsfield	22	3	Durant	Isaac	2			1		2	1		1				7		
Haverhill	145	11	Durton	Thomas		1		1		4	1		1	1			9		
Ipswich	275	42	Dutch	Daniel	1	1		1		2			1				6		
Bradford	124	33	Dutch	Ebenezr			2		2	1	1	1					8		
Salem	207	27	Dutch	John	1		2						1	1			5		
Ipswich	276	5	Dutch	Martha									1				1		
Ipswich	275	41	Dutch	Nathaniel	1					1		1	1	1			5		
Danvers	9	6	Dutch	Samuel				1						1			2		
Marblehead	241	21	Dutton	Peter				1			2			1			4		
Newburyport	164	16	Dutton	Stephen	1			1		1			1				4		
Newbury	119	22	Duty	John		1	1	1		2		2	1				8		
Bradford	126	12	Dwinel	Abigal			1						1	1			3		
Rowley	129	6	Dwinel	Amos	1		1						2				4		
Rowley	130	20	Dwinel	Israel	2		1			1		1	1	1			7		
Topsfield	18	20	Dwinell	John			1	1				1	1	1			5		
Danvers	8	13	Dwinell	Joseph			1	1				1	1	1			5		
Danvers	8	15	Dwinell	Joseph Junr	1	1		1					1	1			5		
Newbury	108	17	Dyke	William			1						1				2		
Beverly	304	6	Dyson	John	1			1		2	2	2		1			9		
Haverhill	145	27	Eames	Samuel		2	1		1	1		1	3	1			10		
Manchester	51	14	Eastcot	Philip	1	1		1		3			1				7		
Haverhill	145	22	Easterbrooks	Hannah	1			1			1			1			4		
Salisbury	27	20	Eastman	Daniel	1			1		2			1				5		
Salisbury	27	23	Eastman	Ephrm	3			1		1			1				6		
Salisbury	27	21	Eastman	Hannah Wd	2	1			1	1				1			6		
Salisbury	27	10	Eastman	Jeremiah		1		1				1	1				5		
Salisbury	27	14	Eastman	Moses	1			1		1			1				4		
Salisbury	27	19	Eastman	Thomas Capt			1					1		1			3		
Salisbury	27	22	Eastman	Wd										2			2		
Salisbury	27	24	Easton	Wheeler			1			1			1				3		
Salisbury	27	1	Eaton	Abel		2		1					1	1			5		
Salisbury	27	6	Eaton	Abigail Wd		1						1	2	1			5		
Haverhill	145	46	Eaton	Amos	1	2		1			1	1		1			7		
Salisbury	27	2	Eaton	Anna Wd										2			2		
Newburyport	164	39	Eaton	Benjamin				1					1	1			3		
Salisbury	27	8	Eaton	Caleb			1	1		1	1	1		1			6		
Salem	204	39	Eaton	Charles	2	1		1		2			1				7		
Marblehead	244	7	Eaton	Hannah	1			2						1			4		
Salisbury	27	7	Eaton	Henry		1	1						1				3		
Marblehead	266	29	Eaton	Israel			1		1			1	1	1			5		
Salisbury	27	3	Eaton	James	1	1	2	1		2	2		1				10		
Beverly	300	25	Eaton	Joseph	1	1		1			1	2	1				7		
Haverhill	145	30	Eaton	Joseph			1	1			1	2	1	1	1		7		
Beverly	303	33	Eaton	Joseph 2nd			1				1	1					3		
Boxford	134	4	Eaton	Peter	2		1			1	1		1		1		7		
Haverhill	145	45	Eaton	Phineas	1	2	1						1				5		
Haverhill	145	33	Eaton	Rebeckah	2		1	1		1	1	3		1			10		
Salisbury	27	5	Eaton	Saml Capt		1	2	2	1				2	2			10		
Newburyport	164	40	Eaton	Stephen	1		1						1				3		
Haverhill	145	29	Eaton	Timothy		1			1				1	1			4		
Methuen	153	19	Eaton	Timothy		1	3		1				2	1			8		
Haverhill	145	37	Eaton	Timothy Jun	2	2	4	1		3			1	1			14		

190

TOWN	PG#	LN#	LAST NAME	FIRST NAME	FREE WHITE MALES under 10	10 to 16	16 to 26	26 to 45	45 and over	FREE WHITE FEMALES under 10	10 to 16	16 to 26	26 to 45	45 and over	TOTAL ALL OTHER	TOTAL SLAVES	TOTALS	DISTRICT/ TOWNSHIP	NOTES
Lynnfield	235	32	Eaton	Timy	1			1		2			1				5		
Haverhill	145	28	Eaton	Ward			3						1				4		
Salisbury	27	4	Eaton	William					1					1			2		
Salem	217	13	Eddy	Margt	2			1		2		1	1				7		
Danvers	11	34	Eden	Mary									1	1			2		
Newburyport	164	38	Edes	Isaac	1			1		2			1				5		
Newburyport	164	25	Edmunds	Barnabas				1						1			2		
Marblehead	247	22	Edney	James	1	1		1		1			1				5		
Beverly	291	25	Edward	Robert				1					1				2		
Newburyport	164	31	Edwards	Abraham	1			1		1		1		1			5		
Wenham	308	18	Edwards	Abraham	2		1	1		2		1					7		
Newburyport	164	32	Edwards	Benjamin	2			1				2					5		
Wenham	308	20	Edwards	Benjamin		2	1	1		3			1	1			9		
Newburyport	164	34	Edwards	Edward	2			1		1			1				5		
Newburyport	164	30	Edwards	John				1					1				2		
Salem	208	49	Edwards	John			1			1			1				3		
Salem	210	34	Edwards	John	2			1				1					4		
Salem	215	25	Edwards	John					1				1	1			3		
Manchester	51	9	Edwards	John 3d	2			1		1	1		1				6		
Salem	215	26	Edwards	John Jr	1			1		1			1				4		
Manchester	51	8	Edwards	John Jun				1			1	1					3		
Manchester	51	6	Edwards	John Junr				1				1					2		
Salisbury	27	15	Edwards	Moses	1			1		1			1				4		
Newburyport	164	36	Edwards	Moses R				2				2	1				5		
Salisbury	27	17	Edwards	Reuben	3	1	2	1			1	1	1				10		
Salisbury	27	16	Edwards	Rise	1			1		1			1	1			5		
Beverly	306	20	Edwards	Robert Jr	1			1		3			1				6		
Manchester	51	5	Edwards	Samll	2		1						1	1			5		
Newburyport	164	33	Edwards	Thomas	1		1						1				3		
Manchester	51	3	Edwards	Willa	3		1			1		1	1				7		
Haverhill	145	42	Edwards	William	2		1	1		1		1	1				7		
Newburyport	164	35	Edwards	William	2	1		1		1	1		1				7		
Manchester	51	7	Edwards	Willm Jun	1		2	1			1	1					6		
Beverly	293	45	Edwards	Asa B	1			1		2			1				5		
Beverly	293	50	Edwards	Jacob		1	2		1		1	1		1			7		
Beverly	293	48	Edwards	John		1	1		1	1	1			1			6		
Haverhill	145	18	Ela	Jacob				1	1	1				1	1		5		
Haverhill	145	21	Ela	Jonathan		1		1		1			1				4		
Salem	195	32	Eldridge	Joshua	1			1				1	1	1			5		
Haverhill	145	20	Eliot	Ephraim	1	1	1	1	1	2			2				9		
Newburyport	164	26	Eliot	Jeremiah				1		2			1	1			5		
Haverhill	145	19	Eliot	Thomas					1		1	1	1				4		
Middleton	17	3	Eliott	Stephen				1					1				2		
Salem	194	8	Eliotte	Mary						3		2		1			6		
Andover	103	25	Elisha	John									1		2		3		
Salem	210	22	Elkins	Henry			1			1			1				3		
Salem	212	50	Elkins	Mary	1					1		1	1	1			5		
Marblehead	243	29	Elkins	Thomas		1	1		1	1		1	1				6		
Marblehead	253	2	Elkins	Thomas				1				1					2		
Gloucester	59	12	Ellery	Abigale Wo								1	1				2		
Gloucester	72	2	Ellery	Benja	2	2	2	1				1	1	1			10		
Gloucester	64	8	Ellery	Esther Wo			1					1	1	1			4		
Gloucester	59	13	Ellery	Nathll	2			1					1				4		
Gloucester	62	10	Ellery	William		1							1				2		
Ipswich	277	44	Ellice	George				1				1		1			3		
Beverly	300	13	Ellinwood	Joanna	1							1		1			3		
Beverly	296	2	Ellinwood	John	2	1	1	1	1				2				8		
Beverly	300	28	Ellinwood	Sarah									1				1		
Beverly	300	21	Ellinwood	Wm			1				1		1				3		
Middleton	17	9	Elliot	Andrew	1		1						1				3		
Middleton	17	12	Elliot	Asa		1		1				1	1	1			5		
Middleton	17	13	Elliot	John			1			1			1				3		
Middleton	16	19	Elliot	Rachel									2				2		
Middleton	17	4	Elliot	Roger	1			1					1				5		
Middleton	17	8	Elliot	Ruth			1			1			1	1			5		
Beverly	290	31	Elliott	Andrew	1		3	1		2			2		1		10		
Beverly	292	5	Elliott	Andrew Jr			1					1					2		
Beverly	297	27	Elliott	James	2	1		1		1			1				6		
Beverly	296	43	Elliott	William	1	1		1		5	1	1	1				11		
Beverly	294	6	Elliott	William 2d	1	1	1	1		5		1	1	1			12		
Marblehead	256	20	Ellis	Francis				1			1		1				3		
Newburyport	164	29	Ellis	Rachael Wido	2					1			1				4		
Salem	219	6	Ellison	John				1						2			3		
Gloucester	71	13	Ellott	Andrew				1						1			2		
Salem	205	37	Ellsy	Hipsabh							1	1	1	1			4		
Newburyport	164	27	Elsworth	Jeremiah		1		1					1	1			4		
Salem	211	10	Elsworth	William	1	1							1				3		
Newbury	113	17	Elwall	Samuel				1					1				2		
Gloucester	85	30	Elwell	Andrew		1	1	1		1		1	1				6		
Gloucester	79	16	Elwell	David			1			2		2					5		
Newburyport	164	28	Elwell	David			1						1				3		
Gloucester	64	11	Elwell	Elias	1	2	1	1				2	1	1			9		
Gloucester	59	15	Elwell	Isaac	1	3	1		1			2		3			11		

191

TOWN	PG#	LN#	LAST NAME	FIRST NAME	M under 10	M 10 to 16	M 16 to 26	M 26 to 45	M 45 and over	F under 10	F 10 to 16	F 16 to 26	F 26 to 45	F 45 and over	TOTAL ALL OTHER	TOTAL SLAVES	TOTALS	DISTRICT/TOWNSHIP	NOTES
Gloucester	85	29	Elwell	Job	2			1		1	2			1			7		
Gloucester	64	5	Elwell	Jona 3d	1			1		1	3			1			7		
Gloucester	84	9	Elwell	Mary Widow	2	2	2						2	1			9		
Gloucester	64	10	Elwell	Robert 3d	1	1	1	1		4			1				9		
Gloucester	64	7	Elwell	Robert Junr			2	1	1			1	1	1			7		
Gloucester	84	29	Elwell	Saml			1						1				2		
Gloucester	64	9	Elwell	Solomon		1			1	1	1						4		
Gloucester	86	21	Elwell	Zebulon	3	2	2		1	2				1			11		
Beverly	306	18	Ely	John Francis		1	2	1	1	1		1	2	1			10		
Haverhill	145	44	Emer	Micah		1								1			2		
Newbury	108	41	Emerey	Samuel	1		1	1	1				2	1			7		
Newbury	108	35	Emerey	Stephen	1	1		1		1	1			1			6		
Newbury	108	32	Emerson	Abel	1			1					2	1			5		
Haverhill	145	35	Emerson	Abraham	1	1	2	1					2	1			8		
Haverhill	145	24	Emerson	Amos	1	1							1				3		
Newburyport	164	21	Emerson	Bulkeley				1					3	1			5		
Newburyport	164	22	Emerson	Bulkeley Jr	4			1			1		1	1			8		
Haverhill	145	38	Emerson	Daniel	4	1		1						1			7		
Methuen	153	22	Emerson	Day	2		1			3			1				8		
Haverhill	145	32	Emerson	Ithamar			2		1	2	1		1				7		
Haverhill	145	40	Emerson	John		1	1		1	1	2		1				7		
Ipswich	282	52	Emerson	John	2			1	1	1			3				7		
Newbury	119	36	Emerson	John		1		1					1				3		
Newburyport	164	24	Emerson	Joseph				1					1	1			3		
Haverhill	145	39	Emerson	Josiah		2		1		1			1	1			6		
Haverhill	145	36	Emerson	Moses	3	1		1		2		1	1				9		
Haverhill	145	34	Emerson	Nathan	2			1		1			1				5		
Haverhill	145	25	Emerson	Nehemiah	2	1	2	1		3			1	1	1		13		
Haverhill	145	43	Emerson	Nehemiah Jun			1						1				2		
Methuen	153	21	Emerson	Oliver		1	2		1	2	1		1				8		
Newburyport	164	23	Emerson	Samuel			2	1					1				4		
Haverhill	145	26	Emerson	Susana			2	1				1		1			5		
Methuen	153	20	Emerson	Timothy	1	1				2		1	1	3			10		
Salem	193	11	Emerston	Ephraim				1			1	1	1				4		
Salem	211	22	Emerton	Jeremiah	1	2		1		1		1	1				7		
Salem	221	23	Emerton	Jeremiah Master Salem	9	2	3	7	23	4	1	6	15	36	19		125		
Salem	220	5	Emerton	John	1		1	1		1	2		1	1			8		
Ipswich	282	9	Emerton	Oliver		1		1		1			1	1			5		
Haverhill	145	23	Emery	Ephraim	1	1		1		1			1				5		
Haverhill	145	31	Emery	John		1	1	1	1		4		1				9		
Newbury	108	25	Emery	Moody	2	1		1					1				5		
Haverhill	145	41	Emery	Moses	2	1		1		1	2		1				8		
Newbury	108	30	Emery	Nathaniel		2		1					1				4		
Newbury	109	4	Emery	Nathaniel			2		1	1	2	2					8		
Newbury	110	20	Emery	Thomas	2	1	1						1				5		
Danvers	13	39	Emmerson	Thomas				1					1		1		3		
Topsfield	21	5	Emmerson	Thomas			3	1	1	2	1		1	1	2		12		
Danvers	13	38	Emmerson	Timothy	2	1	2		1	1	1	1	1				10		
Lynn	225	22	Emmerton	Jeremiah		1				1		1					3		
Ipswich	275	14	Emmons	Daniel		1				1	1		1				4		
Gloucester	63	15	Emons	Daniel			1			1			1				3	West Ward	
Salem	189	35	Endicot	Samuel												5	5		
Danvers	8	17	Endicott	Elias			1	1		2		1	1				6		
Danvers	8	42	Endicott	Israel	1			1					1				3		
Danvers	9	37	Endicott	John		1	1		1				1	2	1		7		
Danvers	9	23	Endicott	John Junr	3	1		1		1			1	1			8		
Danvers	9	36	Endicott	Joseph		1		1					1	2			5		
Danvers	9	16	Endicott	Moses	1	1		1		1	1		1				6		
Beverly	303	8	Endicott	Robert	2	2		1					1	1			7		
Salem	210	39	Endicott	Samuel	1			1		2	1		1				6		
Newburyport	165	1	England	Francis	1	1	1	1						1			5		
Newburyport	165	2	England	Samuel Jr	1			1		2				1			5		
Salem	194	32	Epes	Samuel		1	4		1	1	2			1			10		
Danvers	10	35	Epes	William	1	1		1		3	2	1	1				10		
Salem	188	28	Epes	William	1			1		1		1	1				5		
Salem	202	2	Erving	Geo		1	1	1		1	2			1			7		
Salem	216	4	Erving	Hugh		1							1				2		
Salem	204	27	Erving	John			1			1			1				3		
Newburyport	165	3	Ervins	John	3			1		1	1		1	1			8		
Lynn	226	30	Estes	Mark		1		1					1	1			4		
Salem	200	31	Estes	Nath	2	1		1		1			1	1			7		
Salem	217	34	Estes	William	1		1						1				3		
Lynn	226	31	Estes	Willm		1	1						1				3		
Topsfield	18	12	Estey	Daniel		1		1	1			3	1	2	2		11		
Topsfield	18	21	Estey	Enos									1				1		
Middleton	16	6	Estey	John	1	2	1	1	1	1		2		1			10		
Middleton	15	19	Estey	Samuel		1							1				2		
Salem	213	3	Eusis	Lydia							1	1	1				3		
Salem	193	1	Eustes	Jotham	2	1	2	2		3	2		1				13		
Newburyport	164	37	Eustice	William	1	1		1		1			1	1			6		
Salisbury	27	25	Evans	Benja Esq		1			1	1	1			1			5		
Salisbury	27	18	Evans	David			1			1			1				3		
Marblehead	268	25	Evans	Elizabeth		2					1						4		

192

TOWN	PG#	LN#	LAST NAME	FIRST NAME	FREE WHITE MALES					FREE WHITE FEMALES					TOTAL ALL OTHER	TOTAL SLAVES	TOTALS	DISTRICT/TOWNSHIP	NOTES
					under 10	10 to 16	16 to 26	26 to 45	45 and over	under 10	10 to 16	16 to 26	26 to 45	45 and over					
Salisbury	27	9	Evans	Ezekiel	2	1	1		1		1	1		1			8		
Salisbury	27	11	Evans	John	2			1		2			1	1			7		
Salisbury	27	13	Evans	Jona Colo		1			1		1	1		1			5		
Salisbury	27	12	Evans	Jona Junr				1					1				2		
Gloucester	56	14	Eveleth	Isaac Majo		1		1					1				3		
Gloucester	56	13	Eveleth	Joseph				1						2			3		
Salem	214	47	Eveleth	Joseph	1	2	4	1	2	2	2	2		1			17		
Ipswich	277	22	Eveleth	Samuel		1		1		3	1		1				7		
Ipswich	282	57	Evelett	Aaron	1		3		2	1	1	1		1			10		
Ipswich	282	59	Evelett	Lucy									1		1		2		
Beverly	290	17	Evelith	Anna		1	2				1		1				5		
Marblehead	253	7	Evens	Ebenezer G.	2	1	1	1			2		1				8		
Gloucester	64	6	Everton	Joseph		3			1	2	2	1					9		
Newbury	114	40	Evons	Thomas	2		2	1		2	1		1				9		
Salem	199	39	Fabens	Sarah										1			1		
Salem	189	26	Fabens	Tho	4			1					1				6		
Salem	202	30	Fabens	William	1	1	1	1		2	1	2	1				10		
Hamilton	285	108	Fairfield	Elijah					1					2			3		
Salem	219	19	Fairfield	Eliza			3				1	1					5		
Salem	218	53	Fairfield	John		1						1					2		
Wenham	309	3	Fairfield	Joseph	1	1	1	1			1		1				6		
Salem	212	55	Fairfield	Rebecca		2					1	2	1				6		
Danvers	9	35	Fairfield	Samuel				1					1				2		
Salem	210	20	Fairfield	William	1			1		2			1	1			6		
Salem	189	14	Falen	Esther			1					1	1	1			4		
Newbury	116	16	Fallingbe	Samuel			1						1				2		
Lynn	226	2	Fanington	John					1	1				1			3		
Andover	94	17	Farington	Benja		1				2		1					4		
Andover	94	16	Farington	Phillip		2		1	1	1		2		1			8		
Newburyport	165	4	Faris	William	1		1		1	3	2		2	1			11		
Newburyport	165	11	Farley	Daniel	1	1	1	1		1		1	2				8		
Ipswich	276	11	Farley	Jabez	4	1	3	1		1	1	1			1		13		
Ipswich	278	51	Farley	John			2	1					1				4		
Newburyport	165	12	Farley	John D				1				2					3		
Ipswich	276	51	Farley	Jonathan	3			1		1	2		1				8		
Ipswich	276	29	Farley	Mary			2				1	2					5		
Ipswich	275	43	Farley	Michiel	1		1					1	1				4		
Ipswich	278	38	Farley	Nathaniel				1					1				2		
Ipswich	276	12	Farley	Robert		1		1		3	2		1	1			9		
Salem	208	8	Farlis	Thos	1	2		1			1	2		2			9		
Newburyport	165	32	Farnham	David				1					1				2		
Newburyport	165	31	Farnham	Peter	1			1					1	1			4		
Newburyport	165	29	Farnham	William	3			1		3		2	1		1		11		
Newburyport	165	30	Farnham	Zebedee		1			1		1	1					5		
Andover	94	15	Farnum	Benja Jr		1		1		3		1	1				7		
Andover	94	4	Farnum	Benjmain				1		1	2	1	1				6		
Andover	94	8	Farnum	Daniel			1		1	1	2	1		1			7		
Andover	93	18	Farnum	Isaac		1	1		1	1		3	1				8		
Andover	93	19	Farnum	Isaac Jr			1			1		1					3		
Andover	94	11	Farnum	Jacob		2				1		2					5		
Andover	94	13	Farnum	James	1	1		1		1	1	1		1			8		
Andover	94	9	Farnum	Jedediah		2	1					1	1	1			6		
Andover	94	10	Farnum	Jedediah Jr		1		1		1		1					4		
Andover	94	5	Farnum	John	2			1		1	1		1				6		
Andover	94	12	Farnum	Moses			1										1		
Andover	94	7	Farnum	Peter	3	1		1		1	1		1				8		
Andover	94	6	Farnum	Sarah Wid									1				1		
Andover	94	14	Farnum	Timothy	2	1		1		3	1		1				9		
Methuen	153	26	Farnum	William	1	2	1	1			2	1	1				9		
Lynn	228	40	Farrington	Amos	1			1					1				3		
Lynn	225	8	Farrington	Danl Jr	1		1	1		2			1				6		
Amesbury	39	9	Farrington	Ebenz				1			1		1				3		
Amesbury	39	10	Farrington	Ebenz Junr	1		1	1		2	2	2	1				10		
Amesbury	39	11	Farrington	Saml		2			1	2			1				6		
Lynn	224	33	Farrington	Theph		1		1		3			1				6		
Lynn	228	39	Farrington	Willm		1		1					1				3		
Salem	195	7	Farrinton	Daniel	3			1		2			1				7		
Salem	192	27	Farrinton	William	1			1			1	1					4		
Manchester	51	17	Farriss	Mary Wo								1	1	1			3		
Andover	93	34	Faulkner	Abiel		1	1	1					1	2			6		
Andover	94	20	Faulkner	Daniel			2	1		1			1				5		
Andover	94	19	Faulkner	Hannah Wid							1		1				2		
Salem	204	15	Fauzel	John		1		2					1	1			5		
Newburyport	165	40	Favorer	Daniel				1		1	1		2				5		
Salem	198	13	Faye	Daniel	1		4	1			2	1	1	1			11		
Gloucester	85	24	Fears	Patty Wo		1	2						1				4		
Salem	216	21	Fearson	Margt		1	1						1				3		
Salem	205	22	Feel	Joseph			1						1				2		
Salem	190	24	Felch	Rebecca							1	1	2				4		
Salisbury	27	34	Felch	Samuel	1	1		1				1	1				5		
Salem	203	24	Fell	Geo W.	1		1				1	1					4		
Salem	203	23	Fell	Kathn									1				1		
Marblehead	250	20	Feller	Hannah									1				1		

			HEADS OF HOUSEHOLD		FREE WHITE MALES					FREE WHITE FEMALES									
TOWN	PG#	LN#	LAST NAME	FIRST NAME	under 10	10 to 16	16 to 26	26 to 45	45 and over	under 10	10 to 16	16 to 26	26 to 45	45 and over	TOTAL ALL OTHER	TOTAL SLAVES	TOTALS	DISTRICT/ TOWNSHIP	NOTES
Beverly	302	18	Fellows	Isaac			1			1			1				3		
Ipswich	281	21	Fellows	Isaac	1		1		1				1	1			5		
Ipswich	281	19	Fellows	Israel	2	1		1		2	1	1	1				9		
Ipswich	281	20	Fellows	John			1	1					1	1			4		
Ipswich	280	12	Fellows	Mary									1	1			2		
Ipswich	281	22	Fellows	Nathan	1	1			1	4	4		1				12		
Salisbury	27	35	Fellows	Samuel	1	1		1	1				2	1			7		
Salem	204	5	Felt	Benja			2		1		2	1		1			7		
Salem	216	30	Felt	Benja			5	1		3			1				10		
Salem	205	6	Felt	David			1	1				2					4		
Salem	214	39	Felt	Henry	1		1										2		
Salem	214	37	Felt	James	1		1						1	1			4		
Salem	206	5	Felt	Jane		1				1	1	1					4		
Salem	205	9	Felt	John		3		1		2		1	1				8		
Salem	192	26	Felt	Joseph	3		1	1	2	1		1	1				10		
Salem	205	8	Felt	Joseph		1				1		1	1				3		
Salem	191	37	Felt	Mary	1	1	1	1		1			1	1			7		
Salem	204	40	Felt	Nath	2	1	1	1		3	1	1					10		
Salem	214	38	Felt	Phebe										1			1		
Middleton	17	42	Felton	Amos	2		1	1		2	1		1				8		
Marblehead	257	33	Felton	Daniel				1					1	1			3		
Danvers	12	28	Felton	David		1		1				1	1				4		
Danvers	5	33	Felton	Eunice									2				2		
Marblehead	265	25	Felton	Francis		1						1					2		
Marblehead	260	32	Felton	James	2		1			1		1					5		
Salem	214	41	Felton	James	1	1		1		2		1					6		
Marblehead	251	17	Felton	John H.		1					1						2		
Danvers	10	23	Felton	Jonathan		1	1						2				4		
Danvers	5	30	Felton	Mary								1	1				2		
Danvers	5	28	Felton	Nathl	2			1		1	1		1	1			7		
Newburyport	165	41	Felton	Samuel			1	1					1				3		
Danvers	5	31	Felton	Sarah	1	1				3			1				7		
Marblehead	260	31	Felton	Thomas	1				1	1			1	1			5		
Danvers	5	32	Felton	Timothy		1	2		1		1	1	1	1			8		
Salem	215	20	Fenno	Joseph	1			1		2	1	1	1				7		
Salem	196	20	Ferguson	John	2	1	1						1	1			6		
Lynn	228	22	Fern	Saml	2			1		1	1		1	1			7		
Marblehead	260	2	Fettyplace	Edward			2		1			1		1			5		
Marblehead	250	15	Fettyplace	Edward Junr		3	2		1			1		1			6		
Beverly	298	38	Fielder	John				1		1			1	1			4		
Beverly	298	33	Fielder	John Jr	3			1		1			1				6		
Beverly	298	37	Fielder	Willm H	3	1	1	1					1	1			8		
Danvers	14	24	Finney	Filemon		1		1						1			3		
Newbury	112	45	Finney	George	2			1		2			1				6		
Gloucester	73	13	Fips	Abigal Wo										3			3		
Andover	94	21	Fish	Benjamin	3	1			1	2				1			8		
Marblehead	263	12	Fish	Daniel			1		1		1	1					5		
Newbury	114	48	Fish	Samuel	2			1		2	1		1	3			10		
Wenham	307	12	Fish	Samuel				1						1			2		
Beverly	294	13	Fisher	Anna									1	1			2		
Salem	189	13	Fisher	James	3			1		3	1		1				9		
Salem	213	39	Fisher	James	1	1		1					1				4		
Beverly	289	4	Fisher	Joshua Revd				1				1	1				3		
Salem	193	14	Fisher	Nathl		1	2		1		1			1			6		
Salem	197	21	Fisk	Benja	2			1		1		1	1		1		7		
Andover	93	29	Fisk	John			1	1	1		1						4		
Beverly	293	19	Fisk	John	3	1		1					1	1			7		
Topsfield	19	2	Fisk	Nathaniel			2		1				1	1			5		
Wenham	309	5	Fisk	Samuel Jun			1		1		2						4		
Salem	195	36	Fisk	Sarah		3	1			2		2	1	1			10		
Haverhill	146	6	Fitts	Jeremiah	2			1		2	1		1				7		
Ipswich	276	48	Fitts	Jeremiah				1						1			2		
Salisbury	28	25	Fitts	Joseph		1	1		1		2	3	1	1			10		
Ipswich	275	35	Fitts	Mary	1								1	1			3		
Newburyport	165	6	Fitz	John	2	1		1		2			1	1			8		
Newburyport	165	5	Fitz	Mark		1	2	2	1			1		1			8		
Newburyport	165	7	Fitz	William	2			1					1				4		
Marblehead	261	7	Flack	Martha									2	1			3		
Salem	218	12	Flagg	Josiah				1		2			1				4		
Lynnfield	236	14	Flagg	Theodore	1			1		1			1				4		
Marblehead	256	23	Flaitt	Michael	1			1					1				3		
Salem	193	38	Flanders	Asa			3						1				4		
Salisbury	28	21	Flanders	Benaiah	2			1		1			1	1			6		
Salisbury	28	20	Flanders	Bennet				1			3		1				5		
Salisbury	27	37	Flanders	Betty Wd								1	1	1			3		
Newbury	110	37	Flanders	Daniel	2			1		3	1		1	1			9		
Amesbury	39	1	Flanders	Deborah Wid		1							3	1			5		
Salisbury	28	19	Flanders	Jacob	1	2	1		1	1			1				7		
Newburyport	165	34	Flanders	John			2						1	1			4		
Salisbury	27	36	Flanders	John	1			1		2	1		1				6		
Salisbury	28	14	Flanders	Joseph				1		2			1	1			5		
Salisbury	28	12	Flanders	Merrill	1	1	1							1			4		
Salisbury	28	17	Flanders	Nathan		2	1			1			1				5		
Salisbury	28	18	Flanders	Nathan Junr				1		1			1				3		
Newburyport	165	33	Flanders	Nehemiah	3	1	2		1	1		2	1	1			12		

TOWN	PG#	LN#	LAST NAME	FIRST NAME	FREE WHITE MALES					FREE WHITE FEMALES					TOTAL ALL OTHER	TOTAL SLAVES	TOTALS	DISTRICT/ TOWNSHIP	NOTES
					under 10	10 to 16	16 to 26	26 to 45	45 and over	under 10	10 to 16	16 to 26	26 to 45	45 and over					
Salisbury	28	13	Flanders	Timothy				1		4			1	1			7		
Newburyport	165	36	Fletcher	Nathaniel		1	1						1				3		
Newburyport	165	35	Fletcher	Uriah		1	2		1				1	1			6		
Marblehead	268	35	Fletcher	William	2			1		2			1	1			7		
Danvers	3	21	Flint	Amos		1		1	1	2	2		1				8		
Danvers	2	18	Flint	Elijah	1	2	1	1		1	1		1		1		9		
Marblehead	258	21	Flint	Elizabeth	1								1				2		
Danvers	2	19	Flint	Herzekiah	1	1		2			2		1				7		
Middleton	15	12	Flint	Jeremiah	1	2	3		1	2		1	1	1			12		
Andover	95	11	Flint	John	2	1		1		1		2					7		
Middleton	15	13	Flint	John	1			1	1	2	2	1	1				9		
Salem	212	26	Flint	John	2	1		1		3	2	2	1				12		
Methuen	153	27	Flint	Miles			1	1		2		1		1			6		
Lynnfield	235	26	Flint	Phebe	1						1			1			3		
Andover	95	10	Flint	Samuel				1			1						2		
Danvers	2	21	Flint	Samuel			1					1					2		
Salem	212	25	Flint	Susanna							1		1				2		
Danvers	3	23	Flint	William	4		1			1				1			7		
Salem	200	44	Floid	William	1		1	1		1	1		1				6		
Newbury	113	47	Flood	Aaron		1	2					1					4		
Newbury	106	8	Flood	Enoch				1					1				2		
Newbury	113	43	Flood	James	1		1	1			1	1	1				6		
Newbury	115	22	Flood	John		1	3	1				2	1				8		
Newbury	117	29	Flood	Jonath		1						1					2		
Newbury	106	28	Flood	Joseph		2		1		2		1					6		
Salem	208	59	Flood	Mary									1				1		
Newbury	115	17	Flood	Moses	1	1	1						1				4		
Andover	94	2	Flood	William	1			1		1	1	1		1			6		
Newbury	114	7	Flood	William	2	1	1		1	1		1		1			8		
Marblehead	245	32	Florence	Charles	3	1		1		1	1		1				8		
Marblehead	246	34	Florence	John	1			1		1			1				4		
Lynn	232	31	Florence	Thos			1		1								2	West Parish	
Marblehead	265	24	Florey	Nicholas	1			1		1			1				4		
Marblehead	254	8	Flory	John			1	1				1					3		
Manchester	51	16	Flours	Wm			1			1		1					3		
Manchester	51	18	Flowers	Barthl	1		2		1			1		1			6		
Manchester	51	19	Flowers	John			1	1		4			1				7		
Lynn	225	41	Floyd	Hugh		2		1		2	2		1				8		
Danvers	9	12	Floyd	Stephen				1		2	1	1					5		
Salem	219	31	Floyd	Thos	2			1					1	1			5		
Amesbury	39	4	Fobes	Levi	1		1	1		1		1	1				6		
Salem	201	1	Fobler	Wilson											10		10		
Salem	219	45	Fogg	Joseph				1				1		1			3		
Lynnfield	236	8	Fogg	Nathl	1		1	1		3			1				7		
Boxford	135	41	Folensbee		4	1		1			1		1				8		No first name
Andover	94	3	Follambee	Moody			1										1		
Newburyport	165	10	Follansbee	Amos Jr		1	1										2		
Newburyport	165	9	Follansbee	John N				1		3			1				5		
Newburyport	165	8	Follansbee	Thomas M		1		1	1	2	1		1	1			8		
Amesbury	39	3	Follembe	Berzia Wid						1			1				2		
Amesbury	39	7	Follembe	David Capt	1	1		1				1					4		
Amesbury	39	2	Follembe	Samuel	1	1						1	1	1			6		
Salisbury	28	16	Follensbe	Anna Wd			1			1			1	1			4		
Salisbury	28	23	Follensbe	Benja		2	1		1	1		1		1			7		
Salisbury	28	15	Follensbe	Daniel	1			1		3	1	1					7		
Salisbury	28	24	Follensbe	Joshua		1	1		1		1	1	1				6		
Salisbury	28	8	Follensbe	Robert Capt		1	1						1				3		
Salisbury	27	38	Follensbe	Thos Capt				1				2					3		
Salisbury	28	22	Follensbe	Ws Abl	2					1			1				4		
Newbury	106	39	Follensbee	Jeremiah		1		1		1	2	1	1				7		
Newbury	106	46	Follensbee	John		1	2		1	1	1	1	1				8		
Salem	191	8	Follete	William			1						1				2		
Marblehead	247	31	Follett	Elizabeth									1				1		
Marblehead	264	13	Follett	Elizabeth										1			1		
Marblehead	266	15	Follett	Elizabeth	1		1							1			3		
Marblehead	253	24	Follett	Thomas	2	1	2	1		1	1		1	1			10		
Newbury	116	14	Follingbe	Moody		1		1	1				3	1			7		
Newburyport	165	19	Folsom	Jeremiah		1		1					1				3		
Bradford	125	14	Foot	David	1			2		2			2				7		
Amesbury	39	6	Foot	Ephm	1			1				1					3		
Bradford	124	41	Foot	Rowel	1			1		3			1				6		
Amesbury	39	5	Foot	Theophilus	3	1	1		1			1		1			8		
Gloucester	59	18	Forbes	Eli Revd		1			1		1	1		1			5		
Beverly	302	27	Ford	Charity									1				1		
Beverly	300	42	Ford	Edward			1						1				2		
Salem	217	39	Ford	James			1						1				2		
Gloucester	56	16	Ford	John	1		1		2				1	1			6		
Beverly	305	44	Ford	Sarah	1					2			1				4		
Newburyport	165	39	Ford	Timothy T				1					1				2		
Beverly	293	17	Fornice	David		2	1	1					2	1	1		8		
Beverly	295	43	Fornice	David Jr	2			1		1							5		
Beverly	296	8	Fornice	John				1		1		2					4		
Beverly	296	37	Fornice	William	2		1	1		1			1	1			7		
Salem	217	8	Forrester	Simon	2	1	2		1	2		3		1	1		13		

TOWN	PG#	LN#	LAST NAME	FIRST NAME	FREE WHITE MALES					FREE WHITE FEMALES					TOTAL ALL OTHER	TOTAL SLAVES	TOTALS	DISTRICT/ TOWNSHIP	NOTES
					under 10	10 to 16	16 to 26	26 to 45	45 and over	under 10	10 to 16	16 to 26	26 to 45	45 and over					
Marblehead	263	13	Fortune	Francis	2			1						1			4		
Newburyport	165	37	Foss	John	1			1						1			3		
Ipswich	283	19	Foster	Aaron				1					1	1			3		
Salem	199	30	Foster	Abram		2	1	1				1	1				6		
Ipswich	279	38	Foster	Allen	2		2		1	1		1					7		
Salem	190	25	Foster	Amos	1			1		1			1				4		
Topsfield	19	8	Foster	Amos		1		1					1				3		
Andover	94	27	Foster	Andrew				1				1					2		
Marblehead	253	5	Foster	Annis	1						1						2		
Beverly	305	16	Foster	Benja			1			1		1					3		
Manchester	51	12	Foster	Benja			1			2		1					4		
Manchester	51	11	Foster	Betha Wo			1						1				2		
Gloucester	72	13	Foster	Betty Wo							1		1				2		
Salem	189	37	Foster	Cato											3		3		
Andover	93	24	Foster	Charles		1	1			1	1		1	1			6		
Andover	93	32	Foster	Daniel	1		4	1		2		1	1				10		
Beverly	298	11	Foster	Daniel		1	3	1		2			1				8		
Rowley	130	12	Foster	Daniel	3	3	3	1		1	1		1				13		
Andover	93	20	Foster	Daniel 3d		1	1				2	2	1				7		
Andover	94	26	Foster	Daniel Junr	2		1	1		1		1	1				7		
Andover	93	23	Foster	David		1		1				1		1			4		
Danvers	13	8	Foster	David		1	1	1		1			1				5		
Andover	93	33	Foster	Davis		1		1		1			1				4		
Ipswich	279	46	Foster	Ebenezer	1	1		1		1	1	1					6		
Beverly	290	19	Foster	Edward		1		1		1	2		1				6		
Gloucester	64	16	Foster	Elijah		1		1		3			1				6		
Boxford	134	30	Foster	Ephm	1	1	1		1	1		1		1			7		
Andover	95	7	Foster	Gideon	2			1		1		2		1			7		
Danvers	12	18	Foster	Gideon		1	2		1	1	1		1				7		
Ipswich	279	42	Foster	Hannah									2				2		
Boxford	134	34	Foster	Israel	1	1		1	1	3		1	1		1		10		
Marblehead	247	18	Foster	Israel				1			2		2				5		
Andover	93	30	Foster	Jacob		1	1		2	1	2		2	2			11		
Danvers	6	30	Foster	James			2		1			1		1			5		
Ipswich	275	44	Foster	James				1					1				2		
Boxford	134	37	Foster	Jereh		1	1		1				1				5		
Gloucester	64	14	Foster	Jereh Capt	2	1		1		3	2	1	1				12		
Beverly	297	29	Foster	Jeremiah		1	2		1	2			1				7		
Beverly	297	36	Foster	Jeremiah Jr			1						1				2		
Andover	94	24	Foster	John	1			1		3	1	1	1				8		
Boxford	136	2	Foster	John	2		1	1		1	1	1	1				8		
Haverhill	146	5	Foster	John	1		1	1					1				4		
Rowley	130	13	Foster	John				1					1				2		
Salem	205	50	Foster	John				1			1	1					3		
Salem	213	50	Foster	John	2			1		1	2	2					8		
Andover	94	1	Foster	John 3d			1			1			1				3		
Andover	95	14	Foster	John Junr			1						1				2		
Boxford	134	31	Foster	Jonathan	1			1				1		1			4		
Ipswich	279	50	Foster	Jonathan		1		1				1	1				4		
Boxford	134	40	Foster	Jonathn		1	1	1				1					4		
Andover	93	31	Foster	Joseph			1			1	1		1				4		
Beverly	298	12	Foster	Joseph		2		1				1		1			5		
Danvers	13	26	Foster	Joseph	1			1		1	1	1					6		
Gloucester	64	12	Foster	Joseph Colo			2	1				3	2				8		
Gloucester	64	13	Foster	Joseph Junr Cap	2	1		1		1	2		1	1			9		
Beverly	297	45	Foster	Joshua	2	1	1	1		2	1	1	1				10		
Marblehead	240	11	Foster	Joshua				1			1		1				2		
Beverly	297	40	Foster	Josiah	2	2		1		2	2		1				10		
Beverly	302	26	Foster	Josiah Jr	2			1				1	1				5		
Beverly	300	37	Foster	Mary	3	2						1		1			7		
Ipswich	276	55	Foster	Mary									1				1		
Newbury	108	18	Foster	Mary						1		1	2	2			6		
Newburyport	166	7	Foster	Mary Wido								1	2				3		
Ipswich	279	41	Foster	Mehitable									1	1			2		
Ipswich	283	25	Foster	Moses	3	1	1	2		1		1	1	1			11		
Salem	192	17	Foster	Nath			1	1					1				3		
Andover	94	25	Foster	Nathan	2		1	1		3		1	1				9		
Topsfield	19	36	Foster	Nathaniel	1			1					1				3		
Gloucester	79	17	Foster	Nathl	1	1		1	1	3	1		1				9		
Haverhill	146	2	Foster	Nathll			1			2			1	1			5		
Andover	94	28	Foster	Peter		2	1	1		3			1				8		
Ipswich	279	49	Foster	Philemon				1		1	1		1				4		
Ipswich	279	51	Foster	Philemon Jun		1							1				2		
Boxford	135	32	Foster	Phineas		1							1		1		3		
Marblehead	241	19	Foster	Pompey												5	5		
Topsfield	19	7	Foster	Priscilla			1					1	1				3		
Boxford	135	43	Foster	Richard	1			1	1	3			1				7		
Amesbury	39	8	Foster	Robert			2						1				3		
Salem	196	31	Foster	Robert		2	1		1	1	2		1				8		
Bradford	126	17	Foster	Runnels			1	1		1			1				4		
Beverly	300	36	Foster	Samuel				1		1		1					3		
Newburyport	165	15	Foster	Samuel	2		1		1	2	1		1				8		
Beverly	303	23	Foster	Samuel 2d	1			1		1			1				4		
Newburyport	165	17	Foster	Samuel 3d	1			1	4		1	1					8		

TOWN	PG#	LN#	LAST NAME	FIRST NAME	FREE WHITE MALES					FREE WHITE FEMALES					TOTAL ALL OTHER	TOTAL SLAVES	TOTALS	DISTRICT/ TOWNSHIP	NOTES
					under 10	10 to 16	16 to 26	26 to 45	45 and over	under 10	10 to 16	16 to 26	26 to 45	45 and over					
Newburyport	165	16	Foster	Samuel Jr	1		1	1			1	1					5		
Beverly	295	42	Foster	Sarah		1						1		1			3		
Andover	94	23	Foster	Simeon		1	1	1					1	1			5		
Bradford	125	3	Foster	Stephen	2	1	3	1	1		1	2		1			12		
Ipswich	279	40	Foster	Thomas				1		3	1		1				6		
Ipswich	282	54	Foster	Thomas	1	1		1		3	1		1				8		
Andover	93	28	Foster	William	6	11		1	1			2		1			22		
Hamilton	285	98	Foster	William	1			1					1				3		
Andover	94	22	Foster	William Junr			2	1	1			1		3			8		
Salem	219	14	Foster	Wm			1						1				2		
Salem	201	41	Foster	Zach											4		4		
Ipswich	283	20	Foster	Zebulun	1			1		1			1	1			5		
Marblehead	241	2	Fowle	Mart	1								1				2		
Danvers	9	9	Fowler	Anna						1	2		1				4		
Beverly	303	24	Fowler	Benja	1		1	1						1			4		
Salisbury	28	9	Fowler	Daniel	2		1	1		1			1				6		
Andover	93	22	Fowler	Dolly Wid	1							1		1			3		
Salisbury	28	2	Fowler	Elijah				1		1			2	1			5		
Salisbury	28	1	Fowler	Elijah Junr	1	1		1		3	1		1				8		
Salem	198	26	Fowler	Ezekiel					1				2	1			4		
Salisbury	28	10	Fowler	Ezekiel		1		1					2	1			5		
Salisbury	28	11	Fowler	Ezekiel Junr		1							1				2		
Salem	199	25	Fowler	Ezekl Jr	2	2	1	1		1			1				8		
Manchester	51	13	Fowler	Jacob	2			1		2			1				6		
Salisbury	28	4	Fowler	Jacob	1			1		3	1		1				7		
Danvers	4	37	Fowler	John			2					1					3		
Ipswich	279	37	Fowler	John	1	1	2		2	1	1			1			9		
Marblehead	258	2	Fowler	John		1		1					1	1			4		
Ipswich	273	36	Fowler	Joseph			1	1				1			1		4		
Ipswich	273	38	Fowler	Joseph Jun		1	2	1		1	3		1				9		
Salisbury	28	6	Fowler	Robert	1	2		1		3		1	1				9		
Salem	208	6	Fowler	Robt	1	2	2	1		1	3		1				11		
Salem	216	34	Fowler	Robt	1		1						1				3		
Salisbury	28	7	Fowler	Saml Capt	1	1	1	1			1	1	1				7		
Danvers	9	18	Fowler	Samuel					1	1	1		1				4		
Newburyport	165	18	Fowler	Samuel			1						1				2		
Salem	198	43	Fowler	Samuel				1		1			1				3		
Salem	200	46	Fowler	Samuel		1		1		1							3		
Salisbury	28	5	Fowler	Samuel	3			1		1	2		1				8		
Danvers	9	3	Fowler	Samuel Junr	1		4					1					6		
Marblehead	257	8	Fowler	Thomas		1						1					2		
Salisbury	28	3	Fowler	Thomas		1						1					2		
Wenham	307	18	Fowls	Nathaniel	1		1						1				3		
Salem	213	10	Foy	William	1	3			1	1	1	2	1				10		
Marblehead	241	4	Frail	John		2			1	2	1	1	1				9		
Beverly	293	26	Frances	Aaron	2		2	1				1		1			7		
Middleton	18	13	Frances	Charles											5		5		
Middleton	18	11	Frances	Frank											6		6		
Middleton	18	12	Frances	Snow											3		3		
Beverly	300	1	Franch	Sarah		1	1				1	1		1			5		
Marblehead	242	23	Francis	Abraham		1				2		1					4		
Newburyport	166	4	Francis	Ann Wido								1		2			3		
Marblehead	242	17	Francis	Charles											4		4		
Marblehead	243	8	Francis	Christopher			1			1			1				3		
Newbury	111	31	Francis	Hannah	1					1	1		1				4		
Newburyport	166	3	Francis	Hannah Wido	1	1	2					1		1			6		
Newburyport	166	2	Francis	James	1		1	1		1			1				5		
Salem	188	30	Francis	John	1			1		3	1		1				7		
Salem	193	18	Francis	Peter											7		7		
Marblehead	270	19	Francis	Richard	1	1		1		5			1				9		
Salem	190	20	Francis	Thos		1	1		1				1	1			5		
Newburyport	166	1	Francis	William	2	1	4	6		1	1		1				16		
Salem	211	17	Franks	Joseph		1		1						1			3		
Salem	211	18	Franks	Joseph Jr		1						1					2		
Newburyport	166	6	Frazier	Elizabeth Wido		1	1			1		1	2	1			7		
Gloucester	59	16	Fredericks	Jabez		2	2	1				2		1			8		
Andover	93	26	Freeman	Cato											7		7		
Beverly	306	33	Freeman	Cato Negro											5		5		
Marblehead	243	3	Freeman	Cesar											6		6		
Salem	189	33	Freeman	Fortune											4		4		
Salem	194	3	Freeman	Israel											2		2		
Gloucester	86	22	Freeman	Robt blk											12		12		
Boxford	134	29	Freeman	Simon											2		2		
Wenham	308	35	Freeman	Sippes											4		4		
Marblehead	246	13	Freeto	Francis	3	1	1	1		2	2		1	1			12		
Marblehead	259	3	Freetoe	John				1						1			2		
Wenham	308	33	Freind	Hannah		1							1	1			3		
Wenham	308	34	Freind	Israel			1			1		1					3		
Wenham	308	36	Freind	James		1		1				3		1			6		
Wenham	309	38	Freind	Joseph		1						1					2		
Andover	103	18	Freman	Cesar											7		7		
Salisbury	27	31	French	Amos		1	1		1	2	3			1			9		
Salisbury	27	27	French	Andrew	2			1					1				4		
Salisbury	27	33	French	Benja			2	1				2	1	1			7		

197

TOWN	PG#	LN#	LAST NAME	FIRST NAME	FREE WHITE MALES under 10	10 to 16	16 to 26	26 to 45	45 and over	FREE WHITE FEMALES under 10	10 to 16	16 to 26	26 to 45	45 and over	TOTAL ALL OTHER	TOTAL SLAVES	TOTALS	DISTRICT/ TOWNSHIP	NOTES
Marblehead	257	31	French	Chase W			1			2	1						4		
Salisbury	27	32	French	Eliza Wd									2	1			3		
Andover	95	12	French	Jacob	2	2	1	1			1	1	1				9		
Andover	93	27	French	Jonathan Revd		5	2		1	1		2		2	2		15		
Salem	191	2	French	Joshua		2	4	1		3	1		1			1	13		
Salisbury	27	30	French	Joshua Capt			1			2	1		1				5		
Salisbury	27	29	French	Josiah	2	1	2		1		1	2		1			10		
Salisbury	27	28	French	Mary Wd									2				2		
Salisbury	27	26	French	Nicholas			2		1	1			1				5		
Andover	95	13	French	Peter	1			1		1			1				4		
Newburyport	165	38	French	Samuel Jr	3	1	1	1	1	2	1		1	1			12		
Beverly	305	14	Friend	Caleb			1			1		1					3		
Newburyport	165	28	Friend	Elizabeth Wido			2						1				3		
Beverly	293	31	Friend	Hannah									1				1		
Newburyport	165	26	Friend	Henry				1			1	1					3		
Newburyport	165	27	Friend	John				1					2				3		
Beverly	305	12	Friend	Nathl	1		1		1	3	1	1	1				9		
Gloucester	64	15	Friend	Richard	2	1		1		2	1		1				8		
Beverly	305	18	Friend	William	2	1	1	1			1	1					7		
Haverhill	146	3	Frink	Elizabeth						2			1				3		
Haverhill	146	4	Frink	Samuel	2			1		2	2		1	1			9		
Ipswich	276	60	Frisbie	Levie		1	1		1	1		1	1	1			7		
Beverly	299	29	Froathingham	Ruth		1				1	1		1	1			5		
Beverly	303	16	Frost	Benja	1		1			1		1					4		
Bradford	123	27	Frost	Caleb	2			1		2	2	1					9		
Marblehead	252	9	Frost	Grace		1							1				2		
Danvers	11	41	Frost	John	3	2	1	1		1	1		1				10		
Marblehead	250	3	Frost	Joshua			1			1			1				3		
Marblehead	252	18	Frost	Richard	1			1		4	1		1				8		
Andover	93	21	Frost	William	2	1			1	2	1	1	1				9		
Marblehead	260	25	Frost	William	1		1						1				3		
Newburyport	165	21	Frothingham	Andrew		1	3		1		1	2	1	1			10		
Newburyport	165	22	Frothingham	Andrew Jr		1	1					1	1				4		
Newburyport	165	23	Frothingham	Benjamin				1		3		1	2				7		
Newburyport	165	24	Frothingham	Gilman			1	1			2		2				7		
Salem	203	28	Frothingham	Nath	1		6	1		2			1	1			11		
Newburyport	165	25	Frothingham	Stephen	2	1		1				1	1				6		
Salem	198	1	Frothinham	James	3	2		1		2			1				9		
Newburyport	165	20	Fry	Zachariah	1	2		1					1				6		
Andover	95	4	Frye	Amos			1										1		
Salem	199	5	Frye	Benja	2	2	1		1			3	1				10		
Methuen	153	25	Frye	Daniel		2	1					1					4		
Salem	188	17	Frye	Deborah								2	1	1			4		
Andover	93	35	Frye	Elizabeth Wid									1				1		
Andover	95	3	Frye	Enoch	1		1						1				3		
Andover	94	29	Frye	James			1	1				1		1			4		
Methuen	153	23	Frye	James		1	2	1	1		1		1	1	1		8		
Andover	94	30	Frye	John	1				1		1	2		1			6		
Salem	206	41	Frye	John	2		1		1	1		1					6		
Andover	94	34	Frye	John 3rd	3	1		1		3	2	1	1	1			13		
Andover	94	33	Frye	John Junr	1			1			1	1		2			6		
Andover	95	5	Frye	Joseph			1			1			1				3		
Andover	94	31	Frye	Joshua	1				1	2			1				5		
Salem	198	44	Frye	Moses	1		1			1		1					4		
Andover	94	32	Frye	Peter			1			2			1				4		
Salem	214	32	Frye	Peter			1			2	1		1				5		
Andover	93	25	Frye	Phillip		1	1						2	2			6		
Methuen	153	24	Frye	Robertson	1	1		1		1	1	1	1				7		
Andover	94	37	Frye	Samuel			1						1				2		
Andover	95	2	Frye	Samuel 3rd	2		1			3			1				7		
Andover	94	36	Frye	Samuel Junr	1		1			1			1				4		
Andover	94	35	Frye	Sarah Wid									1				1		
Andover	95	1	Frye	Theophilus	3	2	1		1	2		1		1			11		
Andover	95	6	Frye	Timothy		1		1	1	2			2				7		
Danvers	11	25	Frye	William	1	1						1					3		
Salem	199	14	Frye	William					1		2	3	1	1			8		
Lynn	225	6	Fuller	Abigail	1	1				2	1		1				6		
Andover	94	18	Fuller	Abijah			2		1		1		1				5		
Danvers	9	27	Fuller	Andrew			1			4			1				6		
Middleton	16	14	Fuller	Andrew			1				1		1				3		
Middleton	15	10	Fuller	Betty									1				1		
Ipswich	278	53	Fuller	Daniel			1				1		1				3		
Middleton	15	11	Fuller	Daniel	2			1					2				5		
Gloucester	56	15	Fuller	Danl Revd	1	1	2		1		1	1		1			8		
Middleton	16	25	Fuller	David	1			1					1				3		
Middleton	16	33	Fuller	David 2nd	2	2		1		2	1		2				10		
Middleton	16	5	Fuller	Elijah	1			1					1				3		
Middleton	16	9	Fuller	Elisha			1	1				1					3		
Ipswich	275	52	Fuller	Elizabeth									1				1		
Ipswich	280	10	Fuller	James			1					1					2		
Salem	201	10	Fuller	James	1		1						1				3		
Salem	220	52	Fuller	James	1		1						1				3		
Salem	220	59	Fuller	James					1	2			1				4		

TOWN	PG#	LN#	LAST NAME	FIRST NAME	FREE WHITE MALES					FREE WHITE FEMALES					TOTAL ALL OTHER	TOTAL SLAVES	TOTALS	DISTRICT/ TOWNSHIP	NOTES
					under 10	10 to 16	16 to 26	26 to 45	45 and over	under 10	10 to 16	16 to 26	26 to 45	45 and over					
Middleton	16	24	Fuller	Jerusha								1	1				2		
Middleton	16	15	Fuller	John		2		1		1		1					5		
Rowley	130	46	Fuller	John	2		2					1					5		
Lynn	231	14	Fuller	Jona				1		1		1					3		
Lynn	223	12	Fuller	Joseph 3d	1		1	1				1	1				5		
Lynn	231	13	Fuller	Joseph Jr				2						1			3		
Lynn	229	43	Fuller	Joseph Junr		2	1		2			1		1			7		
Ipswich	277	46	Fuller	Mary										2			2		
Salem	199	40	Fuller	Mary								1					1		
Newbury	110	16	Fuller	Nathan	1			1		2		1	1				6		
Ipswich	278	11	Fuller	Nathaniel	1			1		5	2		1				10		
Salem	189	24	Fuller	Rachel									2				2		
Salem	197	10	Fuller	Samuel	1		2		1	3	2	1					10		
Middleton	16	22	Fuller	Sarah		1	1						2	1			5		
Middleton	17	27	Fuller	Simeon	2		1	1		2			1				7		
Marblehead	242	1	Fuller	Thomas				1					1				2		
Salem	201	14	Fuller	Thos	2	1		1					1				5		
Danvers	6	4	Fuller	Timothy	3	2			1	1	1	2		1	1		12		
Ipswich	278	61	Fuller	William	3			1		1	1		1				7		
Salem	198	2	Fullingham	Jonathn			1	1					2				4		
Marblehead	253	26	Fundy	Nicholas				1		3			1				5		
Newburyport	165	13	Furber	John D		1	1	1		1		1					5		
Andover	95	8	Furbush	Simeon		1		1		1		1					4		
Andover	95	9	Furbush	Solomon	1		1			1			3	1			7		
Newburyport	165	14	Furgeson	Elizabeth Wido	1		2	2		2	1		3	1			12		
Newburyport	166	5	Furlong	Laurence			1		1				1	1			4		
Marblehead	245	28	Furniss	Alice									1				1		
Marblehead	243	24	Furniss	Anthony		1	1		1			2		1			6		
Gloucester	59	20	Gaffnay	Michl	5			1		2	1		1				10		
Bradford	122	34	Gage	Abijah		1			1		1	2		2			7		
Middleton	17	6	Gage	Abraham	2			1			1	1					5		
Beverly	304	31	Gage	Andrew					1			1					2		
Bradford	122	3	Gage	Asa		1		1	1	3		1	1	1			9		
Bradford	121	15	Gage	Daniel		1		1		2		1		1			6		
Haverhill	146	18	Gage	Ebenezer			2	1	1		1						5		
Beverly	304	34	Gage	Henry	1			1		2		1					5		
Bradford	122	9	Gage	Jeremiah		1	1	1					2				6		
Methuen	153	29	Gage	John	1	1	1	1		2	2		2	1			11		
Rowley	130	8	Gage	John	1			1		1		1	1				5		
Newburyport	167	2	Gage	Jonathan				1		2	1		1				5		
Beverly	295	50	Gage	Judith	1							1	2				4		
Methuen	153	28	Gage	Micah	2		1	1		1			1				6		
Andover	95	18	Gage	Nathanael	1		1	1		4		1	1				9		
Rowley	131	26	Gage	Nathll					1			1	1				3		
Bradford	122	2	Gage	Peter			1		1	1	1	2		1			7		
Haverhill	146	17	Gage	Thomas					1		1	4	1	1			8		
Rowley	129	45	Gage	Thos	2		1		1	3		1	1				9		
Rowley	129	48	Gage	Thos	2			1		2		1	1				7		
Rowley	129	49	Gage	Thos		1	1					1					3		
Bradford	122	8	Gage	Uriah			3		1	3	1	1	1	1			11		
Beverly	304	37	Gage	William			1										1		
Beverly	304	35	Gage	Zachariah	1		1		1			1		1			5		
Salem	218	25	Gaines	Eliza									1				1		
Ipswich	275	19	Gains	Thomas				1		2			1				4		
Marblehead	268	15	Gale	Ambrose				1		1		1					3		
Amesbury	39	14	Gale	Beza				1				1					2		
Amesbury	39	13	Gale	Ely Capt		1	3	1		2			1				8		
Haverhill	146	31	Gale	Ephraim	3		1	1		1			1				7		
Amesbury	39	17	Gale	John	1			1		1		1					4		
Beverly	301	9	Gale	Jonas			1					1					2		
Marblehead	263	14	Gale	Mary								1		1			2		
Salem	213	23	Gale	Mary										1			1		
Haverhill	146	14	Gale	Moses			2	1		2	1	1	1				8		
Salem	218	27	Gale	Saml			1		1	1	3		1				7		
Marblehead	268	20	Gale	Samuel	1	2		1		1	1			1			7		
Salem	212	41	Gale	Anna									2				2		
Salem	206	27	Gale	Edmund	1	2			1	3	1	1	1				10		
Salem	210	11	Gale	Samuel	3	2		1		2	1	1	1				11		
Salem	202	37	Galey	William	2			1					1				4		
Newburyport	166	22	Gallishan	Abraham				1					1				2		
Newburyport	166	23	Gallishan	Abraham Jr		1	2	1		1	1	1		1			8		
Marblehead	269	30	Gallison	Henry		1		1					1				3		
Topsfield	20	37	Gallop	Amos		2	1	1		3	3		1				11		
Wenham	309	14	Gallop	Enos				1		1				1			3		
Beverly	301	16	Gallop	William	1		2		1	1	1		1				7		
Topsfield	21	4	Gallop	William				1						3			4		
Ipswich	277	50	Galloway	Abigail							1	1	1				3		
Ipswich	274	21	Galloway	Sarah							2	1					3		
Lynn	232	9	Gallusha	Simeon	1		1					1					3		
Salem	190	5	Gallushe	Jacob	1		3			2		1					7		
Salem	198	42	Gallushe	John	1		1						1				3		
Salem	190	42	Galway	Samuel	1	4		1		1			1				8		
Gloucester	79	26	Gamage	John		2	2	2	1			1		1			9		
Gloucester	79	27	Gamage	John Junr				1		3		1					5		

TOWN	PG#	LN#	LAST NAME	FIRST NAME	M under 10	M 10-16	M 16-26	M 26-45	M 45+	F under 10	F 10-16	F 16-26	F 26-45	F 45+	TOTAL ALL OTHER	TOTAL SLAVES	TOTALS	DISTRICT/TOWNSHIP	NOTES
Marblehead	258	27	Gamey	Margaret										1			1		
Marblehead	268	22	Gardiner	Benjamin		1		1			2	1		1			6		
Salem	195	48	Gardner	Abel	1	2		1		1			1	1			7		
Marblehead	256	4	Gardner	Benjamin		1				1		1					3		
Newburyport	166	25	Gardner	Benjamin	1		1		1	2	2	1		1			9		
Newburyport	166	26	Gardner	Cristopher		1			1	1	1	1					5		
Gloucester	86	12	Gardner	Ebenz	1				1	2				1			5		
Salem	183	3	Gardner	Hannah	1					1	1		1				4		
Salem	195	27	Gardner	Henry		1			1			3	1	1			7		
Salem	200	6	Gardner	James	3			1		1			1				6		
Lynn	229	22	Gardner	James Esq	2			1		1	1		1	1			7		
Beverly	303	38	Gardner	John	1		1			1			2				5		
Danvers	7	12	Gardner	John			1	1					3	1			6		
Danvers	10	5	Gardner	John			5	1	1				1				8		
Marblehead	256	5	Gardner	John			2	1	1					1			5		
Salem	212	1	Gardner	John	3	1		1		1	1	1	2				10		
Wenham	310	1	Gardner	John	1				1		1	1		1			5		
Andover	95	17	Gardner	Jonathan	1	1	2		1				1	4			10		
Salem	212	2	Gardner	Jonathan	1		1	1				1	1		1		6		
Salem	196	7	Gardner	Joseph	3	2		1					1				7		
Salem	210	43	Gardner	Joseph	2		1	1		3	1	2	1				11		
Marblehead	265	21	Gardner	Molly										1			1		
Beverly	306	14	Gardner	Nancy						1			1	2	1		5		
Salem	217	59	Gardner	Nancy	1								1				2		
Salem	208	24	Gardner	Newberry											2		2		
Marblehead	241	20	Gardner	Peter											5		5		
Salem	211	16	Gardner	Richard	1		1	1					2				5		
Gloucester	84	28	Gardner	Robert		1		1						1			3		
Newburyport	166	27	Gardner	Robert	2	1		1		2			2				8		
Bradford	122	36	Gardner	Samuel	1	1	3	1					1				7		
Danvers	3	15	Gardner	Samuel			3		1	1			1				6		
Salem	221	18	Gardner	Samuel			1					1					2		
Beverly	303	2	Gardner	William											2		2		
Marblehead	265	22	Garner	Grace			1					1					2		
Marblehead	257	23	Garney	Thomas	1	3		1		2		2	1				10		
Newbury	112	6	Garrish	Enoch		1		1			3	2					7		
Newbury	112	7	Garrish	Mayhue	2		1			1				1			5		
Newbury	112	9	Garrish	Paul			1							1			2		
Newbury	112	10	Garrish	William			1	1						1			3		
Marblehead	245	17	Garrison	Fanny						1		1					2		
Salem	206	42	Gavet	Jona	2			1		1			1				5		
Salem	192	16	Gavet	Jon		1		1	1	2			1				6		
Salem	209	29	Gavete	James			1			1		1					3		
Salem	188	42	Gavete	John	3	4	3		1	2		2		1			16		
Haverhill	146	13	Gay	Joseph		2		1		1		1					5		
Newburyport	166	30	Gearing	Jabez	1			1					1	1			4		
Gloucester	86	13	Gearix	Edward	1			1	1	1		2		1			6		
Gloucester	86	14	Gearix	Edward Jn	3	0	1						1				5		
Gloucester	72	11	Ged	Willm Capt			3		1	1	1			1			7		
Newburyport	167	10	Geiger	Henry	1		2	1					1				5		
Wenham	308	11	Gently	Molly		3							1				5		
Haverhill	146	7	George	Amos	1	2	1		1	2	1	1		1			10		
Haverhill	146	9	George	Austin	3	1		1		1	1	1	1	1			10		
Newburyport	167	5	George	Benjamin	3		1	1		3	2		1				11		
Salisbury	29	6	George	Ebenz				1		3		1					5		
Marblehead	256	31	George	Hannah	1					1		1					3		
Haverhill	146	10	George	Hezekiah		1				2		1					4		
Newbury	107	4	George	James	1	1		1		2		1		1			7		
Newburyport	167	6	George	James			1			3		1					5		
Haverhill	146	8	George	Lewis	1	1	2		1	2	1	1		1			10		
Salisbury	29	5	George	Nathl		2			1			1		1			5		
Haverhill	146	25	George	Richard	3			1		1			1				6		
Haverhill	146	26	George	Timothy		2		1		1			1				5		
Salem	209	46	Gerde	Benja		1							1				2		
Salisbury	28	33	Gerish	Prudence Wd				1					2	1			4		
Salisbury	28	32	Gerish	Richd	3	1		1		1	1	1					8		
Salisbury	28	34	Gerren	Joseph		1		1		2	1	1					6		
Salem	193	2	Gerrick	Samuel	1	3	1	1		1	1	1	2				11		
Newburyport	166	38	Gerrish	oses		1		1					1				4		
Newburyport	166	39	Gerrish	Stephen		2		1				3		1			7		
Marblehead	261	25	Gerry	Cato												2	2		
Marblehead	252	28	Gerry	Samuel R		1	2		1	1	1	1					7		
Salem	221	21	Getchel	Josiah	1	1						1					3		
Marblehead	265	27	Getchell	Jeremiah	2		1	1		2			1	1			8		
Marblehead	266	4	Getchell	Mary							1			1			2		
Salem	202	44	Getchell	Mary									2	1			3		
Marblehead	265	26	Getchell	Samuel			1	1					1	1			4		
Salem	201	40	Geyer	John												2	2		
Salem	215	41	Gibant	Edwd			1	1				1		1			4		
Methuen	153	30	Gibbon	Samuel	3			1					1				5		
Salem	192	8	Gibbs	Mary	2	1							1	1			5		
Marblehead	263	15	Gibson	Alice	2							1					3		
Newburyport	167	1	Gibson	John	2			1		1			1				5		
Boxford	135	39	Giddens	John	2	2			1			1		1			7		
Ipswich	281	48	Giddings	Aaron		1		1		2	1		1				6		
Hamilton	285	54	Giddings	Abigail										1			1		

TOWN	PG#	LN#	LAST NAME	FIRST NAME	FREE WHITE MALES					FREE WHITE FEMALES					TOTAL ALL OTHER	TOTAL SLAVES	TOTALS	DISTRICT/ TOWNSHIP	NOTES
					under 10	10 to 16	16 to 26	26 to 45	45 and over	under 10	10 to 16	16 to 26	26 to 45	45 and over					
Middleton	17	25	Giddings	Isaac					1					1			2		
Middleton	18	2	Giddings	Isaac Junr	1	1		1		4		1	1				9		
Hamilton	285	85	Giddings	Joshua			1	1			1			1			4		
Ipswich	276	44	Giddings	Joshua	1		2					2		1			7		
Ipswich	281	43	Giddings	Samuel			1	1		2			1				5		
Ipswich	281	47	Giddings	Thomas				1					1				2		
Ipswich	281	42	Giddings	Thomas Junr			1			1			1				3		
Middleton	16	18	Giddings	Zacheus				1		4	3	1	1				10		
Danvers	9	24	Giddins	Solomon	3		1		1				1				6		
Marblehead	260	22	Gifford	*ah	1			1						1			3		
Danvers	6	16	Gifford	Lydia							1			1			2		
Danvers	6	17	Gifford	Sarah						2		1	1				4		
Danvers	7	5	Gifford	Simeon	1	1		1		4	1		1				9		
Salem	188	11	Giffords	Samuel		1				1	1	3	1				7		
Salem	204	30	Gilbert	James	1		1			1		1					4		
Marblehead	243	2	Gilbert	John	1			1				1					3		
Marblehead	244	4	Gilbert	John	1		1					1					3		
Gloucester	56	17	Gilbert	Jona				1		1			1				3		
Gloucester	56	19	Gilbert	Jona Junr	2		1					1					4		
Gloucester	69	9	Gilbert	Moses		1						1					2		
Marblehead	241	5	Gilbert	Thomas	3			1		1		1					6		
Gloucester	56	18	Gilbert	Willa	1		3	1		2	5		1	1			14		
Haverhill	146	24	Gile	Amos	1		1		1	3				2			8		
Haverhill	146	23	Gile	James	1	1			1	2	1			1			7		
Haverhill	146	28	Gile	John R	3			1		1			1				6		
Haverhill	146	29	Gile	Samuel	2			2	1				1	1			7		
Beverly	298	25	Giles	Ebenezer				1			1						2		
Beverly	298	23	Giles	Eleazer		1	1		1	1	1		1				6		
Beverly	298	6	Giles	Hannah			2						1	2			5		
Gloucester	79	29	Giles	Mary Wo	1	2	1				1						6		
Salem	215	30	Giles	Priscilla									1				1		
Marblehead	254	10	Giles	Samuel					1	4			1				8		
Newburyport	166	40	Giles	Samuel	1	1	1	1		1			1				6		
Salem	207	57	Giles	Sarah							1	1	1				3		
Danvers	7	25	Gilford	Aaron				1		1			1				3		
Salisbury	28	37	Gill	Ruth Wd			1				1		1				3		
Salisbury	28	38	Gill	Samuel			1	1					1				3		
Marblehead	266	22	Gilley	William		1	1	1					2				5		
Newburyport	166	37	Gilman	Arthur		1		1		1	1	2		1			7		
Lynn	230	36	Gipson	Mary									1				1		
Marblehead	249	18	Girdler	Benjamin			1	1			1	1	1				5		
Marblehead	250	28	Girdler	Hannah									1				1		
Marblehead	260	27	Girdler	Joseph	3		1			2			1				8		
Marblehead	249	7	Girdler	Lewis	2		1			1			1				5		
Marblehead	239	20	Girdler	Richard	1		1			1		1					4		
Marblehead	260	26	Girdler	Robert			1	1				1	1				4		
Beverly	298	4	Givens	Lydia	2	1						1	1				5		
Ipswich	278	10	Glazer	Benjamin			1			2			1				4		
Ipswich	277	56	Glazer	John	1			1		2			1				5		
Haverhill	146	30	Gleason	David	2		2	1				1	1				7		
Andover	95	32	Gleason	Jonathan		1		1					1	1			4		
Beverly	292	23	Glidden	John	2	1		1					1				5		
Beverly	295	33	Glidden	Joseph					1				1	1			3		
Salem	188	10	Glison	Ichabod		1		1			1	2		1			6		
Gloucester	69	16	Gloucester												4		4		
Beverly	291	15	Glover	Benjamin	2		1			2			1				6		
Marblehead	240	25	Glover	Edmund	2			1				1					4		
Marblehead	245	30	Glover	Hannah									1				1		
Salem	204	17	Glover	Hannah							1	2		1			4		
Beverly	303	31	Glover	John		1				1		1					3		
Salem	201	34	Glover	John	1	1	1	1					1	1			6		
Salem	213	29	Glover	Jona	2		1				1						4		
Marblehead	270	17	Glover	Jonathan		1		1		2	1	1	1				7		
Beverly	294	32	Glover	Peter		1		1	1		3		1				7		
Beverly	301	26	Glover	Peter Jr		1				1			1				3		
Salem	209	26	Glover	Priscilla	1	1				1			1				4		
Marblehead	266	21	Glover	Sarah		1			1	2		1					5		
Danvers	8	14	Gloyad	Hannah										2			2		
Salem	204	22	Godhsaw	William	1	1		1		2		1			1		7		
Haverhill	146	32	Godkins	Stephen	2			1					1				4		
Andover	95	22	Goldsmith	Benja		1	1	1		1	1	2					8		
Marblehead	267	4	Goldsmith	Elizabeth		1						1		1			3		
Manchester	51	22	Goldsmith	Gifford	1	1	1	1	1	3	2	1	1	1			13		
Andover	95	23	Goldsmith	Jeremiah	2			1		4		1	1				9		
Andover	95	29	Goldsmith	John	2	1	1			1		1					6		
Lynn	227	44	Goldsmith	Joseph	1			1				1					3		
Marblehead	249	10	Goldsmith	Lucy		2				2		1					5		
Marblehead	263	22	Goldsmith	Samuel	2			1		2			1				6		
Salem	212	52	Goldsmith	Thos	1		1				1	1		1			5		
Andover	95	19	Goldsmith	William		2	2		1					1			6		
Andover	95	24	Goldsmith	Zacheus	2	1		1		3	1		1				9		
Danvers	12	6	Goldthwait	Benjamin	1			1			2		1				5		
Danvers	14	14	Goldthwait	Daniel				1		1			1				3		
Salem	183	26	Goldthwait	James		1		1				1		1			4		
Danvers	14	15	Goldthwait	John	1			1		2			1	1			6		

TOWN	PG#	LN#	LAST NAME	FIRST NAME	FREE WHITE MALES					FREE WHITE FEMALES					TOTAL ALL OTHER	TOTAL SLAVES	TOTALS	DISTRICT/ TOWNSHIP	NOTES
					under 10	10 to 16	16 to 26	26 to 45	45 and over	under 10	10 to 16	16 to 26	26 to 45	45 and over					
Danvers	14	16	Goldthwait	Nathaniel		1				1	2		1	1			6		
Danvers	13	24	Goldthwait	William					1			2	1	1			5		
Danvers	13	25	Goldthwait	William Jr	1		1						1				3		
Salem	206	20	Goldthwaite	Anna	2	3						1	2		1		9		
Salem	197	11	Goldthwaite	Ezekl	1		1			1		1					4		
Salem	208	32	Gomez	Emanuel	2			1					1				4		
Danvers	7	28	Goodale	Daniel	4		1						1				6		
Danvers	7	9	Goodale	Daniel Junr		1	1			1		1					4		
Danvers	7	24	Goodale	Eleazer		2		1		1		2		1			7		
Salem	199	21	Goodale	Enoch					1					1			2		
Salem	199	20	Goodale	Ezekiel	4		1						1				6		
Danvers	3	12	Goodale	James		1		1	1			1	1	1			6		
Danvers	3	13	Goodale	James Junr		1		3					1				5		
Salem	208	53	Goodale	John			1						1				2		
Salem	191	16	Goodale	Mary	1		1					3	2	1			8		
Danvers	5	29	Goodale	Phebe	1	1				1		1	1	1			6		
Salem	199	11	Goodale	Samuel		1		1		2	1		1				6		
Danvers	6	8	Goodale	Sarah										2			2		
Ipswich	280	4	Goodhue	Aaron	2			1	1	1	1		2	1			9		
Salem	192	22	Goodhue	Abner	2			3		1	2		1				9		
Salem	195	29	Goodhue	Benja		1	1	1	1	1	2	3	1				11		
Ipswich	274	28	Goodhue	Daniel	2			1					1				4		
Newburyport	166	42	Goodhue	Hezekiah			2		1		1	2		1			7		
Ipswich	275	24	Goodhue	Jeremiah	2	1		1		1	1		1				7		
Hamilton	285	15	Goodhue	John				1					1				2		
Hamilton	285	16	Goodhue	John Junr			2		1		1		1				5		
Newburyport	166	41	Goodhue	Joseph	1	2		1		2			1				7		
Ipswich	280	3	Goodhue	Jude		1		1	1			2		1			6		
Ipswich	282	29	Goodhue	Lucy									1				1		
Ipswich	276	17	Goodhue	Moses			2	1					1	1			5		
Ipswich	281	59	Goodhue	Nancy									1	1			2		
Andover	95	27	Goodhue	Phineas	2	1		1		1			1				6		
Salem	218	8	Goodhue	Saml		2		1		3	1		1				8		
Newburyport	166	43	Goodhue	Sarah Wido							1						1		
Gloucester	64	18	Goodhue	Sarah Wo									1				1		
Salem	198	21	Goodhue	Stephn	2			1	1	1	1	1	2		1		10		
Ipswich	274	30	Goodhue	Daniel Jur			1						1				2		
Newbury	113	40	Gooding	Amos	1		3	1					1	1			7		
Newbury	115	31	Gooding	Moses	1		1					1					3		
Newbury	115	30	Gooding	Nath	1	2	2		1			2	1	1			10		
Newbury	113	41	Gooding	Samuel		1							1				2		
Newbury	113	45	Gooding	Stephen	1			1		3	1		1				7		
Newburyport	166	31	Goodrich	Charles				1		2	2	1	1				7		
Newburyport	166	33	Goodrich	Edward	4			1				1	1				7		
Gloucester	69	10	Goodrich	Joseph	1		1	1	1	4							9		
Gloucester	85	9	Goodrich	Mary Wo									1				1		
Newburyport	166	32	Goodrich	Moses	1	1	1	1		1	1		1	1			8		
Amesbury	39	15	Goodrich	Willm	1	1		1	1	2			1	1			8		
Haverhill	146	20	Goodridge	Barnabas	2			1		1			1				5		
Newbury	106	5	Goodridge	Edward		1		1		1	1	1	1				6		
Beverly	292	20	Goodridge	Eliza									1				1		
Beverly	290	21	Goodridge	Hannah			2	1					1				4		
Bradford	124	4	Goodridge	James	3	2	2	1		1		1					10		
Haverhill	146	33	Goodridge	John	1			1		1			1	1			5		
Newbury	119	45	Goodridge	Jonathan	1			1		1			1	1			5		
Newbury	115	29	Goodridge	Joseph	1			1		3			1				6		
Newbury	119	46	Goodridge	Joseph		1	1							1			3		
Salem	208	41	Goodridge	Lydia		1						1					3		
Lynn	228	26	Goodridge	Moses			2	1		2			1				6		
Newbury	106	29	Goodridge	Oliver	1			1				1	1				4		
Beverly	293	7	Goodridge	Samuel		1	1		1	1	3	1					8		
Beverly	292	12	Goodridge	William		1	1	1		2		1					6		
Lynn	225	23	Goodwin	Amaziah			1					1	1				3		
Amesbury	39	24	Goodwin	Ephm	1		1						1				3		
Amesbury	39	28	Goodwin	Ezra			1			1			1				3		
Marblehead	251	28	Goodwin	Hannah	3	1							1				5		
Salisbury	29	3	Goodwin	Henry			2	1						3			6		
Marblehead	257	9	Goodwin	Hephzibah										2			2		
Amesbury	39	26	Goodwin	Isaac				1	1	1		2	1				5		
Amesbury	39	27	Goodwin	Isaac Junr	2	1		1					1				5		
Newburyport	166	34	Goodwin	John		1			1	1			1				4		
Amesbury	39	16	Goodwin	Levi	2	1	1	1		1			1				7		
Beverly	294	2	Goodwin	Mary									1	1			2		
Amesbury	39	23	Goodwin	Mons		1			1				1	1			4		
Beverly	300	22	Goodwin	Nathaniel		3	2	1					1		1		8		
Marblehead	253	3	Goodwin	Samuel		1	1		1		1	2		1			7		
Marblehead	258	24	Goodwin	Samuel	3			1		2			1				7		
Amesbury	39	22	Goodwin	Susanna									1	1			2		
Amesbury	39	29	Goodwin	Thomas			1	1		1	1	1					5		
Amesbury	40	1	Goodwin	Thomas Junr		1		1		2			1				5		
Amesbury	39	25	Goodwin	William	4		1	1		1			1				8		
Marblehead	252	5	Goodwin	William	1		1						1				3		
Marblehead	259	8	Goodwin	William		1							1				2		
Amesbury	39	19	Googin	Richard				1		3							5		

Town	PG#	LN#	Last Name	First Name	FREE WHITE MALES under 10	10 to 16	16 to 26	26 to 45	45 and over	FREE WHITE FEMALES under 10	10 to 16	16 to 26	26 to 45	45 and over	Total All Other	Total Slaves	Totals	District/ Township	Notes
Salem	194	33	Goold	Mary			1			1			1				3		
Newbury	110	13	Gorden	Timothy	3	2		1			1		1				8		
Newburyport	166	29	Gordon	Elisha	2			1		2	1		1				7		
Salem	195	23	Gordon	John	2			1		3			1				7		
Amesbury	39	18	Gordon	Mirriam Wid										1			1		
Marblehead	263	16	Gordon	Nicholas	1			1		1			2	1			6		
Gloucester	79	23	Goss	James Doct	2			1		1			1	1			6		
Marblehead	254	3	Goss	Joshua	2		1		1	1	1	2		1			9		
Marblehead	250	30	Goss	Joshua Jun	1			1		1			1				4		
Marblehead	263	7	Goss	Katherine	1	1				2			1				5		
Gloucester	79	25	Goss	Richard	2			1		1			1				5		
Salem	220	49	Goss	Richard					1				1				2		
Salem	218	4	Goss	Thos	1			1		1	1	2	1				7		
Gloucester	79	24	Goss	William	3			1		1	3		1				9		
Marblehead	253	35	Goss	William			1			2		1					4		
Marblehead	263	17	Goss	William		2	1	1		2			1		5		12		
Newburyport	166	36	Gotham	Edward		1						1					2		
Gloucester	75	27	Gott	Abner		1		1			1	1		1			5		
Gloucester	79	20	Gott	Betty Wo	1	3	1			1				1			7		
Gloucester	76	1	Gott	Charles			1			2		1					4		
Gloucester	77	11	Gott	James			1	1				1					3		
Gloucester	75	16	Gott	James Junr	1			1		2	1		1				6		
Gloucester	79	19	Gott	John	1	1	1	1		1	2		1				8		
Gloucester	77	21	Gott	Joshua	1		2		1	2	1	1	1				9		
Gloucester	79	28	Gott	William	1	1		1		3			1				7		
Lynn	229	39	Goudey	Levi	2			1		1			1				5		
Topsfield	19	21	Gould	Amos	1		1						1				3		
Middleton	18	10	Gould	Andrew			1			1			1				3		
Topsfield	21	17	Gould	Asa				1					1	1			3		
Boxford	135	38	Gould	Cornelus	1			1		3			1				6		
Boxford	135	19	Gould	Daniel	2			1		1	1	3	1				9		
Amesbury	39	21	Gould	Elihu		1		1						3			5		
Topsfield	21	21	Gould	Elijah		1							1				2		
Boxford	135	40	Gould	Jacob		1						1	1	1			5		
Boxford	135	44	Gould	Jacob	1			1		1		1	1				5		
Salem	192	34	Gould	James				1					1				2		
Gloucester	59	19	Gould	John				1		1			1				3		
Topsfield	21	12	Gould	John		1		1		1	1	1		1			6		
Topsfield	21	14	Gould	John Junr	1			1		1	1	1		1			6		
Beverly	304	30	Gould	Joseph	4		1	1		1		1	1				9		
Newbury	118	46	Gould	Joseph	2			1		1	2			1			7		
Topsfield	21	15	Gould	Joseph				1					1				2		
Topsfield	21	16	Gould	Joseph Junr			1			1	1						3		
Salem	211	44	Gould	Josiah				1			1		1				3		
Ipswich	274	9	Gould	Major			1	1					1				3		
Middleton	17	38	Gould	Nathaniel	1	1		1		1			1				5		
Topsfield	21	19	Gould	Nathaniel	3	2		1		2		2	1	1			12		
Amesbury	39	20	Gould	Philip			1	1						3			5		
Boxford	135	47	Gould	Samuel	4		1	1		1	1	1					9		
Salem	201	24	Gould	Sarah	1								1				2		
Newbury	112	1	Gould	Silas	1	1	1						1	2			9		
Topsfield	21	20	Gould	Simon				1					1				2		
Topsfield	21	22	Gould	Simon Junr	1	1		1		1			1				5		
Middleton	17	37	Gould	Solomon				1						1			2		
Salem	216	14	Gould	Solomon	1			1		1			1				4		
Amesbury	39	12	Gould	Theophilus			1							1			2		
Ipswich	274	10	Gould	Thomas	1			1		1			1				4		
Topsfield	21	23	Gould	Zacheus	3	1	1		1		2	2	1	1			12		
Beverly	296	18	Gouldsberry	Asa			1			2			1				4		
Beverly	295	38	Gouldsberry	Joseph		1				1		2					4		
Danvers	8	12	Gowdy	James				1						1			2		
Salem	207	37	Gowen	Charles		2		1				1	1				5		
Lynnfield	237	7	Gowen	Ezra	3	1		1		2		1	1	1			10		
Danvers	6	36	Gowen	Gideon	1			1						2			4		
Lynnfield	236	15	Gowen	Joseph				1				1	1				3		
Lynnfield	237	14	Gowen	Nathl	1			1		2	1		1	1			7		
Salem	209	10	Gower	Eliza									1				1		
Wenham	307	4	Graften	Pattee		2						1	1				4		
Salem	215	31	Grafton	Mary								2		2			4		
Salem	214	18	Grafton	Woodbe	1			1		2	1		1	1			7		
Andover	95	15	Grainger	Sarah Wid									1	1			2		
Marblehead	263	18	Grandy	Mary		1								1			2		
Newburyport	166	28	Granger	Joseph	1			1		3			1				6		
Marblehead	266	7	Grant	Amos	1		1	1		1				2			6		
Marblehead	242	27	Grant	Christopher		1		1		4			1				7		
Salem	197	13	Grant	Elias		2	1	1				1	1				6		
Salem	206	59	Grant	Eliza								2	1	1			4		
Salisbury	28	31	Grant	Eliza Wd										2			2		
Salem	203	44	Grant	John			1	1	1	2		1	1				7		
Beverly	294	20	Grant	Joseph				1		1			1				3		
Salem	183	2	Grant	Joshua Jr	1	1	1		1	3	1		1				9		
Salem	183	11	Grant	Joshua Jr		1		1					1	1			4		
Ipswich	276	38	Grant	Nathaniel				1						2			3		
Marblehead	242	25	Grant	Thomas	2			1		2	1		1				7		

203

TOWN	PG#	LN#	LAST NAME	FIRST NAME	FREE WHITE MALES					FREE WHITE FEMALES					TOTAL ALL OTHER	TOTAL SLAVES	TOTALS	DISTRICT/ TOWNSHIP	NOTES
					under 10	10 to 16	16 to 26	26 to 45	45 and over	under 10	10 to 16	16 to 26	26 to 45	45 and over					
Marblehead	263	19	Grant	Thomas			2		1				1				4		
Marblehead	263	20	Grant	William	1			1		1		1					4		
Boxford	135	45	Grant				1						1				2		No first name
Marblehead	244	26	Grater	Francis	2	1	1		1				1	1			7		
Lynn	228	25	Graves	Benja			1	1					1				3		
Ipswich	275	39	Graves	John	2			1	1				1	1			6		
Lynn	231	24	Graves	Mark	1			1		1			1				4		
Salisbury	28	30	Graves	Mark			2		1				1				4		
Lynn	228	23	Graves	Ran				2						1			3		
Lynn	228	24	Graves	Saml	2	1		1					1				5		
Salem	209	54	Gray	Albert	2	3	2				1		2	1			11		
Salem	189	20	Gray	Benja		1		1		3		1	1				7		
Andover	95	28	Gray	Daniel	4	1		1		1	1		1	1			10		
Andover	95	21	Gray	David	1	1		1		1	1		2				7		
Beverly	305	10	Gray	James	2		1			1		1					5		
Danvers	9	17	Gray	James			1					1					2		
Salem	213	14	Gray	James		1		1					1				3		
Salem	215	47	Gray	John	2		1			2	2		1				8		
Salem	220	50	Gray	John	2		1			1			1				5		
Beverly	303	14	Gray	Molly							1		1				2		
Danvers	5	15	Gray	Rebech Wido									1				1		
Salem	207	10	Gray	Samuel	1	2	2	1			2		1				9		
Salem	213	48	Gray	Saumuel	1	1		1		4	3	1	2				13		
Andover	95	20	Gray	Thomas	2		1	1		1			1				6		
Gloucester	63	6	Gray	William	1			1					1				3	West Ward	
Middleton	16	27	Gray	William	3			1					1				5		
Salem	196	25	Gray	William	1	1						1					3		
Salem	212	23	Gray	William				1				1		1			3		
Salem	217	6	Gray	William	2	1	1	1	1		1	2	1				10		
Salem	202	4	Gray	Willm 4th	1			1		1		1	2				6		
Marblehead	249	13	Gready	Samuel	2	1		1					1				5		
Marblehead	270	23	Greaves	Crispus	1		1					1					3		
Marblehead	254	18	Greaves	Ebenezer	1	1	2		1	1	1	1					8		
Marblehead	254	5	Greaves	Ebenezer Junr			1			1		1	1				4		
Marblehead	255	15	Greaves	John	1	2		1		2		1		1			8		
Marblehead	268	26	Greaves	Joseph	1		1			1		1					4		
Marblehead	270	22	Greaves	Mark		1		1				1		1			4		
Marblehead	249	22	Greaves	Samuel			1			1		1					3		
Marblehead	263	21	Greaves	Samuel			1			2		1					4		
Marblehead	241	8	Greaves	William	2			1		1		1					5		
Haverhill	146	15	Greeley	Clement	1	1		1					1				4		
Haverhill	146	11	Greeley	Joseph				1		1		1	1				4		
Salisbury	28	36	Greely	David		1				1		1					3		
Salisbury	28	35	Greely	John		2		1		1		1					5		
Salisbury	29	4	Greely	Jona		1				1		1	1				4		
Salisbury	29	8	Greely	Judith Wd								1		1			2		
Salem	205	18	Greely	Philip		1				1		1					3		
Salisbury	29	1	Greely	Philip	1	1		1		2	2	1	1	1			10		
Salisbury	29	7	Greely	Samuel		1	1	1		2	1		1				7		
Newburyport	167	7	Greely	Stephen	2		3	2				1		2			10		
Marblehead	249	3	Green	Alexander			1					1					2		
Ipswich	278	5	Green	Benjamin			1			2		1					4		
Marblehead	249	11	Green	Elizabeth						2	1		1				4		
Lynn	230	12	Green	James				1						1			2		
Lynn	225	40	Green	James Jr	1		1						1				3		
Beverly	292	41	Green	Joanna		2							2	1			5		
Beverly	293	16	Green	Joanna 2d	1					2			1				4		
Haverhill	146	21	Green	John				1			1	1					3		
Marblehead	248	37	Green	John	1		2		1	1	1		1				7		
Marblehead	255	3	Green	John			1					1					2		
Marblehead	260	13	Green	John		1		1				1		1			4		
Salem	205	52	Green	John		1	2	1		1	1						6		
Newburyport	167	11	Green	Joseph	2	1		1		2	1		1	1			9		
Beverly	299	35	Green	Lydia						2		1					3		
Marblehead	251	31	Green	Mary	1	1							1				3		
Marblehead	263	23	Green	Mercy										2			2		
Danvers	3	29	Green	Meribah							1		1				2		
Beverly	292	40	Green	Moses	4	1		1		1	1		1	1			10		
Haverhill	146	22	Green	Moses	1			1		1		1	1				5		
Lynn	230	32	Green	Nehh	3	1		1					1				6		
Danvers	3	28	Green	Samuel			1					1					2		
Marblehead	248	32	Green	Sarah								1	1				2		
Salisbury	29	2	Green	Sarah Wd									1				1		
Marblehead	259	25	Green	Thomas		1				2		1					4		
Salem	211	5	Green	William	1	1		1				1					4		
Marblehead	246	29	Green	Peter			1						1				2		
Gloucester	57	34	Greene	Negro											4		4	West Parish	
Marblehead	254	7	Greene	Peter Junr			1			1		1	1				4		
Marblehead	254	9	Greene	Samuel		1				1		1					3		
Newbury	112	2	Greenfield	Nathll			1						1				2		
Newburyport	166	11	Greenleaf	Abel	1	1		1	1	1		1	2	1		2	11		
Newbury	108	33	Greenleaf	Abner	2	1	6	1	1	2	2		1	1			17		
Newbury	118	8	Greenleaf	Abner				1		1	1	1	1				5		
Newburyport	166	12	Greenleaf	Abner				1					1				2		
Haverhill	146	27	Greenleaf	Caleb	2	2		1		1	1	1	1				9		

TOWN	PG#	LN#	LAST NAME	FIRST NAME	FREE WHITE MALES under 10	10 to 16	16 to 26	26 to 45	45 and over	FREE WHITE FEMALES under 10	10 to 16	16 to 26	26 to 45	45 and over	TOTAL ALL OTHER	TOTAL SLAVES	TOTALS	DISTRICT/ TOWNSHIP	NOTES
Newburyport	166	20	Greenleaf	Dorothy Wido		1				2			1				4		
Newbury	111	29	Greenleaf	Ebenezer	1	1		1		1		1	1				6		
Newburyport	166	14	Greenleaf	Edmund C	4	1		1				1	2				9		
Newburyport	166	19	Greenleaf	Elizabeth								1		1			2		
Newburyport	166	16	Greenleaf	Jacob			1					1	1				3		
Newburyport	166	8	Greenleaf	John			1	1	1	1		1	3				8		
Newburyport	166	9	Greenleaf	John Jr	1			1			3	1	1				7		
Newburyport	166	10	Greenleaf	Jonathan				1					1				2		
Newburyport	166	13	Greenleaf	Joshua	1	1		1		2		1	1				7		
Newburyport	166	18	Greenleaf	Lucy Wido						1		1	4	1			7		
Newbury	108	27	Greenleaf	Nathaniel			2	3					1				6		
Newburyport	166	17	Greenleaf	Richard	1			1		3			1	1			7		
Newbury	110	32	Greenleaf	Samuel	2			1		1		1					5		
Haverhill	146	34	Greenleaf	Sarah	1	1				1			1	1			5		
Gloucester	59	21	Greenleaf	William	2			1			1	1		1			6		
Haverhill	146	16	Greenleaf	William	1	1		1	1	3	1	1	1	2			12		
Newburyport	166	15	Greenleaf	Woodbridge	2					1			1				5		
Newbury	112	46	Greenlieff	Thomas			1	1	1					1			4		
Newbury	118	11	Greenliff	Josiah			1			1		1					3		
Bradford	124	11	Greenough	Bayley		1				1		1	2	1			6		
Marblehead	263	25	Greenough	Emanuel				1					1				2		
Bradford	123	31	Greenough	James				1			1	2		1			5		
Bradford	124	21	Greenough	John	2			1			1		2	1			7		
Newburyport	167	4	Greenough	John			1			2		2					5		
Newburyport	167	3	Greenough	Joseph			1	1	1		1	1		1			6		
Bradford	125	40	Greenough	Moses	1		1			2			1				5		
Haverhill	146	19	Greenough	Polly		1								2			3		
Bradford	124	5	Greenough	William	2	1		1		3	2	1	1				11		
Wenham	307	10	Greenwood	Elizabeth										1			1		
Marblehead	240	34	Greenwood	Mary										1			1		
Marblehead	248	38	Gregory	Joseph	4	1		1					1				7		
Marblehead	248	31	Griffen	Alice		1					1	1		1			4		
Gloucester	74	21	Griffen	Andrew	1	2	1	1		3		1		1			10		
Gloucester	74	3	Griffen	Dudly	2			1			1		1	1			6	Squam Parish	
Gloucester	76	12	Griffen	Eliphalet	2			1		3			1				7		
Gloucester	75	5	Griffen	Epes	2		1			1		1					5		
Gloucester	74	15	Griffen	Gustaves		1		1		1		1					4		
Gloucester	74	22	Griffen	James	1		2	1		1	3	3		1			12		
Gloucester	76	29	Griffen	James	1	1	1	1				1		1			6		
Gloucester	76	9	Griffen	Joel	1		1			1		1					4		
Andover	95	16	Griffen	Joseph			1										1		
Gloucester	74	18	Griffen	Mary Wo		1	2						1	1			5		
Gloucester	74	10	Griffen	Nathll	2			1	1	1			1	1			7	Squam Parish	
Gloucester	74	19	Griffen	Oliver		1	1		1		1	1		1			6		
Gloucester	76	8	Griffen	Sam			1	1				1	3	1			7		
Gloucester	59	17	Griffen	William	1			1		4			1	1			8		
Gloucester	76	18	Griffen	William	1			1		1	1	1					5		
Salisbury	28	28	Griffin	Benja Capt			1		1			1		1			4		
Salisbury	28	29	Griffin	Benja Junr Capt	2			1		2		1					6		
Andover	95	31	Griffin	Daniel				2					1				3		
Salisbury	28	27	Griffin	Daniel Capt	1		1					2					4		
Bradford	122	22	Griffin	Ebenezr	1	2		1		1	1	1					8		
Bradford	122	21	Griffin	John		3			1	1				1			6		
Andover	95	25	Griffin	Jonathan	2		1	1		1			1	1			7		
Beverly	302	43	Griffin	Jonathan	2		2	1					1				6		
Methuen	153	33	Griffin	Jonathan	2	1		1					1				5		
Methuen	153	31	Griffin	Joseph			3	1	1		1	1		1			8		
Methuen	153	32	Griffin	Joseph Junr	1	1		1		1			1				5		
Andover	95	30	Griffin	William				1			1	1	1				4		
Marblehead	270	3	Griffin	William	1			1				1					3		
Andover	95	26	Griffin	William Junr			1						1				2		
Salisbury	28	26	Griffin	Wm Capt			1					1					2		
Newburyport	167	8	Griffith	Sarah Wido		2	2			1		1					6		
Newburyport	167	9	Griffith	William	1	2		1		1				2			7		
Marblehead	248	10	Grifle	John					1				1	1			3		
Gloucester	70	19	Grimes	Mark	1	1		1		3			1	1			8		
Gloucester	64	19	Grimes	William			1	1	1			2		1			6		
Gloucester	64	20	Grimes	William Junr				1					1				2		
Beverly	290	10	Grind	Robert	2			1		2		1					6		
Salem	200	28	Groce	Danl			1						1				2		
Salem	197	12	Groce	Obadh	2	1			1	2	1	1					8		
Marblehead	259	17	Grons	Elizabeth		2								1			3		
Beverly	291	40	Grose	George		1		1						1			3		
Beverly	291	38	Grose	George Jun	2			1		1			1				5		
Beverly	301	42	Grover	Abigail							2		2				4		
Lynn	233	23	Grover	Asa	2			1		1		1	1	1			6		
Gloucester	82	31	Grover	E* Wd		1							1				2		
Gloucester	79	21	Grover	Ebenz Junr	1		1	1		1		1		1			6		
Gloucester	64	17	Grover	Eleazer	2			1		3	1		1	1			9		
Beverly	301	41	Grover	John			1					1	1				3		
Lynn	232	27	Grover	John			1			2		1					4	West Parish	
Haverhill	146	12	Grover	Joseph		1	1		1			1					4		
Gloucester	79	22	Grover	Neha Junr	2		1						1				4		
Gloucester	83	18	Grover	Nehemiah			1		1		1	1		1			5		
Salem	193	4	Groves	Thad	1			1	1	2		1		1			7		
Marblehead	265	20	Grow	Jane	1						1		1				3		

205

TOWN	PG#	LN#	LAST NAME	FIRST NAME	M under 10	M 10-16	M 16-26	M 26-45	M 45+	F under 10	F 10-16	F 16-26	F 26-45	F 45+	TOTAL ALL OTHER	TOTAL SLAVES	TOTALS	DISTRICT/ TOWNSHIP	NOTES
Ipswich	274	41	Grow	John				1		1			1				3		
Marblehead	268	33	Grush	Thomas	2	2		1		3	1	1					10		
Beverly	296	21	Grusts	Philip	1		1			1		1					4		
Newburyport	166	21	Gunnison	Ebenezer	1	1	2	1		1	1	1	2				10		
Manchester	51	21	Gurley	George	2	1		1				1	2	1			8		
Manchester	51	20	Gurley	John		1		1		2	2		1				7		
Manchester	53	33	Gurley	Willm			1						1				2		
Newburyport	166	24	Gurney	Elisha	2				1	2			1				6		
Methuen	153	35	Gutterson	James	3			1					2				6		
Methuen	153	34	Gutterson	William	2				2	2	2	1	1				10		
Salem	209	53	Gwynn	Thaddeus	3	2	1	1				1	3	1			12		
Salem	192	35	Hacker	Isaac Jr			1						1				2		
Salisbury	29	13	Hacket	Benja		1	1						1				3		
Salisbury	29	14	Hacket	John		1		1		1	1			2			6		
Salisbury	29	18	Hacket	John Junr	1			1		2			1				5		
Salisbury	29	16	Hacket	Wm Capt			1	1		1		1	3	1			8		
Salisbury	29	19	Hacket	Wm Junr Capt			1			2			1				4		
Marblehead	259	28	Hackleton	John1			1	1				1					3		
Salem	211	12	Hacklin	William			1					1					2		
Haverhill	147	17	Haddack	Dileverc								1	1	1			3		
Haverhill	146	41	Haddack	James	2		1	1		2			1				7		
Gloucester	86	1	Hadley	John				1				1		1			3		
Marblehead	242	15	Hadley	Nathaniel				1		1			1	1			4		
Gloucester	58	8	Hadock	Hannah Wo			1							1			2		
Bradford	121	3	Haggit	Moses		1		1						1			3		
Lynn	233	43	Hakes	Rebekah		1	2			1	3	1	1				9	West Parish	
Salem	205	29	Halden	Charles	1		1						1				3		
Newbury	117	15	Hale	Amos	1		2						2	2			7		
Gloucester	79	31	Hale	Benja	1	1	2		2	3	2	1	1				13		
Rowley	131	34	Hale	Daniel	2	1		1		1		1	2				8		
Newburyport	167	32	Hale	David Wido of								1					1		
Newburyport	167	31	Hale	Ebenezer	3		2	1		1		1	1				9		
Bradford	125	25	Hale	Eliphalet	3		2	1	1	2		1	1	1			12		
Newbury	114	11	Hale	Eliza						1		1	1				3		
Newbury	112	43	Hale	Enoch	4	1		1		1	2		1	1			11		
Newbury	114	37	Hale	Ezra				1		1		1	1				4		
Haverhill	146	43	Hale	Ezzekiel	3	1	1	1		2		1	2				11		
Newbury	117	38	Hale	Isaac			1	1		3	2	1	1				9		
Newburyport	167	27	Hale	Jacob	1		1	1				1		1			5		
Newburyport	167	28	Hale	Jacob Jr	3		1	1		1		1	1				8		
Newbury	117	32	Hale	John				1			1			1			3		
Bradford	125	23	Hale	Jonath	1	1	1	1			1		1	1			7		
Boxford	135	15	Hale	Joseph		1				2		1	1	1			6		
Newbury	105	19	Hale	Joseph	1		3	1	1	1		1	1	1			10		
Newburyport	167	29	Hale	Joseph			1						1				2		
Haverhill	147	15	Hale	Joshua			1						1				2		
Newbury	117	21	Hale	Joshua	1			1		1			1				4		
Gloucester	73	10	Hale	Lydia Wo			1	1					1	1			4		
Beverly	299	25	Hale	Mary	1	1	1				1	1		1			6		
Newbury	112	3	Hale	Moses	1					1	1	1					5		
Newbury	108	24	Hale	Nathaniel				1									1		
Newbury	119	37	Hale	Oliver		2		1					2				5		
Newbury	119	38	Hale	Oliver	2	1	1	1	1		2	2	1	1			12		
Newburyport	167	36	Hale	Paul	3	1		1				1	1				7		
Rowley	129	42	Hale	Pemberton	1		1			1		1					4		
Newburyport	167	38	Hale	Robert			1					1		2			4		
Newburyport	167	30	Hale	Samuel			1			2		1	1				5		
Newbury	110	10	Hale	Thomas	3	3	4	1				1		1			13		
Marblehead	242	16	Halen	Elias	1		1			1	1						4		
Gloucester	59	27	Hall	Aaron	2	3		1		1		1	1				9		
Manchester	51	30	Hall	Abigalk Wo		1					1	3	2	1			8		
Ipswich	276	54	Hall	Charles	1	1			1			1					7		
Andover	96	20	Hall	Christa B. Wid						1			1				2		
Methuen	154	8	Hall	Elizabeth									1	1			2		
Beverly	299	6	Hall	Hugh	5			1				1	1	2			10		
Methuen	154	19	Hall	Jacob	3			1		1		1	1	1			8		
Salisbury	29	15	Hall	Joseph	1			1					1	1			5		
Bradford	121	8	Hall	Moses	1			1		4			1		1		8		
Marblehead	252	13	Hall	Prince									1		1		2		
Lynn	228	38	Hall	Thos	2			1				1	1	1			6		
Gloucester	68	11	Haller	Mary Wo									1	1			2		
Lynn	224	13	Hallowell	Henry		1	2		1	1	2		1				8		
Lynn	224	15	Hallowell	Theoph	1	1	2		1			1	2	1			9		
Lynn	229	16	Halsey	Benj	2	1		1		3	2		1				10		
Newburyport	168	21	Ham	Thomas	2			1		1		1	1				6		
Salem	202	6	Hamills	Stephen	1			1		2	1	2	1				9		
Ipswich	277	30	Hammon	Abigail	2							1		1			4		
Beverly	304	16	Hammon	Eliza		2	1			2			1				6		
Marblehead	243	13	Hammon	Elizabeth									1	1			2		
Beverly	301	18	Hammon	Philip	1			1		2			1				5		
Ipswich	277	8	Hammon	Phillip				1						1			2		
Danvers	12	21	Hammond	Benjamin	1			1						1			3		
Marblehead	263	27	Hammond	Edward	4		1			1			1				7		
Marblehead	247	21	Hammond	Elizabeth	2	1	1						1	1			6		
Marblehead	259	33	Hammond	Jane	1								1				2		

TOWN	PG#	LN#	LAST NAME	FIRST NAME	FREE WHITE MALES					FREE WHITE FEMALES					TOTAL ALL OTHER	TOTAL SLAVES	TOTALS	DISTRICT/ TOWNSHIP	NOTES
					under 10	10 to 16	16 to 26	26 to 45	45 and over	under 10	10 to 16	16 to 26	26 to 45	45 and over					
Danvers	13	32	Hammond	John	2	2		1		2	1		1				9		
Marblehead	245	34	Hammond	John	3			1		1	1		1				7		
Marblehead	249	34	Hammond	John	2			1		1	1		1				6		
Topsfield	22	6	Hammond	Nathaniel		1	1	1		1		1	1	1			7		
Marblehead	260	30	Hammond	Thomas F	1	1	1		1		1			1			6		
Marblehead	257	28	Hammond	William	2			1		1		1					5		
Gloucester	80	2	Hampson	John			1	1				1	1				4		
Marblehead	263	24	Hamson	Henry	2	1	2		1	1	1	1	1				10		
Salem	220	44	Han	Mary	1	2					1		1				5		
Newburyport	168	38	Hand	William		1		1	1		1						4		
Marblehead	256	14	Handley	Joseph				1									1		
Lynn	229	28	Haney	Martin	2			1					1				4		
Beverly	298	34	Hannon	George	2						1		1	1			5		
Gloucester	58	7	Hannon	John			1			2			1				4		
Marblehead	241	9	Hanover	Hannah										1			1		
Salem	219	33	Hanscom	James			1				1	1	1				4		
Salem	217	56	Hanscom	Willm	4		1			1			1	1			8		
Lynn	223	21	Hanson	Bitfield		1	1			1		1					4		
Marblehead	247	29	Hanty	Mary						1		1					2		
Gloucester	74	17	Haraden	James	5		1			1			2				9		
Gloucester	74	4	Haraden	John	1		1			3			1				6	Squam Parish	
Gloucester	74	11	Haraden	Joseph	1	1	2	1		2	1		2				10	Squam Parish	
Salisbury	29	21	Harbert	James		1		1						1			3		
Salisbury	29	22	Harbert	Sarah Wd	1	1	1			2	1		1				7		
Gloucester	68	17	Harday	John		1			1			2		1			5		
Hamilton	285	75	Harden	Isaac			1			2		2					5		
Andover	96	24	Harden	John	1		2			2			1				6		
Newburyport	168	32	Hardin	John	1		1			2		1					5		
Haverhill	146	45	Harding	Jesse	1		1			2		1	1	1			7		
Haverhill	147	3	Harding	Thomas	1		1					1					3		
Salem	197	23	Hardwick	Mehita								1	1				2		
Rowley	127	4	Hardy	Benja	3		2					1					6		
Bradford	125	42	Hardy	David	1	1			1	2	1	1		1			8		
Newburyport	168	33	Hardy	Dudley			1			1			1				3		
Bradford	125	37	Hardy	Elijah	2			1		2			1				6		
Bradford	124	23	Hardy	Enoch	2		2	1	1	2	1	1	1	1			12		
Rowley	127	9	Hardy	Enos	1			1		1			1				4		
Andover	96	18	Hardy	Ezekiel				1						1			2		
Andover	96	33	Hardy	Ezekiel Junr			3	1		1		3	4				12		
Bradford	125	20	Hardy	Henry	2	1		1		3	2		1	1			11		
Bradford	125	38	Hardy	Jacob	1			1		3			3	1			9		
Andover	96	31	Hardy	James		1	1	1						1			4		
Andover	96	32	Hardy	John			1							2			3		
Bradford	125	35	Hardy	Joseph	3		1					1					5		
Bradford	125	2	Hardy	Joshua	2	2		1				2					7		
Bradford	125	32	Hardy	Joshua	1	1	1		2	2			1				8		
Bradford	124	37	Hardy	Parker	1		1			1		1	1				5		
Bradford	123	48	Hardy	Phineas		2	2	1				1	1				7		
Bradford	124	30	Hardy	Reuben	1	1				2	1		1				7		
Bradford	124	12	Hardy	Samuel	2			1				1	2	1			7		
Ipswich	281	45	Hardy	Samuel	3	1			1	1	2			1			9		
Bradford	124	35	Hardy	Silvanus		1				1		1					3		
Bradford	124	38	Hardy	Simon				1					1				3		
Bradford	125	34	Hardy	Simon	1			1					1				3		
Bradford	123	47	Hardy	Solomon		1			1			1		2			5		
Bradford	124	36	Hardy	Timothy				1						1			2		
Gloucester	64	29	Hardy	William			1			1			1	1			4		
Rowley	129	37	Haris	John	1		1		1				2				5		
Rowley	129	38	Haris	Timothy		2	1	1						1			5		
Gloucester	62	18	Harken	Hannah Wd	1		2			1			1	1	1		7		
Newbury	113	23	Harker	Mary	1	1							1	1			4		
Amesbury	40	6	Harket	Joseph			1			1			1				3		
Amesbury	40	2	Harket	Mehitable Wid	3								1				4		
Ipswich	282	18	Harlow	John	4			1		1	2		1				9		
Beverly	299	27	Harmon	John	1	1		1		1			1				5		
Salem	215	15	Harnadan	Jona		1	1			1	1	3	1				9		
Gloucester	64	21	Harradan	David		2	1	2	1			2		1			9		
Salem	192	30	Harredan	Andrew			1						1				2		
Gloucester	64	24	Harrick	Josiah	1			1		2	2		1	1			8		
Haverhill	147	4	Harriman	Joel			1	1	1				2	1			6		
Haverhill	147	18	Harriman	Joseph		1			1	2	1		1				6		
Lynn	233	15	Harrington	Eliza									1				1		
Salem	204	16	Harrington	James			1			1			2				4		
Salem	204	18	Harrington	Joseph			1			1		1					3		
Salem	197	40	Harrinton	Charles	1		1				1		1				4		
Beverly	301	36	Harris	Charles S			1			3			1				5		
Ipswich	277	41	Harris	David	3			1		1			1				6		
Danvers	8	18	Harris	Ephriem			1					2					3		
Newburyport	167	26	Harris	Giles	1			1		1			2	1			6		
Beverly	301	43	Harris	Hannah			1					1	1	1			4		
Methuen	154	16	Harris	Heman			1			1	1	1					4		
Ipswich	275	6	Harris	James	2			1			1			1			8		
Ipswich	274	11	Harris	John	1		3		1	2		3		1			11		
Ipswich	277	36	Harris	John	1		2		1		1		1	1			7		

207

TOWN	PG#	LN#	HEADS OF HOUSEHOLD		FREE WHITE MALES					FREE WHITE FEMALES					TOTAL ALL OTHER	TOTAL SLAVES	TOTALS	DISTRICT/ TOWNSHIP	NOTES
			LAST NAME	FIRST NAME	under 10	10 to 16	16 to 26	26 to 45	45 and over	under 10	10 to 16	16 to 26	26 to 45	45 and over					NOTES
Marblehead	266	30	Harris	John	2	2	1		1		1	1	1				9		
Marblehead	268	5	Harris	John				1				1	1				3		
Methuen	154	14	Harris	John			1	2				1	1	1			6		
Newbury	109	42	Harris	John		1	1	1		2		1	1				7		
Beverly	297	33	Harris	Jonathan	1		1					1					3		
Ipswich	275	40	Harris	Mary				1					1				2		
Marblehead	268	30	Harris	Mason		2	1		1		2	2		2			10		
Ipswich	274	20	Harris	Nathaniel			1			1		1					3		
Methuen	153	44	Harris	Ralph	1	1	2	1		2	1	1	1				10		
Marblehead	268	28	Harris	Robert			1	1				2					4		
Salem	206	21	Harris	Robt		1		1		1							3		
Ipswich	277	37	Harris	Samuel	1				2		1	1	1	1			7		
Methuen	154	13	Harris	Samuel	3	1		1	1	3	1	1	1	1			13		
Ipswich	277	48	Harris	Samuel Jun			1					1		1			3		
Ipswich	277	55	Harris	Tabathy									1	1			2		
Marblehead	241	7	Harris	William	1	1	1	1		2	1	2	1				10		
Marblehead	268	13	Harris	William				1									1		
Marblehead	268	16	Harris	William Revd				1		5	1	1		1			9		
Newburyport	168	3	Harrison	John	1		1			2			2				6		
Newburyport	168	2	Harrod	John		1	1			2	3	1	1		1		10		
Haverhill	146	40	Harrod	Joseph	1	1	1	2		1	4	1	1				12		
Lynnfield	235	36	Hart	Ebenz	2		1			3		1					7		
Lynnfield	235	35	Hart	George	1		1					3		1			6		
Beverly	295	36	Hart	Jacob			1			1		2	1	1			6		
Lynnfield	235	33	Hart	John				1				1	1	1			4		
Lynn	230	1	Hart	Joseph			1	1				2		1			5		
Lynnfield	235	34	Hart	Joseph	1		1			1		1					4		
Lynn	230	21	Hart	Lois										1			1		
Ipswich	273	48	Hart	Mary										1			1		
Manchester	50	23	Hart	Ruth Wo								1					1		
Beverly	301	14	Hart	Sarah								1	2	1			4		
Amesbury	40	19	Hartings	Robert		1		1						1			3		
Gloucester	78	5	Hartly	Saml	2		1	1	1	1		1					8		
Newburyport	168	28	Harton	George C			1			1				1			3		
Salem	203	32	Hartshorn	Joseph	1	1	1							1			4		
Salem	203	20	Hartshorn	Thos				1				1		1			3		
Gloucester	70	22	Harvey	Benja	1	2	2		1	2		2	1				11		
Newburyport	168	30	Harvey	David	2		1						1				4		
Beverly	299	17	Harvey	Dover											6		6		
Amesbury	41	9	Harvey	Jacob	2	1		1		1			1				6		
Salem	207	14	Harvey	John	3		1	1		1	1		1				8		
Newbury	111	19	Harvey	Thomas				1					1				2		
Newburyport	168	29	Harvey	Thomas	3	1	1	2		1	1	1	1	2			13		
Newburyport	168	31	Harvey	William			1			1		1					3		
Salem	202	16	Hasan	Peter		1		1		2		1					5		
Salem	192	31	Hascal	Epes		1	2			1		1					5		
Salem	212	29	Hascol	Elisha				1		2		1	1	1			6		
Salem	188	27	Hascol	William	2			1		2			1				6		
Salem	214	3	Hascoll	Ephm			1			1			1				3		
Methuen	154	17	Hase	Samuel			1	1		2			1	1			6		
Haverhill	146	39	Haseltine	James 4th	1		1						1				3		
Haverhill	146	38	Haseltine	James Jun	1	1	1		1	1	1			1			7		
Methuen	153	43	Haseltine	Mehetable		1	1						1	1			4		
Gloucester	80	1	Haskall	Josiah	2		1	1				1					5		
Beverly	297	3	Haskel	James W	3	1		1		2		1	1				9		
Beverly	296	49	Haskel	Nathaniel		1		1		1				1			4		
Beverly	298	29	Haskel	Robert	3	2		1		3	1		1	1			12		
Beverly	297	2	Haskel	William		1	2	1		1		2					7		
Beverly	303	43	Haskel	William	2			1		1			1				5		
Gloucester	56	22	Haskell	Aaron		2	4	1	1	1	1	1		2			13		
Ipswich	282	55	Haskell	Aaron	1			1		1			1				4		
Gloucester	56	37	Haskell	Abraham	2			1						1			4		
Gloucester	56	33	Haskell	Adonj	1			1		1			1				4		
Newbury	108	9	Haskell	Alexander				1						1			2		
Gloucester	56	39	Haskell	Amoss		1	1	1		1				1			5		
Gloucester	57	1	Haskell	Amoss Junr			1			1			1				3		
Manchester	52	1	Haskell	Benja		1		1				1	1	1			5		
Newburyport	167	13	Haskell	Caleb				1					1	1			3		
Gloucester	57	35	Haskell	Cornelius											12		12	West Parish	
Beverly	300	38	Haskell	Daniel		1						1					2		
Gloucester	56	23	Haskell	Daniel				1					1				2		
Gloucester	56	24	Haskell	Danl Jun	2	1		1		1			1				6		
Ipswich	282	15	Haskell	Ebenezer	1	1		1		3		1	1				8		
Gloucester	56	26	Haskell	Elias	1		2	1		2	2			1			9		
Newburyport	167	37	Haskell	Elizabeth Wido		1						3		1			5		
Gloucester	57	2	Haskell	Enoch	1		1					1					3		
Ipswich	282	14	Haskell	Enoch				1					1	1			3		
Newburyport	167	15	Haskell	Hubbard		1	1			1		1	3	1			8		
Gloucester	64	22	Haskell	Hubbard Dea				1						1			2		
Newburyport	167	16	Haskell	Hubbard Jr	2		1			1			1				5		
Beverly	296	48	Haskell	Isaac		1				2		1					4		
Gloucester	57	33	Haskell	Isaac				1						1			2	West Parish	
Beverly	296	16	Haskell	Israel	1		1			1			1				4		
Newburyport	167	17	Haskell	Jeremiah	3		2	1					1				7		
Gloucester	64	25	Haskell	John	1	1		1		2	1	1	1				8		

208

TOWN	PG#	LN#	LAST NAME	FIRST NAME	FREE WHITE MALES					FREE WHITE FEMALES					TOTAL ALL OTHER	TOTAL SLAVES	TOTALS	DISTRICT/ TOWNSHIP	NOTES
					under 10	10 to 16	16 to 26	26 to 45	45 and over	under 10	10 to 16	16 to 26	26 to 45	45 and over					
Newburyport	167	14	Haskell	John				1		1			1				3		
Gloucester	59	28	Haskell	Josiah	1	1	1		1		2			1			7		
Ipswich	273	22	Haskell	Mark			2	1				1	1	1	1		6		
Gloucester	56	34	Haskell	Moses	3	1	2		1	2	1		1				11		
Beverly	297	1	Haskell	Nathaniel Jr		1				1		1					3		
Gloucester	56	20	Haskell	Nathl Deac				1					1				2		
Gloucester	59	22	Haskell	Nathll	1		1	1		2	1		1				7		
Gloucester	59	24	Haskell	Nathll Junr		1	2		1			1	1	1			7		
Newburyport	167	12	Haskell	Nehemiah		2		1				1	1				5		
Newbury	111	36	Haskell	Solomon	1	2		1		3		1	2				10		
Beverly	298	5	Haskell	Stephen	2	1		1		1			1				6		
Gloucester	56	25	Haskell	Stephen	2			1			3			1			7		
Gloucester	56	35	Haskell	Stephen Junr	1			1			1	1					4		
Gloucester	64	26	Haskell	Thomas	1		1			2		1					5		
Marblehead	269	26	Haskell	Thomas	2			1		1	1		1				6		
Gloucester	56	21	Haskell	William				1					1				2		
Gloucester	64	23	Haskell	William	3	2		1		1	1	1	1				10		
Newburyport	167	18	Haskell	William		1		1		1			1				4		
Gloucester	56	27	Haskell	Zebulon	1		1	2	1	2	2		1				10		
Gloucester	65	7	Haskell	Zebulon	1		1					1					3		
Gloucester	56	28	Haskell	Zebulon Junr	1		1	1		2			1				6		
Gloucester	69	12	Haskell	Josiah Junr	1			1					1				3		
Gloucester	80	3	Haskins	Bennett	2				1				1				4		
Gloucester	79	32	Haskins	John	1			1		2			2				6		
Gloucester	78	30	Haskins	Willm	1		3		1					1			6	Sandy Bay Parish	
Marblehead	269	21	Haskoll	Mark		1		1	1				2	1			6		
Marblehead	269	13	Haskoll	William				1					1				2		
Haverhill	147	19	Hastings	John		1	1					1					3		
Haverhill	147	13	Hastings	Richard	2			1					1				4		
Methuen	154	7	Hastings	Robert		1		1					2				4		
Methuen	153	42	Hastings	Simeon	1			2				1	1				5		
Newburyport	167	40	Hastings	Susannah Wido							1		1				2		
Beverly	296	26	Hatch	Gamaleal		1	1				1						3		
Beverly	296	25	Hatch	John		1					1						2		
Newbury	109	12	Hatch	John			1						1				2		
Marblehead	243	4	Hatch	Naler	1	1	1			1		1					5		
Lynn	224	40	Hatcher	Thos C		1		1		2			2				6		
Marblehead	269	17	Hathaway	John Gardner	3	2	1	1		2	1		1				11		
Salem	211	35	Hathorne	Eliza			1					2		1			4		
Salem	206	31	Hathorne	John		2	1		1	2	2	1		2			11		
Salem	191	10	Hathorne	Mary								1	3				4		
Salem	213	34	Hathorne	Mary							1	1	1				3		
Salem	216	49	Hathorne	Rachel	1			2		2		1	4	1			11		
Salem	190	8	Hathorne	William		1	1			1	3		1				7		
Salem	194	41	Hathorne	William		1	1				4		1				7		
Salem	214	11	Hathorne	William				1				1	1				3		
Salem	198	29	Hawker	Isaac	1	2	1		1	2		1	1				9		
Marblehead	253	20	Hawkes	Benjamin	2			1		1	1		1				6		
Lynn	228	11	Hawkes	Delliverance									2				2		
Lynn	233	41	Hawkes	Ebenz		1		1				1	1				4	West Parish	
Lynn	233	27	Hawkes	Eunice								1	1	1			3	West Parish	
Lynnfield	235	24	Hawkes	John	2				1	3	3		1				10		
Lynn	230	40	Hawkes	John Jr	3		1		2		1		1				8		
Lynn	230	43	Hawkes	Joseph				1	1	1		1					4		
Lynn	234	2	Hawkes	Joseph	2			1		2			1				6		
Lynn	230	39	Hawkes	Mattw		2	1		1	1		2		1			8		
Lynn	233	42	Hawkes	Nathan		1	3		1		1	2		1			9	West Parish	
Lynn	233	44	Hawkes	Nathan		1	3		1		1	2		1			9	West Parish	
Salem	210	28	Hawkins	Samuel		1		1					1				3		
Salem	218	21	Hawks	Benja	1	1	1	1		3			1	1			9		
Newbury	111	49	Hawks	John		1		1			1		1				4		
Marblehead	250	19	Hawks	Willia	1			1		4		1					7		
Andover	96	23	Hawley	William		1	1	1		2			1				6		
Newburyport	168	1	Hawley	William	1				1	2			1				5		
Gloucester	86	18	Haycock	Joseph	1	1		1			1		1	0			5		
Marblehead	263	26	Hayden	William				1					1				2		
Gloucester	59	26	Hayes	James		1	1	1		1	2	1	1				8		
Gloucester	59	30	Hayes	James Junr	1		1					2					4		
Haverhill	147	8	Haynes	Ammi			1	1			3		1				6		
Methuen	154	18	Haynes	James	2	2		1		2			1	1			9		
Haverhill	147	9	Haynes	Jonathan		1	1			3	1	1					8		
Haverhill	147	7	Haynes	Joseph		1	1	2	1			2		1	1		9		
Haverhill	146	42	Haynes	Thomas	1	2			1	2		1	1				9		
Haverhill	147	20	Haynes	Warren	2		1						1	1			5		
Danvers	11	33	Hayward	Archelaus	2			1		1	1		1				6		
Salem	201	7	Hayward	John				1				1	1				3		
Gloucester	83	17	Hayward	Jona Capt	2							1		1			5		
Danvers	5	7	Hayward	Levi		1			1		1	1	1				5		
Andover	96	17	Haywood	Nehemiah		1		1		1	2		1				6		
Andover	96	37	Hazeltine	Botfer							1		1				2		
Haverhill	147	21	Hazeltine	James				1				2		1			4		
Haverhill	147	22	Hazeltine	James 3d	3		3		1	1			1				10		
Haverhill	147	5	Hazeltine	John	2	1	1		1	1	1	2		1			10		
Haverhill	147	6	Hazeltine	Ladd	4	3		1		1	1	1	1				12		
Bradford	122	1	Hazzeltine	Amos	1	1			1	1	2			1			7		

TOWN	PG#	LN#	LAST NAME	FIRST NAME	FREE WHITE MALES under 10	10 to 16	16 to 26	26 to 45	45 and over	FREE WHITE FEMALES under 10	10 to 16	16 to 26	26 to 45	45 and over	TOTAL ALL OTHER	TOTAL SLAVES	TOTALS	DISTRICT/ TOWNSHIP	NOTES
Bradford	122	14	Head	Amos				1		1	1		1				4		
Newburyport	168	37	Head	Richard					2		1			1			4		
Bradford	122	13	Head	Reuben	2	1		1		1	2		1	1			9		
Ipswich	276	41	Heard	John	1	1	1		1	2		3		2	1		12		
Salem	218	16	Heard	Luke	1			1					1				3		
Ipswich	276	16	Heard	Nathaniel		1		1	1					1			4		
Ipswich	279	6	Heard	Nathaniel Jun	2			1		3			1	1			8		
Ipswich	276	13	Heard	Samuel				1	2					2			5		
Methuen	154	15	Heath	Abial	1	1		1		1	1		1				6		
Salem	214	51	Heather	Martha									1				1		
Salem	191	26	Heman	Jos	2			1		4	3		1				11		
Beverly	289	12	Heman	William Esq	2	1			1	2		1	2	1	1		12		
Salem	211	49	Henderson	Benja	2	2		1					1				6		
Salem	189	28	Henderson	Benjn	1			1					1	1			4		
Salem	194	23	Henderson	Joseph	2			1		1			1				5		
Marblehead	256	21	Hendley	Abigail									1				1		
Marblehead	242	32	Hendley	John		1		1					1				3		
Salem	209	14	Hendy	John					1					1			2		
Salem	213	18	Henfield	John				2									2		
Salem	213	26	Henfield	Joseph		2		1			1	2		1			7		
Salem	209	15	Henick	Jona	2	1		1		1			1				6		
Boxford	136	4	Hening	Asa											4		4		
Salem	218	1	Henry	John				1					1				2		
Salem	210	54	Henry	Samuel		1		1				2		1			5		
Newbury	106	16	Henshinfield	John			1							1			2		
Salem	194	46	Hensler	George	1			1			2		1				5		
Newburyport	168	27	Herbett	Charles		2	1	2		1			2	1			9		
Bradford	122	35	Hergeyethine	John	1	1		1		3	1		1				8		
Beverly	300	9	Herick	Jonathan	2		2			2			1				7		
Beverly	305	42	Herick	Joshua	2			1		2	1		2	1			9		
Beverly	291	1	Herrick	Anna			1					1	2	1			5		
Beverly	289	16	Herrick	Asa		1		1	1			1		1			5		
Salem	207	49	Herrick	Barnebas				1					1				2		
Beverly	299	8	Herrick	Daniel		1		1				1	1				4		
Gloucester	56	32	Herrick	Danl		1	1	1		2			1	1			7		
Beverly	290	14	Herrick	Deborah		1							1	1			3		
Boxford	135	52	Herrick	Edmond	1	1		1		3	2		1				9		
Methuen	153	46	Herrick	George D.	1	1		1					1				4		
Newburyport	168	39	Herrick	Hannah Wido	1	1						1	1				4		
Boxford	135	22	Herrick	Israel		1		1	1		1		2	1			7		
Beverly	290	11	Herrick	James				1		1			1				3		
Beverly	296	19	Herrick	James Jr	1		1			3			1	1			7		
Beverly	294	9	Herrick	John	1		1						1				3		
Gloucester	56	29	Herrick	Joseph				1						1			2		
Gloucester	56	30	Herrick	Joseph Junr			1						1				2		
Wenham	307	9	Herrick	Joshua		1	1	1		1	1		1				6		
Beverly	296	22	Herrick	Lemmon			1			1	1		1				4		
Beverly	292	7	Herrick	Mary			1							1			2		
Boxford	135	2	Herrick	Nathll	1	1		1		4			1				8		
Salem	207	50	Herrick	Peter			1	1		2			1				5		
Gloucester	56	38	Herrick	Richard	2			1					1				4		
Beverly	292	8	Herrick	Thomas	2		1	1			1		1				6		
Methuen	153	45	Herrick	Thomas					1			1		1	1		5		
Gloucester	56	36	Herrick	Thos			1				1	1		1			4		
Beverly	292	31	Herrick	William		1	2		1				1	1			6		
Beverly	298	27	Herrick	William 2d	2	1	2	1			1	1	1				9		
Gloucester	56	31	Herrick	Willm A.		2		1		3			2				8		
Ipswich	282	17	Herriden	Sarah			1	1				1	1	1			5		
Bradford	125	36	Herriman	Enoch	2	1		1		2			1				7		
Rowley	127	2	Herriman	Enoch			1	1					1	1	1		5		
Boxford	134	12	Herriman	Jereh		1	1		1	1		1	2	1			8		
Rowley	128	2	Herriman	Jonathn		1	2						1	1			5		
Bradford	125	24	Herriman	Nathll	1			1		1			1				4		
Bradford	125	22	Herriman	Samll				1					1	1			3		
Rowley	128	3	Herriman	Samll		1		1					1	1			4		
Gloucester	76	10	Herring	Thos	1			1		2	1		1				6		
Danvers	6	39	Herrod	Ezra	1				1	3	2		1				8		
Danvers	14	10	Herrod	Jonathan				1						1			2		
Lynnfield	236	24	Hewes	John	1	2	2		1			1		1			8		
Gloucester	59	25	Hibbard	Jacob	2		1	1		1	3	1					9		
Bradford	123	13	Hibbart	Thomas				1		2			1				4		
Methuen	154	12	Hibberd	Ebenezer		1		1	1	1			1	1			6		
Methuen	154	9	Hibberd	John		1		1		1		1	1	2			7		
Methuen	154	11	Hibberd	Nathl	1	1		1				2	3	1			9		
Methuen	154	10	Hibberd	William		1		1					3	1			6		
Salem	183	9	Hibbert	Eliza									2				2		
Salem	218	14	Hice	Sarah	2						1	1	1				5		
Marblehead	269	31	Hichings	Nancy									1				1		
Haverhill	147	1	Hickey	Volentine		1	1	1					1				4		
Newbury	112	37	Hidden	Anny		1							1	1			3		
Newburyport	168	5	Hidden	David			1			1			2				4		
Newbury	112	38	Hidden	Icabod	1		1						1				3		
Newburyport	168	4	Hidden	John	1					1							4		

TOWN	PG#	LN#	LAST NAME	FIRST NAME	FREE WHITE MALES					FREE WHITE FEMALES					TOTAL ALL OTHER	TOTAL SLAVES	TOTALS	DISTRICT/ TOWNSHIP	NOTES
					under 10	10 to 16	16 to 26	26 to 45	45 and over	under 10	10 to 16	16 to 26	26 to 45	45 and over					
Wenham	309	29	Higgans	Timothy		1	1	1			1		1				5		
Gloucester	75	13	Higgens	Edward	1	1	1		1		1	2	1				8		
Newburyport	168	35	Higgins	Josiah	2			1		1			1				5		
Salem	195	37	Higginson	Mehita						1			1	1			3		
Marblehead	259	31	High	John			1		1		1			1			4		
Danvers	8	41	Hilbert	Nathan			1			1		1					3		
Danvers	10	1	Hilbert	William			4					1					5		
Danvers	12	20	Hilbert	William	1		1	1		1		1					5		
Methuen	154	4	Hildrith	Samuel	1	1	1		1	1	1	1		1			8		
Marblehead	269	23	Hiler	Samuel		1		1		1			1				4		
Manchester	51	35	Hill	Benja			1			1			1				3		
Haverhill	147	16	Hill	Edmund				1						1			2		
Beverly	299	18	Hill	Eliza	2		1			2	2	1	2				10		
Haverhill	147	11	Hill	George W.	2	1	1			1		1					6		
Andover	96	1	Hill	John	3		1	1		1	2		1				9		
Manchester	51	33	Hill	John				1		2		2					5		
Newbury	107	7	Hill	Josiah	3	1	5	3		1			3				16		
Manchester	51	36	Hill	Margt Wo								1		1			2		
Haverhill	147	14	Hill	Nathll		1	1					1		1			4		
Beverly	294	30	Hill	Peter	1	1			1	2			1	1			7		
Manchester	51	32	Hill	Sarah Wo	1									1			2		
Newbury	107	27	Hill	Thomas			1					1	1				3		
Andover	96	35	Hill	William	1			1						1			3		
Salem	197	39	Hill	Prince											5		5		
Marblehead	270	31	Hiller	Thomas	2	1		1					1				5		
Marblehead	263	28	Hilliard	George	2			1		1			1				5		
Salem	192	38	Hilliard	Marg									1	1			2		
Newburyport	167	44	Hillier	Caleb	1		1	1		1			1				5		
Newburyport	167	39	Hillier	Edward	2	1		1		2			1				7		
Newburyport	167	43	Hillier	Joshua			2						1				3		
Salem	199	35	Hillor	Joseph		1			1		1	5		1			9		
Newbury	115	33	Hills	Amos	1			1	1	3			1				7		
Newbury	116	7	Hills	Benja	2		1		1	3	2		1				10		
Newbury	118	34	Hills	Benja	2				1	1	3	1	1				9		
Newbury	107	19	Hills	Eliphalet		1							1	1			4		
Newbury	118	31	Hills	Josiah				1	1					3			5		
Newbury	115	32	Hills	Nath	1		2		1	1	1	1	1				8		
Newbury	119	44	Hills	Obediah	3	1	1		1	1	2	2	1				12		
Newbury	107	20	Hills	William			1	1						1			3		
Manchester	51	34	Hilton	Abig Wo	1	1	1			1			1				5		
Manchester	51	37	Hilton	Aphice Wo	1	1						1		1			4		
Beverly	295	26	Hilton	Benjamin			1			2		1	1	1			6		
Beverly	303	12	Hilton	Hale			1										1		
Manchester	51	29	Hilton	Hilton				1		2	2	2	1				8		
Manchester	51	25	Hilton	Nathl Jun	1		1			1		1					4		
Manchester	51	27	Hilton	Nathll Jun		1		1		1	1			1			5		
Marblehead	240	9	Hilton	Richard				1						1			2		
Manchester	51	24	Hilton	Susa Wo										1			1		
Ipswich	277	28	Hinderson	Thomas	2				1				1	1			5		
Newburyport	167	19	Hindson	Henry		2			2		1	1		2			8		
Marblehead	246	10	Hine	John			2		1				1	1			5		
Amesbury	41	7	Hine	Nathan Dr		1		1	1					2			5		
Amesbury	41	8	Hine	Nathan Junr	1			1					1				3		
Marblehead	255	4	Hines	Nancy						1	1		1				3		
Marblehead	262	14	Hinkley	Joseph				1		2	2		2				7		
Salisbury	29	9	Hinkson	John			1			1		1					3		
Marblehead	252	2	Hiram	Richar			1					1					2		
Danvers	15	2	Hires	John			1		1	2			1				5		
Lynn	233	39	Hitchings	Eunice		2						1	1	1			5	West Parish	
Lynn	226	9	Hitchings	Ezra		1	1	1					1	1			6		
Lynn	230	17	Hitchings	Ezra Jr		1	1						1				3		
Lynn	230	15	Hitchings	John	3		1			2			1				7		
Lynn	233	38	Hitchings	Nathan		2			1				1	1			5	West Parish	
Lynn	224	7	Hitchings	Thos	2	2		1		3			1				9		
Salem	219	17	Hitchins	Abijah	2		1			1		1					5		
Salem	220	32	Hitchins	Abijah		5	1			1		2	1				10		
Salem	220	15	Hitchins	Nath		1		1		1	1	2	2				9		
Salem	220	27	Hitchins	Nath Jr			1			1			1				3		
Salem	215	49	Hobart	Noah	2	1		1		2	2		1				9		
Wenham	307	13	Hobb	Jonathan	1	1			1	1	1	1	1				7		
Topsfield	19	40	Hobbs	Abraham			1		1	1		3	3	1			11		
Topsfield	19	38	Hobbs	Benjamin	1	1		1		1		1		1			6		
Topsfield	19	39	Hobbs	David	1	1			2			1	1				6		
Middleton	16	31	Hobbs	Elizabeth									1				1		
Ipswich	279	16	Hobson	Clarek	5			1			1		1	1	5		13		
Rowley	131	6	Hobson	David				1				1		1			3		
Rowley	131	3	Hobson	Humphrey	2			2		1		1	1				8		
Rowley	129	7	Hobson	John				1						4			5		
Rowley	129	1	Hobson	Moses	1			1		1			1				4		
Rowley	129	29	Hobson	Moses	1	1				1			1				4		
Rowley	129	30	Hobson	Samuel	2		1	1		2			1				7		
Rowley	130	10	Hobson	Thomas	1		1			1		1	3	1			8		
Lynn	229	2	Hocker	Martha			2							1			3		
Newburyport	168	24	Hodge	James	1	1	3	1		2		1	1				10		

TOWN	PG#	LN#	LAST NAME	FIRST NAME	FWM under 10	FWM 10 to 16	FWM 16 to 26	FWM 26 to 45	FWM 45 and over	FWF under 10	FWF 10 to 16	FWF 16 to 26	FWF 26 to 45	FWF 45 and over	TOTAL ALL OTHER	TOTAL SLAVES	TOTALS	DISTRICT/TOWNSHIP	NOTES
Newburyport	168	23	Hodge	Michael		1	3		1		2	2	1	1			11		
Newburyport	168	25	Hodge	Nicolas					1				2	2			5		
Newburyport	168	26	Hodge	William			1							1			2		
Salem	217	35	Hodges	Benja		1	1		1	4	2	1	1	1			12		
Salem	217	52	Hodges	Gaml	2	1		1		2		1	1				8		
Salem	216	6	Hodges	Geo	1			1		2	1	1					6		
Salem	191	25	Hodges	Jonathan	2			1		2	2		2				9		
Salem	209	36	Hodges	Priscilla							1		1	1			3		
Ipswich	281	37	Hodgkins	Christopher				1					1	1			3		
Gloucester	59	23	Hodgkins	Jacob	2			1					1	1			5		
Newburyport	167	23	Hodgkins	Jacob		1		1					1				3		
Gloucester	71	5	Hodgkins	James	2	1	1	1					1	1			7		
Ipswich	273	23	Hodgkins	John	1			1					1				3		
Ipswich	274	25	Hodgkins	John 3d		1		1		1		1					4		
Ipswich	275	11	Hodgkins	John Junr	1	1	1	1		3	1	1	1		1		11		
Ipswich	278	39	Hodgkins	Joseph		1	2		2		1	2		1	2		11		
Gloucester	77	29	Hodgkins	Mary Wido		1	1			1		1	1				5		
Gloucester	76	6	Hodgkins	Moses	1			1		3			1				6		
Gloucester	85	6	Hodgkins	Patty Wo	1								1	1			3		
Gloucester	71	4	Hodgkins	Saml	2	1	2		1	1			1	1			9		
Ipswich	276	6	Hodgkins	Sarah									1				1		
Ipswich	278	9	Hodgkins	Sarah								2	1				3		
Ipswich	276	56	Hodgkins	Thomas	1			1		1		1	1				5		
Ipswich	277	35	Hodgkins	Thomas	1			1		3			1				6		
Gloucester	73	24	Hodgkins	Timothy		1		1		1			1	1			5	Squam Parish	
Salem	207	26	Hodgson	Saml			1			1		1					3		
Ipswich	277	58	Hodkins	Abigail		1					1	1		1			4		
Marblehead	240	31	Hodson	Peter				1									1		
Beverly	301	20	Hogins	Thomas	1	2	1	1	3	3							12		
Bradford	124	9	Holden	John	1								1	1			3		
Marblehead	255	28	Holder	Daniel	2			1					1				4		
Lynn	226	17	Holder	Richd	3		3		1	1	1		1				10		
Marblehead	255	29	Holder	Susanna									1	1			2		
Salem	217	48	Holland	Charles			1					1					2		
Ipswich	277	4	Holland	Daniel			1					1					2		
Ipswich	278	3	Holland	Hannah										1			1		
Haverhill	147	2	Holland	Joseph	1	1	1		1	1	2	1					8		
Ipswich	278	21	Holland	Richard				1				1		1			3		
Newburyport	167	42	Holland	Samuel			1					1		1			3		
Newburyport	167	41	Holland	Stephen	2	1		1		1	1	1	1				8		
Newburyport	168	36	Holliday	William			2	2					1	1			6		
Salem	191	6	Holman	Gabriel		1	1	1				1	1				5		
Salem	208	43	Holman	Robt			1						1				2		
Salem	191	7	Holman	Samuel	3		2	1		3			2	1			12		
Salem	194	4	Holman	William			2		1	1	3	2	1				10		
Salem	194	27	Holman	William Jr	1		1			2		1					5		
Ipswich	281	68	Holmes	Nathaniel	1			1		3			1				6		
Rowley	127	1	Holmes	Samuel			1		1			1		1			4		
Ipswich	281	69	Holmes	William	3			1		1		1	1				6		
Andover	96	11	Holt	Abiel					1	1				1			3		
Andover	96	7	Holt	Abiel Junr			1							1			2		
Andover	96	15	Holt	Abigail Wid	2								1				3		
Andover	96	5	Holt	Dane	1		1	1	1			1	1	1			7		
Andover	96	10	Holt	David	1		1		1			1	1	1			6		
Andover	96	25	Holt	David Junr				1						1			2		
Salem	216	51	Holt	Esther		1	2	2					1	1			7		
Andover	96	14	Holt	Ezra	1			1		1			1	1			5		
Andover	96	2	Holt	George	2	1	1	1		4	1		1				11		
Andover	96	16	Holt	Henry	2			1		1	1		1				6		
Andover	96	34	Holt	Isaac				1				1	1				3		
Andover	96	9	Holt	Isaac Junr	2			1	1	3			1	1			9		
Andover	96	27	Holt	James			1		2			1		2			6		
Andover	96	8	Holt	James Junr			1		1	2		2		1			7		
Danvers	10	10	Holt	Job				1						1			2		
Andover	96	21	Holt	John				1					1	2			4		
Andover	96	4	Holt	Jonathan				1				1							
Andover	96	6	Holt	Joseph		1		2		1		1	1				6		
Newburyport	168	34	Holt	Joseph	1			1				1					3		
Andover	96	3	Holt	Joseph Junr	2			1				1					4		
Andover	96	28	Holt	Joshua Esq	1	2		1	1				2	1			8		
Andover	96	22	Holt	Kimball		1							2				3		
Salem	194	19	Holt	Lemuel	3			1	1	1	1	2	2	1			12		
Andover	95	34	Holt	Nathanel Junr	3			1		2			1				7		
Andover	96	26	Holt	Nathl				1						1			2		
Andover	96	13	Holt	Peter		1						1	1				4		
Andover	95	33	Holt	Phebe Wid		1	2						1	1	1		6		
Andover	96	12	Holt	Timothy	1	2			1	1	2		1				8		
Andover	96	29	Holt	Zebadiah	2	2		1		1	1		1				8		
Danvers	5	6	Holt	James	2			1					1				5		
Danvers	2	1	Holten	Samuel			1		1	1		2	1				6		
Salem	213	44	Holyoke	Edwd A			1		1		1		2	1	1		7		
Boxford	135	24	Holyoke	Elizar			1	1				1		2	2		7		
Marblehead	256	11	Homan	Ambrose		1	1										2		

			HEADS OF HOUSEHOLD		FREE WHITE MALES					FREE WHITE FEMALES									
TOWN	PG#	LN#	LAST NAME	FIRST NAME	under 10	10 to 16	16 to 26	26 to 45	45 and over	under 10	10 to 16	16 to 26	26 to 45	45 and over	TOTAL ALL OTHER	TOTAL SLAVES	TOTALS	DISTRICT/ TOWNSHIP	NOTES
Marblehead	254	23	Homan	Benjamin	2			1		2			1	1			7		
Marblehead	246	12	Homan	Edward		1		1		1			1				4		
Marblehead	268	14	Homan	Edward	3	1			1			2		1			8		
Marblehead	246	11	Homan	Hannah										1			1		
Marblehead	267	20	Homan	John	3	2		1		1			1				8		
Marblehead	241	1	Homan	Nathaniel					1			2					3		
Marblehead	242	31	Homan	Richard			1	1	1		1	1		1			6		
Marblehead	246	7	Homan	Thomas	1	1		1		1	1	1	1				7		
Marblehead	258	31	Homan	William	2	2	1	1					1				7		
Ipswich	277	34	Homes	Sarah								1	1	1			3		
Salem	195	41	Homes	Sarah			1							1			2		
Salem	196	2	Homes	Willm		1		1				2	1				5		
Salem	205	31	Honeys	Israel	1			1		3	1		1				7		
Gloucester	62	17	Honners	Robert	1		4		1	1		1		1			9		
Newburyport	168	6	Honniwell	Daniel			3						1	1			5		
Newburyport	168	7	Honniwell	Richard	1			1		1		1	1	1			6		
Lynn	231	35	Hood	Abner	2	1	1			1	1	1		1			9		
Topsfield	20	38	Hood	John				1						1			2		
Topsfield	20	39	Hood	John Junr	3			1		3			1				8		
Wenham	309	1	Hood	Josiah M		1							1				2		
Lynn	226	14	Hood	Martha		1							1	1			3		
Wenham	309	4	Hood	Richard		1		1				2		1			5		
Topsfield	19	11	Hood	Samuel	2	1		1				2	1				7		
Salisbury	29	11	Hook	Anna Wd	1		1			1		3	1	1			8		
Danvers	8	32	Hook	Humphrey		1		1	1		1			1			5		
Salisbury	29	10	Hook	Jonah Capt			1	1					2	1			5		
Salem	191	22	Hook	Robert		2	1						1				4		
Salem	193	41	Hook	William	1		4						1				6		
Wenham	308	15	Hooker	John	1	1			1				1	1			5		
Marblehead	244	27	Hooker	Philip	1		1		1	3	1	2	1				10		
Marblehead	253	33	Hooper	*an	1			1		3	1	1	1				8		
Salem	208	17	Hooper	Abiel									1	1			2		
Marblehead	244	12	Hooper	Asa		1	1	1		3			1				7		
Marblehead	240	37	Hooper	Elizabeth								1		2			3		
Manchester	52	7	Hooper	Jacob		1		1	1			1		1			5		
Manchester	52	5	Hooper	John	1			1					1				3		
Marblehead	240	33	Hooper	John			1			1		2					4		
Marblehead	252	10	Hooper	John	1			1		1			1	1			5		
Marblehead	256	17	Hooper	John	1		1					1					3		
Marblehead	257	7	Hooper	John	1		1	1			2			1			6		
Marblehead	244	13	Hooper	Mary								2	1				3		
Salem	183	6	Hooper	Mary									1				1		
Marblehead	248	4	Hooper	Nathaniel	1		1	1		3	1	1	1				9		
Manchester	52	8	Hooper	Nathll	2			1		1			1				5		
Marblehead	247	15	Hooper	Phillip	1		1		1	3	1	2	1				10		
Marblehead	263	29	Hooper	Robert			1	1	1				2	2			7		
Marblehead	261	28	Hooper	Robert Junr	4			1		2	1	1	1				10		
Marblehead	247	12	Hooper	Samuel			2	1	2	1			1	1			8		
Newbury	108	22	Hooper	Stephen		1	2	1	1		1		1	2			9		
Manchester	52	4	Hooper	William					1			2					4		
Manchester	52	6	Hooper	William Jun	1				1	1			1				4		
Middleton	15	7	Hoping	John	1				1				1				3		
Salem	195	17	Hopkins	Daniel		1			1		1	1	1	1			6		
Bradford	126	8	Hopkinson	Daniel		1	1		1		1			2			6		
Bradford	125	8	Hopkinson	Ebenzr		1	1					1		1			5		
Bradford	126	9	Hopkinson	Nathll		1		1						1			3		
Bradford	125	5	Hopkinson	Silas	2	1	1	2		2		1	1	1			11		
Marblehead	260	12	Horgan	Anna		1				1			1				3		
Marblehead	253	9	Horten	Richard				1					1				2		
Marblehead	253	8	Horten	Richard Junr			1			1			1				3		
Newbury	114	21	Horton	Aaron	2			1		1	2	2					8		
Newburyport	168	12	Horton	Daniel		1	2	1				2		1			7		
Gloucester	69	20	Horton	Elijah Junr	1		1						1				3		
Salem	207	16	Horton	eo	1			1		2			1				5		
Marblehead	254	33	Horton	George	2								1				4		
Newburyport	168	9	Horton	James			2			1			1				4		
Salem	210	5	Horton	Jona	2			1					1				4		
Salem	200	37	Horton	Lemuel	1	4		1		2			1				9		
Newburyport	168	10	Horton	Obadiah					1				2	1			4		
Newburyport	169	11	Horton	Obadiah Jr	1			1		2			1				5		
Marblehead	240	5	Horton	Samuel	2		1		1	4		2	1				11		
Newburyport	168	8	Horton	Samuel	1				1			2	1				5		
Manchester	53	38	Hosman	John		1							1				2		
Manchester	51	31	Hossim	Joseph					1		1	2	1	1			6		
Manchester	52	2	Hossim	Josiah	1			1		3			1				6		
Manchester	51	23	Hossim	Willm			2		1		2		1				6		
Gloucester	59	29	Hough	Benja				1			1	2	1	1			6		
Andover	96	19	Houghton	Euclid	3	1		1		2	1		1				9		
Marblehead	251	20	Houghton	Joseph				1		1		1					3		
Newbury	108	29	House	Thomas	1				1	1				1	2		6		
Salem	219	42	Hovey	Amos				1		1		1					4		
Ipswich	277	32	Hovey	Ebenezer	2			1		1			1				5		
Ipswich	277	43	Hovey	Francis	1		1	1	1		1	3		1			9		
Beverly	305	17	Hovey	Hannah								2		1			3		
Boxford	134	1	Hovey	Hannah		1	5			1		3	2	1	1		14		

213

TOWN	PG#	LN#	LAST NAME	FIRST NAME	FREE WHITE MALES under 10	10 to 16	16 to 26	26 to 45	45 and over	FREE WHITE FEMALES under 10	10 to 16	16 to 26	26 to 45	45 and over	TOTAL ALL OTHER	TOTAL SLAVES	TOTALS	DISTRICT/ TOWNSHIP	NOTES
Topsfield	20	36	Hovey	Ivery	1	1		1				1	1				5		
Boxford	134	5	Hovey	Ivory		2			1	1	2	1					7		
Boxford	133	1	Hovey	John				1					1				2		
Boxford	133	4	Hovey	John	1		1			1		1					4		
Bradford	123	29	Hovey	John		1	1		1				1	2			6		
Boxford	134	7	Hovey	Joseph	1	1	1		1		1	3		1			9		
Boxford	133	3	Hovey	Richard				1					1	1			3		
Bradford	123	11	Hovey	Stephen			1					1					2		
Beverly	290	2	Hovey	Thomas		3	1	1				2		1			8		
Salem	210	36	Hovey	Thos		1	2		1			3		1			8		
Methuen	153	38	How	Abial		1		1					1	1			4		
Methuen	153	39	How	Abial Junr		1	1			3			1	1			6		
Middleton	17	18	How	Asa	2	1	1		1	1	1	1					9		
Newbury	111	23	How	Benjamin	1		1	1			1	1	1				6		
Beverly	302	9	How	Daniel	1	1		1		2			1	1			7		
Haverhill	146	37	How	david	2	2	2	2		1	1	2	2				14		
Middleton	17	19	How	Eunice									1				1		
Rowley	130	45	How	George			1			1			1				3		
Haverhill	147	10	How	Isaac	2	1	2	1		2	2	1	2				13		
Methuen	154	6	How	Jacob		1	1		1	2			1				6		
Methuen	153	41	How	James	1	1	1		1			2	1				9		
Methuen	153	40	How	John		1		1				1	1				4		
Methuen	154	20	How	Jonathan	1		1		1			1		1			5		
Methuen	153	36	How	Joseph				1		2	1		1	1			6		
Methuen	153	37	How	Joseph Junr	4	1		1				1	1				8		
Rowley	130	50	How	Philemon			1				1	1	1				4		
Gloucester	72	7	How	Rachel Wo						1				2			3		
Rowley	130	51	How	Reuben	2	1		1		2	1		1	1			9		
Newbury	110	9	How	Varnum	1	1	2	7		2		1	2				16		
Hamilton	285	28	Howard	Anna									1	1			2		
Lynn	233	30	Howard	Ezekiel	1	2		1		1	1			2			8	West Parish	
Salem	211	42	Howard	John	1	2	3	1		1	3	2		1			14		
Lynn	233	29	Howard	Lydia	2	2							1				5	West Parish	
Newburyport	167	34	Howard	Mary Wido			4	5		1	1		1				13		
Beverly	304	20	Howard	Moses		1						1					2		
Newbury	112	4	Howard	Nathan	1	1		1		3	1		1				8		
Lynn	234	14	Howard	Nathl		1						1					2		
Salem	188	6	Howard	Phebe									1				1		
Marblehead	261	19	Howard	Rachel						2			1				3		
Salem	190	31	Howard	Sarah						1			1				2		
Newburyport	167	33	Howard	Stephen	2	2		1		1	1		1	1			9		
Newburyport	167	35	Howard	William		1		1		1		2		1	1		7		
Newburyport	168	22	Howard	William			1			1			1				3		
Ipswich	279	45	Howe	Elenor		2				1			1	1			5		
Ipswich	279	60	Howe	Jacob		1		1					1	1			4		
Ipswich	279	47	Howe	Joseph	2			1		2			2	1			8		
Ipswich	279	48	Howe	Nathaniel		1	1	1					1				4		
Marblehead	254	6	Howe	Nathaniel			1					1					2		
Salem	200	51	Hower	Isaac											9		9		
Newbury	117	7	Howes	Amos			1			3	1	1		1			7		
Bradford	123	39	Hows	Thos	2	2	2		1	1		1	1	1			11		
Haverhill	149	6	Hoyes	Eliphalet	2			1		1			1				5		
Newbury	117	6	Hoyes	Noah			1	1				1	1				4		
Haverhill	149	5	Hoyes	Parker		2					1	2		1			6		
Newbury	115	28	Hoys	Joseph	1			1					1				3		
Amesbury	40	9	Hoyt	Aaron		1				1		1					3		
Salisbury	29	17	Hoyt	Benja Capt	2			1		1	1		1				6		
Amesbury	40	21	Hoyt	Daniel		1		1		1	2		1				6		
Amesbury	41	4	Hoyt	Daniel		1	1	1			1		1				5		
Newburyport	168	17	Hoyt	David			1						1	1			3		
Newburyport	168	20	Hoyt	Dotothy Wido			1	1				1		1	1		5		
Newburyport	168	16	Hoyt	Ebenezer		1		1		2	1		1				6		
Amesbury	40	11	Hoyt	Enoch		1							1				3		
Amesbury	40	23	Hoyt	Hannah Wid						2			1				3		
Amesbury	41	13	Hoyt	Humphrey		1		1					1				3		
Amesbury	41	14	Hoyt	Jacob	3	1		1					1				6		
Amesbury	41	11	Hoyt	Jacob Junr		1	2						1				4		
Amesbury	41	12	Hoyt	John				1					1				2		
Haverhill	147	12	Hoyt	John	2	1		1		1			1				6		
Amesbury	41	16	Hoyt	John Junr				1					1				2		
Amesbury	41	1	Hoyt	Joseph		1	1	1		3		1	1				8		
Newburyport	168	18	Hoyt	Joseph			1			1			1				3		
Amesbury	40	3	Hoyt	Joseph Capt		2	1	1		1			1				6		
Amesbury	41	15	Hoyt	Joseph Junr	1			1		2			1				5		
Amesbury	40	22	Hoyt	Judith Wid	1									1			4		
Amesbury	40	14	Hoyt	Levi		1		1		2	1	1	1				7		
Amesbury	40	10	Hoyt	Lydia Wid	1					3			1	1			6		
Amesbury	41	6	Hoyt	Matthias		1		1	1	1		1	2	1			8		
Amesbury	40	20	Hoyt	Moses		1		1		1	1		1				5		
Newburyport	168	13	Hoyt	Moses		1	1							4			7		
Salisbury	29	20	Hoyt	Moses	1	1		1		2			1	1			7		
Amesbury	40	12	Hoyt	Moses				1					1	2			4		
Newburyport	168	14	Hoyt	Moses Jr	1		1		1	1		1	1	1			7		

TOWN	PG#	LN#	LAST NAME	FIRST NAME	FREE WHITE MALES under 10	10 to 16	16 to 26	26 to 45	45 and over	FREE WHITE FEMALES under 10	10 to 16	16 to 26	26 to 45	45 and over	TOTAL ALL OTHER	TOTAL SLAVES	TOTALS	DISTRICT/ TOWNSHIP	NOTES
Amesbury	40	8	Hoyt	Moses Junr					1					1			2		
Newburyport	168	15	Hoyt	Nathan		1			1	2	3	2		2			11		
Amesbury	41	10	Hoyt	Robert			2		1				1				4		
Newbury	113	28	Hoyt	Samuel				1	1	1			1				4		
Amesbury	40	24	Hoyt	Sarah Wid		1			1				2	1			5		
Amesbury	40	7	Hoyt	Stephen		1		1		4			1				7		
Amesbury	41	5	Hoyt	Thomas Junr				1					1				2		
Amesbury	41	2	Hoyt	Timothy					1				2				3		
Amesbury	41	3	Hoyt	William			1	1					1	1			4		
Newburyport	168	19	Hoyt	William		1				1			1				3		
Amesbury	40	5	Hoyt	Willoughby					1	1	1		1				4		
Amesbury	40	30	Hoyt	Zenos	1								1				3		
Marblehead	258	17	Hubbard	*tha										1			1		
Methuen	154	1	Hubbard	Daniel	1			1		2		1		1			6		
Marblehead	242	4	Hubbard	Ebenezer Revd	3	2		1		1	2		2				11		
Salisbury	29	12	Hubbard	Joseph			1						1	1			3		
Marblehead	243	18	Hubbard	Ruth									1	1			2		
Marblehead	258	19	Hubbard	Sarah										1			1		
Gloucester	70	9	Hubbard	Sarah Wo			2							1			5		
Salem	203	8	Huddle	William		1					2	1					4		
Gloucester	64	27	Hudgen	John G.	1	1	2	1	1		2	3	1				12		
Lynn	231	4	Hudson	Benj	4	2		1		1		1	1				10		
Lynn	231	8	Hudson	Hannah										1			1		
Lynn	231	6	Hudson	Jona	1		1	1		2			1				6		
Gloucester	69	23	Huffon	Cathr Widw									1	1			2		
Marblehead	243	14	Hulen	Elias				1				1		1			3		
Marblehead	242	29	Hulen	John	3	1		1		1	1		1				8		
Beverly	291	41	Hull	Isaac	2		1	1		2	1		1				8		
Salem	214	45	Hull	John	3	1		1		2		1	1				9		
Amesbury	40	13	Hull	Stephen Revd	1		1						2				4		
Beverly	292	1	Hull	Theophilus				1				2		1			4		
Marblehead	245	25	Humphreys	Amos	3	1		1		1	1		1				8		
Marblehead	261	21	Humphries	Hannah	1		1			1	2			1			6		
Marblehead	266	16	Humphries	John	1	1		1		4	2	1	1				11		
Marblehead	261	22	Humphries	Samuel			1						1				2		
Marblehead	247	26	Humphries	Sarah									1	1			2		
Haverhill	146	36	Hunkins	David	3	2		1			1	2	1				10		
Haverhill	146	35	Hunkins	Jonathan	1		1	1				3		2			8		
Amesbury	40	15	Hunniford	John	1			1					1				3		
Andover	96	36	Hunt	Anna Wid			1							1			2		
Newbury	113	2	Hunt	Bart	2		1						1				4		
Ipswich	277	14	Hunt	Deborah									1				1		
Newbury	111	41	Hunt	Elias	3	1			1	1	2		1	1			10		
Newburyport	167	25	Hunt	Elizabeth Wido	1		5	5		2	4	3	1	1			22		
Marblehead	270	20	Hunt	Job	1	1		1		3			1				7		
Salem	190	43	Hunt	John				1		2			1				4		
Newbury	113	36	Hunt	Josiah	1			1		1			1	1			5		
Salem	213	53	Hunt	Lydia		1	2	1				3	1	1			9		
Salem	203	18	Hunt	Mary		2	3			3		2	1				11		
Amesbury	40	4	Hunt	Merriam Wid								1	1				2		
Newbury	113	4	Hunt	Nathl	2		1			1	1	1					6		
Andover	96	30	Hunt	Reul			1		1		1	1	1				5		
Salem	203	19	Hunt	Sarah										1			1		
Salem	219	52	Hunt	Thos		1				3			1				6		
Newburyport	167	24	Hunt	Zebedee		1	1	1		1	1			1			6		
Amesbury	40	28	Huntington	Amos		1		1					2	1			5		
Topsfield	21	13	Huntington	Asahel Revd	3			1		1	1	1	1				8		
Amesbury	40	26	Huntington	David	1			2					1				4		
Amesbury	40	25	Huntington	Elijah	2	1		1		3	1		1				9		
Amesbury	40	29	Huntington	Isaac				1					1	1			3		
Amesbury	40	27	Huntington	John				1				1	3	1			6		
Amesbury	40	18	Huntington	Moses	2			1				1	1				5		
Amesbury	40	16	Huntington	Willm		2	1	1					1				5		
Amesbury	40	17	Huntington	Willm Junr			1			1			1				3		
Beverly	300	14	Hurly	Abigail	1		1					1		1			4		
Newbury	118	6	Huse	Amos	2	1		1		1			1	1			7		
Methuen	154	5	Huse	Daniel				1			1		1				3		
Gloucester	72	25	Huse	John	2			1	1	2	1		1				8		
Haverhill	146	44	Huse	John	2			1		1			1				5		
Methuen	154	2	Huse	John		1	2	1	1		1	2		4			12		
Newburyport	167	20	Huse	Joseph	1		2	1		1			1				6		
Newbury	111	18	Huse	Samuel	1			1		2		1	1				6		
Newburyport	167	22	Huse	Samuel	2	1	5	1		2			1				12		
Methuen	154	3	Huse	Stephen	1	1		1		1		1	1				6		
Newburyport	167	21	Huse	William	2			1			1		2	1			7		
Gloucester	79	30	Hustens	Saml	2			1		3			1				7		
Gloucester	67	14	Hutching	Benja				1		1			1				3		
Gloucester	64	28	Hutchings	Willm Capt	2	1	1	1			2	2	1				10		
Gloucester	67	15	Hutchins	Rachal Wo			1							1			2		
Danvers	6	11	Hutchinson	Abijah			1						1				2		
Salem	220	6	Hutchinson	Benja	5			1					1				7		
Danvers	6	6	Hutchinson	Ebenezer	2			1		1			1				5		
Danvers	9	13	Hutchinson	Israel					1			1		2			4		
Danvers	9	14	Hutchinson	Israel Junr	2	1		1		3	2		1				10		
Danvers	6	5	Hutchinson	Jeremiah			1	1	1				2				5		

TOWN	PG#	LN#	LAST NAME	FIRST NAME	FREE WHITE MALES					FREE WHITE FEMALES					TOTAL ALL OTHER	TOTAL SLAVES	TOTALS	DISTRICT/ TOWNSHIP	NOTES
					under 10	10 to 16	16 to 26	26 to 45	45 and over	under 10	10 to 16	16 to 26	26 to 45	45 and over					
Danvers	6	10	Hutchinson	Job		1	2					1		1			5		
Danvers	3	8	Hutchinson	John	1		1	1	1	2		1	1	1			9		
Salem	197	14	Hutchinson	John		1			1	1	1	1					5		
Middleton	15	1	Hutchinson	Joseph		1	1	1		3			1				7		
Middleton	15	4	Hutchinson	Josiah	2	1		1		1			1				6		
Middleton	15	2	Hutchinson	Keziah								1		1			2		
Salem	220	7	Hutchinson	Margt			1					2		1			4		
Danvers	5	10	Hutnam	Matthew		1	1	1		4		1		1			9		
Salem	209	5	Hutson	John		1		1		2		2	1				7		
Salem	190	40	Hyer	Elias			1				1	2	1				5		
Newburyport	169	19	Ilsley	David	1			1		1			1				4		
Newbury	115	1	Ilsley	Isaiah		2		1		1	1		1				6		
Newbury	116	3	Ilsley	Jonathan		2			1			2	1				6		
Newbury	115	2	Ilsley	Joshua	2		1						1				4		
Newbury	115	3	Ilsley	Stephen			1						1	1			3		
Gloucester	59	32	Indersol	William	1	1		1				1	1				5		
Newburyport	169	10	Ingalls	Ann Wido	1		1	1		1			1				5		
Salem	201	9	Ingalls	Collins	3			1		2	1		1				8		
Haverhill	147	23	Ingalls	Henry	2		1		1		1	1		1			7		
Methuen	154	21	Ingalls	James	1		1	1	1	3			2				9		
Salem	202	45	Ingalls	James	2	1		1		1	1		1				7		
Marblehead	266	5	Ingalls	John		1		1				1	1	1			5		
Gloucester	65	1	Ingalls	Joseph	1	1		1		1	1		1				6		
Marblehead	269	19	Ingalls	Mary			1						1	1			3		
Newburyport	169	11	Ingalls	Susannah Wido		1	1					1		2			5		
Marblehead	244	23	Ingalls	Thomas	1	1		1		1			1				5		
Marblehead	247	16	Ingalls	Thomas	1	1		1		1			1				5		
Marblehead	263	32	Ingalls	Thomas	1	1		1		1			1				5		
Salem	201	26	Ingalls	Thos			1	1						1			3		
Marblehead	261	5	Ingalls	William			1			2		1					4		
Lynn	227	2	Ingals	Abner	3		1						2				6		
Lynn	226	41	Ingals	Amos				1									1		
Lynn	227	23	Ingals	Edmd	1			1		3	1		1				7		
Lynn	231	40	Ingals	Edmd Junr	3			1		1	1		1				7		
Lynn	231	34	Ingals	Eleazr			1	1				1	1	1			5		
Andover	97	18	Ingals	Elizabeth Wid										2			2		
Andover	97	26	Ingals	Ezra		1	1					1					3		
Andover	97	15	Ingals	Henry		1	1	1				1	1	1	1		7		
Lynn	226	39	Ingals	Henry	4	1		1		1	1		1				9		
Andover	97	20	Ingals	Hutchinson	1			1				4	1				7		
Andover	97	28	Ingals	Isaac				1					1				2		
Lynn	227	22	Ingals	Jacob	1	1		1					1				4		
Andover	97	16	Ingals	John		1		1	1				2	1			6		
Lynn	231	12	Ingals	John	2		1	1		2	2		1				9		
Lynn	227	28	Ingals	Jona			1	1		3			1				6		
Andover	97	17	Ingals	Jonathan	2			1		1		1	1				6		
Andover	97	19	Ingals	Lydia Wid								2	1	1			4		
Lynn	227	24	Ingals	Nathl				1					1				2		
Lynn	227	25	Ingals	Nathl Junr	2			1		1			1				5		
Lynn	227	26	Ingals	Rebekah	1	1				1			1				4		
Middleton	17	23	Ingals	Theodor	2	2	1						1				6		
Gloucester	84	2	Ingersol	Andrew	1	1		1		2	1		1				7		
Gloucester	69	19	Ingersol	Robt Wo		1				1			2				4		
Beverly	303	32	Ingersol	Samuel	2	2		1	1		1	2	1	1			11		
Gloucester	70	24	Ingersol	Samuel	2	1		1		2	1	1					10		
Salem	220	9	Ingersol	Samuel			1	1			1	1		1			5		
Haverhill	147	30	Ingersol	Zebulon		1		1		1	3		1				7		
Gloucester	69	11	Ingersol	Lydia Wo		1	2					1		1			5		
Gloucester	66	12	Ingersole	Abigail Wo		1	1					1	1				4		
Gloucester	62	15	Ingersole	David	1			1		1			1				4		
Danvers	2	3	Ingersoll	Jonathan	1		2	2	1		1	1	2				10		
Ipswich	276	45	Ingersoll	Jonathan				1				1		1			3		
Salem	213	1	Inglish	Andrew		1		1		1	1		1				5		
Salem	213	11	Inglish	Phillip				1		1	1		1				4		
Salem	194	34	Ireland	Jona	1		1		1	1	2		1				7		
Salem	201	4	Ireland	Jona	1	2	2			2	1	1					9		
Salem	205	30	Ireland	Samuel	1					1			1				3		
Lynn	227	17	Ireson	Benj	1	1	3	1		4	2		1				13		
Lynn	227	18	Ireson	Edwd		1						1					2		
Marblehead	257	5	Ireson	Elizabeth									1				1		
Lynn	226	37	Ireson	John Junr	3	1		1					1	1			7		
Marblehead	263	33	Ireson	Joseph	2	1		1		3			1				8		
Marblehead	249	27	Ireson	Robert	1			1		1			1				4		
Lynn	227	16	Ireson	Saml		2	1	1		1		1	1	1			8		
Rowley	129	21	Iselley	Thomas				1						1			2		
Newbury	117	19	Isley	Ansel	2			1		4	2		1	2			12		
Newbury	118	35	Isley	Jonathan		2		1		2			1				6		
Newbury	117	18	Isley	Paul	2			1				1		1			5		
Newbury	117	9	Isley	Stephen			1	1				1		1			4		
Beverly	304	29	Ives	Eliza		1					1	1		2			5		
Salem	200	1	Ives	William	2		1					1	1	1			6		
Marblehead	255	17	Iveson	Benjamin			1						1				2		
Rowley	128	15	Jackman	Anna										1			1		
Newbury	114	24	Jackman	Benja	1			1	1				1				4		
Rowley	128	17	Jackman	Benja			3		1	1		1		1			7		

216

TOWN	PG#	LN#	LAST NAME	FIRST NAME	FREE WHITE MALES					FREE WHITE FEMALES					TOTAL ALL OTHER	TOTAL SLAVES	TOTALS	DISTRICT/ TOWNSHIP	NOTES
					under 10	10 to 16	16 to 26	26 to 45	45 and over	under 10	10 to 16	16 to 26	26 to 45	45 and over					
Newburyport	169	14	Jackman	Benjamin	1			1					1				3		
Newbury	109	21	Jackman	David			4	1					3	1			9		
Salisbury	29	26	Jackman	Eleanor Wd						1	1		1				3		
Newbury	109	17	Jackman	Elias	2	1		1		2		1	1				8		
Newbury	114	15	Jackman	Hannah		1				1		2					4		
Newbury	109	11	Jackman	John				1			1			2			4		
Salisbury	29	25	Jackman	Levi		1		1		2			1				5		
Newbury	109	15	Jackman	Matthias	2		1			2		1					6		
Salisbury	29	24	Jackman	Nathl		1		1					1				3		
Newbury	109	30	Jackman	Richard	1		1	1		2		1	1				7		
Newbury	109	18	Jackman	Stephen	1	1			1		1	1		1			6		
Bradford	125	27	Jackman	Timothy		1	1		1	1		1		1			6		
Newbury	114	13	Jackman	William	2	1		1		1	1		1				7		
Newburyport	169	12	Jackson	Abraham			2		1	3		3	1				10		
Rowley	130	19	Jackson	Caleb	1	1		1		1	1	1					6		
Newburyport	169	13	Jackson	Charles			1			1	1	1					4		
Marblehead	241	23	Jackson	Elizabeth	1	2							1				4		
Lynn	231	31	Jackson	George	1			1		1			1				4		
Marblehead	241	24	Jackson	George				1						1			2		
Salem	193	16	Jackson	John											3		3		
Salem	197	8	Jackson	Joseph	2	2		1		1			1				7		
Boxford	135	10	Jackson	Joshua				1				1	1				3		
Danvers	10	7	Jacobs	Daniel				1						1			2		
Danvers	10	4	Jacobs	Ebenezer	2	2		1				1	1	1			8		
Danvers	10	3	Jacobs	Elizabeth		1				1				1			3		
Danvers	7	19	Jacobs	Henry				1						1			2		
Danvers	7	20	Jacobs	John	1		1	1		2		1	1				7		
Newburyport	169	23	Jacobs	Mary Wido		1				2		1					4		
Danvers	15	11	Jacobs	Primas											4		4		
Newbury	107	2	Jacquish	Samuel	1		1	1		3		2	1	1			10		
Marblehead	254	27	James	Mary		1	1					1	1				4		
Marblehead	250	12	James	Richard				1					1				2		
Salem	197	18	James	Sam											5		5		
Salem	193	30	Janes	John	2		1				1		1				5		
Salem	193	29	Janes	Mary	1	2	2			3	1		1	1			11		
Salem	197	35	Jant	Jona				1					1				2		
Danvers	5	39	Jaques	Nathan			1			3			1				5		
Newburyport	169	21	Jaques	Theophilus	2			1	1	2	1	1	1				9		
Bradford	125	43	Jaquish	Benja		1	1	1				2	1				6		
Newbury	120	9	Jaquish	Enoch	1			1		1	1	1					5		
Newbury	120	8	Jaquish	Joseph	1			1	1			1		1			5		
Newbury	106	35	Jaquish	Moses	1	1			1				4				7		
Bradford	125	44	Jaquish	Noyce	1			1		3			1				6		
Newbury	106	32	Jaquish	Parker			1		1			1	2				5		
Newbury	115	5	Jaquith	Eliphelet					1								1		
Newbury	114	45	Jaquith	Enos		1			1			1	1				4		
Newbury	114	43	Jaquith	John			1	1				1		1			4		
Newbury	115	6	Jaquith	Parker		1	1	1		2	1	1		1			8		
Newbury	115	14	Jaquith	Richard		1		1					1				3		
Newbury	116	24	Jaquith	Stephen	2	1	1	1		2		1	1	1			10		
Newbury	116	37	Jaquith	Stephen		1		1				2	1				5		
Marblehead	247	28	Jarvis	John	3			1		1	1	1	1				8		
Marblehead	263	30	Jarvis	John	3			1		1	1		1				7		
Marblehead	263	31	Jarvis	Manjural	1								1				2		
Salem	220	18	Jefferds	John			1						1				2		
Salem	218	6	Jeffrey	Walter P			1			2	1		1				5		
Salem	206	56	Jeffry	James				2				1		1			4		
Gloucester	85	26	Jeffs	Joseph		1	1			2	1	1	1				7		
Gloucester	73	8	Jeffs	Thos				1						1			2		
Ipswich	276	32	Jefts	John	1		3					1					5		
Salem	218	3	Jenkins	Abigail									1				1		
Andover	97	11	Jenkins	Benja	1	2	1	1		1	1	1					8		
Andover	97	24	Jenkins	Benja Jr	2		2	1		1		1	1				8		
Newburyport	169	16	Jenkins	George		1		1		1		2					5		
Andover	97	12	Jenkins	Joel	2	1	1		1	1	1	1		1			9		
Newburyport	169	15	Jenkins	John			1		1			1	1				4		
Salem	194	11	Jenkins	John				1					1				2		
Newbury	113	48	Jenkins	Lenord				1				1	1				3		
Newburyport	169	17	Jenkins	Mary Wido							1	2	1				4		
Newbury	113	42	Jenkins	Robert	2			1					1				4		
Newburyport	169	18	Jenkins	Ruth Wido						1		1	1				3		
Andover	97	10	Jenkins	Samuel		2							3	1			6		
Salem	216	9	Jenkins	Wm			1			2	1		1				5		
Salem	206	48	Jenks	Daniel			1				1	3	1				6		
Salem	203	2	Jenks	John				1						1			2		
Salem	206	37	Jenks	John		1	1	1		3	2	2	1	1			12		
Bradford	124	8	Jennings	John	4			1		1				1			7		
Methuen	154	23	Jennings	Solomon				1		4			1	1			7		
Newbury	113	24	Jester	Anny								1	1				2		
Rowley	130	5	Jewet	Daniel	1			1					1	1			4		
Rowley	130	7	Jewet	George			1			1			2				4		
Rowley	129	12	Jewet	Jacob	1			1		2	2		2				8		
Rowley	128	16	Jewet	Jeremiah		2		1		1	1		1				6		
Rowley	130	4	Jewet	John				1					1				2		
Rowley	128	34	Jewet	Jonathan	1			1		1			1				4		
Rowley	129	35	Jewet	Jonathn			1				1	3	1	1			7		

TOWN	PG#	LN#	HEADS OF HOUSEHOLD		FREE WHITE MALES					FREE WHITE FEMALES					TOTAL ALL OTHER	TOTAL SLAVES	TOTALS	DISTRICT/ TOWNSHIP	NOTES
			LAST NAME	FIRST NAME	under 10	10 to 16	16 to 26	26 to 45	45 and over	under 10	10 to 16	16 to 26	26 to 45	45 and over					
Rowley	131	37	Jewet	Joseh				1	1				1	1			4		
Rowley	129	8	Jewet	Joseph	2	1	1		1	1		1		1			8		
Rowley	128	42	Jewet	Maximillion		1	1				1	2	1	1			8		
Rowley	131	28	Jewet	Nehemiah	1		2	2	1	1			1	1			9		
Rowley	131	17	Jewet	Paul		1	1		1	1		1	1	1			7		
Rowley	128	38	Jewet	William	1	2	1						1	1			6		
Ipswich	273	9	Jewett	Aaron			2		1	2		1	1				7		
Ipswich	273	10	Jewett	Abigail									4				4		
Ipswich	273	16	Jewett	Abraham			1					1					2		
Ipswich	273	2	Jewett	Edward	2		1		1	1		1					5		
Ipswich	274	8	Jewett	Epes	1	2	1		1	1	1	1		1			8		
Ipswich	276	10	Jewett	John	2	1	1		1	2		1	1				8		
Ipswich	273	37	Jewett	John C.	1	2	1		1			1		1			7		
Salisbury	29	31	Jewett	Joseph	1	1	1	1			1	1					6		
Ipswich	273	13	Jewett	Katharine	1									1			2		
Ipswich	276	47	Jewett	Martha						1		1	1				3		
Ipswich	273	15	Jewett	Mehitable			1										1		
Ipswich	273	53	Jewett	Moses	2		1					1					4		
Ipswich	273	12	Jewett	Nehemiah			1		1				1				3		
Ipswich	273	11	Jewett	Nehemiah Junr			1				1						2		
Ipswich	273	14	Jewett	Purchase		1	1						1				3		
Ipswich	276	3	Jewett	Richard D.	2			1			1	1					5		
Newburyport	169	20	Jewett	Seth		1		1		1	1	1					7		
Rowley	128	28	Jewit	David		1		1		1			1				3		
Newburyport	169	22	Johns	Samuel	2			1			1	1	2				7		
Andover	97	5	Johnson	Asa	2		1		2		1	1					7		
Andover	103	19	Johnson	Benito											5		5		
Lynn	223	59	Johnson	Benj		1	1		1	1			1				5		
Lynn	223	53	Johnson	Benj B.		1	1		2			1					5		
Lynn	223	58	Johnson	Benj Jn	2			1	3			1					7		
Newbury	114	36	Johnson	Benja				1			2		1				4		
Andover	97	3	Johnson	Benjamin	2	1	1	1		1		1	2	1			10		
Marblehead	255	10	Johnson	Benjamin				1					1				2		
Marblehead	266	28	Johnson	Benoice	1	3		1		2			1				8		
Marblehead	244	19	Johnson	Benrice		2		1			1	1					5		
Newburyport	169	1	Johnson	Bradford				1					1				2		
Lynn	231	38	Johnson	Caleb		1			1		1						3		
Marblehead	267	7	Johnson	Charity	1	2							1				4		
Salem	210	2	Johnson	Charles		1					1						2		
Newburyport	169	6	Johnson	Daniel				1					1				2		
Rowley	130	2	Johnson	Daniel		2	1						3				6		
Newburyport	169	7	Johnson	Daniel C	1		2	1	2		1	1					8		
Lynn	223	14	Johnson	David	1	1	1	1			1		1				6		
Andover	97	22	Johnson	Ebenezer				1	1		1		1				4		
Andover	97	7	Johnson	Edmund		1			1		1						3		
Salem	192	19	Johnson	Edmund	2		6		1	1	1						11		
Salem	183	19	Johnson	Edward		1		1	1	2	1	1					7		
Newburyport	169	2	Johnson	Eleazer		1					1						2		
Newburyport	169	3	Johnson	Eleazer Jr	1	2	2				2						7		
Haverhill	147	29	Johnson	Elias		1		1	2			2	1				7		
Salem	198	36	Johnson	Elijah	1	2			1	3			1				8		
Lynn	226	1	Johnson	Enoch	2		1	1		1			1				6		
Salem	219	53	Johnson	Geo	1			1		2			1				5		
Haverhill	147	27	Johnson	Hannah		1				1			1				3		
Lynn	226	34	Johnson	Hannah			1			1				1			3		
Newburyport	169	4	Johnson	Isaac		1		1		1	1		1				5		
Andover	97	25	Johnson	Jacob	1		1		1				2	1			6		
Andover	97	27	Johnson	James	1				1			1	1				4		
Lynnfield	236	19	Johnson	James				1				1	1				3		
Salem	198	34	Johnson	Jedih	1	1	1	1			1	2	1				8		
Newburyport	169	8	Johnson	Joanna Wido								2	2				4		
Gloucester	59	33	Johnson	John	1		2					1	1				5		
Haverhill	147	26	Johnson	John	2		1			1	1		1				6		
Middleton	16	21	Johnson	John	3		1		2	1	1						8		
Newbury	111	43	Johnson	John	2		1		1		1	1					6		
Newburyport	168	43	Johnson	John B	1		1					1					3		
Haverhill	147	28	Johnson	John Jur		1			1		1						3		
Lynn	223	60	Johnson	John L	3	1		1		1		2					8		
Lynn	231	37	Johnson	Jona		1		1					1				3		
Newburyport	169	5	Johnson	Joseph		1	1		1			3		1			7		
Lynn	223	62	Johnson	Joseph	1	1		1		2	1		1				7		
Lynn	231	39	Johnson	Joseph Junr		1		1		2		1	1				6		
Andover	97	4	Johnson	Joshua	3	1	1	1		1	1		1				9		
Andover	97	23	Johnson	Mary		1					1		1				3		
Salem	183	8	Johnson	Micajah	4			1		2			1	1			9		
Rowley	130	6	Johnson	Moses		1							1				2		
Haverhill	147	25	Johnson	Nathll	3		1	1				1					6		
Rowley	129	51	Johnson	Nathll	3		2	1		1	3		1				11		
Newburyport	168	41	Johnson	Nicolas	4	1	1		1		2	3		1			13		
Andover	97	2	Johnson	Peter		1		1					1				3		
Newburyport	168	42	Johnson	Philip	1		1			2			1				6		
Andover	97	29	Johnson	Phillip	3	1			1	1	1		1				8		
Salem	190	44	Johnson	Polly	2					2		1					5		

TOWN	PG#	LN#	HEADS OF HOUSEHOLD		FREE WHITE MALES					FREE WHITE FEMALES					TOTAL ALL OTHER	TOTAL SLAVES	TOTALS	DISTRICT/ TOWNSHIP	NOTES
			LAST NAME	FIRST NAME	under 10	10 to 16	16 to 26	26 to 45	45 and over	under 10	10 to 16	16 to 26	26 to 45	45 and over					
Lynn	223	15	Johnson	Richard				1					1				2		
Lynn	223	64	Johnson	Saml	2	1	1	2				2	1	1			10		
Bradford	123	33	Johnson	Samll				1					1				2		
Andover	97	1	Johnson	Samuel		1		1	1				4	1			8		
Andover	97	6	Johnson	Samuel Jr	1			1					1				3		
Andover	97	8	Johnson	Stephen				1						1			2		
Middleton	15	20	Johnson	Tabitha								1	1	2	1		5		
Haverhill	147	24	Johnson	Thomas	4		1				1		1				7		
Bradford	124	43	Johnson	Thos				1		2		1	1				5		
Lynn	223	63	Johnson	Timy	2		1			1			1				5		
Andover	97	21	Johnson	William	2		2	1		3	1		2				11		
Danvers	8	43	Johnson	William	2		1			1	1		1				6		
Danvers	12	17	Johnson	William			1					1					2		
Newburyport	169	9	Johnson	William		1		1		1	1		1				5		
Newburyport	168	40	Johnson	William P	2	2	1	1				3		1			10		
Haverhill	147	31	Johnston	John		1		1				3	1				6		
Salem	189	32	Johnston	Jonathan				1					1	1			3		
Amesbury	41	20	Jones	Abner		1	1	2		1			1	1			7		
Ipswich	283	37	Jones	Abraham		1				1		1					3		
Newburyport	169	26	Jones	Abraham			1						1	1			3		
Gloucester	62	28	Jones	Agnes Wo	1					1			1				4		
Gloucester	75	7	Jones	Ambrose		2		1		1	4		1				9		
Ipswich	278	36	Jones	Amos		1							1				2		
Manchester	51	4	Jones	Benja			1			1			1				3		
Beverly	302	28	Jones	David	1			1		3	2		1	1			9		
Amesbury	41	18	Jones	Ezekiel				1					1	1			3		
Amesbury	41	17	Jones	Ezekiel Junr			1	1					1				3		
Salem	213	31	Jones	Hannah	1	1				1			2	1			6		
Andover	97	9	Jones	Jacob		1	1	1					2	1			6		
Marblehead	260	35	Jones	James	1			1		1	1		1				5		
Methuen	154	22	Jones	James			1	1		1		2	1	1			7		
Gloucester	59	31	Jones	Joseph	1			1		2			1	1			6		
Manchester	52	3	Jones	Mary									1				1		
Marblehead	270	24	Jones	Mary									1				1		
Salisbury	29	30	Jones	Merrill	2			1		1			1				5		
Andover	97	13	Jones	Nathan	2			1		2	1		1				7		
Ipswich	275	37	Jones	Nathaniel				1						1			2		
Lynn	223	55	Jones	Nathl	1			1					1				3		
Amesbury	41	19	Jones	Philip		1		1		2		1	1				6		
Newburyport	169	24	Jones	Reuben			1						1				2		
Salisbury	29	29	Jones	Richd	1	1		1					1				4		
Newburyport	169	25	Jones	Samuel		2		1					1	1			5		
Marblehead	255	22	Jones	Sarah	1	1							2	1			5		
Ipswich	278	35	Jones	Thomas					1	1			1	1			4		
Danvers	13	10	Jones	William	2			1		1			1				5		
Salem	209	8	Joplin	Mary	1			1		2		1	1	1			7		
Andover	97	14	Jordan	Richard		1		1				1	1				4		
Gloucester	85	10	Joseph	Dorcas Wid	1					1			1				3		
Salem	202	13	Joseph	Fras		1				1		1					3		
Salem	207	34	Joseph	John	1	1				1			1				4		
Gloucester	68	12	Joseph	Mathew			1			1			1	1			4		
Danvers	9	39	Josling	John	1	1		1		4	2		1				10		
Salisbury	29	27	Joy	Benja				1						2			3		
Salisbury	29	28	Joy	Benja Junr		1		2					1				5		
Salisbury	29	23	Joy	David				1						1			2		
Salem	212	40	Joy	Joseph	2	1		1					1				5		
Gloucester	77	12	Jumper	Joseph		1	1	1		2	2	1	1				9		
Gloucester	83	26	Jumper	William				1		2	3		1				7		
Gloucester	74	26	Jusomin	Peter			1						1				2		
Newbury	117	4	Kal*sh	Moses		1				1	1						3		
Salem	188	41	Kane	Eliza		2				1			1				4		
Marblehead	250	27	Kanpp	Samuel	2			1		1			1				5		
Salem	193	10	Karns	Samuel	1	1	1					1	1				5		
Danvers	8	34	Karr	James				1		1	1		1				4		
Danvers	8	33	Karr	James Junr	1			1					1				3		
Salem	201	49	Keeton	Francis												5	5		
Newburyport	170	7	Keezer	Eleazer			1			2			2	1			6		
Newburyport	170	8	Keezer	Nathaniel	3			1		1			1				6		
Newburyport	170	22	Keiff	William	3			1					1				5		
Haverhill	148	1	Kelley	Abijah		1		1				1		1			4		
Salem	189	31	Kelley	Darkes	1	1							1	1			4		
Amesbury	41	24	Kelley	John			2	1					2	1			6		
Methuen	154	24	Kelley	John		1		1					1	1			4		
Haverhill	147	33	Kelley	Joseph		1	1	1					1	2			6		
Amesbury	41	25	Kelley	Louis			1						2	1			4		
Haverhill	147	32	Kelley	Moses	1		1			1			1				4		
Amesbury	41	26	Kelley	Stephen	1	1	3	1		1			1	1			9		
Haverhill	148	2	Kelley	Willm			1	1						1			3		
Amesbury	41	27	Kelly	Anthony	1	1		1	1	1		1	1	1			8		
Marblehead	247	20	Kelly	John	1	1				1		1	1				6		
Newbury	108	4	Kelly	Nathan	1			1					1				3		
Salem	196	14	Kempton	Eliza								2	1				3		
Salem	188	7	Kendal	Abm	2	1	2										6		

TOWN	PG#	LN#	LAST NAME	FIRST NAME	FWM under 10	FWM 10 to 16	FWM 16 to 26	FWM 26 to 45	FWM 45 and over	FWF under 10	FWF 10 to 16	FWF 16 to 26	FWF 26 to 45	FWF 45 and over	TOTAL ALL OTHER	TOTAL SLAVES	TOTALS	DISTRICT/ TOWNSHIP	NOTES
Haverhill	147	44	Kendal	Asaph	2			1		1		1	1				6		
Gloucester	78	16	Kendal	Jona	2			1					1	1			5		
Andover	98	11	Kendall	Ephraim	3	2			1	1	1	2	1				11		
Salem	197	9	Kendinson	Joseph	3	2	1	1		2	1		1				11		
Haverhill	147	41	Kendrick	Abner	2			1	1	2		1	1				8		
Haverhill	147	40	Kendrick	John	5			1					1				7		
Amesbury	41	28	Kendrick	Seth			1		1			2	1	1			6		
Salem	189	16	Kenfield	Eliz	1					3		1	1				6		
Salem	201	31	Kenfield	Peter				1				1	1				3		
Salem	214	50	Kennedy	Andrew				1				1					2		
Salem	205	33	Kennedy	James		1	1	1				2	3				8		
Middleton	16	8	Kenney	Archelaus				1		1			1				3		
Middleton	15	8	Kenney	Asa	1		1			1		2					5		
Middleton	18	8	Kenney	Asa		1		1					1	1			4		
Lynn	228	30	Kenney	Ebenz	1			1		2			1				5		
Middleton	15	9	Kenney	Eunice			1							1			2		
Middleton	18	9	Kenney	Simeon			1	1		1	1		1				5		
Marblehead	253	34	Kenning	*			1	1		1			1	1			4		
Amesbury	41	22	Kenniston	Moses				1						2			3		
Salem	205	5	Kenny	Adam		1		1		1		1					4		
Salem	220	13	Kenny	Danl	2	1	1	2		1	1		1				9		
Salem	215	42	Kenny	Ebenz	1			1		2		1					5		
Salem	208	51	Kenny	Hannah		2						1	1				4		
Salem	205	51	Kenny	John				1		1			1				3		
Danvers	10	30	Kenny	Jonathan			1	2					1	1			5		
Danvers	8	29	Kent	Benjan			2	1						1			4		
Danvers	8	31	Kent	Benjan Junr	2			1		2			1				6		
Newburyport	170	19	Kent	Daniel	2			1		1	1		1	1			7		
Amesbury	41	23	Kent	John	1			1	1	1			1				5		
Newburyport	170	16	Kent	Joseph	1		2		1		2			1			7		
Newburyport	170	17	Kent	Joshua	1			1						1			3		
Beverly	297	44	Kent	Josiah		1				1		1					3		
Haverhill	147	42	Kent	Justin	2			1		2		2	1				8		
Newbury	117	31	Kent	Moses	1		1			1		1		1			5		
Newburyport	170	18	Kent	Moses	1		1	1		2		1	1				7		
Newbury	116	41	Kent	Paul		1		1		1		1	1				5		
Newbury	116	40	Kent	Stephen	1	1		1	1			1		2			7		
Wenham	307	8	Kerbe	Hanna	1					1			1				3		
Salem	219	30	Kerny	Jesse	1			1		1			1				4		
Salem	191	14	Kerrik	William	1	1		1		4			1				8		
Salem	215	52	Kerring	Samuel	1		3	1				1					6		
Newburyport	169	27	Kettell	James		1			1	1	1	1	1				7		
Newburyport	169	28	Kettell	James Jr		1	1	1		1	1	1					6		
Danvers	2	8	Kettell	John	1	2	1		1	2		1					8		
Newburyport	169	29	Kettell	Jonathan		1	1	1		3	1	1					8		
Haverhill	147	43	Kezer	Timothy				1					1				2		
Rowley	129	41	Kilborn	Ebenezr				1				2	3				6		
Newburyport	169	30	Kilborn	George		1	1	1		1	1	1		2			8		
Newbury	118	7	Kilborn	Jedediah				1		1	1	1	1				5		
Ipswich	278	28	Kilborn	Joseph		1	1	1					1				4		
Rowley	131	8	Kilborn	Joseph	1			1		1		1	1				5		
Newburyport	169	31	Kilborn	Robert	2		1				1						4		
Newbury	111	44	Kilburn	Thomas	2		1					1					4		
Beverly	303	36	Kilham	Abraham				1		1		2					4		
Manchester	52	10	Kilham	Joseph				1		3			1				5		
Manchester	52	12	Kilham	William				1			1		1				3		
Salem	194	30	Killam	Asa	2	1	3	1		2			1				10		
Boxford	135	46	Killam	John		1	2	1			1		1				6		
Newbury	118	28	Killey	John				1			1		1				3		
Wenham	309	37	Killham	Daniel		1		1		1			1				4		
Salem	215	5	Killin	Edws				1						1			2		
Amesbury	41	29	Kimbal	John			1							1			2		
Ipswich	276	20	Kimball	Aaron	1	1	1	1		2				2			9		
Bradford	123	3	Kimball	Abel	1			1		2	1	1	1				7		
Bradford	122	10	Kimball	Abraham	1			1				3	1	1			7		
Ipswich	277	9	Kimball	Abraham	1			1		4			1				7		
Boxford	134	26	Kimball	Amos	1	1			1	1	1	1					6		
Bradford	122	43	Kimball	Amos	1		1			2			1				6		
Newburyport	170	3	Kimball	Amos	2		2	1					1	1			7		
Boxford	134	36	Kimball	Asa		1			1				2	1			5		
Bradford	122	7	Kimball	Asa		3	1			2	1		1				8		
Bradford	122	11	Kimball	Benja	1	1				1	1		2				6		
Bradford	122	12	Kimball	Benja	1							1	1	1			4		
Ipswich	279	24	Kimball	Benjamin		1		1					1	2			5		
Newburyport	170	2	Kimball	Benjamin	4		4	1		2			1	1			13		
Topsfield	19	10	Kimball	Benjamin	1	1							1				3		
Ipswich	277	18	Kimball	Benjamin Jr	1			1		1				1			4		
Haverhill	147	48	Kimball	Benjan	3	1	1	1		2			1				9		
Ipswich	279	27	Kimball	Caleb	1			1		2	3		1				8		
Newbury	108	37	Kimball	Caleb		1			1			2		1			5		
Wenham	308	31	Kimball	Caleb				1					1				3		
Haverhill	147	34	Kimball	Cotton	2		3		1	2			1				9		
Andover	98	9	Kimball	Daniel	2	2			1	2	1	1	1				10		
Boxford	134	41	Kimball	Daniel	1	1			1	1				1			5		

TOWN	PG#	LN#	LAST NAME	FIRST NAME	FREE WHITE MALES					FREE WHITE FEMALES					TOTAL ALL OTHER	TOTAL SLAVES	TOTALS	DISTRICT/ TOWNSHIP	NOTES
					under 10	10 to 16	16 to 26	26 to 45	45 and over	under 10	10 to 16	16 to 26	26 to 45	45 and over					
Bradford	122	20	Kimball	Daniel	2	1		1		1	1	1	2	1			10		
Bradford	123	36	Kimball	Daniel			1	1	1					1			4		
Marblehead	253	22	Kimball	Daniel	1		1	1		2			2				7		
Boxford	133	5	Kimball	David			1		1			2	1	1			6		
Boxford	134	39	Kimball	David		3	2		1			2		1			9		
Gloucester	80	6	Kimball	David			1				1	2					4		
Haverhill	147	36	Kimball	David		3	2		1			2		1			9		
Ipswich	276	15	Kimball	Ebenezer					1			1					2		
Ipswich	280	15	Kimball	Ebenezer	5				1		1		1				8		
Newburyport	170	4	Kimball	Edmund	1			1		2		1	1				6		
Bradford	122	28	Kimball	Edward	3	1	2		1	1	2		2				12		
Bradford	123	7	Kimball	Edward	3	1		1	1	2			2				10		
Bradford	122	5	Kimball	Elijah	1		2	1				1	1				6		
Boxford	134	35	Kimball	Enoch	1		2		1	3	1	1		2			11		
Andover	98	10	Kimball	Esther Wid										2			2		
Bradford	123	19	Kimball	Francis	1		1			1	1	1					5		
Bradford	126	19	Kimball	Francis	1	1		1		2	1		1				8		
Wenham	308	32	Kimball	Huldah			1							1			2		
Ipswich	273	46	Kimball	Isaac	1			1		2			1				5		
Bradford	122	47	Kimball	Jacob				1				2	1				4		
Ipswich	278	8	Kimball	Jacob	2			1		2			1				6		
Salem	212	34	Kimball	Jacob				1					1				2		
Topsfield	19	9	Kimball	Jacob		1	1	1	1		1	1		1			7		
Bradford	122	30	Kimball	James	2	1	1		2	2	3	2	1				14		
Ipswich	274	49	Kimball	James	1			1					1				3		
Wenham	308	30	Kimball	James				1				1		1			3		
Bradford	122	18	Kimball	Jereh				1				1		2			4		
Ipswich	273	26	Kimball	Jeremiah	1	1							1				3		
Ipswich	273	34	Kimball	Jeremiah	2	1	1		1	1	1	3		1			11		
Andover	98	7	Kimball	John					1			3		1	1		6		
Boxford	134	28	Kimball	John	1		1				1	1	1				5		
Haverhill	147	38	Kimball	John		1			1					1			3		
Ipswich	278	31	Kimball	John					1		1		1	1			4		
Newbury	108	38	Kimball	John	2			1				1					4		
Salem	191	3	Kimball	John			1					1					2		
Gloucester	75	4	Kimball	Jona	3		1			3	1	1	1				10		
Haverhill	147	47	Kimball	Jonathan	1	2			1	1	2						7		
Haverhill	147	39	Kimball	Jonathan Jnr			1			1		1					3		
Bradford	123	30	Kimball	Jonathn	1	1	2	1	1		3	1	1				11		
Bradford	123	32	Kimball	Joseph	2			3	1	2			3	1			12		
Ipswich	280	11	Kimball	Joseph					1					1			2		
Salem	219	13	Kimball	Mary		1								2			3		
Boxford	133	6	Kimball	Micijah	1			1				2					4		
Andover	98	6	Kimball	Moses			1					1	1	1			4		
Bradford	123	1	Kimball	Moses		1	1				1			1			4		
Haverhill	147	37	Kimball	Moses	1			1		2			1				5		
Middleton	17	20	Kimball	Moses	3			1		1	1		1				7		
Newburyport	170	6	Kimball	Moses	1		2				2	1		1			7		
Andover	98	3	Kimball	Moses Junr					1	2	1	1		1			6		
Boxford	134	33	Kimball	Nathan					1		1			1			3		
Bradford	122	4	Kimball	Nathan	1	2	2	1			1	1	1				9		
Bradford	122	6	Kimball	Nathan				1	1				2	1			5		
Salem	193	32	Kimball	Nathan			1		1		1	4	3	1			11		
Ipswich	274	4	Kimball	Nathaniel		1		1	1	1		2		1			7		
Ipswich	279	35	Kimball	Nathaniel	3	2		1		1	2		1				10		
Wenham	307	5	Kimball	Nathaniel	2			1	1		1		1	2			8		
Bradford	123	5	Kimball	Nathl		1	2			1	2	1		1			8		
Bradford	122	29	Kimball	Obadiah		1	1	1		1			1				5		
Bradford	123	4	Kimball	Phineas		2	1					2	2				7		
Danvers	13	5	Kimball	Richard		1		1	1				1				4		
Haverhill	147	46	Kimball	Richard	2	1	3	1		2			2				11		
Bradford	123	6	Kimball	Richd		1			1			1		1			4		
Boxford	134	38	Kimball	Samuel	1	1	1		1			2	1				7		
Boxford	134	49	Kimball	Samuel	2	1		1		2		1	1				8		
Haverhill	148	3	Kimball	Samuel			1							1			2		
Ipswich	273	33	Kimball	Sarah										1			1		
Haverhill	147	35	Kimball	Solomon	1			1		2			1	1			6		
Boxford	134	32	Kimball	Stephen	1		1			3		1					6		
Andover	98	8	Kimball	Thomas			1			1		1					3		
Ipswich	275	29	Kimball	Thomas	1	2		1		2			1				7		
Newbury	108	39	Kimball	Thomas	2			1		1		1					5		
Wenham	309	20	Kimball	Thomas		1	1		1					1			4		
Wenham	308	28	Kimball	Thomas Jr	1	1		1		3	1		1				8		
Andover	98	4	Kimball	William	1		2						1				4		
Newburyport	170	5	Kimball	William	1			1		2	1		1				6		
Ipswich	275	21	Kindall	Ephraim		2	2	1	1		1	3		1			11		
Ipswich	275	22	Kindall	Ephraim Jur	1			1		1			1				4		
Ipswich	278	7	Kinder	Benjamin			1		1				1	1			4		
Amesbury	41	21	Kindrick	Samuel			1		1					1			3		
Newbury	116	15	Kindrick	Samuel	1		1	1		1		1					5		
Danvers	7	4	King	Amos	1	2			1	2		1	1				9		

TOWN	PG#	LN#	HEADS OF HOUSEHOLD		FREE WHITE MALES					FREE WHITE FEMALES					TOTAL ALL OTHER	TOTAL SLAVES	TOTALS	DISTRICT/ TOWNSHIP	NOTES
			LAST NAME	FIRST NAME	under 10	10 to 16	16 to 26	26 to 45	45 and over	under 10	10 to 16	16 to 26	26 to 45	45 and over					
Salem	203	27	King	Benja		1			1		1	2		1			6		
Danvers	14	30	King	Daniel		1		1			1	1					4		
Salem	212	36	King	Gedney			2		1			1		1			5		
Salem	206	54	King	James		3			1	1	1	4	1	1			12		
Danvers	3	33	King	John	1	1		1		1	1		2				7		
Danvers	14	23	King	Jonathan				1						1			2		
Salem	195	22	King	Nathl	1		1	1		1		2	1				7		
Salem	215	43	King	Saml	1			1		1			1				4		
Danvers	14	32	King	Sarah										2			2		
Salem	212	13	King	Seth	1			1		1			1				4		
Newburyport	170	15	King	Thomas	1			1					1				3		
Danvers	14	19	King	Zachariah Junr	2			1									3		
Danvers	14	31	King	Zacheriah		1	3		1			1		1			7		
Gloucester	65	3	Kingsbury	Aaron					1					1			2		
Gloucester	65	2	Kingsman	Nathaniel					1			2	1	2			6		
Salem	221	13	Kinman	Nath	2			1					1	1			5		
Salem	208	56	Kinman	Thos			1			4			1				6		
Beverly	290	24	Kinneson	Aphria										1			1		
Beverly	294	27	Kinney	Israel		1		1		1		1	1				5		
Ipswich	280	18	Kinsman	Aaron	1		1	1		2		1	1				7		
Ipswich	276	19	Kinsman	Eunice								2					2		
Ipswich	281	32	Kinsman	Jeremiah				1					1				2		
Gloucester	68	7	Kinsman	John			1					1					2		
Hamilton	285	70	Kinsman	Mary								2	1		6		9		
Ipswich	279	18	Kinsman	Mary	1	1				1		1	1				5		
Ipswich	280	25	Kinsman	Moses	2		1		1	4	2	1	1				12		
Ipswich	277	15	Kinsman	Nathaniel		1			1	3		1		1			7		
Ipswich	279	14	Kinsman	Samuel		2			1	1		1		1			6		
Gloucester	65	4	Kinsman	William	1		1	1		1	1		1				6		
Hamilton	285	67	Kinsman	William	1				1	1	1		1				5		
Ipswich	281	33	Kinsman	William			2		1				1				4		
Lynn	227	10	Kippontall	France				1					1				2		
Lynn	230	6	Kirbey	John		1		1		1		2	1				6		
Marblehead	252	1	Kitchens	Lilla									1	1			2		
Marblehead	251	27	Kitchens	Samuel			1						1				2		
Manchester	52	15	Kitfield	Lydia Wo						1			1	1			3		
Andover	98	2	Kitteridge	John	1		1	1					2	1			6		
Andover	98	1	Kitteridge	Thomas			4		1	1	1	1	1	1	4		14		
Newburyport	169	37	Knap	Anthony	1			1		1			1	1			5		
Newburyport	169	43	Knap	Benjamin	1	2	2			1		1	1	1			9		
Newburyport	169	36	Knap	Benoni E				1			1	1		1			4		
Newburyport	169	44	Knap	Ebenezer			1						2	1			4		
Newburyport	169	35	Knap	Hannah Wido			1						1	1			3		
Newburyport	169	34	Knap	Isaac	1			1		1			1				4		
Newburyport	169	38	Knap	John	1			1		2		1	1	1			7		
Salem	209	9	Knap	John	1			1		1			1				4		
Salisbury	29	33	Knap	John		1	1		1	1		1	1	1			6		
Salem	220	19	Knap	Joseph			1			1	1	1					4		
Salem	219	37	Knap	Mary			1			1			1	1			4		
Newburyport	169	32	Knap	Nathaniel		1		2		1		1		1			6		
Newburyport	169	33	Knap	Nathaniel Jr	2	1	1	1		2			1	1			9		
Newburyport	169	40	Knap	Philip C	2	1	1	1		1			1	1			8		
Newburyport	169	39	Knap	Samuel				1						2			3		
Newburyport	170	1	Knap	Tristram			1						1				2		
Newburyport	169	41	Knap	William			1	1				2		2			6		
Newburyport	169	42	Knap	William Jr	1			1				1	1	1			5		
Marblehead	250	25	Knapp	Peter	1			1		3			1				6		
Topsfield	19	32	Kneeland	Aaron	3	1	3	1	1			1	1				11		
Topsfield	19	33	Kneeland	Aaron Jun			1						1				2		
Topsfield	19	34	Kneeland	Daniel			1	1		1			1	1			5		
Andover	98	5	Kneeland	John		2			1				1	1			5		
Gloucester	57	4	Knghts	Thos			1			1			1				3		
Salem	213	36	Knight	Aaron			1						1				2		
Gloucester	59	35	Knight	Abigl Widow		1	1					2		1			5		
Newbury	115	11	Knight	Addams	1		1						1	1			4		
Newburyport	170	11	Knight	Amos			1	2					1	1			5		
Newburyport	170	9	Knight	Ann Wido	2	2					1	1	1				7		
Newbury	112	34	Knight	Barzuliel				1					1				2		
Marblehead	250	21	Knight	Benjamin	3			1		1	1		1				7		
Newburyport	170	12	Knight	Daniel	1			2		2			1	1			7		
Salem	191	9	Knight	Daniel				1						1			2		
Newburyport	170	13	Knight	Daniel Jr			1						1				2		
Newbury	116	30	Knight	Edmund		1		2		1			2	1			7		
Newburyport	170	10	Knight	Elizabeth Wido		2						1	1				4		
Newbury	117	11	Knight	Eunice	1	1	2			2	1	1		2			10		
Marblehead	243	27	Knight	George	1	1			1	4			1				8		
Newburyport	170	14	Knight	Hale	2		1	1					1	1			6		
Gloucester	77	26	Knight	Job	3	1		1		2			1	1			9		
Manchester	52	9	Knight	John	3	2	1	1		1	1	1	1				11		
Newbury	109	33	Knight	John	1			1		4			1	1			8		
Newbury	115	12	Knight	John	1			1	1	1		1	1	1			6		
Gloucester	57	3	Knight	Joseph				1				1		1			3		
Middleton	16	28	Knight	Joseph		2	1							1			4		
Newbury	108	12	Knight	Joseph		1							1				2		
Newbury	112	12	Knight	Joseph			1			1			1				3		
Salisbury	29	32	Knight	Lemuel	1		1	1					1				4		
Salem	196	11	Knight	Nath	1				1				1				3		

TOWN	PG#	LN#	LAST NAME	FIRST NAME	FREE WHITE MALES under 10	10 to 16	16 to 26	26 to 45	45 and over	FREE WHITE FEMALES under 10	10 to 16	16 to 26	26 to 45	45 and over	TOTAL ALL OTHER	TOTAL SLAVES	TOTALS	DISTRICT/ TOWNSHIP	NOTES
Salem	212	47	Knight	Nath	2		1			2	2		1	1			9		
Newbury	117	5	Knight	Richard	1	2			1	3			1				8		
Marblehead	243	26	Knight	Robert			1	1					1				3		
Marblehead	257	29	Knight	Samuel	4		1				1		1				7		
Salem	219	3	Knight	Sarah									1				1		
Gloucester	59	34	Knight	Stephen	2		1					2					5		
Haverhill	147	45	Knight	Stephen			1	1		2		1	1				6		
Gloucester	69	17	Knight	Thomas	3			1				1					5		
Newbury	112	30	Knight	Thomas	2		1			2	1		1				7		
Salem	218	20	Knight	Thos	2		2	1		2		1	1				9		
Newbury	112	32	Knight	Unice										1			1		
Gloucester	80	4	Knight	Willm			1			2			1				4		
Gloucester	71	19	Knight	David	3		1			2			1				7		
Salem	210	27	Knights	Enoch	1		1			1		1					4		
Gloucester	81	29	Knights	Satah Wo	2					1			2	1			6		
Gloucester	80	5	Knights	Thos	1		1			1		1					4		
Lynn	233	40	Knights	Thos K	1	1		1		1				1			5	West Parish	
Marblehead	249	8	Knowland	Andrew	2		1						1				4		
Marblehead	264	1	Knowland	Andrew	2		1			2			1				6		
Marblehead	264	11	Knowland	James	2		1			2			1				6		
Wenham	309	32	Knowlton	Abraham	1		1	1		2	1	1					7		
Wenham	308	19	Knowlton	Anna							1		1				2		
Beverly	295	11	Knowlton	Benja 2nd	1	2		1		1			1				6		
Beverly	295	12	Knowlton	Benjamin	2			1		1			1				5		
Beverly	298	18	Knowlton	Caleb		1						1					2		
Hamilton	284	9	Knowlton	Edmund			2	1	1	1			1	1			7		
Hamilton	285	109	Knowlton	Ephraim	1				1	1		2		1			6		
Hamilton	284	16	Knowlton	Ezra			2	1						1			4		
Gloucester	75	17	Knowlton	John	2		1			1			1	1			6		
Hamilton	284	18	Knowlton	John	2					1			1				4		
Newburyport	170	21	Knowlton	John	1	1	3	1		2			1	1			10		
Beverly	293	32	Knowlton	Jonathan			1			1			1				3		
Wenham	309	30	Knowlton	Jonathan		1	1		1	1	1	1	1				7		
Beverly	302	12	Knowlton	Joseph					1	1		1		1			4		
Beverly	293	21	Knowlton	Mark	1		1			1			1				4		
Hamilton	284	15	Knowlton	Melicah		1	1	1		1			1				5		
Gloucester	57	5	Knowlton	Moses	2		1		1	1	2	1		1			9		
Hamilton	284	13	Knowlton	Nathaniel	1		1	1					1				4		
Gloucester	80	7	Knowlton	Nehemiah	3	1	2	1		2			1				10		
Hamilton	284	14	Knowlton	Nehemiah		1	2		1	1			1	1			7		
Ipswich	277	1	Knowlton	Sarah						1	3			1			5		
Ipswich	275	56	Knowlton	Thomas			1						2				3		
Hamilton	284	23	Knowlton	William			1			1			1				3		
Gloucester	77	28	Knutsford	Stephen	3	1			1	2			1	1			9		
Newburyport	170	20	Kuhn	Jacob		1			1	1	1	2		1			7		
Andover	98	19	Lacy	Ephraim	2		1		1	2	1			1			8		
Andover	98	20	Lacy	John		1			1	1	1	1		1			6		
Haverhill	148	8	Ladd	Dudley				1				1	1	1			4		
Methuen	154	25	Ladd	John		1		1						1			3		
Haverhill	148	4	Ladd	Nathll	3	1		1		1	2		1				9		
Salem	216	31	Lafavor	Daniel	1			1					1				3		
Salem	204	4	Laffege	Peter											2		2		
Salem	204	3	Laffege	Thos											2		2		
Danvers	15	5	Laird	Margaret	1		1							1			3		
Newburyport	170	46	Laird	Robert	1			1		3		1	1				7		
Gloucester	69	13	Lakay	James		1			1		2		2				6		
Gloucester	69	3	Lakay	Lucy Wd	1					1	2		1				5		
Topsfield	21	25	Lake	Eleazer		3	2		1	1			1				8		
Salem	189	39	Lake	John											2		2		
Haverhill	148	5	Lake	Joseph	4			1		1			1				7		
Topsfield	21	26	Lake	Robert	2			1					2				5		
Newburyport	170	36	Lake	John			1						1				2		
Newburyport	170	35	Lakeman	Ann Wido							1			1			2		
Ipswich	277	10	Lakeman	Deborah		1				1	1		1				4		
Lynnfield	236	4	Lakeman	James	1		1						1				3		
Ipswich	274	15	Lakeman	John			1	1					1	1			4		
Ipswich	279	9	Lakeman	Jonas	2	2	1		1	1	1	1		1			10		
Ipswich	278	17	Lakeman	Jonathan				1		1			1		5		8		
Ipswich	274	17	Lakeman	Martha										1			1		
Gloucester	84	3	Lakeman	Nathl Doct				1			1		1				3		
Beverly	301	34	Lakeman	Rachel		2	1						1				4		
Ipswich	278	16	Lakeman	Richard		1		1		1			1				4		
Ipswich	277	12	Lakeman	Richard	1		1	1						1			4		
Ipswich	279	7	Lakeman	Richard Jun	2		1			2			1				6		
Ipswich	278	54	Lakeman	Samuel				1		2			2				5		
Ipswich	278	15	Lakeman	Samuel Junr			1			2	1		1				5		
Ipswich	273	54	Lakeman	William			1			2			1				4		
Ipswich	281	2	Lakeman	William		2		1						1			4		
Ipswich	281	1	Lakeman	William Jr				1		2		1					4		
Salem	204	33	Lamb	Simon Jr	1			1		1	1	1	1				6		
Salem	204	32	Lamb	Simon				1						1			2		
Rowley	129	19	Lambert	Alfia			1			1		2	1				5		
Salem	203	16	Lambert	Jonathan		2	2		1			1		1			7		
Rowley	129	18	Lambert	Jonathn	1			1				1	1		1		5		
Salem	220	26	Lambert	Joseph		1		1		1		1	1	1			6		

TOWN	PG#	LN#	HEADS OF HOUSEHOLD		FREE WHITE MALES					FREE WHITE FEMALES					TOTAL ALL OTHER	TOTAL SLAVES	TOTALS	DISTRICT/ TOWNSHIP	NOTES
			LAST NAME	FIRST NAME	under 10	10 to 16	16 to 26	26 to 45	45 and over	under 10	10 to 16	16 to 26	26 to 45	45 and over					
Salem	183	15	Lambert	Mary										2			2		
Rowley	128	55	Lambert	Nathan		1		1						1			3		
Rowley	129	28	Lambert	Nathan		1		1					1				3		
Salem	203	17	Lambert	Saml	1		1			1		1					3		
Wenham	307	11	Lambord	Priscilla									1				1		
Middleton	16	16	Lamon	Lydia						1		1					2		
Salem	209	30	Lampaul	Hannah								2	1				3		
Hamilton	285	11	Lampen	Abigail									2	1			3		
Salem	194	7	Lamson	Amos	1		1			2			1				5		
Topsfield	19	28	Lamson	Anna									2	1			3		
Beverly	303	29	Lamson	Asa	1		1			1			1				4		
Gloucester	72	12	Lamson	Caleb				1					1				2		
Gloucester	65	8	Lamson	Daniel	1		1			1			1				4		
Hamilton	285	29	Lamson	Edward			1	1				1	1				4		
Beverly	303	17	Lamson	Francis		2		1		3	1		1				8		
Gloucester	73	1	Lamson	Henry		1				1			1				3		
Hamilton	285	31	Lamson	Jonathan		1	1	2				1		1			6		
Beverly	303	41	Lamson	Jonathn	3		1						1				5		
Topsfield	19	29	Lamson	Josiah		2		1		1		1	1				6		
Beverly	298	21	Lamson	Nathan	2	2	2		1	5	1	1	1				15		
Beverly	302	34	Lamson	Samuel	2			1					1				4		
Hamilton	285	30	Lamson	Sarah				1				1	1				3		
Salem	195	11	Lamson	Thos	2	1	2						1				6		
Newburyport	171	6	Lanagin	Ann Wido						1			1				2		
Manchester	50	2	Lanbord	John	3			1		1		1					6		
Newburyport	170	41	Lancaster	Henry	1	2	2	1		1	1		1				9		
Salem	189	43	Lancaster	John											2		2		
Rowley	130	38	Lancaster	Paul				1		1			1				3		
Newburyport	170	42	Lancaster	Thomas		1		1		1		2	1				6		
Rowley	127	42	Lancaster	Thos		1							1				2		
Amesbury	42	13	Lancster	Jacob	1	2		1		3	1		1				9		
Beverly	300	10	Landen	Rebecca				1			1		1				3		
Salem	210	4	Lander	Charles	1			1				1					3		
Newburyport	170	40	Lander	John	1	1		1		1			1				5		
Salem	214	14	Landers	Peter		1	2		1	2	3	3	1				13		
Salem	195	3	Landers	William	3			1		1			1				6		
Gloucester	76	13	Lane	Aaron	1			1		1			1				4		
Gloucester	83	19	Lane	Andrew			1			1		1					3		
Newburyport	170	33	Lane	Benjamin Jr	2			1		2			1				6		
Gloucester	76	11	Lane	Caleb	2	3	1	1		1			1				9		
Gloucester	74	1	Lane	Cornelius	3			1				1	1				6	Squam Parish	
Gloucester	76	37	Lane	David	1	1		1		1	1	2	1	1			9		
Newburyport	170	31	Lane	David		1	1						1				3		
Gloucester	76	36	Lane	David Junr		1				1	1		1				4		
Gloucester	84	4	Lane	Dennison		1							1				2		
Newburyport	170	32	Lane	Francis	3	2		1		1			1				8		
Gloucester	74	12	Lane	Gedeon	2			1		2			1				6	Squam Parish	
Gloucester	76	2	Lane	Gedeon	1			1		1			1				4		
Gloucester	83	25	Lane	George	3			1		2				1			7		
Amesbury	42	8	Lane	Hannah Wid	1					1			1				3		
Marblehead	252	29	Lane	Henry	2	2	1	1		1	1	1					9		
Newbury	113	16	Lane	Humphrey	1		1			1			1				4		
Gloucester	72	8	Lane	James	1			1		2			1				5		
Gloucester	76	38	Lane	John	1			1		2			1				5		
Gloucester	77	2	Lane	Jona			2	1		2	1		1				7		
Gloucester	77	1	Lane	Joseph	1		1	1		2	3	1	1				10		
Gloucester	76	14	Lane	Joseph Junr	1			1		4			1				7		
Gloucester	75	15	Lane	Judith Wo	1	1	1						1	1			5		
Gloucester	75	18	Lane	Lydia Wo			2						1				3		
Gloucester	77	16	Lane	Nathl			1			2			1				4		
Salem	220	22	Lane	Nicholas	1	1			2	5	3	1	1				14		
Salem	202	20	Lane	Salem												6	6		
Gloucester	73	25	Lane	Solomon	1			1		2		1	1	1			7	Squam Parish	
Salem	219	8	Lane	William		1		1		2			1				5		
Salem	209	51	Lang	Edward		1		1	1	1	2		1				7		
Gloucester	69	14	Lang	James	2		1			1		1	1				6		
Salem	195	20	Lang	Richard				1									1		
Salem	193	25	Lang	William		1			1	3	3	1		2	1		12		
Ipswich	281	11	Lano	John	1			1		1			1				4		
Gloucester	77	3	Lansford	John	3	2			1	2		1	1	1			11		
Salem	200	29	Lany	Nath		3		1				1	1				6		
Bradford	124	40	Lapham	King			3	1		1			1				6		
Lynn	230	13	Larabe	Isaac	1	2		1					1				5		
Lynn	226	40	Larabe	Isaac Jr	2			1		1			1				5		
Lynn	228	36	Larabee	Ebenz C	1			1					1				3		
Lynn	228	33	Larabee	Elias			1			1			1				3		
Lynn	232	7	Larabee	Lydia								1	1	1			3		
Lynnfield	235	15	Larabee	Willm	2			1		3	1		1	1			9		
Beverly	297	5	Larcom	Abigail			3			1			1	1			6		
Beverly	295	23	Larcom	Henry		1				1		1	1				4		
Beverly	297	4	Larcom	Juno Negro											11		11		
Beverly	295	22	Larcom	Priscill		1							1				2		
Beverly	297	26	Larcome	Cornelius		1				1		1					3		
Beverly	304	9	Larcome	Jonathan	1		1			1			1				4		
Newburyport	171	11	Larcum	Luke				2					1				3		
Danvers	14	2	Laribee	Anna			2	1				1	1				6		

224

TOWN	PG#	LN#	LAST NAME	FIRST NAME	FREE WHITE MALES under 10	10 to 16	16 to 26	26 to 45	45 and over	FREE WHITE FEMALES under 10	10 to 16	16 to 26	26 to 45	45 and over	TOTAL ALL OTHER	TOTAL SLAVES	TOTALS	DISTRICT/ TOWNSHIP	NOTES
Danvers	3	25	Laribee	Ephraim		1				1		1					3		
Danvers	3	35	Laribee	Ephriem	1		1		1	1			1				5		
Danvers	3	36	Laribee	Ephriem		1				1		1					3		
Danvers	3	24	Laribee	Hannah	1					2	1		1				5		
Danvers	11	22	Laribee	Stephen	3	1	1	1					1				7		
Beverly	303	9	Larnard	David	3	1		1		2			1				8		
Salem	202	15	Larock	John		1								1			2		
Beverly	295	2	Lascome	Francis W			1			2			1				4		
Marblehead	258	3	Lashey	James	1			1					1	1			4		
Marblehead	268	8	Laskey	Benjamin	3			1					1				5		
Beverly	290	26	Laskey	James	1		1						1				3		
Marblehead	264	2	Laskey	Mary	3		1			1			1				6		
Marblehead	267	5	Laskey	William			1						1				2		
Newburyport	170	45	Laurence	David	2	1		1		2			1	1			8		
Gloucester	74	2	Lavall	Thos	3			1				1	1	1			7	Squam Parish	
Gloucester	82	4	Lavell	William	2			1					1				4		
Salem	201	25	Law	Peter	1			1					1				3		
Marblehead	246	16	Lawrece	Joseph H.		1			1		1			1			4		
Salem	206	13	Lawrence	Abel	1	2	2		1	4	1	2	2				15		
Lynnfield	235	17	Lawrence	Ebenr		1	1							1			3		
Manchester	52	21	Leach	Annie Wo										1			1		
Beverly	299	42	Leach	Asa	1	1		1	1		1	2	1				8		
Manchester	52	25	Leach	Benja	1	1		1		2			1				6		
Haverhill	148	14	Leach	Benjamin	2			1		2			1	1			7		
Newburyport	171	8	Leach	Benjamin	2	1			1	1		1	1	1			8		
Manchester	52	19	Leach	Bethh									1				1		
Manchester	52	31	Leach	Daniel	1			1		1	3	1	1				8		
Marblehead	257	16	Leach	Eleazer	2			1					1				4		
Manchester	52	37	Leach	Ezehl		1	3	1		1	2	1	1				10		
Salem	190	15	Leach	Geo				1			3	1	1				6		
Marblehead	259	10	Leach	Henry		1			1	2			1				5		
Salem	194	38	Leach	John	4		2		1	1	1	2	1				12		
Manchester	52	35	Leach	Marian Wo							1	1	1				3		
Salem	213	35	Leach	Mathew		1			1	1			1				4		
Salem	205	27	Leach	Paul	2	1		1		3	1		1				9		
Salem	206	7	Leach	Robt		2			1		2	4		2			11		
Salem	218	24	Leach	Samuel	2	1		1		1			1				6		
Marblehead	267	26	Leach	Sarah										1			1		
Newburyport	171	9	Leach	Sarah Wido		1							1	1			3		
Danvers	5	37	Leach	Timothy				1		1			1	1			4		
Salem	189	25	Leache	Eliza									1	2			3		
Ipswich	276	30	Lealand	John	2			1		2			1				6		
Marblehead	270	28	Lear	Alexander			1						1				2		
Gloucester	78	12	Lears	William	3	1			1	1	3	1					10		
Ipswich	277	13	Leatherland	William	2			1		2			1				6		
Haverhill	148	9	Leborquet	Caleb		1	1	1		1			1		1		6		
Haverhill	148	11	Leborquet	Ebenezr			1			1		1					3		
Haverhill	148	10	Leborquet	John				1		1		1	1	1			5		
Newburyport	170	37	LeBreton	Peter		1	1		1	1		1	1	1			7		
Haverhill	148	13	Lecount	William	1		1	1					1	2			7		
Marblehead	256	16	LeCrane	John	2			1		2			1				6		
Marblehead	256	15	LeCrane	William		2		1		2			1				6		
Marblehead	264	3	LeCrans	Philip		2		1		2	1	2	1	1			10		
Manchester	52	23	Lee	Aaron		1	1	1					1				4		
Wenham	307	20	Lee	Aaron	2			1		1	2	3	1				10		
Manchester	53	5	Lee	Amoss	2		1			3			1				7		
Manchester	52	32	Lee	Andrew		1		1		1			1				4		
Marblehead	251	4	Lee	Elizabeth									1				1		
Manchester	52	20	Lee	Elizabh Wo	1		2				1		1				5		
Manchester	52	17	Lee	Henry			1			5	1	1	1				9		
Manchester	53	3	Lee	Isaac	1	1	2	1	1	1	1		1				9		
Manchester	53	7	Lee	Isaac Junr	2	1		1		2	1		1				8		
Manchester	52	16	Lee	Israel	1	1		1		2			1				6		
Beverly	293	2	Lee	Joanna		3	2			1	1	2	1				10		
Andover	98	12	Lee	John		2		1					1	1	1		6		
Marblehead	247	4	Lee	John	2	1		1			1		1				6		
Manchester	53	4	Lee	John Junr		1				1							2		
Manchester	52	29	Lee	Joseph	1	1		1		3	1	2	1				10		
Manchester	53	2	Lee	Josiah	2	2	1						1				6		
Manchester	52	36	Lee	Lydia Wo									2		1		3		
Manchester	52	30	Lee	Nathan	2	1		1		2			1				7		
Manchester	53	8	Lee	Nathll			1					1		1			3		
Manchester	52	24	Lee	Nathll Junr	2	1		1		2		1	1				8		
Marblehead	270	9	Lee	Richard	2	1	1	1		1			1				7		
Marblehead	264	5	Lee	Samuel			1					2					3		
Manchester	53	1	Lee	Sarah Wo										1	1		2		
Manchester	52	27	Lee	Sol	1	2		1		1			1				6		
Salem	206	38	Lee	Thos		2	1	1	1			2	1	1	1		10		
Manchester	52	28	Lee	William	2			1		2		1					6		
Marblehead	240	32	Lee	William			1			2		1	2				6		
Marblehead	264	4	Lee	William R.		1		1		1		2		2			7		
Manchester	52	18	Lee	Winthrop			1					1					2		
Beverly	304	23	Lee	Joseph				1				4		2	1		8		
Salem	214	43	Leech	Mary										1			1		

225

TOWN	PG#	LN#	LAST NAME	FIRST NAME	M under 10	M 10 to 16	M 16 to 26	M 26 to 45	M 45 and over	F under 10	F 10 to 16	F 16 to 26	F 26 to 45	F 45 and over	TOTAL ALL OTHER	TOTAL SLAVES	TOTALS	DISTRICT/ TOWNSHIP	NOTES
Beverly	299	2	Leech	Nathan					1				1	1			3		
Beverly	303	22	Leech	Nathan 2d	1	1		1		1		1	1				6		
Beverly	299	4	Leech	William	1	1	1	1		2	1	1	1				9		
Beverly	305	13	Leeds	Richard				1									1		
Marblehead	243	9	Lefarrow	Elizabeth	3	3		1		2		1	1				11		
Salem	220	2	LeFavour	Amos	1		1			4		1	1				7		
Salem	219	11	Lefavour	Eliza		1	4	3		1	1	1		1			12		
Topsfield	22	1	Lefavour	John	1	1		1		2			1				6		
Marblehead	267	2	Lefavour	Philip		1							1				2		
Beverly	291	13	Lefeaver	Amos	1			1					1				3		
Beverly	291	12	Lefeaver	Anna		1	1					1	1	1			5		
Marblehead	256	24	LeGron	Philip				1					1				2		
Salem	211	38	Leich	Mary										1			1		
Newburyport	170	34	Leigh	Benjamin	2	1	1		1	1	1	2		1			10		
Gloucester	86	3	Leighton	Esther Wo		2	2	1			1			1			7		
Marblehead	240	23	LeMaster	Thomas	1				1	2	2		1				7		
Beverly	298	24	Lemmon	John	1				1				1				3		
Middleton	15	16	Lemon	Jonathan		1		1	1				2	2			7		
Manchester	53	6	Lendal	Eunice Wo			2			1		1		1			5		
Manchester	52	34	Lendal	John	3	1	2	1		2			1				10		
Newburyport	171	7	Lenox	James					1			1		1			3		
Newburyport	171	1	Leonard	William B					1								1		
Salem	201	28	Lerrock	Ebenz	1			1		2			1				5		
Gloucester	86	4	Letour	Doly Wo								1	1				2		
Salem	208	62	Levans	Richard				1		1		1		1			4		
Gloucester	85	28	Levenear	Lewis1			1			1			1				3		
Amesbury	42	9	Lewin	John	1			1		1		1					4		
Marblehead	256	30	Lewis	Aaron		1		1		1			1				4		
Newburyport	171	2	Lewis	Anthony	2			1					1	1			5		
Lynn	231	44	Lewis	Benj	1	1		1		2			1				6		
Salem	202	28	Lewis	Benja		1				2		2					5		
Lynn	234	10	Lewis	Caleb	4		1			1			1	1			8		
Salem	216	37	Lewis	Ebed	1	1		1			1		1				5		
Lynn	227	40	Lewis	Edmd	1				1	1	3			1			7		
Marblehead	248	8	Lewis	Edmund	1	1			1	2	1	2		1			9		
Marblehead	260	34	Lewis	Edmund	3			1		1		1					6		
Marblehead	260	15	Lewis	Edward	1			1		2			1				5		
Lynn	230	3	Lewis	Hannible											5		5		
Lynn	223	3	Lewis	Isaac			1						1				2		
Marblehead	241	17	Lewis	Jack											2		2		
Lynn	227	42	Lewis	James	1			1		2			1				5		
Lynn	227	43	Lewis	John	3	1	2		1	1			1				9		
Newbury	106	17	Lewis	John	1			1		1	1	1					5		
Newburyport	171	3	Lewis	John	2			1	1	1			3				7		
Lynn	228	1	Lewis	John 3d	1		1						1				3		
Lynn	231	29	Lewis	John Junr	1			1		1			1				4		
Salem	212	7	Lewis	Martha		2				2	1	1					6		
Lynn	227	41	Lewis	Nath	2			1		2			1				6		
Lynn	231	28	Lewis	Nathl Jr	2			1		3			1				7		
Lynn	227	35	Lewis	Robert		1				1			1				3		
Marblehead	264	6	Lewis	Thomas	1			1		3	1		1		1		8		
Lynn	225	1	Lewis	Thos	2	1	1						1				5		
Salem	210	47	Lewis	Thos	2		1						1				4		
Lynn	228	12	Lewis	W Burk				1		1			1				3		
Lynn	227	33	Lewis	Willm	2			1					1				4		
Marblehead	247	33	LeWorthy	Thomas				1					1				2		
Newburyport	171	5	Libby	John	2			1		1	1		1				6		
Gloucester	65	6	Lincoln	Obed Esq		1		1				1	1				4		
Gloucester	60	1	Lincoln	Richard	2			1				1	1				5		
Marblehead	245	14	Lindsey	Joseph	1			1				2	1				5		
Marblehead	270	15	Lindsey	Nathaniel	2			1		1			1	1			6		
Marblehead	270	4	Lindsey	Sarah		3					2	2		1			8		
Ipswich	273	21	Linneus	John Jur		1	1	1					2				5		
Marblehead	256	28	Liscolm	Richard	1			1		1			1				4		
Gloucester	78	3	Liscomb	Gedion	2			1		2			1				6		
Salem	192	7	Liscomb	Jno	2		1						1				4		
Newbury	116	34	Little	Amos		1		1		2	2		1				7		
Newbury	120	14	Little	Amos		1		1		2	2		1				7		
Newbury	116	21	Little	Coleman	1			1		2			1				5		
Newbury	115	21	Little	David	1	1	1	1		2	1		1		1		9		
Newbury	115	36	Little	Edmund					1			1		1			3		
Bradford	124	18	Little	Enoch			4	1		2		2					9		
Newbury	115	37	Little	Enoch					1	1				1			3		
Beverly	304	26	Little	Hannah						2			1				3		
Newburyport	170	44	Little	Hazen			2						1	1			4		
Newbury	110	5	Little	Jacob	3	1		2		2	1	1	1				11		
Amesbury	42	12	Little	John		1	1			2		1					5		
Newbury	114	26	Little	John			2						1				3		
Newbury	115	39	Little	John				1					1				2		
Newbury	115	34	Little	Joseph	1	1		1				1		1			5		
Newbury	120	26	Little	Joshua			1				1		1				3		
Newbury	120	28	Little	Josiah	1	2		1		1		2	1				8		
Newbury	115	38	Little	Moses		1							1				2		
Newbury	120	27	Little	Moses	3	1		1		1	2	1	1				10		
Salem	215	32	Little	Moses		1		1				1	1	1			5		
Newbury	116	35	Little	Nathll	1		1		1	1	1	1		1			7		
Newbury	120	15	Little	Nathll		2			1	1	1	1	1				7		

TOWN	PG#	LN#	LAST NAME	FIRST NAME	FREE WHITE MALES					FREE WHITE FEMALES					TOTAL ALL OTHER	TOTAL SLAVES	TOTALS	DISTRICT/ TOWNSHIP	NOTES
					under 10	10 to 16	16 to 26	26 to 45	45 and over	under 10	10 to 16	16 to 26	26 to 45	45 and over					
Newbury	115	16	Little	Paul		1	1							1			3		
Newbury	115	20	Little	Richard			1	1	3				2	1			8		
Newbury	116	36	Little	Silas	1			1		3	1		1				7		
Newbury	120	16	Little	Silas	1	2		1			1		1				6		
Newbury	110	43	Little	Stephen	2		3	1		1			1	1			9		
Newbury	116	9	Little	Stephen	1		1			1			1				4		
Bradford	126	5	Little	William	1			1					1				3		
Haverhill	148	6	Little	William	1		4	1					1	1			8		
Amesbury	42	11	Little	Willm C		2	1		1		1	1		1			7		
Gloucester	65	5	Littlehale	Richard		1	2	1	1		1	2		1			9		
Marblehead	270	26	Lloyd	Thomas		1		1		2			1				5		
Salisbury	30	4	Locke	James	2			1		1			1				5		
Gloucester	62	22	Locke	Joseph		1		1		1			1				4		
Gloucester	59	39	Logan	John				1						1			2		
Salisbury	30	5	Lombard	Barzilla Capt				1		1	1	1					4		
Andover	98	21	Long	John			1		1			1		2			5		
Andover	98	22	Long	John Junr	1			1		1			1				4		
Haverhill	148	16	Long	Joshua				1			1	1	1				4		
Newburyport	170	39	Long	Judith		1					1			1			3		
Amesbury	42	4	Long	Nathan	3	1	2	2		2		1	1				12		
Boxford	134	23	Long	Nathll		1		1		1	2		1				6		
Newburyport	170	38	Long	Robert	1	3	2		1		3	1		1			12		
Andover	98	23	Long	Stephen					1								1		
Salem	213	51	Long	Willliam	1		1	1		1		2		1			7		
Newbury	106	11	Longfellow	John	2			1		1		1	1	1			7		
Newbury	106	13	Longfellow	Nathan	1		2	1		1			1	1			7		
Rowley	128	13	Longfellow	Stepn		3	2		1	1			1	1			9		
Salem	213	8	Longway	Mary		1				1		1	2	1			6		
Ipswich	274	52	Lord	Aaron	1				1				1	1			4		
Ipswich	281	17	Lord	Aaron Junr		1		1		2	1	1	1				7		
Ipswich	274	16	Lord	Abraham			1						1				2		
Ipswich	273	31	Lord	Benjamin	2			1		1	2		1				7		
Marblehead	243	5	Lord	Benjamin	2	2		1					1				6		
Ipswich	274	57	Lord	Caleb				1					1				2		
Ipswich	273	25	Lord	Charles		1		1	1	1	1		1				6		
Ipswich	273	40	Lord	Daniel			1	1				1	1				4		
Ipswich	274	27	Lord	Daniel	3			1		1			1				6		
Ipswich	274	44	Lord	Daniel	2			1					1				4		
Ipswich	274	54	Lord	Daniel B.	2			1		2			1				6		
Ipswich	273	29	Lord	David	1	2			1	2			1				7		
Ipswich	274	50	Lord	Ebenezer		1			1		1	1		1			5		
Ipswich	279	21	Lord	Ebenezer		1	1		1				1	1			5		
Ipswich	274	43	Lord	Ebenezer Jun	1			1		1			1				4		
Ipswich	273	47	Lord	Elizabeth			1						2	1			4		
Ipswich	274	18	Lord	Elizabeth									1	1			2		
Ipswich	273	45	Lord	Isaac	1		3	1					1	1			7		
Salem	195	12	Lord	Jacob		1	1			1	1						4		
Ipswich	273	41	Lord	John	1			1				1		1			4		
Ipswich	277	2	Lord	John	3			1		1	1		1				7		
Ipswich	274	46	Lord	Joseph	2			1		1	1		1				6		
Ipswich	273	27	Lord	Moses								1					1		
Ipswich	276	7	Lord	Moses Jun	2	1	1	1		1			1	1			8		
Ipswich	274	51	Lord	Nathaniel	1		1		1	2	2		1				8		
Ipswich	279	22	Lord	Phillip				1									1		
Ipswich	274	58	Lord	Robert	1			1		1	1			1			5		
Ipswich	274	6	Lord	Samuel				1			2			1			4		
Ipswich	275	1	Lord	Samuel	1	1		1	1	2			1				7		
Ipswich	274	53	Lord	Samuel 3d				1	1				3	1			6		
Ipswich	274	55	Lord	Samuel 4th	2		2	1		2			1				8		
Ipswich	275	48	Lord	Stephen	2			1		2			1				6		
Ipswich	281	56	Lord	Thomas	2	1	3		1			1	1	2			11		
Newburyport	170	30	Loring	Richard				1		2	1			1			5		
Haverhill	148	15	Loud	William	3			1		1			1				6		
Andover	98	26	Lovejoy	Ebenezer	4			1					1				6		
Andover	98	13	Lovejoy	Isaac					2	1			1	1			5		
Andover	98	16	Lovejoy	Isaac 3rd	3			1	1	1	2	1	1				10		
Andover	98	25	Lovejoy	Isaac Junr	1	2		1	1	2	1		1	1			10		
Andover	98	24	Lovejoy	Jeremiah	1		1		1			1		1			5		
Andover	98	17	Lovejoy	John			1										1		
Andover	98	15	Lovejoy	Joseph		2		1			1	1		1			6		
Andover	98	14	Lovejoy	Joshua				1						1			2		
Andover	103	28	Lovejoy	Momp											3		3		
Andover	98	18	Lovejoy	Nathaniel Esq	1		1		1			1	1				5		
Hamilton	285	45	Lovering	Ebenezer			1	1				1	1	1			4		
Newbury	113	38	Lovering	Enis		2							1				3		
Hamilton	285	46	Lovering	John		1	1			1	1		1				6		
Hamilton	287	1	Lovering	John		1			1			2	1				5		
Hamilton	285	47	Lovering	Joseph	1	1		1		2			1				6		
Newbury	109	45	Lovering	Richard		1	2	1		1		1	1				7		
Beverly	301	8	Lovett	Benja B					1					1			2		
Beverly	303	27	Lovett	Benja Jr	3	3	2	1		2	2	1	2				16		
Beverly	304	38	Lovett	Benjamin		2			1		2	1	2	1			9		
Beverly	301	4	Lovett	Ebenezer		1	1	1		3	1		1				8		

227

TOWN	PG#	LN#	HEADS OF HOUSEHOLD LAST NAME	HEADS OF HOUSEHOLD FIRST NAME	FREE WHITE MALES under 10	10 to 16	16 to 26	26 to 45	45 and over	FREE WHITE FEMALES under 10	10 to 16	16 to 26	26 to 45	45 and over	TOTAL ALL OTHER	TOTAL SLAVES	TOTALS	DISTRICT/ TOWNSHIP	NOTES
Beverly	292	42	Lovett	Eliza		1	1					3	1	1			7		
Beverly	304	1	Lovett	Ezra		1		1		2			1				5		
Beverly	304	2	Lovett	Hannah								1		1			2		
Beverly	304	10	Lovett	Hezekiah	1		1	1		3			1				7		
Beverly	304	3	Lovett	Jeremiah	1	1	1	1		1			1	1			7		
Beverly	301	6	Lovett	Joanna	1									1			2		
Beverly	292	44	Lovett	John	1			1		1	1		2				6		
Beverly	301	28	Lovett	Jonathan		1		1			1		1				4		
Beverly	292	43	Lovett	Jonathan H			1			1			1				3		
Beverly	292	32	Lovett	Joseph			1	1	1			1	1	1			6		
Beverly	297	25	Lovett	Joseph			1		1			1		1			4		
Beverly	294	37	Lovett	Joseph 3d	2			1		2			1				6		
Beverly	301	7	Lovett	Josiah		1						1					2		
Beverly	301	29	Lovett	Judith										1			1		
Beverly	296	39	Lovett	Mary		1							1	1			3		
Beverly	301	44	Lovett	Samuel		1	1			2			1	1			6		
Beverly	303	42	Lovett	William	2			1	1	2				1			7		
Beverly	294	38	Lovett	William 2d	1			1		2	1		1				6		
Rowley	128	1	Lovewell	Shuball	1			1		1			1				4		
Ipswich	282	26	Low	Aaron	2	1	1		1	3			1	1			10		
Danvers	11	40	Low	Caleb			2		1					1			4		
Ipswich	281	70	Low	Daniel	1	1	2	1	1		1	1		1			9		
Manchester	52	26	Low	Daniel	1	1	1	1		3			1				8		
Salem	204	11	Low	Daniel	1		2		1	1	3	2		1			11		
Gloucester	70	6	Low	David Capt	2	1		1		2		2	1				9		
Ipswich	281	35	Low	Ebenezer	1	1	1	1	1					1			6		
Ipswich	283	30	Low	Einice										1			1		
Gloucester	62	11	Low	Elias Junr			1			1		1					3		
Ipswich	281	81	Low	Elizabeth	1					1	1		1				4		
Gloucester	59	37	Low	Frances	1			1						1			3		
Haverhill	148	7	Low	Hannah	2		2			2			1				7		
Ipswich	283	29	Low	Isaac			1					1					2		
Beverly	295	40	Low	John	3	1	1		1	2	2		1				11		
Gloucester	59	38	Low	John Junr	2	1		1		1			1	1			7		
Gloucester	59	36	Low	Jonathan	1	2		2		2			1	1			9		
Gloucester	71	21	Low	Judith Wo									1				1		
Gloucester	65	9	Low	Lydia Wo	2	2				2	1	1					8		
Boxford	135	9	Low	Nathan	1		3	1					1				6		
Ipswich	283	15	Low	Rufus			1			1			1		1		4		
Ipswich	273	52	Low	Sarah									1				1		
Danvers	11	42	Low	Stephen	5			1				1	1				8		
Ipswich	283	14	Low	Stephen				1		1			1				3		
Ipswich	281	57	Low	William	1	2	2		1	2		1	1				10		
Gloucester	71	24	Lowe	Elias	3	1		1		1	2		1				9		
Gloucester	70	7	Lowe	John	2	2	4		1		1	3	1				14		
Newburyport	170	43	Lowe	John	1		1		1					1			4		
Gloucester	80	8	Lowe	Willm	3	2	2		1	1			2	1			12		
Rowley	131	23	Lowel	Solomon	1		1			1			1				4		
Amesbury	42	1	Lowell	Barnard	4	2		1		1			1				9		
Amesbury	42	5	Lowell	David	1	1	1	1				3	1				8		
Newburyport	171	10	Lowell	Ebenezer	1				1					1			3		
Amesbury	42	6	Lowell	Eliphalet					1					1			2		
Amesbury	42	2	Lowell	Ezra Capt					1		1	1	1	1			5		
Amesbury	42	3	Lowell	James Capt	1	1		1					1				4		
Salisbury	30	3	Lowell	Lewis	1			1		2	1		1				6		
Salisbury	30	1	Lowell	Simeon	1		1		1	1	3		1				9		
Salisbury	30	2	Lowell	Stephen			1			1	1						3		
Newbury	117	26	Lowrey	Peter	2			1		2	1		1				7		
Amesbury	42	7	Lowvey	Benj Capt				2					1	1			4		
Amesbury	42	10	Lowvey	Wm Capt	3		2	1				2		1			9		
Gloucester	69	15	Loyd	John	2			1		1				1			5		
Newburyport	171	4	Lucas	Thomas	2			1					1				4		
Salem	201	19	Ludden	Michael	2	1		1				1		1			6		
Ipswich	282	8	Lufkin	Jonathan		1				1		1					3		
Ipswich	282	39	Lufkin	Mary		2						1	1				4		
Gloucester	86	25	Lufkin	Moses	3	2		1			1		1				5		
Ipswich	282	6	Lufkin	Nathaniel				1				1		1	1		4		
Salem	218	58	Lufkin	Solomon	1	1			1		2	1		1			7		
Ipswich	282	7	Lufkin	William	2	1	1		1	2	2			1			10		
Gloucester	69	2	Lufkins	Moses												10	10		
Gloucester	57	6	Lufkins	Thos	2		1	1		1	1	1	1	1			9		
Haverhill	148	12	Luftkin	Mehitable		2						2	1				5		
Beverly	299	34	Lugue	Anthony	2			1					1				4		
Rowley	128	29	Lull	Thomas		2		1	1		1	1		1			7		
Newbury	117	3	Lumbart	Abigail	2						1	1	1				6		
Lynn	224	39	Lummus	Aaron	4			1		1	2		1				9		
Ipswich	274	31	Lummus	Daniel Jur			1	1						1			3		
Ipswich	274	24	Lummus	Isaac		1				1			1				3		
Andover	98	27	Lummus	Joseph	4			1				1		1			7		
Newburyport	170	25	Lunt	Abel	2			1		1			1	3			8		
Newbury	112	47	Lunt	Ambrose	2			1		1			2				6		
Newbury	120	33	Lunt	Amos	1		1			1			1				4		
Newbury	111	46	Lunt	Benja	1			1		1	1	1					5		
Newburyport	170	23	Lunt	Benjamin	2	1		1	1		2	3	1	1			12		
Newburyport	170	27	Lunt	Benjamin S	1		1	1						1			4		

TOWN	PG#	LN#	LAST NAME	FIRST NAME	FREE WHITE MALES under 10	10 to 16	16 to 26	26 to 45	45 and over	FREE WHITE FEMALES under 10	10 to 16	16 to 26	26 to 45	45 and over	TOTAL ALL OTHER	TOTAL SLAVES	TOTALS	DISTRICT/TOWNSHIP	NOTES
Newbury	113	18	Lunt	Elijah	1	1				1	1			1			5		
Newbury	112	20	Lunt	Enoch	1	1			1	3		1	1				8		
Newbury	120	3	Lunt	Enoch			1					1	1				3		
Newbury	115	4	Lunt	Henry	1	1	1		1	1	1		1				7		
Newburyport	170	29	Lunt	Josiah	2			1		3			1				7		
Newbury	112	13	Lunt	Lydia						1				1			2		
Newbury	117	13	Lunt	Nicolas			1	1				4	1	2			9		
Newbury	115	15	Lunt	Paul		1			1	2				1			5		
Newbury	116	32	Lunt	Paul	1				1				1				3		
Newbury	120	12	Lunt	Paul		1	1						1				3		
Newbury	113	44	Lunt	Richard				1		2			1	1			5		
Newbury	112	42	Lunt	Samuel	1			1		2			1	1			6		
Newbury	117	14	Lunt	Samuel				1						1			2		
Newburyport	170	24	Lunt	Samuel		1			1	1	1	2		2			8		
Newbury	110	22	Lunt	Sarah			1					2		1			4		
Newburyport	170	28	Lunt	Silas			1					1		1			3		
Newbury	106	27	Lunt	Stephen	1		1		1				1	1			5		
Newbury	113	21	Lunt	Thomas	1			1		1			1	1			5		
Newbury	112	21	Lunt	Tristam			1						1				2		
Newburyport	170	26	Lunt	William P				1					1	1			3		
Newbury	111	47	Lunt	Woodbridge	2			1		1			1				5		
Gloucester	73	7	Lurvey	Jacob					1					1			2		
Salem	201	22	Luscomb	Benja			1	1		1	3		1				7		
Salem	201	23	Luscomb	Henry	2	2		1		1			1				7		
Salem	205	2	Luscomb	Saml					1					1			2		
Salem	218	10	Luscomb	William	2			1		2			1				6		
Salem	205	15	Luscomb	Willm	1	2			1	1	1			1			7		
Salem	205	16	Luscomb	Willm Jr	2	2	1			2	1	1					9		
Gloucester	85	33	Luteral	Hughes	1			1		2	1	1	1				7		
Salem	183	14	Luther	Nathan			2	1		1			1				5		
Bradford	124	46	Lutice	Joshua	1	2		1	1				4	1			10		
Gloucester	59	40	Lutkin	David	1				1	1	1	3	1	1			9		
Gloucester	80	9	Lutterel	Hughes				1		4			1				6		
Lynn	225	5	Lye	Joseph	2	1	1	1		2	2		1				10		
Lynn	224	10	Lyndsey	Daniel		2			1	3				2			8		
Lynn	232	14	Lyndsey	John	1			1		3			1				6		
Lynn	224	9	Lyndsey	Mary			1							1			2		
Lynn	232	15	Lyndsey	Phebe									1	3			4		
Marblehead	251	24	Lyons	James	4	2		1			1	1	1				10		
Newburyport	172	18	Mace	Abraham	1	1			1	2	1	1		2			9		
Newburyport	172	17	Mace	Bernard				1						1			2		
Newbury	114	8	Mace	Joseph	1	1		1		1			1				5		
Newbury	114	23	Mace	William				1		1		1					3		
Danvers	6	19	Macentire	Aaron	2			1		1			1				5		
Danvers	6	40	Macenture	Judith									1	2			3		
Danvers	9	32	Macintire	John				1				1		1			3		
Danvers	9	30	Macintire	Samuel	1	2		1		2	1		1				8		
Danvers	11	21	Macintire	Solomon			2			1			1				4		
Beverly	304	28	Mackey	Samuel G			1					1					2		
Salem	203	4	Magredge	Rachel		2		1						1			4		
Newbury	111	14	Magridge	John				1			2	2	1				6		
Haverhill	148	36	Mahana	John	1		1	1		1			1				5		
Marblehead	250	26	Maine	William			1	1		1		1	1				5		
Topsfield	21	18	Majery	Hannah										1			1		
Salem	218	42	Major	Susanna						1			1				2		
Andover	99	13	Malcoy	John				1						1			2		
Marblehead	255	23	Maley	Daniel	2	1	2		1	2		1	1				10		
Salem	210	21	Maley	Lydia	1					1		1					3		
Salem	219	46	Mallia	Marcello			1			1		1					3		
Salem	201	36	Maloon	Judy	1					1		1	1				4		
Salisbury	30	27	Manfield	Dudley		2		1						3			6		
Salisbury	30	32	Manfield	John	1		1	2		2	1	1					8		
Salem	188	35	Manfield	Joseph				1				1					2		
Salisbury	30	33	Manfield	Wd										2			2		
Haverhill	148	24	Manfise	Cornelus		2	1	1		1			1	1			7		
Haverhill	148	22	Manfise	Hannah										2			2		
Haverhill	148	23	Manfise	Simon		2	1	1		1		1	1				7		
Beverly	300	19	Mange	Sarah						1		1					2		
Marblehead	270	18	Mann	Abijah	2	1	2	2		1	1						9		
Salisbury	31	4	Mann	Dolly Wd						1		1					2		
Salem	199	10	Mann	Ebenz	3		1	4		1		1	1				11		
Marblehead	241	33	Mann	Lydia	2	1	1			1	1	1					7		
Marblehead	258	14	Mann	Thomas				1						1			2		
Beverly	296	15	Mann	Perez	1	1	1	1		3				1			8		
Salem	205	4	Manning	Anstis									1	1			2		
Ipswich	278	50	Manning	Jacob	1	1			1	2	2			1			8		
Gloucester	80	11	Manning	Jno Doct	1	2		1					2				6		
Ipswich	275	9	Manning	John		1	5		1	2		4		1			14		
Ipswich	281	18	Manning	John 3d				1		1			1				3		
Ipswich	281	13	Manning	John Junr	1		1	1		1	1		1	1			7		
Manchester	53	24	Manning	Prisc Wo	1								2				3		
Salem	216	28	Manning	Richard					2			1		3			6		
Salem	216	48	Manning	Richard Jr	1	3	2	1				1	3	1			12		
Andover	98	35	Manning	Thomas	1	4	1	1					1	1			9		
Andover	99	15	Manning	Thomas Jr			1										1		
Salem	215	12	Manning	Thos	3	1			1	1	3	3	1				13		
Salem	209	4	Manning	William	1		1			1		1		1			5		

229

TOWN	PG#	LN#	LAST NAME	FIRST NAME	FREE WHITE MALES under 10	10 to 16	16 to 26	26 to 45	45 and over	FREE WHITE FEMALES under 10	10 to 16	16 to 26	26 to 45	45 and over	TOTAL ALL OTHER	TOTAL SLAVES	TOTALS	DISTRICT/ TOWNSHIP	NOTES
Beverly	295	31	Manning	Wm S	1	1			1	3			1				7		
Newburyport	172	28	Manser	Samuel			1				1	1					3		
Ipswich	277	47	Mansfield	Abigail								1	1				2		
Danvers	4	6	Mansfield	Andrew		1	1	1	1		1		2				7		
Lynnfield	235	23	Mansfield	Andrw	1		1			1		1	1				5		
Lynn	234	12	Mansfield	Benj	1		2		1		1	1		1			7		
Salem	189	7	Mansfield	Daniel R	1	1		1		1	1	1	1				7		
Newburyport	172	24	Mansfield	David	1			1		1			1				4		
Lynn	227	11	Mansfield	Ebenz	2		1			1		1					5		
Lynn	229	17	Mansfield	Eliza	1		2				1	1		1			6		
Salem	206	43	Mansfield	Ellis			1			2	2	1					6		
Marblehead	264	7	Mansfield	Isaac		1		1		1			2				5		
Gloucester	60	8	Mansfield	James	1		1	1		2	1		2				8		
Salem	214	36	Mansfield	James	2			1		2		1					6		
Lynnfield	235	9	Mansfield	Jane		3				1	3		1				8		
Danvers	4	7	Mansfield	John		1	1					1					3		
Lynn	229	26	Mansfield	Jona		1						1					2		
Salem	207	38	Mansfield	Jona	2			1		1	1	1					6		
Salem	201	30	Mansfield	Joseph	2	2		1			1		1				7		
Salem	206	57	Mansfield	Joseph	1		1					1					3		
Salem	204	42	Mansfield	Mary	2						1	1	1				5		
Salem	206	55	Mansfield	Mathew				1			1	1					3		
Lynn	234	18	Mansfield	Moses		1	2	1				2					6		
Lynn	234	13	Mansfield	Nathl	1		1	1				1					4		
Lynn	234	15	Mansfield	Richard		1	1	1		2		1					6		
Lynn	228	32	Mansfield	Robert	1		4		1	1	1		1				9		
Lynn	225	20	Mansfield	Robt Jr			1					1					2		
Lynn	229	34	Mansfield	Rufus		3		1		1		1					6		
Lynn	229	35	Mansfield	Rufus Jr			1			1		1					3		
Lynn	228	41	Mansfield	Saml		2	1				1		1				5		
Lynn	234	16	Mansfield	Saml	1	2		1				1					5		
Lynn	233	22	Mansfield	Saml 3d	1	2		1	1	3		1					9		
Lynn	234	17	Mansfield	Thomas Jr	1	2	2	1		2	1	1	1				11		
Lynn	233	34	Mansfield	Thos				1				1	1				3	West Parish	
Lynn	229	3	Mansfield	Willm			2	1	1	2	1	1	1				9		
Lynnfield	235	18	Mansfield	Willm		1		1		1	1		1				5		
Lynnfield	236	22	Mansfield	Willm Jr			1					1					2		
Methuen	155	3	Mansur	Elijah	3		1		1			1					6		
Salem	208	30	Manuel	Peter											4		4		
Gloucester	60	2	Marble	Benja	3			1		2			1				7		
Andover	98	29	Marble	Cyrus		1	1	1	1		1	2	1				8		
Danvers	7	10	Marble	Enoch			1										1		
Haverhill	148	48	Marble	John	1			1			1	1	2				6		
Bradford	123	28	Marble	Joseph			2	1				1	1				5		
Haverhill	148	45	Marble	Samuel	1		1					2					5		
Newburyport	171	14	March	Angier		1	3	1		1		2					8		
Andover	98	32	March	Daniel		1											1		
Newbury	114	38	March	Ebenezer		1		1		1		1					4		
Amesbury	42	27	March	Ichabod		1		1					1				3		
Salisbury	30	7	March	John			1	1				1	1				4		
Ipswich	277	21	March	Nathaniel		1		1			1		1				4		
Ipswich	274	36	March	Nathaniel Jun			1			2	1						4		
Salisbury	30	6	March	Samuel		1	1	1		2	1	1	1				8		
Salem	217	28	March	Thos	1		1					1					3		
Newburyport	172	20	Marchant	Samuel		1		1			1	1					4		
Newburyport	171	19	Marchmore	Jeffrey	1			1		1			1				4		
Newburyport	171	20	Marchmore	John		1		1		1			1				4		
Bradford	124	32	Mardin	David				1		1	1	1					4		
Andover	99	8	Mare	Isaac				1				1	1				3		
Andover	99	9	Mare	Jonathan	2			1		1			1				5		
Newburyport	171	23	Margerand	Joseph	1	1			1	2	2	2	1	1			11		
Lynn	232	6	Markpiece	Jona			1			1		2					4		
Danvers	7	22	Marsh	Aaron			1			1	1						3		
Haverhill	148	32	Marsh	Cutting	1			1		1			1				4		
Danvers	7	18	Marsh	Daniel	1		1			2		2					6		
Haverhill	148	26	Marsh	David				3					2				5		
Haverhill	148	28	Marsh	David Junr	1		1					1					3		
Danvers	7	21	Marsh	Ebenezer			1			1							2		
Gloucester	75	12	Marsh	Elles Wo	2						1						3		
Danvers	7	1	Marsh	Ezekiel	1	1		1				2					5		
Danvers	7	2	Marsh	Ezekiel Junr	1			1		1		1					4		
Danvers	14	6	Marsh	John		1							2				3		
Newburyport	171	12	Marsh	Jonathan	1			1			1	1	1				5		
Haverhill	148	27	Marsh	Moses		1	1	1		1	1	1	1				7		
Haverhill	148	33	Marsh	Moses Junr	2		1	1		1	1		1				7		
Danvers	4	28	Marsh	Rhode wife of John Ma:	2							1	1				4		
Haverhill	148	34	Marsh	Robert	2			1					1				4		
Newbury	112	39	Marshal	Isaac			1	1					1				3		
Danvers	11	32	Marshal	Robert	1	1		1		2		1					6		
Salem	199	17	Marshal	Samuel			1	1	1			1		1			5		
Salem	199	19	Marshal	Samuel	1			1		1	1	1					6		
Gloucester	79	18	Marshall	Benja	1	1		1		1	2	1		1			8		
Gloucester	80	10	Marshall	Benja		1				1		1					3		
Andover	99	14	Marshall	Jacob	1	1		1	1			1					6		

TOWN	PG#	LN#	LAST NAME	FIRST NAME	FREE WHITE MALES					FREE WHITE FEMALES					TOTAL ALL OTHER	TOTAL SLAVES	TOTALS	DISTRICT/ TOWNSHIP	NOTES
					under 10	10 to 16	16 to 26	26 to 45	45 and over	under 10	10 to 16	16 to 26	26 to 45	45 and over					
Andover	103	22	Marshall	Jeremiah				1						1	2		4		
Gloucester	60	10	Marshall	John			1	1		1	1	1					5		
Ipswich	281	73	Marshall	Moses	2	2		1		2		1	1				9		
Salem	199	34	Marshall	Rufus			1					1					2		
Gloucester	60	12	Marshall	Samuel				1		3	2		1				7		
Ipswich	283	16	Marshall	Sarah									2	1			3		
Gloucester	60	11	Marshall	Solomon	2			1		1		1	1				6		
Rowley	131	1	Marshall	Thomas	1	1		1		2		1	1				7		
Gloucester	62	30	Marshall	William	3			1					1				5		
Beverly	295	20	Marshel	Timothy	4	1	1	1					1				8		
Methuen	154	35	Marsten	Peter		4		1		2		1	1	2			11		
Manchester	53	17	Marston	Andrew		1							1				2		
Manchester	53	27	Marston	Betty Wo						1		1	1				3		
Newburyport	172	25	Marston	John	1		2			1		1					5		
Salem	191	19	Marston	Mary		1	1			1				1			4		
Salem	204	23	Marston	Mary								1	1				2		
Marblehead	270	8	Marston	Sarah	1	1						2	1	1			6		
Salem	202	43	Marston	William				1					1				2		
Salem	206	23	Marston	William		1	2		1	3							8		
Ipswich	277	7	Martain	Edward	1			1		1	2		1				6		
Ipswich	278	23	Martain	Mary		1						1	2				4		
Ipswich	281	50	Martain	Nathaniel				1					1				2		
Marblehead	252	26	Martin	Ambrose		1	1			1	1	1					5		
Marblehead	243	6	Martin	Amorlold		2	1	1		1			1				6		
Amesbury	42	30	Martin	Aquilla		2		1		2	1	2	1				9		
Marblehead	268	18	Martin	Bartholomew	2			1		3	1		1				8		
Marblehead	250	10	Martin	Ebenezer	2	2	2	1		3		2	1				13		
Amesbury	42	15	Martin	Eliphalet				1					1				2		
Salem	192	28	Martin	Geo W			4			1	1		1				7		
Marblehead	264	8	Martin	Hannah				1				1		1			3		
Amesbury	42	29	Martin	Isaac	1	1	1	1					1	1			6		
Salem	221	20	Martin	Israel		1							1	1			3		
Newbury	105	5	Martin	James				1				1		1			3		
Amesbury	42	14	Martin	John	2		1	1					2	1			7		
Marblehead	239	28	Martin	John		1		1		1	1		1				5		
Marblehead	241	26	Martin	John				1		1			1				3		
Lynn	224	12	Martin	Jonathan		1		1					1				3		
Newbury	105	16	Martin	Jonathan			1			2		1	1				5		
Andover	99	4	Martin	Joseph				1					1				2		
Marblehead	256	1	Martin	Knott				1		1			1				3		
Marblehead	245	23	Martin	Mary		1					1	1	1				4		
Marblehead	257	11	Martin	Mary			1						1				2		
Salem	203	13	Martin	Mary		1	1			1			1				4		
Salem	212	31	Martin	Mary						1		1	1				3		
Newburyport	172	31	Martin	Mary Wido									1	1			2		
Marblehead	251	23	Martin	Nathan B	1		1	1		2			1				7		
Haverhill	148	17	Martin	Oliver	2			2		3	1	1	1				10		
Marblehead	251	21	Martin	Polly	1					1			1				3		
Marblehead	250	11	Martin	Prudence									1	2			3		
Marblehead	245	7	Martin	Richard		1	2		1	2	2	1	1	1			11		
Gloucester	68	20	Martin	Sarah Wo			1						1				2		
Andover	99	6	Martin	Solomon	2			1		3	1		1				8		
Marblehead	267	32	Martin	Thomas	1		1	1				1		1			5		
Marblehead	267	22	Martin	Thomas Junr	1	1	1	1		1	1		1				6		
Salem	208	26	Martin	Thos											2		2		
Salem	214	23	Martin	Thos			1						1				2		
Salem	219	28	Mascol	Hannah				1					1				2		
Salem	219	29	Mascol	Stephen			1			1			1				3		
Gloucester	84	8	Maskell	Joseph	1		1						1	1			4		
Gloucester	60	13	Mason	John	2			1				1		1			5		
Salem	215	11	Mason	Jona	2	1				1	2	1	1				9		
Gloucester	84	16	Mason	Joseph			2	1			2		1				6		
Marblehead	242	22	Mason	Mary									1		2		3		
Andover	99	5	Mason	Robert				1					1				2		
Salem	193	24	Mason	Susanna							1			1			2		
Salem	215	33	Mason	Thos				1				1	1				3		
Marblehead	242	12	Mason	William				1					1				2		
Marblehead	246	1	Mason	William	1	1	1						2	1			7		
Lynn	226	4	Massey	John	1	1	1	1	1	2			1				8		
Lynn	230	18	Massey	Nathl			1				1	1					3		
Gloucester	84	22	Masters	Charles G	2			1		3	1		1				8		
Salem	195	10	Masurey	Thoms	1			1					1				3		
Beverly	303	13	Masury	John	1			1		1			1				4		
Salem	214	46	Masury	Samuel	3			1		2		1	1				8		
Salem	221	17	Masury	Samuel	2	1	1	1		2		1	1				9		
Salem	210	44	Mathews	Abigail									1				1		
Salem	216	11	Matoon	Hubartus				1					1				2		
Amesbury	43	8	Matron	Dorothy Wid						1			1				2		
Beverly	301	31	Matter	John			1				1						2		
Beverly	301	32	Matter	Samuel		1						1					2		
Marblehead	252	14	Matthews	William				1					1				2		
Salem	196	26	Maurey	Hannah		2						1		1			4		
Salem	193	26	Maxcy	Levi	2			1					1				4		
Amesbury	42	17	Maxfield	Judith			1						1	1			3		
Manchester	53	26	May	Annie Wo									1	1			2		
Beverly	295	9	May	James	1			1		2			1	1			6		

			HEADS OF HOUSEHOLD		FREE WHITE MALES					FREE WHITE FEMALES									
TOWN	PG#	LN#	LAST NAME	FIRST NAME	under 10	10 to 16	16 to 26	26 to 45	45 and over	under 10	10 to 16	16 to 26	26 to 45	45 and over	TOTAL ALL OTHER	TOTAL SLAVES	TOTALS	DISTRICT/ TOWNSHIP	NOTES
Manchester	53	19	May	Jon		1			1	1			1				4		
Manchester	53	28	May	Jona Jun		1	1			1			1				4		
Manchester	53	20	May	Sarah Wo	2	1							2	1			6		
Newburyport	171	15	Mayhew	Elijah		1	5				1	1	1				9		
Haverhill	148	41	Mayhew	Nathll			1			3			1	2			7		
Salem	217	24	Mcannister	John A	1		1						1	1			4		
Salem	191	11	McCarthy	Justin	2		1			3			1	1			8		
Manchester	50	16	McCartney	Jas	1	1	1			1			1				5		
Methuen	154	46	McClary	David		2		1					1	1			5		
Andover	93	6	McCrobia	William		1				1		1					3		
Newburyport	172	26	McDaniel	Ruth Wido										1			1		
Salem	219	2	McDonald	Benja			1			2			1	1			5		
Salem	208	22	McElroy	Benja				1						1			2		
Haverhill	146	1	McFarland	Moses	1	1	1		1			2		1			7		
Newburyport	166	35	McGaw	John	1	1		1			1		1				5		
Salem	211	11	McGuay	John	1			1	1	4	1		1				9		
Lynnfield	235	39	McIntire	John	1			1	1	1			1				5		
Salem	204	46	McIntyer	Anger	1	2		1		2			1				7		
Salem	192	39	McIntyer	Eliza									3				3		
Salem	209	22	McIntyer	Eliza				1					1				2		
Salem	204	44	McIntyer	Joseph	1	1		1					1				4		
Salem	202	3	McIntyer	Nath	1			1		2			1				5		
Salem	198	25	McIntyer	Nathl	1			1		4	2		1	1			10		
Salem	205	32	McIntyer	Samuel			1	1		1			2				5		
Salem	204	45	McIntyer	Sarah								2	1				3		
Beverly	289	3	McKeen	Joseph Rvd	1	2		1		1	1	1					7		
Beverly	292	34	McLallan	George			1				2			1			4		
Andover	98	34	McLaughlin	Mary	2								1				3		
Salem	202	26	McMillan	Arch	1	1		1		1	1		1				6		
Salem	212	38	McMillan	John			1		1				1	1			4		
Salem	200	32	McPherson	Duncan		1	1	1						1			4		
Salem	219	12	McPherson	John	1	1		1		1	1	1	1				7		
Haverhill	148	38	McRoy	John	1			1		1			1				4		
Andover	98	31	Meacham	Benja	2	1	1			1			1				6		
Salem	188	40	Mead	Benja			1	1					1				3		
Salem	200	38	Mead	Jacob	1		2						1				4		
Lynnfield	236	10	Mead	John					1					1			2		
Danvers	11	9	Mead	Samuel Revd	1			1		1			1				4		
Ipswich	283	11	Mears	Alexander	3		2		1	1	1		1				9		
Ipswich	283	33	Mears	John			1			1			1				3		
Ipswich	279	32	Medcalf	Joseph				1		1			1				3		
Gloucester	85	18	Medler	Enoch			1			2			1				4		
Gloucester	85	17	Medler	Susa Wo			1			1			1				3		
Gloucester	65	11	Medox	James	1			1		1			1				4		
Gloucester	65	13	Medox	John	2				1				1				4		
Lynn	231	5	Meecham	Ruth										1			1		
Ipswich	281	3	Meedy	Thomas	1	1	1		1	2	1		1				8		
Marblehead	248	13	Meek	Thomas	2	3	3	1		3	1	1	1	1			16		
Salem	190	39	Meek	Timothy	2			1		2			1				6		
Lynn	229	36	Meeks	George			1			1		1					3		
Salem	197	31	Meeks	Tho					1	1			1	1			4		
Marblehead	241	10	Megan	Susannah	3								1	1			5		
Marblehead	252	7	Megear	John				1		1			1				3		
Methuen	155	2	Melone	James	1			1		1			1				4		
Methuen	155	1	Melone	Kendal	1		1	1		1		1					5		
Newbury	116	1	Melton	Silas	1		1			1			1				4		
Marblehead	239	29	Melvill	John		1		1		3				1			6		
Marblehead	258	10	Melzard	George		1	1	1			1			1			5		
Marblehead	261	11	Melzard	John	2	1	2		1	1	1			1			9		
Marblehead	251	11	Melzard	Mary									1				1		
Marblehead	261	16	Melzard	Richard		1							1				2		
Gloucester	75	11	Merchant	Daniel			1			1			1				3		
Gloucester	75	23	Merchant	Daniel				1						1			2		
Gloucester	77	19	Merchant	Daniel Junr		1				1			1				3		
Salem	218	36	Merchant	Nath	3		1			1			1				6		
Gloucester	78	14	Merchant	William	1	1	2			1			1				6		
Gloucester	78	15	Merchant	Willm Junr			1			1			1				3		
Newburyport	172	27	Mercy	Anthony	1			1		1			1				4		
Gloucester	75	6	Merhcant	Jabez	1	1			1	2		2	1	1			9		
Topsfield	20	40	Meriam	John		2		1		1			1				5		
Topsfield	21	2	Meriam	Jonas		1		1		2			1				5		
Middleton	16	7	Meriam	Silas			2	1		3			2				8		
Salem	217	4	Meriam	William	1	4	1			1	1	1	1				10		
Marblehead	255	33	Merrett	Francis	2			1					1				4		
Marblehead	255	20	Merrett	John	1	1	1					1		2			6		
Marblehead	269	2	Merrich	Elizabeth			1							1			2		
Ipswich	278	58	Merrifield	Francis			1	1						1			3		
Ipswich	278	57	Merrifield	Francis Jr				1						1			2		
Ipswich	279	17	Merrifield	Thomas	1		1						1				3		
Newbury	110	25	Merril	Abel		1		1						1			3		
Boxford	134	19	Merril	Dorcas							1	1					2		
Bradford	123	10	Merril	Dortha	2				1		1	2		1			7		
Newbury	109	38	Merril	Henry	1	1	2		2	2	1			1			10		
Newbury	110	40	Merril	Jacob	2				1	1	1			1			6		
Rowley	132	9	Merril	John				1		2	1			1			5		
Newbury	111	13	Merril	Jonathan	1		1							1			3		

TOWN	PG#	LN#	LAST NAME	FIRST NAME	FREE WHITE MALES					FREE WHITE FEMALES					TOTAL ALL OTHER	TOTAL SLAVES	TOTALS	DISTRICT/ TOWNSHIP	NOTES
					under 10	10 to 16	16 to 26	26 to 45	45 and over	under 10	10 to 16	16 to 26	26 to 45	45 and over					
Newbury	110	38	Merril	Joseph	1			1		1			1				4		
Rowley	130	25	Merril	Moses		1		1		2	1		1				6		
Newbury	110	28	Merril	Nathan			2				1	2		1			6		
Newbury	111	12	Merril	Nathan	1		1	1					1				4		
Newbury	110	6	Merril	Olander	3	1		1					1	1			7		
Rowley	128	40	Merril	Thomas		1	1			1	2	1					6		
Rowley	132	8	Merril	Thos		1	2		1	1			1		1		7		
Amesbury	42	18	Merrill	Benja	1		1	1		2	1		1	1			8		
Andover	98	33	Merrill	Benja			1										1		
Salisbury	30	9	Merrill	Benja		2			1	2				1			6		
Newburyport	172	15	Merrill	Daniel		1			1	2				1			5		
Salisbury	30	20	Merrill	Daniel			1		1		1	1	1	2			7		
Andover	98	28	Merrill	Ebenz	1		1	1		2			1	1			7		
Andover	99	10	Merrill	Enoch	1				1	3	2		1				8		
Newburyport	172	16	Merrill	Ezra	1		1						1				3		
Salisbury	30	21	Merrill	Ezra		1	3		1					1			6		
Salisbury	31	1	Merrill	Ezra Capt			1						1				2		
Haverhill	148	47	Merrill	Giles		2	1		1	2	3			1			10		
Amesbury	43	6	Merrill	Hannah Wid										1			1		
Amesbury	42	31	Merrill	Isaac		1	1		1	1	1	1		1			7		
Amesbury	42	26	Merrill	Jacob	1		2	1	1	1	1	1		1			9		
Newbury	118	44	Merrill	Jacub	1	1	2		1				1	1			7		
Newburyport	172	12	Merrill	James		1			1		2	1		1			6		
Andover	99	11	Merrill	John			1		1			3		1			6		
Methuen	154	27	Merrill	John			1		1	1			1		1		5		
Amesbury	43	1	Merrill	John Capt		1	2	1					2				6		
Salisbury	30	13	Merrill	John Capt		1			1					1			3		
Andover	99	12	Merrill	John Junr	1			1		3		1					6		
Salisbury	30	12	Merrill	John Junr	1	1		1		1		1	1				6		
Methuen	154	45	Merrill	Jonathan	2		1	1		2	1		1	1			9		
Newburyport	172	13	Merrill	Jonathan				1		2			1				4		
Haverhill	148	49	Merrill	Jonathn		1		1					1				3		
Amesbury	42	28	Merrill	Joseph	3	1			1	2	1	1	1				10		
Salisbury	30	11	Merrill	Margaret Wd										1			1		
Salisbury	30	34	Merrill	Melatiah				1						2			3		
Salisbury	30	18	Merrill	Moses	1			1		2			1	1			6		
Salisbury	30	29	Merrill	Rhoda Wd									2	1			3		
Newburyport	172	9	Merrill	Robert		1	1	1									3		
Salisbury	31	3	Merrill	Robert		1	2		1				1				5		
Haverhill	148	44	Merrill	Samuel			4	2	1		1			3			11		
Methuen	154	26	Merrill	Samuel	3	1		1	1				2				8		
Salisbury	30	14	Merrill	Samuel			1				1		1				3		
Salisbury	30	19	Merrill	Samuel	1	1		1		2	1	1	1	1			9		
Salisbury	30	10	Merrill	Sarah Wd		2				1	2		1				6		
Newburyport	172	30	Merrill	Sarah Wido										1			1		
Newburyport	172	10	Merrill	Thomas				1		1	1			1			4		
Newburyport	172	11	Merrill	Thomas Jr				1		1	2	1		1			6		
Newburyport	172	14	Merrill	Thomas P	1			1				1					3		
Salisbury	31	2	Merrill	Wm Capt	2			1		1		1					5		
Salem	183	16	Merrit	Samuel		2		1		2			1				6		
Rowley	129	9	Merrit	Thomas			1			1			2	1			5		
Gloucester	73	17	Merritt	James	1		2					1		1			5	Town Parish	
Lynn	229	25	Merry	Sarah	1	1							1	1			4		
Newburyport	171	35	Mersevy	Mary Wido						1		2		1			4		
Salem	217	22	Meservey	Eliza							1		1				2		
Salem	201	44	Meservey	Hannah		1					1	1					3		
Beverly	299	33	Meservey	John	1			1					1				3		
Marblehead	256	33	Meservy	William		2			1					1			4		
Methuen	154	34	Messer	Alpheus	2		2	1			1	1	1				8		
Methuen	154	28	Messer	Asa		1			1		1	2		1			6		
Danvers	14	35	Messer	Asa Swan	1		1	1		1			1				5		
Methuen	154	44	Messer	Cyrus	3		1	1		1			1	1			8		
Methuen	154	32	Messer	Jacob		1		1		1	1	1	1				6		
Methuen	154	37	Messer	Jacob Jun			1					1					2		
Methuen	154	43	Messer	James	2	1			1	2		1					7		
Methuen	154	29	Messer	Nathl	2			1		1		2					6		
Methuen	154	31	Messer	Phineas			1	1	1	4	1	1		1			10		
Methuen	154	30	Messer	William	1		1	1		1	1	1					6		
Marblehead	254	28	Metzard	Benjamin		1				2		1					4		
Salem	218	13	Metzard	Nancy	1					1		1					3		
Andover	103	20	Middleton	Douglas											1		1		
Haverhill	148	39	Middleton	Samuel				1		4		1	1				7		
Newburyport	171	16	Middleton	William	1			1		2		1					5		
Rowley	127	43	Mighill	David	1	1			1		1	1					5		
Rowley	131	19	Mighill	Thos		1			1		2	1					5		
Salem	206	6	Mikels	Andrew			1				1						2		
Newburyport	171	17	Milbery	William	1	1		1		2		1					6		
Haverhill	148	42	Miliken	Susanna			1						1				2		
Gloucester	60	14	Millatt	Thos			1	2		3			1				7		
Beverly	296	45	Miller	Isaac	3		1			1		1					6		
Marblehead	249	9	Miller	John			1				1		1				3		
Marblehead	259	29	Miller	Joseph		1					1						2		
Salem	194	12	Miller	Joseph		1				1		1					3		
Salem	210	16	Miller	Joseph		1				1		1					3		

TOWN	PG#	LN#	HEADS OF HOUSEHOLD		FREE WHITE MALES					FREE WHITE FEMALES					TOTAL ALL OTHER	TOTAL SLAVES	TOTALS	DISTRICT/ TOWNSHIP	NOTES
			LAST NAME	FIRST NAME	under 10	10 to 16	16 to 26	26 to 45	45 and over	under 10	10 to 16	16 to 26	26 to 45	45 and over					
Salem	210	52	Miller	Leonard			1			2		1					4		
Marblehead	259	20	Miller	Patience									1				1		
Salem	192	15	Miller	Peter			1			1		1					3		
Gloucester	72	1	Miller	Sarah Wo						1	1		1				3		
Manchester	53	35	Miller	Simeon		1	1		1	1	1						5		
Marblehead	253	16	Millet	Abigail							2		1				3		
Salem	208	11	Millet	Abram	1		1						1				3		
Salem	216	54	Millet	Benja	1			1		2			1				5		
Salem	203	29	Millet	John	1			1		1				1			4		
Salem	218	30	Millet	Jona	4			1		1							7		
Salem	216	27	Millet	Sarah		2							1	1			4		
Salem	212	45	Millet	William	2			1		4			1				8		
Gloucester	70	18	Millett	Dorcas Wo							1	0	2				3		
Gloucester	62	14	Millett	Isaac	1		1						1				3		
Gloucester	65	12	Millett	James	1	2	1	1		3	1		1				10		
Gloucester	72	18	Millett	Nathl	2	1	1	1					1				6		
Gloucester	70	17	Millett	Susanh Wo									1	1			2		
Marblehead	264	9	Millett	Zebulun	1	2	1	1		3	1		1				10		
Gloucester	71	6	Millette	Anna Wo								2	1				3		
Gloucester	73	20	Millette	Jona		2		1	1			2		1			7	Town Parish	
Lynn	230	24	Milliken	Saml	3	1	1	1		1	1		1				9		
Salem	192	18	Millit	Eliza	1	1							3				5		
Danvers	13	3	Mills	James			1						1				2		
Newburyport	172	1	Mills	Levi		1	1			2			1				5		
Newburyport	171	22	Milton	Charles W Revd	1		1			1	1		2				6		
Lynn	224	37	Minick	John		1						1					2		
Newburyport	172	19	Minor	Francis		1	2						1				4		
Lynnfield	236	16	Miriam	Jona	2		1			2			1				6		
Bradford	124	22	Mitchel	Day		1	1						1				3		
Haverhill	148	46	Mitchel	James		1	1			3	2	2	1	1			11		
Haverhill	152	2	Mitchel	John		1		1				1		1			4		
Haverhill	152	3	Mitchel	John Junr		1							1				2		
Bradford	124	19	Mitchel	Joseph			1			1			1	1			4		
Haverhill	152	4	Mitchel	Mehetable									1	1			2		
Bradford	124	17	Mitchel	Peter			1						1				2		
Newbury	113	31	Mitchel	Stephen				1						1			2		
Marblehead	253	30	Mitchell	*en		1				2		1					4		
Marblehead	266	23	Mitchell	John	1	3		1		1				1			7		
Newburyport	172	22	Mitchell	Josiah		1	1					1	1				4		
Newburyport	172	23	Mitchell	Rachel Wido			2	4	1					1			8		
Gloucester	60	9	Mittell	Joseph	2								1				4		
Andover	99	3	Moary	Thomas	1		1			1			1				4		
Newburyport	171	18	Moffett	Samuel	1		1						1				3		
Salem	212	24	Moley	John			1					1	1	1			4		
Newbury	109	24	Molton	John	2		1			2			1				6		
Newbury	118	40	Molton	Silas	1	1	1						1				4		
Topsfield	21	7	Moneys	William				1						1			2		
Topsfield	21	8	Moneys	William Junr	1		1	1					1				5		
Andover	98	30	Montgomery	Alexander		1	1							1			3		
Newburyport	172	4	Montgomery	Mary Wido						1	1		1				3		
Newburyport	172	5	Montgomery	Moody				1						1			2		
Andover	99	1	Mooar	Isaac		1	1			2				1			5		
Andover	99	2	Mooar	Martha Wid							1		1				2		
Andover	99	7	Mooar	Timothy				1					1				2		
Haverhill	148	29	Moody	Abigail						1				1			2		
Newburyport	171	27	Moody	Benjamin			2	1					1	2			6		
Amesbury	43	3	Moody	Cutting		1		1				1	1				4		
Newbury	111	20	Moody	Cutting		1	2	1					3	1			8		
Newburyport	171	28	Moody	Daniel		3				1			1				5		
Salisbury	30	15	Moody	Daniel		2		1			1			1			5		
Newburyport	171	24	Moody	David			1	1						2			4		
Newbury	111	24	Moody	Enoch		1	1			1			1	1			5		
Newburyport	171	25	Moody	John		1	1						1				3		
Amesbury	43	4	Moody	Joseph		1	2	1				1	1	1			7		
Newburyport	171	26	Moody	Joseph		1	1						1	1			4		
Salisbury	30	17	Moody	Joshua				1					1				2		
Salisbury	30	16	Moody	Judith Wd		1	3			1			1	1			7		
Haverhill	148	18	Moody	Moses		1		1		1			1				4		
Newbury	108	26	Moody	Moses	1			1		1	1	1	1	1			7		
Newbury	111	17	Moody	Moses			1					1	1				4		
Newburyport	171	29	Moody	Moses		1								2			3		
Haverhill	148	30	Moody	Moses Junr	2	2		1		2	1		1				9		
Newbury	116	43	Moody	Nathll	1	1		3		2		1	1	2			11		
Newbury	106	15	Moody	Paul	2		4	1					2	1			10		
Newbury	108	19	Moody	Samuel	1	1	2	1		3			1				9		
Salisbury	30	8	Moody	William	2	1	2		1	2	1	1		1			11		
Topsfield	19	16	Moore	Dominick			1			2	1		1				5		
Salem	201	33	Moore	Jona											6		6		
Topsfield	21	30	Moore	Thomas				1						1			2		
Haverhill	148	35	Moore	Seth H.	3		1			1			1	1			7		
Haverhill	148	25	Moores	Jonathan			1			2	1		1				5		
Newbury	114	44	Moors	John	1	1				1			1				4		
Salem	216	40	Moratty	Deborah		1	1	4		1			1	1			9		
Salem	199	23	More	Alexr		2		1		1	1		1				6		
Gloucester	60	7	Morehead	Samll				1				2	1				4		
Salem	216	56	Morely	Eliza	1	2				2		1	2				9		

TOWN	PG#	LN#	LAST NAME	FIRST NAME	FREE WHITE MALES					FREE WHITE FEMALES					TOTAL ALL OTHER	TOTAL SLAVES	TOTALS	DISTRICT/ TOWNSHIP	NOTES
					under 10	10 to 16	16 to 26	26 to 45	45 and over	under 10	10 to 16	16 to 26	26 to 45	45 and over					
Rowley	128	22	Mores	Elizabeth		1								1			2		
Gloucester	60	5	Morey	Joseph		1		1		1		1		1			5		
Gloucester	60	3	Morey	Thomas	2	2			1		1	3		1			10		
Beverly	291	16	Morgan	Abigail	1		1				1		1	1			5		
Manchester	53	36	Morgan	Anna Wo						1	1		1				3		
Manchester	54	22	Morgan	David	1			1		2			1	1			6		
Manchester	53	31	Morgan	Edward	1			1		1			1				4		
Salem	195	8	Morgan	Eunice			1			1		1	1				4		
Beverly	291	17	Morgan	Israel	1	1		1	1				1				5		
Manchester	53	18	Morgan	Israel	1	2	1	1		1			1				7		
Manchester	53	29	Morgan	Israel			1			1		1					3		
Salem	200	34	Morgan	Israel	1				1				1				3		
Beverly	291	21	Morgan	Josiah				1					2				3		
Manchester	53	30	Morgan	Loes Wo			1					1		1			3		
Gloucester	77	5	Morgan	Nathan F.	1		1						1				3		
Gloucester	77	4	Morgan	Paul	1	2		1		1		2		1			8		
Manchester	53	23	Morgan	Polly Wo	1		1						1				3		
Gloucester	60	4	Morgan	Willa				1			1	1		1			4		
Gloucester	57	32	Morgan	William			1				1	2		2			6	West Parish	
Beverly	290	16	Morgan	William 2d		1		2						1			4		
Beverly	291	22	Morgan	William 3d	2	1	2	1		2			1				9		
Beverly	293	6	Morgan	Zachariah	2	1		1		1		1	1				7		
Beverly	292	2	Morgan	Zachariah 2d	2		1	1					3				7		
Salem	211	24	Moria	Robt			1			1	1		1				4		
Marblehead	270	30	Moriatt	Hugh	1			1					1				3		
Newburyport	171	13	Morland	William		1		1					1				3		
Salem	214	30	Morong	John		1		1		5	1		1	1			10		
Salem	214	33	Morong	John	2		1	1		1		1	1	1			8		
Salem	214	22	Morong	Sus									1	1			2		
Manchester	52	33	Morre	Mary Widw		1						1	1	1			4		
Newbury	109	39	Morril	Enoch	1	2	1	1		2		3	1	1			12		
Rowley	130	27	Morril	Samuel		1		1		2		1					5		
Salisbury	31	16	Morrill	Aaron			1						2	1			4		
Newbury	118	33	Morrill	Able				1	1	1	1				1		5		
Salisbury	30	22	Morrill	Abraham			1		1	1	2	1	1				7		
Amesbury	42	20	Morrill	Adam			2		1			1	1				5		
Salisbury	31	22	Morrill	Amos	2			1		2	1		1				7		
Salisbury	31	26	Morrill	Anhelm			2	1					1				4		
Salisbury	31	25	Morrill	Benja	2			1		1			1				5		
Newburyport	172	8	Morrill	Benjamin				1					1	1			3		
Salisbury	31	20	Morrill	Bradbury	2			1					1				4		
Salisbury	31	21	Morrill	Daniel Dr				1					1				2		
Salisbury	31	15	Morrill	David				1				1	1				3		
Salisbury	31	7	Morrill	David Junr	2	1	1	1		2			1				8		
Salisbury	31	10	Morrill	Elanor Wd				1				1	1				3		
Salisbury	30	30	Morrill	Enoch			1	1	3				2				7		
Salisbury	31	9	Morrill	Ephrm	3			1				1		1			6		
Methuen	154	47	Morrill	Ezekiel		1						1	1	2			5		
Newburyport	172	7	Morrill	Ezekiel		1	4	1				1		1			8		
Haverhill	148	43	Morrill	Israel		1		1					1				3		
Salisbury	30	31	Morrill	Israel Capt	2	1	1	1		2		1	1				9		
Salisbury	31	23	Morrill	Israel Junr			1					1	1				3		
Amesbury	42	22	Morrill	John			1			1		1					3		
Newbury	116	22	Morrill	John		1		1				1	1				4		
Salisbury	31	14	Morrill	John	1	1		1		2	2	1	1				9		
Amesbury	42	24	Morrill	Jona Capt	3	2	1	1				3	1				11		
Salisbury	31	8	Morrill	Jonathn	1	2		1		2	1	1	1				9		
Salisbury	31	24	Morrill	Judith									2				2		
Salisbury	31	12	Morrill	Mary Wd	1		1			2		1	1				6		
Newburyport	172	6	Morrill	Micajah	1			1		2			1				5		
Salisbury	31	13	Morrill	Moses S	1			1		1	1	2	1				8		
Salisbury	30	25	Morrill	Philip	1	1			1	2	2	1	1	1			10		
Salisbury	30	23	Morrill	Samuel 3d	3		1			1			1				6		
Salisbury	30	24	Morrill	Sarah Wd	1								1				2		
Salisbury	31	27	Morrill	Sarah Wd		3							2	1			6		
Amesbury	42	21	Morrill	Sarah Wid									2	1			3		
Salisbury	30	28	Morrill	Stephen	4		1						1				6		
Salisbury	31	17	Morrill	Thomas	1		1						1				3		
Salisbury	31	6	Morrill	Timothy		2	1	1			1	1		1			7		
Salisbury	31	5	Morrill	True				1				1		1			3		
Amesbury	42	23	Morrill	Wid									2				2		
Salisbury	31	11	Morrill	Willm	1	1		1		1	1		1				6		
Salisbury	31	19	Morrill	Wm Junr		2		1				1					4		
Newburyport	171	39	Morris	John	1			1		2			1				5		
Newburyport	171	40	Morris	William			1										1		
Newburyport	171	45	Morrison	Allen				1				1					2		
Newburyport	171	41	Morrison	Ebenezer	1			1					1				3		
Newburyport	171	42	Morrison	Ebenezer Jr	3	1		1		1			1				7		
Amesbury	42	25	Morrison	Michael	1			1		2			2				6		
Newburyport	171	43	Morrison	Thomas	1		1			1			1				4		
Newburyport	171	44	Morrison	William		1						1					2		
Beverly	297	28	Mors	Ebenezer			1				1	1					3		

TOWN	PG#	LN#	LAST NAME	FIRST NAME	FREE WHITE MALES					FREE WHITE FEMALES					TOTAL ALL OTHER	TOTAL SLAVES	TOTALS	DISTRICT/ TOWNSHIP	NOTES
					under 10	10 to 16	16 to 26	26 to 45	45 and over	under 10	10 to 16	16 to 26	26 to 45	45 and over					
Beverly	302	10	Mors	Mark	1	1	1	1					1	1			6		
Beverly	306	16	Mors	Sally								1	1				2		
Beverly	295	24	Mors	William			1				1			1			3		
Newbury	114	42	Mors	Abraham			1			2	1		1				5		
Marblehead	240	7	Morse	Abraham	3	1		1			1		1				7		
Marblehead	266	8	Morse	Abraham	3	1		1		1			1				7		
Methuen	154	39	Morse	Amos	4	2		1		2	1		1				11		
Methuen	154	36	Morse	Asa	3		2	1		3			1	1			11		
Bradford	123	40	Morse	Benja	3	1		1				2	1	1			9		
Bradford	123	46	Morse	Benja	1	1		1		1	3						8		
Methuen	154	41	Morse	Daniel	1			1		3			1				6		
Newbury	107	42	Morse	Daniel	3	3	1		1	1	1	1	1				12		
Haverhill	148	20	Morse	David		1		1		3			1	1			7		
Haverhill	148	40	Morse	David	3		4	1					1	1			10		
Manchester	53	25	Morse	David	1			1		1			1	1			6		
Methuen	154	33	Morse	David		1		1			1			1			4		
Newbury	108	49	Morse	David			1		1	1			1	1			5		
Newburyport	171	31	Morse	Edmund		2		1				1		1			5		
Marblehead	269	22	Morse	Elizabeth										1			1		
Haverhill	148	19	Morse	Henry		1		1						1			3		
Gloucester	63	14	Morse	Humphrey	2	2		1					1				6	West Ward	
Newbury	109	6	Morse	Humphrey		2		1				2		1			6		
Amesbury	43	5	Morse	John	1	1	2		1		1	1		1			8		
Newbury	109	20	Morse	John	2	1		1		2			1	1			8		
Newbury	116	13	Morse	John				1					1	1			3		
Newburyport	171	30	Morse	Jonathan		1	2	1						1			5		
Amesbury	42	16	Morse	Joseph	3	1	1	1				2		1			9		
Methuen	154	40	Morse	Joseph				1		1	1	1		1			4		
Salem	218	57	Morse	Joseph	1		1						1				3		
Salisbury	30	26	Morse	Martha Wd										1			1		
Haverhill	148	37	Morse	Moses	2			2					2				6		
Newbury	108	16	Morse	Moses		1	1						1				3		
Haverhill	148	21	Morse	Oliver		1		1		2			1	1			6		
Methuen	154	38	Morse	Paine	2	1	1		1	1	2	2		1			11		
Salisbury	31	18	Morse	Reuben	2			1					1				4		
Manchester	53	22	Morse	Saml	1			1		2			1				6		
Methuen	154	42	Morse	Samuel	2			1	1	1	1	1		1			8		
Newburyport	171	32	Morse	Samuel N			1			2			1				4		
Newburyport	171	34	Morse	Sarah Wido									1	1			2		
Bradford	126	10	Morse	Stephen		2		1					2				6		
Marblehead	268	10	Morse	Stephen			1			1			1	1			4		
Marblehead	257	22	Morse	Thomas			1			3			1				5		
Manchester	55	1	Morse	William			1			2			1				4		
Newburyport	171	33	Morse	William	2			1					1				4		
Newbury	119	2	Morss	Greenlif	1	1		1	1			1	1	1			7		
Salem	207	33	Moses	Benja				1			1		1				3		
Amesbury	42	19	Moses	David	3		1	1		1				1			7		
Newbury	109	31	Moses	Jonathan	1			1						1			3		
Ipswich	274	47	Moss	Thomas	3	1		1			1		1				7		
Ipswich	279	44	Moss	Timothy		1	1	1						1			4		
Lynnfield	236	12	Mottey	Joseph		1		1			2	1	1				6		
Danvers	3	32	Moulton	Benjamin				1				1		1			3		
Beverly	295	51	Moulton	Billy	1		1			1			1				4		
Wenham	309	19	Moulton	Daniel	1			1					1				3		
Amesbury	43	7	Moulton	David				1						1			2		
Danvers	3	30	Moulton	Ebenezer		1						1		2			4		
Danvers	3	31	Moulton	Ebenezer Jr		1							1				2		
Lynnfield	235	8	Moulton	Eliza	1			1		1			1				4		
Danvers	10	27	Moulton	Elizabeth										1			1		
Lynn	230	10	Moulton	Ezekl	2	1	2		1					1			7		
Lynn	230	16	Moulton	Ezra			1							1			2		
Lynn	228	34	Moulton	Jacob		1							1				2		
Wenham	309	13	Moulton	John	2	1		1					1	1			6		
Amesbury	43	2	Moulton	Jonathan				1		1				1			3		
Newburyport	171	38	Moulton	Jonathan	2			1						1			4		
Wenham	309	18	Moulton	Jonathan				1						1			2		
Lynn	229	18	Moulton	Joseph	1		1	1		1			1				5		
Newburyport	171	36	Moulton	Joseph		2	2	1			1	2	1	1			10		
Newburyport	171	37	Moulton	Joseph Jr	2	1		1		3				1			8		
Lynn	232	8	Moulton	Joshua		2		1		2		1	1				8		
Beverly	300	12	Moulton	Tarbox			1										1		
Salem	207	11	Mous	Ben				1			1		1				3		
Lynn	226	26	Mover	Enoch	1			1		2			1				5		
Lynn	226	18	Mover	John				1						1			2		
Lynn	224	36	Mudge	Enoch	1	1	2		1		2			1			8		
Lynn	224	34	Mudge	John		2	1			1	1	1					6		
Salem	191	31	Mudge	Joseph	1		1						1	1			4		
Lynn	227	6	Mudge	Nathan	3	3	2	1		2	2	1		1			15		
Lynn	227	32	Mudge	Nathl Jr	1		1						1				3		
Danvers	6	12	Mudge	Simon			2					1	2	1			6		
Marblehead	252	23	Mugford	Lidia									1	2			3		
Salem	201	27	Mugford	William	2			1				1	1	1			8		
Salem	205	17	Muley	Rebecca		1								1			2		
Haverhill	148	31	Mullen	Robert	1	1		2			1		1				6		

TOWN	PG#	LN#	LAST NAME	FIRST NAME	FREE WHITE MALES					FREE WHITE FEMALES					TOTAL ALL OTHER	TOTAL SLAVES	TOTALS	DISTRICT/ TOWNSHIP	NOTES
					under 10	10 to 16	16 to 26	26 to 45	45 and over	under 10	10 to 16	16 to 26	26 to 45	45 and over					
Marblehead	261	1	Mulley	Susannah										1			1		
Newburyport	171	21	Mulliken	Samuel			1			1		1					3		
Salem	221	9	Mumford	John											6		6		
Salem	204	29	Munday	William				1		1	1		1				4		
Salem	204	34	Munday	Willm	2		1			1	2	1					7		
Bradford	121	1	Munnds	John			1		1			2		1			5		
Danvers	7	3	Munro	Andrew	2	3	1		1	3	1	1	1				13		
Salem	198	11	Munro	Phips			1			1	1	1					4		
Lynn	223	30	Munroe	Timothy	1		2	1		1			1				6		
Lynnfield	235	25	Munroe	Timy	1				1			1	1	1			5		
Salem	208	42	Munyan	Gabriel				1		2			1				4		
Salem	213	6	Murphy	David		1	2	1		1			1	1			7		
Salem	215	17	Murphy	Margt			1				1	1	1				4		
Danvers	15	12	Murphy	Milon											3		3		
Gloucester	60	6	Murphy	William				1					1				2		
Beverly	296	35	Murray	Eliza			1			1		1					3		
Salem	218	17	Murray	Eliza							1	1					2		
Salem	218	49	Murray	Lydia								1					1		
Salem	220	33	Murray	Mary							1	1					2		
Salem	219	18	Murray	Peter				1			1						2		
Newburyport	172	3	Murry	Elizabeth Wido		1	1							4			6		
Newburyport	172	21	Murry	John	1			1	1	1	2	1	1				8		
Salem	207	12	Muse	Mary	2						1		1				4		
Newburyport	172	2	Myers	James	1		1				1						3		
Salem	214	4	Mylor	Mary									1				1		
Newburyport	172	29	Myrick	Jacob	2	1			1				1	1			6		
Marblehead	264	10	Nantz	Henry			1			1		1					3		
Marblehead	265	30	Nantz	Nicholas			1							1			2		
Rowley	129	5	Narker	Nathan	1			2						2			5		
Beverly	294	7	Nash	Morish			1			2		1		2			6		
Salem	206	12	Neal	Jona	2		1				1	2	1				7		
Salem	191	28	Neale	Benja	1		1			3			1				6		
Salem	196	8	Neale	David			1						1				2		
Salem	196	9	Neale	Jona	1	1		1					1				4		
Marblehead	253	12	Neck	Elizabeth		1							1	1			3		
Lynnfield	235	44	Needham	Daniel	1	1		1		2	1		1				7		
Salem	210	41	Needham	Edmund				1				1	1				3		
Salem	204	1	Needham	Isaac		2	1		2	2	2		1				10		
Danvers	5	12	Needham	John			1	1				1	1		1		5		
Danvers	14	4	Needham	John	1		2		1	1		1	1		1		8		
Danvers	7	14	Needham	John Junr	1			1		1			1				4		
Danvers	7	13	Needham	Lydia								1		1			2		
Salem	190	17	Needham	Nath		1	1	1					1				4		
Danvers	7	15	Needham	Stephen	3	1		1	1			1	1	1			9		
Marblehead	255	27	Neel	John	1		1						1	1			4		
Beverly	293	9	Negro	Philip											2		2		
Newburyport	173	10	Nellage	Duncan			1										1		
Rowley	127	35	Nelson	Amos	1		2		1	1		2		1			8		
Rowley	127	46	Nelson	Amos					1			1		1			3		
Rowley	127	40	Nelson	Asa		1	3	1	1			3		3			12		
Rowley	131	35	Nelson	David		3		1		1			1				6		
Rowley	131	36	Nelson	David		1	1		1				2	1			6		
Rowley	127	45	Nelson	Moses	2		3		1	1		1	1				9		
Rowley	127	34	Nelson	Nathll		1	1		1	2		1	1				7		
Rowley	127	15	Nelson	Paul		1	2										3		
Newburyport	173	21	Nelson	Samuel			1							1			2		
Rowley	127	16	Nelson	Solomon				1						3			4		
Rowley	132	11	Nelson	Solomon				1			1		1	1			4		
Rowley	131	9	Nelson	Stephen		1	1	1		2		1					6		
Gloucester	75	8	Nevans	William	1			1		3			1				6		
Newbury	107	5	Newal	Joseph	1		2	2		1	1	1	2	1			11		
Beverly	292	14	Newbury	Tryphena								2		1			3		
Gloucester	85	11	Newcomb	Mary Wo		1								1			2		
Lynn	224	20	Newhall	Aaron		1	3	1	1			1		2			9		
Lynnfield	235	12	Newhall	Aaron	1		1	1		1		1		1			6		
Lynn	227	7	Newhall	Abijah				1				1	1				3		
Lynn	223	32	Newhall	Allen	2			1		1		1					5		
Lynn	229	20	Newhall	Amos	1		1			2		1					5		
Lynnfield	235	2	Newhall	Amos	1	1	1	1					1				5		
Lynn	232	13	Newhall	Asa			1		1	1	1		1				5		
Lynn	230	4	Newhall	Benj			1			1		1	1				4		
Lynn	228	43	Newhall	Benj Jr			1			1			1				3		
Lynn	230	28	Newhall	Charles	1	1	3	1	1					1			8		
Lynn	229	19	Newhall	Daniel		1	2		1	1				2			7		
Lynn	229	7	Newhall	Daniel AB				1		1			1				3		
Danvers	4	8	Newhall	David	1			1		1			1				5		
Lynnfield	235	1	Newhall	David	1			1					1				3		
Lynn	228	42	Newhall	Ebenzr	1	1	1	1	1		1			2			8		
Lynn	226	19	Newhall	Eliza										2			2		
Salem	212	11	Newhall	Else		1	2						1				4		
Lynn	226	24	Newhall	Estes	2	1	1	1					1	1			7		
Lynnfield	235	14	Newhall	Ezekl		1	2		1		1	2		2			9		
Salem	189	4	Newhall	Gilbert			1					1					2		
Lynn	223	31	Newhall	Hanson					1					1			2		

TOWN	PG#	LN#	LAST NAME	FIRST NAME	FREE WHITE MALES					FREE WHITE FEMALES					TOTAL ALL OTHER	TOTAL SLAVES	TOTALS	DISTRICT/ TOWNSHIP	NOTES
					under 10	10 to 16	16 to 26	26 to 45	45 and over	under 10	10 to 16	16 to 26	26 to 45	45 and over					
Lynn	229	31	Newhall	Increase					1					1			2		
Lynn	229	24	Newhall	Israel	1		1			1		1					4		
Lynn	232	30	Newhall	Jacob			4	2	2				3	1			12	West Parish	
Lynnfield	235	13	Newhall	Jacob	3			1					4	1			9		
Lynn	232	17	Newhall	Jacob 3d	4			1					1	1			7	West Parish	
Lynn	232	19	Newhall	Jacob Jun					1	1	2	1		1			6	West Parish	
Lynn	230	44	Newhall	James 3d				1		2		1					4		
Lynn	234	20	Newhall	James 3d	2			1		3			1				7		
Lynn	230	37	Newhall	James Esq		1	1	2	1			1		1			7		
Lynn	224	14	Newhall	James Jr			1	1		2		1					6		
Lynn	230	19	Newhall	Jedh	2			1		1	2			1			8		
Lynn	229	12	Newhall	Joel	3	1	3		1		1	1	1				11		
Lynn	226	5	Newhall	John			1	1					1				3		
Lynn	225	18	Newhall	John B	1	1		1		3		1					7		
Lynn	225	3	Newhall	John Esq	2	1		1		2			1				7		
Lynn	234	21	Newhall	Jona	1	1		1		1	1		1				6		
Danvers	4	11	Newhall	Joseph	3	1		1		1	1	2					9		
Lynn	224	28	Newhall	Joseph	1			1		1		1					4		
Marblehead	259	4	Newhall	Joseph				1		3			1				5		
Salem	206	26	Newhall	Joseph			4	1		2	1		1				9		
Danvers	4	12	Newhall	Joseph Jun	1		1	1					1				4		
Lynn	223	36	Newhall	Lois						1			1				2		
Lynn	223	39	Newhall	Lois						1			1				2		
Lynn	224	3	Newhall	Mary									1	1			2		
Lynnfield	235	10	Newhall	Matthew				1		1				2			4		
Lynn	224	35	Newhall	Micajah	1	2	3	1		3	1	1	1				13		
Lynn	225	9	Newhall	Nathan		1		1		1				1			4		
Danvers	4	9	Newhall	Nathaniel			1	1						1			3		
Danvers	4	10	Newhall	Nathaniel Jun				1					1				2		
Lynnfield	235	16	Newhall	Noah	1			1		3	2		1				8		
Marblehead	254	34	Newhall	Peter	1		2		1	2				1			7		
Lynn	226	20	Newhall	Pharaoh		1		1	1			1		1			5		
Lynnfield	235	5	Newhall	Phebe										2			2		
Marblehead	257	12	Newhall	Philip	3			1					1				5		
Lynn	229	11	Newhall	Polly	2								1				3		
Salem	207	29	Newhall	Rebecca		1								1			2		
Lynn	223	29	Newhall	Richard			1	1		1			2				5		
Lynn	227	38	Newhall	Rufus	1	2		1		3			1				8		
Lynn	223	27	Newhall	Rufus Jr	1			1		2			1				5		
Lynn	226	21	Newhall	Saml	2	1		1					1				5		
Marblehead	242	5	Newhall	Samuel	2	1	2		1	2	2						10		
Salem	203	15	Newhall	Samuel	1			1				1	1				4		
Lynn	229	5	Newhall	Sarah						1			1				2		
Marblehead	253	27	Newhall	Sarah	2					2	1		1				6		
Salem	188	36	Newhall	Thomas	3	1	1	1					1		1		10		
Salem	213	37	Newhall	Thomas			1				1		1				2		
Lynn	230	38	Newhall	Thos	1		2	1	1		1			2			8		
Lynn	226	35	Newhall	Timy	2			1		1			1				5		
Lynn	230	2	Newhall	Willm	1			1				1	1				4		
Lynnfield	235	6	Newhall	Willm				1		2			1	1			5		
Lynn	230	20	Newhall	Willm 3d	4			1					1	1			7		
Lynn	232	28	Newhall	Willm 5th	3			1					1				5	West Parish	
Lynn	230	23	Newhall	Willm Jr	1	3	2		1	3		2	1	1			14		
Lynn	223	43	Newhall	Winthrop	2			1		1			1				5		
Lynnfield	235	11	Newhall	Wright	3			1		1		1		1			7		
Salem	210	38	Newham	Daniel		2	1		1			1		1			6		
Newburyport	173	29	Newman	Benjamin	1			1		1			1	1			5		
Ipswich	274	33	Newman	Elisha				1			1			1			3		
Newburyport	173	22	Newman	Elizabeth Wido			1				1	1					3		
Gloucester	65	15	Newman	John	1	1	2	1	1	1	1	1	1				10		
Newburyport	173	23	Newman	John	1			1		1		1	1				5		
Newburyport	173	27	Newman	Joseph	1			1		1	1		1				5		
Andover	99	19	Newman	Mark	1	1		1				1	1				5		
Ipswich	276	25	Newman	Michiel				1		1	1			1			4		
Newburyport	173	24	Newman	Nathaniel				1						3			4		
Newburyport	173	25	Newman	Nathaniel Jr			1		1		1	2	2	1			8		
Ipswich	275	7	Newman	Samuel		1		1		1	1			1			5		
Newburyport	173	26	Newman	Samuel			1						1	2			4		
Lynn	231	1	Newman	Thos				1						1			2		
Newburyport	173	28	Newman	Timothy		1		1		2			1				5		
Ipswich	275	8	Newman	William			1			1		1					3		
Ipswich	278	19	Newmarck	Hannah										2			2		
Ipswich	278	22	Newmarck	John			1	1	1		1		1	1			6		
Newburyport	173	20	Newmarsh	Joseph	1	1		1					2				5		
Salem	189	34	Newport	John											7		7		
Salem	206	25	Nicholls	Ichabod	3	2	2		1		2	2		2			14		
Salem	203	6	Nicholls	James	1			1		2		1	1				6		
Salem	208	5	Nicholls	Jno	3		2	1		2	2		1				11		
Salem	198	22	Nicholls	Thos		2			1	1	2			1			7		
Danvers	2	28	Nichols	Andrew	1	1	1	1					1	1			7		
Lynn	224	38	Nichols	Andrew	1			1		1			1				4		
Haverhill	149	4	Nichols	Benjamin			1			1		1					3		
Amesbury	43	11	Nichols	Daniel				1						1			2		
Haverhill	149	2	Nichols	Dottey	2			1				1	1	1			6		

238

TOWN	PG#	LN#	LAST NAME	FIRST NAME	FREE WHITE MALES					FREE WHITE FEMALES					TOTAL ALL OTHER	TOTAL SLAVES	TOTALS	DISTRICT/ TOWNSHIP	NOTES
					under 10	10 to 16	16 to 26	26 to 45	45 and over	under 10	10 to 16	16 to 26	26 to 45	45 and over					
Amesbury	43	12	Nichols	Enoch		1			1	1		1		1			5		
Amesbury	43	14	Nichols	Hezekiah	2	1			1		1	1		1			7		
Salem	198	9	Nichols	Ichabod	1		2	1		1	1	1					7		
Middleton	17	5	Nichols	Jerusha									2				2		
Beverly	303	10	Nichols	John				1					1				2		
Lynn	224	25	Nichols	John	2			1			1						4		
Middleton	18	6	Nichols	John		1	1	1			1		1				5		
Salem	218	5	Nichols	John		1						1	1				3		
Andover	99	22	Nichols	John Junr	2		1			1		1	1	1			7		
Middleton	17	7	Nichols	Joseph			1						3	1			5		
Amesbury	43	10	Nichols	Moses		1	1						1				3		
Andover	99	23	Nichols	Phillip			1			1			1				3		
Haverhill	149	1	Nichols	Phineas				1			1		1	1			4		
Amesbury	43	13	Nichols	Stephen	4			1		2	2		1				10		
Middleton	17	10	Nichols	Stephen	1		1	1		1		2					6		
Salem	183	24	Nichols	Stephen	1		2	1				1	1				6		
Haverhill	149	3	Nichols	Thomas	3			1		2	1	1	1				9		
Andover	99	21	Nichols	John		1		1			1			1			4		
Andover	99	20	Nicholson	Francis				1			1			1			3		
Marblehead	257	32	Nicholson	Thomas	3	2	2	1			2			1			11		
Marblehead	267	19	Nicholson	Thomas	1			1		2			1	1			6		
Marblehead	267	21	Nicholson	William			2	1				1	1	1			6		
Salem	210	49	Nick	Jona	2			1		1			1				5		
Newburyport	173	11	Nicolls	John				1						1			2		
Newburyport	173	12	Nicolls	Mary Wido		1	1					1	1				4		
Marblehead	246	24	Nimblet	Robert			2	1		3				1			7		
Gloucester	85	2	Noble	Benja			1				1		1				3		
Gloucester	86	5	Noble	Daniel	1			1		1			1				4		
Gloucester	80	15	Noble	Francis		1		1		2			1				5		
Gloucester	70	14	Noble	Joseph			1						1				2		
Gloucester	72	23	Noble	Mary Wo	1	1				1	1		1				5		
Salem	214	25	Norfolk	John		1		1						1			3		
Salem	206	50	Norris	Edward	1	1	3	1					1	1			8		
Salem	206	32	Norris	John		1		1		1	1	1					5		
Salem	191	36	Norris	Phillip	1		1			1	1						4		
Newbury	107	39	North	Edmond		1		1				1	3	1			7		
Newbury	105	18	Northern	Samuel	1	4	4	2		1	1		1	1			15		
Salem	206	51	Northey	Abijah		1		1		2		2	1	1			8		
Marblehead	258	25	Northey	John	2			1		2			1				6		
Lynn	228	3	Northey	Willm			2	1		1				1			5		
Newburyport	173	15	Norton	Benjamin	3	2	1	1	2	2			2				13		
Newburyport	173	13	Norton	Bishop	1	1	1	1		1	2	2		1			10		
Newburyport	173	18	Norton	Constantine				1					1				2		
Ipswich	282	33	Norton	George		1	1	1						2			5		
Manchester	53	32	Norton	George			1						1				2		
Newburyport	173	14	Norton	George				1		1		1	1	1			5		
Newbury	110	41	Norton	John		1		1						1			3		
Newburyport	173	16	Norton	John	2	1				1				1			6		
Newburyport	173	17	Norton	Michael	2			1		1			1				5		
Ipswich	283	32	Norton	Oliver	2		1			1			1				5		
Beverly	299	32	Norton	Wm		1	1			1	1						4		
Salisbury	31	31	Norwell	Henry				1						1			2		
Gloucester	80	12	Norwood	Caleb				1					1	1			3		
Manchester	53	34	Norwood	Davd Doct		1	1			1	1	1		1			7		
Gloucester	75	20	Norwood	Eliza Wo		1	2			2	2	1	1				9		
Gloucester	80	16	Norwood	Francis			2	1				1		1			5		
Gloucester	80	14	Norwood	Francis Jr	1	1		1		3	1	1					8		
Gloucester	75	14	Norwood	Gustaves	2	2	1		1	2	2	1					11		
Gloucester	77	20	Norwood	James	1		2	1		1		2					7		
Lynnfield	237	6	Norwood	John	1		2	1		1		1	1	1			8		
Newburyport	173	19	Norwood	Judith Wido	1	2	2	1		2			1				9		
Gloucester	75	24	Norwood	Mary Wo						3		1					4		
Gloucester	76	5	Norwood	Nathan				1		0				2			3		
Gloucester	69	5	Norwood	Solomon	3		1	1		2	2	1					10		
Gloucester	65	14	Norwood	Solomon Junr	2		1			1		1					5		
Gloucester	78	2	Norwood	William	1		1			1		1					4		
Salem	193	6	Nource	Samuel	1		1	2			1	1	1	1			8		
Beverly	299	36	Nours	Rufus	1		1			1			1				4		
Lynn	228	29	Nouse	James	1	3		1		3			1				9		
Newburyport	173	30	Nowell	George	2		1			2		1	1				7		
Newburyport	173	32	Nowell	Joseph			1		1	1	1	1					6		
Newburyport	173	34	Nowell	Joseph Jr	1		1						1	2			5		
Newburyport	173	35	Nowell	Richard		1	1					2					4		
Newburyport	173	33	Nowell	Samuel		1			1	1				1			4		
Newburyport	173	31	Nowell	Silas		1	1	1				2					5		
Newbury	106	43	Noyce	Enoch		1	2	1		2		1					7		
Newbury	106	37	Noyce	Ephraim	2	1		1		1		1					6		
Newbury	106	33	Noyce	Follensbee	3	1				2		1	1				8		
Newbury	106	3	Noyce	John				2				2					4		
Newbury	106	49	Noyce	John		1		1		2	2	1					7		
Newbury	106	47	Noyce	Joseph				1				1					3		
Newbury	105	15	Noyce	Lemuel	1	1	1		2	1		1	2	1			10		
Newbury	107	25	Noyce	Moses			1			1			1	1			4		
Newbury	107	21	Noyce	Stephen			1		1	1	1		1				5		
Newbury	107	29	Noyce	Thomas			1		1	1			1				4		
Newbury	107	11	Noyce	William			1			1		2	1				5		
Andover	99	24	Noyes	Aaron	1	2	1	1		2		1	1	1			10		

TOWN	PG#	LN#	LAST NAME	FIRST NAME	FWM under 10	FWM 10 to 16	FWM 16 to 26	FWM 26 to 45	FWM 45 and over	FWF under 10	FWF 10 to 16	FWF 16 to 26	FWF 26 to 45	FWF 45 and over	TOTAL ALL OTHER	TOTAL SLAVES	TOTALS	DISTRICT/ TOWNSHIP	NOTES
Newbury	119	10	Noyes	Abner				1		1			1				3		
Newbury	118	23	Noyes	Amos				1	1			1	1	1	2		7		
Newburyport	172	42	Noyes	Amos	3	1	1	1					2	1			9		
Ipswich	275	60	Noyes	Daniel	1		1	1	1					1			5		
Newburyport	173	2	Noyes	Dorcas Wido									1				1		
Newburyport	173	6	Noyes	Ebenezer	1	1	5					2	1	1			11		
Salisbury	31	28	Noyes	Edmund Esq				2	1				1	1			5		
Amesbury	43	9	Noyes	Eliphalet			1						1				2		
Newburyport	173	7	Noyes	Eliphalet				1					1	1			3		
Newburyport	173	5	Noyes	Enoch	1	1	1						1				4		
Newbury	119	15	Noyes	Ezekiel	4	3		1		1	1		1				11		
Newbury	119	18	Noyes	Gedion	1	3	1		1	3	2		1				12		
Newburyport	172	40	Noyes	Isaac				1						1			2		
Newbury	118	43	Noyes	Jacob	2			1		1			1				5		
Newburyport	173	1	Noyes	Jacob				1			1		1				3		
Newbury	115	18	Noyes	John			1	1				1					3		
Newbury	116	29	Noyes	John			1	1				1		1			4		
Newbury	120	10	Noyes	John			1	1					1				3		
Newbury	120	35	Noyes	John	1	1	2	1				1					6		
Newburyport	173	3	Noyes	John M	2			1		1			1				5		
Newburyport	172	32	Noyes	Joseph	1		1	2					1	1			7		
Newburyport	172	34	Noyes	Joseph 3	1			1		2			1				5		
Newburyport	172	33	Noyes	Joseph Jr	1			1		2			1	1			6		
Newburyport	172	35	Noyes	Josepth 4th			2			1			1	1			4		
Salisbury	31	29	Noyes	Judith Wd		1							1	1			3		
Newbury	116	38	Noyes	Mary				1		1			1	1			4		
Newbury	120	18	Noyes	Mary			1			1			1	1			4		
Newbury	118	26	Noyes	Nathan			1	1					1	1			4		
Newburyport	173	8	Noyes	Nathan			1						1				2		
Newburyport	172	36	Noyes	Nathaniel	2	2		1		2			1	1			9		
Newbury	118	27	Noyes	Nathll															Enumeration left blank
Andover	99	18	Noyes	Nicholas			1						1				2		
Newbury	116	42	Noyes	Nicolas	1			2				1	2				6		
Newbury	118	47	Noyes	Paul	3	1		1		1			1				7		
Newburyport	173	4	Noyes	Paul			2		2		1		2	1			8		
Newburyport	172	41	Noyes	Richard S.	4			1		1	1		1				8		
Newbury	119	1	Noyes	Samuel	4	1		1		3	1		1				11		
Newbury	120	20	Noyes	Samuel		1	1	1				1	2	1			7		
Newbury	120	21	Noyes	Samuel	2		1			1		1	1				6		
Newburyport	172	37	Noyes	Samuel				1						4			5		
Newburyport	172	38	Noyes	Samuel Jr	2	1	1			2			1				7		
Newbury	115	19	Noyes	Sarah		2						1	2				5		
Newbury	118	21	Noyes	Silas		1		1		2	1						5		
Newbury	118	42	Noyes	Silas				2						1			3		
Salem	210	56	Noyes	Simeon			1						1				2		
Newbury	120	17	Noyes	Stephen		1		1		1	1		1				5		
Newbury	118	22	Noyes	Thomas			2	3	1				1	1			8		
Newbury	119	25	Noyes	Thomas	1			1		2			1				5		
Andover	99	17	Noyes	Timothy			1	1						1			3		
Newburyport	172	43	Noyes	Timothy	3			1					1				5		
Andover	99	16	Noyes	Ward				1	1	2	2	1		1			7		
Newburyport	172	39	Noyes	William			1	1					1				3		
Ipswich	273	17	Nurse	Daniel			1	2	1			1		1			6		
Danvers	4	14	Nurse	Jonathan		1	1		1	1	1			1			6		
Danvers	4	13	Nurse	Nathaniel	1		1	2		1	1	1		1			8		
Salem	220	42	Nutting	Eben				1				1		1			3		
Marblehead	260	18	Nutting	John				1	2	1			2				6		
Salem	198	5	Nutting	John	2			1		1			1				5		
Salem	202	8	Nutting	Joseph	1			1		2			1				5		
Newburyport	173	9	Nutting	William	1			1				2					4		
Salisbury	31	30	Nye	Samuel		2			1	1	1		1				6		
Gloucester	80	19	Oakes	Ebenz		1	1					1		1			3		
Marblehead	264	12	Oakes	Hannah	2			1				1		1			5		
Marblehead	266	13	Oakes	Hannah	2							1		1			4		
Marblehead	249	5	Oakes	Jacob	1	1			1	1	2		1				7		
Gloucester	65	16	Oakes	John	2	1			1	2		2		1			9		
Gloucester	80	18	Oakes	John			1						1				2		
Gloucester	80	17	Oakes	Thos	3		1	1		2		1	1				9		
Gloucester	65	17	Oakes	William	3			1					1				5		
Lynn	230	42	Oakman	Ebenz	2	2		3					1				9		
Salem	202	12	Oakman	Samuel	1			1		2	2	1					8		
Danvers	8	40	Oaks	Caleb	1	2	1			1			1				6		
Newbury	112	31	Obbin	Joseph	1		1	1					1	1			5		
Salem	220	45	Obear	Abigail			1							1			2		
Beverly	296	9	Obear	Eliza	1					1			1				3		
Beverly	295	8	Obear	Isaac	2		1			1			1				5		
Beverly	298	7	Obear	Joseph		1		1		1				1			4		
Beverly	297	17	Obear	Peter			1	1			1		1				5		
Wenham	309	12	Obear	Samuel	1		1	1				1	2	1			7		
Beverly	297	20	Obear	Samuel 2d	1		1			1			1				4		
Salem	202	40	Obear	William	4			1					1				6		
Beverly	293	3	Obear	Zebulon		1	1	2		1	1	2					9		
Gloucester	60	15	Oben	Jona	2	1			1	1	2	2	1				10		
Beverly	301	13	Ober	Andrew	1			1		1			2				5		
Beverly	296	44	Ober	Asa	1			1		2			1				5		
Manchester	54	1	Ober	Benja		1		1			1			1			4		
Beverly	302	44	Ober	Issacher	1		1			1			1				4		
Beverly	297	9	Ober	Jerusha						1			1	1			3		

TOWN	PG#	LN#	LAST NAME	FIRST NAME	FREE WHITE MALES under 10	10 to 16	16 to 26	26 to 45	45 and over	FREE WHITE FEMALES under 10	10 to 16	16 to 26	26 to 45	45 and over	TOTAL ALL OTHER	TOTAL SLAVES	TOTALS	DISTRICT/ TOWNSHIP	NOTES
Beverly	301	39	Ober	Jonathn P			1	1		3			1				6		
Beverly	292	29	Ober	Josiah	1			1		1	2	2	1				8		
Beverly	301	38	Ober	Lydia			1							1			2		
Beverly	297	19	Ober	Mary										1			1		
Beverly	296	6	Ober	Oliver			1						1				2		
Beverly	295	16	Ober	Richard			1		1				1	1			4		
Beverly	301	5	Ober	Richard 2nd		1	1	1					1	1			5		
Beverly	295	17	Ober	Richard 3d	1			1		3	1		1				7		
Beverly	300	35	Ober	Samuel	1	1		1		2	1		1				7		
Ipswich	274	12	Obrian	John				1					1				2		
Newbury	111	38	Obrian	John	2	1	1			1		3	2				11		
Newburyport	173	36	Obrien	John	2	2	2	1	1	2	1	1	1	1			14		
Newburyport	173	37	OBrien	Joseph	2	2		1					2				7		
Salem	208	47	Ocum	Lydia		1							1				2		
Salem	218	7	Odberry	John	2		1	1		1			1				6		
Salem	188	19	Odel	James	1	1		1		1	1		1				6		
Salem	210	48	Odell	Samuel	1		1					1					3		
Beverly	296	7	Odlin	Samuel					1	3			1				5		
Marblehead	264	14	Ogleby	Martha							1		1				2		
Beverly	296	32	Oliver	Anna			1					1	1				3		
Beverly	289	2	Oliver	Daniel Rvd			1		1	4	1		1		2		10		
Marblehead	262	19	Oliver	Elizabeth								2	2				4		
Lynn	226	29	Oliver	Henry	1	2	1		1		1		1				7		
Lynn	223	61	Oliver	Henry Jr	1			1				1					3		
Salem	195	31	Oliver	Hubbard					1	2	1	1					5		
Marblehead	245	8	Oliver	James	2			1				1					4		
Salem	189	41	Oliver	Mary											2		2		
Salem	214	10	Oliver	Mary				2				1		2			5		
Lynn	232	36	Oliver	Saml	3	1		1		1			1				7	West Parish	
Marblehead	249	30	Oliver	Sarah										2			2		
Marblehead	250	4	Oliver	Sarah								2	1	2			5		
Salem	203	41	Oliver	Sarah		3	1			2	4	4	1				15		
Salem	221	5	Oliver	William	2			1		1			2				6		
Lynn	224	17	Oliver	Willm			1	1				1					3		
Marblehead	248	16	Ollyer	John	1			1		1			1				4		
Newburyport	173	42	O'Neill	Mercy Wido								1	1				2		
Haverhill	149	7	Ordway	Benjamin				1			1	1	1				4		
Newbury	109	9	Ordway	Benjamin	1	2	1	1						3			8		
Haverhill	149	12	Ordway	Benjamin Jun	1		1	1	1		2	1	2				9		
Haverhill	149	13	Ordway	Edward	1	1	2		1	1	1		1				8		
Newbury	108	28	Ordway	Eliphalet	1	1	1				1		2				6		
Haverhill	149	8	Ordway	James	1			1					1				3		
Methuen	155	6	Ordway	James	1		1		2	1	1		1				7		
Newbury	109	10	Ordway	James			1			1		1					3		
Newbury	110	11	Ordway	Joseph				1		1		1					3		
Newbury	109	8	Ordway	Peter		1		1			1		1				4		
Amesbury	43	17	Ordway	Saml Dr		1	3		1			2		1			8		
Newbury	116	23	Ordway	Stephen	2	1		1		2	1		1				8		
Lynn	229	6	Organ	Isaac	1			1		3	1		1				7		
Beverly	295	27	Ormon	Asa	2			1				1					4		
Salem	203	42	Orne	Eliza			2				1	1	1	1			6		
Lynnfield	236	6	Orne	John		1	1			2		2		1			7		
Marblehead	242	13	Orne	John	2			1		1		1					5		
Marblehead	245	1	Orne	John	1			1				1					3		
Newburyport	173	41	Orne	John			1	1		1				1			4		
Marblehead	260	3	Orne	Jonathan Junr	2		1			1			1				5		
Marblehead	264	15	Orne	Joshua	1	3	1	1		1			2	1			10		
Wenham	308	24	Orne	Joshua	2			1		1			1				5		
Salem	207	43	Orne	Josiah	3	1		1		1	1	2	1				10		
Wenham	308	25	Orne	Mary			1							1			2		
Newburyport	173	40	Orne	William	1			1		2			1	1			6		
Salem	194	22	Orne	William	2	1		1		2	1		1				8		
Danvers	11	13	Osborn	Aaron	1			1			1						3		
Danvers	11	16	Osborn	Abraham			1	1				1	1				4		
Danvers	15	8	Osborn	Amos	1			1				1					4		
Danvers	10	40	Osborn	Anna									1	1			2		
Danvers	15	10	Osborn	Benjamin		1		1				3	1				6		
Danvers	14	13	Osborn	Caleb	2	1		1		1			1				7		
Danvers	11	6	Osborn	Daniel				2					2				4		
Danvers	13	34	Osborn	Daniel Junr		1	1					1	1				4		
Danvers	11	12	Osborn	James		2		1			1	1					5		
Danvers	13	33	Osborn	James 3rd	2		1			1			1				5		
Danvers	11	3	Osborn	John	1		1	1			1	1	1				6		
Danvers	11	11	Osborn	John Jr	2	1		1		1	2		1				8		
Danvers	13	12	Osborn	John Junr				1					1				2		
Danvers	15	3	Osborn	Jonathan	1	1		1		1	1		1				6		
Danvers	15	7	Osborn	Joseph					1			1	1				3		
Danvers	13	4	Osborn	Joseph Junr		2	1	1		2			2				8		
Danvers	13	9	Osborn	Lydia		1						1	1	1			4		
Danvers	11	15	Osborn	Patience								1	1				2		
Danvers	11	4	Osborn	Paul	1		1	1	1	3	1		1				9		
Danvers	11	10	Osborn	Richard	1			1					1	1			4		
Danvers	11	14	Osborn	Samuel		1	2	1				2	1	1			8		
Danvers	10	41	Osborn	Susanna		1	2			1	1	1	1	1			8		
Danvers	12	29	Osborn	Sylvester	1		2	1	1	1	1		2				9		
Salem	207	20	Osborne	Betsey	1					1		1					3		
Salem	183	21	Osborne	Eliza			1							1			2		

241

TOWN	PG#	LN#	LAST NAME	FIRST NAME	FREE WHITE MALES					FREE WHITE FEMALES					TOTAL ALL OTHER	TOTAL SLAVES	TOTALS	DISTRICT/ TOWNSHIP	NOTES
			LAST NAME	FIRST NAME	under 10	10 to 16	16 to 26	26 to 45	45 and over	under 10	10 to 16	16 to 26	26 to 45	45 and over					
Salem	198	20	Osborne	Eliza										2			2		
Salem	196	22	Osborne	Geo				1				1		1			3		
Salem	199	37	Osborne	Henry			1					1	1				3		
Newburyport	173	43	Osborne	Mary Wido	4						1		1				6		
Salem	198	24	Osborne	Robt	2	1	1	1		2		1	1	1			10		
Salem	191	1	Osborne	Stephen		1			1				2	1			5		
Salem	190	29	Osborne	William			1			1		1	1				4		
Andover	99	34	Osgood	Aaron			1						1				2		
Amesbury	43	16	Osgood	Abel	1			1		2			1				5		
Haverhill	149	9	Osgood	Abigail		1	1	2			2			2			8		
Salisbury	32	5	Osgood	Abigail Wd	1							2		1			4		
Newburyport	173	39	Osgood	Alfred			2	1					1				4		
Salem	207	19	Osgood	Benja				1	1					1			3		
Salem	207	21	Osgood	Benja Jr				1		1	1	1					4		
Methuen	155	4	Osgood	Benjamin	2	1	3		1	1		1	1	1			12		
Salisbury	31	33	Osgood	Benjamin		1		1					1	3			6		
Salem	200	36	Osgood	Chas	1	2	3		1	2		2		1			12		
Salisbury	31	34	Osgood	Elijah				1		1			1				3		
Andover	99	27	Osgood	George	2		2	1		1	1	1					9		
Haverhill	149	11	Osgood	Henry		2		2		1			1				6		
Marblehead	248	15	Osgood	Hooker			1						1				2		
Andover	99	30	Osgood	Huldah Wid										1			1		
Salem	203	43	Osgood	Isaac	2	1		1		1	1	1	1	1			9		
Andover	99	33	Osgood	Jacob		1	2	1				1	1				6		
Salisbury	32	4	Osgood	Jacob Capt	2		1	1		1			1				6		
Salisbury	32	7	Osgood	James				1		2			1				4		
Newbury	107	10	Osgood	John		4	3		1	1		2	1				12		
Salem	209	39	Osgood	John		2	1	1		3	2	1	2	2			14		
Salisbury	32	9	Osgood	John	1	1	1	1		1				1			6		
Danvers	9	33	Osgood	Jonathan			1			1		1					3		
Methuen	155	5	Osgood	Joseph	3		1						1				5		
Salem	192	40	Osgood	Joseph		2	1		1	2	2		1	1			10		
Salem	194	15	Osgood	Joseph	2		1	1			1	1	1				7		
Salisbury	32	12	Osgood	Joseph				1						1			2		
Salisbury	32	11	Osgood	Joseph Capt		1	1	1		1			1				5		
Salisbury	32	6	Osgood	Moses	1		1			1		1					4		
Salisbury	32	2	Osgood	Oliver Capt		2	2	1		1		1	1				8		
Andover	99	25	Osgood	Peter		1	2	1				1	1				6		
Haverhill	149	10	Osgood	Peter	1		1	1		2			1				6		
Salisbury	32	13	Osgood	Peter	1		1						1				3		
Andover	99	28	Osgood	Peter Junr	1	3	1		1	2	2	4	1				15		
Salisbury	31	32	Osgood	Ruth Wd									1	1			2		
Amesbury	43	15	Osgood	Samuel			1			1				1			3		
Andover	99	31	Osgood	Samuel		1					1	1	1				5		
Salisbury	32	3	Osgood	Stephen	1			1		2			1				5		
Andover	99	32	Osgood	Thomas	1		2	1		3			1				8		
Salisbury	32	10	Osgood	Thomas	3			1			1	1					6		
Amesbury	43	18	Osgood	Timothy				1		2	1			1			5		
Andover	99	29	Osgood	Timothy		1	1	1		1	2	1	2				10		
Andover	99	26	Osgood	Timothy Junr	4		1	1		1	2	1	1				11		
Salisbury	31	35	Osgood	Willm		1	1		1			1	1				5		
Salisbury	32	8	Osgood	Willm Junr	2	1		1		1	1		1				7		
Salisbury	32	1	Osgood	Winthrop Dr				1			1			1			3		
Beverly	295	28	Osmond	Jane			1						1				2		
Newburyport	173	38	Otis	Samuel A	2	1		1				2		1			7		
Newburyport	173	44	Over	Rhoda Wido				1		1		1	1	1			4		
Methuen	155	16	Pace	Thomas				1					1				2		
Newburyport	175	37	Packer	Thomas	2	1	1		1			1	1				7		
Marblehead	257	30	Page	*hel	3			1		1	2		1				8		
Haverhill	149	17	Page	Caleb	1			1		1	1		1				5		
Andover	100	28	Page	Daniel				1				1		2			4		
Newburyport	175	41	Page	Daniel	1			1		1			1				4		
Salisbury	32	31	Page	Dorothy Wd						1		2	1	1			5		
Danvers	4	30	Page	Jeremiah			3	1				1	1				6		
Danvers	9	42	Page	Jeremiah Junr		1	2	1				1					5		
Salem	194	40	Page	John	2	1	4	1		1	2		1				12		
Haverhill	149	18	Page	John C.		1	1	1				2		1			6		
Haverhill	149	23	Page	Jonathan		1	1						1				3		
Haverhill	149	22	Page	Joshia Junr			1			1		1					3		
Haverhill	149	20	Page	Joshua		2	1		1	1		3		1			9		
Danvers	5	11	Page	Samuel	1	2			1	1	1	3		1			10		
Haverhill	149	21	Page	Samuel	1			1					1				3		
Haverhill	149	19	Page	Stephen W	1			1		1			1				4		
Salem	208	23	Pain	Dinah											1		1		
Gloucester	63	2	Pain	Richard		1	1	1					1				4	West Ward	
Marblehead	264	17	Paine	James	1			1					1				3		
Marblehead	264	18	Paine	John	1		1	1				1	1				5		
Marblehead	264	16	Paine	Martha			2						1				3		
Newburyport	175	16	Paine	Thomas			1			2		1	1				5		
Salem	217	20	Palfray	Deborah							1		1				2		
Salem	217	25	Palfray	Hemlock		1	1	1					1				4		
Salem	220	36	Palfray	Jona		1		1		2			1				5		
Salem	220	25	Palfray	Richard	2		1	1		1	2	1					9		
Salem	217	19	Palfray	Thos	3	1		1					1				6		
Salem	212	39	Palfry	Richard	1		1			1		1					4		

TOWN	PG#	LN#	HEADS OF HOUSEHOLD LAST NAME	HEADS OF HOUSEHOLD FIRST NAME	FREE WHITE MALES under 10	FREE WHITE MALES 10 to 16	FREE WHITE MALES 16 to 26	FREE WHITE MALES 26 to 45	FREE WHITE MALES 45 and over	FREE WHITE FEMALES under 10	FREE WHITE FEMALES 10 to 16	FREE WHITE FEMALES 16 to 26	FREE WHITE FEMALES 26 to 45	FREE WHITE FEMALES 45 and over	TOTAL ALL OTHER	TOTAL SLAVES	TOTALS	DISTRICT/ TOWNSHIP	NOTES
Newburyport	174	42	Palmer	Andras	1		2	1		1	1		1				7		
Methuen	155	21	Palmer	Asa				1					1	2			4		
Bradford	125	7	Palmer	David					1	2	1	1	1				6		
Haverhill	149	39	Palmer	James	2			1		1			1				5		
Danvers	11	28	Palmer	Jeremiah	1		1			1		1					4		
Boxford	134	25	Palmer	John				1					1				2		
Methuen	155	22	Palmer	John	2	1		1		1	1	1	1				8		
Rowley	132	7	Palmer	John	1		1	1			1	2	1				7		
Salem	198	18	Palmer	Jona			1	2					1	4			8		
Rowley	131	22	Palmer	Moses	1			1				1	1				4		
Salem	197	15	Palmer	Saml	5	2		1		2	2						12		
Bradford	125	49	Palmer	Samuel			2	1	1	1	2		1	1			9		
Rowley	131	24	Palmer	Stephen				1				2					3		
Newburyport	174	41	Palmer	Timothy	1			1					1				3		
Bradford	122	45	Palmer	William			1			1		1	1				4		
Lynn	227	27	Panott	Benja Jun	2			1		3			1				7		
Lynn	227	29	Panott	Benja Jun		1	1	1		1				1			5		
Lynn	228	16	Panott	Danl			1	1		1		1		1			5		
Lynn	228	19	Panott	Eleazr	1		1			2			1				5		
Lynn	227	30	Panott	Jane	1	1		1		1			1				5		
Lynn	228	17	Panott	Joseph	1		1	1		2			1				6		
Newbury	118	12	Papin	Daniel				1			2	2	1	1			7		
Newbury	113	12	Pappen	Anny										1			1		
Newbury	115	8	Pappin	Joseph			1	1					1				3		
Newbury	113	27	Pappon	Moses	1			1		3	1		1				7		
Newburyport	175	44	Parchard	Samuel	2		2			1		2					7		
Newburyport	174	39	Pardee	Aaron	2	1		1		1		1	1				7		
Newburyport	174	43	Paris	Peter				1				1					2		
Newbury	105	4	Parish	Elijah			1	1		1			1		1		5		
Bradford	123	41	Parker	Aaron	1	2	1	1		1		2					8		
Andover	99	35	Parker	Asa		1	2	1		2	1		1	2			10		
Andover	100	31	Parker	Benja				1					1				2		
Bradford	125	39	Parker	Broadst	1	1		1			1		1	1			7		
Andover	100	22	Parker	Carlton	1			1		1	1	1		1			6		
Bradford	124	14	Parker	Chesen	1			1		3			1				6		
Salem	214	17	Parker	Danl	2	1			1	1			1				6		
Lynn	232	34	Parker	David			2		1			2					5	West Parish	
Lynnfield	235	31	Parker	Ebenz	4			1		1			1				7		
Topsfield	20	29	Parker	Edmand	2			1		2			1				6		
Salem	219	26	Parker	Eliph		1		1				2	1				5		
Methuen	155	19	Parker	Elisha	1	2		1		4	1		1				10		
Haverhill	149	14	Parker	Frederick		2		1					1				4		
Newburyport	175	36	Parker	George	1			1			1	1					4		
Andover	100	29	Parker	Isaac	2		1		1	4	3		1				12		
Boxford	134	16	Parker	Jacob	1			1		1			1		1		5		
Andover	100	23	Parker	James				1					1		1		3		
Beverly	297	31	Parker	James	1	1		1		1			1				5		
Methuen	155	18	Parker	John		2		1			1	1	1				6		
Andover	100	30	Parker	Jonathan				1		1		1		2			5		
Methuen	155	20	Parker	Joseph K	4	1		1		1			2				9		
Andover	100	24	Parker	Kendall		1						1					2		
Topsfield	21	9	Parker	Lucy						1				1			2		
Ipswich	278	18	Parker	Mary										1			1		
Andover	99	36	Parker	Michael		1	2	1			1	2	1	1			9		
Bradford	124	13	Parker	Moses									2				2		
Bradford	125	1	Parker	Moses	1	1		1		1	1	1	1				7		
Bradford	123	42	Parker	Nathll			4			1		1		1			7		
Bradford	124	3	Parker	Paul				1		2			1	1			5		
Salem	195	44	Parker	Phil				1		1			1				3		
Marblehead	239	32	Parker	Richard	5			1					1				7		
Salem	204	41	Parker	Saml		1				2		1					4		
Bradford	124	1	Parker	Samuel	1			1		1				1			4		
Bradford	124	10	Parker	Sarah	1								2	1			4		
Newburyport	175	35	Parker	Silas	1	1	1		1			2	1	1			8		
Bradford	124	2	Parker	Stephen	2	1	2	1				2		1			10		
Lynn	234	6	Parker	Timy			1			1			1				3		
Bradford	124	26	Parker	Trace Grove	1		1	1		1		1		1			6		
Boxford	133	2	Parker	William	2			1		2	1			1			7		
Bradford	123	44	Parker	William	1	1	5	1		1		2	1				12		
Bradford	124	27	Parker	William	1		2	1		1	1	1					8		
Lynn	234	5	Parker	Willm			1			1			1				3		
Salem	216	44	Parker	Willm B		2		1				2					5		
Amesbury	44	3	Parker	Willm Dr			1	1		4	4	1	1				12		
Gloucester	81	13	Parkhurst	Willa		1	1			3	1		1				7		
Salem	205	13	Parnell	James	1	2		1					1				5		
Salem	204	6	Parnell	Jonas		2		1					1				4		
Salem	214	12	Parons	Josiah				1				1	1				3		
Lynn	231	23	Parrott	Rufus	2			1				1					4		
Newburyport	175	43	Parry	Samuel H	2			1					1				4		
Andover	100	20	Parson	Abiel	1	1		1		2		1					6		
Newbury	105	7	Parson	Obadiah			1			1				1			3		
Newbury	116	39	Parson	Silas	1		1	1		1	1		1				6		
Newbury	120	19	Parson	Silas	1		1	1	1	1		2	1	2			10		
Gloucester	60	23	Parsons	Aaron Capt	2			1		2			1				6		

243

TOWN	PG#	LN#	LAST NAME	FIRST NAME	FREE WHITE MALES under 10	10 to 16	16 to 26	26 to 45	45 and over	FREE WHITE FEMALES under 10	10 to 16	16 to 26	26 to 45	45 and over	TOTAL ALL OTHER	TOTAL SLAVES	TOTALS	DISTRICT/TOWNSHIP	NOTES
Gloucester	60	24	Parsons	Andrew	2			1		1	1	1		1			7		
Gloucester	83	28	Parsons	Daniel		1		1		1				1			4		
Gloucester	84	15	Parsons	David			2		1					1			4		
Lynnfield	236	13	Parsons	Ebenz	2			1			2		1	1			7		
Gloucester	80	24	Parsons	Ebenz Junr	1		1	1		2		2	1				8		
Gloucester	77	13	Parsons	Eliza Wo		1	1	1			2	1		1			7		
Gloucester	62	21	Parsons	Enoch	1				1				1	1			4		
Gloucester	77	22	Parsons	Esther Wo				1					1				2		
Gloucester	63	9	Parsons	Ezekial	2	1		1		1			1				6	West Ward	
Newburyport	175	18	Parsons	Harry		1		1				1	1				4		
Gloucester	65	24	Parsons	James	1			1		2	1		1	1			7		
Gloucester	80	21	Parsons	James			1					1					3		
Gloucester	81	12	Parsons	Jeffery	1			1		1		1	1				5		
Gloucester	65	19	Parsons	Jereh				1					1				2		
Gloucester	84	17	Parsons	John	4			1		2	1	1	1				10		
Gloucester	60	21	Parsons	Jona	1		1			3		1					6		
Gloucester	80	22	Parsons	Jona P.	3			1		1			1				6		
Gloucester	74	7	Parsons	Jonah				1		1			1				3	Squam Parish	
Newburyport	175	20	Parsons	Jonathan			2						1				3		
Gloucester	62	8	Parsons	Joshua	2	1	1	1		1			1				7		
Gloucester	60	26	Parsons	Michael	1			1		1	1	1	1	1			7		
Gloucester	83	21	Parsons	Moses			1						1				2		
Gloucester	60	25	Parsons	Nehemiah	1	1		1		1	1	1		1			7		
Gloucester	62	12	Parsons	Obed Esq			2		1		2		1				6		
Gloucester	65	27	Parsons	Samuel	2			1		1			1				5		
Marblehead	240	29	Parsons	Samuel					1					1			2		
Gloucester	60	16	Parsons	Solomon					1		2	2		1			6		
Newburyport	175	17	Parsons	Theophilus	2		1	1	1	1	2	3	2	1	1		15		
Newburyport	175	19	Parsons	Thomas	1	1		1		1	1		1				6		
Gloucester	65	20	Parsons	Thomas Capt	1	1	1					2	1				6		
Gloucester	80	23	Parsons	Thos	4			1					1				6		
Manchester	54	2	Parsons	Tyler	1	1	1			1		1					5		
Gloucester	81	11	Parsons	Vinery	3			1		1			1				6		
Manchester	54	9	Part	Richd		1	1	3	1			1	1	1			9		
Manchester	54	8	Part	Samll	2			1					1				4		
Gloucester	65	26	Pasa	Richard G.	2			1		1			1				5		
Salem	221	12	Pascue	Joseph				1				1					2		
Beverly	305	19	Patch	Abigail									2	1			3		
Ipswich	279	5	Patch	Abigail										1			1		
Hamilton	285	106	Patch	Abraham	2	1		1		3			1	1			9		
Hamilton	285	22	Patch	Benjamin	2			1		1			1				5		
Hamilton	285	66	Patch	Benjamin	2		1		1	2	1		1				9		
Hamilton	285	76	Patch	Benjamin	1			1	1	1	1	1		1			6		
Hamilton	285	27	Patch	Edmund	1			1			1	1		1			5		
Hamilton	285	96	Patch	Isaac		1							1				2		
Beverly	291	28	Patch	James	1			1				1		1			4		
Hamilton	284	11	Patch	James				1			1	1					3		
Hamilton	284	20	Patch	James				2					1				3		
Hamilton	285	112	Patch	John				1									1		
Ipswich	280	24	Patch	John			2			1	1						4		
Hamilton	285	113	Patch	John Junr				1					1				3		
Beverly	291	39	Patch	Joseph	3			1		1			1				6		
Hamilton	284	21	Patch	Joseph	1	2		1		1	2		1				8		
Newburyport	175	40	Patch	Joseph	2			1					1				4		
Danvers	2	20	Patch	Mahue	1	1		1		1			1				6		
Hamilton	285	94	Patch	Nehemiah			1		1			1		1			4		
Beverly	290	39	Patch	Nicholas			2	1		1	1		1				6		
Hamilton	285	10	Patch	Paul	1		1						1				3		
Ipswich	281	31	Patch	Samuel			2		1			3		1			7		
Beverly	291	31	Patch	William	2	1		1		2	2		1				9		
Salem	221	15	Paterson	John			1	1		3		1	1				7		
Andover	100	27	Patten	Elijah			1					1	1	1			4		
Marblehead	244	5	Patten	Elizabeth	2	1				1	1	1		1			7		
Amesbury	44	6	Patten	John		1		1	1	2	1		1				6		
Amesbury	43	19	Patten	Jona	3		1	1		2		2					9		
Amesbury	44	7	Patten	Mary Wid	1		1	1		1			1				5		
Amesbury	44	5	Patten	Willis Dr		1	2	1	1		2		1				8		
Amesbury	44	8	Patten	Willis Junr	1			1		2		1					5		
Salem	189	38	Patterson	Isaac											2		2		
Salem	209	43	Patterson	Robt				1					2				3		
Salem	209	27	Patterson	Saml			3			1	1		1				6		
Salem	209	28	Patterson	Thos	2			1		1			1	1			6		
Salem	209	41	Patterson	William	2			1		2			1			1	7		
Salem	202	46	Patterson	Willm	3	1		1		2			1				8		
Amesbury	44	9	Patty	Moody		1		1		1			1				4		
Rowley	131	21	Payson	Moses			1				1	2	1				6		
Rowley	131	18	Payson	Thos			1						1				2		
Bradford	123	26	Payton	Elliot		1	1	3				1	1	1			8		
Middleton	18	4	Peabody	Amos	3	1		1		2		1	1				9		
Bradford	123	34	Peabody	Andrew	1	1			1	3	1	1		1			9		
Middleton	16	39	Peabody	Andrew		1		1		1			2				5		
Boxford	135	25	Peabody	Asa			1			1		1					4		
Middleton	16	29	Peabody	Benjamin			1	1	1	1	1		1	1			7		
Boxford	135	49	Peabody	Bimsley	1		1		1			1		1			5		

TOWN	PG#	LN#	LAST NAME	FIRST NAME	FWM under 10	FWM 10 to 16	FWM 16 to 26	FWM 26 to 45	FWM 45 and over	FWF under 10	FWF 10 to 16	FWF 16 to 26	FWF 26 to 45	FWF 45 and over	TOTAL ALL OTHER	TOTAL SLAVES	TOTALS	DISTRICT/ TOWNSHIP	NOTES
Boxford	133	8	Peabody	Daniel				1						1			2		
Middleton	16	40	Peabody	David		2	1	1		3		2	1				10		
Andover	100	15	Peabody	Deborah Wid										1			1		
Boxford	133	15	Peabody	Ebenezr	1	1	1		1	2	1	2	1	1			11		
Methuen	155	25	Peabody	Ephraim	1	1		1					1	1			5		
Salem	207	58	Peabody	Ezra	2			1		2	1		1				7		
Middleton	18	7	Peabody	Frances Jun		1		1		4			1				7		
Middleton	16	32	Peabody	Francis	1	1	1	1	1		1	2	1	1			10		
Topsfield	20	4	Peabody	Jacob		1	1		1			1		1			5		
Topsfield	20	5	Peabody	Jacob Junr		1		1		4	1		1				8		
Bradford	123	2	Peabody	John	3		1	1		2	1		1				9		
Topsfield	18	13	Peabody	John		1		1				2	1				5		
Topsfield	18	14	Peabody	John Junr	1	1	1	1		2		1	1				8		
Salem	209	6	Peabody	Jona	1	1	1	1		2			1				7		
Newburyport	176	1	Peabody	Jona	1	1	1	1		2	1		1				8		
Haverhill	149	36	Peabody	Jonah G.	1	1		1				1					4		
Haverhill	149	31	Peabody	Joseph	2	1			1	1	1						6		
Middleton	16	41	Peabody	Joseph		1			1				1				3		
Salem	212	4	Peabody	Joseph	2		1	1				2	1	1	1		9		
Middleton	16	34	Peabody	Joseph 2nd					1			3		1			5		
Middleton	17	29	Peabody	Joseph 3rd		1	1	1				1					4		
Haverhill	149	30	Peabody	Josiah	1			2		1			1	1			6		
Andover	100	14	Peabody	Mary									1				1		
Boxford	135	51	Peabody	Moses		1			1	1	2		1				6		
Middleton	16	42	Peabody	Nathaniel	1			1		3	1						6		
Salem	188	29	Peabody	Oliver	1	1	2			1		1					6		
Boxford	135	21	Peabody	Richard		1		1		1	1		1				5		
Boxford	135	27	Peabody	Samll			1					1					2		
Salem	197	34	Peabody	Samuel		2	1	1		1	1		1				7		
Salem	214	2	Peabody	Samuel		1	2	1				2					6		
Boxford	135	20	Peabody	Stephen		1		1		1			1				4		
Danvers	13	35	Peabody	Thomas	1	1		1		2			1				6		
Lynnfield	235	41	Peabody	Willm			1			2			1				4		
Marblehead	242	18	Peach	Abraham F.											4		4		
Marblehead	269	29	Peach	Elizabeth		1	3				1	1		1			7		
Marblehead	248	23	Peach	John	3			1		1		1	1	1			8		
Salem	200	47	Peach	John		1		1			2		1				5		
Marblehead	249	25	Peach	Joseph		1		1					1				3		
Marblehead	249	24	Peach	Thomas				1					2				3		
Marblehead	268	11	Peach	William		1							1				2		
Salem	218	35	Peal	Robt	2		1			1			1				5		
Marblehead	259	24	Pearce	Benjamin				1					1				2		
Marblehead	256	12	Pearce	George	1		1					1					3		
Marblehead	246	2	Pearce	Hannah	1							1					2		
Marblehead	249	33	Pearce	Robert		1			1	1	1		1				5		
Marblehead	269	24	Pearce	Robert	2			1					1				4		
Marblehead	247	38	Pearce	William	3			1			1	1					6		
Marblehead	261	2	Pearce	William	3			1			1	1					6		
Boxford	133	16	Pearl	John	1		2		1	2	2	1		1			10		
Boxford	133	17	Pearl	John	1			1		1	1	1					5		
Methuen	155	9	Pearley	Humphrey				1		1			1	1			4		
Haverhill	149	33	Pearley	Nathan		1	1		1	2	1			1			7		
Salisbury	32	33	Pearly	Ebenzr Capt		1		1		3		2					7		
Salisbury	32	32	Pearly	Samuel		1				1	1	1					4		
Newbury	114	12	Pears	Ebnz	2							1					3		
Newbury	114	14	Pears	John			1			3		1					5		
Newburyport	174	14	Pearson	Amos		1		1		1	1						4		
Newburyport	174	18	Pearson	Benjamin		1		1		1			1				4		
Newburyport	174	13	Pearson	David		1		1		2			1				5		
Salisbury	32	30	Pearson	Ebenezer	1	1		1		3	1	3	1				11		
Salem	202	29	Pearson	Elijah	2	2		1		1		1					7		
Ipswich	276	27	Pearson	Enoch		1		1	1	1	2	3		1			10		
Newburyport	174	20	Pearson	Hannah Wido							1	1	1				3		
Newburyport	174	19	Pearson	Isaac G	1	1	3		1	1	4		3				14		
Newburyport	174	16	Pearson	Jethro	1		3					1					5		
Newburyport	174	9	Pearson	John	1	1		1				1					4		
Newburyport	174	10	Pearson	John Jn	3	1	2	1		2		1	2				12		
Newburyport	174	11	Pearson	Jonathan				1		2	1		1				5		
Ipswich	276	28	Pearson	Lemual	4			1		1	2	1					9		
Marblehead	240	3	Pearson	Lucretia	1	1					1		1				4		
Newburyport	174	15	Pearson	Moses	3	1		1		2		1	1				9		
Newbury	119	11	Pearson	Nathan			1			1		1					3		
Ipswich	273	5	Pearson	Nathan		1		1		1		1		1			5		
Gloucester	65	18	Pearson	Samuel	2			1		2		1					6		
Ipswich	273	6	Pearson	Sarah									1				1		
Newburyport	174	21	Pearson	Simeon	2			1		2	3		1				9		
Ipswich	273	7	Pearson	Stephen	2			1		1		1					5		
Newburyport	174	17	Pearson	Theodore	2		1		1	1	3	1	1				10		
Newburyport	174	12	Pearson	Thomas	1				1	1	2	1					6		
Gloucester	65	21	Pearson	William Cap	1	1	1		2	1	1	2	1				10		
Lynnfield	235	29	Pearsons	Saml	1					2	2		1				7		
Lynnfield	235	7	Peas	James			1			1		1					3		
Salem	205	49	Peas	Jona	1		1					1					3		
Salem	205	25	Peas	Minor	1	1		1		1			1				5		
Salem	205	44	Peas	Richard			1										2		

TOWN	PG#	LN#	LAST NAME	FIRST NAME	FREE WHITE MALES under 10	10 to 16	16 to 26	26 to 45	45 and over	FREE WHITE FEMALES under 10	10 to 16	16 to 26	26 to 45	45 and over	TOTAL ALL OTHER	TOTAL SLAVES	TOTALS	DISTRICT/ TOWNSHIP	NOTES
Salem	205	28	Pease	Samuel	1			1		1			1				4		
Danvers	8	2	Peasley	Ruben		1							1				2		
Marblehead	270	14	Peck	Benjamin			1			3		1					5		
Salem	199	18	Peck	John			1			1		1	1				4		
Salem	214	19	Peck	Jona		1		1				1	1				4		
Haverhill	149	34	Pecker	Daniel			1			5		1					7		
Salisbury	32	25	Pecker	James	2		1	1		3	1	1					9		
Haverhill	149	35	Pecker	Ruth	1		1					1	1	1			5		
Beverly	297	23	Pedrich	Richard			1			2		1	1				5		
Marblehead	242	24	Pedrick	John		1	1			1		1	1				5		
Marblehead	243	19	Pedrick	John				1					1				2		
Marblehead	265	23	Pedrick	Joseph	1	2	1			1		1					6		
Marblehead	264	19	Pedrick	Knott			1	1		1	3	1	1				8		
Marblehead	246	3	Pedrick	Mary	1		1			3		1					6		
Marblehead	252	30	Pedrick	Richard		3	1	2				1	1	1			9		
Marblehead	256	18	Pedrick	Thomas	1		1			2	1	1					6		
Marblehead	244	14	Pedrick	Thomas Junr	1		1					1					3		
Marblehead	239	30	Pedrick	William			1			2		1					4		
Marblehead	257	26	Pedrick	William		2	2	1		1	1	1	1				9		
Newbury	116	11	Peeksbury	Jonathan	3		1			1		1					6		
Salem	216	7	Peele	Geo				1						2			3		
Salem	218	55	Peele	Josh	1		1			1		1					4		
Salem	188	2	Peele	Robert	3			1				1	1				6		
Salem	203	36	Peele	Willard		1		1				1	1				4		
Salem	220	38	Peele	William				1			2			1			4		
Manchester	54	4	Peirce	Abial Wo		1				1			1	1			4		
Gloucester	74	27	Peirce	Andrew	4		1				2		1				8		
Salem	215	9	Peirce	Asa	2	1	1			2		2	2				10		
Beverly	302	38	Peirce	Benja		2				2		1	1				6		
Newburyport	174	30	Peirce	Benjamin		1	1			4		1	1				8		
Salem	191	30	Peirce	Daniel		1	1			1	1	1	1				7		
Newburyport	174	29	Peirce	Enoch	1	1	1	1	3	1		1					10		
Ipswich	281	52	Peirce	George		1	1		1	4	2			1			10		
Newburyport	174	28	Peirce	Henry			1	1					2	1			5		
Salem	188	4	Peirce	Jerath	1	2		1		2		1					8		
Gloucester	76	20	Peirce	John				1						1			2		
Salem	204	31	Peirce	John				1		2		2	1				6		
Salem	220	11	Peirce	John		1	1			3			1				6		
Beverly	294	51	Peirce	John Jr			1						1				2		
Salem	213	17	Peirce	Jona				1						1			2		
Salem	221	1	Peirce	Jona				1						1			2		
Salem	188	16	Peirce	Joshua				1						1			2		
Salem	218	52	Peirce	Lydia		1								1			2		
Wenham	309	7	Peirce	Molly										2			2		
Newburyport	174	26	Peirce	Nathan				1					2	1			4		
Salem	215	10	Peirce	Nathan		1	1	1		1	2	3	1	1			11		
Newburyport	174	27	Peirce	Nathan for the work house	1		2	6		6		1	9	10	1		36		
Beverly	305	20	Peirce	Nathanl		2	1			5	1	1					10		
Newburyport	174	31	Peirce	Nicolas	1	2	1						1				5		
Beverly	304	4	Peirce	Samuel	2		1			1			1				5		
Beverly	294	46	Peirce	William			1					1	1				3		
Gloucester	60	30	Peirce	Will C Col	1	2	5	1		1	1	2	2				15		
Gloucester	60	19	Peirced	David Capt				1		2		3					6		
Marblehead	268	24	Peltro	Hannah	1								1	1			3		
Salem	191	4	Penchard	John	2	1	2	1		2	1		2				11		
Beverly	303	11	Pender	John		1						1	1				3		
Beverly	305	41	Pennel	John	1			1			2			1			5		
Lynn	232	23	Pennison	John	2			2					1				6	West Parish	
Salem	209	34	Penny	Saml				1					1				2		
Salisbury	32	34	Pensen	John				1				1	1				3		
Danvers	4	19	Pepper	John	1			1		1		1	1				5		
Methuen	155	17	Percy	John				1		3			1	1			7		
Gloucester	84	27	Perkens	Richard			1			1	1	1					4		
Ipswich	275	31	Perkins	Aaron		3		1			1	1	1				7		
Ipswich	275	32	Perkins	Aaron Jr	2		1					1					4		
Ipswich	277	51	Perkins	Abraham	1			1		1			1				6		
Ipswich	283	1	Perkins	Abraham		1		1				1	2				6		
Newburyport	174	25	Perkins	Abraham	3	2	1	1					1	1			9		
Ipswich	283	2	Perkins	Abraham Junr				1		1			1		1		4		
Topsfield	20	27	Perkins	Amos				1						2			3		
Middleton	17	40	Perkins	Andrew	1			1		2		1	1				6		
Topsfield	21	34	Perkins	Asa				1		2		1	1				5		
Newburyport	174	23	Perkins	Benjamin				1		1		1	2				5		
Ipswich	278	30	Perkins	Bensley				1						2			3		
Newbury	117	28	Perkins	Bimsley	4			1		1	7		1				14		
Ipswich	278	4	Perkins	Charlotte	1					1			1				3		
Topsfield	18	11	Perkins	Daniel	2	1		1		2	1	1	1				9		
Topsfield	19	41	Perkins	Daniel		1		1						2			4		
Salem	208	14	Perkins	David	3	1	1			2			1	1			10		
Topsfield	22	7	Perkins	David	2	1	1		2	1		1					9		
Topsfield	22	8	Perkins	David Junr	2	1	2	1		1	2	1	1				11		
Topsfield	20	30	Perkins	Deborah			1						1				2		
Wenham	307	14	Perkins	Edward	1	1		1		2	1		1				7		
Salem	207	55	Perkins	Elijah	2			1		2		2	2	1			10		
Topsfield	22	5	Perkins	Elijah	1			1		1			1				4		
Topsfield	22	9	Perkins	Elijah		1	1		1	1		1	1	1			7		

TOWN	PG#	LN#	HEADS OF HOUSEHOLD		FREE WHITE MALES					FREE WHITE FEMALES					TOTAL ALL OTHER	TOTAL SLAVES	TOTALS	DISTRICT/ TOWNSHIP	NOTES
			LAST NAME	FIRST NAME	under 10	10 to 16	16 to 26	26 to 45	45 and over	under 10	10 to 16	16 to 26	26 to 45	45 and over					
Methuen	155	11	Perkins	Elisha		1	1		1			2		1			6		
Ipswich	274	37	Perkins	Elizabeth									2				2		
Ipswich	276	58	Perkins	Elizabeth										1			1		
Salem	188	3	Perkins	Eunice			2		1			1		1			5		
Salem	221	3	Perkins	Isaac				1						1			2		
Salem	221	2	Perkins	Isaac Jr	1		1	1				1	1				5		
Newbury	112	5	Perkins	Jacob				1						1			2		
Newburyport	174	24	Perkins	Jacob	2	1		1		2	1		1				8		
Ipswich	275	20	Perkins	James			1	1		1		1		1			5		
Salem	220	12	Perkins	James			1	1	1	1		1					4		
Lynn	233	14	Perkins	Jenny									1		1		2		
Salem	216	24	Perkins	John			1		1	1		1	1				4		
Salem	220	56	Perkins	John		1	2	1				1	1				6		
Wenham	309	34	Perkins	John	1		1	1	1					1			5		
Lynnfield	235	46	Perkins	John Esq		1	1	1				2		1	1		7		
Lynn	227	8	Perkins	Jona	1			1	1		1						4		
Ipswich	281	67	Perkins	Joseph		1	1	1	2	1	2	2		1			11		
Newbury	113	20	Perkins	Joseph	2	1	1							1			5		
Beverly	294	1	Perkins	Mary										2			2		
Newburyport	174	22	Perkins	Mathew				1						1			2		
Topsfield	18	10	Perkins	Moses				1		1		1		1			4		
Salem	216	18	Perkins	Nathan		1		1					1	1			4		
Ipswich	278	12	Perkins	Nathaniel		1		1					1	1			4		
Wenham	309	35	Perkins	Nehemiah	1			1		2	1		1				6		
Middleton	17	26	Perkins	Oliver Junr	2			1					1				4		
Middleton	17	41	Perkins	Oliver Junr		1	1	1				2	1	1			7		
Topsfield	20	26	Perkins	Robert				1					3	1			5		
Topsfield	20	25	Perkins	Robert Junr	2	2	3	1		1	1	3		1			14		
Salem	220	53	Perkins	Robt	1	1	1	1		2	1	1	1				9		
Topsfield	22	4	Perkins	Samuel		1		1						1			3		
Ipswich	275	30	Perkins	Sarah		1							3	1			5		
Topsfield	21	1	Perkins	Thomas		1		1					2				4		
Topsfield	19	13	Perkins	Thomas Junr	2	1		1		2				1			7		
Middleton	16	20	Perkins	Timothy				1		1				1			3		
Salem	221	19	Perkins	Willm	2	2		1		1	1		1				8		
Topsfield	22	10	Perkins	Zebulon	1			1	1	1	2	1	1				8		
Boxford	135	14	Perley	Aaron	3	2		1	2		1		1	1			11		
Ipswich	279	53	Perley	Allen				1				1	1				3		
Ipswich	279	52	Perley	Allen Jun	3	1		1		1			1				7		
Boxford	135	13	Perley	Amos	3			1		2	1	1	1				9		
Boxford	135	16	Perley	Asa	1		1	1					1	2			6		
Rowley	131	27	Perley	Darius	2	1	2	1		2	1	2	1				12		
Boxford	135	5	Perley	Eliphalet			1						1				2		
Boxford	136	5	Perley	Henry	2	1		1		1	2		1				8		
Ipswich	279	54	Perley	Jacob			1			1			1				3		
Boxford	135	17	Perley	Jesse	3			1					2	1			7		
Ipswich	279	55	Perley	John	1			1		1			1				4		
Rowley	129	26	Perley	John				1		2	1	1		2			7		
Rowley	130	22	Perley	John			1	1						2			4		
Boxford	135	3	Perley	Moody	2					1		1	1	1			6		
Rowley	127	47	Perley	Nathan	2	1		1	1	2	1	1	1				10		
Boxford	135	8	Perley	Nathll		1		1					1	1			4		
Boxford	135	7	Perley	Phineas	2			2		2	1	1	1				9		
Rowley	130	21	Perley	Samuel			2						1	1			4		
Topsfield	21	10	Perley	Stephen				1		2			1				4		
Boxford	136	8	Perley	William			2	1				2	1	1			7		
Rowley	130	11	Perley	William	2		1	1		1			1				6		
Gloucester	58	13	Perrin	Eliza Wo							1	2		1			4		
Bradford	123	12	Perry	David				1					1				2		
Manchester	54	5	Perry	Elizh Wo	2								1	1			4		
Marblehead	250	17	Perry	George		1			1			1					3		
Marblehead	250	16	Perry	Hannah		1								1			2		
Gloucester	71	22	Perry	Hannah Wo		1	1							1			3		
Danvers	5	8	Perry	John				2						1			3		
Lynnfield	236	11	Perry	John				1		2			1				4		
Salem	218	51	Perry	John	2	2		1		1			1	1			8		
Newburyport	175	42	Perry	Joseph	2			1		1			2	1			7		
Beverly	295	13	Perry	Mary			2						1	1			4		
Beverly	295	14	Perry	Robert	1		1						1				3		
Lynnfield	237	17	Perry	Thaddeus		1		1					1				3		
Beverly	304	42	Perry	William		1	1										2		
Newbury	119	21	Perry	William		2		1		2			1				6		
Newbury	106	23	Person	Benjamin	2	1	1		1	1	2	2	1	1			12		
Newbury	106	22	Person	David				1						1			2		
Newbury	109	14	Person	David		2		1		2	1		1				7		
Newbury	106	21	Person	Ebenezer	1		1	1		1			1	1			6		
Rowley	128	8	Person	Isaac	1		1	1		1		1	1				6		
Rowley	128	25	Person	Jacob		1	1	1					1				4		
Newbury	106	31	Person	Jeremiah		1	2	1					1	2			7		
Newbury	111	10	Person	John				1					1	1			3		
Rowley	131	31	Person	John	1			1				1	2	1			6		
Newbury	106	24	Person	Joseph	1		1						1				3		
Rowley	131	33	Person	Reuben		1		1				2		4			8		

TOWN	PG#	LN#	LAST NAME	FIRST NAME	M under 10	M 10 to 16	M 16 to 26	M 26 to 45	M 45 and over	F under 10	F 10 to 16	F 16 to 26	F 26 to 45	F 45 and over	TOTAL ALL OTHER	TOTAL SLAVES	TOTALS	DISTRICT/ TOWNSHIP	NOTES
Rowley	131	29	Person	Solomon			1	1					1	1			4		
Andover	100	1	Peters	Andrew			1	1	2				1		1		6		
Salem	197	46	Peters	Benja				1						1			2		
Salem	188	20	Peters	Eliza			1					1	1	1			4		
Newburyport	175	27	Peters	John			1							1			2		
Salem	212	42	Peters	John	1	1		1		1			2				6		
Salem	197	47	Peters	Jona		1	1	1			2	2		1			8		
Andover	100	2	Peters	Joseph	3			1		1			2	1			8		
Ipswich	274	7	Peters	Mary									1				1		
Newburyport	175	26	Peters	Richard	2	1	1	1					1				6		
Salem	193	34	Peters	Samuel	2			1		1			1	1			6		
Salem	210	53	Peters	Sarah								1		1			2		
Salem	206	18	Peterson	Hanse				1		1	1	1					4		
Marblehead	257	36	Petey	Mary		1	1			1	1	1					5		
Haverhill	149	29	Petingall	Mathew	1		1			3			1	2			8		
Newbury	116	28	Pettengall	Stephn			1					1		1			3		
Newbury	112	23	Pettengill	Benjn	1	2	1			3	1	2		1			11		
Newbury	112	22	Pettengill	David		2		1			3		2	2			10		
Methuen	155	8	Pettery	Edward			1			1			2				4		
Newbury	113	8	Pettingall	Anny			1			1		1		1			4		
Methuen	155	24	Pettingall	Asa	2	1	1			2	1		1				9		
Haverhill	149	37	Pettingall	Jedediah	1		1			1			1				4		
Methuen	155	23	Pettingall	John	1	1	1		1	3	2		1	1			11		
Newbury	114	35	Pettingall	Nicol		1		1	1				1	1			5		
Newbury	113	19	Pettingall	Thomas	2	1		1					1				5		
Newburyport	174	35	Pettingel	Edmund				1				1					2		
Newburyport	174	38	Pettingel	John			1	1			3			1			6		
Salem	195	30	Pettingel	Joseph	1	3	1			1	2		1				9		
Salem	211	34	Pettingel	Joseph	1	1						1					3		
Newburyport	174	36	Pettingel	Joshua		2		1		1	2			1			7		
Newburyport	174	37	Pettingel	Mathew			1	1				1	2	1			6		
Newbury	113	39	Pettingell	Moses	1	2	1	1		1		1		1			9		
Salisbury	32	29	Pettingill	Amos			1	1						1			3		
Salisbury	32	14	Pettingill	Joseph	1		1		1	1		1		1			6		
Newbury	120	7	Pettingill	Sarah				1						1			2		
Haverhill	149	38	Petty	Abigail										1			1		
Gloucester	60	27	Pew	William			1					1					2		
Marblehead	254	14	Peyton	Mary									1				1		
Andover	100	17	Phelps	Elisha				1					1				2		
Andover	100	33	Phelps	Henry		1	1	1				1		1			5		
Gloucester	60	28	Phelps	Henry Doct	1	1		1		2		1		1			7		
Andover	100	25	Phelps	Isaac		1	1				2						4		
Salem	216	35	Phelps	Jonathan									1				1		
Andover	100	16	Phelps	Joseph			1	1					1				3		
Andover	100	21	Phelps	Joseph Junr			1			1			1				3		
Andover	100	32	Phelps	Joshua	2	1		1					1	1			6		
Andover	100	34	Phelps	Mary Wid						1	1		1				3		
Salem	216	23	Phelps	Wm	2		1		1	2			1				7		
Newburyport	175	33	Phillemore	Samuel	1		1						1				3		
Lynn	231	9	Phillips	Alice	1		1	2				1	1	1			7		
Lynn	228	6	Phillips	Anne			1						1	1			3		
Salem	208	1	Phillips	Asa			1	1					1				3		
Lynn	229	33	Phillips	Benj	1	2	1	1		5	1		1				12		
Lynn	226	13	Phillips	Benj H	2	1	1	1		1	1	1	1	1			10		
Lynn	228	5	Phillips	Content								1	1	1			3		
Rowley	130	36	Phillips	David	1			1					1				3		
Marblehead	265	32	Phillips	Jacob	2			1		3			1	1			8		
Andover	100	13	Phillips	John		1		1	1			1	1	1			6		
Lynn	228	2	Phillips	John	3	1	1	2		3	1	1					13		
Marblehead	268	36	Phillips	John	2			1		2		1					6		
Andover	100	12	Phillips	John Junr			4			1	2	2	1	1			11		
Lynn	226	15	Phillips	Jonathan	1		1	1		2			1				6		
Rowley	130	35	Phillips	Nathan			1			1			1				3		
Marblehead	267	10	Phillips	Nathaniel	3	1		1		1	1	1	1				9		
Marblehead	264	20	Phillips	Richard	2	1		1		1	1		1				7		
Salem	189	17	Phillips	Richd	1			1					1				3		
Bradford	121	4	Phillips	Samuel	2			1		2			1				6		
Andover	100	18	Phillips	Samuel Esq Honble		1	2	2	1			1	2	1			10		
Marblehead	248	9	Phillips	Stephen				1					1	1			3		
Salem	215	8	Phillips	Stephen			1	1		1		1					4		
Bradford	121	5	Phillips	Timo	1	1	3	1					1	1			8		
Lynn	231	11	Phillips	Walter		2		1				1	1	1			5		
Salem	200	45	Phillips	Walter		1		1		2		1					5		
Marblehead	265	31	Phillips	William		1						1		1			4		
Newbury	114	22	Phillips	William											3		3		
Lynn	231	10	Phillips	Willm			1						1				2		
Lynn	223	8	Phillips	Zacheus		1		1		3			1				6		
Salem	216	3	Phippen	Anna	1		7			1	1	1					12		
Salem	215	18	Phippen	Anstis									1				1		
Salem	210	40	Phippen	David	1		1			1			1				4		
Salem	219	55	Phippen	Joshua	1	1	7			1		1	1	1			13		
Salem	219	57	Phippen	Joshua Jr			1			1			1				3		
Salem	216	1	Phippen	Mary		1							1	1			3		
Salem	215	29	Phippen	Nath		1		1			1		1				4		
Salem	219	56	Phippen	Nath	2	2		1		2			1				8		
Salem	215	27	Phippen	Thos			3		1		1	1	1				7		
Salem	201	13	Phipps	Eliza	2		1										3		

TOWN	PG#	LN#	LAST NAME	FIRST NAME	FREE WHITE MALES under 10	10 to 16	16 to 26	26 to 45	45 and over	FREE WHITE FEMALES under 10	10 to 16	16 to 26	26 to 45	45 and over	TOTAL ALL OTHER	TOTAL SLAVES	TOTALS	DISTRICT/ TOWNSHIP	NOTES
Gloucester	77	7	Phips	Amos	1			1		1		1					4		
Gloucester	76	32	Phips	John					1	2			1				4		
Gloucester	81	10	Phips	John	1	1				2	1		1				7		
Salem	196	1	Phips	John	2	1	4		1	2	1		1				12		
Gloucester	75	10	Phips	Willm Capt	1			1		2			1				5		
Newbury	113	7	Phurlo	John	1			1		1			1				4		
Newbury	113	3	Phurlo	Paul		1		1		4		1	1				8		
Beverly	292	26	Pickard	Ephraim		1	2		1				2	1	1		8		
Rowley	129	33	Pickard	Francis					1					1			2		
Rowley	129	32	Pickard	Jacob	1			1	1				1	1			6		
Rowley	130	44	Pickard	John		1		1					1	1			4		
Rowley	129	27	Pickard	Joseph	3			1		1	2		1	1			9		
Marblehead	266	14	Pickel	Moses A.				1									1		
Methuen	155	15	Picker	John	1	1	2	1		1	1	1					9		
Marblehead	244	20	Picker	Nicholas	1		1	1		2		2	2				11		
Marblehead	245	11	Picker	Sally									1				1		
Danvers	14	11	Pickering	James	1		1					1					3		
Salem	196	5	Pickering	John	1			1		1	1	1	1				7		
Salem	190	23	Pickering	Joseph	1	3		1		2			1				9		
Salem	190	21	Pickering	William				1	1	1	1	1	1	1			6		
Beverly	290	15	Pickett	John	2	1	1		1			1	2		1		9		
Beverly	289	23	Pickett	Joseph				1		1		1		1			4		
Beverly	289	22	Pickett	Joseph Jr	2			1		1			1				5		
Beverly	303	18	Pickett	Thomas	1	2	2		1	2	2	2		1			13		
Newburyport	175	34	Pickett	William	1	3		1		2		1	1				9		
Salem	213	49	Pickman	Benja Jr	3	1		1		2	1		3				11		
Newburyport	175	22	Pidgeon	Benjamin					2					2			4		
Danvers	5	34	Pierce	Abigail								1	1				2		
Danvers	12	25	Pierce	John		1		1					1				3		
Beverly	294	49	Pierce	Nicholas								2		1			4		
Salisbury	32	20	Pike	Abl Wd								1		1			2		
Topsfield	18	3	Pike	Benjamin	1	1	1		1	4		1	1				10		
Salisbury	32	27	Pike	Caleb		1	1		1	3	1	3	1	1			12		
Salisbury	32	16	Pike	Caleb Junr			1				1			1			3		
Newburyport	175	8	Pike	Daniel				1						1			2		
Newburyport	175	9	Pike	Daniel Jr	3	1		1		1			1				7		
Danvers	11	17	Pike	Eben				1						1			2		
Salisbury	32	18	Pike	Elias				1	1	1	1		1				5		
Salisbury	32	15	Pike	Elias Junr	1		1	1		1	2	1					8		
Newburyport	175	10	Pike	Enoch	1		1	1		1			1				6		
Salisbury	32	22	Pike	Francis		1		1					1				3		
Salisbury	32	19	Pike	Henry				1		4			1				6		
Salisbury	32	21	Pike	Jacob	1			1		2			1				5		
Haverhill	149	16	Pike	James					1					1			2		
Salisbury	32	24	Pike	John	2			1		1			1				5		
Newburyport	175	7	Pike	Joseph	4			1					1				6		
Rowley	131	50	Pike	Joseph	2	1	1	1	1				2	1			9		
Salisbury	32	28	Pike	Joshua		1				1		2	1	2			7		
Newburyport	175	12	Pike	Josiah		1				1	1						3		
Newburyport	175	5	Pike	Martha Wido		2	1					1		1			5		
Newburyport	175	6	Pike	Martha Wido Junr		1				1	1		1	1	1		6		
Salem	191	35	Pike	Mary									1	2			3		
Salisbury	32	23	Pike	Mary Wd		2	1						2	1			6		
Newbury	120	32	Pike	Mathew		1						1	1	1			4		
Salisbury	32	17	Pike	Moses	3	1	1		1				2	1			9		
Newburyport	175	4	Pike	Nicolas		1			1					1	1		4		
Newbury	111	37	Pike	Richard				2		1		1	1				5		
Beverly	299	21	Pike	Sally	1					1	1		1				4		
Methuen	155	7	Pike	Thomas	1			1		1		1					4		
Newbury	105	8	Pike	Thomas			1	1		1			2				5		
Newburyport	175	11	Pike	William		1				1		1					3		
Rowley	128	44	Piker	Thomas		2		1						1			4		
Amesbury	44	12	Pillsbury	Samuel	1			1					1				3		
Newbury	119	8	Pilsbury	Amos		1						1	1	1			5		
Rowley	127	14	Pilsbury	Amos		1		1				1		2			5		
Rowley	132	10	Pilsbury	Amos	1		1					1		1			4		
Newburyport	175	32	Pilsbury	Benjamin	2			1					2				5		
Newbury	107	43	Pilsbury	Chase							1		1	1			3		
Newbury	111	2	Pilsbury	David				1									1		
Rowley	127	7	Pilsbury	Dole		1	1					1		1			4		
Newburyport	175	30	Pilsbury	John	1			1		1	1	2		1			7		
Newburyport	175	31	Pilsbury	Michael	2	1		1		1		1	2	1			9		
Newbury	107	22	Pilsbury	Moses				1		1		2					4		
Newbury	115	40	Pilsbury	Moses	5		1	1				2	1				10		
Newbury	111	26	Pilsbury	Samuel				1									1		
Newburyport	175	28	Pilsbury	Samuel		1		1	1	1			1	1			6		
Rowley	131	11	Pilsbury	Samuel		1	1	1				1	1				5		
Newburyport	175	29	Pilsbury	Samuel Jr	2			1		2	1		1				7		
Newbury	119	7	Pilsbury	Semion	2			1		1			1				5		
Newbury	107	6	Pilsbury	Silas		1				1		1					3		
Newbury	111	4	Pilsbury	Timo	2	1						1	1	1	1		7		
Newbury	107	23	Pilsbury	William			1						1				2		
Bradford	123	43	Pimberton	Abel	1	2		1					2				6		
Ipswich	276	34	Pinder	Moses	1			1		1			1				4		
Danvers	9	34	Pinder	Samuel	1		1			1		1					4		

TOWN	PG#	LN#	LAST NAME	FIRST NAME	FWM under 10	FWM 10 to 16	FWM 16 to 26	FWM 26 to 45	FWM 45 and over	FWF under 10	FWF 10 to 16	FWF 16 to 26	FWF 26 to 45	FWF 45 and over	TOTAL ALL OTHER	TOTAL SLAVES	TOTALS	DISTRICT/ TOWNSHIP	NOTES
Danvers	9	22	Pinder	Simon	1		1		1		1	1		1			6		
Bradford	125	15	Pine	David		1	1	1				1	1	1			6		
Rowley	130	23	Pingree	Asa	1			1	1	1		1		1			6		
Rowley	130	29	Pingree	Asa				1						1			2		
Rowley	130	30	Pingree	Asa	1			1		1			1				4		
Rowley	130	24	Pingree	Clement		1				1		1					3		
Rowley	130	17	Pingree	Daniel	1			1					2	1			5		
Newburyport	175	39	Pingree	Daniel R	1			2					1				4		
Rowley	130	15	Pingree	Francis			1		1			2		1			5		
Methuen	155	12	Pingrey	Job		1			1			1		1			4		
Methuen	155	13	Pingrey	John	2		2	1		1		1	1				8		
Methuen	155	14	Pingrey	Moses				1				1	1				3		
Newbury	119	3	Pinny	Moses	1		2			1		1	1				6		
Newbury	116	12	Pinny	Samuel	1		1		1	1	2	3		1	1		11		
Gloucester	60	37	Piper	Marth Wd		1						1		2			4		
Newburyport	174	32	Piper	Walter		1	2		1	1		2		1			8		
Newburyport	174	33	Piper	Walter Jr	2	1		1		2			1				7		
Newburyport	174	34	Piper	William		1				1		1					3		
Newbury	112	15	Pirce	Henry	2	1		1		1		1					6		
Newbury	111	3	Pirce	John	1	1		1			1		1				5		
Lynn	226	33	Pitcher	Robert		1	1		1				1	1			5		
Andover	100	26	Pitcher	Wm						3		1					4		
Marblehead	255	9	Pitman	Benjamin	2			1		2			1				6		
Salem	201	16	Pitman	John			1	1		1	1	1	1				6		
Salem	199	2	Pitman	Michael	4		1	1		1		1	1				9		
Salem	216	32	Pitman	Sarah									1				1		
Marblehead	246	20	Pitman	Thomas			1	1		1			1				3		
Marblehead	264	21	Pitman	Thomas	2			1		2	1		1				7		
Salem	198	40	Pitman	William	1		1	1				1					4		
Salem	190	28	Pitam	Hannah	1			1		1	1		1				5		
Salem	195	45	Pitam	Mark			1			1		1					3		
Salem	195	47	Pitam	Polly									2				2		
Salem	209	33	Pitam	William	3			1					1				5		
Salem	211	43	Pittman	William		1	1					1	2				5		
Marblehead	245	19	Plaisted	Lucy									1				1		
Newburyport	175	38	Platt	Thomas	1	2			1				1				5		
Bradford	126	14	Platts	Abigal									2				2		
Rowley	132	5	Platts	John		1	1	1		2	1		1				7		
Gloucester	84	12	Plumer	Mary Wo		1	2	1				1		1			6		
Newbury	105	21	Plumer	Nathaniel	1			1		1	1	1	2				7		
Haverhill	149	25	Plummer	Asa	1	1		1		1	1	1	1				7		
Newbury	117	41	Plummer	Benja				1				1	1				3		
Newbury	117	42	Plummer	Benja	1		3	1				3					8		
Newburyport	174	3	Plummer	Daniel		1	2						2				5		
Gloucester	65	23	Plummer	David		2	3			1	2	1	1				10		
Newbury	118	4	Plummer	David	1	2					1	3	1				8		
Newburyport	174	5	Plummer	Enoch	1	1		1		1		2					6		
Newbury	117	37	Plummer	Hannah								2		1			3		
Newbury	117	22	Plummer	Isaiah	1		1			2		1		1			6		
Amesbury	44	11	Plummer	John				1									1		
Newbury	118	3	Plummer	John	2		1			1			1				5		
Newbury	117	12	Plummer	Jonath			1	1	1			1		1			5		
Newbury	117	43	Plummer	Joseph	1	1		1		1			1				5		
Newburyport	174	1	Plummer	Joseph		1	2		1			1					5		
Amesbury	44	10	Plummer	Joshua				1			1		1				3		
Newburyport	174	2	Plummer	Josiah				1				1	1				3		
Newbury	118	2	Plummer	Mark				1					1				2		
Amesbury	44	4	Plummer	Moses	2	1		1		1	1	1		1			8		
Gloucester	71	15	Plummer	Moses	3			1					1				5		
Newburyport	174	7	Plummer	Nathan				1		1			2				4		
Salem	196	23	Plummer	Oliver		3	1				1	2	1				8		
Newbury	117	30	Plummer	Paul	1	1	1		1		1	1	1	1			8		
Newbury	117	36	Plummer	Paul			1			2	2	1					6		
Newbury	117	24	Plummer	Richard			1		1	1		1	1				5		
Newburyport	174	4	Plummer	Samuel	2	1			1	2	2			1			9		
Rowley	127	48	Plummer	Samuel			1	1				1		1			4		
Rowley	127	49	Plummer	Samuel									1				1		
Rowley	129	50	Plummer	Samuel			1		1	2		2		1			7		
Newbury	117	33	Plummer	Seth				1		1	1	1					4		
Newburyport	174	8	Plummer	Seth	2	1	1					2					6		
Haverhill	149	27	Plummer	Silas	1	2	1	1		2		1	1				9		
Haverhill	149	26	Plummer	Thomas		2	1			1	2	1	1				8		
Newburyport	174	6	Plummer	Tristram		1	1			1	2		3				8		
Ipswich	273	39	Poiles	Charles			1					1					2		
Ipswich	283	10	Poland	Abner					1			1	1				3		
Ipswich	283	9	Poland	Abner Junr	2	2		1		1		1	2	1			10		
Hamilton	285	4	Poland	Francis				1				1		1			3		
Beverly	294	47	Poland	Joseph				1			1	2	1				5		
Beverly	299	12	Poland	Joseph	1		1	1		1		1					5		
Hamilton	285	6	Poland	Joseph			1	1	1	2	1		1				7		
Ipswich	281	46	Poland	Josiah	3			1		2			1				7		
Hamilton	285	83	Poland	Nathan		1	1	1		2			1				6		
Hamilton	287	4	Poland	Nehemiah			1			1	1	1					4		
Hamilton	285	5	Poland	Samuel		1		1					1				3		
Ipswich	273	19	Poller	John Jur	1	2		1		3	1		1				9		
Gloucester	81	7	Pool	Aaron	2			1				1					4		

TOWN	PG#	LN#	LAST NAME	FIRST NAME	FREE WHITE MALES under 10	10 to 16	16 to 26	26 to 45	45 and over	FREE WHITE FEMALES under 10	10 to 16	16 to 26	26 to 45	45 and over	TOTAL ALL OTHER	TOTAL SLAVES	TOTALS	DISTRICT/ TOWNSHIP	NOTES
Gloucester	81	1	Pool	Abraham	2	2		1		3			1				9		
Gloucester	81	3	Pool	Ebenz Junr		1		1			1		1				4		
Danvers	12	9	Pool	Elizabeth			1	1				1		1			4		
Gloucester	80	32	Pool	John	2			1	1	2	1	2	1				10		
Gloucester	80	33	Pool	John Junr	2			1		2	1	1	1				8		
Gloucester	81	4	Pool	Joseph			1						1				2		
Gloucester	81	6	Pool	Mark				1		2			1				4		
Gloucester	81	5	Pool	Mark Maj		2		1	1	1			1				6		
Danvers	15	13	Pool	Milo											4		4		
Gloucester	81	8	Pool	Moses		1	1	1		1	1		1				6		
Gloucester	83	31	Pool	Rachel Wo								1	1				2		
Gloucester	80	20	Pool	Sarh Widow		1	1			1	1		1				5		
Gloucester	81	2	Pool	Stephen Junr	2	2	1	1		2			1				9		
Lynn	234	4	Pool	Susanna		1	1	1				1	1				5		
Lynn	233	47	Pool	Thos		1				1		1					3	West Parish	
Danvers	13	28	Pool	Ward	2		2	1				1	1				7		
Gloucester	80	30	Pool	Caleb		1			1	1	1		1				5		
Gloucester	80	31	Pool	Caleb Junr	1		1			1		1					4		
Gloucester	80	25	Pool	Ebenz	1		1	1			1	3	1				8		
Gloucester	80	27	Pool	Francis		3		1	1	1	1		1				8		
Gloucester	80	26	Pool	Isaac		1		0	1	2		1	2				7		
Gloucester	80	28	Pool	Jona	1	1	2		1	2			1				8		
Gloucester	80	29	Pool	Stephen				1					2				3		
Andover	100	4	Poor	Abraham		1	2		1	1	2			1			8		
Newbury	119	12	Poor	Amos			1					1	1				3		
Newbury	119	31	Poor	Benja		7		1				3	3				14		
Rowley	128	41	Poor	Benja	2		1			2		1					6		
Andover	100	19	Poor	Daniel	6	3		1		1	2		1		1		15		
Newbury	107	26	Poor	Daniel	1			1		1	1		1				5		
Rowley	132	16	Poor	Daniel				1		1	1	1					4		
Rowley	128	11	Poor	David	2			1		2			1				6		
Rowley	132	15	Poor	David				1		1		1	1				4		
Andover	100	7	Poor	Ebenz	3		1	1		1			1				7		
Rowley	128	19	Poor	Eliphalet				1					1	1			3		
Andover	100	5	Poor	Isaac	3			1		2			1				7		
Danvers	11	2	Poor	James	2				1	2		1	1				7		
Rowley	128	12	Poor	Jeremiah		1		1	1	1	1		1				6		
Haverhill	149	28	Poor	John		1		1		2			1				6		
Marblehead	240	35	Poor	John		1						1					2		
Newbury	119	26	Poor	John		1		1		1	1	1					5		
Andover	100	3	Poor	John Junr		2	2	2			2		2				10		
Newbury	117	45	Poor	Jonathan		1		1	1			1					4		
Danvers	14	34	Poor	Joseph	2			1				1	1				5		
Danvers	14	43	Poor	Joseph	2	2	2	1		1	1	2		1			12		
Rowley	128	9	Poor	Joseph	1			1		1		1	1	1			6		
Andover	100	9	Poor	Lemuel	1	1		1		1			1				5		
Newbury	119	28	Poor	Micajah	1	1		1	1		1	1		2			8		
Newbury	119	29	Poor	Moses	1		1	1		4			1				8		
Rowley	128	10	Poor	Moses		1						1					2		
Andover	103	29	Poor	Nancy											2		2		
Newburyport	175	13	Poor	Nathan		2	1	1		1			1				6		
Andover	100	10	Poor	Peter				1					1				2		
Newbury	119	27	Poor	Samuel			1			2			1				4		
Andover	100	8	Poor	Stephen	1	1		1		1		1	1				6		
Newbury	117	40	Poor	Stephen	1	2		1		2	2	2	1				11		
Andover	100	11	Poor	Susanna									1				1		
Andover	100	6	Poor	Theodore	1			1		3		1					6		
Methuen	155	10	Poor	Thomas		1	2	1			1		2				7		
Haverhill	149	15	Poor	Timothy				1		1			1				3		
Newburyport	175	14	Poor	William			1	1	1	1			3				7		
Marblehead	244	17	Poorhouse	Keeper of	2				12	1		1	1	37			54		
Salem	198	12	Pope	Eleazer	2		1	1		2	1		1				8		
Danvers	7	16	Pope	Elijah	1			1	1	3			2	1			9		
Salem	198	14	Pope	Enos	1			1	1			1	1				5		
Salem	198	10	Pope	Gertrude						1			1				2		
Salem	208	13	Pope	James		1	1	1		1	1		1				6		
Marblehead	256	34	Pope	Joseph				1				1					2		
Marblehead	260	6	Pope	Joseph		1					1						2		
Salem	188	32	Pope	Folger	2	3	3	1			1		1				11		
Salem	183	1	Pope	John	3	1			1	1		1	2	1			10		
Salem	183	20	Pope	Joshua	3	1	3	2		1		1	1	1			13		
Salem	191	23	Popes	Ebenz		3	2	1	1	1	2	1	1	1			13		
Salem	200	50	Porter	Aaron	1	2	1	1		2		1	1				9		
Danvers	8	24	Porter	Abigail				1				1	1				3		
Marblehead	251	15	Porter	Abigail									1				1		
Salem	209	3	Porter	Abigail								1	1				2		
Danvers	8	25	Porter	Abijah			1			1			1				3		
Topsfield	20	8	Porter	Asa				1					1				2		
Danvers	5	20	Porter	Benjamin				1					1				2		
Beverly	293	30	Porter	Billy Esq				1					1				2		
Danvers	9	8	Porter	Daniel				1		3		1	1				6		
Topsfield	18	4	Porter	Daniel	1		2	1	1		1	2		1			9		
Salem	215	4	Porter	Duddy	2		2	1		1			1				7		
Hamilton	285	82	Porter	Dudley	2			1					1				4		
Haverhill	149	32	Porter	Dudley				1			1	1					3		
Beverly	289	19	Porter	Hannah									1				1		
Danvers	4	26	Porter	Hannah									1				1		

TOWN	PG#	LN#	LAST NAME	FIRST NAME	FREE WHITE MALES under 10	10 to 16	16 to 26	26 to 45	45 and over	FREE WHITE FEMALES under 10	10 to 16	16 to 26	26 to 45	45 and over	TOTAL ALL OTHER	TOTAL SLAVES	TOTALS	DISTRICT/ TOWNSHIP	NOTES
Wenham	309	9	Porter	Hannah								1	1	2			4		
Danvers	4	35	Porter	Hitte	1					1		1					3		
Wenham	307	3	Porter	Isaac	1			1	1	1			1	2			7		
Danvers	8	23	Porter	Israel		1		1				1	1				4		
Danvers	8	22	Porter	Israel Junr			1	1		3			1				6		
Danvers	9	5	Porter	James				1					1				2		
Beverly	290	8	Porter	John			1	1				1	1				4		
Wenham	307	17	Porter	John 2nd	1			1		1	1		1				5		
Danvers	8	21	Porter	Jonathan 3rd	1		1					1	1				4		
Danvers	8	10	Porter	Jonathan Junr	1			1	1	2	1		1	1			8		
Danvers	8	20	Porter	Joseph					1				1	1			3		
Danvers	7	43	Porter	Joseph Junr		1		1				1					3		
Boxford	134	24	Porter	Mary							1	1	1	2			5		
Boxford	134	13	Porter	Moses			1	1	1			1		1			5		
Bradford	122	31	Porter	Moses	1			1		1			1				4		
Beverly	305	1	Porter	Nathan	1	3		1		1			1				7		
Wenham	309	8	Porter	Nathaniel		2		1				1	1				5		
Wenham	307	1	Porter	Paul	1		1			1		2					5		
Beverly	298	32	Porter	Rachel		1	1					1		2			5		
Beverly	299	5	Porter	Robert		2	2	1			1		1				7		
Salem	213	40	Porter	Ruth	2	1				1	2	1	1				8		
Danvers	8	19	Porter	Ruth Widow										2			2		
Hamilton	285	104	Porter	Samuel	1	1	2		1		2		1				8		
Marblehead	252	3	Porter	Thomas	1	2		1		2			1				7		
Lynn	227	31	Porter	Thos	1	1	2						1				6		
Wenham	307	16	Porter	Tyler Esquire				1					2		1		4		
Beverly	298	31	Porter	William	1	2	3	1					1				8		
Danvers	5	19	Porter	Zorubbable	2		4	1		1			1	1			10		
Danvers	12	16	Porters	Mary									1	1			2		
Salem	196	12	Portsmouth												5		5		
Wenham	309	6	Potter	Benja	3		1					1					5		
Ipswich	281	8	Potter	Daniel Jun	1			1	1	1	1	1					6		
Ipswich	279	57	Potter	Ezekiel				1					1				2		
Ipswich	280	1	Potter	Ezekiel Jun		1		1					1				3		
Salem	191	38	Potter	Hannah									1				1		
Ipswich	279	59	Potter	Isaac	3			1		2			1				7		
Newburyport	175	25	Potter	James		2	1				1	1					5		
Ipswich	273	32	Potter	John				1					1	1			3		
Ipswich	281	10	Potter	Jonathan	4			1					1				6		
Hamilton	285	115	Potter	Nathaniel	2			1					1				4		
Ipswich	279	58	Potter	Nathaniel	1		1	1			1						4		
Newburyport	175	15	Potter	Thomas	2	1	1		1	1	1	4		1			12		
Hamilton	285	105	Potter	William	3	3	1			1		1	1	1			10		
Newburyport	175	24	Potter	William	1		1						1				3		
Beverly	296	27	Poulling	Edward			1			1			1				3		
Beverly	306	7	Pouslas	John	1		2	1		3	1	1	1				10		
Beverly	306	8	Pouslas	John Jr	2		1			1			1				5		
Beverly	300	20	Pouslin	Thomas			1						1				2		
Salem	208	44	Powell	Abigail		1						1		1			3		
Marblehead	247	14	Powers	John		1	1	1		2	3		1				9		
Marblehead	248	36	Powers	John	1		1	1					1				4		
Marblehead	264	23	Powers	Sarah			2							1			3		
Marblehead	264	22	Powers	Thomas	1	2		1		3	2		1				10		
Salem	208	29	Poynton	Nelly											1		1		
Rowley	131	16	Prang	Mary	1						1		1				3		
Salem	197	48	Pratt	Caesar											2		2		
Salem	201	20	Pratt	Jas		1		1					1	1			4		
Lynn	223	6	Pratt	John	2	1	1	1		1	1	1	1				9		
Salem	202	23	Pratt	John	1	1	1			1		1					5		
Lynn	229	40	Pratt	Joseph				1		2			1				4		
Lynn	229	41	Pratt	Nathn G	1			1		2			1				5		
Lynn	223	50	Pratt	Richd Jn	2			1		1	2		1				7		
Salem	221	6	Pratt	William	3			1		1	1		1				7		
Marblehead	247	37	Prebble	Nathaniel		1							1				2		
Marblehead	256	32	Prebble	Nathaniel		2	1		1			1		1			6		
Marblehead	251	9	Prebble	Nehemiah	1		1			2			1				5		
Manchester	50	6	Prentice	Jana	1		1			1			1				4		
Marblehead	248	3	Prentiss	Henry	2	1		1		3			1	1			9		
Marblehead	251	29	Prentiss	Joshua	1	2		1		2			1				7		
Marblehead	268	1	Prentiss	Joshua				1						1			2		
Salem	195	40	Prescott	William	1	1		1		1		3	1				8		
Gloucester	81	14	Presse	Willm		1				1		1					3		
Beverly	294	42	Presson	Allice	1						1		2	1			5		
Beverly	294	43	Presson	Benjamin	1			1		2			1				5		
Manchester	54	3	Presson	Isaac	1			1		1			1				4		
Salem	217	47	Presson	Mary		1	1					1	1	1			5		
Salem	220	55	Presson	Sarah	2	1				1	1		1				6		
Gloucester	60	17	Presson	William		1				1		1	1	1			5		
Beverly	294	52	Preston	Elizabeth			1							1			2		
Salem	203	9	Preston	Hannah	2	1	1			1		1	1	1			8		
Danvers	2	5	Preston	John		1	2		1	1	1	2		1			9		
Danvers	3	2	Preston	Levi	3	1	1	1	1	2	1	1	1				12		
Danvers	5	27	Preston	Moses	1	1				1		1	1				5		
Beverly	294	53	Preston	Richard			1					1					2		

TOWN	PG#	LN#	LAST NAME	FIRST NAME	FREE WHITE MALES					FREE WHITE FEMALES					TOTAL ALL OTHER	TOTAL SLAVES	TOTALS	DISTRICT/ TOWNSHIP	NOTES
					under 10	10 to 16	16 to 26	26 to 45	45 and over	under 10	10 to 16	16 to 26	26 to 45	45 and over					
Beverly	294	44	Preston	Thankfull										1			1		
Beverly	295	21	Preston	Thomas	1			1		1		1					4		
Newbury	112	29	Price	Elizabeth		2							1				3		
Beverly	294	23	Price	Joanna									1				1		
Beverly	294	45	Price	John				1					1				2		
Salem	218	15	Price	Thos		1		1			1		1				4		
Salem	219	54	Price	Thos	1	1		1			1	2					6		
Salem	204	19	Price	William	1		1					1					3		
Beverly	297	7	Pride	Peter	1			1		1	1	2		1			7		
Gloucester	73	14	Priestly	James	2					1			1	1			6		
Beverly	297	37	Prince	Abigail									1				1		
Marblehead	264	25	Prince	Anna							1		1				2		
Beverly	297	34	Prince	Brackbry	2	2		1		1	1		1				8		
Danvers	7	32	Prince	Caleb		1	1	1					1				4		
Marblehead	241	16	Prince	Cato											5		5		
Newburyport	175	2	Prince	Ezekiel	2	1	2	1		3	1		2				12		
Salem	217	18	Prince	Henry	2	1		1		1	1	1	1				8		
Danvers	6	1	Prince	James	4			1			1		1				7		
Newburyport	175	1	Prince	James	1		3		1	1	2	2	2	1			13		
Beverly	290	33	Prince	John	2			1		1	1		1				6		
Marblehead	264	24	Prince	John	1			1		2			1				5		
Newburyport	175	3	Prince	John	2			1		1			1				5		
Salem	194	42	Prince	John	1	2	1		1		1	1	1				8		
Danvers	7	31	Prince	Joseph		1		1				1		2			5		
Beverly	292	11	Prince	Mary			1						1				2		
Marblehead	248	11	Prince	Richard	2	1		1		2	2	1	1				10		
Salem	208	54	Prince	Richard	1			1		1			1				4		
Manchester	54	6	Prince	Samll	1		1				1						3		
Gloucester	65	22	Prindle	Eldad					1				2				3		
Gloucester	65	25	Prindle	Eliakim	3	1		1		1	1	1	1				9		
Newbury	111	25	Printice	Stanton	2	2			1		1			1			7		
Marblehead	240	8	Pritchard	Benjamin				1			1						2		
Marblehead	244	9	Pritchard	Elizabeth	2	1	2							1			6		
Newburyport	174	40	Pritchard	Hugh		2	1		1		1			1			6		
Marblehead	244	8	Pritchard	John	3	1		1		1			1				7		
Danvers	13	11	Procter	Daniel Junr			1						1				2		
Gloucester	60	29	Procter	Danl & Epes	1	1		1		3	1		2				9		
Danvers	10	16	Procter	David	2	1		1		2	1		1				8		
Danvers	15	9	Procter	Esther	1				1		1			2			5		
Danvers	7	7	Procter	Frances	2			1					1	1			5		
Manchester	54	7	Procter	Francis	1	3	1		1	4			1	1			12		
Gloucester	60	18	Procter	Isaac		2			2			1		1			6		
Danvers	7	8	Procter	Johnson	2		1	1		2		1	1				8		
Danvers	7	11	Procter	Jonathan	1	1	1		1			1	1	2			8		
Danvers	10	18	Procter	Jonathan Junr			1			1			1				3		
Gloucester	60	20	Procter	Joseph		1	2	1				2		1			7		
Danvers	7	6	Procter	Keziah		1						1		1			3		
Danvers	13	16	Procter	Mehitable							2		1				3		
Danvers	10	17	Procter	Sarah									1				1		
Danvers	10	15	Procter	Stephen		1		1		1	1	1					5		
Danvers	13	15	Procter	Sylvester		1	1						1				3		
Gloucester	57	12	Procter	Willm	1	1	1	1						2			6		
Marblehead	253	25	Procter	*us			1				1		1				3		
Salem	216	55	Procter	Daniel			1				1	1					3		
Salem	198	39	Procter	Ebenz		2		1			1			1			5		
Lynn	231	32	Procter	Isaac	2			1					1				4		
Marblehead	269	16	Procter	John	3		1				1						5		
Marblehead	242	14	Procter	Jonathan	1				1				1				3		
Lynn	231	30	Procter	Joseph					1								1		
Marblehead	253	18	Procter	Joseph	1	1	1		1	1	1	1					7		
Marblehead	249	36	Procter	Mary									1				1		
Salem	183	23	Procter	Robert		1	2		1	1		1	1				7		
Ipswich	282	4	Procter	Samuel				1	1	3		1	1	1	1		9		
Marblehead	270	27	Procter	Thomas				1		4		1	1				7		
Marblehead	255	7	Procter	William	2			1					1	1			5		
Salem	183	12	Procter	William	1	2	1	1		2		1	1				9		
Lynn	231	25	Procter	Willm			1				1		1				4		
Lynn	231	26	Procter	Willm Jr	2			1					1				4		
Amesbury	44	2	Propey	Chalare		2				1			1				5		
Amesbury	43	23	Propey	Hezekiah	1	1		1					1				4		
Amesbury	43	21	Propey	John	3	1		1		1	1		1				8		
Amesbury	43	20	Propey	Jona				1					1				2		
Amesbury	43	22	Propey	Joseph			1					1	1				3		
Newburyport	175	23	Prout	William M		1	1				1	2			1		6		
Amesbury	44	1	Prouter	Nathl		2	1						1				4		
Gloucester	57	10	Pulcifer	Daniel	2			1		1			2				6		
Gloucester	58	4	Pulcifer	Edmand	1			1		1		1		1			5		
Gloucester	57	9	Pulcifer	Jabez		1		1					1				3		
Gloucester	57	8	Pulcifer	Jacob		1						1					2		
Gloucester	57	7	Pulcifer	Nathl		2	1		1	1			1				6		
Gloucester	58	14	Pulcifer	Nathll Junr			1					1					2		
Gloucester	57	11	Pulcifer	Taba Wd			1				1	1		1			4		
Gloucester	71	14	Pulcifer	William	1	1		1	0				1				4		
Salem	207	5	Pulling	Mary						1		1	1				3		
Newburyport	174	44	Pulsifer	Ebenezer			1						1				2		

TOWN	PG#	LN#	HEADS OF HOUSEHOLD LAST NAME	FIRST NAME	FREE WHITE MALES under 10	10 to 16	16 to 26	26 to 45	45 and over	FREE WHITE FEMALES under 10	10 to 16	16 to 26	26 to 45	45 and over	TOTAL ALL OTHER	TOTAL SLAVES	TOTALS	DISTRICT/ TOWNSHIP	NOTES
Salem	209	52	Pulsifer	Fras	1	1	3	1		3	1		1				11		
Ipswich	277	52	Pulsipher	Anna			1				1	1					3		
Ipswich	277	53	Pulsipher	Bickford	1		1					1					3		
Ipswich	275	34	Pulsipher	David	2		1			2			1				6		
Ipswich	277	45	Pulsipher	Lucey									1				1		
Salem	194	13	Punchard	Benja	1			1			1		1				4		
Salem	195	13	Punchard	James		1	1				1	1	1				5		
Salem	209	56	Punchard	Samuel	2		1			2	1	2	1				9		
Salem	194	28	Punchard	William	2		1			1	2		1				7		
Salem	211	36	Purbeck	Aaron	1		1			1			1				4		
Danvers	11	31	Purington	Abijah			1			1	1		1				4		
Danvers	11	29	Purington	Amos		1		1		1			1	1			5		
Danvers	11	30	Purington	Samuel		1		1					1	1			4		
Salem	197	28	Purinton	Daniel				1					1				2		
Lynn	223	16	Purinton	Jedh	1	1	2		1	2	1		1				9		
Salem	183	18	Purinton	Mathew	1			1					1	1			4		
Salisbury	32	26	Purrington	Wd			1							2			3		
Newburyport	175	21	Putman	Billings	2		2		1	2	1						8		
Marblehead	242	8	Putman	Jacob	2	1	1	1		2	1	1	1				10		
Middleton	16	23	Putman	Joseph	1	1		1					1				4		
Haverhill	149	24	Putman	Oliver	2	1			1	2	1	1	1				9		
Danvers	5	17	Putnam	Aaron		1	1		1	1	1	1		2			8		
Danvers	5	4	Putnam	Amos		1		1	2			2		3			9		
Danvers	6	9	Putnam	Asa	1			1		1			1	1			5		
Salem	209	49	Putnam	Barthl		1		1			1		1				4		
Danvers	7	44	Putnam	Benja		1		1		2	2		1				7		
Danvers	2	6	Putnam	Daniel	1	1	1			1			1	1			6		
Danvers	4	22	Putnam	Daniel Junr	1			2				2					5		
Danvers	8	5	Putnam	David	1	2		1	2	1		1		2			10		
Danvers	7	39	Putnam	Eben	1			1		2			1				5		
Salem	207	40	Putnam	Ebenz	2		1		1	1	1	1					7		
Danvers	5	3	Putnam	Edmund Junr	2			1		1		2					6		
Danvers	3	4	Putnam	Eleazer	2	1	1	1			2		1				8		
Danvers	6	14	Putnam	Elisha				1			3		2				6		
Danvers	5	25	Putnam	Ezra				2			1						3		
Salem	193	36	Putnam	Fred	2		1					1					4		
Danvers	4	29	Putnam	Gideon	1		1		1	1			1				5		
Danvers	7	37	Putnam	Hannah									1				1		
Danvers	4	27	Putnam	Henry				1					1				2		
Salem	201	2	Putnam	Isaac		1					1						2		
Danvers	4	21	Putnam	Israel				1				1	2				4		
Danvers	2	22	Putnam	Israel Jur	2			1	1			1					5		
Danvers	5	21	Putnam	Israel3rd		2		1	1	1			2	1			8		
Danvers	2	16	Putnam	James		1			1	1	1		1				5		
Lynnfield	236	5	Putnam	James		1					1						2		
Danvers	9	7	Putnam	Jeremiah			1			1	1	1					4		
Danvers	4	24	Putnam	Jethro	2		1	1		2		1					7		
Danvers	4	23	Putnam	Joseph	1		1		1	1		1					5		
Danvers	2	30	Putnam	Joseph 3rd		1		1		1			1				4		
Danvers	7	41	Putnam	Mary	1						1	1	2				5		
Danvers	9	15	Putnam	Nathaniel		1	1		1	4	1	1	1				10		
Danvers	9	2	Putnam	Nathaniel Jr		1		1		1	1	1					5		
Danvers	7	33	Putnam	Peter			1		1	2			1				5		
Danvers	2	29	Putnam	Phinehas					1				1		1		3		
Danvers	7	40	Putnam	Porter			1	1		1			1				4		
Danvers	9	20	Putnam	Rachel							1		1				2		
Danvers	7	42	Putnam	Rebecca									1				1		
Beverly	305	15	Putnam	Rufus	3			1					1				5		
Danvers	7	34	Putnam	Ruth									1	1			2		
Lynnfield	237	5	Putnam	Saml			3	1		2			1				7		
Salem	193	39	Putnam	Samuel	1			1		1	1	1			1		7		
Danvers	8	1	Putnam	Sarah			1						1	1			3		
Danvers	8	4	Putnam	Stephen		3	3	1	1	1	1	1		2			13		
Marblehead	248	14	Putnam	Stephen			1				1	1					3		
Danvers	8	39	Putnam	Thomas	5			1				1	2				10		
Danvers	4	25	Putnam	Timothy	2	1	3	1				1					9		
Danvers	7	38	Putnam	William	1		1		1	1		1	2				7		
Danvers	4	1	Putney	Stephen	4			1					1				6		
Hamilton	285	107	Quales	Francis					1		1	1	1				4		
Hamilton	285	97	Quales	Hipsabah								2					2		
Gloucester	66	1	Qualls	William	1			1		2			1				5		
Salem	215	24	Quarles	William	1		1	1	1	2	2		1				9		
Marblehead	246	27	Quill	Robert		2			1				1				4		
Newbury	109	5	Quimby	Henry		1		1		1							3		
Newburyport	176	2	Quimby	Henry	1		1	1		2			1				6		
Newbury	108	42	Quimby	Moses	1			1		2			1				5		
Newbury	108	10	Quimby	Phillip		1	1			1			1				4		
Ipswich	282	3	Quincy	Samuel	3	2		1		2	1	1	1				11		
Marblehead	240	27	Quinen	Henry		1				2	1						4		
Beverly	299	39	Quiner	Abraham Jr	2		1			2			1				6		
Beverly	303	15	Quiner	Abrahm				1				2		1			4		
Lynn	229	42	Quiner	John			1	1									2		
Beverly	300	41	Quiner	Mary	1							1					2		

254

TOWN	PG#	LN#	LAST NAME	FIRST NAME	FREE WHITE MALES under 10	10 to 16	16 to 26	26 to 45	45 and over	FREE WHITE FEMALES under 10	10 to 16	16 to 26	26 to 45	45 and over	TOTAL ALL OTHER	TOTAL SLAVES	TOTALS	DISTRICT/ TOWNSHIP	NOTES
Marblehead	269	8	Quiner	Nicholas		2			1	2	1		1				7		
Marblehead	260	28	Quinner	Peter					1				1	1			3		
Wenham	308	10	Quoles	Jerusha			1			1			1				3		
Newburyport	176	3	Raboteau	Charles C				1		2	1		2				6		
Newburyport	176	6	Racklyeth	Benjamin	1	1	2	1		1	1			2			9		
Ipswich	278	56	Radford	Benjamin	1			1					1				4		
Beverly	300	34	Rae	Ebenz	2		1	1		1	2		1				8		
Beverly	300	43	Rae	Gideon	2	1		1		1		1	1				7		
Beverly	300	44	Rae	Isaac			1						1				2		
Beverly	296	40	Rae	John	2			1				3		1			7		
Beverly	300	33	Rae	Mehitable									1				1		
Lynn	228	28	Ramsdel	Abijah Jn	2	1	1	1		2			1				8		
Lynn	227	1	Ramsdel	Eliza	1	1		1					1				4		
Lynn	232	10	Ramsdel	Giddeon			1			1	1		1	1			5		
Lynn	228	44	Ramsdel	Joseph	1	1	1	1		2			1				7		
Lynn	230	5	Ramsdel	Nathl			1	1		3		1	1	3			10		
Lynn	230	25	Ramsdel	Nehh			1						1				2		
Lynnfield	237	18	Ramsdel	Timy				1					1				2		
Lynn	228	27	Ramsdel	Willm	1	1		1		4			1				8		
Lynn	225	43	Ramsdel	Eliza									1				1		
Lynn	224	27	Ramsdell	Kimbal	1			1					1				3		
Marblehead	258	33	Ramsdell	Phillip	3		1	1		2			1				7		
Salem	215	46	Ramsdell	William	2			1		1		1	1				6		
Salem	208	45	Ramsden	Anthony	2			1		2			1				6		
Marblehead	264	26	Ramsdile	James	3	1		1		2	1		2				10		
Amesbury	44	17	Ramsey	Charles	1			1					1				3		
Newbury	113	29	Ramsey	William	1			1		4			2				8		
Andover	101	11	Rand	Ebenz				1						1	1		3		
Newburyport	176	7	Rand	Edward		2	1	1		1	1	1	1				8		
Lynn	230	26	Rand	Ezekiel			1					1					2		
Lynn	230	27	Rand	Ezra			1					1					2		
Salem	203	21	Rand	Mary			1			1			1	1			4		
Gloucester	66	5	Rand	Thomas	1		1	1				3	1				7		
Amesbury	44	13	Randall	Isaac Capt				1					1				2		
Lynn	228	18	Randel	Abijah		2		1				1		2			6		
Salem	219	20	Ransom	Cato											6		6		
Newburyport	176	32	Rappal	George	1		1	1				2	1				6		
Salem	218	46	Ravel	Thos	3	2	2	1			2		1				11		
Salem	200	42	Rawson	John				1					1				2		
Beverly	296	23	Raymond	Benjamin		1	1	1					1				4		
Beverly	306	6	Raymond	David			1		1	2			1				5		
Beverly	306	5	Raymond	George				1	1								2		
Beverly	306	2	Raymond	Hannah									1	1			2		
Beverly	306	1	Raymond	John			1			3		1	1				6		
Beverly	306	4	Raymond	Joseph					1		1		1	1			4		
Beverly	290	23	Raymond	Mary						2			1				3		
Beverly	304	43	Raymond	Nathan				1		1	2		1				5		
Beverly	296	3	Raymond	Thomas		1	1					2					4		
Beverly	296	33	Raymond	William	3	4	1	1		1		1	1				12		
Newburyport	176	18	Raynes	John	1			1					1				3		
Danvers	5	26	Rea	Archelaus			1	1					1				3		
Andover	101	9	Rea	Daniel		1						1					2		
Marblehead	241	32	Rea	Henry	2		1			1			2				6		
Topsfield	18	18	Rea	Israel	1		1	1		2	1		2	1			9		
Topsfield	18	19	Rea	John	1			1		1		2	1				6		
Middleton	17	15	Rea	Jonathan Frye		1					1						2		
Boxford	136	1	Rea	Joshua		1	1	1		1	1	1	2				8		
Danvers	10	9	Rea	Mary									1				1		
Salem	206	46	Rea	Mary		2				1	3		1				7		
Salem	216	33	Read	Martha	1	1		2		1	2		1				8		
Salem	205	53	Rebour	Peter L	1		1	1				1	1	1			6		
Lynn	233	46	Redding	Benj		1	3	1						1			6	West Parish	
Lynn	233	48	Redding	John	1		2	1		1			1				6	West Parish	
Lynn	232	21	Redding	Thos	1		1	1		1			1				5	West Parish	
Salem	201	46	Reddington	James												5	5		
Salem	208	36	Redfield	James				1		1		1	1				4		
Gloucester	66	9	Reding	William	1			1	1	2	1		1				7		
Wenham	309	15	Redington	Adams	2			1		1			1				5		
Marblehead	242	7	Redrick	James												5	5		
Marblehead	242	6	Redrick	Thomas		1	1	1	1				1				5		
Marblehead	240	15	Reed	Annie									1				1		
Danvers	13	23	Reed	Benjamin	1		1						1				3		
Danvers	12	44	Reed	Daniel			1				1			1			3		
Danvers	12	43	Reed	Daniel Junr			1			1			1				3		
Danvers	14	44	Reed	Desiah		1								1			2		
Marblehead	240	10	Reed	Elizabeth										1			1		
Lynnfield	235	27	Reed	Isaac	1		1					1	1				4		
Salem	199	24	Reed	Jacob				1				1					2		
Marblehead	240	2	Reed	John	4		1			1	1		1				8		
Newburyport	176	4	Reed	Joseph	1		1			1			3	1			7		
Marblehead	247	10	Reed	Mary		3					1	1	1	1			8		
Marblehead	258	28	Reed	Nancy	1								1				2		
Danvers	9	38	Reed	Nathan		2	1			2		1	1				7		
Newbury	110	15	Reed	Phillip	2		1			2		1					6		
Lynn	223	37	Reed	Thomas			1			1			1				3		
Lynn	223	40	Reed	Thomas			1			1			1				3		
Salem	191	12	Reed	Thos	1		1			1		1					4		

TOWN	PG#	LN#	LAST NAME	FIRST NAME	FREE WHITE MALES					FREE WHITE FEMALES					TOTAL ALL OTHER	TOTAL SLAVES	TOTALS	DISTRICT/ TOWNSHIP	NOTES
					under 10	10 to 16	16 to 26	26 to 45	45 and over	under 10	10 to 16	16 to 26	26 to 45	45 and over					
Salem	192	13	Reed	Thos	4		5	3			2			1			15		
Danvers	13	22	Reed	William	2				1	1	1		2				7		
Newbury	114	18	Reed	William	3			1		1		1					6		
Salem	196	45	Reeves	Asa	1			1		1			1				4		
Salem	198	3	Reeves	John	1		1					1					3		
Salem	214	52	Reeves	Nath			1			1		1					3		
Danvers	10	29	Reeves	Samuel				1					1				2		
Newburyport	176	19	Remick	William			1			1		1		1			4		
Newbury	111	16	Remmix	Samuel		1	1	1		4	1		1				9		
Beverly	300	4	Remmond	Robert	2	1		1		1			1				6		
Salem	192	4	Repes	Nathl	1			1		2	1	1	1	1			8		
Marblehead	250	23	Rexford	Jordan	1			1		1			1				4		
Marblehead	253	15	Reynolds	Andrew	1			1		2	1		1				6		
Marblehead	261	23	Reynolds	Nathaniel		3		1		1	1			1			7		
Marblehead	264	27	Reynolds	William H.	2	1	1		1	1	2		1				9		
Lynn	229	27	Rhodes	Amos	2			1	1	2	1		2				9		
Lynn	229	4	Rhodes	Ezra			1				5		1				4		
Lynn	229	13	Rhodes	Jesse	1		1	1		1	3		1				8		
Lynn	225	17	Rhodes	John			1		1	1	1	1					6		
Lynn	228	20	Rhodes	Jona	1		1		1	1		1					5		
Lynn	229	29	Rhodes	Jona Jr	1		1						1				3		
Lynn	232	5	Rhodes	Joseph	1		1						1				3		
Lynn	230	41	Rhodes	Josiah			1		1	2			1				5		
Lynn	225	38	Rhodes	Thos		2	2		1	1		1		1			8		
Lynn	223	9	Rich	James	3			1		1	1		1				7		
Lynn	226	28	Rich	Robert			1					1					2		
Lynn	226	27	Rich	Thos			1	1		2			1				5		
Rowley	129	17	Richard	John		1			1	1		1					4		
Rowley	129	25	Richard	Joshua				1	1	1	2	2		1			7		
Rowley	129	16	Richard	David	1	2		1	1	3			2				10		
Salem	202	42	Richards	Benja	1	1	1	1					1	2			7		
Lynn	223	23	Richards	Crispus			1		1		1		1				4		
Newburyport	176	22	Richards	Daniel		1	1		1		1		1				5		
Salem	204	8	Richards	David	2	3			1		1			1			8		
Lynn	231	20	Richards	Henry	2	1		1		2	1		1	1			9		
Newburyport	176	23	Richards	James	1			1					1				3		
Manchester	49	19	Richards	John			1			2		1					4		
Salem	208	61	Richards	Jona	1	1		1		1	1		1				6		
Lynn	231	21	Richards	Joseph	2	1		1		1	1	1					8		
Salem	188	9	Richards	Joseph		1	1			2	1	1					6		
Rowley	129	10	Richards	Moses		2		1					1				4		
Salem	195	42	Richards	Richard			1						1				2		
Salem	197	36	Richards	Richard				1				1		1			3		
Lynn	231	19	Richards	Richd			2	1				1	1				5		
Lynn	223	28	Richards	William			1			2		1					4		
Andover	101	10	Richardson	Abigail	1								1				2		
Salem	196	19	Richardson	Addison		1	3	1				1	1				7		
Salem	196	29	Richardson	Addison Senr			1	1	1	1			1				5		
Andover	103	23	Richardson	Allen											6		6		
Newburyport	176	26	Richardson	Ann Wido		2				2			1				5		
Andover	101	1	Richardson	Caleb	1			1		2		1	1				6		
Bradford	126	11	Richardson	Daniel					1	1	1	1	1				5		
Bradford	126	15	Richardson	Dorithy	1					1			1	2			5		
Lynn	232	2	Richardson	Ebenz	1	2			1	1		1		1			6		
Methuen	155	35	Richardson	Edward	3			1	3	2			2	1			12		
Lynn	228	31	Richardson	Eleazr	1			1		1		1					4		
Lynnfield	236	3	Richardson	Elias			1			1			1				3		
Methuen	155	33	Richardson	Elisha	1	1		1		2	1		1				7		
Salem	211	32	Richardson	Eunice		2	1			1	1	1		1			7		
Methuen	155	32	Richardson	Francis	1	1		1	1			2		1			7		
Danvers	11	18	Richardson	James				1					2				3		
Salem	199	12	Richardson	James		1		1					1				3		
Danvers	5	36	Richardson	Jedediah			1			3			1				5		
Salem	209	48	Richardson	Jesse		1				1		2					4		
Marblehead	248	6	Richardson	John	3	1		1				1	1	1			8		
Methuen	155	30	Richardson	John	3	1				1	2			3			11		
Middleton	15	6	Richardson	John	1			2		1	1		1				6		
Newbury	106	34	Richardson	Joseph	2			1			1	1		1			6		
Salem	215	21	Richardson	Josiah		1	2	1			1	3		1			9		
Middleton	15	5	Richardson	Mary	1	3	1				2		1	1			9		
Beverly	304	11	Richardson	Philip		1			1		1	1	1				5		
Salem	192	12	Richardson	Phin			1										1		
Salem	219	51	Richardson	Robt		1	4		1	1		3		1			11		
Danvers	10	39	Richardson	Samuel			1	1		1		1					4		
Methuen	155	34	Richardson	Samuel	2	1	1		1	1	2	1		1			10		
Newburyport	176	24	Richardson	Samuel			1	3		1		1	1		2		9		
Danvers	9	41	Richardson	Seth	1	1		1		1	1		1				6		
Gloucester	81	26	Richardson	Simeon		1		1		1		1					4		
Middleton	15	3	Richardson	Stephen	2	2	1		1			1		2			9		
Methuen	155	31	Richardson	Thomas			3	1		2		1		1			8		
Newburyport	176	25	Richardson	Thomas	1			1		3			1				6		
Andover	101	5	Richardson	William	2	1		1		2			1				8		
Salem	212	3	Richardson	William	2	1		1		4	1	1	1				11		
Salem	215	28	Richrdson	Josiah Jr	1		1	1		1		1	1				6		
Marblehead	240	28	Riddan	John			1	1					1				3		

TOWN	PG#	LN#	LAST NAME	FIRST NAME	M under 10	M 10-16	M 16-26	M 26-45	M 45+	F under 10	F 10-16	F 16-26	F 26-45	F 45+	TOTAL ALL OTHER	TOTAL SLAVES	TOTALS	DISTRICT/ TOWNSHIP	NOTES
Marblehead	244	3	Riddan	Rachel			1							1			2		
Ipswich	274	32	Ridge	John		2		1		3				1			7		
Newbury	110	12	Ridgeway	Joseph	4		3	1					1	1			10		
Salem	202	35	Riding	Jacob		1		1				1	1				4		
Salem	191	15	Ridor	Joseph				1				1	2	1			5		
Gloucester	57	19	Riggs	Aaron	2		1						1				4		
Gloucester	70	16	Riggs	Aaron	1	2	2		1	1	2			1			10		
Gloucester	66	10	Riggs	Asa				1					1				2		
Gloucester	70	21	Riggs	Mary Wo									1				1		
Gloucester	70	20	Riggs	Pela Widow										2			2		
Gloucester	70	23	Riggs	Saml Capt	1	1		1					1				4		
Gloucester	73	16	Riggs	Sarah									1	2			3	Town Parish	
Gloucester	71	17	Riggs	Sarah Widw									1	2			3		
Salem	192	1	Rileman	Benjamn		1	1		1			2	1	2			8		
Ipswich	274	35	Rindge	Mary										1			1		
Salisbury	33	7	Ring	Abner		1			1			1		1			4		
Salisbury	33	6	Ring	Daniel					1			1		1			3		
Amesbury	44	15	Ring	David					1				1	1			3		
Salisbury	33	8	Ring	Nathl	1	1		1	1	1		1	1	1			8		
Salisbury	33	1	Ring	Page		2		1				2	1	1			7		
Salisbury	33	2	Ring	Reuben F.	2			1		1			1				5		
Salem	216	29	Ring	Seth				1		3		1					5		
Ipswich	274	22	Ripley	Kimball				1		3				1			5		
Lynnfield	236	1	Riplon	John	1			1			1	1	1	1			6		
Marblehead	247	30	Roads	Henry				1			1			1			3		
Marblehead	264	28	Roads	Henry				1						1			2		
Marblehead	241	6	Roads	Samuel	3			1					1				5		
Danvers	9	31	Robbins	Jonathan	1		1	1		1			1	1			6		
Gloucester	58	1	Robbins	Nathl		1	3	1	1	1	1			2			10		
Beverly	295	25	Roberts	Andrew	1		1	1		3	3	1					10		
Hamilton	285	92	Roberts	David				1		1			1				3		
Ipswich	276	37	Roberts	Easter										2			2		
Gloucester	57	38	Roberts	Eliphalet	1	1	1		1					1			5	West Parish	
Gloucester	57	15	Roberts	Ephm	1			1					1				3		
Gloucester	58	3	Roberts	Estr Wo							1	1		1			3		
Hamilton	284	4	Roberts	Francis		1			4	3	1			1			10		
Gloucester	57	14	Roberts	Jacob	1			1					1				3		
Gloucester	58	2	Roberts	Jeru Wo								1		2			3		
Gloucester	57	17	Roberts	John	3	2	1		1				1				8		
Hamilton	287	8	Roberts	Joseph		2	1	1					2	1			7		
Gloucester	57	16	Roberts	Levi	1	1	1		1	1			1				6		
Manchester	51	15	Roberts	Marcy Wo		1						1	2	1			5		
Gloucester	58	9	Roberts	Mary Wo							1	1	1				3		
Beverly	291	33	Roberts	Nathaniel	1			1				1	1				4		
Hamilton	285	93	Roberts	Samuel		1		1		1			1				4		
Gloucester	81	17	Roberts	Thomas			1	1				1		1			4		
Gloucester	81	16	Roberts	Thos Junr	4	1		1		2	2		1				11		
Ipswich	277	25	Roberts	William	1		1						2	1			5		
Beverly	291	32	Roberts	Mary						1	1			1			3		
Beverly	290	30	Robertson	John			1					1		1			3		
Haverhill	149	40	Robertson	Joseph				1				1	1		1		4		
Beverly	301	19	Robertson	Rawling		1		1		1			1				4		
Salem	192	3	Robey	Thos				1			1			1	1		4		
Gloucester	81	27	Robins	Nathll	2		1						1				4		
Boxford	134	3	Robinson	Aaron	1			1		1			1	1			5		
Gloucester	68	10	Robinson	Abigal Wo										1			1		
Gloucester	71	10	Robinson	Abigal Wo			1					2	1				4		
Gloucester	77	10	Robinson	Abraham	1			1					1				3		
Gloucester	66	7	Robinson	Andrew	2	1		1					1				5		
Boxford	134	20	Robinson	Benj	2			1		2			1				6		
Marblehead	251	25	Robinson	Benjamin		1	1	1		3			1				7		
Newburyport	176	21	Robinson	Daniel				1						1			2		
Marblehead	243	11	Robinson	Elizabeth									1				1		
Marblehead	258	9	Robinson	Elizabeth									1				1		
Newbury	113	9	Robinson	Isaac	3			1					1				5		
Lynn	229	23	Robinson	James Esq	3	1	1	2		1	1	2					11		
Gloucester	60	39	Robinson	Jno Junr	1	1		1		1			1	1			6		
Andover	100	35	Robinson	John	1	2	1	1	1	1		2	1	1			11		
Boxford	134	2	Robinson	John		1		1				2	2				6		
Marblehead	270	6	Robinson	John											4		4		
Newburyport	176	20	Robinson	John		1		1	1	1			1	1			6		
Salem	214	24	Robinson	John				1					1				2		
Salem	215	38	Robinson	John				1		1			1				3		
Andover	101	12	Robinson	John Junr		1						1					2		
Gloucester	63	4	Robinson	Jona	1			1		1			1	1			5	West Ward	
Gloucester	76	28	Robinson	Jona					1				1				2		
Gloucester	86	11	Robinson	Jona 3d			1	1			1	1	1				5		
Gloucester	76	33	Robinson	Jona Junr	2	2		1		3	1	1	1				11		
Salem	208	37	Robinson	Mary						1			1	1			3		
Salem	207	60	Robinson	Patty	1	2	1			2			1	1			8		
Gloucester	60	33	Robinson	Samuel				1	1	1			1	1			5		
Salem	207	4	Robinson	Samuel			3	1		1	1		1				7		
Gloucester	84	24	Robinson	Stephen	2			1			1		1				5		
Danvers	14	8	Rodes	Edmund			1	1						1			5		

257

TOWN	PG#	LN#	HEADS OF HOUSEHOLD		FREE WHITE MALES					FREE WHITE FEMALES					TOTAL ALL OTHER	TOTAL SLAVES	TOTALS	DISTRICT/ TOWNSHIP	NOTES
			LAST NAME	FIRST NAME	under 10	10 to 16	16 to 26	26 to 45	45 and over	under 10	10 to 16	16 to 26	26 to 45	45 and over					
Danvers	14	9	Rodes	Joseph				1		1			1				3		
Danvers	14	12	Rodes	Samuel	1			1	1	4		2	1				10		
Newbury	119	20	Rogers	Aaron	1	1		1		3	2		1				9		
Newburyport	176	16	Rogers	Amos				1			1		1				3		
Newburyport	176	10	Rogers	Benjamin				1					1				2		
Newburyport	176	11	Rogers	Benjamin Jr	2		1			1			1				5		
Gloucester	60	34	Rogers	Charles Capt	1	2		1		3		3					10		
Gloucester	60	35	Rogers	Daniel			3					2			1		6		
Ipswich	275	59	Rogers	Daniel		1	2	1		3	2		1				10		
Amesbury	44	16	Rogers	Enoch		1		1				1	1	1			5		
Newbury	118	25	Rogers	Ester				1						2			3		
Newburyport	176	12	Rogers	George W	1		1	1		2			1				6		
Haverhill	149	45	Rogers	Hannah								1	1	1			3		
Rowley	128	45	Rogers	Jacob		1	1	1		1	1	1	1				7		
Gloucester	66	4	Rogers	John	1	2		1		1	1	1	1				8		
Newbury	106	6	Rogers	John	4	1		1		2		2	1				11		
Gloucester	60	38	Rogers	John Maj	3			1		2	1	1	1				9		
Salem	220	8	Rogers	Joseph	1		1						1				3		
Newbury	115	24	Rogers	Mary	1					1		1		1			4		
Salem	211	28	Rogers	Mary	1	3				1	3	2	2				12		
Newburyport	176	13	Rogers	Mary Wido						4		1	1				6		
Newburyport	176	14	Rogers	Moses Wido of									1				1		
Newburyport	176	15	Rogers	Moses Wido of Jr			2	3			1		1				7		
Rowley	132	2	Rogers	Nathll		1	1						3				5		
Manchester	51	28	Rogers	Nathll				1									1		
Newbury	109	32	Rogers	Peter		2	1	1		2	1		1				8		
Gloucester	60	36	Rogers	Rachel Wd		5		1		1	2	3		1			13		
Newburyport	176	8	Rogers	Robert				1			1		1				3		
Newburyport	176	9	Rogers	Robery Jr	3	1	1	1			2		1				9		
Newbury	110	3	Rogers	Samuel	1		4	1		1			1				8		
Amesbury	44	14	Rogers	Sarah Wid	2								1	1			4		
Gloucester	70	8	Rogers	William	2	1		1		2	1	1	1				9		
Marblehead	253	13	Rogers	William	2	1	1						1				6		
Marblehead	264	29	Rogers	William	2	1	1						1				6		
Newbury	113	14	Roges	Budley	1		1						1		1		4		
Beverly	302	42	Roggers	Benja		1				1		1					3		
Beverly	302	41	Roggers	Ebenezer				1					1				2		
Salem	202	33	Roland	Jacob	1	1		1				1	1				5		
Marblehead	267	16	Roles	Jeremiah		1		1				1	1				4		
Danvers	12	12	Roles	Rebecca			1					1	1				3		
Marblehead	246	33	Rolf	Samuel				1					1				2		
Newburyport	176	29	Rolf	Samuel				1		3			1				5		
Salem	196	27	Rolle	James	1	1	4	1		2		1	1				11		
Bradford	124	16	Rollings	Eliphalet	1		1						1				3		
Bradford	124	24	Rollings	Joseph	1		1	1		1	1	1					6		
Gloucester	81	18	Rollins	John	1	1		1		1		2	1				7		
Haverhill	149	41	Rollins	John	1		2					3					6		
Newbury	119	41	Rollins	Joseph		1	1					1		1			4		
Marblehead	242	21	Rolls	Alden	2		1						1				4		
Lynn	232	35	Root	Eliza		1							1				2	West Parish	
Salem	196	42	Ropes	Benja		1	1						1				3		
Salem	212	8	Ropes	Dan			1						1				2		
Salem	217	42	Ropes	Danl	1	1		1		1			1				5		
Salem	206	28	Ropes	David	3	2	2	1		1		1	1				11		
Salem	206	11	Ropes	John	1	1	1	1		2	1	1	1				9		
Salem	201	15	Ropes	Jonathn		1	1	1			1	2	1				7		
Salem	207	42	Ropes	Joseph		1		1		1			2				5		
Salem	210	55	Ropes	Priscilla									1				1		
Salem	211	47	Ropes	Ruth									1				1		
Salem	220	24	Ropes	Samuel	1	2	1	1		2	1		1				9		
Salem	205	42	Ropes	Susanna								1	1				2		
Salem	195	39	Ropes	Timothy	1		1				1	1					4		
Salem	212	35	Ropes	William	1		2	1		3	1		2				10		
Beverly	294	33	Rose	Benjamin											2		2		
Salem	207	54	Rose	Brackly	1			1		2	1		1				6		
Newburyport	176	28	Rose	Eber	2			1		2			1				6		
Rowley	131	39	Rose	Paul	2			1		1	1		1				6		
Lynn	224	18	Rose	Willm		1	3	1			1		1				7		
Ipswich	276	39	Ross	Daniel				1		2	1	2	1				7		
Salem	209	55	Ross	Hannah		2						1		1			4		
Ipswich	279	62	Ross	Jabez	1	1	1		1	1		1	2				8		
Ipswich	275	49	Ross	Jeremiah	3			1		1			1				6		
Salem	193	9	Ross	Josep	2			1		1		1					5		
Marblehead	257	14	Ross	Rebecca			2					1	1				4		
Ipswich	275	53	Ross	Samuel	1			1		1			1				4		
Ipswich	275	54	Ross	Sarah								1	2	2			5		
Marblehead	260	1	Ross	Sarah								1	1	1			3		
Ipswich	282	58	Ross	Timothy	1			1		2	2		1				7		
Rowley	127	5	Ross	William	2	3		1		2	1		1				10		
Marblehead	245	20	Rotch	George			1					1					2		
Marblehead	252	20	Roundey	Francis	2			1		2		1					4		
Marblehead	252	22	Roundey	John	1		1					1	1				4		
Marblehead	265	5	Roundey	John		1	1			1	1		1				5		
Marblehead	252	17	Roundey	Jonathan Junr		1	1	1		1	1		1				6		
Marblehead	241	12	Roundey	Joseph		1	1			1		1	1				6		
Marblehead	264	31	Roundey	Joseph	5	1		1					1				8		
Marblehead	264	32	Roundey	Samuel	3			1					1				5		

TOWN	PG#	LN#	LAST NAME	FIRST NAME	M under 10	M 10 to 16	M 16 to 26	M 26 to 45	M 45 and over	F under 10	F 10 to 16	F 16 to 26	F 26 to 45	F 45 and over	TOTAL ALL OTHER	TOTAL SLAVES	TOTALS	DISTRICT/ TOWNSHIP	NOTES
Marblehead	267	15	Roundey	Thomas	1	1		1		2			1				6		
Beverly	292	9	Roundy	Benja			1	1					1				3		
Marblehead	254	29	Roundy	Elizabeth									1				1		
Marblehead	252	6	Roundy	Jonathan Junr			1						1				2		
Beverly	304	21	Roundy	Nehemiah	2	1	1		1	1	1		1				8		
Beverly	302	35	Roundy	Nehemiah 2d		2		1					1				4		
Beverly	292	16	Roundy	Robert				1									1		
Beverly	295	35	Roundy	Stephen	2			1					2	2			7		
Marblehead	241	28	Rousland	William	1	1		1		2			1	1			7		
Salem	217	43	Row	Benja				1		3		1					5		
Beverly	298	41	Row	Seth				1		1		1					3		
Gloucester	85	23	Row	James		1		1					1				3		
Gloucester	86	6	Row	Abra 3d	1			1			1		1				4		
Gloucester	66	8	Rowe	Abraham			2		1	1			1	1			6		
Gloucester	68	23	Rowe	Abraham		1		1						2			4		
Gloucester	68	24	Rowe	Abraham Junr	1			1		2			1				5		
Gloucester	81	24	Rowe	Benja		1		1		2	1		1				6		
Gloucester	81	28	Rowe	Daniel	1		1						1				3		
Gloucester	66	2	Rowe	David	1	1	1		1				1				5		
Gloucester	85	21	Rowe	David	1			2		1			1	1			6		
Gloucester	81	21	Rowe	Ebenzr	3	1		1		1			1	1			8		
Gloucester	81	25	Rowe	Isaac		2	1	1		2			1	1			8		
Gloucester	81	19	Rowe	Jabez Deac	1	1		1		1			1	1			6		
Gloucester	81	20	Rowe	Jabez Junr	2			1		2			1				6		
Gloucester	70	5	Rowe	John Esq	1	1		1		1	1	2	1				8		
Gloucester	78	7	Rowe	John Majr		1	1		1				1	1			5		
Gloucester	66	3	Rowe	Joseph	1	1		1					2				5		
Gloucester	86	2	Rowe	Robert				1		2			1				4		
Gloucester	84	13	Rowe	Solomon	2	1	1	1					1	1			7		
Gloucester	81	22	Rowe	Thomas		2			1				1	1			5		
Gloucester	81	23	Rowe	Thos Junr	2			1					1				4		
Gloucester	66	6	Rowe	William	2	1		1		2			1				7		
Gloucester	81	15	Rowe	Willm	3	1	1	1		1	1		1				9		
Salem	196	34	Rowell	Adam	3	1			1	2	1	2	1				11		
Salem	203	30	Rowell	Eliza			2			2	1		1	1			7		
Salisbury	33	3	Rowell	Jacob			2	1	1				1	1			6		
Salisbury	33	5	Rowell	Mark		1	1					1		1			4		
Newburyport	176	17	Rowell	Olive Wido		1				1			2				4		
Salisbury	33	4	Rowell	Philip	1			1		1			1				4		
Salem	218	40	Roxan	Maria									1				1		
Salem	204	36	Ruck	Mary	1								1				2		
Salem	213	9	Rue	Anna		1							1	1			3		
Salem	216	26	Rufus	Geo	3	1		1		2			1	1			9		
Newbury	117	20	Rummer	Simion			1	1	1			3	1	2			9		
Boxford	133	14	Runnels	Enos	2	1	3	1		2	1	1	1	1			13		
Haverhill	149	42	Runnels	Hannah							1		1	1			3		
Boxford	133	13	Runnels	Jonathan			1			1			1				3		
Boxford	133	12	Runnels	Samuel		1	2		1			1	1	1			7		
Haverhill	149	43	Runnels	Thomas	1		1	1		3			1				7		
Methuen	155	26	Runnels	William		1	1		1	1		2		1			7		
Methuen	155	28	Russ	John			1	1				1		1			4		
Methuen	155	27	Russ	William			2		1		1	1		1			6		
Andover	101	6	Russel	Abigail Wid										2			2		
Salem	216	2	Russel	Benja			2			1			1				4		
Beverly	297	14	Russel	Ceaser											6		6		
Salem	213	33	Russel	Edward	2			1		1		1	1				6		
Andover	101	2	Russel	John			1		1	1		2		1			6		
Andover	101	4	Russel	John Junr	1		1						1				3		
Andover	101	8	Russel	Prudence Wid								1	1				2		
Andover	101	7	Russel	Sarah Wid									1				1		
Andover	101	3	Russel	Uriah			1	3		1		1	1				8		
Salem	214	8	Russel	William	1	1	1	1		2		1	1		1		9		
Danvers	6	20	Russell	Benjamin				1					2				3		
Marblehead	258	16	Russell	Benjamin		2		1					1				4		
Danvers	6	21	Russell	Benjamin Junr	1			1		1	1		1				7		
Ipswich	277	20	Russell	Daniel	3			1					1				5		
Middleton	15	14	Russell	David	1			1			1	1		1			5		
Marblehead	244	24	Russell	Elizabeth	1						2		1				4		
Marblehead	247	17	Russell	Elizabeth	1						2			2			5		
Marblehead	264	30	Russell	Elizabeth	1					1		1	1				4		
Danvers	6	23	Russell	Enoch			1						1				2		
Manchester	54	11	Russell	Isaac	1		1			1		1	1	1			6		
Methuen	155	29	Russell	Isaac				1						1			2		
Boxford	135	48	Russell	James	1	2	1	1		2			1				8		
Danvers	6	18	Russell	Jethro			1		1			1		1			4		
Danvers	6	22	Russell	John				1					1				2		
Haverhill	149	44	Russell	John	1			1					1	1			4		
Marblehead	241	31	Russell	John	1			1		1			1	1			5		
Marblehead	247	19	Russell	John			2	1			1	1		1			6		
Marblehead	264	34	Russell	John	3		2	1		1	2	1					10		
Newbury	120	13	Russell	John			1						1	2			4		
Newburyport	176	31	Russell	John			1			1	1	1	1				5		
Salem	191	29	Russell	John	2			1		2			1				6		
Danvers	6	24	Russell	John Junr	2		1						1				4		
Haverhill	149	46	Russell	Joseph	1		1	1				1	1				5		
Marblehead	265	1	Russell	Joseph		2		1					1				4		
Middleton	15	15	Russell	Joseph	2			1					1				4		

TOWN	PG#	LN#	LAST NAME	FIRST NAME	FREE WHITE MALES					FREE WHITE FEMALES					TOTAL ALL OTHER	TOTAL SLAVES	TOTALS	DISTRICT/ TOWNSHIP	NOTES
					under 10	10 to 16	16 to 26	26 to 45	45 and over	under 10	10 to 16	16 to 26	26 to 45	45 and over					
Newbury	116	33	Russell	Joseph				1					2	1			4		
Marblehead	249	32	Russell	Martha										1			1		
Bradford	124	28	Russell	Peter				1		1	2			1			5		
Marblehead	258	12	Russell	Richard	1	1		1		2		1	1				7		
Marblehead	254	20	Russell	Samuel	3			1		2			1				7		
Ipswich	273	35	Russell	Stery		1		1					1	1			4		
Ipswich	273	30	Russell	Story Jun	1	1		1		2	1		1				7		
Marblehead	256	19	Russell	Thomas	2			1		3			1				7		
Manchester	54	10	Russell	William	1	1		1		2			2	1			8		
Marblehead	264	33	Russell	William	2	1		1		2		1		1			8		
Newburyport	176	30	Russell	William		1	1	1	1			1	2		1		8		
Marblehead	248	33	Russell	Wilson H.	2			1					1	1			5		
Gloucester	57	20	Rust	Anna Wd									1	1			2		
Gloucester	57	13	Rust	Benja	2	1	1	1			2		1				8		
Hamilton	285	100	Rust	Daniel	2			1		2			1				6		
Salem	206	29	Rust	Henry				1			1	2		1			5		
Salem	207	47	Rust	Henry	1	1		1		2		2	1				8		
Gloucester	57	18	Rust	Israel	2		1			3		2		1			9		
Salem	203	14	Rust	Jacob	3		1				1	1					6		
Gloucester	60	31	Rust	John				1						2			3		
Salem	207	51	Rust	John		1		1		1		1	2				6		
Gloucester	60	32	Rust	Morey		1	2	1		1			1	1			7		
Ipswich	278	33	Rust	Nathanl	1	1	3	1	1				2		1		10		
Gloucester	71	8	Rust	Nathl				1		2			1				4		
Ipswich	281	60	Rust	Parker				1									1		
Ipswich	282	46	Rust	Robert	1		1			1			1				4		
Salem	208	12	Ruste	Danl				1		2		1	1				5		
Newburyport	176	33	Rutherford	Alexander				1					2				3		
Newburyport	176	34	Rutherford	John	1			1						1			3		
Newburyport	176	35	Rutherford	Joseph	2			1		1		1	1	1			7		
Newburyport	176	27	Rutley	Henry	1			1		1			2	3			8		
Salem	218	39	Rutlidge	Winslow	2			1		1				1			5		
Salem	204	13	Ryan	Anna		1	1	1					1				4		
Newburyport	176	5	Ryan	Augustus	1	1		1		1			1	1			6		
Salem	188	18	Ryan	James	1		1	1						1			4		
Ipswich	273	28	Safford	Ebenezer				1		1	1		1				4		
Beverly	305	30	Safford	John		1	1			1		1	1				6		
Newbury	112	24	Safford	John			1	1					1				3		
Salem	214	9	Safford	Nath	1	2	1	1		1		1					7		
Hamilton	285	21	Safford	Samuel	1	2	1		1				1	1			7		
Ipswich	276	31	Safford	Simeon	2	2			1			2		1			8		
Salem	216	38	Safford	Thos	3	1		1		1			1				7		
Salem	213	32	Safford	William	1		5	1					3	1			11		
Salem	217	53	Sage	Danl	1	1		1		2		1	1				7		
Salem	217	32	Sage	William		1	1										2		
Danvers	13	1	Saivl	Curtis	1			1					1				3		
Marblehead	261	29	Salkins	Thomas	1	1	2			1	1			1			7		
Newburyport	178	16	Salter	Ebenezer	1			1					1				3		
Newburyport	178	15	Salter	Francis			1			2			1				4		
Marblehead	246	17	Salter	Joseph				1						1			2		
Marblehead	246	21	Salter	Joseph	1	2		1		2			1				7		
Marblehead	250	2	Salter	Mary		1	1						1				3		
Danvers	10	6	Saltmarsh	Seth			1					1	1				3		
Haverhill	150	27	Saltonstall	Nathll	1	2	1		1			3	1	1			12		
Newburyport	178	24	Sanborn	Enoch		2	2	1		2				1			8		
Marblehead	265	2	Sanden	William				1				1		1			3		
Salem	190	30	Sander	Abigail							1	1		1			3		
Rowley	129	34	Sanders	David			1			1		1	1				4		
Beverly	300	8	Sanders	John			1			1		1					3		
Bradford	126	7	Sanders	Moses	1	1		1	4				1		1		9		
Haverhill	150	1	Sanders	Samuel				1						1			2		
Haverhill	150	16	Sanders	Subtle	2		1	1		1		2	1	1			9		
Haverhill	150	5	Sanders	Timothy		2		1		1				1			5		
Salem	199	38	Sanderson	David	1		1	1		1			1	1			6		
Salem	194	36	Sanderson	Elijah	1	1	3	1	1	3			1	1			12		
Salem	194	37	Sanderson	Jacob	1	1	4	1		1		1	1	1			11		
Salem	196	6	Sanderson	James	1			1		1		1	1				5		
Wenham	309	39	Sands	Isaac				1					1	1			3		
Hamilton	285	81	Sands	Susanna									1				1		
Ipswich	277	26	Saniford	Ebenezer	1			1		1	1		1				5		
Marblehead	259	5	Sanitt	Samuel	2	1		1		1			1				6		
Andover	101	16	Sargeant	Benja	2	1		1		3			1				8		
Marblehead	248	24	Sargeant	Francis	1		1						1				3		
Amesbury	45	13	Sargent	Amasa	1	3		1				1		1			8		
Amesbury	45	12	Sargent	Amos	4	3	2	1		1			2				13		
Haverhill	150	3	Sargent	Amos				1		2		1	1				5		
Newburyport	178	19	Sargent	Amos	1			1		2			1				5		
Amesbury	45	8	Sargent	Christopher Esqr			1	1				2		1			5		
Amesbury	45	33	Sargent	Christopher Junr	3		1						1				5		
Amesbury	45	1	Sargent	Dorothy Wid									2	1			3		
Newburyport	178	18	Sargent	Ebenezer					1	4		1		2	1		9		
Haverhill	149	48	Sargent	Elias		1		1				1	1				4		
Amesbury	45	11	Sargent	Ezekiel	1	2		1		3			1				8		
Amesbury	45	23	Sargent	Hezekiah		1	1	1		1	1		1				6		
Amesbury	44	26	Sargent	Ichabod	3	1		1		1		1	1				8		
Amesbury	45	18	Sargent	Jacob	1			1		3	1		1				7		

TOWN	PG#	LN#	LAST NAME	FIRST NAME	FREE WHITE MALES under 10	10 to 16	16 to 26	26 to 45	45 and over	FREE WHITE FEMALES under 10	10 to 16	16 to 26	26 to 45	45 and over	TOTAL ALL OTHER	TOTAL SLAVES	TOTALS	DISTRICT/ TOWNSHIP	NOTES
Methuen	156	4	Sargent	Jacob	1			1		1	1		1				5		
Methuen	155	38	Sargent	James				1	1	1			1	1			5		
Methuen	155	45	Sargent	James Jun	1			3	1			1		1			7		
Methuen	155	44	Sargent	John	3	1	1		1	1		3		1			11		
Amesbury	45	24	Sargent	Jona	2			2		1	1		1				7		
Amesbury	45	22	Sargent	Jona Junr	1			2					1				4		
Haverhill	150	18	Sargent	Jonathan				1	2				1	1			5		
Amesbury	45	14	Sargent	Joshua	2	2	2	1		2			1	1			11		
Amesbury	45	20	Sargent	Joshua					1					1			2		
Amesbury	45	19	Sargent	Joshua Junr	2			1			1		1				5		
Amesbury	45	7	Sargent	Josiah					1		1	1	1				4		
Haverhill	150	17	Sargent	Judith Wid							1	2	1				4		
Haverhill	150	26	Sargent	Mary							1	2	1				4		
Amesbury	45	4	Sargent	Moses			2		1	3	1	2		1			10		
Haverhill	150	31	Sargent	Moses	1			1		1			1				4		
Amesbury	45	5	Sargent	Moses Junr	1	1		1		2	2	1	1	1			10		
Methuen	155	46	Sargent	Nathl	3			1					1	1			6		
Amesbury	45	9	Sargent	Nehemiah				1					1				2		
Amesbury	45	10	Sargent	Nehemiah Junr	3			1			1		1	1			7		
Amesbury	45	2	Sargent	Orlando Esqr		1		1					2	2			6		
Amesbury	45	3	Sargent	Orlando Junr	1			1		1			1				4		
Amesbury	45	6	Sargent	Robert Capt	1			1		2			1				5		
Haverhill	150	9	Sargent	Sarah						1				1			2		
Amesbury	45	15	Sargent	Sarah Wid								1	2				3		
Amesbury	45	21	Sargent	Seth	1			1					1				3		
Amesbury	44	27	Sargent	Stephen	2		1	1				1					5		
Amesbury	45	16	Sargent	Thomas	1		2	1		3	1		1				9		
Amesbury	45	1	Sargent	Zebulon	1			1				2	1				5		
Gloucester	81	31	Sargent	Aaron				1				1	1				3		
Gloucester	61	19	Sargent	Abimh	2			1		2		1	1				7		
Gloucester	76	25	Sargent	Andrew	1	1			1					2			5		
Gloucester	76	23	Sargent	Benja	2		1			1		1					5		
Gloucester	67	1	Sargent	David					1					1			2		
Gloucester	75	9	Sargent	David		1		1	1					1			4		
Gloucester	76	19	Sargent	David Junr	2			1		1		1					5		
Gloucester	57	27	Sargent	Dudlay	1			1		1		1					4	West Parish	
Gloucester	76	26	Sargent	Epes	2		1			1		1					5		
Gloucester	66	24	Sargent	Fit* W. Capt	2			1	1	4	1		2	1			12		
Gloucester	74	16	Sargent	Gustaves			1			1		1					6		
Gloucester	66	13	Sargent	Ignatius Majr	2			1		1		3					7		
Gloucester	75	19	Sargent	John Lane	2			1		1			1	1			6		
Gloucester	76	27	Sargent	Jona					1					1			2		
Gloucester	66	21	Sargent	Jonan		2	3		1	1	1			1			9		
Gloucester	74	24	Sargent	Michael	1		1			1		1					4		
Gloucester	61	6	Sargent	Nathll					1		1	2	1				5		
Gloucester	76	31	Sargent	Peter		1	2	1		1				1			6		
Gloucester	76	24	Sargent	Samll	1		1	1		1				1			5		
Gloucester	76	22	Sargent	Solo	2			1						1			4		
Gloucester	76	21	Sargent	Solo Junr	2		1			3			1				7		
Gloucester	57	21	Sargent	Thos Doct	3			1		1				1			4	West Parish	
Gloucester	76	35	Sargent	Winthrop	2		2	1		2	3		1				11		
Rowley	128	51	Sarle	Mehitabel							1	1	1				3		
Danvers	13	19	Sarle	Richard			1					1					2		
Salem	214	31	Saul	Joseph	3	1			1			1	1				7		
Rowley	132	6	Saunders	Benja	2			1		1				2			6		
Rowley	132	17	Saunders	Benjamin	2			1	1	1				1			6		
Gloucester	62	23	Saunders	Bradbury				1				2	1				4		
Salem	199	9	Saunders	Daniel	1		1	1		1		1	1				6		
Salem	206	39	Saunders	Daniel	1	1			1		1			1			5		
Salem	189	10	Saunders	Daniel R	1		1			2			1				5		
Rowley	129	46	Saunders	Edward	2		1	1		1	1		1				7		
Gloucester	78	10	Saunders	George	1		1					1					3		
Danvers	13	6	Saunders	John			1						1				2		
Gloucester	78	9	Saunders	John	1		1	1		4	2		1				10		
Rowley	129	43	Saunders	John		1	3		1			2	1				8		
Gloucester	66	16	Saunders	John Capt			2		1					1			4		
Gloucester	61	8	Saunders	Joseph Capt				1			1	1	1				4		
Gloucester	66	22	Saunders	Joseph Junr	3	2		1		1	1		1				9		
Gloucester	62	13	saunders	Nath	2			1		1			1				5		
Salem	206	47	Savage	Ezekiel	2			1		1	2	1	1				8		
Marblehead	251	8	Savage	John	2		1						1				4		
Marblehead	261	27	Savage	John	1			1				1					3		
Gloucester	75	30	Savell	James				1		1		1					3		
Gloucester	75	29	Savell	Jese			2	1	1	1	1		1				7		
Bradford	125	10	Savory	Benja	3			1	1	1	1		1				8		
Amesbury	45	34	Savory	Daniel	1	1		1		1			1	1			8		
Amesbury	45	36	Savory	Daniel Junr			1						1				2		
Newbury	120	31	Savory	Ebenzr			1	1		3			1	1			7		
Bradford	125	11	Savory	Eliphalet		1		1					1				3		
Bradford	125	9	Savory	John	1	1	1	1		1	1	1	1				8		
Bradford	125	45	Savory	Thomas		1	3					2	1	1			8		
Bradford	125	50	Savory	Thomas	3			2	1	3		1	1	1			12		
Methuen	155	48	Sawyer	Aaron			1	1		3				1			6		
Amesbury	45	30	Sawyer	Aaron Dr			1		1					1			3		

TOWN	PG#	LN#	HEADS OF HOUSEHOLD		FREE WHITE MALES					FREE WHITE FEMALES					TOTAL ALL OTHER	TOTAL SLAVES	TOTALS	DISTRICT/ TOWNSHIP	NOTES
			LAST NAME	FIRST NAME	under 10	10 to 16	16 to 26	26 to 45	45 and over	under 10	10 to 16	16 to 26	26 to 45	45 and over					
Gloucester	60	40	Sawyer	Abraham		1		1				1		1			4		
Gloucester	60	22	Sawyer	Abraham Jun		1		1		1	1		1				5		
Beverly	295	49	Sawyer	Amasa	1	1	2			1			1				6		
Haverhill	150	13	Sawyer	Amos	2	1			1	1		1		1			7		
Gloucester	84	21	Sawyer	Anna Wo		1							1	1			3		
Methuen	155	47	Sawyer	Benjamin	1			1		3			1	1			7		
Newbury	119	47	Sawyer	Bootfield					1			1		1			3		
Methuen	155	42	Sawyer	Caleb			1	1					2				4		
Newbury	110	17	Sawyer	Elijah		1		1					2				4		
Newbury	110	36	Sawyer	Elijah	1		1					1					3		
Newbury	107	28	Sawyer	Enoch		1		1			1	2					5		
Newbury	110	21	Sawyer	Enoch	2	1	1	1		2	1		3				11		
Gloucester	84	18	Sawyer	George			1			1		1					3		
Newbury	111	35	Sawyer	George											2		2		
Salisbury	33	28	Sawyer	George	2		1			1		1					5		
Ipswich	275	16	Sawyer	George W.		1		1					1				3		
Newbury	109	7	Sawyer	Hannah	2					1	1	1					5		
Newbury	110	18	Sawyer	Hannah		1							1	1			3		
Gloucester	61	16	Sawyer	James	2		1	1	1		1	1		1			8		
Gloucester	61	21	Sawyer	James Junr	1	1		1		2	1		1				7		
Newburyport	178	26	Sawyer	Jeremiah		1		1					1				3		
Amesbury	45	29	Sawyer	John	2			2		2	3		1				10		
Salisbury	33	14	Sawyer	John		1	1						1	3			6		
Amesbury	45	26	Sawyer	John Capt		1		1	1	2			1				6		
Newbury	107	45	Sawyer	Joseph	1				1	2	2	1					7		
Newbury	109	36	Sawyer	Joseph			1			1		1	1	1			5		
Haverhill	150	4	Sawyer	Joshua		2		1		1				1			5		
Rowley	128	20	Sawyer	Lydia				2					2				4		
Newbury	108	14	Sawyer	Mary								1	2				3		
Newbury	119	30	Sawyer	Micajah	1	2		1		3			1				8		
Newburyport	178	25	Sawyer	Micajah		1		1		2	1		2		1		8		
Amesbury	45	27	Sawyer	Michl		1	1	1					1				4		
Haverhill	150	23	Sawyer	Ruth									1	1			2		
Ipswich	277	31	Sawyer	Samuel		1	2	1		1		2	1				8		
Amesbury	45	31	Sawyer	Stephen	1			1		3			1				6		
Haverhill	150	33	Sawyer	William	1	1	2		1	1	3	1	1				11		
Amesbury	45	28	Sawyer	Willm	1		1						1				3		
Beverly	290	41	Saxby	James		1	1	1					1	1			5		
Gloucester	66	25	Sayward	Daniel			1			3	1		1				6		
Gloucester	66	15	Sayward	Henry		1							1	1			3		
Gloucester	66	17	Sayward	James Junr	1			1		2	1		1				6		
Gloucester	66	23	Sayward	James S. Capt				1		3				1			5		
Gloucester	67	3	Sayward	John	1			1		2			1	1			6		
Gloucester	69	18	Sayward	Steven	1			1		1		1	1	1			6		
Gloucester	66	28	Sayward	William	1	1		1		1			1				4		
Marblehead	244	25	Scobie	James	2			1		2		2					7		
Haverhill	150	15	Scoffield	James	1	1		1		3	1		1				8		
Marblehead	259	7	Scores	Edward	1			1		3			1				6		
Rowley	131	12	Scot	Moses			1	1					1	1			4		
Ipswich	279	25	Scott	Benjamin	1	1		1		2	2		1				8		
Newburyport	177	21	Scott	Joel	2			1		3			1				7		
Marblehead	243	10	Scott	John				1						1			2		
Marblehead	258	8	Scott	John				1						1			2		
Rowley	131	25	Scott	Samuel	2		1	1		1			1				6		
Salem	208	16	Seagar	Nath	1		1	1		1		1	1				6		
Lynn	230	22	Seargant	Salley	1	1	1						1	1			5		
Lynn	233	2	Seargant	Saml				1		1	1	1		1			6		
Methuen	156	3	Searl	John		1	2	1					3	1			8		
Rowley	132	3	Searle	Jereh			1						1	1			3		
Salem	220	14	Searle	John	1	1		1		1				2			6		
Salem	220	43	Searle	John	1		1						1				3		
Rowley	131	44	Searle	Joseph	2	2	1				1	1	1				8		
Newburyport	177	41	Searle	Mary Wido	1	1				2	3		1				8		
Lynn	231	18	Seegar	Willm	1	1	1			1		1	1	1			8		
Gloucester	86	24	Segurs	John				1						1			2		
Wenham	307	15	Seirley	Eleanor		1				1			1				3		
Gloucester	62	19	Selah	Mathew				1		1			1	1			4		
Danvers	5	13	Seldon	Elizabeth	1					1		1	1				4		
Marblehead	251	30	Selman	Archa	4	1		1			1	1					8		
Beverly	300	18	Selman	Jacob				1		2			1				4		
Marblehead	251	33	Selman	John		3		1		2			1	1			8		
Marblehead	239	21	Selman	Joseph	2			1					1				4		
Marblehead	257	17	Selman	Joseph	2	1	2		1	1	1			1			9		
Marblehead	259	19	Selman	Mary										1			1		
Salem	219	34	Selsbee	Sarah			2	1		1	1		1	1			7		
Beverly	302	4	Sergant	John		1							1				2		
Boxford	133	11	Sessions	Nathll			1						1	1			3		
Ipswich	277	11	Sevard	John		1		1		3			1				6		
Marblehead	260	21	Seveny	Joseph				1		1			1				3		
Marblehead	250	14	Severance	Sarah									1	1			2		
Marblehead	249	21	Severy	Clement	2	1		1		1			1				6		
Marblehead	251	3	Severy	Mary						2			3	1			6		
Marblehead	259	26	Severy	Nicholas					1					2			3		
Newburyport	178	28	Sevier	Joseph		3		1		3	1		1				9		
Marblehead	269	10	Sewall	Samuel	2	2		1		3			1	1			10		
Ipswich	278	60	Seward	Abraham	2					1	1		1				6		

TOWN	PG#	LN#	LAST NAME	FIRST NAME	FREE WHITE MALES					FREE WHITE FEMALES					TOTAL ALL OTHER	TOTAL SLAVES	TOTALS	DISTRICT/ TOWNSHIP	NOTES
					under 10	10 to 16	16 to 26	26 to 45	45 and over	under 10	10 to 16	16 to 26	26 to 45	45 and over					
Beverly	302	8	Seward	Henry	2			1					1				4		
Salem	189	40	Seward	Jack											6		6		
Ipswich	278	6	Seward	John	1				1	2	2			1			7		
Newburyport	177	19	Seward	Samuel Wido of	2		3	4	1	2		1		1			14		
Lynn	226	7	Seylon	James	1			1		2			1				5		
Gloucester	61	22	Shackelford	Willm	1			1		4			1				7		
Newburyport	178	20	Shackford	Levi	2	1		1		1			1	1			7		
Beverly	304	14	Shale	Andrew	1				1	2	1	1	1				7		
Newburyport	177	43	Shanks	Benjamin		1		1					1				3		
Newbury	114	41	Shannon	Robert	1	2			1	1	1			1			7		
Ipswich	275	33	Shatswell	Martha									1				1		
Wenham	308	26	Shatten	John	1			1					1				3		
Andover	102	4	Shattuck	Isaac	2			1	1				1	2			7		
Andover	101	38	Shattuck	Isaac Junr	3	2		1		1	1		1				9		
Andover	102	3	Shattuck	Jebadiah		2			1			2		2			7		
Andover	102	5	Shattuck	Joseph	2			1		1			1				5		
Andover	102	6	Shattuck	Peter	1		1	1		1		1		1			6		
Newburyport	178	40	Shaw	Andrew		1		1		2		1	1				6		
Danvers	14	28	Shaw	Esther									1	1			2		
Salem	207	1	Shaw	John	4			1		2		1					8		
Danvers	14	29	Shaw	Joseph	1	1	1	1		3	1	1		1			10		
Beverly	306	10	Shaw	Peter	1		1	1		3			1				7		
Newburyport	178	39	Shaw	Samuel	1	1			1	2				1			6		
Danvers	14	7	Shaw	William		2			1	2		2		1			8		
Salem	189	22	Shebrock	Abigl										1			1		
Salem	217	21	Shed	Cathr	1					2			1				4		
Salem	195	24	Shed	Henry			1			1	1	1					4		
Salem	219	22	Sheehan	Danl	2			1		2			1				6		
Danvers	3	16	Shelden	Amos		2		1		2	1		1				7		
Danvers	5	16	Shelden	Amos 2nd	2			1	1	2		1	1				8		
Danvers	3	17	Shelden	Elisabeth									2				2		
Salem	208	2	Shelden	Ephm		1			1	1	1	1					5		
Lynnfield	235	30	Shelden	Jerh	1		1	1		2		1	1				7		
Danvers	8	3	Shelden	Jonathan		1		2		3			1	1			8		
Salem	200	25	Sheldon	Ephrm	1		1						1				3		
Marblehead	269	33	Sheldon	Francis			1						1	1			3		
Beverly	306	24	Sheldon	John	5	1	1	1		2	1	1	1				13		
Salem	216	19	Shelty	James			1			1			1				3		
Amesbury	44	25	Shepherd	Samuel				1					1				2		
Salem	210	23	Sheppard	David			1					1					2		
Salem	211	46	Sheppard	Jeremiah	1	2	4		1			2		1			11		
Salem	214	16	Sheppard	Jona			1					1					2		
Lynnfield	235	42	Sherman	Hannah										2			2		
Lynnfield	235	40	Sherman	Nathl		1			1					1			3		
Salem	196	32	Sherry	Francis	1				1	2	1			1			6		
Salem	190	12	Shillaber	Benja	1		1		2	1	1	1	1				8		
Salem	194	39	Shillaber	Ebenz	2	1		1			2		1				7		
Salem	198	41	Shillaber	John	1			1		3	3		1				9		
Danvers	11	38	Shillaber	Robert		1		1	1			1		1			5		
Salem	190	7	Shillaber	Walter			1		1	3				1			6		
Danvers	11	39	Shillaber	William		1		1				1		2			5		
Salem	199	13	Shillaber	William		1		1					1				3		
Salem	213	7	Shipen	Sarah	1	2								2			4		
Salem	214	28	Shippen	Atwater				1					1				2		
Marblehead	253	4	Shirley	William	1	2			1	3	1	1		1			10		
Amesbury	44	23	Shoars	Matthew			1						1				2		
Salem	209	24	Shool	Priscilla		1							1				2		
Lynn	223	57	Shorey	Miles	1			1		1			1				4		
Amesbury	45	32	Short	David	2			1		1			1				5		
Newburyport	178	30	Short	Elizabeth Wido	1					2		1	1				5		
Newbury	116	44	Short	Henry		1	1		1			1		1			5		
Salem	215	36	Short	James				1		1			1				3		
Newburyport	178	31	Short	Joseph	3	1		1		1			1				7		
Newbury	115	23	Short	Moses	2	1	1	1					1				6		
Newbury	116	46	Short	Richard		1	1		1	1	1	1		1			7		
Newburyport	178	29	Short	Sarah Wido	2				1			1		1			5		
Newbury	116	45	Short	Silas		1	1		1	1	1	1	1				8		
Newburyport	178	32	Short	William	1	1			1	2	1		1				7		
Ipswich	273	44	Shotswell	Moses	1			1		2			1				5		
Ipswich	273	43	Shotswell	Nathaniel				1		1		1	1				4		
Ipswich	273	42	Shotswell	Richard				1				1		1			3		
Danvers	12	22	Shove	Squiers	2		4		1	2	1		1				11		
Bradford	124	29	Shuff	John		1		1			1		1				4		
Newburyport	179	2	Sillaway	Daniel	2	1		1		2			1				7		
Newburyport	179	1	Sillaway	John				1		2	1	1	1				6		
Haverhill	149	47	Silleway	Reuben				1					1				2		
Salem	206	15	Silsbee	Enoch				1		1	1	1					4		
Salem	217	54	Silsber	Saml		1		1	1		1	1		1			6		
Salem	217	33	Silsber	Saml Jr	3	2	6	1			2		1				15		
Salem	197	26	Silver	Benjamin		1				1		1	1				4		
Haverhill	150	40	Silver	Daniel	1			1		2			1				5		
Salem	197	44	Silver	James	1			1		1		1	1				5		
Haverhill	150	41	Silver	John	2			1		1			1				5		
Haverhill	150	46	Silver	John Junr	1	1						1					3		
Salem	200	9	Silver	Samuel	1			1		1		1					4		
Salem	207	36	Silver	Sarah			1							1			2		
Haverhill	150	42	Silver	Susanna										2			2		

TOWN	PG#	LN#	LAST NAME	FIRST NAME	FREE WHITE MALES under 10	10 to 16	16 to 26	26 to 45	45 and over	FREE WHITE FEMALES under 10	10 to 16	16 to 26	26 to 45	45 and over	TOTAL ALL OTHER	TOTAL SLAVES	TOTALS	DISTRICT/ TOWNSHIP	NOTES
Salem	197	27	Silver	William				1		3	1		1				6		
Manchester	54	17	Simmons	Andrew	2			1				1					4		
Salem	204	2	Simmons	John											4		4		
Haverhill	150	35	Simmons	Nehemiah		1	1		1	1		1		1			6		
Haverhill	150	36	Simmons	Nehemiah Junr	1		1					1					3		
Manchester	54	18	Simmons	Ruth Wo								1		1			2		
Marblehead	254	30	Simonds	Daniel	2		1					1					4		
Beverly	293	4	Simonds	Thomas			1	1			2		1				5		
Andover	103	24	Simpson	Cesar											2		2		
Newburyport	178	4	Simpson	David	1		1			2			1	1			6		
Haverhill	150	20	Simpson	James	1	2	1			1			1				6		
Manchester	54	16	Sinnett	Willm			1			2			1	1			5		
Salem	200	5	Skerry	Ephrm			1	1	1				1	1			5		
Salem	214	7	Skerry	Henry	2	2	1	1		1	1		1				9		
Salem	200	8	Skerry	John	1		1		1	3			1	1			8		
Salem	210	37	Skerry	Samuel	1		1					1	1				4		
Danvers	8	37	Skidmore	Richard	1		2		1	2	1		1				8		
Danvers	4	33	Skidmore	Richard Jr			1			2			1	1			5		
Danvers	10	2	Skilson	Seth			1					1					2		
Lynn	230	11	Skinner	Abigail			1							1			2		
Marblehead	255	12	Skinner	John	1	1	1			1	1		1				6		
Marblehead	255	18	Skinner	Richard	2		1			1	1		1				6		
Marblehead	248	7	Skinner	William			1					1	1				3		
Lynn	230	14	Skinner	Willm	2		1	1				1	1				6		
Newbury	113	15	Slarter	Thomas				1					1				2		
Gloucester	61	14	Slatery	Henry	2		1					1					4		
Salem	206	19	Slewman	Margt		1	2	1		1			1				6		
Salem	201	48	Slewman	Simon	1	1		1		2			1				6		
Salem	218	47	Slocum	Ebenr	1		1			1	1		1				5		
Gloucester	82	5	Slownan	Josiah			1			4			1				6		
Newburyport	177	42	Small	Elisha	2		1						1	1			5		
Danvers	3	7	Small	George		1		1				1	1				4		
Middleton	17	1	Small	Samuel			1	1		1	1		1				5		
Salem	197	30	Smally	Samuel			1			1	1		1	1			5		
Marblehead	263	4	Smethurst	Alice										1			1		
Marblehead	240	17	Smethurst	John	1		1			2			1				5		
Marblehead	251	1	Smethurst	John	3	1	1			3	1		1				10		
Haverhill	150	34	Smiley	James		2	1	1		1			1	1			7		
Bradford	122	42	Smiley	John	2	1	2	1					1				7		
Haverhill	150	30	Smiley	Mary			2							2			4		
Haverhill	150	10	Smiley	William	1	1	3		1		1			1			8		
Beverly	290	1	Smith	*	1		1						1				3		
Ipswich	276	22	Smith	Aaron	1		1			1			1				4		
Ipswich	278	42	Smith	Aaron		2	1				1	1	1				6		
Methuen	155	43	Smith	Aaron				1					1				2		
Salem	189	42	Smith	Aaron												1	1		
Lynnfield	235	37	Smith	Abigail									1				1		
Lynn	233	25	Smith	Abram				1					1				2	West Parish	
Ipswich	280	20	Smith	Adam		1	1	1				1	1				5		
Ipswich	274	48	Smith	Annie			1				1		1				3		
Rowley	128	47	Smith	Anthony			1						2				3		
Beverly	290	20	Smith	Asa	2		1			1							4		
Ipswich	280	22	Smith	Asa	3	1		2		3		1	1				11		
Manchester	54	19	Smith	Barly	1		1						1				3		
Rowley	129	31	Smith	Benja		1	1			1			1				4		
Beverly	296	1	Smith	Benjamin	1		1						1	1			4		
Marblehead	240	18	Smith	Benjamin	1			1		2			1				5		
Salem	196	18	Smith	Benjamin				1		1		1	1				4		
Gloucester	66	26	Smith	Benjm Jun	1		1			1			1				4		
Salem	188	38	Smith	Caleb	1	2			1	1		2	2	1		1	11		
Gloucester	61	12	Smith	Charles	3		1						2				6		
Gloucester	85	12	Smith	Charles	1		1						1	1			4		
Gloucester	69	6	Smith	Daniel					1					1		1	3		
Ipswich	274	42	Smith	Daniel B.	2	1		1		1	3		1				9		
Beverly	300	17	Smith	Daniel G	1		1			2			1				5		
Salem	188	43	Smith	David	2		1						1				4		
Amesbury	45	25	Smith	David Revd	1		1			2	2		1				7		
Beverly	304	24	Smith	Ebenezer Jr		2	3	1		1		2					9		
Beverly	292	13	Smith	Ebenz		1		1						1			3		
Salem	193	8	Smith	Ebenz	1			1		2				1			5		
Salem	189	30	Smith	Edward			1			1	1		1				4		
Andover	101	37	Smith	Eliakim	2		1	1					1				5		
Beverly	302	21	Smith	Elias				1						1			2		
Danvers	14	22	Smith	Elizabeth									1	1			2		
Ipswich	280	2	Smith	Elizabeth							1			1			2		
Newburyport	177	5	Smith	Elizabeth Wido			2	2		2				1			7		
Salem	192	23	Smith	Emmons			1						1				2		
Salem	221	7	Smith	Emmons	2		2		1				1				6		
Newbury	115	42	Smith	Enoch	3			1						2			6		
Lynn	229	9	Smith	Ephm					1	1			1				3		
Danvers	8	38	Smith	Epriem	2			1		1		1	1				6		
Beverly	293	15	Smith	Ezra			1			3							4		
Lynn	233	26	Smith	Frances	1	1		1		1			1				5	West Parish	
Beverly	289	21	Smith	Francis		1	1		1				1	1			5		
Beverly	292	4	Smith	Francis Jun	3			1		2			1				7		

264

TOWN	PG#	LN#	LAST NAME	FIRST NAME	FREE WHITE MALES					FREE WHITE FEMALES					TOTAL ALL OTHER	TOTAL SLAVES	TOTALS	DISTRICT/ TOWNSHIP	NOTES
					under 10	10 to 16	16 to 26	26 to 45	45 and over	under 10	10 to 16	16 to 26	26 to 45	45 and over					
Salem	190	18	Smith	Geo		1	1	1			1		1				5		
Salem	205	36	Smith	Geo			1			1		1					3		
Salem	207	35	Smith	Geo					1	1			1				3		
Danvers	2	23	Smith	George G				1		2			1				4		
Gloucester	70	12	Smith	George G Cao	3			1	1	1	1	1	1				9		
Salem	189	12	Smith	Hannah			3			1			1	1			6		
Salem	196	4	Smith	Hannah		2	1			2		2		1			9		
Salem	213	22	Smith	Hannah										1			1		
Salem	216	13	Smith	Hannah										1			1		
Beverly	289	20	Smith	Hasadiah					1				1	1			3		
Gloucester	66	27	Smith	Henry Cap	1	1		1		3	1		1	1			9		
Haverhill	150	11	Smith	Hezekiah		1		1				2		1			5		
Beverly	297	15	Smith	Isaac	1	1		1		2	2		1	1			9		
Ipswich	273	18	Smith	Isaac	3			1		2			1				7		
Rowley	128	54	Smith	Isaac		1	1	1		1			1		2		7		
Rowley	130	43	Smith	Isaac	1		2		1			1		1			6		
Salem	210	46	Smith	Isaac				1			1	1	1				4		
Beverly	295	4	Smith	Isaac W				1		1		1					3		
Danvers	8	16	Smith	Israel	1				1	3			1				6		
Danvers	12	1	Smith	Jabez	1	3	2						1				7		
Gloucester	61	11	Smith	Jacob	2	1	3	1		2	1	1	1	1			13		
Beverly	290	3	Smith	James		2	1				2		1				6		
Gloucester	83	6	Smith	James					1				1				2		
Gloucester	85	14	Smith	James					1								1		
Ipswich	277	29	Smith	James	2	1		1			1		1	1			7		
Ipswich	279	39	Smith	James		1		1				1		1			4		
Marblehead	265	3	Smith	James			1			1	1	1					6		
Newbury	115	41	Smith	James	2			1		1			1				5		
Newburyport	177	2	Smith	James			2		1		1			2			6		
Rowley	128	53	Smith	James	1			1		1			1				4		
Ipswich	277	57	Smith	Jeremiah	1			1				1					3		
Marblehead	261	3	Smith	Jeremiah			1					1					2		
Salem	190	10	Smith	Jesse	1			1		1	1	1	1	1			7		
Newbury	113	34	Smith	Joanna	1	1						1					3		
Beverly	292	25	Smith	Job		1		1					1				3		
Hamilton	285	110	Smith	Job			2			1	1		1				5		
Boxford	136	10	Smith	John		1			1	2	1		1				6		
Bradford	125	16	Smith	John		1		1					1		1		4		
Gloucester	66	19	Smith	John			1		1	1			1				3		
Hamilton	285	36	Smith	John	1		1					1					3		
Haverhill	150	44	Smith	John		1		1					1				3		
Ipswich	280	9	Smith	John		1		1					1				3		
Ipswich	281	58	Smith	John			1		1	1			1				4		
Ipswich	283	44	Smith	John				1				1	1				3		
Lynn	225	19	Smith	John	2			1					1				4		
Marblehead	255	25	Smith	John	2			1		2			1				6		
Marblehead	260	23	Smith	John	1		1						1				3		
Marblehead	261	17	Smith	John			1		1					2			4		
Newbury	113	13	Smith	John	3	1		1		1			1	1			8		
Newbury	114	1	Smith	John		1		1		1	2	1					7		
Newbury	114	47	Smith	John															Enumeration left blank
Newbury	116	26	Smith	John	2		2	1			1	1		1			8		
Newbury	120	4	Smith	John	1	1		1					1				4		
Newbury	120	5	Smith	John	2		1					1					5		
Rowley	132	14	Smith	John				1	1			1	1				4		
Salem	190	33	Smith	John	1	1		1		1	2	3	1				10		
Salem	215	48	Smith	Jona		1	2	1				1	1	1			7		
Salisbury	33	11	Smith	Jona Colo	2		1		1	2	2	3	1				12		
Beverly	295	29	Smith	Jonathan	1	1		1		2			1				6		
Haverhill	150	29	Smith	Jonathan				1		1			1				3		
Beverly	292	24	Smith	Joseph	4		1	1					1				7		
Boxford	135	34	Smith	Joseph		1	1			1		1					4		
Danvers	9	19	Smith	Joseph					1					1			2		
Gloucester	61	13	Smith	Joseph	2			1					2				5		
Gloucester	81	30	Smith	Joseph	1	1		1		2			1	1			7		
Rowley	129	24	Smith	Joseph	3	1		1		1	1		1				8		
Salem	209	47	Smith	Joseph		1		1		1	1		1				5		
Ipswich	275	18	Smith	Joshua		1		1	1	1	1		1				7		
Ipswich	279	33	Smith	Josiah			1			1			1				3		
Newburyport	177	1	Smith	Josiah		1	1		1	1	2	1		1			8		
Amesbury	44	18	Smith	Judith Wid									1	1			2		
Newburyport	176	37	Smith	Leonard		3	4		1	1		2		3			14		
Newbury	114	39	Smith	Lydia								1	1				2		
Beverly	290	6	Smith	Mary						1		1					2		
Danvers	6	15	Smith	mAry										2			2		
Ipswich	282	35	Smith	Mary				1				1		1			3		
Ipswich	282	36	Smith	Mary							3	1		1			5		
Marblehead	255	6	Smith	Mary							2		1	1			4		
Gloucester	86	7	Smith	Mary Wo	2							2	2	1			7		
Newburyport	177	3	Smith	Michael	1		1	1		1			1				5		
Ipswich	278	29	Smith	Moses			2		1	3	1		1				8		
Marblehead	247	3	Smith	Moses	2			2		1	1		1				7		
Salem	195	9	Smith	Moses		1	1	1				1					4		
Ipswich	275	12	Smith	Nathaniel		1			1			3		1			6		
Newburyport	176	39	Smith	Nathaniel	1			1				2					5		

TOWN	PG#	LN#	LAST NAME	FIRST NAME	under 10	10 to 16	16 to 26	26 to 45	45 and over	under 10	10 to 16	16 to 26	26 to 45	45 and over	TOTAL ALL OTHER	TOTAL SLAVES	TOTALS	DISTRICT/ TOWNSHIP	NOTES
Gloucester	68	19	Smith	Nathl				1		1	1	1					4		
Boxford	135	33	Smith	Nathll					1			1	2				4		
Beverly	293	14	Smith	Nehemiah			2		1					1			4		
Beverly	295	3	Smith	Nellie								1	2				3		
Newbury	115	46	Smith	Parker	1	1			1			2	1				6		
Gloucester	82	15	Smith	Polly Wo								1			1		2		
Danvers	12	42	Smith	Richard			1					1	2				4		
Newbury	114	46	Smith	Richard	1	1		1		1	1		1				6		
Newburyport	176	38	Smith	Richard				1						1			2		
Salem	190	2	Smith	Robert											4		4		
Salem	211	1	Smith	Robert				1				1		1			3		
Hamilton	285	35	Smith	Ruben	1		1	1	1			1		1			6		
Salisbury	33	15	Smith	Rufus	2			1		1			1				5		
Lynn	225	37	Smith	Saml	2	1		1		1			1				6		
Ipswich	275	25	Smith	Samuel	1	2		1		2	1		1				8		
Ipswich	281	16	Smith	Samuel	2		1	1		2		1	1	2			10		
Marblehead	254	13	Smith	Samuel	1	2			1	3	1		1				9		
Newburyport	177	4	Smith	Samuel			1						1				2		
Salem	195	14	Smith	Samuel	2		1	1				1	1	1			7		
Salem	197	7	Smith	Samuel	1		1			1			1	1			5		
Salem	198	15	Smith	Samuel		2		1					1				4		
Ipswich	273	51	Smith	Simon			2		1		1		1	1			6		
Lynnfield	236	21	Smith	Stephen	1			1		3			1	1			7		
Lynn	223	56	Smith	Stephn	1	1		1					1				4		
Manchester	54	12	Smith	Stephn	2	1	1						1				5		
Gloucester	84	26	Smith	Susa Wo									1	1			2		
Danvers	3	18	Smith	Susanna	1	1	1			3	1	1	1				9		
Beverly	296	4	Smith	Thomas	2			1		1	1	1					6		
Marblehead	246	19	Smith	Thomas	1		1						1				3		
Newbury	105	1	Smith	Thomas	1		1			1	1	1	1				6		
Newburyport	176	40	Smith	Thomas	2			1		1			1				5		
Marblehead	245	26	Smith	Thomas G.			1						1				2		
Gloucester	73	18	Smith	Thos	1			1					1				3	Town Parish	
Haverhill	150	45	Smith	Walker		1	1		1	3	2			1			9		
Lynnfield	235	38	Smith	Walter		1	1					1					3		
Gloucester	81	32	Smith	Willa	1	1	1	1		1			1	1			7		
Gloucester	82	6	Smith	Willa Junr	1		1			1			1				4		
Beverly	292	10	Smith	William	2		1			1			1				5		
Haverhill	150	24	Smith	William	2	1	1	1		1	1		1				8		
Salem	205	26	Smithers	Tobias					1		1			1			3		
Salem	195	1	Smithhurst	Micha	1				1	2	1	1	2				8		
Salem	204	38	Smithurst	Peter		1		1		3	2		1	2			10		
Salem	202	17	Smithurst	Thos	2	1		1		2			1				7		
Danvers	12	7	Smothers	Sarah			3					1	1	1			6		
Marblehead	247	6	Snell	Joseph		1	1							1			3		
Marblehead	248	12	Snell	Martha									2				2		
Marblehead	250	22	Snell	Samuel	3	2		1					1				7		
Marblehead	250	18	Snell	Stephen	1			1		2	1	1	1				7		
Marblehead	249	17	Snelling	Abigail										1			1		
Salem	211	48	Snelling	John				1			1		1				3		
Danvers	13	36	Snow	Asa	2			1		1		1	1				6		
Salem	201	5	Snow	James	1	1				5		1	1				10		
Marblehead	248	30	Snow	Mary										1			1		
Marblehead	248	29	Snow	Samuel	3	2		1		1			1				8		
Haverhill	150	22	Soley	Nathll	2	1		1					1				5		
Newbury	112	11	Somerbe	Henry	1		1	1		1	1			1			6		
Newbury	111	7	Somerbe	Nathan	1		1	1		1	1		1	1			7		
Newburyport	178	10	Somerby	Abraham				1					1				2		
Newburyport	178	12	Somerby	Benjamin	2		1	1		2	3		1	1			11		
Newburyport	178	11	Somerby	Daniel	2	1	1		1	2				1			8		
Newburyport	178	14	Somerby	Enoch			1			3			2	1			7		
Newburyport	178	7	Somerby	John				1			1		1				3		
Newburyport	178	8	Somerby	John F	2	1	1			1		1	2	1			9		
Newburyport	178	22	Somerby	Margaret Wido	1								1				2		
Newburyport	178	13	Somerby	Moses	3	1		1				1	1				7		
Newburyport	178	9	Somerby	Sarah Wido									1	1			2		
Newburyport	178	5	Somerby	Thomas		1		1		1			1				4		
Newburyport	178	6	Somerby	Thomas Jr				1			1			1			3		
Gloucester	66	18	Somes	Abigal Widw		1		2		2	1		1				7		
Gloucester	66	20	Somes	John 3d	4		1	1		1		1	1				9		
Gloucester	61	17	Somes	John 4th Capt	1			1	1	1			1	1			6		
Gloucester	61	9	Somes	John Capt		1			1	1			2				5		
Gloucester	61	18	Somes	John Jun	1			1		1			1				4		
Gloucester	68	9	Somes	John Junr	3	1		1		3	1		1				10		
Gloucester	84	6	Somes	Reba Wo	1									1			2		
Gloucester	67	26	Sorey	Nancy Wo	1		1						1	1			4		
Haverhill	150	21	Sortridge	William		2				2			1				5		
Danvers	12	33	Souter	Sally		1							1				2		
Amesbury	44	22	Souter	Samuel	2	1		1		1	1		1				7		
Haverhill	150	32	Souther	Jonathan	2	1		1		1	1		1				7		
Haverhill	150	28	Souther	Samuel	1	1	1		1	1			2				7		
Ipswich	278	32	Southier	Timothy	3			1		1			2				7		
Salem	216	36	Southward	Geo		1		1	1			3		1			7		
Salem	218	56	Southward	Geo	2	2		1		2			1	1			9		
Salem	216	17	Southward	Lydia							1		1				2		
Danvers	14	18	Southwick	Ebenz		2		1			1		1	1			6		
Danvers	12	31	Southwick	Edward	3		1	1		2			2				9		

266

TOWN	PG#	LN#	LAST NAME	FIRST NAME	FREE WHITE MALES					FREE WHITE FEMALES					TOTAL ALL OTHER	TOTAL SLAVES	TOTALS	DISTRICT/ TOWNSHIP	NOTES
					under 10	10 to 16	16 to 26	26 to 45	45 and over	under 10	10 to 16	16 to 26	26 to 45	45 and over					
Salem	198	4	Southwick	Eliza			1					1		1			3		
Danvers	6	32	Southwick	George				1		1				1			3		
Danvers	14	21	Southwick	George 3rd	1			1		2		1	1				6		
Danvers	6	34	Southwick	George Junr	1	2		1		1	1		1	1			8		
Danvers	6	35	Southwick	Hannah	1					1				2			4		
Danvers	15	1	Southwick	Hepsy	1								1	1			3		
Danvers	14	26	Southwick	James			1			2	2		1				6		
Danvers	14	17	Southwick	James Junr	3	1	1	1		1			2		1		10		
Salem	198	6	Southwick	John	2			1					1				4		
Salem	208	52	Southwick	John			1	1									2		
Salem	212	28	Southwick	John	1			1				1	1				4		
Danvers	12	35	Southwick	Joseph			1			1		1					3		
Danvers	6	33	Southwick	Nathan		1	1			2		1					5		
Danvers	12	19	Southwick	Sarah									1	1			2		
Danvers	13	17	Southwick	Simon	2			1		2			1				6		
Danvers	14	27	Southwick	Stephen	1	1		1		1	1		1				6		
Danvers	14	25	Southwick	William	3	1		1	1	1	1	1		1			10		
Newburyport	178	44	Soward	Henry			1					1		1			3		
Methuen	156	2	Spafford	Amos	1			1		1			1				4		
Newburyport	178	42	Spafford	Daniel	1	1	2	1		2			1	2			10		
Andover	101	26	Spafford	Isaac	3	1	1	1		1			1	1			9		
Andover	101	25	Spafford	Moody	3		1		1	2	1	1	1				10		
Newburyport	178	43	Spalding	Jeptha	1	1			1				1	1			5		
Salem	205	24	Spalding	Joshua	2			1		1		1	1				6		
Marblehead	241	25	Sparhawk	John	3			1		1			1				6		
Beverly	304	45	Spencer	William	3	1	2	1		1		1					9		
Newbury	109	34	Spillar	Josiah	3		1			1		1		1			7		
Ipswich	278	59	Spiller	Henry					1		1		2	1			5		
Newburyport	177	20	Spiller	Henry					1	4		1		2			8		
Ipswich	276	42	Spiller	Jeremiah				1					1				2		
Ipswich	278	2	Spiller	John	4	1		1		1			1				8		
Ipswich	277	38	Spiller	Mary							1	1	1				3		
Ipswich	276	4	Spiller	Moses	2		1						1				4		
Rowley	131	42	Spiller	Samll	3		1	1		1	1						7		
Ipswich	281	38	Spiller	Thomas	6		1		1		1			1			10		
Ipswich	274	14	Spiller	William	1			1		2			1		7		12		
Lynn	224	8	Spinney	Thos	1		1			2			1				5		
Boxford	134	44	Spofford	Amos				1					2				3		
Rowley	127	25	Spofford	Amos	3	2	2	1			1	2	1				12		
Boxford	135	12	Spofford	Benja		2		1		2			2				7		
Rowley	127	26	Spofford	Daniel				1					1				2		
Rowley	127	23	Spofford	Jacob	1	1		1		2	1	2	1				9		
Rowley	127	19	Spofford	Joseph	1			1		2	1		1				6		
Rowley	127	22	Spofford	Moody		1	2		1		2	1		1			8		
Rowley	127	17	Spofford	Moses			2		1	1	2			1			7		
Rowley	127	27	Spofford	Moses Dole			1			1		2					4		
Boxford	135	1	Spofford	Parker	5	2		1		2	1	1	1				13		
Boxford	134	46	Spofford	Samuel		1		1	1				1				4		
Boxford	134	47	Spofford	Stephen		1			1	1				1			4		
Boxford	134	45	Spofford	Thos	2			1					1				4		
Rowley	127	20	Spofford	William	1	1	2		1	1	1	1					9		
Rowley	127	21	Spofford	Zach		1			1	1	1	2	1				7		
Haverhill	150	6	Spollet	Henry	2				1	1			1				5		
Newburyport	178	27	Spooner	Bartholomew				1			4	1	1				7		
Danvers	13	20	Sprague	Betsy						1		1	1				3		
Danvers	12	23	Sprague	Ebenezer				1					1				2		
Danvers	12	24	Sprague	Ebenezer Jr		1	1	1			1		1				5		
Salem	196	21	Sprague	Joseph			1	1				1	1	2			6		
Newburyport	176	36	Spring	Samuel Revd	5	1		1			1	2	1				11		
Ipswich	276	33	Stacey	Edward		1		1		1	1	2		1			7		
Marblehead	251	10	Stacey	Edward	3			1		1	1		1				7		
Marblehead	249	2	Stacey	Elizabeth									1				1		
Marblehead	256	9	Stacey	Elizabeth									1				1		
Marblehead	248	27	Stacey	John	2			1				1					4		
Marblehead	251	16	Stacey	John		2			1	1			1				5		
Marblehead	252	16	Stacey	John		1	1	1					1				5		
Marblehead	256	8	Stacey	John	1	2			1	2	1	1		1			9		
Marblehead	243	21	Stacey	Mary			2				1		1				4		
Marblehead	265	4	Stacey	Mary			1			3	1		1				6		
Marblehead	266	19	Stacey	Rebecca	1					1		1	1				4		
Marblehead	266	10	Stacey	Samuel	2			1		1			1				5		
Marblehead	243	20	Stacey	William	3			1					1				5		
Gloucester	61	5	Stacy	Benja	3	1		1				1		1			7		
Gloucester	67	2	Stacy	John Capt	1			1		2		1	1				6		
Gloucester	61	4	Stacy	Lucy Wd			2			1	1	2		1			7		
Gloucester	61	1	Stacy	Nymphus Dea				1					1				2		
Marblehead	244	28	Standley	Peter	2		1	1		2		1					7		
Marblehead	268	6	Standley	Thomas		1	2	1		1			1				6		
Marblehead	244	29	Standley	William	2	1	1	1		3	1	1	1				11		
Beverly	302	15	Standly	Andrew	1			1		1		1					4		
Beverly	292	28	Standly	Benja	1	2		1		2			1				7		
Beverly	303	44	Standly	Betsy			1				2		1				4		
Beverly	291	43	Standly	David	1			1				1		1			4		
Beverly	297	24	Standly	David	1		1	1		2		1					6		
Beverly	294	50	Standly	George				1					1				2		

TOWN	PG#	LN#	LAST NAME	FIRST NAME	FREE WHITE MALES					FREE WHITE FEMALES					TOTAL ALL OTHER	TOTAL SLAVES	TOTALS	DISTRICT/ TOWNSHIP	NOTES
					under 10	10 to 16	16 to 26	26 to 45	45 and over	under 10	10 to 16	16 to 26	26 to 45	45 and over					
Beverly	291	35	Standly	John	1			1		1			1	1			5		
Beverly	295	1	Standly	Jonathan			1	1			1	1		1			5		
Beverly	295	5	Standly	Nehemiah	1			1		2		1					5		
Beverly	303	45	Standly	Peter	2	1		1			1		1				6		
Beverly	290	42	Standly	Robert		1	1		1		1			1			5		
Beverly	294	54	Standly	Robert 2nd	5			1		1	2		1				10		
Beverly	291	34	Standly	Sands	2			1		3			1				7		
Beverly	293	22	Standly	Thomas			1						1				2		
Beverly	291	27	Standly	Timothy	2			1		1			1				5		
Beverly	306	28	Standly	Wells			1			1		1	1				4		
Beverly	291	26	Standly	William		2		1						1			4		
Beverly	291	36	Standly	William Jur	2	1		1		1			1				6		
Amesbury	44	24	Standring	Benja	1	1		1		2			1				6		
Ipswich	275	23	Staniford	Aaron		1			1	2	1		1				6		
Ipswich	275	15	Staniford	James			1					1					2		
Ipswich	277	27	Staniford	Jeremiah		1		1		1			1				4		
Ipswich	275	36	Staniford	Jeremiah Jur				5		2	1	1	1				10		
Ipswich	275	26	Staniford	Thomas	1		1					1					3		
Marblehead	243	16	Stanley	Thomas			1						1				2		
Lynn	228	4	Stanley	Thos	1	1	3	1		4			2				12		
Newburyport	177	14	Stanwood	Abel		1		1		2	1	1	1				7		
Ipswich	276	57	Stanwood	Isaac	2			1		1	1		1				6		
Ipswich	277	49	Stanwood	John		1			1		1		1	1			5		
Newburyport	177	17	Stanwood	John	2	2		1		1		1					7		
Newbury	108	20	Stanwood	Joseph		2	4		3	4	1	3	1	1			19		
Newburyport	177	13	Stanwood	Joseph	3	1		1		1	2		1				9		
Manchester	55	3	Stanwood	Mary				1				2	1				4		
Ipswich	277	59	Stanwood	Nathaniel	1	1		1		1			1				5		
Newburyport	177	16	Stanwood	Nathaniel			1					1					2		
Newburyport	177	18	Stanwood	Philip	1			1		1			1				4		
Newburyport	177	15	Stanwood	Thomas	2	1		1		3	1		1				9		
Newbury	113	25	Stanwood	William	3		1			1		1					6		
Gloucester	61	2	Stanwood	Aaron		1	1						1	1			4		
Gloucester	72	5	Stanwood	David	1		1			1		1					4		
Gloucester	71	12	Stanwood	Goss	1		1			1		1					4		
Gloucester	73	9	Stanwood	John	1		1			1		1		1			5		
Gloucester	62	20	Stanwood	Lemuel				1					1				2		
Gloucester	73	2	Stanwood	Nehemiah	1			1		1			1	1			5		
Gloucester	72	22	Stanwood	Susa Wo			1					1		1			3		
Gloucester	61	23	Stanwood	Thos	1	1	1			1			1	1	1		7		
Gloucester	61	7	Stanwood	Zebulon	1	2	2	1	1		2		1				10		
Gloucester	57	25	Stanwood	Zebulon Junr			1			1	1	1					4	West Parish	
Manchester	54	27	Stares	Philip			1					1	1				3		
Gloucester	61	15	Steal	James	3	2		1		1	1		1				9		
Haverhill	150	17	Stearns	Benjamin	1		1						1				3		
Salem	189	5	Stearns	William	1	5	1		1	4		1	2				15		
Gloucester	57	24	Steel	Danl	1		1	1		2		1	1				7	West Parish	
Gloucester	57	23	Steel	John	1			1		1				1			4	West Parish	
Gloucester	57	26	Steel	Joseph	1		1			1	1	1	1				6	West Parish	
Gloucester	57	22	Steel	Sarah Wd			2	1						1			4	West Parish	
Newburyport	178	21	Steele	Ebenezer			1					1	1				3		
Salem	210	19	Steele	Robert			1					1					2		
Marblehead	254	19	Stenness	Samuel	2		1					2					5		
Beverly	289	7	Stephens	Anne				2				2	1				5		
Danvers	10	33	Stephens	Benjamin		1	2	1		1			1				6		
Haverhill	150	43	Stephens	Ephraim	1	1		1		3	1		1				8		
Beverly	300	26	Stephens	George				1					1				2		
Methuen	156	1	Stephens	Jeremiah	3		2	1		2		2	2				12		
Beverly	289	8	Stephens	John	1	1		1		2	1		1				7		
Danvers	15	4	Stephens	Jonas			1					1					2		
Haverhill	150	7	Stephens	Judith	1					1			1				3		
Methuen	155	41	Stephens	Noah	1		1			3		2	1	1			9		
Andover	101	35	Stevens	Abigail								1	1				2		
Andover	101	23	Stevens	Amos		2	2	1				1	1	1			8		
Salisbury	33	9	Stevens	Benja				1		1	1		1				4		
Marblehead	252	8	Stevens	Benjamin	1	1						1	1				5		
Gloucester	84	25	Stevens	Bethh Wo	1					1			1				3		
Marblehead	255	19	Stevens	Christopher			1			1	1	1					4		
Gloucester	61	20	Stevens	Cyrus	1	1		1		1		2					6		
Andover	101	31	Stevens	David	1			1		1		1					4		
Andover	101	33	Stevens	Ebenz		1			1	1	1			1			5		
Gloucester	57	39	Stevens	Ebenz				1					1	1			3	West Parish	
Andover	101	28	Stevens	Edward	2			1		2			1				6		
Gloucester	61	3	Stevens	Eliza Wd			1				2	4	1				8		
Marblehead	261	10	Stevens	Francis			1			1		1					3		
Salisbury	33	25	Stevens	Jacob		1	1			1	2		1				6		
Andover	101	15	Stevens	James	2	1	2	1		1	1	1					9		
Salisbury	33	23	Stevens	Jeremiah				1		1	1			1			4		
Marblehead	247	35	Stevens	John				1		1	1			1			4		
Salisbury	33	12	Stevens	John	1			1		2				1			5		
Salisbury	33	26	Stevens	John Junr	1			1			1			1			4		
Salisbury	33	17	Stevens	Jona	2	1		1					1				5		
Andover	101	24	Stevens	Jonathan	3	1			1		1	2		1			9		
Bradford	124	25	Stevens	Jonathan	2	2	3		1			2		1			11		

TOWN	PG#	LN#	LAST NAME	FIRST NAME	FREE WHITE MALES					FREE WHITE FEMALES					TOTAL ALL OTHER	TOTAL SLAVES	TOTALS	DISTRICT/ TOWNSHIP	NOTES
					under 10	10 to 16	16 to 26	26 to 45	45 and over	under 10	10 to 16	16 to 26	26 to 45	45 and over					
Andover	101	22	Stevens	Jonathan Junr	1		1	1		2			1				6		
Andover	101	29	Stevens	Joseph	1		1	1			1	1		1			6		
Gloucester	84	31	Stevens	Joseph	0	2		1		3		0	1				7		
Marblehead	250	7	Stevens	Joseph				1		2			1				4		
Marblehead	270	1	Stevens	Joseph					1		3			1			5		
Salisbury	33	10	Stevens	Joseph	2			1		2	2		3				10		
Andover	101	34	Stevens	Joseph Junr	3			1				1	1				6		
Andover	102	2	Stevens	Joshua	3	1		1		2	2		1				10		
Andover	101	13	Stevens	Lydia Wid		1								2			3		
Marblehead	239	24	Stevens	Mary		3		1				1					5		
Salem	218	23	Stevens	Mary						1	1		1				3		
Andover	101	14	Stevens	Mary Wid										1			1		
Manchester	54	20	Stevens	Moses	1		1					1					3		
Salem	192	42	Stevens	Nath		1						1					2		
Gloucester	82	1	Stevens	Oliver	1		1			1		1	1				5		
Andover	101	18	Stevens	Peter	2	1		1		1	1		1				7		
Andover	101	19	Stevens	Phebe									1				1		
Andover	101	21	Stevens	Phillip			1			1			1				3		
Gloucester	82	7	Stevens	Robert	1			1		1		1					4		
Salisbury	33	24	Stevens	Ruth Wd						2		1		1			4		
Salisbury	33	13	Stevens	Samuel				1						1			2		
Andover	102	1	Stevens	Samuel Junr	2	1	3	1	1				1	1			10		
Salisbury	33	20	Stevens	Samuel Junr				1		2			1				4		
Marblehead	247	27	Stevens	Sarah	1	1	2			3	1	1		2			11		
Marblehead	247	34	Stevens	Silvester			1						1				2		
Andover	101	39	Stevens	Simeon		1		1	1	2		1	1	1			8		
Andover	101	32	Stevens	Thomas	1				1					1			3		
Marblehead	256	2	Stevens	Thomas	1	1		1		1	1		1	1			7		
Andover	101	17	Stevens	Timothy			1		2	2		1	1	1			8		
Gloucester	61	10	Stevens	Zacha	2	1		1		1	1	2	2				10		
Newburyport	178	41	Stevens	Samuel	2	1		1					1	1			6		
Marblehead	266	31	Stevenson	David	2	1			1	2		3	1	1			11		
Newburyport	178	17	Stevenson	Robert				1			1		3				5		
Newburyport	178	33	Stewart	James	1			1		2		1					5		
Salem	216	47	Stewart	James		1						1					2		
Beverly	296	24	Stewart	Mary						1		2					3		
Andover	102	7	Stickney	Abraham	3	1	2	1		1		2	1				11		
Newburyport	177	39	Stickney	Alice Wido	1	1	1					1					4		
Newbury	114	33	Stickney	Amos			1	1						1			3		
Rowley	128	37	Stickney	Amos	1			1	1			1	1	1	1		7		
Boxford	134	54	Stickney	Ariel		1		1		1		1					4		
Danvers	4	36	Stickney	Asa	1	1	1		1	3		1		1			9		
Newbury	114	29	Stickney	Benja	2			1		1			1				5		
Rowley	131	46	Stickney	Benja		1	2	1	1			1	1	2			9		
Bradford	125	41	Stickney	Daniel	1			1		2	1		1				6		
Newbury	111	22	Stickney	David	1		1		1	1			1				5		
Rowley	131	52	Stickney	Dudley	1			2				1		1			5		
Newburyport	177	35	Stickney	Ebenezer	1			1		2			1				5		
Bradford	125	31	Stickney	Ebenzr		1	1		1			1		1			5		
Lynn	223	54	Stickney	Enoch			1			1		1					3		
Newburyport	177	37	Stickney	Gideon W		1	1			1		1					4		
Newbury	113	5	Stickney	Hannah							1	1	1				3		
Rowley	131	4	Stickney	Hannah										2			2		
Newburyport	177	33	Stickney	Jacob	1			1		1			1				4		
Newburyport	177	34	Stickney	Jacob Jr			2			2		1					5		
Boxford	134	53	Stickney	Jedidiah				1			1			1			3		
Rowley	131	45	Stickney	Jedidiah		1	1	1				1	1	1			6		
Haverhill	150	14	Stickney	Jeremiah		2		1		3	1		1				8		
Andover	101	27	Stickney	John		1	1					1		1			5		
Newburyport	177	30	Stickney	John		2			1			1		1			5		
Newburyport	177	31	Stickney	John Jr	2			1		4			1				8		
Newburyport	177	28	Stickney	Jonathan		1	1	1						1			4		
Newburyport	177	29	Stickney	Jonathan Jr				1		3	2		1				7		
Beverly	302	32	Stickney	Joseph	3			1		1			1				6		
Salisbury	33	16	Stickney	Joseph				1		1			1				3		
Rowley	131	5	Stickney	Josiah	2		1	1		1	1		1				7		
Salem	213	52	Stickney	Judith		2	2	2				1	1	1			9		
Newburyport	177	32	Stickney	Moses	1	1		1		2	1		1				7		
Rowley	131	49	Stickney	Moses		1				1		1					3		
Rowley	128	5	Stickney	Paul		2		1						1			4		
Newbury	112	25	Stickney	Rebecca								1	2				3		
Newbury	114	30	Stickney	Richard	1			1		1		1					4		
Beverly	303	25	Stickney	Samuel	1		3	1		2	1	2					10		
Beverly	305	26	Stickney	Samuel	1	2		1				1		1			6		
Newburyport	177	38	Stickney	Sarah Wido								1		2			3		
Newburyport	177	40	Stickney	Sarah Wido Jr				1		1	2	2	1				7		
Newbury	114	31	Stickney	Theoder		1	1						1	1			4		
Newburyport	177	36	Stickney	Thomas	3		1	1						2			7		
Bradford	125	4	Stickney	Thos			1	1	1			2	1	1			7		
Newbury	114	28	Stickney	William	2			1		1		1	1				6		
Newburyport	177	26	Stickney	William			2		1	1		2	1				7		
Newburyport	177	27	Stickney	William Jr		1		1		3			1				6		
Beverly	293	1	Stickny	Seilas	2			1		2							5		
Middleton	17	31	Stiles	Daniel			2	1				1	2				6		
Marblehead	255	31	Stiles	Desire								1		1			2		
Boxford	135	26	Stiles	John				2						1			3		

TOWN	PG#	LN#	LAST NAME	FIRST NAME	FWM under 10	FWM 10 to 16	FWM 16 to 26	FWM 26 to 45	FWM 45 and over	FWF under 10	FWF 10 to 16	FWF 16 to 26	FWF 26 to 45	FWF 45 and over	TOTAL ALL OTHER	TOTAL SLAVES	TOTALS	DISTRICT/ TOWNSHIP	NOTES
Middleton	16	17	Stiles	John	1			1		1			1				4		
Middleton	17	30	Stiles	Mary			1						1	1			3		
Middleton	17	32	Stiles	Meriam		2	2	1				1	1	1			8		
Bradford	123	23	Stiles	Samll	1	1		1		2			1	1			7		
Boxford	135	50	Stiles	Simeon			2		1	1		2	1				7		
Manchester	54	26	Stiles	Thomas	1	1		1		2			1				6		
Salem	209	17	Still	Mary		1							1				2		
Gloucester	82	3	Stilman	Danl		1	1	1		1		4	1				9		
Gloucester	82	2	Stilman	Peter	2			1		1			1				5		
Salem	183	27	Stimpson	Thadeus	1	1	1	1		1	1						6		
Danvers	11	27	Stinson	John			2		1	2				3			8		
Lynn	232	38	Stocker	Amos			1				1		1				3	West Parish	
Lynn	232	37	Stocker	Amos Junr	1		2	1		1			1	1			7	West Parish	
Newbury	111	32	Stocker	Ebenezer		1	2	1		2	2		3	1			12		
Lynn	233	3	Stocker	Ebenz	1	2	1		1	2			2				9		
Lynn	232	39	Stocker	John			1						2		2		5	West Parish	
Ipswich	274	1	Stocker	Robert	1		1	1		1			1	1			6		
Lynn	232	40	Stocker	Ruth									2				2	West Parish	
Newbury	112	16	Stocker	Samuel	2			1					1				4		
Lynn	233	1	Stocker	Susanna							1	1	1	1			4		
Newburyport	179	3	Stockman	John	1		1						2	1			5		
Salem	219	32	Stoddard	Ebed	3	2		1		1	1	1					9		
Salem	201	12	Stoddard	Richard	1		1			1		1					4		
Newbury	113	26	Stodder	Daniel				1				1		1			3		
Danvers	12	3	Ston	Benjamin	2	1	1	1					1				6		
Beverly	299	41	Stone	Abigail									1	1			2		
Beverly	293	24	Stone	Abner C	2			1		2	1		1				7		
Manchester	54	24	Stone	Abraham	2	1		1		1			1				6		
Newburyport	177	11	Stone	Benjamin	1			1		1			1				4		
Salem	197	42	Stone	Benjamin	3			1					1				5		
Lynn	227	45	Stone	Caleb	4		2	1		1	1		1				10		
Newburyport	177	10	Stone	Daniel		1	1						1				3		
Newburyport	177	9	Stone	Ebenezer	2	1				2	1	1	1				9		
Danvers	12	37	Stone	Edmund Junr		1		1		4	2		1				9		
Danvers	13	14	Stone	George	1		1			3	1		1				7		
Marblehead	270	12	Stone	Hannah	2	1	2			2		1	1				9		
Newburyport	177	8	Stone	Isaac		1	2	1				1	1				6		
Newburyport	177	7	Stone	Jacob	1			1				1	1				4		
Marblehead	266	1	Stone	James	2	2		1		1				1			7		
Beverly	293	20	Stone	Joanna			1				1	1		1			4		
Beverly	304	39	Stone	John	1	2	2	1		3			1	1			11		
Hamilton	284	5	Stone	John		1	1					1	1	1			5		
Lynn	225	21	Stone	John		1							1	1			3		
Newburyport	177	6	Stone	John			3			1			1				5		
Salem	205	7	Stone	John		1				1			1				3		
Beverly	291	23	Stone	Josiah				1					1				2		
Beverly	291	24	Stone	Josiah Jun	1	1		1		3	1		1				8		
Beverly	303	20	Stone	Mary			1						1	1			3		
Beverly	293	23	Stone	Mary 2d									1	1			2		
Marblehead	265	29	Stone	Nehemiah	1		2	1				1	1	1			7		
Beverly	295	41	Stone	Rachel		1				1	2		1				5		
Danvers	14	20	Stone	Robert	2	2	1						1				6		
Ipswich	274	23	Stone	Robert	1		1			2			1				5		
Salem	218	31	Stone	Robt	1		1		1	2		3		1			9		
Ipswich	277	16	Stone	Samu				1			1			1			3		
Manchester	54	23	Stone	Samuel	1			1		3		1					6		
Salem	197	41	Stone	Samuel				1						1			2		
Ipswich	278	14	Stone	Samuel Junr	2			1		2			1				6		
Newburyport	177	12	Stone	Sarah Wido								1		1			2		
Manchester	54	21	Stone	Willa Senr			1			1	1		1				4		
Ipswich	277	39	Stone	William	1			1		1		1					4		
Newbury	108	11	Stonewood	Peter	1		1			2			1				5		
Gloucester	68	28	Storey	Amos			1			1			1	1			4		
Ipswich	283	35	Storey	Anna									1	1			2		
Ipswich	283	43	Storey	Deborah									1	1			2		
Ipswich	283	40	Storey	Ebenezer		1		1					1	1			4		
Ipswich	283	38	Storey	Elisha	1			1		2	2		1		1		8		
Ipswich	283	3	Storey	Elizabeth	1							1	1	1			4		
Ipswich	283	27	Storey	Elizabeth		1							1	1			3		
Ipswich	283	34	Storey	Hannah			1						1	1			3		
Manchester	54	15	Storey	Henry Maj	1	2		1		2			1	1			8		
Ipswich	282	50	Storey	Jacob	3	1	2	1		3			1				11		
Gloucester	77	25	Storey	James	2	1		1		3	1		1				9		
Ipswich	283	26	Storey	Jesse	1			1		1				1			4		
Gloucester	68	18	Storey	John	1		1			2			1	1			6		
Ipswich	282	56	Storey	Jonathan	2	2		1				3		1			9		
Ipswich	283	39	Storey	Jonathan	2			1		1			1				5		
Ipswich	283	21	Storey	Nathan		1	1	1		1	1		1				6		
Manchester	54	13	Storey	Nathll			1			1			1				3		
Ipswich	283	22	Storey	Nehemiah			1							1			2		
Ipswich	283	28	Storey	Stephen	3	1		1				1	1				7		
Salisbury	33	18	Storkman	Joseph				1				1	1				3		
Salisbury	33	19	Storkman	Joseph Junr	1		1			1			1				4		
Marblehead	248	19	Story	Abiel			1						1	1	1		4		
Marblehead	245	21	Story	Elisha	3		1		1	2	2	2	1				12		
Marblehead	244	18	Story	Isaac Revd				1		1		1	3				7		

TOWN	PG#	LN#	LAST NAME	FIRST NAME	FWM under 10	FWM 10 to 16	FWM 16 to 26	FWM 26 to 45	FWM 45 and over	FWF under 10	FWF 10 to 16	FWF 16 to 26	FWF 26 to 45	FWF 45 and over	TOTAL ALL OTHER	TOTAL SLAVES	TOTALS	DISTRICT/ TOWNSHIP	NOTES
Salem	215	44	Story	Saml		1	1							1			3		
Marblehead	242	3	Story	William			1			1		2					4		
Newburyport	179	4	Story	William		1				1		2	1	1			7		
Lynn	223	13	Stover	John Junr			1	1		1			1				4		
Newburyport	178	37	Stover	Sarah Wido	4		2	1				1	1	1			10		
Newburyport	178	36	Stover	William			1						1				2		
Newburyport	178	35	Stoves	David				1		1	1		1				4		
Amesbury	45	35	Stowker	Marshal		1		1					1				3		
Haverhill	150	25	Straw	Abigail		1				1	1		1	1			5		
Haverhill	150	12	Straw	Sherburn	1			1		2			1				5		
Beverly	298	16	Strickland	Allin	3			1		2	1		1				8		
Marblehead	253	17	Striker	Samuel			1						1				2		
Marblehead	245	5	Strong	William	2			1		1			1				5		
Salem	217	1	Strout	Joseph	3	1		1					1				7		
Beverly	304	18	Sugden	Lucy						1			1				2		
Gloucester	66	11	Sullivan	Michael	1			1					1				3		
Ipswich	279	23	Summers	Daniel				1			1	2		1			5		
Ipswich	278	26	Summers	William	2	1		1		1			2				7		
Beverly	298	1	Sumner	Benja C	3	2		1		2	1		1				10		
Newburyport	178	34	Sumner	Ebenezer	1		2	1		2	1	1		1			9		
Beverly	298	13	Sumner	James	3	1		1		1			1				7		
Gloucester	70	15	Survey	Abigal Wo			2						1	1			4		
Ipswich	281	39	Sutton	Ebenezer			1	1				1		1			4		
Salem	194	45	Sutton	Rebecca										2			2		
Ipswich	277	19	Sutton	Richard				1		1			1				3		
Newburyport	178	23	Swain	Edward Wid of	2		2			2		2		1			9		
Salisbury	33	21	Swain	Roger				1		1	1		1	1			5		
Marblehead	270	21	Swan	Aaron				1				1		1			3		
Methuen	155	36	Swan	Dorcas	1	1				1	1	1		1			6		
Haverhill	150	2	Swan	Francis	3	1		1		2	1		1				9		
Methuen	155	40	Swan	John	1		1	1		3			1	1			8		
Marblehead	265	6	Swan	John P.	1		1	1		3	1		2				9		
Methuen	155	39	Swan	Joshua	1	1		1		3	1						8		
Andover	101	36	Swan	Robert			2		1	4		1	1				9		
Marblehead	265	7	Swan	Robert	1	1		1		1	1	1					6		
Salem	200	15	Swan	Robt	1	4	3	1				2		1			12		
Salem	197	2	Swan	Sarah	1	2					1			1			5		
Methuen	155	37	Swan	William	2	2		1		3		2	1				11		
Newburyport	177	22	Swasey	Edward	3	1		1		3	2	1	1				12		
Ipswich	279	8	Swasey	Joseph	1						1	1	1	2			7		
Newburyport	177	23	Swasey	Joseph		1	1		1			2	1				6		
Newburyport	177	24	Swasey	Joseph Jr	1			1		2			1				5		
Salem	202	41	Swasey	Rachel	3						2	2	1				8		
Salem	203	12	Swasey	Richd	1	2	1	1				1	1				7		
Salem	217	26	Swasey	Samuel			2		1	1		1	1	1			7		
Newburyport	177	25	Swasey	Stephen		1			1	1		1		1			5		
Marblehead	253	32	Swasey	Susannah									1				1		
Marblehead	251	22	Swaysey	Samuel		1				2		1					4		
Salisbury	33	22	Sweat	Aaron	1			1	1	1		1					5		
Amesbury	44	20	Sweat	Benja				1					1				2		
Amesbury	44	19	Sweat	Enoch	3			1		2			1				7		
Salisbury	33	29	Sweat	Saml Junr	2			1					1				4		
Salisbury	33	30	Sweat	Samuel				1						1			2		
Amesbury	44	21	Sweat	Willm				1		2		1					4		
Salisbury	33	27	Sweat	Willm	1	1		1		2		1		1			7		
Haverhill	150	39	Sweesy	Appleton	1			1				1		1			4		
Ipswich	278	1	Sweet	Aaron	1			1					1				3		
Ipswich	273	50	Sweet	Jabez					1			1		1			3		
Ipswich	278	13	Sweet	John		1		1			2	2		1			7		
Marblehead	268	4	Sweet	Nathaniel	1			1		3			1				6		
Salem	206	16	Sweeten	James				1				1		1			3		
Lynn	233	32	Sweetser	Asa	2			1		2	1		1				7	West Parish	
Lynn	234	7	Sweetser	Benj			1	1			2		1				5		
Lynn	233	49	Sweetser	Ephm		1						1					2	West Parish	
Lynn	233	33	Sweetser	Joseph	1	1		1		3			1				7	West Parish	
Lynn	233	37	Sweetser	Saml		1		1				1		1			4	West Parish	
Lynn	233	36	Sweetser	Saml Junr			1						2				3	West Parish	
Salem	209	20	Sweetser	Samuel	1	1		1		2	1	2	1	1			10		
Newburyport	178	45	Sweetser	Seth				1		1	1	1					4		
Lynn	233	7	Sweetser	Willm	2	1		1		1	1	2	1				9		
Lynn	233	45	Sweetser	Willm			1		1				1	1			4	West Parish	
Marblehead	250	6	Swetland	Benjamin			1				1	1					3		
Haverhill	150	37	Swett	Abraham		1	1	1				1		1			5		
Haverhill	150	38	Swett	Daniel			1			3	1	1		1			6		
Newburyport	178	1	Swett	Edmund		2	1		1	1	1	1		1			8		
Newburyport	178	3	Swett	Jacob	2	2	1	1				2					8		
Haverhill	150	19	Swett	Nathan		1						1					2		
Newburyport	178	2	Swett	Samuel		1	1					2					4		
Andover	101	30	Swift	Jonathan	1	3	1					1	1				7		
Danvers	7	27	Swinerton	Ede										1	1		2		
Danvers	7	30	Swinerton	James			1	1				2	1				5		
Danvers	3	9	Swinerton	John	1		1		1			1		1			5		
Danvers	7	26	Swinerton	John Junr	1	1		1		3		2					8		
Danvers	7	29	Swinerton	Ruth	1			1		1		1		1			5		
Lynnfield	235	43	Swinnerton	Lucy									1				1		
Newburyport	178	38	Sylvester	Adam	1			1		2			1				5		
Salem	221	22	Symes	Pely D	1		3	3				1	1				9		

TOWN	PG#	LN#	HEADS OF HOUSEHOLD		FREE WHITE MALES					FREE WHITE FEMALES					TOTAL ALL OTHER	TOTAL SLAVES	TOTALS	DISTRICT/ TOWNSHIP	NOTES
			LAST NAME	FIRST NAME	under 10	10 to 16	16 to 26	26 to 45	45 and over	under 10	10 to 16	16 to 26	26 to 45	45 and over					
Marblehead	266	6	Symmes	John			1			1		1					3		
Andover	101	20	Symmes	William Revd		1		1		1		1		1	1		5		
Salem	196	40	Symonds	Abigail			1			3			1				5		
Salem	200	11	Symonds	Benjamin				1		2	1			1			5		
Salem	196	39	Symonds	Ebenz	4		1	1			1		1				8		
Salem	196	41	Symonds	Eliza			1						1	1			3		
Salem	210	58	Symonds	Eliza										1			1		
Salem	196	44	Symonds	Hannah			1	1					1	1			4		
Salem	200	27	Symonds	Jacob			1						1				2		
Topsfield	20	2	Symonds	Jacob		1	1		1	1	1			1			6		
Salem	197	6	Symonds	James		1			1	1				1			4		
Salem	197	22	Symonds	John			1			3	1		1				6		
Salem	200	10	Symonds	John	1		2					1	1	1			6		
Salem	200	14	Symonds	John			1							1			2		
Salem	200	24	Symonds	John	2			1		1	1		1				6		
Salem	200	12	Symonds	Jonathan	1	2	1		1	3				1			9		
Boxford	135	53	Symonds	Joseph	1		1	1		1	3	1	1	1			10		
Middleton	16	38	Symonds	Joseph	1		1	1		4			1	1			9		
Salem	190	27	Symonds	Joseph	1	1	1		2				1	2			8		
Salem	196	37	Symonds	Lydia										1			1		
Salem	200	4	Symonds	Mary			2					2	1	1			6		
Salem	200	26	Symonds	Mehitl	1								1	1			3		
Salem	200	23	Symonds	Nancy										1			1		
Salem	197	20	Symonds	Nath	3			1		2	3	1		2			12		
Danvers	13	7	Symonds	Samuel	2		1			1	1		1				6		
Salem	196	33	Symonds	Samuel	3		1			1			1				6		
Boxford	135	35	Symonds	Stephen	1		1	1				2		1			6		
Salem	196	36	Symonds	Thorndike	3	1		1		2		1		1			9		
Salem	197	1	Symonds	Thos				1	1			3	1	1			7		
Salem	196	43	Symonds	William	1		1					1	1				4		
Salem	197	5	Symonds	William	1	3		1		1	1			1			9		
Salem	202	34	Symonds	Willm	4	1		1				1		1			8		
Gloucester	67	7	T*	Marry Widw			1							1			2		
Salem	218	41	Tabor	David	1			1						1			3		
Newburyport	180	15	Talbot	Nathaniel			1						1				2		
Salem	209	57	Taley	William	3			1					1				5		
Danvers	2	17	Tapley	Amos	2	2	1		1	1	1	1	1	1			11		
Danvers	2	15	Tapley	Asa	2	2	1	1		1	1		1				9		
Danvers	13	41	Tapley	Betsy	2								1	1			4		
Danvers	5	2	Tapley	David			1	1		2			1	1			6		
Danvers	3	10	Tapley	Gilbert				1			1		1				3		
Haverhill	151	3	Tapley	William				1						1			2		
Newbury	109	40	Tappan	Enoch	2		1	1		2		1	1	1			8		
Gloucester	61	29	Tappan	James	1			1		3	1	2					8		
Newbury	111	39	Tappan	Samuel	1			1		1	1		1				5		
Newbury	109	41	Tappan	Stephen	2	1	2		1	2	1	1					10		
Manchester	54	28	Tappon	Ebenz	4			1		1	1		2	1			10		
Lynnfield	235	3	Tarbel	Jona				1					1				2		
Lynnfield	235	4	Tarbel	Jona Junr				1		1	1		1				4		
Beverly	294	39	Tarbell	William	2			1					1		1		5		
Gloucester	67	8	Tarbox	Benja		1		1				2		1			5		
Beverly	302	33	Tarbox	Daniel	1			1		1			1				4		
Lynn	228	15	Tarbox	David	5		1	1					1	1			9		
Gloucester	72	15	Tarbox	Dorcas Wo			1							1			2		
Lynn	232	11	Tarbox	Ebenz		3		1		3	1			1			9		
Gloucester	72	14	Tarbox	Esther Wo		1				2		1					4		
Lynn	229	37	Tarbox	Nathl			1		2		1	2		2			8		
Salem	208	57	Tarbox	Thos				1		1			1				3		
Newburyport	180	17	Tarbox	William			1			1	1			1			3		
Lynn	229	32	Tarbox	Willm	2	1		1					1				5		
Gloucester	67	10	Tarr	Abraham	2			1						1			3		
Gloucester	82	12	Tarr	Andrew	1			1				1		1			4		
Gloucester	83	7	Tarr	Anna Wo				1		1				1			3		
Gloucester	82	8	Tarr	Benja		1		1		1			1	1			5		
Gloucester	82	23	Tarr	Benja 3d	1	1	1			1		1	1				6		
Gloucester	82	9	Tarr	Benja Junr			1	1		1		1	1	1			5		
Gloucester	83	22	Tarr	Betty Wo		1		1						1			3		
Gloucester	83	23	Tarr	Charles			1			1		1					3		
Gloucester	82	14	Tarr	Danl B.	1	1		1		1	1		1				6		
Gloucester	61	28	Tarr	David	2	1		1					1				5		
Gloucester	82	13	Tarr	David	1	1		1		2	1		1				7		
Gloucester	82	16	Tarr	Ebenz	2	2	1		1	2	1	2	1				12		
Gloucester	82	20	Tarr	Epes	1			1					1				3		
Gloucester	83	24	Tarr	Eunice										2			2		
Gloucester	82	11	Tarr	Francis	2		1			1	1	1					6		
Gloucester	82	10	Tarr	Jabez	1	1		1		4	2	1	1				11		
Gloucester	83	5	Tarr	James				1					1				2		
Gloucester	82	19	Tarr	Job	2		1	1		3	1		1				9		
Gloucester	82	24	Tarr	John	4			1			1	2	1				9		
Gloucester	82	21	Tarr	Jona	3			1		1			1	1			7		
Gloucester	82	17	Tarr	Nathl	3	1		1				1	1	1			8		
Gloucester	82	18	Tarr	Oliver	1			1				1	1	1			5		
Gloucester	82	25	Tarr	Saml	2				1	3	1	1	1				9		
Gloucester	69	4	Tarr	Solomon	1	1		1		1	1	1					6		
Salem	190	14	Tarrant	Susanna									1	1			2		
Salem	188	15	Tate	Thos	2			1		2			1				6		
Salem	214	20	Tatum	Jas	2			1		2			1				6		

272

TOWN	PG#	LN#	LAST NAME	FIRST NAME	FREE WHITE MALES					FREE WHITE FEMALES					TOTAL ALL OTHER	TOTAL SLAVES	TOTALS	DISTRICT/ TOWNSHIP	NOTES
					under 10	10 to 16	16 to 26	26 to 45	45 and over	under 10	10 to 16	16 to 26	26 to 45	45 and over					
Salem	205	14	Tay	Benja				1		1		2					4		
Salem	201	29	Tay	Ebenz		1	1						1	1			4		
Beverly	290	18	Tayler	Asa			1						1				2		
Danvers	3	19	Tayler	Daniel			1	2	1					1			5		
Danvers	3	22	Tayler	Daniel Junr	1		1	1		3			1				7		
Danvers	3	20	Tayler	Samuel			1			1			1				3		
Gloucester	61	26	Tayler	Thomas			1			1	1	1					4		
Gloucester	85	7	Tayler	William				1					1	1			3		
Amesbury	46	4	Taylor	Archibald Capt		1		1		1	1		1	1			6		
Salem	195	2	Taylor	Geo	1	1		1		1			1	1			6		
Rowley	131	38	Taylor	Jonathan	1		1	1					2				5		
Salem	210	1	Taylor	Samuel			1			2			1				4		
Salem	208	7	Teague	Wm	2		1	1		1	2		1				8		
Newburyport	180	1	Teed	Nathaniel	1			1		1		1		1			5		
Newburyport	180	9	Teel	John Wido of			1			1		1		1			4		
Newburyport	180	8	Teel	Joseph		1	2				1	2		1			7		
Salem	197	24	Telford	William	2	2			1	1			1				7		
Marblehead	257	24	Tenly	Thomas	1			1		1		1					4		
Bradford	125	48	Tenn	Silas	2	1		1		1			1				6		
Bradford	122	16	Tenney	John				1			1	1		2			5		
Rowley	128	14	Tenney	Oliver	1	1		1					1				4		
Topsfield	18	6	Tenney	Thomas	3	1		1			2		1				8		
Rowley	127	8	Tenny	David	1			1			1		1				4		
Rowley	128	46	Tenny	David		1		1		2			1	1			6		
Ipswich	279	43	Tenny	Elijah		1						1					2		
Rowley	131	51	Tenny	Nathl	1	1		1	1	1	1	3		1			10		
Rowley	128	31	Tenny	Oliver	2		1	1	2		1		1	2			10		
Newburyport	180	13	Tenny	Richard	1		2	2				2					7		
Rowley	132	4	Tenny	Richard	1		2		1				2	1			7		
Bradford	125	13	Tenny	Samuel	1	2		1	1	2	1	1					9		
Newburyport	180	14	Tenny	Samuel	1		1			1	1						4		
Bradford	122	32	Tenny	Shubal			3		1		1	1		1			7		
Bradford	125	19	Tenny	Solomon		2		1	1			1	1	1			7		
Bradford	125	46	Tenny	William		1		1		1			1				4		
Bradford	125	47	Tenny	William		1		1				2		1			5		
Amesbury	46	11	Tewksbury	Daniel		1		1		2	2			3			9		
Danvers	13	31	Tewksbury	Henry			1	1		2	1	1					6		
Amesbury	46	8	Tewksbury	Isaac	3		1		1		2	2	1				10		
Marblehead	246	4	Tewksbury	James			1	1		2			1	1			6		
Amesbury	46	9	Tewksbury	John			1		1			1					3		
Salem	197	43	Tewksbury	Mary	2	1			1	1			1	1			7		
Amesbury	46	10	Tewksbury	Moses	1		1	1		2	2		1				8		
Manchester	54	35	Tewxbury	Jacob Deac				1					1				2		
Manchester	54	36	Tewxbury	Jacob Junr	1			1					1				3		
Salem	195	28	Thayer	Benja				1		1	1	1					4		
Marblehead	265	8	Thayer	Isaac	1		1					1					3		
Marblehead	269	6	Thayer	Jeremiah				1				2		1			4		
Salem	195	43	Thayer	Stephen	1		2	1					1				5		
Rowley	129	36	Theyar	Samuel		1			2		1		1				5		
Newburyport	180	16	Thing	Josiah	1		1	1				1					4		
Beverly	291	8	Thissel	Ebenezer		1	1		1	1		1	1	1			7		
Beverly	302	2	Thissel	Hannah	1								1				2		
Beverly	297	10	Thissel	James		2			1		1	2		1			7		
Beverly	297	12	Thissel	James Jr			1					1					2		
Beverly	290	36	Thissel	Jeffrey	1	1	2	1		1	1	1	1				9		
Beverly	297	13	Thissel	John	1			1		1		1					4		
Beverly	297	11	Thissel	Lucy		1	1			2	2	1	1	1			9		
Beverly	300	32	Thissel	Lydia		1	1			2	1	1					6		
Beverly	290	40	Thissel	Mary								1	1	2			4		
Beverly	290	35	Thissel	Paul	2			1		1		1					5		
Beverly	290	37	Thissel	Sarah		1								1			2		
Beverly	290	43	Thissel	Sarah 2d	1					3	1						5		
Gloucester	68	13	Thomas	Anna Wo		1	1					2		1			5		
Beverly	302	36	Thomas	David	1			1		3		1					6		
Salem	216	10	Thomas	Eliza		2						2	1				5		
Marblehead	241	18	Thomas	Isaac											3		3		
Middleton	15	18	Thomas	Israel		1		1						1			3		
Salem	197	32	Thomas	Jethro			1						1				2		
Newbury	114	32	Thomas	Joseph				1					1				2		
Marblehead	269	4	Thomas	Martha		1	1						1	1			4		
Salem	199	4	Thomas	Mary									1				1		
Salem	210	7	Thomas	Moses		2	2	1		3	1	1					10		
Gloucester	58	26	Thomas	Nehemiah	1		1			1		1					4		
Middleton	15	22	Thomas	Rebecca									1				1		
Marblehead	263	3	Thomas	Reddin			1			1		1					3		
Marblehead	249	4	Thomas	Redding			1			1		1					3		
Middleton	16	10	Thomas	Richard	3	2			1					1			7		
Gloucester	86	16	Thomas	Samuel			1					1					2		
Gloucester	86	17	Thomas	Sara Wo	1	2								1			4		
Newburyport	180	20	Thomas	Thomas	1			1			1	1	1				5		
Gloucester	67	5	Thomas	William	1	1	1	1			1	2	1				8		
Middleton	16	26	Thomas	William				1						1			2		
Newburyport	180	19	Thomas	William	1		1	1					1				4		
Marblehead	252	25	Thompson	Abigail										1			1		
Manchester	54	32	Thompson	Benja	1		1					1					3		

TOWN	PG#	LN#	LAST NAME	FIRST NAME	M under 10	M 10 to 16	M 16 to 26	M 26 to 45	M 45 and over	F under 10	F 10 to 16	F 16 to 26	F 26 to 45	F 45 and over	TOTAL ALL OTHER	TOTAL SLAVES	TOTALS	DISTRICT/TOWNSHIP	NOTES
Marblehead	259	34	Thompson	Benjamin				2						1			3		
Marblehead	246	15	Thompson	Benjn 3rd			1			1		1					3		
Newburyport	179	25	Thompson	Charles			1			2			1				4		
Marblehead	260	17	Thompson	Cornelius			1							1			2		
Marblehead	246	32	Thompson	George	1		1			1		1					4		
Beverly	303	1	Thompson	James	2		1						1	1			5		
Gloucester	67	11	Thompson	James	1	1	1			2		1	1				7		
Andover	102	9	Thompson	John				1		2			1				4		
Marblehead	267	23	Thompson	John	1	2	1	1		1	1	1	2				10		
Salem	205	3	Thompson	Joseph	1	2		1		3		1	1				9		
Salem	213	43	Thompson	Mary	1		1					2	1				5		
Beverly	298	3	Thompson	Peter				1						1	1		3		
Marblehead	254	16	Thompson	Richard	2	1				1		1	1	1			7		
Marblehead	251	32	Thompson	Samuel	4		1	1			1	2	1				10		
Newburyport	179	24	Thompson	Samuel Wido of			3			1		2					6		
Marblehead	265	9	Thompson	Thomas	4	1		1		1	1		1				9		
Newburyport	179	23	Thompson	Thomas		1	2	1				2	1	2			9		
Marblehead	254	1	Thompson	William	1	1		1		2	2		1				8		
Marblehead	260	16	Thompson	William		1		1		2	1		1				6		
Beverly	303	7	Thomson	Jacob	1			1		2			1	1			6		
Salem	215	37	Thorn	William			1			1			1				3		
Beverly	303	5	Thorndike	Eleanor		1	1					1	1				4		
Beverly	300	31	Thorndike	Elizabeth									1	1			2		
Beverly	292	45	Thorndike	Henry	1	1		1		4	2		1				10		
Beverly	289	1	Thorndike	Israel Esq	6	3			1				3		1		14		
Beverly	300	39	Thorndike	Jeremiah			1					1					2		
Ipswich	275	47	Thorndike	Mary						1			2	1			4		
Beverly	303	6	Thorndike	Nicholas	2		1			2		1	1				7		
Marblehead	270	10	Thorner	Sarah	1								1	1			3		
Marblehead	270	11	Thorner	Sarah		2								1			3		
Danvers	3	34	Thornton	John	2		1	1					1				5		
Ipswich	274	45	Thornton	Lydia									2				2		
Salem	203	11	Thornton	Thos				1					2				3		
Gloucester	86	20	Thorp	Sarah Wo	1			1		1				1			4		
Marblehead	243	17	Thrasher	Sarah									2				2		
Rowley	128	21	Thurlow	Eliphalet	1		1			1			1	1			5		
Newbury	120	2	Thurlow	Enoch	2		1						1				4		
Rowley	128	32	Thurlow	John			1					1	1	1			4		
Newbury	112	17	Thurlow	Joseph	3	2	1			1			2	1			10		
Newbury	112	18	Thurlow	Lydia	1	1	1		1	1	1	1	1				8		
Rowley	128	23	Thurlow	Mark	1	1	1		1	2	1	1		1			9		
Newbury	115	43	Thurlow	Samuel		1	1					1	1	1			5		
Newbury	106	25	Thurlow	Simeon			1					1	2	1			5		
Beverly	306	21	Thursting	Enoch	1		1						1				3		
Gloucester	83	4	Thurston	Ambrose	3	1	1			1	2		1				9		
Newbury	118	1	Thurston	Benjamin		2		1		1	1		1				6		
Bradford	123	22	Thurston	Daniel		1	1	1		3	1		1				8		
Bradford	123	25	Thurston	Daniel		1		1		1		1		1			5		
Ipswich	276	36	Thurston	Daniel				1					1				2		
Gloucester	82	30	Thurston	Danl	3			3	1				2	1			10		
Danvers	8	36	Thurston	Ebenezer		1				1		1					3		
Newburyport	180	12	Thurston	Enoch	1		3	1		2			1	1			9		
Salem	189	45	Thurston	Henry											3		3		
Newbury	118	5	Thurston	John	2		1	1		1			1	1			7		
Gloucester	83	2	Thurston	Joseph				1						1			2		
Gloucester	83	3	Thurston	Joseph Junr		2		1			1			1			5		
Bradford	123	24	Thurston	Nathll	2	1	1	1	1				3				9		
Gloucester	83	1	Thurston	Saml	1		1			1			1				4		
Gloucester	77	23	Thurston	Stephen	1			1		1	3	1					7		
Newbury	105	2	Thurston	Stephen		1	1	1		3	3						9		
Andover	102	21	Thurton	Stephen	1			1		2			1				5		
Salem	209	31	Tibbet	Henry	1	2		1		1			1				6		
Ipswich	276	14	Tibbets	Timothy	1	1		1					1				4		
Newbury	116	27	Tictcomb	Joseph		2	1	1	1	1		2	1				9		
Newbury	106	10	Tictman	Caleb	1		1	1		4	2		1				10		
Newbury	106	9	Tictman	Simeon	3	1		1		1	1	1	1	1			10		
Marblehead	239	31	Tidder	John	1		2			1			1	1			6		
Marblehead	247	8	Tidder	Volentine		2		1					1	1			5		
Bradford	124	20	Tilden	Niles	2	1		1					1				5		
Lynn	227	15	Tilsbe	Henry		2		1				2					5		
Lynn	223	18	Tilsbe	Nehemiah	2		1	1					1				5		
Lynn	223	17	Tilsbe	Saml			1					1					2		
Lynn	223	19	Tilsbe	Sarah		1		1					3	1			6		
Ipswich	279	12	Tilton	Anna		1							1	1			3		
Amesbury	46	7	Tilton	Samuel	1		1			3			1				6		
Salem	204	12	Tink	Thos	1	2	1			1			1				6		
Salem	213	13	Tiplady	Elizabeth	2								1				3		
Methuen	156	9	Tippet	John	2	2		1	1	3	1	1	1	1			13		
Marblehead	249	12	Tishoe	John		3		1		1	2		1				8		
Marblehead	254	24	Tishoe	Peter				1						1			2		
Beverly	303	4	Tisser	Abigail		1							1	1			3		
Newburyport	179	44	Titcomb	Ann Wido		2							2	1	1		6		
Newburyport	179	36	Titcomb	Benariah				1				1	3	1			6		
Newburyport	179	38	Titcomb	Enoch		3	1		1	3		2	1				11		
Newburyport	179	41	Titcomb	Henry	2			1				1	1				5		
Newburyport	179	34	Titcomb	John B	2		1			1		1	1	1			7		
Newburyport	179	35	Titcomb	John L	3	1		1		1				1			7		

TOWN	PG#	LN#	LAST NAME	FIRST NAME	FREE WHITE MALES					FREE WHITE FEMALES					TOTAL ALL OTHER	TOTAL SLAVES	TOTALS	DISTRICT/ TOWNSHIP	NOTES
					under 10	10 to 16	16 to 26	26 to 45	45 and over	under 10	10 to 16	16 to 26	26 to 45	45 and over					
Newburyport	179	28	Titcomb	Jonathan				1		1		2		1			5		
Newburyport	179	29	Titcomb	Jonathan Jr	2			1		1	1		1				6		
Newbury	120	6	Titcomb	Joseph		2			1	1	1	2		1			8		
Newburyport	179	39	Titcomb	Joshua					1	2	1	2		1			7		
Newburyport	179	42	Titcomb	Mary Wido				1					1	1			3		
Newburyport	179	26	Titcomb	Michael					1			2		2			5		
Newburyport	179	27	Titcomb	Michael Jr					1			1		1			3		
Newburyport	179	37	Titcomb	Nicolas	1	1	4			3		2		1			12		
Newburyport	179	30	Titcomb	Richard					1				2				3		
Newburyport	179	31	Titcomb	Richard Jr	2		1					1					4		
Newburyport	179	40	Titcomb	Samuel			1	1	1	1	1		1	2			8		
Newburyport	179	43	Titcomb	Sarah Wido								1		1			2		
Newburyport	179	32	Titcomb	William	1	1	1		1	1	1	1		2			9		
Newburyport	179	33	Titcomb	William Jr	2			1		1			1				5		
Amesbury	46	6	Titromb	Anna Wid									1	1			2		
Amesbury	46	5	Titromb	Ichabod	1			1		2		1					5		
Beverly	303	37	Tittle	John		2	1		1	3		1	1	1			10		
Andover	103	26	Toby	Dinah											2		2		
Rowley	129	23	Todd	Benja		3	2		1	1	1	1					9		
Salem	217	58	Todd	Benja			1			2		1	1				5		
Rowley	131	20	Todd	Daniel			1		1			1	1				4		
Rowley	129	52	Todd	David	1		1		1	1	1			2			7		
Rowley	129	20	Todd	George	1	1			1	1	1			1			6		
Rowley	131	41	Todd	James			2	1			1	1		1			6		
Newburyport	179	19	Todd	Jeremy		3		1		1	1	1		1			8		
Newburyport	179	20	Todd	Joanna Wido	2		3	2		1			1	1			10		
Rowley	129	22	Todd	Jonathn	1	1			1	1	1			1			6		
Rowley	129	53	Todd	Nathan			1	1		1	1		1				5		
Rowley	130	9	Todd	Nelson		1	1	2		1	1	2	1				9		
Gloucester	82	22	Todd	Sarah Wo	2		1			1		1		1			6		
Newburyport	179	18	Todd	William	4	2			1		1	1		1			11		
Rowley	130	1	Todd	William	1		1	1	1	1		1		1			7		
Newburyport	179	21	Todd	William Wido of									1	1			2		
Newbury	108	23	Tomb	Samuel			1	1		3	1		2				8		
Haverhill	150	47	Tomkins	Isaac		1		1		2		2					6		
Marblehead	246	28	Topham	James			1	1				1	1				4		
Newburyport	179	13	Toppan	Abner	2	1	2		1	1		1		1			9		
Newburyport	179	11	Toppan	Amos	1		4	1			1	1		1			9		
Newburyport	179	6	Toppan	Benjamin	3	1			1	1	1	1	1	1			10		
Newburyport	179	7	Toppan	Benjamin H	1			1				1					3		
Newburyport	179	12	Toppan	Edward	3	1		1		1	2	1		1			10		
Newburyport	179	17	Toppan	Elizabeth Wido								1	1				2		
Newburyport	179	9	Toppan	Enoch		1	1	3		5		1	1				12		
Newburyport	179	15	Toppan	John	2			1		2	1		1	1			8		
Newburyport	180	21	Toppan	John Wido of								1	1	1			3		
Newburyport	179	10	Toppan	Joseph	1	2	1		1		1	2		1			9		
Newburyport	179	8	Toppan	Joshua	3			1		2	1			1			8		
Newburyport	179	16	Toppan	Samuel	2			1		2			1				6		
Newburyport	179	5	Toppan	Sewell	2			1		1		2		1			7		
Newburyport	179	14	Toppan	William	1	2		1		4				1			9		
Gloucester	66	14	Torres	Benj Capt				1					2				3		
Danvers	12	10	Torry	Joseph	2			1					1		1		5		
Newbury	115	13	Tory	John	1	1		1		1			1	1	1		7		
Beverly	292	38	Toutam	Ruth						1			2				3		
Andover	102	16	Town	Aaron				1				1		1			3		
Andover	102	17	Town	Aaron Junr	1			1		1		1					4		
Salem	196	10	Town	Amos	1			1					1				3		
Andover	102	10	Town	Asa	4	1	5		1	1		1	1				14		
Methuen	156	8	Town	Benjamin		1	3		1	1	1			1			8		
Andover	102	18	Town	Elijah	2	1	1			1		1					6		
Boxford	135	54	Town	John	2		2	1				1	1				7		
Boxford	136	3	Town	John		1	1		1	1		1		1			6		
Andover	102	20	Town	Mary						1		1		1			3		
Andover	102	13	Town	Nathan	1	2			1		1	1	1				7		
Andover	102	14	Town	Peter		1	3			1	2		1				9		
Andover	102	15	Town	Simeon				1		3		1	1				6		
Topsfield	21	35	Towne	Daniel				1					1				2		
Topsfield	18	1	Towne	David		1	2	1				2	1				7		
Topsfield	19	5	Towne	Elijah				1				1					2		
Topsfield	18	7	Towne	Ephriem			1	1				1		1			4		
Topsfield	19	1	Towne	Jacob Junr	1	2		1				1		2			7		
Topsfield	18	17	Towne	Joseph				1		2			1	1	1		5		
Topsfield	19	3	Towne	Joshua	2	1	1		1	1	1	1	1				9		
Salem	208	9	Towne	Saml	1			1		1		1					4		
Danvers	5	14	Towne	Samuel	1			1		1		1	1				6		
Danvers	8	11	Towne	Thomas	1			1	1				1	1			5		
Danvers	2	10	Towne	William		1			1				1	1			4		
Danvers	11	36	Towne	William			1			1		1					3		
Newbury	114	4	Townsen	Anny	1							1					2		
Andover	102	24	Townsend	Dennis	2	1		1		3			1				8		
Salem	210	31	Townsend	Pen				1		2		1	1				5		
Salem	217	49	Townsend	Samuel	2	1		1		1		1					6		
Salem	204	28	Townsend	Thos				1		3		1					5		
Lynnfield	236	23	Townshend	Daniel	3			1		2			1				7		
Salem	220	10	Towsend	Martha										1			1		
Salem	219	43	Towsend	Moses			1	1		2	2	1	1	1			9		

275

TOWN	PG#	LN#	LAST NAME	FIRST NAME	FREE WHITE MALES					FREE WHITE FEMALES					TOTAL ALL OTHER	TOTAL SLAVES	TOTALS	DISTRICT/ TOWNSHIP	NOTES
					under 10	10 to 16	16 to 26	26 to 45	45 and over	under 10	10 to 16	16 to 26	26 to 45	45 and over					
Salem	216	20	Towser	Ebenzr			1	1	1	2				1			6		
Newburyport	180	6	Tracy	John	2	1	1	1	2	3	1	2	1				14		
Newburyport	180	5	Tracy	Mary Wido	1		1			1	3	3		1			10		
Newburyport	180	4	Tracy	Merian Wido				1				1	1	1			4		
Newburyport	180	7	Tracy	Nicolas		1		1		2			2				6		
Newburyport	180	18	Trainer	James				1		1			1				3		
Marblehead	261	13	Trasher	John		1	2		1	4	1	1	1				11		
Gloucester	61	24	Trask	Abigal Widw						1		1	1	1			4		
Gloucester	62	29	Trask	Abigal Wo	1	1				2	1		1				6		
Beverly	294	16	Trask	Barnabas		1	1	1						1			4		
Beverly	293	40	Trask	Bartholomew	1		2		1			1		1			6		
Salem	201	3	Trask	Ben	1	2	2			1		1					7		
Beverly	292	19	Trask	Benja			1					1					2		
Salem	199	16	Trask	Benja		1	1	1		1		1					5		
Danvers	11	37	Trask	Daniel			1										1		
Beverly	294	15	Trask	Deborah	1							1		1			3		
Beverly	305	28	Trask	Ebenezer	1	1		1				2		1			6		
Beverly	305	29	Trask	Ebenezer Jr	4			1		2			1				8		
Gloucester	57	28	Trask	Ebenz		2		1		1		1					5	West Parish	
Beverly	304	22	Trask	Eliza										1			1		
Danvers	6	37	Trask	Ezra				1									1		
Bradford	122	44	Trask	Ezzra				1		4	1	1	1				8		
Danvers	11	26	Trask	Henry			1			1		1					3		
Gloucester	67	9	Trask	Israel Cap	2			1		3	1		1				8		
Beverly	292	22	Trask	Jeremiah	4	3	1	1		1	1		2				13		
Beverly	304	44	Trask	John	1		1	1		2	1			1			7		
Danvers	13	13	Trask	John	1		1							1			3		
Danvers	12	32	Trask	Jonathan	1	1			1	1			1	1			6		
Danvers	12	34	Trask	Joseph			1	1					2				4		
Salem	219	36	Trask	Joseph			1		2			1					4		
Danvers	11	35	Trask	Lydia	1							1	1	2			5		
Salem	197	33	Trask	Mary	1					2		1	2				6		
Salem	204	24	Trask	Mary									2				2		
Danvers	12	4	Trask	Mehitable				1					1				2		
Beverly	295	19	Trask	Molly	1									1			2		
Beverly	299	22	Trask	Nehemiah			1			1		2					4		
Beverly	290	27	Trask	Osman			3		1	2			3	1			10		
Beverly	292	36	Trask	Osman 2d		2	2		1			1		1			7		
Beverly	292	18	Trask	Retire	1				1				1	1			4		
Bradford	122	39	Trask	Samuel				1					1	1			3		
Bradford	122	40	Trask	Samuel		1	2		1	1				1			6		
Beverly	305	22	Trask	William		1		1						1			3		
Danvers	9	4	Trask	William		1		1		1	1						4		
Danvers	12	5	Trask	William	1			1					1				3		
Beverly	296	28	Trask	William 2d	2			1					1				4		
Ipswich	278	25	Treadwell	Aaron			1	1		1			1				4		
Ipswich	278	27	Treadwell	Aaron Junr			1			1			1				3		
Ipswich	278	55	Treadwell	Jabez	1	1	1	1						1			5		
Ipswich	275	45	Treadwell	Jacob	2	1			2	2			2		1		10		
Salem	190	38	Treadwell	John			1	1		1	1	1					5		
Salem	195	35	Treadwell	John			1	1		1	1		1				5		
Ipswich	276	23	Treadwell	Lidia	1	1						1	2				6		
Ipswich	275	46	Treadwell	Moses		1	1		1	1	2		1				7		
Ipswich	275	4	Treadwell	Nathaniel	1			1		1		1	1				5		
Ipswich	275	17	Treadwell	Nathaniel Jr	1		1					1			1		4		
Beverly	299	30	Treadwell	Nathl	1		1	1		1	1		1	1			7		
Ipswich	280	14	Treadwell	Nathl	2			1						1			4		
Ipswich	276	24	Treadwell	Priscilla										1			1		
Ipswich	276	1	Treadwell	William			1						1	1			3		
Marblehead	249	28	Trefry	Edward	1	1			1	1				1			5		
Marblehead	249	31	Trefry	Elizabeth										1			1		
Marblehead	253	21	Trefry	James	1			1		1				1			4		
Marblehead	243	22	Trefry	John	2			1		2				1			6		
Marblehead	244	11	Trefry	Sarah	1	1								1			3		
Marblehead	257	19	Trefry	William	2			1		1				1			5		
Marblehead	260	19	Trefry	William	1	1		1		1	2		1				7		
Ipswich	273	8	Tresser	Daniel		1		1						1			3		
Lynn	227	37	Trevitt	Richd					1			1		1			3		
Gloucester	61	25	Trewboday	John	1			1	2	1			2	1			8		
Wenham	307	19	Trivett	Samuel R		2	2	1		1		1		1			8		
Ipswich	281	7	Troop	Lucy	1		1					3	2	1			8		
Salem	198	7	Trosater	Samuel	3		1			2			1				7		
Beverly	295	7	Trout	Abraham	2			1		3	1		1				8		
Andover	102	25	Trow	Dudley	1			1		1	1		1				5		
Andover	102	22	Trow	John	3	1	1	1		2	2		2				12		
Andover	102	19	Trow	John Junr	1		1	1		3	1		1	1			9		
Beverly	293	36	Trow	Josiah	1			1						1			3		
Salem	219	35	Trow	Nath	1		1			1			1				4		
Danvers	9	10	True	Corier				1					1				2		
Salisbury	34	2	True	David	1		1	1		3			1				7		
Salisbury	34	4	True	Dudley		1		1	1			1	1	1			6		
Salisbury	33	33	True	Jabez	1	1		1		1			2				6		
Salisbury	34	3	True	Moses			1		1					2			4		
Salisbury	33	32	True	Saml Junr	1	1		1		3			1				7		
Salisbury	33	31	True	Samuel Dr			1	1					2				5		

276

TOWN	PG#	LN#	LAST NAME	FIRST NAME	FREE WHITE MALES					FREE WHITE FEMALES					TOTAL ALL OTHER	TOTAL SLAVES	TOTALS	DISTRICT/ TOWNSHIP	NOTES
					under 10	10 to 16	16 to 26	26 to 45	45 and over	under 10	10 to 16	16 to 26	26 to 45	45 and over					
Newburyport	180	11	Truesdale	Richard	1		1	1					1				4		
Newburyport	180	10	Truesdale	Samuel	1			1		1	1		1				5		
Andover	102	23	Trull	Levi				1		1		1					3		
Salem	191	40	Trumbel	Nath	2	3	1			1			1				8		
Amesbury	46	3	Trupell	Henry		1			1					1			3		
Amesbury	46	2	Trupell	Moses			1			1			1				3		
Manchester	54	34	Tuck	John			1		1	1	2		1				6		
Manchester	54	33	Tuck	John Junr	1			1		1		1	1				5		
Manchester	54	29	Tuck	Samll	2			1		1			1				5		
Manchester	54	31	Tuck	William Esq	2	1	1		1		1		2				8		
Beverly	294	31	Tuck	Samuel	2				1	1			1	1			6		
Marblehead	254	4	Tucker	Andrew			1			1		1					3		
Salem	198	8	Tucker	Andrew	3		1					2	1				7		
Wenham	308	29	Tucker	Barnard				1					1	1			3		
Ipswich	276	40	Tucker	David	2			1		1				1			5		
Marblehead	250	31	Tucker	Deborah								2					2		
Salem	199	6	Tucker	Desire		1						1	3	1			6		
Salem	199	8	Tucker	Edward		3	2	1	1	2			2	1			12		
Amesbury	46	12	Tucker	Elisha		1				1		1					3		
Marblehead	261	6	Tucker	Elizabeth	2	1	2			1		1		1			8		
Salem	198	23	Tucker	Geo			3	2	1	1	1	1		1			10		
Marblehead	247	23	Tucker	George		1	1		1	1	1			1			6		
Newburyport	179	47	Tucker	George		1		1		3			1				6		
Marblehead	247	32	Tucker	George Junr	1			1					1	1			4		
Beverly	291	42	Tucker	Henry	1			1		2			1				5		
Haverhill	150	48	Tucker	Henry	1			1					1				3		
Haverhill	151	2	Tucker	Ihabod			1	1		2	1		1				5		Probably Ichabod
Newbury	110	24	Tucker	Jacob		1	1					1		1			4		
Newburyport	179	46	Tucker	John		1	1						1	1			4		
Gloucester	67	4	Tucker	John Maj		1			1	2	1	1					6		
Gloucester	73	6	Tucker	Joseph				1			1		2				4		
Gloucester	82	28	Tucker	Joseph	1			1		2			1				5		
Salem	203	26	Tucker	Lewis	1		2	1		1		1	1				7		
Andover	102	12	Tucker	Martha Wid								1	1				2		
Salem	203	5	Tucker	Mary		1				1	1	1		1			5		
Gloucester	71	26	Tucker	Mary Wo						1	1		1				3		
Gloucester	61	27	Tucker	Nathl	1		1		1	2			1	1			7		
Gloucester	72	4	Tucker	Nathl		2		1		2			1				6		
Marblehead	240	20	Tucker	Nicholas		1	2		1	1	2		1				8		
Marblehead	240	19	Tucker	Nicholas Junr		1				1		1					3		
Gloucester	71	3	Tucker	Pegy Wo	1		1					1		1			4		
Salem	201	35	Tucker	Robt	3			1		1			1				6		
Salem	202	11	Tucker	Saml	2	1	1			1			1				6		
Danvers	11	43	Tucker	Sarah							1		1	1			3		
Newbury	114	34	Tucker	Sarah									2	2	1		5		
Salem	193	7	Tucker	Susanna		1	1						1				3		
Gloucester	82	29	Tucker	Willa	2			1		2			1				6		
Andover	102	11	Tucker	William	1	1	1			3			1				7		
Gloucester	71	2	Tucker	William	3	2		1	1			1	1				9		
Newburyport	179	45	Tucker	William				1		3			1				5		
Lynn	233	21	Tudors	Willm Family in Lynn		1	1						1		1		4		
Haverhill	150	8	Tuexbury	Jonathan		1				1		1					3		
Lynn	225	44	Tuffts	David	3			1		1	1		1	1			8		
Lynn	226	8	Tuffts	Grimes	1			1				1					3		
Salem	201	43	Tuffts	Grimes	1		1	1				1					4		
Salem	209	21	Tuffts	Ivory	1		2			1		1					5		
Newburyport	180	3	Tufts	Abigail Wido	1									1			2		
Lynn	223	22	Tufts	Anne	2		1			3		1		1			8		
Newburyport	180	2	Tufts	John	1		2		1		1			1			6		
Salem	193	27	Tufts	Richd	2			1		2			1				6		
Salisbury	34	6	Tukesbury	Daniel	1	1		1		2	1		1				7		
Salisbury	34	5	Tukesbury	David Dr		1	1		1				2	1			6		
Beverly	293	12	Turkin	Abigail		1							1	1			3		
Gloucester	70	13	Turner	Daniel	1			1		3			1				6		
Salisbury	34	1	Turner	Ebenz Dr	1		2		1			3		1			8		
Newbury	119	17	Turner	Israel				1	1	2	3		1				8		
Gloucester	82	27	Turner	John		2		1						1			4		
Gloucester	82	26	Turner	John Junr				1		2	1			1			5		
Marblehead	265	10	Turner	Samuel	1	1	3	1		3	3						12		
Salisbury	33	34	Turner	Samuel	1			1		2			1				5		
Newbury	119	16	Turner	William				1					1				2		
Gloucester	85	15	Turner	Willm			1			1		1					3		
Salem	209	38	Tussel	Joseph	2	2			1	2	1	2	1				11		
Salem	210	3	Tuttle	Edward	1		1			2	1	1					6		
Salem	192	21	Tuttle	Eliza								1		1			2		
Salem	198	32	Tuttle	James C.		1	1						1				3		
Hamilton	285	65	Tuttle	John		1	1							2			5		
Lynn	232	20	Tuttle	Thomas	1	1	1			1			1				5	West Parish	
Lynn	234	1	Tuttle	Willm			1			3	1		1	1			7		
Beverly	290	22	Twess	Robert		1			1			2	1	1			6		
Marblehead	255	13	Twisden	Samuel	2	2		1		1	1	1	1				9		
Marblehead	255	14	Twisden	Sarah			2					1		1			4		
Beverly	305	6	Twiss	Benjamin	1		1			2			1				5		
Beverly	294	18	Twiss	Dimon C				1		1			1				3		
Danvers	4	17	Twiss	Joseph					1	1			1	1			4		
Beverly	290	25	Twiss	Mehitable									1	1			2		
Danvers	4	5	Twiss	Peter			1		1	2			1				5		

TOWN	PG#	LN#	LAST NAME	FIRST NAME	M<10	M10-16	M16-26	M26-45	M45+	F<10	F10-16	F16-26	F26-45	F45+	TOTAL ALL OTHER	TOTAL SLAVES	TOTALS	DISTRICT/ TOWNSHIP	NOTES
Salem	221	10	Twist	John				1						1			2		
Boxford	134	50	Tyler	Abraham	1		1	1			1	1	1				6		
Boxford	133	9	Tyler	Broadst	3	1	1	1			1	2	1				10		
Gloucester	67	6	Tyler	James	1			1						1			3		
Boxford	134	27	Tyler	John	1	1	2	1		3		1	2	2			13		
Gloucester	63	13	Tyler	John	2	1		1				1		1			6	West Ward	
Andover	102	8	Tyler	Jonathan			1	1		3	1	1					7		
Newburyport	179	22	Tyler	Joseph	2			1		1	1		1				6		
Boxford	133	10	Tyler	Joshua			2			1		2					5		
Bradford	124	45	Tyler	Samuel	1		1	1		1		2					6		
Boxford	136	6	Tyler	Stephen	2	1		1		2			1				7		
Methuen	156	6	Tylor	Jacob	5				1	1	2		1				10		
Methuen	156	7	Tylor	Jacob Junr	2		2	1		1			1				7		
Methuen	156	5	Tylor	Jesse	3	1			1	2	1	1		1			10		
Haverhill	150	49	Tylor	Job	1	1			1	4		1	1		1		10		
Haverhill	151	1	Tylor	Joseph	1		1					1	1				4		
Newbury	109	43	Tyng	Dudley	2	1		1		2			1	2			9		
Gloucester	78	11	Tyork	Tammy Widw						2			1				3		
Ipswich	281	14	Underhill	Jeremiah			1			1			1	1			4		
Salem	217	44	Underwood	Sarah			1			1			1	1			4		
Andover	102	26	Upton	Abiel	3	1		1			1		2				8		
Danvers	6	25	Upton	Asa		1		1			1		2				5		
Salem	190	41	Upton	Edmund	2	2		1		2	1		1				9		
Danvers	6	26	Upton	Eli	1		2			1		1	1				6		
Danvers	15	6	Upton	Elizabeth			2			1		1	1				5		
Salem	208	28	Upton	Flora											6		6		
Danvers	2	24	Upton	George				1					2	1			4		
Salem	215	3	Upton	Jed	2	2	1	1				2		1			9		
Middleton	17	28	Upton	Jeremiah	1		1	1		1	1		1	1			7		
Danvers	6	27	Upton	Jesse	3		2	2					2	1			10		
Danvers	12	41	Upton	John		1	1	1						1			4		
Danvers	12	39	Upton	John Junr	1			1		1			1				4		
Salem	200	48	Upton	Paul	3	3	2	1				2	1				12		
Marblehead	249	23	Upton	Thomas	4	2		1		1	1		1				10		
Danvers	8	27	Usher	Daniel	1			1		1			1				4		
Marblehead	252	19	Valentine	Andrew	3	1		1		2	2		1				10		
Salem	207	18	Valpey	Abram	4	1		1					1				7		
Salem	207	25	Valpey	Joseph	4			1					1				6		
Salem	198	38	Vanderford	John	2			1					1				4		
Marblehead	259	6	Veal	Charles			1					1	1				3		
Salem	209	32	Veal	Mich		1				1		1					3		
Marblehead	240	1	Venning	Mary					1					1			2		
Salisbury	34	7	Verner	Thomas	3		1			1			1				6		
Danvers	14	1	Verry	Amos	1		1			2			1	1			6		
Danvers	12	27	Verry	Ephriem	3		1						1				5		
Danvers	5	38	Verry	Joseph			1	1						1			3		
Danvers	12	26	Verry	Joseph		2		1				1					4		
Beverly	290	29	Verry	Mary	3								1				4		
Danvers	4	18	Verry	William	2			1		2	2	1		1			9		
Salem	195	38	Very	Eliza		1						1	1	1			4		
Salem	210	15	Very	Isaac	3		1			1			1	1			7		
Salem	209	2	Very	James	1		1			1	1		1				5		
Salem	207	17	Very	Jona				1					1	1			3		
Salem	217	36	Very	Mary	1		1					1	1				4		
Salem	199	28	Very	Samuel	1		1	1		2	1	2	1				9		
Salem	212	48	Very	Samuel	2			1		1			1				5		
Newburyport	180	22	Vezie	Lydia									1	1			2		
Beverly	298	35	Vickeree	John			1	1		1	2		1				6		
Beverly	298	26	Vickeree	Knot	1	1	1	1		3	2		1				10		
Beverly	298	28	Vickeree	Richard	4			1		1			1				7		
Beverly	298	30	Vickeree	William	1			1		3			1				6		
Marblehead	240	16	Vickery	Alice	1	1				1			1	1			5		
Salem	198	30	Vickery	David	2	3		1		2			1	1			10		
Marblehead	247	7	Vickery	Eli				1					1	1			3		
Marblehead	265	11	Vickery	Samuel	2			1		1	1	1	1				7		
Marblehead	244	1	Vickery	William	2			1		1			1				5		
Marblehead	245	33	Vikery	Elisabeth										1			1		
Salem	211	20	Vincent	Joseph			3	1				1	1	1			7		
Salem	211	26	Vincent	Joseph			2	1			1	1	1	3			9		
Salem	217	51	Vincent	Mathew	2	2		1		1			1	1			8		
Lynn	233	24	Vinning	Saml		2	1	1					2				6		
Marblehead	253	10	Vinsent	John				1						1			2		
Beverly	304	33	Wadden	Hannah		1							1	2			4		
Beverly	302	5	Wadden	Isaac		1							1				2		
Marblehead	246	5	Wadden	Jacob		1							1	1			3		
Marblehead	254	32	Wadden	John B.	3			1		1	1		1				7		
Ipswich	278	48	Wade	John	1	1	1	1		2			1				7		
Ipswich	278	45	Wade	Nathaniel	1	1		1	1	1	1	1	1				8		
Ipswich	278	47	Wade	Ruth									2				2		
Ipswich	278	46	Wade	Thomas	3			1		1			1				6		
Salisbury	34	14	Wadleigh	Adams	1			1		1			1	1			5		
Salisbury	34	29	Wadleigh	Anna Wd								1	1				2		
Salisbury	34	28	Wadleigh	Benja	3	1		1		2	1		1				9		
Salisbury	34	31	Wadleigh	Ephrm	1	1	1	1		3		1	1	1			10		
Salisbury	34	13	Wadleigh	Joseph Capt	3		1	1		2		1		2			10		
Salisbury	34	30	Wadleigh	Philip	2	1	2	1		2		2	1				11		
Danvers	2	2	Wadsworth	Benjm Revd	2			1					2		1		6		

278

TOWN	PG#	LN#	LAST NAME	FIRST NAME	FREE WHITE MALES					FREE WHITE FEMALES					TOTAL ALL OTHER	TOTAL SLAVES	TOTALS	DISTRICT/ TOWNSHIP	NOTES
					under 10	10 to 16	16 to 26	26 to 45	45 and over	under 10	10 to 16	16 to 26	26 to 45	45 and over					
Gloucester	83	29	Wainright	Thomas	3			1		1		1					6		
Amesbury	46	20	Wait	Daniel	1				1	2	1		1				6		
Amesbury	46	17	Wait	John	1			1		1	1	1					5		
Amesbury	46	22	Wait	Sylvanus	1		1					1					3		
Ipswich	280	13	Waite	Aaron	3	1		1		2	1		1	1			10		
Salem	190	4	Waite	Edmund	2			1		2			1	1			7		
Ipswich	276	2	Waite	Judith		2	2				1			1			6		
Salem	195	33	Waitt	Aaron			1	1	1	1			1	1			5		
Marblehead	258	32	Waitt	Elias			1			1			1				3		
Lynn	228	8	Waitt	Jabez	1			1					1				3		
Marblehead	240	12	Waitt	Jacob					1	3	3	1	1				9		
Marblehead	248	21	Waitt	John		2	2	1	1		1	2		1			10		
Marblehead	267	28	Waitt	John	1	2		1		3		1	1				9		
Danvers	4	34	Waitt	Jonathan	2			1		1	1		1				6		
Marblehead	265	12	Waitt	Peter	1		1			1		1					4		
Marblehead	269	32	Waitt	Sarah	1					1			1				3		
Marblehead	248	18	Waitt	William				1						2			3		
Salem	208	39	Wakefield	John	2	1		1		1	2	2	1				10		
Beverly	299	44	Wakefield	Nathl	1	1	1			1			1				5		
Newburyport	181	19	Wakefield	William			1			2		1					4		
Danvers	7	17	Walcut	John	3	1		1	1		1		1	1			9		
Salem	211	21	Walden	Joseph	3	1		1		1			1				7		
Lynn	225	32	Walden	Nathl	4			1		1			1				7		
Salem	193	42	Waldo	Jona Jur			1						1				2		
Salem	189	9	Waldo	Jonathan		2	1		1	1	1	1	1				8		
Beverly	296	20	Wales	David	2			1		1	1						5		
Beverly	301	3	Wales	John			1					1					2		
Beverly	297	38	Wales	Mary						1				1			2		
Marblehead	246	8	Walfrey	John	1			1					1				3		
Andover	103	4	Walker	Abbot	1			1		1			1				4		
Bradford	123	18	Walker	Benjamin	2	1		1	1		1	1	1				8		
Lynn	226	3	Walker	David				1				1	1				3		
Haverhill	151	4	Walker	James		1			1				1				3		
Haverhill	152	1	Walker	John	2			1					1				4		
Marblehead	265	15	Walker	Mary	3								1				4		
Marblehead	240	21	Walker	Moses			1	1					1				3		
Haverhill	151	6	Walker	Nathll		2	1	1	1			3		1			9		
Andover	103	21	Walker	Prince											3		3		
Bradford	123	20	Walker	Richard		1	1		1	1			3				7		
Haverhill	151	21	Walker	Samuel	1				1				1				3		
Salem	220	35	Walkins	Saml					1				1				2		
Gloucester	67	21	Wallace	David		1			1			1		1			4		
Gloucester	72	16	Wallace	John					1			1					2		
Gloucester	57	29	Wallace	Joseph	3	1		1		1	2	1	1				10	West Parish	
Newburyport	181	28	Wallace	Robert	1		1		1	1				3			7		
Gloucester	72	17	Wallace	Saml		1			1	3			1				6		
Newburyport	181	27	Wallace	Samuel			1						1				2		
Ipswich	280	6	Wallice	Aaron	2			1		4			1				8		
Hamilton	285	14	Wallice	David		1		1		3	1		1				7		
Ipswich	280	7	Wallice	Robert	1				1					2			4		
Rowley	127	11	Wallingford	Benja	1				1					2			4		
Bradford	126	13	Wallingford	James			1						2				3		
Bradford	126	2	Wallingford	Nathll		1	1			1		1		1			5		
Beverly	296	31	Wallis	Barthm	1	1	2		1	1	1			1			8		
Beverly	298	15	Wallis	Bartholomew Jr		1				1		1					3		
Beverly	298	40	Wallis	Benja				1		1	1	1					4		
Beverly	304	25	Wallis	Daniel		1	1	1	1		1	1	1	1			8		
Danvers	12	36	Wallis	Dennison		2	1	1			1	2					7		
Beverly	296	17	Wallis	Ebenezer	1		1	1		2			1				6		
Beverly	300	6	Wallis	Eleazer	1	2		1			1		2				7		
Beverly	296	12	Wallis	Hannah	2	2	2		1	2	1		1				11		
Beverly	295	44	Wallis	Hezekiah	1			1		4	1		1				8		
Beverly	293	13	Wallis	James	2			1		1			1				5		
Beverly	296	11	Wallis	John		2	1	1		3	1	1	1				10		
Hamilton	285	18	Wallis	Lidia								1		1			2		
Beverly	294	24	Wallis	Mary			2					1		1			4		
Salem	191	39	Wallis	Moses			1					1					2		
Beverly	300	11	Wallis	Nathl			1				1		1	1			5		
Salem	196	24	Wallis	Robt	1	1		1		1			1				5		
Beverly	302	24	Walls	Thomas	1	2		1					1				5		
Newburyport	180	31	Walsh	Michael	1			1		2	3		1				8		
Newburyport	180	32	Walsh	Richard	1		1		1	1	1	1	1	1			7		
Lynnfield	235	22	Walton	Josiah	3			1		1			1				6		
Lynnfield	235	20	Walton	Nathan					1	1			1	1			4		
Salisbury	34	8	Walton	Saml Capt				1		1			1	1	1		5		
Lynn	230	29	Walton	Willm	1	1	1	1					1				5		
Salem	202	10	Ward	Andrew	1			1				1					3		
Salem	213	20	Ward	Andrew		1			1		1			1			4		
Salem	220	30	Ward	Andrew	3			1		1			1				6		
Salem	209	1	Ward	Benja										1			1		
Salem	212	49	Ward	Benja	1				1					1			3		
Salem	211	3	Ward	Eben B.	1	1	1	1		1	1		1				7		
Salem	214	15	Ward	Geo	1			1		1			1				4		
Salem	203	37	Ward	James			1						1				2		
Salem	206	9	Ward	Joshua				1			1	2		1			5		
Salem	206	10	Ward	Joshua Junr		1				1	1	1					5		
Salem	213	38	Ward	Nath	1			1				1					3		

279

TOWN	PG#	LN#	HEADS OF HOUSEHOLD LAST NAME	FIRST NAME	FREE WHITE MALES under 10	10 to 16	16 to 26	26 to 45	45 and over	FREE WHITE FEMALES under 10	10 to 16	16 to 26	26 to 45	45 and over	TOTAL ALL OTHER	TOTAL SLAVES	TOTALS	DISTRICT/ TOWNSHIP	NOTES
Salem	192	10	Ward	Richd	1		2		1	1		2	2	2	1		12		
Salem	192	5	Ward	Saml	3			1				1	1				6		
Salem	209	7	Ward	Samuel	1	3	2		1	2		2	1	1			13		
Beverly	298	10	Ward	William				1			1			2			4		
Salem	188	31	Ward	William	1	1		1		1	2	1	1				8		
Salem	199	33	Ward	Nath	1			1				1					3		
Salem	190	19	Warden	John				1				1		1			3		
Newburyport	181	29	Warden	Martha Wido	1							2	1				4		
Salem	199	7	Wardwell	Abiel				1		1			1				3		
Andover	103	2	Wardwell	Daniel			1					1	1				3		
Andover	103	3	Wardwell	Ezekiel	1		1		2	1	1			2			8		
Andover	103	8	Wardwell	Jeremiah			1										1		
Andover	103	10	Wardwell	John	2			1				2					5		
Andover	103	6	Wardwell	Joshua	1			1						1			3		
Andover	102	29	Wardwell	Nathan	2			1		3			1				7		
Andover	103	7	Wardwell	Ruth									1				1		
Andover	102	30	Wardwell	Simon	3	2	2		1	3			1	1			13		
Newburyport	180	39	Warker	Charles	2	1		1					1	1			6		
Manchester	54	37	Warner	Abrm			1			1			1				3		
Marblehead	266	18	Warner	Elizabeth	1		2			1	2		1	1			8		
Newburyport	180	40	Warner	Groye	2	1		1					1	1			6		
Newbury	111	6	Warner	Lucy	1	1		1				1	1				5		
Ipswich	277	3	Warner	William					1			1		1			3		
Ipswich	280	5	Warner	William	2	1	2	1				1	1	2			10		
Gloucester	67	16	Warren	Danl Colo				1	2			1	1				5		
Marblehead	265	18	Warren	John	1			1		1							3		
Rowley	127	18	Warren	Jonas				1		2			1				4		
Salem	215	1	Warren	Sarah	1	1				1				1			4		
Gloucester	67	12	Warren	Willm Capt	1			1					1				3		
Newburyport	181	17	Waterman	Luther			2	1				2					5		
Salem	211	2	Waters	Esther	1									1			2		
Salem	211	45	Waters	John	1			1				1					3		
Salem	209	42	Waters	Joseph	2			1		2	2	2		1			10		
Danvers	9	40	Waters	Lydia										1			1		
Salem	215	14	Waters	Mary								1		1			2		
Salem	191	13	Waters	Robert	2			1		1		1	1	2			8		
Salem	208	46	Waters	Sarah						2			1				3		
Beverly	305	33	Waters	Silus	1				1	1	1		1				5		
Beverly	299	14	Waters	Stephen					1	1	1						3		
Salem	219	5	Waters	Thos	1		1					1					3		
Salem	203	34	Watkins	Benja			3	1				1					5		
Newburyport	181	26	Watkins	William			1	1				1		3			6		
Gloucester	68	25	Watson	John			1					1					2		
Salem	216	43	Watson	John	1	1		1		2	2	1	1				9		
Salem	188	23	Watson	Nath			1			1		1					3		
Gloucester	67	18	Watson	Robert	1	2		1		1			1				6		
Lynn	226	42	Watts	Daniel	5	1		1		1			1				9		
Salem	192	41	Watts	Hannah										1			1		
Lynn	227	3	Watts	Jacob	1			1		1			1				4		
Lynn	231	15	Watts	John			1	1					1	1			4		
Lynn	227	4	Watts	John Junr			1			1		1					3		
Middleton	18	3	Watts	Mary									1				1		
Salem	212	21	Webb	Ben	3	2		1		1	1	1	1				10		
Salem	208	50	Webb	Benja			1				1						2		
Salem	212	10	Webb	Benja	1	1	7	4	2	4		1	1		1		22		
Haverhill	151	23	Webb	Daniel				1					1				2		
Salem	211	30	Webb	Hannah			1				1		1	1	1		4		
Salem	212	43	Webb	Henrh			1			2			1				4		
Salem	197	25	Webb	Joanna	1								2				3		
Salem	219	38	Webb	John				1					1				2		
Salem	219	21	Webb	Joseph			1			3	1		1				6		
Salem	220	1	Webb	Joshua	1		1	1					1				4		
Salem	207	52	Webb	Michael	2	1		1		1	1	1	1				8		
Danvers	4	31	Webb	Nathl	2	1	2		1	3		1	1				11		
Amesbury	46	18	Webb	Samuel			1					1					2		
Salem	217	30	Webb	Samuel	1			1		2		1		1			6		
Salem	209	40	Webb	Stephen		1	1	1		1	1	2	1				8		
Salem	217	41	Webb	Stephen			1			3			1				5		
Salem	217	55	Webb	Thos			1					1					2		
Salem	218	22	Webb	Wm	2			1		2			1				6		
Gloucester	62	1	Webber	Benja	2	3		1		1	1	2	1				11		
Methuen	156	13	Webber	Benjamin	1	1	2		1	1	1		1	1			9		
Methuen	156	14	Webber	Daniel	3			1		3			2				9		
Wenham	309	16	Webber	Elizabeth	1						1	1					3		
Marblehead	269	18	Webber	George	1			1		1		1					4		
Gloucester	62	2	Webber	Ignatius	2	1		1		1	2	1	1				9		
Salisbury	34	22	Webber	Joseph Capt			1					1					2		
Beverly	290	5	Webber	Nathll			1			2		1					4		
Beverly	299	20	Webber	Samuel	1		1	1		1		1					5		
Beverly	306	3	Webber	William	2	2	1		1	1	1	1		1			10		
Beverly	304	32	Webber	William Jr	2		1					1					4		
Marblehead	266	24	Webster	Ambrose			1			1		1					3		
Haverhill	151	47	Webster	Caleb	2	3		1		2			1				9		
Salisbury	34	24	Webster	Daniel		1	2	1						1			5		
Salisbury	34	21	Webster	Daniel Junr	1			1					1				3		
Amesbury	46	13	Webster	David	1		1			2			1				5		
Haverhill	151	42	Webster	David		1			1	1		1		2			6		

TOWN	PG#	LN#	LAST NAME	FIRST NAME	FREE WHITE MALES					FREE WHITE FEMALES					TOTAL ALL OTHER	TOTAL SLAVES	TOTALS	DISTRICT/ TOWNSHIP	NOTES
					under 10	10 to 16	16 to 26	26 to 45	45 and over	under 10	10 to 16	16 to 26	26 to 45	45 and over					
Salisbury	34	25	Webster	Enoch			1	1		2			1				5		
Haverhill	151	46	Webster	Isaac	1		1		1		1		1				5		
Salisbury	34	17	Webster	John	1			1		1		1					4		
Salisbury	34	16	Webster	Jona	1			2		1		1		1			6		
Haverhill	151	37	Webster	Jonathan		2		1			1	1		1			6		
Gloucester	83	12	Webster	Joshua	3			1		1	2		1				8		
Haverhill	151	39	Webster	Joshua	5	2	1		1	1		1	1				12		
Ipswich	283	18	Webster	Josiah				1					1				2		
Bradford	122	23	Webster	Moses		1		1		2		1	1				6		
Haverhill	151	38	Webster	Moses			2		1			2	1		1		7		
Salisbury	34	23	Webster	Moses	2			1		1			1				5		
Haverhill	151	40	Webster	Moses Junr		1	2		1			2		1			7		
Bradford	122	27	Webster	Samuel		1		2		1	1	1	1				7		
Salisbury	34	20	Webster	Samuel			1	1						1			3		
Beverly	304	19	Webster	Sarah			1							1			2		
Haverhill	151	43	Webster	Stephen	2	1	1	1	1	1			1				8		
Haverhill	151	41	Webster	Stephen 3d	1		1	1	1		1			2			7		
Haverhill	151	45	Webster	Stephen 4th	2			1					1				4		
Amesbury	46	16	Webster	Stephen Capt	2			1			1	1					5		
Haverhill	151	44	Webster	Stephen Junr	2		2		1	1	2	1		2			11		
Bradford	122	26	Webster	Thomas			1	1		1		1					4		
Amesbury	46	23	Weed	Charles				1		2		1		1			5		
Amesbury	46	28	Weed	David		1	1		1			1		1			5		
Amesbury	46	24	Weed	Elijah			1			1			1				3		
Amesbury	46	26	Weed	Ephm				1						1			2		
Amesbury	46	25	Weed	Ephm Capt		1	2	1	1			1		1			7		
Amesbury	46	27	Weed	Isaac			1		1			2		1			5		
Newburyport	181	31	Weed	William	1	1	1	1		2			1				7		
Danvers	9	11	Welch	Betty	1		2			1				1			5		
Salem	192	20	Welch	Thos			1	1					1				3		
Newbury	114	6	Weld	Daniel			1		1	1		1	1				5		
Amesbury	47	4	Weld	Elias Dr.			1			1			1				3		
Marblehead	242	30	Weld	Payson	2		1					1					4		
Salem	193	19	Wellman	Ezekl	1	1		1	1			2		1			7		
Salem	196	16	Wellman	Mary									1	1			2		
Salem	213	4	Wellman	Mary	1	1					1	1	1	1			6		
Salem	219	27	Wellman	Mary								1		1			2		
Salem	219	49	Wellman	Timo	1	1	1	1		3	1	2	1				11		
Salem	214	5	Wellman	Timothy	3	1		1		1		1	2	1			10		
Salem	219	44	Wellman	Timothy			1					1					2		
Newbury	112	35	Wells	Daniel			1						1				2		
Haverhill	151	15	Wells	David				1			1			1			3		
Newburyport	180	35	Wells	David				1		2				1			4		
Ipswich	274	13	Wells	Elizabeth										2			2		
Ipswich	279	15	Wells	John	1			1				1		1			4		
Newburyport	180	33	Wells	John		1		1				1	1				4		
Newburyport	180	34	Wells	John Jr	1	1	1	1			1	1	1				7		
Ipswich	277	5	Wells	Jonathan			1			1		1					3		
Salisbury	34	18	Wells	Joseph		1		1		1	2	1	1				6		
Newburyport	180	36	Wells	Moses	2		1			1	1	1					6		
Beverly	302	37	Wells	Nathaniel	1			1		1		1					4		
Ipswich	280	23	Wells	Nathaniel		1			2			1	1	1	1		6		
Marblehead	267	25	Wells	Polly						1			1				2		
Salisbury	34	19	Wells	Thomas	2	1	1	1			1	1	1				8		
Danvers	8	35	Wells	Willebie	2	1	1					2					6		
Lynn	229	30	Welman	Caleb	1			1						1			3		
Lynnfield	235	21	Welman	Jona				1				2	1				4		
Lynnfield	237	2	Welman	Mehetable								1	2	2			5		
Marblehead	265	16	Welsh	Deborah		1						1		1			3		
Amesbury	46	21	Welsh	Jonathan			2					1		1			4		
Newburyport	181	2	Wessell	James Wido of			3			1	1		1				6		
Lynn	224	19	Wesson	George	2		1			1			1				5		
Beverly	291	30	West	Anna	1	2	2					2		2			9		
Gloucester	62	7	West	Benja	1	2	1	1	1	5	1	2		1			15		
Salem	215	23	West	Benja		1	1	1			2	1					6		
Salem	206	53	West	Edward	1		1			1	1	2	1				7		
Haverhill	151	12	West	Henry	1		2		1	2	1		1	2			10		
Bradford	122	33	West	Isaac			1	1					1				3		
Manchester	55	2	West	John	2			2		2				1			7		
Haverhill	151	13	West	Mary			3	1					1	1			6		
Salem	207	9	West	Nath	1	3		1		2	1	1	3				12		
Haverhill	151	31	West	Richard	1		1			1		1					4		
Haverhill	151	48	West	Thomas	2	1		1		2			1				7		
Salem	206	52	West	William				1					2	2			5		
Salem	192	11	Weston	Nathl	2	1		1		2	3	1	1				11		
Gloucester	77	6	Whalen	Michael	1			1		1	1	1					5		
Gloucester	73	5	Wharfe	Abraham		1			1	3			1	1			7		
Gloucester	84	20	Wharfe	Abraham Junr	1	1		1		2	1		1				7		
Gloucester	73	4	Wharfe	Arther					1					1			2		
Gloucester	72	24	Wharfe	David	3	1				2	2	1	1	1			11		
Gloucester	62	3	Wharfe	Isaac	1				1	2	1		1	1			7		
Gloucester	85	1	Wharfe	John		2		1		2		1	1	1			8		
Gloucester	85	5	Wharfe	Noby Wo	W		1						1	1			3		
Gloucester	71	11	Wharfe	Saml		1		1				1		1			4		
Gloucester	59	4	Wharfe	Sarah Widw	2							2		1			5		
Gloucester	84	32	Wharfe	Sarah Wo	2							2					4		
Gloucester	76	34	Wheeler	Aaron	2	2		1	1	1		2	1	1			11		

281

TOWN	PG#	LN#	HEADS OF HOUSEHOLD		FREE WHITE MALES					FREE WHITE FEMALES					TOTAL ALL OTHER	TOTAL SLAVES	TOTALS	DISTRICT/ TOWNSHIP	NOTES
			LAST NAME	FIRST NAME	under 10	10 to 16	16 to 26	26 to 45	45 and over	under 10	10 to 16	16 to 26	26 to 45	45 and over					
Gloucester	77	33	Wheeler	Benja		1	1		1					1			4		
Gloucester	77	34	Wheeler	Daniel		1	1						1				3		
Gloucester	77	35	Wheeler	John D.	2	1		1		1		1					6		
Rowley	128	35	Wheeler	Jonathn		1		1				1		1			4		
Salem	197	37	Wheeler	Joseph	1			1		1	1		1				5		
Gloucester	77	31	Wheeler	Moses		1	2	1		4		1	1	1			12		
Newburyport	180	26	Wheeler	Moses	1	1		1				1		1			5		
Marblehead	265	19	Wheeler	Richard		1		1		1			1	1			5		
Wenham	307	2	Wheeler	Ruben	2			1		2	1		1				7		
Gloucester	78	1	Wheeler	Saml	2	1		1		1			1				6		
Newburyport	180	27	Wheeler	Samuel	3	1		1		2			1				8		
Salem	197	17	Wheeler	Thos	3	1		1		1	2		1				9		
Newburyport	180	41	Wheelwright	Abraham	3	1	1		1	2		1	1	2			12		
Newbury	111	33	Wheelwright	Ebenezer	2	1		1		4	1		2				11		
Newburyport	181	34	Whelpley	Anson			1						1				2		
Gloucester	67	28	Whipple	David	1		1			2			1				5		
Hamilton	285	74	Whipple	John	1		1		1			1	1	1			6		
Hamilton	285	78	Whipple	John		1		1		1		1		1			5		
Hamilton	285	64	Whipple	Jonathan	3		1		1	1	2	1		1			10		
Danvers	5	23	Whipple	Marey									1	1			2		
Hamilton	285	73	Whipple	Matthew		2		1	1				1				5		
Hamilton	285	77	Whipple	Nathaniel		1		1					3	1			6		
Hamilton	285	88	Whipple	Samuel	1			1					1				3		
Hamilton	285	79	Whipple	Sarah										2			2		
Hamilton	284	1	Whipple	William		1	1		1	1	4			1			9		
Haverhill	151	36	Whitaker	Peter	2			1	1	1			1				6		
Haverhill	151	35	Whitaker	William	2	1		1		2			1				7		
Newburyport	181	5	Whitcher	Elizabeth Wido										2			2		
Rowley	129	13	White	Anna	1		1						1	1			4		
Gloucester	73	12	White	Anna Wo	2	2	1			1			2	1			9		
Salem	213	5	White	Chrisr											7		7		
Methuen	156	16	White	Elizabeth	1	1	1	2		3	1	1		1			11		
Newburyport	181	25	White	Gilman	3		1	1		1	1	1	1				9		
Beverly	299	37	White	Henry	1	1	1		1	2	1		1				8		
Gloucester	78	4	White	Henry		1		1		1				1			4		
Gloucester	72	21	White	James	1		1			3			1				6		
Danvers	3	3	White	John	1	2	1		1				1	1			7		
Gloucester	68	5	White	Jos Doct	1		1			2			1	1			6		
Danvers	8	7	White	Joseph	2		1			2			1				6		
Salem	212	12	White	Joseph			2	1					1	1	1		6		
Haverhill	151	8	White	Leonard	1			2		3	3	2	1		1		15		
Danvers	12	13	White	Lucreece		1				3			1				5		
Salem	218	50	White	Margt										1			1		
Danvers	6	7	White	Samuel	3		1			2	1		1				8		
Haverhill	151	7	White	Samuel		2	2	1				2	1	1			9		
Haverhill	151	11	White	Samuel Junr		1		1		4			1				7		
Haverhill	151	33	White	Thomas M.			1						1		1		3		
Gloucester	85	8	White	William		1		1	1	1			1				5		
Hamilton	285	95	White	William	2			1		1			1				5		
Salem	203	1	Whitefoot	Sarah	2	3							1				6		
Newburyport	181	32	Whitehouse	Stephen	3		1						1				5		
Newbury	110	19	Whitemore	Ebenezer	2					2			1				6		
Hamilton	285	26	Whitfield	Thomas				1		1			1				3		
Salem	218	54	Whitford	John		1							1				2		
Salem	189	2	Whitford	Samuel	1		1			1	1		1				5		
Middleton	18	1	Whitford	William	1		1	1					1				4		
Gloucester	77	32	Whitham	Jonah	2			1		1			1				5		
Haverhill	151	28	Whiting	John				1					1	1			3		
Newburyport	181	24	Whiting	Joseph			1					1					2		
Lynn	234	8	Whitman	Joseph	1			1		2			1				5		
Hamilton	285	111	Whitmarsh	Zakariah			1						1				2		
Newbury	111	9	Whitmore	Amos		1		1		1	2	1					6		
Newbury	109	13	Whitmore	Daniel		1		1					3	1			6		
Newburyport	180	25	Whitmore	Jonathan		1		1					1	1			4		
Newburyport	180	24	Whitmore	Joseph	2		1							1			4		
Newburyport	181	18	Whitney	Elisha		1		1					2	1	1		6		
Beverly	304	5	Whitney	Elisha Eaq	2	1		1		2	1	2	2				12		
Lynn	232	32	Whitney	Isaiah			1			1							3	West Parish	
Salem	206	1	Whittamore	Saml	1	1		1				2		1			6		
Danvers	10	31	Whittemore	Daniel			1						1				2		
Middleton	18	5	Whittemore	Edmund				1									1		
Danvers	10	8	Whittemore	Hannah								1		1			2		
Salisbury	34	10	Whittemore	Jacob	2	1	1	2	1	1		1	1	1			11		
Danvers	10	32	Whittemore	Joseph				1				1		1			3		
Newburyport	180	23	Whittemore	Joseph		1		1		1	1		1				6		
Gloucester	62	5	Whittemore	Joshua	1			1		1	1	1					6		
Salem	218	37	Whittemore	Mary		1								1			2		
Gloucester	61	30	Whittemore	Samll Esq		1	1	1	1	1	3	1		2			11		
Lynn	228	37	Whittemore	Willm			1							1			2		
Amesbury	46	14	Whitten	Rhoda Wid						1			1				2		
Danvers	6	2	Whitten	William Jr	2		1	2				1	1				7		
Gloucester	74	8	Whitteredge	Oliver	1		1						1				4	Squam Parish	
Gloucester	74	9	Whitteredge	Richd			1			2			1	1			5	Squam Parish	
Haverhill	151	32	Whittier	Daniel	3			1					1				6		
Amesbury	47	5	Whittier	Isaac Major	2	2	1		1	1	1	1					9		
Methuen	156	18	Whittier	John			2		1	1	2			1			8		

TOWN	PG#	LN#	LAST NAME	FIRST NAME	FREE WHITE MALES under 10	10 to 16	16 to 26	26 to 45	45 and over	FREE WHITE FEMALES under 10	10 to 16	16 to 26	26 to 45	45 and over	TOTAL ALL OTHER	TOTAL SLAVES	TOTALS	DISTRICT/ TOWNSHIP	NOTES
Haverhill	151	5	Whittier	Joseph		1		3				2	1	1			8		
Amesbury	47	8	Whittier	Maurice		1			1				1	1			4		
Methuen	156	11	Whittier	Nathl	1	2	1	1		2	1		1				9		
Haverhill	151	14	Whittier	Thomas		1	1		1		1	3		1			8		
Haverhill	151	34	Whittier	Thomas Junr	1		2						1				4		
Haverhill	151	30	Whittier	William	1		1						1	1			4		
Methuen	156	17	Whittier	William				1					1	1			3		
Methuen	156	19	Whittier	William 3d	1	1	1						2				5		
Methuen	156	10	Whittier	William Junr	1	1		1		3		2	1				9		
Salisbury	34	26	Whittier	Wm Capt	1	1		1		2			1				6		
Newburyport	181	20	Whittleton	William	3			1		1	1			1			7		
Salem	220	54	Whittmore	James	1			1					1				3		
Beverly	298	45	Whittridge	Livemore		1		1			1	2		1			6		
Beverly	299	1	Whittridge	Livemore Jr	2			1		2		1					6		
Beverly	298	22	Whyer	Joseph				1			1			1			3		
Ipswich	277	17	Whyett	Stephen	1			1		1			1	1			5		
Danvers	2	25	Wiatt	George			1	1					2				4		
Ipswich	277	42	Wickins	Abraham	1		1						1				3		
Salem	211	31	Widen	Charles			1			1		1					3		
Manchester	55	14	Widgen	Joseph	3		1			1			1				6		
Marblehead	245	29	Widger	Thomas	1		1						1				3		
Marblehead	248	20	Widger	William		1						1					2		
Marblehead	261	8	Widger	William	2	1		1		1	1	1		1			8		
Haverhill	151	17	Wied	Joshua			1				1		1				3		
Salem	205	47	Wiggins	Joseph	2	2	1		1	1		1	1				9		
Newburyport	180	42	Wigglesworth	Michael			2			3		1	1	1			8		
Andover	103	5	Wight	John				1						1			2		
Amesbury	47	7	Wilcomb	Hezekiah Wid	1	1								1			3		
Salem	219	24	Wild	Michael	1		1			1		2	2				7		
Topsfield	20	28	Wildes	Daniel	1		1			1		1					4		
Topsfield	19	37	Wildes	Dudley		1	2	1			1			2			7		
Topsfield	20	13	Wildes	Ephriem			1	1						2			4		
Topsfield	21	33	Wildes	Mary									2	1			3		
Topsfield	20	23	Wildes	Moses	1	1	3	1				1	1				8		
Topsfield	21	32	Wildes	Sylvanus		2		1		1	2	3		2			11		
Beverly	299	9	Wiles	Michael		1							1				2		
Marblehead	265	17	Wilford	George	1	2		1		1			1				6		
Hamilton	285	90	Wilkins	Abijah			1			2	1	1					5		
Middleton	15	21	Wilkins	Benjamin		2		1			1	1		1			6		
Middleton	16	37	Wilkins	Elias		1	2	1		2		1					7		
Middleton	17	39	Wilkins	Elijah	2	1		1		4			1				9		
Middleton	16	1	Wilkins	Enos		1		1				1		1			4		
Middleton	17	16	Wilkins	Icabod				1				1	1				3		
Middleton	15	17	Wilkins	Jonathan			1	1				1	1	2			6		
Middleton	17	14	Wilkins	Jonathan			1	1					1	1			4		
Andover	103	15	Wilkins	Moses	1		1	1		3		2					8		
Middleton	17	2	Wilkins	Nehemiah	1	1		1				1	3	1			8		
Middleton	16	2	Wilkins	Pelatiah			1			1		1					3		
Salem	197	19	Wilkins	Reuben	4		2	1		1	1		1				10		
Middleton	17	17	Wilkins	Samuel		1	1	1		1	2	1	1				8		
Middleton	16	11	Wilkins	Solomon			1	1				1		1			4		
Beverly	293	49	Wilkins	Sylester			1			1		1					3		
Marblehead	240	22	Wilkins	William			1			2		1					4		
Danvers	8	8	Wilkins	Zadock	2		1	1	1	4			1	1			11		
Newburyport	180	43	Willard	Josiah			2					1	1				4		
Marblehead	246	35	Willard	Thomas			1				1	1					3		
Ipswich	275	2	Willcomb	Sarah										1			1		
Ipswich	275	3	Willcomb	William	1			1		2	1		1				6		
Ipswich	281	12	Willett	John		1	1	1	1				2	1			7		
Lynnfield	236	9	Willey	Benj	1	3		1					1	1			7		
Lynnfield	237	8	Willey	Ephm	2	1		1					2				6		
Gloucester	85	20	William	Abraham	1			1				2	1	1			6		
Marblehead	241	15	Williams	Abigail	1		1			1			1	1			5		
Salem	216	45	Williams	Abigail			1						1	1			3		
Gloucester	68	1	Williams	Abraham	2		2			1	1		1	1			8		
Salem	202	22	Williams	Andrew											5		5		
Salem	208	40	Williams	Anna	1							1	1	1			4		
Amesbury	47	3	Williams	Dorothy Wid			1						1	1			3		
Newbury	110	42	Williams	Eliphalet				1		3			1				5		
Newburyport	181	4	Williams	George	1		1						1				3		
Rowley	130	16	Williams	Gilbert T	3			1		1			1				6		
Marblehead	257	10	Williams	Hannah			1						1				2		
Danvers	4	16	Williams	Henry	1		2			1			1				5		
Salem	210	13	Williams	Henry	1	1			1			1		1			5		
Salem	203	40	Williams	Isaac				1				3	1	2			7		
Haverhill	151	27	Williams	Isaac F.			1			2	2		1				6		
Beverly	299	15	Williams	James						2	1		1	1	1	1	7		
Lynn	228	21	Williams	James	1	1	1		1	1			1	1			7		
Lynn	223	52	Williams	Jerusha		2				3			1				6		
Danvers	5	9	Williams	John				1						1			2		
Marblehead	261	18	Williams	John	1	1		1		2	1		1				7		
Salem	203	3	Williams	John		1	1						2	1			5		
Salem	205	48	Williams	John			1						1				2		
Salem	219	25	Williams	John		1		1				1	1	1			5		
Lynn	225	24	Williams	John Junr	1			1	1	2			1				6		

283

			HEADS OF HOUSEHOLD		FREE WHITE MALES					FREE WHITE FEMALES									
TOWN	PG#	LN#	LAST NAME	FIRST NAME	under 10	10 to 16	16 to 26	26 to 45	45 and over	under 10	10 to 16	16 to 26	26 to 45	45 and over	TOTAL ALL OTHER	TOTAL SLAVES	TOTALS	DISTRICT/ TOWNSHIP	NOTES
Haverhill	151	22	Williams	John M.			1		1	1	1						4		
Lynn	232	4	Williams	Joseph					1					1			2		
Newburyport	181	6	Williams	Joseph	2	2		1		1		2		1			9		
Salem	200	43	Williams	Joseph	1			1		2			1	1			6		
Ipswich	275	10	Williams	Joshua				1						1			2		
Newburyport	181	7	Williams	Lucy Wido		1	1						1				3		
Salem	212	6	Williams	Lycia							1	2		1			4		
Marblehead	245	13	Williams	Mary									2	1			3		
Salem	188	5	Williams	Mehitable		1	2						3	1			7		
Gloucester	67	24	Williams	Nathl	2			1		1	1		1				6		
Newburyport	181	3	Williams	Richard			2				1		1	1			5		
Salem	199	32	Williams	Samuel				1				1		1			3		
Beverly	299	38	williams	Thomas				1			1		1				3		
Newbury	108	40	Williams	Thomas				1		1	1	3	2				8		
Beverly	293	5	Williams	Thomas 2d			1										1		
Salem	216	50	Williams	Thos			1			2		1	1				5		
Amesbury	47	6	Williams	William		2		1					1	1			5		
Rowley	131	30	Williams	William	1		1		1	1			1				5		
Salem	195	34	Williams	Israel			1			2	1	1	1				6		
Salem	191	42	Williamson	Saml								1		1			2		
Danvers	11	19	Willington	Thaddeus	1	1		1		3	1	3	1				11		
Haverhill	151	9	Willis	Benjamin		2		1		1	2			2			8		
Haverhill	151	10	Willis	Benjan Junr	4	1	1	1		1		1					9		
Lynn	228	35	Willis	John				1					1				2		
Salem	211	53	Willis	John	1	1		1		1			1				5		
Marblehead	252	24	Willisten	Thomas		2	1	1		1							5		
Marblehead	258	5	Williston	Thomas Junr			1						1				2		
Marblehead	256	13	Wills	Elizabeth		1	1						1				3		
Lynn	233	35	Willson	Benj	2	1		1		1	1		1				7	West Parish	
Danvers	11	1	Willson	Benjamin		1		1					2	1			5		
Methuen	156	20	Willson	Benjamin	1			1					1				3		
Danvers	10	42	Willson	Clark	1			1		1			1				4		
Danvers	10	36	Willson	Elisha	1		1					1					3		
Danvers	10	21	Willson	Isaac	1	1		1		2	2	2	1				10		
Danvers	11	5	Willson	Isaac				2					2				4		
Beverly	299	7	Willson	James	1	1		2					1				5		
Methuen	156	12	Willson	James			1	1	1			1		1			5		
Methuen	156	15	Willson	John	1	1		1					1				4		
Salem	205	1	Willson	John	2		1						1				4		
Danvers	10	19	Willson	Jonathan	3	1		1		2	2		1				10		
Danvers	10	26	Willson	Newhall	2		1			1	2						6		
Danvers	10	24	Willson	Robert			1						1				2		
Salem	204	26	Willson	Robt	1			1		1			1				4		
Danvers	10	25	Willson	Sarah		1	1			1		2		1			6		
Danvers	10	22	Willson	Sarah Junr		1	1			2			1				5		
Danvers	12	8	Willson	William	3			1		1	2	1					8		
Hamilton	285	24	Wilredge	John		1		1	1	1				1			5		
Newburyport	181	33	Wilson	Andrew	1			1		1			1				4		
Salem	197	4	Wilson	James											4		4		
Haverhill	151	18	Wilson	John	1		1	1		2		1		1			7		
Marblehead	247	9	Wilson	Joseph	1	1		1		2			1	1			7		
Andover	102	27	Wilson	Joshua	2	3		1				1	1	3			11		
Salem	199	15	Winchester	Jacob	4	2		1				2		1			10		
Gloucester	62	6	Winchester	John	3			1					1				5		
Andover	103	13	Winchester	Samuel	2	1		1		2	2		1				9		
Salisbury	34	15	Wines	Thomas				1						1			2		
Salem	206	49	Wing	Cornielius			1	1				1	1				4		
Salem	220	23	Wing	William			1			2			1				4		
Newburyport	181	36	Wingate	Edmund	1				1	1	1	1	1				6		
Haverhill	151	26	Wingate	Moses			1			1			1				3		
Haverhill	151	25	Wingate	Paine	2		1	1		2			1				7		
Haverhill	151	24	Wingate	William			1					1					2		
Haverhill	151	19	Winn	David	1	1	1	1		2			1				7		
Salem	206	24	Winn	John			1						1				2		
Salem	211	41	Winn	Joseph	2			1		2			1	1			7		
Danvers	10	34	Winn	Joshua		2	1	1				1		1			7		
Lynn	229	14	Winship	Saml	2	1	2	1				1	1				8		
Gloucester	68	4	Winter	William	1		1			1		1		1			5		
Marblehead	245	9	Wipping	George	3			1				3	1				8		
Newbury	109	16	Wise	David	1		1		1	2		1		1			7		
Ipswich	274	3	Wise	Elizabeth			1							1			2		
Newbury	111	11	Wise	Jonathan		1		1					1				3		
Ipswich	274	2	Wise	Joseph			1						1				2		
Newbury	112	19	Wise	William	1		1		1		1		1				5		
Newburyport	181	35	Wise	William	1			1		1			1				4		
Gloucester	68	3	Witham	Abraham		1				1			1				3		
Gloucester	67	22	Witham	Benja	1	1			1				1				4		
Gloucester	67	23	Witham	Benja 3d			1			1			1				3		
Gloucester	71	16	Witham	Benja 4				1				2		1			4		
Gloucester	67	20	Witham	Danl		1	2		1	2		1		1			8		
Gloucester	67	19	Witham	Dorcas Wo			3			2				1			6		
Gloucester	81	9	Witham	Ebenz		1		1						1			3		
Gloucester	67	13	Witham	Edward			2		1			1		1			5		
Gloucester	83	9	Witham	Henry	1	1			1			1		1			5		
Gloucester	83	10	Witham	Henry Junr			1					1					2		
Gloucester	83	13	Witham	Joshua	1		1			2		1					5		
Gloucester	83	27	Witham	Mark			1										1		
Marblehead	239	27	Witham	Susanna		2				2			1				5		

| TOWN | PG# | LN# | HEADS OF HOUSEHOLD | | FREE WHITE MALES | | | | | FREE WHITE FEMALES | | | | | TOTAL ALL OTHER | TOTAL SLAVES | TOTALS | DISTRICT/ TOWNSHIP | NOTES |
			LAST NAME	FIRST NAME	under 10	10 to 16	16 to 26	26 to 45	45 and over	under 10	10 to 16	16 to 26	26 to 45	45 and over					
Newburyport	181	30	Witham	Thomas	3	1		1						1			6		
Gloucester	68	2	Witham	Thos	1		1				1		1				4		
Gloucester	83	14	Witham	Thos	1		2			1		1					5		
Gloucester	83	8	Witham	Zebulon	1	1		1		1	1		1				6		
Lynn	224	30	Witt	Benj			1		1	1	1			1			5		
Lynn	225	7	Witt	Danl P				1		1			1				3		
Marblehead	250	32	Wittam	John			1		1			1		1			4		
Beverly	299	43	Wittemore	Joseph	1	1		1		4	2	1	1				11		
Salem	198	27	Wittridge	Tho	2		1	1		1		1	1				7		
Newburyport	181	14	Woart	William				1		1		2	1				5		
Gloucester	67	27	Wonson	Charles	2		1						1				4		
Gloucester	83	15	Wonson	Patience Wo										1			1		
Gloucester	68	26	Wonson	Saml	1				1	2				2			6		
Gloucester	67	25	Wonson	Saml Junr	2		2			2		2					8		
Newburyport	181	8	Wood	Abner	2	1	1	1		2	1		2				10		
Salem	221	14	Wood	Anna					1	2		1		1			5		
Gloucester	85	31	Wood	Charles	2		1			1		1	1				4		
Beverly	301	17	Wood	Cornelius			1	1					1	1			4		
Andover	103	9	Wood	David					1		1	1	1				4		
Newburyport	181	10	Wood	David			1	2	1	2	1		2				10		
Beverly	304	36	Wood	Eliza		3							1				4		
Marblehead	248	5	Wood	Elizabeth	1					1		1					3		
Salem	202	31	Wood	Hannah						1	1	1		1			4		
Danvers	10	13	Wood	Israel	1			1		2	2		1				7		
Andover	103	11	Wood	John	1			1		2	2		1				7		
Boxford	136	11	Wood	John	1				1	2			1				5		
Rowley	128	6	Wood	John		1	1						1				3		
Newburyport	181	9	Wood	John Jr	1		1	1				1	1				5		
Rowley	130	39	Wood	Jonathan	1	2		1				2		1			7		
Rowley	130	40	Wood	Jonathn					1		1			1			3		
Boxford	133	19	Wood	Joseph		1			1				1	1			4		
Boxford	133	20	Wood	Joseph			1			1		1					3		
Newburyport	181	12	Wood	Joseph			1			1			1				3		
Beverly	289	17	Wood	Judith										1			1		
Boxford	134	6	Wood	Lemuel	2		1		1	2	1			1	1		9		
Boxford	135	18	Wood	Margret							1		1				2		
Salem	213	16	Wood	Mary		1	2	1					1				5		
Boxford	134	52	Wood	Moses	2		2		1	2	3	1	1				12		
Bradford	126	1	Wood	Moses		1		1					1				3		
Boxford	134	51	Wood	Nathan					1				1				2		
Salem	201	45	Wood	Nathan		3	1		3	1							8		
Andover	103	12	Wood	Obadiah		1			1				1				3		
Salem	220	58	Wood	Phalie		1		1					1				3		
Marblehead	266	32	Wood	Richard					1				1				2		
Gloucester	72	9	Wood	Ruth	1								1	2			4		
Salem	215	45	Wood	Sarah									1				1		
Boxford	135	4	Wood	Solomon		1		1		3	1		1				7		
Bradford	126	3	Wood	Thomas			3		1	1	1			1			8		
Newburyport	181	11	Wood	Thomas	2	1		1		1			1				6		
Newburyport	181	13	Wood	William	3	1	1	1		1			2	1			10		
Beverly	289	15	Wood	Joseph		1	2		1			1		1			6		
Bradford	125	12	Wood	Samuel	4		1	1	1	2	3	1	1				15		
Beverly	296	47	Woodberry	Anna										1			1		
Beverly	292	33	Woodberry	Asa	1		2		1	1	3			2			10		
Beverly	306	30	Woodberry	Benja 2d	2	1			1					1			5		
Beverly	290	4	Woodberry	Benja 3d	2		1					1					4		
Beverly	296	42	Woodberry	Benjamin		1		1					1	1			4		
Beverly	306	31	Woodberry	Daniel	1			1		1			1	1			5		
Beverly	301	40	Woodberry	Elisha				1		1		1					3		
Beverly	297	42	Woodberry	Eliza									1	1			2		
Beverly	292	39	Woodberry	Esther									1				1		
Beverly	301	10	Woodberry	Freeborn	1			1		1			1				4		
Beverly	294	19	Woodberry	Hannah		1	2				1		1				5		
Beverly	295	6	Woodberry	Hannah						1		1		1			3		
Beverly	297	8	Woodberry	Hephzibah		3						1		1			5		
Beverly	306	19	Woodberry	Isaac		1	2	1		3	1		1				9		
Beverly	295	18	Woodberry	James				1					1				2		
Beverly	294	40	Woodberry	Jeremiah			1					1					2		
Beverly	305	40	Woodberry	John		1		1				1	1	1			5		
Gloucester	62	4	Woodberry	John	1			1		2		1	1				6		
Beverly	293	25	Woodberry	Joseph		1	2	1	1		1		1				7		
Beverly	295	32	Woodberry	Joseph		1						1					2		
Beverly	299	26	Woodberry	Joseph 2d					1					2			3		
Beverly	296	46	Woodberry	Joseph 3d	2			1		1			1				5		
Salem	194	10	Woodberry	Josiah	2	2	1		1	2	1	1	1				11		
Beverly	292	27	Woodberry	Lucy		1							1	1			3		
Beverly	295	15	Woodberry	Malachi		1					1	2	1	1			7		
Beverly	300	40	Woodberry	Mark	1			1		2			1				5		
Beverly	292	37	Woodberry	Martha										1			1		
Beverly	294	41	Woodberry	Martha								1		2			3		
Beverly	302	7	Woodberry	Nathl					1								1		
Beverly	296	41	Woodberry	Obed	3			1		1			1				6		
Beverly	305	25	Woodberry	Peter					1				1	1			3		
Gloucester	77	24	Woodberry	Peter	1			1		1			1				4		
Beverly	297	39	Woodberry	Priscilla									2	2			4		

285

TOWN	PG#	LN#	LAST NAME	FIRST NAME	FREE WHITE MALES					FREE WHITE FEMALES					TOTAL ALL OTHER	TOTAL SLAVES	TOTALS	DISTRICT/ TOWNSHIP	NOTES
					under 10	10 to 16	16 to 26	26 to 45	45 and over	under 10	10 to 16	16 to 26	26 to 45	45 and over					
Beverly	301	2	Woodberry	Richard	1			1					1				3		
Beverly	295	10	Woodberry	Robert	2	1			1		1	3		2			11		
Andover	103	14	Woodberry	Wm			1	1					1	1			4		
Beverly	293	8	Woodberry	Zebulon			1			1			1				3		
Gloucester	83	11	Woodbery	Andrew		1		1			1	1		1			5		
Manchester	54	39	Woodbery	Andrew				1						1			2		
Gloucester	73	23	Woodbery	Asa	1	1		1		2			1				6	Squam Parish	
Beverly	290	34	Woodbery	Curtice			1		1			2		1	2		7		
Manchester	54	38	Woodbery	David	1			1		3	1	1					7		
Gloucester	77	17	Woodbery	Epes		0				3		1					5		
Beverly	301	24	Woodbery	Gideon	3			1		1		1					6		
Gloucester	68	6	Woodbery	Joshua	2	1		1		1		1	1				7		
Beverly	301	33	Woodbery	Josiah		2	1	2					1				6		
Beverly	301	23	Woodbery	Martha									1				1		
Beverly	291	19	Woodbery	Mary		1							1	1			3		
Manchester	55	15	Woodbery	Mary Widow								1		1			2		
Beverly	301	27	Woodbery	Myhill	1			1					3				5		
Beverly	290	32	Woodbery	Nicholas		2	3		1	2	1			2			11		
Beverly	303	21	Woodbery	Peter	3		2	1		1			1				8		
Beverly	302	40	Woodbery	Samuel				1					1				2		
Beverly	291	4	Woodbery	Sarah	3	2	1			1		2	1				10		
Gloucester	57	31	Woodbery	Seth			1					1		1			3	West Parish	
Gloucester	77	15	Woodbery	Susannah Wo		1	1	2		2		1		1			8		
Beverly	289	10	Woodbery	Thomas		1		1		1	2		1				6		
Beverly	289	11	Woodbery	Thomas Jun	1		1			1	1						4		
Gloucester	77	18	Woodbery	Walter		1		1		5			1				8		
Beverly	291	20	Woodbery	William			1					1					2		
Beverly	295	47	Woodbery	Willm C	1			1		2			1				5		
Gloucester	57	30	Woodbery	Winthrop	1		1			1	1	1		1			6	West Parish	
Andover	102	31	Woodbridge	Benja	3	1		1		1	2		1				9		
Salem	215	7	Woodbridge	Darkis	1							1		1			3		
Andover	103	1	Woodbridge	Dudley	2	1		1		2			1				7		
Hamilton	285	1	Woodbury	Andrew	1	1		1		2	1		1				7		
Hamilton	284	25	Woodbury	Barnet		1		1		1			1				4		
Hamilton	284	7	Woodbury	Benjamin			1	1			1		1				4		
Salisbury	34	9	Woodbury	Caleb		1	2	1				2	1				7		
Hamilton	284	10	Woodbury	Eliot		2				2	1						5		
Haverhill	151	16	Woodbury	Hannah	2	1				3	1						7		
Hamilton	284	22	Woodbury	Isaac	1			1		2	1		1				6		
Hamilton	284	8	Woodbury	Isiah	1			1			1	2	1				6		
Hamilton	284	24	Woodbury	James	1			1		3			1				6		
Hamilton	284	6	Woodbury	John	2		1	1					1				5		
Lynn	231	3	Woodbury	John	1			1		1	2		1				6		
Hamilton	284	19	Woodbury	John Jun	2	1		1		3			1				8		
Salem	189	29	Woodbury	Josiah	1	1	1		1	1	1		1				7		
Ipswich	279	1	Woodbury	Major		1		1		1			1	1			5		
Salem	183	17	Woodbury	Nath		2	1		1	1			1	1			7		
Hamilton	287	9	Woodbury	Nicholas	1		1	1					1				4		
Marblehead	244	6	Woodfine	Richard L.	3	1		1	1	2			1				9		
Newbury	106	20	Woodman	Abner	1	1	1		1					1			5		
Newbury	107	12	Woodman	Edward		1		1	3			2	1	1			9		
Beverly	294	11	Woodman	Hannah									1	1			2		
Newbury	106	4	Woodman	Jewel		1		1		1		2	1				6		
Newburyport	180	28	Woodman	Jonathan		2	1		1	1			1	1	1		8		
Newbury	117	44	Woodman	Joseph	3	1		1		2	1		1				9		
Newburyport	180	29	Woodman	Joseph H	3		1			2		1	1				8		
Newbury	107	40	Woodman	Mark	2	1		1		1	2	1					9		
Newbury	109	37	Woodman	Merriam									1	1			2		
Salisbury	34	27	Woodman	Nathl	4			1			1		1				7		
Bradford	123	21	Woodman	Phineas			1	1	3				1	1			7		
Bradford	126	18	Woodman	Richard	1		1	1		1		2	2				8		
Newbury	116	17	Woodman	Samuel		1	1					2	1				5		
Newbury	106	19	Woodman	William			1	1			1	1	1				5		
Newburyport	180	30	Woodman	William		1	1	1					1				4		
Marblehead	240	38	Woodridge	John	2	2		1		1	1	1	1				9		
Marblehead	243	1	Woodridge	Mary								1		1			2		
Andover	102	28	Woods	John			1				1	1					3		
Newbury	107	24	Woods	Lenord Revd	1		1				2	1					5		
Marblehead	239	13	Woodward	Abraham		1		1					1	1			4		
Marblehead	239	14	Woodward	Abraham Junr	1			1			1		1				4		
Newbury	112	27	Woodwell	Gideon	1		1		1	1	2	2	1	1			10		
Newburyport	181	1	Woodwell	Jacob			1			1		2					4		
Newbury	112	26	Woodwell	John	1	3		1		1			4				10		
Marblehead	260	10	Wooldridge	Benjamin	2		1	1									4		
Marblehead	241	29	Wooldridge	Margaret								2		1			3		
Marblehead	243	25	Wooldridge	Robert	1			1				1		1			5		
Marblehead	265	14	Wooldridge	Thomas	2	2		1		1			1				7		
Marblehead	268	31	Wooldridge	William	3	1		1		2	1		1				9		
Newburyport	181	16	Work	John			2						1				3		
Newburyport	181	15	Work	William	1	1	4	1		1	1	1					10		
Salem	208	35	Worldly	William			1				1	1					3		
Gloucester	84	34	Worley	William	1									2			3		
Marblehead	254	2	Wormstead	Benjamin		1		1					1	1			4		
Beverly	299	31	Worrly	James		1					1		1				4		
Marblehead	254	15	Wortey	Elizabeth				1		2	1		1				5		
Salisbury	34	11	Worthen	Amos	1		1			2	1		1				6		

TOWN	PG#	LN#	LAST NAME	FIRST NAME	FREE WHITE MALES					FREE WHITE FEMALES					TOTAL ALL OTHER	TOTAL SLAVES	TOTALS	DISTRICT/ TOWNSHIP	NOTES
					under 10	10 to 16	16 to 26	26 to 45	45 and over	under 10	10 to 16	16 to 26	26 to 45	45 and over					
Salisbury	34	12	Worthen	Ezekiel				1		1			1				3		
Amesbury	46	19	Worthen	Ezekiel Capt	2	1			1					1			5		
Amesbury	46	15	Worthen	Ezra		1	1		1				2	1			6		
Amesbury	47	2	Worthen	George	1	1	2		1				1	1			7		
Amesbury	46	30	Worthen	Hannah Wid									1	1			2		
Amesbury	47	1	Worthen	Thomas		1		1				1	1				4		
Amesbury	46	29	Worthen	Willm	1			1		2			1				5		
Gloucester	62	25	Wotton	Henry	1			1		3	3	1	1				10		
Gloucester	62	26	Wotton	Joseph	1				1			1	1	1			5		
Salem	200	40	Wright	David			1						1				2		
Salem	210	29	Wright	James			1	1					1		1		4		
Middleton	16	30	Wright	Joseph				1		2			1				4		
Salem	211	54	Wright	Mary									2	2			4		
Wenham	309	23	Wyat	Abraham				1					1				2		
Beverly	294	48	Wyat	George		1		1		3	1		1				7		
Wenham	309	27	Wyat	Jane	1	1				1				1			4		
Wenham	309	26	Wyat	Jonathan	1			1				1	1				4		
Wenham	309	24	Wyat	Simon	2			1		2	1		1				7		
Wenham	309	28	Wyat	Thankful	2								1				3		
Wenham	309	25	Wyat	William	3			1		2		1					7		
Newburyport	180	37	Wyatt	Benjamin	1			1		2	2		1	2			9		
Newburyport	180	38	Wyatt	Josiah	1		1						1				3		
Newburyport	181	23	Wyer	Nathaniel			1	1		1			1				4		
Beverly	304	15	Wyer	William	2			1		1			1				5		
Newburyport	181	21	Wyer	William		1	1	1		1			1	1			6		
Newburyport	181	22	Wyer	William Jr	2	1		1		2			1	1			8		
Bradford	122	46	Wyman	Daniel	1		2	2					2				7		
Lynn	229	38	Wyman	Ebenz		1				1		1					3		
Danvers	12	30	Wyman	Francis	1			1		1	1		1				5		
Marblehead	265	13	Wyman	Isaac			1	1						1			3		
Haverhill	151	20	Wyman	Jacob				1						1			2		
Beverly	293	39	Wyman	Joshua	4			1		3			1				9		
Haverhill	151	29	Wyman	Reuben			1						1				2		
Danvers	13	2	Wyman	Solomon				1						1			2		
Lynn	230	35	Yell	John			1			1			1				3		
Salem	207	32	Yell	Mehihl										1			1		
Salem	207	28	Yew	Eliza	1							1	1	1			4		
Salem	207	13	Yew	Mosis			1			2		1					4		
Gloucester	83	16	York	Thos	1		1			2	1	1					6		
Gloucester	84	14	Youlen	John				1						3			4		
Salisbury	34	32	Young	Banja Major	3	1			1		1			1	18		25		
Gloucester	77	8	Young	Daniel	1			1				1					3		
Gloucester	77	9	Young	Heteh Wo	2	2								1	1		6		
Newburyport	181	37	Young	Israel	2			1		1			1				5		
Newburyport	181	38	Young	Jonathan	1	1	1	1	1			1		1			7		
Newburyport	181	39	Young	Joseph	2			1		2			1				6		
Salem	213	41	Young	Joseph	1		1	1		2			1				6		
Salem	217	31	Young	Margt										1			1		
Newburyport	181	40	Young	Reuben				1					2				3		
Beverly	297	41	Young	William	3	1		1		2	1		1				9		
Gloucester	84	33	Younger	Willard	1			1					1	2			5		
Marblehead	241	14	Youngs	Stephen				1					1				2		
Lynn	234	22		Alexander a Black Man										1	1		2		
Andover	103	27		Boos											5		5		
Gloucester	83	20		Dick Negro				0						0	2		2		
Beverly	290	38		Pompe Negro											4		4		
Beverly	294	36		Pompe Negro											7		7		
Marblehead	261	24		Simon											4		4		Last name left blank

287

NOTES

www.ingramcontent.com/pod-product-compliance
Lightning Source LLC
Chambersburg PA
CBHW080243290526
45790CB00005B/1680